DATE DUE

W9-ACA-436

Bob Jones University
hereby gratefully acknowledges
a gift of $25 from

Miss Debora Ann Andrews

for the building of
the new library addition
dedicated September, 1980,
to the glory of God.

CATALOGUE OF
ENGLISH BIBLE TRANSLATIONS

CATALOGUE OF
ENGLISH BIBLE TRANSLATIONS

A Classified Bibliography of Versions and Editions Including Books, Parts, and Old and New Testament Apocrypha and Apocryphal Books

William J. Chamberlin

016.2205
C355

MACK LIBRARY
BOB JONES UNIVERSITY
GREENVILLE, SC

Bibliographies and Indexes in Religious Studies, Number 21

Greenwood Press

New York • Westport, Connecticut • London

84485846

Library of Congress Cataloging-in-Publication Data

Chamberlin, William J.
  Catalogue of English Bible translations : a classified
bibliography of versions and editions including books, parts, and
Old and New Testament Apocrypha and Apocryphal books / William J.
Chamberlin.
    p. cm.—(Bibliographies and indexes in religious studies,
  ISSN 0742-6836 ; no. 21)
  Includes bibliographical references and index.
  ISBN 0-313-28041-X (alk. paper)
    1. Bible. English—Versions—Bibliography. 2. Apocryphal books—
Bibliography.   I. Title.   II. Series.
Z7771.E5C43   1991
[BS455]
016.2205'2—dc20   91-27497

British Library Cataloguing in Publication Data is available.

Copyright © 1991 by William J. Chamberlin

All rights reserved. No portion of this book may be
reproduced, by any process or technique, without the
express written consent of the publisher.

Library of Congress Catalog Card Number: 91-27497
ISBN: 0-313-28041-X
ISSN: 0742-6836

First published in 1991

Greenwood Press, 88 Post Road West, Westport, CT 06881
An imprint of Greenwood Publishing Group, Inc.

Printed in the United States of America

The paper used in this book complies with the
Permanent Paper Standard issued by the National
Information Standards Organization (Z39.48-1984).

10 9 8 7 6 5 4 3 2 1

AAD-6714

To my wife, Elaine, who is a loving helpmate to me, a gentle mother to our children and grandchildren, and an enthusiastic supporter of the ministry to which God has called me. She is a virtuous, valiant woman.

Contents

Preface

The entries in this Bible Bibliography contain more than
what may be perceived by some ministers and lay people as
Bible books, the accepted books of the Bible Canon. But,
where are the limits of inclusion? The Jews believe that
the Bible stops with Malachi. The Christians include the
New Testament, and some believe that the Apocrypha is a
part of the Bible. The King James Bible always included
a version of the Apocrypha, even though most Catholic
translations don't include 2nd Esdras and the Prayer of
Manasses. The books that were not specifically included
- - The Pseudepigrapha (Apocryphal, both the Old
Testament and New Testament) - - need to be "available"
in order to examine their important value in early
Christian teachings.

As for the New Testament, the Syriac claim that
Revelations and some short books preceding are not part
of the canon. Some Church Fathers have accepted other
titles such as the Shepherd of Hermas. And the old
Unicals included 1st. Clement and others.

Some ministers and lay people believe that paraphrases should not be included in this work, because some of these paraphrases take extreme liberties with the text. Josephus' "Antiquities of the Jews" can be classified as a padded paraphrase of the historical portions of the Old Testament. What we are to include or exclude in a Bible Bibliography is not an easy task.

It must be remembered that to some lay people and students, "Bible History," as researched by modern scholarship, doesn't do more than intrigue one's curiosity. Many of them want to examine the ancient written evidence themselves. Modern viewpoints in "Theology" interest them less than what it is based on. Many of them want to know about beliefs that were felt back when the first manuscripts were penned.

Where there is no full equivalency between languages, variant translations seem the ideal way of understanding the opinions of what was originally written. Thus we need literal translations that better reveal how the original expressed itself, translations that express the thought that the translator "understood." Paraphrases which bring out the opinions of what scholars conclude was understood by the original readers.

That is the reason for this attempt to list all English

translations of the Bible and parts thereof. This
bibliography consists of complete Bibles; Old and New
Testaments; portions of the Bible; single books; single
chapters; single verses; commentaries with their own
translation; theology books that contain the author's own
translation of biblical quotations; children's Bibles, if
a new translation or a close paraphrase; Apocrypha books;
Old and New Testament Apocryphal books (Pseudepigrapha);
and the Koran.

Several additional features of this bibliographical
reference work are as follows:

A.   The titles are conveniently listed according
     to the date of publication, with those undated
     or where the date is unknown listed first.

B.   Many early translations were, unfortunately,
     published anonymously. Many translators felt
     that listing their name with the version would
     give glory to them instead of God. Some, such
     as William Tyndale, were fearful for their
     lives, especially if it was known who
     translated the version.

     In some cases it has been determined, over
     time, who likely did the translation. Because
     a person using this reference work would not

have this information, and thus would not be
able to find it by means of the translator's
name, the title is listed under <u>Anonymous</u>.
However, the translator's name, when known, is
listed within the entry in square [] brackets.

C.   The index contains

1.   all known translator's names,

2.   all names by which the translation
itself may be known (such as Revised
Version, New American Version, King
James II, etc.).

Acknowledgements

I am grateful to many people for their encouragement in preparing this work, among them are Arnold D. Ehlert, former Graduate Studies Librarian at Biola College and past editor of "The Bible Collector" magazine; George D. Brown, Rare Book Dealer, Toledo, Ohio; and Carl Johnson, Publisher and Editor of the "Bible Collectors' World" magazine; Dr. Gerald Bergman; and finally Robert Guillery, a good friend from W. Bloomfield, MI.

Special thanks are due to Evangelist William E. Paul, who has spent many hours proof-reading this work. Paul, a graduate of Midwestern School of Evangelism in Ottumwa, Iowa, was the editor of "News and Truths," published from 1955 to 1970, and editor of "Impact For Christ," published from 1971 to 1981. Evangelist Paul has, also, published a book, several booklets, and numerous tracts. I am in his debt for his generous encouragement and untiring support.

I acknowledge a very great debt to Mr. David Simonton, who passed away in August, 1975. Mr. Simonton had a life-long hobby that consumed literally thousands of hours compiling a Bible Bibliography on index cards. His file, primarily a concentration of private translations and commentaries with translations by the commentators, contained approximately 5200 cards. It was loaned to me by Arnold D. Ehlert and Gerald Studer. This file brought my bibliography to approximately five times the level of entries of different English translations and versions than both M. Hill's and A.S. Herbert's work combined.

I also want to thank several people at Oakland University who came through for me when my computer broke down. They are: Gerard Joswiak (Manager of Academic Computer Services), Jeff Marraccini (Computer Resource Administrator), and especially Steven E. Grevemeyer and Walid M. Elsady (Computer Technologists).

In addition, thanks go to Blaine Aldrich and Jodi Bentley of The American Speedy Printing Center, located in Clarkston, MI. They contributed their time, equipment, and material in printing the many copies of this work required for proof-reading.

A special acknowledgement goes to four people who have made a difference in my life: My mother, Mary Chamberlin; my brother who has always stood by me, Arthur F. Chamberlin, Jr.; Father Charles E. Cushing; and Father Louie Braatz, S.J.

Last but not least, I want to thank my wife, Elaine; my children, William Jr., Suzanne (DeFratis), Annette (Fox), Denise (McReynolds), and Paul Fox for all my time they gave up so that I could complete this work.

Introduction

No book in history has influenced the world, and is still influencing history and thought, more than the Bible. The Bible is not only the best known book in the world, but it is also quoted with more frequency than all the works of Shakespeare combined. Surveys consistently show that four out of five Americans believe in some way that the Bible is the inspired word of God (Gallup, 1990). For most of the rest of the population, this extraordinary book is held, at the very least, to be a source of inspiration and a valuable record of history.

Eric Fromm (1966:7), one of the premiere American psychologists, acknowledged that he does not believe that the Bible is the word of God, yet he acknowledged that it was to him a most extraordinary book that expresses "the Genius of a people." Well known atheist Isaac Asimov, in his two volume <u>Asimov's Guide to the Bible,</u> concludes that "the most influential, the most published, the most widely read book in the history of the world is the Bible. No other book has been so studied and so analyzed, and it is a tribute to the complexity of the Bible and the eagerness of its students that after thousands of years of study, there are still endless books that can be written about it" (1981:7). Asimov states that his own massive work on the Bible (716 pages on the Old Testament and 637 on the New) is not a scholarly compendium but only a very readable summary of its contents.

For those and other reasons, the Bible is still the world-wide best seller of all time. The American Bible Society alone has distributed more than three-billion Bibles since its founding in 1816. It has been translated into almost 2,000 languages and virtually every person on the Earth has at least a portion of it in his or her native tongue.

The Bible's importance is such that it is often the first book translated into a new language. For many languages, linguists have developed a written form just so that the Bible could be translated into the language of the people. (An example of this is the first translation of the Bible by an American ever made (1663), that by John Eliot into the Algonquian Indian language. He first had to invent a dictionary for their language -- the Algonquian language had never before been written.)

Bible translations have been especially important since the beginning of the Reformation in the 1500s. Luther, Calvin, and Wesley all stressed the critical importance of personal Bible Study and Scriptural knowledge. According to the teachings of most Protestant denominations, salvation is an individual matter. This required more than just a passing familiarity with the Scriptures -- one should experience them directly. Such knowledge can be achieved <u>only</u> by translating the Bible in the tongue of the many peoples of the Earth.

The Great Commission to preach the gospel to all the world, found at Matthew 28:19-20, consequently requires the Bible to be translated into thousands of languages. Unfortunately, therein also lay the source of the schisms that have been occurring ever since Luther. Many argue, and some quite persuasively, that the proliferation of literally thousands of Protestant sects and cults in modern times has occurred partially because of a superficial knowledge of the Scriptures on the part of the population in general. This lack of knowledge makes it easy for people to fall prey to all sorts of demagogues and ignorant leaders, many of whom more than make up for their lack of knowledge by their charisma. Studies have adequately demonstrated the ignorance of the American population on Biblical knowledge -- in one Gallup poll (1980) only four out of ten knew that it was Jesus who delivered the Sermon on the Mount and a similar percentage could not name the four Gospels. Another study found that only half of all Americans could identify five of the Ten Commandments (Gallup 1990).

The problem of interpretation and the misuse of the Scriptures has likewise proven venerable fodder for those who have concluded that civilization would have been better off without the Bible. Joseph Lewis, in his book The Bible Unmasked (1940), argues that the Bible teaches a story of a brutal, barbarous God and has spurred on religious wars that have taken the lives of millions of innocent people. Others who believe the word of the Bible counter that often the problem is that the Bible is not properly understood. This requires much knowledge of its historical context, and a realization that the meanings of individual words, and especially a whole sentence, goes well beyond mere words. Words cannot be translated, only ideas, yet most translators endeavor to maintain fidelity to the original.

This is all the more a problem in that the Bible was written in what are now dead languages, and translating them into a modern language such as English is no easy task. Some translators have attempted to translate consistently each Greek, Hebrew, or Aramaic word with one word in English. This attempt often fails ludicrously. A good example is the Hebrew word yom, often translated into English as day. Does a specific use of yom refer to a work day (which could be six hours, eight hours, twelve hours, fourteen hours, or more) or to an astronomical day of twenty-four hours? Many people use the word day to refer to the daylight period, others to refer to a long time period, such as in the expression _in my father's day_. It can also refer to a specific event in the past or future, such as implied in the expression _in the day of our Lord_.

Admittedly, one's own preconceptions usually influence how one decides to translate a particular verse or expression. Herein lies the problem. For this and other reasons, the student, who studies the Bible in depth, has always relied upon several versions of the Bible, those from his or her own heritage and versions of contrasting heritages. The four major heritages are Protestant, Catholic, Eastern Orthodox, and Judaism, but within these broad traditions fall many others. Even many of the smaller Protestant denominations and sects have their own versions. These include the Jehovah's Witnesses, Mormons, Seven-Day Adventists, and Christian Scientists.

The difficulty of translating the Bible, and thus the need to rely upon several versions, is also illustrated by the fact that most books were authored by one writer, and translation requires the knowledge of only one person's writing and usage style. The Bible, though, had forty independent authors, representing about twenty occupations living in ten countries during at least a 1,500 year span. These forty authors worked in a total of three different languages and used a cast of at least 2,930 characters in almost as many events that occurred in over 1,550 places. It is written in almost all literary forms -- history, mystery, prose, poetry, even romance, biography, and science. A major problem is that we know very little about the authors, who often refer to events that they assume the readers know about and understand (and which many readers today do not). Although many were well educated priests, physicians, kings, and statesmen, the cast also includes farmers, fishermen, sheep herders, and persons about whom we know so little that we cannot even classify their occupation.

Arguments over the variances of interpretation of the Bible's meaning show no sign of letting up today. Controversies between fundamentalists and modernists still rage with enormous force in the United States and in many other countries. This war is partially due to the enormous reverence that the American population has for the Bible. The previously mentioned Gallup poll found that only a mere one percent believe that God had nothing to do with the Bible. Even the fourteen percent who saw the Bible as a book of fables, legends, and moral precepts believe that the wisdom of God is in this ancient work.

As long as there is controversy about the Bible,

translations will be made that reflect different views about that controversy. And as long as languages continue to change and our knowledge of Biblical times continues to grow (and it has grown phenomenally in the past several decades), a need will exist for newer translations. A quick review of the original King James Bible reveals that what many people have today in their homes is a far cry from the original King James Version.

As society becomes more educated, many have predicted that the Scriptures will lose their weight and promise. The Soviet Union's great experiment in atheism, which recently formally ended in failure, well illustrates that people have a need to answer questions such as "Where did we come from?" and "What is the purpose for our existence?" with answers that posits the weight of a divine authority. Although many intellectuals have heaped scorn on the Scriptures, many highly educated persons still hold it to be a valid source of information about spiritual matters. The growth of conservative Protestantism and movements such as Creationism among scientists well illustrate this.

Many claim that the Scriptures speak to them, and they say that when they read a passage they achieve both more understanding of God and our purpose on the Earth. The Bible is, to many, the mouthpiece of God, and God speaks

to them through its words. It is to them the channel by
which humankind is connected with God and the means that
God has of helping us understand His will for us on Earth
today. And God communicates, many believe, more than just
by what is said there. He also communicates through words
that allow the reader's direct communication with God. As
many put it, "God speaks to me through the Scriptures,
just as some people speak to others via the telephone. It
is not the telephone doing the speaking, but the person
at the other end. The Bible is only the means by which
God speaks to us." Woodrow Wilson, the twentieth
president of the United States, once said that "when you
have read the Bible with an openness to its message in
your heart, you will know that it is the word of God"
(Kroll, 1988:1).

In 1975 a magazine called <u>Biblical Archeology Review</u> was
begun. The magazine has grown enormously, as have the
number of Biblical archeologists. Their research has
yielded enormous fruits. Archeologist Bryant Wood (1990),
in a recent evaluation of the data, concludes that the
Biblical account of the fall of the walls of Jericho is
fully correct. The author, a renown archeologist at the
University of Toronto, is not arguing for its
infallibility, but simply that, in this case, the account
is correct. Although many scholars believe that the
destruction was caused by an earthquake, even this

conclusion is based on the Biblical record (from the account of the temporary damming of the Jordan River). Much of the Biblical record is still being researched or debated, and herein lies part of its importance.

So many translations exist because people believe different things about this book. If a person believes that every word is inspired by God, he or she may take great pains to translate every word correctly. On the other hand, if a person believes that the Gospels can and should be read like any good book for new ideas and insight, he or she will endeavor to translate it this way. This philosophy has motivated a translation style called **paraphrase**, where the author takes more liberties with the text, endeavoring to translate what he or she believes the original author <u>meant</u>, not what the original author <u>said</u>.

Even those who condemn this approach often admit that an enormous amount of insight can be gleaned from it. Two of the better examples of this approach are <u>The Living Bible</u> (1971), and <u>The Good News Bible (1976)</u>. Others have endeavored to develop scientific methods of translation such as the <u>Concordant Literal New Testament</u> (1926) and Ivan Pann's <u>Bible Numerics</u> (1914). By analyzing such things as the original word order, sentence structure, or even the number of letters in various words, scholars and charlatans alike have come up with an amazing variety of interpretations and conclusions. They often color their own translation. These versions, too, can teach us much about the Bible. Some of the mathematical relationships that the translators have discovered defy probability to a degree that many feel that this approach proves its inspiration.

If the past is any guide, the current proliferation of new translations will continue. To make sense of the enormous number now available, this work is an invaluable reference guide. Some translations appear to be new and unique, when actually they are a reprint of an older version that has become part of the public domain. Mr. Chamberlin's work will help the researcher determine not only this information but also data on the publishing history, when the translation was originally completed, and certain notable features about it. It contains a wealth of data, and its completeness guarantees that it will become the standard work in this field. This information enables it to be used as a major source for a number of studies, the development of language, for example, or historical changes in various religious views and how they are reflected in translation trends.

This reference work is primarily for those who are interested in doing research related to the Bible, as

are included in many modern Bible translations) and other
Apocryphal books. The use of these for the historian and
theologian alike is enormous.

This compilation, as a reference work, does not make
judgments as to what properly belongs in the scriptural
canon, but includes works that were at one time or
another regarded as part of it, or at least were felt to
be important in the early history in the development of
Christianity.   The   same   problems   relative   to
interpretation also exist with the Apocryphal books, and
the same advantage of comparing translations. The bulk of
this work is on translations of the Old and New
Testaments, a list that is of enormous use for further
studies -- such as on historical patterns of translations, the free versus literal translations, and the
particular books of the Bible that scholars have
preferred to translate into English. It includes all
translations published in British, American, Australian,
New Zealand, and other variations of the English
language.

In researching subjects that range from the history of
translations to the translations themselves, and for
Biblical research in which several translations can be
used to help elucidate the meaning of a passage, this
volume can be enormously helpful. It is the first

well as for Bible scholars. As Richard Elliot Friedm

professor of Hebrew and comparative literature at

University of California at San Diego, and author

several books on the Bible, claimed that men and w

become Bible scholars, for the most part, because eac

his or her own way feels the riches, the power,

beauty, the spirit, the relevance, the value of the b

An awareness of the enormousness of the task

understanding the Bible and its complexity helps the

feel that their individual contributions can help

only small pieces of the puzzle. As a result of t

Friedman concludes that those who research the

develop a special kind of humility towards it.

This leads us to this enormous work of twenty-three

in the making, Cataloque of English Bible Translat

A Classified Bibliography of Versions and Edi

Including Books, Parts, and Old and New Test

Apocrypha and Apocryphal Books.

A life-long collector and scholar of Bible translat

Mr. Chamberlin has accomplished in his work a va

service for scholars. This comprehensive annotated

of translations of the Bible into English include

Old and New Testaments, and it includes translati

the Apocrypha (those books that have been accep

part of the Canon by the Catholic and other churche

comprehensive work to list every translation in English
that could be considered "published." It is far more
exhaustive than any other work of its type, and far more
useful for the serious scholar and those endeavoring to
do more exhaustive research in other areas.

Mr. Chamberlin's work is far more comprehensive even then
the most authoritative and comprehensive works, that by
Margaret T. Hills, The English Bible in America (1777-
1957), published by the American Bible Society, and A.S.
Herbert, Historical Catalogue of Printed Editions of The
English Bible 1525-1961, published by the British and
Foreign Bible Society. It includes about five times as
many different translations as these works combined, a
comparison that indicates its level of increased
comprehensiveness over other works. The annotations in
this work are especially valuable. They include data that
is useful in understanding the significance and
usefulness of the work. They also include information
relative to revisions and various editions that are
available, information that is important for the scholar
and collector alike.

This Bibliography is more useful than either the National
Bible Union Catalogs or the British Library Catalogs for
several reasons.

     First, the above catalogs do not identify in their

entries as to whether the book is a new translation or not.

Second, neither set of volumes contains all translations, especially those private translations published locally and those contained in magazines, in theology books, and so forth, under the listing "Bible."

Third, these volumes are incredibly unwieldy to use.

Fourth, neither two sets of volumes _identifies_ the various editions of an entry. In fact, when viewing an entry, one does not know if the entry at hand is the first edition, or the second, or the third.

Fifth, _if_ a book is listed, it is listed only by the publication and edition information. This bibliography, on the other hand, lists it according to the date of the first publication, and then the publication history is given. In addition, many valuable annotations (information about the translation, its advantages, merits, and publication history) are provided.

Extremely close attention has been paid to accuracy in this work, and this includes both the unique spelling of the original (many of which show variations in spelling due to the period of history in which they were printed) and other nuances. This strict attention to accuracy will facilitate this work becoming widely recognized as the accurate and authoritative reference work that it is. Unfortunately, some authors do not pay close attention to accuracy, and various errors creep in -- a problem that can mar a work considerably. This volume utilizes, in many cases, the original work for the bibliographic data, facilitating a high level of accuracy for the various translations included. In addition, different bibliographies were compared and other reference works were utilized to insure that bibliographic information is as accurate as humanly possible.

Jerry Bergman, Ph.D.

Northwest Technical College

Archbold, Ohio 43502

REFERENCES

Asimov, Isaac. 1981. *Asimov's Guide to the Bible; Two Volumes in One, the Old and New Testaments.* New York, NY: Avennel Books.

Beegle, Dewey M. 1960. *God's Word Into English.* New York, NY: Harper and Brothers, Publishers.

Fromm, Erich. 1966. *You Shall Be As Gods; A Radical Interpretation of the Old Testament and Its Tradition.* New York, NY: Holt, Rinehart and Winston.

Gallup, George and David Poling. 1990. Americans and the Bible. *Bible Review,* 6:37-38.

_____. 1980. *The Search for America's Faith.* Nashville, TN: Abingdon Press.

Kroll, Paul. 1988. Who Really Wrote the Bible? *Plain Truth.* 53:7-10.

Lewis, Joseph. 1940. *The Bible Unmasked.* New York, NY: The Free Thought Press.

Wallis, Ethel Emily and Mary Angela Bennett. 1959. *Two Thousand Tongues to Go; The Story of the Wycliffe Bible Translators*. New York, NY: Harper and Brothers, Publishers.

Wood, Bryant. 1990. Did the Israelites Conquer Jericho? *Biblical Archaeology Review*. 17:44-57.

Explanatory Notes

<u>DATES</u>:

The listings are chronological by year with the undated entries first. The date is placed before each entry. Books, which were issued over several years, are listed under the earliest date. Books issued in volumes are listed under the date of the earliest volume. Books that bear more than one date (such as second, third, fourth... editions, reprints, etc.) are listed under the earliest date. The other dates are given in the description. Question marks (????, 19??) indicate unknown or undated publications.

ENTRIES:

The titles, in each entry, are given exactly as in the work. However, the titles used in this work do not necessarily reproduce the original type style, line breaks, punctuation, or capitalizations.

The name of the translator(s) is printed in boldface type next to the date for convenience. If the translator's name is not provided in the title, then it is listed as "Anonymous." If the translator(s) have been identified at a later date, then the name is given in square [ ] brackets in the entry. The complete title, when known, is listed next. Where no title was accessible, the contents of the translation is indicated within square brackets. The place of publication is shown next, followed by the publisher (or printer) and date.

ANNOTATIONS:

The annotations given are either taken from the Prefaces, Introductions, or dust covers to that particular version of the Bible, or are derived from one of the entries listed in the bibliography

located at the end of this book. Otherwise, the
author has provided his own annotations.

INDEX

The page numbers listed in boldface indicate the
entry name is listed on that page in bold print. The
non-bold page numbers indicate the entry is listed
on that page in either non-bold print only or both.

Parentheses in the index has several purposes.

1. The name in the parentheses may identify
    the initials that were used in the
    translation entry.

2. The name(s) inside the parentheses may be
    other names or initials that translation
    is known as.

3. When no page number accompanies an entry
    with a parentheses, the name in the
    parentheses is where the page number will
    be found.

THE HISTORICAL CATALOGUE

1

Bibles

COMPLETE BIBLE LISTINGS

???? **Priestly, Timothy**   The New Evangelical Family Bible... Paraphrased, [179?].

1388 **Wycliffe, John**   The Holy Bible. c1388
    1390 A Revision of Wycliffe's Bible. 1390?
        [There are only 150 copies still known to exist, all having been written before 1430.]

    1850 The Holy Bible...in the earliest English versions made from the Latin Vulgate by John Wycliffe and his followers; edited by the Rev. Josiah Forshall...and Sir Frederic Madden... 4 Vols. Oxford: University Press.
        Reprinted; New York: Ams Press, 1982.

    1877 A New Biblia Pauperum, being thirty-eight wood cuts illustrating the life, parables & miracles of our Blessed Lord and saviour Jesus Christ, with the proper descriptions thereof, extracted from the translation of the New Testament, by John Wiclif. London: Unwin Bros.
        Another edition; A Smaller Biblia Pauperum..., 1884.

    1881 The Books of Job, Psalms, Proverbs, Ecclesiastes and the Song of Solomon... Oxford: Clarendon Press.
        [Reprinted from the edition of 1850.]

    Also; MS. Bodey 959; Genesis-Baruch 3.20 in the earlier version of the Wycliffite Bible.

Edited by Conrad Lindberg. 6 Vols. Stockholm: Almquist & Wiksell, 1959.

1388 **Purvey, John**   See John Wycliffe, The New Testament 1380.

1390 **Hereford, Nicholas de**   See John Wycliffe, The Holy Bible, 1380.

1535 **Coverdale, Myles**   Biblia. The Bible, that is, The holy Scripture of the Olde and New Testaments faythfully and truly translated out of the Douche and Latyn into English. Zurich: Froschouer, 1535.
      [Known as 'Treacle' Bible. Jeremiah 8:22 states, "Is there no treacle in Gilead?". Also, this work has an error at Psalm 91:5 which reads, "So y thou shalt not nede to be afrayed for the bugges by night...".]

Another edition; 1st. folio Bible printed in England, 1537.

Again; 1st. quarto Bible printed in England, 1537.

Reprinted; London: Samuel Bagster & Sons, 1838.

Also, 1847.

Reprint; The Hexaplar Psalter: being the Book of Psalms in six English versions. Edited by William Aldis Wright... Cambridge: University Press, 1911.
      [Contains Coverdale's Psalms as printed in the Bible of 1535.]

Another; The Coverdale Psalter... Chicago: Printed for the Caxton Club, 1935. [This is a facsimile taken from the Coverdale Bible of 1535.]

Also; Our Prayer Book Psalter; containing Coverdale's Version from his 1535 Bible and the Prayer Book version by Coverdale from the Great Bible 1539-1544; Printed side by side. With an Introduction and Notes on the Sources of Coverdale's rendering by Ernest Clapton... London: Society for Promoting Christian Knowledge, 1934.

Reprinted; The Coverdale Bible 1535; with an Introduction by the Rev. Professor S.L. Greenslade, D.D., F.B.A. Kent, England: Wm. Dawson & Sons, Ltd., 1975.

1537 **Matthew, Thomas**   The Byble which is all the holy Scripture: In whych are contayned the Olde and Newe

Testament truly and purely translated into Englysh
by Thomas Matthew. Esaye.j. Hearcken to ye heauens
and thou earth geaue eare: For the Lorde speaketh.
M,D,XXXVII, Set forth with the Kinges most gracyous
lycece. [Antwerp: Printed for R. Grafton and E.
Whitchurch of London, 1537.]
>[Thomas Matthew is commonly treated as a pseudonym of
>John Rogers. This work is Tyndale's version and
>Coverdale's version edited by Matthew. Includes Roger's
>translation of the Prayer of Manasses.]

>[1538 edition is reported but no known copies exist.]

Reprinted; London: Thomas Raynalde, and William
Hyll..., 1549. [Also; University Microfilm, No.
1821.]

Reprinted; Nicolas Hyll, 1551.

Reprinted; ...Modern spelling, punctuation and
introduction by John Sawyer. The Martyrs Bible
Series. Vol. Two. Milford, OH John the Baptist
Printing Ministry, 1989.

>[See Anonymous, The Byble, 1549; edited by Edmund
>Becke.]

1537 **Nycolson, James**   Biblia. The Byble, that
is the holy Scrypture of the Olde and New Testament,
faythfully translated in Englysh, and newly ouersene
& corrected. M.D.XXXVII. S. Paul. II. Tessa. III.
Praye for vs, that the worde of God maye haue for
passage and be glorified. S. Paul. II. Colloss. III
Let the worde of Christ dwell in you plenteously in
al wysedome. Josue. I. Let not the Boke of this lawe
departe out of thy mouth, but exercyse thy selfe
therin daye and nyght, that thou mayest kepe and do
euery thynge accordyng to it that is wrytten therin.
Imprynted in Sowthwarke for James Nycolson. 1537.

1539 **Great Bible (Cranmer's Bible)**   The Byble in
Englyshe, that is to saye the content of all the
holy scrypture, bothe of ye olde and newe testament,
truly translated after the veryte of the Hebrue and
Greke textes, by ye dylygent studye of dyuerse
excellent learned men, expert in theforsayde tonges.
Prynted by Rychard Grafton & Edward Whitchurch. Cum
priuilegio ad imprimen- dum solum. 1539.
>[Published under the auspices of Thomas, Lord Crumwell;
>finished in Apryll 1539. This work is often referred to
>erroneously as "Cranmer's Bible". This is a revision by
>Coverdale of Matthew's Bible. Between 1539 and 1541,
>this work was revised four times. This was the first
>Bible authorized to be read in the Churches. Usually
>called the "Great Bible" for its great size (337x235).
>Also called the "Chained Bible."]

4

3BIBLES

[The Deity is rendered "Jehovah" at Psalm 33:12;
"Iehouah" at Psalm 83:18.]

Other editions; 1549, 1550, 1552, 1553, 1553
(quarto edition), 1561, 1562, 1566, 1568.

Another edition; 1569.
[There are at least three 1569 editions, while
generally agreeing so closely as to read together
page for page, do differ in many small points, and
are distinct issues.]

1539 The new testament in Englysche traslated
after the text of master Erasmus.
Roterodame in Anno. 1539. Let the worde
of Chryst dwell in you plenteously in all
wysdome. Collo, iii.c. London: R.
Grafton & E. Whitchurch.
Other editions; 1540, 1546, 1547, 1548,
1550, 1551.

1540 The Byble in Englyshe...
[A reprint in smaller sixe (287x197) of
1539 1st edition with some correction and
revision.]

1540 Second Edition. (337x233)
1540 Third Edition. (337x237)
1541 Fourth Edition. (348x237)
1541 Fifth Edition. (340x236)
1541 Sixth Edition. (354x238)
1541 Seventh Edition. (335x237)

Also; The Psalter of the Great Bible of 1539...
Edited with introduction and notes by John
Earle... Cambridge: J. Palmer; London: for
Macmillan and Co., 1894.

[See Psalms, 1911 William Aldis Wright, Hexapla
Psalter; See New Testament, 1962 Luther Weigle, N.T.
Octapla; See New Testament, 1841 English Hexapla.]

1539 **Taverner, Richard** The Most Sacred Bible, Whiche
is the holy scripture, conteyning the old and new
testament, translated into English, and newly
recognised with great diligence after most faythful
exemplars, by Rychard Teverner Harken thou heuen,
and thou earth gyue eare: for the Lorde speaketh.
Esaie. i. Prynted at London in Fletestrete at the
sygne of the sonne by John Byddell, for Thomas
M.D.XXXIX. (1539)
[A slight revision of Matthew's Bible of 1537.]

Reprinted; 2 Vols. Ann Arbor, MI: University
Microfilms, 1972.

[Also; See Complete Bibles, 1549 Anonymous, The ByBle, [Edmund Becke] for a revision of Taverner.]

1549 **Anonymous**   The Byble, that is to say, al the holy Scripture conteined in the olde & new Testament, faythfully set furth according to ye Coppy of Thomas Mathewes trauslacio, wherunto are added certaine learned Prologes, & Annotacios for the better vnderstanding of many hard places thorowout the whole Byble. Esay. i. Hearken to ye heauens, & thou earth geue eare: for the Lorde speaketh. Imprinted at London by Ihon Day dwellyng ouer Aldersgate. Cum gratia et priuilegio ad-imprimendum solum. Anno a. M.D.Li. (1549-1551)
> [The title is misleading. The Old Testament and Apocrypha are a revised edition of Taverner's version, apparently prepared by Edmund Becke, the editor of this Bible.]
>
> [This 1551 edition also has the 'wife-beater' note at I Peter 3.]

1549 The second parte of the ByBle, containyng these Bookes followyng The boke of Josua...The boke of Hiob.
> [Taverner's version edited by Edmund Becke.]

1549 The volume of the bokes called Apocripha: Coteining these bokes folowing. The thyrd boke of Esdras...The . iii . boke of Machabees.
> [Herbert lists this as Taverner's version. The text actually agrees with Taverner's version, as revised by Becke, and published by Day in his folio Bible of 1551. According to Lea Wilson, the books 3 Esdras, Tobit, and Judith are an entirely new translation. 3 Maccabees appears here for the first time in English.]

1550 The thyrde parte of the Byble conteynynge these bokes The Psalter. The Prouerbes. Ecclesiastes. Cantica Canticoru.
> [Taverner's version as revised by Edmund Becke.]

1550 The Boke of the Prophetes. Esaye...Malachi.
> [Taverner's version as revised by Edmund Becke.]

1551 The fyrste parte of the Bible called the . v . bookes of Moses translated by . W T . wyth all his prologes before euery boke, and certeine learned notes vpon many harde wordes. Genesis. Exodus.

Leuiticus. Numeri. Deuteronomium. Anno
Dom. M.D.L.I. (1551)
[Taverner's version as revised by Edmund
Becke.]

1549 **Anonymous**   The ByBle, that is to say all the holy
Scripture: In whych are cotayned the Olde and New
Testamente, truly & purely traslated into English,
& nowe lately with greate industry & diligece
recongnised. Esaye. i. Hearken to ye heauens, and
thou earthe geue eare: For the Lorde speaketh.
Imprynted at London by Jhon Daye, dwelling at
Aldersgate, and William Seres, dwelling in Peter
Colledge. Cum gratia et Priuilegio ad Imprimendum
solum. xvii. day of August. M.Ḋ.XLIX.
[A reprint of Matthew's Bible of 1537, with notes, etc.,
revised, edited by Edmund Becke.]

[This translation is often called the 'Bugge' Bible even
though the error first appeared in Coverdale's Bible of
1535 (see listing no. 277). Psalm 91:5 reads "So y thou
shalt not nede to be afrayed for the Bugges by
night..."]

[Also known as the 'Wife-beater' Bible. The note at 1
Peter 3 reads "And if she be not obedient and helpful
unto him, endeavoreth to beat the fear of God into her
head."]

1553 **Jugge, Richard**   The whole Byble, That is
the holye Scripture, of the olde and new Testament,
faithfullye translated into Englyshe by Miles
Couerdale, and newly ouersene and correcte.
M.D.Liii. ij. Tessa. iij. Praye...glorifiyed.
Prynted at London by Rycharde Jugge, dwellynge at
the North dore of Powles, at the synge of the Byble.
1553.

1560 **Geneva Version**   The Bible and Holy Scriptvres
conteyned in the Olde and Newe Testament. Translated
according to the Ebrue and greke, and conferred With
the best translations in diuers languages. With
moste profitable annotations vpon all the hard
places, and other things of great importance as may
appeare in the Epistle to the Reader.   At Geneva.
Printed by Rouland Hall. M.D.LX. [1560]
[This was the earliest English Bible to be printed in
Roman letters and with verse divisions. Translated by W.
Whittingham, Anthony Gilby, Thomas Sampson, M.
Coverdale, and others. They used the Great Bible for the
O.T. (1550 edition) with help from the Hebrew and Latin
texts. The N.T. is a careful revision of Whittingham's
Testament of 1557 due to a further comparison with
Beza's Latin translation. Whittingham also began another
practice which was continued to the Revised Version,
that of italicized words, inserted to complete the sense
of a passage, but which was lacking in the original
languages. Tomson's revision of the N.T. began to be

incorporated in Geneva Version in 1576. The blackletter type was used for all Geneva Bibles not having Tomson's N.T. By 1644, this work had gone through 140 editions, with various and sundry changes. The Geneva Bible rivaled even the KJV in popularity after 1611, Influenced the KJV more than any other version. Calvinistic in tone. The second edition is known by various names: 'Breeches Bible': 'Whig Bible'; 'Place-Maker's Bible' (Mt.5:9 reads "Blessed are the Place-makers." Also has an error at Luke 26 "Christ condemnth the poore widdowe." The Deity is rendered "Iehouah" at Genesis 22:14 & Psalm 83:18.]

1557 The Psalmes of David Translated accordyng to the veritie and truth of the Ebrue, with annotations moste profitable.

1560 The Newe Testament of ovr Lord Iesvs Christ Conferred Diligently with the Greke, and best approued translations in diuers languages. Geneva.
     [First edition of Geneva N.T. published separately.]

     Other editions; 1575, 1576, 1619.

1580 The Third Part of the Bible, (after some division) conteyning fiue excellent bookes, most commodious for all Christians: Faithfully translated... with... Annotations... Imprinted at London by Christopher Barker, printer to Queenes Maiestie. 1580. Cum gratia & priuilegio. Again, 1583, 1614.

1842 The New Testament... A facsimile reprint of the Genevan Testament, 1557; with the marginal annotations and references, the initial and other wood cuts, prefaces and index. London: for S. Bagster & Son.

Also; A facsimile of the 1560 edition, with an introduction by Lloyd E. Bery. Madison: University of Wisconsin Press, 1969.

[See N.T. listing - 1576 Lauerence Tomson, The New Testament; See N.T. listing - 1962 Luther Weigle, N.T. Octapla; See N.T. listing -1841 English Hexapla; See Psalms listing - 1911 William Aldis Wright, Hexapla Psalter.]

[Between 1560 and 1644 there have been at least 140 editions of the Geneva Version. Some are dated 1562, 1570, 1576, 1577, 1578, 1579, 1580, 1581, 1582, 1583, 1584, 1585, 1586, 1587, 1588, 1589, 1590, 1591, 1592, 1593, 1594, 1596, 1597, 1598, 1599, 1600, 1601, 1602, 1603, 1605, 1606, 1607, 1608, 1609, 1610, 1611, 1614, 1615.]

[See Complete Bibles, 1599 Geneva-Thomson-Junius, The Bible; See New Testament, 1602 Geneva-Thomson-Junius, The N.T.]

1568 **Bishops' Bible**   The.holie.Bible. conteynyng the olde Testament and the newe. London: R. Jugge, 1568.

[The Bishops' Bible was a revision of the Great Bible. It is sometimes referred to as "Parker's Bible" out of acknowledgement of Matthew Parker, Archbishop of Canterbury one of the foremost Reformation Leaders in England. This work was undertaken at his request, with the assistance of many Bishops and well-known Biblical Scholars, and carried on under his inspection and published at his expense. The first major revision, still retaining Title of Bishops' Bible, was issued in 1572; its next major revision was 1611 when it became the Authorised Version, or King James Version. It went through approx. 20 editions between 1568-1611, with each edition altered or varying from all the former. These were mainly printer alterations, but a number being printers efforts to revise.]

   Some of the Revisors:
W. Alley (Bishop of Exeter)
R. Davies (Bishop of St. David's)
E. Sandys (Bishop of Worcester)
T. Bentham (Bishop of Lichfield & Coventry)
R. Cox (Bishop of Ely)
A. Pierson (Prebendary of Canterbury)
A. Perne (Dean of Ely)
R. Horne (Bishop of Winchester)
E. Grindal (Bishop of London)
J. Parkhurst (Bishop of Norwich)
E. Guest (Bishop of Rochester) replaced by Thomas Bickley
G. Goodman (Dean of Westminster)
W. Barlow (Bishop of Chichester)
E. Scambler (Bishop of Peterborough)
N. Bullingham (Bishop of Lincoln)
H. Jones (Bishop of Llanduff)
T. Cole
T. Beacon

Other editions; 1569 (Contains traces of revisions.), 1572 (N.T. Revised), 1573?, 1574, 1575, 1576, 1577, 1578, 1584, 1585, 1588, 1591, 1595, 1602.

1568? The New Testament. [The earliest known edition of the N.T. of the Bishops' version.]

1572 The Newe Testament... London: Richard Watkins.
   [Agrees with N.T. in Bishops' Bible (1572 edition).]

   Other editions; 1573?, 1575, 1578?, 1579, 1581, 1582, 1595, 1596, 1598, 1600, 1605, 1606, 1608, 1613, 1614, 1615, 1617.

[See New Testament listing, 1589 William Fulke, The N.T.; See New Testament listing, 1962 Luther A. Weigle, N.T. Octapla; See Psalms, 1911 William Aldis Wright, Hexapla Psalter.]

1599 **Geneva-Tomson-Junius Bible**   The Bible, that is... With ...Annotations... Imprinted at London by the Deputies of Christopher Barker... 1599

[This work contains the Genevan Old Testament; Laurence Tomson New Testament except Revelation; Francis Junius Revelation which was translated by Thomas Barbar.]

Other editions; 1603, 1610, 1611 [contains an error at John 6:67 "Judas" for "Jesus"], 1612, 1615, 1616, 1633, 1640, 1644.

Also; The New Testament of ovr Lord Iesvs Christ, Translated out of Greeke by Theod. Beza: With briefe Summaries... Englished by L. Tomson. Together with the Annotations of Fr. Junius vpon the Reuelation of S. John. Imprinted at London by Robert Barker, Printer to Queenes most Excellent Maiestie. Anno 1602.
Also, 1610.

1609 **Douay-Rheims Version**

1582 The Nevv Testament of Iesvs Christ, translated faithfvlly into English, out of the authentical Latin, according to the best corrected copies of the same, diligently conferred vvith the Greeke and other editions in diuers language: Vvith Argvments of bookes and chapters, Annotations, and other necessarie helpes, for the better vnderstanding of the text, and especially for the discouerie of the Corrvptions of diuers late translations, and for cleering the Controversies in Religion, of these daies: In the English College of Rhemes. Psalm 118...That is, Al things that are readde... Printed at Rhemes, by Iohn Fogny. 1582.

[Translated from the Vulgate by Gregory Martin, under the supervision of William Allen and Richard Bristow.]

Second edition; Printed at Antvverp by Daniel Vervliet, 1600.

Third edition; Printed at Antvverp by James Seldenslach, 1621.

Fourth edition, 1630.

Reprint; Ilkley: Scholar Press, 1975.

1609 [Vol. I]   The Old Testament, translated
     from the Latin Vulgate, by the Roman
     Catholic College of Douay. L. Kellam.
     [Genesis - Job] [Sometimes called 'Rosin' Bible.
     Jeremiah 8:22 "Is there no rosin in Galand?"]
     Second edition, 1635.

1610 The Holie Bible faithfvlly translated
     into English, ovt of the avthentical
     Latin. Diligently conferred with the
     Hebrew, Greege, and other Editions in
     diuers languages. With Argvments of the
     Bookes,   and   Chapters: Annotations:
     Tables: and other helps, for better
     vnderstanding of the text: for
     discouverie of Corrvptions in some late
     translations: and   for   clearing
     Controversies in Religion. By the English
     College of Doway. Hauriets aquas in
     gaudio de fontibus Saluatoris. Isaiae.
     12. You shal draw waters in ioy out of
     the Sauiours fountaines. 2 Vols. Printed
     at Doway by Lavrence Kellam, at the signe
     of the holie Lambe. M. DC. X.
          [Vol. 2; Psalms-4 Esdras]

Another Edition; 5 Vols. in 3. Revised.
"Clementin Edition", 1750.

[See New Testament listing, 1841 English Hexapla; See
New Testament listing, 1962 Luther Weigle, N.T.
Octapla.]

[Many reprints.]

1611 **Authorised Version**   The Holy Bible, Conteyning
     the Old Testament, and the New: Newly Translated out
     of the Originall tongues: & with the former
     Translations diligently compared and reuised, by his
     Maiesties speciall Comandement. Appointed to be read
     in Churches. Imprinted at London by ·Robert Barker,
     Printer to the Kings most Excellant Maiestie. Anno
     Dom. 1611.
          [This is more commonly referred to as the AV or KING
          JAMES VERSION, (and on occasion as the St. James
          Version!). It is recognized that from 1611 to 1614
          there are two distinct series of editions in various
          sizes, which differ in many minor points of typography,
          and are generally distinguished by the names 'He' Bible
          and 'She' Bible. In fact, the KJV text usually differs
          in minor points from edition to edition, printer to
          printer. The 'She' Bible came to be the accepted wording
          or text. This work has been revised a numberless amount
          of times, moreover all the revisions, corrections and
          alterations which have been proven of interest and value
          will be listed here. Revised in 1613, 1629, 1638 and
          1683 by Dr. Scattergood. Revised in 1769 by Dr. Blayney

and Oxford Press, who attempted to modernize the diction of the KJV. A minor revision of major importance for its influence. (See Benjamin Blayney, 1769.]

SPECIAL EDITIONS;

- 1613 Folio edition with small print (362X225)
- 1613 1st. black-letter quarto edition (199X138)
- 1616 A new form of quarto in roman type (199x136)
- 1616 1st. small folio edition (roman type) (292x178)
- 1617 3rd. distinct folio edition, printed in large black-letter (362x232)
- 1618 The earliest duodecimo edition (140x69)
- 1629 1st. Cambridge edition (256x167)
- 1630 1st. quarto edition printed at Cambridge (211x149)
- 1633 1st. Edinburgh: edition (158x93)
- 1634 4th. distinct folio printed in large black-letter (364x230)
- 1634 1st. duodecimo edition printed in Scotland (138x71)
- 1637 2nd. octavo edition printed in Scotland (159x99)
- 1638 See Anonymous, Holy Bible (329x205)
- 1640 Last folio edition in large black-letter between 1611-1640 (363x230)
- 1642 KJV with notes of the Geneva Bible and Junius' Annotations on Revelation (327x198)
- 1653 'Quakers' Bible' (London: for Giles Calvert, and are to be sold at the Sign of the Black-spread-Eagle, near the west end of Pauls.)
- 1659 Diglot; KJV and Beza's Latin Testament.
- 1675 1st. English Bible printed at Oxford.
- 1679 2nd. edition printed at Oxford.
- 1833 Reprint in roman type of 1st edition of 1611 (30x23.5)
- 1896 A miniature facsimile edition of 25,000 copies. (4.5x3)
- 1904 The 91st Psalm: reprint from the King James version. Hingham Centre, Mass.: Village Press.

Again; Hingham Centre, Mass.:
Sold by W. Dwigging, 1906.

CURIOUS EDITIONS;
1611 Great "He" Bible. The first issue of
the first edition. Ruth iii:15 "and
he went into the city".

1611 Great "She" Bible. The second issue
of the first edition. Ruth iii: 15
"and she went into the city".

1611 "Judas" Bible. Misprints of "Judas"
for "Jesus" at Matthew xxvi:36.

1631 "Wicked" Bible. This Bible is so-
called "Wicked" because the negative
is left out of the Seventh
Commandment at Exodus xx:14.

1638 "Forgotten Sins" Bible. See Luke
vii:47.

1641 "More Sea" Bible. From Rev.xxi:1.
"And there was more sea".

1653 "Unrighteous" or Field's Bible. This
work was printed by John Field and
contains many errors. Some of them
are; I Corinthians vi:9, "Know ye
not that the unrighteous shall
inherit the kingdom of God?"; Matt.
vi:24, "Ye cannot serve and Mammon"
omitting "God".

1702 "Printers" Bible. Psalms 119:161
states, "Printers (instead of
'Princes') have persecuted me
without cause."

1711 "Profit" Bible. A Oxford edition, at
Isaiah lvii:12 states, "I will
declare thy righteousness, and thy
works: for they shall profit thee"
instead of "Shall not profit thee."

1716 "Sin On" Bible. The first English
Bible printed in Ireland contains in
Isaiah: "Sin on more" for "Sin no
more". This error was not discovered
until the entire impression of 8,000
copies were bound and partly
distributed.

1717 "Vinegar" Bible. This work received its name from an error in the headline of St. Luke xx, which reads: "The Parable of the Vinegar" instead of the "Vineyard".

1746 "Sting" Bible. Mark vii:37, "The sting of his tongue" and not "string".

1792 "Denial" Bible. An Oxford edition in St. Luke xxii:34, where Philip, instead of Peter, is named to deny Jesus.

1801 "Murderers" Bible. St. Jude 16, the word "murderers" is used instead of "murmurers".

1802 "Discharge" Bible. 1 Tim. v:21 states, "I discharge thee before God" for "I charge thee".

1804 "Lions" Bible. This Bible pre-eminently distinguished for its many errors. A few of them are; Numbers xxxv:18, " The murderer shall surely be put together" for "to death"; I Kings vii:19, "Out of thy lions" instead of "loins"; and Gal.v:17, "For the flesh lusteth after the spirit" for "against".

1805 "To-Remain" Bible. This was published by the Bible Society at Cambridge, having the words "to remain" inserted in Galatians iv:29, instead of a comma.

1806 "Standing Fishes" Bible. From Ezekiel xlvii:10, "the fishes shall stand" and not "fishers".

1807 "Ears to ear" Bible. Matthew xiii:43 reads, "Who hath ears to ears", instead of "hear"; and Hebrews ix:14 states, "How much more shall the blood of Christ...purge your conscience from good works (should be 'dead works') to serve the living God?"

1810 "Wife-Hater" Bible. Luke xiv:26 reads, "If any man come to me, and hate not hid father...yea, and his own wife (should be 'life') also, he cannot be my disciple."

1823 "Camels" Bible. Misprint at Genesis xxiv:61, "And Rebekah arose, and her camels", for "damsels".

1829 "Large Family" Bible. Oxford's version has at Isaiah lxvi:9, "Shall I bring to the birth, and not cease (instead of 'cause') to bring forth."

n.d. "Fool" Bible. In an edition printed during the reign of Charles I, the text of Psalm xiv:1 reads, "The fool hath said in his heart there is a God." For which error, the printers were fined 3000 Pounds and all copies suppressed.

[There are many other editions with errors in them, but the above curious Bibles are the most well known and collectible.]

1629 **Anonymous**   The Holy Bible... Cambridge: University of Cambridge, Thomas and John Buck, 1629.
> ["...the text appears to have undergone a complete revision, although...no record of such having been done by authority..."]

1638 **Anonymous**   Holy Bible...Cambridge: Printers to the University of Cambridge; Buck and Roger Daniel, 1638.
> ["The authentique corrected 'Cambridge Bible', revised Mandato Regid, by the learned Doctor Ward, Doctor Goad of Hadley, Mr. Boyse, Mr. Mead, &". "The revisers took special pains to render uniform the use of italics; and they also introduced a certain number of new readings..." This remained the standard text until Dr. Paris' Cambridge edition of 1762.]

1657 **Haak, Theodore**   The Dutch Annotations upon the whole Bible: or, all the Holy Canonical Scriptures of the Old and New Testament, together with, and according to their own Translation of all the Text: as both the one and the other were ordered and appointed by the Synod of Dort, 1618, and published by Authority, 1637. Now faithfully communicated to the use of Great Britain, in English. Whereunto is prefixed an exact Narrative touching the whole Work, and this Translation. By Theodore Haak, Esq. 2 Vols. London: Henry Hills, for John Rothwell, Joshua Kirton and Richard Tomlins, 1657.

1709 **Wells, Edward**   An Help for the more Easy and Clear Understanding of... Oxford: Printed at the Theater. And sold by Will. Wells Bookseller in Oxford: James Knapton at the Crown, and Jonah Bowyer at the Rose in St. Paul's Church Yard, London. 1709-1715.

    1713 An Help...The Epistle to the Hebrews.
    1715 An Help...The Catholic Epistles.
    1716 An Help...Daniel.
    1717 An Help...The Revelation of St. John.
    1718 An Help...St. Matthew & St. Mark.
    1719 An Help...St. Luke & the Acts.
    1719 An Help...St. John's Gospel.
    1718 An Help...A Treatise on the Harmony of the four Gospels, with a table.
    1723 An Help...The Twelve Lesser Prophets.
    1724 An Help...(Pentateuch), 1724-1725.
    1725 An Help...Exodus, Leviticus, Numbers, and Deuteronomy.
    1725 An Help...Joshua, Judges, and Ruth.
    1726 An Help...The Two books of Samuel and two of Kings.
    1727 An Help...Chronicles, Ezra, Nehemiah, and Esther.
    1727 An Help...Job, Psalms, Proverbs, Ecclesiastes, and Canticles.
    1728 An Help...Isaiah, Jeremiah, and Lamentations.
    1728 An Help...Ezechiel.

1715 **Anonymous**   Bible (O.T. & N.T.) with annotations wherein mistakes in the present version were corrected. (from a sample page on the wall at Arvada, Colorado. Seen by Seth Wilson in 1974)

1718 **Wells, Edward**   The Common Translation Corrected. Oxford: 1718-1724.

    1719 New Testament, Greek and English with a paraphrase and annotations by Edward Wells.

    1724 Old Testament, Hebrew and English with a paraphrase and annotations by Edward Wells.
       [KJV corrected with paraphrase and notes.]

1724 **Harris, B.**   The Holy Bible...Done into Verse, 1724.

1749 **Challoner, Richard**   The Holy Bible, translated from the Latin Vulgat...first published by the English College at Douay, Anno 1609. Newly revised, and corrected, according to the Clementin Edition of the Scriptures. With annotations for clearing up the principal difficulties of Holy Writ... 4 Vols. [Dublin?] 1750.

1749 N.T. First revision.
[Incorporates most of the changes of the 1738 edition (Richard Challoner & Francis Blyth).]

1750 O.T. First revision. (2 Vols.)

1750 N.T. Second revision. (1 Vol.)

1752 N.T. Third revision. (2 Vols.)

1763 - 1764 O.T. Second revision. (4 Vols.)

1764 N.T. Fourth revision.

1772 N.T. Fifth revision.

1790 The Holy Bible... 2 Vols. Philadelphia: Carey, Stewart & Co., 1790.
[1st. American edition based on Challoner's Second Edition, 1763-64.]

1796 The Holy Bible... 4 Vols.   Edinburgh: John Moir, 1796.

1942 The New Testament... Rheims...1582. As revised by Dr. Challoner, London, A.D. 1752... New York: The Douay Bible House.
[Pope states, "This edition is the best text in the American tradition."]

1762 **Anonymous**   The Holy Bible... Cambridge: J. Bentham, 1762.
["The 'Standard' edition prepared by Dr. F.S. Paris. In this Bible a serious attempt was made to correct the text of the King James Version..."]

1764 **Purver, Anthony**   A new and literal translation of all the books of the Old and New Testament; with notes critical and explanatory. By Anthony Purver... 2 Vols. London: Printed by W. Richardson and S. Clark; and sold by William Johnston, 1764.
[A portion of Purver's translation was published in parts about 1742 by Felix Farley, but received little support. In 1763, Dr. John Fothergill purchased the copyright from Purver, and published a folio.]

[Purver's Bible is often referred to as "The Quaker Bible".]

1766 **Anonymous**   The Universal Bible...Old and New Testament. Illustrated with parallel Scriptures and notes... The whole intended and accommodated to the use and understanding of every Christian and the benefit of all families. Edinburgh: John Reid, 1766.
[The N.T. title page states that it was edited by John Guyse.]

1769 **Blayney, Benjamin**   The Holy Bible... Oxford: T. Wright and W. Gill, 1769. [Folio]
> [Blayney and Oxford Press produced the KING JAMES BIBLE in a revised text used as a standard ever since. This was an attempted to modernize the diction of the KJV. Blayney followed the lines of Dr. Paris' Cambridge edition of 1762 and incorporated most of Paris' improvements, increased his marginalia, and repeated not a few of his errors. A minor revision of major importance for its influence. Also known as the "Oxford Standard Edition". Also, See Complete Bibles, 1611 Authorised Version.]

> Another edition; 1769. [Quarto]

> Other editions; 1776, 1790.

> N.T. Reprinted; 1792.

> Revised; 2 Vols.   Cambridge: Archdeacon & Burges, 1796.

> Reprint of the Apocrypha Books; Arranged in paragraphs and parallelisms, by T.W. Coit... Cambridge: Printed & Published by Manson & Grant..., 1835.

1773 **Southwell, Henry**   The Universal Family Bible: or Christian's Divine Library... Illustrated with notes &c. Wherein the mistranslations are corrected by... Henry Southwell London: for J. Cooke.
> [H. Southwell lent his name to this work for a fee. The real compiler was Robert Sanders. Also published in 1775.]

1778 **Fellows, John**   The Bible in Verse. 4 Vols., 1778.

1785 **Cruttwell, Clement** (Editor)   The Holy Bible; containing the Books of the Old and New Testaments, and the Apocrypha. Carefully printed from the First Edition (compared with others) of the Present [KJV] Translation. With notes by the Right Reverend father in God, Thomas Wilson, D.D. Lord Bishop of Sodor and Man. And various renderings, collected from other Translations by the Reverend Clement Cruttwell, the editor. 3 Vols.   Bath: Printed by R. Cruttwell, 1785.
> [The Editor translated Third Maccabees.]

1786 **Anonymous**   The Holy Bible...with explanatory notes ...by ... Clement XIV... Translated from the Latin by An English Divine... London: G. Kearsley, 1786.
> [The AV with notes at the bottom of the pages which are falsely attributed to Pope Clement XIV.]

1791 **Fitzpatrick, H.** Douay-Rhemish Bible...Newly Revised
     and Corrected. Dublin: Richard Cross, 1791.
     [This is the Douay Bible that received the expressed
     sanction of Dr. Troy and is often known in its various
     editions as 'Troy Bible'.]

1791 **MacMahon, Rev. Bernard**   The Holy Bible... Dublin:
     Reilly, 1791.
     [This is MacMahon's first revision of the O.T., second
     revision of the N.T., called "the fifth edition".]

     Also; MacMahon's second revision of the O.T.,
     third revision of the N.T., called "the sixth
     edition". Dublin: Reilly.

     Also; The Holy Bible, translated from the Latin
     Vulgate...   with   annotations   by   ...Dr.
     Challoner,   together   with   references...
     London: Richardson & Son, 1847?
     [A composite text from the various Challoner
     editions and MacMahon's revisions.]

1794 **Butler, Joseph**   The Christian's New and Complete
     ...Universal Family Bible, 1794.

1799 **Anonymous**   A Revised Translation and Interpretation
     of the Sacred Scriptures, after the Eastern manner,
     from   concurrent   authorities   of   the   critics,
     interpreters, and commentators, copies and versions:
     showing that the inspired writings contain the seeds
     of valuable sciences, being the source whence the
     ancient philosophers derived them, also the ancient
     histories and greatest antiquities, and are the most
     entertaining as well as instructing to both the
     curious   and   the   serious.   With   an   appendix...
     London: G. Robinson and Co., 1799.
     [Orme (p.303) and Horne (p.260) ascribe this version to
     David Macrae (or McRae) whose name is also given as J.M.
     Ray.]

     Another edition; Revised, corrected & improved,
     "with philosophical and medical commentary". 3
     Vols.   Glasgow: Printed for R. Hutchinson &
     Co., 1815.

1800 **Kendall, John**   The Holy Scriptures of the Old and
     New Testament by way of Abstract... 2 Vols. London:
     William Phillips, 1800.
     [An abbreviation with some alteration to words and
     expressions of the KJV.]

1802 **Reeves, John**   The Holy Bible... 10 Vols. London:
     J. Crowder and Others, 1802.
     [Known as "Reeves' Bible". "The text is a careful
     reprint of Blayney's Bible of 1769 with certain
     changes."]

Another edition; 4 Vols. [Without the Apocrypha and Explanatory Notes.], 1802.

Also; Without the Apocrypha, Explanatory Notes, and other matter. This is a smaller Edition. London: Printed for J. Reeves by C. Whittingham, at the Chiswick Press, 1811.

1808 **Thomson, Charles**   The Holy Bible, containing the Old and New Covenant, Commonly Called the Old and New Testament: Translated from the Greek, by Charles Thomson, Late Secretary to the Congress of the United States. 4 Vols.   Philadelphia: Printed by Jane Aitken, 1808.
    Vol. I.   Genesis - I Samuel
    Vol. II.   II Samuel - Psalms
    Vol. III. Proverbs - Malachi
    Vol. IV.   New Testament

1811 **Haydock, George Leo**   The Holy Bible, translated from The Latin Vulgate... With useful notes... selected from the most eminent commentators... By...Geo. Leo Haydock... Enriched with... engravings. 2 Vols. Manchester: T. Haydock, 1811-14.
    Again; 1831.

Another edition; The Holy Bible, translated from the Latin Vulgate... With Useful Notes... by the Rev. George Leo Haydock... New York: Edward Dunigan and Brother, 1852.
    [First issued in 38 parts. Editing started by Rev. J.R. Bayley & completed by Rev. J. MacMahon. While many corrections were made, some errors remained.]

    Again, 1856.

1811 **Haydock, Thomas**   The Holy Bible, translated from the Latin Vulgate: Diligently compared with the Hebrew, Greek, and other editions in divers Languages. The Old Testament, first published by the English College at Doway, A.D. 1609. And the New Testament, first published by the English College at Rhemes, A.D.1582. With annotations, references, and an historical and chronological index. Manchester: 1811-1814.
    [The O.T. is substantially Challoner's first edition (1750) and the N.T. that of the third edition (1752). However, while reproducing Challoner's third ed., he followed MacMahon's edition of 1783, 1791, 1794, 1803, and 1810, where these differ from that of 1752. In other words, he used the seven to eight hundred "improvements" MacMahon made over Challoner. Haydock does have some independent renderings. Pope stated,"...Haydock's was essentially an eclectic text..."]

Second edition; By George Leo Haydock, 1813. [The first edition (1811-1814) was followed by a second before the first ed. was completed.

Third edition; Hamil's edition. Dublin, 1822-1824. [Abridged and full of errors]

Fourth edition; London, Edinburgh & Glasgow, 1845-1848; New York, 1852.

Fifth edition; With notes abridged by Husenbeth, 1853.
        Again, 1854.

Sixth edition; with a very valuable Introduction, by Oakeley and Law, 1874-1878.

Also; The Holy Bible... By George Leo Haydock. New York: T. Kelly, n.d. [1885] [This claims to be the "only correct and unabridged edition now issued".]

1817 **Boothroyd, Benjamin**   A New Family Bible, and improved version, from corrected texts of the originals; with notes critical and explanatory, and short practical reflections ...with a general introduction...By the Rev. B. Boothroyd... 3 Vols. Huddersfield: Printed for the Author, and others, by William Moore, 1817.
        Again, 1824.

New edition, revised, 1835.

An Abridged Edition; London: James Duncan, 1836.

Another edition; Translated from Corrected Texts. London: Partridge & Oakey, 1853.

1818 **Bellamy, John**   The Holy Bible, newly translated from the original Hebrew: with notes critical and explanatory...
        [See Old Testament Selections for the complete entry.]

1822 **Hamil, Rev. Dr.**   The Holy Bible, translated from the Latin Vulgate: Diligently compared with the Hebrew, Greek, and other editions in divers... by... Haydock...inaccuracies of former edition corrected ...2 Vols. Dublin: Thomas Haydock, 1822.
        [Roman Catholic]

1825 **Alger, Israel**   The Pronouncing Bible. The Holy Bible, containing the Old and New Testaments; Translated out of the Original Tongues, and with the former Translations diligently compared and revised. The proper Names of which, and numerous other words,

being accurately accented in the Text and divided into syllables, as they ought to be pronounced, according to the Orthoepy of John Walker, as contained in his critical pronouncing Dictionary and Key to the Classical pronunciation of Greek, Latin, and Scripture proper Names. By Israel Alger, Jun., A.M. Boston: Printed and Published by Lincoln & Edmands, No. 59 Washington-Street (53 Cornhill). Stereotyped by T.H. Carter & Co., 1825.
[Reissued with a new title in 1826 by the same Publishers.]

Other editions, 1829, 1848, 1855.

1825 **Murray, Daniel**   The Holy Bible... with Annotations, etc. The whole revised and diligently compared with the Latin Vulgate. The Stereotype Edition. With an Historical and Chronological Index to both Testaments; Tables of References and of the Epistles and Gospels for Sunday and Holy Days. Dublin: Printed by Richard Coyne, Bookseller, Printer, and Publishers, to the Royal College of St. Patrick, Maynooth, 1825.
[A revision of Challoner.]

1833 **Webster, Noah**   The Holy Bible containing the Old and New Testaments, in the common version; with emendations of the language; by Noah Webster... New Haven: Published by Durrie & Peck, Sold by Hezekiah Howe and Co., and A.H. Maltby, 1833.
[Webster considered this work more important than his work on the dictionary.]

Second edition, 1841.

Other editions; The New Testament, 1839, 1840, 1841.

Reprinted; Grand Rapids: Baker Book House, 1987.

1834 **Townsend, George**   The Holy Bible...arranged in historical and chronological order, in such a manner that the whole may be read as one connected history in the words, of the authorized translation. By...George Townsend... New edition with select notes...indexes, and a table dividing the sacred volume into 365 portions, for daily reading throughout the year. 2 Vols. London: Gilbert and Rivington, for J.G. & J. Rivington, 1834.
[A new edition of Townsend's O.T. and of his N.T. of 1825.]

1838 **Denvir, Dr**.   Holy Bible.
[Roman Catholic. Mainly revisions of Challoner. Dr. Denvir was responsible for at least nine editions of the

entire Bible and as many more separate editions of the
New Testament.]

1841 **Conquest, J.T.**   The Holy Bible, containing
the authorised version... with twenty thousand
emendations.   London: Longman, Brown and Co.;
Bungay: John Childs & Son, 1841.
    [The Deity is rendered "Jehovah" at Psalm 83:18 only.]

Also; Sabbath School Teacher's Edition, 1842.

Another edition, 1843.

1842 **Anonymous**   The Holy Bible; Being the English
Version of the Old and New Testaments, Made by Order
of King James I. Carefully Revised and Amended, the
meaning of the sacred original being given, in
accordance with the best translations and the most
approved Hebrew and Greek lexicographers; By Several
Biblical Scholars... Philadelphia: Stereotyped by L.
Johnson. [Kay and Brothers, Printers] Published for
David Bernard, by J.B. Lippincott, 1842.
    [The O.T. is an anonymous revision. Dr. George Riply
    Bliss was among the translators. The New Testament was
    the work of Dr. A.C. Kendrick, a Baptist Scholar. An
    immersion version. Copyrighted by David Bernard.]

Second edition, 1842.

Another Edition;   The Holy Bible...Carefully
Revised and Amended, by Several Biblical
Scholars.   Sixth   Edition.   Mannaville,
Jefferson Co., New York: Published by D.S.
Dean and Rhodes Barker, Philadelphia: J.P.
Lippincott & Co., Stereotyped by L. Johnson,
1847.

1844 **Hussey, Rev. T.J.**   The Holy Bible...and
the Apocrypha accompanied throughout with a brief
hermeneutic and exegetical commentary and revised
version, by T.J. Hessey, D.D., Rector of Hayes,
Kent... 3 Vols. London: H. Colburn, 1844-1845.
    [Contains 3rd, 4th & 5th Maccabees.]

1847 **Roger, Charles**   A Collation of the Sacred
Scriptures. The Old Testament from the translations
of John Rogers, the Bishops, the Genevan, and
present Authorized Version; the New Testament from
Wiclif, Rogers, the Rhemes, or Roman Catholic...the
Genevan, the present Authorized, and Gilbert
Wakefield, 1795...with a historical account of all
the English versions, and also an account of the
more ancient MSS. and editions. And Memoirs of the
Principal Translators. By Charles Roger. Dundee:
M'Cosh, Park and Dewars, 1847.

1848 **American Bible Society**   The Holy Bible...1848-1851.
>   1848 The Holy Bible... With Canne's Marginal
>   References ... and a Key Sheet of
>   Questions... The Text Corrected According
>   to the Standard of the American Bible
>   Society. Troy [New York]: Merriam, Moore
>   & Co.
>
>   1850 The New Testament... New York: American
>   Bible Society.
>>   [1st of a series of "Standard Editions".
>>   James McLane was collator of a committee of
>>   seven   for   this   work.   His   collation
>>   disclosed 24,000 variations between the
>>   current ABS publication and editions
>>   currently from Cambridge, Oxford, London,
>>   Edinburgh and one of the 1611 editions.]
>
>   1852 The Holy Bible... New York: American
>   Bible Society.
>>   [This is referred to as "Bourgeois
>>   Reference Octavo", the first official
>>   edition with the new American Bible Society
>>   Standard Text. A correct edition, 1868.]

1848 **Nourse, James**   The Holy Bible...the text of the
common translation arranged in paragraphs, such as
the sense requires...   New York: American and
foreign Bible Society, 1848.
>   [This is evidently the AV paragraphed. The extent of any
>   revisions or changes of words is questionable.]

1849 **Kenrick, Francis Patrick**   The Holy Bible. 7 Vols.
1849-1862.
>   1849 The Four Gospels, translated from the
>   Latin Vulgate, and diligently compared
>   with the Original Greek Text, being a
>   revision of the Rhemish translation, with
>   notes critical and explanatory. By The
>   Right Rev. Francis Patrick Kenrick,
>   Bishop of Philadelphia...   New York:
>   Edward Dunigan & Brother.
>>   ["A few years ago, a new version of the
>>   Four Gospels, made directly from the
>>   Greek... was published in English by...Dr.
>>   [John] Lingard... I have freely availed
>>   myself of his labors..."]
>
>   1851 The Acts of the Apostles, the Epistles of
>   St. Paul, the Catholic Epistles, and the
>   Apocalypse. Translated from the Latin
>   Vulgate, and diligently compared with the
>   Greek text, being a revision of the
>   Rhemish Translation, with Notes Critical
>   and Explanatory by Francis Patrick
>   Kenrick. Bishop of Philadelphia ... New
>   York: Edward Dunigan & Brother.

1857 The Psalms, Books of Wisdom, and Canticle of Canticles. Translated from the Latin Vulgate; diligently compared with the Hebrew and Greek, being a Revised and Corrected Edition of the Douay Version, with Notes Critical and Explanatory, by Francis Patrick Kenrick, Archbishop of Baltimore... Baltimore: Lucas Brothers, 1857?
[This work contains Psalms, Proverbs, Ecclesiastes, Canticle of Canticles, Wisdom and Ecclesiasticus.]

1859 The Book of Job, and the Prophets, Translated from the Vulgate, and Diligently Compared with the Original Text, being a Revised Edition of the Douay Version, with Notes Critical and Explanatory, by Francis Patrick Kenrick, Archbishop of Baltimore... Baltimore: Kelly, Hedian & Piet, Publishers.
[This work contains Job, Jeremiah, Lamentations, Baruch, Ezekiel, Daniel, and the twelve Minor Prophets.]

1860 The Pentateuch. Translated from the Vulgate, and Diligently Compared with the Original Text, Being a Revised Edition of the Douay Version. With Notes, Critical and Explanatory. By Francis Patrick Kenrick, Archbishop of Baltimore... Baltimore: Kelly, Hedian & Piet, Publishers.

1860 The Historical Books of the Old Testament. Translated from the Latin Vulgate, Diligently Compared with the Original Text, being a revised Edition of the Douay Version. With Notes, Critical and Explanatory, by Francis Patrick Kenrick, Archbishop of Baltimore... Baltimore: Kelly, Hedian & Piet, Publishers.
[This work contains Joshua, Judges, Ruth, 1, 2, 3 and 4 Kings, 1 and 2 Paralipomenon, Esdras, Nehemiah, Tobias, Judith, Esther and 1 and 2 Maccabees.]

1862 The New Testament. Translated from the Latin Vulgate, and Diligently Compared with the Original Text. With Notes, Critical and Explanatory, by Francis Patrick Kenrick... Second Edition, Revised and Corrected... Baltimore: Kelly, Hedian & Piet, Publishers.

[See The Four Gospels (1849) and The Acts
of the Apostles (1851) for the 1st edition
of part of the N.T.]

1850 **Ellis, Alexander John**   The Holy Bible...according
to the authorised version. Arranged in paragraphs
and parallelisms, and printed phonetically. London:
for F. Pitman; Bath: Isaac Pitman, 1850.
Another edition; The New Testament...according to
the authorised version. Printed phonetically
by Alexander John Ellis.   London: for Fred
Pitman, Phonetic Depot; Bath: A.J. Ellis,
1849.

1850 **Forshall, Josiah and Sir Fredrick Madden**   (Editors)
The Holy Bible; The New Testament,1388,1380.
[See New Testament, 1380 John Wycliffe; See Complete
Bibles, 1388 John Wycliffe.]

1852 **Bayley, J.R.**   (Editor)   The Holy Bible, 1852.
[See George Leo Haydock, The Holy Bible, 1811.]

1860 **Sawyer, Leicester Ambrose**   The Holy Bible,
Containing the Old and New Testament...
[See Old Testament Selections for the complete entry.]

1863 **Young, Robert**   The Holy Bible, containing the
Old and New covenants, literally and idiomatically
translated out of the original languages. By Robert
Young. Edinburgh: A. Fullarton and Co., 1863.
[The Deity is rendered "Jehovah" many times.]

Second edition; revised, 'translated according to
the   letter   and   idioms   of   the   original
languages'. Edinburgh: G.A. Young and Co.,
1863.

Other editions; 1871, and 1898.

Another edition; London & Glasgow: Pickering and
Inglis, [1929].

Revised edition; Young's Literal Translation of
the Holy Bible by Robert Young. Youngstown,
Ohio: W.J. Schnell Co., 1953.

Also; Grand Rapids, Michigan: Baker Book House,
1958.

1864 **Lange's Commentaries**
The following are translators:

Charles A. Aitken	Samuel Ralph Asburg
George Ripley Bliss	Charles Augustus Briggs
John A. Broadus	Talbot Wilson Chambers
Thomas Creran	Howard Crosby
George E. Day	Charles Ellicott

Llewelyn J. Evans   Patrick Fairbairn
William Findlay   John Forsyth
A. Gosman   Horatio B. Hackett
James B. Hammond   Edwin Harwood
William H. Hornblower   John Flectcher Hurst
Samuel T. Lowrie   S. Manson
Charles Marsh Mead   James G. Murphy
Joseph Packard   Daniel W. Poor
James Frederick McCurdy

1867 **Smith, Joseph, Jr.**   Holy Scriptures, Translated
and corrected by the Spirit of Revelation, by Joseph
Smith, Jr. the Seer... Plano, Illinois: Published
by the Church of Jesus Christ of Latter-Day Saints.
Joseph Smith, I.L. Rogers, E. Robinson Publishing
Committee, 1867.
> [The New Testament and the Book of Mormon were published
> together in 1892 and titled, 'The two Records'.]

> [The Deity is rendered "Jehovah" only at Psalm 83:18.]

Reprinted;   Inspired   Version.   The   Holy
Scriptures, Corrected   by the   Spirit of
Revelation by Joseph Smith, Jr. Published by
the Board of Publication of the Reorganized
Church of Jesus Christ of Latter Day Saints.
Independence, Missouri: Herald   Publishing
House, 1936.

Also; Holy Scriptures. Containing the Old and
New Testaments. An Inspired Revision of the
Authorized Version, by Joseph Smith, Junior. A
new corrected edition. Published by the
Reorganized Church of Jesus Christ of Latter
Day Saints. Independence, Missouri: Herald
Publishing House, 1944.

Second edition; 1947.

Joseph Smith's "New Translation" of the Bible.
Independence, Mo.: Herald Publishing House,
1970.
> [This is a parallel-column edition: KJV and
> Inspired Version.]

[From 1881-1891, (after headquarters was moved from
Plano, Illinois) Lamoni, Iowa appears on the title page,
but the copyright date is 1867. From 1892 to 1921,
Lamoni, Iowa: Published by the Reorganized Church of
Jesus Christ of Latter Day Saints. From 1921, it is
published in Independence, Missouri. The Church split
after Smith died. The Reorganized Church won a court
case over ownership of the translation. The Utah group
continued to use the KJV.]

1869 **Clapp, Otis**   The Word of the Lord; The Old and
New Testaments. Boston: n.p., 1869.

1870 **Anonymous**   The Holy Bible, according
to the AV, arranged in paragraphs and sections, with
emendations of the text... London: Printed for The
Religious Tract Society by Eyre & Spottiswoode,
1870.
> [Contains the KJV, with emendations inserted within
> brackets in the text. The O.T. was edited by F.W. Gotch,
> and the N.T. by G.A. Jacob. No date given. Published
> originally in parts between 1868-1871.]

1870 **Newberry, Thomas**   The Englishman's Bible. 1870-
1884.

> 1870 The New Testament, according to the AV,
> with analysis, notes, etc. London: Sold
> for the Author by S. Bagster and Sons.
>> ["...brief footnotes, giving more correct
>> renderings of certain phrases..."]
>
> Another edition, 1882.

> 1882 The English-Greek Testament; uniting the
> precision of the original Greek with the
> text of the Authorized Version... By
> Thomas Newberry. London: S. Bagster &
> Sons.

> 1884 The Englishman's Bible, giving the
> accuracy, precision and certainty of the
> original hebrew and greek scriptures on
> the page of the Authorized Version...
> London: Hodder & Stoughton.
>> [Marginal notes give a more accurate
>> rendering of very many words and phrases.]

> 1886 The Englishman's Bible; designed to
> give...the accuracy, precision and
> certainty of the ... Hebrew and Greek
> Scriptures on the page of the Authorized
> version... By Thomas Newberry. Large
> print edition. Three Volumes. London:
> Hodder & Stoughton.
>> [Known as the Newberry Bible. The extensive
>> revision in the margin constitutes the
>> 'Newberry Bible'.]
>
> Also; London:, 1890.

1871 **Cook, Frederick Charles** (Editor)   The Speaker's
Commentary. 12 Vols. Cambridge: University Press,
C.J. Clay; London: W. Clowes & Sons, for J. Murray;
New York: Scribner, Armstrong & Co., 1871-1888.
> 1873 The Holy Bible, according to the
> authorized version (A.D. 1611); with an
> explanatory and critical commentary, and
> a revision of the translation; by Bishops

and other Clergy of the Anglican Church.
Edited by F.C. Cook... 1873-1881.

1873 - - Genesis

1875 - - Isaiah   (Vol. V)

1880 - - Psalms

1888 - - Apocrypha... In Two Volumes. Edited
by Henry Wace. London: John Murray.

[Known as "The Speaker's Commentary" because the Speaker
of the House of Commons first suggested the undertaking.
"It was decided to reprint the authorised English
Version, without alterations, from the edition of 1611,
with the marginal references and renderings; but to
supply in the notes amended translations (...distinctive
type) of all passages proved to be incorrect."   O.T. in
six volumes. The N.T. in four volumes.]

1876 **Cheyne, T.K. and Others** (Editors)   The Holy Bible
...Variorum Edition. Edited with Various Renderings
and Readings from the Best Authorities. By T.K.
Cheyne, S.R. Driver, R.L. Clarke and A. Goodwin.
London: Eyre & Spottiswoode, 1876 - 1892.
     1876 The Holy Bible...edited with various
          readings from the best authorities...

        1880 The Sunday School Century Bible (or
             Variorum Teachers Bible)

        1882 The Variorum Teacher's Edition of the
             Holy Bible.
             Also, 1885 and 1886.

        1888 The Variorum Reference Bible.
             Also, 1893, 1894, and 1898.

        1892 The Ecclesiastical or Deutero - Canonical
             Books of the Old Testament commonly
             called the Apocrypha. Edited   with
             Various Renderings and Readings from the
             best authorities by ...C.J. Ball.

        [KJV, with various renderings and readings printed below
        the text.]

1876 **Smith, Julia Evelina**   The Holy Bible containing
the Old and New Testaments; Translated Literally
from the Original Tongues.   Hartford, Conn.:
American Publishing Co., 1876.
        [Julia Smith was the first woman to translate the whole
        Bible.   She   was   a   member   of   the   Sandemanian
        (restorationist) Church of Scotland. The work was very
        literal and concordant, resulting in an unnatural

English. It follows the Palestinian Jewish canon in the
O.T. order of books. This is a 'Immersionist' version.]

1877 **Revised English Bible**   Revised English Bible.
The Holy Bible according to the Authorised Version,
compared with the Hebrew and Greek texts, and
carefully revised; arranged in paragraphs and
sections, with supplementary notes, references...
chronological tables, and maps. London: Printed for
the Editor by Eyre and Spottiswoode, 1877.
> [The Pentateuch was edited by F.W. Gotch; the balance of
> the O.T. was edited by Benjamin Davies and Joseph
> Gurney; and the N.T. was edited by G.A. Jacob and S.G.
> Green. The design "is to correct what may be considered
> indisputable errors and inadequate renderings in our
> present English Bible..."]

1881 **English Revised Version**   (ERV & RV) The Holy Bible
...translated out of the original tongues: being the
version set forth A.D. 1611 compared with the most
ancient authorities and revised... 5 Vols. Oxford:
University Press, 1881-1885.

> The following were translators:

Henry Alford	Joseph Angus
Edward Bickersteth	John Birrell
Joseph William Blakesley	David Brown
Edward Harold Browne (CO-Chairman)	
Frank Chance	T.K. Cheyne
George E. Day	Samuel Rolles Driver
John Eadie	C.J. Ellicott
F.W. Gotch	Horatio B. Hackett
Benjamin Hall	Roswell D. Hitchcock
Fenton John Anthony Hort	William Gilson Humphrey
Benjamin Hall Kennedy	William Lee
Joseph Barber Lightfoot	George Moberly
William Fiddian Moulton	Samuel Newth
Edwin Palmer	

> [Also called the "Canterbury Version". A monumental work
> by 97 British and American scholars and finished by 77.
> Basis for the American Standard Version (1901).]

> [Also called the "Revised Version".]

1881 The New Testament of our Lord and Saviour
Jesus Christ translated out of the Greek:
being the version set forth A.D. 1611
compared with the most ancient
authorities and revised A.D. 1881.
Printed for the Universities of Oxford
and Cambridge. Cambridge: University
Press, 1881.

1885 The Old Testament... Revised A.D. 1885. 4
Vols.
> American Edition; The Revised Version
> of the Old Testament with marginal
> notes and the readings preferred by

the American revisers printed as footnotes. In four parts...Harper's American Edition. New York: Harper's Franklin Square Library, Harper and Bros., 1885.

The following were some of the revisors:

Robert Lubbock Bensley   Thomas Chenery
Andrew Bruce Davidson   Benjamin Davies
Patrick Fairbairn   Frederick Field
John Dury Geden   Christian D. Ginsburg
Benjamin Harrison   Arthur Charles Hervey
William Kay   Stanley Leathes
Joseph Rawson Lumby   J. McGill
Alfred Ollivant   Edward Plumptre
George Cunningham Monteath Douglas
John James Stewart Perowne

1885 American Edition; The Holy Bible... Being the Version Set Forth A.D. 1611... Revised... New York: Harper & Bros.

1895 The Apocrypha, translated out of the Greek and Latin tongues, being the version set forth A.D. 1611, compared with the most ancient authorities and revised A.D. 1894. Printed for the Universities of Oxford and Cambridge. Oxford: University Press, 1895.

1898 The Holy Bible...being the revised version set forth A.D. 1881-1885, with revised marginal references. Printed for the Universities of Oxford and Cambridge. Cambridge, Mass., U.S.A.: The Riverside Press; New York:for the Oxford University Press, American Branch, and the Cambridge University Press, James Pott and Co., Agents.

1898 The Holy Bible... Being the Revised Version Set Forth 1881-1885. With the Readings and renderings Preferred by the American Revision Companies Incorporated in the Text, and with Copyright Marginal References. [Electrotyped and printed at the Riverside Press, Cambridge, Mass.] ...for the Universities of Oxford and Cambridge. New York: Oxford University Press, American Branch, and Cambridge University Press, James Pott & Co., Agents.
     [This is the first edition of the ERV issued in which the American preferences are incorporated in the text and in the

margins, while the corresponding English renderings are placed in the Appendix.]

[The Deity is rendered "Jehovah" at Exodus 6:2-3 & Psalm 83:18.]

[Reprinted many times.]

1881 **Sharpe, Samuel**   The Holy Bible translated by Samuel Sharpe ...a revision of the Authorised English Version.   London: Williams & Norgate, 1881.
[The Deity is rendered "Jehovah" many times.]

Other editions; London: 1883, 1904.

1884 **Oakeley, F. and T.G. Law**   The Holy Bible, Translated from the Latin Vulgate... With Notes... Selected...by the Rev. George Haydock. Revised and Corrected Under the Superintendence of the very Rev. Frederick Canon Oakeley ... With the Approbation of his Eminence the Cardinal Archbishop of Westminster. And Imprimatur John Cardinal M'Closkey, Archbishop of...   New York: P.F. Collier, Publisher, 1884.

1885 **Alexander, William**   The Holy Bible, a Revision of the Authorised Version, with Notes.   York: W. Alexander and Son, 1885.

1890 **Pitman, Isaac**   The Holy Bible...lithographed in the easy reporting style of phonography. London: I. Pitman & Sons, 1890.   [see 1904]

1895 **International Critical Commentary**   International Critical Commentary. (45 Vols. Proposed) New York: Charles Scribners and Sons, 1895-
[Not certain this work was ever completed. This work was done under the editorship of Charles Augustus Briggs, Samuel R. Driver and Alfred Plummer. The leading scholars of the era were asked to contribute to this work which has made it a long standing popular commentary and translation with notes and original text. The translators known to have completed work for this commentary and translation will be listed by name and referred to here.]

1895 **Moulton, Richard Green**   The Modern Reader's Bible: The Books of the Bible with Three Books of the Apocrypha. Presented in Modern Literary Form... Edited with Introductions and Notes by Richard G. Moulton... 22 Vols. New York: The Macmillan Co.; London: Macmillan & Co. Ltd., 1895-1923.
["the text...is one construed specially for this work for which the Editor is solely responsible. It is based on the English Revised Version, with choice between the readings of the text and margin, and such slight changes of wording as are involved in the adaptation to modern literary structure."]

[The Deity is rendered "Jehovah" at Psalms 68:4 & 83:18; Exodus 6:2-9 & 22:14; Jeremiah 16:20; Isaiah 12:2 & 26:4.]

One volume edition; New York (1907), and often thereafter.
        Another; 1914.

Also; The Modern Reader's Bible for School. The Old Testament. By Richard G. Moulton... New York: Macmillan Co., 1928. (Abridged).

1896 The Book of Job, with an Introduction and Notes, by Richard G. Moulton. New York: Macmillan.

1897 Genesis; edited with an introduction and notes by Richard G. Moulton... New York: The Macmillan Co.; London: Macmillan & Co. Ltd.

1898 The Psalms and Lamentations; edited, with an introduction and notes by Richard G. Moulton... New York: The Macmillan Co.; London: Macmillan & Co. Ltd.

Also; A revision of the Revised version, 1906.

[Reprinted many times.]

1897 **Rotherham, Joseph Bryant**   The Emphasised Bible. A New Translation, Designed to Set Forth the Exact Meaning, the Proper Terminology and the Graphic Style of the Sacred Originals; Arranged to Show at a Glance Narrative, Speech, Parallelism, and Logical Analysis, Also to Enable the Student Readily to Distinguish the Several Divine Names; and Emphasised Throughout After the Idioms of the Hebrew and Greek Tongues. With Expository Introduction, Select References, and Appendices of Notes... By Joseph Bryant Rotherham... 4 Vols. in Two. Cincinnati: The Standard Publishing Co., 1897-1902.
    [The Old Testament was adjusted to the newly revised "Massoretical-critical" text of Dr. Ginsburg; and the New Testament adjusted to the critical text of Drs. Westcott and Hort.]

[The Deity is rendered "Yahweh" many times.]

Another edition; London and Tonbridge: Bradbury, Agnew, and Co.; London: for H.R. Allenson, 1902.

Also; [Old Testament] The Emphasised Bible, a New Translation Designed to Set Forth the

Exact Meaning...Joseph Bryant Rotherham... 3 Vols. New York, Chicago, Toronto: Fleming H. Revell, 1902.

Also; Four Vols. in One. Cincinnati: Standard Publishing Co., 1916.

Reprinted; Grand Rapids: Kregel Publications, 1961.

[This work has been reprinted many times.]

1898 **American Revised Version**   The Holy Bible containing the Old and New Testaments translated out of the Original Tongues being the Revised Version set forth A.D. 1881-1885; with the readings and renderings preferred by the American Revision Companies incorporated in the text, and with copyright marginal references. Printed for the Universities of Oxford and Cambridge. Cambridge: The Riverside Press, 1898.

1899 **Ballantine, Frank Schell**   The Modern American Bible: The Books of the Bible in Modern American Form and Phrase with Notes and Introduction. By Frank Schell Ballantine. Five Vols.   New York: Thomas Whittaker, 1899-1901.
  Pt. 1   1899?   S. Mark
  Pt. 2   1899?   S. Matthew, S. Peter, S. Jude, and S. James
  Pt. 3   1899?   S. Luke (Gospel and Acts)
  Pt. 4   1901?   S. Paul (Thessalonians, Corinthians, Galatians, Romans, Colossians, Ephesians, Philemon, Philippians, I Tim., Titus, II Tim., and Hebrews)
  Pt. 5   1901?   S. John (Gospel, Letters, Revelation)

1899 **Murphy Bible**   Holy Bible... The Whole Revised and diligently compared with the Latin Vulgate. published with the Approbation of His Eminence James Cardinal Gibbons, Archbishop of Baltimore. Baltimore, New York: John Murphy, [1899]
    ["This edition is the basis of almost all subsequent American editions, some of which, however, adopted a few more readings from Challoner's revision of 1752; this edition, through Washbourne's reprint of 1900, is likewise the basis of most current British editions." "This important edition was often reprinted with the imprints of various publishers; it was the most common Bible in America during the first quarter of the twentieth century, and like most 8vo Bibles published since that time, it appeared with and without illustrations."]

1901 **American Standard Version**   The Holy Bible
     containing the Old and New Testaments translated out
     of the original tongues. Being the version set forth
     A.D. 1881-1885. Newly edited by the American
     Revision Committee A.D. 1901. Standard Edition. New
     York: Thomas Nelson and Sons, 1901.
              O.T. Committee consists of:
                    C.A. Aiken (Princeton)
                    T.W. Chambers(New Brunswick)
                    T.J. Conant (Rochester)
                    G.E. Day (Yale)
                    J. DeWitt (New Brunswick)
                    W.H. Green (Princeton)
                    T. Lewis (Union)
                    C.M. Mead (Andover)
                    H. Osgood (Rochester)
                    C.E. Stowe (Andover)
                    J. Strong (Drew)
                    G.E. Hare (Philadelphia)
                    C.P. Krauth (Philadelphia)
                    J. Parkard (Alexandria)
                    C.V.A.VanDyck (Beirut, Translator of the Arabic B)

     [The Deity is rendered "Jehovah" many times.]

     [See New Testament listing, 1962 Luther Weigle, N.T.
     Octapla.]

1901 **Fenton, Ferrar**   The Bible in Modern English. By
     Ferrar Fenton. London: Bradbury, Agnew, and Co., for
     Messrs. S.W. Partridge and Co., 1901-1903.
              1901 The Five Books of Moses, being volume the
                   first of the Bible in modern English,
                   translated   direct   from   the   Hebrew,
                   Chaldee,   and   Greek   languages   into
                   English, by Ferrar Fenton.

              1902 The Bible in Modern English. Vol. II: The
                   History of the People of Israel, by
                   Isaiah-Ben-Amos, the Prophet...from the
                   conquests of Joshua to the death of King
                   Hezekiah. (In VI Books) Translated direct
                   from the Hebrew into English, with a
                   critical   introduction   and   notes,   by
                   Ferrar Fenton... 1902?

              1902 The Bible in Modern English. Vol. III:
                   containing the Books of the Prophets,
                   direct from the Hebrew into English, and
                   in verse, in the Hebrew metres of the
                   prophets, or in prose, as originally
                   written; translated by Ferrar Fenton...
                   with a critical introduction and notes.
                   1902?

              1903 The Bible in Modern English. Vol. IV:
                   containing the Psalms, Solomon, and

Sacred Writers, in the original Hebrew order of the books, translated direct from the Hebrew and Chaldee texts into English by Ferrar Fenton... with an introduction and critical notes.

1903 The Holy Bible in Modern English, containing... the Old and New Testaments, translated into English direct from the Hebrew, Chaldee, and Greek languages, by Ferrar Fenton... with an introduction and critical notes.

Another Edition; 4 Vols. Carefully Revised, 1906.

Fenton's Bible revised throughout, 1910.

Another edition; The Holy Bible in Modern English (second revision of the whole Bible) 1913. [Published 1919.]
Reprinted; New York: A.S.C. Black, 1938.

Reprint edition, 1966.

1902 **Ballantine, Frank Schell**   The American Bible... The Books of the Bible in Modern English for American Readers. Five Vols. Scranton: Good News Publishing Co., 1902?.
Vol. I   Matthew, Peter, Jude, James, Hebrews
Vol. II   Mark
Vol. III   Luke (Gospel and Acts)
Vol. IV   John (Gospel, Letters, Revelation)
Vol. V   Paul

[Ballantine used "Jehovah" seventeen times in Romans; five times in I Corinthians; one time in II Corinthians.]

1903 **Anonymous**   The Holy Bible...With the Marginal Readings Adopted by General Convention. Authorized to be read in Churches... New York: [Printed by Norwood Press, Norwood, Mass.] Thomas Nelson & Sons, 1903.
["In order to provide an English Bible preserving the AV text but reflecting modern scholarship and changes in the English language, the General Convention...appointed a Commission...to consider marginal readings that could be "authorized for instruction of our people". Copyrighted by Arthur C.A. Ball and Charles W.E. Body, members of the committee. Sometimes called the Episcopal Marginal Bible.]

1903 **Scrivener, F.H.**   The English Bible containing the Old Testament & the New translated out of the original tongues by special command of His Majesty King James the First and now reprinted with the text revised...and edited by...F.H. Scrivener... 5 Vols. London: Doves Press, 1903-1905.

        1903 Vol. I.   Genesis-1 Samuel
        1903 Vol. II.   2 Samuel-Song of Solomon
        1904 Vol. III. Isaiah-Malachi
        1904 Vol. IV.   Apocrypha
        1905 Vol. V.   New Testament

    [Only 500 copies were printed.]

1904 **Pitman, Isaac**   The Holy Bible, containing the Old and New Testaments. Authorised version. Lithographed in the easy reporting style of Pitman's shorthand. Twentieth century edition. London: Sir I. Pitman & Sons, 1904.   [see 1890]

1911 **Anonymous**   The 1911 Tercentenary Commemoration Bible. The Holy Bible, containing the Old and New Testaments translated out of the original tongues...1611; the text carefully corrected and amended by American Scholars, 1911. New York: Oxford University Press, American Branch.
      [Supposes to be a 'corrected' rather than revised or retranslated text, by 34 eminent Hebrew and Greek scholars. It is, however, a severe revision of the AV.]

1913 **American Baptist Publication Society** The Holy Bible containing the Old and New Testaments. An Improved Version (based in part on the Bible Union Version). Philadelphia: The American Baptist Publication Society, 1913.
      [The New Testament has a separate title page: The New Testament... American Bible Union Version. An Improved edition revised and corrected, 1912.]

      [The Deity is rendered "Jehovah" many times.]

      O.T. Committee consists of:
          Bernard C. Taylor (Crozer Theological Seminary) - Job, Genesis, Psalms, Proverbs, Joshua, Ruth, 1 & 2 Samuel, and 1 & 2 Kings.

          J.R.   Sampey   (Southern   Baptist   Theological Seminary) - Chronicles, Ezra, Nehemiah, Esther, Ecclesiastes, Song of Solomon, and Lamentations.

          William R. Harper (University of Chicago) - Isaiah, and Minor Prophets.

          Ira M. Price (University of Chicago) - Jeremiah, Daniel, and Ezekiel.

          J. M. Powis Smith (University of Chicago) - Proof read Dr. Harper's section.

1913 **Westminster Version** [The Westminster Version of the Bible] General editors: Cuthbert Lattey and Joseph Keating. London: Longmans, Green and Co. 1913-1953.

1913 The New Testament...Westminster Version.
4 Vols. London: Longmans, Green and Co.,
1913-1935.

Vol. I   pt.1 St. Matthew by Joseph
               Dean, 1928.
          pt.2 St. Mark by Joseph Dean,
               1916.
          pt.3 St. Luke by Joseph Dean,
               1935.

Vol. II   pt.1 St. John by W.S. Reilly,
               1929.
          pt.2 The Acts by C. Lattey,
               1933.

Vol. III pt.4 Romans by C. Lattey, 1920.
          pt.2 1 Corinthians by C.
               Lattey, 1914.
          pt.3 2 Corinthians by C. Lattey
               and J. Keating, 1920.
          pt.4 Galatians by Alexander
               Keough, 1920.
          pt.5 Ephesians and Colossians
               by Joseph Rickaby;
               Philippians and Philemon
               by Alban Goodier, 1914.
          pt.1 1 and 2 Thessalonians by
               C. Lattey, 1913.

Vol. IV   pt.1 Hebrews by Patrick Boylan,
               1924.
          pt.2 1 and 2 Timothy, Titus, 1,
               2 and 3 John [bound with a
               reprint of the Apocalypse] by
               Francis Gigot, 1924;
               James, 1 and 2 Peter and
               Jude by W.H. Kent, 1924.
          pt.3 The Apocalypse of St. John
               by Francis Gigot, 1915.

Four Vol. New Testament Edition;
1921 Vol. III Epistles of St. Paul
                    Second edition, 1927.
                    Third edition, revised,
                    1939.
1928 Vol. I   Synoptic Gospels Second
               edition; Revised, 1938.
1931 Vol. IV   Hebrews, Pastoral and
               Catholic Epistles, and
               Apocalypse
                    Second Edition;
                    Revised, 1938.
1936 Vol. II   St. John and Acts

[A one-volume edition containing the entire Revised New Testament text, but with shorter introductions and notes by Lattey appeared in 1948.]

1934 The Old Testament...Westminster Version. London: Longmans, Green and Co., 1934-

   1934 Malachy by C. Lattey.
   1935 Ruth by C. Lattey.
   1937 Nahum and Habakkuk by H. Bevenot.
   1938 Jona by T.E. Bird.
   1939 Psalms i-xli by C. Lattey.
   1944 Psalms by C. Lattey. London & Glasgow: Sands and Co.
   1948 Daniel by C. Lattey. Dublin: Browne and Nolan.
   1953 Obadiah, Micah, Zephaniah, Haggai and Zechariah by Sebastian Bullough. London: St. Catherine Press.

   [The Deity is rendered "Jehovah" many times.]

1926 **Master Library**   The Master Library by Walter Scott Athearn. 9 Vols. Cleveland, Ohio; Springfield, Mass.; Kansas City, MO: The Foundation Press Inc., 1926.
   ["Only in well-defined instances has there been modification of (The KJV) text herein. Whenever obsolete words occur, they have been superseded by words of present day usage..."]

1926 **Moffatt, James**   The Holy Bible... A new translation by James Moffatt. Garden City, New York: Doubleday, Doran & Co.; New York: George H. Doran Co., [1926]
   Another edition; The Shorter Moffatt Bible. New York & London: Harper & Bros., 1935.

1929 **MacLean, Charles**   A Homiletical and Exegetical Version of the Bible. By Charles MacLean. Completed by June, 1929.
   [Unpublished]

1931 **Goodspeed, Edgar J. and J.M. Powis Smith**   The Bible. An American Translation. The Old Testament Translated by a Group of Scholars Under the editorship of J.M. Powis Smith. The New Testament Translated by Edgar J.Goodspeed. Chicago: University of Chicago Press, 1931.
   [The Deity is rendered "Yahweh" at Exodus 3:15 & 6:3; "Yah" at Isaiah 12:2 & 26:4.]

   Another edition, 1935.

Also; The Short Bible. An American Translation. Edited by Edgar J. Goodspeed and J.M. Powis Smith.   Chicago: University of Chicago Press, 1931.
> Another Edition, 1933.

In addition; The Junior Bible. An American Translation. Edited by Edgar J. Goodspeed. Illustrated by Frank Dobias.   Chicago: University of Chicago Press, 1936.

Another edition; The Complete Bible. An American Translation. The Old Testament Translated by J.M. Powis Smith and a Group of Scholars. The Apocrypha and the New Testament Translated by Edgar J. Goodspeed.   Chicago: University of Chicago Press, 1939.
> Another; 1948.

1933 **Ogden, Charles K.**   The Bible in Basic English. 1933-1949.

> 1933 Stories from the Bible Put into Basic English. By C.K. Ogden.   London: Kegan Paul & Co.

> 1934 Micah and Habakkuk Put into Basic English.

> 1935 The Basic St. Mark. [Edited by C.K. Ogden] London: Kegan Paul & Co.

> 1938 The Basic St. John. [Edited by C.K. Ogden]

> 1941 The New Testament in Basic English. Cambridge: University Press in Association with Evans Bros.

> 1949 The Bible in Basic English.   Cambridge: University Press & Evans Bros.
> > [The Deity is rendered "Yahweh" at Psalm 83:18; Exodus 6:2, 3, 6 & 8; "Jah" at Isaiah 12:2 &26:4.]
>
> > First American Edition; New York: E.P. Dutton & Co., 1950.

[This work was done under the direction of S.H. Hooke. Restricted to 1,000 words.]

1935 **Moffatt, James**   A New Translation of the Bible, containing Old and New Testaments. James Moffatt. London: Hodder & Stoughton, 1935.

[This is 'the revised and final edition'. The translator reviewed the entire work 'in order to make the English more exact, more telling, or more idiomatic.']

Another edition; New York: Harper & Bros., 1935.

1939 **Darby, John Nelson**   The 'Holy Scriptures' a New Translation from the original languages, by J.N. Darby.   London: Stow Hill Bible and Tract Depot, 1939.
[A reprint of the editions previously published with a few corrections. The footnotes were rewritten in order to put the Hebrew and Greek words into Roman characters or translated.]

[The Deity is rendered "Jehovah" many times.]

1948 **Anonymous**   The Holy Bible. Translated from the Original Languages with Critical Use of All the Ancient Sources by Members of the Catholic Biblical Association of America. Sponsored by the Episcopal Committee of the Confraternity of Christian Doctrine... Paterson, New Jersey: St. Anthony Guild, 1948-1961. [Confraternity Version]
1948 The Book of Genesis.

   1950 The Book of Psalms and the Canticles of the Roman Breviary.

   1952 [Vol. One] Genesis to Ruth.
            [Genesis is a reprint of the 1948 edition with some errors (Gen. 2:12, Lev. 11:30. The errors were corrected in the 1953 reprint.]

   1969 [Vol. Two] Samuel to Maccabees.

   1955 [Vol. Three] The Sapiential Books, Job to Sirach.

   1961 [Vol. Four] The Prophetic Books, Isaia-Malachia.

   1949 The New Catholic Edition of the Bible, Translated from the Latin Vulgate. The Old Testament, Douay Version, with Newly Edited Annotations of Bishop Challoner and a New Translation of the Book of Psalms from the New Latin Version Approved by Pope Pius XII and the New Testament Confraternity Edition, A Revision of the Challoner-Rheims Version Edited by Catholic Scholars under the Patronage of the Episcopal Committee of the Confraternity of Christian

Doctrine... New York: Catholic Book Publishing Co.

1950 The Holy Bible. Old Testament, Douay Version, With Psalms from the New Latin Version Authorized by Pope Pius XII. New Testament, Confraternity Edition, with the Encyclical Letter "On the Study of the Holy Scriptures" by Pope Leo XIII; Also a Presentation of the Essence of the Encyclical Letter "On Biblical Studies" by Pope Pius XII; and a Preface by William H. McClellan... Also an Appendix Containing an... Index, Table of References and Maps... New York, Boston, Cincinnati, Chicago, San Francisco: Benziger Bros., Inc.

1952 The Holy Bible translated from the original languages with critical use of all ancient sources by Members of the Catholic Biblical Association of America. Sponsored by the Episcopal Committee of the confraternity of Christian Doctrine. Paterson, N.J.: Confraternity of Christian Doctrine.

1954 The New Catholic Edition of the Bible. The Old Testament. Confraternity Douay Version with the New Confraternity of Christian Doctrine Translation of the First Eight Books, and a New Translation of the book of Psalms from the New Latin Version. Approved by Pope Pius XII. And the New Testament Confraternity Edition. A Revision of the Challoner-Rheims Version Edited by Catholic Scholars under the Patronage of the Episcopal Committee of the Confraternity of Christian Doctrine. New York: Catholic Book Publishing Co.

[See New Testament listing, 1941 Anonymous, The New Testament... Confraternity.]

1949 **Anonymous**   The Bible in Basic English.
[See Complete Bibles, 1933 Charles K. Ogden, The Bible in Basic English.]

1950 **Watchtower Bible & Tract Society**
The New World Translation of the Holy Scriptures; Rendered from the Original Languages by the New World Bible Translation Committee. Brooklyn, New York: Watchtower Bible and Tract Society of New

York, Inc., International Bible Students Association,The New World Translation of the Holy Scriptures; Rendered from the Original Languages by the New World Bible Translation Committee. Brooklyn, New York: Watchtower Bible and Tract Society of New York, Inc., International Bible Students Association, 1950-1961.

    1950 The New World Translation of the Christian Greek Scriptures...
        Revised edition, 1951.

    1953 Vol. 1 New World Translation of the Hebrew Scriptures... (Genesis through Ruth)

    1955 Vol. 2 New World Translation of the Hebrew Scriptures... (1 Samuel through Esther)

    1957 Vol. 3 New World Translation of the Hebrew Scriptures... (Job through Song of Solomon)

    1958 Vol. 4 New World Translation of the Hebrew Scriptures... (Isaiah through Lamentations)

    1960 Vol. 5 New World Translation of the Hebrew Scriptures... (Ezekiel through Malachi)

    1961 The New World Translation of the Holy Scriptures; Rendered from the Original Languages by the New World Bible Translation Committee. Revised A.D. 1961. Brooklyn, New York: Watchtower Bible and Tract Society of New York, Inc., International Bible Students Association, 1961.

    1963 The New World Translation of the Holy Scriptures; Rendered from the Original Languages by the New World Bible Translation Committee. A.D. 1953-1960. Brooklyn, New York: Watchtower Bible and Tract Society of New York, Inc., International Bible Students Association, 1963. [Volumes 1-5 bound together in one volume with the Christian Greek Scriptures.]

Other editions; 1970, 1971, 1981, 1984.

[For the Deity, this translation used "Jehovah" throughout, even the New Testament.]

[The WB&TS also published the KJV, ASV, B. Wilson's 'Emphatic Diaglott', Steven T. Byington's 'Bible in Living English' and the .]

1952 **Revised Standard Version** The Holy Bible. Revised Standard Version, containing the Old and New Testament... Being the Version set forth A.D. 1611. Revised...1881-1885 and...1901...and Revised A.D. 1952. Toronto, New York: & Edinburgh: Thomas Nelson & Sons, 1952.
[The 1946 New Testament was revised. See Luke 24:28.]

[The RSV, which was published in 1960 and afterwards, received 85 changes; about half were in punctuation, capitalization, or footnotes. It was not announced as a revised edition. The "Second Edition" appeared in 1971. The introduction to the "Second Edition" states, "Profits from textual and linguistic studies published since the RSV of 1946. Certain passages omitted because of dispute in the earlier version are restored though separated from the rest of the text and their problems noted. Notes are also added which indicate significant variations or omissions in the ancient manuscripts. Published in USA."]

Catholic Edition, 1966.
[Two of the revisers were R.C. Fuller and Dom Bernard Orchard]

Another Edition; Revised, 1971.

[See New Testament listing, 1962 Luther Weigle, N.T. Octapla; 1946 Revised Standard Version, N.T.]

[See Old Testament listing, 1952 Revised Standard Version, O.T.]

[See Apocrypha listing, 1957 Revised Standard Version, Apocrypha]

[See Complete Bibles, 1990 New Revised Standard Version.]

1956 **Anonymous** The Holy Bible newly translated from the Latin Vulgate in Light of the Hebrew and Greek Originals Authorized by the Hierarchy of England and Wales and the Hierarchy of Scotland. [By Ronald A. Knox.] 3 Vols. New York: Sheed & Ward, 1956

1957 **Lamsa, George M.** The Holy Bible from Ancient Eastern Manuscripts, containing the Old and New Testaments, Translated from the Peshitta, The Authorized Bible of the Church of the East. By George M. Lamsa. Philadelphia: A.J.Holman Co., 1957.
[The N.T. of this edition is a revised edition of the 1940.]

MACK LIBRARY
BOB JONES UNIVERSITY
GREENVILLE, SC

1959 **Berkeley Version**   The Holy Bible. The Berkeley
    Version in Modern English, containing the Old and
    New Testaments. Translated afresh from the original
    languages and diligently compared with previous
    translations, with numerous helpful non-doctrinal
    notes to aid the understanding of the reader. Gerrit
    Verkuyl, Ph.D., Editor-in-chief and translator of
    New Testament section. Grand Rapids, MI: Zondervan
    Publishing House, 1959.
        The following are some of the translators:
        David E.Culley   Leonard Greenway
        Howard A.Hank   S.Lewis Johnson, Jr.
        James B.Keefer   William Sanford LaSor
        J.Barton Payne

    Revised edition; The Holy Bible. The New Berkeley
    Version in Modern English. A Completely New
    Translation From the Original Languages With
    Informative Notes to Aid the Understanding of
    the Reader. Gerrit Verkuyl, Ph.D. Editor-in-
    chief.   Grand Rapids, Michigan: Zondervan
    Publishing House, 1969.

    [See New Testament listing, 1945 Berkeley Version, N.T.]

1960 **New American Standard Bible**   The New American
    Standard Bible. 1960-1971.
        [A fresh translation based on the ASV of 1901.]

        1960 New American Standard Gospel of John.
            Produced by the Lockman Foundation. La
            Habra,   California: The   Lockman
            Foundation.

        1962 New American Standard Gospels. La Habra,
            California: The Lockman Foundation.

        1963 New   American   Standard   Bible: New
            Testament. La Habra, California: The
            Foundation Press, Publisher for The
            Lockman Foundation.
                Another Edition; Nashville, TN:
                Broadman Press, 1963.

        1971 New American Standard Bible. Carol
            Stream, Illinois: Creation House, Inc.
                Another Edition; New York: New York
                Bible Society International, 1971.

            Other editions, 1972, 1973, 1975.

            Another edition; "Minor revisions and
            refinements, recommended over the
            last several years, are presented in

this edition". Chicago: Moody
Press, 1977.

Also; Red letter edition,
Paragraphed. Nashville: Holman Bible
Publishers, 1977.

1961 **New English Bible** The New English Bible. 1961-1970.
The New English Bible. The New Testament.
Oxford: Oxford University Press, 1961.
["This new version is a completely new translation
from the original texts. Representatives of eight
denominations, the British and Scottish Bible
Societies, and various Councils of Churches in the
British Isles worked on this version. C.H. Dodd
served as the General Director of the whole
translation and as the convener of the N.T.
committee. T.H. Robinson was the convener of the
O.T. committee.]

[The British and Foreign Bible Society in
association with the University Presses, published
an edition of St. John, pp.62; and St. Luke, pp.
64 in 1963.; St. Matthew, pp. 62 and St. Mark, pp.
62 in 1962. B&FBS also issued a Missionary Edition
of the N.T. in 1962, not to be sold in the United
Kingdom, the United States of America, Canada,
Australia, New Zealand and South Africa.]

Second Edition, 1970.

The New English Bible: Old Testament. Oxford
and Cambridge: University Presses, 1970.

The New English Bible: the New Testament. 2nd
edition. 1970.

The New English Bible. Oxford and Cambridge:
University Presses, 1970.
[Contains the 2nd ed. of the N.T.]

[The Deity is rendered "Jehovah" on page XVI; at
Genesis 4:26f; Exodus 3:15-16, 33:19, 34:5-6 &
35:31f.]

[For a radial revision, see Revised English Bible,
1989.]

1962 **Anonymous**   Modern King James Version of the Holy
Bible. New York, Toronto, London: McGraw-Hill Book
Co., Inc., 1962.
[Copyright by Jay Green]

1962 **Taylor, Kenneth N.**   The Living Bible Paraphrased.
Wheaton, Illinois: Tyndale House, Publishers, 1962-
1971.
[The Deity is rendered "Jehovah" many times.]

1962 Living Letters. The Paraphrased Epistles by Kenneth N. Taylor.

1965 Living Prophecies. The Minor Prophets Paraphrased with Daniel and The Revelation.

1966 Living Gospels. The Four Gospels and The Book of Acts Paraphrased by Kenneth N. Taylor.

1967 Words of Wisdom from Living Psalms and Proverbs, Paraphrased.

1967 The Living New Testament Paraphrased.

1968 Living Lessons of Life and Love: Ruth, Esther, Job, Ecclesiastes, and Song of Solomon, Paraphrased. Billy Graham Evangelistic Association. Crusade edition.

1969 Living Books of Moses.

1970 Living History of Israel; a Paraphrase of Joshua, Judges, I and II Samuel, I and II Kings, I and II Chronicles, Ezra and Nehemiah.

1971 The Living Bible Paraphrased.
       British edition; London: 1974.

1972 The Children's Living Bible: Paraphrased. Illustrations by Richard and Francis Hook. Wheaton, IL: Tyndale House Publishers; London, England: Coverdale House Publishers Ltd., 1972.
       [Same as the Living Bible, 1971.]

1982 The Living Bible with Deuterocanonical Books Paraphrased.

Revised Edition; The Book. Tyndale House, 1985.

[Also, See Children's Bibles, 1970 Kenneth N. Taylor, Taylor's Bible Story Book; 1971 The Bible in Pictures...; 1972 The Children's Living Bible; 1990 Anonymous, The Holy Bible. Simplified Living Bible.]

1963 **Traina, A.B.**   The Holy Name Bible; containing the Holy Name Version of the Old and New Testaments; Critically compared with ancient authorities and various manuscripts. By A.B. Traina. Brandywine, Maryland: The Scripture Research Association, Inc., 1963.

[The Deity is rendered "Yahweh" many times.]

Another edition, 1971.

Revised edition, 1974.

1964 Anchor Bible   Anchor Bible includes commentary.
[61 vols. thus far.]   Garden City, New York:
Doubleday & Co., 1964
[The Deity is rendered "Yahweh" many times.]

Translators are:

Francis I. Anderson	John A. Bailey
Markus Barth	Robert G. Boling
John Bright	Raymond E. Brown
George Wesley Buchanan	E.F. Campbell, Jr.
Mordechai Cogan	Frank Moore Cross
Mitchell Dahood	Alexander A. Di Lella
Joseph A. Fitzmyer	J. Massyngberde Ford
Victor P. Furnish	H.L. Ginsberg
Jonathan A.Goldstein	Moshe Greenberg
Louis F. Hartman	Delbert R. Hillers
Leander E. Keck	Baruch A. Levine
Abraham J. Malherbe	C.S. Mann
J. Louis Martyn	S. Dean McBride, Jr.
P. Kyle McCarter	John L. McKenzie
George E. Mendenhall	Carol L. Meyers
Eric M. Meyers	Jacob Milgrom
Carey A. Moore	Johannes Munck
Jacob M. Myers	Kevin G. O'Connell
William F. Orr	Marvin H. Pope
Jerome D. Quinn	Bo Ivar Reicke
John Reumann	R.B.Y. Scott
Patrick W.Skehan	E.A. Speiser
Hayim Tadmor	James Arthur Walther
Moshe Weinfeld	David Winston
G. Ernest Wright	

[For the books they translated, see the individual listing.]

1965 Amplified Bible   Amplified Bible containing
the Amplified Old Testament and the Amplified New
Testament. Grand Rapids: Zondervan Publishing House,
1965.
Revised edition; The Amplified Bible: Expanded
Edition... Grand Rapids: Zondervan Publishing
House, 1987.

1966 Jerusalem Bible   The Jerusalem Bible...
1966 The New Testament of the Jerusalem Bible.
Garden City, New York: Doubleday &
Company, Inc.

1966 The Jerusalem Bible. Garden City, New
York: Doubleday & Company, Inc.; London:
Darton, Longman & Todd.

1969 The Jerusalem Bible. Genesis, the First
     Book of Moses; Wood engravings by Hermann
     Fechenbach. London: A.R. Mowbrary.

1969 Jerusalem Bible: Old Testament, with
     abridged introduction and notes. London:
     Darton, Longman and Todd.

1985 The New Jerusalem Bible. Garden City, New
     York: Doubleday & Company, Inc.

[A Catholic translation with minor revisions from the
French Version, "La Bible de Jerusalem" published by Les
Editions du Cerf, Paris, 1961, (modified in the light of
the subsequent revised fasciculi edition) under the
general editorship of Pere Roland de Vaux, O.P. This is
the first Catholic Bible to use the familiar book titles
and nomenclature. Clear, contemporary English. Alexander
Jones was the General Editor.]
     The following were translators:
Joseph Leo Alston   Florence Bennett
Joseph Blenkensopp   David Joseph Bourke
Douglas Carter   Aldhelm Dean
Illtud Evans   Kenelm Foster
Ernest Graf   Prospero Grech
Edmund Hill   Sylvester Houedard
Leonard Johnston   Alexander Jones
Anthony J. Kenny   James Lloyd
James McAuley   Alan Neame

[The Deity is rendered "Yahweh" many times.]

1967 **New Scofield Reference Bible**   The New Scofield
     Reference Bible. Holy Bible; Authorized King James
     Version. With introductions, annotations, subject
     chain references, and such word changes in the text
     as will help the reader. Editor C.I. Scofield, D.D.
     Editorial Committee of the New Edition: E. Schuyler
     English... Chairman, Frank E. Gaebelein..., William
     Culbertson..., Charles L. Feinberg..., Allan A.
     MacRae..., Clarence E. Mason Jr..., Alva J.
     McClain..., Wilbur M. Smith..., John F. Walvoord...
     New York: Oxford University Press, 1967.

1969 **Anonymous**   The Bible Reader, and Interfaith
     Interpretation with Notes from Catholic, Protestant,
     and Jewish Traditions. New York: Bruce Publications
     Co., 1969.
          [The RSV with selections from other translations, old
          and new.]

1969 **New International Version**   ...New International
     Version. 1969-1978.
          1969 The Gospel according to John. A
               contemporary translation by New York
               Bible Society.

Another   Edition;   Grand   Rapids:
Zondervan, 1973.

1973 The   Holy   Bible: New   International
Version: New Testament.   Grand Rapids:
Zondervan Bible Publishers.

1975 Isaiah.

1976 The Book of Daniel.

1977 Proverbs and Ecclesiastes.

1978 The   Holy   Bible: New   International
Version.   Grand Rapids: Zondervan Bible
Publishers.

Another   Edition;   The   NIV   Triglot   Old
Testament.   Grand Rapids: Zondervan Publishing
House, 1981.
   [Unpaged. Measures 11 X 9 inches, and is 2 1/2
   inches thick.]

Another Edition, 1984. [Slightly revised. See Acts
10:43.]

1970 **Anonymous**   The Restoration of Original Sacred Name
Bible containing the Old and New Testaments. The
Restoration of Original Sacred Name Bible is
designed to restore to the scriptures the Sacred
Name of the MOST HIGH and His Son from the Sacred
Original on the Basis of the Rotherham Version.
Revised by Missionary Dispensary Bible Research.
Buena Park, Calif.: Missionary Dispensary Bible
Research, 1970.
   [See New Testament listing, 1968 Anonymous, The New
   Testament]

   [The Deity is rendered "Yahweh" many times.]

1970 **New American Bible**   The New American Bible.
Translated from the Original Languages with Critical
Use of All the Ancient Sources by Members of the
Catholic Biblical Association of America. Sponsored
by the Bishop's Committee of the Confraternity of
Christian Doctrine...   New York: Catholic Book
Publishing Co., 1970.
   [The translation is simple, clear and straight forward
   and reads smoothly. "It is good American English... It
   is not as pungent and colorful as the New English Bible.
   Its translations are not striking but neither are they
   clumsy. It is more faithful to the original." Reportedly
   issued by twelve different publishers. The World edition
   is in three columns, others are in two columns. Some
   arrangement of verses occur in Ezekiel, and there is
   confusion in that no reference is made to where the

sequence is to be found. The Kenedy edition has good
print, but the verse numbers are too small. It is not
really the "first complete American version of Holy
Scripture translated directly from the original Hebrew,
Aramaic and Greek" as advertized. The N.T. is the
Confraternity version revised.]

[The N.T. was revised 1987.]

1971 Anonymous   King James II Version of the Bible.
Byron Center, MI: Associated Publishers and Authors,
Inc., 1971.
　　　[Copyright by Jay Green]

1972 Byington, Steven T.   The Bible in Living
English, translated by Steven T. Byington. Brooklyn:
Watchtower Bible and Tract Society of New York,
1972.
　　　[The Deity is rendered "Jehovah" many times.]

1973 Common Bible   The Holy Bible: Revised Standard
Version, containing the Old and New Testament with
Apocrypha/ Deutercanonical Books. An Ecumenical
Edition. New York: William Colling Sons, 1973.
　　　Also; New York, Nashville & Camden: Thomas
Nelson, Inc., 1973.

1976 Anonymous   Holy Bible. Today's English Version.
New York: American Bible Society, 1976.
　　　[Also published as "Good News Bible". See Anonymous,
　　　Today's English Version, 1966; Anonymous, The Psalms,
　　　1970; Anonymous, "Tried and True" Job, 1971; Anonymous,
　　　Wisdom for Modern Man (Proverbs and Ecclesiastes), 1972;
　　　Anonymous, Justice Now! (Hosea, Amos and Micah), 1975.]

　　　[The 'Good News Bible' used "Lord" for the Deity. In the
　　　footnote for Exodus 6:3, it used "Jehovah".]

　　　Another edition; ...with Deuterocanonical/
Apocrypha, 1979.

1976 Beck, William F.   The Holy Bible in the Language
of Today, An American Translation, by William F.
Beck. New Haven, Mo.: Leader Publishing Co., 1976.
　　　Another edition; The Holy Bible in the Language
　　　of Today, An American Translation, By William
　　　F. Beck. Stylistic alterations and other
　　　changes dictated by the latest MS evidence
　　　made by Elmer B. Smick and Erich H. Kiehl.
　　　Nashville: Holman Bible Publisher, 1976.

1976 Green, Jay (General Editor and Translator)
The Interlinear Hebrew/Greek English Bible. 4 Volume
Edition. Wilmington, Delaware: Associated Publishers
and Authors, 1976-1979.
　　　1976 Vol. 1 (Genesis - Ruth)

1976 Vol. 2   (1 Samuel - Psalms)
1978 Vol. 3   Psalms 56 - Malachi
1979 Vol. 4   (The New Testament)
           Second and Revised edition; The New
           Testament, 1984.

    Second Edition; Four Volume Set, 1985.

    [The Deity is rendered "Jehovah" many times.]

    [A 72-page sample of this Interlinear Bible was
    published in 1976 titled, "The Book of Judges.]

1977 **Anonymous**   The Psalms. A New Translation
for Worship, Pointed for Singing to Anglican Chant.
Published in cooperation with church information
office by Collins. [English text by David L. Frost,
John A. Emerton, Andrew A. MacIntosh]   London:
Collins Liturgical Publications, 1977.
    Also; The Psalms, a New Translation for Worship
    prepared by David L. Frost and a panel of
    Hebrew and Biblical Scholars. London: Collins
    Liturgical, 1977.

1979 **New King James Bible**   The New King James Bible.
1979-1982.
    1979 The New King James Bible: New Testament.
    Nashville, Tenn.: Thomas Nelson.

    1982 Holy Bible: the New King James Version.
    Nashville, Tenn.: Thomas Nelson.

1981 **Anonymous**   The Sacred Scriptures, Bethel Edition.
Premier Publication. Bethel, Pa.: Assemblies of
Jahweh, 1981.
    [Used "Yahweh" in both the Old & New Testament.]

1982 **Word Biblical Commentary**   Word Biblical Commentary.
[Book of the Books]   Waco, TX: Word Books,
Publisher, 1982-Present.
    [The translators known to have completed work for this
    commentary and translation will be listed by name and
    referred to here. There are approx. 52 vols. projected.]

1983 **Open Bible**   Holy Bible Containing The Old and New
Testaments. The New King James... The Open Bible,
Expanded Edition with Read-along References, Read-
along Translations, Biblical Cyclopedic Index,...
Nashville, Camden & New York: Thomas Nelson
Publishers, 1983.
    Another Edition; 1985.

    Revised Edition; 1990.

1987 **Anonymous**   The Holy Bible: English Version for the
Deaf.   Grand Rapids: Baker Book House, 1987.
[See New Testament listing, 1978 Anonymous, The New
Testament... for the Deaf.]

1988 **Anonymous**   Christian Community Bible. Translation,
presented   and   commented   for   the   Christian
communities of the Philippines and the Third World;
and for those who seek God. Complete text translated
from   Hebrew   and   Greek.   Pastoral   Edition.   [Co-
Published   in   the   Philippines   by]   Claretian
Publications, St. Paul Publications [and] Divine
Word Publications, 1988.
Second Edition; Catholic Pastoral Edition, 1988.

1989 **Revised English Bible**   The Revised English
Bible with the Apocrypha.   Oxford University Press;
Cambridge University Press, 1989.
[A revision of the 'New English Bible' of 1961.]

1990 **Anonymous**   The Holy Bible. Simplified Living Bible
Text.   Wheaton,   Illinois: Tyndale   House   Publishers,
Inc., 1990
[Text by Mark Norton and Kenneth N. Taylor.]

1990 **New Revised Standard Version** (NRSV)   Holy Bible.
New Revised Standard Version. containing the Old and
New Testaments.   Grand Rapids, MI: Zondervan Bible
Publishers, 1990.
[See Complete Bibles, 1952 Revised Standard Version.
Also, see Apocrypha listing, 1989 New Revised Standard
Version.]

1991 **Anonymous**   The Bible for Today's Family, 1991–
1991 The   Bible   for   Today's   Family   –   New
Testament.   New   York: American   Bible
Society.

[The Old Testament portion is scheduled to be released
by 1996.]

ABRIDGED BIBLES

???? **Formby, Henry**   Pictorial Bible and Church history
Series, from the Beginning of the World down to the
Present Time.   New York: The Catholic Publication
Society, n.d. [188?].
["Complete   in   Seven   Separate   Parts,   forming   Five
Volumes".   Includes   lengthy   quotes   from   the   Douay
version.]

???? **Schuster, Ignacius**   Illustrated Bible History of the Old and New Testaments for the Use of Catholic Schools..., [189?].
> Another edition; - - Revised by Mrs. J. Sadlier and carefully Improved by Several clergymen. Fifteenth edition, with new illustrations and two colored maps. St. Louis, Mo. & London: B. Herder Book Co., 1922.
>
> Another edition, With 82 illustrations by Philipp Schumacher, 1955.
>> [Described by British Museum Cat. as "a condensed translation of 'Handbuch zur biblischen Geschichte des alten and neuen Testaments.'"]
>
> Also; The practical Commentary on Holy Scripture for those who Teach Bible History by Frederick Justus Knecht, D.D... Translated and adapted from the sixteenth German Edition. Preface by the Very Rev. Canon M.F. Glancey...
>> ["The narrative in the Practical Commentary is Dr. Schuster's Bible History..."]
>
> - - First English Edition, 1894.
> - - Second English Edition, 1901.
> - - Third English Edition, 1910.
> - - Fourth English Edition, 1923.

1200 **Anonymous**   The Sowlehele, or Salus Animae. Bodley: Veron MS.
> ["...a metrical summary of the leading events of Bible history... Warton thinks this was made before the year 1200, and several of them, including the story of Lazaras and other Gospel stories, have been copied for the E.E.T.S...."]

1548 **Paynell, Thomas**   The Piththy and moost notable Sayinges of al Scripture gathered by Thomas Paynel after ye maner of como places, very necessary for al those that delite in cosolacions of the Scriptures, newly augmeted & corrected. Imprinted at London by me Wyllyam Copland for John Waley, 1548.
> Another edition; Imprinted...for Richard Jugge, 1549.
>
> Also; Imprinted at London by Thomas Gaultier at the costes and charges of Robert Toye, 1550.

1553 **Taverner, Richard**   Commo places of scripture ordrely and after a comendious forme of teaching, set forth with no little laboure, to ye great profit & help of all suche studentes in Gods word as haue not had longe exercise in the same, by the right excellent clerke Eras. Sarcarius. Translated in to

Englysh by Richard Taverner. Imprinted at London by
Nycolas Hyll, 1553.

1596 **Clapham, Henoch**   A Briefe of the Bible; drawne
first into English Poesy, and then illustrated by
apte Annotations together with some other necessary
Appendices.   Edinburgh: Printed by Robert Walde-
Graue, 1596.
> Another edition; ...whereunto is now added a
> Synopsis of the Bibles Doctrines.   Imprinted
> at London for I.N., 1603.
>
> Third Edition; in sundrie things amended and
> enlarged. Imprinted at London by R.B. for
> Nathaniell Butter, 1605.
>
> Fourth Edition; London: Printed by Thom. Harper
> for Nathaniell Butter, 1639.

1602 **Pagit, Evsebius**   The History of the Bible, Briefely
collected by way of Question and Answer. Written by
Evsebius Pagit, and by him corrected. Printed at
London by I.L. and are to be sold by Ihon Waterson,
1602.

1614 **Anonymous** Verbum Sempiternae. [John Taylor] Printed
at London by Jo. Beale for John Harman, 1614.
> [Subsequent editions: Verbum Sempiternum]
>
> [Stone lists 14 editions of Taylor's "Thumb Bible", the
> latest by Longman & Co., London, in 1849. An edition
> dated 1693, Preface reads:"Heere, Reader, maist thou
> read / (for little cost) How thou wast ransomed, / when
> thou quite wast lost. Mans gracelessness,/ and Gogs
> exceeding Grace Thou heere maist read and see,/ in
> little space."]

1623 **Wastel, Simon**   A Trve Christians daily delight:
being The Summe of euery Chapter of the Old & New
Testament, set downe Alphabetically, in English
Verse, that the Scripture we reade may more happily
be remembered, and the things forgotten more easily
recalled by Simon Wastel.   London: Printed by G.
Eldd and M. Flesher, for Robert Mylbourne, 1623.
> Another edition; Microbiblion or the Bibles
> Epitome: In Verse. Digested according to the
> Alphabet, that the Scripture we reade...
> London: Printed for Robert Mylbourne, 1629.
>
> Another edition; The Divine Art of Memory: or,
> The Sum of the Holy Scriptures delivered in
> Acrostick Verses, so that the contents of the
> whole Bible may readily be remembered, and in
> what chapter each particular passage is
> recorded. Written originally in Latine by the

Reverend and Learned John Shaw, and made English by Simon Wastel. London: Printed for Nath. Ponder, 1683.

1633 **Exon, Jos.**   A Plaine And Familiar Explication (by way of Paraphrase) of All the Hard Texts of the whole Divine Scripture of the Old and Nevv Testament. By Jos. Exon. [Joseph Hall] London: printed by Miles Flesher, for Nath. Bvtter, at the Signe of the Pyde Bull at S.Austins Gate. M DC XXXIII. (1633)

1649 **Roberts, Francis**   Clavis Bibliorum. The Key to the Bible, Unlocking the Richest Treasure of the Holy Scriptures &c with Addition of the Scripture Songs, Metrically translated out of the Hebrew. By Francis Roberts. London: Printed for George Calvert, 1649.

1671 **Anonymous**   A Good Help of Weak Memories; Or, the Contents of every Chapter in the Bible In Alphabetical Dysticks. By J.L. [John Lloyd] London: Printed for Thomas Helder, 1671.

1690 **Clarke, Samuel**   The Holy Bible... With Annotations and Parallel Scriptures. To which is annex'd the Harmony of the Gospels: as also the Reduction of Jewish Weights Coins and Measures, to our English Standards. And a table of the Promises in Scripture. London: J. Rawlins for Richard Chiswell and Jonathan Robinson, 1690.
        [...in some passages he has use of the marginal readings (of the AV), and in one case he has an independent rendering...]

        Another Edition; London: J. Fuller, 1760.

1690 **Nesse, Christopher**   A compleat history and mystery of the Old and New Testaments, 1690-1696.

1700 **Ellwood, Thomas**   Sacred History: or the Historical Part of the Holy Scriptures of the Old and New Testament; Digested into Due Method with Respect to Order of Time and Place... 3 Vols. London: c1700.
        [The Preface to the seventh edition of Vol. 3 indicates that it was done by a Quaker primarily for Juveniles. Being a synoptic of the Gospels and the addition of Acts. It is primarily an AV with a running embellishment plus slight changes. The Preface also indicates that Volumes 1 & 2 will be published when volume 3 had been disposed of. I don't know if vols 1 & 2 were ever published. No listing of this work can be found anywhere.]

        From the first American, compared with the last London Edition; Mount Pleasant, Ohio: Enoch & Emily M. Harris, 1853.

1701 **Wesley, Samuel**   The History of the Holy Land by
      Samuel Wesley. 3 Vols. London: 1701-1716.
       1701 The History of the New Testament.
                Representing the Actions and Miracles of
                our Blessed Saviour and His Apostles,
                Attempted in Verse. And Adorn'd with CLII
                Sculptures... The Cutts done by J. Sturt.
                For Charles Harper.

       1716 The History of the Old and New Testament
                Attempted in Verse: And Adorn'd with
                three hundred & thirty Sculptures.
                Written by S. Wesley, A.M. The Cuts done
                by J. Sturt. 2 Vols. Printed for John
                Hooke.

                Vol. II. The History of the Holy Bible,
                From the Revolt of the Ten Tribes to the
                end of the Prophets, with sculptures.

1736 **Smith, S.**   The Compleat History of the Old and New
      Testament: or, a Family Bible. With Critical and
      Explanatory Annotations, Extracted from the writings
      of the most Celebrated Authors, Ancient and Modern,
      by S. Smith... London: W. Rayner, 1736.

1737 **Stackhouse, Thomas**   A New History of the Holy
      Bible, by Thomas Stackhouse. 1737.

1772 **Wynne, Richard**   Bible, adapted to the use of
      schools and private families by Richard Wynne.
      London: for J. Wilkie, 1772.
        ["From this edition certain portions of the text are
        excluded."]

1803 **Priestley, Joseph**   Notes on all the Books
      of Scripture, for the use of the Pulpit and Private
      Families   by   Joseph   Priestley.   4   Vols.
      Northumberland: Andre Kennedy, 1803.
        ["In some cases observations in the form of Notes are
        not sufficient to give a clear and connected view of the
        meaning of the sacred writers. In these cases I had
        recourse to a paraphrase..." from the preface.]

1807 **Anonymous**   A Short History of the Bible
      and Testament, with 48 Neat Engravings, Designed by
      Alfred Wells. London: Bublished [sic] by W. Darton
      & J. Harvey... and J. Harris, 1807.

1814 **Reeve, J.**   The History of the Holy Bible,
      interspersed with Moral and Instructive Reflections,
      Chiefly taken from the Holy Fathers. From the
      French. 2 Vols. New York: J. Seymour, 1814.
        ["An abridgment (paraphrase) of the Historical Books of
        the Old and New Testaments."]

1868 **Tiffany, Osmond**   Sacred Biography and History,
Containing Descriptions of Palestine, Ancient and
Modern: Lives of the Patriarchs, Kings and Prophets,
Christ and the Apostles, Edited by Osmond Tiffany.
Springfield, Mass.: Bill, Nichols & Co.;   Chicago,
Ill.: Hugh Heron, 1868.
     [Apparently pirated from John Fleetwood (See 1815) and
     revised.]

     Another edition, 1873.

1869 **Anonymous**   The Bible Manual: An Expository
and Practical Commentary on the Books of Scripture,
Arranged in Chronological Order; forming a Handbook
of Biblical Elucidation, for the use of families,
schools, and students of the Word of God. Translated
from the German Work edited by the late Rev. Dr.
T.C. Barth...   London: James Nisbet & Co., 1869.
     ["The received version has been altered only where this
     was necessary for a correct understanding of the
     passage..."]

1870 **Murray, John A**.   Bible Lyrics, by John A. Murray...
New York & Cincinnati: C.F. Vent;   Chicago: J.S.
Goodman & Co., 1870.
     ["...the work consists of a metrical versification of
     what may properly be termed the Poetry of the
     Bible...together with the entire Book of Job, arranged
     in the form of a Sacred Drama." The Psalms appear
     complete in verse form.]

1873 **Foster, Charles**   The Story of the Bible
from Genesis to Revelation. Told in Simple Language
Adapted to all Ages, But especially to the Young.
Philadelphia: 1873.
     ["Although simplified in language, the spirit of the
     Scripture narrative is most carefully preserved, and the
     incidents of the Bible story...are told in an
     interesting and continuous form."]

     Another edition; Philadelphia: Charles Foster
     Publications, 1884.

     Also; Philadelphia: Macrae Smith Co., 1911.

1880 **Bindel, A. and F.W. Weiskotten**   Biblical History
in the Words of Holy Scripture, with Engravings,
Maps, Questions and Notes. A Lesson-Book for Sunday
and Week-53

          Thirty-eight edition; Reading, Pa: Pilger Book
          Store. nd.

          [The wording is patterned after the KJV, but with many
          revisions and abridgements.]

1883 **Anonymous**   Sacred Scriptures of the World;
     Being Selections of the Most Devotional and Ethical
     Portions of the Ancient Hebrew and Christian
     Scriptures, to which have been Added Kindred
     Selections from other Ancient Scriptures of the
     World; Designed for Common use in Churches, Schools,
     and Homes, or Wherever else the Devout and Moral
     Teachings of the World may be Needed for Purposes of
     Religious Inspiration or of Ethical Instruction;
     Compiled, Edited, and in Part Retranslated by a
     Clergyman. [Martin K. Schermerhorn]   New York &
     London: G.P. Putnam's Sons, 1883.
          New edition, 1898.

          [Spine is entitled 'Ancient Sacred Scriptures Compiled
          for the 20th Century.' Outside cover is entitled 'The
          Old Religion in Modern Words.' From the General Preface,
          "...the translator has ventured to adapt what are known
          as free renderings in place of the common (professedly)
          literal renderings..." Includes extensive selections
          from the Old and New Testaments; also selections from
          Persian, Egyptian, Hindu, Buddhist, Chinese, Grecian,
          Roman and Arabian Scriptures.]

1886 **Bartlett, Edward T. and John P. Peters**
     Scriptures Hebrew and Christian arranged and edited
     for Young Readers as an Introduction to the Study of
     the Bible. By Edward T. Bartlett and John P. Peters.
     3 Vols.   London & New York: G.P. Putnam's Sons,
     1886-1893.
          1886 ...Vol. I. Hebrew Story, From Creation to
               Exile, Comprising material from the
               following books of the O.T.: Genesis,
               Exodus, Deuteronomy, Joshua, Judges, I.
               Samuel, II. Samuel, I. Kings, II. Kings,
               I. Chronicles, II. Chronicles, Psalms,
               Proverbs, Isaiah, Jeremiah, Ezekiel,
               Hosea, Amos, Micah, Nahum, Zephaniah.
                    Another edition, 1887.

          1889 ...Vol. II. Hebrew Legislation, Tales,
               Poetry, and Prophecy.

          1893 ...Vol. III. Christian Scriptures,
               comprising the greater portion of the
               Books of the N.T.

          ["The story is told in the words of the Bible, but with
          considerable condensation and rearrangement... glosses
          In our translation we have preserved, for the most part,
          the wording of either the AV or the recent Canterbury
          Revision; making, however, a considerable number of
          minor changes..."]

1894 **Mosher, Jennie M.**   Story of the Bible in Rhyme by
Jennie M. Mosher. Independence, Iowa: Independence
Book Co., 1894.
[A gross condensation.]

1896 **Oort, Dr. H. and Dr. I. Hooykaas**   The Bible for
Learners by Dr. H. Oort...and Dr. I. Hooykaas... 3
Vols. Boston: Roberts Brothers, 1896-1898.
[The Deity is rendered "Yahweh" a few times.]

1899 **Gibson, Margaret Dunlop**   Studia Sinaitica No.
VII... A Treatise on the Triune Nature of God with
translation by Margaret Dunlop Gibson. London: C.J.
Clay & Sons; Cambridge University Press, 1899.
[From an eighth or ninth century ms in the Convent of
St. Catherine on Mount Sinai; contains many
miscellaneous passages from the Old & New Testament.]

1900 **Sanders, Frank Knight and Charles Foster Kent**
The Messages of the Bible. Edited by Professor Frank
K. Sanders...and Professor Charles Foster Kent. 11
Vols. New York: Charles Scribner's Sons, 1900-1920.
> 1909 Vol. I   The Messages of the Earlier
> Prophets freely rendered in paraphrase.
> By Frank Knight Sanders and Charles
> Foster Kent.
>
> 1908 Vol. II   The Messages of the Later
> Prophets freely rendered in paraphrase.
> By Frank Knight Sanders and Charles
> Foster Kent.
>
> 1902 Vol. III   The Messages of Israel's
> Lawgivers... By Charles Foster Kent.
>
> 1909 Vol. IV   The Messages of the Prophetic
> and Priestly Historians... By John Edgar
> McFadyen.
>
> 1909 Vol. V The Messages of the Psalmists...
> By John Edgar McFadyen.
>
> Vol. VI The Messages of the Sages (never
> published).
>
> 1911 Vol. VII   The Messages of the Dramatic
> Poets: the Books of Job and Canticles and
> some Minor Poems in the Old Testament
> with Introduction, Metrical Translations
> and Paraphrases. By Nathaniel Smith.
>
> 1909 Vol. VIII   The Messages of the
> Apocalyptical Writers... By Frank
> Chamberlin Porter.

1901 Vol. IX   The Messages of Jesus According
     to the Synoptists... By Thomas Cuming
     Hall.

1908 Vol. X   The Messages of Jesus According
     to the Gospel of John... By James
     Stevenson Riggs.

1900 Vol. XI   The Messages of the Apostles...
     By George Barker Stevens.

1907 Vol. XII   The Messages of Paul... By
     George Barker Stevens.

[Free rendering in paraphrase.]

[The Deity is rendered "Jehovah" many times in the Old
Testament and many times in Vol. XI, 'The Messages of
the Apostles'.]

1904 **Brun, N.C.**   Bible History and Brief Outlines of
     Church History by Volrath Vogt, Formerly Principal
     of the Cathedral School, Christiania, Norway.
     Revised According to the New translation of the
     Bible by the Publishing Committee of the Norwegian
     Lutheran Church. From the Norwegian by N.C.Brun,
     1904.
          Another edition, 1916. [Includes the Old and New
          Testaments, compressed into 84 pages.]

1904 **Marshall, Logan**   The Wonder Book of Bible Stories;
     Edited and Arranged by Logan Marshall.   Chicago,
     Philadelphia, Toronto: John C. Winston, 1904.

1906 **Hall, Newton Marshall, and Irving Francis Wood**   The
     Bible Story. The Golden Book. Arranged and edited by
     Newton Marshall Hall and Irving Francis Wood...
     Springfield, Massachusetts: The King-Richardson Co.,
     1906.
          [KJV. "Obsolete words are modernized."]

     Another edition, 1917.

1907 **Pierce, Ulysses G.B.**   The Soul of the Bible; Being
     Selections from the Old and New Testaments and the
     Apocrypha, Arranged as Synthetic readings by Ulysses
     G.B. Pierce; Introduction by Edward Everett Hale.
     Boston: American Unitarian Association, 1907.
          ["...some verbal changes, and the omission of whatever
          would distract the attention, offend the moral sense, or
          start a divergent line of thought." Based on the ASV.]

     Another edition; Boston: American Unitarian
     Association, 1908.

Also; Boston: The Beacon Press, n.d.

1908 **Kent, Charles Foster**   The Historical Bible.
By Charles Foster Kent. 6 Vols. New York: Charles
Scribner's Sons, 1908-1916.
> 1909 Vol. I   The Heroes and Crises of Early
> Hebrew History from the Creation to the
> Death of Moses.
>
> 1908 Vol. II   The Founders and Rulers of
> United Israel from the Death of Moses to
> the Division of the Hebrew Kingdom.
>
> 1909 Vol. III   The Kings and Prophets of
> Israel and Judah from the Division of the
> Kingdom to the Babylonian Exile.
>
> 1911 Vol. IV   The Makers and Teachers of
> Judaism from the Fall of Jerusalem to the
> Death of Herod the Great.
>
> 1913 Vol. V   The Life and Teachings of Jesus
> According to the Earliest Records.
>
> 1916 Vol. VI   The Work and Teachings of the
> Apostles.
>
> ["...a simple, dignified idiomatic translation... based
> on the oldest and best readings of the Hebrew, Greek,
> Syriac and Latin texts..." The O.T. closely follows
> Kent's "Students O.T.', 1904. Contains a "condensed
> paraphrase".]

1911 **Evans, Adelaide Bee**   Easy Steps in the Bible Story.
Takoma Park, Washington, D.C.: Review & Herald
Publication Society, 1911.
> ["Though the book is written in easy words, it is
> nevertheless put in good strong English..." mostly KJV.]

1915 **Canton, William**   The Bible Story, Illustrated.
London: Hodder & Stoughton, 1915.

1915 **Tichenor, Henry M.**   The Life and Exploits of
Jehovah by Henry M.Tichenor. St.Louis, MO: Published
by Phil Wagner, 1915.
> ["To those who, through religious prejudice, may attempt
> to deny some of the legends and wonders found in 'The
> Life of Jehovah', the writer would state that there is
> not a single story narrated but what has its source in
> the ancient Scriptural and Rabbinical writings. The
> writer has simply put them in popular language..."]

1918 **Anonymous**   Comprehensive Bible History. St. Louis,
Mo: Concordia Publishing House, 1918.

["Some additions and changes in the text of the stories were made..." Text is KJV with frequent paraphrase and condensation.]

Another edition; Advance Bible History in the Words of Holy Scripture With Illustrations, Maps, and Notes. By A.C. Stellhorn. St. Louis, Mo.: Concordia Publishing House, 1936.

1918 **Kent, Charles Foster**   The Shorter Bible. Translated and Arranged by Charles Foster Kent, with the collaboration of Charles Cutler Torrey, Henry A. Sherman, Frederick Harris and Ethel Cutler. Two Volumes. New York: Charles Scribner's Sons, 1918-1922.
    1918 The New Testament.
         Another edition, 1925.

    1922 The Old Testament.
         Second edition, revised, 1922.
         Third edition, Revised, 1934.

    ["In the translation the aim has been to translate the original Hebrew, Aramaic, and Greek idioms into their modern English equivalent – that is, to make it literal rather than literalistic, and to present the thought of the Biblical writers so simply that it can be easily understood by all." Gospels are harmonized. Approximately two-thirds of the O.T. and one-third of the N.T. are omitted.]

    [The Deity is rendered "Jehovah" many times.]

    Also published; London: Hodder & Stoughton, date unknown.

1919 **Tyler, John Williamson**   Beautiful Story of the Bible in Simple Language; Containing Nearly Three Hundred Stories from the Holy Book; A Fascinating, Inspiring and Instructive Historical Narrative of the Old and New Testament Times, Including the Lives of the Prophets, of the Rulers, and the Beautiful Stories of Jesus and His Disciples; Designed as a Course of Instruction for the Fifty-two Weeks of the Year, or for Daily Reading. Followed by a Series of Questions which Simplify the Stories, and Emphasize Their Important Truths... Embellished With Nearly Two Hundred Fine Illustrations, Including Sixteen Magnificent Full Color Plates. Cincinnati, Ohio: The S.A. Mullikin Co., 1919.

1922 **Egermeier, Elsie E.**   Egermeier's Bible Story Book. Gospel Trumpet Co., 1922.
    Another Edition; Bible Story Book. A Complete Narration from Genesis to Revelation for Young

and Old. By Elsie E. Egermeier. Anderson, Indiana: The Warner Press, 1923.

Other editions, 1927, 1934, 1935, 1938.

New and Revised Edition; 1939, 1947, 1955 & 1965.

Another edition; Picture-Story Life of Jesus by Elsie E. Egermeier. Story Revision by Arlene S. Hall. Adopted from Egermeier's Bible Story Book. Anderson, Indiana: Warner Press, 1963.

1923 **Hall, Newton Marshall, and Irving Francis Wood**   The Book of Life; Arranged and Edited. 8 Vols. Chicago: John Rudin, 1923.
    [KJV with obsolete words modernized.]

1923 **Hay, Florence E.**   Bible Stories in Rhyme; Rhymes and Illustrations by Florence E. Hay.   Chicago & Philadelphia: The Rodeheaver Co., 1923.

1923 **Jefferson, Thomas and R.F. Weymouth**
    The Thomas Jefferson Bible; undiscovered teachings of Jesus; reported by his first four biographers; arranged by Thomas Jefferson; translated by R.F. Weymouth; printed in modern form; designed as an aid to the practice of social intelligence, and the creation of a science of society, edited by Henry E. Jackson... New York: Boni and Liveright, 1923.
        Another Edition; Edited by O.I.A. Roche. NY: Clarkson N. Porter, Inc., 1964.   [Photographic reproduction.]

1923 **Loon, Hendrik William Van**   The Story of the Bible, Written and Drawn by Hendrik William Van Loon. New York: Boni & Liveright, 1923.
    [An abbreviated paraphrase.]

1924 **Vedder, Henry C.**   The Essence of the Bible Selected and Edited by Henry C. Vedder.   Girard, Kansas: Haldeman-Julius Company ["Little Blue Book No. 600"], 1924.
    [Contains many unique renderings.]

1925 **Hurlbut, Jesse Lyman**   Bible Stories Everyone Should Know. Chicago, Philadelphia & Toronto: John C. Winston Co., 1925.

1928 **Browne, Lewis**   The Graphic Bible. From Genesis to Revelation in Animated Maps and Charts by Lewis Browne. New York: The Macmillan Co., 1928.
    [Many times reprinted, as late as 1944.]

    ["The main incidents in (the Bible) are recounted in the text in this book... I have sought to follow the

Scriptures quite literally..."   Also; The Adventures
of Ancient Israel: From Abraham to the Dispersion in
Maps and charts. (Publisher and date unknown.]

1928 **Cambridge Shorter Bible**   The Cambridge Shorter
Bible... [A. Nairne, T.R.Glover, and A. Quiller-
Couch] Cambridge: University Press, 1928.
[Text is generally AV or ERV with "...further   slight
alterations...for the sake of lucidity."]

1928 **Hall, Bolton**   The Living Bible. Being the Whole
Bible in its Fewest Words. Edited from the KJV. By
Bolton Hall.   New York: 1928.
Revised edition; Cleveland & New York: The World
Syndicate Pub Co., 1937.

Revised edition; Cleveland, New York: 1938.

["The words of the text almost throughout are those of
the KJV. Every interpolation or substitution and every
transposition not otherwise indicated are inclosed in
brackets."]

1931 **Inge, William Ralph**   Every Man's Bible. An
Anthology Arranged with an Introduction. By William
Ralph Inge.   New York & Toronto: Longmans, Green &
Co., 1931.
["In this book most of the extracts are from the AV, but
in a few instances the ERV has been preferred. I have
also taken the liberty of altering a very few archaisms
and obsolete spellings of words."]

1931 **Johnson, George and Others**   Bible History. A
Textbook of the Old and New Testament for Catholic
Schools. Rev. George Johnson... Rev. Jerome D.
Hannan... Sister M. Dominica...   New York,
Cincinnati, Chicago and San Francisco: Benziger
Bros., 1931.
Another edition; 1936.

1932 **Browne, Lewis**   Stranger Than Fiction. A
Short History of the Jews From Earliest Times to the
Present Day. By Lewis Browne...   New York: The
Macmillan Co., 1932.
[An abridged paraphrase.]

1934 **Vos, Catherine F.**   The Child's Story Bible by
Catherine F. Vos. 3 Vols. Grand Rapids, Michigan:
William B. Eerdmans Publishing Co., 1934-1936.
New Edition; (8th) One Vol., 1949.

1936 **Faris, Lillie A.**   [Bible] Stories Retold for
Children. 2 Vols. New York: Platt & Munk Co., 1936.
Vol. 1.   O.T. Stories Retold for Children

Vol. 2.   N.T. Stories Retold for Children

1937 **Brooks, J. Barlow**   Th' amazin stories o' the'
    Bible... Stalybridge, Lancashire: George Whittaker
    & Sons, 1937.

1937 **Knox, Ronald Arbuthnott**   The Holy Bible. An
    abridgement and rearrangement. By Ronald A. Knox.
    London: Sheed & Ward; New York: Sheed & Ward, 1937.

1937 **Newton, William L. and Ellamay Horan**   The First
    Book of the Kingdom of God Series. Bible Lessons.
    New York, Chicago: W.H. Sadlier, Inc., 1937.
        ["The stories are written in simple language and may be
        used as early as the third grade."]

1940 **Roney, Charles P. and Wilfred G. Rice**   Beautiful
    Bible Stories. By Rev. Charles P. Roney..., Rev. G.
    Rice, Collaborator. Inspirational, Entertaining,
    Fascinating, Educational,... Wichita, Kansas: The
    John A. Hertel Co., 1978.
        [Previous copyrights: 1940 by C.P. Roney; 1948 by The
        John A. Hertel Co.; 1967 by The John A. Hertel Co.; 1976
        by DeVore & Sons, Inc. This information came from the
        Preface.]

1940 **Welsch, Howard**   The Bible (A Condensed Version) by
    Howard Welsch. [No place or name.], 1940.
        [A very gross condensation.]

1943 **Hogner, Dorothy Childs**   The Bible Story...
    Illustrated by Nils Hogner.   London, New York &
    Toronto: Oxford University Press, 1943.
        [An abridged Bible with many unique renderings.]

1946 **Werner, Elsa Jane**   The Golden Bible for Children
    by Elsa Jane Werner.   New York: Simon & Schuster,
    1946-1953.
            1946 - - Stories from the Old Testament
                selected and arranged by Elsa Jane
                Werner;   Illustrated   by   Feodor
                Rojankovsky.

            1953 - - The New Testament edited and arranged
                by Elsa Jane Werner; Illustrated by Alice
                and Martin Provenson.

        Another Edition; The Holy Bible selected and
        arranged by Elsa Jane Werner and Charles
        Hartman. The Old Testament illustrated by
        Feodor   Rojankousky.   The   New   Testament
        illustrated by Alice and Martin Provensen.
        New York: Guild Press, 1946.
            [1 Vol. edition. Title taken from the 1960
            edition.]

        Reprinted; New York: Guild Press, 1960, 1965.

1947 **Nordgren, J. Vincent**   A Bible History for Schools, Confirmation Classes and Homes; Prepared by J. Vincent Nordgren; Under the Direction of the Board of Parish Education of the Evangelical Augustana Synod of North America.   Rock Island, Illinois: Augustana Book Concern, 1947.
> [Selections; "A considerable part of the Bible text...is from the RSV..."]

1947 **Schoolland, Marian M.**   Marian's Big Book of Bible Stories... Illustrated in Full Color by Dirk Gringhuis. Grand Rapids: Wm. B. Eerdmans Publishing Company, 1947.
> ["...selected and simplified for very young children..."]

> Another edition, 1952

> Reprint; July, 1988.

1949 **Barnhart, Nancy**   The Lord is My Shepherd; Stories from the Bible pictures in Bible lands, arranged and illustrated by Nancy Barnhart.   New York: Charles Scribner's, 1949.
> [Many abbreviated paraphrases linking passages from the AV.]

1950 **Morrow, Louis LaRavoire**   My Bible History in Pictures. Complete Edition Old and New Testament. By the Most Reverend Louis LaRavoi Morrow... Kenosha, Wisconsin: My Mission House, 1950.

1951 **Briggs, G. W., G. B. Caird, and N. Micklem**   The Shorter Oxford Bible. Abridged and edited.   London, New York & Toronto: Geoffrey Cumberledge, Oxford University Press, 1951.
> [Text is generally the AV; ERV for the Apocrypha; "...with some exceptions..."]

1951 **Ross, Peter V.**   Bible in Brief; a digest of the King James version, by Peter V. Ross.   New York: Grosset & Dunlap, 1951.
> [Contains a paraphrase.]

1951 **Rowe, Mortimer**   A Golden Treasury of the Bible; I. from the Old Testament and Apocrypha; II. from the New Testament. Selected and edited by Mortimer Rowe with the assistance of Herbert McLaclan and Dorothy Tarrant.   Boston: The Beacon Press, 1951.
> [The AV has been used "...uncorrected, in the whole of the great narrative section from Genesis to Nehemiah and Maccabees, except that some short poetic passages (printed in verse) are given in a corrected and more rhythmic form. But one cannot adhere strictly to the AV beyond this point if respect [is to be] shown for the actual words of the prophets, poets and sages, since the AV, for all its beauty, is a defective translation based

upon a defective text... Where the Septuagint and other ancient versions seem to offer a more probable reading of an obscure word or phrase, these variants have been freely but not irresponsibly adopted..." Preface is dated 1934.]

1952 **Ballou, Robert O.**   The Living Bible. A shortened version for modern readers based on the King James Translation. Edited by Robert O. Ballou. New York: Viking Press, 1952.
["...with the exception of the Song of Songs and the Logoi..the AV of the KJ translation has been used. Some liberties, in addition to that of shortening it, and that of rearranging the order of the books and in a number of cases ignoring divisions into books entirely, have been taken with the well-known text..."]

1955 **Fanchiotti, Margherita**   Stories from the Bible, Illustrated by Joan Kiddell-Monroe. London: Oxford University Press, 1955.
["All the stories in this book are taken from the Bible, and no doubt you will want to look them up for yourself..."]

Reprinted, 1957 and 1959.

1955 **Ford, Alvy E.**   The Bible in Verse; a bird's-eye view of every Bible chapter as observed through the eyes of the poet.   Santa Cruz, California: Monte Vista Press, 1955.
[Each chapter of each book of the Bible is represented by a four-line stanza of couplet verse. Mr. Ford calls himself "The Blind Poet".]

1956 **Gaer, Joseph and Chester C. McCown**   The Bible for Family Reading with Introductions and Notes; The Old Testament prepared by Joseph Gaer - The New Testament by Joseph Gaer and Chester C. McCown. Boston & Toronto: Little, Brown and Company, 1956.
["...approximates the KJV more closely than any other version... All obscurities and archaisms are eliminated... every chapter is accounted for... The Gospels according to Matthew, Mark and Luke have been combined into a single story... this is followed by the Acts of the Apostles, the Apostolic Letters... the Revelation of John; and ends with the Gospel according to John..."]

Another edition; The Jewish Bible for Family Reading, with Introduction and Notes.   New York & London: Thomas Yoseloff, 1957.
[O.T. only]

1956 **Hodges, Turner and Elizabeth McLean** (Editors)   The Bible Story Library; the Holy Scriptures retold in story form for the young and as an explanation and commentary for all, based on traditional texts and

illustrated with the most famous Biblical art. 8
Vols. New York: Educational Book Guild Inc., 1956.
[Based on copyright information only; publication is
uncertain.]

Another edition; 8 Vols. New York: American
Handbook & Textbook Co., Inc., 1963.

1957 **Cox, Lilan**   Mirror to Today; Paraphrases and
reflections. Naperville, Ill.: SCM Book Club, 1957.
[Paraphrases of Old and New Testament passages, only
vaguely related to the original texts.]

1957 **Gibson, Katherine**   The Tall Book of Bible Stories
Retold ...Illustrations by Ted Chaiko.   Harper &
Bros., 1957.
["...most familiar stories of the Old & New Testament,
retold for the youngest children in simple and lovely
prose."]

1958 **Fanchiotti, Margherita**   A Beginner's Bible.
A Shortened Bible in Modern English. By Margherita
Fanchiotti with the advice and assistance of
Nathaniel Michlem.   London, New York, Toronto:
Oxford University Press, 1958.
[Several times reprinted.]

1958 **Mand, Ewald**   Men of Tomorrow. Stories from the
Bible for Youth Today by Ewald Mand, Illustrated by
John Lear.   Philadelphia: The Westminster Press,
1958.
["The author does not attempt to give a continuous story
of the Bible. He has selected certain men used of God in
a special way and brings them on the stage of our
imaginations..." Preface is signed M.G.H.]

1960 **Kirby, Ralph**   The Bible Story with Living
Pictures... Editorial Consultants E.O. James. Harold
Roberts, Sebastian Bullough.   New York: Harper &
Bros., 1960.
["Retold in simple vivid narrative..."]

1960 **Korfka, Dena**   My Picture Story Bible...
Illustrations by Dirk Gringhuis. Grand Rapids, MI:
Zondervan Publishing House, 1960.
["The author knows how to reach the minds and hearts of
children, for she has told these stories daily for more
than 30 years..." Many times reprinted.]

1961 **Price, Eugenia** Beloved World; the Story of God and
People as told from the Bible; Illustrated by Dirk
Gringuis.   Grand Rapids, MI: Zondervan Publishing
House, 1961.

1961 **Woodward, Daphne**   The Living World of the Bible by
     Daphne Woodward.   Cleveland: World Publishing Co.,
     1961.

1962 **Weigle, Oscar**   Bible Stories to Read
     Aloud; Compiled by Oscar Weigle; Illustrated by Ann
     Brewster.   New York: Wonder Books, 1962.
         ["...in language that is easy to understand. Most of the
         great dramatic pieces of both the Old and New Testaments
         will be found in this collection."]

1963 **Hall, Arlene S**.   Picture-Story of Jesus by Elsie
     E. Egermeier.   Story Revision by Arlene S.Hall.
     Adopted from Egermeier's Bible Story Book. Anderson,
     Indiana: Warner Press, 1963.
         [See Elsie Egermeier, Egermeier's Bible Story, 1922.]

     Again; 1965.

1965 **Badley, J.H.**   The Bible as Seen Today. Selected and
     rearranged in Historical Sequence, with a Commentary
     by J.H. Badley... 3 Vols.   Reading, England:
     Berkshire Printing Co., Ltd., 1965.
         ["It is written in simplified language... The text of
         the O.T. is based on the RV, but with some further
         modernization of archaic modes of expression. For the
         N.T. Dr. R.F. Weymouth's Translation in every day
         English has been adopted, with a few slight changes for
         the sake of further simplicity"]

1965 **Garhart, Marjorie**   The Book of the Promises of
     God. By Marjorie Garhart, Illustrated by Tom Irons,
     Gustav K. Wienke, Editor.   Philadelphia: Lutheran
     Church Press, 1965.
         [Abridged Paraphrase and commentary. Some direct quotes
         from the RSV.]

1966 **Anonymous**   Beginner's Bible 1966.
         ["Beginner's Bible is the authorized English edition of
         Katholische Schulbibel published and copyrighted by
         Patmos-Verlag, Dusseldorf, Germany 1957." "Copyrighted
         1966 by The Order of St. Benedict, Inc., Collegeville,
         Minnesota. Printed in U.S.A." (An abridged version).]

     Another Edition;   The Holy Bible, Hospital
     Edition. Collegeville, Minn.: The Liturgical
     Press. (nd).

1966 **Heineman, Thea**   Bible Stories from the Old and
     New Testaments; Based on the Story of the Bible by
     Charles Foster; Edited by Thea Heineman; Illustrated
     by Huntley Brown. Racine, Wisconsin: Whitman
     Publishing Co., [1966]

1968 **Richards, Jean Hosking**   The Richards Bible Story
     Book; Illustrations by Dorothy Teichman.   Grand
     Rapids, Michigan: Zondervan Publishing House, 1968.

["Adapting Bible Stories for Children means more than simplifying the vocabulary. It also involves selections of stories and details...it implies interpretation."]

1971 **Gross, Arthur W.**   Concordia Bible Story Book. St. Louis, London: Concordia Publishing House, 1971.
["...in simple yet dignified present-day English..."]

1973 **Hoth, Iva**   The Picture Bible for All Ages. Script by Iva Hoth. Illustrations by Andre Le Blanc. Bible Editor, C. Elvan Olmstead, Ph.D. 6 Vols.   Elgin, Ill.: David C. Cook Publishing Co., 1973.

Vol. 1	Creation. Genesis 1:1-Exodus 19:20
Vol. 2	The Promised Land. Exodus 20:1-1 Samuel 16:19
Vol. 3	Kings and Prophets. 1 Samuel 16:23-1 Kings 21:8
Vol. 4	The Captivity. 1 Kings 21:9-Malachi
Vol. 5	Jesus. Matthew-John
Vol. 6	The Church. Acts-Revelation

[Second edition done in color pictures, one vol., 1978.]

1973 **Peale, Norman Vincent**   Bible Stories Told by Norman Vincent Peale. With Illustrations by Gabrainski. New York: Franklin Watts Inc., 1973.

1975 **Edington, Andrew**   The Word Made Fresh, compiled by Andrew Edington. 3 Vols.   Atlanta: John Knox Press, 1975-1976.

1975 Volume one of the Old Testament, containing the books of Genesis through Kings.

1975 Volume Two of the Old Testament, containing the books of Chronicles through Malachi.

1976 Volume Three. The New Testament.

Second Printing; 1977.

1977 **Andrew**   Andrew's Holy Bible, for the Layman. Dallas, Tx.: B & B Foundation Inc., 1977.
[The Deity is rendered "Jehovah" & "Yahweh" many times.]

1980 **Brooke, Avery and Others**   The Vineyard Bible. A Central Narrative and Index. Edited by Avery Brooke; Assistant Editors: Eleanor Allen, Katheryne M. Fincke, Elizabeth Moynahan, Rose E. Hoover.   New York: The Seabury Press, 1980.
["The narrative index is made up of quotations from the KJV of the Bible. These lines are often abridged and paraphrased..."]

BIBLE SELECTIONS

???? **Ainsworth, Henry**   MS form of Hosea, Matthew and Hebrews, was never published. [16??]

???? **Anonymous**   Hortus Animae; or, Garden of the Soule: Being a Manual of Spiritual Exercises and Instructions, as commonly used by Christians who, living in the World, aspire to devotion, To which are added many devotions of recent practice and approved by the church. With a Supplement Containing the Gospels and Epistles, in Latin and English, for all the Sundays and Chief Festivals of the Year. London: Burns & Oates, [188?].
  [Bible passages appear to be from the Douay version, but with many minor revisions, especially in the penitential Psalms.]

???? **King James I**   His version of 26 Psalms, the Lord's Prayer and the Song of Moses, into English Meeter; These three Books written with the King's own Hand. British Museum: Reg. MS. 18.B.XVI   [16??].

???? **Sawyer, Leicester Ambrose**   (The Bible) Analyzed, translated, and Accompanied with Critical Studies, Published in Parts of Books, Single Books, and Collections of Books, by Leicester Ambrose Sawyer, translator of the Scriptures. Whitesboro, New York: Published by the author, [188?]-1891.
  1889 – – Introduction
  188? – – Early Generations. Genesis 1 – 11
  1884 – – Abraham, Genesis 12:1 – 25:11
  1883 – – Job
  1887 – – Isaiah [Copyright 1884]
  1888 – – Esther and the Song of Songs [Copyright 1844]
  1883 – – Daniel [Copyright 1882]
  1885 – – Gospel according to John. [Copyright 1884.]
  1883 – – Revelation of John. [Copyright 1883.]
  1891 – – [The New Testament] The Bible: Analyzed, Translated and Accompanied with Critical Studies, Published in parts of Books, Single Books and Collections of Books, by Rev. Leicester A. Sawyer... Whitesboro, New York: [T.J. Griffiths, Printer, Utica], 1891.
      [This work contains a new translation with improved renderings in a different arrangement of the order of books.]

["The author's first translation of the New Testament was published in Boston in 1858, and was followed by translations of several Old Testament books embracing Daniel in 1864. He then became dissatisfied with all his previous translations, and determined to re-translate the whole, and to complete his translation of the entire Bible, with several valuable improvements that he had not before contemplated...he has now accomplished this task, and now proposes to publish the whole..." from the preface to Daniel, 1883. Apparently publication was never completed. The publication of "The Five Letters of Paul" was advertised in Daniel, 1883, but has not been confirmed. Also see: Leicester Ambrose Sawyer, New Testament, 1858.]

???? **Tafel, Leonard, Rudolph L. Tafel and L.H. Tafel** Interlinear Translation of the Sacred Scriptures, with Grammatical and Critical Notes, by Dr. Leonard Tafel...Dr. Rudolph L. Tafel...Prof. L.H. Tafel. New York: E. & J.B. Young & Co., [187?].
[Pentateuch, Gospels, Acts and Revelation.]

Another Edition; New York; 1873?

670 **Caedmon**   Songs sung by an illiterate herdsman of Whitby. c670 AD
["His Song was of the creation of the world, of the birth of man, of the history of Genesis. He sang too, the Exodus of Israel from Egypt and their entrance into the promised land, and many other narratives of Holy Scripture. Of the incarnation also did he sing, and of the passion; of the resurrection and ascension into heaven; of the coming of the Holy Spirit, and the teaching of the Apostles." Bede's Ecclesiastical History.]

1483 **Anonymous**   The Golden Legende... the legende named in latyn legenda aurea, that is to saye in englysshe the golden legende... [William Caxton] westmestre the twenty day of nouembre/the yere of our lord MCCCClxxxxiij. [1483]
["Caxton's translation included passages from the Bible which he paraphrased. They were not included in the French version by Jean de Vigny, on which he based his translation, nor in the original Latin text, Legenda Aurea, which was compiled about 1265 by Jacobus de Voragine...".]

A translation into English of nearly the whole of the Pentateuch an a great deal of the Gospels. Together with much apocryphal matter, from the Latin of James deVoragine, c1265.

Another edition; Westmestre: By me Wyllyam Caxton, 1487.

Another edition (numerous variations). London, flete strete: Wynkyn de Worde, 1527.

Reprinted; F.S. Ellis (Editor)   7 Vols., 1900.

1535 **Anonymous**   Storys and prophesis out of the
holy scriptur gary-shede with faire ymages and with
deuoute praeirs and thanck-geuings vnto God. With
grete diligence oursien and aprouued by the
inqisitor of the christen faithe maester Nycholas
Coppyn de Montibus Deane of Saincte Peters and
Chacelor of the Vniuersitie of Louen. Anno
M.CCCCC.XXXV. Colophon: This boke is prentyd in
Andwarpe...By me Symon Cowke. Anno xxxvi.

1536 **Anonymous**   Thys prymer in Englyshe and in Laten is
newly traslatyd after the Laten texte. [Imprinted
in Rowen the yere of our Lorde 1536.]
    [Contains N.T. selections after Tyndale and 15 Psalms,
    mostly after Joye.]

1538 **Anonymous**   Here begynneth the pystles and gospels,
of euery Sonday, and holy daye in the yere. M.D.xxx
xviii   Imprinted at Paris or Rowen. [1538]
    [N.T. selections are drawn from Tyndale, but certain
    O.T. epistles are apparently given in a new and
    independent version. Third part of 'Thys prymer in
    Englysh and in Laten', many times reprinted.]

1539 **Anonymous**   The Manual of prayers or the prymer in
Englyshe & Laten set out at lenght, whose contentes
the reader by ye prologue next after the Kaleder
shal sone perceaue, and there shall se brefely the
order of the whole boke... Set forth by Ihon by
Goddes grace, & the Kynges callyng, Bysshoppe of
Rochester at the comaundemente of the ryghte
honorable lorde Thomas Crumwell... [John Hilsey]
[Imprinted at Lodo in fletestrete by me Iohan
Wayland...M.D.xxxix] [1539]
    ["... with the Epistles and Gospels thorowe out the
    whole yere."]

1543 **Anonymous**   Ane Compendious Booke of Godly and
Spiritualll Songs. [John Wedderburn] 1543.
    [Commonly known as 'The gude and godlie Ballates'.]

1550 **Anonymous**   Certayne Chapters of the Prouerbes of
Salomon drawen into metre by Thomas Sternholde, late
Grome of the Kynge's Magesties Robes. [John Hall]
London: by John Case, for Willyam Seres, 1550.
    [Cotton lists an edition by E. Whitchurch, 1550. Henry
    E. Hunting Library, San Marino, Calif., has a photocopy
    of an edition without title-page or colophon, which is
    tentatively dated 1549. It contains 'Prouerbes, chapters
    i-xi; three Chapters of Ecclesiastes; the .vi. chapter
    of Sapientia; the .ix. Chapter of Ecclesiasticus;
    Certayne Psalmes of Dauyd (xxxiii, liii, cxi, cxiii)]

Another edition; Certayn chapters take out of the Prouerbes of Salomo, wyth other chapters of holy Scripture, and certayne Psalmes of Dauid, translated into English metre, by John Hall. Whych Prouerbes of late were set forth, Imprinted and untruely entituled, to be the doynges of Mayster Thomas Sternhold, late grome of the Kynges Maiesties robes, as by thys Copye it maye be perceaued. M.D.L. Imprinted at London...by Thomas Raynolde.
>   [Includes: 'Prouerbes i-xi; The .vi.chapter of the Boke of Wysdom called Sapientia; The .xi. chapter of Ecclesiasticus; The .iii. chapter of thee second Epistle of S. Paule, to the Thessalonians; Certayne Psalmes of Dauid, drawen in metre.' (xxi, xxxiii, liii, lxiiii, cxi, cxii, cxiii, cxliiii) Another in 1565 Titled: The Court of Virtue.]

1560 **Tysdale, John**   The bryfe somme of the Byble. Licensed to John Tysdale in 1560.

1578 **Anonymous**   The Lectures or daily Sermons, of that Reuerend Diuine, D. Iohn Caluine...vpon the prophet Ionas, by N.B. Student of Diuinitie. Whereunto is annexed and excellent exposition of the last Epistles of S. Iohn, Done in Latin by that worthy doctor, August. Marlorate, and englished by the same N.B. [Nathaniel Baxter]   London: Imprinted for Edward White, 1578.
>   Another edition; ...newly corrected and amended, 1580.

1591 **Fravnce, Abraham**   The Countess of Pembroke's Emanuel. Conteining the Natiuity, Passion, Buriall, and Resurrection of Christ: together with certeine Psalmes of Dauid: All in English Hexameters. Imprinted at London: for William Ponsonby, 1591.

1611 **Graile, Edmund**   A Summary Relation of the Historical Part of Holy Scripture in Meeter. London: 1611.

1612 **Broughton, Hugh**   The Works of the Great Albionean Divine, Renowned in Many Nations for Rare Skill in Salem's and Athen's Tongues and Familiar Acquaintance with all Rabbinical Learning, 1662.
>   Another edition; Edited by John Lightfoot, 1825.

1630 **Usher, Ambrose**   ["All of the O.T.; and of the New, the four 1st chapters of St. John's Gospel, Romans, I Corinthians, St. James, 1st. & 2d. epistles of St. John, and Revelation, Translated..."]   Dublin: Library of Trinity College, MS, c1630.

1643 **Anonymous**   The Souldiers Pocket Bible: Containing most (if not all) those places contained in the Holy Scripture, which doe shew the qualifications of his inner man, that is a fit Souldier to fight the Lordes Battels, both before the fight, in the fight, and after the fight; Which Scriptures are reduced to severall heads, and fitly applyed to the Souldiers severall occasions, and so may supply the want of the whole Bible, which a Souldier cannot conveniently carry about him: And may bee also usefull for any Christian to meditate upon, now in this miserable time of Warre. Imprimatur, Edm. Calamy. Printed at London by G.B. and R.W. for G.C., 1643.
["The selections from Scripture are, in almost every case, taken from the Genevan Version; but in some cases, a very few, KJV has been used. In a few cases, the phraseology varies slightly from all the English Versions which I have examined." This quotation from George Livermore, Esq, is taken from Hannah Conant's 'The English Bible...']

The Christian Soldier's Penny Bible... London: R. Smith, 1693.
[The Scriptures are KJV with some fresh texts added.]

The Souldier's Pocket Bible...reproduced in facsimile ...by Francis Fry. London: Willis and Sotheran, 1862.

The Christian Soldiers Penny Bible..., 1862.

1644 **Anonymous**   A Good Help for Weak Memories... Sum of the Bible in Verse. "J.L." 1644.

1644 **Brightman, Thomas**   The Revelation with Daniel chapter XI, verses 36-45. Amsterdam: T. Stafford, 1644.

1647 **Jackson, John**   An abridgement of the histories, of Noah, Joseph, Moses, Joshuah, Hezekiah, and the taking of the Ark. With meditations and prayers, upon each history... London: Printed by J. Legatt, 1647.

1648 **Boyd, M. Zachary**   The Songs of the Old and New Testament in Meeter. Glasgow: Heirs of G. Anderson, 1648.

1651 **Fairfax, Thomas**   A Paraphrase of the Psalms and Other Parts of Scripture, 1651.

1652 **Ainsworth, William**   Medulla Bibliorum, the Marrow of the Bible, or, a Logico - theological Analysis of every several Book of the holy Scripture, together with so many English Poems Containing the Contents of every several Chapter in every such Book by William Ainsworth. 1652.

1659 **Gell, Robert**   An Essay toward the Amendment of the last English-Translation of the Bible; or, a proof by many instances, that the last Translation of the Bible into English, may be improved. London: by R. Norton for Andrew Crook, 1659.
> ["...the last translation is wrested and partial, speaking the language of one sect or part (the Calvinistic), and the better renderings have usually been relegated to the margin..."]

1685 **Cleeve, C.**   The Songs of Moses and Deborah paraphras'd ...by C. Cleeve.   London: for Luke Meredith, 1685.

1685 **Simson, Patrick**   Spiritual Songs or Holy Poems. A Garden of True Delight, Containing All the Scripture-Songs that are not in the Book of Psalms, together with several sweet Prophetical and Evangelical Scriptures, meet to be composed into Songs. Translated into English meeter, and fitted to be sung with any of the common tunes of the Psalms. "Done at first for the Authors own Recreation:" But since Published (before in part, and now more compleat) to be, as a Supplement to the Book of Psalms, out of the same rich Store-house, a further Help to the Spiritual Solace of his Christian Friends. - And Digested into Six Books, according to the Order and Distinction of the Boks of Scripture, out of which they are taken. By Patrick Simson. Edinburgh: Printed   by   the   Heir   of   Andrew Anderson..., 1685.
> [Includes "The Dedication of the First Edition of the Song of Solomon, with some of the rest of these Spiritual Songs, then published with it." Apparently published earlier. British Museum Catalogue attributes to Patrick Symson; Wilson, to Andrew Symson (see 1701).]

1688 **Poole, Matthew**   Annotations upon the Holy Bible. Wherein the sacred text is inserted, and various annex'd, together with the parallel scriptures... By the late Reverend and learned divine Mr. Matthew Poole.   London: Printed by Robert Roberts, for Thomas Parichurst..., 1688.
> Third edition; 2 Vols. 1696.

> Fourth edition; 2 Vols. 1700.

1691 **Keach, Benjamin**   Spiritual Melody; viz. Psalms and Hymns from the Old and New Testament. London: J. Hancock, 1691.

Another edition; A Feast of Fat things Full of Marrow. Containing several Scripture songs taken out of the Old and New Testament. With others, composed by the author. London: B.H., 1696.
  [Includes 17 Psalms.]

Also; Spiritual Songs; being the Marrow of the Scripture in Songs of Praise to Almighty God from the Old and New Testament...with a Hundred Divine Hymns on Several Occasions, 2d edition. London: Printed for John Marshall, 1700.

1694 **Anonymous**   The Historical Parts of the Old and New Testaments in Verse, with One Hundred and Twenty Cuts, being the best use of Poetry and Sculpture. London: Printed for Samuel Keble, 1694.

1698 **Thwaites, Edward**   Heptateuchus, liber Job, et evangelium Nicodemi, Anglo-Saxonice, historiae Judith fragmentum, Dano-Saxonice. Edidit nunc primum ex MSS., 1698.
  [The Anglo-Saxon.]

1700 **Anonymous**   Scriptural Poems. Being several portions of Scripture digested into English verse. Viz. I. The Book of Ruth. II. The History of Sampson. III. Christ's Sermon on the Mount. IV. The Prophecy of Jonah. V. The Life of Joseph. VI. The Epistle of James. By John Bunyan.   London: J.Blare, 1700.
  [The ascription to Bunyan is false.]

1706 **Kennett, Basil**   An Essay Towards a Paraphrase on the Psalms, in English Verse. To which is added a Paraphrase on the Third Chapter of the Revelations. London: Printed by J.H. for B. Aylmer, 1706.
  [Contains 28 Psalms.]

1707 **Lloyd, B.**   Sacred Miscellanies, Several Psalms and Chapters from the Old and New Testaments in Verse, 1707.

1707 **Watts, Isaac**   Hymns and Spiritual Songs. In Three Books. I. Collected from the Scriptures. II. Compos'd on Divine Subjects. III. Prepared for the Lord's Supper. With an Essay Towards the Improvement of Christian Psalmody, by the Use of Evangelical Hymns in Worship, as well as the Psalms of David. By I. Watts.   London: By J. Humphreys for John Lawrence, 1707.

Second Edition; Corrected and Much Enlarged. - - J.H. for John Lawrence, 1709.

Sixteenth Edition; London: Printed by R. Ware, T. Longman, C. Hitch, J. Hodges, J. Oswald, J. Davidson, J. Buckland, J. Ward, and M. Cooper, 1748.

[Many changes in intervening editions.]

1710 **Anonymous** Biblia Americanum. The Sacred Scriptures of the Old and New Testaments, 1710.

1717 **Anonymous**   An Essay for a New Translation of the Bible, Wherein is shewn From Reason, and the Authority of the best Commentators, Interpreters and Criticks, that there is a Necessity for a New Translation. In Two Parts by H.R. a Minister of the Church of England. [Hugh Ross] London: for John Nutt, 1717.
> ["...it renders a great many places of scripture more truly and clearly than they have formerly been expressed by any version..." From the preface, signed by H.Ross, who translated from the French of Charles le Cene.]

Second edition; By Hugh Ross. London: 1727.

[Essays for a New Translation of the Bible. London: 1702. Not known whether this work contains translations.]

1737 **Wesley, John**   A Collection of Psalms and Hymns by John Wesley. Charleston: 1737.
> [Includes "...Psalms and Hymns by Dr. Watts...his father's (Charles Sr.'s) hymn...John Astin's hymns from the 'Devotions', Addison's hymns from the 'Spectator', and his own, translated from the German..." from 'A History of Methodism' by W.J. Townsend, H.B. Workman and George Eayrs; London: Hodder & Stoughton, 1909. The date of Wesley's first edition is not clear; Oxford – 1738; Prothro – 1740.]

Another edition; Hymns and Sacred Poems. By John & Charles Wesley. London: W. Strahan, 1740.

Also; A Collection of Psalms and Hymns. The Third Edition Enlarged. By John & Charles Wesley. London: W. Strahan, 1744.

Another edition; revised by Mr. Whitfield & Mr. Madan. Bristol: 1755.

Again; Short Hymns on Selected Passages of Scripture. By Charles Wesley. Bristol: 1762.

Another edition; Hymns on the Trinity. By Charles
Wesley. Bristol: 1767.

[1762 & 1767 editions based on 'Charles Wesley
Evangelist and Poet' F. Luke Wiseman; New York,
Cincinnati & Chicago: Abingdon Press, 1932.]

1743 **Marchant, John**   The Holy Bible; With an Exposition
in which several mis-translations are rectified. 2
Vols. London: 1743-1745.

> 1745 - - The Old Testament. London: R.
> Walker.

> 1743 An Exposition of the Books of the New
> Testament Extracted from the Writings of
> the Best Authors, Antient and Modern; in
> which difficult Texts are explain'd, many
> Mis-translations rectify'd, and seeming
> Contradictions reconcil'd. The Whole
> render'd of singular Advantage to Persons
> of every Religion and Capacity; and
> designed to promote the Knowledge of the
> Scriptures, and the Practice of Sincere
> Piety and Virtue. John Marchant, Gent.
> MDCCXLIII.   London: Printed for the
> author.

[Text is KJV, rectifications in the exposition.]

1745 **Anonymous**   The Scottish Paraphrase. Translations
and Paraphrases of Several Passages of Sacred
Scriptures. Collected and Prepared by a Committee
appointed by the General Assembly of the Church of
Scotland. And by the Act of the Last General
Assembly, transmitted to Presbyteries for their
Consideration. Edinburgh: Printed by Robert Fleming
and Company, Printers to the Church of Scotland,
MDCCXLV. [1745]
[The Deity is rendered twice as "Jehovah".]

The following committee worked on the Paraphrases:

Joseph Addison	Philip Doddridge
Isaac Watts	Thomas Blacklock
John Morison	Naham Tate
William Robertson	Michael Bruce
Hugh Blair	William Cameron
Thomas Randall	John Logan
Samuel Martin	Robert Blair
John Ogilvie	Some Anonymous

Second edition, 1751.

Third Edition; Revised and corrected according to
Appointment of the General Assembly 1749.
Printed in the Year M,DCC,LIV., 1754.

[The 3rd edition was reprinted as an appendix to a Pamphlet entitled "Remarks on the Innovations in Public Worship of God proposed by the Free Presbytery of Hamilton, " Edinburgh: Bell & Bradfute, 1854.]

Another edition; Translations and Paraphrases in Verse on Several Passages of Sacred Scripture; Collected and Prepared by a Committee of the General Assembly of the Church of Scotland, in order to be sung in Churches. Edinburgh: Printed and Sold by J. Dickson, 1790, 1797.
["All the Translations and Paraphrases have been revised with care..."]

Also; Translations and Paraphrases... With an improvement now to each. (Future Punishment under the notion of War). Glasgow: N. Douglas, 1815.

Another edition; An Account of their History, Authors, and Sources, together with the Minutes of the General Assembly and Extracts from Presbytery Records Relative thereto; Reprints; 1745, 1751 and 1781. Information Regarding Hymns Contemporary with the Paraphrases; and some Account of the Scripture Songs of 1706, by Douglas Maclagan. Edinburgh: Andrew Elliot, 1889.
[A good summary of this type of publication from "The Songs of the Old and New Testament" Appended to Zachary Boyd's Work, The Garden of Zion, in 1644, and Passages of Scripture Paraphrased in 1745 on down to the present volume. The selections cover from the creation to the last Judgment. Various versions are printed in parallel columns with variations noted. See 1790]

[See Psalms, 1650 Anonymous, The Psalms of David.; see Psalms Selections, 1872 Free Church Version.]

1747 **Manal, Nicholas** Critical Notes on Some Passages of Scripture Correcting the Translation...London: 1747.

1749 **Glass, John (Glas)**   Christian Songs, 1749.
[The Hymn-Book of the Glassite Church; frequently revised, enlarged and reprinted.]

Another edition; ...To which is prefixed, The Evidence and Import of Christ's Resurrection versified for the help of memory. The Sixth Edition, 1784.

The Thirteenth Edition, 1847.

1751 **Anonymous**   Sacred Poems: or A Collection of Translations and Paraphrases from the Holy

Scripture. By various authors. [David Dalrymple]
Edinburgh: Printed for Hamilton, Balfour and Neill,
1751.
> [Contains 29 Pieces, some selections, some originals.
> Although the dedication is "...inscribed by the
> Editors."]

1754 **Erskine, Ralph**   Scripture Songs. In Three Parts.
I. Old Testament Songs: or, Songs upon several
passages in the Old Testament.   II. New Testament
Songs: or, Songs upon several passages in the New
Testament.   III. Songs upon several Parts of
Scripture; some whereof are in the Old Testament and
some in the New.   Glasgow: 1754.
> [Posthumously edited by Henry Erskine, his son. Part I.
> contains 20 Songs; Part II., 26; Part III., 40.]

> [Reprinted in Erskine's Works,"Scripture Songs. In Two
> Books."   Glasgow: 1766. Book I. consists of Old
> Testament Songs, and is divided into Six Parts –(1)
> containing 14 Poems upon passages from Genesis to Job;
> (2) containing Job's Hymns; (3) A New Version of the
> Song of Solomon; (4) 21 Poems from Ecclesiastes, Isaiah,
> and Jeremiah; (5) A Short Paraphrase upon the
> Lamentations of Jeremiah; (6) 6 Poems from the Minor
> Prophets. Book II. consists of New Testament Songs, and
> divided into Three Parts –(1) 17 Songs from the
> Evangelists; (2) 24 Songs from Apostolical Epistles; (3)
> 16 Songs from the Book of Revelation.]

Also; Scripture Songs from the Old and New
Testament. Edinburgh: Gavin Alston, 1771.

1756 **Anonymous**   Select Passages of the Old and New
Testaments Versified. [Edward Perronet]   London:
H.Cock, 1756.

1757 **Anonymous**   Some Scriptural Hymns, selected
from sundry Passages of Holy Writ, Intended for the
service of the Church in Secret or Society, as may
be thought agreeable. By a Minister of the Church of
Scotland. [John Forbes]   Aberdeen: Sold by John
Mitchell and George Lauraunce, Merchants of Old
Deer, 1757.
> [Old and New Testament hymns, many reminiscent of the
> Rising of 1745. Popularly known as "Pitneycadell's
> Psalms."]

1759 **Maxwell, James**   Hymns and Spiritual Songs by James
Maxwell. Birmingham: 1759.
> [See James Maxwell's Book of Psalms, 1773, for 'Divine
> Hymns or Scripture Songs' (51 Songs).]

1765 **Anonymous**   Miscellaneous Pieces of Poetry.
Edinburgh: Printed for W. Gray, 1765.
> [This work contains a number of Original Paraphrases and
> Hymns. Also, contains selections from various Eminent
> Authors.]

1765 **Erskine, Ralph**   A Paraphrase of Song of Solomon: also Scripture Songs... A New Version of Song of Solomon, with other Poetical Parts of the Bible in Verse. Glasgow: R. Urie, 1765.
Again, 1788.

Another edition; London: H. Howell, 1830?.

1767 **Barclay, John**   A Select Collection of New Original Spiritual Songs, Paraphrases and Translations by John Barclay, 1767-1776.
1767 Rejoice Evermore: or, Christ All in All. An Original Publication; consisting of Spiritual Songs, collected from the Holy Scriptures; and several of the Psalms, together with the whole Song of Solomon, paraphrased. To which are also prefixed, three Discourses relative to those subjects; with a Letter concerning the Assurance of faith. By John Barclay, Preacher of the Gospel. Glasgow: Printed by W.Bell for the Author.
[Includes "Part of the Psalms (I - XXXIV, CXLIX) Paraphrased and Applied to Christ", "The Song of Solomon Paraphrased in a literal Manner", and numerous selections from the O.T. & N.T.]

1776 A Select Collection of New original Spiritual Songs, Paraphrases, and Translations; together with the most Useful and Agreeable of these formerly published under the title of 'Rejoice Evermore or Christ All in All'. By John Barclay, A.M., Minister of the Berean Assembly in Edinburgh. Edinburgh: James Donaldson.
[Includes 285 Spiritual Songs, of which 32 are versions of Psalms. At the end is "The Song of Solomon, paraphrased in a literal manner."]

1768 **Merrick, James**   The Lord's Prayer, Benedicite, Nunc Dimittis and the Blessing of Balaam from Numbers 24:5-9. Oxford: Clarendon Press, 1768.

1769 **Guyse, John** (Editor)   The Family Bible, or an Illustration of the Scriptures containing the sacred texts at large... with annotations... Selected from the best Commentators, wherein Mistakes in the present [KJV] Translation are corrected; difficult texts explained. 2 Vols. Aberdeen: J. Bruce & J. Boyle, 1769-1771.

1771 **Erskine, Ralph**   Scripture Songs from the Old and New Testaments. Edinburgh: Gavin Alston, 1771.

1772 **Gibbons, T.**   Poetical Versions of Several Parts of Scripture.   London: printed in 'The Christian Minister', 1772.

1772 **Rowe, Elizabeth**   Miscellaneouc Works. 1772.
> [Contains: Job 38 (metrical), p.61-61; Psalm 23 (metrical), p. 74-77; Psalm 63 (metrical), p.124-125; Psalm 72 (metrical), p. 126-127; Psalm 146 (metrical), p. 128-129; Song of Solomon 5 (metrical), p. 137-139; Song of Solomon 8:6, p. 130; Revelation 16 (metrical), p. 79-80. All the above are from vol. 1.]

1778 **Brown, John**   The Self-interpreting Bible: Containing the Old and New Testament; to which are annexed an extensive introduction; marginal references and illustrations, an exact summary of the several books; A paraphrase of the most obscure or important parts; An analysis of the contents of each chapter, explanatory notes, evangelical reflections; &c. By the late John Brown. 2 Vols. London: 1778.
> [This title is taken from the Third Edition. The basic text is KJV. The paraphrases represent Bible selections only.]

Second Edition, 1789?

London reprint, 1791.

Another edition; New York: Printed by Hodge & Campbell, 1792.

Third Edition; With many additional references and illustrations.   London: Printed for David Ogilvy..., 1806.

Another edition; Edinburgh: Blair & Bruce, 1808.

Another edition; The N.T. of our Lord and Saviour Jesus Christ... Bungay: Printed and Published by T. Webster, 1810.

Revised edition; Revised...by the Rev. Thomas Raffles. 2 Vols.   London: Barnard and Farley, for Walker & Edwards, etc., 1817.

[First published in America 1792 by subscription (500 subscribers?). George Washington being the first to subscribe. This work, under the name usually of Brown's Family Bible has enjoyed immense popularity both in England and America, having been reprinted a vast number of times, in various forms.]

1781 **Mitchell, David**   A Select Number of Spiritual Hymns Taken from the most Strong, Plain, and Suitable Texts in the Old and New Testament. Having the general Scope or Meaning at the beginning of each Hymn... By David Mitchell, Schoolmaster in Glasgow. To which is added, St. Augustine's Hymn. Glasgow: William Smith for the Author, 1781.

1782 **Southwell, Henry**   Bible; with notes, &c., wherein the mis-translations are corrected by Henry Southwell. London: for J. Cooke, 1782.

1783 **Barclay, John**   The Experience and Example of the Lord Jesus Christ; Illustrated and Improved for the Consolation of the Church; Making A Copious Variety of Subjects for the Purpose of Divine Praise; Introduced by a Close Examination into the Truth of several Received Principles... By John Barclay. Edinburgh: printed for the Author by J. Donaldson, 1783.
> [Includes: Psalm versions, 53 pages;, The Lord's prayer, 1 page; The Epistle to the Hebrews Paraphrased, 100 pages; Miscellaneous Paraphrases and Hymns, 72 pages.]

1784 **Anonymous**   The New-England Psalter or Psalms of David: with the Proverbs of Solomon, and Christ's Sermon on the Mount, being an Introduction for the Training up Children in the Reading of the Holy Scriptures. Boston: Benjamin Edes & Sons, 1784.

1785 **Anonymous**   Select Passages of Sacred Scripture Rendered into Metre after the Manner of the Psalms of David: wherein (To accommodate Persons of every Capacity) Particular care has been taken To Retain the Scripture Expressions as much as possible. [Andrew Laurie?] Edinburgh: Mundell & Wilson, 1785.

1786 **Steuart, James**   Sacred Songs and Hymns on Various Passages of Scripture; Selected for the Congregation at Anderstoun, by James Steuart. Glasgow: Printed by David Niven, 1786.
> [Steuart's collection, with the additions of Messrs Hutchison (of Paisley) and Dun (of Glasgow)]

> Another edition; - - approved by the Synod of Relief, and recommended to be sung in the congregations under their inspection. Glasgow: Printed by J. Mennons, 1794.

1790 **Anonymous**   Translations and Paraphrases in Verse of Several Passages of Sacred Scripture, Collected and Prepared by a Committee of the General Assembly of the Church of Scotland in order to be sung in churches. Glasgow: Printed for J. Dickson, 1790.

1790 **Belcher, W.**   The Galaxy. Consisting of a variety of
sacred and other poetry... by W. Belcher and others.
London: James Evans, 1790.
> [Versions of the Psalms, in twelve large odes. – Version
> of the Apocalypse, in twenty odes. – Detached versions
> of the Prophets, etc.]

1791 **Anonymous**   An Introduction to Reform Singing: being
an essay to sing the Holy Scriptures; or repeat them
melodiously   in   Churches,   instead   of   singing
erroneous rhymes and human compositions. Containing
those parts of the Psalms that are most agreeable to
the Gospel, and many sacred portions of the N.T.;
disposed   into   long,   common   and   short   metre...
Likewise specimens in Hebrew, Greek, Latin, etc...
by o os I o pi o .   London: The Author, 1791.

1793 **Hill, Aaron**   Habakkuk 3, Part of Psalm 14; Matthew
6; Song of Moses; David's Lamentation over Saul; and
Psalm 104 paraphrased in verse.   In Anderson's
British Poets. Edinburgh: 1793.

1794 **Anonymous**   Remarks on the Book of Daniel, and on
the Revelations. Whereby it appears, That Daniel had
visions of eight great temporal monarchies: That the
three last of Daniel being future when John wrote,
he only had visions of the three last great temporal
powers. That the prophetic periods of Daniel and
Jogn, all terminate in 2520 years from the first of
Cyrus, and 1890 from the birth of Christ, so far as
temporal powers are concerned. That the end of
temporal powers, designates an end of mankind in the
flesh;   the   commencement   of   the   millenium;   the
resurrection of the Just, and the restitution of all
things. Revelations III. "Because thou hast kept the
word of my patience...   New York: Printed at
Greenleaf's Press, April 19, A.D. 1794.
> [The Book of Daniel, pp. 1-28; Revelations begin at p.
> 272, but the text is not printed like that of Daniel,
> but with remarks intercalated.]

1794 **Anonymous**   Sacred Songs and Hymns on Various
Passages of Scripture, approved by the Synod of
Relief,   and   Recommended   to   be   sung   in   the
Congregations under their inspection.   Glasgow:
Printed by J. Mennons, 1794.

1799 **Anketell, John**   A Versification of the
Book of Job, and Christ's Sermon on the Mount. John
Anketell. Dublin: Printed for the Author by William
Porter, 1799.
> ["In consequence of my wishing to adhere very closely to
> the words of the original, I have avoided amplification
> as much as possible in the poetical garb with which I
> have presumed to exhibit it."]

1803 **Tomlinson, Robert**   A new Translation of the Bible; an Attempt to preserve the Holy Scriptures from their Disrepute with Free-Thinkers, and their misapplication to certain Tenets, by a new and correct Translation of controverted Passages, illustrated with Notes and the Opinion of the Ancients. London: Hor. W. Baynes, 1803.
Another edition, 1805.

1815 **Wemyss, Thomas**   Biblical Gleanings; or a Collection of passages of scripture, that have been generally considered to be mistranslated in the received English version, with proposed corrections; also the important various readings in both Testaments and occasional notes.   York: Ogle & Baynes, 1815.

1817 **Raffles, Thomas**   See John Brown, The Self-Interpreting Bible, 1778.

1818 **Horne, Thomas Hartwell**   An Introduction to the Critical Study and Knowledge of the Holy Scriptures, 1818.
[Anglo-Saxon]

Second edition, 1821.

Seventh edition, 1834.

Eighth edition, 1839.
[Contains a comprehensive bibliography of Bible Commentaries, many of which include English Translations.]

New edition from the 8th London Edition; Corrected and Enlarged. 2 Vols. New York: Robert Carter & Bros., 1850.

Eleventh edition; Revised and Brought Down to the Present Time. Edited by Thomas Hartwell Horne, John Ayre, and Samuel Prideaux Tregelles. 4 Vols.   London: Longman, Green, Longman, Roberts & Green, 1863.

1819 **Anonymous**   Musae Biblicae; or, The Poetry of the Bible. A Selection of the Most Elegant Poetical Translations, Paraphrases & Imitations of the Sacred Scriptures. London: Printed for the editor and sold by Longman & Co. & J. Hatchard, 1819.
[Selections run from the creation to the last judgement, with the majority from the Old Testament. They are chiefly from renounced authors, some anonymous. Some are not too closely tied to the text, but expand the theme. A number of Parnell's Psalms are included.]

1820 **Neligan, James** Sacred Poetry; parts of the Old and New Testaments paraphrased in verse. By James Neligan. Dublin: for the author, 1820.

1834 **Anonymous** The Christian's Golden Harp; or the Promises of the Scripture, in verse. By W.C.D. London: Hamilton, Adams & Co., 1834.

1835 **Morgan, C.** The Psalms in Metre...with Translations and Paraphrase of Several Passages of Scripture. London: 1835.

1836 **Anonymous** Book of Public Worship, for the use of The New Church signified by The New Jerusalem in the Revelation. Prepared by order of the General Convention. [T.B. Hayward] 1836.
> [Contains many Bible selections, including the Ten Commandments, the Sermon on the Mount and about 100 Psalms, "Much pains were taken to make the translation literal; but no alterations were attempted, unless a manifest improvement could be made. The names Jehovah and Jah, heretofore translated Lord, have been invariably restored..."]

Another edition; Boston: Published by Otis Clapp, 1848.

1837 **Clapp, Otis** The Holy Bible...[Swedenborgian Bible] Boston: O. Clapp, 1837.
> [Omitted the books Swedenborg regarded as not having "an internal sense." Omitted Ruth, Chronicles, Ezra, Nehemiah, Esther, Job, Proverbs, Song of Solomon, Acts, and all the epistles from the New Testament.]

1844 **Anonymous** Commentaries [on the books of the Bible] by John Calvin. Translated from the original Latin, and collated with the author's French version [Latin & English] Edinburgh: Calvin Translation Society, 1844-1856. 45 vols.

> 1847-50 ...Genesis [Text is KJV] John King. (2 Vols.) Reprinted, 1948.

> 1852-55 ...The Four Last Books of Moses, arranged in the form of a harmony... C.W. Bingham. (4 Vols.) Reprinted, 1950.

> 1854 ...the Book of Joshua... Henry Beveridge. Reprinted, 1949.

> 1845-49 ...the Book of Psalms... James Anderson. (5 Vols.) [Arranged in parallelism]
> Vol. 2 George McCrie and James McLean. Reprinted, 1949.

1850-53   ...the Prophet Isaiah... William
               Pringle. (4 vols.)   Reprinted, 1948.

1850-55   ...Jeremiah and Lamentations...John
               Owen. (5 vols.)   Reprinted, 1950.

1849-50   ...the Prophet Ezekiel... Thomas
               Myers. (2 vols.)   Reprinted, 1948.

1852-53   ...the Prophet Daniel...   Thomas
               Myers. (2 vols.)   Reprinted; Grand
               Rapids: Wm. B. Eerdmans Publishing
               Co., 1948; Grand Rapids: Baker Book
               House, 1981.

1846-49   ...the Twelve Minor Prophets...John
               Owen. (5 vols.)   Reprinted, 1950.

1845-46   ...Harmony of the Evangelists...
               William Pringle.   (3 vols.)
                   Reprinted, 1949.

1847   ...The Gospel according to John...
               William Pringle. (2 vols.)
                   Reprinted, 1949.

1844   ...The Acts of the Apostles... Henry
               Beveridge. (2 vols.) Reprinted, 1949.

1849   ...Romans... John Owen.
                   Reprinted, 1947.

1848-49   ...Corinthians... John Pringle. (2
               vols.)   Reprinted, 1948.

1854   ...Galatians &   Ephesians..
               William Pringle.   Reprinted, 1948.

1851   ...Philippians, Colossians and
               Thessalonians... Wm. Pringle.
                   Reprinted, 1948.

1855   ...The Catholic Epistles... John
               Owen.   Reprinted, 1948.

1856   ...Timothy, Titus and Philemon...
               William Pringle.   Reprinted, 1948.

1853   ...Hebrews... John Owen.
                   Reprinted, 1948.

Reprinted; 45 Vols. Grand Rapids: Wm. B.
Eerdmans Publishing Co., 1947-1950.

1848 **Asher, David**   ...The Way of Faith, or The Abridged Bible: containing selections from all the books of Holy Writ. By Dr. M. Budinger; translated from the Fifth German Edition by David Asher specially sanctioned by the Rev. Adler, Chief Rabbi of the United Congregations of the British Empire. Intended for the use of Jewish Schools and Families. London: Samuel Bagster & Sons, [1848].
[Contains selections from the O.T. in an original version.]

1855 **Paul, J.D.**   Bible Illustrations; or, The Harmony of the Old and New Testament, Arranged... To Which is Added a Paraphrase of the Book of Esther, by J.D. Paul. London: H. Elliot, 1855.

1856 **Iliffe, F.**   A Plea for a Revisal of the Bible Translation of 1611 with a plan for gradual introduction of changes as suggested in the select portions of the church service for the ensuing year, commencing Advent Sunday, 1856. Sunderland: J. Williams, 1856.

1857 **D'Alton, Charles**   Select Passages of the Old and New Testaments, newly translated from the Hebrew and Greek. With notes critical and explanatory. London: Barritt & Co., 1857.

1860 **Ingraham, J.H.**   The Throne of David. From the consecration of the Shepherd of Bethlehem to the Rebellion of Prince Absalom... Chicago: M.A. Donohue & Co., 1860.
[This work is an attempt to illustrate the grandeur of Hebraic history, when the "People of God" had attained, under the reigns of David and Solomon, the height of their power and glory as a nation.]

Another Edition; Roberts Brothers, 1887.

Reprinted; Elgin, IL: David C. Cook Publishing Co., 1899.

1863 **Ayre, John and Samuel Prideaux Tregelles**   (Editor) See Thomas Hartwell Horne, An Introduction to the Critical Study and Knowledge of the Holy Scriptures, 1818.

1873 **Riggs, Elias**   Suggested Emendations of the [AV/RV]. Andover: Warren F. Draper, 1873-188?
1873 Suggested Emendations of the Authorized English Version of the Old Testament.

188? Suggested modifications of the Revised Version of the New Testament.

["...he gives in one column the passages of the Common Version (of the O.T.; of the ERV for the N.T.) which need revision, and in the opposite column his 'suggested emendations.'" Baptist Quarterly.]

1879 **Marquess of Bute, John**   The Roman Breviary: Reformed by order of the Holy Ecumenical Council of Trent, Published by order of Pope St. Pius V, and Revised by Clement VIII and Urban VIII, together with the offices since granted. Translated out of the Latin into English. 2 Vols.   Edinburgh and London: William Blackwood & Sons, 1879.
[Includes some Psalms.]

1880 **Malet, Arthur**   The Books of Job, Ecclesiastes, and Revelation. 1880-1883.
1880 The Book of Job in Blank Verse, by Arthur Malet. Ashcott [Bridgewater]: Privately centographed.
[Only eight copies centographed.]

1880 The Book of Revelation, metrically arranged, by Arthur Malet. Ashcott: privately centographed.
[Only eight copies centographed.]

1880 Koheleth. Ecclesiastes Arranged in Verse, by Arthur Malet. Ashcott: privately centographed.

1883 The Books of Job, Ecclesiastes, and Revelation Rendered into English Verse; also, Solomon and his Bride: a Drama from the Song of Songs, by Arthur Malet. London: Nisbet & Co., 1883.

1888 **Expositor's Bible**   The Expositor's Bible. Edited by the Rev. W. Robertson Nicoll... New York: A.C. Armstrong & Son; London: Hodder & Stoughton, 1888-1903.
[The text in the following books only are different translations by those indicated:]

189? The Book of Job (Fragmentary Translation) by Robert A. Watson.

1903 The Psalms by A. McLaren. 2 Vols.

1890 The Book of Ecclesiastes. With a new translation by Samuel Cox.

1889 The Book of Isaiah (Fragmentary Translation) by George Adam Smith. 2 Vols.

189? The Prophecies of Jeremiah by C.J. Ball.
2 Vols.

1896 The Book of the Twelve Prophets... by
George Adam Smith. 2 Vols.

1893 The Epistle of St. Paul to the Romans
(2nd ed., 1894) by Handley C.G. Moule.

1888 The Epistle to the Galatians by C.G.
Findlay.

1892 The Epistle to the Ephesians by C.G.
Findlay.
["The text...is, with very few exceptions,
that of the ERV, or its margin."]

1889 The Epistles of St. John by William
Alexander.
[Includes Greek text, Latin, AV, RV, &
Alexander's translation in parallel
columns.]

Another edition of the Expositor's Bible; 48 Vols.;
New York: Eaton & Mains; Cincinnati: Jennings
& Graham, n.d.

1891 **Anonymous**   The Numerical Bible; being a Revised
Translation of the Holy Scriptures with Expository
Notes: Arranged, Divided, and Briefly Characterized
According to the Principles of Their Numerical
Structure. [F.W. Grant] 7 Vols. New York: Loizeau
Brothers, 1891-1931.
1891 - - The Books of Law. (Genesis to
Deuteronomy)

1894 - - The Covenant History - - Joshua to
(2) Samuel.

1896 - - The Psalms.

1897 - - The Gospels.

1901 - - Acts to II Corinthians.

1903 - - Hebrews to Revelation.

1931 - - Ezekiel. The Text of the Whole Book
and the Notes on Chaps 1 to 37 by the
late F.W.Grant. Notes on Chapters 38 to
48, with a Historical Chart of the
Prophets, Plans Illustrating the Temple,
and the Future Division of the Land, by
J. Bloore.

[The Deity is rendered "Jehovah" many times.]

1895 **Anonymous**   Woman's Bible. 2 vols.   New York:
     European Publishing Co., 1895-1898.
        [Chaired by Elizabeth Cady Stanton. "...the Revising
        Committee Referred to a Woman's translation of the Bible
        (Julia E. Smith, 1876 edition) as their ultimate
        authority for the Greek, Latin and Hebrew text..."]

        The following was the revising committee:

        Millie Devereaux Blake   Olympia Brown
        Frances Ellen Burr   Lucinda B. Chandler
        Augusta Chapin   Clara Bewick Colby
        Ellen Battelle Dietrick   Matilda Joslyn Gage
        Helen H. Gardiner   Ursala N. Gestefield
        Phebe A. Hanaford   Josephine K. Henry
        Mary Seymour Howell   Mrs. Robert G. Ingersoll
        Clare B. Neyman   Louisa Southworth
        Elizabeth Cady Stanton   Catherine F. Stebbins
        Sarah A. Underwood   Charlette Beebe Wilbour

        ["The object is to revise only those texts and chapters
        directly referring to women, and those also in which
        women are made prominent by exclusion."]

        1895 ..Part I. Comments on Genesis, Exodus,
             Leviticus, Numbers and Deuteronomy.
             Third Thousand, 1898.

        1898 ..Part II. Comments on the Old & New
             Testament from Joshua to Revelation.

        Reprinted; 2 Vols. in 1. New York: Arno Press,
        1972.

1897 **Margoliouth, G.**   The Palestinian Syriac Version
     of the Holy Scriptures. Four recently discovered
     portions. Together with verses from the Psalms and
     the Gospel of St. Luke. Edited in photographic
     facsimile, from a unique MS. in the British Museum,
     with a transcription, translation, introduction,
     vocabulary, and notes. London: Society of Biblical
     Archeology, 1897.
        [Syriac & English.]

1898 **Cook, Albert Stanburrough**   Biblical Quotations in
     Old English Prose Writers, edited with Vulgate and
     other Latin originals, Introduction on Old English
     Biblical versions, Index of Biblical Passages, and
     Index of Principle Words by A.S. Cook.   London:
     Macmillan & Co.; New York: The Macmillan Co., 1898.

1900 **Ellis, F.S.** (Editor)   See Anonymous, The Golden
     Legende... the legende named in latyn legenda aurea,
     that is to saye in englysshe the golden legende,
     1483.

1903 **Bagshawe, Edward Gilpin**   The Psalms and Canticles
in English Verse. London, Paris: Sands & Co., 1903.
Another edition, St. Louis: Herder, 1903.

1906 **Anonymous**   Prophetic Suggestions; Being Expository
of the Books of Revelation and Daniel.   London:
Dogby, Long & Co., 1906.
["Although the ERV has been used as the text, I...have
shown mainly on the authority of Dean Alford and the
Emphatic Diaglott, along with the RV..." Signed
"Kalomos"]

1906 **Hart, Charles**   A Manual or Bible History by Charles
Hart. 2 Vols.   New York, Cincinnati and Chicago:
Benziger Bros., 1906-1908.
             Vol. 1   The Old Testament.
             Vol. 2   The New Testament.

             [Interwoven into the narrative is the Sacred Text which
             was "compiled chiefly from the text and notes of
             Haydock's Douai Bible; but for the Part between the two
             Testaments- that is, from the end of the Books of the
             Machabees- The Jewish Historian Josephus is the one
             authority".]

1909 **Porter, Frank Chamberlin**   The Messages of the
Apocalyptical   Writers...,   1909.   [Daniel   and
Revelation]
             [See Abridged Bibles, 1900 Frank Knight Sanders and
             Charles F. Kent, The Messages of the Bible, Vol. VIII.]

1910 **Cunard, F.W.**   The First Judgment of the Christians
by the Spirit, Alpha and Omega. An Authorised
Revision of St. Matthew, and the History of the
Planet, from the First Strata to the End. Written
for the Spirit at Command. By F.W. Cunard.
Liverpool: Cunard & Sons, 1910.
             [Genesis I and Matthew printed in two columns; the left-
             hand column consists of the KJV with some words
             modernized; the right-hand column carries some eccentric
             commentary and painfully obvious definitions: e.g., "Le
             means look, see."]

1913 **Anonymous**   The Fourth Gospel...and Genesis. By
F.W.H. London: Newnham, Cowell & Gripper, 1913-1914.
             1913 Genesis as originally compiled...by the
             author of 'God's Week of Creation'...

             1914 The Fourth Gospel...and Genesis, a new
             translation shewing the...connection that
             exists between both books by F.W.H.

1913 **Oxford Church Bible Commentary**   Oxford Church Bible
Commentary. (General Editor of the Old Testament -
C.F. Burney; General Editor of the New Testament -
Leighton Pullan [A New Translation]   Two Volumes.
London: Rivingtons, 1913-1915.

1913 Book of Wisdom Edited by A.T.S. Goodrick.
1915 St. Mark, Translated by W.C. Allen.

[Only two books published.]

1914 **Clegg, Alfred**   The Bible within the Bible,
including the Apocrypha. Edited by...Alfred Clegg...
London: Headley Bros., [1914].
["With the omission of all unnecessary and unhelpful
Words and passages."]

1915 **Root, Seth Benson**   Treasures of verse; a collection
of original poems embracing a versification of the
last twenty-one books of the Old Testament, by Seth
B. Root.   Saratoga Springs: The Saratogian, 1915.

1918 **Anonymous**   Bible Stories from the Old and the New
Testaments; a textbook for use in the intermediate
department of Sunday schools. Rock Island, Illinois:
Augustana Book Concern, [1918].

1923 **Hall, Newton Marshall**   The Golden Book. A Modern
Bible. The Heart of the Holy Scriptures, arranged
and edited especially for family reading by Rev.
Newton Marshall Hall... Springfield, Massachusetts:
The King-Richardson Co., 1914.

1924 **Anonymous**   The Road to Real Success. London:
Simpkin, Marshall; Portsmouth: W.H. Barrell, 1924.
[Translation of the Four Gospels, the Epistles of James,
John 1, and The Book of Jonah.]

1926 **O'Neill, George**   Scripture Readings for Times
of Retreat. Selected...and translated by George
O'Neill.   New York & Cincinnati: Frederick Pustet
Co., 1926.

1927 **Gollancz, Israel**   The Caedmon Manuscript of
Anglo-Saxon Biblical Poetry.   Oxford: 1927.

1930 **Kent, Charles Foster**   The Social Teachings of the
Prophets and Jesus.   New York: Charles Scribner's
Sons, 1930.
["The chief aims, therefore, of this volume are to
single out the important social teachings of the Bible,
to translate them into clear English, and then to
classify and present them..."]

1931 **Pridgeon, Charles**   Is Hell Eternal or Will God's
Plan Fail? Pittsburgh: 1931.
[Contains many Universalist translations.]

1932 **Meecham, Henry G.**   The Oldest Version of the Bible:
'Aristeas' on its traditional origin. A study in

early apologetic. With translation and appendices.
London: Holburn Publishing House, 1932.

1934 **Hansen, H.C.**   The Bible in Song; selected passages.
By H.C. Hansen. Minneapolis: 1934.

1935 **Loveland, Seymour**   Illustrated Bible Story Book.
One-volume edition. Based on The Illustrated Bible
Story Books (Old and New Testaments) by Seymour
Loveland. Adapted by Edith Patterson Meyer. Pictures
by Milo Winter. NY, Chicago & San Francisco: Rand
McNally & Co., 1935.
   Another Edition; 1943.

1937 **Bates, Ernest Sutherland**   The Bible designed to be
read as literature, edited and arranged by Ernest
Sutherland Bates.   London: Heinemann, 1937.
   [The AV has been used , except in the case of Proverbs,
   Job, Ecclesiastes and the Song of Songs, where the RV
   has been followed. The spelling and punctuation are
   modernized.]

   Reprinted; London: The Folio Society, 1958.

1938 **Richards, James**   Bits from de Old Book. Being
bits from each of de sixty six books of de Bible.
Put into de Sussex tongue by Jim Cladpole. [James
Richards] 2 Parts Turnbridge Wells: James Richards,
1938.

1939 **Ballou, Robert O.**   The Bible of the World, edited
by Robert Ballou...Friedrich Spieclesers... Horace
L. Friess. New York: Viking Press, 1939.
   [A compilation of Scriptures representative of the
   "Best" in Hinduism, Buddhism, Judaeo-Christianity, etc.
   The text of the latter (which comprises more than half
   of the book) is unidentified.]

1939 **Copp, Zed Hopeful**   The Book of Life. Home Library.
The Interwoven Gospels, The Acts, Revelation, The
Epistles, and Gems from Proverbs by Zed Hopeful
Copp. Volume one-Home Library.   Philadelphia,
Chicago & Toronto: The John C. Winston Company,
1939.
   [AV with some modifications and paraphrase of Gospels.]

1940 **Neer, Maude Jessamine**   The Story of the Christ
of the Bible; In Verse. By Maude Jessamine Neer.
Glendale, California: Published at Glendale Union
Academy Press, 1940.
   [A devotional paraphrase of selections from the O.T. &
   N.T.]

1943 **MacDonald, Wilson**   Greater Poems of the Bible;
Metrical Versions, Biblical Forms and Original Poems

by Wilson MacDonald.   Buffalo, New York: The
Broadway Press, 1943.
[An edition limited to one thousand copies.]

["...I have made no metrical versions of many poems of
the Bible, but have presented them unchanged except in
form. The reason is that these poems are such pure
poetry in the St. James version, and so devoid of
obscure or archaic phrasing that no metrical enhancement
could add to their strength or beauty."]

Also; Toronto: Macmillan, 1944.

1946 **Dodd, C.H.**   The Bible Today by C.H. Dodd...
Cambridge: at the University Press, 1946.
["Quotations from the Old and New Testaments usually
follow the Revised Version, but not scrupulously. I have
sometimes silently altered it, and sometimes made my own
translation." Many times reprinted.]

1949 **Gray, Nicolete**   Jacob's Ladder; a Bible Picture
Book from Anglo-Saxon and 12th Century English MSS
by Nicolete Gray. London: Faber & Faber, 1949.

1949 **Niebuhr, Hulda**   One story, by Hulda Niebuhr.
Philadelphia: Presbyterian Board of Christian
Education, 1949.

1949 **Waddell, Helen**   Stories from Holy Writ. Helen
Waddell. London: Constable, 1949.
Reprinted; Westport, Connecticut: Greenwood
Press, Publishers, 1975.

1953 **Klein, Hyman**   Encyclopedia of Biblical
Interpretation, 1953.

1955 **Ford, Alvy E.**   The Old Testament in Verse: Genesis
to Job, from the Bible in Verse, by Alvy E. Ford.
Lincoln, Neb.: Back to the Bible Broadcast, 1955.

1957 **Anonymous**   Bible Poetry in Modern Verse... [Norman
Veeder typed.] 1957?

1959 **Klaperman, Libby M. and Others**   Stories from the
Bible. The Old Testament. Illustrated in full color
by H. Duport. Written and adapted by Libby M.
Klaperman. Selected and arranged by Jorn Sann and
Ralph Shonberg. London: Macdonald, 1959.

1959 **Wolverton, Basil**   The Bible Story by
Basil Wolverton. 6 Vols. Pasadena, CA: Published by
Ambassador College Press, 1959-1964.
         Vol. 1   1961
         Vol. 2   1959, 1960, 1961
         Vol. 3   1961, 1962

        Vol. 4   1962, 1963, 1964
        Vol. 5   1964, 1965, 1966
        Vol. 6   1964, 1965, 1966, 1967, 1968

1960 **Anonymous**   The Twentieth Century Encyclopedia of Catholicism. New York: Hawthorn Books, 1960-1964.
    1960 ...Vol. 66. The Prophetes by Joseph Dheilly; Translated from the French by Rachel Attwater.
       [Selections]

    196? ...Vol. 68. The Life of Our Lord. [Gospel harmonies.]

    196? ...Vol. 70. St. Paul and His Message.

    1964 ...Vol. 71. The O.T. Apocrypha, by Catherine Dimier; Translated from the French by S.J. Tester.

    1960 ...Vol. 72. The N.T. Apocrypha, Translated from the French by Wulston Hibberd.

1962 **Blessing, Rev. William L.**   Blessing Version of the Bible, 1962.
    ["Showers of Blessing", 499th Issue, July, 1962: contains the first four chapters of Genesis. "Showers of Blessing", 500th Issue, August, 1962: contains the first two chapters of Matthew.]

1962 **Casey, Francis J.**   Staging the Bible; Readings from Holy Scripture arranged for dramatic and Choral Recitation by Francis J. Casey, C.SS.R. With a Preface by Edward J. Crowley... Westminster, Maryland: The Newman Press, 1962.

1962 **Napier, Davie**   Song of the Vineyard. A Guide through the Old and New Testament. A Theological Introduction to the Old Testament. B. Davie Napier... New York: Harper & Bros., Publishers, 1962.
    Revised edition; Song of the Vineyard. A Guide through the Old Testament. Davie Napier. Revised Edition. Philadelphia: Fortress Press, 1981.
      ["Although I have not always felt justified in modifying the RSV in this regard, my own language in this revision is consistently inclusive."]

1962 **Putz, Louis J.**   The Kingdom of God. A Short Bible. Translations, explanations and paraphrases under the direction of Louis J. Putz, C.S.C. Notre Dame, Indiana: Fides Publishers, Inc., 1962.
    [The basic translation is taken from the Confraternity Version and some translations from the Douay Version.

The paraphrases are in smaller type. Examples: Pages 21,
26, 35, 39, 40-41, 42-43, 44-47.]

1963 **Oesterreicher, John M.** The Israel of God on the
Old Testament Roots of the Church's Faith. John M.
Oesterreicher... Englewood Cliffs, NJ: Prentice-
Hall, Inc., 1963.
["Quotations from Holy Scripture follow in the main the
Confraternity version... Occasionally, however, the
author has made his own translation."]

1965 **Martin, Frances** The Inspired Word; Scripture in
the Light of Language and Literature by Luis Alonso
Schokel, S.J. Translated by Frances Martin. New
York: Herder & Herder, 1965.
["The translation of the Old Testament, when they are
not original, are taken from the Confraternity of
Christian Doctrine version. The New Testament
translation, when they are not original, are taken from
the New English Bible...Whenever patristic and other
texts are not my own translation, credit is given in the
footnotes."]

1966 **Anonymous** Listen... The Lord is Speaking: The
Bible in Simplified English. Collegeville, Minn.:
The Liturgical Press, 1966.
[The poetic books, duplicated historical material, and
the Epistles are not included.]

1966 **Bullock, Michael** The Bible Story Retold by
Stefan Andres, Illustrated by Gerhard Oberlander;
Translated from the German by Michael Bullock. New
York: McGraw - Hill Book Co. Printed in West
Germany, 1966.

1966 **Burke, Carl F.** God is For Real, Man:
Interpretations of Bible passages and stories, as
told by some of God's bad-tempered angels with
busted halos to Carl F. Burke, Chaplain of Erie
County Jail, Buffalo, N.Y.. New York: Association
Press, 1966.
[Paraphrases]

1966 **Hurlbut, Jesse Lyman** Hurlbut's Story of
the Bible. The complete Bible Story, running from
Genesis to Revelation, told in the simple language
of today for Young and Old... By Rev. Jesse Lyman
Hurlbut... Westwood, NJ: Fleming H. Revell Co.,
1966.

1966 **McNamara, Martin** The New Testament
and the Palestinian Targum to the Pentateuch. Rome:
Pontifical Biblical Institute, 1966.
[Analecta Biblia 27.]

1966 **Seerveld, Calvin G.**   Take Hold of God and Pull; Moments in a College Chapel. Translations of Scripture with Accompanying Meditations, by Calvin Seerveld. Palos Heights, Ill.: Pennyasheet Press, 1966.
> [Selections range from Genesis to John, mostly from the Old Testament.]

1968 **Rachleff, Owen S.**   Great Bible Stories and Master Paintings. A Complete Narration of the Old and New Testaments by Owen S. Rachleff. Illustrated with One Hundred and Four Works of Art from Giotto to Corot. New York: Abradale Press, 1968.
> ["It attempts to provide, for young and old alike, a basic narrative of Bible text..." Most of the direct quotations appear to be KJV.]

1969 **Burke, Carl F.**   God is Beautiful, Man; Interpretations of Bible passages and stories, as told by some of God's bad-tempered angels with busted halos to Carl F. Burke.   New York: Association Press, 1969.
> [Paraphrases]

1971 **Aaron, David**   Aaron's Riming Bible, by David Aaron. Philadelphia: Dorrance & Co., 1971.

1971 **Buck, Pearl Sydenstryker**   The Bible Story by Pearl S. Buck. n.p.: Bartholomew House Ltd., 1971.
> [The O.T. & N.T. retold in seventy-two 'story-sections' in the language of today. An Abridged version.]

1973 **Anonymous**   Psalm Praise. Chicago: G.I.A. Publications, 1973.
> ["We have sought to provide a metrical balance without always attempting to rhyme the verses; we have sought to keep closely to the thought and thrust of the Psalms."]

1975 **Waddy, Lawrence**   The Bible as Drama by Lawrence Waddy. New York, Paramus, & Toronto: Paulist Press, 1975.
> [90 Bible stories presented as plays.]

1979 **Fishbane, Michael**   Text and Texture; Close Readings of Selected Biblical Texts. Michael Fishbane. New York: Schocken Books, 1979.
> ["All translations found herein are my own."]

1984 **Harper, H.B. George** H.B. & His/Her Bible Adventures (Human Being) by H.B. George Harper. Helena, Montana: H.B. Publications, 1984-1988.
>   Vol. 1   "A God in the Bush is Worth Two in the Hand", 1984.   [Pentateuch]
>
>   Vol. 2   "Promises, Promises", 1985.
>   [Joshua, Judges, Ruth, I & II Samuel]

MACK LIBRARY
BOB JONES UNIVERSITY
GREENVILLE, SC

Vol. 3   Kings of the Hill, 1985.   [I & II Kings, I & II Chronicles, Ezra, Nehemiah]

Vol. 4   The Race to Grace, 1985.   [Esther, Job, Psalms, Proverbs, Ecclesiastes, Song of Solomon]

Vol. 5   An Idol a Day Keeps God Away, 1984. [Isaiah, Jeremiah, Lamentations]

Vol. 6   Prophet Potourri, 1986.   [Ezekiel, Daniel, Hosea, Joel, Amos, Obadiah, Jonah, Micah, Nahum, Habakkuk, Zephaniah, Haggai, Zechariah, Malachi]

Vol. 7   Jesus: The Whole in One, 1986. [Gospels]

Vol. 8   Tough Acts to Follow, 1987.   [Acts, Romans, I & II Corinthians, Galatians, Ephesians, Philippians, Colossians, I & II Thessalonians, I & II Timothy, Titus, Philemon]

Vol. 9   End of the Beginning, 1988. [Hebrews, James, I & II Peter, I, II & III John, Jude, Revelation]   [The Apocrypha including I & II Esdras and Letter of Jeremiah]

1984 **Holtz, Barry W.** (Editor)   Back to the Sources. Reading the Classic Jewish Texts. New York: Summit Books, 1984.
[Contains some original translations.]

1986 **Bensen, D.R.**   Biblical Limericks. Old Testament Stories Re-Versed by D.R. Bensen. Introduction by Isaac Asimov. Illustrations by Albrecht Durer. New York: Ballantine Books, 1986.

1990 **Roche, Paul**   The Bible's Greatest Stories. Paul Roche. Signet Books, 1990.
["A brilliant new rendering in contemporary language-from the Creation to the Resurrection."]

Another Edition; A Mentor Book, 1990.

CHILDREN'S BIBLES

???? **de Vries, Anne**   The Children's Bible as Retold for Children by Anne de Vries. St. Louis, MO: Concordia Publishing House, [19??].

???? **Mark, Thiselton**   The Bible for Children.
Bible Stories in Bible Language. New York, Chicago,
Toronto, London, and Edinburgh: Fleming H. Revell
Co., [192?].
> ["Only a word is changed now and then to make the
> meaning easier, for, as you know it is three hundred
> years since this translation which we call the AV was
> made."]

???? **Marshall-Taylor, Geoffrey**   The Illustrated
Children's Bible. Retold by Geoffrey Marshall-
Taylor. Illustrated by Andrew Allof, Jon Davis, Dick
Eastland, Colin Shearing, Barrie Thorpe. Cathay
Books, Printed in Hong Kong, n.d.
Also; Octopus Books Ltd., 1980.

???? **O'Gorman, Rev. Denis**   Scriptural Dramas for
Children. Twelve Musical Plays. Text and Songs,
Denis O'Gorman. Accompaniment; Jim Brand and
Elizabeth Copeman-Hill. New York: Paulist Press,
n.d.

???? **Pierson, Mrs. Helen W.**   Bible Stories in Easy Words
by Mrs. Helen W. Pierson. New York: McLoughlin
Bros., n.d.

1765 **Anonymous**   An abridgement of Scripture history
designed for the amusement and improvement of
children: wherein the most striking actions in the
Old Testament are made plain to the youngest
capacities: adorned with Head pieces, Expressive of
the subject of each narrative. Curiously engraved on
60 copper plates; and dedicated to the infant Bishop
of Osnaburg, by an Eminent Divine. London: Printed
& Sold by Edward Ryland, 1765.

1823 **Anonymous**   Scripture Histories; for the Instruction
of Youth: Translated from the French Version of the
original German of M.Hubner. Hamburgh. [Ms]

1834 **Anonymous**   The Children's Bible with Plates.
By a Lady of Cincinnati. Philadelphia, New York,
Baltimore & Boston: Fisher & Brother, 1834.
> ["This little book, dear children, is not the Bible, but
> only a brief history of it." About 2 inches square.]

1838 **Anonymous**   The Child's Own Bible: being a selection
of narratives of the leading events of revealed
religion, in the language of Holy Writ...London:
Longman, Orme, Brown, Green, & Longmans; J. Hatchard
& Son, 1838.
> [O.T. series only; no more published.]

1855 **Child, Isabella**   The Child's Picture Bible, by
Isabella Child. New York: 1855.

[Text may be a paraphrase. Covers Old Testament only.]

1873 **Rogers, William**   The School and Children's Bible;
prepared under the superintendence of the Rev.
William Rogers... London: Longman, Green, and Co.,
1873.
> ['adapted for the use of children'. The AV is retained
> except the Psalms is the P.B. version.]

1889 **Pollard, Josephine**   Young Folk's Bible in Words of
Easy Reading: The Sweet Stories of God's Word in the
Language of Childhood... by Josephine Pollard...
n.p.: R.S. Peale & Co., 1889.
> Another Edition; With an introduction by Rev.
> W.H. Milburn... Chicago and New York: The
> Werner Co., 1889.

1890 **Church, Alfred J.**   Stories from the Bible,
Illustrated. n.p.: The Macmillan Co., 1890.

1892 **Mackail, John William**   [The Holy Bible for Young
Readers] 1892.
> 1892 Biblia Innocentium, being the story of
> God's Chosen People before the coming of
> our Lord, Jesus Christ, upon the earth.
> Written anew for Children. Hammersmith:
> Kelmscott Press.
> > [O.T. selections]
>
> 1892 Biblia Innocentium, The N.T. Being the
> Story of God's Chosen People after the
> Coming of our Lord Jesus Christ upon the
> Earth. Together with Stories of Saints
> and Martyrs.

["This is a distinguished version of the N.T... Instead
of four parallel Gospels, the N.T. has been made into
one consecutive story. Passages difficult to explain
have been clarified, repetitions have been eliminated,
and the whole story has been couched in language of rich
simplicity."]

Other editions, 1900, 1905, 1910.

Another Edition; Biblia Innocentium: part
second, being the story of God's chosen people
after the coming of Our Lord Jesus Christ upon
earth, written anew for children by J.W.
Mackail.   London, New York, and Bombay:
Longmans, Green and Co., 1901.

Another edition; The Holy Bible for Young
Readers. The New Testament. Being the story of
God's chosen people after the coming of Our
Lord Jesus Christ upon earth together with

stories of saints and martyrs written by J.W. Mackail... Mount Vernon, New York: The Peter Pauper Press, [c.1950].

Also; Biblia Innocentium, The N.T. Being the Story of God's Chosen People after the Coming of our Lord Jesus Christ upon the Earth. Together with Stories of Saints and Martyrs. Written by J.W. Mackail and Illustrated by Fritz Kredel. Mount Vernon, New York: Peter Pauper Press.

Also; London: Mayflower Publishing Co., 1958.

1898 **Lathbury, Mary Artemisia**   Children's Story of the Bible, by Mary A. Lathbury. Boston: DeWolfe & Fishe Co., 1898.

1901 **Jones, Harriet Newell**   The Young People's Bible; or, The Scriptures connected, explained, and simplified, by Harriet Newell Jones. Philadelphia: American Book and Bible House, [1901].

1902 **Gilder, Mrs. J.B.**   The Children's Bible. New York: 1902.

1916 **Alcott, Francis Jenkins**   Bible Stories to Read and Tell, Arranged by Francis Jenkins Alcott. Houghton Mifflin Co., 1916.

1922 **Sherman, Henry A. and Charles Foster Kent**
The Children's Bible; Selections from the Old and New Testaments translated and arranged by Henry A. Sherman and Charles Foster Kent. New York: Charles Scribner's Sons, MCMXXII [1922].
["The 'Children's Bible' provides, in simple English, a translation of selections from both the Old and New Testaments... the text is that of the Bible itself, but in the language of the child..."]

[The Deity is rendered "Jehovah" many times.]

Another edition, 1925, 1930.

Another edition; Bible stories every child should know, selections from the Old and New Testaments, translated and arranged. New York: Published by Doubleday, Doran & Co. for The Parents Instruction, 1941.

1924 **Fryer, Jane Eayre and John G. Fryer**   The Bible Story Book for Boys and Girls, by Jane Eayre Fryer and John G. Fryer. Oakland, Calif.: The Smithsonian Company; Philadelphia, Pa.: The John C. Winston Co., 1924.

["Nowhere has there been a conscious departure from the plain meaning of the Biblical narrative, or anything added not clearly contained therein. For the sake of vividness, some of the characters have been allowed to tell their stories in the first person."]

1924 **Nairne, Alexander and Others**   The Older Children's Bible, by Alexander Nairne, T.R. Glover, and Arthur Quiller-Couch.   New York: Macmillan, 1924.
["The text used is in general that of the AV, with here and there the change of a word or the adaption of an old spelling to that more commonly used in school."]

1924 **Nairne, Alexander and Others**   The Little Children's Bible, by Alexander Nairne, T.R. Glover, and Arthur Quiller-Couch.   New York: Macmillan, 1924.

1925 **Anonymous**   The Great Stories of the Bible for Children. Cleveland & New York: The World Publishing Co., 1925.

1929 **De La Mare, Walter**   Stories from the Bible by Walter De La Mare. Illustrated by Theodore Nadejen. New York: Cosmopolitan Book Corp., 1929.
Another Edition; Stories from the Bible by Walter De La Mare. Illustrated by Edward Ardizzone. New York: Alfred A.Knoff, 1961.

1934 **Bowie, Walter Russell**   The Story of the Bible; Retold from Genesis to Revelations in the Light of Present Knowledge for Both the Young and the Mature. Walter Russell Bowie.   New York & Nashville: Abingdon Press, 1934.

1934 **Cohen, Lenore**   Bible Tales For Very Young Children by Lenore Cohen. Cincinnati, Ohio: The Union of American Hebrew Congregations, 1934-1936.
1934 Book 1 (Pentateuch).
1936 Book 2 (Joshua to Daniel) With many
    illustrations by Penina Kishore.

1934 **Smith, Lloyd Edwin**   The Story of Jesus. Retold for Children by Lloyd Edwin Smith. Illustrated by Henry E. Vallely.   Racine, Wis.: Whitman Publishing Co., 1934.
Another Edition; 1941.

1943 **Andruss, Bessie Edmond**   Rarely Told Bible Stories for Bigger Children by Bessie Edmond Andruss. Illustrated by Priscilla Pointer. New York: Coward-McCann Inc., 1943.
Another Edition; 1946.

1945 **Beebe, Catherine**   The Story of Jesus for Boys and Girls, Told by Catherine Beebe. Pictured by Robb Beebe. Milwaukee: The Bruce Publishing Co., 1945.

1946 **Doane, Pelagie**   A Small Child's Bible. By Pelagie Doane. New York: Henry Z. Walck, Inc., 1946.
[A collection of Bible stories for younger children...]

Another edition; London: Oxford Univ. Press.

1946 **Hartman, Charles**   A Catholic Child's Bible, 1946.

1948 **Becker, May Lamberton**   The Rainbow Book of Bible Stories. The Old Testament and New Testament edited, with an introduction... Illustrated by Hilda Van Stockum. Cleveland & New York: The World Publishing Co., 1948.
["The words in which these stories are told come as closely as circumstances permit to those of the AV of the English Bible."]

1948 **Medary, George P.**   Child's Bible In Rhyme, by George P. Medary. [No place or name] 1948.
["I use no flowery language - I would not if I could - But try to talk so simple, it Is easy understood."]

1951 **Bowie, Walter Russell**   The Bible Story for Boys and Girls; New Testament. Walter Russell Bowie. New York & Nashville, Abingdon-Cokesbury Press, 1951.
Also; Englewood Cliffs, N.J.: Prentice - Hall, 1951.

1953 **Maxwell, Arthur S.**   The Bible Story. More then 400 Stories in Ten Volumes covering the entire Bible from Genesis to Revelation. Mountain View, California: Pacific Press Club Publication Association, Copyright 1953 by the Review & Herald Publishing Association, 1953.

1955 **Anonymous**   Bedtime Bible Stories, Illustrated by Bruno Frost. Racine, Wisconsin: Whitman Publishing Co., 1955.

1955 **Anonymous**   Crusade. The Story of the Bible Retold for Catholic Children. Written by the Maryknoll Sisters. Chicago: John J.Crawley & Co., 1955.
[Based on the Confraternity Version. Consisted of 21 pamphlets.]

1955 **Armstrong, April Oursler**   Stories from the life of Jesus, Adapted by April Oursler Armstrong from "The Greatest Book Even Written" by Fulton Oursler. Illustrated by Jules Gotlieb. Garden City, New York: Garden City Press Books, 1955.

1955 **Fiorentino, Dante Del**   The Catholic Bible
in Pictures edited by the Right Reverend Monsignor
Dante Del Fiorentino. New York: Greystone, 1955.

1955 **Graham, Lorenz**   The Story of Jesus. Adapted
by Lorenz Graham. Illustrated by William A. Walsh.
Classic Illustrated, Special Issue, No. 129, 1955.

1957 **Worm, Piet**   More Stories from the Old Testament
from Joseph to the Prophets. New York: Published by
Sheed and Ward, Inc. Published in Holland, 1957.

1959 **Anonymous**   Children's Bible. Baltimore, Maryland:
Helicon Press, 1959.
        [Text by W. Hillmann, Illustrated by Johannes Gruger,
        Translated by Lawrence Atkinson.]

        Another Edition; Collegeville, Minnesota: The
        Liturgical Press, St. John's Abbey, 19??

1960 **Green, Jay**   The Children's 'King James' Bible: New
Testament. The wording by Jay Green.   Evansville:
Modern Bible Translations, 1960.
        [Purports to be the AV, however it is a highly altered
        text. Only the N.T. has appeared to date.]

1962 **Anonymous**   The Children's Version of the Holy
Bible. New York, Toronto, London: McGraw-Hill Book
Co., Inc., 1962.
        [Copyright by Jay Green]

1962 **Anonymous**   The Teen-Age Version of the Holy Bible.
New York, Toronto, London: McGraw-Hill Book Co.,
Inc., 1962.
        [Copyright by Jay Green]

1964 **Haughton, Rosemary**   The Family God Chose. Written
and Illustrated by Rosemary Haughton.   New York:
P.J. Kenedy & Sons, 1964.

1964 **Sellew, Catharine F.**   Adventures with Abraham's
Children by Catharine F. Sellew. With Illustrations
by Steele Savage. Boston & Toronto: Little, Brown
& Co., 1964.

1965 **Anonymous** The Children's Bible; The Old Testament;
The New Testament. New York: Golden Press, 1965.
        Editorial Advisory Board:
          Joseph A. Grispino
          Samuel Terrien
          David H. Wice

        ["All the truth, beauty, and poetry of the Bible have
        been preserved in this new version for children."
        Selections only; Includes five of the Psalms (in the

KJV), Gospels are harmonized. Sumptuous illustrations in color show Jesus as a blue-eyed blonde.]

1966 Martin, Patricia Summerlin Bible Stories That Live by Patricia Summerlin Martin. Nashville, TN: The Southwestern Co., 1966.

1967 Cocagnac, A.-M. and Rosemary Haughton Bible for Young Christians; The New Testament. By A.-M. Cocagnac and Rosemary Haughton. Illustrations by Jacques Lescauff. Translation by A.M. Cocagnac and Rosemary Houghton. 2 Vols. New York: The Macmillan Co., 1967.
> ["...based on the RSV...simplified and adapted where necessary to the understanding of children..."]

1967 Edwards, Anne A Child's Bible. London: Puff Publishers Ltd., 1967.
> Another edition; The Bible for Young Readers. The Old Testament Rewritten for Young Readers by Anne Edwards. New York: Golden Press, 1968.

[Consists of O.T. selections in simplified English]

1968 Bradford, Barbara Taylor (Editor) Children's Stories of the Bible from the Old and New Testament. Edited by Barbara Taylor Bradford; Illustrated by Laszlo Matulay. Old Testament stories by Merle Burnick. Manchester & London: The GR Book Company & The World Distributors Ltd., 1968.
> ["...carefully checked for accuracy and has been approved by reliable consultants comprising of clergymen from the Protestant, Catholic and Jewish faiths."]

Another Edition; New York: Playmore, Inc., 1968.

1968 Catholic Children's Bible in Colour Catholic Children's Bible in Colour. Feltham, England: Hamlyn Pub. Group, 1968.

1968 Kossoff, David Bible Stories Retold by David Kossoff. Illustrated by Gino D'Achille. Forward by William Barclay. Chicago & New York: Follett Publishing Co., 1968.

1969 Anonymous The Taize Picture Bible. Stories from the Scriptures, adapted from the text of the Jerusalem Bible. With Illustrations by Brother Eric de Saussre of the Taize Community. Philadelphia: Herder; NY: Fortress Press, 1969.
> ["The Bible Story for Children" in Great Britain.]

1969 Edwards, Anne and Shirley Steen A Child's Bible. 1969-1973.

Vol. I ...The Old Testament. Re-written for Children by Anne Edwards. Illustrated by Charles Front and David Christian. London: Pan Books Ltd., 1973.

Vol. II ...The New Testament Re-written for Children by Shirley Steen... Great Britain: Wolfe Pub. Ltd., 1969.

Another Edition; A Child's Bible in Colour. Re-written for Children by Shirley Steen. Illustrated by Charles Front. New York, New Jersey, and Toronto: Paulist Press, 1973.

1970 **Taylor, Kenneth N.**   Taylor's Bible Story Book. Wheaton, Illinois: Tyndale House; London: Coverdale House; Toronto: Home Evangel Books, 1970.
["...told clearly, directly, in everyday English familiar to children."]

1971 **Palmer, Peter**   Beautiful Bible Stories for Little Eyes and Ears, by Peter Palmer. Grand Rapids, MI: Associated Authors and Authors, Inc., 1971.

1971 **Taylor, Kenneth N.** The Bible in Pictures for Little Eyes by Kenneth N. Taylor, 1971.
["A multi-media educational experience for the preschooler and primary. Includes 190 Bible stories and full-color pictures, plus 16 child-proof records."]

1972 **Taylor, Kenneth N.**   The Children's Living Bible: Paraphrased. Illustrations by Richard and Frances Hook.   Wheaton, IL: Tyndale House Publishers; London, England: Coverdale House Publishers, 1972.
[May be the same as the Living Bible, 1971. See Kenneth Taylor, The Living Bible, 1962.]

1973 **Allen, J.T. and Others**   Nelson's Picture Bible. Text by J.T. Allen, Lane Easterly, Bernice Rech and Elmer T. Towns. Pictures by Carlo Tora. Nashville, New York: Thomas Nelson, Inc., 1973.
[The Bible Paraphrased for Children... More than 185 Short Stories (Old & New Testaments)... for your Youngsters Ages 4-11.]

1973 **Hadaway, Bridget and Jean Atcheson**   The Bible for Children Retold by Bridget Hadaway and Jean Atcheson.   London: Octopus Books Ltd.;   New York: Distributed in U.S.A. by Cresent Books, 1973.
[Abridged - Bible stories from the Old and New Testaments, 304 pages.]

Reprinted; New York: Derrydale Books, 1985.

Reprinted, 1986, 1987.

1973 **Hirsh, E.B.R.**   Illustrated Children's Bible.
Adapted by E.B.R.Hirsh; Illustrated by Gwen Green.
Miami, FL: P.S.I. & Associates, Inc., 1973.
     Another Edition, 1988.

1973 **Samuels, Ruth**   Bible Stories for Jewish Children
from Joshua to Queen Esther by Ruth Samuels.
Illustrated by Laszio Matulay. KTAV Publishing
House Inc., 1973.

1974 **Christie-Murray, David**   Hamlyn Bible for Children,
1974.
     Another Edition; The Illustrated Children's
     Bible, 1976.

     Also; The Illustrated Children's Bible. David
     Christie-Murray. Illustrated by Ken Petts,
     John Berry, Neville Dear and Norma Burgin.
     New York: Publishers, Grosset & Dunlap, 1982.

1974 **Easterly, R. Lane**   Illustrated Great Bible Stories
for Children; Paraphrased in Today's English. Text
by R. Lane Easterly. Illustrated by Carlo Tora and
Alvaro Mairani. Nashville, TN: Royal Publishers,
Inc., 1974.

1977 **Behnke, John**   Stories of Jesus; Words by John
Behnke of the Paulist Fathers. Pictures by Betsy
Roosen Sheppard. New York, New York/Ramsey, N.J.:
Paulist Press, 1977.
     ["In contemporary language, for today's children, John
     Behnke of the Paulist Fathers retells the classic
     stories of the life of Jesus."]

1977 **Jahsmann, Allan Hart** (Editor)   The Holy Bible
for Children: A Simplified Version of the Old and
New Testament edited by Allan Hart Jahsmann.
Illustrations and Maps by Don Kueker. St. Louis:
Concordia Publishing House, 1977.
     ["A simplified retelling...of selected portions of the
     book of the Bible."]

1977 **Paolini, Mary and Others**   The Storyteller's
Bible. Mary S. Paolini, Louis M. Savary, William E.
Frankhauser. Illustrated by Dolores T. Kirwan. New
York: The Regina Press, 1977.

1978 **Anonymous**   My Book of Bible Stories. Brooklyn,
NY: Watch Tower Bible & Tract Society, 1978.

1979 **Gaines, M.C.** (Editor)   Picture Stories from the
Bible; the Old Testament in Full-color Comic strip
Form, edited by M.C. Gaines... New York: Scarf
Press, 1979.

1980 **Forsee, Aylesa**   They Trusted God. Bible Stories Retold by Aylesa Forsee. Illustrations by Hank Ziol. Boston, Mass.: The Christian Science Publishing Society, 1980.

1980 **Gaines, M.C.**   (Editor)   Picture Stories from the Bible. The New Testament in comic-strip form. Edited by M.C. Gaines. Illustrations by Don Cameron; Scripts by Montgomery Mulford and Edward L. Wertheim. New York: Ballantine Books, 1980.

1980 **Hannon, Ruth**   (Editor)   My First Bible. Edited by Ruth Hannon. Illustrations by P. Ghijsens. New York: The Regina Press, 1980.

1980 **Horn, Geoffrey and Arthur Cavanaugh**   Bible Stories for Children Retold by Geoffrey Horn and Arthur Cavanaugh. Illustrated by Arvis Stewart. New York: Macmillan Publishing Co., 1980.

1980 **Pellowski, Michael J.**   A Child's Book of The Bible. Retold by Michael J. Pellowski. Edited by Malvina G. Vogel. New York: Playmore, Inc. Publishers, 1980.

1981 **Alexander, Pat**   Illustrated Children's Bible, Stories from the Old and New Testaments retold by Pat Alexander. Illustrated by Lyndon Evans. Nashville, Tn.: Ideals Publishing Corp., 1981.
      Another Edition; The Nelson Children's Bible. Stories from the Old and New Testaments retold by Pat Alexander. Illustrated by Lyndon Evans. Nashville: Thomas Nelson Publishers, 1981.

1981 **Knowles, Andrew**   Fount Children's Bible. Glasgow: William Collins Sons & Co.; London: Fount Paperbacks, 1981.
      Reprinted; The Crossroad Children's Bible. Andrew Knowles. Illustrated in full color by Bert Bouman. New York: Crossroad, 1989.

1981 **Wangerin, Walter, Jr.**   The Bible-Its Story for Children by Walter Wangerin, Jr. Chicago, New York & San Francisco: Rand McNally & Co., 1981.
      Another Edition; The Bible for Children by Walter Wangerin, Jr. New York: Checkerboard Press, 1981.

1983 **Ife, Elaine and Rosalind Sutton**   Now You Can Read ...Stories from the Bible. Stories Retold by Elaine Ife and Rosalind Sutton. Illustrated by Eric Rowe, Russell Lee and George Fryer. Nashville, Camden, New York: Thomas Nelson Publishers, 1983.

1983 **Lovasik, Lawrence G.**   St Joseph Children's
Bible. Popular Bible Stories from the Old and New
Testaments. By Lawrence G. Lovasik... New York:
Catholic Book Publishing Co., 1983.

1983 **Lovasik, Lawrence G.**   Catholic Picture Bible. By
Lawrence G. Lovasik... New York: Catholic Book
Publishing Co., 1983.
    [Over 150 Bible stories retold in simple words.]

1983 **Stoddard, Sandol**   The Doubleday Illustrated
Children's Bible by Sandol Stoddard. Paintings by
Tony Chen. New York: Doubleday & Co., Inc., 1983.

1983 **Theola, Sister Mary**   The Catholic Children's
Bible by Sister Mary Theola... Illustrated by J.
Verleye. The Regina Press, [1983].

1984 **Weed, Libby** (Editor)   Read-n-Grow Picture Bible.
Edited by Libby Weed, Illustrated by Jim Padgett.
Worthy Publishing, 1984.
    [Copyright by Sweet Publishing Co.]

1985 **Batchelor, Mary**   The Children's Bible in
365 Stories by Mary Batchelor. Illustrated by John
Haysom.   Belleville, MI: Lion Publishing Corp.,
1985.
    Another Edition; Tring-Batavia-Sydney: A Lion
    Book, 1985.

1985 **Grant, Amy**   Heart to Heart Bible Stories. By Amy
Grant. Fortworth, Tx: Sweet Publishing, 1985.

1986 **Anonymous**   Holy Bible. International Children's
Bible. New Century Version. Fort Worth, TX: Sweet
Publishing, 1986.
    [Unknown if same text as the New Century Version, 1984.]

    [See Anonymous, International Children's Version, 1978.]

1986 **Brown, Alice & Pat Kirk**   Jesus, His Story
for Children As Told by Alice Brown and Pat Kirk.
Illustrated by Sue Roby/Creative Studios I.   Fort
Worth, TX: Brownlow Publishing Co., Inc., 1986.

1987 **Hayward, Linda**   Bible Stories from the Old
Testament. Retold by Linda Hayward. Illustrated by
Katherine Dietz Coville.   New York: Publishers-
Grosset & Dunlap, 1987.

1987 **Hughes, Ray**   The Illustrated Bible for Children.
Re-told by Ray Hughes. Illustrations by Nino Musio.
Published in the United States and Canada: Joshua
Morris Publishing Co., 1987.

3rd printing, 1990.

1987 **Kyles, Rev. David**   Classic Bible Stories for
Children.   Re-told by   David Kyles...   New York:
Derrydale Books, 1987.

1987 **Wolf, Donald D.**   Bible Stories for Young People.
Edited by Donald D. Wolf. Design and Layout by
Margot L. Wolf. Engravings by Gustave Dore.   New
York: Published by Lexicon Publications, Inc., 1987.
    ["The Holy Scriptures retold for Young People based on
    traditional texts..."]

1988 **Hayes, Wanda**   A Child's First Book of Bible Stories
by Wanda Hayes. Illustrations by Kathryn Hutton/
Heidi Petach. Cincinnati, OH: Standard Publishing,
1988.

1989 **Bach, Alice and J. Cheryl Exum**   Moses' Ark. Stories
from the Bible. Alice Bach and J. Cheryl Exum.
Illustrated by Leo & Diane Dillon.   New York:
Delacorte Press, 1989.

1989 **Couch, James F., Jr.**   Children's Bible in Story.
Retold by James F. Couch, Jr. Illustrated by Michael
Codd. Nashville, TN: Ideals Children's Books, 1989.

1989 **Henley, Karyn**   The Beginner's Bible.
Timeless Children's Stories as told by Karyn Henley
illustrated by Dennis Davis.   Sisters, OR: Questar
Publishers, Inc., 1989.

1989 **Hurlbut, Jesse Lyman**   The Bedtime Bible Story
Book by Jesse Lyman Hurlbut. Edited by Toni Sortor.
Illustrations by Kathy Arbuckle.   Westwood, NJ:
Barbour & Co., Inc., 1989.

1989 **Rossel, Seymour**   A Child's Bible. Lessons From the
Prophets and Writings. Seymour Rossel. W.Orange, NJ:
Behrman House, 1989.

1989 **Willis, Geoffrey**   Classic Bible Stories Retold
for Today's Child by Geofrrey Willis. Illustrated by
Mike Dodd. London: The Hamlyn Publishing Group,
Ltd.; New York City: Gallery Books, 1989.

2
Hebrew Scriptures (Old Testaments)

HEBREW SCRIPTURES LISTINGS

1630 **Usher, Ambrose**   ["All of the O.T.; and of the New, the four 1st chapters of St. John's Gospel...
[See Bible Selections, 1630 Ambrose Usher, ["All of the O.T...]

1743 **Marchant, John**   The Holy Bible; With an Exposition in which several mis-translations are rectified...
[See Bible Selections for the complete entry. Includes the O.T.]

1765 **Wesley, John**   Explanatory Notes upon the Old Testament. By John Wesley. Bristol: William Pine, 1765.
[See Bible Selections for the complete entry.]

1774 **Bayly, Anselm**   The Old Testament, English and Hebrew, with remarks, critical and grammatical, on the Hebrew, and corrections of the English [AV] by Anselm Bayly. 4 Vols. London: George Bigg & Edward Cox, 1774.

1788 **Orton, Job**   A Short and Plain Exposition of the Old Testament, with devotional and practical Reflections, for the use of families, subjoined to each, somewhat in the manner of Dr. Doddridge's Family Expositor. Published from the author's Manuscripts, by Robert Gentleman. 6 Vols. Shrewbury: J. & W. Eddowes, 1788-1791.
["The sacred text is printed in Roman letters, and corrected from the valuable edition of the [KJ] Bible published at Oxford in the year 1772..." "My great business as been, to connect the text and exposition together..." "The attentive reader will perceive that the work is not uniformly a paraphrase, but has criticisms and other remarks (frequently taken from

Clark's Annotations) intermingled." From R. Gentleman's
Preface.]

First American, from the Second London Edition; 6
Vols. Charlestown: Printed and sold by Samuel
Etheridge, 1805.

1792 **Geddes, Alexander**   The Holy Bible, or the
Books accounted sacred by the Jews and Christians
otherwise called the Books of the Old and New
Covenants: faithfully translated from corrected
texts of the originals. With various readings,
explanatory notes, and critical remarks. By
Alexander Geddes. 3 Vols. London: Printed for the
Author by J. Davis, 1792-1800.
         1792 ...Volume I.   Genesis thru Joshua
         1797 ...Volume II.   Judges   thru   Chronicles
                              [Ruth and Manasseh]
         1800 ...Volume III. Critical Remarks

["I could have made my revision often more clear, and,
I believe more elegant; if I had not, with some
reluctance, adhered too strictly to the rigid rules of
verbal translation..." The work was produced "...without
the assistance of any one person, to share in the
ungrateful labour."]

[Lowndes lists the following constituents of the work:
         1786 Prospectus; Glasgow
         1787 Appendix, London
         1788 Proposals, London
         1790 General answer to the Queries, London
         1792 Vol. I
         1793 Address to the Public
         1797 Vol. II
         1800 Critical remarks to the Hebrew Scriptures]

[For Geddes' Psalms, see Psalms, 1807 Alexander Geddes,
A New Translation.. Psalms.]

1808 **Thomson, Charles**   The Old Covenant, commonly
called the Old Testament : Translated from the
Septuagint by Charles Thomson Late Secretary to the
Congress of the United States. 3 Vols. Philadelphia:
Jane Aitken, 1808.
         Revised edition; 2 Vols. By S.F. Pells.   London:
Skeffington & Son, 1904.

Another edition; As edited, revised and enlarged
by C.A. Muses. Colorado: Falcon's Wing Press,
1954.

Another edition, 1956.

1821 **Townsend, George**   The Old Testament, arranged
in historical & chronological order (on the basis of
Lightfoot's Chronicle) in such manner that the

Books, Psalms, Prophecies, &c. may be read as one connected history, in the words of the Authorized Translation...By...George Townsend. 2 Vols. London: Printed for F.C. & J. Rivington, 1821.
Another edition, 1826.

1st. American Edition; The Old Testament, Arranged in Historical and Chronological Order, on the Basis of Lightfoot's Chronicle, in such a Manner that the Books, Chapters, Psalms, Prophecies, &c. May be Read as One Connected History, in the Words of the Authorized Translation. With Notes and Copious Indexes. By the Rev. George Townsend... Revised, Punctuated, Divided into Paragraphs and Parallelisms... By the Rev. T.W. Coit... Boston: Published by Perkins and Marvin; Philadelphia: Henry Perkins, 1838.
Reprinted, 1839.

1822 **Alexander, A.**   The Holy Bible, Hebrew and English, the English a New Translation by A. Alexander. London: for L. Alexander, 1822.
[Presumably the O.T. only.]

1823 **Asher-Budinger**   Old Testament, 1823.

1838 **Coit, T.W.**   See George Townsend, The Old Testament, 1821.

1844 **Brenton, Sir Lancelot Charles Lee**   The Septuagint Version of the Old Testament, according to the Vatican text, translated into English; with the principal various readings of the Alexandrine copy, and a table of comparative chronology; by Sir Lancelot Charles Lee Brenton, Bart... 2 Vols. London: Samuel Bagster & Sons, 1844.
[An undated and unidentified reprint under the Title:] The Septuagint Version of the Old Testament with an English Translation and with various readings and critical notes, current from S. Bagster and Sons, London; Harper and Bros. New York.

Another edition, 1870.

Also; The Septuagint Version of The Old Testament; and with Various Readings and Critical Notes. London: Samuel Bagster and Sons, 15, Paternoster Row, 1879.

Another edition; The Septuagint Version of the O.T., with Apocrypha; With an English

Translation and with Various Readings and
Critical Notes, 1879.

Another edition (as 1879 with Apocrypha); London:
Samuel Bagster and Sons, Ltd.;   New York:
Harper & Brothers, 1966.

Also; Grand Rapids: Zondervan, 1970, 1972.

Reprinted; Peabody, MA: Hendrickson Publishers,
1986.

1851 **Benisch, Abraham** ...Jewish School & Family Bible...
newly translated under the supervision of... the
Chief Rabbi, by Dr. A. Benisch. of the United
Congregations of the British Empire. London: James
Darling, 1851 - 1861.
[4 Vols. bound in two Volumes.]

Vol. 1 The Pentateuch. Published by J.Darling,
1851.
Second edition; revised and improved, 1852.
Another edition; 1864.

Vol. 2 Containing the Historical Parts.
Published by Longmans & Co., 1852.
Another edition; 1864.

Vol. 3 Containing the Books of Isaiah,
Jeremiah, Ezekiel and the Twelve Minor
Prophets. Published by Trubner & Co. and
Jewish Chronicle Office, 1856.

Vol. 4 Containing the Hagiography. Published
by Jewish Chronicle Office, 1861.

[The American Bible Society has a complete set of four
volumes dated 1852 - 1864.]

1853 **Leeser, Isaac**   ...[The Old Testament] The
Twenty-Four Books of the Holy Scriptures: Carefully
Translated According to the Masoretic Text, on the
Basis of the English Version, after the Best Jewish
Authorities; and Supplied with Short Explanatory
Notes. By Isaac Leeser. Philadelphia: [L. Johnson],
1853.
[Herbert dates as 1854.]

Other editions; 1857, 1878, 1880, 1884.

Revised; London: John Childs & Co. for Trubner
& Co., 1865.

Another edition; Hebrew and English. 4 Vols. New York: Hebrew Publishing Co., 1912.

Also; English Only. 1 Vol. New York: Hebrew Publishing Co., 1912?

[Other editions as late as 1958.]

1858 **Vance, Alexander**   The Authorised Version of the Old Testament Scriptures; revised, condensed, corrected and reformed by Alexander Vance.   London: Holyoake & Co., 1858.
[" ...the first step taken towards the completion of the present volume was...to withdraw...one of all such portions as proved to be a second time inserted..."]

[KJV revised and condensed.]

Another edition; The Authorized Version of the Old Testament Scriptures Harmonized, Classified, Revised with notes critical and explanatory. By Alex. Vance.   London: Printed for the Author by G. Phipps, 1864.

Also; Hellenica Sacra -- Scripture as divested of Jewish Incrustation.   Dublin: Moffat & Co.; London: Hamilton, Adams, 1868.

1859 **Wellbeloved, Charles and Others**
The Holy Scriptures of the Old Covenant, in a revised translation by the late...Charles Wellbeloved..., George Vance Smith..., and John Scott Porter. 3 Vols.   London: Longman, Brown, Green, Longman, and Roberts, 1859-1862.
        1859 - - Vol. I   Genesis to Ruth
        1861 - - Vol. II Samuel to Psalms
        1862 - - Part III Proverbs to Malachi

["They have assumed the Common Version as the basis, and have departed from it only where, in their judgement, the text was clearly corrupt, the rendering inaccurate, or the phraseology obsolete or obscure." They followed the Masoretic text of Van der Hooght.]

[The Deity is rendered "Jehovah" many times.]

Reprinted, 1962.

1865 **Anonymous**   The first book of Moses called Genesis [- Malachi] translated out of the original tongues ...20 parts.   London: 1865.
[Not clear whether this is a new translation; Advocates give no further information.]

1865 **Biblical Commentary**   [and Translation of Old Testament Books]   ...by Keil and Delitzsch...

Translated from the German. 25 Vols. Edinburgh:: T.
& T. Clark, 1865-1880.

1866-67 The Pentateuch   James Martin
        3 Vols.

1865 Joshua, Judges, Ruth   James Martin

1866 The Book of Samuel   James Martin

1867 The Book of Kings   James Murphy

1868 The Book of Chronicles   Andrew Harper

1879 Ezra, Nehemiah, Esther   Sophia Taylor

1866 The Book of Job   Francis Bolton
     2 Vols.

1871 The Book of Psalms   Francis Bolton
     3 Vols.

1874 Proverbs of Solomon   M.G. Easton
     2 vols.

1877 The Song of Songs & Ecclesiastes
     M.G.Easton

1867 The Prophecies of Isaiah James Martin
-69   2 Vols.

1880 The Prophecies of Jeremiah
        David Patrick and James Kennedy
        2 Vols.

1876 The Prophecies of Ezekiel   James Martin
     2 Vols.

1877 The Book of Daniel   M.G. Easton

1868 The Twelve Minor Prophets   James Martin
     2 Vols.

[Most of the volumes do not give a continuous biblical
text.]

Reprinted; 25 Vols. Grand Rapids: Eerdmans, 1949
- 1950.

1865 **Heinfetter, Herman**   A Collation of an English
     Version of the Old Testament from the text of the
     Vatican Manuscript with the Authorized English
     Version, by Herman Heinfetter. London: Evan Evans,
     1865.
        [This work did not go beyond Genesis.]

Another edition; An English Version of the Old
and New Testament on Definite Rules..., 1865.

1865 **Sharpe, Samuel**   The Hebrew Scriptures, translated
by Samuel Sharpe, being a revision of the Authorized
English Old Testament... 3 Vols. London: Whitfield,
Green & Son, 1865.
> Second   edition;   3   Vols.   London: Billing,
> Guildford for J. Russell Smith, 1871.

[Several other editions were printed.]

1880 **Gollancz, Hermann**   The Holy Bible, containing
the Pentateuch, the Hagiographa, and the Former and
Latter Prophets; translated out of the original
tongues; and with the former translations diligently
compared and revised. Revised by Rev. Hermann
Gollancz... For Jewish Families.   London: J.G.
Murdoch & Co.; L. Schaap, 1880.
> ['it has been deemed advisable to adhere as closely as
> possible to the excellent Anglican version of the 17th
> century.' A slight revision of the KJV, with Apocrypha.]

Reprint, 1882.

1881 **Friedlander, Michael**   The Jewish Family Bible in
Hebrew and English.   London: W. Rider & Son, 1881.
> [The English translation is the AV revised; O.T.]

Another edition; 1884.

Another edition; The Hebrew Bible with English
Translation...   Sanctioned by the Rabbinate.
Jerusalem, London, New York: Jerusalem Bible
Publishing Co. Ltd., 1953.
> ["...facsimile of the Jewish Family Bible issued
> in London in 5645-1884."]

Another edition; The Illustrated Jerusalem Bible.
English Translation. Edited by M. Friedlander,
with   2000   Pictures.   2   Vols.   Jerusalem,
London, New York: Jerusalem Bible Publishing
Co. Ltd., 19??
> [The present edition of the Scriptures is a
> reduced facsimile of the Jewish Family Bible
> issued in London in 5645-1884, edited by Dr. M.
> Friedlander.]

1885 **Darby, John Nelson**   The Holy Scriptures commonly
called the Old Testament. A new translation from the
original Hebrew. London: G. Morrish, 1885.
> [Published in four parts between 1883 and 1885
> comprising only the O.T.]

[The Deity is rendered "Jehovah" many times.]

Another edition; 1890.

Also; London: G.Morrish, 1920.

Another Edition; 1961.

1885 **Spurrell, Helen**   A translation of the Old Testament
Scriptures from the Original Hebrew; by Helen
Spurrell. London: James Nisbet, MDCCCCLXXXV [sic].
["...the translation is made from the unpointed Hebrew;
that being the original..." i.e., B. Boothroyd's
unpointed 'Biblia Hebraica'. Also, the actual date reads
1985 which was a misprint.]

[The Deity is rendered "Jehovah" many times.]

Reprinted; [Grand Rapids:] Kregel Publications,
[1988].

1904 **Pells, S.F.**   (Editor)   See Charles Thomson, The Old
Covenant, 1808.

1907 **Taylor, R. Bruce**   Ancient Hebrew Literature.
4 Vols. London: J.M. Dent & Co.;   New York: E.P.
Dutton & Co., [1907].
["The text is that of the AV 'changed only when that
rendering was obviously wrong'." This work forms part of
the series of 'Everyman's Library' edited by Ernest
Rhys.]

1915 **Harkavy, Alexander**   ...The Twenty-Four Books of the
Old Testament. Hebrew Text and English Version with
Illustrations. Translation revised by Alexander
Harkavy. New York: Hebrew Publishing Co., 1915-1916.
   1915 The Book of Genesis with Haphtaroth;
        Hebrew Text and English Authorized
        Versions, Translation revised by
        Alexander Harkavy. With Notes.
            Also; The Book of Genesis with Bible
            Comments for Home Reading by Rabbi
            Herbert S. Goldstein..., 1928.   [The
            translation was revised by Harkavy.]

   1915 The Book of Psalms...with exegetical
        notes by the reviser.

   1916 - - Vol. I. The Pentateuch, the Earlier
        Prophets

   1916 - - Vol. II. The Later Prophets, The
        Hagiographa

["The English translation accompanying the Hebrew text
is the AV... Among the passages amended are all those
which have been mistranslated or colored to suit

Christian dogma." "In changing phrases or sentences, the reviser has followed the general style of the language of the AV."]

[The Deity is rendered "Jehovah" at Exodus 6:4; Psalm 83:18; Isaiah 12:2.]

Also; One Volume edition, 1917.

Another edition; 2 Vols. 1926.

Also; The Holy Scriptures Revised in Accordance with Jewish Tradition and Modern Biblical Scholarship, 1930. [One vol.; revised.]

Another edition; The Holy Scriptures (O.T.). English Version... 1936.

Another edition, 1939.

1917 **Jewish Publication Society**   The Holy Scriptures According to the Masoretic Text. A New Translation with the Aid of Previous Versions and with Constant Consultation of Jewish Authorities... Philadelphia: Jewish Publication Society, 1917.

[Max Margolis was editor-in-chief. "In preparing the MS for consideration by the Board of editors, Professor (Max) Margolis took into account the existing English versions, the standard commentaries, ancient and modern, the translations already made by the JPSA, the divergent renderings of the RV prepared for the Jews of England, the marginal notes of the RV, and the changes of the American Committee of Revisers..." The 'translations already made' were the following:

Genesis	Max Landsberg
Obadia, Jonah	J. Voorsanger
Exodus, Lev.	L.N. Dembitz
Micah	Maurice H. Harris
Numbers	David Philipson
Nahum	L. Mayer
Deuteronomy	F. de Sola Mendes
Habakkuk	R. Grossman
Joshua	Joseph H. Hertz
Zephaniah	M. Schlesinger
Judges	Steven S. Wise
Haggai	S. Mendelsohn
II Samuel	Bernard Drachman
Malachi	D. Davidson
Jeremiah	Sabato Morais
Job	Marcus Jastrow
Ezekiel	H.W. Schneeberger
Ruth	Joseph Krauskopf
Joel	Oscar Cohen
Ecclesiastes	Gustav Gottheil
Amos	H. Pereira Mendes
Esther	William Rosenau
Psalms (1903)	Kaufman Kohler
I & II Chronicles	M. Mielziner

[Abridgments were made for the armed forces of both
World Wars: Readings from the Holy Scriptures for Jewish
Soldiers and Sailors, 1918. Readings from the Holy
Scriptures prepared for the use of Jewish Personnel of
the Army of the United States, 1942. A peace-time
abridgment, The Holy Scriptures... for use in the Jewish
School and Home, 1931 and 1945.]

[Many reprints.]

1924 **Czarnomska, Elizabeth**   The Authentic Literature of
Israel: freed from the disarrangements, expansions
and comments of early native editors; edited with
introductions ... 2 Vols. New York: Macmillan Co.,
1924-1928.
Part 1 From the Exodus to the Exile.

Part 2 From the Exile to the Recovery of
Israel's Independence.

["The text is the AV with some modifications, notably
the use of Yahweh for the Tetragrammaton. The
arrangement of the text aims to show the results of the
work of Driver, Haupt, Kent, et al, in simple form,
without notes, and in chronological order beginning with
the Decalogue. All the text is included at some point."]

1924 **Moffatt, James**   The Old Testament. A
new translation by James Moffatt. 2 Vols. London:
Hodder & Stoughton, [1924-1925]
         1924 Vol. 1 Genesis - Esther
         1925 Vol. 2 Job - Malachi

Another edition; New York: George H. Doran Co.,
1924-1925.

1927 **Smith, John Merlin Powis and Others**   The Old
Testament. An American Translation. By J.M. Powis
Smith,...; Theophile, ...; Alex R. Gordon,...; and
Leroy Waterman,... Edited by J.M. Powis Smith.
Chicago: University of Chicago Press, 1927.

1936 **Soncino Books of the Bible**   Soncino Books of the
Bible; Editor: Rev. Dr. Abraham Cohen,... London:
The Soncino Press, 1936-1952.
         [With pointed Hebrew Text, English Translation, and a
         verse-by-verse Commentary.]

         1936 The Pentateuch and Haftorahs...J.H. Hertz
         5 Vols.   Oxford: University Press;
         Soncino, 1 Vol., 1937.
                  [The Pentateuch & Haftorahs first appeared
                  in 1929, but the text of that edition was
                  the ERV, with marginal renderings (q.v.)
                  "When (The JPS version) presents
                  difficulties, the most probable translation
                  and interpretation are suggested (in the

notes) without resort to textual emendation."]

Another Edition; One Vol., 1960.

Another edition; The Soncino Chumash. Five Books of Moses with Haphtaroth ...Edited by the Rev. Dr. A. Cohen ... 1947. [This work uses the Jewish Publication Society's translation of 1917.]

1947	Genesis	H. Freedman
1947	Numbers & Deuteronomy	S. Fisch
1946	Lamentations & Esther	S. Goldman
1950	Joshua and Judges	A. Cohen (Editor)
1951	Samuel I & II	S. Goldman
1950	Kings I & II	Israel W. Slotki
1952	Chronicles I & II	Israel W. Slotki
1946	The Five Megilloth	A. Cohen (Editor)
1946	Job	Victor E. Reichert
1945	The Psalms [Also, 1958.]	A. Cohen
1945	Proverbs	A. Cohen
1940	Isaiah [Also, 1949]	Israel W. Slotki
1949	Jeremiah	H. Freedman
1950	Ezekiel	S. Fisch
1948	The Twelve Prophets	A. Cohen (Editor)
1951	Daniel, Ezra, Nehemiah	Judah J. Slotki
1948	Obadish, Jonah & Micah	S. Goldman

1948 **Knox, Ronald Arbuthnott**   The Old Testament newly translated from the Vulgate Latin by Msgr. Ronald Knox at the request of His Eminence The Cardinal Archbishop of Westminster...2 Vols. New York: Issued by Sheed and Ward, Inc., 1948-1950.

> [Also contains an alternative version of the Psalms based on the Latin text of the Pontifical Biblical Institute (Rome, 1945), printed in smaller type.]

[The Deity is rendered "Jave".]

Another edition; London: Burne, Oates, 1949.
> [This was a one volume revised edition.]

Also, 1955.

1952 **Revised Standard Bible - O.T.**   The Holy Bible. The Old Testament. 2 Vols. New York, Toronto & Edinburgh: Thomas Nelson & Sons, 1952.

> In additional to Dr. Weigle, Dr. Moffatt and Dr. Burrows, the following scholars were active on the O.T. Committee:
> W.F. Albright (Johns Hopkins)
> G. Dahl (Yale)

J.P. Hyatt (Vanderbilt)
W.A. Irwin (U of Chicago)
J. Muilenburg (Pacific)
H.M. Orlinsky (Jewish Institute of Religion)
W.L. Sperry (Harvard Divinity)
W.R. Taylor (Toronto)
L. Waterman (U of Chicago)
K.M. Yates (So. Baptist)

[See Revised Standard Version, N.T., 1946.]

[See Revised Standard Version, Holy Bible, 1952.]

[See Revised Standard Version, Apocrypha, 1957.]

1954 **Muses, C.A.**   The Septuagint Bible. The Oldest
Version of the Old Testament in the Translation of
Charles Thomson...As Edited, Revised and Enlarged by
C.A. Muses.   Indian Hills, Colorado: The Falcon's
Wing Press, 1954.
> ["In several instances we have corrected Thomson's
> wording. Where the oldest surviving MS of any feasible
> length for the basis of rescension — the Codex
> Vaticanus, No. 1209...is lacking, best readings have
> been supplied from the next oldest portion of the MS
> tradition, depending for principle authority in this
> respect on the Sinaitic and Alexandrine Codices, and the
> editors of the Sixtine text..." See 1808 Charles
> Thomson, The Old Covenant.]

Second edition; Revised, 1960.

1955 **Jewish Publication Society**   The Holy Scriptures
According to the Masoretic Text. A New Translation
with the Aid of Previous Versions and with Constant
Consultation of Jewish Authorities... [New Edition]
2 Vols. Philadelphia: Jewish Publication Society,
1955.
> [No changes were made in the text except for
> topographical errors and identification of "Haftorah".]

[There is a 1 volume edition and a 2 volume edition.]

1962 **Amplified Old Testament**   Amplified Old Testament.
2 vols. Grand Rapids: Zondervan Publishing House,
1962-1964.
> [Part 2 was published 1962; Part 1 was published 1964.]

1962 **Jewish Publication Society**   A new translation of
The Holy Scriptures according to the Masoretic text.
1962-1982.
> [Harry Orlinsky was assisted by the following: H.L.
> Ginsberg, Max Artz, Harry Freedman, Ephraim A. Speiser,
> Bernard J. Bamberger, and Solomon Grayzel.]

    1958 The Book of Genesis...Draft Version.
         Another edition; Genesis. The N.J.V.
         Translated. Introduction by Harry M.

Orlinsky. New York: Harper & Row;
Philadelphia: Jewish   Publication
Society, 1966. ["...practically the same
as that of the 1962 edition...modified for
the sake of uniformity of style or in order
to   bring   the   English   closer   to   the
Hebrew..."]
[See   Jewish   Publication   Society,
Genesis, 1966.]

1962 The Torah. The Five Books of Moses. First
Section. Philadelphia: Jewish Publication
Society.
Another edition; 1967.

["Dr. Orlinsky prepared a draft translation which was
circulated among the seven working members, each of whom
made comments and suggested changes... the present
rendering is not a revision, but essentially a new
translation. Obsolete words and phrases were avoided;
and Hebrew idioms were translated, in so far as
possible,   by   means   of   their   normal   English
equivalents..."]

1969 The Five Megilloth and Jonah. A New
Translation.   Philadelphia: Jewish
Publication Society.
[When "The Torah" (1962) was published, it
was announced that the next step would be
the publication of a volume for home and
synagogue use, containing the Torah and
Haftaroth, in Hebrew and English. To be
completely useful in the synagogue, such a
volume called for the inclusion of the Five
Megilloth and the Book of Jonah, each of
which   is   read   in   connection   with   the
services on holidays and special occasions
in the Jewish calendar. The translation of
the entire volume was completed, but, its
publication was delayed. It was decided to
issue at once this rendering of the six
shorter books of the Bible.]

Revised edition,1974.

1972 The Book of Psalms. A New Translation
According to the Traditional Hebrew text.
Philadelphia: Jewish Publication Society.

1973 The Book of Jeremiah. A new translation,
with   woodcuts   by   Nikos   Stavroulakis.
Introduction by Bernard J. Bamberger.

1973 The Book of Isaiah, a new translation
with   Drawings   by   Chaim   Gross.
Introduction   by   H.L.   Ginsberg.
Philadelphia: Jewish Publication Society.

1978 The Prophets. NEVI'IM. Philadelphia:
     Jewish Publication Society.

1972 The Book of Psalms. A New Translation
     According to the Traditional Hebrew text.
     Philadelphia: Jewish Publication Society.

1973 The Book of Isaiah, a New Translation,
     with Drawings by Chaim Gross.
     Introduction by H.L. Ginsberg.
     Philadelphia: Jewish Publication Society.

1980 The Book of Job: a new translation
     according to the traditional Hebrew text;
     with Introductions by Moshe Greenberg,
     Jonas C. Greenfield, Nahum M. Sarna.
     Philadelphia: Jewish Publication Society.

1982 The Writings. KETHUBIM. Philadelphia:
     Jewish Publication Society.

1985 TANAKH. A New Translation of The Holy
     Scriptures According to the Traditional
     Hebrew Text. Philadelphia: Jewish
     Publication Society.
          [This work is a one volume edition of the
          Torah, The Writings and The Prophets (1962-
          1982) with revisions.]

     [See Jewish Publication Society, The Holy Scriptures,
     1973.]

1969 **Bowker, John**   The Targums and Rabbinic Literature.
     An Introduction to Jewish Interpretations of
     Scripture. John Bowker... Cambridge: at the
     University Press, 1969.

1972 **Schedl, Claus**   History of the Old Testament. Claus
     Schedl. Staten Island, New York: Alba House, 1972-
     1973.
          1973 Vol. 1   The Ancient Orient and Ancient
                         Biblical History.

          1973 Vol. 2   God's People of the Covenant.

          1972 Vol. 3   The Golden Age of David.

          1972 Vol. 4   The Age of the Prophets.

          1973 Vol. 5   The Fullness of Time.

          [Can not identify the translation, may be his own.]

1973 **Jewish Publication Society**   The Holy Scriptures according to the Masoretic Text. New and Revised edition. Chicago: Menorah Press, 1973.
[See Jewish Publication Society, A New Translation..., 1962.]

1974 **Magil, Joseph**   The Englishman's Hebrew-English Old Testament: Genesis-2 Samuel by Joseph Magil. Grand Rapids: Zondervan, 1974.

1976 **ArtScroll Tanach Series**   ArtScroll Tanach Series. A traditional commentary on the Books of the Bible. Rabbis Nosson Scherman/Meir Zlotowitz - General Editors.
Another edition; ... An Allegorical Translation based upon Rashi with a Commentary Anthologized from Talmudic, Midrashic and Rabbinic Sources. New York: Published by Mesorah Publications, Ltd., 1976-

    1977 Genesis (2 Vols.)   Meir Zlotowitz.
    1976 Ruth.   Meir Zlotowitz.
    1976 Esther.   Meir Zlotowitz.
    1977 Psalms (3 Vols.)   Avrohom Chaim Feuer.
    1976 Ecclesiastes.   Meir Zlotowitz.
    1977 Song of Songs.   Meir Zlotowitz.
    1976 Lamentations.   Meir Zlotowitz.
    1977 Ezekiel   Moshe Eisemann &
                             Nosson Scherman.
    1979 Daniel   Hersh Goldwurm.
    1978 Jonah   Meir Zlotowitz.

1976 **Birnbaum, Philip**   The Concise Jewish Bible. Edited and translated by Philip Birnbaum. New York: Sanhedrin Press, 1976.

1976 **New International Commentary on the Old Testament** Edited by R.K. Harrison. Grand Rapids, MI: Wm. B. Eerdmans Publishing Co., 1976-
[The volumes are listed under the translator's name. Some of the translators are: V.P. Hamilton, G.J. Wenham, P.C. Craigie, M.H. Woudstra, R.L. Hubbard, F.C. Fensham, J.E. Hartley, J.N. Oswalt, J.A. Thompson, L.C. Allen, O.P. Robertson, P.A. Verhoef.]

1977 **Fisch, Harold**   [The Jerusalem Bible - Title on the Cover] The Holy Scriptures. The English text revised and edited by Harold Fisch. Jerusalem, Israel: Koren Publishers Jerusalem Ltd., 1977.

1979 **Kohlenberger III, John R.**   The NIV Interlinear Hebrew-English Old Testament. Edited by John R. Kohlenberger III. 4 Vols. Grand Rapids, Michigan: Zondervan Publishing House, 1979.

1987 **Aramaic Bible**   The Aramaic Bible. Wilmington,
    Delaware: Michael Glazier, Inc., 1987–
        [A parapharastic or expanded translation of the Hebrew
        Bible.]

    1988 Vol. 6   The Targum Onkelos to Genesis.
                    Translated with a Critical
                    Introduction, Apparatus, and
                    Notes by Bernard Grossfeld.

    1988 Vol. 7   The Targum Onkelos to Exodus.
                    Translated with a Critical
                    Introduction, Apparatus, and
                    Notes by Bernard Grossfeld.

    1988 Vol. 8   The Targum Onkelos to
                    Leviticus. Translated with a
                    Critical   Introduction,
                    Apparatus, and Notes by Bernard
                    Grossfeld.

    1988 Vol. 9   The Targum Jonathan of
                    Deuteronomy.   Introduction,
                    Translation and   Notes by
                    Daniel J. Harrington, S.J. and
                    Anthony J. Saldarini.

    1987 Vol. 10   The Targum Jonathan of the
                    Former Prophets. Introduction,
                    Translation and   Notes by
                    Daniel J. Harrington, S.J. and
                    Anthony J. Saldarini.

    1987 Vol. 11   The Isaiah Targum.
                    Introduction, Translation and
                    Notes by Bruce D. Chilton.

    1987 Vol. 12   The   Targum   of   Jeremiah.
                    Translated with a Critical
                    Introduction, Apparatus, and
                    Notes by Robert Hayward.

    1987 Vol. 13   The   Targum   of   Ezekiel.
                    Translated with a Critical
                    Introduction, Apparatus, and
                    Notes by Samson H. Levey.

ABRIDGED HEBREW SCRIPTURES

1549 **Anonymous**   The images of the old testament, Lately
    expressed, set forthe in Ynglishe and Frenche with

a playn and brief exposition. Printed at Lyons, by
Iohan Frellon..., 1549.

1569 **Samuell, William**   An Abridgement of all the
Canonical books of the olde Testament, written in
Sternholdes meter. By William Samuell.   London:
William Seres, 1569.

1869 **Levinsky, Jacob Levi**   ...Abridged School and
Family Bible in Hebrew and English. Three Parts...
Elaborated by Jacob Levi Levinsky, with the
cooperation of Rev. Dr. H. Vidaver, and other Hebrew
Theologians. 3 Vols.   New York: L.H. Frank Co.,
1869-1871.
>   1869 - - Part I.   Pentateuch
>   1869 - - Part II   Earlier Prophets. Joshua.
>   Judges.   Ruth.   Samuel.
>   Kings.
>   1871 - - Part III.   Selections from the Later
>   Prophets. Hagiographa, and
>   Apocrypha.

>   [Based on Leeser's Translation, with "Lord" rendered
>   "Eternal".]

>   1871 English Text of the Abridged School and
>   Family Bible... New York: The Printing
>   Co.
>   [Also includes abridged versions of Esther,
>   Ezra,   Judith,   Tobit,   Serach,   and   I
>   Maccabees.]

1890 **Harris, Maurice H.**   The People of the Book;
A Bible History for School and Home; With Appendix
containing Description of the Bible Books,
Scriptural Quotations, the Canon, Examination
Questions... In Three Volumes by Maurice H. Harris.
New York: Bloch Publishing Co., 1890.
>   [Narrative is interspersed with O.T. quotes in a unique
>   rendering.]

>   Rewritten, 1896.

>   Other editions, 1912, 1923.

1896 **Montefiore, Claude Goldsmid**   The Bible for Home
Reading; Edited with comments and reflections for
the use of Jewish Parents and Children by C.G.
Montefiore. 2 Vols. London: Macmillan & Co. Ltd.;
New York: Macmillan & Co., 1896-1899.
>   1896 - - First Part, to the second visit of
>   Nehemiah to Jerusalem.

>   1899 - - Second Part, containing selections
>   from the Wisdom Literature, the Prophets,

and the Psalter together with extracts from the Apocrypha.

["The AV is the basis of the translation, but I have frequently corrected it..."]

Reprinted, 1900, 1907, 1914.

1904 **Kent, Charles Foster**   The Student's Old Testament Logically   and   Chronologically   Arranged   and Translated by Charles Foster Kent. 6 Vols.   New York: Charles Scribner's Sons;   London: Hodder & Stoughton, 1904-1927.

> 1904 Vol. I   Narratives of the Beginnings of Hebrew History from the Creation to the Establishment of the Hebrew Kingdom.
>
> 1905 Vol.   II   Israel's   Historical   and Biographical   Narratives   from   the Establishment of the Hebrew Kingdom to the End of the Maccabean Struggle...
>
> 1910 Vol. III   The   Sermons,   Epistles   and Apocalypses of Israel's Prophets from the Beginning of the Assyrian Period to the End of the of the Maccabean Struggle...
>
> 1907 Vol.   IV   Israel's   Laws   and   Legal Precedents from the Days of Moses to the Closing of the Legal Canon...
>
> 1914 Vol. V   The Songs, Hymns and Prayers of the Old Testament.
> [The   Deity   is   rendered   "Jehovah"   many times.]
>
> 1927 Vol. VI   Proverbs and Didactic Poems

[This work was done with the collaboration of Charles Cutler Torrey and F.C. Porter. "...a clear, vivid, dignified translation, which will represent not merely the words but also the ideas, the spirit, and the beauty of the original..."]

1907 **Blaine, Harriet S.**   Stories from the Old Testament. Duffield & Co., 1907.

1912 **Smith, James**   Patriarchs and Prophets. Old Testament stories in modern English.   London: Macmillan & Co., 1912.

1913 **Glazebrook, M.G.**   The Layman's Old Testament, comprising the major part of the Old Testament with selections from the Apocrypha, arranged from the Revisor's version and edited with Brief notes by

M.G. Glazebrook.   London & Edinburgh: Oxford
University Press, 1913.
> ["The text...is that of the ERV, amended by the use of
> many of the marginal renderings... In five or six
> places, indeed a conventional word has been substituted
> for one which offends modern ears..."]

1916 **Olcott, Frances Jenkins**   Bible Stories to Read
and Tell; 150 Stories from the Old Testament with
References to the Old and New Testaments; Selected
and Arranged Illustrations by Willy Pogany. Boston:
& New York: Houghton, Mifflin Co., 1916.
> ["In editing the stories, a few words unsuitable for
> children have been omitted, and other expressing the
> same meaning have been inserted. Where an occasional
> passage from the AV is not clear, corrections have been
> made, following either the English and American RV's or
> that of Isaac Leeser."]

1929 **Mare, Walter de la**   Stories from the Bible by
Walter de la Mare.   London: Faber & Gwyer, 1929.
> ["My own versions of...the O.T. stories is no more than
> my own conception of them..." Edited and rewritten in
> narrative form.]

1930 **Dalby, Ezra C.**   Land and Leaders of Israel; Lessons
in the Old Testament by Ezra C. Dalby.   Salt Lake
City: Desert Book Co., 1930.

1940 **Clarke, W.K. Lowther** Old Testament – Shorter Bible,
1940.

1941 **Bible Students**   The Word of Faith – A Simplified
Scripture. Arranged for Study, Devotions, Church,
School and Other Public Readings, by Bible Students
of Concord, Massachusetts. Concord, Mass.: The
Concord Press, 1941.
> ["A rearrangement of Old Testament and Apocryphal
> Writings, in condensed and comprehensible form."]

1946 **Cohen, Mortimer J.**   Pathways through the Bible
by Mortimer J. Cohen. Illustrations by Arthur Szyk.
Philadelphia: The Jewish Publication Society, 1946.
> [A modernized version of the text of the Jewish
> Publication Society (O.T., 1917). This is an abridgement
> of the O.T. printed in regular prose form.]

1947 **Anonymous**   Old Testament Stories. Written in easy
English for native pupils with a small vocabulary.
by the Sisters of the Cross, Melanesian Mission,
etc. London: Sheldon Press, 1947.

1955 **Dower, Pauline**   Old Testament Stories... Told and
Illustrated. Oxford: University Press, 1955.
> Other editions, 1956, 1957.

1955 **Greenlees, Duncan**   The Gospel of Israel...Edited and for the most part Newly Translated from the Hebrew, Greek and other Original Tongues of the Jewish Scriptures and various ancient Apocrypha... with   Historical   Introduction,   Explanatory Commentary, Full Annotations and an Appendix by Duncan   Greenlees,...   Adyar,   Madras,   India: Theosophical Publishing House, 1955.
[The Deity is rendered "Yahweh" many times.]

1965 **Jones, Cyrus W.**   Old Testament Anecdotes in Rhyme, Diligently Condensed and Revised, and Translated into the Vernacular, by Cyrus W. Jones. New York: Exposition Press, 1965.

1968 **Dell'Isola, Frank**   The Old Testament for Everyone, edited and re-arranged in a continuous narrative by Frank Dell'Isola. New York: Meredith Press, 1968.

1972 **Dale, Alan T.**   Winding Quest: the Heart of the Old Testament in Plain English.   London: Oxford University Press,1972.

HEBREW SCRIPTURES SELECTIONS

???? **Anonymous**   Tales from the Old Testament.   New York: F.M. Lupton Pub. Co., [189?].

???? **Anonymous**   Bible Cartoons. Illustrations of Scripture history, from designs by John Franklin. Containing sixteen scenes from the lives of Adam, Noah, Abraham, Joseph, and Moses. With descriptions in the words of the Bible. New York: Francis & Co., [185?].

???? **Bush, Frederic W.**   Word Biblical Commentary. Ruth, Song of Songs, Esther. Frederic W. Bush. Waco, Tx: Word Books, Publishers, [198?].
[See Complete Bibles,   1982 Word Biblical Commentary, Vol. 9.]

???? **Byrne, Laurence E.**   The History of Israel by Laurence E. Byrne. Milwaukee: The Bruce Publishing Co., [195?].

???? **Davis, Arthur and Herbert Adler**   Service of the Synagogue; New Year and Day of Atonement. A New Edition of the Festival Prayers with an English Translation in Prose and Verse; Reprinted from the

latest and best London Edition. New York: Hebrew
Publishing Co., [19??].
[Includes 25 Psalms and a revised translation of the
Book of Jonah, together with other O.T. selections.]

???? **Judaica Press Publications**   The Judaica Books
of the Prophets... A New English Translation of the
Text, Rashi and a Commentary...   New York: The
Judaica Press, Inc., [198?].
    1989 The Book of Joshua.
    1987 The Book of Judges.
    1988 The Book of I Samuel.
    1989 The Book of II Samuel.
    1988 The Book of I Kings.
    1985 The Book of II Kings.
    1982 The Book of Isaiah Vol. 1.
    1983 The Book of Isaiah Vol. 2.
    1986 The Book of the Twelve Prophets.
    1985 Jeremiah Vol. 1.
    1985 Jeremiah Vol. 2.
    1988 The Book of Proverbs.
    1989 The Book of Job.

???? **Schliebe, R.H.**   Epitome, n.d.
[Old Testament - metrical synopsis. Unpublished.]

[Schliebe used "Jehovah" for the Deity.]

???? **Stern, M.**   ...The Five Books of Moses; With
Haptorath and Five Megiloth and Sabbath Prayers...
[See Pentateuch listing for the complete entry.]

???? **Translator's Old Testament**   Translator's
Old Testament. London: The British & Foreign Bible
Society, [19??].
    Exodus   93 pages
    Deuteronomy   59 pages
    Proverbs   66 pages
    Jeremiah   Chapters 1-20, 30-31, 46-52 77 pages
    Amos   43 pages

[The aim of this translation is to help translators who
use English as a second language. There may have been
more books translated.]

???? **Weedon, Lucy L.**   Old Testament stories, re-told by
Lucy L. Weedon... London: E. Nister, [190?].

???? **White, Joseph**   Letter to Bishop Randolph with
specimens of a new critical edition of the Hebrew
Bible... accompanied with an English translation and
notes, n.d.

875 **Alfred the Great**   O.T. portions translated.
[Anglo-Saxon.]

1100 **Anonymous**   Metrical Paraphrase of the Old
     Testament. c1100.
              A Middle English Metrical Paraphrase of the
              Old Testament, edited...and examined in an
              introduction... Edited by Herbert Kalen and
              Urban Ohlander. Gotheborg: Elanders Boktr,
              1923-72. [Studies in English. Editor Frank
              Behre...]

              ... Vol.1.   1923   Gotheborg: Elanders Boktr
              ... Vol.2.   1955   Stockhold: Almkvist   &
                                     Wiksell
              ... Vol.3.   1961   Gotheborg
              ... Vol.4.   1963   Gotheborg
              ... Vol.5.   1972   Glossary.   Stockhold:
                                     Almkvist & Wiksell

              ["The poem...which is here printed for the first time,
              is preserved in two mss: Ms Seiden Supra 52 (here
              edited) which is in the Bodelian Library... and Ms
              Longeat 257 in the private possession of the Marquis of
              Longeat."]

1534 **Joye, George**   Jeremy the Prophete, translated
     into Englisshe: by George Joye:... The songe of
     Moses is added in the ende to magnifie our Lorde for
     the fall of Pharao the bishop of Rome. [Antwerp:
     Widow of Christopher of Endoven alias C. van
     Ruremund], And MD and XXXIIII. in the monethe of
     Maye. [1534]
              [Includes Jeremiah, Lamentations, Prayer of Jermy and
              song of Moses.]

1540 **Clifford, Henry**   Poetical translation of some
     Psalms and of the Song of Solomon, with other Divine
     poems, by that noble and religious Soule now sainted
     in heauen, the Right Honourable Henry Earle of
     Cumberland, Lord Clifford, Vipont Brumflet and
     Vessey, Lord of Westmoreland and the honour of
     Skipton. [Bodleian MS] 1540?
              [First printed in Holland's 'Psalmists of Britain',
              1843.]

1540 **Coverdale, Myles**   The Psalter; or, booke of the
     Psalmes, wher vnto are added certayne other deuoute
     praiers...
              [See Psalms listing for the complete entry.]

1550 **Hunnis, William**   Certayne Psalmes chosen out of
     the Psalter of Dauid, and drawen furth into English
     meter by William Hunnis servant to the ryght
     honorable syr Wyllyam Harberde knight. Newly
     collected and imprinted. Imprinted at London...by
     the wydowe of John Herforde for John Harrington the
     yeare of our lorde M.D. and L. (1550)

[Includes Psalms 51, 56, 57, 113, 117 & 147; Song of Zachary; the Song of the Three Children; a thanksgiving to God for delivery from adversitie; Ecclesiasticus the last; the Complaint of a Sinner. All in four line stanzas, except for the 'Compliant' which is in 6-line stanzas.]

Another edition; Seven Sobs of a Sorrowfull Soul for Sinne, comprehending those Seven Psalmes of the Princelie Prophet David, commonly called Penitentiall, reduced into Meeter. [Publisher and date are unknown.]

Also; - - Wherunto are also annexed his Handfull of Honisuckles... London: H.L. [Humphrey Lownes], 1618.

Another edition; London: A.I., 1629.

1551 **Copland, William**   The Bookes of Solomon, Proverbia &c... London: 1551.

1568 **Pierson, Andrew**   Ezra, Nehemiah, Esther, Job, 1568.
[See Complete Bibles, 1568 Bishops' Bible.]

1580 **Barker, Christopher (Geneva)**   The Third Part of the Bible - After Some Diuision, Conteining the Fiue Excellent Books... Faithfully Translated out of the Ebrew, and Expounded with Most Profitable Annotations upon the Harder Places,etc. (1. The Book of Job...) by Christopher Barker. London: 1580.
Other editions; 1583, 1614, 1616, 1626.

Another edition; Edinburgh: Evan Tyler, 1642.

1600 **Broughton, Hugh**   Books of David, Ecclesiastes, Lamentations, Job, 1600.

1616 **Ainsworth, Henry**   Pentateuch, Solomon's Song and Psalms. Amsterdam: 1616-1623.

1621 **Wither, George**   The Hymnes and Songs of the Chvrch, 1621-1623.
     1621 The Songs of the Old Testament, translated into English measures; to euery song is added a new and easie tune, and a short Prologue by George Wither. London: T.S. [Thomas Snodham].
          [Contains fourteen of those versions of Scripture which afterwards were entitled "Hymns and Songs of the Church".]

     1623 The Hymnes and Songs of the Chvrch, Diuided into two Parts. The first part comprehends the Canonicall Hymnes, and such parcels of Holy Scripture, as may properly be sung: With some other ancients Songs and Creeds. The second Part consists of Spirituall Songs, appropiated to the severall Times and Occasions, observable in the Church of England. Translated and Composed by G.W. London: Printed by the Assignes of George Wither.

> [Among the 'Songs' are 'Song of Solomon divided into Ten Canticles' and 'Lamentations of Jeremiah'.]

Reprinted; in 'Hymns and Songs of the Church' edited by Edward Farr. London: John Russell Smith, 1856.

1623 **Anonymous** Saxon-English Remains of the Pentateuch, Joshua, Judges, Ruth, etc., out of sir Robert Cotton's MSS. of most revered antiquity, now first new Englished and set out by W.L. [William L'Isle] 1623.

> Another edition; The Old English Version of the Heptateuch: Aelfric's Treatises on the Old & New Testament, and His Preface to Genesis. Printed from both MSS, along with a translation by the Reformation Scholar, William L'Isle. Edited by S.J. Crawford. London: Early English Text Society, Original Series No. 160, 1922.

1636 **Sandys, George** A Paraphrase upon the Divine Poems. 1636-1641.

> 1636 A Paraphrase upon the Psalmes of David and upon the Hymnes dispersed throughout the Old and New Testaments. By G.S. London: Andrew Hebb.
>
> > [See Psalm listing — 1636 Anonymous, A Paraphrase...Psalmes.]
>
> 1638 A Paraphrase upon the Divine Poems. London: [Printed by Ihon Legatt 1637.]
>
> > [Includes: A paraphrase vpon Iob; A paraphrase vpon the Psalmes of David by G.S. Set to new Tunes for private devotions: And a thorow Base, for Voice, or Instrument by Henry Lawes...; A Paraphrase vpon Ecclesiastes; A Paraphrase vpon the Lamentations of Ieremiah; A Paraphrase vpon the Songs collected ovt of the Old & New Testament.]
>
> 1641 A Paraphrase upon the Song of Solomon. By G.S. London: Iohn Legatt.

1648 A Paraphrase vpon the Divine Poems, Second Edition. [London]
>   Third edition; London: Printed by J.M. for Abel Roper, 1648.

>   Another edition; Carefully Revised and Corrected...by John Playford. London: Printed by W. Godbid, 1676.
>   [The Deity is rendered "Jehovah" many times.]

[Reprinted in 'The Poetical Works of George Sandys. R. Hooper, editor. London: John Russell Smith, 1872.]

1644 **Boyd, M. Zachary**   The Garden of Zion... By Zachary Boyd. Glasgow: Printed by George Anderson, 1644-1646.

> 1644 The Garden of Zion; Wherein the life and death of godly and wicked men in scriptures are to be seene, from Adam unto the last of the Kings of Judah and Israel, with the good uses of their life and death... The Second Volume of the Garden of Zion: the bookes of Job, Proverbs, Ecclesiastes and Song of Songs all in English verse.

> 1645 The Holy Songs of the Old and New Testaments: Dedicated to the Royall Lady Mary, his Majesties Elder Daughter, Princess of Orange, 1645.
> [The 1st volume of the Garden of Zion.]

> 1646 The Psalmes of David in Meeter; with the Prose [KJV] interlined. The Songs of the Old and New Testaments in meeter. Glasgow: Printed by the Heirs of George Anderson, 1646.
> [Includes Song of Solomon made in praise of Christ and his Church, the Song of Moses, Deborah, David, Isaiah, Hezekiah, the Lamentations of Jeremiah, the Song of Jonah, Habakkuk, Mary, Zacharius and Simeon. One song added since 1645.]

> Another edition; The Psalms of David in Meeter; With the Prose [KJV] interlined. The Songs of the Old & New Testament in meeter. Printed at Glasgow: by the Heirs of George Anderson, 1648.

1650 **Anonymous**   The Psalms, Hymns and Spiritual Songs of the Old & New Testament, faithfully translated into English meeter. For the Edification and Comfort of the Saints in publick and private, especially in

New England. [Henry Dunster and Richard Lyon]
London. 1650.
> [This is a revision of the Bay Psalm Book of 1640.
> Includes the Songs of Moses, of Deborah and Barak, of
> Hannah, David's Elegy, the whole Song of Songs, the
> Songs of Isaiah, the Lamentations of Jeremiah, the
> Prayer of Habakkuk, and the Song of the Virgin. This
> version went through numerous editions in British
> America, and was reprinted in England and Scotland.]

1653 **Slater, Samuel**   Epithalmium; or, Solomons Song,
Together with the Songs of Moses... the Song of
Deborah... the Song of Hannah... the Church Song.
Isaiah 26. Digested into meeter, by Samuel Slater.
London: J. Moxon, for W.Lugg[a]r & L. Chapman, 1653.
> [AV in margin.]

1659 **Barton, William**   Six Centuries of Select Hymns and
Spiritual Songs by William Barton. 1659 - 1688.
> 1659 A Century of Select Hymns Collected out
> of S. Scripture. London?
>
> 1670 Two Centuries of Select Hymns and
> Spiritual Songs. Collected out of several
> Chapters of the Holy Bible. All to be
> Sung in six or seven Tunes commonly known
> and practised. By W.B., M.A. and Minister
> of the Gospel of St. Martins in
> Leicester. Printed for the Author.
> London: by W. Godbid.
>
> 1672 Two Centuries of Select Hymns Collected
> out of the Psalms. By W.B., M.A. and
> Minister of the Gospel at St. Martins in
> Leicester. London: Printed by W. Godbid,
> for Francis Tyton.
>
> 1688 Four Centuries of Select Hymns
>
> 1688 Six Centuries of Select Hymns and
> Spiritual Songs Collected out of the Holy
> Bible. Together With a Catechism, The
> Canticles, and a Catagloue of Vertuous
> Women...The Fourth Edition, with above a
> third part of Additions. London: Printed
> by J. Heptinstall for William Cooper.

> ["...he collected 100 Hymns and published them...Anno
> 1659. ... He then collected ...another century of
> Chapter-Hymns (for so he called them to distinguish them
> from the Psalm-Hymn which he afterwards published)... he
> composed two centuries more of Psalm -Hymns, which four
> centuries unpollished and as yet not methodized ...were
> serruptitiously printed without knowledge or consent of
> the author (in 1668)... But after that he did then
> methodize and polish them...and in the year 1670 he
> published two centuries of Chapter-Hymns; and in the

year 1672 he set forth the two centuries of Psalm-
Hymns... He collected a third century more out of the
chapters of the Old & New Testament, and another out of
the Psalms, which he compleated, together with a
Catechism, the Book of Canticles... (etc.)... and then
declared to his Children, Relatives and Friends that He
had finished all he designed...; within a short time
after he sickened and (died in 678)... and now this
present year 1688 is published the rest of his works
carefully preserved ever since his death." To the Reader
by Edward Barton.]

1676 **Anonymous**   The Book of the Song of Solomon
(and the Book of Jonah) in Meeter. With Some Brief
Observations from the Text, something pleasant, but
more profitable to the Unprejudiced Reader, who
loves the knowledge of God, and hath his heart
inflam'd with the Love of the Lord Jesus. By T.S.
London: Printed for Francis Smith, 1676.

1683 **Mason, John**   Spiritual Songs, or, Songs of Praise
to Almighty God Upon Several Occasions, Together
with the Song of Songs Which is Solomon's, First
Turn'd, then Paraphrased in English Verse. London:
Richard Northcott, 1683.
         [Of this work, A. Moody Stuart said, "The most
         remarkable feature in this Paraphrase appeared to us to
         consist in the number of editions it had gone through,
         from which however we apprehend that we must undoubtedly
         have overlooked some of its excellencies."]

Another edition, 1694.

Also; - - To which may be added, Penitential
Cries. The Fifth Edition, Corrected, with an
addition of Sacred Poem on Dives and Lazarus.
London: Printed for Thomas Parkhurst, 1696.

Twelfth edition, 1725

1699 **Chamberlaine, James**   Lamentations of Jeremiah and
Eighteen of David's Psalms, paraphrased. London:
A.Bettsworth, 1699.

1700 **Blackmore, Sir Richard**   A Paraphrase on the Book of
Job: as likewise on the Songs of Moses, Deborah and
David: on four select Psalms: some chapters of
Isaiah, and the third chapter of Habakkuk
paraphrased [in Verse]. By Sir Richard Blackmore.
London: Awnsham & John Churchill, 1700.
         Second edition; Revised. London: for Jacob
         Tonson, 1716.
              [With 'Six Select Psalms'.]

1717 **Pyle, Thomas**   A Paraphrase with Short and Useful
Notes on the Books of the Old Testament after the

Manner of Dr. Clarke on the Evangelists. 4 Vols.
London: John Wyatt, 1717-1725.
Second Edition; London: J. Osborn, 1738.

[Genesis through Esther only.]

1727 **Broome, Rev. W.**   Habakkuk 3; Part of 38th and 39th
Chapters of Job; and Ecclesiasticus 43, paraphrased
in Metre. London: B. Lintot, 1727.

1727 **Patrick, Symon**   Commentary on Historical Books of
the Old Testament...by ...Symon Lord Bishop of Ely.
2 Vols. London: for John Darby, and others, 1727.
[Genesis through Esther. The Preface is dated 1694.]

[A long series of paraphrases in which the text and
notes are mixed together.]

Another Edition; 1738-1743.

1727 **Pitt, Christopher**   Job 3 and 25; also Song of Moses
and six Psalms, paraphrased. London: 1727.

1755 **Green, William**   A New Translation of the Prayer of
Habakkuk, the prayer of Moses (Psalm 90) and CXXXIX
Psalm; with a commentary on each... also Psalm CX by
William Green. Cambridge: J. Bentham, 1755.

1761 **Fawkes, T.**   David's Lamentations over Saul,
Ecclesiastes 12:1-7; Proverbs 31; Nathan's Parable
and Song of Deborah in verse. London: T. Fawkes,
1761.

1773 **Bate, Julius**   A New and Literal Translation, from
the Original Hebrew of the Pentateuch of Moses, and
of the Historical Books of the Old Testament to the
end of the Second Book of kings; with Notes Critical
and Explanatory. By Julius Bate. London: W. Faden,
1773.
["It is most certainly a new translation, and so very
literal as to be really unintelligible to a plain
English reader." Monthly Review OS, Vol. 1.]

1781 **Green, William**   Poetical Parts of the Old
Testament newly translated from the Hebrew, with
notes critical and explanatory: Being
          The Blessing of Noah, Gen. IX
              of Isaac, - XXVII
              of Jacob, Gen. XLIV
              and of Moses, Deut. XXXII
          The Song of Moses, Exod. XV
              of the same, Deut. XXXII
              of Deborah, Judges V
              of Isaiah, Chap. V
              of the Jews, - XXVI

and of Solomon VIII Chapters
The Parables of Balaam, Num. XXIII, &c
of the Jews, Isaiah XIV
and of the Nations, Hab. II
The Thanksgivings of Hannah, I Sam. II
of Hezekiah, Isaiah XXXVIII
and of Jonah, Chap. II
The Lamentations of David, 2 Sam. II
and of Jeremiah, V Chapters
The last words of David, 2 Sam. XXIII
The Prayer of Habakkuk, Chap. III

and other poetical pieces: Newly translated
from the Hebrew, with notes, critical and
explanatory.   Cambridge: Printed   by   J.
Archdeacon, for J. Dodsley, London, 1781.

1785 **Alexander, A.**   The First [through Fifth] book of
Moses [with the Haphtaroth and the Megilloth]...
[See Pentateuch listing for the complete entry.]

1787 **Gregory, G.**   Lectures on the Sacred Poetry of the
Hebrews; Translated from the Latin of the Right Rev.
Robert Lowth... By G. Gregory... To which are added,
the Principal Notes of Professor Michaelis, and
Notes by the Translator and Others. Vol. I & II.
London: Printed for J. Johnson, 1787.
["Presuming that it would be more agreeable to give the
literal translation of the Hebrew from works of
Established reputation, I have taken many of them from
our author's excellent version of Isaiah (1778), from
Mr. Blayney's Jeremiah (1784), from Bishop Newcome's
Minor Prophets (1785), Mr. Heath's Job (1756), and from
Dr. Hodgson's translation of the Canticles (1786)...
Where these did not furnish me with a translation, I
have endeavored myself to produce one as faithful to the
original as my knowledge of the language would admit."
Includes a translation of much of the Book of Psalms in
verse. Cotton attributes a translation of the whole book
of Psalms in English verse from Lowth's 'Praelectiones
Hebraicae'.]

Second Edition; Corrected, 1787.

Facsimile Edition; London: Garland Publishing,
Inc., 1971.

1787 **Kennicott, B.**   Exodus 11,15; Deuteronomy 32;
Numbers 21; Judges 5; II Samuel 23.   Oxford: D.
Prince, 1787.
[Published in "Remarks on Select Passages of the Old
Testament", Dunigan & Bros. Also in "Remarks"
translations of Thirty two Psalms.]

1787 **Levi, David**   The First [thru Fifth] Book of Moses
[with the Haphtaroth and Megilloth]...in Hebrew,
with the English translation on the Opposite Page.

With notes...by Lion Soesmans, corrected, and translated, by David Levi. 5 Vols. London: Lion Soesmans & Co., 1787.
Another edition, 1789.

1794 **Roberts, W.H.**   Corrections of various passages in the English Version of the Old Testament. By W.H. Roberts. London: J. Nichols, 1794.
["...to reduce the number of italicised supplementary words which occur in the AV."]

1800 **Newcome, William**   [MS material for a revised Old Testament] Lambeth Castle, c1800.

1805 **Browne, Theoph**   Ezra and Nehemiah, 1805.

1810 **Clarke, George Somers**   Hebrew Criticism and Poetry; or, The Patriarchal Blessings of Isaac and of Jacob, Metrically Analyzed and translated; with Appendixes of Readings and Interpretations of the Four Greater Prophets, interspersed with Metrical Translation and Composition; and with A Catena of The prophecies of Balaam and of Haba'kuk, of The songs of Debo'rah and Hannah, and of the Lamentations of David over Saul, Jonathan, and Abner, Metrically Translated; also with The table of First Lessons for Sundays, Paged with References. By George Somers Clarke. London: Printed by Richard Taylor and Co... and Sold by J. White and Co., 1810.

1818 **Bellamy, John**   The Holy Bible, newly translated from the original Hebrew: with notes critical and explanatory. By John Bellamy. London: Printed for the Translator. Published by Longman, Longman, Hurst, Rees, Orme & Brown, 1818 - 1867.
[Ten or more vols. 1818 - 1869. The translator contends that he was the only man to make a translation of any part of the Bible from the pure Hebrew text since 128 A.D.]

1818-42 [Genesis thru Canticles only.]

1863 The Book of Daniel. Translated from the original Hebrew and Chaldee Text by John Bellamy. London: Simpkin, Marshall & Co.

1867 The Minor Prophets; containing Obadiah, Jonah, Micah, Nahum, Habakkuk, Zephaniah and Haggai. Translated from the original Hebrew Text by John Bellamy. [Edited by Peter Stuart]

[The latter two editions were edited by Peter Stuart, Bellamy having died in 1842. Stuart's preface to Daniel states, "...the translation proceeded as far as the Book of Psalms (Actually thru Canticles, as confirmed by the British Museum) when it was suspended for want of means. But since the decease of Mr. Bellamy, the whole of his manuscripts have come into my possession, amongst which, translated and ready for the press, are the whole of Prophets..." Bellamy wrote several works criticizing the KJV translators for translating from translations, insisting that only Hebrew should be used as a basis. He translated "Lord" uniformly as "Jehovah".]

1819 **Gell, John** An exposition of the Old Testament, in which are recorded the origin of mankind, of the several nations of the world, and of the Jewish nation in particular; in the exposition of which it is attempted to give an account of the several books, and the writers of them, a summary of each chapter and the genuine sense of every verse; and throughout the whole, the origin... 6 Vols. Philadelphia: Published by William W.Woodward, 1819.

1819 **Wellbeloved, Charles** The Holy Bible, a new translation with introductory remarks, notes explanatory and critical, and practical reflections; designed principally for the use of families by C. Wellbeloved. 3 Vols. London: Smallfield & Son, 1819-1838.

    1819 - - Part 1, Pentateuch
    1838 - - Part 3, Job-Song of Solomon

    One Vol. Edition; 1838.

    [The relationship between this work and the O.T. of 1859-1862 is not known.]

1820 **Perrin, W.** Hebrew Canticles, or, a Poetical Commentary, or paraphrase, on the Various Songs of Scripture; including Solomon's Song, Lamentations, &c. and a Few Miscellaneous Pieces, by W. Perrin. Philadelphia: J. Maxwell, 1820.

1820 **Taylor, C.** The Holy Minstrel, being the Song of Solomon, and other parts of Scripture in metre, 1820.

1823 **Christie, James** Holy Bible. Dublin: 1823 - 1824.
    [Christie had intended to publish a reprint of Macmahon's 1791 edition, but was so impressed by the faulty character of the translation, he drew up a list of Forty passages, which he corrected by the Latin text. Only thirty weekly numbers appeared. Genesis - Isaias 13:2 only.]

1826 **Conybeare, John J.** Illustrations of Anglo-Saxon Poetry. London: 1826.
    [Genesis, pages 356-378; Exodus, pages 447-463, 489-494; with translations in Latin.]

1827 **Anonymous**   Translations from the Old Testament...
explaining the causes of solidarity and perpetual
motion. Bideford: J. Wilson, 1827.

1828 **Nordheimer, Isaac**   A Grammatical Analysis
of Selections from the Hebrew Scriptures, with an
Exercise in Hebrew Composition, by Isaac Nordheimer.
New York: Wiley & Putnam; Boston: C.C. Little &
Co.; Philadelphia: Henry Perkins; New Haven:
Durrie & Peck, 1828.
          [A literal, word-for-word translation and analysis of
          Genesis I-XII, Deuteronomy I-III, and various other O.T.
          passages.]

1830 **Anonymous**   The Holy Bible, according to
the established version; with the exception of the
substitution of the original Hebrew names, in place
of the English words, Lord and God: and of a few
corrections thereby rendered necessary by Keseph.
London: F. Westley & A.H. Davis, 1830.
          [Genesis thru 2 kings XIX only; NNAB has a copy ending
          with Job.]

1832 **Thorpe, Benjamin**   Caedmon's Metrical Paraphrase of
Parts of the Holy Scripture, in Anglo-Saxon; with an
English Translation, Notes and a verbal Index, by
Benjamin Thorpe. London: Society of Antiquaries,
1832.
          [Genesis, Exodus and Daniel; Lamentations of the fallen
          angels, the Harrowing of Hell, and the Temptation.]

          Another edition; London: William Pickering, 184?

1838 **Jackson, Thomas**   Paraphrase on the Eleven First
Chapters of Exodus, with Annotations...Job; or the
Gospel Preached to the Patriarchs,Being a Paraphrase
of the Last Ten Chapters of the Book of Job, 1838.

1839 **Newman, Selig**   Emendations of the AV of the Old
Testament. London: B. Wertheim, 1839.

1842 **Hodgson, F.**   Sacred Lyrics; or, Extracts
from the prophetical and other scriptures of the Old
Testament; adapted to Latin versification, in the
principle metres of Horace.   London: Taylor &
Walton, 1842.

1843 **Bialloblotzky, Dr.**   Specimen of an edition of the
Hebrew Bible, with the Greek of the Septuagint, and
a literal English rendering interlinearly arranged
by Dr. Bialloblotzky. Cheshunt: Printed at the
private press of Dr. Bialloblotzky, 1843.

1844 **Horsley, Samuel**   Biblical Criticism on the First
Fourteen Historical Books of the Old Testament: also

on the First Nine Prophetical Books. Second Edition, Containing Translations by the Author, Never Before Published, Together with Copious Indexes. 2 Vols. London: 1844.

1845 **Tregelles, Samuel Prideaux**   Hebrew Reading Lessons: consisting of the first four chapters of Genesis, and the eighth chapter of Proverbs. With a grammatical praxis, and an interlineary translation ...to which is added exercises with interlineary pronunciation and translation; [Genesis XII.1-10, XXII.1-8; Deuteronomy IX.25-X.5; Proverbs XXIII.19-26] London: Samuel Bagster & Sons Ltd., 1845.
     [The Deity is rendered "Jehovah" many times.]

     Twentieth Edition, n.d. [1888?]

     Reprinted; 1967.

1847 **Barrett, R.A.F.**   A Synopsis of Criticisms upon those Passages of the Old Testament in which Modern Commentators have Differed from the Authorized Version; Together with an Explanation of Various Difficulties in the Hebrew and English Texts. 3 Vols. in 5 parts (or more.) London: n.p., 1847.

1848 **Barham, Francis**   The Bible Revised; a carefully corrected translation of the Old and New Testaments. By Francis Barham. London: Houlstone & Stoneman, 1848 - 1850.
          1848 ...Part 1. Ecclesiastes
          1848 ...Part 2. Song of Solomon
          1850 ...Part 3. Micah

1854 **Anonymous**   The Songs and Small Poems of the Holy Scriptures: also the Lamentations of Jeremiah. New and literal translations from the Hebrew text of Vander Hooght, 1705. London: Thomas Hatchard, 1854.

1855 **Wolfe, J.R.**   The Messiah, as predicted in the Pentateuch and Psalms; being a new translation and critical exposition of these ancient oracles by J.R. Wolfe. London: 1855.
          [Contains the Messianic portions only.]

1857 **Smith, George Vance**   The prophecies relating to Nineveh and the Assyrians; translated from the Hebrew, with historical notes, exhibiting the principle results of the recent discoveries. London: 1857.

1858 **Anonymous**   The Pentateuch, Haphtorahs, and Sabbath morning service, in Hebrew and English. 5 Vols. London: P. Vallentine, 1858.

1860 **Ingraham, J.H.**   The Pillar of Fire; or, Israel in Bondage. Chicago: M.A. Donohue & Co., 1860.
[This work takes up the Hebraic history at the time of the sale of Joseph into Egypt, and closes it with the promulgation of the Two Tables of the Divine Law at Sinai.]

[It has been reported that Pudney and Russell may have published this work in 1859.]

Another Edition; Roberts Brothers, 1887.

Also; Elgin, IL: David C. Cook Publishing Co., 1899.

1860 **Sawyer, Leicester Ambrose**   The Holy Bible, Containing the Old and New Testament. Translated and Arranged, with Notes; By Leicester Ambrose Sawyer. 3 Vols.   Boston: Walker, Wise and Company, 1860-1862.
> 18?? Vol. I [See note below]

> 1861 Vol. II.   The Later Prophets. [12 Minor Prophets, Isaiah, Jeremiah, Ezekiel]

> 1862 Vol. III.   The Hebrew Poets. [Psalms, Proverbs, Job, Canticles, Lamentations, Ecclesiastes]

> [Translated from the Hebrew Bible of Hahn, "...into the recent improved style of the times..." preserving "...Jehovah and Jah as proper names of God..." and with the arrangement of "...the books according to their times..."]

> [Simms states that "'The Holy Bible translated and arranged with notes' was published in three volumes in 1860-62." but no further clue can be found to the existence or contents of any Vol I.]

1868 **Delgado, Isaac**   Genesis, Leviticus, Numbers and Deuteronomy accompanied by a revised and corrected translation, and a very valuable commentary. London: Abrahams & Son, 1868.

1872 **Hooper, R.**   (Editor)   See George Sandys, A Paraphrase ...Poems, 1636.

1874 **Proby, W.H.B.**   The Ten Canticles of the Old Testament Canon...newly translated with notes... by the Rev. W.H.B.Proby...Edinburgh: T. & A. Constable; London: for Rivington , 1874.
[Songs of Moses, Deborah, Hannah, Isaiah, Hezekiah, Jonah and Habakkuk.]

1876 **Polano, H.** The Talmud, Selections from the Contents of that Ancient Book, its Commentaries, Teachings,

Poetry and Legends; also Brief Sketches of the Men
who made and commented upon it. Translated from the
Original, by H. Polano. Philadelphia: Leary, Stuart
& Co., 1876.
> [Includes selections from various O.T. historical
> narratives and was a very much interpolated version of
> the book of Esther; also many Rabbinical works and
> sayings.]

1879 **Heilprin, Michael**   The Historical Poetry of the
Ancient Hebrews, Translated and Critically Examined.
2 Vols. New York & London: D. Appleton & Co., 1879-
1880.

1879 **Taylor, Sophia**   Ezra, Nehemiah, Esther...
> [See Old Testament listing, 1865 Biblical Commentary.]

1883 **Hunt, Theodore W.**   Caedmon's Exodus and Daniel.
Edited from Grein. Boston: Ginn & Co., 1883.
> [Anglo-Saxon.]

Second edition, 1885.

Third edition, 1888.

Another edition, 1889.

1883 **Roberts, Alexander**   Old Testament Revision: A
Handbook for English Readers, by Alexander Roberts.
New York: Charles Scribner's Sons, 1883.
> ["I have embodied...a number of what appear to me
> improved translations of Old Testament passages..."]

1885 **Wrangham, Digby S.**   Lyra Regis. The Book of Psalms,
and other Lyrical poetry of the Old Testament,
rendered literally into English metres by Digby S.
Wrangham.   Leeds: J.S. Flectcher & Co.;   London:
Simpkin, Marshall & Co., 1885.
> [Includes Lamentations, Song of Solomon, and
> songs from other books. "...the translation
> must be rigidly literal... the peculiar
> character of the Hebrew poetry must be kept in
> sight by the translator. Rhymeless and
> metreless, it is a system of parallelism of
> idea..."]

1887 **Crane, Oliver T.**   The Targums on the Books of Ruth
and Jonah, literally translated from the Chaldee by
Oliver T. Crane. New York: Jenkins & McCowan, 1887.

1888 **Pollard, Josephine**   History of the Old Testament
in Words of One Syllable... with Eighty-Eight
Illustrations, by Josephine Pollard.   New York:
George Routledge & Sons, Ltd., 1888.

1890 **Singer, S.** The Authorised Daily Prayer Book of the United Hebrew Congregations of the British Empire, with a new translation, by S.Singer. London: Eyre & Spottiswoode, 1890.

> ["...in the translation of the various Biblical passages the RV (text or margin) has throughout been adopted as a basis. Several changes have, however, been made, chiefly in the direction of greater literalness. These are chiefly the work of Mr. Claude G. Montefiore." Includes 78 of the Psalms and numerous passages from the Pentateuch, in Hebrew and English.]

American Edition, 1920.

1890 **Summer, Sam** The Form of Prayers for the Feast of the New-Year, According to the Custom of the German & Polish Jews. With an English Translation, Carefully Revised by Sam Summer. Vienna 5650-1890. 2 Vols. Vienna: Published by Joseph Schlessinger Bookseller, 1890.

1895 **Baldwin, James** Old Stories of the East. New York & Cincinnati: American Book Co., 1895.

1895 **Dillon, Emile Joseph** The Skeptics of the Old Testament. Job; Koheleth; The Sayings of Agur; with English Text translated for the first time from the Primitive Hebrew as Restored on the Basis of Recent Philological Discoveries, by E.J. Dillon. London: Isbister and Company Limited, 1895.

> [Job is translated from a Saidic ms., first published by Agostino Ciasca, in Rome; also known as the Thebaic Version. Not known whether the translation was revised in 1905.]

Another edition; The Original Poem of Job translated from the Restored Text, by E.J. Dillon... to which is appended the Book of Job According to the AV. London: Fisher Uncoin, 1905.

[Also; The Bible Collector notes an edition (identical to the 1895 edition) issued in 1885.]

Reprinted; New York: Haskell House, 1973.

1897 **Gwilliam, G.H.** The Palestinian Version of the Holy Scriptures. Five more fragments recently acquired by the Bodleian Library. Oxford: Clarendon Press, 1897.
[Syriac & English]

1898 **Sacred Books of the Old and New Testament** The Sacred Books of the Old and New Testament. A New English Translation with Explanatory Notes and Pictorial Illustrations. Prepared by Eminent

Biblical scholars of Europe and of America, and edited with the assistance of Horace Howard Furness, by Paul Haupt... ["The Polychrome Bible"] London: James Clarke & Co.; New York: Dodd, Mead, and Co.; Stuttgart: Deutsche Verlags-Anstalt, 1898-1899.

    1898 Part 3. The Book of Leviticus.
                    S.R. Driver

    1899 Part 6. The Book of Joshua.
                    W.H. Bennett

    1898 Part 7. The Book of Judges. G.F. Moore

    1898 Part 10. Isaiah   T.K. Cheyne

    1899 Part 12. The Book of Ezekiel.
                    C.H. Toy

    1898 Part 14. The Book of Psalms.
                    Horace Howard Furness.

[The Polychrome Bible is sometimes called the "Rainbow Bible". English text is based on the companion Hebrew texts, printed originally in Germany (16 Vols.). Overprint colors distinguish the various sources to which sections the text is assigned. Although a larger number of the Polychrome series appeared in Hebrew, only these six appeared in English. Only parts 3, 6, 7, and 10 were "Printed in Colors Exhibiting the Composite Structure of the Book."]

1899 **Pollard, Josephine**   Ruth, A Bible Heroine; and Other Stories Told in the Language of Childhood, by Josephine Pollard. New York; Akron, Ohio; Chicago: The Werner Co., 1899.
[Also includes abbreviated stories of Job, Samuel, David & Saul, Solomon the Wise Man, Elijah, Elisha, Jonah the Man Who Tries to Hide from God, Daniel and the Good Queen Esther.]

1901 **Glanville, J.U.**   The Acrostic Poems of the Old Testament: an English Version, Metrical and Alphabetical. London: Skeffington & Son. 1901.

1902 **Kent, Charles Foster**   The Messages of Israel's Lawgivers..., 1902.
[See Abridged Bibles, 1900 Frank K. Sanders and Charles F. Kent, The Messages of the Bible, Vol. III.]

1905 **Heller, Nachman**   Daniel and Ezra, the Canonized Aramaic Text, Translated into Hebrew, Yiddish and English, and supplemented with footnotes and marginal comments. New York: Press of A.H.Rosenberg, 1905.
[In parallel columns.]

1906 **Anonymous**   An American Commentary on the
     Old Testament. Philadelphia: The American Baptist
     Publication Society, 1906-1939.
          [Text is KJV and RV in parallel columns except for the
          following, which contain original translations by the
          commentators.]

          1906 - - The Book of the Prophet Jeremiah. By
               Prof. Charles Rufus Brown, D.D.

          1939 - - The Book of Ezekiel.   I.G. Matthews.

          1934 - - The Book of Psalms.
               George Ricker Berry.

1906 **Anonymous** The Wisdom of Solomon. Being a transcript
     in verse of passages from the Books of Proverbs,
     Ecclesiastes, and Wisdom. Bedford: F. Hockliffe;
     London: Simpkin, Marshall, 1906.

1907 **Blackburn, Francis A.**   Exodus and Daniel, Two
     Old English Poems Preserved in MS. Junius 11 in the
     Bodleian Library of the University of Oxford,
     England. Boston & London: 1907.

1908 **Carter, George**   Old Testament History narrated
     for the most part in the words of the Bible. Oxford:
     Clarendon Press, 1908.

1909 **Kent, Charles Foster**   The Junior Bible for the
     Jewish School and Home, 1909.

1909 **Williams, O.T.**   Short Extracts from Old English
     Poetry. Banger, 1909.
          [Contains part of Genesis, Exodus, and Daniel.]

1910 **Sheffield, Alfred Dwight**   The Old Testament
     Narrative. Separated out, set in connected order and
     edited by Alfred Dwight Sheffield... Boston & New
     York: Houghton, Mifflin Co.; London: Constable &
     Co.; Cambridge, Mass.: Printed by the Riverside
     Press, 1910.
          ["I have...cut out palpable glosses, restored (in Sam
          XIV.41 and elsewhere) original renderings that have been
          dropped out of the Hebrew but are preserved in the
          Greek, and used corrected renderings where the received
          version is seriously misleading."]

          Another edition; London: Constable and Co.;
          Boston & New York: Houghton Mifflin Co., 1911.

1910 **Torrey, Charles Cutler**   Ezra Studies, by Charles
     Cutler Torrey. Chicago: The University of Chicago
     Press, 1910.
          [Contains an English translation of selections from Ezra
          and Nehemiah.]

Reprinted; New York: KTAV Publishing House,
1970.
[Contains his translation of most of Ezra.]

1911 **King, Edward George**   Early Religious Poetry of the
Hebrews by E.G. King. Cambridge: at the University
Press, 1911.
["In my translation I have done my best to imitate the
rhythm of the Hebrew... I have translated the
Tetragrammaton by Jahve..." Contains translations of
many poetic O.T. passages.]

1911 **Smith, Nathaniel**   The Messages of the Poets: the
Books of Job and Canticles and some Minor Poems in
the Old Testament with Introductions, Metrical
Translations and Paraphrases, by Nathaniel Smith.
New York: Scribner's Sons, 1911.
[See Abridged Bibles, 1900 Frank Knight Sanders and
Charles Foster Kent, The Messages of the Bible, Vol.7.]

1912 **Gordon, Alexander R.**   The Poets of the Old
Testament. London: Hodder & Stoughton, 1912.
[Includes a translation from Kittel's standard Biblia
Hebraica of selections from: Job, Proverbs, the Thoughts
of the Wise, Song of Songs, Vanity, the Songs of Moses
and Deborah, and a few Psalms. The Deity is rendered
"Jahweh."]

Other editions, 1913, 1919.

1912 **Rutland, James R.**   Old Testament; edited for use in
secondary schools, by James R. Rutland. Boston, New
York & Chicago: Silver, Burdett & Co., 1912.
["...comprising at least the chief episodes in Genesis,
Exodus, Joshua, Judges, Samuel, Kings, and Daniel,
together with the books of Ruth and Esther... The text
is that of the King James or AV... the reader may note
a few paraphrases."]

1913 **Batten, Loring W.**   A Critical and Exegetical
Commentary on The Books of Ezra and Nehemiah by
Loring W. Batten... Edinburgh: T. & T. Clark, 1913.
[See Complete Bibles, 1895 The International Critical
Commentary.]

1913 **Sampey, J.R.**   Chronicles, Ezra, Nehemiah, Esther,
Ecclesiastes, Song of Solomon and Lamentations,
1913.
[See Complete Bibles, 1913 American Baptist Publication
Society, The Holy Bible.]

1913 **Taylor, Bernard C.**   Genesis, Job, Psalms, Proverbs,
Joshua, Judges, Ruth, 1 & 2 Samuel, 1 & 2 Kings,
1913.
[See Complete Bibles, 1913 American Baptist Publication
Society, The Holy Bible.]

1914 **Anonymous**   The War Bible Of the Moment, Written
into Colloquial English and Pure Slang. The Five
Books of Moses With Sidelights on the Book of Job,
Hindoo Version of the Creation of Woman, ye Cloister
Version of the Transformation of Man, Unfolding The
Grand Old Story with Cloister Soliloquies, Smiles
and Tears. [James Austin Murray ("Cloisterman")]
Chicago: James Austin Murray, 1914.
> ["Ye Cloisterman writeth ye book and sticketh ye type.
> Is also responsible for ye meter and cadence, if any."
> Consists of deletions paraphrased in couplets.]

> Third edition, 1915.

1916 **Kennedy, Charles W.**   The Caedmon Poems Translated
into English Prose by C.W. Kennedy.   London: G.
Routledge & Sons, 1916.
> [From Caedmon's Anglo-Saxon Paraphrase of Genesis,
> Exodus and Daniel.]

1916 **Smith, Nora Archibald**   Old, Old Tales from the
Old, Old Book by Nora Archibald Smith. Illustrated.
Garden City, New York: Doubleday, Doran & Co., Inc.,
1916.
> Another edition, 1929.

1917 **James, Montague Rhodes**   The Biblical Antiquities
of Philo. Now First Translated From the Old Latin
Version by M.R. James... London: S.P.C.K., 1917.
> ["Phrases and sentences in italics mark quotations from
> the Old Testament."]

> [The Library of Biblical Studies. Edited by Harry M.
> Orlinsky.]

> Reprint; Prolegomenon by Louis H. Feldman.   New
> York: KTAV Publishing House Inc., 1971.

1920 **Books of the O.T. in Colloquial Speech**   Books of
the Old Testament in Colloquial Speech. Edited by G.
Currie Martin, M.A., B.D. and T.H. Robinson, M.A...
London: National Adult School Union, 1920-1934.
> ["Literary elegance has been sacrificed to clearness of
> expression and simplicity of language."]

> 1920   1.   The Book of Amos. Translated into
>   Colloquial English by Theodore H.
>   Robinson.   Revised, 1927.

> 1922   2.   The Book of Genesis... Theodore H.
>   Robinson.   Revised, 1923.

> 1923   3.   The Book of Jeremiah. Adam C. Welch.
>   Revised, 1928.   Reprinted; 1958.

    1924 4. The   Books   of   Ruth and Jonah.
                Constance Mary Coltman.

    1924 5. The   Books   of   Joel   (J. Garrow
                Duncan), Nahum (G. Currie Martin),
                and   Obadiah   (Constance   Mary
                Coltman).

    1924 6. The Book of Hosea. J.W. Povah.
                Reprinted; 1964.

    1925 7. The Book of Samuel. John Skinner.
                Reprinted; 1 & 2 Samuel, 1964.

    1930 8. The   Book   Of   Isaiah.   Vol.   I.
                (Chapters   1-39)   J.B.   Allan.
                Reprinted; 1958.

    1932 9. The Book of Deuteronomy. Cecil John
                Cadoux.

    1934 10 The Books of Micah (John Naish), and
                Habakkuk (R.B.Y. Scott).

    [13 1/2 O.T. books; no more published. Dates are taken
    from the printer's marks in the back of each volume.]

1922 **Bewer, Julius A.**   The Literature of the Old
    Testament. By Julius A. Bewer. New York: Columbia
    University Press, 1922.
    Second edition; slightly revised, 1933.

    Third   edition;   Completely   Revised   by   Emil
    Kraeling.   New   York: Columbia   University
    Press, 1962.

    ["...material on sources of error in ms transmission was
    omitted and replaced with material about the Dead Sea
    Scrolls." Contains   translations   of   many   O.T.
    selections.]

1922 **Mansfield, Clarimond**   The Book of Yahweh (The
    Yahwist Bible) Fragments from the Primitive Document
    in Seven Early Books of the Old Testament. By An
    Unknown Genius of the Nineth Century, B.C. Arranged
    by Clarimond Mansfield ... Boston & New York: The
    Cornhill Publishing Co., 1922.
    [The Deity is rendered "Yahweh".]

1923 **Craige, W.A.**   Specimens of Anglo-Saxon Poetry. I.
    Biblical and Classical Themes. Edinburgh, 1923.
    [Contains part of Genesis, Exodus, and Daniel.]

1923 **Evans, Lawton**   Heros of Israel by Lawton Evans.
Illustrated by Clara M. Burd. Springfield, Mass.:
Milton Bradley Co., 1923.

1923 **Kalen, Herbert and Urban Ohlander** (Editors)
See Anonymous, A Middle English Metrical Paraphrase
of the Old Testament, c1100.

1924 **Anonymous**   The Bible Story in Bible Words.
Cincinnati: Department of Synagog and School
Extension of the Union of American Hebrew
Congregations, 1924-1930.
    1924 Book One. The Story of Genesis. Adele
    Bildersee.

      1925 Book Two. Out of the House of Bondage.
      Adele Bildersee.
          [Selections from the remainder of the
          Pentateuch.]

      1927 Book Three. Into the Promised Land. Jacob
      D. Schwarz.
          [Selections from Joshua, Judges, I & II
          Samuel, First Kings and I & II Chronicles]

      1928 Book Four. In the Land of the Kings and
      Prophets. Jacob D. Schwarz.
          [Selections from I & II Kings, Isaiah,
          Jeremiah, Ezekiel, Amos and II Chronicles.]

      1929 Book Five. The Voice of the Prophets.
      Mamie G. Gamoran.

      1930 Book Six. With Singer and Sage. Mamie G.
      Gamoran.
          [Selections from Psalms, Proverbs, Job,
          Songs, Ruth, Lamentations, Ecclesiastes,
          Esther, Daniel, Ezra and Nehemiah.]

    ["...the Jewish Publication Society translation has been
    followed throughout, due allowance having been made for
    adaption to the needs of children..."]

1924 **Cooke, W.J.**   Israel's Songs and Meditations.
Preston: R. Seed & Sons, 1924.

1924 **Schwarz, Jacob D.**   Into the Promised Land, 1924.
        [See Old Testament Selections, 1924 Anonymous, The Bible
        Story in Bible Words.]

1924 **Schwarz, Jacob D.**   In the Land of Kings and
Prophets, 1924.
        [See Old Testament Selections, 1924 Anonymous, The Bible
        Story in Bible Words.]

1927 **Gordan, Robert K.**   Anglo-Saxon Poetry.   London
and Toronto, 1927.
   [Contains part of Genesis, Exodus, and Daniel.]

1928 **Harkavy, Alexander**   The Pentateuch with Haptaroth
and Five Megiloth...
   [See Pentateuch for the complete entry.]

1929 **Hertz, Joseph Herman**   The Pentateuch and
Haftorahs...
   [See Old Testament Selections for the complete entry.]

1929 **Richmond, Charles E.**   A Metrical Version of
Ruth and Other Bible Stories by Charles E. Richmond.
Butler, Penn.: the author, 1929.

1929 **Rosenbaum, M. and A.M. Silbermann**   Pentateuch with
Targum Onkelos... Sabbath...
   [See Old Testament Selections for the complete entry.]

1930 **Gamoran, Mamie**   With Singer and Sage, 1930.
   [See Old Testament Selections, 1924 Anonymous, The Bible
   Story in Bible Words.]

1930 **Richardson, Charles E.**   Bible Stories (of the O.T.)
and Miscellaneous Verse, by Charles E. Richardson.
Boston: Chrisopher Publishing House, 1930.

1931 **Anonymous**   Before Jesus Came. A Shortened Edition
of the Old Testament in Bible words... Translated
from the original Hebrew. Sukkar: R.H. Weastern &
L.K. Junkison, 1931.

1931 **Sprengling, Martin and William Creighton Graham**
Barhebraeus' Scholia on the Old Testament . Part I:
Genesis- II Samuel.   Chicago,   Illinois: The
University of Chicago Press, 1931.
   [Includes photo-copies of Barhebraeus' Syriac text dated
   1272 and an English translation . More published?]

1933 **Ish-Kishor, Sulamith**   Children's History of
Israel. From the Creation to the Present Time. A New
Presentation By Sulamith Ish-Kishor. In 3 Vols.
Illustrated. New York: The Jordon Publishing Co.,
1933-1937.
   1937 Vol. One From   the   creation   to   the
              passing of Moses.

   1933 Vol. Two From   Joshua   to   the   Second
              Temple.

   1932 Vol. Three From the Second Temple to the
              Present Time.

1936 **Albright, Lelands**   One Hundred Bible stories; The gist of the Old Testament in continuous narrative. Harper and Bros., 1936.

1936 **James, Lionel**   Songs of Zion.   London: 1936.

1938 **Oesterley, William Oscar Emil**   Ancient Hebrew Poems Metrically Translated, with Introductions and Notes by W.O.E. Oesterley.   London: S.P.C.K.;   New York: Macmillan, 1938.
> [Includes Deuteronomy 32:1-43 and 33:2-29; Exodus 15:1-18 is rendered on pages 18-23.]

1943 **Horowitz, David**   The Bible in the Hands of Its Creators; Biblical Facts As They Are; A Biblical Research by Moses Guibbory; The English Translation of which, in its Greater Part, was Written down from his Mouth in Jerusalem and Brought out from the Power into Execution by his Secretary at his left David Horowitz. Jerusalem, New York: The Society of the Bible in the Hands of its Creators, 1943.
> ["...I was compelled to write my Book in both the Hebrew and the English tongues... the time in my hands for the creation of this Book was not sufficient for the translation of every word in the whole Bible. That is the function of volume II of my Book." Apparently Volume II was never published.]
>
> [This 1978 page tome contains an exceedingly prolix and eccentric commentary, interspersed with innumerable passages from the Old Testament (and a few from the N.T. - the N.T. passages are from the KJV). Guibbory apparently considered himself a prophet, "And it shall come to pass, if ye be willing and hearken unto My voice, unto the voice of Moses Guibbory, the author of this Book... the good of the land shall ye eat; but if ye refuse and rebel - see, I have this day caused the heavens and the earth to be witness against you - by the sword, pestilence, famine, and thirst shall ye be devoured..." A hand-written Scripture Index of this work (1978 pages) was made by and is available from the editor of this present Bible Bibliography.]

1946 **Goldman, Solomon**   Lamentations & Esther, 1946.
> [See Old Testament listing, 1936 Soncino Books, The Five Megilioth.]

1946 **North, Christopher R.**   The Old Testament Interpretation of History. By Christopher R. North ...London: The Epworth Press, 1946.
> ["Translations from the Hebrew poetry are for the most part my own."]
>
> Reprinted, 1953.

1946 **Sutcliffe, Edmund Felix**   The Old Testament and the Future Life. By Edmund Felix Sutcliffe... London: Burns Oates & Washbourne Ltd., 1946.

[The Bellarmine Series VIII]

["The translations given throughout this book are the author's except where the source of the translation is named."]

Second Edition, 1947.

1947 **Pack, Elizabeth**   My Own Bible. A Child's Old Testament, by Elizabeth Pack. London: Independent Press, 1947.

1949 **Flight, John W. and Sophia L. Fahs**   The Drama of Ancient Israel. Boston: Beacon Press, 1949.
> ["...twenty-one stories covering the period from the Amarna Age to Solomon, embodying Biblical and archaelogical material..."]

1950 **Newell, William R.**   Old Testament Studies: Volume 1; Lessons given at Union Bible Classes in the United States and Canada...Genesis to Job, by William R. Newell. Chicago: The Moody Press, 1950. New Edition; Revised, Enlarged. Chicago, n.d.

1950 **Zeligs, Dorothy F.**   A Child's History of the Hebrew People. From the Nomadic Times to the Destruction of the Second Temple. By Dorothy F. Zeligs. New York: Bloch Publishing Co., 1950.

1951 **Samuel, Maurice**   Sholem Asch. Moses translated by Maurice Samuel. New York: G.P. Putnam's Sons, 1951.
> [A story about Moses with history and fiction interwoven.]

1951 **Silverman, Morris**   ...High Holiday Prayer Book; Rosh Hashanah - New Year's Day; Yom Kippeur - Day of Atonement; With a New Translation and Explanatory Notes, together with Supplementary Prayers, Meditations, and Readings in Prose and Verse; compiled and arranged by Morris Silverman. Hartford: Prayer Book Press, 1951.
> [Includes 25 Psalms and the Book of Jonah, together with various other O.T. selections, mostly revisions of the JPS version of 1917.]

1951 **Slotki, Judah J.**   Daniel, Ezra & Nehemiah. Hebrew Text & English Translation. With an Introduction and Commentary, by J.J. Slotki. London: The Soncino Press, 1951.
> [See Old Testament listing, 1936 The Soncino Books of the Bible.]

1954 **Eldad, Dr. Israel and Moshe Aumann** (Editors) Chronicles: News of the Past. 3 Vols. Jerusalem, Israel: The Reubeni Foundation, 1954.

Vol. 1   In the Days of the Bible. (From
          Abraham to Ezra, 1726-444 BCE.)
                    [The Story of the Bible, Set Against
                    the Background of the Ancient World,
                    and Uniquely Retold - in the Form of
                    a Modern Daily Newspaper.]

Vol. 2   The Second Temple; Dispersion; Rise
          of Christianity. (From 165 BCE to
          1038CE)
                    [From   the   Maccabees   to   Spanish
                    Jewry's Golden Age, 165 BCE - 1038
                    CE. The Unparalleled Survival of a
                    People Deprived of Normal Existence
                    in its Land and the Interplay of its
                    Turbulent   History   with   that   of
                    Christianity and Islam - Presented
                    Here, for the First Time, in the Form
                    of a Modern daily Newspaper.]

Vol. 3   The Dawn of Redemption (From the
          Crusades to Herzl's Vision of the
          Jewish State, 1099-1897)
                    [A Tortured, Persecuted People Draws
                    Inspiration,   and   the   Strength   to
                    Survive, from an Age-old Dream that
                    Finally   Begins   to   Take   Shape.
                    Saladin, Marco Polo, Luther, Henry
                    VIII, Chaucer, Napoleon, Jefferson
                    and a Host of Other History-makers
                    also "Come Alive" in this Unique
                    Journalistic   Presentation   of   the
                    Recorded Annals of Man.]

Another edition; 1970.

1954 **Humphreys, Agnes**   From Abraham to Solomon. London:
S.C.M. Press, 1954
          ["This little book, written by a teacher of Scripture,
          is designed for lower forms. It selects some of the
          salient incidents of the Biblical story and wither
          recounts them simply or presents them in brief plays for
          the children to act."]

1954 **Moriarty, Frederick L.**   Foreward to the Old
Testament Books by Frederick L. Moriarty... Weston,
Mass.: Weston College Press, 1954.
          ["Wherever possible I have used the new and excellent
          translation of the Old Testament which is published
          under the auspices of the Confraternity of Christian
          Doctrine. In other places the translation is my own."]

1954 **Orlinsky, Harry M.**   Understanding the
Bible Through History and Archaeology. Harry M.
Orlinsky... Cornell University Press, 1954.
          ["The translations of the passages from the Prophets and
          the Writings are mine..."]

Again, 1960.

Also; **Jewish** Publication Society of America, 1962, 1967.

Another edition; New York: KTAV Publishing House, Inc., 1972.

1954 **Torrey, Charles Cutler**   The Chronicler's History of Israel; Chronicles-Ezra-Nehemiah Restored to its Original Form by Charles Cutler Torrey. New Haven: Yale University Press; London: Oxford University Press, Geoffrey Cumberledge, 1954.
["The Hebrew Text, Baer's edition, is presented complete, after transposition..."]

1955 **Coppens** O.T. Selections for Catholic Schools, 1955.

1955 **Hermans, Mabel C**.   (The Academy Classics) Stories from the Old Testament selected and edited by Mabel C. Hermans... Boston:, New York, Chicago, Atlanta, San Francisco & Dallas: Allyn & Bacon, 1955.

1955 **Hooke, B.E.**   Nineveh and the Old Testament. Andre Parrot... (Translated by B.E. Hooke from the French) London: SCM Press Ltd., 1955.
[Studies in Biblical Archaeology No. 3]

["Translator's Note. Throughout this volume biblical quotations are not taken from any of the recognized English versions of the Bible, but are translated from the French."]

1955 **Jones, Alexander and Thomas Cummins**   Old Testament Selections for Catholic Schools. By the Sisters of St. Joseph Calasanctius, Vorselaar, under the direction of Canon Coppens...Translated by Alexander Jones and Thomas Cummins. London: Thomas Nelson & Sons, 1955.

1956 **Anonymous**   The Psalms: A New Translation. Translated from the Hebrew and arranged for singing to the Psalmody of Joseph Gelineau. [The Grail: Gall Schuon, Albert Derzelle, Hubert Richards, Philippa Craig, and Gregory Murray.] 1956-1963.
    1956 Twenty-Four Psalms and a Canticle. London: The Grail.

    1958 [A further 30 Psalms and two Canticles (Nunc Dimitis, and the Song of the Three Children)]

    1963 The Psalms.. London & Glasgow: Fontana Books.
        [The whole Book of 150 Psalms.]

Another edition; London: Collins, 1963.

Another edition. Philadelphia: Westminster Press, 1964.

Also; The Psalms. An inclusive language version based on the Grail translation from the Hebrew. London: The Grail, 1983. Again, 1986.

1956 **Vawter, Bruce**   A Path Through Genesis, by Bruce Vawter, C.M. New York: Sheed & Ward, 1956.
["The text of Genesis reproduced in this book is from 'The Holy Bible, translated from the original languages...by members of the Catholic Biblical Association of America", 1952. ...Other quotations from the OT are either from this version or my own translation."]

1957 **Anonymous**   Concordant Literal Old Testament. Concordant Publishing Concern, 1957-
  1957 Concordant Version of the Hebrew Scriptures "In the Beginning" commonly called "Genesis". Unsearchable Riches, Vol. XLVIII, No. 4, July, 1957.

  1957 In a Beginning - Genesis. Concordant Version, International Edition. The Sacred Scriptures. An Idiomatic, Consistent, Emphasized Version. Conforming to the basic laws of language, in that, as far as feasible, each expression constantly represents its closest equivalent in the Original, each word of which is given a standard exclusive English rendering. Unavoidable shortcomings due to English idiom are largely overcome by the use of lightface type for words not found in the original, boldface for emphasis, and the rectifications of words and of grammar by means of letters or signs. Common figures of speech are indicated. Maps, illustrations, Hebrew names and their meaning, carefully selected references and the structural skeleton are in the margin. Preface is signed A.E.K.] [A.E. Knoch] Saugus, California, USA.

  1962 Isaiah. Concordant Version. The Sacred Scriptures. (Remainder of title as in Genesis above.) [A.E. Knoch] Saugus, Califorina, USA.

  1965 [Psalm XXIII] The Shepherd Psalm by A.E.K. [Adolph Ernst Knoch].

Unsearchable Riches, Vol. 56, No. 3, May, 1965.

1968 Concordant Literial Old Testament. The Book of Daniel. Saugus, Califorina, USA.
["The third fascicle of the Concordant Literal O.T. which is being published in installments."]

1972-1973 Psalms. Unsearchable Riches, Vol. LXIII, No. 1, January, 1972 to Vol. LXXIV, No. 4, July, 1983. [The Journal printed Psalms 1 to Psalms 94. Unknown whether further Psalms were published in the Journal.]

1973 Hebrew Scriptures Study Sheets. Concordant Version of Jeremiah and Lamentations. [E.H. Clayton] Canyon Country, Ca USA.
["...a facsimile reproduction of typewritten copy... originally prepared on half sheets by our late Brother E.H. Clayton of Sheffield, England..."]

1977 Concordant Version of the Old Testament. The Book of Ezekiel.

[The Deity is rendered "Ieve" (pronounced Yahweh) many times.]

[Also see New Testament Selections, 1914 Concordant Version.]

1957 **Armstrong, April Oursler**   The Book of God; Adventures from the Old Testament by April Oursler Armstrong. Adapted from The Greatest Book Ever Written by Fulton Oursler... Garden City, New York: Garden City Press Books, 1957.

1958 **Anonymous**   Stories from the Old Testament...from Adam to Joseph. Pictures by Piet Worm. London and Glasgow: Collins, 1958.
Another edition; Sheed & Ward, nd.

1959 **Gottwald, Norman K.**   A Light to the Nations; An Introduction to the Old Testament. Norman K. Gottwald... New York: Harper & Bros., Publishers, 1959.
["Biblical quotations are for the most part taken from the Revised Standard Version of the Bible, but I have not hesitated to make my own translation whenever a specific purpose is better served."]

1959 **Lindberg, Conrad** (Editor)   MS. Bodey 959; Genesis-Baruch 3.20 in the earlier version of the Wycliffite Bible...

[See Complete Bibles, John Wycliffe, The Holy Bible, 1388.]

1959 **Weitzner, Emil**   Humanist Meditations and Paraphrases by Emil Wetzer.   New York: 1959-1965.
> 1959 Meditations of a Humanist.   New York: Behrman.   [Includes Ecclesiastes & Selected Psalms.]
> 1960 The Book of Job; A Paraphrase.
> 1961 The Book of Jonah; A Paraphrase.
> 1962 The Song of Songs; A Paraphrase.
> 1963 The Book of Amos; A Paraphrase.
> 1965 Humanist Meditations and Paraphrase. New York: Random House. [Includes all the above, plus Micah.]

> ["I write as a Jew revering the tradition, yet seeking (and finding) within it values compatible with a religion rooted in skepticism and humanism."]

1960 **Cox, Ronald**   Waiting for Christ, based on the translation of the Old Testament messianic prophesies by Ronald Knox, arranged in a continuous narrative with explanations.   New York: Sheed & Ward, 1960.

1960 **Moriarty, Frederick L.**   Introducing The Old Testament. Frederick L. Moriarty, S.J.   Milwaukee: The Bruce Publishing Co., 1960.
> ["The author has frequently let the sacred writers speak for themselves in the belief that use of the Old Testament is the best way to acquire that savor for its enduring message, and to realize what the ancient Hebrew meant when he called the God of the Bible 'a living God.'"]

1960 **Scott, Patrick Hepburne**   The Old Testament Selections, Narrative and Commentary by M. Fargues, Translated from "L'Histoire Sainte", by Patrick Hepburne Scott.   London: Darton, Longman & Todd, 1960.

1961 **Silver, Abba Hillel**   Moses and the Original Torah. Abba Hillel Silver.   New York: The Macmillan Co., 1961.
> ["The author has used the RSV as well as the translation of the Jewish Publication Society in quoting biblical scources.   Occasionally   he   has   given   his   own translation."]

1962 **Kraeling, Emil G.**   The Literature of the Old Testament..., 1962.
> [See Julius Bewer, The Literature of the Old Testament, 1922.]

1962 **Old Testament Library**   The Old Testament
Library... A Commentary. Philadelphia: Westminster
Press; London: S.C.M. Press Ltd., 1962-1968.
    1962 - - Martin Noth; Exodus J.S. Bowden
    1965 - - Martin Noth; Leviticus
        J.E. Anderson
    1968 - - Martin Noth; Numbers
    1966 - - Gerhard von Rad; Deuteronomy
        Dorothea Barton
    1964 - - H.W. Hertzberg; I & II Samuel
        J.S. Bowden
    1964 - - I & II Kings   John Gray
    1962 - - Artur Weiser; The Psalms
        Herbert Hartwell
    1969 - - C.Westermann; Isaiah 40-66
        D.M.G. Stalker
    1965 - - Daniel   Norman W. Porteus

    [Translation based on the RSV, revised as necessary to
    coordinate with the commentary.]

1962 **Schwartzman, Sylvan D. and Jack D. Spiko**
The Living Bible. A Topical Approach to the Jewish
Scriptures by Rabbi Sylvan D. Schwartzman... and
Rabbi Jack D. Spiko... Illustrated by Bruno Frost.
New York: Union of American Hebrew Congregations,
1962.

1963 **MacKenzie, R.A.F.**   Faith and History in the Old
Testament. R.A.F. MacKenzie, S.J. Minneapolis:
University of Minnesota Press, 1963.
    ["The translations from original texts are my own."]

1963 **Sandmel, Samuel**   The Hebrew Scriptures; an
introduction to their literary and religious ideas,
by Samuel Sandmel ... New York: Alfred A. Knopf,
1963.
    [Includes many miscellaneous passages; "...my renderings
    are not translations as much as they are paraphrases."]

    Another edition; New York: Oxford University
    Press, 1978.

1964 **Schofield, J.N.** Introducing Old Testament Theology.
J.N. Schofield... London: SCM Press, Ltd., 1964.
    ["Except in a few places where I have given my own
    translation of the Hebrew text, the quotations are from
    the American Revised Standard Version."]

1965 **Barnes, O.L.**   A New Approach to the Problem of
the Hebrew Tenses and its Solution without Recourse
to Waw-Consecutive. Illustrated by New Translations
of Various Old Testament Passages with an Analysis
of each Verb by O.L. Barnes. Oxford: Published by
J. Thornton and Son, University Booksellers, 1965.

1965 **Brin, Ruth Firestone**   Interpretations for the Weekly Torah Reading by Ruth F. Brin. Introduction by Jerome Lipnik. Drawings by Sharon Lerner. Minneapolis: Lerner Publications Co., 1965.
[Torah selections and commentary on opposite pages. "...the JPS...1917 version...has been largely followed, with occasional changes to facilitate its recitation responsively by the congregation..."]

1965 **Myers, Jacob M.**   Ezra, Nehemiah. Introduction, Translation, and Notes, by Jacob M. Myers. Garden City, New York: Doubleday & Co., 1965.
[See Complete Bibles, 1964 Anchor Bible, Vol. 14.]

1966 **Altmann, Alexander**   Biblical Motifs; Origins and Transformations Edited by Alexander Altmann. Cambridge, Massachusetts: Harvard University Press, 1966.
[Philip W. Lown Institute of Advanced Judaic Studies, Brandeis University. Studies and Texts: Volume III]

["All transliterations of cuneiform words and texts are given according to Thureau-Dangin's system, which is generally accepted. Within quotations from ancient texts (both transliterations and translations),..."]

1966 **Dean, Dom Aldhelm**   God and His Image. An Outline of Biblical Theology. Dominique Barthelemy, O.P. Translated by Dom Aldhelm Dean... New York: Sheed and Ward, 1966.
["Passages from scripture are largely taken from the Revised Standard Version but depart from it occasionally in order to conform to the author's own French translation."]

1966 **Dicken, E.W. Trueman**   The Problem of the Hexateuch and other essays. Gerhard von Rad. Translated by Rev. E.W. Trueman Dicken, D.D. Introduction by Norman W. Porteous... Edinburgh & London: Oliver & Boyd, 1966.
["All biblical references to the Old Testament,...are given here according to the numbering of the Revised Standard Version of the Bible, and the text of this version has also been followed wherever possible in biblical quotations. It should be noted, however, that many instancesoccur in which Professor von Rad's exegesis of a passage preludes the interpretation suggested by the Revised Standard Version. In such cases the text of the translation has necessarily been modified, and a note added to indicate this fact when it is of significance to the main argument."]

1967 **Sanders, J.A.**   The Dead Sea Psalms Scroll, by J.A. Sanders. Ithaca, New York: Cornell University Press, 1967.
[Includes 38 Psalms, or portions; also parts of Sirach and II Samuel. Hebrew and English; facsimiles.]

1969 **Berkouits, Eliezer**   Man and God. Studies in
Biblical Theology by Eliezer Berkouits... Detroit:
Wayne State University Press, 1969.
   ["Our study is based entirely on the Masoretic text. The
   English translation we use is in general the Jewish
   Publication Society edition of 1916 and, occasionally,
   the Revised Version. Where we depart from these
   translations, as is often the case, we usually indicate
   our reasons for our disagreement. For technical reasons
   it was impossible to employ any of the usual methods for
   the transliteration of Hebrew words. Wherever practical
   the transliteration was put on a phonetic basis without
   seeking or achieving complete consistency."]

1969 **Hillers, Delbert R.**   Covenant: The History of a
Biblical Idea. Delbert R. Hillers.   Baltimore &
London: The John Hopkins Press, 1969.
   ["Translations of Hebrew texts are my Own."]

1969 **Wright, G. Ernest**   The Old Testament and Theology
by G. Ernest Wright. New York, Evanston, and London:
Harper & Row, Publishers, 1969.
   ["Scripture translations are my own except where
   noted."]

1972 **Gray, George Buchanan**   The Forms of Hebrew Poetry
considered with special reference to the criticism
and interpretation of the Old Testament by George
Buchanan Gray...Prolegomenon by David Noel Freedman.
KTAV Publishing House, 1972.
   [The Library of Biblical Studies. Edited by Harry M.
   Orlinsky.]

1974 **Kohl, Margaret**   Anthropology of the Old Testament.
Hans Walter Wolff. (Translated by Margaret Kohl from
the German) Philadelphia: Fortress Press, 1974.
   ["The biblical quotations have been taken from the RSV,
   but its wording has been modified where this was
   necessary for a correct rendering of the author's
   text."]

1976 **Gordis, Robert**   The Word and the Book. Studies in
Biblical Language and Literature by Robert Gordis.
New York: KTAV Publishing House Inc., 1976.

1978 **Austin, Carl C.**   The Christian Bible: Integrated
Version: based on the King James Version, with
corrected translations from the Greek reinterpreted
in the light of these corrections, including several
newly recognized testaments not previously
authenticated, each passage comprehensively
explained and cross-referenced. Compiled and
interpreted by Carl C. Austin.   Whispering Pines,
NC: C.C. Austin, 1978.

1978 **Green, David E.**   Old Testament Theology in Outline
by Walther Zimmerli. Translated by David E. Green.
Atlanta: John Knox Press, 1978.
["All Scripture translations in this book are by the
author."]

Another edition; Edinburgh: T. & T. Clark Ltd.,
1983.

1978 **Kohl, Margaret**   The Prophets. Volume One. The
Assyrian Period. Klaus Koch. (Translated by Margaret
Kohl from the German) Philadelphia: Fortress Press,
1978.
["In a quotation, a Hebrew word followed by the RSV
reading in brackets and inverted commas indicates that
the English reading is only approximate, and that the
correct meaning of the Hebrew is explained in the
text."]

1980 **Freedman, David Noel**   Pottery, Poetry, and
Prophecy. Studies in Early Hebrew Poetry. David Noel
Freedman. Winonalake, Indiana: Eisenbrauns, 1980.

1980 **Marks, John H.**   God at Work in Israel. Gerhard von
Rad. Translated by John H. Marks.   Nashville:
Abingdon, 1980.
["The lectures are presented here in two groups. The
first contains critical paraphrases of biblical
passages..."]

1980 **Tsevat, Matitiahu**   The Meaning of the Book of Job
and Other Biblical Studies. Essays on the Literature
and Religion of the Hebrew Bible by Matitiahu
Tsevat. New York: Ktav Publishing House, Inc.;
Dallas, TX: Institute for Jewish Studies, 1980.

1981 **Eaton, J.H.**   Vision in Worship. The Relation
of Prophecy and Liturgy in the Old Testament. J.H.
Eaton. London: SPCK, 1981.
["In the nature of the case, it seemed right to cite
many of these passages generously and in a fresh
translation."]

1981 **Kugel, James L.**   The Idea of Biblical poetry;
Parallelism and its History. James L. Kugel. New
Haven & London: Yale University Press, 1981.
["Hebrew words that appear frequently in the body of the
text have been transcribed into Latin characters."
"Elsewhere Hebrew characters have been used, followed by
English translations."]

1983 **Miscall, Peter D.**   The Workings of Old Testament
Narrative. Peter D. Miscall.   Philadelphia,
Pennsylvania: Fortress Press; Chico, California:
Scholars Press, 1983.
["Quotes are generally from the RSV; at times I do
change the translation to a more 'literal' rendering or

to a rendering that better displays a parallel with another text."]

1983 **Vawter, Bruce**   Job and Jonah, Questioning the Hidden God, by Bruce Vawter. New York: Paulist Press, 1983.

1984 **Crenshaw, James L.**   A Whirlpool of Torment. James L. Crenshaw. Philadelphia: Fortress Press, 1984.
["Translations of biblical material are the author's unless otherwise noted."]

1985 **Alter, Robert**   The Art of Biblical Poetry. Robert Alter. New York: Basic Books, Inc., Publishers, 1985.

1985 **Carmichael, Calum M.**   Law and Narrative in the Bible. The Evidence of the Deuteronomic Laws and the Decalogue. Ithaca and London: Cornell University Press, 1985.
["In quoting biblical texts I have relied on the King James Authorized Version of 1611, but made changes where these were called for. I have used the AV because it is almost a more literal rendering of the Hebrew original than any other translation. The texts that I quote, though sometimes paraphrased, constitute but a convenient selection of the more pertinent ones."]

1985 **Fishbane, Michael**   Biblical Interpretation in Ancient Israel. Michael Fishbane. Oxford: Clarendon Press, 1985.
[Contains his own translations.]

1985 **Sternberg, Meir**   The Poetics of Biblical Narrative; Ideological Literature and the Drama of Reading. Meir Sternberg. Bloomington: Indiana University Press, 1985.
["My translations are literal enough, and the transliterations simple enough, to enable even the Hebrewless reader to follow the textual analysis as well as the drift of my argument."]

1985 **Tigay, Jeffery H.**   Empirical Models for Biblical Criticism. Edited by Jeffery H.Tigay. Philadelphia: University of Pennsylvania Press, 1985.
["Translations of biblical texts, often in modified form, are based on The Torah, The Prophets, and The Writings..."]

1985 **Williamson, H.G.M.**   Word Biblical Commentary. Ezra, Nehemiah. H.G.M. Williamson. Waco, TX: Word Books, Publisher, 1985.
[See Complete Bibles, 1982 Word Biblical Commentary, Vol. 16.]

1986 **Barton, John**   Oracles of God: Perceptions
of Ancient Prophecy in Israel after the Exile. John
Barton. London: Darton, Longman and Todd, 1986.
  ["Quotations are taken from commonly used translations,
  though sometimes I have made small changes without
  calling attention to them."]

1987 **Ollenburger, Ben C.**   Zion the City of the Great
King. A Theological Symbo of the Jerusalem Cult. Ben
C. Ollenburger. Sheffield: JSOT Press, 1987.
  [Journal for the Study of the Old Testament. Supplement
  Series 41.]

1989 **Bach, Alice and J. Cheryl Exum**   Moses' Ark.
Stories from the Bible. Alice Bach & J. Cheryl Exum.
Illustrated by Leo and Diane Dillon. [New York:
Bantam Doubleday Dell Publishing Group, Inc.]
Delacorte Press, 1989.

1989 **Trible, Phyllis**   "Bringing Miriam out of the
Shadows". Bible Review, Vol. V, No. 1, Pages 14-25,
34, Feb., 1989.
  ["In this article, Bible translations are by P. Trible
  or are adapted by P. Trible from the RSV."]

HEPTATEUCH

1000 **Aelfric**   West Saxon translation of Genesis-Judges,
1000.
  [British Museum Cotton Clauduis B.iv (B) Bodleian
  (Oxford) Laud Misc.509 (6)]

1200 **Anonymous**   Old English Version of the Heptateuch;
Aelfric's Treatise of the Old and New Testament. Ms.
  [First published, 1922. Another edition, 1969. Both
  published in London: EETS.]

1688 **Thwaites, Edward**   Versio Heptateuchi Saxonica,
praeter alia quaedam Aelfrici Abbatis, 1688.

1922 **Anonymous**   Old English Version of the Heptateuch;
Aelfric's treatise on the Old and New Testament.
London: Early English Text Society, 1969.
  [Originally published 1922.]

  [See Anonymous, Old English Version..., 1200.]

1922 **Crawford, S.J. and N.R. Ker**   The Old English
Version of the Heptateuch; Aelfric's Treatise on the
Old and New Testament and His Preface to Genesis.
Edited together with a reprint of 'A Saxon Treatise

Concerning the Old and New Testament: Now First
Publishedin Print with English of Our Times by
William L'isle of Wilburgham (1623)' and the Vulgate
Text of the Heptateuch by S.J. Crawford, with the
Text of Two Additional Manuscripts Transcribed by
N.R. Ker... Bungay, Suffolk: Printed by Richard
Clay & Sons Ltd., 1922.   [Anglo-Saxon]
   Reprinted; London, New York & Toronto: Published
   for Early English Text Society by the Oxford
   University Press, 1969.

HEXATEUCH

1892 **Addis, W.E.**   The Documents of the Hexateuch
translated and arranged in Chronological order with
introduction and notes by W.E. Addis. 2 Vols.
London: David Nutt, 1892-1898.
        1892 - - Part I. The Oldest Book of Hebrew
              History.

        1898 - - Part II. The Deuteronomical Writers
              and the Priestly Documents.

        ["In translating, it has been my habit to make my own
        translation of each verse, and then to adapt it as
        closely as I could to that of the Revised English
        Version." In Part I, Jahvist and Elohist sources are
        indicated by distinctive type.]

1974 **Dodwell, C.R. and Peter Clemoes** (Editors)   The Old
English Illustrated Hexateuch: British Museum Cotton
Claudius B. iv   Edited by C.R.Dodwell and Peter
Clemoes. Copenhagen: Rosenkilde of Bagger, 1974.
        [Anglo-Saxon]

1985 **Smith, Andrea B.**   The Anonymous Parts of the Old
English Hexateuch: A Latin - Old English/Old English
- Latin Glossary. Andrea B. Smith. Cambridge: D.S.
Brewer, Printed and Bound in Great Britian by Short
Run Press Ltd., Exeter, 1985.

3

Pentateuch

PENTATEUCH LISTINGS

???? **Stern, M.** ...The Five Books of Moses; With Haptorath and Five Megiloth and Sabbath Prayers. A New Edition Revised by M. Stern. New York: Star Hebrew Book Co., [193?].
>[Includes the Pentateuch, Solomon's Song, The Book of Ruth, The Book of Lamentations, The Book of Ecclesiastes, The Book of Esther, and extensive other Old Testament selections, in Hebrew and English. The spine is entitled, "Pentateuch – Haftorath – Harkavy." The version is extensively revised from Harkavy's translation. Possibly "A new revised edition" refers merely to Harkavy's O.T. (q.v., 1915).]

???? **Tafel, Leonard, Rudolph L. Tafel and L.H. Tafel** Interlinear Translation of the Pentateuch, with Grammatical and Critical Notes, by Dr. Leonard Tafel... Dr. Rudolph L. Tafel... Prof. L.H. Tafel. New York: E. & J.B. Young & Co., [187?].
>[See Bible Selections for the complete entry.]

1483 **Anonymous**   The Golden Legende... the legende named in Latyn legenda...
>[See Bible Selections for the complete entry. Includes most of the Pentateuch.]

1530 **Tyndale, William**   The fyrste boke of Moses call Genesis ...[Then follows the rest of the books of the Pentateuch, each with its own title page.] Emprinted at Marlborow in the lande of Hesse, by me Hans Luft [i.e., Antwerp: Hoochstraten], 1530.
>[The Deity is rendered "Jehovah" at Gen. 15:2; Ex. 6:2; Ex. 13:17; Deut. 3:23.]

> Another edition; - - Newly correctyd and amendyd by W.T. MDXXXIII [1533]

[This is the second edition, possibly 1534; Only
Genesis is 'amendyd'; the other books remain the
same.]

Other editions; London: John Day, 1551, 1552.

Also; William Tyndale's Five Books of Moses,
called the Pentateuch, being a verbatim
reprint of the edition of M.CCCCC.XXX Compared
with Tyndale's Genesis of 1534, and the
Pentateuch in the Vulgate, Luther, and
Matthew's Bible, with Various Collations and
Prolegomena. Edited by the Rev. J.I. Mombert.
New York: Anson D.F. Randolph & Co.; London:
Samuel Bagster & Sons, 1884.

Another edition; – – And Newly Introduced by
F.F. Bruce. Carbondale, Illinois: Southern
Illinois University Press, 1967.

1549 **Anonymous**   The Fyve Bokes of Solomon, with the
Story of Bel. London: Edward Whitchurche, 1549.

1616 **Anonymous**   Annotations upon the [Pentateuch]
Wherein the Hebrew words and sentences, are compared
with, and explayned by the ancient Greek and Chaldee
versions: but chiefly by conference with the Holy
Scriptures. By H.A. [Henry Ainsworth] [5 Parts.
Amsterdam] 1616-1619.
       1616 ..the first book of Moses, called
            Genesis.   Another Edition; 1639.

       1617 ..the second book of Moses, called
            Exodus.

       1618 ..the third book of Moses, called
            Leviticus.

       1619 ..the fourth book of Moses, called
            Numbers.

       1619 ..the fifth book of Moses, called
            Deuteronomie

       Re-issued; 1622, 1627 with the Song of Solomon,
       1639.

1623 **Anonymous**   Saxon-English Remains of the Pentateuch,
Joshua, Judges, Ruth...
       [See Old Testament Selections for the complete entry.]

1639 **Ainsworth, Henry**   Annotations vpon the Five Books
of Moses, the Psalms, and the Canticles, translated
by Henry Ainsworth. London: M. Parsons, 1639.

1694 **Kidder, Richard**   A Commentary on the Five Books
of Moses, with a dissertation concerning the Author
or Writer of the said Books, and a general argument
to each of them. 2 Vols. London: J. Heptinstall,
1694.

1748 **Anonymous**   A Critical and Practical Exposition of
the Pentateuch, with notes... To which are subjoin'd
two dissertations, the first on the Mosiac history
of the creation, the other on the destruction of the
seven nations of Canaan. [Robert Jameson] London:
J. & P. Knapton, 1748.

1763 **Durrell, D.**   The Hebrew Text of the Parallel
Prophecies of Jacob and Moses relating to the Twelve
Tribes; with a Translation and Notes: and the
Various Lections of Near Forty MSS. To which are
added: I. The Samaritan-Arabic Version of those
Passages, and part of another Arabic Version made
from the Samaritan Text; neither of which have been
before printed: II. A Mao of the Land of Promise;
and III. An Appendix containing four Dissertations
on Points connected with the Subject of these
Prophecies. Oxford: Clarendon Press, 1763.

1785 **Alexander, A.**   The First [through Fifth] book
of Moses [with the Haphtaroth and the Megilloth] in
Hebrew and English... with Remarks Critical and
Grammatical on the Hebrew... By A.Alexander. 6 Vols.
London: A. Alexander and Son, 1785.
      [Apparently the first Pentateuch in Hebrew and English.
      It is not known whether this is the same version as that
      in the O.T., 1822.]

1787 **Levi, David**   The First [thru Fifth] Book
of Moses [with the Haphtaroth and Megolloth] ...in
Hebrew, with the English translation on the Opposite
Page. With notes...by Lion Soemans, corrected, and
translated by David Levi. 5 Vols.   London: Lion
Soesmans & Co., 1787.
      Another Edition; 1789.

1789 **Delgado, Isaac**   A New English Translation of
the Pentateuch: being a thorough correction of the
present translation, wherever it deviates from the
genuine sense of the Hebrew expressions, or where it
renders obscure the meaning of the text; or, lastly,
when it occasions a seeming contradiction: proving
the validity of such emendations by critical remarks
and illustrations... together with a comment on such
passages as cannot be sufficiently understood by a
mere Translation... By Isaac Delgado.   London:
Printed for the author, and sold by W. Richardson,
1789.

[Corrects the KJV "...wherever it deviates from the genuine sense of the Hebrew expressions, or where it renders obscure the meaning of the text, or, lastly, when it occasions a seeming contradiction..." According to Walter Coslet (a Bible Collector), "...does not present more than the passage being corrected. The set in 1868 is the full text of the Pentateuch."]

Another edition; Pentateuch & Megilloth. 5 Vols. (Hebrew & English)   London: Printed and Published by Abraham & Son, 35, St. Mary Axe, City, 1868-5628.
> [The title of Exodus reads: Exodus: Being the second of the five books of Moses, with the Haptorath and the five Megilloth, arranged according to the German and Portuguese rituals, accompanied by a revised and correct translation, and a very valuable commentary, containing critical, grammatical, and explanatory notes, by the late Isaac Delgado. To which is added the Sabbath evening, morning and additional service. (Of the Megilloth, this volume contains only Esther.)]

1818 **Clapham, Samuel**   The Pentateuch; or, the Five Books of Moses illustrated: being an explication of the phraseology incorporated with the text, for the use of Families and Schools. By the Rev. Samuel Clapham. London: J. Harris, 1818.

1819 **Wellbeloved, Charles**   The Holy Bible, a new translation with introductory remarks, notes explanatory and critical, and practical reflections; designed principally for the use of families...
> [See Old Testament Selections for the complete entry. Includes the Pentateuch.]

1828 **Alexander, William**   The Pentateuch; or, The Five Books of Moses, Principally Designed to Facilitate the Audible or Social Reading of the Sacred Scriptures; Illustrated with Notes, Historical, Geographical, and Otherwise Explanatory, and also pointing out the Fulfillment of the Prophecies. By William Alexander.   York: Printed and Published by W. Alexander and Son; London: Harvey & Darton...; Birmingham: R. Peart; Derby: H. Mozley; Edinburgh: W. Whyte & Co.; Dublin: D.F. Gardiner, 1828.
> [Herbert: 'The Holy Bible...In three volumes − − Vol.1.', apparently a half − title for the above work. The text consists of the KJV with numerous minor revisions; also an occasional 'lineal rendering' intended to '...facilitate the audible of social reading...'. Alexander's preface expressed the intention to complete the entire O.T.; apparently this was not accomplished.]

1835 **Ablett, Joseph**   The Book of the Law from the Holy Bible, in which the mind and the memory are

powerfully impressed with the ordinances and commandments of Almighty God. Translated by Joseph Ablett. Liverpool: George Smith, 1835.
[The Pentateuch.]

1845 **Leeser, Isaac**   [The Torah in Hebrew and English] The Law of God... Edited, and with former Translations diligently compared and revised, by Isaac Leeser. 5 Vols. Philadelphia: Printed by C. Sherman for the Editor, 1845-1846.
[The Pentateuch; The Hebrew text of Wolf Heidenheim (1818-1821) and Leeser's translation are printed on facing pages.]

1852 **Bingham, Charles William**   Commentaries on the four last Books of Moses arranged in the form of a Harmony by John Calvin. Translated from the original Latin, and compared with the French edition, with annotations,etc., by Charles William Bingham. 4 Vols. Edinburgh: Calvin Translation Society, 1852-1855.
[See Old Testament Selections, 1844 Anonymous, Commentaries on the Books of the Bible.]

1853 **Anonymous**   The Holy Bible in Hebrew and English. With the portions of the prophets as read in synagogue. To which are added the explanatory, critical, and grammatical notes of the late David Levi. 5 Vols. London: S. Solomon, 1853.
[Pentateuch only.]

1855 **Howard, Henry Edward John**   [The Pentateuch] according to the version of the LXX. Translated into English, with notices of its omissions and insertions, and with notes on the passages in which it differs from our authorised translation, by...Henry E.J. Howard. Cambridge: Macmillan & Co., 1855-1857.
    1855 - - The Book of Genesis...
    1857 - - The Book of Exodus and Leviticus...
    1857 - - The Books of Numbers and
             Deuteronomy...

1861 **MacHale, John**   An Irish Translation of the Holy Bible from the Latin Vulgate version, chiefly from the Douay... Vol. 1. Dublin: James Duffy, 1861.
[Pentateuch only; no more published.]

    Another Edition; 1868.

1862 **Etheridge, J.W.** The Targums of Onkelos and Jonathan ben Uzziel on the Pentateuch; with the Fragments of the Jerusalem Targum from the Chaldee. 2 Vols. London: Longman, Green, Longman, and Roberts, 1862-1865.

["...I have followed upon Onkelos, the Aramaic text of
Walton, carefully collated with the last edition of the
Targums, published at Wilna..."]

Another edition; New York: KTAV, 1968.

1866 **Martin, James**   The Pentateuch, 1866.
     [See Old Testament, 1865 Biblical Commentary.]

1871 **Deutsch, Solomon**   A Key to the Pentateuch:
     Explanatory of the Text and the Grammatical Forms...
     Part I. Genesis.   New York: Holt & Williams, 1871.
          [Hebrew and a word-for-word English translation; more
          published?]

1884 **Mombert, J. Isidor**   William Tyndale's Five Books of
     Moses, called the Pentateuch, being a verbatim
     reprint of the edition of M.CCCCC.XXX Compared with
     Tyndale's Genesis of 1534, and the Pentateuch in the
     Vulgate, Luther, and Matthew's Bible, with Various
     Collations and Prolegomena...
          [See William Tyndale, The fyrste boke of Moses, 1530.]

1884 **Moses, Adolph and Isaac S. Moses**   The Pentateuch,
     or the Five Books of Moses. (School and Family
     Education.) Milwaukee, Wis., 1884.
          Another edition; Cincinnati & Chicago: The Bloch
          Publishing and Printing Co., n.d.

1899 **Magil, Joseph**   Magil's Linear School Bible
     -or- The Hebrew Bible in its Original Language Self
     Taught. -for- Teachers and Students in Schools,
     Colleges, and Universities, as well as for Self
     Instruction. A New and Easy Method for Popularising
     the Study of the Original Hebrew Bible by Means of
     a Linear Translation. By Joseph Magil, Formerly
     Instructor in Higher Hebrew at the Hebrew Education
     Society's School and in the B'ne Zion School,
     Philadelphia, Pa.2 Vols. New York and Philadelphia:
     Joseph Magil's Publishing Co., 1899-1905.
          1899 - - Genesis I-XXVIII. Philadelphia:
               Joseph & Myer Magil.
                    [It is not known whether additional
                    portions of the translations were published
                    prior to the whole Pentateuch in 1905. CFT
                    has a 1910 edition of Exodus, copyright
                    1899.]

          1905 - - The Five Books of Moses (1 Vol.)
                    Fifteenth Edition; Philadelphia: Joseph
                    Magil, 1927. Sixteenth Edition; New
                    York: Hebrew Publishing Co., n.d.

                    Reprinted; Magil's Linear School Bible
                    by Joseph Magil. Hebrew Text and
                    English Translation. The Five Books

of Moses. New York: Hebrew
Publishing Co., n.d.

1908 – – Genesis [Complete Genesis]
Other editions; 1910, 1913.

["...there are places where the English must be
sacrificed for the sake of literalness of the Hebrew,
and the Hebrew order of words followed instead of that
of English."]

1914 **Anonymous**   The War Bible Of the Moment Written into
Colloquial English and Pure Slang; The Five Books of
Moses, With Sidelights on the Book of Job, Hindoo
Version of the Creation of Woman. Ye Cloister
Version of the Transformation of Man, Unfolding The
Grand Old Story with Cloister Soliloquies, Smiles
and Tears...
[See Old Testament Selections for the complete entry.]

1928 **Harkavy, Alexander**   The Pentateuch with Haptaroth
and Five Megiloth; English translation revised by
Alexander Harkavy. Music Notes arranged by M.
Nathanson. New York: Hebrew Publishing Co., 1928.
Another edition; The Pentateuch with Haptaroth
and Five Megiloth; English translation revised
by Alexander Harkavy, including Sabbath
morning prayers. Music Notes arranged by M.
Nathanson. New York: Hebrew Publishing Co.,
1933.

1929 **Hertz, Joseph Herman**   The Pentateuch and Haftorahs;
Hebrew text, English Translation and Commentary.
Edited by Joseph Herman Hertz. 5 Vols. New York:
Oxford University Press, 1929–1936.
["Wherever the RSV brings more than one translation of
a difficult passage, the rendering most in accord with
Jewish tradition has been chosen." This commentary,
accompanied by the JPS translation of 1917 (with
modifications) was published, with the rest of the O.T.
in 1936; qv.]

Second Revised Edition; The Pentateuch and
Haftorahs; Hebrew text, English Translation
and Commentary edited by The Chief Rabbi (Dr.
J.H. Hertz). 5 Vols. London & New York: 1940–
1951.

[See Old Testament listings, 1936 Soncino Books of the
Bible.]

1929 **Rosenbaum, M. and A.M. Silbermann**   Pentateuch with
Targum Onkelos, Haphtaroth and prayers for Sabbath,
and Rashi's Commentary, translated into English and
annotated by M. Rosenbaum and A.M. Silbermann in

collaboration with A. Blashki and L. Joseph. 5 Vols.
London: Shapiro, Valentine & Co., 1929.
[note]["This works aims at giving, so far as is possible, a
literal translation into English of the Hebrew text of
Rashi's commentary on the Pentateuch. For this reason,
no striving has been made after elegance of diction, and
in all cases this has been sacrificed, and frequently
ruthlessly so, to the needs of literalness..." Text in
Hebrew and English.][/note]

Another edition, 1946.

1943 **Allis, Oswald T.**   The Five Books of
Moses. A Reexamination of the Modern Theory that the
Pentateuch is a Late Compilation from Diverse and
Conflicting Sources by Authors and Editors Whose
Identity is Completely Unknown. By Oswald T.
Allis...   Philadelphia: The Presbyterian and
Reformed Publishing Co., 1943.

1944 **Hershon, Jerome**   Torah Readings; a simplified
translation of the Five Books of Moses, for home,
synagogue, school and camp. Translated and edited by
Jerome Hershon. New York: Junior Publications, 1944.
["...not a simplified literal translation, but an
interpretative translation of the text... The term
'Eternal' is used for the commonly accepted terms of
'Lord', 'Yahve', or 'Jehovah'."]

1944 **Scharfstein, Ben-Ami**   ...The Five Books of Moses
Selected and Translated for Jewish Youth, by Ben-Ami
Scharfstein. New York: Shilo Publishing House, 1944.
["...aims at being clear and simple... The stories are
translated almost completely... But extreme repetition
has been eliminated, and unsuitable parts omitted..."]

Second Edition, Revised (n.d.)

1949 **Isaiah, Abraham ben and Others**   The Pentateuch
and Rashi's Commentary; a linear translation into
English by Abraham ben Isaiah and Benjamin Sharfman,
in collaboration with Harry M. Orlinsky and Morris
Charner. 5 Vols.   Brooklyn: S.S. & R. Publishing
Co., 1949-1950.
         1949   - - Genesis
         1950   - - Exodus
         1950   - - Leviticus
         1950   - - Numbers
         1950   - - Deuteronomy

1953 **Freedman, Harry** (Editor)   Encyclopedia of Biblical
Interpretation... A millennial anthology by Menehem
M. Kasker translated under the editorship of Harry
Freedman [and Hyman Klein].   New York: American
Biblical Encyclopedia Society, 1953-1966.

["Generally speaking the version of the JPS has been used... However, where the Rabbinic saying clearly presupposes a different rendering, it is given straight in the text..." A commentary on the Pentateuch, with a "...sound, scholarly translation in masterful English prose..."]

1955 Schonfeld, Solomon   The Universal Bible, being the Pentateuchal texts at first addressed to all nations (Torat b'nai No'ach) Teachings of the Sons of Noah. Translation and notes, by Solomon Schonfeld. London: Sidgwick & Jackson, 1955.

["The translator has naturally based his renderings on existing translations from the AV of 1611, to the most recent translation, the RSV of 1952."]

1956 Levy, Isaac   The Pentateuch, Translated and Explained by Samson Raphael Hirsch... rendered into English by Isaac Levy. 6 Vols. London: Printed by L. Honig & Sons, 1956-1962.

["...literal, almost word for word, translation of the great work of my Grandfather, S.R. Hirsch 'Der Pentateuch, ubersetzt und erlantert', which was first published in Frankfort between 1867 and 1878."]

1959 - - Vol. I   Genesis

1956 - - Vol. II   Exodus

1958 - - Vol. III Leviticus (Part I)

1958 - - Vol. III Leviticus (Part II)

1960 - - Vol. IV   Numbers

1962 - - Vol. V   Deuteronomy

Second edition; [Completely revised] 5 Vols. London: 1962-1967.

Another Edition; 7 Vols. New York: Judaica Press, 1976.   [Vol. 7 is titled, "The Haphtoroth Translated & Explained by Dr. Mendel Hirsch eldest son of Samson Raphael Hirsch. Rendered into English by Isaac Levy. Gateshead: Judaica Press, Ltd., 1979."]

1962 Freedman, Harry   Pentateuch, 1962.
[See Old Testament, 1962 Jewish Publication Society.]

1962 Grayzel, Solomon   Torah, 1962.
[See Old Testament, 1962 Jewish Publication Society.]

1963 Kahane, Charles   Torah Yesharah, a traditional interpretative translation of the Five Books of Moses, and an introduction to each Haftorah, based

on Talmudic and Madrishic sources, as well as from
medieval and modern commentaries. Translated and
edited by Charles Kahane. 2 Vols. New York: Torah
Yesherah Publications, Solomon Rubinowitz Book
Concern, 1963-1964.

1970 **Duckworth, D., J.G. Mongredieu & N. Ryder** (Editors)
Pentateuch: Genesis, Exodus, Leviticus, Numbers,
Deuteronomy. London: The General Conference of the
New Church, 1970.
> [An independent translation of the MT without any
> emendations.]

1980 **Klein, Michael L.** The Fragment-Targums of
the Pentateuch According to their Extant Sources. 2
Vols. Rome: Biblical Institute Press, 1980.
> Vol. 1   Texts, Indices and Introductory
>   Essays.
> Vol. 2   Translation

> [Analecta Biblia 76.]

1981 **Kaplan, Aryeh** The Living Torah: The Five Books
of Moses: a New Translation based on traditional
Jewish sources with notes, introduction, maps,
tables, charts, bibliography, an index by Aryeh
Kaplan. New York: Maznaim Publishing Corp., 1981

1982 **Greenfield, Moses** The Five Books of Moses; With
a newly revised contemporary English translation.
n.p.: Atereth Publishing, 1982.

1986 **Hirschler, Gertrude** The Pentateuch with
a translation by Samson Raphael Hirsch and excerpts
from the Hirsch Commentary. Edited by Ephraim Oratx.
English Translation from the original German by
Gertrude Hirschler. New York: The Judaica Press,
Inc., 1986.

PENTATEUCH SELECTIONS

1619 **Ainsworth, Henry** Numbers and Deuteronomy
Translated. Amsterdam: G. Thorp, 1619.
> Second edition; London, 1622.

1662 **Hughes, George** An Analytical Exposition of
the Whole first Book of Moses. Called Genesis, and
of XXIII Chapter of his Second Book, called Exodus.

Wherein, the various Readings are observed, the Original Text explained, doubts resolved, Scriptures parallelled, the Scripture Chronology from the Creation of the World to the giving of the Law at Mount Sinai cleared, and the whole illustrated by Doctrines collected from the Text. Delivered in a Morning Exercise on the Lord's Day. Printed Anno Domini M.DC.LXXII. [1662]
[Colophons indicate that Genesis was finished in 1659, and Exodus in 1662. Translation appears to be based upon Ainsworth, 1616.]

1852 **Bingham, Charles William** Commentaries on the four last Books of Moses arranged in the form of a Harmony by John Calvin. Translated from the original Latin, and compared with the French edition, with annotations,etc., by Charles William Bingham.4 Vols. Edinburgh: Calvin Translation Society, 1852-1855.
[See Anonymous, Commentaries on the Books of the Bible, 1844.]

1855 **Kalisch, Marcus Moritz** A Historic and Critical Commentary on the Old Testament, with a new translation by M. Kalisch... London: 1855-1872.
> 1858 - - Genesis. London: Longman, Brown, Green, Longmans & Roberts. Again, 1879.
>
> 1855 - - Exodus. London: Longman, Brown, Green, Longmans & Roberts.
>
> 1867 - - Leviticus. Part I. Containing Chapters I-X... London: Longman, Green, Reader & Dyer.
>
> 1872 - - Leviticus. Part II. Containing Chapters XI-XXVII... London: Longman, Green, Reader & Dyer.

["...the language of the English version is frequently obsolete, and not seldom obscure and unintelligible; we have altered such passages, without, however, destroying the old venerable hue; we have designedly preserved a coloring of antiquity...". No more was published. Hebrew and English.]

1855 **Wolfe, J.R.** The Messiah... Pentateuch...
[See Old Testament Selections for the complete entry.]

1868 **Delgado, Isaac** Genesis, Leviticus, Numbers and Deuteronomy accompanied by a revised and corrected translation...
[See Old Testament Selections for the complete entry.]

1871 **Kelly, William** Lectures Introductory to the Study of the Pentateuch. London: W.H. Broom, 1871.
[Pentateuch selections.]

1872 **Anonymous**   The mystical sense of the
Sacred Scriptures; or, The books of the Old and New
Testaments... with explications and reflections...by
Madame Guion... Glasgow: J. Thomson, 1872.
[Only the Pentateuch. The translator was Thomas Watson
Duncan.]

Reprinted, 1886.

1896 **Mendes, Henry Pereira**   Jewish History ethically
presented for private or Sunday-School use. The
Pentateuch; by H.Pereira Mendes. New York: Published
by the author, 1896.
[Copyrighted 1895.]

1917 **Dembitz, L.N.**   Exodus and Leviticus, 1917.
[See Jewish Publication Society, The Holy Scriptures,
1917.]

1937 **Widdowson, B.C.**   A New Presentation of the Bible
by B.C. Widdowson. 2 Vols.   Telscombe Cliffs: B.C.
Widdowson, 1937-1938.
[Genesis to Numbers XII, typed.]

1944 **Scharfstein, Ben-Ami**   ...The Five Books of Moses
Selected and Translated for Jewish Youth, by Ben-Ami
Scharfstein. New York: Shilo Publishing House, 1944.
["...aims at being clear and simple... The stories are
translated almost completely... But extreme repetition
has been eliminated, and unsuitable parts omitted..."]

Second Edition, Revised (n.d.)

1947 **Fisch, S.**   Numbers and Deuteronomy, 1947.
[See Soncino Books of the Bible, The Chumash, 1936.]

1947 **Flight, John W. and Sophia L. Fahs**   Moses, Egyptian
Prince, Nomad Sheikh, Lawgiver by John W. Flight and
Sophia L. Fahs, Collaborator. Boston: Beacon Press,
1947
["Twelve short simply written chapters tell the story in
the writer's own words, and after each chapter the Bible
passage on which the chapter is based is given in the
(ASV)"]

1966 **Simon, Solomon and Morrison David Bial**
The Rabbis' Bible. Vol. one: Torah; by Solomon Simon
and   Morrison   David   Bial.   With   the   editorial
assistance of Hannah Grad Goodman. Woodcuts by Irwin
Rosenhouse.   New York: Behrman House, Inc., 1966.
[Abridged]

1975 **Brueggemann, Walter and Hans Walter Wolff**
The Vitality of Old Testament Traditions by Walter
Brueggemann and Hans Walter Wolff.   Atlanta: John
Knox Press, 1975.

["Unless otherwise indicated, scripture quotations are translations of the respective author."]

Second edition, 1982.

1975 **Chiel, Arthur A.**   Pathways Through the Torah by Rabbi Arthur A. Chiel. 2 Vols. KTAV Publishing House Inc., 1975.

1987 **Segal, Lore and Leonard Baskin**   The Book of Adam to Moses. Lore Segal and Leonard Baskin. New York: Schocken Books, 1987.

1990 **Rosenberg, David**   The Book of J; Translated from the Hebrew by David Rosenberg, Interpreted by Harold Bloom. New York: Grove Weidenfeld, 1990.

GENESIS

???? **Anonymous**   Genesis Chapter 2.1-4   (MS), n.d.

???? **Kellner, Maximilian Lindsay**   The Deluge in the Izdubar Epic. Cambridge: Episcopal Theological School, [19??].   [Genesis selections]

???? **Mercer, Samuel Alfred Browne**   The Book of Genesis for Bible Classes and private Study, by Samuel A.B. Mercer.   London: A.R. Mowbray & Co.;   Milwaukee, Wis.: Morehouse Publishing Co., [192?].
["Biblical & Oriental Series."]

???? **Sawyer, Leicester Ambrose**   (The Bible) Analyzed, translated ... Early Generations. Genesis 1 - 11...
[See Bible Selections for the complete entry.]

???? **Stuart, Moses**   A Commentary on Genesis, by Moses Stuart. [189?].
Another edition; - - edited and revised by R.D.C. Robbins.   Andover: Warren F. Draper, 189?

???? **Weigle, Luther A.** (Editor)   The Genesis Octapla; Eight English Version of the Book of Genesis in the Tyndale-King James Tradition. Edited by Luther A. Weigle. Edinburgh, New York, Toronto: Thomas Nelson & Sons, [19??].
[Contains: Tyndale: Five Books of Moses (1530), Great Bible (1540), Geneva Bible (1602), Bishop's Bible (1602), Douay Bible (1609), KJV (1873), ASV (1901) and RSV (1952).]

670 **Caedmon**   Songs sung by an illiterate...

[See Bible Selections for the complete entry Includes songs from Genesis.]

1400 **Trevisa, John**   Be Bygynnyng of þe World and þe Ende of Worldes.   MSS. Harl. 1900; Add 37049 St. John's College, Cambridge, c1400.
[Includes a paraphrase of parts of Genesis.]

Dialogus inter Militem at Clericum, Richard Fitz-Ralph's Sermon: 'Defensio Curatorum' and Methodius: 'þe Bygynnyng of þe World and þe Ende of Worldes' by John Trevisa, Vicar of Berkeley, Now first edited from the MSS. Harl. 1900, St. John's College, Cambridge, H.1, Add. 24194, Stowe 65, and Chetham's Library... London: Published for the Early English Text Society by Humphrey Milford, Oxford University Press, 1925.

1533 **Joye, George**   Genesis.   Holland, 1533.
[One page only. It was sent to King Henry VIII for permission to continue work on a translation of the Bible. Permission was never obtained.]

1578 **Tymme, Thomas**   A Commentarie of John Caluine, vpon the firste booke of Moses called Genesis: Translated out of the Latine into English by Thomas Tymme, Minister.   Imprinted at London, for Iohn Harison and George Bishop, 1578.

1578 **Hunnis, William**   A Hyue Full of Hunnye, Contayning the Firste Booke of Moses, called Genesis, Turned into English Meeter... Seene and allowed, accordinge to the Order appointed.   Imprinted at London by Thomas Marsh, 1578.

1595 **Hunnis, William**   The Life and Death of Joseph; in metre... London: P.S. for William Jaggard, 1595.

1616 **Ainsworth, Henry**   Genesis Translated. 1616.
[No further information available.]

1646 **Hammond, John**   The Creation of the World, being the First Chapter of Genesis [in verse]. London: John Hammond, 1646.

1655 **Junius, Francis**   Caedmonis monachi paraphrasis Genesos ac praecipuarum sacrae paginae historiarum, abhinc annos MLXX Anglo-Saxonice conscripta, et nunc demum edita... Amsterdam: 1655.
[Anglo-Saxon]

1662 **Hughes, George**   An Analytical Exposition of the Whole first Book of Moses. Called Genesis, and of XXIII Chapter of his Second Book, called Exodus...

[See Pentateuch Selections for the complete entry.]

1676 **Lesly, George**   Joseph Revived; or, The Last VI
Chapters of Genesis Metaphras'd, by G. Lesly.
London: 1676.

1679 **Anonymous**   Order and disorder: or, The world made
and undone. Being meditations upon the creation and
the fall; as it is recorded in the beginning of
Genesis. London: Printed by Margaret White for Henry
Mortlock..., 1679.
          [Paraphrases]

1682 **Anonymous**   Cabbalistical Dialogue, in Answer
to the Opinion of a Learned Doctor in Philosophy and
theology... to Which is Subjoyned a Rabbinical and
Paraphrastical Exposition of Genesis I. Written in
High-Dutch by the Author of the Foregoing Dialogue,
first Done into Latin, but now made English [by F.M.
van Helmont] London: Benjamin Clark, 1682.

1684 **Lesly, George**   Divine Dialogues, viz.: Dives's
Doom, Sodom's Flames, Abraham's Faith, Containing
the Histories of Dives and Lazarus, the Destruction
of Sodom, and Abraham's Sacrificing His Son. [In
Verse] To which is added, Joseph Revived; or, The
History of His Life and Death [In Verse] by G.
Lesly. 2nd Edition. 2 Parts. London: 1684.

1697 **Helmont, Franciscus Mercurius van**   Some Premediate
and Considerate Thoughts Upon the Four First
Chapters of the First Book of Moses, Called Genesis,
Delivered by Franciscus Mercurius van Helmont.
Translated from the Latin. Amsterdam & London:
Printed for Samuel Clark, 1697.

1700 **Anonymous**   Scriptural Poems. Being several
portions of Scripture digested into English verse.
Viz. I. The Book of Ruth. II. The History of
Sampson. III. Christ's Sermon on the Mount. IV. The
Prophecy of Jonah. V. The Life of Joseph. VI...
          [See Bible Selections for the complete entry.]

1702 **Anonymous**   The Fall of Adam and Eve... Written
originally by an Eminent Divine in Amsterdam;
Translated into English. London: Printed for T.
Osborne, and Sold by J. Nutt, 1702.
          [Paraphrases]

1705 **Simson, Andrew**   Tripatriarchicon; or, The lives
of the three patriarchs Abraham, Isaac and Jacob.
Extracted forth of the sacred story, and digested
into English verse, by Andrew Symson... Edinburgh:

Printed by the Author and sold by II Knox [etc], 1705.

> [Paraphrases.]

1738 **Lookup, John**   Genesis. By - - - - Lookup. London: Wm. Rayner, 1738.

> Also; Berashith; or the first Book of Moses, call'd Genesis. Translated from the original... By John Lookup. London: Printed for J. Roberts, 1740.

1746 **Bland, John**   An essay in a method never before attempted, towards a new version of the Old Testament into English from the original Hebrew, by throwing it into short lines, as it is stopped or pointed, by the major accent points. for the Author, 1746.

> [Genesis translated.]

1754 **Anonymous**   First Chapter of Genesis. <u>Gentleman's Magazine</u>, Aug. 1754.

> [Said to be translated by an old man who sold fruit in Clare Court. Thus the name, "Fruitseller's Bible". A portion appeared in Gentleman's Magazine and was reprinted in Cotton's Editions of the Bible and again in Simms' "Bible in America". There seems to be only two copies of this extant. One in the British Museum (?) and the other held by an anonymous collector in England, who refuses to allow it to be copied.]

> [The following is the excerpt from Cotton: "Aelohim, beginning, created Lucide and Illucide matter. 2. And the illucide, void of co-adjunct co-hesion, was unmodified, and distinguishableness was nowhere upon the face of the chaos: And the Ruach of Aelohim emanated over the periphery of the fluctuation. 3. Until Aelohim saw the light was good, when it was become a separation from obscurity. 5. And Aelohim deemed this daylight, and the obscurity was yet as night, which was light, and obscuration the consummation of the first day."]

1760 **Anonymous**   The history of Joseph. Compiled in an easy and familiar way, for the entertainment and instruction of youth. Interspersed with moral reflections. Adorned with cuts. Coventry: Printed and sold by Luckman & Suffield, [ca. 1760?].

> [Paraphrases]

1763 **Dawson, Abraham**   A New English Translation, from the Original Hebrew of the First Three Chapters of Genesis, with Marginal Illustrations, and Notes Critical and Explanatory. London: 1763-1786.

> 1763 ... The Three first chapters...
> 1772 ... The Fourth and Fifth Chapters...
> 1786 ... The six[th] and Eleven following
> chapters...

1763 **Greenwood, W.**   An Essay on Genesis 1 with a
Paraphrastical Exposition, by W. Greenwood, 1763.

1788 **Drysdale, Rev. William**   Genesis 1, 2, 3, a New
Translation with Notes, by Rev. William Drysdale.
Newcastle on Tyne. 1788.

1789 **Anonymous**   Genesis. Chapter III, and part of IV.
Worcester: Isaiah Thomas. November, 1789.
        ["This is a specimen accompanying a sheet of proposals
        issued by Mr. Thomas for publishing by subscription, his
        4to edition of the Bible."]

1794 **Anonymous**   Arcana Coelestia: or Heavenly Mysteries
contained in the Sacred Scriptures, or Word of the
lord, Manifested and Laid open; beginning with the
book of Genesis. Interspersed with Relations of
Wonderful Things seen the World of Spirits and the
Heaven of Angels: Translated from the Original Latin
of Emanual Swedenborg. Printed at the Apollo Press
in Boston, by Joseph Belknap, 1794.
        [Vol. I. Genesis, Chapter I. No more was published.]

1800 **Anonymous**   The Story of Joseph and His Brethren...
Philadelphia: Printed by B. & J. Johnson, 1800.

1800 **Anonymous**   The Fall of Adam. Philadelphia:
Printed by B. & J. Johnson, 1800.

1805 **Macgowan, John**   The Life of Joseph, the Son of
Israel. In Eight Books. Briefly designed to allure
young minds to a love of the Sacred Scriptures. By
John Macgowan. Printed at Greenfield, Massachusetts:
By John Denio, 1805.

1810 **Anonymous**   The Fall of Adam, our first parent,
with some account of the creation of the world, etc.
[London: Howard & Evans, printers], 1810?
        [Paraphrases]

1810 **Clarke, George Somers**   Hebrew Criticism and
Poetry...
        [See Old Testament Selections for the complete entry.]

1812 **Oxoniensis**   Genesis 49, a new version. <u>Gentleman's
Magazine</u>, 1812.

1816 **Matthews, Arthur**   Paraphrase on the Book
of Genesis; a poetical essay. By Arthur Matthews.
Providence [R.I.]: Goddard & Mann, 1816.

1818 **Anonymous**   The attributes of God: an account
of the creation; and the story of Joseph and his
Brethren, taken from scripture: adorned with cuts.
New Haven: Sidney Press for J. Babcock & Son, 1818.

[Paraphrases]

1819 **Anonymous**   A New Version of the first three
chapters of Genesis; accompanied with dissertations
illustrative of the Creation, the Fall of Man, the
Principles of Evil, and the Plagues of Egypt. To
which are annexed strictures on Mr. Bellamy's
translation. By Essenus. [Pseud.] London: Rowland
Hunter, 1819.
    [The British Museum identifies Essenus with John Johns,
    a Unitarian minister.]

1819 **Walworth, William Thackwray**   Paraphrases. (Exodus
XX.1-17), 1819.

1826 **Conybeare, John J.**   Illustrations of Anglo-Saxon
Poetry...
    [See Old Testament Selections for the complete entry.
    Includes Genesis.]

1828 **Anonymous**   The Book of Genesis in English-
Hebrew; Accompanied by an Interlinear translation,
substantially the same as the authorized English
version; with notes, and a grammatical introduction.
By the editor of the Comprehensive Bible. [William
Greenfield] London: John Taylor, 1828.
    ["Text is that of Everard Vander Hooght"; The 'English-
    Hebrew' is in Roman characters.]

    [The Deity is rendered "Jehovah" many times.]

    Second edition; corrected. London: Printed for John
    Taylor, 1831.

    Third edition; London: for Taylor & Walton, 1836.

    Fourth edition; London: 1843.

    Another Edition; London: Printed for Taylor,
    Walton & Maberly, 1848.

1828 **Nordheimer, Isaac**   A Grammatical Analysis of
Selections from the Hebrew Scriptures...
    [See Old Testament Selections for the complete entry.
    Includes Genesis I-XII.]

1829 **Anonymous**   The Life of Moses, the meekest man. New
York: Printed and Sold by Mahlon Day, [ca. 1829].
    [Paraphrase]

1830 **Anonymous**   A help to the Book of Genesis on the
lesson system of teaching; containing the text, with
explanations, forming a paraphrase, a catechetical
exercise, and practical lessons. Edinburgh: J.
Call, 1830.

Another Edition, 1831.

1832 **Thorpe, Benjamin**   Caedmon's Metrical Paraphrase...
[See Old Testament Selections for the complete entry. Includes Genesis.]

1836 **Bennett, Solomon**   ...Specimen of a New Version of the Hebrew Bible, translated from the original text, and comprising selected chapters...arranged in three Columns, viz., the AV, the New Version, and the Original Hebrew Text. By Solomon Bennett. London: the author, 1836.
[See F. Barham, The Hebrew and English Holy Bible, 1841.]

[Diglot edition; contains Genesis i-xli only.]

1841 **Barham, Francis**   The Hebrew and English Holy Bible ... The English Versions... Revised by the Late Solomon Bennett...Edited by Francis Barham. London: Printed for the Family of the Late Solomon Bennett, 1841.
[2 parts. Genesis 1-41:30 only were published.]

1844 **Anonymous**   A Paraphrase in Verse on the First, Second, and Third Chapters of Genesis; with a Poem to the Monsoon in India, a Dialogue [the dedication signed Scribbler], 1844.

1844 **DeSola, D.A., I.L. Lindenthal and Morris J. Raphall**
...The Sacred Scriptures in Hebrew and English. A new translation, with notes... Vol. 1   London: S. Bagster & Sons, 1844.
[Genesis only.]

1845 **Tregelles, Samuel Prideaux**   Hebrew Reading Lessons: consisting of the first four chapters of Genesis...
[See Old Testament Selections for the complete entry. Also includes Genesis XII.1-10, XXII.1-8.]

1847 **Anonymous**   The First Bible Reader; containing the history of the creation, the origin of sin, the death of Abel, the flood, the dispersion, the offering of Isaac, and the life of Joseph; with the words of the lessons previously arranged in columns, divided into syllables, and accented, and the pronunciation of the proper names given all to a new pronouncing alphabet. New Haven: 1847.
[Binder's title: James P. Hart.]

1847 **King, John**   Commentaries on the First Book of Moses called Genesis by John Calvin. Translated from the original Latin, and collated with the author's French version. 2 Vols. Edinburgh: Calvin Translation Society, 1847-1850.

[Text is KJV]

[See Bible Selections, 1844 Anonymous, Commentaries on the Books of the Bible.]

1852 **Jervis, John-Jarvis White**   Genesis Elucidated. A new translation, from the Hebrew compared with the Samaritan Text and The Septuagint and Syriac Versions, with Notes. By John Jervis-White Jervis... London: Samuel Bagster & Sons, 1852.
Another Edition; 1858.

1852 **Paul, William** Analysis and critical Interpretation of the Hebrew text of the Book of Genesis, preceded by a Hebrew Grammar, and dissertation on the Genuineness of the Pentateuch and on the structure of the Hebrew language, by William Paul. Edinburgh & London: William Blackwood & Sons, 1852.

1854 **Putnam, Catherine Hunt**   The Gospel of Moses, in the Book of Genesis; or, the Old Testament Unveiled. By C.H. Putnam.   New York: Edward H. Fletcher, 1854.

1855 **Heywood, James**   An Introduction to the Book of Genesis, with a Commentary on the Opening Portion, from the German of Peter von Bohlen. Edited by James Heywood. 2 Vols. London: John Chapman, 1855.
[The Commentary and Translation of Genesis i-xi:9 is extracted from Bohlen's "Die Genesis Historisch-kritisch Erlautert".]

1858 **Kalisch, Marcus Moritz**   A Historic and Critical Commentary on Genesis...
[See Pentateuch Selections, 1855 Marcus Moritz Kalisch, A Historic and Critical Commentary...]

1860 **Bosenquet, W.H.F.**   The Fall of Man; or, Paradise Lost, by Caedmon [Extracted from his Paraphrase of Genesis] translated in verse from the Anglo-Saxon, with a new Metrical Arrangement of the Lines of Part of the Original Text, and Introduction on the Versification of Caedmon, by W.H.F. Bosenquet. London: Longman and Co., 1860.

1861 **Pratt, H.F.A.**   The Genealogy of Creation, Newly Translated Unpointed Hebrew Text of the Book of Genesis, Showing the General Scientific Accuracy of the Cosmogony of Moses and the Philosophy of Creation, by H.F.A. Pratt. London: John Churchill, 1861.
[With the text of Genesis i-ii.4, and with an Appendix Containing Genesis ii.5-iii.]

1863 **Anonymous**   Cottage Readings in Genesis. London: Book Society, 1863.

[By the Author of 'Cottage Readings in Exodus'. A Paraphrase.]

A New Edition. London: S.W. Partridge & Co., 1880.

1863 **Murphy, James G.**   A Critical and Exegetical Commentary on the Book of Genesis, with a New Translation. Edinburgh: T. & T. Clark, 1863.
  The American Edition; with a preface by J.P. Thompson. Boston: Draper & Halliday, 1867, 1873, 1887.

1864 **Browne, Robert George Suckling**   The Mosaic Cosmogony; a Literal Translation of the First Chapter of Genesis, with Annotations and Rationalia, by R.G. Suckling Browne. London: n.p., 1864.

1865 **Anonymous**   The History of Joseph and His Brethren: Genesis Chapters XXXVII. XXXVIII. XL. London: Day & Son, 1865.
  [This work was possibly done by Owen Jones.]

1865 **Anonymous**   A literal translation of the Old Testament on definite rules of translation, from the text of the Vatican manuscript, Herman Heinfetter. [Frederick Parker] London: Evan Press, 1865.
  [Genesis only.]

  [Some believe that Herman Heinfetter is a pen name for F. Parker. Nothing is known about F. Parker/Herman Heinfetter.]

  Another edition; An English Version of the O.T. on definite rules..., 1865.

  Also; A collation of an English version of the O.T., from the text of the Vatican manuscript, with the authorized English version..., 1865.

1865 **Lewis, Evan**   God's Week of Work; being an Examination of the Mosaic Six Days...Together with an Exposition of Genesis Chap. i and Chap. ii., 1-4; and a new Translation, by Evan Lewis. London: F. Pitman, 1865.

1866 **American Bible Union**   The Book Of Genesis. The Common version revised for the American Bible Union, with explanatory and philological notes, by Thomas J. Conant. New York: American Bible Union, 1866-1868.
    1866 "The following sheets are printed as a specimen of the revised translation of Genesis..."

1868 ...with Explanatory Notes. New York: American Bible Union; London: Trubner & Co.

1868 **Delgado, Isaac**   Genesis, Leviticus, Numbers and Deuteronomy accompanied by a revised and corrected translation...
[See Old Testament Selections for the complete entry.]

1869 **Anonymous**   Joseph: the Hebrew Prince of Egypt. In Bible language. With nine illustrations. Philadelphia: Presbyterian Publishing Committee; New York: A.D.F. Randolph & Co., 1869.

1869 **Wright, Charles Henry Hamilton**   The Pentateuch; or, The five Books of Moses in the AV; with a critically revised translation, a collation of various readings translated into English, and of various translations; together with a critical and exegetical commentary... by Charles Henry Hamilton Wright. London: Williams and Norgate, 1869.
[A specimen, containing only Gen. i–iv.]

1873 **Tafel, Leonard, Rudolph L. Tafel and L.H. Tafel** Interlinear Translation of the Book of Genesis, with Grammatical and Critical Notes, by Leonard Tafel... Rudolph L. Tafel... L.H. Tafel... London & Leipzig: David Nutt, 1873.
[Hebrew and English.]

Another printing, 1873.

1876 **Sweet, Henry**   An Anglo-Saxon Reader. Oxford, 1876.
[Contains part of Genesis.]

9th. edition; Revised by C.T. Onions, 1922.

1878 **Garland, G.V.**   Genesis, with notes by G.V. Garland. London: Rivingtons, 1878.
[Hebrew and English]

1881 **Bartram, Richard**   Stories from the Book of Genesis, by Richard Bartram.   London: Sunday School Association, 1881.

1881 **Grote**   Genesis 1–11; an Essay on the Bible Narrative of Creation. 2nd Edition, Revised with Additions. New York: Asa K. Butts, 1881.
[Contains an Anglicized Hebrew text and the English version in parallel columns.]

1883 **Hershon, Paul Isaac**   The Pentateuch according to the Talmud. Genesis: with a Talmudical commentary... London: Bagster, 1883.
[Including an English rendering of much of Genesis.]

1883 **Warleigh, H.S.**   Genesis in Advance of Present
Science; a Critical Investigation of Chapters I to
IX, by a Septuagenarian Presbyter, H.S. Warleigh.
London: Kegan Paul, Trench, 1883.
>   Another edition; London: Simpkin, Marshall,
>   Hamilton, Kent; Worthing: Henry A. Foyster,
>   Royal Library, 1883.

>   [Paraphrase of Genesis 1-9.]

1884 **Hellmuth, J.**   Biblical Thesaurus; or a Literal
Translation and Critical Analysis of Every Word in
the Original Languages of the Old Testament.
London: Hodder & Stoughton, 1884.
>   [Genesis only.]

1884 **Sawyer, Leicester Ambrose**   (The Bible) Analyzed,
translated... Abraham, Genesis 12:1 - 25:11...
>   [See Bible Selections for the complete entry.]

1886 **Anonymous**   The Book of Genesis. A Translation
from the Hebrew, in which the constituent elements
of the text are separated, to which is added an
attempted restoration of the original documents used
by the latest reviser, by Francois
Lenormant...translated from the French with an
introduction and notes by the author of 'Mankind,
their origin and destiny'. [Arthur Dyot Thomson]
London: Longmans & Co., 1886.

1886 **Lenormant, Francis**   The Book of Genesis...by
Francis Lenormant. London: Longmans & Co., 1886.
>   [A translation from the French.]

1886 **Rae, R.R.**   A Plea for a Pure English Bible,
Freed from Felt Corruptions and Errors...by R.R.
Rae. London: Elliot Stock, 1886.
>   [A specimen translation of Genesis i-iv]

1888 **Taylor, Sophia**   A New Commentary on Genesis, by
Franz Delitzsch... Translated by Sophia Taylor. 2
Vols. Edinburgh: T. & T. Clark; New York: Scribner
& Welford, 1888-1889.
>   Another edition, 1899.

1889 **Younghusband, Francis**   The Story of Genesis; being
Part I of the Story of the Bible, told in Simple
Language for Children by Francis Younghusband.
London: Longmans, Green & Co., 189?

1890 **Rother, Fr.**   ...Revelation of Genesis. "The Lost
Ages". From Ethiopian manuscripts of an anonymous...
Translated from Amharic in English by Fr. Rother.
First Volume. Cambridge: Harvard Print Co., 1890.

1891 **Bright, James W.**   An Anglo-Saxon Reader. New York,
     1891.
          [Contains part of Genesis.]

          4th. edition; 1917.

1892 **Bacon, Benjamin Wisner**   The Genesis of Genesis; a
     Study of the Documentary Sources of the First Book
     of Moses in Accordance with the Results of Critical
     Science Illustrating the Presence of Bibles within
     the Bible   ..., by B.W. Bacon. London & Hartford:
     Student Publishing Co., 1892.
          ["A Few conjectural readings and ammendments...and in a
          small number of cases, a new translation suggested by
          the analysis, and an arrangement of the text in
          verses..." Part II is entitled, "The Text of Genesis in
          the RV, presented in varieties of type to exhibit the
          theory of documentary sources..." Also; ...with
          corrections, 1893.]

1892 **Bissell, Edwin Cone**   Genesis Printed in Colors;
     showing the Original Sources from which it is
     Supposed to have been Compiled, with an Introduction
     by Edwin Cone Bissell. Hartford: Belknap & Warfield,
     1892.

1893 **MacLean, G.E.**   An Old and Middle English Reader.
     New York, 1893.
          [Contains part of Genesis based on Zupitza.]

1896 **Wade, G. Woosung**   The Book of Genesis; Edited with
     Introduction, Critical Analysis and Notes... by G.
     Woosung Wade... With Two Maps. London, New York, &
     Bombay: Longmans, Green, and Co., 1896.
          ["The translation is based upon the AV, which has been
          adhered to as closely as the plan of the book would
          allow..." The Priestly and Jehovist accounts appear in
          parallel columns.]

          [The Deity is rendered "Jehovah" many times.]

1902 **Chainey, G.**   The Unsealed Bible; or, Revelation
     Revealed, Disclosing the Mysteries of Life and
     Death, by G. Chainey. London: Kegan Paul, 1902.
          [Vol. 1 was all that was published. Genesis.]

1904 **Driver, Samuel Rolles**   The Book of Genesis with
     introduction and notes, 1904.
          [Includes "...a careful paraphrase of the text..."]

          12th edition; enlarged. London: Macmillan & Co.,
          1926.

1906 **Pratt, H.B.**   Studies on the Book of Genesis...
     Translated from the Spanish by H.B. Pratt. Boston,
     New York, Chicago: American Tract Society, 1906.

1908 **Magil, Joseph**   Magil's Linear Abridged Bible
in the Original Language and Style of the Bible with
an English Translation in the new Linear System, by
Joseph Magil. [Genesis] Philadelphia: J.Magil, 1908.
> Another edition; Numerical Abridged Bible in the
> Original Language and Style of the Bible with
> an English Translation in the new Number
> System., by Joseph Magil. [Genesis]
> Philadelphia: J. Magil, 1908.

1909 **Williams, O.T.**   Short Extracts from Old English
Poetry...
> [See Old Testament Selections for the complete entry.
> Includes part of Genesis.]

1911 **Ramsay, F.P.**   An Interpretation of Genesis;
Including a Translation into Present-day English, by
F.P. Ramsay.   New York & Washington: The Neale
Publishing Co., 1911.
> ["...an interpretative translation, intended, as a part
> of the present interpretation of Genesis, to replace, in
> what is hoped a more readable form, a mass of critical
> and exegetical notes."]

1912 **Anonymous**   ...Genesis...Issued for the General
Conference of the New Church. London: James Speirs,
1912.
> [A new version prepared by Swedenborgians.]

1912 **Rutland, James R.**   Old Testament...use in secondary
schools...
> [See Old Testament Selections for the complete entry.
> Includes the chief episodes in Genesis.]

1913 **Anonymous**   Genesis as originally compiled...by the
author of 'God's Week of Creation'...
> [See Bible Selections, 1913 Anonymous, The Fourth
> Gospel...and Genesis.]

1913 **Hampdon-Cook, Ernest**   Joseph and His Brothers
in Modern Speech, translated from Hebrew by Ernest
Hampdon-Cook.   London: J. Clark and Co., 1913.

1913 **Klaeber, Fr.**   The Later Genesis and Other Old
English and Old Saxon Texts Relating to the Fall of
Man. Heidelberg: 1913.
> [Contains also Genesis A, pages 852-964, and the Old
> Saxon text of Genesis, pages 791-817.]

1915 **Mason, Lawrence**   Genesis A. Translated from the Old
English by Lawrence Mason. New York: H. Holt & Co.,
1915.
> [Yale Studies in English. No. 48.]

1916 **Kennedy, Charles W.** The Caedmon Poems Translated...

[See Old Testament Selections for the complete entry.
Includes Genesis.]

1916 **Robertson, Eric Sutherland**   The Bible's prose epic
of Eve and her sons; the "J" stories in Genesis, by
Eric S. Robertson... London: Williams & Norgate,
1916.

1917 **Landsberg, Max**   Genesis, 1917.
[See Old Testament, 1917 Jewish Publication Society.]

1919 **Wyatt, Alfred J.**   An Anglo-Saxon Reader. Cambridge,
1919.
[Contains part of Genesis.]

1921 **Cameron, Henry P.**   Genesis in Scots, with Glossary,
by Henry P. Cameron.   Paisley: Alexander Gardner,
1921.
[Biblical and Oriental Series.]

1921 **Maeder, J.D.**   The Story of Joseph, by J.D. Maeder;
being a Literal Translation of Genesis, Chapters 37,
39-50, Without Notes or Comment.   Kingwood, N.J.:
1921.

1922 **Anonymous**   The Book of Genesis. [Edited by Michael
Friedlander] New York: Bureau of Jewish Education,
1922.
["Friedlander Series of Juvenile Classics" It is not
known whether any more of this proposed series was
published. "...the text follows carefully the American
Jewish translation of the Bible published by the JPS.
(Actually there are numerous minor variations in
wording.) In abridging the text, lists of names and
genealogies have been omitted, together with passages
that either in content or in language are beyond the
grasp of a child's mind."]

1922 **Robinson, Theodore H.**   The Book of Genesis.
Translated into Colloquial English, by Theodore H.
Robinson.   London: National Adult Sunday School
Union, 1922.
[See Old Testament Selections, 1920 Books of the Old
Testament in Colloquial Speech.]

Revised, 1923.

1923 **Craige, W.A.**   Specimens of Anglo-Saxon Poetry...
[See Old Testament Selections for the complete entry.
Includes Part of Genesis.]

1924 **Bildersee, Adele**   The Story of Genesis, 1924.
[See Old Testament Selections, 1924 Anonymous, The Bible
Story in Bible Words.]

1925 **Fagnani, Charles Prospero**   The Beginnings
of History, According to the Jews; the First Eleven

Chapters of Genesis; A New Translation from a Revised Text with Notes, A Contribution to the Discussion of Fundamentalism, by Charles Prospero Fagnani... New York: Albert & Charles Boni, 1925.

1925 **Marshall, F.H.**   Old Testament legends from a Greek poem on Genesis and Exodus by Georgios Chumnos, edited, with introduction, metrical translation, notes and glossary, from a manuscript in the British Museum, by F.H. Marshall. Cambridge, England: The University Press, 1925.
[Paraphrases]

1925 **Waton, Harry**   The Bible; Genesis - Chapter I to IX..., translated and interpreted... (Typewritten MS), 1925.

1926 **Wyatt, Alfred J.**   The Threshold of Anglo-Saxon. New York, 1926.
[Contains part of Genesis.]

1927 **Gordan, Robert K.**   Anglo-Saxon Poetry...
[See Old Testament Selections for the complete entry. Includes part of Genesis.]

1927 **Turk, Milton H.**   An Anglo-Saxon Reader. New York, 1927.
[Contains part of Genesis.]

1928 **Lowe, James H.**   "Rashi" on the Pentateuch; Genesis, translated and annotated by James H. Lowe. London: The Hebrew Compendium Publishing Co., 1928.
["...the ONLY object...is and remains to supply the BEGINNER with as LITERAL a translation of Rashi as possible, so that he may follow the text word for word..."]

1929 **Krapp, George P. and Arthur G. Kennedy**   An Anglo-Saxon Reader. New York, 1929.
[Contains part of Genesis.]

1929 **Powys, Theodore Francis**   An Interpretation of Genesis, by Theodore Francis Powys. London: Chatto & Windus, 1929.
[An abridged, eccentric paraphrase, attributed to the "Lawgiver of Israel", interspersed with commentary attributed to "Zetetes". The deity is rendered "Truth".]

1934 **Anonymous**   Arcana Coelestia (The Heavenly Arcana) Which are Contained in the Holy Scriptures or Word of the Lord Disclosed from the Latin of Emanuel Swedenborg. London: Swedenborg Society, 1934-1949.
   1934 Vol.I.   Genesis, Chap I-VII   James R. Randell
   1936 Vol. II.   Genesis, Chap VIII-XII   L. Gilbey

1939 Vol. III. Genesis, Chap XIII-XVII   H.
               Goyder Smith
1949 Vol.IV.   Genesis, Chap XVIII-XX   P.H.
               Johnson

["...a pocket edition intended to run to 20 volumes...
owing to the 1939-45 war; this edition ceased with Vol.
IV and we decided not to continue..."]

1934 **Randell, James R.**   Genesis Chapters I-VII, 1934.
[See Anonymous, Arcana Coelestia (Vol. I), 1934.]

1936 **Gilbey, L.**   Genesis Chapters VIII-XII, 1936.
[See Anonymous, Arcana Coelestia (Vol. II), 1934.]

1937 **Widdowson, B.C.**   A New Presentation of the Bible...
[See Pentateuch Selections for the complete entry.
Includes Genesis.]

1938 **Marlowe, Alexander**   The Book of Beginnings; a
New Translation of the Book of Genesis with Special
Attention to its Poetic Values, by Alexander
Marlowe. Grand Rapids, Michigan: Wm. B. Eerdmans
Publishing Co., 1938.

1938 **Petersham, Maud (Fuller)**   Joseph and His Brothers;
from the story told in the Book of Genesis.
Philadelphia: Winston, 1930.
[Paraphrases.]

1939 **Smith, H. Goyder**   Genesis, Chap XIII-XVII, 1939.
[See Anonymous, Arcana Coelestia (Vol. I), 1934.]

1941 **Martin, William Wallace**   The Book of Genesis
Complete. The Ephramean Version, its Author a
Descendent of the Northern Kingdom; The Judean
Version, its Author a Descendent of the Southern
Kingdom. Reconstructed and Retranslated by William
Wallace Martin. Nashville: The Parthenon Press,
1941.

1942 **Leupold, Herbert Carl**   Exposition of Genesis,
with a New Translation, by H.C. Leupold. 3 Vols.
Columbus, Ohio: Wartburg Press, 1942.
Another edition; 2 Vols. Grand Rapids, Michigan:
Baker Book House, 1950, 1958.

1944 **Anonymous**   Genesis, the First Book of Moses.
Drawings by Saul Raskins. [New York: Academy Photo
Offset], 1944.
["English Translation revised by I.M.Rubin". Hebrew
text & translation in Parallel columns.]

1944 **Fillmore, Charles**   Mysteries of Genesis. Kansas
City, Mo: Unity School of Christianity, 1944.

1947 **Freedman, Harry**   Genesis, 1947.
   [See Old Testament, 1036 Soncino Books, The Chumash.]

1949 **Johnson, P.H.**   Genesis, Chapters XVIII-XX, 1949.
   [See Anonymous, Arcana Coelestia (Vol. IV.), 1934.]

1951 **Levene, A.**   The Early Syrian Fathers on Genesis,
   from a Syriac Manuscript on the Pentateuch in the
   Mingana Collection. London: Taylor's Foreign Press,
   1951.
   ["Dr. Levene prints a facsimile and offers a translation
   of the first eighteen chapters of a Nestorian ms..."]

1957 **Anonymous**   Concordant Literal Old Testament...
   [See Old Testament Selections for the complete entry.
   Includes Genesis.]

1958 **Jewish Publication Society**   The Book of Genesis
   of the Holy Scriptures, According to the Masoretic
   Text. Draft Version of the Revised Translation.
   Philadelphia: Jewish Publication Society, 1958.

1958 **Mueller, J. Theodore**   Commentary on Genesis
   [by Martin Luther]. A new translation by J.Theodore
   Mueller. 2 Vols. Grand Rapids, Michigan: Zondervan
   Publishing House, 1958.

1958 **Orlinsky, Harry M.**   Genesis, 1958, 1961.
   [See Jewish Publication Society, 1962.]

1958 **Pelikan, Janoslav** (Editor)   Lectures on Genesis,
   edited by Janoslav Pelikan. 8 Vols. Saint Louis:
   Concordia Publishing House, (Luther's Works... 54
   Vols.), 1958.
   ["in translating Luther's translations," the editors,
   where possible, have used "...an existing English
   version - KJV, Douay, or Revised Standard..." otherwise
   they have supplied their own translation.]

1959 **Fletcher, John C.**   Creation and Fall. A Theological
   Interpretation of Genesis 1-3. London: SCM Press,
   1959.
   [Translation of "Schopfung und Fall" by Dietrich
   Bonhoffer.]

1960 **Fish, Sidney Meshulam**   The Weekly Torah Reader...
   Parshet Hashavua. Book of Genesis... A survey of the
   Weekly Torah Readings, with Commentaries based on
   Rabbinic Sources and Selections from the Midrash.
   New York: Block Publishing Co., 1960.
   [A close paraphrase and commentary for students.]

1961 **Abrahams, Israel**   A Commentary on the Book of
   Genesis, by U. Cassuto...translated from the Hebrew
   by Israel Abrahams. 2 Vols. Jerusalem: Magnes Press,
   The Hebrew University, 1961-1964.

1961 ..Part I   From Adam to Noah: Genesis I-V
18.

1964 ..Part II   From Noah to Abraham: Genesis
V.19-XI 32; With an Appendix: A Fragment
of Part III.

["Generally...I have followed the rendering of the RSV
as the basis of my Bible translation, deviating from it
whenever required by Cassuto's interpretation."]

1961 **Custance, A.C.**   From Adam to Noah. Part 1. Ottawa:
1961.
[Genesis 1:1-25, Genesis 2: 1-4]

1962 **Blessing, Rev. William L.**   Blessing Version...
[See Bible Selections for the complete entry. Includes
the first four chapters of Genesis.]

1962 **Pamplin, Brain Randall**   A Draft for The Book of
Creation, by Brain Randall Pamplin... Durham City:
The Paperback, 1962.

1963 **Findlay, Ian F.**   Joseph in Egypt. Translated [from
'Joseph in Agypten' by Rudolph Otto Wiener]. London
& Gutersloh: Macmillan & Co., 1963.

1963 **Watts, J. Wash**   A Distinctive Translation of
Genesis by J. Wash Watts. Grand Rapids, Michigan:
William B. Eerdmans Publishing Co., 1963.
["An effort is made in this translation to reproduce
distinctive features of the Hebrew text not incorporated
in any existing translation."]

1964 **Renckens**   Israel's Concept of the Beginning; The
Theology of Genesis 1-3. New York: Herder & Herder,
1964.
[Contains his translation of Genesis 1-3.]

1964 **Speiser, Ephraim A.**   Genesis. Introduction,
Translation, and Notes by E.A. Speiser.   Garden
City, New York: Doubleday and Co., Inc., 1964.
[See Complete Bibles, 1964 Anchor Bible, Vol. 1.]

1966 **Jewish Publication Society**   Genesis; the N.J.V.
Translation. Introduction by Harry M. Orlinsky. New
York: Harper, 1966.
[Harper Torchbooks. The Temple Library. Revised version
of the First Book of the Torah, published in 1962 by the
Jewish Publication Society of America.]

[See Jewish Publication Society, A New Translation...,
1962.]

1966 **Moose, H.**   In the Beginning, [translated] by H.
Moose. New York: [Baruch Publishing Corp.], 1966.

[Genesis 1-11. "An astounding new translation-explanation of the Bible, revealing unsuspected levels of meaning..."]

1966 **Ross, Kenneth**   Genesis: Last Chapter. American Forests, August, 1966.
[Genesis 1:1-2:2]

1966 **Ryskind, Morrie**   How Double Talk Began, by Morrie Ryskind. Human Events Magazine, 6-11-66.
[Paraphrase of Genesis 11: 4-7]

1966 **Young, Edward J.**   Genesis 3, a Devotional and Expository Study, by Edward J. Young. London: Banner of truth trust, 1966.

1967 **Lindsay, Gordon**   The Rhyming Bible [i.e., Genesis]. By Gordon Lindsay. Dallas, Texas 75216: Christ for the Nations, 1967.
[Freely paraphrased doggerel.]

1971 **McEvenue, Sean E.**   The Narrative Style of the Priestly Writer. Sean E. McEvenue, S.J... Rome: Biblical Institute Press, 1971.

1972 **Richie, Dwight C.**   A Bride for Isaac. The Mount Zion Reporter, June, 1972.
[Poetical paraphrase of Genesis 24th chapter.]

1972 **Tubbs, Edward J.**   The Book of Genesis, for the use of Divinity students; history, prophecy and wisdom, samples of the Divine word, translated and transliterated from the Hebrew, by Edward J. Tubbs. Newport, England: Starling Press; Distributed by Miles Bullivant Associates, 1973.

1975 **Anonymous**   The story of creation: Genesis 1:1-2:4a Illustrated by Holly and Ivar Zapp. Plainfield, NJ: Logos International, 1975.

1976 **Aberbach, Moses and Bernard Grossfeld**   Targum Onqelos on Genesis 49. Translation and Commentary by Moses Aberbach and Bernard Grossfeld. Missoula, Montana: Published by Scholars Press for The Society of Biblical Literature, 1976.

1976 **Nutt, Ben**   Train Up a Child. Part 1. Genesis, paraphrased for children by Ben Nutt. Chicago: Adams Press, 1976.

1977 **Zlotowitz, Meir**   Genesis. Vol. 1, 1977.
[See Old Testament, 1976 ArtScroll Tanach Series.]

1978 **Zlotowitz, Meir**   Genesis. Vol. 2, 1978.
[See Old Testament, 1976 ArtScroll Tanach Series.]

1982 **Aberbach, Moses and Bernard Grossfeld**   Targum
Onkelos to Genesis. A critical Analysis Together
With An English Translation of the Text (Based on A.
Sperber's Edition) by Moses Aberbach and Bernard
Grossfeld. KTAV Publishing House Inc. Center for
Judaic Studies, University of Denver, 1982.

1983 **Fox, Everett**   In the Beginning: A New English
Rendition of the Book of Genesis. Translated with
Commentary and Notes by Everett Fox. New York:
Schocken Books, 1983.
      [The Deity is rendered "YHWH" many times.]

1983 **Graves, Robert and Raphael Patai**   Hebrew Myths:
The Book of Genesis. Robert Graves and Raphael
Patai. New York: Greenwich House, Distributed by
Crown Publishers, Inc., 1983.

1983 **Rand, Harry**   The Beginning of Things. Translations
by Harry Rand. Watercolors by Mindy Weisel.
Washington, D.C. & San Francisco: Dryad Press, 1983.

1987 **Wenham, Gordan J.**   Word Biblical Commentary.
Genesis. 2 Vols. Gordan J. Wenham. Waco, Tx: Word
Books, Publishers, 1987.
      [See Complete Bibles, 1982 Word Biblical Commentary,
      Vol.1 & 2.]

1987 **Friedman, Richard Elliott**   Who Wrote the Bible?
Richard Elliott Friedman. N.Y.: Summit Books, 1987.
      [Contains his own translation (Genesis 6:5-8:22).]

1988 **Grossfeld, Bernard**   Genesis, 1988.
      [See Old Testament, 1987 Aramaic Bible, Vol. 6.]

1990 **Hamilton, Victor P.**   The Book of Genesis: Chapters
1-17, 1990.
      [See Hebrew Scriptures listings, 1976 New International
      Commentary on the O.T.]

1990 **Rosenberg, David**   The Book of J...
      [See Pentateuch Selections for the complete entry.]

GENESIS AND EXODUS

???? **Anonymous**   The Middle English Genesis and
Exodus. [Ms. C.C.C.C.444] [12??].
          ...re-edited from Ms. C.C.C.C.444 with
          Introduction, Notes and Glossary by Olof
          Arngart. (Lund Studies in English, 36) Lund,
          Sweden: Gleerup, 1968.

???? **Anonymous**   Arcana Coelestia – – The Heavenly
Arcana contained in the Holy Scriptures, or word of
the Lord. Unfolded in an exposition of Genesis and
Exodus...from the Latin of Emanuel Swedenborg. [A.H.
Searle] 12 Vols.   London: The Swedenborg Society,
[188?].
>   Another edition, 1903.

???? **Mills, Samuel and Others**   Arcana Coelestia...
Rotch Edition. 19 Vols. Boston: New Union Church;
New York: New Church Board of Publications, [189?].
>   [The translators of this work were: Samuel Howard
>   Worchester, Samuel C. Eby, A.L. Kip, Theodore F. Wright
>   and Horace W. Wright.]

1250 **Anonymous**   The Story of Genesis and Exodus. [Ms.]
c1250.
>   ...an early English song about A.D. 1250. Now
>   first edited from a unique MS. in the Library
>   of Corpus Christi College, Cambridge, by
>   Richard Morris.   London: Published for the
>   Early English Text Society, by Trubner & Co.,
>   1865.

1662 **Hughes, Obadiah** (Editor)   An Analytical
Exposition of the Whole first Book of Moses. Called
Genesis, and of XXIII Chapter of his Second Book,
called Exodus. Wherein, the various Readings are
observed,   the   Original   Text   explained,   doubts
resolved, Scriptures parallelled, the Scripture
Chronology from the Creation of the World to the
giving of the Law at Mount Sinai cleared, and the
whole illustrated by Doctrines collected from the
Text. Delivered in a Morning Exercise on the Lord's
Day. [Edited by Obadiah Hughes, the Elder] Printed
Anno Domini M.DC.LXXII (1662)
>   [Colophons indicate that Genesis was finished in 1659,
>   and Exodus in 1662. Translation appears to be based upon
>   Ainsworth, 1616.]

1783 **Anonymous**   Arcana Coelestia; or, Heavenly Mysteries
Contained in the sacred Scriptures, or Word of the
Lord, manifested and laid open... Now translated
from theoriginal Latin of Emanuel Swedenborg by a
Society of Gentlemen... [John Clowes] 13 Vols.
London: R. Hindmarsh, 1783–
>   Reprinted; London: J.& E. Hodson, 1802-1816.

>   Also; Arcana Coelestia; or, Heavenly Mysteries
>   Contained in the sacred Scriptures, or Word of
>   the Lord, Unfolded, in an exposition of
>   Genesis and Exodus:...by Emanuel Swedenborg.
>   Being a translation of his work... In Twelve
>   Vols.   London: Published by the Swedenborg
>   Society, 1861.

Another edition; Revised by J.R. Rendell. London:
Swedenborg Society, 187?-188?

1837 **Anonymous**   Arcana Coelestia...First American
Edition (Revised). 12 Vols. Boston: 1837-1847.
[Genesis and Exodus with a commentary. Vol.1-4, Boston
Printing Society. Remainder, Otis Clapp, for the
Proprietors.]

1849 **Klipstein, Louis F.**   Analecta Anglo-Saxonia. Vol.
II. New York, 1849.
[Contains Genesis and Exodus.]

1857 **Harrison, George**   Arcana Coelestia. 12 Vols.
London: Longmans, Green & Co., 1857.
[Genesis and Exodus, with the commentary of Emanuel
Swedenborg.]

        [- - Vol 11 retranslated by Rudolph Tafel. London:
        1890.]

1861 **Warren**   Arcana Coelestia by Warren. 10 Vols.
London: Swedenborg Society, 1861-
[Genesis and Exodus, with the commentary of Emanuel
Swedenborg.]

1865 **Morris, Richard**   See Anonymous, The Story of
Genesis & Exodus, 1250.

1870 **March, Francis A.**   Introduction to Anglo-Saxon. An
Anglo-Saxon Reader, with Philological Notes, a Brief
Grammer, and a Vocabulary. NY, 1870.
[Contains part of Genesis and Exodus.]

1872 **Alford, Henry**   The Book of Genesis, and Part of
the Book of Exodus; a Revised Version, with Marginal
References, and an Explanatory Commentary, by Henry
Alford. London: Strahan and Co., 1872.
Another edition, 1874

1875 **Carpenter, Stephen H.**   An Introduction to the Study
of the Anglo-Saxon Language. Boston, 1875.
[Contains part of Genesis and Exodus.]

1896 **Berry, George Ricker**   The Interlinear Literal
Translation of the Hebrew Old Testament, with the
King James Version and the Revised Version
Conveniently Placed in the Margins for Ready
Reference and with Explanatory Textual Footnotes
Supplemented by Tables of the Hebrew Verb, and the
Hebrew Alphabet. By George Ricker Berry... Genesis
and Exodus. Harrisburg, Pa: Handy Book Corporation,
1896.
        [No more published.]

        [The Deity is rendered "Jehovah" many times.]

Other editions; New York: Hinds & Noble, 1897; Chicago: Wilcox & Follett, 1943, 1946, 1951 and 1959; Grand Rapids: Kregel Reprint Library, 1970.

1902 **Cook, Albert Stanburrough and Chauncey B. Tinker**
Select Translations from Old English Poetry. Boston, 1902.
[Contains part of Genesis and Exodus.]

1905 **Potts, John Faulkner**   Arcana Coelestia, the Heavenly Arcana contained in the Holy Scriptures, or Word of the Lord Unfolded beginning with the Book of Genesis together with wonderful things seen in the world of the spirits and in the heaven of angels; translated from the Latin of Emanual Swedenborg, thoroughly revised and edited by the Rev. John Faulkner Potts. (XII Vols.) New York: American Swedenborg Printing & Publication Society, 1905-1910.
[Genesis and Exodus with a commentary.]

1909 **Kent, Charles Foster and Eugene H. Lehman**
The Junior Bible for the Jewish School and Home... Prepared by Prof. Charles F. Kent, Ph.D... Eugene H. Lehman, M.A... Published by arrangement with Charles Scribner's Sons, New York. New York: Bloch Publishing Co. "The Jewish Book Concern", 1909.
1909 - - Part I, From Abraham to Moses; Nos. 1-19

[Selections from Genesis and Exodus in a new translation; unknown if more was published.]

1921 **Spaeth, J. Duncan** Old English Poetry. Translations into Alliterative Verse, with Introductions and Notes. Princeton, 1921.
[Contains Genesis (with slight omissions) and Exodus.]

1948 **Goldman, Solomon**   The Book of Human Destiny: 1948-1958.
1948 1.   The Book of Books: An Introduction. New York: Harper & Bros.

1949 2.   In the Beginning. New York: Harper & Bros.
["Chapter two consists of selections from (Genesis) in a translation based on the Hebrew text and several ancient, medieval, and modern versions."]

1958 3.   From Slavery to Freedom. (Edited by Harry Orlinsky) London & New York: Abelard-Schuman; published in behalf

of the Solomon Goldman Memorial
Foundation.
[Selections from Exodus]

1958 **Orlinsky, Harry M.**   (Editor)   See Solomon Goldman,
The Book of Human Destiny, 1948.

1968 **Anonymous**   See Anonymous, The Middle English
Genesis and Exodus, 12??.

EXODUS

???? **King James I**   His version of 26 Psalms, the Lord's
Prayer and the Song of Moses...
[See Bible Selections for the complete entry.]

???? **Milman, W.H.**   Miriam's song of triumph; soprano
solo and chorus, with piano accompaniment. English
version from the German of Grillparzer and Exodus,
chapter XV, by W.H. Milman. n.p.: n.p., n.d.
[Exodus selections]

???? **O'Connell, Kevin G.**   Exodus. A New Translation with
Introduction and Commentary by Kevin G. O'Connell.
Garden City, New York: Doubleday & Co., Inc.,
[19??].
[See Complete Bibles, 1964 Anchor Bible, Vol. 2.]

???? **Younghusband, Francis**   The Story of Exodus,
told in Simple Language for Children by Francis
Younghusband. London: Longmans, Green & Co., [189?].

670 **Caedmon**   Songs sung by an illiterate...
[See Bible Selections for the complete entry. Includes
songs from Exodus.]

1534 **Joye, George**   Jeremy the Prophete, translated...
[See Old Testament Selections for the complete entry.
Includes the Song of Moses.]

1617 **Ainsworth, Henry**   Exodus Translated. Amsterdam:
G. Thorp, 1617.
Second edition, 1621.

1621 **Ainsworth, Henry**   Annotations upon the First
(second) Book of Moses, Called Genesis (Exodus).
Amsterdam: 1621-1622.

1662 **Hughes, George**   An Analytical Exposition... XXIII
Chapter of his Second Book, called Exodus...

[See Pentateuch Selections for the complete entry.]

1685 **Cleeve, C.**   The Songs of Moses and Deborah...
        [See Bible Selections for the complete entry.]

1699 **Lesly, George**   Israel's Troubles and Triumph; or,
        The History of Their Dangers and Deliverance out of
        Egypt, as it is Recorded...in Exodus and Turned into
        English Verse. London: N. Wolf, 1699.

1727 **Pitt, Christopher**   Job 3 and 25...Song of Moses...
        [See Old Testament Selections for the complete entry.]

1740 **Anonymous**   The Song of Moses, Exodus, Chapter 15;
        Paraphrased in Verse. Gentleman's Magazine, Vol.x,
        Page 566, 1740.

1784 **Hopkins, William**   Exodus, a corrected Translation
        with Notes, Critical and Explanatory. By William
        Hopkins. London: J. Johnson, 1784.
                ["...where it could be done with propriety, (or where
                the readings of the Samaritan copy would permit it)," he
                has adopted "the English vulgar translation..." Cotton
                dates it 1782.]

1787 **Kennicott, B.**   Exodus 11,15...
        [See Old Testament Selections for the complete entry.]

1793 **Hill, Aaron**   Habakkuk 3, Part of Psalm 14;
        Matthew 6; Song of Moses...
        [See Bible Selections for the complete entry.]

1826 **Conybeare, John J.**   Illustrations of Anglo-Saxon
        Poetry...
                [See Old Testament Selections for the complete entry.
                Includes Exodus.]

1832 **Thorpe, Benjamin**   Caedmon's Metrical Paraphrase...
                [See Old Testament Selections for the complete
                entry. Includes Exodus.]

1838 **Jackson, Thomas**   Paraphrase on the Eleven First
        Chapters of Exodus...
                [See Old Testament Selections for the complete entry.]

1855 **Kalisch, Marcus Moritz**   Exodus, 1855.
                [See Pentateuch Selections, 1855 Marcus Moritz Kalisch,
                A Historical and Critical Commentary...]

1866 **Murphy, James G.**   A Critical and Exegetical
        Commentary on the Book of Exodus. With a New
        Translation. By James G. Murphy. Edinburgh: T. & T.
        Clark; London: Hamilton Adams & Co.; Dublin: J.
        Robertson; Belfast: C. Aitchison, 1866.
                ["...designed to be a mere revision of the AV."]

Other editions; Andover: W.F. Draper; Boston:
W.H. Halliday..., 1868; Boston: Estes &
Lauriat, 1874; Andover: Warren F. Draper,
1881; New York: I.K. Funk & Co., n.d.

1867 **Anonymous**   Cottage Readings in Exodus, by the
author of 'Cottage Readings in Genesis.' London: J.
Nisbet & Co., 1867.
       [A paraphrase. See Anonymous, Cottage...Genesis, 1863.]

       Another Edition; Cottage Readings in Exodus.
London: S.W. Partridge & Co., 1880.

1874 **Proby, W.H.B.**   The Ten Canticles of the O.T...
       [See Old Testament Selections for the complete entry.
       Includes the Song of Moses.]

1883 **Hunt, Theodore W.**   Caedmon's Exodus and...
       [See Old Testament Selections for the complete entry.]

1894 **Bacon, Benjamin Wisner**   The Triple Tradition of
the Exodus. A Study of the Structure of the Latter
Pentateuchal Books, Reproducing the Sources of the
Narrative, and further illustrating the presence of
Bibles within the Bible. Benjamin Wisner Bacon.
Hartford: The Student Publishing Co., 1894.

1903 **Johnson, William S.**   Translation of the
Old English Exodus. Journal of English and Germanic
Philology, Vol. 44-57, 1903.

1903 **Schlesinger, Jos.**   The Five Books of Moses with
the Haphtaroth, and Prayers for Sabbath. Exodus.
Vienna: Published by Jos. Schlesinger, 1903.

1907 **Blackburn, Francis A.**   Exodus and Daniel...
       [See Old Testament Selections for the complete entry.]

1909 **Williams, O.T.**   Short Extracts from... Poetry...
       [See Old Testament Selections for the complete entry.
       Includes part of Exodus.]

1912 **Gordon, Alexander R.**   The Poets...Old Testament...
       [See Old Testament Selections for the complete entry.
       Includes the Song of Moses.]

1912 **Rutland, James R.**   Old Testament; edited for use
in schools...
       [See Old Testament Selections for the complete entry.
       Includes the chief episodes in Genesis, Exodus.]

1916 **Kennedy, Charles W.**   The Caedmon Poems Translated
into English Prose...
       [See Old Testament Selections for the complete entry.
       Includes Exodus.]

1917 **Dembitz, L.N.**   Exodus and Leviticus, 1917.
      [See Old Testament, 1917 Jewish Publication Society, The
      Holy Scriptures.]

1922 **Sedgefield, W.J.**   An Anglo-Saxon Verse Book.
      Manchester, 1922.
      [Contains part of Exodus.]

1923 **Craige, W.A.**   Specimens of Anglo-Saxon Poetry...
      [See Old Testament Selections for the complete entry.
      Includes part of Exodus.]

1927 **Gordan, Robert K.**   Anglo-Saxon Poetry...
      [See Old Testament Selections for the complete entry.
      Includes part of Exodus.]

1927 **Grimmelsman, Henry J.**   The Book of Exodus; A Study
      of the Second Book of Moses with Translation and
      Concise Commentary. Rev. Henry J. Grimmelsman.
      Norwood, Cincinnati, Ohio: The Seminary Book Store,
      1927.

1937 **Widdowson, B.C.**   A New Presentation of the Bible...
      [See Pentateuch Selections for the complete entry.
      Includes Exodus.]

1938 **Oesterley, William Oscar Emil**   Ancient... Poems...
      [See Old Testament Selections for the complete entry.
      Includes Exodus 15:1-18.]

1947 **Rabbinowitz, J.**   Exodus, 1947.
      [See Old Testaments, 1936 Soncino Books, The Chumash.]

1962 **Bowden, J.S.**   Exodus, 1962.
      [See Old Testament Selections, 1962 O.T. Library.]

1964 **Cross, Frank Moore, Jr.**   Exodus. Introduction,
      Translation, and Notes by Frank Moore Cross. Garden
      City, New York: Doubleday &. Co., 1964.
      [See Complete Bibles, 1964 Anchor Bible, Vol. 2.]

1967 **Abrahams, Israel**   A Commentary on the Book
      of Exodus by Umberto Cassuto. Translated from the
      Hebrew by Israel Abrahams. Jerusalem: Magnes Press,
      1967.

1975 **Anonymous**   Exodus "Let My People Go". Exodus
      in Today's English version. New York: American Bible
      Society, 1975.

1977 **Owens, John Joseph**   Analytical Key to the Old
      Testament. Exodus. John Joseph Owens. Published in
      San Francisco by Harper & Row, Publishers, 1977.
      [The Deity is rendered "Yahweh" many times.]

1977 **Watts, J. Wash**   A Distinctive Translation
of Exodus with an interpretative outline by J. Wash
Watts.   South Pasadena, California: Jameson Press,
1977.

1987 **Durham, John I.**   Word Biblical Commentary. Exodus.
John I. Durham.   Waco, TX: Word Books, Publisher,
1987.
    [See Complete Bibles, 1982 Word Biblical Commentary,
    Vol. 3.]

1988 **Grossfeld, Bernard**   Exodus, 1988.
    [See Complete Bibles, 1987 Aramaic Bible, Vol. 7.]

1990 **Rosenberg, David**   The Book of J; Translated from
the Hebrew...
    [See Pentateuch Selections for the complete entry.]

LEVITICUS

???? **Hartley, John E.**   Word Biblical Commentary.
Leviticus.   Waco, Tx: Word Books, Publishers,
[198?].
    [See Complete Bibles, 1982 Word Biblical Commentary,
    Vol. 4.]

???? **Milgrom, Jacob**   Leviticus; Introduction,
Translation, and Notes, by Jacob Milgrom.   Garden
City, New York: Doubleday & Co., [19??].
    [See Complete Bibles, 1964 Anchor Bible, Vol. 3.]

1618 **Ainsworth, Henry**   Leviticus Translated. Amsterdam:
G. Thorp, 1618.

1872 **Murphy, James G.**   A Critical and Exegetical
Commentary on the Book of Leviticus, with a New
Translation. Andover: W.F. Draper, 1872.
    Another Edition;   London: Trubner & Co.;
    Edinburgh: T. & T. Clark; Dublin: John
    Robinson, 1872.

    Also; Andover: W.F. Draper, 1874.

1898 **Driver, Samuel Rolles**   The Book of Leviticus,
a new English Translation Printed in Colors
Exhibiting the Composite Structure of the Book, with
Explanatory Notes and Pictorial Illustrations, by
S.R. Driver. New York: Dodd, Mead, and Co., 1898.
    [See Old Testament Selections, 1898 Sacred Books of the
    Old and New Testaments, Part 3. The Polychrome Bible.]

1947 **Lehrman, S.M.**   Leviticus, 1947.
      [See Old Testaments, 1936 Soncino Books, The Chumash.]

1965 **Anderson, J.E.**   Leviticus, 1965.
      [See Old Testament Selections, 1962 O.T. Library.]

1979 **Wenham, Gordon J.**   The Book of Leviticus, 1979.
      Reprinted; 1981.

      [See Hebrew Scriptures listings, 1976 New International
      Commentary on the O.T.]

1988 **Grossfeld, Bernard**   Leviticus & Numbers, 1988.
      [See Old Testaments, 1987 Aramaic Bible, Vol. 8.]

NUMBERS

???? **Levine, Baruch A.**   Numbers. A New Translation
      with Introduction and Commentary by Baruch A. Levine.
      Garden City, New York: Doubleday & Co., Inc.,
      [19??].
      [See Complete Bibles, 1964 Anchor Bible, Vol. 4.]

???? **Mendenhall, George E.**   Numbers; Introduction,
      Translation, and Notes, by George J. Mendenhall.
      Garden City, New York: Doubleday & Co., [19??].
      [See Complete Bibles, 1964 Anchor Bible, Vol. 4.]

1550 **Bale, John**   Numbers, Chapter 30, with Exposition.
      London: John Daye, 1550.

1619 **Ainsworth, Henry**   Numbers and Deuteronomy
      Translated...
      [See Pentateuch Selections for the complete entry.]

1787 **Kennicott, B.**   Exodus 11,15... Numbers 21...
      [See Old Testament Selections for the complete entry.]

1868 **Delgado, Isaac**   Genesis, Leviticus, Numbers and
      Deuteronomy...revised and corrected translation...
      [See Old Testament Selections for the complete entry.]

1912 **Gray, George Buchanan**   A Critical and Exegetical
      Commentary on Numbers by George Buchanan Gray...
      Edinburgh: T. & T. Clark, 1912.
      [See International Critical Commentary (Numbers), 1895.]

1917 **Philipson, David**   Numbers, 1917.
      [See Old Testaments, 1917 Jewish Publication Society.]

1937 **Widdowson, B.C.**   A New Presentation of the Bible...
      [See Pentateuch Selections for the complete entry.
      Includes Numbers I-XII.]

MACK LIBRARY
BOB JONES UNIVERSITY
GREENVILLE, SC

1947 **Fisch, S.**   Numbers and Deuteronomy, 1947.
     [See Old Testaments, 1936 Soncino Books of the Bible,
     The Chumash.]

1968 **Old Testament Library**   Numbers, 1968.
     [See Old Testament Selections for the complete entry.]

1984 **Budd, Philip J.**   Word Biblical Commentary. Numbers.
     Philip J. Budd.   Waco, TX: Word Books, Publisher,
     1984.
     [See Complete Bibles, 1982 Word Biblical Commentary,
     Vol. 5.]

1990 **Rosenberg, David**   The Book of J...
     [See Pentateuch Selections for the complete entry.]

DEUTERONOMY

???? **Christensen, Duane L.**   Word Biblical Commentary.
     Deuteronomy. Duane L. Christensen.   Waco, Tx: Word
     Books, Publishers, [198?].
     [See Complete Bibles, 1982 Word Biblical Commentary,
     Vol. 6.]

???? **McBride, Jr., S. Dean**   Deuteronomy; Introduction,
     Translation, and Notes, by S. Dean McBride, Jr.
     Garden City, New York: Doubleday & Co., [19??].
     [See Complete Bibles, 1964 Anchor Bible, Vol. 5.]

???? **Stalker, David**   Studies in Biblical Theology
     No. 9. Studies in Deuteronomy by Gerhard Von Rad.
     London: S.C.M. Press Ltd., [195?].

???? **Weinfeld, Moshe**   Deuteronomy. A New Translation
     with Introduction and Commentary by Moshe Weinfeld.
     Garden City, New York: Doubleday & Co., Inc.,
     [19??].
     [See Complete Bibles, 1964 Anchor Bible, Vol. 5.]

1583 **Golding, Arthur**   The sermons of J. Calvin upon
     Deuteronomie, 1583.

1619 **Ainsworth, Henry**   Numbers and Deuteronomy...
     [See Pentateuch Selections for the complete entry.]

1723 **Lindsay, John**   A Paraphrase on the XXVIII. Chapter
     of Deuteronomy.   Chester: W. Cooke, 1723.
     [In Verse.]

1787 **Kennicott, B.**   Exodus 11,15; Deuteronomy 32...

[See Old Testament Selections for the complete entry.]

1811 **Oxoniensis**   Deuteronomy 32 and 33, literally
translated. Gentleman's Magazine, 1811.

1828 **Nordheimer, Isaac**   A Grammatical Analysis of
Selections from the Hebrew Scriptures...
[See Old Testament Selections for the complete entry.
Includes Deuteronomy I-III.]

1845 **Tregelles, Samuel Prideaux**   Hebrew Reading
Lessons...
[See Old Testament Selections for the complete entry.
Includes Deuteronomy IX.25-X.5.]

1868 **Delgado, Isaac**   Genesis, Leviticus, Numbers and
Deuteronomy accompanied by a revised...
[See Old Testament Selections for the complete entry.]

1899 **Girdlestone, R.B.**   The Student's Deuteronomy. A
Corrected Translation with Notes and with References
in Full to the Preceding and Later Books, by R.B.
Girdlestone. London: Eyre & Spottiswoode, 1899.

1900 **Martin, William Wallace**   The Tora of Moses; Being
a Critical Study of Deuteronomy: Its Separation into
Two Copies of the Tora; a Refutation of Higher
Criticism, by William Wallace Martin.   Nashville,
Tenn. & Dallas, Texas: Publishing House of the M.E.
Church, South; Barbee & Smith, Agents, 1900.
["I have followed as closely as possible the AV."]

1902 **Driver, Samuel Rolles**   A Critical and Exegetical
Commentary on Deuteronomy. By Rev. S.R. Driver...
Edinburgh: T. & T. Clark, 1895.
[See Complete Bibles, 1895 International Critical
Commentary (Deuteronomy).]

Second Edition, 1896.

Third Edition, 1902.

Reprinted; 1908, 1925.

1912 **Wiener, Harold M.**   Pentateuchal Studies by Harold
M. Wiener...Oberlin, OH: Biblotheca Sacra Co., 1912.
[Contains a probable text of the LXX for Deu. 17:14-20.]

1917 **Sola Mendes, F. de**   Deuteronomy, 1917.
[See Old Testaments, 1917 Jewish Publication Society.]

1932 **Cadoux, Cecil John**   The Book of Deuteronomy,
translated into Colloquial English, by Cecil John
Cadoux. London: National Adult School Union, 1932.
[See Old Testament Selections, 1920 Books of the Old
Testament in Colloquial Speech.]

1938 **Oesterley, William Oscar Emil**   Ancient... Poems...
      [See Old Testament Selections for the complete entry.
      Includes Deuteronomy 32:1-43 and 33:2-29.]

1947 **Fisch, S.**   Numbers and Deuteronomy, 1947.
      [See Old Testaments, 1936 Soncino Books of the Bible,
      The Chumash.]

1966 **Barton, Dorothea**   Deuteronomy, 1966.
      [See Old Testament Selections, 1962 O.T. Library.]

1976 **Craigie, Peter C.**   The Book of Deuteronomy by Peter
      C. Craigie... [Grand Rapids:] William B. Eerdmans
      Publishing Co., 1976.
        ["The translation is neither absolutely literal nor
        particularly literary..."]

        [See Hebrew Scriptures listings, 1976 New International
        Commentary on the O.T.]

1988 **Grossfeld, Bernard**   Deuteronomy, 1988.
      [See Old Testaments, 1987 Aramaic Bible, Vol. 9.]

1990 **Rosenberg, David**   The Book of J...
      [See Pentateuch Selections for the complete entry.]

DECALOGUE

???? **Anonymous**   The Ten Commandments... Revised by the
      Committee of Publication of the American Sunday-
      School Union. Philadelphia: American Sunday-School
      Union, [183?].

1836 **Anonymous**   Book of Public Worship...
      [See Bible Selections for the complete entry. Includes
      the Ten Commandments.]

1981 **Feuer, Avrohom Chaim**   The ArtScroll Mesorah
      Series. Expositions on Jewish liturgy and thought.
      Rabbis Nosson Scherman / Meir Zlotowitz General
      Editors. Aseres Hadibros. The Ten Commandments/A New
      Translation with a Commentary Anthologized from
      Talmudic, Midrashic, and Rabbinic Sources.
      Translation by Rabbi Avrohom Chaim Feuer. An
      Overview / "Prelude to Sinai," by Rabbi Nosson
      Scherman. Published by Mesorah Publications, Ltd.,
      1981.

4

Historical Books

HISTORICAL BOOKS AND SELECTIONS

1568 **Davies, Richard**   Joshua, Judges, Ruth, 1568.
    [See Complete Bibles, 1568 Bishops' Bible.]

1579 **Marbeck, Ihon**   The Holie Historie of King
Dauid, Wherein is chieflye Learned These Godly and
Wholsome Lessons, that is: to haue sure Patience in
Persecution, due Obedience to our Prince Without
Rebellion; and also the True and Most Faithfull
Dealings of Friends. Drawne into English Meetre for
the Youth to Reade by Ihon Marbeck.   At London:
Printed by Henrie Middleton, for Ihon Harison, 1579.
    [Cotton lists as 1578.]

    [A Paraphrase of Passages from I and II Samuel and I
Kings.]

1770 **Tans'ur, William**   The Life of Holy David, King of
Israel, in forty five poetical Cantos, Concordant to
the Holy Scriptures &c.   Cambridge: Printed by J.
Archdeacon, 1770.

1865 **Martin, James**   Joshua, Judges, Ruth, 1865.
    [See Old Testaments, 1865 Biblical Commentary.]

1878 **American Bible Union**   The Books of Joshua, Judges,
Ruth. The Common Version revised for the American
Bible Union. [Thomas J. Conant]   New York: American
Bible Union, 1878.

1884 **American Bible Union**   The Books of Joshua, Judges,
Ruth, 1 and 2 Samuel, 1 and 2 Kings. The Common
Version revised with an Introduction and Occasional
Notes. [Thomas J. Conant] Philadelphia: American
Baptist Publication Co., 1884.

1888 **Moses, Adolph and Isaac S. Moses**   The Historical
Books of the Bible. School and Family Edition.
Cincinnati & Chicago: The Bloch Publishing and
Printing Co., 1888.

1895 **Hill, Henry**   The Story of the Kings of Israel and
Judah. A compilation of Bible narratives arranged
consecutively. London: Elliot Stock, 1895.
   [The wording of the revised version has been generally
   adopted.]

1950 **Cohen, Abraham** (Editor) Joshua and Judges. Hebrew
Text & English Translation with an Introduction and
Commentary by The Rev. Dr. A. Cohen... London: The
Soncino Press, 1950.
   [See Old Testament listings, 1936 The Soncino Books of
   the Bible.]

1954 **Torrey, Charles Cutler**   The Chronicler's History
of Israel; Chronicles-Ezra-Nehemiah Restored to its
Original Form by Charles Cutler Torrey. New Haven:
Yale University Press; London: Oxford University
Press, Geoffrey Cumberledge, 1954.

1957 **Pfeiffer, Robert H.**   The Hebrew Iliad; The History
of the Rise of Israel Under Saul and David. Written
during the reign of Solomon Probably by the Priest
Ahimaaz. Translated from the original Hebrew by
Robert H. Pfeiffer. With general and chapter
introductions by William G. Pollard. New York:
Harper & Bros., 1957.
   [The text in the two appendices consists of edited
   selections from the AV of Judges – Kings, although the
   Song of Deborah is further edited "...in a rather free
   translation of my own..."]

1982 **Fensham, F. Charles** The Books of Ezra and Nehemiah,
1982.
   [See Hebrew Scriptures Listing, 1982 New International
   commentary on the O.T.]

JOSHUA

???? **Judaica Press Publications**   The Judaica Books of
the Prophets... Joshua...
   [See Old Testament Selections for the complete entry.]

1578 **Anonymous**   A Commentarie of M. Iohn Caluine, vpon
the Booke of Iosue, finished a little before his
death: Translated out of the Latine into Englishe by
W.F. Wherevnto is added a table of principall

matters. [William Fulke?]   Imprinted at London, [by Thomas Dawson] for George Bishop, 1578.

1623 **Anonymous**   Saxon-English Remains... Joshua...
    [See Old Testament Selections for the complete entry.]

1685 **Cleeve, C.**   The Songs of Moses and Deborah...
    [See Bible Selections for the complete entry.]

1724 **Anonymous**   A Paraphrase on Part of the Book of Joshua, in Three Canto's, by J.M., S.T.C.D. Dubline: P. Rider & T. Harbin; W. Smith, 1724.

1854 **Beveridge, Henry**   Commentaries on the Book of Joshua by John Calvin. Translated from the Original Latin, and collated with the author's French Version.   Edinburgh: Calvin Translation Society, 1854.
    [See Bible Selections, 1844 Anonymous, Commentaries on the Books of the Bible.]

1899 **Bennett, W.H.**   The Book of Joshua, a new English Translation Printed in Colors Exhibiting the Composite Structure of the Book, with Explanatory Notes and Pictorial Illustrations, by W.H. Bennett. New York: Dodd, Mead and Company, 1899.
    [See Old Testament Selections, 1898 Sacred Books of the Old and New Testament (Part 6). The Polychrome Bible.]

    [The Deity is rendered "JHVH" many times.]

1912 **Rutland, James R.**   Old Testament...schools...
    [See Old Testament Selections for the complete entry. Includes the chief episodes in Genesis, Exodus, Joshua.]

1917 **Hertz, Joseph Herman**   Joshua, 1917.
    [See Old Testaments, 1917 Jewish Publication Society, The Holy Scriptures.]

1918 **Anonymous**   ...The Book of Joshua with English Translation; Linear System. [Joseph Magil] New York: Hebrew Publishing Co., 1918.
    ["The translation is very simple and as literal as possible within the bounds of English grammar..."]

1950 **Freedman, Harry**   Joshua, 1950.
    [See Old Testaments, 1936 Soncino Books of the Bible. Bound with Judges by J.J. Slotki.]

1969 **Oratz, P.**   The Book of Joshua; a New English Translation of the Text and Rashi with a Commentary Digest. Sidney B. Hoenig, Editor; Translation of the Text by Rabbi P. Oratz. Rashi Translation and commentary Digest by Rabbi A.J. Rosenbert and Rabbi Sidney Shulman.   New York: Judaica Press, 1969.

1972 **Wilson, J.A.**   J.A. Soggin: Joshua. Translated by
J.A. Wilson. London: S.C.M. Press, 1972.
[The RSV text is reproduced, emended where necessary.]

1981 **Woudstra, Marten H.**   The Book of Joshua by Marten
H. Woudstra. Grand Rapids, MI: William B. Eerdmans
Publishing Co., 1981.
["A choice had to be made between Bible translation,
itself a form of Bible exposition, and Bible Commentary.
The commentary took precedence part of the time, but at
other times the translation simply had to take
priority." See the New International Commentary on the
Old Testament, 1976.]

1982 **Boling, Robert G.**   Joshua. A New Translation with
Notes and Commentary by Robert Boling. Garden City,
New York: Doubleday & Co., Inc., 1982.
[See Complete Bibles, 1964 Anchor Bible, Vol. 6.]

1983 **Butler, Trent C.**   Word Biblical Commentary. Joshua.
Trent C. Butler. Waco, TX: Word Books, Publisher,
1983.
[See Complete Bibles, 1982 Word Biblical Commentary,
Vol. 7.]

JUDGES

???? **Anonymous**   The Book of Judges, with English
Translation, Linear System [by Joseph Magil]. New
York: Hebrew Publishing Co., [191?].
Magil's Linear-Bible; Book of Judges... The
Hebrew Bible in its Original Language and
Completeness Self-Taught by Means of a Linear-
Translation; For Teachers and Students, In
Schools, Colleges and Universities, as well as
for Self-Instruction, 1928.

???? **Armerding, Carl Edwin**   Word Biblical Commentary.
Judges. Carl Edwin Armerding. Waco, Tx: Word Books,
Publishers, [198?].
[See Complete Bibles, 1982 Word Biblical Commentary,
Vol. 8.]

???? **Judaica Press Publications**   The Judaica Books
of the Prophets... Judges...
[See Old Testament Selections for the complete entry.]

1564 **Anonymous**   Most Fruitful and Learned Commentaries
of Peter Martir Vermil...with a Very Profitable
Tract of the Matter and Places... London: John Day,
1564.

[Commentary on the Book of Judges with the text, translated from the Latin of Peter Martyr or Vermigli.]

1623 **Anonymous**   Saxon-English Remains...Judges...
[See Old Testament Selections for the complete entry.]

1631 **Quarles, Francis**   The History of Sampson, paraphrased in verse. London: 1631.

1700 **Anonymous**   Scriptural Poems... The History of Sampson...
[See Bible Selections for the complete entry.]

1753 **Green, William**   The Song of Deborah, David's Lamentation over Saul with new translation... Cambridge: J. Bentham, 1753.

1768 **Coleridge, John**   The Book of Judges, Chapters 17 & 18. London: 1768.

1781 **Davies, Dr. Sneyd**   The Song of Deborah in verse, 1781.

1787 **Kennicott, B.**   Exodus 11,15...Judges 5...
[See Old Testament Selections for the complete entry.]

1806 **Cumberland, Richard**   Song of Deborah in verse. London: Lackington & Co., 1806.
[In Memoirs of R. Cumberland.]

1874 **Proby, W.H.B.**   The Ten Canticles...Canon...
[See Old Testament Selections for the complete entry. Includes the Song of Deborah.]

1895 **Moore, George Foot**   A Critical and Exegetical Commentary on Judges by the Rev. George F. Moore... Edinburgh: T. & T. Clark, 1895.
[See Complete Bibles, 1895 International Critical Commentary (Judges).]

Reprinted; 1898, 1903, 1908, 1918, 1949.

1898 **Moore, George Foot**   The Book of Judges, a New English Translation Printed in Colors Exhibiting the Composite Structure of the Book, with Explanatory Notes and Pictorial Illustrations, by G.F. Moore. London: James Clarke & Co.; New York: Dodd, Mead, and Co., 1898
[See Old Testament Selections, 1898 Sacred Books of the Old and New Testaments, Part 7. The Polychrome Bible.]

[The Deity is rendered "JHVH" many times.]

1903 **Burney, C.F.** The Book of Judges with Introduction and Notes. By C.F.Burney. 1903.
Another edition; London: Rivingtons, 1918.

Second edition; London: Rivingtons, 1920.

Reprint; The Book of Judges, with Introduction and Notes, and Notes on the Hebrew Text of the Book of Kings, with an Introduction and Appendix. Prolegomenon by William F. Albright. 2 Vols. in 1. New York: KTAV Pub. House, 1970.
[The Library of Biblical Studies. Reprint of 1918 edition, first published in 1903. Contains his own variations from the King James.]

1912 **Gordon, Alexander R.**   The Poets of the Old Testament...
[See Old Testament Selections for the complete entry. Includes the Song of Deborah.]

1912 **Rutland, James R.**   Old Testament...schools...
[See Old Testament Selections for the complete entry.]

1917 **Wise, Steven S.**   Judges, 1917.
[See Old Testaments, 1917 Jewish Publication Society, The Holy Scriptures.]

1950 **Slotki, Judah J.**   Judges. Hebrew Text & English Translation. With an Introduction and Commentary, by J.J. Slotki. London: The Soncino Press, 1950.
[See Old Testaments, 1936 The Soncino Books of the Bible. Bound with Joshua by H. Freedman.]

1962 **Shunary, J.**   An Arabic Taesir of the Song of Deborah. Textus, Vol.2, 1962.
[Judges IV: 23-31.]

1975 **Boling, Robert G.**   Judges. Introduction, Translation, and Commentary by Robert Boling. Garden City, New York: Doubleday & Co., Inc., 1975.
[See Complete Bibles, 1964 Anchor Bible, Vol. 6a.]

1981 **Woudstra, Marten H.**   The Book of Joshua, 1981.
[See Hebrew Scriptures listings, 1976 New International Commentary on the O.T.]

RUTH

???? **Bush, Frederic W.**   Word Biblical Commentary. Ruth, Song of Songs...
[See Old Testament Selections for the complete entry.]

???? **Cox, Samuel** The Book of Ruth. A Popular Exposition. London: The Religious Tract Society, [187?].
[Includes a translation slightly modified from the AV.]

Another edition; ...A Devotional Commentary. New
& Revised edition, 1910.
[Contains two texts: the AV and one that is
apparently his.]

1597 **Anonymous**   The Reward of Religion. Deliuered in
sundry lectures vpon the Booke of Ruth, wherin the
godly may see their dayly both inward and outward
trials, with the presence of God to Assist them, and
his mercies to recompence them. Verie profitable for
this present time of dearth, wherein many are most
pittifully tormented with want; and also worthy to
be considered in this Golden age of the preaching of
the worde, when some vomit up the loathsommenes
therof, and others fal away to damnable securitie...
Seene and allowed. [Edward Topsell] London: Printed
by Ihon Windet, 1597.
[Cotton lists under 1596.]

Other editions, 1601, 1931.

1623 **Anonymous**   Saxon-English Remains of the
Pentateuch, Joshua, Judges, Ruth, etc., out of Sir
Robert Cotton's MSS. of most revered antiquity, now
forst new Englished and set out...
[See Old Testament Selections for the complete entry.]

1700 **Anonymous**   Scriptural Poems. Being several
portions of Scripture digested into English verse.
Viz. I. The Book of Ruth. II. The History of
Sampson. III. Christ's Sermon on the Mount. IV. The
Prophecy of Jonah. V. The Life of Joseph. VI. The
Epistle of James...
[See Bible Selections for the complete entry.]

1818 **Anonymous**   A Poetical Paraphrase of the
Book of Ruth; with Other Poems. London: the Author,
1818.

1850 **Cadogan, Lady Augusta**   The Book of Ruth,
Illustrated by the Lady Augusta Cadogan. London: J.
Cundell, 1850.
[The Text is the KJV, but included for its
illustrations.]

1860 **Robson, Joseph Philip**   The Book of Ruth in the
Northumberland dialect; from the authorised English
version, by J.P. Robson. [London: George Barclay]
Impensis Ludovici Luciani Bonoparte, 1860.

1876 **American Bible Union**   The Book of Ruth. The Common
Version Revised for the American Bible Union...for
the Promotion of the cause of a pure Bible [Horatio
B. Hackett] New York: American Bible Union; London:
Trubner & Co., 1876.

1887 **Crane, Oliver T.**   The Targums on the Books of Ruth
and Jonah...
     [See Old Testament Selections for the complete entry.]

1899 **Pollard, Josephine**   Ruth, A Bible Heroine; and
Other Stories Told in the Language of Childhood...
     [See Old Testament Selections for the complete entry.]

1912 **Rutland, James R.**   Old Testament, edited for use
in secondary schools...
     [See Old Testament Selections for the complete entry.
     Includes the chief episodes in Genesis, Exodus, Joshua,
     Judges, Samuel, Kings, and Daniel, together with the
     Book of Ruth.]

1912 **Steuart, R.H.J.**   The Book of Ruth, a Literal
Translation from the Hebrew, with Full Grammatical
Notes and Vocabularies, by R.H.J. Steuart. London:
David Nutt, 1912.

1917 **Krauskopf, Joseph**   Ruth, 1917.
     [See Old Testaments, 1917 Jewish Publication Society.]

1920 **Books of the O.T. in Colloquial Speech**   Books of
the Old Testament in Colloquial Speech. The Books of
Ruth and Jonah...
     [See Old Testament Selections for the complete entry.]

1929 **Richmond, Charles E.**   A Metrical Version of Ruth
and Other Bible Stories...
     [See Old Testament Selections for the complete entry.]

1931 **Grimmelsman, Henry J.**   The Book of Ruth; A
Translation and Commentary for Schools and Colleges.
By Henry J. Grimmelsman. Chicago, Dallas, Atlanta,
New York: Scott, Foresman & Co., 1931.
     ["The translation is directly from the Hebrew. It is
     literal at a sacrifice of literary finish..."]

1935 **Lattey, Cuthbert**   Ruth, 1935.
     [See Complete Bibles, 1913 Westminster Version.]

1936 **Richards, James**   De Story of Ruth, a Gell from
de Couutry [sic]. Put into de Sussex dialect by Jim
Cladpole. [James Richards] Turnbridge Wells: James
Richards, 1936.

1946 **Slotki, Judah J.**   The Five Megilloth. [Ruth] Hebrew
Text & English Translation with an Introduction and
Commentary, by J.J. Slotki.   London: The Soncino
Press, 1946.
     [See Old Testaments, 1936 The Soncino Books of the
     Bible.]

1955 **Myers, Jacob M.**   The Linguistic and Literary Form
of the Book of Ruth, by Jacob M.Myers. Leiden: E.J.
Brill, 1955.

1958 **Goldin, Grace**   Come under the Wings; A Midrash on
Ruth, by Grace Goldin.   Philadelphia: Jewish
Publication Society of America, 1958.
    ["I wrote this poem to round out the rabbis' version of
    the story and to illustrate their point of view... My
    chief sources were the Midrash Rabbah on Ruth, and Louis
    Ginsberg's Legends of the Jews..."]

1968 **Sola Pool, David de**   The Book of Ruth.
Introduction by Henri Baruk. Essay by Andre Neher.
Commentaries by Leon Askenazi. English translation
by David de Sola Pool.   Paris? 1968?
    [Hebrew and English.]

1973 **Levine, E.**   The Aramaic Version of Ruth. Rome:
Pontifical Biblical Institute, 1973.
    [Analecta Biblia 58. Text and translation.]

1975 **Campbell, Edward F., Jr.**   Ruth. A New Translation
with Introduction, Notes, and Commentary by E.F.
Campbell.   Garden City, New York: Doubleday & Co.,
Inc., 1975.
    [See Complete Bibles, 1964 Anchor Bible, Vol. 7.]

1976 **Zlotowitz, Meir**   Ruth, 1976.
    [See Old Testaments, 1976 ArtScroll Tanach Series.]

1979 **Sasson, Jack M.**   Ruth, a new translation with
a philological commentary and a formalist-folkorist
interpretation. Jack M. Sasson.   Baltimore: John
Hopkins University Press, 1979.

1979 **Wallace, James S. and Others**   Interlinear of the
Book of Ruth, Hebrew-English Old Testament
translated by James S. Wallace, Ulysses S. Wallace,
Frederick J. Schwartz.   Kaual, Hawaii: Universal
Missionary Publications, 1979.

1988 **Hubbard, Robert L.**   The Book of Ruth, 1988.
    [See Hebrew Scriptures Listings, 1976 New International
    Commentary of the O.T.]

SAMUEL

???? **Judaica Press Publications**   The Judaica Books
of the Prophets. The Book of I Samuel...
    [See Old Testament Selections for the complete entry.]

???? **Judaica Press Publications**   The Judaica Books
of the Prophets. The Book of II Samuel...
   [See Old Testament Selections for the complete entry.]

1684 **Oldham, John**   David's lamentation over Jonathan
and Saul paraphrased in verse.   London: 1684.

1749 **Grey, Richard**   The Last Words of David, II
Samuel 23 ...metre. London: William Bower, 1749.

1787 **Kennicott, B.**   Exodus 11,15; Deuteronomy 32;
Numbers 21; Judges 5; II Samuel 23...
   [See Old Testament Selections for the complete entry.]

1866 **Martin, James**   The Books of Samuel, 1866.
   [See Old Testaments, 1865 Biblical Commentary.]

1874 **Proby, W.H.B.**   The Ten Canticles of the Old
Testament Canon... newly translated with notes...
   [See Old Testament Selections for the complete entry.
   Includes the Song of Hannah.]

1899 **Pollard, Josephine**   Ruth, A Bible Heroine; and
Other Stories Told in the Language of Childhood...
   [See Old Testament Selections for the complete
   entry. Includes abbreviated stories of Job, Samuel,
   David & Saul.]

1899 **Smith, Henry Preserved**   A Critical and Exegetical
Commentary on The Books of Samuel by Henry Preserved
Smith...   Edinburgh: T. & T. Clark, 1899.
   [See Complete Bibles, 1895 International Critical
   Commentary (I & II Samuel).]

   Reprinted; 1904, 1912.

1912 **Rutland, James R.**   Old Testament, edited for use
in secondary schools...
   [See Old Testament Selections for the complete entry.
   Includes the chief episodes in Genesis, Exodus, Joshua,
   Judges, Samuel.]

1917 **Drachman, Bernard**   II Samuel, 1917.
   [See Old Testaments, 1917 Jewish Publication Society.]

1925 **Skinner, John**   The Book of Samuel. Translated into
Colloquial English by John Skinner. London: National
Adult School Union, 1925.
   [See Old Testament Selections, 1920 Books of the Old
   Testament in Colloquial Speech.]

   Another edition; 1 and 2 Samuel, translated by
   John Skinner.   London: National Adult School
   Union, 1964.

1928 **Magil, Joseph**   Magil's Linear-Bible; First
and Second Book of Samuel... The Hebrew Bible in its
Original Language and Completeness Self-Taught by
Means of a Linear-Translation; For Teachers and
Students In Schools, Colleges and Universities, as
well as for Self-Instruction.   New York: Hebrew
Publishing Co., 1928-1929.
> 1928 - - The First Book of Samuel...
> 1929 - - Second Book of Samuel...

1951 **Goldman, Solomon**   I & II Samuel. Hebrew Text
and English Translation with an Introduction and
Commentary by S. Goldman. London: Soncino Press,
1951.
> [See Old Testaments, 1936 Soncino Books of the Bible.]

> [See Old Testament Selections, 1962 O.T. Library.]

1964 **Bowden, J.S.**   I & II Samuel, a Commentary
[translated by J.S. Bowden from the German Die
Samuelbuecher (Das Alte Testament Deutsch,10) 2d
rev. ed.]   London: SCM Press, 1964.
> ["...translation has proved the simplest course to print
> an English equivalent of the Author's German text,
> checked against the Hebrew and Greek, based on the RSV
> but deviating from it whenever this is necessary".
> Preface page 12.]

> [See Old Testament Selections, 1962 O.T. Library.]

1980 **McCarter, P. Kyle, Jr.**   I Samuel. A New Translation
with Introduction, Notes, and Commentary by P. Kyle
McCarter, Jr.   Garden City, New York: Doubleday &
Co., 1980.
> [See Complete Bibles, 1964 Anchor Bible, Vol. 8.]

1983 **Klein, Ralph W.**   Word Biblical Commentary.
1 Samuel. Ralph W.Klein. Waco,TX: Word Books,
Publisher, 1983.
> [See Complete Bibles, 1982 Word Biblical Commentary,
> Vol. 10.]

1984 **McCarter, P. Kyle, Jr.**   II Samuel. A New Translation
with Introduction, Notes, and Commentary by P. Kyle
McCarter, Jr.   Garden City, New York: Doubleday &
Co., 1984.
> [See Complete Bibles, 1964 Anchor Bible, Vol. 9.]

1985 **Kort, Ann and Scott Morschauser** (Editors)
Biblical and Related Studies to Samuel Iwry edited
by Ann Kort and Scott Morschauser.   Winona Lake,
Indiana: Eisenbrauns, 1985.

1989 **Anderson, A.A.**   Word Biblical Commentary.
2 Samuel. A.A. Anderson. Word Books, Publishers,
1989.

[See Complete Bibles, 1982 Word Biblical Commentary,
Vol. 11.]

KINGS

???? **Judaica Press Publications**   The Judaica Books
of the Prophets...I & II Kings...
[See Old Testament Selections for the complete entry.]

1867 **Murphy, James**   The Book of Kings, 1865.
[See Old Testaments, 1865 Biblical Commentary.]

1904 **Anonymous**   The III. and IV. Books of Kings. A
revised version, with old notes by Bishop Challoner
and new notes by Father Kent. London: Burns & Oates,
1904.

1904 **MacLagan, Henry**   The Two Books of Kings Explained.
By Henry Maclagan.   London: New Church Press, 1904?
[Contains two versions; one looks like a modification of
the KJV; the other an expanded paraphrase.]

1950 **Slotki, Israel W.**   I & II Kings. Hebrew
Text & English Translation. With an Introduction and
Commentary, by I.W. Slotki.   London: The Soncino
Press, 1950.
[See Old Testaments, 1936 The Soncino Books of the
Bible.]

1951 **Montgomery, James A. and Henry Snyder Gehman**
A Critical and Exegetical Commentary on The Books of
Kings by James A.Montgomery...edited by Henry Snyder
Gehman...   Edinburgh: T. & T. Clark, 1951.
[See Complete Bibles, 1895 International Critical
Commentary (Kings).]

1964 **Gray, John**   I & II Kings, 1964.
[See Old Testament Selections, 1962 Old Testament
Library.]

1985 **DeVries, Simon J.**   Word Biblical Commentary.
1 Kings. Simon J. DeVries.   Waco, TX: Word Books,
Publisher, 1985.

[See Complete Bibles, 1982 Word Biblical Commentary,
Vol. 12.]

1985 **Hobbs, T.R.**   Word Biblical Commentary.
2 Kings. T.R. Hobbs.   Waco, TX: Word Books,
Publisher, 1985.

[See Complete Bibles, 1982 Word Biblical Commentary, Vol. 13.]

1988 **Cogan, Mordechai and Hayim Tadmor**   II Kings. A New Translation with Introduction, and Commentary by Mordechai Cogan and Hayim Tadmor. Garden City, New York: Doubleday & Co., Inc., 1988.
[See Complete Bibles, 1964 Anchor Bible, Vol. 11.]

CHRONICLES

1588 **James, King, VI of Scotland**   I Chronicles, chapter 15: 25-29...by King James VI. Edinburgh: H. Charteris, 1589.

1868 **Harper, Andrew**   The Books of Chronicles, 1868.
[See Old Testaments, 1865 Biblical Commentary.]

1910 **Curtis, Edward Lewis and Albert Alonzo Madsen** A Critical and Exegetical Commentary on The Books of Chronicles by Edward Lewis Curtis... and Albert Alonzo Madsen... Edinburgh: T. & T. Clark, 1910.
[See Complete Bibles, 1895 International Critical Commentary (Chronicles.]

1917 **Mielziner, M.**   I & II Chronicles, 1917.
[See Old Testaments, 1917 Jewish Publication Society.]

1952 **Slotki, Israel W.**   I & II Chronicles. Hebrew Text & English Translation. With an Introduction and Commentary, by I.W. Slotki.   London: The Soncino Press, 1952.
[See Old Testaments, 1936 The Soncino Books of the Bible.]

1954 **Torrey, Charles Cutler**   The Chronicler's History of Israel; Chronicles-Ezra-Nehemiah Restored to its Original Form...
[See Old Testament Selections for the complete entry.]

1965 **Myers, Jacob M.**   I Chronicles. Introduction, Translation, and Commentary, by Jacob M. Myers. Garden City, New York: Doubleday & Co., 1965.
[See Complete Bibles, 1964 Anchor Bible, Vol. 12.]

1965 **Myers, Jacob M.**   II Chronicles. Translation and Notes, by Jacob M. Myers. Garden City, New York: Doubleday & Co., 1965.
[See Complete Bibles, 1964 Anchor Bible, Vol. 13.]

1986 **Braun, Roddy**   Word Biblical Commentary.
1 Chronicles. Roddy Braun. Waco, TX: Word Books,
Publisher, 1986.
[See Complete Bibles, 1982 Word Biblical Commentary,
Vol. 14.]

1987 **Dillard, Raymond B.**   Word Biblical Commentary.
2 Chronicles. Raymond B. Dillard. Waco, TX: Word
Books, publisher, 1987.
[See Complete Bibles, 1982 Word Biblical Commentary,
Vol. 15.]

EZRA

1805 **Browne, Theoph**   Ezra and...
[See Old Testament Selections for the complete entry.]

1873 **Davies J.**   The Book of Ezra: with notes. London:
G. Philip & Son, 1873.

1879 **Taylor, Sophia**   Ezra, Nehemiah, Esther...
[See Old Testament Selections, 1865 Biblical
Commentary.]

1905 **Heller, Nachman**   Daniel and Ezra, the Canonized
Aramaic Text, Translated into Hebrew, Yiddish and
English, and supplemented with footnotes and
marginal comments...
[See Old Testament Selections for the complete entry.]

1910 **Torrey, Charles Cutler**   Ezra Studies...
[See Old Testament Selections for the complete entry.]

1913 **Batten, Loring W.**   A Critical and Exegetical
Commentary on The Books of Ezra and Nehemiah...
[See Old Testament Selections for the complete entry.]

1954 **Torrey, Charles Cutler**   The Chronicler's History of
Israel; Chronicles-Ezra-Nehemiah Restored to its
Original Form...
[See Old Testament Selections for the complete entry.]

1965 **Myers, Jacob M.**   Ezra, Nehemiah. Introduction...
[See Old Testament Selections for the complete entry.]

1982 **Fensham, F. Charles**   The Books of Ezra..., 1982.
[See Historical Books and Selections, 1982.]

1985 **Williamson, H.G.M.**   Word Biblical Commentary. Ezra,
Nehemiah...
[See Old Testament Selections for the complete entry.]

NEHEMIAH

1585 **Pilkington, Iames**   A Godlie Exposition
vpon Certeine Chapters of Nehemiah, Written by that
Worthy Byshop and Faithfull Pastor of the Church of
Durham Master Iames Pilkington, and now Newlie
Pvblished. [James Pilkington] Imprinted by Thomas
Thomas printer to the Vniuersitie of Cambridge,
1585.
> [Includes the text through chap V.13.   Reprinted in
> 'The Works of James Pilkington', by the Parker Society.
> Cambridge: The University Press, 1842.]

1805 **Browne, Theoph**   Ezra and Nehemiah...
> [See Old Testament Selections for the complete entry.]

1879 **Taylor, Sophia**   Ezra, Nehemiah, Esther...
> [See Old Testaments, 1865 Biblical Commentary.]

1910 **Torrey, Charles Cutler**   Ezra Studies...
> [See Old Testament Selections for the complete entry.
> Includes Nehemiah.]

1913 **Batten, Loring W.**   A Critical and Exegetical
Commentary on The Books of Ezra and Nehemiah...
> [See Old Testament Selections for the complete entry.]

1954 **Torrey, Charles Cutler**   The Chronicler's History...
> [See Old Testament Selections for the entire
> entry.]

1965 **Myers, Jacob M.**   Ezra, Nehemiah. Introduction...
> [See Old Testament Selections for the complete entry.]

1982 **Fensham, F. Charles**   The Books of Ezra..., 1982.
> [See Historical Books and Selections, 1982.]

1985 **Williamson, H.G.M.**   Word Biblical Commentary. Ezra,
Nehemiah...
> [See Complete Bibles for the complete entry.]

ESTHER

???? **Bush, Frederic W.**   Word Biblical Commentary. Ruth,
Song of Songs, Esther...
> [See Old Testament Selections for the complete entry.]

1621 **Quarles, Francis**   Hadassa; or, The History of
Queene Ester, with Meditations Thereupon, Divine and
Morall (In verse). Oxford: n.p., 1621.

Other editions, 1638, 1717.

1784 **Maxwell, James**   The Book of Esther; Paraphrased
in Blank Verse by James Maxwell.   Glasgow: for the
author, 1784.

1844 **Sawyer, Leicester Ambrose**   (The Bible) Analyzed,
translated...Esther and the Song of Songs...
[See Bible Selections for the complete entry.]

1855 **Paul, J.D.**   Bible Illustrations; or, The Harmony
of the Old and New Testament, Arranged... To Which
is Added a Paraphrase of the Book of Esther...
[See Bible Selections for the complete entry.]

1876 **Polano, H.**   The Talmud... Poetry and Legends...
[See Old Testament Selections for the complete entry.
Includes a very much interpolated version of the book of
Esther.]

1879 **Taylor, Sophia**   Ezra, Nehemiah, Esther. Edinburgh:
T. & T. Clark, 1879.
[See Old Testaments, 1865 Biblical Commentary.]

1885 **Anonymous**   The Book of Esther, a new translation;
with critical notes, excursuses, maps and plans, and
illustrations. By the Lowell Hebrew Club. Edited by
Rev. John W. Haley. [John W. Haley, Owen Street,
William P. Alcott and John M. Greene] Andover:
Warren F. Draper, 1885.
["The text as it appears in this volume is in no sense
the revision of another translation, but a rendering of
the Hebrew de novo. We are the joint authors of the
Translation..."]

1888 **Bernstein, Aaron**   An Explanatory Commentary
on Esther, with Four Appendices, Consisting of the
Second Targum translated from the Aramaic with
Notes, Mithra, the Winged Bulls of Persopolis, and
Zoroaster. By Professor Paulus Cassel... Translated
by Aaron Bernstein. Edinburgh: T. & T. Clark, 1888.
[Clark's Theological Library, new series, v. 34. "The
second Targum covers pages 263-344, and is much too long
to be called even a paraphrase. Perhaps it should be
called an expanded paraphrase, for it does retell the
story with considerable additional material."]

1899 **Gill, William Hugh**   Esther; A Drama of Jewish
History, being the Story of the Book of Esther
Elucidated by Interpolation for Popular Use, by
William Hugh Gill. Philadelphia: George W. Jacobs
& Co., 1899.

1899 **Pollard, Josephine**   Ruth, A Bible Heroine...
[See Old Testament Selections for the complete entry.
Includes abbreviated stories of Job, Samuel, David &
Saul, Solomon the Wise Man, Elijah, Elisha, Jonah the

1903 **Magil, Joseph**   Magil's Linear Book of Esther, by
Joseph Magil. New York: Hebrew Publishing Co., 1903.
    Another edition, 192?

1908 **Haupt, Paul**   The Book of Esther, 1908.

1908 **Paton, Lewis Bayles**   A Critical and Exegetical
Commentary on the Book of Esther by Lewis Bayles
Paton... Edinburgh: T. & T. Clark; New York: Charles
Scribners, 1908.
    [See Complete Bibles, 1895   International Critical
    Commentary (Esther).]

    Reprinted, 1951.

1912 **Rutland, James R.**   Old Testament... schools...
    [See Old Testament Selections for the complete entry.
    Includes the chief episodes in Genesis, Exodus, Joshua,
    Judges, Samuel, Kings, and Daniel, together with the
    books of Ruth and Esther.]

1917 **Rosenau, William**   Esther, 1917.
    [See Old Testaments, 1917 Jewish Publication Society.]

1923 **Haschande, Jacob**   The Book of Esther in the
Light of History by Jacob Haschande. Philadelphia:
The Dropsie College for Hebrew and Cognate Learning,
1923.
    [Translation intermixed with commentary.]

1955 **Kolatch, Alfred J.**   Scroll of Esther, with Modern
Translation by Rabbi Alfred J. Kolatch. New York:
The Jonathan David Co., 1955.
    ["The present translation...(takes) the liberty of
    presenting a freer translation than has been done
    heretofore. But, actually, to remain as true as possible
    to the Hebrew text this has been done only where a
    literal translation cannot convey the thought expressed
    in the original Hebrew." Text in Hebrew and English.]

1960 **Cotton, Ella Earls**   Queen of Persia; the Story
of Esther Who Saved Her People by Ella Earls Cotton.
Illustrated by Stina Nagel. New York: Exposition
Press, 1960.

1963 **Scammon, John H.**   The Book of Esther: a
brief introduction and a new translation by John H.
Scammon.   Newton Centre, Mass.: Andover Newton
Theological School, 1963.

1971 **Moore, Carey A.** Esther. Introduction, Translation,
and Notes, by Carey A. Moore.   Garden City, New
York: Doubleday & Co., 1971.
    [See Complete Bibles, 1964 Anchor Bible, Vol. 7b.]

[See Complete Bibles, 1964 Anchor Bible, Vol. 7b.]

1974 **Gordis, Robert**   Megillat Esther: The Masoretic
     Hebrew text, with introduction, new translation, and
     commentary by Robert Gordis.   New York: Rabbinical
     Assembly: distributed by Ktav Publishing House,
     1974.

1976 **Zlotowitz, Meir**   Esther, 1976.
          [See Old Testaments, 1976 ArtScroll Tanach Series.]

5

Megilloth

???? **Anonymous**   The V Megilloth, or, Books of the Song of Solomon, the Book of Ruth, the Lamentations, the Book of Ecclesiastes, and the Book of Esther. In Hebrew and English, with notes. London: [185?].

???? **Stern, M.**   ...The Five Books of Moses; With Haptorath and Five Megiloth and Sabbath Prayers...
[See Pentateuch listing for the complete entry.]

1785 **Alexander, A.**   The First [through Fifth] Book of Moses [with the Haphtaroth and the Megilloth]...
[See Pentateuch listing for the complete entry.]

1787 **Levi, David**   The First [thru Fifth] Book of Moses [with the Haphtaroth and Megilloth]...
[See Old Testament Selections for the complete entry.]

1928 **Harkavy, Alexander**   The Pentateuch... Five Megiloth...
[See Pentateuch for the complete entry.]

1952 **Cohen, Abraham** (Editor)   The Five Megilloth. Hebrew Text & English Translation with an Introduction and Commentary by The Rev. Dr.A.Cohen...London: The Soncino Press, 1952.
[See Old Testaments, 1936 The Soncino Books of the Bible.]

1956 **Fishman, Isidore**   The Megillah, Translated and Interpreted by Isidore Fishman. London: J. Martin, 1956.

1969 **Ginsberg, H.L.** (Editor) The Five Megilloth..., 1969.
[See Old Testaments, 1962 Jewish Publication Society.]

1973 **Grossfeld, Bernard**   The Targum to the Five
     Megilloth. Edited with an introduction by Bernard
     Grossfeld. New York: Hermon Press, 1973.

1983 **Schwartz, Avraham and Yijroel Schwartz**
     The Megilloth and Rashi's commentary with Linear
     translation.   New York: Hebrew Linear Classics,
     1983.
          [Esther, The Song of Songs and Ruth.]

1984 **Friedlander, Albert H.** (Editor) The Five Scrolls;
     Hebrew texts, English translations, introductions,
     and new liturgies. Translations edited by Rabbi
     Albert H. Friedlander. Introductions co-edited by
     Rabbi Herbert Bronstein and Rabbi Albert H.
     Friedlander. Liturgies edited by Rabbi Herbert
     Bronstein. Research, development, and editorial
     services by Dr. Yehiel Hayon. Illustrated and
     designed by Leonard Baskins. New York, New York:
     CCAR Press, Central Conference of American Rabbis,
     1984.
          [Ecclesiastes, Esther, Song of Songs, Ruth and
          Lamentations.]

6

Wisdom and Poetical Books

WISDOM AND POETICAL BOOKS AND SELECTIONS

???? **Croke, John**   Thirteen Psalms, and the first chapter of Ecclesiastes, translated into English verse by John Croke. MS. 154?
> Another Edition; ...by John Croke, in the reign of Henry VIII. London: Printed by the Percy Society, by T. Richards, 1844.

1550 **Anonymous**   The Fyve Bokes of Salomon and of Jesus the Sonne of Syrach. London: William Copland, 1550.
> [Wisdom Books]

1568 **Perne, Andrew**   Ecclesiastes & Song of Songs, 1568.
> [See Complete Bibles, 1568 Bishops' Bible.]

1579 **Rogers, Thomas**   A Golden Chaine, taken out of the rich Treasure house, the Psalms of King David; also, the pretious Pearles of King Salomon, by Thomas Rogers. London: by Henrie Denham, 1579.

1597 **Anonymous**   Ecclesiastes, Othervvise Called the Preacher. Containing Solomon's Sermons or Commentaries (as it may probably be collected) vpon the 49. Psalms of Dauid his father. Compendiously abridged, and also paraphrastically dilated in English poesie, according to the analogie of Scripture, and consent of the most approued writers thereof. Composed by H.L.Gentleman. Whereunto are annexed sundrie Sonets of Christian Passions heretofore printed, and now corrected and augmented, with other affectionate Sonets of a feeling conscience, of the same Authors. [Henry Lok] London: Printed by Richard Field, 1597.
> [Includes: 'Sundry Psalmes of Dauid translated into verse, as briefly and significantly as the scope of the text will suffer, by the same author.' (Psalms 27, 71, 119, 121, 130) and the Lord's Prayer.]

[Poetical Books Selections]

1609 **Hall, Joseph**   Salomon's Divine Arts, of 1.
Ethickes, 2. Politickes, 3. Oeconomickes; that is
the Government of 1. Behaviour, 2. Commonwealth, 3.
Familie, drawne into Method out of his Proverbs and
Ecclesiastes. With an open and plaine Paraphrase
upon the Song of Songs. London: Printed by H.L. for
E. Edgar & S. Macham, 1609.
        [Poetical Books Selections]

1657 **Leigh, Ed.**   Annotations on the Five Poetical
Books of the Old Testament.   London: 1657.
        [Poetical Books Selections]

1659 **Hammond, Henry**   A Paraphrase and Annotations
upon the books of the Psalms, briefly explaining the
difficulties thereof. London: R. Norton for Richard
Royston, 1659.
        Another edition;   –   – Also A Paraphrase &
        Annotations On the Ten First Chapters of the
        Proverbs. The Second Edition [of the Psalms]
        Corrected and Amended. London: Printed by T.
        Newcomb & M. Flesher, for Richard Royston,
        1683.

        Also; A Paraphrase and Annotations upon the
        book of the Proverbs, Chapters 1 to 10,
        briefly explaining the difficulties thereof.
        London: Newcome & Flesher, 1684.

        [Poetical Books Selections]

        Also; A new edition, edited by Thomas Brancker.
        Oxford: University Press, 1850.

1679 **Patrick, Symon**   The [Poetical Books] Paraphrased.
London: 1679-1685.
        1679 The Book of Job Paraphras'd. London: B.
            Flesher for R. Royston.
                Second Edition Corrected; London: T.
            Macock for R. Royston, 1685.

            Reissue of the 1679 edition, 1697.

            Third edition corrected, 1727.

        1680 The Book of Psalms paraphras'd with
            arguments to each Psalm.
                Second Edition Corrected; London: J.H.,
            for L. Meredith, 1691.

1683 The Proverbs of Solomon Paraphrased, with the Arguments of Each Chapter Which Supply the Place of a Commentary. London: Printed by M. Flesher for R. Royston.

>Another edition; London: Printed by J.H. for Luke Meredith, 1694.

1685 A Paraphrase upon the Books of Ecclesiastes and the Song of Solomon. With arguments to each chapter, and annotations thereupon. London: for Rich. Royston, 2 parts.

The Books of Job, Psalms, Proverbs, Ecclesiastes, and the Song of Solomon, paraphras'd, with Arguments to each Chapter and Annotations. London: For J. Walthoe..., 1707, 1710, 1731, 1743, 1766.

Books of Job, Proverbs, Psalms, Ecclesiastes, and Song of Solomon, Paraphras'd: with Arguments to each Chapter, and Annotations Thereupon. By the Right Reverend Father in God, Symon, Late Lord Bishop of Ely. London: 1727.

1680 **Anonymous** The Councels of Wisdom; or, a Collection of the Maxims of Solomon, Most Necessary for a Man towards the gaining of Wisdom: With Reflections vpon the Maxims. Faithfully Translated out of French. London: Printed by J. Shadd, for M. Turner, 1680.

>[The Epistle Dedicatory is signed "E.S."; A translation of "les Conseils de la sagesse", compiled by Michel Boutauld; in 2 parts; Consists of selections from Proverbs and Ecclesiastes in Latin, followed by a Paraphrase and then by a Reflection.]

Another Edition; The Councils of Wisdom: a Collection of the maxims of Solomon. Most necessary for a man wisely to behave himself. With reflections on those maxins. Rendered into English by T.D. [Thomas Dare] Amsterdam: for Stephen Smart, 1683.

Also; The Counsels of Wisdom. Or, a Collection of Such Maxims of Solomon as are Most Necessary for the Prudent Conduct of Life. With Proper Reflections upon Them. Written Originally in French by Monseigneur Fouquet [or rather, by Michel Boutault. With 'The Sequel of the Counsels of Wisdom' by M.Boutault]...

Done into English by a Gent. With Some
Account of the Illustrious Author.
[J.Leake] Oxford: The Theater, 1736.

1706 **Anonymous**   Select Moral Books of the Old
Testament and Apocrypha, Paraphras'd. Viz. Proverbs,
Ecclesiastes, Wisdom, Ecclesiasticus. [Philip
Bedingfield or John Locke] London: A. & J.
Churchill, 1706.
[Contains KJV and the "Paraphrase" in parallel columns;
also a new translation in paragraphs.]

1732 **Fenton, Thomas**   Annotations on the Book of Job
and the Psalms. London: 1732.
[Poetical Books Selections]

1738 **Tans'ur, William**   Heaven on Earth; or, the Beauty
of Holiness. In Two Books. Containing I. The Whole
Book of Proverbs of King Solomon, composed in
English Verse; II. The Song of Songs, which is the
Song of Solomon... London: S. Birt, Author, 1738.
[Poetical Books Selections]

1739 **Mawer, John**   Proposals for Publishing the Psalms
& Solomon's Song... Oxford: 1739.
[Poetical Books Selections]

1763 **Holden, Lawrence**   A Paraphrase on the Books of
Job, Psalms, Proverbs and Ecclesiastes, with Notes
Critical, Historical, and Practical by Lawrence
Holden. 4 Vols. London: C. Henderson, 1763.
Another edition, 1764.

1772 **Durrell, D.**   Critical Remarks on the Books of
Job, Proverbs, Psalms, Ecclesiastes, and Canticles.
Oxford: Clarendon Press, 1772.
["...transcribers...have not given us true Copies of the
Original Text. To correct these Errors, has been my
chief Aim; and I flatter myself that not a few passages
will be found to be restored to their primitive
Genuineness..."]

1776 **Barclay, John**   Additional Versions of Several
Psalms and a Paraphrase of Solomon's Song. Vol.3
Edinburgh: J. Donaldson, 1776.
[Poetical Books Selections]

1780 **Farrer, John**   A Selection of Hebrew Poems
translated [from the O.T.] Kendal: for the author,
1780.

1791 **Dimock, Henry**   Notes, Critical and Explanatory, on
the Book of Psalms [and Proverbs] Gloucester: 1791.

1819 **Wellbeloved, Charles**   The Holy Bible...

[See Old Testament Selections for the complete entry. Includes Job-Song of Solomon.]

1827 **Noyes, George R.** A New Translation of [the Poetical O.T. Books] with Introductions, and Notes, Chiefly Explanatory, by George R. Noyes... 1827-1846.
> 1827 An Amended Version of the Book of Job, with an Introduction, and Notes Chiefly Explanatory. By George R. Noyes. Cambridge: From the University Press Hilliard, Metcalf & Co.
> > Second Edition; A New Translation of the Book of Job... Second Edition, with corrections and additions. Boston: James Munroe & Co, 1838.

> 1831 A New Translation of the Book of Psalms, with an Introduction, and Notes, chiefly explanatory. By George R. Noyes... Boston: Published by Gray & Bowen; Cambridge: Hilliard & Brown.
> > Second edition; ["carefully revised"]. Boston: James Monroe & Co.; London: Chapman, Brothers. Reprinted, 1846.

> 1846 - - The Proverbs, Ecclesiastes, and the Canticles... Boston: James Monroe & Co.; London: Chapman, Brothers.

> - - Psalms and...Proverbs...Third Edition [Psalms revised]. Boston: American Unitarian Association, 1867.

> - - Job, Ecclesiastes, and the Canticles ... Fourth Edition [of Job] carefully revised... Boston: American Unitarian Association, 1868.

> - - Job, Ecclesiastes, and the Canticles ...Fifth Edition [of Job] carefully revised... Boston: American Unitarian Association, 1868.

> - - Job, Ecclesiastes, and the Canticles ...Sixth Edition [of Job] carefully revised... Boston: American Unitarian Association, 1890.

> - - Psalms and Proverbs, Eighth Edition [Psalms revised]. Boston: American Unitarian Association, 1890.

1845 **Anonymous** A Metrical Version of the Song of Solomon, and other poems (Miscellaneous poems:

consisting chiefly of Paraphrases of some of the
Psalms, and sonnets from the Spanish and Italian) by
a Late Graduate of Oxford. [Frederick K. Naghten]
London: Smith, Elder & Co., 1845.

1850 **McClure, Samuel**   The Psalms of David, and Song of
Solomon in metre, by Samuel McClure. Lewiston, PA:
Samuel McClure; Harrisburgh: Hickock & Barrett,
1850.
     ["He has not attempted anything like a literal version
     for the purpose of praise, but a metrical explanation or
     paraphrase of the scriptural Psalms, and also the Song
     of Solomon, to read for private edification and
     instruction." Poetical Books Selections]

1860 **Sawyer, Leicester Ambrose**   The Holy Bible...
     [See Old Testament Selections for the complete entry.]

1870 **Barham, Francis**   The Writings of Solomon;
Comprising the Book of Proverbs, Ecclesiastes, Song
of Songs, and Psalms LXXII, CXXVII. Translated by
Francis Barham. Printed both in phonetic and in
customary spelling [With 'Rhythmic Version of the
Song of Solomon' by Isaac Pitman]   London: F.
Pitman; Bath: I. Pitman, J. Davies, 1870.

1879 **Benthall, John**   Songs of the Hebrew Poets in English
Verse... Songs illustrating the Life of David. By
John Benthall. London: Sampson, Low & Co., 1879.

1888 **Morgan, Bishop William**   The Book of Job.
Translation by Bishop William Morgan. Oxford: J.G.
Evans, 1888.

1890 **Anonymous**   Poetical Parts of the Old Testament.
1890-1893.
          1890 The Book of Job and the Song of Solomon.
          Translated into English metre. By Talmid.
          Edinburgh: James Thin, Publisher to the
          University.
               [The Deity is rendered "Jehovah" many
               times.]

          1893 Poetical Parts of the Old Testament,
          translated into English rhythm, by
          Talmid. Edinburgh: James Thin.

1891 **Davie, James**   The Poetical Books of the Bible,
rendered according to their literary structure.
Edinburgh: James Davie, 1891.

1901 **M'Swiney, James**   Translation of the Psalms
and Canticles with Commentary by James M'Swiney....
London: Sands & Co.; Dublin: M.H. Gill & Son; St.
Louis, MO: B. Herder, 1901.

[A translation of the Hebrew in one column and a translation of the Vulgate in the other column. Uses YaHWeH for the Tetregrammation.]

[Poetical Books selections.]

1915 Scott, David Russell   Pessimism and Love in Ecclesiastes and the Song of Songs, with Translations from the Same, by David Russell Scott. London: James Clarke & Co., 1915.
  [Contains a translation of the Song of Songs and Selections from Ecclesiastes.]

[Poetical Books selections.]

1916 McFadyen, John Edgar   [The Poetical Books of the O.T.] in Modern Speech and Rhythmical Form. By John Edgar McFadyen. Boston: The Pilgrim Press; London: James Clarke & Co., 1916-1917.
  1916 The Psalms in Modern Speech and
       Rhythmical Form... Second edition, 1917.
       ["This translation aims at reproducing, in modern speech, something of the impression created by the rhythmic form of the Hebrew Psalter."]

       [The Deity is rendered "Jehovah" many times.]

  1917 The Wisdom Books (Job, Proverbs,
       Ecclesiastes) also Lamentations and the
       Song of Songs, in Modern Speech and
       Rhythmical Form... [1917]
       ["In this volume, as in the other, I have endeavored to let the writers speak to us in the language of to-day, and also with something of the music which haunts their words in their original form."]

  [James Clarke & Co. published an undated volume entitled, 'The Problem of Pain; A Study in the Book of Job', of which McFadyen said, "...I have ventured to present it, or most of it, in a fresh translation... I hope soon to publish a continuous translation of the book." Presumably this is the version which appeared in 1917.]

1929 Martin, William Wallace   The Book of Job, in Two Versions: A Judean Version, an Ephramean Version; and the Book of Ecclesiastes. Reconstructive Studies. Separated, arranged, and translated, by William Wallace Martin. Nashville: Press of the Methodist Publishing House, 1929.
  [Poetical Books Selections]

1936 Smith, Walter Bernard   A New Church Psalter. Being the Church of England Prayer Book Version of the Canticles and Psalms with certain omissions and

variations, and added explanatory notes.   London:
Oxford University Press, 1936.
[Poetical Books Selections]

1937 **O'Neill, George**   The Psalms and the Canticles of
the Divine Office, a new English translation based
selectively on the Hebrew, Greek, and Vulgate Texts,
with Introduction and Notes, by George O'Neill....
Milwaukee: The Bruce Publishing Co., 1937.
[Poetical Books Selections]

1941 **Merritt, Alice Haden**   Psalms and Proverbs; A Poetic
Version, by Alice Haden Merritt.   Philadelphia:
Dorrance & Co., 1941.
[Poetical Books Selections]

1955 **Wanefsky, David**   The Hebrew Scriptures Reappraised,
by David Wanefsky. Vol. I   New York: Shulsinger
Bros., 1955.
      [Includes a translation of Psalms, Proverbs and Job;
      other volumes published?]

1965 **Scott, R.B.Y.**   Proverbs and Ecclesiastes.
Introduction, Translation, and Notes, by R.B.Y.
Scott.   Garden City, New York: Doubleday & Inc.,
1965.
      [See Complete Bibles, 1964 Anchor Bible, Vol. 18.]

1972 **Anonymous**   Wisdom for Modern Man. Proverbs
and Ecclesiastes from the Old Testament in Today's
English Version.   New York: American Bible Society,
1972.

JOB AND SELECTIONS

???? **Clines, David J.A.**   Word Biblical Commentary.
Job. 2 Vols. David J.A. Clines.   Waco, Tx: Word
Books, Publishers, [198?].
      [See Complete Bibles, 1982 Word Biblical Commentary,
      Vol. 17 & 18.]

???? **Cox, Samuel**   The Book of Job. A New Translation
by Samuel Cox. (Printed for Private Circulation)
Nottingham: R.B. Earp, Printer, [18??].

???? **Franklin, Benjamin**   A Portion of Job..., [????].
      [Mr. Franklin "left a model translation of a few verses
      of the first chapter of Job..." Simms in his "Bible in
      America" gives a specimen.]

      [Printed in: Our Roving Bible. Tracking its Influence
      through English and American Life. By Lawrence E.

Nelson... New York & Nashville: Abingdon–Cokesbury Press, 1945. (page 136)]

???? Judaica Press Publications   The Judaica Books of the Prophets...Job...
[See Old Testament Selections for the complete entry.]

???? Schliebe, R.H.   Job, n.d.
[Condensed metrical paraphrase. Unpublished.]

???? Watson, Robert A.   The Book of Job. With a new translation. New York: A.C. Armstrong & Son; London: Hodder & Stoughton, [189?].
[See Bible Selections, 1888 The Expositor's Bible.]

1340 Rolle, Richard   Part of the Book of Job. By Richard Rolle. MS c1340.

1574 Golding, Arthur   Sermons of Master Ihon Caluin, vpon the Booke of Iob. Translated out of French by Arthur Golding.   [London]: Imprinted by Lvcas Harison and George Byshop, 1574?

1580 Barker, Christopher (Geneva)   The Third Part of the Bible...
[See Old Testament Selections for the complete entry. Contains the Book of Job.]

1589 Anonymous   Iob Expovnded by Theodore Beza, partly in manner of a Commentary, partly in manner of a Paraphrase. Faithfully translated out of Latine into English. London: Printed by Iohn Leggatt, 1589.
[Beza's preface is dated 1587.]

Another edition; Cambridge: sold by A. Kitson, 1589.

1596 Holland, Henry   Job. 1st and 2d Chapters with an exposition by Henry Holland. London: 1596.

1600 Broughton, Hugh   Books of David... Job...
[See Old Testament Selections for the complete entry.]

1607 Humfry, R.   The Conflict of Job, By Way of Dialogue, Being as it were a Paraphrase on the Book of Job, 1607.

1610 Broughton, Hugh   Iob. To the King. A Colon-Agrippina studie of one moneth, for the metrical translation: but of many yeres, for Ebrew difficulties, by Hugh Broughton. [London] 1610.
[Reprinted with Ecclesiastes, Lamentations and Daniel.]
London: N.Ekins, 1662.

1615 **Sylvester, Joshua**   A divine and true trag-comedy;
Job triumphant in his triall, by Joshua Sylvester.
1615.

1624 **Quarles, Francis**   "Job Militant"; (the history of
Job) in verse. London: Felix Kingston, 1624.

1636 **Sandys, George**   A Paraphrase...Divine Poems...
[See Old Testament Selections for the complete entry.
Includes Job.]

1640 **Abbott, George**   The Whole Book of Iob Paraphrased,
or, Made Easie for any to Understand, by George
Abbott. London: Printed by Edward Griffin for Henry
Overton, 1640.
["A Paraphrase (and not a commenterie) is the thing that
I endeauour, which is a bare rendering of the sense
plaine and easu, the better to enable the Reader to be
a commentator to himselfe."]

1645 **Caryl, Joseph**   An Exposition of...IV, V, VI, and
VII chapters of Job. London: G. Miller, 1645.
[Bound with An Exposition...The First Three Chapters of
Job.]

1647 **Caryl, Joseph**   Job, with Exposition by Joseph
Caryl. 10 Vols. London: H. Overton, 1647 - 1666.

1648 **Anonymous**   A Paraphrase upon Job; written in French
[by J.F.Senault]. London: For Robert Bostock, 1648.
[Translated into English.]

Another edition; The Pattern of Patience in the
Example of Holy Job; a Paraphrase upon the
Whole book of Job... London: Joseph Cranford,
1648. Also, 1657.

1652 **Manley, Thomas**   The Affliction and Deliverance
of the Saints; or, The Whole Booke of Iob Composed
into English Heroicall Verse, Metaphrastically, by
Thomas Manley. London: W.H. for John Tey, 1652.

1661 **Brett, Arthur**   [Patientia Victrix; or] The Book
of Job, in Lyrick Verse, by Arthur Brett. London:
for Richard Gammon, 1661.

1679 **Patrick, Symon**   The Book of Job Paraphras'd...
[See Wisdom and Poetical books and Selections, 1679
Symon Patrick, The [Poetical Books] Paraphrased.]

1685 **Clark, William**   The Grand tryal; or, Poetical
Exercitations upon the Book of Job, by William
Clark. Edinburgh: n.p., 1685.
[Contains a poetical version of the entire book.]

1698 **Thwaites, Edward**   Heptateuchus, liber Job...
[See Bible Selections for the complete entry.]

1700 **Anonymous**   The Book of Job in Meeter, by R.P.,
Minister of the Gospel. London: Thomas Parkhurst,
1700.
[Extracts from Job, with selections from other parts of
the Scripture.]

1700 **Anonymous**   The Book of Job in Meeter, as to Several
of those Excellent Things Contain'd Therein...
London: 1700.

1716 **Anonymous**   A Short Paraphrase on the Book of Job
with arguments to each chapter, by a Presbyter of
the Church of England. London: S. Keble, 1716.

1717 **Young, Edward**   A Paraphrase on Part of the Book of
Job, by Edward Young. Oxford: 1717.
Second edition; London: Jacob Tonson, 1719.

Another edition; Dublin: Cincinnati: Thomas
Whitehouse, 1726.

Third edition; A Specimen for Subscribers...
London: Printed by W. Wilkins, 1727.

Another edition; - - The Complaint; or, Night
thoughts. London: Printed for Thomas Tegg,
1812.

1721 **Boyse, Samuel**   Job Chapter 3 in Verse, 1721.

1726 **Thompson**   A Poetical Paraphrase on Part of the Book
of Job in Imitation of the Style of Milton. London:
Tho. Warrall, 1726.
[Chapters xl-xlii]

1727 **Broome, Rev. W.**   Habakkuk 3; Part of...
[See Old Testament Selections for the complete entry.
Includes part of Job.]

1727 **Pitt, Christopher**   Job 3 and 25...Song of Moses...
[See Bible Selections for the complete entry.]

1732 **Fenton, Thomas** Annotations on the Book of Job...
[See Wisdom and Poetical Books and Selections for the
complete entry.]

1734 **Anonymous**   The Complaint of Job, a Poem. London:
Richard Wellington, 1734.

1736 **Anonymous**   Job Chapter 38. Gentleman's Magazine,
Vol.VI, page 544, 1736.

1741 **Anonymous**   Job; Chapter 38; Paraphrased in verse.
Gentleman's Magazine, Vol.xi, Page 384, 1741.

1743 **Anonymous**   Job; Chapter 3; Paraphrased in Verse.
Gentleman's Magazine, Vol.XIII, Page 437, 1743.

1748 **Anonymous**   The Book of Job; Paraphrased in Verse.
London: Webb, 1748.
[Supposed to be in "Gentleman's Magazine" for August.]

1748 **Bellamy, D.**   A Paraphrase on the Sacred History, or
Book of Job, with observations from various authors,
by D. Bellamy. London: J. Hart, 1748.

1752 **Chappelow, Leonard**   A Commentary on the Book
of Job, in which is inserted the Hebrew text and
English translation, with a paraphrase from the
third verse of the third chapter, where it is
supposed the metre begins; to the seventh verse of
the forty second chapter, where it ends. 2 Vols.
Cambridge: J. Bentham, 1752.
["A mere paraphrase, verbose, and without annotations."]

1753 **Anonymous**   Job; Chapter 28. Gentleman's Magazine,
Vol. XXIII, Page 241, 1753.

1753 **Erskine, Ralph**   Job's Hymns; Or a Book of Songs
on the Book of Job. Glasgow: for J. Newlands, 1753.
[Contains 100 hymns. (Job selections).]

[Reprinted in Erskine's Works, "Scripture Songs. In Two
Books." Glasgow: 1766.]

1756 **Heath, Thomas**   An Essay Towards a New English
Version of the Book of Job from the Original Hebrew,
with a Commentary and Some Account of his Life, by
Thomas Heath. London: for A. Millar, 1756.

1760 **Langhorne, William**   Job, a Poem. In three
Books. By William Langhorne. London: Printed for R.
Griffiths, 1760.
["The greatest part of this work is a free Paraphrase of
the Book of Job... the Author has sometimes omitted
Images unsuitable to our times, and sometimes has
ventured to add to that sublime Composition." Cotton
dates 1759.]

1771 **Scott, Thomas**   The Book of Job in English Verse;
Translated from the Original Hebrew with Remarks,
Historical, Critical and Explanatory, by Thomas
Scott. London: W. Strahan, 1771.
[A close and exact translation, as far as a metrical
version can be.]

Second edition; London: James Buckland, 1773.

1772 **Rowe, Elizabeth**   Miscellaneouc Works...
[See Bible Selections for the complete entry. Includes
Job 38.]

1778 **Anonymous**   Job, Chapter 38. Chesterfield: J.
Bradley, 1778.

1793 **Anonymous**   Job 39:19 "D.G.". Gentleman's Magazine,
October, 1793.

1793 **Anonymous**   Job 39:19, Newly Translated. Gentleman's
Magazine, Page 891, 1793.

1795 **Devens, Richard**   Job. A Paraphrase on Some Parts
of the Book of Job. Boston: Samuel Hall, 1795.

1796 **Bernard, V.L.**   A Sacred Poem in Four Books. Being
a paraphrase on the Book of Job, by V.L.Bernard.
Norwich: Stevenson & Matchett, 1796.
     Another edition, 1800.

1796 **Garden, Charles**   An Improved Version Attempted
of the Book of Job; a Poem, with a Preliminary
Dissertation and Notes, Critical, Historical and
Explanatory. Oxford: J. Cooke, 1796.

1799 **Anketell, John**   A Versification...Job...
     [See Bible Selections for the complete entry.]

1805 **Stock, Joseph**   The Book of Job: metrically arranged
according to the Masora, and newly translated into
English; With notes, critical and explanatory,
accompanied on the opposite page by the authorized
English version. By Joseph Stock.   Bath: Richard
Crutwell, 1805.
     [A new translation with the AV on opposite pages.]

1806 **Lee, Chauncy**   The Trial of Virtue, a Sacred
Poem; Being a Paraphrase of the Whole Book of Job,
and Designed as an Explanatory Comment upon the
Devine Original, Interspersed with Critical Notes
upon a Variety of its Passages – In Six Pts. – to
Which is Annexed, a Dissertation upon the Book of
Job by Chauncy Lee. Hartford, [Conn.]: Printed by
Lincoln and Gleason, 1806.

1810 **Smith, Elizabeth**   The Book of Job; translated
from the Hebrew, by the late Miss Elizabeth Smith,
Author of "Fragments in Prose and Verse"; With a
preface, and annotations, by F. Randolph.   Bath:
Printed by Richard Crutwell, 1810.
     ["This work, so creditable to the fair authoress...was
     completed before her twenty-sixth year, with little
     help, except from Parkhurst's Lexicon, and the revision
     of her friend Dr. Randolph, who annexed to it a few
     critical notes." Page 206 is misnumbered as 188. The
     translation occupies pp. [1]-144.]

1812 **Good, John Mason**   The Book of Job, literally
translated from the original Hebrew, and restored to
its natural arrangement; with notes, critical and
illustrative; and an introductory dissertation on
its scene, scope, language, author and object. By
John Mason Good. London: R. Watts, Brokbourn Press,
for Black, Parry & Co., 1812.

1825 **Hunt, George**   The Book of Job, translated from the
Hebrew. By George Hunt.   Bath: Wood & Cunningham,
1825.

1825 **Rowley, Abraham**   Ten Chapters of The Book
of Job, rendered from the Common Translation, into
Verse. By Abraham Rowley... The pencil of the holy
Ghost hath laboured more in describing the
afflictions of Job, than the felicities of Solomon.
Lord Beacon.   Boston: Printed by J.H.A. Frost...,
1825.

1827 **Fry, John**   A New Translation and Exposition of the
very ancient Book of Job; with notes, explanatory
and philological, by John Fry.   London: Printed for
James Duncan, 1827.

1827 **Noyes, George R.**   An Amended Version... Job...
[See Wisdom and Poetical books and Selections, 1827
George R. Noyes, A New Translation of [the Poetical O.T.
Books]...]

1828 **Laurence, Richard**   The Book of Job; in the Words of
the AV, Arranged and Pointed in General Conformity
with the Masoretic Text.   By Richard Laurence.
Dublin: for W. Curry, 1828.
[The words of the English translation have been retained
throughout, except where a slight alteration was
rendered necessary by the change in their collation, in
which the order of the Hebrew is followed as closely as
the difference of language will permit.]

1831 **Anonymous**   It is reported that there is
an anonymous translation of the Book of Job in The
Christian Observer for 1831.
[Reported by Wemyss.]

1836 **Gray, John Hamilton**   A New Version of the Book of
Job; with expository notes and introduction on the
spirit, composition and authority of the book; by D.
Fredrich Wilhelm Carl Umbreit. Translated from the
German by John Hamilton Gray. 2 Vols.   Edinburgh:
Thomas Clark, Biblical Cabinet or Hermeneutical
Exegetical and Philological Library, Vol. 16, 19,
1836-1837.

1837 **Lee, Samuel**   The Book of the Patriarch Job, translated from the Hebrew, as nearly as possible in the terms and style of the Authorised English Version, to which is prefixed an introduction, on the history, times, country, friends, and Book of the Patriarch; with some strictures and statements of Bishop Warburton, and of the Rationalists of Germany, on the same subjects. And to which is appended a commentary, critical and exegetical, containing elucidations of many other passages of Holy Writ. Inscribed, by Permission, to His Royal Highness the Duke of Sussex. By Samuel Lee. London: James Duncan, 1837.
   ["The object of the present undertaking has been to present to the public as literal a Translation of the Book of Job as the idiom of our language would allow... The language of the AV has been adopted as far as possible..."]

1838 **Anonymous**   Paraphrase [Poetical, on the last 10 Chapters of Job]   London: 1838.
   [Reported by The Bible Collector.]

1838 **Anonymous**   Job; or, The Gospel Preached to the Patriarchs; being a Paraphrase of the Book of Job, by the Widow of a Clergyman of the Church of England [in verse]. [Mrs. Walter Birch]   London: for Rivingtons, 1838.
   [Job selections]

1838 **Jackson, Thomas**   Paraphrase on the Eleven First Chapters of Exodus, with Annotations...Job; or the Gospel Preached to the Patriarchs, Being a Paraphrase of the Last Ten Chapters of the Book of Job...
   [See Old Testament Selections for the complete entry. Includes Last Ten Chapters of the Book of Job.]

1838 **Noyes, George R.**   A New Translation of the Book of Job, with an Introduction and Notes Chiefly Explanatory. By George R. Noyes. Boston: J. Munroe & Co., 1838.
   Third edition; Carefully Revised.   Boston: J. Munroe & Co., 1861.

1839 **Wemyss, Thomas**   Job and his times; or, a picture of the patriarchal age during the period between Noah and Abraham, as regards the state of religion and morality, arts and sciences, manners and customs, &c. And a new version of that most ancient poem, accompanied with notes and dissertations. The whole adapted to the English Reader. By Thomas Wemyss... London: Jackson & Walford, 1839.
   ["...making perspicuity his main object, and avoiding scholastic language as far as possible..."]

1841 **Jenour, Alfred**   The Books of the Old Testament (or, Covenant) Translated from the Hebrew and Chaldee, being the AV revised and compared with other translations, ancient and modern. By ...Alfred Jenour. Volume II.   London: R.B. Seeley & W. Burnside, 1841.
[Actually includes only Job. No more of Vol. II. was published.]

1844 **Barnes, Albert**   Notes Critical, Illustrative, and Practical on the Book of Job: with a new translation [and the KJV] and an introductory dissertation. By Albert Barnes. 2 Vols. London: Wiley & Putnam, 1844.
Another edition; New York: Leavitt, Trow & Co., 1844.

Third edition, 1845.

Also; Carefully Revised by John Cummings. 2 Vols.   London: George Routledge, 1847.

Also; Glasgow: Blackie & Son, 1847.

Another edition; "printed from the Author's Revised Edition" with a preface by E. Henderson. 2 Vols.   London: Partridge & Oakley, 1851.

Also; New Improved Edition by Albert Barnes. 2 Vols.   New York: Leavitt Allen, 1853.

Another edition; Leavitt & Allen, 1854.

Another edition; 1857.

7th. edition; Carefully Revised by John Cummings. 2 Vols.   London: Routledge, Warne and Routledge, 1860.

Reprinted;   2 Vols.   Grand Rapids, Michigan: Baker Book House, 1967.

1845 **Anonymous**   Morals on the Book of Job, by S. Gregory the Great, the First Pope of that Name, Translated, with Notes and Indices In Three Volumes [James Bliss]   Oxford: John Henry Parker; London: J.G.F. and J. Rivington, 1845-1850.
["For the translation, the Editors are indebted to a friend who prefers concealing his name." The text is interspersed with the commentary. Part of The Library of the Fathers of the Holy Catholic Church, Anterior to the Division of East and West. Translated by Members of the English Church. 1839-53, 37 vols.]

1846 **Tattam, Henry**   The Ancient Coptic Version of the Book of Job, the Just, translated into English and Edited by Henry Tattam. London: William Straker, 1846.
   [The text is in English and Coptic.]

1847 **Cummings, John**   Notes Critical, Illustrative, and Practical on the Book of Job: with a new translation and a introductory dissertation... Carefully Revised by John Cummings. 2 Vols. London: Routledge, 1847.
   [Barne's Work Revised.]

   [See Albert Barnes, Note Critical... Book of Job, 1844.]

1852 **Anonymous**   A Metrical Version of the Book of Job: in two parts. Part the first [Chap i-xx; no more published.] [S.H. Fox] London: C. Gilpin, 1852.

1854 **Porteous, M.**   Job Paraphrased; a Poem by M. Porteous. Maybole: n.p., 1854.

1855 **American Bible Union**   Specimen of a Revision of the English Scriptures of the Old Testament, from the original Hebrew, on the basis of the common English version compared with the earlier ones upon which it was founded, by Thomas J. Conant. New York: Holman and Gray; for the American Bible Union, 1855.
   [The specimens are taken from the earlier chapters of Job.]

1855 **Anonymous**   The History of Job; a Tale, illustrative of the dispensations of the Almighty; Reconstructed in the English Language to accord with the long-lost Arabic.   With   brief   comments   and explanations...Edited and for Sale by L.M. Arnold. Poughkeepsie, N.Y. "The Author Chooses not to be Announced". Washington City, D.C.: Samuel Reeve, 1855.

1856 **American Bible Union**   The Book of Job, a Translation from the Original Hebrew on the Basis of the Common and Earlier English Versions, with an Introduction and Explanatory Notes for the English Reader. For the American Bible Union by Thomas J. Conant. New York: American Bible Union; Louisville, Ky: Bible Revision Association; London: Trubner & Co., 1856.
   Part First, containing the Hebrew Text, the Common English Version, and a Revised Version, with a Critical Introduction, and Critical and Philological Notes.

   [Part Second] A Translation from the Original Hebrew on the basis of the Common and Earlier

English Versions. With an Introduction and Explanatory Notes for the English Reader...

Also; The Book of Job, from the Original Hebrew on the Basis of the Common and Earlier Versions. By Thomas J. Conant. New York: American Bible Union, 1856.
[This work has 63 pages; another edition dated 1866 has 99 pages.]

Another edition; The Book of Job; the common English version, the Hebrew text, and the revised version of the American Bible Union, with an introduction and philological notes... 1856. [165 pages.]   Also; without notes, 1866.

1858 **Carey, Carteret Priaulx**   The Book of Job, Translated from the Hebrew on the Basis of the Authorized Version: Explained in a large body of notes critical and exegetical and Illustrated by extracts from Various Works of antiquities, geography, science, etc... and a map; with six preliminary dissertations, an analytical paraphrase, and Meisner's and Doederlein's selection of the various readings of the Hebrew text, from the collation of Kennicott and DeRossi. By Carteret Priaulx Carey. London: Wertheim, Macintosh & Hunt, 1858.

1859 **Stather, W.C.**   The Book of Job in English Verse. Translated from the Original Hebrew: with Notes, Critical and Explanatory, by W.C. Stather. London: 1859.
Another edition; Bath: Binns & Godwin, 1860.

1860 **Anonymous**   The Poem of the Book of Job done into English verse, by the Earl of Winchelsea (Late Viscount Maidstone) [Finch-Hatton] London: Smith, Elder & Co., 1860.

1862 **Davidson, Andrew Bruce**   A Commentary, Grammatical and Exegetical, on the Book of Job; with a translation. By A.B. Davidson. Vol. 1   London: Williams & Norgate, 1862.
[Chapters 1-14 only; no more published.]

1863 **Croly, George**   The Book of Job. Edinburgh: 1863.

1864 **Adams, Henry W.**   The Book of Job in Poetry; or, A Song in the Night, by Henry W. Adams. New York: Robert Craighead, 1864.

1864 **Bernard, H.H.**   The Book of Job, 1864.
[Translation of his work.]

1864 **Chance, Frank**   ...The Book of Job as Expounded
to his Cambridge Pupils by the Late Herman Hedwig
Bernard... Edited, with a Translation and Additional
Notes by his Friend and Former Pupil, Frank Chance.
London: Hamilton, Adams & Co., 1864.
> [Vol. 1 Containing the whole of the original work; no
> more published. The 1884 edition gives the date of the
> 1st ed. as 1863.]

1864 **Rodwell, J.M.**   ...The Book of Job; translated
from the Hebrew, by Rev. J.M. Rodwell. London: for
Williams & Norgate; Hertford: Stephen Austin, 1864.
> Second edition, 1868.

1866 **Green, Rev. William Bachelder**   A new version of
Job. Boston: 1866.

1868 **Bolton, Francis**   Biblical Commentary on the
Book of Job, by Franz Delitzsch...Translated from
the German by Francis Bolton. 2 Vols.   London:
Williams & Norgate, 1868.
> [Clark's Foreign Theological Library, Ser.4, v.10,11.]

> [See Old Testaments, 1865 Biblical Commentary.]

1869 **Anonymous**   The Book of Job in metre, according
to   the   most   approved   commentaries...   [William
Meikle]   Falkirk: William Meikle, 1869.
> Another edition; signed "W.M.", 1871.

1869 **Coleman, John Noble**   The Book of Job,
translated from the Hebrew, with notes, explanatory,
illustrative and critical by the Rev. J.N. Coleman
... London: J. Nisbet & Co.; Edinburgh: T.Constable,
1869.
> Second edition; The Poem of Job; The most ancient
> Book in the Universe; the first written
> revelation which God vouch-safed to Man. With
> a statement of the country where Job resided,
> and an enumeration of some of the lands which
> Job gave to his three daughters for an
> inheritance amidst their brethren, and which
> were called after their own names. Translated
> from the Hebrew, with notes, explanatory,
> illustrative and critical, by John Noble
> Coleman. Printed for private circulation [by
> T. and A. Constable, at the Edinburgh
> University Press], 1871.

1871 **Barham, Francis**   The Book of Job; newly translated
from the original by Francis Barham. Printed both in
Phonetic and in the customary spelling, by A. Elzas.
London: F. Pitman;   Bath: I. Pitman; J. Davies,
1871.

1872 **Elzas, A.**   The Book of Job, translated from the Hebrew Text, with an introduction and notes, critical and explanatory by A. Elzas.   London: Trubner & Co., 1872.
> Again, 1873.

> Another edition; The Book of Job. As Translated from the Original by Rabbi Abraham Elzas; with some Comments on the Poem by Elbert Hubbard. Done into a book at the Roycraft Shop which is in East Aurora, New York, U.S.A. MDCCCXCVII (1897).
>> [This was a limited edition with only 350 autographed copies.]

1872 **Lewis, Taylor**   The Book of Job, a Rhythmical Version with Introduction and Annotations, by Taylor Lewis. New York: Scribner's Sons, 1872.
> [Bound with 'A Commentary on the Holy Scriptures...By Peter Lange' Vol. VIII. See 1864.]

1873 **Smith, John Frederick**   Commentary on the Book of Job with Translation by the late Dr. George Heinrich August von Ewald. Translated from the German by J. Frederick Smith. London: Williams & Norgate, 1873.
> [The Theological Translation Fund Library, Vol. xxvii]

> Another edition, 1882.

1875 **Halsted, Oliver S.**   The Book called Job. From the Hebrew. With footnotes. By Oliver S. Halsted. Published by the Author, Lyon's Farms, New Jersey, September, 1875. Newark, NJ: Printed by Jennings & Hardham, 1875.

1877 **Cowles, Henry**   The Book of Job, with notes, critical, explanatory and practical, designed for both pastors and people. With a New Translation Appended. By Rev. Henry Cowles...   New York: D. Appleton & Co., 1877.
> Another Edition, 1881.

1878 **Raymond, Rossiter W.**   The Book of Job; Essays, and a Metrical Paraphrase. By Rossiter W. Raymond. With an Introductory Note by the Rev. T.J. Conant..., and the Text of the Revised Version Prepared by Dr. Conant for the American Bible Union [1856]   New York: D. Appleton & Co., 1878.
> [The Deity is rendered "Jehovah" a few times.]

1879 **Anonymous**   The Book of Job, translated from the Hebrew Text with an introduction, a summary of each chapter and brief notes in explanation of obscure passages, by John, Bishop of Frederication,

and Metropolitan of Canada. [John Medley] St. John, New Brunswick: J. & A. McMillan, printers, 1879.
> ["...made after repeated examination of the Hebrew Text, aided by such of the learned commentaries of eminent scholars, both German and English, as have fallen within my reach..." American Bible Society attributes to John Lee Watson.]

1879 **Kelly, William**   Notes on the Book of Job with a new version. By William Kelly. London: G. Morrish, 1879.
> Another edition; London: F.E. Race, 1913?

1880 **Clarke, Henry James**   The Book of Job. A metrical translation, with introduction and notes. London: Hodder & Stoughton, 1880.

1880 **Cox, Samuel**   A Commentary on the Book of Job with a translation. By Samuel Cox. London: C. Kegan Paul & Co., 1880.
> ["...to correct certain obvious errors of the Press."]

> Second Edition; London: Kegan Paul, Trench, Trubner & Co., 1885.

> Third Edition; Chapter translations interspersed, 1894

1880 **Malet, Arthur**   The Book of Job in Blank Verse...
> [See Bible Selections, 1883 for the complete entry.]

1880 **White, G. Cecil**   The Discipline of Suffering. Nine short readings on the history of Job... (Part 2. The Conversation in blank verse.) London: W. Skeffington & Son, 1880.
> [i.e., the text of Job.]

1881 **Purvey, John**   The Books of Job [etc.] According to the Wycliffe Version Made by Nicholas de Herford... and Revised by Purvey...Formerly Edited by Josiah Forshall... and Sir Fredrick Maden, ...and now Reprinted. Oxford: Clarendon Press, 1881.

1883 **Sawyer, Leicester Ambrose**   Job: Analyzed, Translated and Accompanied with Critical Studies, by Rev. Leicester A. Sawyer, translator of the Scriptures, etc. Whitesboro, New York: Published by the author, 1883.

1883 **Wright, G.H. Bateson**   The Book of Job. A new critically revised translation with essays on Scansion, Date, etc, by G.H.Bateson Wright... London & Edinburgh: Williams & Norgate, 1883.

1887 **Curry**   The Book of Job (According to the Version of 1885) with an Expository and Practical Commentary, Enriched with Illustrations from some of the most Eminent Modern Expositors and a Critical Introduction.   N. Phillips & Hunt;   Cincinnati: Cranston & Stowe, 1887.

1887 **Russell, Mrs. W.W.**   The Book of Job with Explanations and Reflections Regarding the Interior Life. Translated from the French [of Madam Guyon]. Boston: B.B. Russell, 1887.

1887 **Smith, George Vance**   Chapters on Job (for young readers) by G. Vance Smith.   London: The Sunday School Association, 1887.

1888 **Morgan, Bishop William**   The Book of Job. Translation by Bishop William Morgan.   Oxford: J.G. Evans, 1888.

1889 **Anonymous**   The Book of Job Translated from the Hebrew. With a Study upon the Age and Character of the Poem. By Ernest Renan (Member of the French Academy). Rendered into English by A.F.G. and W.M.T. [Henry Frederick Gibbons and William M. Thomson] London: W.M. Thomson, [1889].
>   ["...the translators have been careful to render both the text and metrical portion as closely as possible to M.Renan's language..." [i.e., the French of his 'La Livre de Job', 1859.] The translation is attributed to Gibbons and Thomson by British Museum Catalogue, but we note that Gibbons' first name is not in accord with the initials.]

>   [The Deity is rendered "Jehovah" a few times.]

1889 **Gilbert, George H.**   The Poetry of Job. By George H. Gilbert. Chicago: A.C. McClurg and Company, 1889.
>   [Includes: Part I. A Rhythmical Translation of Job. and Part II. Interpretation of the Poem. "The text that has been translated is that edited by L. Baer and Franz Delitzsch, Liepzig, 1875."]

1890 **Anonymous**   The Book of Job... Solomon...
>   [See Wisdom and Poetical books and Selections, 1890 Anonymous, Poetical Parts of the Old Testament.]

1891 **Genung, John Franklin**   The Epic of the Inner Life being the Book of Job translated anew, and accompanied with notes and an introductory study by John F. Genung.   London: Clarke & Co., 1891.
>   ["Having made the translation (from the Hebrew) with care, I have then preceded to treat it as if it were an English poem... I have discarded the old division of the poem into chapters and verses..."]

[The Deity is rendered "Jehovah" in the footnote on page 134 in the 1893 edition.]

Other editions; Boston & New York: Houghton, Miffin & Co.; Cambridge: The Riverside Press, 1892, 1893, 1894, 1895, 1900, 1919, 1930.

1894 **Sydenstricker, H.M.**   The Epic of the Orient, an Original Poetical Rendering of the Book of Job, by H.M. Sydenstricker. Hartford: Student Publishing Co., 1894.

1895 **Dillon, Emile Joseph**   The Skeptics...Job; Koheleth...
        [See Old Testament Selections for the complete entry.]

1897 **Anonymous**   The Book of Ayub: known in the West as Job. [R.Sadler]   London: Sheppard & St. John, 1897.
        [Translated, with notes.]

1897 **Tattersall, John**   The Poem of Job, Rendered in English Metre, by John Tattersall. London: Bernard Quaritch, 1897.

1898 **Cary, Otis**   The Man who Feared God for Nought, being a Rhythmical version of the Book of Job, by Otis Cary. London: Elliot Stock, 1898.
        Another edition; The Man who feared God; being a Rhymical Version of the Book of Job. New York & Chicago: Revell, 1898.
            [Also; printed at the Okayama Orphan Asylum, Okayama, Japan.]

1898 **Fenton, Ferrar**   The Book of Job. Translated direct from the Hebrew text into English by Ferrar Fenton. Assisted by Henrik Borgstrom... Rendered into the Same Metre as the Original Hebrew Word by Word and Line by Line.   London: Elliot Stock, 1898.
        Another edition; London and New Haven, Conn., Published for the Translator, [1901].

        Also; London: H. Marshall and Son, [1902].

1898 **Fielding, George Hanbury**   The Book of Job, a Revised Text, with Introduction and Notes, by George Hanbury Fielding... London: Elliot Stock, 1898.

1899 **Pollard, Josephine**   Ruth, A Bible Heroine...
        [See Old Testament Selections for the complete entry. Includes abbreviated stories of Job.]

1901 **Wilkinson, F.H.**   The Book of Job. Translated and annotated. By F.H. Wilkinson... London: Skeffington & Son, 1901.

1903 **Anonymous**   The Book of Job. A
Rhythmical Translation with the Structure, and Brief
Explanatory and Critical Notes. Eyre & Spottiswoode,
1903.

1903 **Bullinger, E.W.**   The Book of Job. Part 1,
the oldest lesson in the world. Part 2, a rhythmical
translation, with the structure; and a brief,
explanatory and critical notes, by E.W. Bullinger.
London: Eyre & Spottiswoode, 1903.
   Another edition, 1904.

1903 **Lund, Emil**   Job. Rock Island: Augustana Book
Concern, 1903.
   [Recorded by Simms.]

1903 **Pritchard, M.**   The Poem of Job. Being an attempt
to obtain a clearer glimpse into the ancient poem of
the Book of Job; After a careful study of
translations, commentaries and notes made by some of
the best students of later times; and by elimination
of certain passages now deemed by many such students
to have been added to the original work; A Version
Prepared by M. Pritchard, with Introduction and
Notes. London: Kegan Paul, Trench, Trubner & Co.,
1903.

1905 **Hirsch, Samuel Abraham**   A Commentary on the Book
of Job from a Hebrew Manuscript in the University
Library, Cambridge... [Edited by William Aldis
Wright].   London: Published for the Text &
translation Society by Williams & Norgate, 1905.
   [The translation is printed in heavy black type,
   interspersed in the commentary.]

1908 **Brown, Charles Reynolds**   The Strange Ways of
God; A Study in the Book of Job by Charles Reynolds
Brown.   Boston, New York, & Chicago: The Pilgrim
Press, 1908.
   ["In the main I have used the translation given in the
   RV and the literary arrangement found in Moulton's
   Modern Readers Bible. Here and there, I have used my own
   Paraphrase."]

1911 **Barton, George Aaron**   The Book of Job By G.A.
Barton. (The Bible for Home and School, Edited by S.
Matthews.) 1911.
   [From the bibliography of M.H.Pope's "Job" in the Anchor
   Bible.]

1911 **Blake, Buchanan**   The Book of Job and the Problem
of Suffering [With the Text Translated into Verse
and Re-arranged] by Buchanan Blake.   London, New
York & Toronto: Hodder & Stoughton, 1911.

Another edition; London: Eyre & Spottiswoode, 1911.

1911 **Smith, Nathaniel** The Messages of the Poets...
[See Old Testament Selections for the complete entry.]

1912 **Gordon, Alexander R.** The Poets of the Old Testament...
[See Old Testament Selections for the complete entry. Includes Job.]

1912 **Jennings, William** The Dramatic Poem of Job; a close metrical translation with critical and explanatory notes ...by William Jennings... London: Methuen & Co., 1912.

1912 **Myers, Isadore** (Metric Translation of Job) MS, 1912.
["My metric translations of the Psalms and of Job have been completed, which I trust will not stay in their unpublished form as long as this work has had to remain." From the Preface to Myers' Proverbs, 1912.]

1912 **Wilson, Peter** The Book of Job, Translated into English Verse by the Rev. Peter Wilson. Edinburgh: James Thin, 1912.

1913 **Sprague, Homer B.** The Book of Job; The Poetic Portion Versified, with due regard to the language of the AV. A closer adherence to the sense of the revised versions, and a more literal translation of the Hebrew original, with an introductory essay advancing new views and explanatory notes quoting many eminent authorities, by Homer B. Sprague. Boston: Sherman, French & Co., 1913.
[The Deity is rendered "Jehovah" many times.]

1913 **Strahan, James** The Book of Job, Interpreted by James Strahan... Edinburgh: T. & T. Clark, 1913.
Second edition, 1914.

1914 **Anonymous** The War Bible of the Moment...Job...
[See Old Testament Selections for the complete entry.]

1914 **Freegard, Edwin** The Book of Job, a Transcription, by Edwin Freegard. St. Louis: The Freegard Press, 1914.

1914 **King, Edward George** The Poem of Job translated in the metre of the Original by Edward G. King. Cambridge: University Press, 1914.

1915 **Noyes, G.A.** Job, a Translation in the Hebrew Rhythm by G.A. Noyes. London: Luzac & Co., 1915.
["The following translation comprises that portion of the Book of Job to which the Massorites assigned the

accentuation known as the 'Poetical', i.e., the portion which commences with Chapter III., verse 2, and ends with Chapter XLII., verse 6."]

1915 **Shove, H.P.**   Job, by H.P Shove. Kirkwood, Mo: n.p., 1915.

1916 **Rothwell, Fred**   A Modern Job; An Essay on the Problem of Evil, by Etienne Giren, with Introduction by Archbishop Lilley, Authorised Translation by Fred Rothwell.   Chicago and London: The Open Court Publishing Co., 1916.

1917 **Jastrow, Morris**   Job, 1917.
          [See Old Testaments, 1917 Jewish Publication Society.]

1917 **McFadyen, John Edgar**   The Wisdom Books...
          [See Wisdom and Poetical books and Selections, 1916 John Edgar McFadyen, [The Poetical Books of the O.T.]...]

1917 **Watch Tower Bible & Tract Society**   Studies in the Scriptures... Series VII. The Finish Mystery... Brooklyn: International Bible Students Association, 1917.
          [Job 40:15-41:34; Pages 84-86.]

1918 **Anonymous**   The Book of Job. [Walter Runciman] East Sheen: Temple Sheen Press, 1918.
          [Prefatory Note signed "W.R."]

1918 **Kallen, Horace Meyer**   The Book of Job as a Greek Tragedy, Restored with an Introductory Essay on the Original Form and Philosophic Meaning of Job... And an Introduction by Professor George Foot Moore.   New York: Moffatt, Yard & Co., 1918.
          ["The text used for the present edition of the Book of Job is that of the American Revised Version. Very few departures from it have been made, and those were compelled by the necessities of accuracy..."]

     Another edition; New York: Hill & Wang, 1959.

1920 **Jastrow, Morris**   The Book of Job, its Origin, Growth and Interpretation, Together with a New Translation based on a Revised Text by Morris Jastrow...   Philadelphia & London: J.B. Lippincott Co., 1920.

1921 **Driver, Samuel Rolles and George Buchanan Gray**
     A Critical and Exegetical Commentary on the Book of Job, Together with a New Translation by Samuel Rolles Driver... and George Buchanan Gray... Edinburgh: T. & T. Clark, 1921.
          [See Complete Bibles, 1895 International Critical Commentary.]

Reprint, 1950.

1922 **Ball, C.J.**   The Book of Job, a revised text and version by C.J. Ball. With a preface by C.F.Burney. Oxford: Clarendon Press, 1922.

1922 **Buttenweiser, Moses**   The Book of Job, by Moses Buttenweiser. London & Norwood. Mass.: Hodder & Stoughton, 1922.
["The reconstruction of chapters 16-37...is based upon very careful study covering many years... my translations...in not a few places are radically different not only from those in the English Bible but also from those prevailing in modern commentaries..." Text is printed in Hebrew (an amended version) and in English.]

Another edition; New York: Macmillan, 1922.

Also, 1925.

1923 **Clements, Colin C.**   Job. A Play in One Act. Adopted by Colin C. Clements. New York & London: Samuel French, 1923.

1923 **Mumford, Alfred Harold**   The Book of Job; A metrical version, by A.H. Mumford. With an Introductory Essay "The Significance of the Book of Job" By A.S. Peake, D.D. New York: George H. Doran, 1923.
["...for the most part this metrical version is independent of any literary aid save the AV to which the debt is unspeakable."]

Another edition; London: Hodder & Stoughton, 1923.

1929 **Jordan, William George**   The Book of Job: Its Substance and Spirit by W.G. Jordan. New York:...The Macmillan Co., 1929.
[Based upon a Rhythmic Version by Dr. Taylor Lewis, 1874.]

1929 **Martin, William Wallace**   The Book of Job...
[See Wisdom and Poetical books and Selections for the complete entry.]

1933 **Nesfield, Vincent**   Let Cockle Grow instead of Barley, by Vincent Nesfield. London: A.J. Davies, 1933.
[The Book of Job.]

1934 **Neumann, Robert**   The Book of Job; A Metrical Translation with a Critical Introduction. Burlington, Iowa: The Lutheran Literary Board, 1934.
Another edition; London: Printed for Thomas Tegg and Sons, 1836.

1935 **Nairne, A.**   The Book of Job, Edited with an Introduction, by A. Nairne. Cambridge: At the University Press, 1935.
["The text will be taken from the English R.V., but its marginal renderings will be adopted without comment where necessary."]

1936 **Richardson, Jacob W.**   Out of the Whirlwind; a Dramatized Version of the Book of Job. Based on Dr. Moffatt's translation, by Jacob W. Richardson. London: Epworth Press, 1936.

1937 **Dimnent, Edward D.**   The Book of Job; The Poem, An Epic Version in English by Edward D. Dimnent... Foreword by Samuel M. Zwemer, D.D...   New York, London, and Edinburgh: Fleming H. Revell Company, 1937.

1938 **Kraeling, Emil G.**   The Book of the Ways of God, by Emil G. Kraeling. London: S.P.C.K.; New York: Charles Scribner's, 1938.
[Commentary interspersed with selections translated from Job.]

1938 **O'Neill, George**   The World's Classic Job; Translation from Original Texts, with Introduction and Notes by George O'Neill... Milwaukee: The Bruce Publishing Co., 1938.
Another edition; Job. Translation from original Texts, with Introduction and Notes by George O'Neill,... Milwaukee: The Bruce Publishing Co., 1938.

1939 **Kissane, Edward J.** The Book of Job. Translated from a Critically Revised Hebrew Text with Commentary by Rev. Edward J. Kissane... Dublin: Browne & Nolan Ltd., The Richview Press, 1939.
Another edition; New York: Sheed & Ward, 1946.

1941 **Strauss, Dorothy**   The Book of Job Rendered so 'that he who runs may read', by Dorothy Strauss. 1941.
[A paraphrase, written in collaboration with Mr. Lazer Grossman.]

1942 **Minn, H.R.**   The Burden of this Unintelligible World; or, The Mystery of Suffering, being a Rhythmical Version of the Book of Job, Annotated by H.R. Minn.   Auckland, Wellington, Christchurch, Dunedin, Invercargill, N.Z., Sydney, Melbourne & London: Printed by Whitcombe & Tombs Ltd., 1942.

1944 **Hurwitz, Nathan**   The Immortal Drama of Life (The Book of Job). The Mystery Book of More than 3000 Years. Translated from the original. [Cape Town: Stewart Publishing Co.] 1944.

1946 **Lassen, A.L.**   The Commentary of Levi ben Gerson
(Gersonides) on the Book of Job, by A.L. Lassen.
New York: Bloch Publishing Co., 1946.
["Gersonides goes through each section of Job three
times: first he explains the meaning of difficult
passages, next he gives a paraphrase of the passage as
a whole, and finally he considers the general
philosophical principles underlying the section."]

1946 **Reichert, V.E.**   Job with Hebrew Text an[d] English
translation, by V.E. Reichert.   Hindhead, Surrey,
n.p., 1946.
[Unknown whether this is the same as that published by
Soncino Press with the same date.]

1946 **Reichert, Victor E.**   The Book of Job. Hebrew Text
and English Translation with an Introduction and
Commentary by Victor E. Reichert.   London: Soncino
Press, 1946.
[See Old Testaments, 1936 Soncino Books of the Bible.]

1947 **Stevenson, William Barron**   The Poem of Job;
A Literary Study with a New Translation, by W.B.
Stevenson. (The Schweich Lectures of the British
Academy, 1943.)   London: Published for the British
Academy by Geoffrey Cumberlege, Oxford University
Press, 1947.
["His translation is based on a freely corrected form of
the only available ancient Hebrew text (MT)... A
modified rhythmic form, similar to that of the original
has been employed..."]

Second edition; 1948.

1951 **Peterson, Russell A.**   The God that Job had; a
Reading of the Book of Job, by Russell A. Peterson.
Minneapolis, Minn.: Colwell Press, 1951.
["The language here used is basic English; the text
followed is that of the original tongue, the Hebraic
mind."]

1954 **Bennett, William**   The Trials of Job, by William
Bennett. Georgetown, Conn.: Glenburgh Co., 1954.
[In Verse.]

1954 **Robinson, W.H.**   Job and His Friends, by W.H.
Robinson.   London: S.C.M. Press, 1954.
[In chapters I and II the AV has been closely followed;
in later chapters, I have ventured to offer an
independent rendering, occasionally noting variations
from the traditional Hebrew text, and sometimes quoting
the Septuagint..."]

[Consists of selected passages interspersed with
commentary.]

1955 **Wanefsky, David**   The Hebrew Scriptures
Reappraised...

[See Wisdom and Poetical Books and Selections for the complete entry. Includes Job.]

1957 **Terrien, Samuel**   Job: Poet of Existence. Indianapolis, New York: Bobbs-Merrill, 1957.
["...Substantially in accordance with the KJV, which has been conservatively amended whenever errors or obscurities warranted a change."]

1957 **Torczyner, H.**   The Book of Job, a New Commentary by N.H. Tur-Sinai (H. Torczyner) Jerusalem: Kiryath Sepher Ltd., 1957.
["...English translation of the text...follows the Authorized and the Revised Version, but deviates from them as far as the new findings require." The English and Hebrew texts appear on facing pages, above the commentary.]

1958 **Ellison, H.L.**   From Tragedy to Triumph: The Message of the Book of Job, by H.L. Ellison. Grand Rapids, MI: Wm. B. Eerdmans Publishing Co., 1958.
["The text printed at the beginning of Chapters or sections is that of the R.V., with the substitution of the marginal renderings, when these are generally accepted as superior."]

1958 **Freehof, Solomon**   Book of Job; a Commentary, by Solomon Freehof. New York: Union of American Hebrew Congregations, 1958.
[The Jewish Commentary for Public Readers.]

1959 **Blackwood, Andrew W.**   Devotional Introduction to Job, by Andrew W.Blackwood. Grand Rapids: Baker Book House, 1959.
[Selections; "...the AV, with occasional modifications to clarify the meaning."]

1959 **Crook, Margaret Brackenbury**   The Cruel God; Job's Search for the Meaning of Suffering, by Margaret Brackenbury Crook. Boston: Beacon Press, 1959.
["The author, in translating passages from the Bible, is frequently indebted to the ERV, sometimes to the KJV, and the RSV..."]

1960 **Carey**   The Book of Job, Arranged for Stage. Anchorage, KY: Children's Theatre Press, 1960.

1960 **Weitzner, Emil**   The Book of Job, a Paraphrase, by Emil Weitzner. New York: the author, 1960.
[See Old Testament Selections, 1959 for the complete entry.]

1963 **Crawford, Harriet A.** A Libretto for Job, by Harriet A. Crawford. Boston: Christopher Publishing House, 1963.
[AV and a 20th Century paraphrase in parallel columns.]

1963 **Donn, Thomas M.**   The Divine Challenge; being a Metrical Paraphrase of the Book of Job in Four-line Stanzas of Anapaestic Tetrameters in Rhyme, by Thomas M. Donn. Inverness, Engl.: Printed by Robert Carruthers & Sons "Courier Office", 1963.

1965 **Gordis, Robert**   The Book of God and Man; a Study of Job. By Robert Gordis.   Chicago: University of Chicago Press, 1965.

1965 **Minn, H.R.**   The Book of Job, A Translation With Introduction and Short Notes, by H.R. Minn. [Auckland, New Zealand: Printed and Bound at the University of Auckland Bindery.] 1965.
> ["The Massoretic or standard Hebrew text has been generally, but not blindly followed." A work distinct from that of 1942.]

1965 **Pope, Marvin H.**   Job. Introduction, Translation and Notes, by Marvin H. Pope.   Garden City, New York: Doubleday and Co., Inc., 1965.
> [See Complete Bibles, 1964 Anchor Bible, Vol. 15.]

Third Edition; 1973.

1967 **Knight, Harold**   A Commentary on the Book of Job, by E. Dhorme. Translated (from the French) by Harold Knight, with Prefatory Notes by H.H. Rowley. London: Nelson, 1967.

1968 **Guillaume, A.**   Studies in the Book of Job, with a new Translation by A. Guillaume. Edited by John Macdonald.   Leiden: E.J. Brill, 1968.
> [The Annual of Leeds University Oriental Society, Supplement 2.]

1971 **Anonymous**   Job for Modern Man. Today's English Version. New York: American Bible Society, 1971.
> [Cover bears title: "Tried and True" Job for Modern Man]

1972 **Etheridge, Eugene W.**   The Man from Uz; A Paraphrastic Drama of the Book of Job in Blank Verse. Francestown, NH: Golden Quill Press, 1972.

1972 **Neiman, David N.**   The Book of Job; a Presentation of the Book with Selected Portions Translated from the Original Hebrew Text, by David N. Neiman. Jerusalem: Masada, 1972.

1976 **Carlisle, Thomas John**   Journey with Job, by Thomas John Carlisle.   Grand Rapids: Wm. B. Eerdmans, 1976.

1977 **Rosenberg, David**   Job Speaks, Interpreted from the Original Hebrew Book of Job, by David Rosenberg. A Poet's Bible.   New York: Harper & Row, 1977.
[Selected passages poetically paraphrased]

Also; Job Speaks. The New Republic, April 16, 1977.
[Third chapter only.]

1978 **Gordis, Robert**   The Book of Job, Commentary, New Translation and Special Studies. New York: Jewish Theological Seminary of America, 1978.

1979 **Mitchell, Stephen**   Into the Whirlwind: A Translation of Job, by Stephen Mitchell. Garden City, New York: Doubleday & Co., 1979.
Another edition; The Book of Job; Translated and with an Introduction by Stephen Mitchell. San Francisco: North Point Press, 1987.

1980 **Ceresko, Anthony R.**   Job 29-31 in the Light of Northwest Semitic. A Translation and Philological Commentary. Anthony R. Ceresko...   Rome: Biblical Institute Press, 1980.
[Job selections]

1980 **Jewish Publication Society**   The Book of Job. A New Translation According to the Traditional Hebrew Text. With Introductions by Moshe Greenberg, Jonas C. Greenfield, and Nahum M. Sarna.   Philadelphia: Jewish Publication Society, 1980.

1980 **Tsevat, Matitiahu**   The Meaning...Book of Job...
[See Old Testament Selections for the complete entry.]

1983 **Vawter, Bruce**   Job and Jonah, Questioning the...
[See Old Testament Selections for the complete entry.]

1988 **Hartley, John E.**   The Book of Job, 1988.
[See Hebrew Scriptures Listing, 1976 New International Commentary on the O.T.]

1989 **Rosenberg, A.J.**   Job, 1989.
[See Old Testament Selections, ???? Judaica Press Publications.]

PSALMS

???? **Anonymous**   The Psalter or Book of Psalms in Latin and English. Worcester: Stanbrook Abbey, [19??].
Second edition, 1901.

???? **Blayney, Benjamin**   Psalms, [179?].
[Not published; location of MS unknown. Mentioned by
Herbert, under Jeremiah and Lamentations, 1784.]

???? **Keeper, John**   Psalter in Metre. London: John Day,
154?

???? **Nicolas, Sir Harris**   See Christopher Davison
& Others, Divers...Psalms, 1620.

700 **Aldhelm**   Translation of Psalter, 700.
["There is no real evidence that any such version ever
existed..."]

700 **Guthlac**   The Psalter (In Anglo-Saxon). MS now lost,
700.
["...there is no real evidence that any such version
ever existed..."]

1150 **Anonymous**   The Shaftesbury Psalter. Cotton MS.
Nero C.4, c1150.
[Anglo-Saxon]

1170 **Eadwine**   The Canterbury Psalter, also known
as the Cambridge Psalter. Contains Jerome's Gallican
Psalms with a Latin Gloss, the Roman version with an
Anglo-Saxon Gloss, and the Hebrew version with a
Norman-French gloss. Trinity College, Cambridge:
Psalterium Triplex MS 1170.
[See F. Harsley, 1889.]

1250 **Anonymous**   Psalter; Latin Text with a
Thirteeth Century Anglo-Saxon Gloss. Royal Library,
Paris. MS. (4.A.xiv), 1250?

1320 **Schorham, William de**   (Vicar of Chant-Sutton near
Leeds in Kent) Psalter in Latin and English, verse
by verse, 1320.

1340 **Anonymous**   The Psalter and Canticles in Latin and
English. MSS: BM, Add. Mss. 17376; Trinity College,
Dublin, Ms. A.4.4 (formerly h.32); Cambridge,
Magdelene College, Pepys 2498.
    The Earliest Complete English Prose Psalter.
    Together with the Eleven Canticles and a
    Translation of the Athanasian Creed, Edited
    from the only Two Mss. in the Libraries of the
    British Museum and Trinity College, Dublin,
    with a Preface, Introduction, Notes and
    Glossary. Edited by Karl D. Bulring (?), 1891.

    Reprinted; Millwood, New York: Kraus Reprint,
    1975.

1340 Rolle, Richard   Psalter in Latin & English. c1340
[English   in   the   Northumbrian   Dialect.]
British Museum: Royal MS. 18.D.i

[English in the Southern Dialect] Arundel MS.
158

["In this worke I seke no straunge Ynglys, bot lightest
and communest, and swilk that is most like vnto the
Latyne, so yt thai that knawes noght ye Latyne be the
Ynglys may com to many Latyne wordis. In ye Translacione
I felogh the letter als-mekille as I may, and thor I
fyne no proper Yngys I felogh ye wit of the wordis, so
that thai that shall rede it them thar not drede
errynge. In the expowndyng I felough holi Doctors..."]

[The work was originally written in the Northumbrian
dialect, but was popular all over the Kingdom, some
38mss remaining.]

The Psalter or Psalms of David, and certain
Canticles, with a Translation and Exposition
in English by Richard Rolle of Hampole. Edited
from manuscripts by ...H.R. Bramley. With an
introduction and glossary.   (Univ. Coll.
Oxford. MS 64) 1884.

1530 Aleph, Johan   The Psalter of David in English,
1530.

1530 Anonymous   The Psalter of Dauid in Englishe
purely ad faithfully traslated aftir the text of
ffeline: euery Psalme hauynge his argument before /
declarynge brefly thentente & substance of the wholl
Psalme. [George Joye] [Emprinted at Argentine in
the yeare of oure lorde 1530. the .16. daye of
Ianuary by me Francis foxe]
['The Argentine Psalter', Preface signed "Johan Aleph".
Translated from the Latin of Friar Felix (Martin Bucer),
an augustinian Monk; printed 1515. Joye's work was
actually printed at Antwerp by Merten de Keyser.]

Another edition; Dauid's Psalter; diligently and
faithfully traslated by George Joye with breif
Arguments before euery Psalme; declaringe the
effecte thereof (Thus endeth the text of the
Psalmes translated oute of Latyne by George
Joye. The year of oure Lorde M.D.xxxiiii. Je
monethe of Auguste. Antwerp: Martyn Emperowr.)

Another edition; - - Whereunto is annexed in
thenede certayne godly prayers thoroweoute the
whole yere commonly called collettes. London:
Imprinted by Edward Whitchurch, 1547.

Reprint; The Psalter of David, 1530; Aretius Felinus; translated from the Latin by George Joy. 1st. Edition. Reprinted; Introduction by G.E.Duffield. Appleford, Sutton Courtenay Press, 1971. [250 numbered copies.]

1532 **Anonymous** The Psalter of Dauid in Englyshe, purely and faythfully traslated after the texte of Felyne: euery Psalme hauynge his argument before/ declarynge brefely thentente & substance of the hole Psalme. Printed at London by Thomas Godfray, 1532?
[Apparently a different work than that ascribed to Joye, 1530 and 1534. The only known copy is in the University Library, Cambridge.]

1535 **Anonymous** A Paraphrasis vpon al the Psalmes of Dauid made by Johannes Capensis, reader of Hebrue lecture in the vniuersitie of Louane, and traslated out of Latyne into Englishe. [Myles Coverdale] Antwerp: The Widow of Christopher van Endhoven. 1535.
Another edition; A Paraphrasis vpon all the Psalmes of Dauid... Pryntes in the house of Thomas Gybson, 1539.

1540 **Anonymous** The Psalter, Translated from the Latin Version of Feline. Edward Whitchurch. 1540.
[Possibly an edition of Joye's Psalter of 1530. Cotton.]

1540 **Coverdale, Myles** The Psalter; or, Booke of Psalmes both in Latyn and Englyshe. Translated into Englyshe out of the como texte of the Latyne, which customably is redde in the churche. London: Ricardus Grafton excudebat, 1540.
[...wyth a Kalender and a Table the more eassyer and lyghtlyer to Fynde the psalmes contayned therein. Ricardus Grafton, M D x l]

1540 **Coverdale, Myles** The Psalter; or, booke of the Psalmes, wher vnto are added certayne other deuoute praiers Psalmes, wher vnto are added certayne other deuoute praiers take out of the Byble. First Prynted in Southwarke by James Nicolson, 1540.
Reprinted; London: Faber & Gwyer, 1926.

Another reprint; The Book of Psalms from the version of Miles Coverdale...; with an introduction by Francis Wormald... London: Haymarket Press, 1930.

1540 **Grafton, R.** Psalter in Latin and English... Translation from the Vulgate. London: 1540.

1547 **Anonymous**   [The First Scottish Metrical Psalter]
     1547-1565.
      1547 Certayne Psalmes chose out of the Psalter
          of David; drawe into Englishe metre, by
          Thomas Sternhold, Grome of ye Kynges
          Maiesties roobes. [19 Psalms] Londini:
          Execubat Edouardus Whitchurche.

      1549 Al suche Psalmes of Dauid, as Thomas
          Sternehold late grome of ye Kynges Robes
          didde in hys lyfe tyme drawe into
          Englyshe metre. Newly emprinted [37
          Psalms] London: E. Whitchurche.
          Other editions, 1551 and 1553.

      1557 [with another seven Psalms by John
          Hopkins]

      1560 Psalmes of David in English metre by T.
          Sternholde and others: conferred with the
          Ebrue and the note ioyned withall, newly
          set forth and allowed [67 Psalms] London:
          J. Daye.
          Another edition, 1561.

      1561 Foure score and seuen Psalmes of Dauid in
          English mitre by Thomas Sterneholde and
          others; conferred with the Hebrewe, ad in
          certeine places corrected, as the sese of
          the Prophet requireth. Whereunto are
          added the Songe of Simeon, the ten
          Commandements and the Lords Prayer. [With
          musical notes.] [London: John Daye]

      1564 The Forme of Prayers and Ministration of
          the Sacraments etc. used in the English
          Church at Geneva, approved and received
          by the Church of Scotland, whereunto
          besydes that was in the former bokes, are
          also added sondrie other prayers, with
          the whole Psalmes of Dauid in English
          meter... Edinburgh: Robert Lekpreuik

      1565 The Psalmes of David in Metre According
          as they are sung in the Kirk of Scotland.
          Together, vvith the Conclusion, or Gloria
          Patria, eftir the Psalme and alsua ane
          Prayer eftir euerie Psalme, agreeing
          vvith the mening thairof. Prented at
          Edinbvrgh be Henrie Charteris.

[More than a hundred of the Psalms in the Anglo-Genevan
Version (see 1556) also occur in the Scottish Psalter of
1564, which differs chiefly in the inclusion of a rather

large number of Psalms by Kethe, Craig, Whittingham and Pont. Rathmell.]

[After 1601, some 40 Psalms were used in variants, chiefly by Pont. (Pollard)]

1611 The Psalmes of David in Prose and Meeter. With Godly Prayers &c. Edinburgh: Andro Hart.

['The whole Psalmes of David' remained the offical Psalter of the Scottish Church until it was superseded in 1650 by 'The Psalmes of David in Metre'. According to Kerr, the 1564 version "...contained all the 'old version' by Sternholde, Whittingham, and Kethe, 37 by Hopkins, 19 more by Kethe, 6 by Robert Pont, and 15 by 'I.C.' (i.e. Ihon Craig).]

1549 **Anonymous**   The Book of Common Prayer and Administration of the Sacraments, and other Rites and Ceremonies of the Church of England. 1549.
[This work includes the Psalms, in the translation of the Great Bible of 1539, but with a great variety of minor alterations throughout. It also contains many selections from the Gospels and Epistles and a few from the OT; these selections were based upon the Bishop's Bible until 1662, at which time the translation of the AV was substituted.]

1549 The First Prayer Book of King Edward VI. London: Edward Whitchurch.

1552 The Second Prayer Book of King Edward VI. London: Edward Whitchurch.

1559 The Prayer-Book of Queen Elizabeth. London: Richard Grafton.

1604 The Prayer-Book of King James I. London: Robert Barker.

1633 The Prayer-Book of King Charles I. London: Robert Barker.

1637 Laud's Scottish Prayer-Book. Edinburgh: For Robert Young.

1662 The Prayer-Book of King Charles II.

Another edition; Our Prayer Book Psalter, Containing Coverdale's Version from his 1535 Bible and the Prayer Book Version by Coverdale from the Great Bible 1539-41 Printed side by side. With an Introduction and Notes on the Sources of Coverdale's Renderings by Ernest Clapton, with a Foreward by the Rev. G.C. Richards... 1934.

[In the 1859 edition, the Deity is rendered in the
Psalter as "Jehovah" at Psalm 33:12; 83:18; "Jeh" at
68:4. In the section of Psalms which is different than
the Psalter, the name "Jehovah" is used in the
selections from XLIII, LXVIII, XCVI, XCVII, XCIX, CIV,
CVII, CXXXI, CXLV, CXLVII.]

[Reprinted many times.]

1549 **Crowley, Robert**   The Psalter of David newly
translated into Englysh metre in such sort that it
maye the more decently, and wyth more delyte of the
mynde, be reade and songe of al men. Whereunto is
added a note of partes, wyth other thynges, as shall
appeare in the Epistle to the readar. Translated and
Imprinted by Robert Crowley in the yeare of our
Lorde M.D.xlix. the xx. daye of September. And are
to be solde in Cleyrentes in Holburne. London: R.
Crowley, 1549.
  [This was the first complete Psalter into metre in the
  English language. In addition to the Psalms, the work
  includes; 'The songe of Simon, The songe of Zacharie,
  The songe of the iii children, The songe of Nicetus the
  bishope, The credo or belyfe of Athanatius'.]

1556 **Norton, Thomas** The Whole Booke of Psalmes..., 1556.

1556 **Sterneholde, Thomas and I. Hopkins**   [The Anglo-
Genevan Metrical Psalter: Sternhold and Hopkins]
1556-1562.
  1556 One and Fiftie Psalmes of David in metre;
       whereof 37 were made by T. Sterneholde,
       ad the rest by others; Coferred with the
       Hebrewe, and corrected, as the text and
       sens of the prophete required. Geneva: by
       J. Crespin.
         [Pt. 2 of 'The forme of prayer vsed in the
         English   congregation   at   Geneva.'   has
         musical notes. Includes 37 Psalms by
         Sterneholde, 7 by Hopkins, together with 7
         by Whittingham, who also introduced
         revisions of the other Psalms. This work
         was based upon the Psalter listed under
         1547 as the 1st Scottish Psalter.]

  1558 - - [with an additional 9 Psalms by
       Whittingham, 2 by Pullain; 62 total.]

  1560 - - [with 3 more Psalms; 65 total.]

  1562 The Whole Booke of Psalmes, collected
       into Englysh metre by T. Starnhold, I.
       Hopkins, & others: conferred with the
       Ebrue, with apt Notes to synge th withal,
       Faithfully perused and alowed according
       to theordre appointed in the Quenes

maiesties Iniunstions. Very mete to be
vsed of all sortes of people priuately
for their solace & comforte: laying apart
all vngodly Songes and Ballades, which
tends only to the norishing of vyse, and
the corrupting of youth. Lodon: Ihon
Day.

>   [This last work was largely the work of
>   John Marchant, who restored the original
>   wording of Sternhold. "The Whole Booke of
>   Psalmes", although of little or no poetic
>   merit, was soon employed throughout the
>   country, being acceptable to both Anglican
>   and Puritan. By 1828, it had achieved more
>   than 600 editions.]

1564 The   first   parte   of   the
     Psalmes...whereunto   is   added   the
     catechisme,   and   also   a   short
     introduction...   Imprinted at London by
     John Day, 1564.

1569 The Whole Booke of Psalmes, collected
     into Englishe metre by T. Sternhold, I.
     Hopkins and others, conferred with the
     Ebrue, vvith apt Notes to synge them
     vvithall. Faithfully perused and allovved
     according to thorder appointed in the
     Quenes   Maiesties   Iniunctions...   At
     Geneva,   Printed   by   Ihon   Crespin,
     M.D.LXIX.   [Published with the Geneva Bibles.]

1628 The Whole Booke of Davids Psalmes, Both
     in Prose and Meetre. With Apt Notes to
     sing them withall. London: Printed for
     the Company of Stationers.

1557 **Anonymous**   The Psalmes of David Translated
Accordyng to the Veritie and Truth of th' Ebrue,
wyth   Annotacions   Moste   profitable...M.D.LVII.
[Anthony Gilby?] [Geneva: Conrad Badius?], 1557.
>   [The only copy of this edition is in the Bodleian
>   Library.]

1559 **Denham, Henry**   The Psalmes... London: 1559.

1559 **Hall, Rouland**   The Book of Psalms and godly
Prayers. Geneva: 1559.

1565 **Anonymous**   The Forme of Prayer and Ministration
of the Sacraments, etc., used in the English Church
at Geneva, approved and received by the Church of
Scotland whereunto besydes that was in the former
bokes, are also sundrie other prayers, with thw
whole Psalmes of David in English meter. The

contents of this boke are conteined in the page
following...Printed at Edinburgh by Robert Leprevik,
MDLXV.

1567 **Anonymous**   The Psalter in Verse. [by ABP. Parker]
1567.

1567 **Anonymous**   The whole Psalter translated
into English Metre, which contayneth an hundreth and
fifty Psalmes. the first [thru third] Quinquagene.
[Matthew Parker]   Imprinted at London by Ihon Daye,
1567?
    [With collects and four-part musical settings by Thomas
    Tallis. Parker's name appears as an acrostic in a
    preface to Psalm 119. Wilson and Cotton date this work
    as 1557.]

1568 **Bickley, Thomas**   Psalms?, 1568.
    [See Complete Bibles, 1568 Bishops' Bible.]

1571 **Anonymous**   The Psalmes of Dauid and others, with
M. John Caluin's Commentaries. Anno.Do.M.D.LXXI.
[Arthur Golding] [Imprinted at London by Thomas East
and Henry Middleton: for Lucas Harison and Gorge
(sic) Byshop] 2 parts., 1571.
    Another edition; A Commentary on the Psalms of
    David. 3 vols. London: Thomas Tegg, 1840.

    Also; - - Edited by Richard G. Barnes.   San
    Francisco: The Arion Press, 1977.

1575 **Church of Scotland**   The Psalms in Metre...used
in the Church of Scotland...Compiled by Robert Pont.
Edinburgh: Thomas Bassandine, 1575.

1575 **Pont, Robert**   CL Psalms of David, in English Metre,
by Robert Pont. Edinburgh: Thomas Bassendyne, 1575.

1577 **Bull, Henry**   The Psalms of Degrees with Luthers
Commentary... London: Thomas Vautrollier, 1577.

1579 **Rogers, Thomas**   A Golden Chaine...
    [See Wisdom and Poetical books for the complete entry.]

1580 **Buchanan, George**   Paraphrasis Psalmorum Davidis
Poeticae Eiusden Buchanis Tragedia quae Inscribitur
Jepthes.   London: Th. Vatrollenus, 1580.
    [This is the finest Latin translation of the Psalms ever
    published.]

1580 **Gilbie, Antonie**   The Psalmes of Dauid, Trvely
Opened and Explaned by Paraphrasis, According to the
Right Sense of Euery Psalme. With large and Ample
Arguments before Euery Psalme, Declaring the True
Vse Thereof. To the VVhich is Added a Briefe Table,

Shewing Wherevnto Euery Psalme is Particularly to be
Applied, According to the Direction of M. Beza and
Tremelivs. Set foorth in Latine by that Excellent
Learned man Theodore Beza. And Faithfully Translated
into English by Antonie Gilbie. At London: Printed
by Ihon Harison and Henrie Middleton, 1580.
> Another edition;...newlie purged from sundrie
> faultes escaped in the first print. London:
> Henrie Denham, 1581.

> Another edition; London: Printed by Richard
> Yardley and Peter Short, for the Assignes of
> W. Seres, 1590.

1586 **Anonymous**   A right godly and learned Exposition
vpon the whole book of the Psalmes [by T.W.] [Thomas
Wilcox] London: by Tho. Man and W. Brome, 1586.
> Another edition; A very godly and learned
> exposition... T. Orwin for T. Man, 1591.

1588 **Bird, W.**   Psalmes, Sonnete... London: Thomas East,
1588.

1592 **Anonymous**   The Whole Book of Psalms...compiled
by 10 Sundry Authors. London: Thomas East, 1592.

1599 **Allison, Richard**   The Psalmes of David in Metre.
London: Printed by William Barley, 1599.

1600 **Anonymous**   Psalmes with Musical Notes. British
Museum: MS. Add. 22,597   1600.

1600 **Anonymous**   A Paraphrasticall Version of the
Booke of Psalmes in Meeter. British Museum:
MS.Harl.6905.   1600.

1600 **Sidney, Philip and Mary Herbert**   The Psalmes
of David translated into divers and sundry kindes of
verse. More rare and excellent for the Method and
Varitie than ever yet hath been done in English, by
Philip Sidney and Mary Herbert. MS, c1600.
> [The Deity is rendered "Jehovah" at Psalm 83:18;
> "Jehova" many times.]

> Another edition; - - Begun by the noble and
> learned Gent. Sir Philip Sidney, Knt. and
> finished by the Right Honorable the Countess
> of Pembroke his sister. Now first printed from
> a Copy of the Original Manuscript, transcribed
> by John Davies, of Hartford, in the reign of
> James the First. Edited by Samuel W. Singer.
> London: From the Chiswick Press by C.
> Whittingham for Robert Triphook, 1823.

Reprinted; The Psalms of Sir Philip Sidney and the Countess of Pembroke. Edited with an introduction by J.C.A. Rathmell. New York University Press, 1963; Garden City, New York: Anchor Books, 1964.

1612 **Anonymous**   The Book of Psalmes: Englished both in Prose and Metre. With Annotations, opening the words and sentences, by conference with other scriptures, by H.A. [Henry Ainsworth] Amsterdam: Giles Thorpe, 1612.
[With musical notes.]

[Also known as the 'Pilgrim Psalter'.]

Second edition; Annotations upon the Book of Psalmes by H.Ainsworth. [Amsterdam?] 1617.

Another edition; Annotations upon the five books of Moses and the booke of Psalmes. By H.A. [Amsterdam?] J.Haviland and B.Fisher, 1622.

Also; Same as 1622 but with Songs. London: M.Flesher for John Bellamie, 1627.

Other editions; London: M. Parsons for J. Bellamie; Amsterdam, 1644; Glasgow: Blackie & Son (2 vols.), 1843.

1613 **Johnson, William**   The Psalms in Metre. Amsterdam: 1613.
[This work is now lost. Mentioned in LeLong's Bibliotheca Sacra.]

1615 **Hart, Andro**   The CL Psalms of David...Meeter, also The Song of Moses... Edinburgh: 1615.

1616 **Anonymous**   Dauids Musick: or, Psalmes of that Royall Prophet...vnfolded Logically, Expounded Paraphrastically, and then Followeth a more Particylar Explanation of the Words...by R.B. and R.A.. [Richard Bernard] London: Felix Kyngston, for Edmund Weauer, 1616.

1620 **Anonymous**   Al the Psalmes of Dauid: with certeine songes & Canticles of Moses, Debora, Isaiah, Hezekiah & others not formerly extat for song: & manie of the said Psalmes, dayly omitted, & not song at all, because of their defficult tunes. Now faithfully reduced into easie meeter, fitting our common tunes. [Henry Dod], 1620.
[The KJV appears in the margin. It is not known whether Dod's 'Certeine Psalmes reduced into English Meter', 1603, were incorporated into this work.]

1621 **Rauenscroft, Thomas**   The Whole Booke of Psalmes,
with the Hymnes Evangelicall, And Songs Spiritvall.
Composed into 4 parts by Sundry Authors, to such
seuerall Tunes, as haue beene, and are vsually sung
in England, Scotland, Wales, Germany, Italy, France
and the Nether-lands: Neuer as yet before in one
volumne published. Also: 1. A briefe Abstract of the
Prayse, Efficacie, and Vertue of the Psalmes. 2.
That all Clarkes of the Churches, and the Auditory,
may know what Tune each proper Psalme may be sung
vnto. Newly corrected and enlarged. London: for the
Company of Stationers, 1621.

1624 **Davies, John**   Metaphrase of the Psalms. London:
1624.
      [Reprinted in Grosart's "The Complete Poems of Sir John
      Davies", 1876.]

1629 **Top, Alexander**   The Book of Prayses, Called
The Psalmes. The Keyes and Holly Things of David.
Translated out of the Hebrew, According to the
Letter, and the Mystery of them. And According to
the rule and Methode of the Compile-er. Opened in
Proper Arguments upon every Psalme, following the
same. T'Amstelredam: Ian Fredericksz Stam, 1629.

1631 **King James**   The Psalmes of King David, translated
by King James. Oxford: W. Turner, 1631.
      [In prose metre.]

      [The Deity is rendered "Iehovah" at Psalm 83:18. In the
      K.J. manuscript, King James used "Jehouas" many times.]

1632 **Anonymous**   Paraphrase on the Psalms Translated
by King James. London: 1636.

1632 **Anonymous**   All the French Psalm Tunes Generally
vsed in the Reformed Churches of France and Germany,
Perused and Approved by Judicius Divines, both
English and French.   London: Printed by Thomas
Harper with permission of the Company of Stationers,
1632.
      Another edition; All the French Psalm Tunes with
      English Words. Being a collection of Psalms
      accorded to the verses and tunes generally
      vsed in the Reformed Churches of France and
      Germany... London: Thomas Harper, 1632.

      Another edition, 1650.

1632 **Wither, George**   The Psalmes of David translated
into Lyrick-Verse, according to the scope of the
Original, and Illustrated, with a short Argument,
and a briefe Prayer, or Meditation; before, & and
after, every Psalme. By George Wither. Imprinted in

the Netherlands: Cornelius Gerrits and Breughel,
1632.
>Facsimile; Manchester: The Spencer Society,
>1881.

>[See Anonymous, The Psalms of David, 1650.]

1636 **Anonymous**   A Paraphrase upon the Psalmes of
David. And upon the Hymns dispersed throughout its
old and new Testaments. By G.S. [George Sandys]
London at the Bell in St. Paul's Church yard [Andrew
Webb], 1636.

1636 **King James**   The Psalms of King David Translated by
King James, 1636.
>[Greatly altered from the 1631 edition.]

1636 **Sandys, George**   A Paraphrase...Divine Poems...
>[Old Testament Selections for the complete entry.
>Includes all of the Psalms in paraphrase.]

1638 **Anonymous**   The Booke of Psalms in English Metre.
Rotterdam: for Henry Tutill, 1638.
>["The Rotterdam Version"; an alteration of Sternhold and
>Hopkins.]

1638 **Anonymous**   The Psalmes of David, the King and
Prophet, And Of other holy Prophets, paraphras'd in
English: Conferred with the Hebrew Veritie, set
forth by B.Arias Montanus, together with the Latine,
Greek Septuagint, and Chaldee Paraphrase. By R.B.
[Richard Brathwaite]   London: Printed by Robert
Young, for Francis Constable, 1638.
>[Metrical version; Fish attributes to R. Burnaby.]

1638 **Burnaby, R.**   Psalms of David and other Holy
Prophets in Verse. London: Robert Young, 1638.

1638 **Lawes, Henry**   A Paraphrase upon the Psalms, 1638.
>[Printed at the end of George Sandy's 'Paraphrase of
>Divine Poems, 1636'.]

1639 **Ainsworth, Henry**   The Books of Psalms literally
translated with other Books of Scripture.   London:
M. Parsons for John Bellamie, 1639.

1639 **Rowallan, Mure of**   See Anonymous, The Psalms of
David in Meeter, 1650.

1640 **Anonymous** (Bay Psalm Book)   The Whole Booke
of Psalmes Faithfully Translated into English Metre.
Whereunto is prefixed a discourse declaring not only
the lawfullnes, but also the necessity of the
heavenly Ordinance of singing scripture Psalmes in

the Churches of God... Imprinted 1640. Cambridge:
Massachusetts: Stephen Daye. [1640]
[Only eleven copies of the first edition are known to
exist. This was the first book to be printed in North
America. This was primarilly the work of Rev. Richard
Mather, Rev. Thomas Welde and Rev. John Eliot. The
Publisher is said to be Stephen Daye.]

[The Deity is rendered "Iehovah" a few times.]

2nd edition; Somewhat amended. Cambridge:
Stephen Daye, 1647.

3rd edition; amended and revised by President
Dunster of Harvard and Henry Lyon; titled: The
New England Version of the Psalms. Published
by Samuel Green, 1650.
        Again; for Hezekiah Usher of Boston,
    1665.

Fourth Edition, 1671.

Fifth Edition, 1680.

Another edition; ...The New-England Psalm Book
revised and improved... with an addition of
fifty other hymns... Boston: D. Henchman, S.
Kneeland, 1758.
    [A revision by Thomas Prince.]

Reprint; American Book-Stratford Press, Inc.,
New York, n.d.

A Literal Reprint of the Bay Psalm Book...
Boston: Riverside Press, 1862.

The Bay Psalm Book; Being a Facsimile Reprint
of the First Edition, Printed by Stephen Daye
at Cambridge in New England in 1640; Edited by
Wilberforce Eames 1903. Prepared for the New
England Society in the City of New York.

The Enigma of the Bay Psalm Book with a
facsimile reprint edited by Zoltan Haraszti. 2
Vols. Chicago: University of Chicago Press,
1956.

1640 **Anonymous**   Book of Psalms. MS [1640]
        [An Anonymous Version in the Bodleian Library - MS.]

1641 **Rous, Francis**   See Anonymous, The Psalms of David
        in Meeter, 1650.

1641 **Rous, Francis**   The Psalmes of David in English
Meeter, by Francis Rous... London: Printed by R.Y.
for Philip Nevil, 1641.

> Another edition; - - set forth by Francis Rous...
> The Order of the House of Commons, for the
> publication, dated Aprill 17. 1643. Signed
> Ihon White. I do appoint Philip Nevill and
> Peter Whaley to print these Psalmes. London:
> Printed by R.Y. for Philip Nevill, 1643.
>> [A revision approved by the Westminster Assembly
>> of Divines.]

> Again revised; London: Printed by Miles Flesher,
> for the Company of Stationers, 1646.
>> ["...the whole hath been conferred carefully with
>> the originall, which hath been strictly followed,
>> and the last translation in concurrence with it,
>> from which few places have been altered, except
>> where some very probable cause hath appeared." KJV
>> appears in the margin; the Scottish Psalter of
>> 1650 largely based in Rous.]

1644 **Anonymous**   The Book of Psalms in Metre; close and
proper to the Hebrew: Smooth and pleasant for the
Metre: Plain and easie for the tunes. With Musicall
Notes, Arguments, Annotations, and Index fitted for
the ready use, and understanding of all good
Christians. [William Barton] London: Printed by
Matthew Simmons for the Companie of Stationers,
1644.

> Another edition; The Book of Psalms in Metre,
> Lately translated, with many whole ones, and
> choice Collections of the old Psalms added to
> the first Impression. Printed by Order of
> Parliament. And now much augmented and amended
> with the cream and flower of the best
> Authours, all following the common Tunes at
> this day used in, and about London. VVith the
> approbation of more than fourty eminent
> Divines of the City, & most of them of the
> Assembly. By William Barton, Mr of Arts, and
> Minister of Iohn Zacharies, London, 1645.
> London: Printed by G.M.; Sold by S.
> Gellibrand.

> Also; The Book of Psalms in Metre. Close and
> proper to the Hebrew: Smooth and pleasant for
> the metre: To be sung in usual and known
> Tunes. Newly translated with amendments and
> addition of many fresh metres. Fitted for the
> ready use, and understanding of all good
> Christians. By William Barton, MR of Arts, as
> he left it finished in his life time. London:
> Printed for the Companie of Stationer, 1682.

Another edition; Appends a variant version of
eighteen of the Psalms "...added out of Mr.
Barton's last translation." Dublin: Joseph
Ray, for E.Dobson, and M.Gunn, 1697.

Another edition; From Ms, left at his death.
London: Printed by Anne Snowden for the
Companie of Stationers, 1705.

Also; The Psalms of David in Metre. Newly
Translated. With Amendments. By William
Barton, M.A. and Set to the best Psalm Tunes,
by Thomas Smith. Dublin: Printed by J.
Bracas, 1706.

1644 **Boyd, M. Zachary**   The Garden of Zion...
[See Old Testament Selections for the complete entry.
Includes all of the Psalms.]

1644 **Hatton, Lord Christopher**   The Psalter... Oxford:
L. Litchfield, 1644.

1645 **Glanville, John**   A Paraphrase Upon the Psalms of
David. British Museum MS. Eg. 2590, 1645.

1646 **Boyd, M. Zachary**   The Psalms of David in Meter.
By Mr. Zachary Boyd, Preacher of God's Word. The
Third Edition.   Printed at Glasgow by George
Anderson, 1646.

1648 **Hughes**, J.   The Psalms of David in various verse,
Plainely and upon the text.   British Museum: MS.
Add. 30270, (1648)

1649 **Anonymous**   ...The Book of Hymns or Praises. Viz.
the Book of Psalms, translated immediately out of
the Hebrew in meter and analytically expounded by
F.R.D.D. [Francis Roberts] London: George Calvert,
1649.
[From the 'Clavis Bibliorum'. Third edition, diligently
revised, 1665. London.]

1650 **Abbott, George**   The Whole Book of Psalmes
Paraphrased, or, made Easier for any to Understand,
by George Abbott. London: William Bentley, 1650.
[An expansive paraphrase, with KJV text in a parallel
column.]

Another edition; Brief Notes Upon the whole Book
of Psalms. Put forth for the help of such who
desire to exercise themselves in them, and
cannot understand without a Guide. Being a
pithie and clear opening of the Scope and
Meaning of the text, to the capacities of the
weakest. London: 1651.

1650 **Anonymous**   The Psalms of David in Meeter:
Newly translated, and diligently compared with the
Originall Text and former Translations: More plaine,
smooth   and   agreeable   to   the   Text,   than   any
heretofore. Allowed the authority of the Generall
Assembly of the Kirk of Scotland and appointed to be
sung in Congregations and Families.   Edinburgh:
Printed by Evan Taylor..., 1650.
> [A new version based upon those by Francis Rous and is
> the first edition of the Scottish Psalms.]

> The presently used Scottish Psalter; commonly found in
> the back of Bibles and Testaments; based upon the
> following, taking various portions from each:
> Henry Dod   1620   Francis Rous   1641
> George Wither   1632   Mure of Rowallan   1639
> Zachary Boyd   1648   William Barton   1644
> Westminster Version   1647?

> Another edition; Translations and Paraphrases, in
> Verse... 1745.   [See Anonymous, The Scottish
> Paraphrases, 1745.]

> Another edition; The Psalms of David in Metre
> According to the Version approved by the
> Church of Scotland With an Introduction by
> William Allan Nielson. Cambridge: Washburn &
> Thomas, 1928.

1650 **Anonymous**   The Psalms, Hymns and Spiritual Songs...
> [See Old Testament Selections for the complete
> entry. Includes all of the Psalms.]

1650 **Dunster of Harvard**   See Anonymous, (Bay Psalm
Book), 1640.

1650 **Lyon, Henry** See Anonymous, (Bay Psalm Book), 1640.

1650 **Rous, Francis**   The Psalms of David in meeter
for the Church of Scotland by Sternhold and Hopkins
but now newly translated on the basis of a
translation made by Francis Rous. 1650.

1651 **Anonymous**   The Psalmses of David, from the
New Translation of the Bible turned into meter. To
be sung after the old tunes used in the Churches.
[Henry King] London: Printed by Edward Griffin;
sold by Humphrey Moseley, 1651.
> [Preface signed "H.K., B.C.".]

> Another edition; Unto which are newly added the
> Lord's   Prayer,   the   Creed,   the   Ten
> Commandments: With some other Ancient Hymnes,
> 1654, 1655 (1678; Cruttwell) London: Printed
> by S.G. to be sold by Humphrey Moseley.

Also; Poems and Psalms by Henry King, D.D.,
sometime Lord Bishop of Chichester. Edited by
the Rev. J. Hannah. London: William Pickering,
184?.

1651 **Fairfax, Thomas**   A Paraphrase of the Psalms...
[See Bible Selections for the complete entry.]

1653 **Anonymous**   The Psalms with a Paraphrase. London:
1653.

1654 **Barton, William**   The Book of Psalms in Metre.
London: By Roger Daniel & Wm. Du-Gard, 1654.
[This is entirely different from that of 1644 and 1645,
of which no notice is taken in the Imprimatur or in his
preface to the reader.]

1655 **White, John**   Davids Psalms in Metre. Agreeable
to the Hebrew, To be sung in usuall Tvnes. To the
benefit of the Churches of Christ by John White.
London: Printed by S. Griffin for J. Rothwel, 1655.
[Published posthumously by Stanley Gower.]

1659 **Anonymous**   Psalter [for the Gaelic-speaking
Presbyterians of Scotland]. 1659-1826.
1659 Fifty Psalms [Issued by the Synod of
Argle.]

1684 [First complete Gaelic translation.] by
Robert Kirk.

1694 [The second complete Gaelic translation
was that of the Synod Argle.]

1753 [An ammended and altered edition by
Alexander MacFarlane, M.A.]

1787 [A further improved edition of the Argle
translation.]

1807 [Another amended translation] by Thomas
Ross, M.A.

1826 The Psalms of David, along with the Hymns
drawn from the holy Scriptures, to be
sung in the worship of God. Improved and
published by authority of the General
Assembly of the Church of Scotland at the
command and expense of the Horourable
Society for propagating Christian
Knowledge through Gaeldom and the Islands
of Scotland. Edinburgh: Printed by
Duncan Stevenson.

[This work was the first with the full and definite authority of the General Assembly.]

1659 **Hammond, Henry**   A Paraphrase and Annotations upon the Books of the Psalms...
[See Wisdom and Poetical books and Selections for the complete entry.]

1662 **Anonymous**   David's Harp strung and tuned; or, an Easie Analysis of the Whole Book of Psalms, cast into such a Method that the Summe of Every Psalm may be Quickly Collected and remembered. With a Devout Meditation or Prayer at the end of every Psalm, Framed for the Most Part out of the Words of the Psalms, and Fitted for Several Occasions. William [Nicholson] London: William Leake, 1662.

1664 **Anonymous**   The Psalms Paraphrased... in verse. Londom: T. Garthwaite, 1664.

1667 **Woodford, Samuel**   A Paraphrase upon the Psalms of David. By Samuel Woodford. London: R. White, for Octavian Pullein, 1667.
["... I have endeavoured to...give, as near as I could, the true sense and meaning of the Psalms, and in as easy and obvious terms as was possible. Suiting them to the Capacities of the meanest: which I found myself the better able to do, by having the difficulties resolved to my hands by the labors of that truly Pious and Learned Divine Dr. Henry Hammond..." In verse.]

Second edition; corrected by the Author. London: J.M., for John Martyn, 1678.

1668 **Smyth, Miles**   The Psalms of King David Paraphrased. And turned into English Verse, according to the common Metre, as they are usually Sung in Parish Churches. London: Printed for T. Garthwiat, 1668.
["Comparing therefore, and making use, as well of the Old Liturgick, as the New-Bible-Translation, with the assistance of the Learned Dr. Hammond. (whose Paraphrase he chose for his guide) he undertook, and went through with them, and now hath adventured them aboard to the world."]

1676 **Playford, John**   See George Sandys, A Paraphrase upon the Divine Poems, 1636.

1677 **Downe, Thomas**   Psalms of Prayer and Praise. London: John Hancock, 1677.

1680 **Patrick, Symon**   The Book of Psalms Paraphras'd...
[See Wisdom and Poetical books and Selections, 1679 Symon Patrick, The [Poetical Books] Paraphrased.]

1682 **Goodridge, Richard**   The Psalter Paraphras'd in Verse, 1682-1684.

      1682 The three first Books of the Psalms, and so much of the Fourth as make up a Century, Paraphras'd in Verse. London: Printed for A. Churchill.

      1684 The Psalter or Psalms of David Paraphras'd in Verse Set to new Tunes. The Second Edition, wherein the whole Number is Compleated. London: Printed by L. Lichfield.

      Another edition; London: Clavel, 1685.

1684 **Kirk, Robert**   See Gaelic Translation, Psalter, 1659.

1688 **Ford, Simon**   A New Version of the Psalms of David, together with all the Church hymns, into metre, smooth, plain and easie to the most ordinary capacities...   London: J.H., for Brabazon Aylmer, 1688.

1688 **Leusden, John**   The Book of Psalms. By John Leusden. Utrecht: Van de Water, 1688.
      [Hebrew and English.]

1692 **Baxter, Richard**   Mr. Richard Baxter's Paraphrase on the Psalms of David in Metre, with other hymns. London: Printed for T. Parkhurst & Jonathan Robinson, 1692.
      Another edition; A Paraphrase on the Psalms of David in Metre, with other Hymns. By M. Rich Baxter. Left fitted for the Press under his own hand, Licensed June 2d 1692.   London. (Published posthumously by Matthew Sylvester)

1694 **Argyle, Synod of**   See Anonymous, Psalter, 1659.

1694 **Chiswell, A.**   Psalms and Hymns in Metre... London: 1694.

1695 **Playford, John**   The Whole Book of Psalms with all the Ancient and proper Tunes composed by John Playford. London: E. Jones, 1695.
      Also, 1715.

      Another edition; The whole Book of Psalms: With the Hymns and Spiritual Songs. Composed in Three Parts, Cantus, Medius and Bassus... by John Playford. London: W. Pearson, 1719.

1695 **Tate, Nahum and Nicholas Brady**   A New Version of
the Psalms of David, by Nahum Tate and Nicholas
Brady. 1695-1696.

> 1695 An Essay of a New Version of the Psalms
> of David: consisting of the first Twenty
> Fitted to the Tunes used in Churches.
> London: Printed for the Company of
> Stationers.

> 1696 A New Version of the Psalms of David,
> fitted to the tunes used in churches.
> London: Printed by M. Clark, for the
> Company of Stationers.

Another edition; London: Printed by T. Hodgkin,
for the Company of Stationers, 1698.

Second edition corrected;   London: Printed by M.
Clark, for the Company of Stationers, 1698.

[After 1700, Tate and Brady's Psalms were usually
accompanied by 'A Supplement to the New Version of the
Psalms.' (See 1700). Many times reprinted, often bound
with Bibles and Prayer-Books.]

[See Anonymous, Scottish Paraphrase, 1745.]

1696 **Anonymous**   A New Version of the Book Of Psalms
of David, fitted to the tunes used in churches.
[Nicholas Brady and Nahum Tate] London: Printed by
M. Clark, for the Company of Stationers, 1696.

> Another edition; London: Printed by T. Hodgkin,
> for the Company of Stationers, 1698.

Second edition; corrected. London: Printed by M.
Clark, for the Company of Stationers, 1698.

[This version was altered a number of times in its
various and many editions. After 1700, Tate and Brady's
Psalms were usually accompanied by 'A Supplement to the
New Version of the Psalms.' Many times reprinted, often
bound with Bibles and Prayer-Books.]

1697 **Anonymous**   The Psalms of David in Meeter, Newly
Translated, 1697.
[Bodlean Library]

1698 **Milburne, Luke**   The Psalms of David in English
Metre; translated from the original and suited to
all the tunes now sung in churches, with the
additions of several New. London: for W. Rogers,
1698.

1700 **Anonymous**   The Psalms of David [in prose],
translated from the Vulgat. [by Mr. Caryll, created

Lord Dartford by the Pretender].   Paris: M.DCC.
[1700]
> [Some ascribe to C. Caryll. This is a prose version from
> the Vulgate taking Bellarmine as a guide.]

Second edition; The Psalms of David, tanslated
from the Vulgate. The Second Edition review'd
and corrected.   St. Germain en Laye: William
Weston, Printer and Stationer to the king's
most excellent Majesty of Great Britian [that
is, to the Pretender] for his household and
chapel, 1704.

> [Another edition; same as above except SECOND EDITION is
> capitals and "Printed in the Year", 1704. It does not
> list the place and printer.]

1700 **Anonymous**   Psalms, Newly Translated, in Metre.
London: Thomas Parkhurst, 1700.
> [Scottish Version.]

1701 **Allix, Dr. P.**   The Psalms; with the Argument of
each Psalm. London: John Taylor, 1701.

1704 **Darby, Charles**   The Book of Psalms in English
metre. The newest version fitted to the common
tunes. London: Tho. Parkhurst, 1704.

1705 **Barton, William**   The Psalms in Metre Close and
Proper to the Hebrew, Smooth and Pleasant for the
Metre, Newly Translated, with Amendments, by William
Barton, M.A. as Left in His Life-time. London: Ann
Anowden for the Company of Stationers, 1705.

1707 **Johnson, J.**   Psalms by J. Johnson. London: 1707.

1707 **Nicholls, William**   A Paraphrase on the Psalter
or Psalms of David, by William Nicholls. London: J.
Holland, W. Taylor, 1707.
> [This listing is based upon the entry of "The Book of
> Common Prayer..." published in 1709 (2nd ed), but
> containing the above Psalter with a separate title page,
> dated 1707.]

Also; A Comment on the Book of Common-Prayer,
and Administration of the Sacraments, &c.
Together with the Psalter or Psalms of David.
Being a Paraphrase on the Sunday and Holiday-
Services, Epistles and Gospels throughout the
Year... With a Paraphrase on the whole Book of
Psalms, according to the Common-Prayer-Book
Translation. The Text of the Whole being
Compared and Amended, according to the Sealed
Books; and the Psalms Compared with the
Translation of the Great Bible.   London:

Printed for R. Bonwicke, W. Freeman, T. Goodwin, J. Walthoe, M. Wotton, S. Manship, J. Nicholson, R. Parker, B. Tooke, and R. Smith, 1710.

1714 **Burgess, Daniel**   Psalms, Hymns and Spiritual Songs by the Late Daniel Burges. London: John Clarke, 1714.

1714 **Denham, Sir John**   A Version of the Psalms of David, Fitted to the Tunes Used in Churches. London: Printed for J. Bowyer, H. Clements, T. Varnum & J. Osborn, 1714.
> ["...I have kept as near as possibly I could to the Letter, and never willingly vary'd from the sense, unless it be to make it plainer to English ears than the Original..."]

1718 **Anonymous**   Psalterium Americanum. The Book of Psalms in a Translation Exactly Conformed unto the Original; But all in Blank Verse, fitted unto the Tunes commonly used in Our Churches. Which Pure Offering is Accompanied with Illustrations, Digging for Hidden Treasures in it; and Rules to Employ it upon the Glories and Various Intentions of it. Whereto are added, some other portions of the Sacred Scripture, to enrich the Cantional. [Cotton Mather] Boston: in N.E. Printed by S. Kneeland, for B. Eliot, S. Gerrish, D. Henchman, and J. Edwards, 1718.

1719 **Anonymous**   The Psalms, by Several Hands. Published in "The Singing-Masters Guide". Oxfordshire: William Turner, 1719.

1719 **Anonymous**   The Book of Psalms made fit for the Closet; with Collects and Prayers out of the Liturgy of the Church of England, and other pious meditations. [Philip Beddingfield?] London: R. Wilkin, 1719.
> [A paraphrase based on the Prayer Book version.]

1719 **Watts, Isaac**   The Psalms of David Imitated in the Language of the New Testament. And apply'd to the Christian State and Worship by Isaac Watts. London: Printed for J.Clark, R.Ford, and R.Cruttenden, 1719.
> New edition; corrected.   Salisbury: Collins & Johnson, 1776.

> Another edition; An Abridgement of Dr. Watt's Psalms by William Wood. Birmingham: Piercy & Jones, 1790.

[Many times published in various editions; also see
Barlow's edition, 1875; Dwight's, 1802; and Conder's,
1851.]

1721 **Blackmore, Sir Richard**   A New Version of the Psalms
of David, fitted to the tunes used in churches by
Richard Blackmore. London: Printed by I. March, for
the Company of Stationers, 1721.

1725 **Anonymous**   The Psalms, Hymns and Spiritual Songs
of the Old and New Testament, Faithfully Translated
into English Metre, for the Use, Edification, and
Comfort of the Saints in Publick and Private,
Especially in New-England.   London: Osborn &
Longman, 1725.
   [See 1758]

1732 **Fenton, Thomas**   Annotations on the Book...Psalms...
   [See Wisdom and Poetical books and Selections for the
   complete entry.]

1740 **Powell, S.**   The Psalms of David in Metre,
collected from the principle versions now in use...
Dublin: 1740.
   [Alteration of Patrick, Tate & Brady, Denham and
   others.]

1744 **Mudge, Zachary**   An Essay towards a New English
Version of the Book of Psalms from the Original
Hebrew, by Zachary Mudge. London: Printed for S.
Birt, 1744.
   [Strong indicates that Mudge may also have authored 'A
   Specimen of a New Translation', 1733.]

1745 **Tans'ur, William**   The Royal Pfalmodift Compleat:
or, the Universal Harmony. Being a whole Body of
Church-Musick. Containing above One Hundred and
fifty of the very beft Tunes, both Old and New;
adapted to the moft felect Portions of every one of
the whole Book of Psalms. Extracted from the beft
Masters, both ancient and modern; and correctly fet
in Four Parts, according to the nifest Rules, for
Voices, or Organ, &c. and so neat as to be fung in
Two or Three Parts, when Voices can't be had; and
exempt from the leaft Difallowance; and fitted for
all Teachers, Learners, and Mifical Societies, &c.
To which is added, a new Jubilate, and Magnificant:
With Variety of Hymns, Anthems, and Canons, &c.,
with   compendious   Inftructions   to   the   whole.
Engraved, and Printed by and for the Author, 1745.

1751 **Anonymous**   The Book of Psalms in metre. Fitted to
the various tunes in common use, wherein Closeness
to the Text, and Smoothness of the verse, are
prefer'd to Rhyme. With a Prefatory Account of the

Present Attempt, and some thoughts on singing in
Social Worship. [Samuel Pike] London: J. Oswald,
1751.
> Other editions; London: Printed for G. Leighton,
> 1819; London: Waney, 1838. [Title is similar to a
> work attributed to James Downes, 1799.]

1751 **Kent, H.**   The Book of Psalms in Metre. London:
Samuel Pike, 1751.

1752 **Barnard, John**   A New Version of the Psalms
of David; fitted to the tunes used in churches: with
several hymns, out of the Old & New Testaments by
John Bernard.   Boston: Printed by J. Draper for
T.Leverett, 1752.
> [Also contains: The Song of Moses, Exodus, Chapter XV,
> Deuteronomy, Chapter XXXII; The Song of Deborah, Judges,
> Chapter V; Proverbs, Chapter VIII (abridged); and parts
> of Isaiah, Chapters II, IX, XLV, LIII, LV. Paraphrased
> in Verse.]

1753 **MacFarlane, Alexander**   See Gaelic Translation,
Psalter, 1659.

1754 **Cradock, Thomas**   A Poetic Translation of the Psalms
of David from Buchanan's Latin into English verse.
By Rev. T. Cradock. London: R. Ware, 1754.
> Another edition; London: for Mrs. A. Cradock of
> Wells, 1754.

1754 **Wheatland, Stephen and Tipping Sylvester**
The Psalms of David, Translated into Heroic Verse,
In as Literal a Manner, as Rhyme and Mtere will
allow. With Arguments to each Psalm and Explanatory
Notes. By Stephen Wheatland & Tipping Sylvester.
London: Printed for S. Birt, J. Buckland, 1754.

1755 **Edwards, Thomas**   A New English Translation
of the Psalms, from the original Hebrew, reduced to
Metre by the late Bishop Hare; with notes critical
and explanatory; illustrations of many passages
drawn from the classics; with a preliminary
dissertation in which the truth and certainty of the
learned prelate's happy decisions is stated and
provided at length. Cambridge: J. Bentham, 1755.
> [Designed "...to make Bishop Hare's discovery of the
> Hebrew metre better known."]

Another edition; London: 1850.

1755 **Edwards, Timothy**   The Psalms translated from Bishop
Hare's arrangement of the text... Cambridge: J.
Bentham, 1755.

1757 **Fox, John**   Sternhold's 20th edition, with improvements and additions. (The Psalms) London: R. Brown, 1757.

1758 **Anonymous**   The Psalms, Hymns and Spiritual Songs of the Old and New Testament, Faithfully Translated into English Metre, being The New-England Psalm Book revised and improved... with an addition of fifty other hymns... [Thomas Prince] Boston: D. Henchman, S.Kneeland, 1758.
> [See 1640 Anonymous (Bay Psalm Book) The Whole Booke of Psalmes Faithfully Translated into English Metre...]

1759 **Fenwick, George**   The Psalter in its original Form; or, the Book of Psalms reduced to lines, in a easy and familiar style, and a kind of blank verse of unequal measurements, answering for the most part to the original lines, with arguments pointing out the general design of each Psalm, and notes, accounting for some passages in the translation; opening and explaining also, in some places, the prophetic views...To which is added a plain translation of the last words of David, with notes. London: T. Longman, 1759.
> [Anonymous?]

1762 **Green, William**   A New Translation of the Psalms from the original Hebrew, with notes critical and explanatory. To which is added, a Dissertation on the last prophetick words of Noah. Cambridge: Joseph Bentham, 1762.
> [In measured prose.]

> Another edition; London: 1763.

1763 **Bradbury, C.**   Psalms and Hymns, in Metre.   London: M. Lewis, 1763.

1765 **Anonymous**   Psalms carefully suited and applied to the Christian State and Worship; designed as an improvement on the old versions of the Hebrew Psalter. [Charles Collum and T.Vance] Dublin: A. Ewing, J.A. Husband, 1765.
> [Principally taken, with alterations, Rous's version (see 1641). Another edition; With translations and paraphrases of several passages in Holy Scriptures, (later date) Dublin: for W. Gilbert.]

1765 **Merrick, James**   The Psalms, Translated or Paraphrased in English Verse by James Merrick. Reading, England: J. Carnan & Co., 1765.
> Second edition, 1766.

MACK LIBRARY
BOB JONES UNIVERSITY
GREENVILLE, SC

Another Edition; A Version of the Psalms by James Merrick... with Explanatory Heads... by W.D. Tattersail. London: Longman..., 1822.

1765 **Smart, Christopher**   A Translation of the Psalms of David, attempted in the spirit of Christianity, and adapted to the divine service, by Christopher Smart. London: Printed by Dryden Leach, for the author, 1765.
> ["In this translation, all expressions, that seem contrary to Christ, are omitted..." Includes 'Hymns and Spiritual Songs for the Fasts and Festivals of the Church of England'.]

1767 **Anonymous**   The Psalms of David, with the Ten Commandments, Creed, Lord's Prayer, &c. In Metre. Also, the Catechism, Confession of Faith Liturgy, &c. Translated from the Dutch. For the use of the Reformed Protestant Dutch Church of the City of New-York. [Francis Hopkinson]   New-York: Printed by James Parker, 1767.
> ["...some of the Psalms being transcribed verbatim from (Tate & Brady's) version, and others altered, so as to fit them to the Music used in the Dutch Churches."]

Another edition; A Collection of the Psalms and Hymn Tunes, Used by the Reformed Protestant Dutch Church of the City of New-York, agreeable to the Psalm Book, published in English. In four parts, viz. Tenor, Bass, Treble, and Counter. New-York: Printed by Hodge and Shober, 1774.

1767 **Scott, George**   The Psalms of David in Metre ... Diligently compared with the Original Text and former Translations. More Plain, Smooth, and Agreeable to the Text, by George Scott. Edinburgh: Printed for the author, 1767.
> Another edition, 1768.

1768 **Anonymous**   A Paraphrase and Exposition of the Book of Psalms; designed principally for the use of the unlearned reader. By a Clergyman. London: J. Newbery, 1768.

1768 **Barton, William**   The Psalms in Metre... Cambridge: Fletcher & Hodson, 1768.

1771 **Anonymous**   A Commentary on the Book of Psalms, in Which Their Literal or Historical Sense, as They Relate to King David, and the People of Israel, is Illustrated; and their Application to Messiah, to the Church, and to Individuals, as Members thereof, is pointed out: With a view to render the Use of the Psalter pleasing and profitable to all Orders and

Degrees of Christians, by George, Lord Bishop of Norwich. [George Horne] 2 vols. Oxford: at the Clarendon Press, 1771.
> [The text is the AV with minor alterations; commentary includes paraphrases taken from Merrick, Ogilvie, etc.; Underwent numerous editions.]

1771 **Anonymous**   The Psalms; Scottish Version; with Translations and Paraphrases of Several Passages of Scripture, Collected and Prepared by a Committee. Colin McFarqunar, 1771.

1772 **Waddel, Andrew**   G. Buchanan's Paraphrase of the Psalms of David, Translated into English Prose, as Near the Original as the Different Idioms of the Latin and English Languages will Allow, with the Latin Text and Order of Construction in the Same Page. By Andrew Waddell. Edinburgh: Printed and Sold by J. Robertson, 1772.
> [It is said that this translation first was published in Maryland, America in 1754. No copy has been found.]

Another edition; Edinburgh: by J. Oxphoot, 1815.

1773 **Anonymous**   A Course of Singing-Psalms, in Metre. London: 1773.

1773 **Maxwell, James**   A New Version of the Whole Book of Psalms in Metre. To which is added, a Supplement of Divine Hymns, or Scripture Songs. All fitted to the common Psalm Tunes; and adapted to the present State of the Christian Church.. by James Maxwell... Glasgow: Printed by William Smith for the Author, 1773.

1775 **Anonymous**   The Book of Common Prayer Reformed... London: for J. Johnson, 1775.
> [Includes the Psalms in prose, altered in many places from the version of the Prayer Book. There are also several Psalms in meter in the collection at the end of the volume.]

1775 **Anonymous**   The Psalms (In Prose Altered in many places from the Version in the Prayer Book). London: J. Johnson, 1775.

1775 **Brown, John**   The Psalms of David, in Metre, Translated and Diligently Compared with the Original Text and Former Translations; More Plain, Smooth, and Agreeable to the Text than any heretofore: Allowed by the Authority of the General Assembly of the Kirk of Scotland, and approved to be sung in Congregations and Families. By John Brown. London: n.p., 1775? 1818?
> [A revision of the Scottish Psalter of 1650.]

Other editions; 1798, 1821, 1825.

1776 **Barclay, John**   The Psalms Paraphrased according to the New Testament Interpretation and adapted to the Common Church tunes. With an illustration at the beginning of each Psalm, or else a reference to its Parallels; and an Introductory Verse expressive of its Spirit and Scope. To the Whole is Prefixed a General Preface. By John Barclay.   Edinburgh: J.Donaldson for the Author, 1776.
> [Vol. 1 of a three volume work. The 2nd col. contains additional versions of several Psalms, and a paraphrase of Solomon's Song. The 2nd vol. is apparently "A Select Collection of New Original Spiritual Songs."]

1776 **Horne, George**   The Psalms. 2 Vols. Oxford: Clarendon Press, 1776.
> [Psalms are Slightly altered from his previous work.]

1780 **Collum, Charles and T. Vance**   Psalms in verse with translations of several passages of Holy Scripture. Dublin: W. Gilbert, 1780.

1781 **Williams, Benjamin**   The Book of Psalms, as Translated, Paraphrased, or Imitated by some of the most eminent English Poets, viz. Addison, Blacklock, Brady... and several others and adapted to Christian worship by Benjamin Williams. Salisbury: Printed & Sold by Collins & Johnson, 1781.

1784 **Anonymous**   The New-England Psalter...
> [See Bible Selections for the complete entry.]

1784 **Anonymous**   The Book of Psalms, in metre; from the original, compared with many versions in different languages. [Robert Boswell] London: for the Editor, sold by J. Johnson, 1784.
> Another edition; The British Psalter; or the Book of Psalms, in metre from the original, compared with many versions in different languages.
>
> Second edition; London: for the Editor, sold by J. Matthews, 1786.

1785 **Anonymous**   The Psalms of David selected from various versions, and adapted to public worship. [Richard Cecil] London: J. Matthews, W. Flexney; printed for the Welsh Charity, 1785.
> [A metrical version many times reprinted.]

1785 **Barlow, Joel**   Doctor Watt's Imitation of the Book of Psalms, Corrected and Enlarged by Joel Barlow. To which is added a Collection of Hymns; The whole applied to the State of the Christian Church in General. Hartford: Printed by Barlow and Babcock, 1785.

Another edition; Psalms carefully suited to the Christian Worship in the United States of America. Being an Improvement of the Old Versions of the Psalms of David. Allowed by the reverend synod of New-York and Philadelphia to be used in churches and private families. Philadelphia: Printed by Francis Bailey, 1787.
["...the Psalms which (Watts) omitted have been supplied by Mr. Barlow, nearly in the same spirit and stile...".]

Another edition; Hartford: N. Patten, 1791.

Also; The Psalms of David in the Language of the NT, and apply'd to the Christian State and Worship. Corrected, and accomodated to the use of the Church of Christ in America. Norwich: Printed by Bushnell & Hubbard, for Benjamin Larken of Boston, 1793.
["The Psalms considerably altered are the 21st, 60th, 67th, 75th, 124th, 147th; those omitted by Dr. Watts are the 28th, 43rd, 52nd, 54th, 59th, 64th, 70th, 79th, 88th, 108th, 137th, 140th.".]

Another edition; Psalms Carefully Suited to the Christian Worship in the United States of America. Being an Improvement of the Old Version of the Psalms of David. Hudson: Printed for William E.Norman, 1805.

Another edition; Philadelphia: Woodward, 1814, 1817.

Also; Pittsburgh: R. Patterson & Lambden, 1824.

1786 **Anonymous**   The Book of Psalms; illustrated by an Improved translation of the proper Psalms, more Conformable to the Hebrew Original, and a poetical version of each; by a Layman. [W.S.Towers]   London: for Robinsons, 1786.
Another edition; A Version of the Psalms, By the late William Samuel Towers, Esq. Printed at the very particular request of several of the Author's friends. London: Printed by H.Reynell, 1811.

1786 **Lewelyn, William**   Psalms of David. By William Lewelyn. Leominister: Haris, 1786.
[Metrical version.]

1787 **Smith, John**   See Gaelic Translation, Psalter, 1659.

1788 **Wesley, Charles**   A Poetical Version of some of
the Psalms of David by Charles Wesley. MS, 1788.
> 1st. Edition; A Poetical Version of Nearly the
> Whole of the Psalms of David by the Rev.
> Charles Wesley M.A.   Edited, with a brief
> introduction, by Henry Fish M.A.   London:
> Printed for the Editor. Sold by John Mason and
> Alexander Heylin, 1854.
>> ["Charles Wesley's Poetical Version of the Psalms
>> never saw the light until 1854, when they were
>> published by Rev. Henry Fish...who discovered the
>> ms in a second hand book shop." From 'The Journal
>> of the Rev. John Wesley...' Edited by Nehemiah
>> Curnock; London: Epworth Press, 1938.]

> Second edition, 1854.

> Reprinted; The Wesleyan Psalter... Edited by
> Thomas O. Summers.   Nashville, Tenn.: E.
> Stevenson & F.A. Owen, Agents for the ME
> Church, South, n.d.

1789 **Anonymous**   Psalms, in Metre, fitted to the Tunes
used in the Churches; selected from the Psalms of
David, for the use of the Protestant Episcopal
Church in the United States &c. Philadelphia and
London. 1789.
> Another edition; The Whole Book of Psalms, in
> metre: with Hymns, suited to the feasts and
> fasts of the Church. New York: Hugh Gaine,
> 1793.

> Another edition; New York: Sherman & Trevett,
> 1839.

1789 **Tattersall, W.D.**   A Version or Paraphrase of the
Psalms, originally written by the Rev. James Merrick
A.M.   Divided into Stanzas, and Adapted to the
purposes of Public or Private devotions. London:
for Thomas Payne & Son, Benjamin White & Son, Robson
& Clarke, G.G.J. & J. Robinson, Mr. Fletcher & Mr.
Prince; Joseph Bence, 1789.
> ["Although it has been printed nearly two years, the
> Editor was unwilling to offer it to the Public, till he
> had collected the sentiments of the Rulers of the
> Church... the principle objection to its admission into
> the Parish Churches appears to be the difficulty of
> adapting several of the best old tunes to a meter
> differing from the ancient version..." The Preface is
> dated 1791.]

> Another edition; Improved Psalmody and arranged
> with new music. London: for Rivingtons, 1794.

> Another edition, 1797.

1790 **Anonymous**   A Book of Common Prayer, and
Adminstration of the Sacraments, and other Rites and
Ceremonies of the Church..., 1790.
> Another edition; New York: Delisser & Procter,
> 1859.

1790 **Street, Steven**   A new literal version of the Book
of Psalms, with a preface and notes. By the Rev.
Steven Street. 2 Vols. London: Printed by J. Davis
for B. White and Son, 1790.
> ["The whole that is aimed at in the present performance,
> is to give a closely literal translation, and, by
> endeavouring to restore the original form of these
> compositions, to exhibit them in their ancient
> semblance..."]

1791 **Dimock, Henry**   Notes, Critical and Explanatory...
> [See Wisdom and Poetical Books and Selections for the
> complete entry.]

1793 **Wake, William Robert**   A Liberal Version
of the Psalms into modern language, according to the
liturgy translation; With copious Notes and
Illustrations, partly original, and partly selected
from the best commentaries: calculated to render the
Book of Psalms intelligible to every capacity, by
William Robert Wake. 2 Vols. Bath: by R. Crutwell,
1793.

1794 **Anonymous**   The Psalms of David. A new and improved
version. London: M. Priestley and J. Matthews, 1794.
> [From the Swedish Translation of J.A. Tingstadius; prose
> version.]

1794 **Travell, F.T.**   An Attempt to render the daily
readings of the Psalms more intelligible to the
unlearned; with a paraphrase selected from the best
commentators, and illustrated with occasional notes
by F.T. Travell.   Gloucester: R. Raikes; Oxford:
1794.
> [With the Prayer Book text.]

1795 **Seabury, Samuel** Morning and Evening Prayer with the
Psalter, by Samuel Seabury. New London, Conn.: 1795.
> [The imprecatory Psalms are softened down greatly, by
> substituting the future tense for the imperative mood.]

1797 **Anonymous**   Psalms of David; Versified from
a new translation, and adapted to Christian Worship,
for the use of such Christians as believe in the
Universal Love of God. To which is added a
collection of hymns, by various authors. [Elhanan
Winchester?] London: the author, 1797.

1799 **Anonymous**   The Book of Psalms in Metre for
closeness to the Hebrew and smoothness of verse to

be preferred to Rhyme. [James Downes]   London:
Griffiths, 1799.
> [Title is similar to an anonymous work attributed to
> Samuel Pike, 1751.]

1800 **Dwight, Timothy** (1752-1817) Dr. Isaac Watts Metrical
Version of the Psalms; Revised and Completed, 1800.

1802 **Dwight, Timothy** (1752-1817)   The Psalms of David,
imitated in the language of the New Testament, and
applied to the Christian use and worship, by I.
Watts, D.D.; A new edition, in which the Psalms
omitted by Dr. Watts are versified, local passages
are altered, and a number of Psalms are versified
anew, in proper metres. To the Psalms is added a
selection of Hymns... Approved and allowed by the
General Assembly of the Presbyterian Church of the
United States of America. Second Edition.   New
Brunswick: A. Blauvelt, 1804.
> First edition, 1802?

> Another edition; New York: Charles Stair, 1822.

> Also; Hartford: P.B. Gleason & Co. for Collins
> & Hannay, 1830.

1805 **Anonymous**   A Version of the Psalms of David...
to which are added, Translations and Paraphrases of
Several Passages in Sacred Scripture.   Dublin:
Gilbert and Hodges, 1805.

1805 **Cottle, Joseph**   A New Version of the Psalms of
David attempted in Metre...Second Edition.   London:
printed for T.N. Longman & O. Rees, by Biggs & Co.,
Bristol, 1801.
> ["...in the year 1801, I published a version of the
> Psalms... although I have named the present, a second
> edition, it is in reality a new work." See 1801
> edition.]

1807 **Geddes, Alexander**   A New Translation of the Book
of Psalms, from the original Hebrew; with various
readings and notes. By Alexander Geddes. London: J.
Johnson, 1807.
> ["The doctor's version extends only to the eleventh
> verse of Psalm cxviii; the rest is added from an
> interleaved copy of Bishop Wilson's Bible, corrected by
> Dr. G., who professes to have confined himself to the
> direct and literal meaning of the inspired authors."
> Edited posthummously by John Disney and Charles Butler.]

1807 **Ross, Thomas** See Gaelic Translation, Psalter, 1659.

1808 **Dennis, Thomas**   A New Version of the Psalms
in blank verse: with a Latin version of the eighth
Psalm in Alcaic verse. London: J. White, 1808.

1809 **Anonymous**   A Version of the Psalms of David,
     attempted to be closely accomodated to the text of
     Scripture; and adapted...to all the music used in
     the versions of Sternhold and Hopkins and of Brady
     and Tate. By a Lay-Member of the Church of England.
     [John Stow] London: F.C. & J. Rivington, 1809.
>   Another edition; A Selection from a version of
>   the Psalms of David, intended for Family use,
>   by a Lay-Member of the Church of England.
>   London: 1821.
>
>   Second edition; (complete Psalms), 1842.
>
>   Third edition, 1844.

1811 **Baker, Richard**   The Psalms Evangelized. London:
     1811.
>   Another edition, 1882.

1811 **Goode, William**   An Entire New Version of
     the Book of Psalms; in which an attempt is made to
     accommodate them to the Worship of the Christian
     Church, with original Prefaces, and Notes Critical
     and explanatory. 2 Vols. London: Printed for the
     Author, 1811.
>   ["...he has at least endeavoured to...keep as closely as
>   possible to the Originals...(and) to preserve the utmost
>   simplicity of language..." a metrical version.]
>
>   Also; In a variety of measures now in general
>   use... Third Edition. London: [by C. Baldwin],
>   1816.

1812 **Davidson, R.**   A New Metrical Version of the whole
     Book of Psalms; in various measures; more free,
     plain and harmonious, and more in the language of
     the New Testament, than former translations; with
     occasional   notes   and   illustrations.   Carlisle
     [Penna]: Printed by Alexander Phillips, 1812.
>   ["This version will be found to agree with the old in
>   many places, and to preserve the scripture as much as
>   possible. Although it is called a free translation, it
>   is notwithstanding in a multitude of places nearly
>   literal."]

1813 **Davis, Abijah**   An American Version of the Psalms
     of David, suited to the State of the Church in the
     Present Age of the World, by Abijah Davis.
     Philadelphia: Printed for the author by D. Heartt,
     1813.
>   ["...a free verse translation of the Psalms."]

1815 **Anonymous**   The Book of Psalms in metre; fitted to the tunes in common use; with notes. [Mrs. S. Pike?] London: for T. Boosey, 1815.
Another edition; London: for G. Leighton, 1819.

1815 **Guildford, R. Donald**   The Psalms of David..., 1815.

1815 **Horsley, Samuel**   The Book of Psalms; translated from the Hebrew: with Notes, Explanatory and Critical by Samuel Horsley. 2 Vols. London: Printed for F.C. & J. Rivington ...and Longman, Hurst, Rees, Orme, & Browne, 1815.
[The Deity is rendered "Jehovah" many times.]

Second edition, 1816.

[This posthumous work, edited by Heneage Horsley, contains many fanciful applications of the Psalms to the Messiah.]

1816 **Anonymous**   Psalms carefully suited to the Christian Worship in the United States of America; being an improvement of the old version of the Psalms of David... Albany: Printed by Websters & Skinners, 1816.

1817 **Goodwin, Edward**   A Version of the Psalms, 1817.
["...altogether by no means devoid of merit." (Holland); never published.]

1817 **Pierce, Samuel Eyles**   The Book of Psalms, with practical Annotations, by Samuel Eyles Pierce. London: n.p., 1817.

1819 **Fry, John**   Lyra Davidis; or, a New Translation and Exposition of the Psalms; Grounded on the Principles Adopted in the Posthumous Work of the late Bishop Horsley. By...John Fry. London: Ogle, Duncan & Co., 1819.
[Like Horsley, Fry believed that the Psalms have for the most part an immediate reference to Christ.]

Second edition, 1842.

1819 **Pruen, T.**   The Psalms; arranged on a new plan by T. Pruen. London: for Rivingtons, 1819.

1820 **Anonymous**   The Book of Psalms in verse; with a short explanatory preface to each verse, taken from the writers on the Psalms, but chiefly from Bishop Horne's Commentary. London: 1820.
Another edition; London: Printed by the Philanthropic Society for Rivingtons, 1822.

1820 **Neligan, James**   The Psalms of David Versifies.
     Boston: James Neligan;   Dublin: printed for the
     author, 1820.

1821 **Reid, John**   ...The Book of Psalms Without Points;
     Corrected from the Edition of Vander Hooght, with a
     Key, Grammar, Literal English Version, and Lexicon,
     upon an Improved Plan, by John Reid.   Glasgow: M.
     Ogle, Wardlaw & Cunninghame, University Press, 1821.

1821 **Sherriffe, Sarah**   Practical Reflexions on the
     Psalms, to Which is Added a Prayer Adapted to Each,
     by Sarah Sherriffe. 2 Vols. London: Strong, 1821.

1823 **Singer, Samuel W.**   See Philip Sidney and Mary
     Herbert, The Psalmes of David, 1600.

1823 **Usher, James**   A New Version of the Psalms;
     principally from the text of Bishop Horne by James
     Usher.   London: for the author, 1823.
          [Metrical version.]

          [The first 30 Psalms only; not clear whether or not the
          1823 edition is complete.]

          Another edition; - - from their Original Text...
          Part First. London: Printed for the editor,
          and published by C.G. Dyer, 1827.

1824 **Mant, Richard**   The Book of Psalms, in
     an English metrical version; founded on the basis of
     the authorized Bible translation, and compared with
     the original Hebrew. With notes, critical and
     illustrative. Oxford: J. Parker, 1824.

1824 **Turner, B.N.**   Songs of Solyma; or, a New Version of
     the Psalms of David: the long ones being compressed,
     in general into two parts, or portions of Psalmody,
     comprising their prophetic evidences and principle
     beauties.   London: C. & J. Rivington, 1824.
          [Metrical version.]

1825 **Anonymous**   A literal translation of the Psalms
     of David, solely upon the authority of the Rev. John
     Parkhurst.   London: printed for the translator by J.
     Johnson, 1825.

1825 **Sankey, Matthew**   A New Version of the Psalms of
     David. London: C. & J. Rivington, 1825.
          [Metrical version]

1826 **Anonymous**   The Psalms of David, attempted in verse,
     regular, irregular, in the way of paraphrase...by
     Senex, a Clergyman. [Edward Rowland]   Carlisle:
     Charles Thurnam, 1826.

1826 **Anonymous**   A Version of the Psalms, with
a comprehensive selection of hymns, chosen from the
best authors.   [C.Bassano]   Leamington: Rose and
Owen, 1826.

1826 **Balfour, J.**   The Psalms of David according to the
Coptic Version, accompanies by a literal translation
into English, and by the version of the Latin
Vulgate, with copious notes... London: MS. British
Museum, 1826.

1828 **Patullo, Margaret**   The Christian Psalter; a new
version of the Psalms of David, calculated for all
denominations of Christians.   Edinburgh: for the
author by Oliver & Boyd, 1828.
        [This version, not proving satisfactory to the friends
        of the authoress, was bought up and suppressed.]

1829 **Cadell, T.**   The Spirit of the Psalms, a compressed
version... London: 1829.

1829 **Wrangham, W.**   A New Metrical Version of the Psalms:
adapted to devotional purposes. By W. Wrangham.
London: Printed for W. Simpkin & R. Marshall by
Jackson, Lowth, 1829.

1830 **Anonymous**   The Book of Psalms according to the AV,
metrically arranged after the Original Hebrew, and
disposed in Chronological Order.   London: Samuel
Bagster, 1830.

1830 **French, William and George Skinner**   A new
translation of the Book of Psalms from the original
Hebrew with explanatory notes by William French...
and George Skinner... Cambridge: J. Smith; London:
Printed by John Murray, 1830.
        [The text, taken for their standard by the
        translators...is that of Vander Hooght; from which,
        utterly disregarding all conjectural emendations, they
        have rarely departed.]

        Also; A new edition with corrections and
        additions; London: J.W. Parker, 1842.

1831 **Anonymous**   A New Metrical Psalter. By a Clergyman
of the Established Church. [W.J. Tower] London: A.
Hatchard & Son, 1831.
        Revised and Republished; Oxford: J. Parker & Co.,
        1875.

1831 **Bartholomew, Alfred**   Sacred Lyrics:
being an attempt to render the Psalms of David more
applicable to parochial psalmody. By Alfred
Bartholemew. London: Rivingtons, 1831.

1831 **Noyes, George R.**   A New Translation... Psalms...
     [See Wisdom and Poetical books and Selections, 1827
     George R. Noyes, A New Translation of [the Poetical O.T.
     Books]...]

1832 **Gahagan, Henry**   A Rhyme Version of the "Liturgy"
     Psalms. London: C.J.G. & F. Rivington, 1832.

1832 **Marsh, Edward Garrard**   The Book of Psalms,
     translated into English verse, and illustrated with
     practical and explanatory notes by Edward Garrard
     Marsh...   London: Printed for R.B. Seeley and W.
     Burnside; Sold by L.B. Seeley and Sons, 1832.

1832 **Scurray, Francis (or Skurray)**   A Metrical Version
     of the Book of Psalms, by Francis Scurray. 1832-
     1843.
            1832 Forty Five Specimens of Psalms in Metre.
            In "The Shepherd's Garland"

            1843 A Metrical Version of the Book of Psalms.
            Composed for private Meditation or Public
            Worship. London: William Pickering.

1833 **Anonymous**   The Christian Psalmist: being
     a collection of Psalms, Hymns, and Spiritual Songs,
     compiled from the most approved authors, and
     designed as a Standard Hymn Book, for public and
     social worship. Philadelphia: 1833.
            [Psalms are collected from Watts, Tate & Brady, Spirit
            of the Psalms, Wragham, Pratt's Collection, Newton, Mrs.
            Steele, Montgomery, Addison, Barlow, Kelly, Dwight,
            Doddridge, Merrick, etc. "The compilers have
            occasionally met with hymns requiring some slight
            alterations, which they conceived themselves justified
            in making..."]

            Pew Edition; Philadelphia: James Kay, Jun. &
            Bros.; Pittsburgh: John I. Kay, 1836.

1833 **Bartrum, Joseph P.**   The Psalms Newly Paraphrased,
     for the use of the Sanctuary. By Joseph P. Bartrum.
     Boston: Russell, Odione & Co., 1833.

1833 **Ducarel, P.J.**   A Paraphrase of the Psalms,
     executed in blank verse: with strict attention to
     the notes and commentaries of Bishops Horsley,
     Horne, etc. and closely approximated to the text of
     the AV of the Old Testament and the Liturgy.
     London: Hamilton Adams & Co., 1833.

1833 **Musgrave, George**   The Book of the Psalms of
     David in English Blank Verse. Being a new poetical
     arrangement of the sweet Songs of Israel: adapted to
     the use of General readers, by George Musgrave.

London: Printed by W. Porter for G.J. & F. Rivington, 1833.
>Another edition; Yeovil: for Rivingtons, n.d.

1834 **Atwood, H.A.S.** A New Version of the Psalms, adapted to Congregational Psalmody. Coventry: J. Turner, 1834.

1835 **Allen, William**   Psalms and Hymns for Public Worship, containing all the Psalms and hymns by Dr. Watts, which are deemed valuable, together with a new version of all the Psalms, and many original hymns, besides a large collection from other writers. William Allen. Boston: Wm. Peirce, 1835.

1835 **Anonymous**   Psalms and Hymns, adapted to public worship, and approved by the General Assembly of the Presbyterian Church of the USA.   Philadelphia: J. Wethan, 1835.
>Another edition; Psalms and Hymns adapted to Social, Private, and Public Worship in the Presbyterian Church in the United States of America. Philadelphia: Presbyterian Board of Publication, [1843].

1835 **Blackhall, Elizabeth** Psalms & Hymns and Spiritual Songs. Twelve Psalms in Verse. Dublin: William Cury, Junior & Co., 1835.

1835 **Morgan, C.**   The Psalms in Metre...
>[See Bible Selections for the complete entry.]

1835 **Nourse, James**   The Book of Psalms: being the AV metrically arranged, by James Nourse.   Boston: Perkins, Marvin & Co., 1835.

1835 **Thorpe, Benjamin**   Libri Psalmorum versio antiqua Latina cum paraphrasi Anglo-Saxonica, partim soluta oratinoe, partim metrice composita, nunc primum e codice MS. in Bibliotheca Parisiensi adservato, descripsit et edidit.   Oxford: University Press, 1835.

1836 **Dee, Thomas**   The Lyre of David; or, an analysis of the Psalms, critical and practical; to which is added a Hebrew and Chaldee grammar, by Victorinus Bythner, formerly Hebrew professor in the University of Oxford. Translated by the Rev. Thomas Dee, A.B., Ex-scholar T.C.D. To which are added, by the translator, a praxis of the first eight Psalms, and tables of the imperfect verbs... Dublin: John Cumming; London: Whittaker & Co., 1836.

[Includes a literal phrase—by—phrase translation from the Hebrew of "Lyra Davidis Regis", by Victorini Bythneri, London, 1650.]

New Edition; Most carefully revised, collated, freed of the errors of its predecessors, with numerous improvements, preliminary remarks, additions to the text and tables, by N.L.Benmohel, A.M., T.C.D. Dublin: Cumming & Ferguson; London: Whittaker & Co.

1836 **Eadie, John** Translation of Buchanan's Latin Psalms into English Verse. Glasgow: for the author, 1836

1836 **Farr, Edward** A New Version of the Psalms of David, in all the various metres suited to Psalmody, divided into subjects, and designated according to Bishop Horne, &c. London: Published by B. Fellowes, 1836.
Second edition, 1847.

1837 **Anonymous** Christian Psalmody: comprising a version of all the Psalms, and a selection of hymns, adapted to the services and festivals of the Church of England. By several clergymen. Liverpool: Joseph Davenport, 1837.
[Robert Bruce Boswell.]

Second edition, 1841.

1837 **Clowes, John** The Psalms: A New Translation from the Hebrew, with the internal sense and exposition from the writings of the Hon. Emamuel Swedenborg, together with observations... J. Clowes... The Editors. Manchester: H. Smith, 1837.
Another edition; London: 1849.

1837 **Cole, H.** The Psalms translated from Martin Luther's Manual. London: Seely's, 1837.

1837 **Drake, Nathaniel** The Harp of Judah; or, the Songs of Sion: being a Metrical Translation of the Psalms, constructed from the most beautiful parts of the best English Versions: With an introduction and Notes Critical and Explanatory. London: J.G. & F. Rivington, 1837.

1837 **Walford, William** The Book of Psalms. A new translation, with notes, explanatory and critical by William Walford... London: by R. Clay, for Jackson and Walford, 1837.

1838 **Anonymous**   The Book of Psalms, arranged for family
devotion; with prefaces and collects. [J. Molony?]
London: J. Hatchard & Son, 1838.

1838 **Anonymous**   A New Metrical Version of the Psalms
of David. By C.F. and E.C. [Catherine Foster and
Elizabeth Colling] London: Simpkin, Marshall & Co.;
Printed by W. Stephenson; Hull, 1838.

1838 **Holmes, James**   Psalms and Hymns; original and
selected by James Holmes. Harrowgate: 1838.

1839 **Anonymous**   The Psalter, or Psalms of David;
in English verse; by a member of the University of
Oxford. Adapted, for the most part, to tunes in
common use; and dedicated, by permission, to the
Lord Bishop of Oxford. [John Keble] Oxford: John
Henry Parker; London: J.G. & F. Rivington, 1839.
    Another edition, 1840.

        Reprinted; "Master's Christian Classics" edited
        by Vernon Staley. London: S.C. Brown, Langham
        & Co, Ltd., 1904.

1839 **Burgess, George**   The Book of Psalms; Translated
into English Verse. By George Burgess. New York:
F.J. Huntington & Co., 1839.
        ["...the author has endeavored...to be so literal, as to
        give the very sentiment and, if possible, the spirit of
        the original, and yet so free as not to inflict pain on
        the reader of taste..."]

1839 **Darnell, W.N.**   An Arrangement and Classification
of the Psalms, with a view to render them more
useful for private devotion. London: J.G.F. & J.
Rivington, 1839.
        [Prayer Book Version, amended by that of 1611.]

1840 **Anonymous**   A New Version of the Psalms of David
as used in the Church of England. London: Renshaw
& Kirkman, 1840?

1841 **Eden, John**   The Book of Psalms in Blank Verse;
with practical reflections... With a brief memoir
and a portrait. London: Hamilton, Adams & Co.:
Printed by J. Chilcott; Bristol, 1841.

1841 **Reichart, J.C.**   ...The Book of Psalms, Carefully
revised, by J.C.Reichart. London: A.Macintosh, 1841.
        [Hebrew and English]

1842 **Anonymous**   The Psalms Translated by a lay member
of the Church of England. London: 1842.
        [See Anonymous, A Version of the Psalms, 1809.]

1843 **Cox, Samuel H.**   Church Psalmist; or Psalms and Hymns, for the Public, Social, and Private use of Evangelical Christians. New York: Mark H. Newman, 1843.

> [Approved by the General Assembly of the Presbyterian Church of the United States of America. "In the arrangement of the Psalms, Dr. Watts is the leading author. Many other versifications of high merit have been selected from Doddridge, Steele, Kenn, Newton, Montgomery, Conder and others... Few alterations have been made in arrangement or expression... Most of the changes which have been adopted, are those which were necessary to conform to the principles (of the work)."]

1843 **Cresswell, Daniel**   The Psalms of David, with notes. London: 1843.

1843 **Cumming, John**   The Psalms of David, with a Paraphrase. London: 1843.

> Another edition; London: Hall, 1848.

1843 **Holland, John**   The Psalmists of Britain: Records of upwards of 150 authors, who have rendered the whole or part of the Book of Psalms into English verse; with specimens... 2 Vols. London: 1843.

> [This contains a number of Psalms which have not since, or were ever previously in print. Cotton drew heavily upon this work for his Edition of the bible and Parts therof.]

1843 **Stevenson, Joseph**   (Editor)   Anglo-Saxon and Early English Psalter: now first printed from manuscripts in the British Museum, edited by J. Stevenson. 2 Vols. Durham: Surtees Society, 1843.

> Other editions; 1844, 1847.

1843 **Sutcliffe, Joseph**   The Union Version of the Psalms, in various metres. By Joseph Sutcliffe. London: William Aylott, 1843.

1844 **Anonymous**   The Psalms of David, metrically paraphrased, for the inmates of the Cottage. By a Cambridge Master of Arts. [Edward Feilde] London: Whittaker & Co., 1844.

1844 **Barrett, J.T.**   Course of Psalms. By J.T. Barrett. London: Leslie, 1844.

> [Metrical version.]

1844 **Fairbairn, P. and J. Thompson**   Commentary on the Psalms, by E. Hengstenberg...Translated [from the German] by P. Fairbairn and J. Thompson. Edinburgh: Thomas Clark, Biblical Cabinet V. 1, 2, 12, 1844-1848.

1844 **Montagu, M.**   The Psalms. In a new version. 1844-
     1851.
          1844 The Seven Penitential Psalms in verse;
               being specimens of a new version of the
               Psalter, with an appendix of correlative
               matter and notes. London: T. Hatchard.

          1851 The Psalms. In a new version. Fitted to
               the Tunes used in Churches. With notes in
               examination   of   difficult   passages.
               London: T. Hatchard.

          [Contains   "...useful   references   to   the   versions
          published..."]

1845 **Anderson, James** Commentaries on the Book of Psalms
     by John Calvin. Translated from the original Latin,
     and collated with the author's French Version [Latin
     & English] 5 Vols. Edinburgh: Calvin Translation
     Society, 1845-49.
          [See Bible Selections, 1844 Anonymous, Commentaries [on
          the books of the Bible].]

1845 **Anonymous**   A Metrical Version of the Hebrew
     Psalter: with explanatory notes. [Thomas Spalding]
     London: Ward & Co., 1845.

1845 **Anonymous**   Psalms and Hymns for Church Use
     and Worship; Prepared and Set Forth by the General
     Association of Connecticut. [Horace Hooker and
     Oliver E. Daggett] 1845.
          Another edition; New Haven: Durrie & Peck;
          Boston: Charles Tappan; N-Y: Clark & Austin;
          Philadelphia: Loomis & Peck; Utica: G. Tracy;
          Rochester: Alling, Seymour & Co., 1851.

1845 **Anonymous**   The Interlineary Hebrew and English
     Psalter. In which the construction of every word is
     indicated, and the root of each is distinguished by
     the use of hollow and other types. [S.P. Tregelles]
     London: S. Bagster & Son, 1845.
          ["Whilst we have no definite information it is likely
          that this is at least partly the work of Samuel Prideaux
          Tregelles, LL.D..." Letter from Bagsters, 1966.]

          [The Deity is rendered "Jehovah" many times.]

1845 **McCrie, George and James McLean**   Commentaries on
     the Book of Psalms by John Calvin. Translated from
     the original Latin, and collated with the author's
     French   version.   4   Vols.   Edinburgh: Calvin
     Translation Society, 1845-1849.
          [See Anonymous, Commentaries on the Books of the Bible,
          1844.]

1846 **Anonymous**   Anthologia Davidica; or, a Metrical
Translation of the whole Book of Psalms, selected
from our published versions, with alterations... by
Presbyter Cisestrensis. [Henry Latham] London: F.&
J. Rivington, 1846.

1846 **Jebb, John**   A Literal Translation of the Book
of Psalms; intended to illustrate their poetical and
moral structure; to which are added dissertations on
the word Selah, and on the authorship, order,
titles, and poetic features of the Psalms. By John
Jebb... 2 Vols. London: Longmans & Co., 1846.
   [Vol.1 Text with footnotes; Vol. 2 Dissertations.]

1846 **Pearson, George**   See Miles Coverdale, Goostly
Psalmes, 1539.

1847 **Anonymous**   The Book of Psalms in Metre; compared
with the Hebrew Original and from former versions
revised, for public and private devotions. Glasgow:
for the author, by Robertson, 1847.
   ["...in some cases giving a happier rendering than the
   AV..."]

1847 **Cole, Benjamin and Thomas Halcott**   The Psalms
of David: a New Metrical Version. London: Seely,
Burnside & Seely, 1847.

1847 **Irons, Joseph** Judah. The Book of Psalms paraphrased
in spiritual songs... London: the Author, 1847.

1847 **Woodruff, Hezekiah** An Exposition and Versification
of the Psalms of David; together with original hymns
by Hezekiah Woodruff.   Elmira [New York]: C.G.
Fairman, Printer, Republican Office, 1847.
   ["A literal version of the Psalms of David in poetry,
   without rhyme."]

1848 **Anonymous**   An Entirely New Metrical Version of the
Psalms, written for the music of that in common use.
By W.H.B. [William Henry Blake] London: John
Rodwell, 1848.

1849 **Connelly, H.**   The Psalms of David in Metre, Allowed
by the authority of the Kirk of Scotland, and used
in several branches of the Presbyterian Church in
the   United   States;   with   verbal   amendments.
Newburgh, New York: H. Connelly, 1849.
   ["In these amendments, a suitable word from the Prose
   language of the Psalms has been preferred to any
   other."]

1850 **Alexander, Joseph Addison**   The Psalms Translated
and Explained by Joseph Addison Alexander. 2 Vols.

Philadelphia: Presbyterian Board of Publications, 1850.
[The Deity is rendered "Jehovah" many times.]

Another edition; New York: Baker and Scribner, 3 vols., 1850.

Other editions; New York: Scribners, 1859; Edinburgh, 1864; Grand Rapids: Baker Book House, 1977.

1850 **Brancker, Thomas**   See Henry Hammond, A Paraphrase ...Psalms, 1659.

1850 **Edwards, Joseph**   A devotional exposition of the Book of Psalms: containing an argument to each Psalm, a paraphrase, suggestive remarks, and parallel Scriptures in words at length.   London: James Darling, 1850.
[With the AV.]

1850 **Fysh, Frederic**   A Lyrical, Literal Version of the Psalms. 2 Vols. London: Seeleys, 1850-1851.

1850 **McClure, Samuel**   The Psalms of David...
[See Wisdom and Poetical books and Selections for the complete entry.]

1851 **Conder, Josiah**   The Psalms of David Imitated in New Testament Language, by Rev. Isaac Watts: together with his three books of hymns and Spiritual Songs, re-arranged in one series. The whole carefully revised... London: n.p., 1851.

1852 **Champney, Henry M.**   A Textual Commentary on the Psalms. London: n.p., 1852.

1852 **Weiss, Benjamin**   A New Translation, Exposition, and Chronological Arrangement of the Book of Psalms; with critical notes on the Hebrew text. By Benjamin Weiss... Edinburgh: W. Oliphant & Sons, 1852.
Another edition; London: Hamilton, Adams and Co.; Glasgow: George Gallie, 1852.

1853 **Anonymous**   The Book of Psalms Translated into English Verse ...Original Hebrew...by a Layman. London: F. & J. Rivingtons, 1853.
Another edition; A Metrical Translation of the Psalms, from the original Hebrew, compared with ancient versions: to which is added, an introduction to each Psalm, shewing the historical and spiritual sense. Second edition, revised and enlarged, 1858.

1853 **Jones, Abner**   The Psalms of David, rendered into English verse of various measures, divided according to their musical cadences, and comprised in their own limits: in which their responsive lines are kept unbroken, the devout and exalted sentiments with which they everywhere abound, expressed in their own familiar and appropriate language, and the graphic imagery, by which they are rendered vivid, preserved entire. Boston: 1853.
> Another edition; New York: Mason Bros., 1854.

> ["...the author has made many stanzas to conform to an able and lucid translation of the Psalms by Prof. J.A. Alexander..." (1850)]

1853 **Ryland, Robert H.**   The Psalms restored to Messiah, a Commentary, by Robert H. Ryland.   London: n.p., 1853.

1854 **Churton, Edward**   The Book of Psalms in English Verse, in measure suited for sacred music.   Oxford & London: John Henry Parker, 1854.
> ["Cleveland Psalter"]

1854 **Good, John Mason**   The Book of Psalms; a new translation, with notes critical and explanatory; by ...John Mason Good...edited by the Rev.E. Henderson. London: Seeleys, 1854.

1854 **Turner, Thomas**   A Metrical Version of the Book of Psalms by Thomas Turner. 1854-1859.
> 1854 An Essay towards a New Metrical Version of the Psalms of David. Fourteen Psalms. London: Rivingtons.

> 1859 A Metrical Version of the Book of Psalms. London: Rivingtons.

1856 **Mombert, J. Isidor**   A translation and commentary on the book of Psalms, for the use of the ministry and laity of the Christian Church by Augustus F. Tholock ... translated from the German, with a careful comparison of the Psalm-Text with the original tongues. London: J. Nisbet & Co.; Leeds: J. Heaton & Son, 1856.
> Another edition; Philadelphia: William S. & Alfred Martien, 1858.

1857 **Anonymous**   A New Metrical Translation of the Book of Psalms. Accentuated for Chanting.... London: Samuel Bagster & Sons, 1857.

1857 **Hawkins, Ernest**   The Book of Psalms with Notes by Ernest Hawkins.   London: 1857.

1857 **Riddell, Henry Scott**   The Book of Psalms in
Lowland Scotch; from the authorized English version,
by Henry Scott Riddell.   London: Robson, Levey &
Franklyn; Impensis Ludovici Luciani Bonoparte, 1857.

1858 **Anonymous**   A Critical Translation of the Psalms in
Metre. London: 1858.

1858 **Bowring, Edgar Alfred**   The Most Holy Book
of Psalms, literally rendered into English verse,
according to the   Prayer Book version. By E.A.
Bowring.   London: J.W.Parker and Son, 1858.

1858 **Crane, John**   The Book of Psalms. A New Version.
London: Simpkin, Marshall; Birmingham: R. Matthison,
1858.

1858 **Jowett, Benjamin Jr**.   A New Metrical Translation
of the Book of Psalms, accentuated for chanting by
Benjamin Jowett, Jr. London: S Bagster & Sons, 1858.

1858 **Kay, William and Krishnamohana Vandyopadhyaya**
The Book of Psalms, newly translated in Bengali and
English.   Calcutta: 1858.

1858 **Sheppard, William**   The Sweet Psalmist of Israel;
or, the Life of David, King of Israel, illustrated
by his own Psalms newly versified in various metres,
by William Sheppard.   London: n.p., 1858.

1859 **Anonymous**   The True Psalmody; or the
Bible's Psalms the Church's only manual of praise.
Philadelphia: 1859.

1859 **Anonymous**   Hebrew Lyrics, by an Octogenarian.
[Hans Busk Sr.] London: Saunders, Oatley & Co.,
Wetheim, Macintosh & Hunt, 1859.

1860 **Anonymous**   Psalms and Hymns as sung in the Parish
Church, Rugby.   Rugby: Crossly & Billington, 1860.

1860 **Anonymous**   The Psalms. A new version by Lord
Congleton. [John Vesey Parnell]   London: William
Yapp, 1860.
        ["...'The Book of Psalms in Hebrew, Metrically Arranged,
        with Selections from the Various readings of Kennicott
        and DeRossi, and from the Ancient Versions', by
        J.Rogers, M.A., 1848, has been taken as the basis of
        this version..."]

        Also; A new edition, revised. With notes
suggestive of interpretation. London: James
E.Hawkins, 1875.

1860 **Anonymous**   The Psalter, or Psalms of David, in English Verse. By A Member of the University of Cambridge. [Benjamin Hall Kennedy]   Cambridge: Deighton, Bell & Co., 1860.
Another edition; by Benjamin Hall Kennedy, Canon of Ely, 1875.

Also; "...a few corrections are made...", 1876.

1860 **Cayley, C.B. (Coyley?)**   The Psalms in Metre with Notes. London: Longman & Co., 1860.
[Strong attributes to Charles Bagot Cogley.]

1860 **Duffield, T.**   Metrical Psalms. MS. c1860.
[Mentioned in "A Metrical Version of the Psalms", Beveridge, 1865.]

1860 **Lord, Eleazer**   The Psalter Re-adjusted in its Relations to the Temple and the Ancient Jewish Faith. New York: Anson D. F. Randolph, 1860.

1860 **Wilson, William**   The Book of Psalms, with an Exposition, evangelical, typical, and prophetical, of the Christian dispensation. By William Wilson. 2 Vols. London: J. Nisbet & Co., 1860.

1861 **Oliver, Andrew**   A Translation of the Syraic Peshito Version of the Psalms of David; with notes, critical and explanatory, by Andrew Oliver. Boston: E.P. Dutton & Co.;   London: Trubner & Co., 1861.
Also; New York: James Pott, 1867.

1862 **Yonge, W.C.**   A Version of the Whole Book of Psalms, in various metres; with pieces and hymns suggested by N.T. quotations; also an appendix of Various translations. By W.C. Yonge. London: Jackson, Walford & Hodder, 1862.

1863 **Coleman, John Noble**   Psalterium Messianicum Davidis Regis et Prophetae. A revision of the authorized English Version of the Book of Psalms with notes, original and selected, vindicating, in accordance with the interpretation of the New Testament, and with pre-Reformation authorities, their prophetic manifestation of Messiah by the Rev. John Noble Coleman....   London: for   J.   Nisbet   &   Co.; Edinburgh: T. Constable; 1863.

1863 **Fayre, Richard**   First Leaves [Mid-Leaves & Last Leaves] of the Psalter; or, the... Psalms of David metrically rendered.   3 Vols.   Fakenham: G.N. Stewardson; London: William Ridgeway, 1863-1872.

1863 **Kay, William**   The Psalms, translated from the
Hebrew, with notes chiefly exegetical. By W. Kay...
Calcutta: R.C. Lepage and Co., 1863.
["The translation has not undergone any material
alteration..."]

Another edition; Oxford: 1864.

Also; London, Oxford, & Cambridge: Rivingtons,
1871.

Other editions; London: Rivingtons, 1874, 1884.

1863 **Malet, Arthur**   A Metrical Version of the Psalms.
London: Rivingtons; 1863.
Revised; Ashcott: Privately centographed (8
copies) 1880.

1863 **Milligan, William**   A Revised Edition of the Psalms
and Paraphrases: to which are added one hundred and
fifty short hymns, selected by William Milligan.
Edinburgh: Maclaren, 1863.

1863 **Young, Robert**   Proposed Emendations of the Metrical
version of the Psalms used in Scotland by Robert
Young. Edinburgh: 1863.

1864 **Anonymous**   The American Metrical Psalter. [George
Burgess] New York: F.J. Huntington, 1864.
[An extraction and alteration from 18 different
versions.]

1864 **Livingstone, Neil**   Scottish Metrical Psalter. By
Neil Livingstone. Glasgow: Maclure, 1864.

1864 **Perowne, John James Stewart**   The Book of Psalms;
a new translation, with introductions and notes
explanatory and critical, by J.J. Stewart Perowne.
2 Vols. London: Bell & Daldy, 1864-1868.
["I have adhered more closely than is usual in the
English Version, to the order of words in the Hebrew...
The text of the LXX which I have followed is that of
Tischendorf's last edition. For the other Greek
versions, Montfaucon's edition of Origen's Hexapla has
been used."]

Second edition; revised, 1870, 1871, 1877.
[In revising my translation, I have
approached...more nearly to the AV..."]

Third Edition; Revised. London: G. Bell & Sons,
1873-1874.

Third London Edition; Andover: Warren F. Draper,
1885.

Fourth Edition, Revised. London: G. Bell & Sons,
1878-1879.
["...does not differ materially from those that
have preceded it..."]

Fourth edition reprinted; Grand Rapids, Michigan:
Zondervan Publishing House, 1966.

1865 **Anonymous**   A Metrical Psalter, Compiled from the
MSS. of the Late Viscount Massareene and Farrard.
"The Honorable L.P."   Dublin: McGlashan and Gill,
1865.

1865 **Anonymous**   A Metrical Version of the Psalms,
in various measures, selected and arranged by a
Committee of the General Assembly of the United
Presbyterian Church. [Thos. Beveridge, Committee
Chairman] Pittsburgh: United Presbyterian Board of
Education by W.S. Haven, 1865.
["They have consulted upwards of twenty versions... and
have selected and emended such versions of particular
Psalms as appeared to possess some poetic excellence...
They have selected a large number from two different
editions of a metrical version by George Burgess... T.
Duffield...allowed us the free use of a MS version by
him..."]

1867 **Alexander, William H.**   The Book of Praises; the
Psalms, with Notes.   London: 1867.

1867 **Anonymous**   The Psalms chronologically arranged.
An amended version with historical introductions and
explanatory notes by Four Friends.   [A.W. Plotts,
F.E. Kitchener, J.S. Phillpotts, and C.T. Arnold]
London & Cambridge: Macmillan & Co., 1867.
Another edition; The Golden Treasury Psalter;
Being an edition with briefer notes.   London:
Macmillan & Co., 1870.

Second edition, 1870.

Reprinted, 1876, 1891, 1927.

1867 **Hapstone, Dalman**   The Ancient Psalms in appropriate
metres; a strictly literal translation from the
Hebrew, with explanatory notes. Edinburgh: William
Oliphant & Co., 1867.
["I have been careful...to render each Hebrew term,
wherever it occurs bearing the same sense, by the same
English word, as far as metre would allow..."]

1868 **Anonymous** The Book of Psalms, rendered into common
metre verse, from the Authorized English Version;
with a repetition of Psalms I to L in miscellaneous
metres. [James Keith] London: J. Nisbet & Co., 1868.

New edition; Improved. Edinburgh & Glasgow: J.
Menzies & Co., 1893.

1868 **Hawley, M.L.**   The Psalms in Meter.   New York:
Published for the Author by Carlton & Lanahan, 1868.
["In attempting to change the Psalms to Christian
Lyrics, it is frequently necessary to substitute the
appellation Christ for that of the Lord or Jehovah..."]

1869 **Anonymous**   The Psalms; as an Illustration of Texts
... by G.V.W., c1869.

1869 **Carter, Charles**   The Book of Psalms; translated
from the Hebrew by Charles Carter.   London: Yates
and Alexander, 1869.

1870 **Anonymous**   The Psalms; As an Illustration
of Texts in (the so-called) Elohistic and Jehovistic
Scriptures. [George Vicesimus Wigram] London: G.
Morrish, 1870?
["Commenced Aug. 24, 1869... The translation is strictly
that of the AV; only the original names of Elohim, El,
Jehovah, Jah, Adonay, etc., as found in the Hebrew are
retained... I print the Psalms as poetry; they are so in
Hebrew."]

1870 **Slater, Thomas**   A Metaphrasis: a Metrical
Version of the Book of Psalms, made by Apollinarius
... Translated by Thomas Slater.   London: Simpkin,
Marshall & Co., 1870.

1871 **American Bible Union**   The Psalms. The Common
Version Revised for the American Bible Union, with
an introduction and occasional notes. By Thomas J.
Conant.   New York: American Bible Union; London:
Trubner & Co., 1871.
[Another edition, 1885.

1871 **Anonymous**   The Book of Psalms, the Scottish Version
Revised, and the New Versions Adopted by the United
Presbyterian Church of North America.   Pittsburgh:
United Presbyterian Board of Publication, 1871.
Second edition, 1871.

1871 **Anonymous**   The Book of Psalms. Translated from the
Latin Vulgate. Being a revised edition of the Douay
Version. [N.P.S. Wiseman and W.J.B. Richards]
London: Burns, Oates & Co., 1871.
[Preface, dated 1871, signed by Henry Edward (Manning),
Archbishop of Westminster; "This English version of the
Book of Psalms may be regarded as one more of the many
gifts bequeathed to us by (Cardinal Wiseman). One half,
at least, of the Psalms were revised by his own hand,
and have been inserted in our chief manuals of devotion,
such as 'Garden of the Soul', the 'Golden Manual', and
others".]

Another edition; The Book Of Psalms, Translated
from the Latin Vulgate. Revised in great part
by His Eminence Cardinal Wiseman. Completed
and edited by Walter J.B. Richards, D.D.
Oblate of St. Charles. Sixth edition. London:
Burns & Oates, Ltd.; New York: Catholic
Publication Society, [1884]

1871 **Barham, Francis and Edward Hare**   The Book
of Psalms, translated from the Hebrew and Syriac:
Francis Barham & Edward Hare. London: Fred Pitman;
Bath: I. Pitman; J. Davies, 1871.
    [Barham translated through Psalm lviii before his death;
    Hare completed the work, 'by collating the Latin
    translation of the Syriac given in the edition of
    Erpenius with the Latin version of the Syriac in
    Walton's Polyglot.']

1871 **Bolton, Francis**   The Book of Psalms. 3 Vols.
Edinburgh: T. & T. Clark, 1871.
    [See Old Testaments, 1865 Biblical Commentary.]

1871 **Burton, John**   The Book of Psalms in English Verse:
a New Testament Paraphrase. By John Burton. London:
John Snow & Co., 1871.

1871 **Linton, Henry P.**   The Psalms of David and
Solomon with Explanations. By Henry P. Linton.
London: 1871.

1871 **Waddell, P. Hately**   The Psalms: frae Hebrew
intil Scottis. By P. Hately Waddell. Edinburgh: J.
Menzies & Co.; Glasgow: T. & J.Lochead & William
Love, 1871.
    ["His own work is done directly from the Original, which
    he has attended to with utmost care — Scotch for Hebrew,
    with utmost fidelity..."]

    Another edition, 1877.

    Revised edition, 1881.

    Another edition, 1882.

1872 **Conant, Thomas J.**   The Psalms, by Carl B. Moss.
Translated from the German with Additions by Charles
A. Briggs, John Forsyth, James B. Hammond (and) J.
Fred McCurdy. Together with a New Version of the
Psalms and Philological Notes by Thomas J. Conant.
New York: Scribner, Armstrong & Co., 1872.
    [See Complete Bibles, 1864 Lange's Commentary, Vol. IX.]

    [The Translation "...is substantially the same as that
    prepared by the author for the American Bible Union
    (1871) but differs from it by numerous corrections in
    the renderings...and certain changes in form..."]

1874 **Birks, Thomas R.**   The Companion Psalter: or four hundred and fifty versions of the Psalms, selected and original, for public or private worship. By T.R. Birks. London: Seeleys & Co., 1874.

1875 **Anonymous**   The Book of Psalms "of David the King and Prophet"...disposed according to the rhythmical structure of the original. With three essays: I. The Psalms of David Restored to David; II. The External Form of Hebrew Poetry; III. The Zion of David Restored to David. With Map and Illustrations. By E.F. [Edward Faulkner]   London: Longmans, Green, and Co., 1875.

1875 **Murphy, James G.**   A Critical and Exegetical Commentary on the Book of Psalms, with a New Translation. Edinburgh: T. & T. Clark, 1875.
     Another edition; Andover: 1876.

1877 **Anonymous**   The Book of Psalms, literally rendered into verse. By the Marquis of Lorne. [i.e. John Edward Henry Douglas Sutherland Campbell , 9th Duke of Argyle] London: Macmillan & Co., 1877.

1877 **Jennings, A.C. and W.H. Lowe**   The Psalms, with Introductions and Critical Notes by Rev. A.C. Jennings... Assisted in Parts by Rev. W.H. Lowe... 2 Vols. London: Macmillan and Co., 1877.
          - - Books I. and II. Psalms I to LXXII
          - - Books III. IV. and V. (Psalms LXXIII. to CL.)

     [Strong's date of 1875-1877 appears to be in error.]

     Second edition; Revised, 1884-1885.

1878 **McLaren, Donald Campbell**   The Book of Psalms: Versified and Annotated by Donald Campbell McLaren. Rochester, New York: Clague & Cophin, 1878.

1879 **Gell, John Philip**   The Psalmes from the Hebrew: translated and arranged as an English comment on the Prayer Book Psalter. By John Philip Gell. London: Printed for Private Circulation. R. Clay, Sons & Taylor, 1879.

1879 **Sinclair, William Macdonald**   The Psalms: The AV in the Original Rhythm, by William Macdonald Sinclair. London: Hatchard, 1879.
          ["To modern taste it does not seem metrical; but, of course, the Hebrew poetical systems were different from ours... The ancient division of Books is followed..."]

1880 **Cunningham, G.H.S.**   The Book of Psalms. London: Murray, 1880.

1880 **Johnson, E.**   Commentary on the Psalms. By the late Dr. G. Heinrich A.v. Ewald... Translated from the German by E. Johnson. 2 Vols.   London: Williams & Norgate, 1880-1881.
> ["Commentary on the Poetical Books of the O.T. Division I.]

1880 **Warren, Samuel**   The Five Books of Psalms, with Marginal Notes by Samuel Warren.   London: 1880.

1881 **Anonymous**   The Book of Psalms in Metre and the Scottish Hymnal with accompanying tunes. Published for use in churches by Authority of the General Assembly. The Harmonies of the tunes revised by W.H. Monk... Edinburgh: Thomas Nelson & Sons; London & New York:, 1881.
> [The Deity is rendered "Jehovah" ten times in the Book of Psalms and four times in the hymnal.]

1882 **Seymour, W.D.**   The Hebrew Psalter...Commonly called the Psalms of David. A new metrical translation, by W.D. Seymour. London: Longmans & Co., 1882.

1883 **Anonymous**   The Book of Psalms in English Blank Verse Using the Verbal and Lineal Arrangements of the Original. "Ben-Tehillim".   Edinburgh: Andrew Elliot, 1883.

1883 **M'Laren, David**   The Book of Psalms in metre, according to the version approved by the Church of Scotland. Revised by David M'Laren. Edinburgh: David Douglas, 1883.

1884 **Bramley, H.R.**   See Richard Rolle, The Psalter or Psalms of David, 1340.

1884 **Cheyne, T.K.**   The Book of Psalms, Translated by T.K. Cheyne. London: Kegan Paul & Co., 1884.
> ["...with numerous corrections which do not, I Trust, materially affect the style... I trust that I need not defend myself for deviating so often from the Massoretic text... Where long reflexion has convinced me that the mutilations of time have rendered exegesis impossible, I have either left a blank in my version, or else sought for a worthy rendering, based upon some natural emendation."]

> [The Deity is rendered "Jehovah" many times.]

> Another edition; The Book of Psalms or The Praises of Israel; A New Translation, with Commentary.   London: Kegan Paul, Trench, & Co., 1888.

Another edition; 2 Vols., 1904.
[The Deity is rendered "Yahwe" many times.]

1884 **DeWitt, John**   Praise-Songs of Israel. A new
rendering of the Book of Psalms by John DeWitt...
New York: Richard Brinkerhoff, 1884.
[The translator has attempted "...to render it into
simple idiomatic and rhythmical English. The preference
has always been given to the AV, but we have not
hesitated to forsake it whenever the sense or rhythm
seemed to require a change."]

[The Deity is rendered "Jehovah" many times.]

New and revised edition; New York & London: Funk &
Wagnalls, 1886.

Also; "...a second revised edition", 1889.

1885 **Lansing, John G.** (Editor)   American Version; The
Book of Psalms, Translated out of the Hebrew. Being
the version set forth A.D. 1611, compared with the
most ancient authorities and revised A.D. 1885 with
the readings and renderings preferred by the
American Committee of Revision incorporated in the
text. Those retained or adopted by the English
Committee being specified in the Appendix.   New
York: Fords, Howard & Hulbert, 1885.
[A spurious edition of the ASV of the Psalms. See the
discussion in the Preface to the ASV, 1901.]

1885 **Wrangham, Digby S.**   Lyra Regis. The Book of
Psalms, and other Lyrical poetry of the Old
Testament, rendered literally...
[See Old Testament Selections for the complete entry.]

1885 **Young, Robert**   Grammatical Analysis of the Chaldee,
and Greek Scriptures, consisting of the original
text unabridged, the parsing of every word...and a
literal English rendering. By Robert Young.
Edinburgh: G.A. Young & Co., 1885.
[Psalms in Hebrew and English; no more published.]

1887 **Easton, M.G.**   The Book of Psalms, 1887.
[See Old Testaments, 1865 Biblical Commentary.]

1887 **Eaton, David and James E. Duguid**   A Biblical
Commentary on the Psalms. by Franz Delitzsch, D.D...
From the latest Edition, specially Revised by the
Author. In three volumes... Translated [from the
German] by the Rev. David Eaton, and the Rev. James
E. Duguid. London: Hodder & Stoughton (The Foreign
Biblical Library), 1887-1889.
[Duguid assisted Eaton on volume 1 only.]

Third Thousand, 1894.

Another edition; A Commentary on the Book of
Psalms. By Professor Franz Delitzsch, D.D. of
Leipzig. New York: Funk and Wagnalls, n.d.

1887 **Livius, T. and Others**   Explanation of the
Psalms and Canticles in the Divine Office. By S.
Alphonsus Liguori... Translated by T. Livius, &c.
London: Burns & Oates, 1887.
[Text in Latin and English.]

1888 **Coles, Abraham**   A New Rendering of the Hebrew
Psalms into English verse. With notes Critical,
Historical and Biographical, including an historical
sketch of the French, English and Scotch metrical
versions. New York: D. Appleton & Co., 1888.

1889 **Anonymous**   The Keys Psalter, 1889.
[Authorized by the Synod of the Reformed Presbyterian
Church of North America mentioned in their "Book of
Psalms", 1950.]

1889 **Cask, C.E.**   The Book of Psalms Rendered in Metre,
1889.

1889 **Harsley, F.**   Eadwine's Canterbury Psalter, edited
with introduction and notes from the MS. in Trinity
College, Cambridge.   London: Early English Text
Society, Original Series, No. 92, 1889.
[See Eadwine, 1170.]

1891 **Anonymous**   The Earliest Complete English
Prose Psalter, Together with Eleven Canticles and a
Translation of the Athanasian Creed. Edited from the
only Two MSS. in the Libraries of the British Museum
and Trinity College,... with Preface, Introduction,
Notes and Glossary. By Karl D. Bulring.   London:
Published for the Early English Text Society by
Kegan, Trency, Trubner & Co., 1891.
[Early English Text Society – Original series, no. 97]

[See Anonymous, The Earliest Complete English Prose
Psalter, 1340.]

Reprinted; [Millwood, New York: Kraus Reprint
Co., 1973.]

1891 **DeWitt, John**   The Psalms. A New Translation with
Introductory Essay and Notes by John DeWitt.... New
York: Anson D.F. Randolph & Co., 1891.
["...the text has been so thoroughly rewrought (from
that of 1884-1889) that it may fairly be called a new
translation." The name "Jehovah" is used many times.]

1893 **M'Lachlan, Peter**   Book of Psalms, by Peter
M'Lachlan.   Glasgow: M'Callum, 1893.
[Metrical version, edited by M'Naught.]

1894 **Paterson, H.A.**   The Bard of Bethlehem: his Psalms and Songs. Translated in metre from the Hebrew, with annotations. By H.A. Paterson. Edinburgh: Andrew Elliot, 1894.

1895 **Anonymous**   The Golden Treasury Psalter [Four Friends]. London: 1895.

1896 **Strong, James**   The Student's Commentary. The Book of Psalms Containing a Free Metrical Rendering, a Rhythmical Translation, an Extended Introduction, and a Tabular Analysis of the Entire Book, also a Logical, Exegetical, and Practical Exposition, and Lexical, Grammatical, and Vindicatory Notes on Psalms I-XVII... With a Prefatory Memoir of the Author by Henry A. Butts... New York: Eaton & Mains; Cincinnati: Curts & Jennings, 1896.
   [Also includes an exhaustive bibliography of Psalm versions and commentaries.]

1898 **Anonymous**   Interlineary Hebrew and English Psalter, in which the Construction of Every Word is Indicated, and the Root of each Distinguished by the use of Hollow and other Types. London: S.Bagster & Sons, 1898.
   [In this edition it is stated it was first published ca. 1850. Apparently no American library has this edition. There are editions dated 1900, 1907, and 1911. The latter was in the Hebrew student's manual. Bagster has kept this in print for many years.]

1898 **Anonymous**   The Psalter: A Revised Edition of the Scottish Metrical Version of the Psalter, with additional Psalm Versions. Prepared and published by Authority of the General Assembly of the Presbyterian Church of Ireland. Oxford: University Press; London: Oxford Univ. Press, 1898.
   [The above title and publisher are taken from an edition bound with an undated KJV Bible. The date is taken from the preface to Furneaux's 'The Book of Psalms', 1923, which quotes its purpose, "...to remove by emendations of those portions where there are erroneous renderings, errors of syntax, etc...". Young reports an edition; Edinburgh: Henry Frowde, 1898.]

1898 **Barton, William E.**   The Psalms and Their Story; a study of the Psalms as related to University history; with a Preliminary of Hebrew Poetry and Music. By William Barton. 2 vols. Boston & Chicago: The Pilgrim Press, 1898.
   ["The text given is that of the RV, but the author has preferred the readings of the American committee...substituting uniformly 'Jehovah' for 'Lord'... In a very few cases the author has given a rendering of his own..."]

1898 **Driver, Samuel Rolles**   The Parallel Psalter
being the Prayer-Book Version of the Psalms and a
new version arranged on opposite pages with an
introduction and glossaries by the Rev. S.R.
Driver... Oxford: at the Clarendon Press, 1898.
> ["My general style and phraseology I have modeled as far
> as was feasible, on those of the Prayer-Book Version
> itself, and of the Authorised Version."]

> [The deity is rendered "Jehovah" many times.]

> Second edition, 1904.

1898 **Furness, Horace Howard**   The Book of Psalms, a new
English Translation, With Explanatory Notes, and an
appendix on the music of the ancient Hebrews by J.
Wellhausen,... English Translation of the Psalms by
Horace Howard Furness. English Translation of the
Notes by John Taylor. English Translation of the
Appendix by J.A. Paterson. London: James Clarke &
Co.; New York: Dodd, Mead and Company, 1898.
> [See Old Testament Selections, Sacred Books of the Old
> and New Testament, Part 14, 1898. The Polychrome Bible.]

1898 **Jebb, Arthur Trevor**   A Book of Psalms, rendered
into English verse by Arthur Trevor Jebb. London:
George Allen, 1898.
> ["A generally close adherence to the diction of the
> Bible, with a careful fidelity to its meaning...a
> certain genuine simplicity of style..." from the
> prefatory note by R.C. Jebb.]

1898 **King, Edward George**   The Psalms in Three
Collections. Translated with notes. By E.G. King.
Cambridge: Deighton Bell and Co.; London: George
Bell & Sons, 1898-1905.
> 1898 - - Part I First Collection (Ps. I-XLI)
>   with a Preface by the Bishop of Durham

> 1902 - - Part II Second Collection (Books II &
>   III, Ps. XLII-LXXXIX)

> 1905 - - Part III Third Collection (Books IV &
>   V, Ps. XC-CL)

> [The deity is rendered YHVH.]

1899 **Boys, Thomas**   A Key to the Psalms; Being a Tabular
Arrangement by Which the Psalms are Exhibited to the
Eye According to the General Rule of Composition
Prevailing in the Holy Scriptures, by Thomas Boys;
Edited with Introduction, Notes, and Appendix on the
Structure of the Psalms as a Whole, by E.W.
Bullinger. London: Eyre and Spottiswoode; New York:
E. and J.B. Young, 1899.

1899 **Carr, Arthur**   The Prayer-Book Psalter for Church
and School; with renderings of difficult passages
from the Revised Version... and short explanations
by the Rev. Arthur Carr...   London: Society for
Promoting Christian Knowledge, 1899.

1899 **Eisenstein, J.D.**   The Classified Psalter arranged
by subjects. The Hebrew Text with a new English
translation on opposite pages... Reader for Hebrew
Schools. New York: Press of A. Ginsberg, 1899.

1899 **M'Neill, P.**   Psalms of David, by P. M'Neill.
Tranent: M'Neill, 1899.
      [Metrical]

1899 **Robertson, J.A.**   A Metrical Version of the Psalms,
by J.A. Robertson. London: Elliot Stock, 1899.

1901 **Benson, R.M.**   The War-Songs of the Prince of Peace;
A Devotional Commentary on the Psalter. By R.M.
Benson. London: John Murray, 1901.
      Vol. I   Helps for using the Psalter.

      Vol. II   A Translation of the Psalter,
      metrical and literal, with Explanatory Notes
      and Hints for Spiritual Instruction.

      [In this literal, metrical translation from the Hebrew,
      "Especial care has been taken with reference to the
      names of God. Jehovah is invariably rendered by the
      English equivalent, 'Lord'. Elohim always by 'God'. El
      by 'Godhead'. Adonai by 'Master'. Jah is retained. It is
      spelt with a Y... Eloah is 'Deity', or else it is
      retained. Elyon is 'Most High'. Shaddai is 'Almighty'.
      Sabaoth is 'Hosts'".]

1901 **M'Swiney, James**   Translation of the Psalms... and
Canticles...
      [See Wisdom and Poetical books and Selections for the
      complete entry.]

1902 **Anonymous**   The Book of Psalms, in metre. Edinburgh:
Waterston, 1902.
      [Glasite Church version. "... attention is given to the
      RV, AV, particularly that of Robert Boswell of
      Edinburgh, 1785..." Preserves 'Jehovah' and 'Elohim'.]

1903 **Anonymous**   The Book of Psalms. [Kaufman Kohler]
Philadelphia: Jewish Publication Society of America,
1903.
      [False title page reads, "...The Twenty-Four Books of
      the Holy Scriptures Translated from the Massoretic Text
      for the Jewish Publication Society of America." This
      version is not the same as that which appeared in the
      JPS O.T. of 1917.]

1903 **Bagshawe, Edward Gilpin** The Psalms and Canticles...

[See Bible Selections for the complete entry.]

1903 **Cree, E.D.**   The Prayer Book Psalms relieved of obscurities, and made smoother for chanting, with scarcely noticeable alteration. London: Macmillan & Co., 1903.

1903 **Eames, Wilberforce** (Editor)   See Anonymous, Bay Psalm Book, 1640.

1903 **Jewish Publication Society**   Book of Psalms. Philadelphia: Jewish Publication Society, 1903.
   [Dr. Morris Jastrow (Chairman 1891–1903) and Dr. Solomon Schechter (Chairman 1903–1917) were involved in selecting scholars to undertake independent translation of the various books. Only the Book of Psalms, translated by Kaufman Kohler and revised by the committee, was issued during the period from 1901 to 1908.]

1903 **McLaren, Alexander**   The Psalms, by A. McLaren. 2 Vols. New York: A.C. Armstrong & Son; London: Hodder & Stoughton, 1903.
   [See Bible Selections, 1888 The Expositor's Bible.]

1904 **Anonymous**   The Psalms. A New Version with short notes. [Rev. & Mrs. William Kelly] London: T. Weston, 1904.
   Another edition; London: F.E. Race, 1913?

1904 **Cheyne, T.K.**   The Book of Psalms. 2 Vols. London: Kegan Paul, Trench, Trubner & Co., 1904.
   ["...Translated from a revised text, with Notes and Introduction, in place of a Second Edition of an earlier work (1888) by the same author. By Rev. Canon T.K. Cheyne...2 Vols."]

   Another edition, 1905.

1904 **Staley, Vernon** (Editor) See Anonymous, The Psalter, 1839.

1905 **Cobb, W.F.**   The Book of Psalms, with introduction and notes by W.F.Cobb...London: Methuen & Co., 1905.
   ["The writer...has not felt able to do more than suggest emendations where the condition of the present text speaks plainly of corruption.]

1906 **Anonymous** A New Translation of the Psalms prepared by the Committee...of the ...General Convention of the New Jerusalem in the United States of America. Philadelphia: 1906.

1906 **Briggs, Charles Augustus and Emilie Grace Briggs**
   A Critical and Exegetical Commentary on the Book of

Psalms by C.A. Briggs ...and E.G. Briggs, B.D. (In
Two Vols.) Edinburgh: T. & T. Clark, 1906-1907.
    1906 Vol. 1 Psalms 1-50 Reprinted; 1907, 1909,
        1925.
    1907 Vol. 2 Psalms 51-150   Reprinted; 1907,
        1909, 1925.

    [Unknown if the same as the International Critical
    Commentary (Ps), 1895.]

1906 **Noyes, Isaac P.**   The Psalms poetically rendered
in Rhyme. Edward VIth version. Washington: Pearson
Printing Office, 1906.
    ["In order to make a rhyme I have often been obliged to
    transpose lines, and sometimes to substitute lines from
    other verses, or even to create something additional."
    Based on the Prayer Book Version.]

1907 **Craven, Charles E.**   The Psalms: New Metrical
Version (1911), 1907.

1908 **Lund, Emil**   The Psalms, Translated and Commented
Upon by Emil Lund.   Rock Island, Ill.: Augustana
Book Concern, 1908.
    [Preface. This translation and commentary have for its
    aim to give to the readers of the Holy Scriptures a
    brief interpretation of our old, dear Psalter in a
    scientific though popular form... The translation is as
    literal as possible.]

    [The Deity is rendered "Yahve" many times.]

1909 **Anonymous**   The New Metrical Version of the
Psalms prepared under the supervision of the General
Assembly's Permanent Committee on Psalmody.
Submitted to the General Assembly of the United
Presbyterian Church at its meeting in Knoxville,
Tennessee, Mat 26, 1909. Pittsburgh, Penna: The
United Presbyterian Board of Publication, 1909.
    [D.A. McClenahan, D.R. Miller, John McNaugher, William
    J. Reid, W.E. McCullough, and W.I. Wishart]

    ["...with some slight retouching. This version contains
    a number of Psalms from Collier's 'Lyrics from the
    Psalter', 1907.]

    Another edition; The Psalter With Responsive
    Readings, 1912.

1909 **McFadyen, John Edgar**   The Messages of the
Psalmists..., 1909.
    [See Abridged Bibles, 1900 Frank Knight Sanders and
    Charles Foster Kent, The Messages of the Bible, Vol. V.]

1910 **Mann, A.H.**   The Psalter - Revised Version - pointed
for chanting. By A.H. Mann. London: Robert Culley,
1910.

1911 **Anonymous**   The Psalms; New Metrical Version with Tunes New and Old. [Henry Van Der Werp] [Country of Origin The Netherlands], 1911.

1911 **Bernard, John Henry**   The Psalter in Latin and English. With an introduction. By J.H. Bernard. London & Oxford: A.R. Mowbray, 1911.

1911 **Hexapla Psalter** The Hexapla Psalter: being the Book of Psalms in six English versions. Edited by William Aldis Wright... Cambridge: University Press, 1911.
>[Coverdale's Bible (1535), Great Bible (1539), Geneva Bible (1560), Bishops' Bible (1568), AV (1611), and the RV (1885).]

1911 **Rotherham, Joseph Bryant**   Studies in the Psalms. By Joseph Bryant Rotherham. London: H.R. Allenson, J. George Rotherham, 1911.
>[Includes a "diligent revision" of the text. A posthumous edition.]

1912 **Fillion, L.C.** The New Psalter of the Roman Breviary Text & Translation, by L.C. Fillion.   St. Louis & London: B. Herder, 1912?
>[Second edition ?.]

>Third English edition; St. Louis & London: B. Herder Book Co., 1923.

>Another edition, 1942.

1912 **Myers, Isadore**   Metric Translation of the Psalms. MS, 1912.
>["My metric translations of the Psalms and of Job have been completed, which I trust will not stay in their unpublished form as long as this work has had to remain." From the Preface to Myers' Proverbs, 1912.]

1912 **Snowdrop** King David's Psalms. Revised by Snowdrop. London: C.W. Daniel, 1912.

1913 **Taylor, Bernard C.**   Psalms, 1913.
>[See Old Testaments for the complete listing, Genesis, Job, Psalms...]

1914 **Anonymous** The Psalter with the Doctrinal Standards and Liturgy of the Christian Reformed Church. Grand Rapids: Eerdmans-Sevensma Co., 1914.

1915 **Clarke, Edward** The Book of Psalms. The Prayer-Book version corrected. London: Smith, Elder & Co., 1915.

1915 **Stryker, Melancthon Woolsey**   The Psalms of Israel in Rhymed English Metre, by Melancthon Woolsey Stryker. Clinton, New York: for the Author, 1915.

["Nearly every Psalm has been metred with some
particular tune in mind."]

[The Deity is rendered "Jehovah" many times.]

1916 **Anonymous**   The Prayer-Book Psalter. Revised
in accordance with the proposals of a Committee
appointed by the Archbishop of Canterbury. London:
S.P.C.K., 1916.

1916 **Coxe, Seymour R.**   The Psalms of Penitence: A
Metrical Rendering.   London: 1916.

1916 **Hielscher, Helen Hughes**   Songs of the Son of
Isai. A Metrical Arrangement of the Psalms of David.
Boston: French & Co., 1916.

1916 **McFadyen, John Edgar**   The Psalms...Modern Speech...
[See Wisdom and Poetical Books and Selections for
the complete entry under 1916, John Edgar McFadyen, [The
Poetical Books of the O.T.]

1917 **Kohler, Kaufman**   Psalms, 1917.
[See Old Testaments, 1917 Jewish Publication Society.]

1918 **Lauritzen, Johannes Rudolph**   The Capitalized Book
of Psalms by Johannes Rudolph Lauritzen. Knoxville,
Tenn.: 1918?
[Whether or not this is a unique translation by
Lauritzen has not been established. It appears to have
been issued bound with his N.T., q.v. Courtesy of Don
Heese. Lakewood Co.]

1919 **Anonymous**   The Book of Psalms. 1919. 1929?
[Authorized by the Synod of the Reformed Presbyterian
Church of North America; mentioned in their 'Book of
Psalms', 1950.]

1920 **Boylan, Patrick**   The Psalms. A Study of the Vulgate
Psalter in the Light of the Hebrew Text by Rt. Rev.
Monsignor Patrick Boylan.... A New Translation and
Commentary by Patrick Boylan. 2 Vols.   Dublin: M.H.
Gill & Son Ltd., 1920-1924.
[Latin & English]

Another edition; 2 Vols. 1948.

1921 **Anonymous**   The Psalter. Together with the Canticles
According to the Use of the Church of Ireland. APCK.
Dublin, Belfast & Limerick: Assn for Promoting
Christian Knowledge, 1921.
["The text of the Psalms contained in this book is that
which the General Synod of the Church of Ireland, in its
session of 1921, ordered to be printed in all subsequent
editions of the Book of Common Prayer according to the
use of the Church of Ireland. It is a revision of the
translation by Coverdale in the Great Bible of 1539-41,

adopted by both Houses of the Convention of Canterbury, in the year 1920. This revision was carried out on very conservative principles; and in a considerable number of the Psalms the text has been altered hardly at all."]

Another edition; Edited & Pointed for Chanting, 1930.

Third edition; 1956.

1921 **Kirkpatrick, A.F.**   The Book of Psalms. Edited by A.F. Kirkpatrick... Cambridge: at the University Press, 1921.
[Cambridge Bible for Schools and Colleges. "The text adopted in this edition is that of Dr. Scrivener's Paragraph Bible. A few variations from the ordinary text, in the spelling of certain words, will be noticed."]

[The Deity is rendered "Jehovah" at Psalm 83:18.]

1922 **Peters, John P.**   The Psalms as Liturgies; Being the Paddock Lectures for 1920. New York: The Macmillan Co., 1922.
[Contains the KJV and a new translation in parallel columns.]

1923 **Anonymous**   The Peerless Poems of David, the King; In a New Metrical Version by "J.C." [Jane Copley] Long   Beach,   California: The   International Fishermen's Club; Fundamental Bible Books, 1923.
[The Deity is rendered "Jehovah" a few times.]

Another edition; Los Angeles, Calif.: Biola Book Room, 1923.

1923 **Furneaux, William Mordaunt**   The Book of Psalms. A revised version. By W.M. Furneaux. London: Hodder & Stoughton, [1923].
["...a translation intended for devotional use may well be less literal than the RV and less slavish in its adherence to the Ancient versions..."]

1923 **Vaughan, J. Jones**   The Brotherhood Psalter by J. Jones Vaughan. London: Congregational Union, 1923.
[Metrical version.]

1924 **Sugden, Edward H.**   The Psalms of David, translated into English verse in accordance with the Metres and Strophic Structure of the Hebrew, by Edward H. Sugden. Melbourne: Macmillan & Co. in association with the Melbourne University Press, 1924.
["My one object is to help the English reader to study the Psalms from a fresh point of view."]

1926 **Bielsky, Frederick Joseph**   Psalms from Aramaic. [Or The   Psalms according to Wisdom's Rule ?] by

Frederick Joseph Bielsky. Boston, U.S.A.: The Christopher Publishing House, 1926.

1926 **Smith, John Merlin Powis**   The Psalms. By J.M. Powis Smith. Chicago: 1926.

1927 **Bird, Thomas E.**   A Commentary on the Psalms. By Rev. T.E. Bird... 2 Vols. London: Burns, Oates & Washbourne Ltd., 1927.
["The Psalterium Breviarii Romani has been copied out with the punctuation as in the Editio Typica of 1912. With this has been compared, word for word, the Massoretic Text of Kittel's Biblica Hebraica..." Latin & English translation.]

1928 **Alexander, T.T.**   The Psalms in Braid Scots. Edinburgh: 1928.

1928 **Martin, William Wallace**   The Psalms Complete. Their Prayers, their Collects, their Praises, in three Books. Separated, arranged and translated by William Wallace Martin. Nashville, Tennessee: Press of Marshall & Bruce Co., 1928.
Another edition; - - with notes. Nashville, Tennessee: Parthenon Press, 1940.

1928 **Wales, Frank H.**   The Psalms... by F.H. Wales. 5 Parts. London: Oxford University Press, 1928-1930.
["...a plain and rhythmic expression of the original even at the expense of the letter..."]

New edition; The Psalms, A Revised Translation by F.H. Wales. London: Oxford University Press, 1931.

Second edition; 1935.
["...without the notes, and with certain changes and corrections of words..."]

1929 **Callan, Fr. Charles Jerome and John A. McHugh**
The Psalms Explained for Priests & Students. With Introductions, Paraphrases and Notes. By The Rev. Charles J. Callan... and The Rev. John A. McHugh... New York: Joseph F. Wagner, Inc.; London: B. Herder, 1929.
["...the English paraphrase and the text of the Latin Vulgate...in parallel columns on each page..."]

1929 **Gowen, Herbert H.**   The Psalms or the Book of Praises, a New Transcription and Translation; Arranged Strophically and Metrically From a Critically Reconstructed Text; with Introduction, Textual Notes, and Glossary, by Herbert H. Gowen. London: A.R. Mowbray & Co.; Milwaukee, Wis.: Morehouse Publishing Co.; <u>Biblical & Oriental Series</u>, 1929.

["...we may attempt the very radical re-editing of the text of the Psalter which I have suggested in the following transcription, and thereafter make from the reconstructed text an entirely new translation."]

[The Deity is rendered "Yahweh" many times.]

Another edition; London: Student Christian Movement Press, 1930.

1929 **Way, Arthur S.**   The Psalms. A verse translation. By Arthur S. Way. London: Epworth Press, 1929.

1930 **Douglas, Winfred, and Others**   Prayer Book. The American Psalter; The Psalms and Canticles according to the use of The Protestant Episcopal Church; Pointed and Set to Anglican Chants together with the Choral Service; Prepared by the Joint Commission on Church Music, under authority of General Convention. New York: The H.W. Gray Company, 1930.
   ["...sets forth the revised Psalms and Canticles of the Prayer Book of 1929, pointed for chanting, and accompanied with suitable chants."]

[This work was done by Winfred Douglas, Miles Farrow, Walter H. Hall, T. Tertius Noble, and Wallace Goodrich]

[The Deity is rendered "Jehovah" at Psalm 83:18 only.]

1931 **Dalton, John Neale**   The Psalms, a suggested revision of The Prayer Book Version and Twelve Old Testament Canticles ... Cambridge: At The University Press, 1931.
   ["...it will be evident how often recourse has had to the earlier Coverdale (1535), and how surprisingly modern are some of his renderings of the rocky terseness of the original..."]

1932 **Krapp, George Philip** (Editor),   The Paris Psalter and the Meters of Boethius. Edited by George Philip Krapp. New York: Columbia University Press, 1932.
   [Anglo-Saxon Paraphrases.]

1933 **Oesterley, William Oscar Emil**   The Psalms Translated with Text-Critical and Exegetical Notes by W.O.E. Oesterley. 2 Vols. London: S.P.C.K., 1933-1936.
   [Translation is based on the Masoretic, LXX, Peshitta & Vulgate. "But...in a very large Number of places we are forced to guess at what the original text was."]

1 Vol. Edition; 1939, 1953, 1955, 1959, 1962.

1934 **Anonymous**   Psalter Hymnal; Doctrinal Standards and Liturgy of the Christian Reformed church. [Wm. Kuipers, Dewey Westra, B. Essenburg, S.G. Brondsema, L.J. Lamberts, Edward A. Collier, Thomas R. Birks,

M.E. Thalheimer (Miss), M. Scott-Haycroft (Mrs.)]
Grand Rapids: Michigan Publication Committee of the
Christian Reformed Church, 1934.

1934 **Berry, George Ricker**   The Book of Psalms, 1934.
        [See Old Testament Selections for the complete entry,
        1906 Anonymous   An American Commentary on the Old
        Testament...]

1934 **Clayton, Ernest**   See Miles Coverdale, Biblia, 1535.

1934 **Hull, Marion McHenry**   Two Thousand Hours
        in the Psalms. Chicago, Illinois: John A. Dickson
        Publishing Company, 1934.
        ["I have transliterated the Hebrew into English script,
        so that the ordinary English reader may know the
        original language is, and have interlined with it, using
        largely the KJV, making a few changes, where it seemed
        to clarify the thought of the original."]

1935 **Curtiss, Anthony**   The Psalms, a new Translation
        and Commentary. By Anthony Curtiss. Brooklyn, New
        York: Guide Printing Co., 1935.
        ["...although I have followed the Vulgate in many ways,
        I have used some freedom in regard to the tenses...
        where both Latin Vulgate and Greek Septuagint seemed
        hopelessly obscure, I have not hesitated to follow the
        Hebrew."]

1935 **Moffatt, James**   The Book of Psalms, A New
        Translation, by James Moffatt. New York: Harper &
        Bros., Publishers, 1935.

1937 **O'Neill, George**   The Psalms and the Canticles...
        [See Wisdom and Poetical books and Selections for the
        complete entry.]

1938 **Anonymous**   De A B C Psalms put into the
        Sessex Dialect and in dere Proper ABC fashion. [Jim
        Cladpole (James Richards)] Typescript. 1938.

1938 **Buttenweiser, Moses**   The Psalms
        chronologically treated with a new translation by
        Moses Buttenweiser.   Chicago, Il: University of
        Chicago Press, 1938.
            Reprinted;   Prolegomenon by N.M. Sarna. New
            York: Ktav, 1969.
                [The Library of Biblical Studies edited by H.M.
                Orlinsky.]

1939 **Cooke, G.A.**   The Prayer Book Psalter Revised.
        Oxford: Clarendon Press, 1939.

1939 **Lamsa, George M.**   The Book of Psalms according
        to the Eastern Version. Translated from Original
        Aramaic Sources by George M. Lamsa. Philadelphia:
        A.J. Holman Co., 1939.

["I used this (the Peshitta text published from
manuscripts by the Presbyterian and Congregational
Missions in Urmiah in 1852) in my translation. I have
also used the Codex Ambrosianus (a sixth century ms in
the Ambrosian Library at Milan, Italy) and compared it
with Jacobite mss and printed texts." The translation is
not the same as that which appears in Lamsa's Bible,
1959.]

[The Deity is rendered "Jehovah" at Ps 83:18.]

1940 **Grieve, Nichol**   The Scottish Metrical Psalter of
1650; A revision by Nichol Grieve. Edinburgh: T. &
T. Clark, 1940.
    ["...The mode followed in this experiment is as follows:
    (1) Only those portions which are entirely suitable for
    Christian worship are printed. (2) Emendations have been
    made in certain portions thus rendering them suitable.
    (3) The Most familiar and best beloved items have been
    left untouched, with changes here and there in
    punctuation. (4) There have been provided additional
    versions in other metres..."]

1940 **Mayer, Harry H.**   The Lyric Psalter. The Modern
Reader's Book of Psalms Edited by Harry H. Mayer.
New York: Liveright Publishing Corp., 1940.
    ["The poems of this book have all specifically written
    for inclusion in this publication." Contributions were
    made by 61 different poets.]

Another edition, 1944.

1941 **Merritt, Alice Haden**   Psalms and Proverbs...
    [See Wisdom and Poetical books and Selections for the
    complete entry.]

1943 **Jewish Publication Society**   Psalms from
the Jewish Holy Scriptures, prepared for emergency
Use by Jewish Personnel in Air Force Life Rafts.
Published under the direction of the Chief of
Chaplains. United States Government Printing Office:
Washington [D.C.], 1943.
    [Issued in a waterproof jacket with matching editions of
    Matthew for use by Protestant Personnel (AV) and for use
    by Roman Catholic Personnel (Douay). The packet is
    marked "Scriptures / Protestant / Catholic / Jewish".]

1944 **Callan, Fr. Charles Jerome**   The Psalms Translated
from the Latin Psalter, in the Light of the Hebrew,
of the Septuagint and Peshitta Versions, and of the
Psalterium Juxta Hebraeas of St. Jerome. With
introductions, critical notes and spiritual
reflections.   New York: Joseph F. Wagner, Inc.;
London: B. Herder, 1944.
    ["The translation is based on the Latin Psalter, and
    endeavors to follow the Latin faithfully, except where
    the Hebrew or some other principal reading is obviously
    better..."]

1944 **Lattey, Cuthbert**   Psalter, 1944.
[See Complete Bibles, 1913 Westminster Version.]

1945 **Cohen, Abraham**   The Psalms. Hebrew Text & English
Translation with an Introduction and Commentary by
The Rev. Dr. A. Cohen... London: The Soncino Press,
1945.
[See Old Testaments, 1936 Soncino Books of the Bible.]

Another edition; 1958.

1946 **Anonymous**   The Psalms; A Prayer Book; Also
the Canticles of the Roman Breviary; New English
Translation   with   Ecclesiastical   Approbation;
Including the New Latin Version from the Hebrew, by
the Professors of the Pontifical Biblical Institute;
Authorized by Pope Pius XII; Also Containing
Preface,   Explanatory   Introductions,   Verse
Commentaries and Topical Guides. [Wm. H. McClellan,
John F. Rowan, James E. Coleran, Dom Bede Babo and
Francis P. Le Buffe] New York, Boston, Cincinnati,
Chicago, San Francisco: Benziger Brothers, 1946.

1946 **Fletcher, Frank Pearl**   Harp and Psaltery: a Group
of Paraphrases of Favorite Psalms.   Concord, New
Hampshire: 1946.

1947 **Eerdmans, B.D.**   The Hebrew Book of Psalms. Leiden:
Oudtestamentische Studien, 1947.
[A   translation   of   the   Masoretic   Text,   with   an
introduction and commentary.]

1947 **Frey, Joseph B.**   My Daily Psalms Book; The Book
of Psalms Arranged for Each Day of the Week; New
English Translation from the New Latin Version, by
Rev. Joseph B. Frey, Director of the Confraternity
of the Precious Blood.   Brooklyn, New York:
Confraternity of the Precious Blood, 1947.
["The new version has greatly clarified many of the
obscure passages of the old version."]

1947 **Knox, Ronald Arbuthnott**   The Psalms. A New
Translation by Ronald Knox.   New York: Sheed and
Ward, 1947.
[Includes the Canticles of the Roman Breviary.]

[Printed, with a few changes in the O.T. (q.v.) 1948.]

Also; The Book of Psalms in Latin and English,
with the Canticles used in the Divine Office,
1947.
["...the Latin text is taken from the new
translation published by the Pontifical Biblical
Commission...1945."]

Other editions, 1950, 1955.

1948 **Grimes, Willard M.**   The Unquenched Cup. A
Paraphrase of the Psalms of David. Preface by Henry
C. Kittridge.   New York City: Lifetime Editions,
1948.
> ["I have merely set forth, in what seemed to me an
> appropriate form, what I as an individual soldier
> obtained from the Bible during one of the most critical
> periods in human history."]

1948 **Peterson, Russell A.**   The Modern Message of the
Psalms. The Psalms in Basic English. Boston: Meador
Publishing Co., 1948.

1948 **Riley, Harold**   The Revision of the Psalter. An
essay in liturgical reform. London: S.P.C.K., 1948.

1949 **Brown, Ray F.**   The Oxford American Psalter.
The Psalms and Canticles according to the use of the
Protestant Episcopal Church in the United States of
America. Pointed & set to Anglican chants by Ray F.
Brown... New York: Oxford University Press, 1949.

1949 **Callan, Fr. Charles Jerome**   The New Psalter of Pius
XII in Latin & English, with introductions, notes
and spiritual reflections...   New York: Joseph F.
Wagner, Inc., 1949.
> [The first edition of 1944 (q.v.) was based upon the old
> Latin Psalter. "In translating this new text,...we have
> endeavored to keep as closely to the Latin as good
> English would seem to permit."]

1949 **Leslie, Elmer A.**   The Psalms. Translated and
Interpreted in the Light of Hebrew Life and Worship.
Elmer A. Leslie.   New York & Nashville: Abingdon-
Cokesbury Press, 1949.
> Another Edition; 1968. (Paperback)

1950 **Caskey, C.E., David M. Carson, and G. Mackay Robb**
The Book of Psalms; Rendered in Metre and Set to
Music; Authorized by the Synod of the Reformed
Presbyterian Church of North America...   Printed at
Chicago, Ill.: The Trustees of the Synod of the
Reformed Presbyterian Church of North America,
Pittsburgh, Penna, 1950.
> ["the Committee appointed to deal with the text of the
> Psalter became convinced that an effort should be made
> to smooth out some expressions found in earlier Psalters
> without altering their meaning... In addition to these
> changes, the committee decided to include (versions of
> Psalms 117, 131, and 134) found in the 1889 Psalter, but
> not retained in any later revisions. (the second
> versions of Psalms 86 and 121) that had no place in any
> previous Psalters have also been placed in the new
> one."]

1950 **Cummings, D.**   Commentary on the Psalms of David and
the Nine Odes of the Church by Apostolos Makrakis...

Translated out of the Original Greek, by D.Cummings. Chicago, Ill.: Orthodox Christian Education Society, 1950.
["My translation was made directly from the original Greek text of the LXX furnished by A. Makrakis...I made no attempt to translate the Psalms and the Odes metrically, it being my sole aim to express the meaning of the Greek exactly in plain English without deviating further than necessary from the AV."]

1950 **Dawson, A.M.P.**   A New Metrical Version of the Psalter. By A.M.P. Dawson. Willingdon: The Author, [1950].

1951 **Silverman, Morris**   ...High Holiday Prayer Book...
[See Old Testament Selections for the complete entry. Includes 25 Psalms.]

1952 **Crim, Keith R.**   The Royal Psalms. Richmond, Vir.: John Knox Press, 1952.

1953 **Kissane, Edward J.**   The Book of Psalms. Translated from a critically revised Hebrew text. With a commentary by Monsignor Edward J. Kissane... 2 Vols. Dublin: Browne & Nolan Ltd., 1953-1954.
[The Deity is rendered "Yahweh".]

Another edition; Westminster, MD: Newman Press, 1953-1954.

1954 **Brown, James Rossie**   The Murrayfield Psalms; a New Metrical Version and notes,...With a Forward by Professor H.J. Paton, D.Litt., LL.D., F.B.A., and the Right Hon. the Earl of Selkirk, O.B.E., A.F.C. James Rossie Brown.   Murrayfield, Edinburgh: Published for the Kirk Session of Murrayfield Parish Church by the Church of Scotland Committee on Publications, 1954.
["Seeking to go behind the AV to the original Hebrew as interpreted by modern commentators, he wished to produce new versions which could be sung by a Scottish congregation without feeling that there was a complete break with the past." Also includes an appendix with 13 Psalms, plus parts of five others, set to special metres.]

1954 **Hugh-Ensor, Henry**   The Psalms. Newly Translated in the Original Metres from a Revised Hebrew Text. With Introductions and Notes. [Yeovil, Typewritten] 1954.
[The Deity is rendered "Yahweh" many times.]

1954 **Kleist, James A. and Thomas J. Lynam**
The Psalms in Rhythmic Prose; Translation based on the authorized Latin version rendered from the original texts by members of the Pontifical Biblical Institute. Translated by James A.Kleist...and Thomas

J. Lynam... Milwaukee: The Bruce Publishing Co., 1954.

1955 **Anonymous**   The Psalms; Fides Translation — Introduction and notes by Mary Perkins Ryan. Chicago, Illinois: Fides Publishers Association, 1955.
> ["The Fides translation of the Psalms has been made in accordance with the New Roman Psalter. Its special purpose is to provide a clear, modern translation..."]

1955 **Tubbs, Edward J.**   The Psalms Transliterated and Translated from the Hebrew Text, by Edward J. Tubbs. 2 Vols. London: Printed for the Author by Norman, Hopper & Co., Ltd., 1955-1958.
> 1955 — — Vol. I... Book I Being Psalms I to XLI for Diploma Students, etc.

> 1958 — — Vol. II... Books II, III, IV, & V Being Psalms XLII to CL Inclusive.

> ["This work is progressive — I transliterate (letter for letter) [Hebrew to English] and translate (thought for word) each Hebrew word as it occurs; the next time it occurs I do not transliterate it..."]

1955 **Wanefsky, David**   The Hebrew Scriptures...
> [See Wisdom and Poetical books and Selections for the complete entry. Includes Psalms.]

1956 **Anonymous**   The Psalms: A New Translation...
> [See Old Testament Selections for the complete entry.]

1956 **Haraszti, Zoltan** (Editor) See Anonymous, (Bay Psalm Book), 1640.

1956 **Whitehouse, H.E.**   Psalms, Set to Meter, Rime and Verse. By H.E. Whitehouse.   Oakland, CA: H.E. Whitehouse, 1956.
> ["...it was sometimes necessary to transpose and re-arrange, to add or take away parts or words or substitute words of the same meaning. The KJV is used... All that I have done...is to set the Psalms to meter and put a rimming word at the end of every thirteen syllables, in harmony and meaning with the Psalm..." Mr. Whitehouse states that, "As far as records show, this is the first time Psalms has been set to true meter, rime and verse." — — to what 'records' did he refer??]

1957 **Anonymous**   Concordant Literal Old Testament...
> [See Old Testament Selections, Concordant O.T., Psalms, 1965 and 1972-73.]

1959 **Anonymous**   The Salisbury Psalter. London: Published for The Early English Text Society by Oxford University Press, 1959.
> [Anglo-Saxon.]

1959 **Leupold, Herbert Carl**   Exposition of Psalms, with a New Translation, by H.C. Leupold. Columbus, Ohio: Wartburg Press, 1959.

1960 **Hirschler, Gertrude**   The Psalms; Translation and Commentary by Rabbi Samson Raphael Hirsch. New York: Published for the Samson Raphael Hirsch Publication Society, by Phillip Feldheim, 1960-1966.
[Hebrew & English]

      1960 - - Vol. I. Books 1 and 2
      1966 - - Vol. II. Books 3, 4, and 5

New Corrected Edition; 1978.

1960 **Richardson, R.D.**   The Book of Psalms. Revised, rearranged and adapted for use in public and private worship as Christian prayers and praises. Warminster: Coates & Parker, 1960.

1961 **Anonymous**   The Revised Psalter, 1961-1963.
      1961 The First Report of the Commission to Revise the Psalter appointed by the Archbishop of Canterbury and York. Book I: Psalms 1-41. London: SCM.

      1963 The Final Report of the Commission to Revise the Psalter...as presented to the Convocations of Canterbury and York, May 1963. London.

      Members of the Commission:
            J. Dykes Bower   F.D. Cogean
            G.A. Chase   Donald Ebor
            T.S. Eliot   Gerald H. Knight
            C.S. Lewis   D. Winston Thomas

      Another edition; The amended text as approved by the Convocations of Canterbury and York in October 1963 with a view to legislation for its permissive use. London: S.P.C.K., 1964.

1961 **Byington, Steven T.**   The Book of Psalms, Translated by Steven T.Byington. Boston: Bruce Humphries, 1961.
      [Copyrighted 1957.]

1961 **Harrison, Roland Kenneth**   The Psalms for Today; A New Translation from the Hebrew into Current English by Roland Kenneth Harrison. Grand Rapids, Michigan: Zondervan Publishing House, 1961.
      [Bound with Olaf M. Norlie's Simplifed N.T. in Plain English for Today's Reader; "The present writer has undertaken an entire retranslation of the Psalms from the Massoretic text, and has paid particular attention to the archaeological discoveries at Ras Shamra

(Ugarit), which have thrown considerable light on hitherto obscure expressions and allusions."]

1962 **Ap-Thomas, D.R.**   The Psalme in Israel's Worship, (Translated from Mowinckel's Norwegian ed., 1951) by D.R.Ap-Thomas. Oxford: Basil Blackwood. 2 vols.
Another edition; New York and Nashville: Abingdon, 1962.

1962 **Hartwell, Herbert**   Psalms, 1962.
[See Old Testament Selections, 1962 The O.T. Library.]

1964 **Hadas, Gershon**   The Book of Psalms for the Modern Reader; A New Translation by Gershon Hadas. New York: Jonathan David Publishers, 1964.

1964 **Noli, Metropolitan Fan S.**   The Psalms; A Metrical English Version Translated from the Original Hebrew Diligently Compared with the Greek Septuagint and other translations by Fan S. Noli. Boston, Massachusetts: Published by the Albanian Orthodox Church in America, 1964.

1964 **Rathmell, J.C.A.** (Editor)   See Philip Sidney and Mary Herbert, The Psalmes of David, 1600.

1965 **Oster, Edward**   Psalms. Massachusetts: 1965.

1965 **Parker, T.H.L.**   Commentary on the Psalms, by Calvin. 2 Vols, 1965-1968.

1966 **Anonymous**   The Holy Psalter: The Psalms of David from the Septuagint. Madras: The Diocesan Press, 1966.

1966 **Brandt, Leslie F.**   Psalms, by Leslie F. Brandt. St. Louis: n.p., 1966-1973.
> 1966 Psalms 20, paraphrase. <u>This Day</u>, Oct.1966, p.50.12

> 1967 Good Lord, Where are You? Prayers for the 20th Century based on the Psalms.

> 1969 God is Here, Let's Celebrate! In 39 Meditations Based on the Psalms.

> 1972 The Lord Rules, Let's Serve Him. Meditations on the Psalms.

> 1973 Psalms Now, by Leslie F. Brandt, with art by Corita Kent.

1966 **Dahood, Mitchell**   Psalms. Introduction,
Translation, and Notes by Mitchell Dahood. Garden
City, New York: Doubleday & Co., Inc., 1966-1970.
     1966 Vol. 1   Psalms 1-50
     1968 Vol. II Psalms 51-100
     1970 Vol. III Psalms 101-150

     [The Deity is rendered "Yahweh" many times.]

     [See Complete Bibles, 1964 Anchor Bible, Vols. 16, 17,
     & 17a.]

1966 **Lazarus, Fr.** The Holy Psalter; the Psalms of David
from the Septuagint (Translated by Fr. Lazarus).
Madras: the author c/o The Diocesan Press, 1966.

1967 **Anonymous**   The Vespasian Psalter... Copenhagen:
Rosenkilde & Bagger, 1967.   [Anglo-Saxon]

1967 **Sanders, J.A.**   The Dead Sea Psalms Scroll...
     [See Old Testaments for the complete entry.]

1968 **Hanson, Richard S.**   The Psalms in Modern Speech for
Public & Private Use by Richard S. Hanson. 3 Vols.
Philadelphia: Fortress Press, 1968.
     Also; 2 vol. edition, 1968.

1969 **Jerusalem Bible**   The Jerusalem Bible. The Psalms
for Reading and recitation. London: Darton, Longman
and Todd, 1969.
     [This new version has been considerably re-worded.]

1970 **Anonymous**   The Psalms for Modern Man; Today's
English Version. N.Y.: American Bible Society, 1970.

1972 **Freer, Coburn**   Music for a King; George Herbert's
style and the Metrical Psalms. Coburn Freer.
Baltimore & London: The John Hopkins University
Press, 1972.

1972 **Seymour, Peter** (Editor)   The Life of Christ in
Poetry and Prose, Illustrated with Famous Paintings
and Drawings. Portrait of Jesus. Edited by Peter
Seymour. [Kansas City, MO]: Hallmark Crown Editions,
1972.

1973 **Maria, Mother (Lydia Gysi)**   The Psalms:
an Exploratory Translation. Mother Maria. Filgrave,
Newport Pagnell, Buckinghamshire, England: Published
by The Greek Orthodox Monastery of the Assumption,
1973.
     [The Deity is rendered "Jahwe" many times.]

1975 **Zerr, Bonaventure**   The Psalms by the monks
of Mount Angel Abbey; translated from the Hebrew by

Bonaventure Zerr... Revised Edition. St. Benedict, OR: Mount Angel Abbey, 1975.

1976 **Levi, Peter**   The Psalms translated from the Hebrew by Peter Levi; with introduction by Nicholas de Lange. London: Penguin Books, 1976. [1977?]

1976 **Shepherd, Massey Hamilton, Jr.**   A Liturgical Psalter for the Christian Year.   Minn.: Augsburg Publishing House, 1976.

1977 **Barnes, Richard G.** (Editor) The Psalms, 1977.
     [See Anonymous, The Psalmes of David, 1571.]

1977 **Feuer, Avrohom Chaim**   Psalms, 1977-1979.
     [See Old Testaments, 1976 ArtScroll Tanach Series.]

1978 **Berrigan, Daniel**   Uncommon Prayer – A Book of Psalms. New York: The Seabury Press, 1978.

1979 **Kimmens, Andrew C.** (Editor)   The Stowe Psalter edited by Andrew C. Kimmens.   Toronto & Buffalo: Published in Association with the Centre for medieval Studies, University of Toronto, by University of Toronto Press, 1979. [Anglo-Saxon]

1979 **Zerr, Bonaventure**   The Psalms: a new translation by Bonaventure Zerr, OSB.   New York, Ramsey & Toronto: Paulist Press, 1979.

1980 **Brown, Joseph E.**   Jesus Sings the Psalms in Your Heart. Joseph E. Brown, S.J. St.Louis, Missouri: We and God Spirituality Center, 1980.

1984 **Anonymous**   The Psalter. Monks of the Brotherhood of Saint Francis, ed. Cambridge, NY: New Skete Monastery, 1984.

1986 **Koeblitz, Roy**   The Psalms. A new version. Palm, 1986.

1986 **Schreck, Nancy and Maureen Leach**   Psalms Anew: In inclusive Language. Nancy Schreck... and Maureen Leach...   Winona, Minnesota: Saint Mary's Press, Christian Bros. Publications, 1986.

1989 **Chamberlain, Gary**   The Psalms: A New Translation for Prayers and Worship translated by Gary Chamberlain. Nashville, TN: Upper Room, 1989.

1989 **Porter, J.R.**   The Living Psalms. Claus Westermann. Translated by J.R. Porter. Grand Rapids, MI: Wm. B. Eerdmans Publishing Co., 1989.

PSALM SELECTIONS

???? **Agee, Lee**   Lambs of Ebon from Psalm XXIII by Lee
Agee. The Lamb Magazine, Page 14, n.d.
[A metrical expanded paraphrase.]

???? **Anonymous**   Unity Version of the Twenty-Third Psalm.
Prosperity, page 9, n.d.   Reprinted; The King's
Business, 57:45, November, 1966.

???? **Anonymous**   23rd Psalm. Shepherd's Version, n.d.

???? **Anonymous**   A Collection of Psalms and Hymns,
extracted, revised, and published for the use of the
Congregation of High Wycombe: Bucks, [180?].
4th. edition; High Wycombe: R.H. Pontifex, 1807.

???? **Anonymous**   Lazy Man's 23rd Psalm. The Bible
Collector, No.2, April-June, 1965. [A parody version.]

???? **Anonymous**   One and forty Divine Odes Englished,
Set to King David's Princely Harpe. By S.P.L.
London: Printed by M.F., n.d.

???? **Anonymous**   Psalms and Hymns for the use of
the German Reformed Church in the United States of
America, [18??].
49th edition; Chambersburg, Pa.: M. Kieffer &
Co., 1862.

???? **Anonymous**   Psalm of the Addicts. Register, Santa
Ana, Ca., n.d.   [A parody version.]
Also; The Bible Collector, No. 22, April-June,
Page 2, 1970.

???? **Anonymous**   The Twenty-Third Psalm. "Showers of
Blessing", [196?].

???? **King James I**   His version of 26 Psalms...
[See Bible Selections for the complete entry.]

???? **Cotterill, Thomas**   A Selection of Psalms and
Hymns for Public Worship. [183?].
Nineteenth edition; London: for T. Cadell [by A.
& R. Spottiswoode], 1833.

???? **Davis, Arthur and Herbert Adler**   Service of the
Synagogue... the Festival Prayers...
[See Old Testament Selections for the complete entry.]

???? **De Wette**   Rhythm of Gradation. [n.p.: n.p., n.d.]
[Psalms of degrees.]

???? **Downing, Ruth Eloise**   Psalms 23, metrical. [????].
[Biola College has a half-sheet from some magazine.]?

??? **Earl of Stirling**   Psalm XXIII. [16??].

???? **Hunt, George**   An Indian version of the 23rd Psalm. Custer, SD: American Indian Mission, Inc., n.d.
[Another copy by the same publisher (n.d.) has Isabel Crawford as translator.]

???? **Knox, William**   Psalm XXIII. [18??].
[See 1922 Arthur Pollok Sym, The Twenty-Third Psalms.]

???? **Newton, B.W.**   Psalms II. London: Sovereign Grace Advent Testimony (The Nations in Relation to Christ as in the Second Psalm– Pamphlet), n.d.
[The Deity is rendered "Jehovah".]

???? **Personeus, Florence L.**   Looking to God – Psalm 121. n.p.: n.p., n.d.

???? **Rawson, George**   Psalm XXIII. [18??].
[See 1922 Arthur Pollok Sym, The Twenty-Third Psalm.]

???? **Schliebe, R.H.**   Twenty-Third Psalm. In Poetic Paraphrase. Burbank, CA: Distributed by Burbank Community Church, n.d.

???? **Summers, Thomas O.**   The Wesleyan Psalter...
[See Psalms, 1788 Charles Wesley, A Poetical Version ...Psalms.]

???? **Tate, Marvin E.**   Word Biblical Commentary. Psalms 51–100. Marvin E. Tate.   Waco, Tx: Word Books, Publishers, [198?].
[See Complete Bibles, 1982 Word Biblical Commentary, Vol. 20.]

???? **Wharton, Mrs.**   Psalms and Hymns, [176?]. Second edition; with appendix. London: Sold at Lock-Hospital, 1763.

900 **Alfred the Great**   Portions of the Paris Psalter.
[MS – 11th. Century in the National Library in Paris.]

1350 **Anonymous**   Jerome's Psalterium Abbreviation; translated from the Latin. MS. Hatton 111, c1350; MS. Bodleian 416, c1400.

1414 **Brampton, Thomas**   A paraphrase on the seven penitential Psalms, in English verse, together with a Legendary Psalter in Latin and English verse. 1414 (MS)
[Also, see W.H. Black, 1842.]

1420 **Anonymous**   The Prymer or Lay Folks Prayer Book.
MS. Dd.11,82; Cambridge.
  [Also, along with several facsimiles, edited by Henry
  Littledale from the MS.Dd.11.82.ab., 1420–1430 A.D. in
  the Library of the Univ. of Cambridge. London: E.E.T.S.,
  Original series #105. Part 1 contains 52 Psalms, 1895.]

1505 **Fyssher, Johan**   The Fruytful Saynges of Davyde,
in the seven penitential Psalmes; devyded in seven
sermons, by Johan Fysscher. London: R. Pynson, 1505.
  [Several times reprinted.]

1519 **Anonymous**   Fyther's seven Penitencial Psalms.
London: J.Day, 1519.

1523 **Anonymous**   Horae [S.T.C. 15935]   London: Peter
Kaetz, 1523.

1523 **Anonymous**   Horae [S.T.C. 15934] London: Wynken
De Worde, 1523.

1530 **Anonymous**   Ortulus anime. The garden of
the soule: or the englisshe primers (the which a
certaine printer lately corrupted /& made false to
the great sclaunder of the author & greter desayte
of as many as boughte and red the) newe corrected
and augmented.
       Firste there is a Kalenderie
       the passion of oure savioure Christe...
       A fruteful instructio for childre
       A christe dialogue ful of lerning
       A general confession before god
       Ther is psalm. added to the euesong...
       The seuene psalmes
       The psalmes of the passion
       The commendacions
       Al the psalmes newe corrected
       [Emprinted at Argentine in the yeare of ower
       lorde .1530. By me Francis Foxe.]

1533 **Anonymous**   The Prymer of Salisbury use. Paris:
Thylman Kewer, 1533.
  Another edition; Paris: Thielman Kewell, 1534.

1534 **Anonymous**   A Prymer in Englysshe, with certeyne
prayers & godly meditations, very necessary for all
people that vnderstonde not the Latyne tongue.
[Wyllyam Marshall] [Imprinted   at   London   in
Fletestrete by Iohan Byddell, 1534.]
  [Includes 48 Psalms, mostly revised from Joye's
  Hortulus.]

  Another edition; A goodly prymer in englyshe, new
  corrected and printed, with certeyne godly
  meditations and prayers added to the same,

very necessarie & profitable for all them that
ryghte assuredly vnderstonde not ye Latine &
greke tongues. 1535 [Imprinted at london in
Fletestrete by me Iohan Byddell...for Wyllyam
Marshall/the yere of oure lorde god M.D.xxxv.
the xvi. day of Iune.

1534 **Anonymous**   A Prymer in Englysshe / with dyuers
prayers & godly meditations.   [Imprinted at London
by Thomas Godfray, 1534.]

1535 **Anonymous**   Prayers of the Byble take out
the olde testament and the newe, as olde fathers
bothe men and women were wont to pray in tyme of
tribulation / deuyded in vi partes. [Imprinted at
London in Fletestrete by me Robert Redman, 1535.]
        [Includes 38 Psalms after Joye.]

1535 **Anonymous**   This prymer of Salsbery vse / bothe
in Englyshe and Laten, is set out a longe without
serchyng. [Imprinted at London, in Fletestrete...by
me Robert Redman]

1535 **Byddel, John**   Psalm LI... London: William Marshall,
1535.

1539 **Coverdale, Myles**   Goostly psalmes and spirituall
songes drawen out of the holy Scripture, for the
coforte and consolacyon of such love to rejoyse in
God and his worde... London: Imprinted by me Johan
Gough, 1539?
        [Nearly all of the poems are free translation or
        adaption of German Hymns, or translation of Psalm, some
        of which are by Luther.]

        [Reprinted in; 'Remains of Myles Coverdale' Cambridge:
        Univ. Press, 1846.]

        Reprinted; Myles Coverdale's 'Goostly Psalmes
        and Spirituall Songes' und das Deutsche
        Kirchenlied... Druck: Heinrich Poppinghaus,
        1935.

1540 **Clifford, Henry**   Poetical translation...Psalms...
        [See Old Testament Selections for the complete entry.]

1541 **Petyt, Thomas**   Psalms LI and XXX... London: 1541.

1541 **Wiat, Thomas**   See A.K. Foxwell, The Poems of Sir
Thomas Wiat, 1964.

1542 **Anonymous**   David's Harpe ful of most delectable
armony, newly strynged and set in tune by Theodore
Basille. An exposition of some of the Psalms by

Thomas Becon and imprinted at London...by Iohn
Mayler for Iohn Gough Anno Dni 1542.
> [Containing Psalms CXV and CXLV. Theodore Basille is a
> pen-name of Beacon, Thomas.]

1544 **Anonymous**   Psalms, or Prayers, taken out of Holy
Scripture. London: Tho. Berthelet, 1544.
> ["...they are only pious breathings, and do not pretend
> to be exact translations, or even Paraphrases..."]

1545 **Anonymous**   The Primer, set foorth by the Kinges
maiestie and his Clergie, to be taught lerned, and
read: and none other to be vsed throughout all his
dominions. Imprinted at London...by Richard Grafton,
1545.
> [Includes 41 Psalms and a variant version of the Lord's
> Prayer; the first officially printed litany in English;
> especially designed by Henry VIII's order for "our
> people and subiects whiche haue no understadyng in the
> Latin tong and yet haue the knowledge of reading..."]

Another edition, 1546.

Reprinted without any alterations, 1710.

1546 **Hertforde, John**   Psalms LI and XXX...Oxford: Christ
Church, 1546.

1547 **Cope, Sir Anthony**   A godly meditacion vpon .XX.
Select and chosen Psalmes of the Prophet David, as
wel necessary to al them that are desirous to haue
ye darke wordes of the Prophet declared and made
playn: as also fruitfull to such as delyte in the
contemplacio of the spiritual meanyng of them.
Compiled and setfurth by Sir Anthony Cope Knight.
Imprinted at London...by John Daye. Anno. .M.Dxlvii
(1547).

1548 **Elizabeth, Queen**   Psalm XIV in verse. 1548.
> [H.A. Glass, The Story of the Psalter. London: Kegan
> Paul, Trench & Co., 1888, quoting Ritson's Bibligraph
> Poetica says this is Psalm 13 and he indicates his
> awareness that Cotton lists this as Psalm 14, I have
> followed Cotton.]

1548 **Tudor, Elizabeth**   Psalm XIV, in verse. 1548.
> [In "A Godly Meditation of the Christian Soul".]

1549 **Smith, Thomas**   Certaine Psalmes or Songues of
David, translated by Sir Thomas Smith, Knt., then
prisoner in the Tower of London; with other Prayers
and Songues by him made to pas the tyme there.   MS
1549.
> [First printed in John Holland's 'Psalmists of Britain',
> 1843.]

1549 **Wyatt, Thomas**   The Seven Penitential Psalmes drawen into English Meter by Thomas Wyatt, 1549.

1550 **Anonymous**   Certayne Chapters of the Prouerbes...
[See Bible Selections for the complete entry. Includes Psalms 21, 33, 53, 64, 111, 112, 113, 123 and 144.]

1550 **Hunnis, William**   Certayne Psalmes chosen...
[See Old Testament Selections for the complete entry.]

1552 **Bale, John**   Psalms XXIII and CXXXII in Metre. London: John Daye, 1552.

1553 **Anonymous**   Certayne Psalmes select out of the Psalter of Dauid, and Drawen into Englyshe Metre, wyth Notes to euery Psalme in iiij parts to Synge, by F.S. [Francys Seager] Imprinted at London by VVyllyam Seres, 1553.
[Includes 17 Psalms.]

1555 **Fisher, Bishop**   The Seven Penitential Psalms. Thomas Marsh, 1555.
[Again, 1714.]

1555 **Pole, Cardinall**   An uniforme and Catholyke Prymer in Latin and Englishe, set forth by certayne of the cleargye with the assente of the moste reverende father in god, the Lorde Cardinall Pole hys grace. &c. London: John Waylande, 1555.

1556 **Huggarde, Miles**   A Short Treatise...Psalm CXXIX, 1556.

1556 **Knox, John**   Psalm vi... Geneva, 1556.

1557 **Forreste, William**   Certayne Psalmes of Davyd, in meeatre, added to Maister Sternholdes and others. MS.
[First printed in John Holland's 'Psalmists of Britain,' 1843.]

1558 **Kethe, William**   Psalm XCIV in metre. Geneva, 1558.

1563 **Anonymous**   Medivs: Psalmes fourer parts which may be song to all musicall instrumentes, set forth for the increase of vertue and abolishying of other vayne and triflying ballods. W.P. London: John Daye, 1563.
[British Museum has only fragments of this work.]

1563 **Beacon, Thomas**   Psalms CIII and CXII... London: John Daye, 1563.

1566 **Anonymous**   The Kynges Psalmes. Imprinted London, by A.Wykes, 1566.

[Selected Psalms, bound with 'The Queenes praiers'.]

1570 **Edwardes, Roger**   A Boke of very Godly Psalmes and Prayers: dedicated to the Lady Letice, Viscountesse of Hereforde. Imprinted at London by Wylliam Griffith, 1570.
> [Herbert's notice is from the Stationer's register. The Epistle describes it as compacted and devised as a recreation during "sickely solitarinesse." The Psalms are in prose.]

1574 **Keeper, John**   Select Psalms of David set to music ...edited by John Keeper. Oxford: Mary Hall, 1574.

1574 **Tirwit, Lady**   Divers Psalmes, Hymnes..., 1574.

1575 **Gascoigne, George**   Psalm CXXX in Metre. Published in 'Posies and Flowers". London: for Richard Smith, 1575.

1577 **Bull, Henry**   A Commentarie vpon the Fiftene Psalmes, Called Psalmi Graduum, that is, Psalmes of Degrees: Faithfvlly copied ovt of the Lectvres of D. Martin Luther, very frutefull and comfortable for all Christian afflicted consciences to reade. Translated out of Latine into English. Imprinted at London by Thomas Vautrollier, 1577.
> Another edition; London: Printed by Richard Field, 1615.

1578 **Anonymous**   Ane Copendious Buik of godlie Psalmes and Spirituall Sangis, 1578.

1578 **Anonymous**   The gude and godly Ballates. [John Wedderburn] Edinburgh: John Ross, 1578.

1579 **Dawson, Thomas**   Psalm LXXXVII... London: 1579.

1580 **Hooper, Bishop John**   Psalms XXIII. LXII. LXXIII. LXXVII... London: H. Middleton, 1580.

1582 **Robinson, Richard**   ...the harmonie of King Dauid's Harpe. That is to say, an exposition of...Psalmes of the Princely Prophet Dauid...Done into the learned Reuerend Doctor Victorinus Strigelius... Translated into English. By Richard Robinson. London: 1582-1596.
> 1582 - - Conteining the first XXI. Psalmes... Printed by John Wolfe.
>
> 1591 - - from the 22. vnto the 35. Psalme... Printed by John Wolfe.

1593 - - from the xxxiiij. to the xlv. Psalme... Printed by I.C., for Abraham Kitson.

1595 - - beginning with the 45. and ending with the 61. Psalme. Printed by Valentine Sims.

1596 - - beginning with the 62. and ending with the 67. Psalme. Printed by Valentine Sims.

1582 **Robinson, Richard** The First 21 Psalms, translated by Robinson from the Latin Version of Victorinus Strigelius; Sub-title "Part of the Harmony of King David's Harp." London: 1582.
["I have only departed from the AV where that version appeared to me to fail to bring out correctly and intelligibly the meaning of the original."]

1585 **Cosyn, John** Sixty Psalms in Metre... 1585.

1585 **Hunnis, William** Seven Sobs of a Sorrowfull Soule for Sinne. London: H. Denham, 1585.
[Seven Penitential Psalms]

1585 **James I, King, of England, VI of Scotland** The CIV (listed CIIII) Psalm; Translated...out of Tremellius, by King James I. Edinburgh: Thomas Vautrollier, 1585.

1590 **Gilbie. Antonie** Fourteen Psalms from the Old and New Testament Paraphrastically Explained from the Latin of Beza. London: R. Yardley & P. Short, 1590.

1591 **Fravnce, Abraham** The Countess of Pembroke's Emanuel.. certeine Psalmes of Dauid...
[See Bible Selections for the complete entry.]

1594 **Mundy, John** Songs and Psalmes; Composed into 3, 4, and 5 Parts; for the Use and Delight of All Such as Either Love or Learn Musicke. London: by Thomas East, 1594.
["This is a strange mixture. It contains some metrical Psalms, differing from Sternhold's version."]

1597 **Anonymous** Ecclesiastes, Othervvise Called the Preacher. Containing Solomon's Sermons or Commentaries (as it may probably be collected) vpon the 49. Psalms of Dauid...
[See Wisdom and Poetical books and Selections for the complete entry.]

1597 **Lok, Henry** Sundry Psalms... London: Richard Field, 1597.

1600 Blak, David   Psalm XXXII... Edinburgh: Robert
Wald-Grave, 1600.

1600 Lumisdon, Charles   An Exposition vpon some select
Psalmes of David &c. written by that faithfull
servant of God, M. Robert Rollok, sometime Pastour
in the Church at Edinburgh: and translated out of
Latine into English by C. Lumisdon. Edinbvrgh:
Printed by Robert Walde-Graue, 1600.

1602 Cosowarth, Michael   Another version of Some Select
Psalms into verse. British Museum: MS. Harl. 6906,
(Farr, Von Rohr-Sauer) 1602.
> [First printed in John Holland's 'Psalmists of Britain',
> 1843.]

1603 Anonymous   Certeine Psalmes reduced into English
Meter by H.D. [Henry Dod] London: R. Waldegrave,
1603.
> ['Nine of the Singing Psalms tuerned into easie meter
> for the use of my family and some godly learned
> friends.' Also see, 'Al the Psalmes of Dauid' 1620.]

1606 Anonymous   The Mindes Melodie. Contayning certayne
Psalmes of the Kinglie Prophete Dauid, applyed to a
nevv pleasant tune, verie comfortable to euerie one
that is rightlie acquainted therwith. [Alexander
Montgomery] Edinburgh: Printed be Robert Charteris,
1606.
> ["The Psalms that are contened in this Booke are these
> 1, 4, 6, 15, 19, 23, 43, 57, 101, 117, 121, 125, 128.
> Simeon's Song, and the Gloria Patri."]

1607 Anonymous   Some Fewe of Dauid's Psalms Metaphrased,
for a taste of the rest. by J.H. [Joseph Hall] 1607.
> [From 'Holy Observations...']

Another edition; 1624 [10 Psalms].

Also; London, 1633.

> [Reprinted in his works, 1808, 1837, London, Oxford;
> Works, Vol ix, edited by Philp Wynter, 1863 (Ps 4, 25,
> 33, 34, 65, 111-115, 130, 137.)]

1612 Davies, John   The Penitential Psalms
paraphrastically... verse. London: 1612.

1613 Leighton, Sir William The Tears or Lamentations of
a Sorrowful Soule (The Penitential Psalms). London:
Knight, 1613.

1615 Anonymous   Sacred Hymns. Consisting of Fifti Select
Psalms of David and others, Paraphrastically turned
into English Verse. And by Robert Tailovr, set to be
sung in five parts, as also to the Viola, and the

Lute or Orph-arion. Published for the vse of such as
delight in the exercise of Mvsic in hir original
honour. [Edwin Sandys?] London: Printed by Thomas
Snodham by the Assignment of the Company of
Stationers, 1615.

1615 **Sandys, George**   Fiftie Select Psalms of David and
Others, 1615.

1616 **Ainsworth, Henry**   Pentateuch, Solomon's Song and
Psalms...
> [See Old Testament Selections for the complete entry.
> Includes some Psalms.]

1620 **Davison, Christopher, Francis Davison, J.Bryon and
R.Gipps**   Divers selected Psalms of David (in
verse) differently translated [of a different
composure?] from those used in the Church. British
Museum: MSS Harl. 6930 & 3357. 1620.
> [Reprinted in "Davison's Poetical Rhapsody. 1814. 3
> Vols. Includes, "Psalms, translated by Francis and
> Christopher Davison".]

Also; The Psalms. London: 1826.

Another edition; Davison's Poetical Rhapsody.
Edited by Sir Harris Nicolas. London: William
Pickering, 184?

1625 **Bacon, Francis**   Certaine Psalmes in English
Verse by Francis Lord Verulam. London: for Street
& Whitaker, 1625.
> [Reprinted in 'Miscellanies of the Fuller Worthies'
> Library. (Edited by Grosart) London, 1871.]

1627 **Anonymous**   An Assay, or Bvchanan His Paraphrase
on the First Twentie Psalmes of David. London:
printed by R.Y. for Richard Moore, 1627.

1629 **Mure, William**   1629 Version of the 23rd Psalm.
By Sir William Mure. Rambles Round Kilmarnock by
Archibald R. Adamson, 1629.

1630 **Anonymous**   Certain of David's Psalms, intended for
Christmas Carrols fitted to the most common but
solempne tunes everywhere familiarly used.
> [Bodleian: R. Smith's MS list in Hearne's Collectanea.]

1631 **Vicars, John**   England's Hallelujah for God's
Gratious Benediction; with some Psalms of David in
verse by John Vicars. London: 1631.
> [Contains 19 Psalms.]

1632 **Herbert, George**   Seven Psalms in verse... In Jo.
Playford's Psalms, Hymns, etc. 1632.

1633 **Donne, John**   Psalm CXXXVII in verse. London: M.F.,
1633.

1633 **Fletcher, Phineas**   Psalms I, XLII, LXIII, CXXVII,
CXXX, CXXXVII. Metaphrased in Verse.   Printed in
Purple Island, Cambridge, 1633.

1635 **Hawkins, John**   The Seven Penitential Psalms, a
paraphrase, translated out of the Italian.   Paris:
1635.
        [Roman Catholic]

1639 **Anonymous**   Some Psalmes Translated and presented
for proof to publick view, whereby to discerne of
the whole being conformed to this essay; by a
weilwiller to the work of Reformatioun, who makes
humble offer of his weak endeavours. [William Mure]
MS.
        [Reprinted in 'The Works of Sir William Mure', edited by
        William Tough. Edinburgh: 1898.]

1640 **Carew, Thomas**   Certaine Psalmes of David Translated
into English Verse. 1640.
        [Reprinted in "The Poems of Thomas Carew", edited by
        J.W. Epworth. London: n.p., 1893.]

        Also; The Poems of Thomas Carew, with his
        Masque Coelum Britanicum, edited by Rhodes
        Dunlap. Oxford: Clarendon Press, 1949.

        [Includes Psalms: 1, 2, 51, 91, 104, 113, 114, 119,
        137.]

1642 **Anonymous**   Psalmes, or Songs of Sion; turned into
the language and set to the tunes of a strange land.
By W.S. [William Slatyer] Intended for Christmas
Carols. London: by Robert Young, 1642.
        [Psalms I-XXII, in Hebrew, Greek, Latin & English.
        Another edition; The Psalmes of David in 4 languages and
        in 4 parts. Set to ye Tunes of our Church. by W.S.
        London: Printed by Tho. Harper for George Thomason &
        Octavian Pullen, 1643.]

1644 **Anonymous**   The Book of Praises...Psalms XC to
CVI in Verse. 1644.

1645 **Milton, John**   Nineteen Psalms paraphrased. 1645-
1673.
        1645 Poems of Mr. John Milton, Both English
            and Latin, Compos'd at several times.
            Printed by his true Copies. The Songs
            were set in Musick by Mr. Henry Lawes
            Gentleman of the Kings Chappel, and one
            of His Maiesties Private Musick...
            Printed and published to Order, by John

Milton.   London: Printed by Ruth Raworth
for Humphrey Moseley.
> [Includes "A Paraphrase on Psalm 114. This
> and the following Psalm (136) were done by
> the Author at fifteen years old."]

1673 Poems, &c. upon Several Occasions. By Mr.
John Milton: Both English and Latin, & c.
Composed at several times. With a small
Tractate of Education to Mr. Hartlib.
London: Printed for Thomas Dring at the
Blew Anchor.
> [Contains "Psalm I (through VIII) Done into
> Verse, 1653." and "Nine of the Psalms done
> into Metre, wherein all but what is in a
> different Character, are the very words of
> the Text, Translated from the Original.
> Psalm LXXX (-LXXXVIII)"]

1935 The Poetical Works of John Milton; Edited
after the Original Texts by the Reverend
H.C. Beeching, M.A. New York: Oxford
University Press.
> [Contains reprints of Psalms 1-8, 80-88,
> 114, 136.]

1647 **Westminster Version**   See Psalms, 1650 Anonymous,
The Psalms of David.

1648 **Crashaw, Richard**   Psalm XXIII and CXXXVII in metre.
London: H. Moseley, 1648.

1650 **Cnobbart, Mrs. John**   The Seven Penitential Psalms
altered from Douay...   Antworpe: James Thompson,
1650.

1651 **Anonymous**   A Paraphrase of a great part of the
Psalms in verse. [British Museum; MS. Harl. 6637]

1656 **Cowley, Abraham**   Psalm CXIV in verse. London: 1656.

1656 **Davis, John**   A Short Introduction to the Hebrew
Tongue, being a translation of... J. Buxtorfius'
Epitome... Whereunto is annexed an English
interlineall interpretation of some Hebrew texts of
the Psalms, for ...beginners...   London: Roger
Daniel, for Humphrey Moseley, 1656.

1659 **Barton, William**   Six Centuries of Select Hymns...
> [See Old Testament Selections for the complete
> entry. Includes some Psalms.]

1661 **Leigh, Samuel**   Samuelis Primitiae: or, an
Essay towards a Metrical Version of the whole Book
of Psalmes. Composed, when attended with the
Disadvantageous circumstances of Youth, and

Sickness. By Samuel Leigh. London: Printed by Tho. Milbourn for the Author, 1661.
[Selected Psalms.]

1679 **Patrick, John**   Century of select Psalms, And Portions of the Psalms of David. Especially those of Praise. Turned into Meter, and fitted to the usual Tunes in Parish Churches. For the use of the Charter-House, London. London: Printed by J.M. for Richard Royston, 1679.
Another edition; The Psalms in meter, 1684.

Also; A Century of Select Psalms... The Fifth Edition Corrected. London: Printed by J.H. for L. Meredith, 1691.

Another edition; The Psalms of David in meter: fitted to the tunes in parish-churches. (Hymns taken out of the N.T.) London: A. & I. Churchill, L. Meredith, 1694.

Other editions, 1698, 1715.

Seventh Edition; London: Printed for D. Brown, 1729.

Eighth Edition; London: Printed for D. Brown, 1742.

1681 **Anonymous**   The Ascents of the Soul: or, David's Mount towards God's House. Being Paraphrases on the Fifteen Psalms of Degrees, written in Italian, by the Illustrious Gio. Francesco Loredano, a Noble Venetian, 1656. Render'd into English (By Henry Lord Coleraine.) [Henry Hare]   London: for R. Harford, 1681.
[Some give the title as, 'A Scale of Devotions, musical and Gradual; or, Decants on the Fifteen Psalms of Degrees.']

1682 **Goodridge, Richard**   The three first Books of the Psalms, and so much of the Fourth as make up a Century, Paraphras'd in Verse. London: Printed for A. Churchill.
[See Psalms for the complete entry.]

1683 **Oldham, John**   Psalm CXXVII paraphrased... London: J. Hindmarsh, 1683.

1687 **Norris, John**   Four Psalms in verse. Oxford: 1687.

1688 **Anonymous**   Psalms sung in the Parishes of St. Martins and St. James. London: 1688.

1689 **Cotton, Charles**   Psalm VIII in Verse. London: 1689.

1689 **Vilant, William**   Psalms, Hymns, and Spiritual Songs. In Two Parts. By Mr. William Vilant, The Author of the Gospel-Call in Meeter.   Edinburgh: 1689.

1691 **Fleming, Robert**   Several Psalms Diversely rendered. See 'The Mirrour of Divine Love, 1691.

1691 **Keach, Benjamin**   Spiritual Melody; viz. Psalms...
    [See Bible Selections for the complete entry.]

1695 **Anonymous**   Family-Hymns Gathered (mostly) out of David's Psalms, By M.H. London: Printed for Tho. Parkhurst, 1695.

1695 **Anonymous**   An Essay of a New Version of the Psalms of David: consisting of the first Twenty Fitted to the Tunes used in Churchs. [Nicholas Brady and Nahum Tate]   London: Printed   for   the   Company   of Stationers, 1695.

1697 **Anonymous**   Select Psalms and Hymns for the use of the Parish-Church, and Tabernacle of St. James's Westminster.   London: J.   Heptinstall,   for   the Company of Stationers, 1697.
    Another edition, 1708.

    Also; Select Psalms and Hymns for the use of the Parish Church and Chappels belonging to the Parish of St.James's Westminster. London: Printed by W. Pearson for the Company of Stationers, 1709.

    Another edition; Select Psalms and Hymns for the use of the Parish Church and Chappels belonging to the Parish of St.James's Westminster. With proper tunes in three parts. London: Printed for the Company of Stationers; sold by B. Creake, 173?

1698 **Phillips, John**   Davideos, or a specimen of some of David's Psalms in Meter, with remarks on the Latin translations, by John Phillips. London: for W. Keble-White, 1698.
    [Erroneously dated 1798; 23 Psalms.]

1699 **Chamberlaine, James**   Lamentations... Psalms...
    [See Old Testament Selections for the complete entry.]

1700 **Blackmore, Sir Richard**   A Paraphrase...Songs of...
    [See Old Testament Selections for the complete entry. Includes four select Psalms.]

1700 **Tate, Nahum and Nicholas Brady**   A Supplement to the New Version of the Psalms; Containing,   I. The

usual Hymns, Creed, Lord's Prayer, Ten Commandments, all set to their proper Tunes; with additional Hymns for the holy Sacrament, &c. II. Select Hymns... III. A Set of Tunes, by Nahum Tate and Nicholas Brady. London: Printed by J. Heptinstall for D. Brown, J. Wild..., 1700.
>   Another edition; London: for Daniel Brown, 1702.

>   [These Bible selections were usually bound with Tate & Brady's Psalms.]

1701 **Gibbs, Dr. James**   The First XV Psalms Translated into Lyric Verse by Dr. [James] Gibbs. London: J. Matthews, 1701.

1706 **Kennett, Basil**   An Essay Towards... the Psalms...
[See Bible Selections for the complete entry.]

1707 **Addison, Mr.**   Psalmes XIX & XXIII Paraphrased in Metre, 1707.

1707 **Anonymous**   Paraphrase on the Psalm CXXXVII, Published in "Oxford and Cambridge Miscellany Poems". Fenton. 1707.

1707 **Bate, Mr.**   Paraphrase on Psalm XLII. Published in Oxford and Cambridge Miscellany Poems, 1707.

1707 **Cobb, Samuel**   Psalms CIII, CXX, and CXLVIII in verse. London: 1707.
[In his 'Poems on Several Occasions'.]

1707 **Lloyd, B.**   Sacred Miscellanies, Several Psalms...
[See Bible Selections for the complete entry.]

1709 **Chudleigh, Lady**   Psalm XV paraphrased in Verse. London: Bernard Lintot, 1709.

1710 **Norris, John**   Psalms CXLVIII, CXIV, CXXVII, CXXXIX, paraphrased in verse. London: 1710.

1712 **Addison, Joseph** [English Essayist]   Psalm XXIII. The Spectator, July 26, 1712.

1713 **Anonymous**   Psalm XXIX Paraphrased in Verse. London: 1713.

1714 **Anonymous**   Psalm XCVII in Paraphristic Verse. "Mr. S." Published in "Poems and Translations" page 185. London: J. Oldmixon, 1714.

1718 **Brown, Jonas**   A Song of Thanksgiving, part of Psalm XCVIII Paraphrased. In Poems Amorus, Moral and divine. London: n.p., 1718.

1720 **Brown (Browne), Simon**   Hymns and Spiritural
Songs (20 Psalms). London: 1720.

1722 **Coney, Thomas**   The Devout Soul...metrical version
of the eighteen Psalms. London: R. Walker, 1722.

1722 **Daniel, Richard**   A Paraphrase of Some Select
Psalms. London: For Bernard Lintot, 1722.
    ["I have singled out about fifty Psalms which I design
    to Paraphrase. I now publish fifteen of them, and in
    some time, God willing, shall finish the rest."]

    Another edition; A Paraphrase on Some Select
    Psalms by Mr. Richard Daniel, Archdeacon of
    Armagh. Dublin: George Grierson, 1722.

    Also; The Royal Penitent, paraphrase of the
    Seven Penitential Psalms. London: B. Lintot,
    1727.

1727 **Harte, Walter**   Psalms CIV and CVII. Paraphrase in
Metre. London: B. Lintot, 1727.

1727 **Pitt, Christopher**   Job 3 and 25... Six Psalms...
    [See Old Testament Selections for the complete entry.]

1727 **Pitt, Christopher**   Psalms VIII, XXIV, XXIX, XLVI,
XC, CXXXIX, and CXLIV, paraphrased. London: B.
Lintott, 1727.

1727 **Pitt, Christopher**   Poems and Translations, 1727.
    [Contains some Psalms. Recorded by Fish.]

1730 **Atwood, George**   Psalm CXIX paraphrased in verse.
London: W. Innys, 1730.

1733 **Anonymous**   Psalm XC Paraphrased in Verse.
Gentleman's Magazine, vol.III, page 542, 1733.

1733 **Costard, G.**   A Specimen of a new translation of
the Psalms...[Gentleman of Wadham College] London:
1733.

1734 **Anonymous**   Psalm CXXXIX Paraphrased in Verse.
Gentleman's Magazine, Vol.IV, page 44, 1734.

1736 **Anonymous**   Psalm CXXIX in Verse. Gentleman's
Magazine, Vol.VI, page 610, 1736.

1736 **Anonymous**   Psalm I & II in Blank Verse. "A.B.".
Gentleman's Magazine, Vol.VI, page 644.

1736 **Burton, Jo.**   Psalm CIV and CXXXVII in Verse.
Oxford: n.p., 1736.

1736 **Facio, N.**   Psalms I and II in Blank Verse.
Gentleman's Magazine, Vol. VII, page 148, 1736.

1736 **Philomel**   Psalm LXVIII in verse. Gentleman's
Magazine, Vol. VI, Page 419, 1736.

1736 **Purver, Anthony**   Psalm LXVIII translated literally
from Hebrew.   Gentleman's Magazine, Vol. VI, Page
95, 1736.

1737 **Anonymous**   Psalm VII in Blank Verse. Gentleman's
Magazine, Vol.VII, Page 695, 1737.

1737 **Anonymous**   Psalm XXII Paraphrased in Verse.
Gentleman's Magazine, Vol.VII, page 629, 1737.

1737 **Colman, George**   Psalm XXXIX in Blank Verse.
London: 1737.
        [In his Miscellaneous Works.]

1737 **Wesley, John**   A Collection of Psalms and Hymns...
        [See Bible Selections for the complete entry.]

1738 **Anonymous**   Psalm CVII Paraphrased in Verse.
Gentleman's Magazine, Vol.VIII, page 153, 1738.

1738 **Anonymous**   "A Collection of Hymns" of the
Brethren's Church (19 Psalms), 1738.
        Another edition, (24 Psalms), 1754.

1738 **Gambold, John**   A Collection of Psalms...for
Moravian Worship. London: 1738.

1739 **Mawer, John**   Proposals for Publishing...Psalms...
        [See Wisdom and Poetical books and Selections for
        the complete entry.]

1740 **Anonymous**   Psalm VIII; Paraphrased in Verse.
Gentleman's Magazine, Vol.x, Page 462, 1740.

1740 **Wesley, Charles**   Hymns and Sacred Poems. By John
and Charles Wesley. London: Strahan, 1740.
        [See Bible Selections, 1737 John Wesley, A Collection of
        Psalm.]

1741 **Dodsley, ?**   Psalm CIV, paraphrased in verse.
Gentleman's Magazine, March, 1741.

1744 **Anonymous**   Psalm CXXI in Verse. Gentleman's
Magazine, Vol.XIV, Page 328, 1744.

1749 **Blacklock, Thomas**   Psalm CIV Paraphrased in Verse.
Gentleman's Magazine, page 514, 1749.
            [This was done at the age of 13, shortly afterwhich
            Blacklock went blind. John Wesley stated: "Perhaps one

of the finest pieces of Poetry in the English
language."]

1750 **Gibbons, T.**   Psalms XIX, XXIII, XXIV, LXXX, XC,
CXXXIX, CXLVIII, in verse. In Juvenilia. London: J.
Buckland, 1750.

1751 **Doddridge, Philip**   Hymns (Contain some Psalms),
1751.

1752 **Allen, E.**   Hymns for the Use of the Congregation
in Grey Eagle St., Spitalfields. [contains Psalms
XI, XLV, XLVI, CIII, CX, CXLVII.]   London: 1752.

1752 **Boyse, Samuel**   Psalms IV and XLII Paraphrased in
Verse. In a Poem Entitled: The Deity, 1752.

1752 **Browne, Moses**   Psalms CXXX and CXXXIX in Metre.
Sunday Thoughts, 1752.
        Again; 1764 and 1781.

1753 **Anonymous** Part of Psalm XVIII Paraphrased in Verse.
Gentleman's Magazine, Vol.XXIII, Page 92, 1753.

1754 **Anonymous**   Psalm XXIII in Verse. In a collection
of Hymns for the use of the Congregation in Margaret
St. London: Oxford Market, 1754.

1755 **Green, William**   A New Translation of... Psalm...
        [See Old Testament Selections for the complete entry.]

1756 **Anonymous**   A select Collection of the Psalms (in
verse) imitated or paraphrased by the most eminent
English Poets. [Henry Dell] London: for the editor,
1756.
        [Taken from Mr. Addison, Mr. Blacklock, Mr. Barton, Mr.
        Daniel, Sir John Denham, Dr. Gibbs, King James I, Mrs.
        Leapor, Milton, Mrs. Masters, Mrs. Rowe, Sir Philip
        Sidney, Dr. Trapp, Mrs. Tollett, Dr. Woodford, and
        several others. Together with some originals never
        before printed.]

1756 **Leapor, Mrs.**   See Anonymous, A select Collection
...Psalms, 1756.

1757 **Anonymous**   An American Gentleman; A Paraphrase
on Psalms CXIX, CXLIII, CXLII, CXX, XIII, CXLIV and
CXXX. London: Rivingtons, 1757.

1758 **Masters, Mrs. Mary**   Familiar Letters and Poems,
1758.
        [Contains several Psalms.]

1759 **Anonymous**   Psalm XXIII in Verse. Gentleman's
Magazine, Page 229, 1759.

1760 **Anonymous**   Poems on subjects chiefly devotional, by Theodosia. [Anne Steele]   London: J. Buckland, 1760.
> [Includes 'Sundry Psalms in metre, with Hymns founded chiefly on passages of scripture.' Fish puts the number of Psalms at 47, and the date at 1765. Also, 'Miscellaneous pieces in prose and verse', 1780.]

1760 **Anonymous**   Psalm CXIV in Verse. Gentleman's Magazine, Page 355, 1760.

1761 **Anonymous**   Psalm CXXXVII Paraphrased in Verse. Gentleman's Magazine, Page 328, 1761.

1761 **Anonymous**   Psalm CXXXVII Paraphrased in Verse. Gentleman's Magazine, Page 375, 1761.
> [This is another version of the above Psalm. Same Vol., different Page.]

1761 **Cruden, William**   Hymns on a Variety of Divine Subjects. By William Cruden, A.M. Minister of the Gospel at Loggie-Pert.   Aberdeen: printed by J. Chalmers, 1761.
> [Includes versions on a number of Psalms.]

1761 **Robson, John**   The First Book of the Psalms of David translated into English Verse of Heroic Measure with Arguments and Notes, by John Robson. London: Printed for W. Sanby, 1761.
> [The first 41 Psalms.]

1762 **Anonymous**   Psalm XIX in Metre in Contrast to Mr. Merrick's Version. Gentleman's Magazine, Page 234, 1762.

1762 **Merrick, James**   Psalms CXXVIII and XIX in verse. Gentleman's Magazine, p. 37 & 85, 1762.

1763 **Anonymous**   A new collection of Psalms, for the use of the Protestant Dissenters at Liverpool. Liverpool: for the Society, 1763.

1764 **Fanch, James**   A Paraphrase on a select number of the Psalms of David; done from the Latin of Buchanan. To which are added some occasional pieces. London: G. Keith, 1764.

1766 **Chandler, Samuel**   XVII Psalms; translated with notes.   London: for Buckland & Coote, 1766.
> [In his 'Life of David'; Strong lists only seven, and dates it 1776.]

1766 **Kennicott, Benjamin**   Psalms XLII and XLIII, 1766.

1767 **Barclay, John**   A Select Collection... Paraphrases
and Translations...
> [See Bible Selections for the complete entry. Includes
> several Psalms.]

1770 **Flexman, R.**   A collection of Psalms, &c. London:
by J. Waugh, 1770.

1772 **Rowe, Elizabeth**   Miscellaneouc Works...
> [See Bible Selections for the complete entry. Includes
> Psalm 23, 63, 72, and 146.]

1773 **Franklin, Benjamin and Francis Dashwood**
Abridgement of the Book of Common Prayer. London:
for Wilkie, 1773.
> ["I abridged by retaining of the Catechism only the two
> questions: 'What is your duty to God?' 'What is your
> duty to your neighbor?' with answers. The Psalms were
> constructed by leaving out the repetitions (of which I
> found more than I could imagined), and imprecations,
> which appeared not to suit well the christian doctrine
> of forgiveness of injuries and doing good to enemies.
> The book...was never much noticed. Some were given away,
> very few sold, and I suppose the bulk became waste
> paper." Benjamin Franklin, by Carl Van Doren.]

1774 **Anonymous**   Psalms, Hymns and Anthems, Used in
the Chapel of the Hospital for the Maintenance and
Education of Exposed and Deserted Young Children.
London: 1774.
> [29 Psalms]

1776 **Barclay, John**   Additional Versions...Psalms...
> [See Wisdom and Poetical books and Selections for the
> complete entry.]

1776 **Kennicott, Benjamin**   [Translation of xxxii Psalms]
Oxford: for D. Prince, 1776.
> [This translation is contained in Dr. Kennicott's
> "Remarks".]

1776 **Ogilvie, John**   Psalm CXLVIII paraphrased in verse.
Printed in Mornes Verses. Oxford: 1776.

1776 **Toplady, Augustus**   Psalms and Hymns for public
worship; collected (for the most part) and published
by Augustus Toplady. London: for E. & C.Dilly, 1776.
> [The subsequent editions were arranged and much altered
> by the respective deacons of his chapel.]

1777 **Young, Matthew**   [Psalms i-cxlii, with notes]
[Dublin: University Press Privately printed]
> [Cotton describes as "The Psalms; a new translation,
> with notes... an unfinished work, suppressed; no title;
> date uncertain." He lists it under 1777.]
>
> [British Museum Catalogue describes it as, "The AV of
> the Psalms revised..." and dates it "1800?"]

1778 **Anonymous**   Psalm CXIV in Verse. <u>Gentleman's</u> <u>Magazine</u>, Page 328, 1778.

1779 **Anonymous**   Psalm XVIII, Paraphrased..."J.W. of Newport Pagnell". <u>Gentleman's Magazine</u>, Page 152, 262, 1779.

1779 **Anonymous**   Psalm CIX, Literally Translated from the Hebrew. <u>Gentleman's Magazine</u>, Page 540, 1779.

1779 **Anonymous**   Psalm XXIII, Paraphrased in Verse. <u>Gentleman's Magazine</u>, Page 368, 1779.

1779 **Pembroke, Countess of**   Certain Psalms in verse. In Harrington's Nugae Antiquae. 1779.

1780 **Anonymous**   Sacred Odes: or Psalms of David, paraphrased from the original Hebrew.   London: W. Oliver, 1780.
    Another edition; London: G. Wilkie & G. Keith, 1782.

1780 **Oliver, W.**   Sacred Odes...from Original Hebrew. (Psalms I, II, XX, XLIX, CXVII, CXXXVI and part of XC.) London: 1780.

1782 **Cowper, William**   Psalm CXXXVII in verse.   London: 1782.
    [In his Poems.]

1783 **Barclay, John**   The Experience and Example... **Divine Praise**...
    [See Bible Selections for the complete entry. Includes some Psalms.]

1784 **Gibbons, Thos.**   Hymns Adapted to Divine Worship. London: 1784.
    [Includes 14 Psalms]

1787 **Gregory, G.**   Lectures on the Sacred Poetry...
    [See Old Testament Selections for the complete entry. Includes most of the Psalms.]

1787 **Keen, Rev. Mr.**   Psalms XV and part of CXXXIX. In Miscellaneous Pieces by a clergyman of Northamptonshire.   London: 1787.

1788 **Geddes, Alexander**   Specimen, contains translation of Psalm XIV.   London: Faulder, 1788.

1788 **Walker, G.**   Psalms and Hymns; unmixed with the disputed doctrines of any sect; collected by G. Walker. Warrington: by W. Eyres, 1788.

1789 **Anonymous**   The Psalms and Hymns of David, with Hymns and Spiritual Songs, Also the Catechism, Confession of Faith, and Liturgy of the Reformed Church in the Netherlands. For the use of the Reformed Dutch Church in North-America. [John H. Livingston] New-York: Printed by Hodge, Allen & Campbell, 1789.
> ["...a selection from the Versions of Dr. Brady and Mr. Tate, Dr. Watts and the Book at present in use in the Dutch Church of the City of New York; with such alterations as may be found necessary..."]

> Revised, 1812.

> Another edition; New York: George Forman, 1814.

> Revised, 1847.

> Another edition; The Psalms and Hymns, with the Doctrinal Standards and Liturgy of the Reformed Dutch Church in North America. New York: Board of Publication of the Reformed Protestant Dutch Church, 1859.

1790 **Belcher, W.**   The Galaxy...poetry...
> [See Bible Selections for the complete entry. Includes some Psalms.]

1790 **May, Thomas**   Psalms XXXIII, XXXIX and XCVII Paraphrased ...London: 1790.

1791 **Anonymous**   An Introduction to Reform Singing...
> [See Bible Selections for the complete entry.]

1791 **Cotton, Nathaniel**   Psalms XIII & XLII in verse. London: 1791.

1792 **Anonymous**   A Selection of Psalms, with Occasional Hymns. [Robert Smith and Henry Purcell] Charleston: Printed for W.P. Young, 1792.

1793 **Hill, Aaron**   Habakkuk 3, Part of Psalm 14...
> [See Bible Selections for the complete entry.]

1794 **Mickle, W.J.**   Psalm LXVIII in verse. London: 1794.

1795 **Belknap, Jeremy**   Collection of Psalms and Hymns, 1795.

1795 **Kippis, A.**   A Selection of Hymns and Psalms; selected and prepared by Dr. A. Kippis and others. Gentlemen's Magazine, vol. lxv, P. 321 & lxvi, P. 925. 1795.
> [Altered from Dr. Watt's version.]

1797 **Mason, William**   The Psalms (in metre) taken from
the old version; revised and altered for the Parish
of Aston, 1797.
> [Twenty-Five Psalms revised and altered from the Old
> Version, and a metrical version of fifteen, 1797.]

> [Not published until 1811.]

1800 **Burns, Robert**   Psalm 1 in English verse. In various
editions of his works.   Liverpool: n.p., 1800.

1801 **Belknap, Jeremy**   Sacred Poetry. Consisting of
Psalms and Hymns; Adapted to Christian Devotion, in
Public and Private. Selected from the best Authors,
with Variations and Additions ...Third edition, with
Improvements.   Published   according   to   Act   of
Congress.   Boston: For Thomas & Andrews and West &
Greenleaf, 1801.
> [...with additional hymns. Boston: Published by Thomas
> Wells, 1820.]

1801 **Cottle, Joseph**   A New Version of the Psalms of
David.   London: printed for T.N. Longman & O.Rees,
by Biggs & Co., Bristol, 1801.
> [In the 2nd edition, 1805, Cottle describes the 1st
> edition as "...a version of the Psalms, in which I did
> not profess to give the literal sense...a short
> Paraphrase on particular parts of Psalms..."]

1801 **Cumberland, Richard**   A Poetical Version of Certain
Psalms of David. Turnbridge Wells: J. Sprange, 1801.
> ["I have rendered into English metre fifty of the Psalms
> of David, which were printed by Mr. Strange (sic) of
> Turnbridge Wells, and upon which I flatter myself I have
> not in vain bestowed my best attention."]

1804 **Harrington, Sir John**   Psalm xxiv, cxii & cxxxvii,
in verse. London: 1804.
> [Printed in "Nugae Antiquae."]

> [According to Cotton, "Sir John Harrington versified the
> entire Psalter. His version is in the collection of Mr.
> Douce, at Oxford.]

1804 **Henry, Earl of Surrey**   Psalms LXXXVIII, LXXIII and
LV in verse. In Harrington's Nugae Antiquae. London:
Thomas Park, 1804.

1804 **Pembroke, Countess of**   Psalms CXXXVII and CXII in
verse. In Harrington's Nugae Antiquae. 1804.

1806 **Anonymous**   A Collection of Psalms , extracted
from various versions with an original version of
several Psalms: adapted to each Sunday in the year,
according to the order of the Church of England: to
which are added select hymns for the Principal
festivals, &c.   London: The Editor, 1806.

1806 **Eveleigh, J.**   Psalms XXXVII; a New Version. Oxford: 1806.

1806 **Middleton, Erasmus**   Versions and Imitations of the Psalms, selected from various authors, and adapted to the public worship of the Church of England, by Erasmus Middleton. London: R. Wilson, 1806.
    [Selected Psalms.]

1810 **Anonymous**   The Psalms of David and other portions of the Holy Scriptures, arranged according to the order of the Church of England for every Sunday in the Year, by B.W. [Basil Woodd?] London: Watts & Bridgewater, 1810.
    Another edition; A new Metrical version of the Psalms of David; with an appendix of select Psalms and Hymns... London: E. Bridgewater &c, 1821.

1810 **Hamilton, William**   Psalm LXV... In Chalmer's Collection of English Poets, 1810.

1810 **Jebb, John**   Psalm CVII, a New Version. In the Christian Observer. 1810.

1811 **Aston, Henry**   Select Psalms in Verse, by Bishop Lowth & Others, Illustrative of the Beauties of the Sacred Poetry. London: Printed for J.Hatchard, 1811.

1811 **Dixon, R.**   Psalms LXVIII and CX. Oxford: 1811.

1811 **Wolseley, Robert**   A Poetical Paraphrase of a Select Portion of the Book of Psalms by Robert Wolseley. Lichfield: T.G. Lomax, 1811.

1814 **Anonymous**   Psalm II; a New Version. Gentleman's Magazine, Page 221, 1814.

1815 **Anonymous**   Horae Davidicae: or a New Translation of the Book of Psalms. [Unfinished, contains the first 14 Psalms.] 1815.

1815 **Donald, R.**   The Psalms of David, on Christian experience. Guildford Press: Printed for the author, by S. Russell & Co., 1815.
    [Selected Psalms only]

1815 **Henry, Earl of Surrey**   Certain Psalms... London: Longman and Co., 1815.
    [Psalm 8 for the first time, the others are reprints of 1804.]

1816 **Anonymous**   Translation of Psalm XVIII. With
observations. The Jewish Expositor and Friend of
Israel, 1:77-79, Feb., 1816.

1818 **Bowler, John**   Four Psalms Paraphrased in Verse.
Published in His Select Pieces in Prose and Verse.
2 Vols. London: n.p., 1818.

1819 **Anonymous**   A Choice Selection of Psalms, Hymns,
and Spiritual Songs, for the use of Christians.
[John Mackenzie, Benjamin Putnam, Christopher W.
Martin, and Jasper Hazen.] Woodstock: Printed by
David Watson, 1819.

          [Watts's version, revised.]

1819 **Harvey, W.C.**   Psalm CXLVIII in Verse. Gentleman's
Magazine, Part 1, p. 562, 1819.

1820 **Anonymous**   Additional Psalmody;...more than Thirty
Psalms by various unnamed Authors. Edinburgh: 1820.

1820 **Lowe, Henry**   Psalms & Hymns, 1820.
          [Twenty Psalms.]

1821 **Anonymous**   Psalm XIII in Verse."J.A.G."
Gentleman's Magazine, September, 1821.

1821 **Anonymous**   A Selection from a Version of the
Psalms of David... [John Stow] 1821.

1821 **Coldwell, William**   The Book of Praises. The Psalms
or sacred odes of the Royal Psalmist David, and
others,the Prophets of Jehovah; in Metre. Halifax:
by R. Sugden, for Baldwin, Cradock & Joy, London,
1821.
          [Psalms i-xli only; in blank verse.]

1821 **Dale, Thomas**   Specimens of a New Translation
of the Psalms. London: 1821.
          [In his 'Irad and Adam']

1822 **Montgomery, James**   Songs of Zion by James
Montgomery. London: Longman, 1822.
          [Contains a metrical version of 59 Psalms; frequently
          reprinted.]

1823 **Anonymous**   A Collection out of the Book of Psalms,
Extracted from Various versions, with an Original
Version of several Psalms. London: 1823.
          [Preface signed "I.S."]

1823 **Murray, Davis**   Paraphrase of Psalm CIV. Edinburgh:
Andro Hart, 1615.
          Reprinted, 1823.

1828 **Anonymous** Psalms XLIII, LXX, C, and CXXI in Verse. Published in "A Collection of Prayers for Household Use."

1828 **Cottle, Joseph** Hymns and Sacred Lyrics in Three Parts. London: 1828.
[Part 2, "Hymns Suggested by, or founded upon, Portions of the Psalms." Relationship to his "New Version..." of 1801 is not known.]

1828 **Muir, Sir William** Psalms XV, XXIII and CXXII in metre, 1828.
[In the "Historie of the House of Rowallane".]

1828 **Mutter, George** Psalms for Public Worship, Original and selected. London: 1828.

1828 **Sutcliffe, Joseph** Psalms and Hymns, by J. Sutcliffe. 1828.
Second impression; London: n.p., 1828.

1829 **Anonymous** The Spirit of the Psalms, or, a compressed version of Select Portions of the Psalms of David, adapted to Christian Worship. [Harriet Auber] London: Printed by A. & R. Spottiswoode, for T. Cadell, 1829.
[Also; See Anonymous, The Christian Psalmist, 1833.]

1831 **Bathurst, W.(illiam) H.(iley)** Psalms and Hymns for Public and Private use. London: Hatchard & Sons; Leeds: J.Y. Knight, 1831.
Another edition, 1832.

1832 **Anonymous** Metrical Versions of Ten Psalms, by Various Authors...Published in "British Magazine", 1832.

1833 **Anonymous** Psalms LXXX in Verse. Saturday Magazine, Vol.II, Page 71, 1833.

1834 **Beaumont, John** Original Psalms; or Sacred Psalms Taken from the Psalms of David, and imitated in the language of the New Testament, in Twenty different metres. Adapted to the Tunes now in general use in the British Churches with a new set of Christian Doxologies, suited to the various measures. Shewsbury: Printed for the author and sold by him, 1834.

1834 **Beaumont, John** Two New Versions of the Seven Pentitential Psalms. Shrewsbury: Hulbert & Davies, 1834.

1834 **Bush, George** A Commentary on the Book of Psalms; on a Plan Embracing the Hebrew Text, with a

New Literal Version..To be published in periodical
numbers... New York: n.p., 1834? 1838?
   [No. 1. Psalms I-III. It is not known whether this plan
   was completed. James Strong's "Student's Commentary",
   196?, lists the basic title under 1838, possibly
   indicating the publication of some of the remainder of
   the work.]

1834 **Dickson, Thomas**   Paraphrases and Hymns. A Metrical
Version of Several of (14) the Psalms. Berwick:
Printed for the author by D. Cameron, 1834.
   [A metrical paraphrase of 14 Psalms included.]

1834 **Judkin, Thomas James**   Church and Home Melodies;
being a New Version of the more Devotional parts of
the Psalms; together with a version of the Collects,
&c. London: Hatchard & Son, 1834.

1834 **Lyte, Henry Frances**   The Spirit of the Psalms,
or the Psalms of David adapted to Christian Worship,
by Henry F. Lyte. Brixham: Printed by W. King, 1834.
   [A collection of Hymns and Psalms, drawn from various
   sources, but mainly his own.]

   Second edition; London: William Marsh, 1834.

   Fourth edition; corrected and enlarged. London:
   Rivington, 1836.

   Also; With some additional Psalms and Hymns,
   Third Edition, 1864.

1835 **Herbert, George**   Psalm XXIII in verse. Printed
in his Works. 2 Vols. London: W. Pickering, 1835.

1836 **Anonymous**   Psalms LXXX, XCVI and CXXXIX in Verse.
In "Poems Original and Translated", 1836.

1836 **Anonymous**   Book of Public Worship...
   [See Bible Selections for the complete entry. Includes
   about 100 Psalms.]

1837 **Conder, Josiah**   Certain Psalms in verse. 1837.
   [In 'The Choir and the Oratory'.]

1838 **Rusling, J.**   Portions of the Psalms and other parts
of scripture, in verse. Designed as a Companion for
the Christian. By J. Rusling. Philadelphia: Sold by
the Publisher, 1838.
   ["...he has attempted to place a portion (99) of the
   Psalms and other parts of scripture in plain and
   unpretending verse..."]

1839 **Anonymous**   Psalms, &c [John Hookham Frere] London:
W. Nicol, 1839?

[Metrical paraphrase of selected Psalms and portions of
the N.T.]

1839 **Grant, Sir Robert**   Sacred Poems. London: Saunders
& Otley, 1839.
[Contains seven Psalms; Fish.]

1839 **Hare, Julius Charles**   Portions of the Psalms in
English Verse by Julius Charles Hare, 1839.

1839 **Scott, Robert Allan**   Metrical paraphrases of
selected portions of the Book of Psalms; generally
adapted to the purposes of public worship or private
devotion, by Robert Allan Scott.   London: for
Rivingtons, 1839.

1840 **Anonymous**   Psalms and Hymns [William Vernon
Harcourt]   York: R. Sumter, 1840.

1841 **Alleyn, Edwards**   Psalm CXIII in Verse. Published
in Memoirs of Him by J. Payne Collier, 1841.

1842 **Black, W.H.**   A Paraphrase on the Seven Penitential
Psalms in English Verse Supposed to be Written by
Thomas Brampton D.D. in 1414; with Notes. London:
Percy Society, 1842.

1842 **Muir, Sir William**   Psalms I and XXII in verse.
Specimens from a MS. Edinburgh: D. Laing, 1842.

1843 **Russell, Frederick**   A metrical version of Fifty
Psalms, Frederick Russell. London: n.p., 1843.

1844 **Croke, Sir Alexander**   Thirteen Psalms and first
chapter of Ecclesiastes XXX ...Vulgate by John Croke
Esq. in the reign of King Henry VIII. London: Percy
Society, 1844.

1844 **Montagu, M.** The Seven Penitential Psalms in verse;
being specimens of a new version of the Psalter,
with an appendix of correlative matter and notes.
London: T. Hatchard.
[See Psalms listing for the complete entry.]

1844 **Morton, Joseph Washington**   Inspired Psalms,
selected and literally translated, (From the Hebrew)
on   an   original   plan   of   Versification,   with
explanations   and   appropriated   music,   by   Joseph
Washington Morton. Freedom, Pa.: Published by the
Author; Printed by John Grant, Pittsburgh, 1844.

1845 **Anonymous**   A Metrical Version of the Song of
Solomon ...some of the Psalms...
[See Wisdom and Poetical books and Selections for the
complete entry.]

1846 **Coverdale, Myles**   Remains of Myles Coverdale.
    Cambridge: Printed at The Univ. Press, M.DCCC.XLVI.
    Reprinted; Johnson Reprint Co., for Parker
    Society.

        [The work contains the only copy of this translation of
        the 23rd Psalm by Coverdale.]

1848 **Burrow, E. B.**   Select Psalms in English Verse.
    London: 1848.

1848 **Harrison, W.**   Psalms and Hymns. London: Guillaume,
    1848.

1848 **Wait, Rev. Dr.**   A Selection from the Psalms;
    prepared for congregational use, from the Hebrew by
    Rev. Dr. Wait. London: 1848.

1854 **Fish, Henry**   See Charles Wesley, A Poetical
    Versions ...Psalms, 1788.

1854 **Stuart, James Park**   A Liturgy for the New Church,
    by James Park Stuart. 1854.
        ["The parts of Sacred Scriptures used in this work are
        translated anew... We have one hundred and thirty-six
        Selections for chanting, about half the number in
        Liturgy in 1854." Contains 32 Psalms. A Swedenborgian
        work.]

    Another edition; Philadelphia: J.B. Lippincott &
    Co., 1876.

1855 **Wolfe, J.R.**   The Messiah, as predicted...
        [See Old Testament listing for the complete entry.]

1857 **Bonar, Horatius**   Hymns of Faith and Hope, 1857.
        [... Third Series; New York: Robert Carter and Brothers,
        1871. The first and Second Series have not been seen;
        date from Webster's Biographical Dictionary. Third
        Series contains 47 Psalms in a metrical version.]

1858 **Anonymous**   The Pentateuch, Haphtorahs, and...
        [See Old Testament listing for the complete entry.]

1862 **Strong, James**   Psalms 17-19. Beauty of Holiness
    in Heart and Life, 13:113, pages 144-145, 184, 1862.
        [The Deity is rendered "Jehovah".]

1864 **Williams, Isaac**   The Psalms interpreted of
    Christ by Isaac Williams. London: 1864.
        [Vol. 1; Psalms i-xxvi; no more published.]

1866 **Anonymous**   Paraphrase of Psalm LXI. The British
    Herald, August 1, 1866.

1868 **Baker, Henry Williams**   Psalm XXIII. <u>Hymns Ancient and Modern, Supplement</u>, 1868.

1869 **Didham, Richard Cunningham**   A New Translation of the Psalms: with a plea for revisal of our versions. By R. Cunningham Didham... 2 Vols. London: Williams & Norgate, 1869-1870.
     [Part 1 & 2; Psalms 1-xxxvi; no more published.]

          1870 Psalms 1 - 36; A New Translation, made by means of Arabic Lexicons, Syriac N.T. Words, the Ancient Versions, Bishop Lowth's Parallelisms, and Parallel Places, whereby the Scriptural Messianic Canon that Our Lord Christ is the Key to the Psalms is upheld. London.

1869 **Hiller, O. Prescott**   Notes on the Psalms, chiefly explanatory of the spiritual sense. With a new translation from the Hebrew. London: James Speirs, 1869.
     [Vol. 1. Psalms 1-lxxvii; no more published.]

1872 **Anonymous**   Revised collection of Psalm versions, paraphrases & Hymns. General Assembly of the Free Church. <u>Church Hymnary</u>, No. 578, and <u>Scottish Hymnal</u>, No. 129.
     [Contained new renderings as alternative forms for 40 Psalms. Called the "Free Church Version".]

1874 **Roberts, Captain John**   The Pilot's Psalm, 1874.
     [Published in Leslie Baily's Log Book, entitled: "A Nice Bit of Fish."]

1877 **Twining, William**   The Antiphonal Psalter, in parallel readings, corresponding to the responsive parallelism of Hebrew Poetry, according to the renderings of the best authorities in Hebrew criticism. To which are added Liturgies, in aid of Congregational worship. Also special services for burials, baptisms and Sunday Schools by William Twining. St. Louis: Slawson & Pierrot, 1877.
     [Includes 120 Psalms.]

1879 **Marquess of Bute, John**   The Roman Breviary...
     [See Bible Selections for the complete entry. Includes some Psalms.]

1883 **MacKellar, Thomas**   Faith, Hope, Love, these Three ... Hymns and Metrical Psalms, by Thomas MacKellar. Philadelphia? 1883.
     [Includes nine Psalms.]

        Third Edition; Philadelphia: Perter & Coates, 1893.

["Revised and Enlarged" Five Psalms added.]

1888 **Mielziner, M.**   A Selection from the Book of Psalms, for School and Family Use. Arranged by Rev. Dr. M. Mielziner. Published by the Hebrew Sabbath-School Union of America.   Cincinnati, Ohio: From the American Hebrew Printing House, The Bloch Publishing and Printing Co., 1888.
> [Contains a prose version of 66 Psalms; the ERV modified.]

1890 **Onslow, F.P.**   A Metrical Version of the Psalms of David regarded as prophecy shewn by reference to the New Testament narrative to have been fulfilled... London: F.V. White & Co., 1890.

1890 **Singer, S.**   The Authorised Daily Prayer Book...
> [See Old Testament Selections for the complete entry. Includes 78 Psalms.]

1893 **Epworth, J.W.**   (Editor)   See Thomas Carew, Certaine Psalmes, 1640.

1894 **Betts, John Thomas**   Juan de Valdes' commentary on the first book of the Psalms, now for the first time translated from the Spanish, having never before been published in English, by John T. Betts. Edinburgh: Privately printed, 1894.

1895 **Gregory, Benjamin**   The Sweet Singer of Israel: selected Psalms Illustrative of David's Character and History with Metrical Paraphrases by Benjamin Gregory...   London: Charles H. Kelly, 1895.

1895 **Littledale, Henry Anthony**   (Editor)   See Anonymous, The Prymer, 1420.

1896 **Anonymous**   Dr. David Einhorn's ...Book of Prayers for Jewish Congregations... New Translation after the German Original. [Ernest G. Hirsch]   Chicago, Ill.: Press of S. Ettlinger Printing Co. Copyright Julie Einhorn, 1896.
> [Contains 52 Psalms and various other O.T. selections; Hebrew and English.]

1897 **Anonymous** The Presbyterian Book of Praise: Approved and commended by the General Assembly of the Presbyterian Church of Canada; Part I. Selections from the Psalter; Part II. the Hymnal, revised and enlarged. [William Gregg and W.B. McMurrich] Oxford: University Press; London: Henry Frowde, 1897.
> [Contains 122 Psalms (or portions) "...for the most part, taken from the Scottish Metrical Version. Some changes have been made in order to bring the meaning into closer conformity with the original text, and to remove imperfections in the metre."]

1897 **Margoliouth, G.**   The Palestinian Syriac Version...
[See Bible Selections for the complete entry.]

1899 **Gray, Isabella Anderson**   Border Rhymes, 1899.
[Contains Psalm XXIII.]

1900 **Dickson, William Bradford**   Psalms of Soul
by William Bradford Dickson. South Bend, Indiana:
Tribune Company, Publishers, 1900.
[The 23rd Psalms and poems]

1900 **Perowne, E.H.**   Savonarola; Meditations on Psalm
LI and Part of Psalm XXXI in Latin, with an English
Translation by E.H. Perowne... London: C.J. Clay
and Sons, 1900.

1902 **Pope, Hugh**   Fifty-Two Psalms selected from
the Psalter, and edited with notes, by Hugh Pope.
London: Catholic Truth Society, 1902.
["In many passages the Douay version is very obscure,
and in such cases we have not hesitated to make
corrections with the aid of St. Jerome's translation of
the Psalter from the Hebrew."]

1907 **Bright, James Wilson and R.L. Ramsay**   Liber
Psalmoium. The West-Saxon Psalms, being the prose
portion, or the "First-Fifty" of the so-called Paris
Psalter, edited from the MS. Boston: n.p., 1907.
[Anglo-Saxon]

1907 **Cohen, Mrs. Nathaniel L.** The Children's Psalm Book:
a Selection of Psalms with explanatory comments,
together with a prayer-book for home use in Jewish
families. London: G. Routledge & Sons, 1907.
[Hebrew and English]

1907 **Collier, Edward A.**   Lyrics from the Psalter; a
metrical rendering of selections from the Psalms.
Pittsburgh: The United Presbyterian Board of
Publication, 1907.
[The Deity is rendered "Jehovah".]

1912 **Eaton, Robert D.**   Sing Ye to the Lord. Exposition
of Fifty Psalms. St. Louis: B. Herder, 1912.

1912 **Gordon, Alexander R.**   The Poets of the O.T...
[See Old Testament Selections for the complete entry.
Includes a few Psalms.]

1912 **Sullivan, W.** A New Version of the Psalms. 119-150.
By W. Sullivan. London: J. Lovejoy & Son, 1912.
[Metrical]

1915 **Berry, E. Sylvester**   Commentary on the Psalms;
Psalms I-L. New York, Cincinnati & Chicago: Benziger
Bros., 1915.

1915 **Berry, E. Sylvester**   Commentary on the Psalms;
Psalms I–L. New York, Cincinnati & Chicago: Benziger
Bros., 1915.
  ["...explanation in which the meaning is usually brought
  out by means of a paraphrase."]

1916 **Brooke, Stopford**   Psalm XXIII. 1916.
  [See Arthur Pollok Sym, The Twenty-Third Psalm, 1922.]

1916 **Cooke, W.J.**   The Psalms: meditative and militant.
A New Paraphrase. Conway: W.J. Cooke, 1916.
  [Psalms 1–41, metrical.]

1919 **Anonymous**   Psalm XXIII. Quarterly Record of the
Bible Society for Scotland, July, 1919.
  ["Lines in possession of a young Scottish soldier who
  fell in France.]

1919 **Finch, R.G.**   The Longer Commentary of R. David
Kimhi on the first Book of Psalms (I–X, XV–XVII,
XIX, XXII, XXIV) Translated from the Hebrew... With
an introduction by G.H. Box... London: S.P.C.K.;
New York: The Macmillan Co., 1919.

1922 **Sym, Arthur Pollok**   The Twenty-Third Psalm;
An Anthology of Metrical Versions, Collected and
composed by the Reverend Arthur Pollok Sym; With an
Introductory Essay and Biographical Notes. London,
Edinburgh & New York: Marshall Bros., Ltd., [1922].
  ["The author has ventured to add a few versions composed
  by himself in various metres..."]

1924 **Cameron, Duncan**   Songs of Sorrow and
Praise; Studies in the Hebrew Psalter by Rev. Duncan
Cameron ... Edinburgh: T. & T. Clark, 1924.

1925 **Askwith, E.H.**   The Psalms; Books IV and V.
Rendered into English in a Rhythm Consonant with
that of the Original Hebrew by E.H. Askwith. London:
M. Hopkinson & Co., 1925.

1928 **Millard, William Barrett**   The Supplementary Bible.
An Anthology of the greatest literature of the
Christian Era reflecting the spirit of the Bible and
restating its immortal truths. Edited by Rev.
William Barrett Millard... With cooperation of a
Board of Associate Editors.   Chicago: Buxton-
Westerman Co., 1928.   [Includes some Psalms.]

1931 **Hodgson, Geraldine**   Office Psalms from Rolle's
Psalter and S. Augustine's Ennarations. Rendered and
edited... London: Oates & Co., 1931.

1936 **Anonymous**   A Book of English. Psalms, etc. [Ernest
Walder] Broadway: E. Walder, 1936.

1936 **Smith, Walter Bernard**   A New Church Psalter...
    [See Wisdom and Poetical Books and Selections for
    the complete entry.]

1937 **Laux, John Joseph**   Songs of Sion; Selections
    from the Book of Psalms. By John J. Laux. New York,
    Cincinnati, Chicago: Benziger Brothers, 1937.
    [A revision of 87 of the Douai Psalms.]

1938 **Anonymous**   Twenty-Third Psalm, an American Indian
    version. "Christ and the Fine Arts" by Cynthia Peal
    Mans, 1938.

1939 **Lattey, Cuthbert**   Book of Psalms, 1939.
    [See Complete Bibles, 1913 Westminster Version.]

1939 **Snaith, Norman H.**   Five Psalms (I, XXVII, LI,
    CVII, XXXIV). London: Manuals of Fellowship, Series
    2, no. 13, 1939.

1942 **Wilmot, Christopher J.**   The Priest's Prayer Book.
    A handbook to the Breviary. The Breviary Psalms for
    Sundays and festivals, together with translation,
    notes and meditations... London: Burns, Oates and
    Washburne, 1942.

1946 **Hughson, S.C.**   The Gloria Psalter; Arranged by S.C.
    Hughson. West Park, New York: Holy Cross Press,
    1946.
        ["In weaving certain high points in each Psalm with its
        accompanying Gloria Patri..."]

1949 **Dunlap, Rhodes** (Editor) See Thomas Carew, Certaine
    Psalmes, 1640.

1949 **Taylor, Cyril**   The Broadcast Psalter; Selections
    from the Psalter together with twelve Canticles as
    used by the British Broadcast Corporation. London:
    S.P.C.K., 1949.
        [67 Psalms.]

1950 **Paterson, John**   The Praises of Israel.
    Studies Literary and Religious in the Psalms by John
    Paterson... New York: Charles Scribner's Sons, 1950.
        ["In the citation of the songs the AV has been used...
        Frequently, where a more exact sense was required, the
        translation has been made directly from the Hebrew."]

1952 **Terrien, Samuel**   The Psalms and Their Meaning for
    Today, by Samuel Terrien. Indianapolis, New York:
    The Bobbs-Merrill Co., Inc., 1952.
        [Includes a translation of 112 of the Psalms.]

        [The Deity is rendered "Yahweh" many times.]

1953 **Johnson, Christopher**   A Mountaineer's version of
the 23rd Psalm, 1953.
>   [See K.H. Strange, Psalm 23, page 47, 1969.]

1955 **Engel, Milton B.**   The Psalmery; Selections
of Old Testament Psalms Revised and Re-arranged with
Additions.   Redwood   City,   California: Western
Publishing Co., 1955.
>   ["Mr. Engel uses the greatest of the Psalms and, taking
>   considerable liberties, he paraphrases and edits them
>   and adds verses of his own." Based on the KJV. Includes
>   96 groupings, made up from various Psalms.]

1955 **Sublette, Ethel Riner**   Songs from One
Hundred Psalms, by Ethel Riner Sublette. New York:
Exposition Press, 1955.
>   ["Portions of verses from the RSV...(and) An American
>   Translation ...(32) poems included in this work
>   previously appeared...in the Bluefield (West Va.) Daily
>   Telegraph..." A Rhymed version.]

1955 **Whitfield, Mr.**   See Bible Selections, 1737 John
Wesley, A Collection of Psalms.

1957 **Ryan, Mary Perkins**   Key to the Psalms,
by Mary Perkins Ryan. Collegeville, Minnesota: The
Liturgical Press, 1957.

1959 **Weitzner, Emil**   Humanist Meditations...
>   [See Old Testament Selections for the complete entry.]

1960 **Hebgin and Corrigan**   St. Augustine on the Psalms,
Translated and Annotated. Ancient Christian Writers,
1960-1961.
>   1960 - - Vol. 1: Psalms 1-29
>
>   1961 - - Vol. 2: Psalms 30-37

1960 **Ward, Archbald F.**   Seasons of the Soul by Archbald
F. Ward. Richmond, Virginia: John Knox Press, 1960.
>   ["I have employed the French as the primary source of
>   this rendering...I have relied upon the German also,
>   using the translation of the Bible by Martin Luther..."
>   98 Psalms.]

1961 **Hadas, Gershon**   The Weekday Prayerbook. New York:
Jonathan David, 1961.

1962 **Dalglish, Edward R.**   Psalm Fifty-one in the Light
of Ancient Eastern Patternism by Edward R. Dalglish
... Leiden: E.J.Brill, 1962.
>   [Chapter N contains 'An English Translation of Psalm
>   li'.]

1962 **McKillop, Sybil L.**   Twenty Psalms for Schools from
the Prayerbook and Scottish Psalter, and a Fresh

translation; selected and arranged for singing at morning worship. London: 1962.

1962 **Turl, Austin**   Praises Through Sorrow and Praises in Faith: A Rendering in Modern English Verse of the Fifth Book of the Psalms of King David and the Penitential Psalms, by Austin Turl. London: The Mitre Press, 1962.
          [Includes Psalms 6, 23, 32, 38, 51, 102, and 107-150.]

1963 **Kendon, Frank** Thirty-Six Psalms, an English Version (I-XXXIV, XL-XLI). By Frank Kendon. Cambridge: University Press, 1963.

1964 **Foxwell, A.K.**   The Poems of Sir Thomas Wiat, edited from the MSS. and early editions by A.K. Foxwell... Vol. I Preface and Text. New York: Russell & Russell Inc., 1964.

1964 **Zeller, Hubert van**   The Psalms in other words: a presentation for beginners, by Hubert van Zeller. Templegate, Springfield, Illinois: 1964.
          ["...I am aiming at only an abstract or digest."]

1965 **Anonymous**   Psalm 23, a Translation of the Japanese version, 1965.
          [Broadcast by Rev. Eric Frost on May 4, 1965, from London.]

1965 **Deiss, Lucien**   Biblical Hymns and Psalms by Lucien Deiss... 2 Vols. Cincinnati: World Library of Sacred Music, 1965.
          Second edition; 1971.

1965 **Knoch, Adolph E.**   The Shepherd Psalm (Psalm 23). Unsearchable Riches, May, 1965.
          Again; The Bible Collector, No. 7, Page 2, July-Sept., 1966.

1966 **Brandt, Leslie F.**   Psalms 20, paraphrase. This Day, Oct. 1966...
          [See Psalms listing for the complete entry.]

1967 **Anonymous**   Japanese 23rd Psalm. Methodist Recorder, Oct. 19, 1967.

1968 **Burke, Carl F.**   Treat Me Cool, Lord; Prayers - Devotions -Litanies; as prepared by some of God's bad-tempered angels with busted halos, with the help of Carl F. Burke, Author of God is for Real, Man. New York: Association Press, 1968
          [Paraphrases]

1968 **Hylander, Herman**   My Psalm from David. The Voice of Peace, May, 1968.

[Psalm 23. A paraphrase interspersed with KJV.]

1968 **Oosterhuis, Huub and Others.**   Fifty Psalms;
An Attempt at a New Translation. Huub Oosterhuis,
Michel van der Plas, Pius Drijvers, Han Renckens,
Frans Josef van Beeck, David Smith, Forrest Ingram.
New York: Herder and Herder, 1968.
      [This is a work from Dutch into English is by Frans
      Josef van Beeck in collaboration with David Smith and
      Forrest Ingram.]

      Another Edition; New York: Seabury Press, 1973.

1969 **Brandt, Leslie F.**   God is Here, Let's Celebrate!
In 39 Meditations...
      [See Psalms listing, 1966 for the complete entry.]

1969 **Miyashina, Toki**   A Translation of the Japanese
Version of the 23rd Psalm.
      [See K.H. Strange, Psalm 23, 1969.]

1969 **Ryan, Mary Perkins**   Psalms '70; A New Approach to
Old Prayers, by Mary Perkins Ryan... Dayton, Ohio:
Pflaum Press, 1969.
      [35 Psalms. "I used the Fides translation as a basis,
      selecting and rephrasing as seemed necessary... I have
      used the Hebrew 'Yahweh' rather than ...'Lord'".]

      Second printing, 1970.

1969 **Strange, K.H.**   Psalm 23; Several versions collected
and put together by K.H. Strange.   Edinburgh: The
Saint Andrew Press, 1969.

1970 **Margolis, Max L.**   Psalm 29. _Biblica_, Vol. 51, Pages
334-335, 1970.
      [The Deity is rendered "Yahweh".]

1971 **Anonymous**   The 23rd Channel. _Rebirth_, 1:1,
October, 1971.
      [A parody version.]

1971 **Haysman, Frederick** Psalm 150. _Decision_, Dec., 1971.
      [F.H. is from Godalming, Surrey. This work was done at
      the British School of Christian Writing held at
      Hildenborough Hall at Kent.]

1971 **Higginbottom, Martin**   Psalm 116. _Decision_, Nov.,
1971.
      [M.H. is from Kendal, Westmorland, England. This work
      was done at the British School of Christian Writing held
      at Hildenborough Hall in Kent.]

1971 **Hodges, Carol A.**   Psalm 30. _Decision_, Nov., 1971.
      [C.A.H. is from Harrow, Middlesex, England. This work
      was done at British School of Christian Writing held at
      Hildenborough Hall in Kent.]

1971 **MacCauley, Sister Rose Agnes**   Vision 20/20;
Twenty Psalms for the Twentieth Century [Interpreted
by] Sister Rose Agnes MacCauley, S.C.   Notre Dame,
Ind.: Fides Publishers, 1971.

1971 **Newman, Marjorie**   Psalm 139. <u>Decision</u>, Nov., 1971.
[M. Newman is from Southampton. This work was done at
the British School of Christian Writing held at
Hildenborough Hall in Kent.]

1971 **Woodfield, Arthur J.**   Psalm 12. <u>Decision</u>, Nov.,
1971.

1971 **Yule, Robert T.**   Psalm 51. Translated by Robert T.
Yule. Edinburgh: June, 1971. <u>Decision</u>, Nov., 1971.

1972 **Anonymous**   Concordant Literal Old Testament...
Psalms...
[See Old Testament Selections, 1957 Anonymous,
Concordant Literal Old Testament.]

1972 **Seerveld, Calvin G.**   Psalm 5, Translated by Calvin
Seerveld. <u>Perspective Newsletter</u>, Vol. 16, No. 3,
May, 1972.
[Published by the Association for the Advancement of
Christian Scholarship.]

[The Deity is rendered "Yahweh".]

1973 **Anonymous**   Psalm Praise...
[See Bible Selections for the complete entry. Includes
some Psalms.]

1973 **Baker Joshua**   The Commentary of Rabbi David Kimchi
on Psalms CXX-Cl. Edited and Translated by Joshua
Baker. New York: Cambridge University Press, 1973.

1973 **Frost, David L. and A.A. MacIntosh**
Twenty-five Psalms from a modern liturgical Psalter.
Translations by D.L.Frost and A.A.MacIntosh.
London: Church Information Office, 1973.

1973 **Taylor, Charles L.**   Layman's Guide to Seventy
Psalms. Nashville: 1973.

1974 **Campbell, A.P.**   The Tiberius Psalter
edited by British Museum MS Cotton Tiberius C vi by
A.P.Campbell. Ottawa: University of Ottawa Press,
1974.
[Interlinear Latin/Anglo-Saxon.]

1975 **Morris, Henry M.**   139th Psalm. <u>Acts and Facts</u>,
Vol. 4, No. 10, page iii, December, 1975.

1976 **Rosenberg, David**   Blues of the Sky, Interpreted
from the original Hebrew Book Psalms, by David
Rosenberg.   New York: Harper & Row, 1976.
[Selected passages poetically paraphrased]

1982 **Brokamp, Sister Marilyn**   Psalms for Children.
By Sister Marilyn Brokamp.   Cincinnati: St. Anthony
Messenger Press, 1982.
["New – a refreshing collection of 25 Old Testament
Psalms skillfully put into a child's own language."]

1983 **Allen, Leslie C.**   Word Biblical Commentary.
Psalms 101–150. Leslie C. Allen.   Waco, TX: Word
Books, Publisher, 1983.
[See Complete Bibles, 1982 Word Biblical Commentary,
Vol. 21.]

1983 **Craigie, Peter C.**   Word Biblical Commentary.
Psalms 1–50. Peter C. Craigie.   Waco, TX: Word
Books, Publisher, 1983.
[See Complete Bibles, 1982 Word Biblical Commentary,
Vol. 19.]

1983 **Sullivan, Francis Patrick**   Lyric Psalms: Half
a Psalter. Frances Patrick Sullivan.   Washington,
D.C.: The Pastoral Press, 1983.

1985 **Craghan, John F.**   The Psalms; Prayers for the
Ups, Downs and In–Betweens of Life. A Literary-
Experiential Approach. John F. Craghan.   Wilmington,
Delaware: Michael Glazier, Inc., 1985.

1987 **Sullivan, Francis Patrick**   Tragic Psalms.
Washington, D.C.: The Pastoral Press, 1987.

1988 **Kraus, Hans–Joachim**   Psalms 1–59. Minneapolis:
Augsburg Publishing House, 1988.

1988 **Oswald, Hilton C.**   Psalm 1–59; A Commentary.
Hans–Joachim Kraus. Translated by Hilton C. Oswald.
Minneapolis: Augsburg Publishing House, 1988.
["For each Psalm the Reader will find: bibliography,
fresh translation of the Hebrew text..."]

PROVERBS

???? **Judaica Press Publications**   The Judaica Books
of the Prophets... (The Book of Proverbs)...
[See Old Testament Selections for the complete entry.]

???? **Kelly, William**   The Proverbs, with a New
     Translation. By William Kelly. [19??].
     [Printed in The Bible Treasury, Kelly's magazine.]

     Reprint edition; Denver, Co: Wilson Foundation,
     1971

???? **Scott, Rachel**   Who can find a virtuous woman?
     Proverbs 31. n.p.: n.p., n.d.
     [From a clipping; source is unknown.]

???? **Sterneholde, Thomas**   Certayne Chapters of
     the Proverbes of Salomon, Drawn into Metre by Thop.
     Sterneholde. John Cafe, n.d.

???? **Youngblood, Ronald F.**   Word Biblical Commentary.
     Proverbs. Ronald F. Youngblood. Waco, Tx: Word
     Books, Publishers, [198?].
     [See Complete Bibles, 1982 Word Biblical Commentary,
     Vol. 22.]

900 **Anonymous**   The Proverbs, c900.
     [A fragmentary Kentish Gloss. Anglo-Saxon.]

1300 **Anonymous**   be Prouerbis of Salamon. MS. Cambridge
     Gg.I.32, f.3b   1300?

1534 **Anonymous**   Pverbes of Solomon, newly translated
     into Englyshe. [George Joye?]   [London: Thomas
     Godfray, 1534?]
     [The only known copy, belonging to A.J.P.Howard, Sussex,
     is bound with Ecclesiastes. Pollard dates 1532; Herbert,
     1534.]

1539 **Taverner, Richard**   Prouerbes or adagies with
     newe addicions, gathered out of the Chiliades of
     Erasmus, by Richard Taverner. 1539.

1550 **Anonymous**   Certayne Chapters of the Prouerbes of
     Salomon drawen into metre...
     [See Bible Selections for the complete entry. Includes
     chapters i-xi.]

1580 **Anonymous**   A Godly and learned Exposition vpon the
     Prouerbes of Solomon: Written in French by Maister
     Michael Cope, Minister of the Woorde of God, at
     Geneua: And translated into English, by "M.O."
     [Marcelline Outred]   Imprinted at London by Thomas
     Dawson for George Bishop, 1580.

1589 **Anonymous**   A short yet sound commentarie; on
     the prouerbes of Salomon. [Thomas Wilcox] London: T.
     Orwin for T. Man, 1589.
          Another edition; London: widow of Orwin, 1597

1592 **Anonymous**   A Commentarie vpon the Booke of the
Proverbes of Salomon. Published for the edification
of the Church of God... [Peter Muffet] At London:
Printed by Richard Field for Robert Dexter, 1592.
["I have translated the text as faithfully as I could,
looking into the translations of the best writers both
old and nevve, but especially into the Hebrue copie..."
The Epistle Dedicatorie is signed P.M.]

Another edition; The second time perused, much
enlarged, and newly published for the
aedification of the Church of God. Wherevnto
is Newly Added an Exposition of the fewe
Choise and excellent Proverbs scatteringly set
downe here and there in the scriptures. At
London: Printed by Robert Robinson for Robert
Dexter, 1596.

1606 **Dod, Iohn and Robert Cleaver**   A Plaine and Familiar
Exposition of the...Prouerbes of Salomon. London:
various printers for Thomas Man et al, 1606-1615.
        1614 --First and Second Chapters

        1606 --Ninth and Tenth Chapters   Revised,
        1608, 1612.

        1607 --Eleuenth and Twelfth Chapters

        1608 --Thirteenth and Fourteenth Chapters
        Revised, 1609.

        1609 --Fifteenth, Sixteenth and Seuenteenth
        Chapters

        1610 --Eighteenth, Nineteenth and Twentieth
        Chapters
                Revised, 1611.

        1614 Bathshebaes Instructions to her Sonne
            Lemuel: Containing a Fruitfull and Plaine
            Exposition of the last chapter of the
            Prouverbes... Penned by a godly and
            learned man, now with God, Perused and
            published for the vse of God's Church.

        1615 A Plaine and Familiar Exposition of the
            whole Booke of Prouerbs of Salomon.
            Robert Cleaver. Imprinted by Flex
            Kyngston for Thomas Man and Roger
            Iackson.

1607 **Hinde, William** ...The Prouerbes of Salomon, 1607.

1609 **Hall, Joseph**   Salomon's Divine Arts...

[See Wisdom and Poetical books and Selections for the complete entry.]

1621 **Granger, Thomas**   A Familiar Exposition or Commentarie on Ecclesiastes. Werein the world's vanity, and the true felicitie are plainely deciphered. London: Printed by T.S. for Thomas Pauier, 1621.

1638 **Iermin, Michael**   Paraphrasticall Meditations, by Way of Commentarie, upon the Whole Booke of the Proverbs of Solomon. Written by Michael Iermin. London: R. Badger for Philemon Stephenson & Christopyer Meredith, 1638.

1655 **Cotton, John**   A Brief Exposition With Practical Observations Upon the whole Book of Canticles. Never before Printed. By that late Pious and Worthy Divine Mr. John Cotton Pastor of Boston in New England. Published by Anthony Tuckney D.D. Master of Saint Johns Colledge in Cambridge. London: Printed by T.R. & E.M., for Ralph Smith, 1655.
    ["A distinct treatise (from that of 1642) differing in arrangement, and containing nearly twice as much as the former."]

1655 **Taylor, Francis**   An Exposition with Practicall Observations upon [certain] chapters of the Proverbs: Grammaticall and Theologicall, as they were delivered in several expository lectures at Christ-Church in Canterbury, by Francis Taylor. London: E.C., for Henry Snowden, 1655-1657.
    1655 - - The first three chapters...
    1657 - - The 4, 5, 6, 7, 9 chapters...

1666 **Anonymous**   Solomon's Proverbs, alphabetically collected out of his Proverbs and Ecclesiastes, for help of Memory. With an additional Collection of other Scripture-Proverbs out of the Old and New Testaments. By H.D. [Henry Danvers] London: 1666.
    Another edition with Latin text. London: J.R. for William Redmayne, 1676.

    Other editions, 1689, 1699, 1704.

    Another edition; Solomon's Proverbs English and Latin, alphabetically collected for help of Memory. In English by H.D. And since made Latin by S. Perkins, late School-master of Christs-Church Hospital. Fitted for the use of Schools. Very much corrected and amended... London: for George Motlock, 1714. Another edition, edited by P. Selby, 1728.

1683 **Hammond, Henry**   A Paraphrase and Annotations
upon the books of the Psalms...
    [See Wisdom and Poetical books and Selections for the
    complete entry.]

1706 **Anonymous**   Select Moral Books of the O.T...
    [See Wisdom and Poetical books and Selections for the
    complete entry.]

1722 **Dykes, [Oswald]**   The Royal Marriage. King Lemvel's
Lesson of 1. Chastity, 2. Temperance, 3. Charity, 4.
Justice, 5. Education, 6. Industry, 7. Frugality, 9.
Marriage, &c. Practically Paraphras'd with Remarks,
Moral and Religious, upon the Virtues and Vices of
Wedlock. London: for the author sold by P. Meighan,
1722.
    [The Book of Proverbs, paraphrased.]

1723 **Anonymous**   The Proverbs of Solomon,
Newly Translated out of the Original Tongues, Very
Necessary for the Use of Young Children. Edinburgh:
The Widow and Assign of James Watson, 1723.
    Another edition; Glasgow: Printed by John and
    James Robertson, 1774.

    Another Edition; The Proverbs of Solomon, Newly
    Translated out of the Original Tongue, Very
    Necessary for the Use of Young Children.
    Edinburgh: Doig & Stirling, 1816.

1736 **Leake, J.**   See Anonymous, The Counsels of Wisdom,
1680.

1738 **Tans'ur, William**   Heaven on Earth...I. The Whole
Book of Proverbs of King Solomon...II. The Song of
Songs...
    [See Wisdom and Poetical books and Selections for the
    complete entry.]

1753 **Anonymous**   The Wisdom of Solomon; Paraphrased
in Verse. <u>Gentleman's Magazine</u>, Vol.XXIII, Page 92,
1753.

1754 **Anonymous**   The Proverbs of Solomon, Son of David,
King of Israel. Dublin: G.A. Grierson, 1754.

1761 **Fawkes, T.**   David's Lamentations over Saul,
Ecclesiastes 12:1-7; Proverbs 31...
    [See Old Testament Selections for the complete entry.]

1775 **Hunt, Thomas**   Observations of the Book of Proverbs.
Oxford: 1775.
    [Contains proposed emendations of the text.]

1784 **Anonymous**   The New-England Psalter...

[See Bible Selections for the complete entry.]

1788 **Hodgson, Bernard**   The Proverbs of Solomon,
Translated from the Hebrew by Bernard Hodgson.
Oxford: Printed at the Clarendon Presss [sic], 1788.

1791 **Dimock, Henry**   Notes, Critical... Psalms...
[See Wisdom and Poetical Books and Selections for the
complete entry.]

1799 **Anonymous**   Solomon's Ethics, or the Book of
Proverbs made easy; a school book,... Air: J. & P.
Wilson, 1799.
[The text is based on the KJV, but is greatly expanded.]

1799 **Dalrymple, William**   Solomon's Ethics, or, the Book
of Proverbs made easy; a school book and seasonable
Present for the Youth of both Sexes, from such as
can spare. Air: J. & P. Wilson, 1799.
[The Text is the KJV with an explanatory paraphrase
inserted in italics.]

1803 **Good, John Mason**   The Book of Proverbs. [Not
published; locatio of MS unknown] 1803?
[Mentioned by Herbert under Song of Songs, 1803.]

1815 **Connellan, Thaddeus**   ...The Proverbs of Solomon, in
Irish and English. Dublin: Graisberry & Campbell,
1815.

1819 **Caldecott, C.**   Sared Ethica; or, The Proverbs
of Solomon, in Verse, with a short life of Solomon
prefixed. By C. Caldecott. London: the author, 1819.
Another edition; Horae Sacrae, Divine Ethics; or,
The Proverbs of Solomon, in verse. By C.
Caldecott.   Blackfriars: T.   Harvey,   n.d.
(1830?)

1831 **French, William and George Skinner**
A new Translation of the Proverbs of Solomon from
the original Hebrew with explanatory notes by
William French... and George Skinner... Cambridge:
Printed by J. Smith; London: John Murray, 1831.

1835 **Brown, Thomas**   Brown's Edition of the Proverbs
of Solomon; or, Wisdom Revived, Wherein the Sounds,
Accents, and Suspensions are Carefully Marked,
Exercises Affixed to Each Chapter... Published by
Thomas Brown. Edinburgh: Oliver & Boyd, 1835.

1839 **Newman, William**   The Proverbs of Solomon:
an Improved Version by ...William Newman. Edited by
George Pritchard. London: George Wightman, 1839.
Another edition, 1872.

1840 **Anonymous**   The Book of Parables, Commonly Entitled
the Book of Proverbs, Paraphrased in Metre, from the
Original, Compared with Many Versions in Different
Languages, by the Author of the British Psalter.
[Robert Boswell] Pinang: Mission Press, 1840.

1845 **Tregelles, Samuel Prideaux** Hebrew Reading Lessons..
[See Old Testament Selections for the complete
entry. Also includes Proverbs XXIII.19-26.]

1846 **Noyes, George R.**   A New Translation of the Book of
Psalms, the Proverbs, Ecclesiastes...
[See Wisdom and Poetical books and Selections, 1827
George R. Noyes, A New Translation of [the Poetical O.T.
Books]...]

1850 **Cobbold, Richard** A Father's Legacy to his Children:
the Proverbs of Solomon in prose and verse. By
Richard Cobbold. London: W.E. Painter, 1850.

1852 **Stuart, Moses** A Commentary on the Book of Proverbs,
by Moses Stuart. New York: M.W. Dodd, 1852.
[With a new translation.]

Another edition; - - Edited and revised, by
R.D.C. Robbins. Andover: Warren F. Draper,
189?

1860 **Brooks, J.W.**   A New Arrangement of the Proverbs
of Solomon, Classified According to the Subject of
Each, Together with critical and Explanatory
Remarks, Various Readings, &c, by J.W. Brooks.
London: Seeley, Jackson & Halliday, 1860.
[May be a King James, but included for its altered
arrangement.]

1862 **Day, William**   The House of the forest of Lebanon;
or the Proverbs of Solomon, a poetical commentary.,
1862.

1866 **Muenscher, Joseph**   The Book of Proverbs,
in an Amended Version, with an Introduction and
Explanatory Notes. Gambier, Ohio: Western Episcopal
Office, 1866.
["In the rendering of the text, it has been the aim of
the writer not to depart unnecessarily from our
excellent standard version."]

1871 **Elzas, A.**   The Proverbs of Solomon, translated
from the Hebrew Text, with notes, critical and
explanatory by A. Elzas. Leeds: Charles Goodall,
1871.

1872 **American Bible Union**   The Book of Proverbs:
Part First; The Hebrew Text, King James Version, and
a Revised Version, with introduction and critical

and philological notes. By Thomas J. Conant. Part
Second; The Revised Version, with introduction and
explanatory notes. For the American Bible Union. New
York: Sheldon & Co., 1872.
[London: Trubner & Co. 141 pages]

1872 **Miller, John**   A Commentary on the Proverbs with
a New Translation, and with some of the Original
Expositions Re-examined in a Classified List. New
York: Anson D.F. Randolph & Co., 1872.
[Metrical text and paraphrase in parallel columns. AV
phraseology is retained except where it conflicts with
the author's attempt to give a literal rendering.]

Another edition, 1873.

Also; London: J. Nisbet & Co., 1874.

1874 **Easton, M.G.**   Proverbs of Solomon, 1874.
[See Old Testaments, 1865 Biblical Commentary.]

1874 **Szold, Benjamin** [Imre Binah]   The Proverbs of
Solomon; In Hebrew, English and German, Arranged
According to different Subjects, forming a
Proverbial Companion for every day in the year. By
Benjamin Szold.   Baltimore: Printed by C.W.
Schneidereith, 1874.

1876 **Briscoe, Josiah**   The Book of Proverbs Versified, by
Josiah Briscoe.   London: Houlston & Sons, 1876.
[Reprinted from 'Pearls from the Golden Stream'.]

1877 **Stock, John**   Inspired Ethics; being a Revised
Translation and Topical Arrangement of the Entire
Book of Proverbs, by John Stock.   London: Elliot
Stock; Huddersfield: J. Crossley & Co., 1877.

1895 **Kent, Charles Foster**   The Wise Men of Ancient Israel
and Their Proverbs, by Charles Foster Kent.   New
York, Boston, Chicago: Silver, Burdett & Co., 1895.
["The text or marginal readings of the RV shall be
employed except where this manifestly fails to bring out
the original meaning of the Hebrew text, as revised by
the aid of the LXX and other versions."]

1899 **Toy, Crawford H.**   A Critical and Exegetical
Commentary on The Book of Proverbs by Crawford H.
Toy... Edinburgh: T. & T. Clark, 1899.
[See Complete Bibles, 1895 International Critical
Commentary.]

Reprinted; 1904, 1914, 1948.

1905 **Lund, Emil**   The Book of Proverbs, Translated and
Commented upon, by Emil Lund. Rock Island: Augustana
Book Concern, 1905.

1906 **Anonymous**   The Wisdom of Solomon...
[See Old Testament Selections for the complete entry.]

1909 **Cheston, James**   Kosoms; a Poem from the Proverbs
of Solomon, Son of David, who ruled in Israel;
Translated from the Van Ess edition of the
Septuagint version, and compared with the American
Revised version of the Proverbs of Solomon I - IX;
Arranged by James Cheston. Philadelphia: McCalla &
Co., 1909.

1912 **Gordon, Alexander R.**   The Poets of the O.T...
[See Old Testament Selections for the complete entry.
Includes Proverbs.]

1912 **Myers, Isadore**   ...The Proverbs of Solomon or
The Words of the Wise In Verse, Translated from the
Massoretic Text of the Hebrew Bible...   New York:
Bloch Publishing Co., 1912.
["...I now offer this versified and rhymed translation
made from the original Hebrew Massoretic text, feeling
assured that this novel and appropriated setting will
appeal and commend itself to a large number of the
reading public. I may add that it has been my endeavor
to employ the simplest language and to make the
translation accurate and as literal as possible."]

1913 **Moon, Edgar L.**   New Minted Gold; an Arrangement of
the Book of Proverbs, by Edgar L. Moon. Cincinnati:
Jennings and Graham;   New York: Eaton and Mains,
1913.

1916 **Paterson, T. Whyte**   The Wyse-Sayin's o' Solomon.
The Proverbs Rendered in Scots, by T.Whyte Paterson.
With a Glossary. Paisley: Alexander Gardner, [1916].
[Herbert dates it 1916.]

1917 **Elmslie, W.A.L.**   Studies in Life from Jewish
Proverbs, by W.A.L. Elmslie. London: James Clarke
& Co., [1917].
["In translating the Proverbs the RV has been used as a
basis, but liberty has been exercised in making any
alterations that seemed necessary..."]

1917 **McFadyen, John Edgar**   The Wisdom Books...
[See Wisdom and Poetical Books and Selections, 1916 John
Edgar McFadyen, [The Poetical Books of the O.T.]....]

1918 **Wightman, F.A.**   Golden Words from the Book of
Wisdom; a New Arrangement of the Book of Proverbs,
by F.A. Wightman. Boston: The Gorham Press, 1918.

1925 **Hood, Francis**   The Proverbs of Solomon in Metre,
by Francis Hood. Hebden Bridge, Kershaw & Ashworth,
1925.

1939 **Copp, Zed Hopeful**   The Book of Life...
     [See Bible Selections for the complete entry.]

1941 **Merritt, Alice Haden**   Psalms and Proverbs...
     [See Wisdom and Poetical books and Selections for the
     complete entry.]

1945 **Cohen, Abraham**   The Proverbs. Hebrew Text & English
     Translation with an Introduction and Commentary by
     The Rev. Dr. A. Cohen... London: The Soncino Press,
     1945.
     [See Old Testaments, 1936 Soncino Books of the Bible.]

1949 **Anonymous**   The Proverbs of Solomon, The Son
     of David, King of Israel [A New Conflatation with
     Introduction, Notes, Glossary and Index] [A.D.
     Power] London, NY, Toronto: Longmans, Green & Co.,
     1949.
     ["My chief object in this conflatation...has been to
     adhere as closely as possible to the language of the AV,
     to express the sense of the original as nearly as I
     could in English words, and to make obscure passages
     clear... some of the alternatives are emendations and
     ...others are such free translations, or even
     conjectures, that they are almost unrecognizable."]

1950 **Cox, A.M.**   The Book of Canticles, Translated by
     A.M. Cox. London: 1950.

1955 **Wanefsky, David**   The Hebrew Scriptures...
     [See Wisdom and Poetical books and Selections for the
     complete entry. Includes Proverbs.]

1965 **Scott, R.B.Y.**   Proverbs and Ecclesiastes...
     [See Wisdom and Poetical books and Selections for the
     complete entry.]

1965 **Whybray, R.N.**   Wisdom in Proverbs; The Concept
     of Wisdom in Proverbs 1 - 9 by R.N. Whybray.
     Naperville, Ill.: Alec R. Allenson, Inc., 1965.

1966 **Sperka, Joshua S.**   Proverbs to Live By; Arranged
     by Topics, And the Book of Proverbs in a Modern
     Translation with Resumes Preceeding Each Chapter.
     Translated, Edited, and Compiled by Rabbi Joshua S.
     Sperka. New York: Bloch Publishing Co., 1966.
     ["I have translated this book from the original Hebrew
     with the aid of the most scholarly and traditional
     commentators..."]

1972 **Anonymous**   Wisdom for Modern Man...
     [See Wisdom and Poetical Books and Selections for the
     complete entry.]

ECCLESIASTES

???? **Croke, John**   Thirteen Psalms...Ecclesiastes...
[See Wisdom and Poetical Books and Selections for the
complete entry.]

???? **Maharba, Z.**   See A. Zuckerman, The Treasures of
Ecclesiastes, 1933.

???? **Short, Robert L.**   A Time to be Born - A Time to Die.
The Images and Insights of Ecclesiastes for Today,
by Robert L. Short.   New York: Harper & Row, [197?].

1534 **Anonymous**   Here foloweth the boke of Solomo
called Ecclesiastes (which is to say in Englishe a
precher).   [George Joye?]   Imprynted at London by
Tho. Godfray, 1534.
[The only known copy is bound with Proverbs. See
Anonymous, The Pverbes of Solomon, 1534?]

1535 **Coverdale, Myles**   A paraphrase...with Ecclesiastes,
1535.

1550 **Anonymous**   Certayne Chapters of the Prouerbes...
[See Bible Selections for the complete entry. Includes
three chapters of Ecclesiastes.]

1550 **Anonymous**   Poore Shakerley, His Knowledge of good
and evill, called otherwise Ecclesiastes, by him
turned into meeter. Printed by Robert Crowley for
John Case. 1550.

1573 **Anonymous**   An Exposition of Salomons Booke called
Ecclesiastes or the Preacher [By Martin Luther]
London: Ihon Day, 1573.

1585 **Woodstock, Ihon**   A Godlie and learned Commentarie
vpon the excellent book of Solomon, commonly called
Ecclesiastes, or the Preacher: In the Which
Commentarie are briefely and plainly layde downe the
methode, sense, and vse of that most profitable
sermon, on the which, yet there hath neuer bin set
forth any exposition in the English tong before this
time, in such large and profitable manner. Written
in Latin by Ihon Serranvs, and newly turned into
English by Ihon Woodstock. London: Printed by Ihon
VVindet for Ihon Harrison the younger, 1585.

1586 **Anonymous**   Solomon's Sermon on Mans Chief Felicite;
Called in the Hebrew Koheleth, in Greke and Latin
Ecclesiastes; with a Paraphrase [by T. Pie],
Gathered out of the Lectures of A.C[orranus]
Oxford: Joseph Barnes, 1586.

1590 **Spenser, Edmund**   Ecclesiastes. (Lost) 1590.

1593 **Anonymous**   Ecclesiastes, or the Preacher.
     Solomon's sermon made to the people, teaching euery
     man howe to order his life, as they may come to true
     and euerlasting happines. With a Paraphrase, or
     short exposition thereof, made by Theodore Beza.
     Translated out of Latine into English. Cambridge:
     Printed by Ihon Legatt, 1593?

1597 **Anonymous**   Ecclesiastes, Othervvise Called the
     Preacher...
         [See Wisdom and Poetical books and Selections for the
         complete entry.]

1600 **Broughton, Hugh**   Books of David, Ecclesiastes...
         [See Old Testament Selections for the complete entry.]

1605 **Broughton, Hugh**   A Comment upon Coheleth or
     Ecclesiastes, Framed for the Instruction of Princf
     (sic) Henri our Hope, by Hugh Broughton. Amsterdam?
     London? 1605.
         [Reprinted with Job, Lamentations & Daniel.] London:
         N. Ekins, 1662.

1609 **Hall, Joseph**   Salomon's Divine Arts...Proverbs
     and Ecclesiastes...
         [See Wisdom and Poetical books and Selections for the
         complete entry.]

1628 **Pemble, W.**   Ecclesiastes, with an exposition.
     London: n.p., 1628.

1636 **Sandys, George**   A Paraphrase upon...Divine Poems...
         [See Old Testament Selections for the complete entry.
         Includes Ecclesiastes.]

1639 **Jermin, Michael**   A Commentary upon the Whole
     Booke of Ecclesiastes or the Preacher, Wherein the
     Originall Hebrew Text is Carefully Examined, our
     Owne English Translation and Others are Duely Viewed
     and Compared...by Michael Jermin. London: Ric.
     Hodgkinsonne for John Clark, 1639.

1645 **Quarles, Francis**   Solomon's Recantations, Entituled
     Ecclesiastes, Paraphrased. With a Soliloquie or
     Meditation upon every Chapter. Very seasonable and
     Vsefull for the times... Pous posthumum. Never
     before imprinted. With a Short Relation of his Life
     and Death.   London: Printed by M.F. for Richard
     Royston, 1645.
         [Strong's "Student's Commentary" (1893) and Power's
         "Ecclesiastes" (1952) erroneously attribute this work to
         John Quarles.]

Another edition of the 1645 work; London: L. Hinde, 1739.

1652 **Cotton, John**   A brief exposition upon Ecclesiastes, 1652.

1685 **Patrick, Symon**   A Paraphrase upon the Books of Ecclesiastes and the Song of Solomon. With Arguments to...
[See Wisdom and Poetical books and Selections, 1679 Symon Patrick, The [Poetical Books] Paraphrased.]

1691 **Anonymous**   The Design of Part of the Book of Ecclesiastes; or, the Vnreasonableness of Mens Restless Contentions for the Present Enjoyments, Represented in an English Poem. [William Wollaston] London: Printed for James Knapton, 1691.

1701 **Yeard, F.**   A New Paraphrase upon Ecclesiastes, with an Analysis and Notes. Proving that the Preacher introduces a refined sensualist, to oppugn and invalidate his penitential animadversions and exhorations. By F. Yeard. London: Tho. Bennet, 1701.

1706 **Anonymous**   Select Moral Books of the O.T...
[See Wisdom and Poetical books and Selections for the complete entry. Includes Ecclesiastes.]

1712 **Hill, Abraham**   The Book of Ecclesiastes Paraphrased; a divine Poem by A. Hill. Newcastle Upon Tyne: J. White, 1712.

1760 **Desveaux, A.V.**   A Philosophical and Critical Essay on Ecclesiastes. Wherein the Author's Design is stated; his Doctrine vindicated; his Method explained in an Analytical Paraphrase annexed to a New Version of the Text from the Hebrew; and the Differences between that new Translation and the Received Version accounted for in Philological Observations. London: for G. Hawkins, 1760.

1761 **Fawkes, T.**   David's Lamentations over Saul, Ecclesiastes 12:1-7; Proverbs 31; Nathan's Parable and Song of Deborah...
[See Old Testament Selections for the complete entry.]

1765 **Anonymous**   Choheleth, or Ecclesiastes; Paraphrased in Blank Verse. [J. Dennis Furley]   London: for the Author, for J. Wallis, 1765.
Another edition; London: 1768.

Also; A Paraphrase of the Book of Ecclesiastes: First Published in the year 1768, and entitled "Choheleth, or the Royal Preacher; a poem." With   notes   philological,   critical,   and

explanatory. To which are added, the text of the AV, supplementary notes, corrections and improvements by Nathaniel Higgins.   London: by Whitchurch, for Rivingtons, 1810.
> Other editions, 1821; London: C. & J. Rivington, 1824.

1768 **Anonymous**   Choheleth, or the Royal Preacher, a Poetical Paraphrase of the Book of Ecclesiastes. Most humbly inscribed to the King. [- - Brodick] London: Printed for J. Wallis, 1768.
> [Ascribed to 'Brodick, a Lisbon Merchant' by James Strong.]

> Another edition; Salop: 1824.

1781 **Anonymous**   Ecclesiastes, in three parts. A New Translation, with a paraphrase. To which is added a new translation of other passages of scripture with notes, and reflections on the present fashion of correcting the Hebrew text by conjecture. [Stephen Greenway] Leicester: George Ireland, 1781.
> Another edition; London: 1787.

1790 **Hodgson, Bernard**   Ecclesiastes, a new Translation from the Original Hebrew, by Bernard Hodgson. Oxford: Prince & Cooke; London: Rivington, Elmsly & Faulder, 1790.
> Another edition; London: 1791.

1804 **Henry, Earl of Surrey** Ecclesiastes 1-5 paraphrased in verse. In Harrington's Nugae Antiquae.   London: Thomas Park, 1804.

1810 **Higgins, Nathaniel**   See Anonymous, Choheleth, or Ecclesiastes; Paraphrased in Blank Verse, 1765.

1822 **Holden, George**   An Attempt to Illustrate the Book of Ecclesiastes, by George Holden.   London: F.C. & J. Rivington, 1822.
> [A kind of paraphrase, similar to that in Doddridge's Family Expositor...taking the AV as his basis, from which he has departed only when necessary.]

1832 **Anonymous**   The Biblical Annual; containing a fourfold translation of the Book of Ecclesiastes, or the Preacher; viz. (1) The common English version, (2) A new translation from the original Hebrew, (3) ...from Greek of the Septuagint, (4) ...from the Latin Vulgate. With illustrative notes.   London: Hamilton, Adams & Co., Stockton-on-Tees; W. Robinson, 1832.
> [Preface signed 'T.W.']

1844 **Preston, Theodore**   ...The Hebrew Text
and a Latin Version of the Book of Solomon, called
Ecclesiastes; with original notes, philological and
exegetical, and a translation of the commentary of
Mendelssohn from the Rabbinical Hebrew. Also a newly
arranged English version of Ecclesiastes with
introductory analysis of the sections; to which is
prefixed a preliminary dissertation.   London:
Hamilton Adams Co., 1844.
   Another edition: London: J.W. Parker; Cambridge:
   J. & J.J. Deighton, 1845.

1846 **Noyes, George R.**   A New Translation of The
Proverbs, Ecclesiastes, and the Canticles...
   [See Wisdom and Poetical books and Selections, 1827
   George R. Noyes, A New Translation of [the Poetical O.T.
   Books]...]

1848 **Barham, Francis**   The Bible Revised; a
carefully corrected translation of the Old and New
Testaments...
   [See Old Testament Selections for the complete entry.
   Includes Ecclesiastes.]

1851 **Stuart, Moses**   A Commentary on Ecclesiastes. By
Moses Stuart. New York: George Putnam, 1851.
   Another edition; - - edited and revised by R.D.C.
   Robbins. Andover: Warren F. Draper; Boston:
   Gould & Lincoln;   New York: John Wiley;
   Philadelphia: Smith, English & Co., 1862.

1856 **MacDonald, James M.**   The Book of Ecclesiastes
Explained. New York: 1856.

1856 **Morgan, Aaron Augustus**   ...The Book of Solomon,
called Ecclesiastes: or, the Preacher, Metrically
Paraphrased, and Accompanied with an Analysis of the
Argument. Being a Retranslation of the Original
Hebrew, According to the Interpretation of the
Rabbinic Commentary of Mendelssohn, the Criticisms
of Preston, and Other Annotators. The subject newly
Arranged, with Analytical Headings to the Sections.
London: Thomas Bosworth, 1856.
   [In rhymed couplets.]

1856 **Weiss, Benjamin**   New Translation and exposition
of the book of Ecclesiastes: with critical notes on
the Hebrew text. By Benjamin Weiss. Dundee: 1856.
   Another edition; Edinburgh: William Oliphant &
   Co.; London: Hamilton, Adams & Co., 1858.

1860 **Simon, D.W.**   Commentary on Ecclesiastes, with
other Treatises. By E.W. Hengstenberg... Translated
from the German by D.W. Simon. Edinburgh: T. & T.

Clark; London: Hamilton, Adams; Dublin: John Robertson, 1860.

> Another edition; Philadelphia: Smith, English, and Co.; New York: Sheldon & Co.; Boston: Gould & Lincoln, 1860.

1861 **Ginsburg, Christian D.** Coheleth, Commonly Called the Book of Ecclesiastes: Translated from the Original Hebrew, with a Commentary, Historical and Critical, by Christian D. Ginsburg. London: Longman, Green, Longman, and Roberts, 1861.

> [The translation is entitled, "The Words of Coheleth, Son of David, King of Jerusalem." "...the translation of the important Chaldee Paraphrase, the collation (selections] of the...Syriac Version with the original, and the discovery of the Version from which Coverdale made his translation [are] given in the Appendices."]

1866 **Coleman, John Noble** Ecclesiastes; a new translation, with notes, explanatory, illustrative and critical by Rev. J.N. Coleman... Edinburgh: Printed for private circulation by T. Constable, 1866.

> Second edition; rev. and enlarged. Edinburgh: Andrew Elliot, 1867.

1868 **Cox, Samuel** The Quest of the Chief Good: expository lectures on the Book of Ecclesiastes, with a new translation, by Samuel Cox. London: Arthur Miall, 1868?

> [A Commentary for Laymen.]

> Also; The Book of Ecclesiastes, with a New Translation, by Samuel Cox. London: Hodder & Stoughton, 1890. (Expositor's Bible).

1870 **Anonymous** Metrical Version of Koheleth, by the American Editor. [Taylor Lewis]

> [Bound with Vol. X of Lange's Commentary, 1864]

> Another edition; Ecclesiastes, or, Koheleth. American Edition edited, with Annotations, Dissertations on Leading Ideas. Together with a New Metrical Version and an Introduction Thereto, by Taylor Lewis. Translated by William Wells. New York: Charles Scribner's Sons, 1909. [Bound with Proverbs.]

1873 **Dale, Thomas Pelham** A Commentary on Ecclesiastes, by Thomas Pelham Dale. London, Oxford, Cambridge: Rivington, 1873.

> [The KJV and Dale's translation are printed on facing pages, with the commentary beneath.]

1874 **Lloyd, J.** An Analysis of the Book of Ecclesiastes: with reference to the Hebrew Grammar of Gesenius, and with notes, critical and explanatory. To which is added the Book of Ecclesiastes in Hebrew and English, in parallel columns. London: S. Bagster & Sons, 1874.

1874 **Proby, W.H.B.**   Ecclesiastes for English Readers. The Book called by the Jews Koheleth, newly translated with introduction, analysis, and notes; by Rev. W.H.B. Proby... London: Pardon & Son, for Rivingtons, 1874.

1874 **Tyler, Thomas**   Ecclesiastes, a Contribution to its Interpretation, Containing an Introduction to the Book, and Exegetical Analysis, and a Translation with Notes. By Thomas Tyler. London: Williams & Norgate, 1874.
      New Edition; London: D. Nutt, 1899.

1880 **Kalisch, Marcus Moritz**   Ecclesiastes. 1880.
      [Power mentions this work. No more is known.]

1880 **Malet, Arthur**   Koheleth. Ecclesiastes Arranged in Verse...
      [See Bible Selections, 1883 Arthur Malet, The Books of Job, Ecclesiastes, and Revelation Rendered into English Verse.]

1883 **Wright, Charles Henry Hamilton**   The Book of Koheleh, Commonly Called Ecclesiastes, Considered in Relation to Modern Criticism, and to the Doctrines of Modern Pessimism, with a Critical and Grammatical Commentary and a Revised Translation, by Charles Henry Hamilton Wright. London: Hodder & Stoughton, 1883.
      [The Donnellan Lectures for 1880-1.]

      ["...the ruggedness of the original must occasionally reflect itself in the translation."]

1886 **Garstang, Walter**   My Heart's Fruit-Garden. Wherein are Divers Delectable Adages and similes of the Prince of Doctrinal Ethics: A Translation out of the Ancient Biblical Hebrew, of the Book of Koheleth, else, "Ecclesiastes, or the Preacher". London: Simpkin, Marshall; Liverpool: Edward Howell, 1886.

1890 **Anonymous**   Cohelet, or, the Preacher. Translated from the Hebrew. With a Study on the Age and Character of the Book, by Ernest Renan (Member of the French Academy.). London: Mathieson & Co., 1890.

1890 **Cox, Samuel**   The Book of Ecclesiastes. With
a new translation. By Samuel Cox... New York: A.C.
Armstrong & Son; London: Hodder & Stoughton, 1890.
[See Bible Selections, 1888 The Expositor's Bible.]

1893 **Strong, James**   Student's Commentary; a complete
Hermeneutical Manual on the Book of Ecclesiastes;
consisting of a corrected Hebrew Text, an Ample
Critical Apparatus, a Free but Terse Metrical
Rendering, a Modernized and Metrically Arranged
Translation, an Extended Introduction, a Detailed
Tabular Analysis, the AV Amended, the American
Revised Version, a Closely Literal Metaphrase, a
Copious Logical, Exegetical and Practical
Exposition, and Full Lexical, Grammatical and
Vindicatory Notes; Adapted to Readers, Preachers and
Scholars of Every Stage of Progress and of Every
Denomination, by James Strong. New York: Hunt &
Eaton; Cincinnati: Cranston & Curts, 1893.
[Also includes an exhaustive bibliography of versions
and commentaries.]

1904 **Genung, John Franklin**   Ecclesiastes;
Words of Koheleth, Son of David, King of Jerusalem;
Translated anew, Divided According to Their Logical
Cleavage, and Accompanied with a Study of Their
Literary and Spiritual Values, and a Running
Commentary, by John Franklin Genung. Boston & New
York: Houghton, Miffin & Co.; Cambridge: Riverside
Press, 1904.

1904 **McNeile, A.H.**   An Introduction to Ecclesiastes,
with Notes and Appendices, and a translation... by
A.H. McNeile. Cambridge: University Press, 1904.
[Includes a translation of the text.]

1905 **Haupt, Paul**   The Book of Ecclesiastes;
A new metrical Translation with an introduction and
explanatory notes by Paul Haupt... Baltimore: The
Johns Hopkins Press, 1905.
[Reprinted from the American Journal of Philology, No.
102. "The arrangement of the text is practically that
which I made in 1890, a specimen of which was published
in the Johns Hopkins University Circulars for June,
1891, and reprinted in the Oriental Studies (Boston;
Ginn & Co., 1894.)"]

1906 **Anonymous**   The Wisdom of Solomon. Being a
transcript in verse of passages from the Books of
Proverbs, Ecclesiastes, and Wisdom...
[See Old Testament Selections for the complete entry.]

1906 **Forbush, William Byron**   Ecclesiastes in the Metre
of Omar. With an Introductory Essay on Ecclesiastes
and the Rubaiyat, by William Byron Forbush. London:
A. Constable & Co., 1906.

Another edition; Boston & New York: Houghton, Mifflin & Co.; Cambridge: The Riverside Press, 1906.

1908 **Barton, George Aaron**   A Critical and Exegetical Commentary on the Book of Ecclesiastes, by George Aaron Barton... Edinburgh: T. & T. Clark, 1908.
[See International Critical Commentary (Ecc.), 1895.]

1909 **Wells, William**   See Anonymous, Metrical Version of the Koheleth, 1870.

1912 **Roe, George**   Kokeleth; a Metrical Paraphrase of the Canonical Book of Ecclesiastes...with an Introduction and Many Notes Comparing the Philosophy of Koheleth, the Hebrew with that of Omar Khayyam, the Astronomer-poet of Persia. By George Roe. New York: Dodge Publishing Co., 1912.

1915 **Scott, David Russell**   Pessimism and Love in Ecclesiastes and the Song of Songs, with Translations...
[See Wisdom and Poetical books and Selections for the complete entry.]

1916 **Harrison, Louis**   Ecclesiastes or Coheleth, in Metrical Form, Translated Direct from the Hebrew, by Louis Harrison. New York: Hebrew-American Press, 1916.
[The text is presented in Hebrew and English.]

1917 **Gottheil, Gustav**   Ecclesiastes, 1917.
[See Old Testaments, 1917 Jewish Publication Society.]

1917 **McFadyen, John Edgar**   The Wisdom Books (Job, Proverbs, Ecclesiastes)...
[See Wisdom and Poetical books and Selections, 1916 John Edgar McFadyen, [The Poetical Books of the O.T.]...]

1919 **Jastrow, Morris, Jr**.   A Gentle Cynic; Being a Translation of the Book of Koheleth. Commonly Known as Ecclesiastes, Stripped of Later Additions; Also, its Origin, Growth and Interpretation, by Morris Jastrow, Jr.... Philadelphia & London: J.B. Lippincott Company, 1919.
["I have felt entirely free to choose my own wording, with no sense of being bound by the "authorized" version, which as a classic of English literature will, of course, always retain its place, but which, as a translation of a text better understood after a lapse of three hundred years, can be improved upon almost every page."]

Orile Editions; New York: 1972.

1922 **Burkitt, Francis Crawford**   Ecclesiastes rendered into English Verse, by F. Crawford Burkitt. London: S.P.C.K. (Society for Promoting Christian Knowledge); New York & Toronto: The Macmillan Co., 1922.
> Also; New York, Toronto: Macmillan, 1922.

1924 **Aaronson, Lionel E.Z.**   Qoheleth, the Record of the Lectures Given by the Son of David, who was King of Jerusalem. A New and Original Translation and Paraphrase of the Book of Ecclesiastes, by Lionel E.Z.Aaronson. Berlin: Trowitzsch & Son, 1924.
> [With Hebrew]

1929 **Martin, William Wallace**   The Book of Job, in Two Versions: A Judean Version, an Ephramean Version; and the Book of Ecclesiastes. Recontrructive Studies. Separated, arranged, and translated...
> [See Wisdom and Poetical books and Selections for the complete entry.]

1933 **Zuckerman, A.**   The Treasure of Ecclesiastes Reopened... A Guide to Modern Life by A. Zuckerman. n.p.: n.p., 1933.
> [Based on the Hebrew, this translation "...aims to make the book more helpful in modern life by rearrangement of the text and the new translation of certain key words as a result of much study of the Hebrew Text."]
>
> [U.S. Library of Congress copy appears identical to that attributed to "A. Zuckerman" except that the KJV has been added at the end, and the date "1933" has been altered by pen to "1938" and the name "Z. Maharba" has been annotated "pseudonym" (presumably for "A. Zuckerman") by what authority is not known.]

> Another edition; Z. Maharba, n.d.

1944 **Brooks, J. Barlow**   Ecclesiastes in Lancaster Dialect, by J. Barlow Brooks. Headington: the Author, 1944.

1945 **Gordis, Robert**   The Wisdom of Ecclesiastes. New York: Behrman, 1945.
> ["In this book, a new interpretation of Eccl. is presented, together with a fresh translation of the original text into the idiom of our day."]

> Other editions; London: Horowitz Publishing Co., 1950; New York: Published for the Jewish Theological Seminary, 1951; New York: Block Pub. Co., 1955.

1946 **Edman, Irwin**   Ecclesiastes, with an Essay by Irwin Edman. New York: Odyssey Press, 1946.

1946 Reichert, Victor E. and A. Cohen   Ecclesiastes...
[See Old Testaments, 1936 Soncino Books of the Bible.]

1949 Ma Than E   Ecclesiastes, 1949.
[See Complete Bibles, 1933 Charles K. Ogden, Basic Bible.]

1950 Gordis, Robert   The Wisdom of Koheleth; A New Translation with a Commentary and an Introductory Essay. London: East & West Library, 1950.
["...this volume is based on an essay which appeared in the Menorah Journal in 1943, which was subsequently expounded into a volume entitled, "The Wisdom of Ecclesiastes" (NY, 1945). The present book however, is different from both earlier versions... a score of changes in the translation and the Introductory Commentary..."]

Another edition; Koheleth - the Man and His World. New York: Published for the Jewish Theological Seminary of America [by Maurice Jacobs, Inc.] "Texts & Studies of the Jewish Theological Seminary of America, Vol. XIX, 1951.

Also; Second Augmented edition, 1955.

In addition; 3rd Augmented edition. New York: Schocken Books, 1968.

1952 Power, A.D.   Ecclesiastes; or, the Preacher. A New Translation, with Introduction, Notes, Glossary and Index, by A.D. Power.   London, New York, Toronto: Longmans, Green and Co., 1952.

1959 Weitzner, Emil   Humanist Meditations and Paraphrases...
[See Old Testament Selections for the complete entry.]

1963 Eickhorn, David Max   Musings of the Old Professor; the Meaning of Koheles; A New Translation of and Commentary on the Book of Ecclesiastes. New York: Jonathan David, 1963.
["...a free, but accurate translation..."]

1965 Scott, R.B.Y.   Proverbs and Ecclesiastes. Introduction, Translation...
[See Wisdom and Poetical books and Selections for the complete entry.]

1972 Anonymous   Wisdom for Modern Man. Proverbs and Ecclesiastes...
[See Wisdom and Poetical books and Selections for the complete entry.]

1972 **Sperka, Joshua S.**   Ecclesiastes. Stories to live
     by; A modern translation with a story illustrating
     each verse. Translation, Edited and Compiled by
     Rabbi Joshua S. Sperka... New York City: Bloch
     Publishing Co., 1972.

1976 **Zlotowitz, Meir**   Ecclesiastes, 1976.
     [See Old Testaments, 1976 ArtScroll Tanach Series.]

1978 **Levine, E.**   The Aramaic Version of Qohelet.
     New York, 1978.
          [Text and translation.]

SONG OF SOLOMON

???? **Anonymous**   The Song of Songs which is Solomon's;
     Decorations by Aldren Watson for the Peter Pauper
     Press, Mount Vernon, New York, [19??].

???? **Bush, Frederic W.**   Word Biblical Commentary...
          [See Old Testament Selections for the complete entry.]

???? **Clarke, Adam**   The Book of Canticles, a literal
     transcription from a Fourteenth Century (circa 1360)
     MS, anonymous, (attributed mainly to Wycliff) mainly
     from the Vulgate.
          [The Targum of Chaldee Paraphrase on the Song of Songs.
          Both of these appear in Clarke's Commentary, Vol.III,
          The Methodist Book Concern, New York, undated but
          current reprints available. So far as is known these
          have appeared since his commentary was first published
          in 8 Vols., for J. Butterworth in London, 1825. Adam
          Clarke, also, did a translation of the entire Bible
          prefatory to his commentary, but his translation was
          never published. He also expressed a considerable
          distaste for all paraphrased portions of scripture,
          calling them by unkind names.]

???? **Clarke, Arthur G.**   The Song of Songs, by Arthur G.
     Clarke. Kansas City, Kansas: Walterich, [197?].
          [Contains his own Paraphrase (Translation).]

???? **Darby, John Nelson**   The Song of Songs, a New
     Translation from the Hebrew Original, by J.N. Darby.
     London: G. Morrish, n.d.
          [Partly corrected by Wm. Kelly.]

1540 **Clifford, Henry**   Poetical translation...the Song...
          [See Old Testament Selections for the complete entry.]

1549 **Baldwin, William**   The Canticles or Balades of
     Salomon, phraselyke declared in Englysh metres, by

William Baldwin. [London: William Baldwin, servaunt with Edwarde Whitchurche], 1549.
[With a prose version.]

1575 **Smith, Jud**   A Misticall Deuise of the Spirituall and Godly Love Betwene Christ the Spouse and the Church or Congregation. Firste Made by the Wise Prince Salomon, and now Newly set Forth in Verse by Jud Smith. Whereunto is annexed certeine other briefe stories. And also a Treatise on Prodigalitie [1st ed, 1573], most fit and necessarie for to read and marked od all estates. Imprinted at London: by Henry Kirkham, 1575.
[Paraphrase of a portion of the Song of Solomon; to which is added 'A Coppie of the Epistle of Jeremye sent unto the Jewes, which were led away Prisoners by the King of Babilon, wherein he certifyeth them of the thinges which was commaunded him of God.' being a paraphrase of the 6th chapter of Baruch. Also 'The Commaundements of God our Creator, geuen by Moyses, Exod. XX.'; 'The commaundements of Sathan, put in practice dayly by the Pope.' and 'This is also that which God speaketh by his holy Prophet Zacharias II.']

1578 **Harmer, John**   The First Three Chapters of the Canticles. Oxford: Joseph Barnes, 1587.

1583 **Andreas, Bartineus**   Solomon's Song, Chapter V Sermons on it. Robert Waldegrave, 1583.

1585 **Anonymous**   An Exposition vppon the Booke of the Canticles, otherwise called Schelomons Song. Published... by T.W. [Thomas Wilcox. With the text.] London: [Robert Waldegrave] for Thomas Man, 1585.

1586 **Fletcher, Robert**   Solomon's Song; Translated into English Verse, with Annotations, by Robert Fletcher. London: T. Chard, 1586.

1587 **Anonymous**   The Song of Songs, that is, the most excellent song which was Solomons, translated out of the Hebrue into Englishe meeter, with as little libertie in departing from the wordes, as any plaine translation in prose can vse: and interpreted by a short commentarie. [Dudley Fenner]   Middelbvrgh: Imprinted by Richard Schilders, 1587.
Another edition; Middelbvrgh: 1594.

1590 **Spenser, Edmund**   Canticles. (Lost) 1590.
["Among the several other Papers that have been lost of the Excellent and Divine Edmund Spenser... I bewail nothing me-thinks so much, as his Version of the Canticles..." From the preface to Woodford's Canticles, 1679. Also mentioned by Farr.]

1591 **Anonymous**   The Harmonie of the Church. Containing
     the Spirituall Songs and Holy Hymns, of Godly Men,
     Patriarkes and Prophetes: All, Sweetly Sounding, to
     the Praise and Glory of the Highest. How (newlie)
     reduced into sundry kinds of English Meeter: Meete
     to be read or sung, for the solace and comfort of
     the Godly. By M.D. [Michael Drayton]   London:
     Richard Jhones, 1591.
         [Includes the Song of Songs.]

         Reprinted; London: T. Richards for the Percy
         Society, 1842.

1596 **Anonymous**   The Poem of Poems. Or, Sions muse
     Contayning the diuine Song of King Salomon, deuided
     into eight Eclogues. [Jervase Markham]   At London:
     Printed by Iames Roberts, for Mathew Lownes, 1596.

1598 **Gyffard, George**   Fifteene Sermons vpon the Song of
     Salomon. Written by George Gyffard. [With the text]
     London: Felix Kingston for Thomas Man, 1598.
         Another Edition; At London: Printed by Ihon
         Windet for Thomas Man, 1600.

         Also; London: W.S. [William Stansby] for George
         Norton, 1612.

1602 **Clapham, Henoch**   The Song of Songs. London: 1602 -
     1606.
             1602 The Song of Songs. the first through
                  third parts expounded. London: V. Sims.

             1603 Three parts of Salomon his Song of Songs
                  expounded. London: V. Sims for E. Mutton.

             1606 The fourth and fifth parts of Salomons
                  Songe of Songs expounded.   London: R.
                  Braddock for N. Butter.

1609 **Hall, Joseph**   Salomon's Divine Arts, of 1.
     Ethickes, 2. Politickes, 3. Oeconomickes; that is
     the Goverment of, 1. Behaviour, 2. Commonwealth, 3.
     Familie, drawne into Method out of his Proverbs and
     Ecclesiastes...
         [See Wisdom and Poetical books and Selections for the
         complete entry.]

1609 **Hall, Ios.**   An Open and Plaine Paraphrase vpon the
     Song of Songs, which is Salomons, by Ios.Hall, 1609.

1613 **Dove, Iohn**   The Conversion of Salomon. A direction
     to holinesse of life; Handled by way of Commentarie
     vpon the whole Booke of Canticles. Profitable for
     young men which are not yet mortified, for old men

which are decrepit, and have one foote in the graue,
and for all sorts of men which haue an intent to
renounce the vanities of this world, and to follow
Iesis Christ.   London: Printed by W. Stansby for
Iohn Smethwick, 1613.

1615 **Beale, J.**   Solomon's Song. London: W. Gouge, 1615.

1615 **Gouge, William**   An Exposition of the Song of
Solomon: Called Canticles. Together with Profitable
Obseruations, Collected Out of the Same. Perused and
Published by William Gouge, Preacher of Gods Word in
Black-Friers, London.   London: Printed by Ihon
Beale, 1615.
> ["Solomon's Song is twice runne ouer in this booke:
> first the sense is deliuered, then obseruations
> collected from thence. In expounding the Text, the
> author hath held himself close to the Hebrewe."]

1621 **Anonymous**   The Song of Songs, Which Was Salomons,
Metaphrased in English Heroiks by way of Dialogue.
With certayne of the Brides ornaments, viz.
Poeticall Essays vpon a Divine Subject. Whereunto is
added a Funerall Elegie, consecrate to the memorie
of that euer honoured Lord, Ihon, late Bishop of
London. By R.A. [Richard Argall] London: Printed by
William Stansby, 1621.
> [Ascribed to R. Azlett by Pollard.]

1621 **Wither, George**   The Hymnes and the Songs of the
Chvrch...
> [See Old Testament Selections for the complete entry.
> Includes the Song Of Solomon.]

1623 **Ainsworth, Henry**   Solomon's Song of Songs.
In English metre: with annotations and references to
other Scriptures, by Henry Ainsworth.   [Amsterdam?]
> [With a prose version slightly altered from that of the
> AV.]

1625 **Quarles, Francis**   Sions Sonets. Sung By Solomon the
King, And Periphras'd. London: Printed by W. Stansby
for Thomas Dewe, 1625.
> ["It is the Song of Songs, I here present you wuth: The
> mysticall, the diuinest subjects: The Speakers, Christ,
> the Bridegroome; the Chvrch, the Bride; the end, to
> invite you all to the wedding. Farewell."]

Reprinted; Cambridge, Mass.: Riverside Press,
1905.

1627 **Ainsworth, Henry**   Pentateuch, Solomon's Song...
> [See Old Testament Selections 1616 for the complete
> entry.]

1637 **Anonymous**   The Loves of the Lord with His Troth-
plight Spouse. Contained in the Song of Songs,
paraphrased with severall soliloquies and particular
petitions upon every division of the said song.
Edinburgh: Robert Young, 1637.
>   [Preface signed: "D.W."   This entry is based upon a
>   bibliography of the Songs by A. Moody Stuart, confirmed
>   by a letter from the Edinburgh University Library.]

1641 **Anonymous**   A Paraphrase upon the Song of Solomon.
By G.S. [George Sandys] London: Printed by Ihon
Legatt, 1641.
>   Another edition; London: for H.S. & W.L., 1642.
>
>   [See Psalms listings, 1636 George Sandys, A Paraphrase
>   upon the Divine Poems.]

1642 **Cotton, John**   A Brief Exposition of the whole
book of Canticles, or, Song of Solomon. London: for
Philip Nevil, 1642.

1644 **Boyd, M. Zachary**   The Garden of Zion...
>   [See Old Testament Selections for the complete entry.
>   Includes Song of Solomon.]

1650 **Anonymous**   The Psalms, Hymns...Spiritual Songs...
>   [See Old Testament Selections for the complete entry.
>   Includes Song of Solomon.]

1653 **Slater, Samuel**   Epithalmium; or, Solomons Song...
>   [See Old Testament Selections for the complete entry.]

1654 **Anonymous**   The Discipline of Gathered Churches,
with the Covenant taken by Each Member; and a
Confession of Faith professed by the Church of
Christ at Martins Vintry; together with the
Spiritual Hymns by Way of Paraphrase upon the Whole
Book of Canticles by them sung at their breaking of
bread. London: for R. Ibbitson, 1654.

1658 **Guild, William**   Solomon's Song. London: W.Wilson,
1658.

1662 **Anonymous**   The Canticles; or, Song of Solomon,
Reduced into a Decasyllable; Together, with the Song
of Moses in Meeter, by R.K.   Printed in the yeare
1662.

1672 **Hildersham, Arthur**   The Canticles, or Song of
Solomon Paraphrased; and Explained by divers other
Texts of Scriptures, very useful. By the Learned,
Reverend, and Faithful Minister of Christ Mr. Arthur
Hildersham, of Ashby-Dela-Zouch. As also the same,
together with the two Songs of Moses, and the song

of Deborah, Collected into meeter. London: Printed by T. Milbourn for Robert Clavel, 1672.

1676 Anonymous   The Book of the Song of Solomon...
[See Old Testament Selections for the complete entry.]

1679 Woodford, Samuel   A Paraphrase upon the Canticles and Some Select Hymns of the New and Old Testaments, with Other Occasional Compositions in English verse, by Samuel Woodford. London: Printed by J.D. for John Baker & Henry Brome, 1679.
["...I have in my Paraphrase left, at least endeavored to leave it, as I found it, and even in those places, where I have taken the greatest Liberty, have not gone far from the literal Sence..." Includes: 'The Legend of Love, the Six Great Hymns of Luke, the Eight great Hymns of the Apocalyps, three Psalms according to the Ordinary Metre', and various Old Testament songs.]

1681 Anonymous   Shir ha - shirm; or, Solomon's Song paraphras'd; a Pindarick Poem [John Lloyd]. London: Printed by H. Hills for Henry Faithorne & John Kersey, 1681.
Another edition; Shir ha Shirim... or the Song of Songs: being a Paraphrase Upon the most Excellent Canticles of Solomon in a Pindarick Poem. By John Lloyd A.M. Vicar of Holy Roods in Southampton, formly of Wadham Oxon; 1682.

1681 Hills, H.   Song of Solomon. London: 1681.

1683 Patrick, Symon   The Proverbs of Solomon Paraphrased, with the Arguments of each Chapter Which Supply the Place...
[See Wisdom and Poetical books and Selections, 1679 Symon Patrick, The [Poetical Books] Paraphrased.]

1684 Reeve, John   Spiritual Hymns upon Solomon's Song; or, Love in the Right Channel. Wherein that Divine Part of Scripture is Paraphras'd, and the dark Places expounded: and may be vocally Sung in the Ordinary Tunes of Singing Psalms. London: Northcott, 1684.
[Title taken from 1693 edition.]

Another edition; London: Printed for the author, and are to be sold by John Hancock, 1693.

1687 Beverley, T.   An Exposition of the divinely prophetic Song of Songs, Which is Solomon's; Composed into Verse, by T. Beverley. London: for the Author, 1687.

1688 Ager, Thomas   A Paraphrase on the Canticles, or, Song of Solomon, by Thomas Ager. London: Printed by A. Godbin & J. Playford; Sold by S. Sprint, 1688.

1691 **Fleming, Robert**   The Mirrour of Divine Love unvail'd, in a Poetical Paraphrase of the High and Mysterious Song of Solomon. Whereunto is added a Miscellany of several other Poems Sacred and Moral, Together with some few Pindariques in the close. 2 Parts   London: Printed by J.A.[Stwood] for John Salusbury, 1691.
> [Includes 'Several (11) Psalms Diversely rendered and on Divers Occasions' and translations of four odes of Pindar.]

1700 **Anonymous**   The Song of Solomon, rendered into English verse, by R.S.   Edinburgh: 1700.

1700 **Stennett, Joseph**   A Version of Solomon's Song; Together with the 45th Psalm in verse, by Joseph Stennett. London: for D.Brown and Andrew Bell, 1700.
> The second edition; Corrected. London: I. Darby, 1709.

1701 **Symson, Andrew**   The Song of Solomon in Meeter, by Andrew Symson.   Edinburgh: James Watson, 1701.

1703 **Anonymous**   The Wise or Foolish choice; or, the Wisdom of Choosing Christ, and the Folly of Choosing the World for our Portion, Discovered and Asserted by Solomon the Wise; in a Paraphrase on the Song of Solomon, and an Abstract of the Book of Solomon called Ecclesiastes... both done in Metre by one of the Ministers of the Gospel in Glasgow, I.C. [James Clark] Edinburgh: 1703.

1707 **Patrick, Symon**   The Books of Job, Psalms, Proverbs, Ecclesiastes, and the Song of Solomon...
> [See Wisdom and Poetical books and Selections, 1679 Symon Patrick, The [Poetical Books] Paraphrased.]

1720 **Anonymous**   The Fair Circassian, a Dramatic Performance. Done from the Original by a Gentleman-Commoner of Oxford. [Samuel Croxall]   London: Printed for J. Watts, 1720.
> [The Song of Songs.]

1720 **Anonymous**   Song of Songs A Divine Pastoral Poem, Written in the first Language by Solomon King of Israel, The inspired Manuensis of the holy Ghost, Justly acknowledged by the Church of God under both Dispensations to be a portion of the Sacred Canon. [Alexander Pennecuik]   Edinburgh: Printed by John Mosman & Co., 1720.
> [Bound with a book of poetry by Pennecuik, published in Edinburgh, 1721.]

1724 **Gell, John**   An Exposition of the Book of Salomon's Song, Commonly called Canticles; Wherein

the Authority of it is Established and Vindicated,
Against Objections both Ancient and Modern, Several
Versions Compared with the Original Text; the
Different Sense, both of Jewish and Christian
Interpreters Considered; and the Whole Opened and
Explained in Proper and Useful Observations. To
which is Added the Targums, or Chaldee Paraphrase
upon the Whole Book, Faithfully Translated Out of
the Original Chaldee by John Gell; Together with
Some Explanatory Notes Upon It. 1724.
[Title taken from the second edition.]

Another Edition, 1728.

Another edition; The Second Edition with
additions. London: Printed for John Ward &
George Keith, 1751.

Another edition; An Exposition of the Book of
Solomon's Song... Wherein the authority of it
is... Vindicated... Several Versions Compared
with the Original Text... and the Whole Opened
and Explained, by John Gill. 3rd. edition.
London: George Keith, 1768.

Also; 4th. edition with many additions, 1776.

1736 **Erskine, Ralph**   A Paraphrase or Large
Explicatory Poem upon the Song of Solomon, Wherein
the mutual love of Christ and His Church Contained
in that Old Testament Song is imitated in the
language of the New Testament, and adapted to the
Gospel- dispensation. By the Reverend Mr. Ralph
Erskine... Edinburgh: Printed by Tho. Lumisden and
Jo. Robertson, for James Beugo..., 1736.
[British Museum Catalogue gives the publisher as
"Dunfermline; James Bengo & Edinburgh: Gideon
Crawford".]

[A. Moody Stuart mentions a Second Edition; 1742.]

Another edition; A New Version of the Song of
Solomon, in Common Metre, Together with A New
Edition of a Paraphrase or Large Expository
Poem upon the Book, Wherein the mutual love of
Christ and His Church contained in that Old
Testament Song is imitated in the language of
the New Testament, and adopted to the Gospel-
dispensation. To which is subjoined The ten
Plagues of Egypt, named and justify'd, The Ten
Commandments abridg'd and versify'd. Glasgow:
John Newlands, 1752.

Also; Paraphrase...A new Edition revised and
corrected... London: Edward Dilly, 1758.

Another edition; Paraphrase...another edition.
Glasgow: Robert Duncan, 1770.

1738 **Tans'ur, William**   Heaven on Earth; or, the
Beauty of Holiness...I. The Whole Book of Proverbs
of King Solomon...II. The Song of Songs...
[See Wisdom and Poetical books and Selections for the
complete entry.]

1739 **Mawer, John**   Proposals for Publishing the Psalms
& Solomon's Song...
[See Wisdom and Poetical books and Selections for the
complete entry.]

1739 **Rowe, Elizabeth**   Paraphrase on the Canticles, by
Elizabeth Rowe. 1739.
[A. Moody Stuart describes as, "The breathings of a
poetic temperament combined with spiritual affections,
but too ardent for our taste." Possibly part of Mrs.
Rowe's 'Miscellaneous Works'.]

1744 **Anonymous**   Solomon a Seranata taken from the
Canticles. Set to Musick by Mr. Boyce, Composer to
his Majesty. [Edward Moore] London: Printed by John
Moore, MDCCXLIV. [1744]

1750 **Bland, John**   A Grammatical Version, from
the original Hebrew; of the Song of Solomon, into
English blank verse. The Persons speaking, and
spoken to, are distinctly described and set forth;
which is impossible every where to be distinguished
in any Version extant, either ancient or modern. The
Whole Being a Drama, in Seven Scenes: Both a Scheme
of the Audience, and Dramatic Personae are prefix'd.
To which is added, A Supplement from the Forty-fifth
Psalm; The Song of Moses from Deut. XXXII. and the
Lamentation of David over Saul and Jonathan, from 2
Sam. Chap. I. likewise Grammatically translated from
the Hebrew, into Blank Verse, with Notes on the
Whole. By J. Bland. London: Printed for,and sold by
J. Wren, 1750.

1751 **Anonymous**   A Dissertation on the Song of Solomon,
with the Original [Hebrew] Text divided according to
the Metre, With a Poetical Version. [Andrew Gifford]
London: A. Millar, 1751.

1751 **Johnson, Charles**   The Song of Solomon Paraphrased
in Lyrick Verse by Charles Johnson. London: for W.
Johnston, 1751.

1754 **Erskine, Ralph**   Scripture Songs... I. Old
Testament Songs: or, Songs upon several passages in
the Old Testament. II. New Testament Songs: or,

Songs... III. Songs upon several Parts of Scripture;
some whereof are in the Old Testament...
[See Bible Selections for the complete entry. Includes
a new version of the Song of Solomon.]

1761 **Anonymous**   The Song of Solomon, in Metre; with
a paraphrase, and some Spirityal Songs &c. 16th.
Edition. London: for C. Hitch &c., 1761.

1764 **Anonymous**   The Song of Solomon, Newly
Translated (in Prose) from the Original Hebrew; with
a Commentary and Annotations. [Thomas Percy] London:
Printed for R. & J. Dodsley, 1764.
     Another Edition; Song of Songs, newly translated
     (in prose) from the original Hebrew, with a
     Commentary and Annotations. Glasgow: 1765.

1765 **Erskine, Ralph**   A Paraphrase of Song of Solomon:
also Scripture Songs... A New Version of the Song of
Solomon...
     [See Bible Selections for the complete entry.]

1767 **Barclay, John**   The Song of Solomon Paraphrased
in a Literal Manner, by John Barclay, 1767.
     [See Bible Selections for the complete entry.]

1772 **Rowe, Elizabeth**   Miscellaneouc Works...
     [See Bible Selections for the complete entry. Includes
     Song of Solomon chapter 5 and 8:6.]

1775 **Anonymous**   The Song of Solomon, Paraphrased: with
an introduction, containing some remarks on a Late
Translation [i.e., Thomas Percy, 1764] of this
sacred poem, also a commentary and notes, critical
and practical.   Edinburgh: for Drummond, 1775.

1775 **Bowler, Mrs**.   Song Of Solomon Paraphrased; with an
Introduction, also a Commentary and Notes, Critical
and Practical, 1775.
     [Anonymous?]

1775 **Drummond**   Song of Solomon paraphrased. Edinburgh:
by Drummond, 1775.

1776 **Barclay, John**   Additional Versions of Several
Psalms and a Paraphrase of Solomon's Song...
     [See Wisdom and Poetical books and Selections for the
     complete entry.]

1781 **Francis, Ann**   A Poetical Translation of
the Song of Solomon, from the Original Hebrew; with
a Preliminary Discourse and Notes, Historical,
Critical, and Explanatory by Anne Francis. London:
J. Dodsley, 1781.

["The translatress has chiefly followed the plan and illustrations of Mr. Harmer. Her version is elegantly executed."]

1786 **Hodgson, Bernard**   Solomon's Song Translated from the Hebrew by Bernard Hodgson. Oxford: Clarendon Press, 1786.
[In this work, the literary meaning only is illustrated, there being not the slightest allusion to its mystical meaning... Horne dates it as 1785.]

1795 **Doederlein, J.C.**   The Song of Solomon; a Literal Version of a Dutch Translation, by J.C. Doederlein, 1795.

1801 **Williams, Thomas**   The Song of Songs, which is by Solomon. A New Translation: with a commentary and notes, by T. Williams. London: Printed by C. Whittingham, for T. Williams, 1801.
[A very literal translation, based upon the AV.]

Another edition; Philadelphia: William W. Woodward, 1803.

1803 **Good, John Mason**   Song of Songs; or, Sacred Idyls, translated from the original Hebrew, with notes, critical and explanatory. By John Mason Good. London: For G. Kearsley by Wilks and Taylor, 1803.
[Includes two versions; one in prose, the other in couplet verse,]

1811 **Fry, C.**   Canticles... London: Haychard, 1811.

1811 **Fry, John**   Canticles; or Song of Solomon: a New Translation, with Notes: An Attempt to Interpret the Sacred Allegories Contained in the Book. To Which is Added an Essay on the Name and Character of the Redeemer, by Rev. John Fry. London: J. Hatchard, 1811.
Second edition; London: J. Duncan, 1825.

1817 **Davidson, William**   A Brief Outline of an Examination of the Song of Solomon in which Many Beautiful Prophecies Contained in that Inspired Book of Holy Scripture are Considered and Explained; with Remarks, Critical and Expository. London: for the author, 1817.
["...at the end of his volume he has divided the text in a poetic translation into hemistiches according to Dr. Kennicott's mode of Printing the poetical parts of the O.T.]

1818 **Miller, Thomas**   The Song of Solomon... in Eight Parts. Fitted to be Sung with Tunes on Common Measure. Edinburgh: Thomas Turnbull, 1818.

1820 **Perrin, W.**   Hebrew Canticles, or, a
Poetical Commentary, or paraphrase, on Various Songs
of Scripture...
      [See Old Testament Selections for the complete entry.]

1820 **Taylor, C.**   The Holy Minstrel, being the Song of
Solomon...
      [See Old Testament Selections for the complete entry.]

1824 **Anonymous**   Song of Songs; or, Sweet Effects of
Union and Communion between Christ and His Church.
Hailsham: Breads, 1824.
      [A metrical version]

1838 **Taylor, Charles**   Fragments of Calmet [Canticles]
1838.
      [A. Moody Stuart's Song of Songs', 1857, extols this
      "...translation and arrangement of the Song of Songs..."
      Calmet apparently refers to Augustin Calmet, an 18th
      Century French commentator.]

1839 **Anonymous**   Solomon's Song of Songs; a
new translation. [Wm. Newman] London: Ball and Co.,
1839.

1841 **Irons, Joseph**   Nymphas. Bride and Bridegroom
communing. A paraphrastic exposition of the Song of
Solomon, in blank verse. London: the Author, 1841.
      Second edition, 1844.

1888 **Sawyer, Leicester Ambrose**   (The Bible) Analyzed...
Esther and the Song of Songs [copyright 1844]...
      [See Bible Selections, ???? Leicester Ambrose Sawyer
      (The Bible) Analyzed.]

1845 **Anonymous**   A Metrical Version of the Song
of Solomon, and other poems (Miscellaneous poems:
consisting chiefly of Paraphrases of some of the
Psalms...
      [See Wisdom and Poetical books and Selections for the
      complete entry.]

1846 **Noyes, George R.** A New Translation of The Proverbs,
Ecclesiastes, and the Canticles...
      [See Wisdom and Poetical books and Selections, 1827
      George R. Noyes, A New Translation of [the Poetical O.T.
      Books]...]

1848 **Anonymous**   The "Song of Songs," Spiritually
contemplated as a sacred dialogue between Christ and
His Church, and briefly rendered into verse. To
which is added, the Stronghold of Bigotry; a poetic
version. London: Partridge & Oakely, 1848.

1848 **Barham, Francis**   The Bible Revised; a
carefully corrected translation of the Old and New
Testaments... Part 2. Song of Solomon.
> [See Old Testament Selections for the complete entry.
> Includes the Song of Solomon.]

1848 **Westwood, John**   A Short Paraphrase of the Song of
Solomon, by John Westwood. London: Simpkin, Marshall
& Co., 1848.

1850 **McClure, Samuel**   The Psalms of David, and Song of
Solomon...
> [See Wisdom and Poetical books and Selections for the
> complete entry.]

1853 **Anonymous**   The Song of Solomon, translated into
English verse. By the Author of "The Book of Psalms
translated   into   English   Verse."   ["A   Layman"]
London: Rivingtons, 1853.
> Revised edition; London: 1858.

1853 **Burrowes, George**   A Commentary on the Song of
Solomon by George Burrowes.   Philadelphia: William
S. Martien, 1853.
> Reprinted; London: The Banner of Truth Trust,
> 1958.

1853 **Clay, Edmund**   The Song of Solomon.   London: J.
Davies, 1853.

1856 **Anonymous**   Metrical Meditations on the
Sacred Book of Canticles. 2d ed. London: Wertheim &
Macintosh, 1856.

1856 **MacPherson, Peter**   The Song of Songs shewn to
be constructed on architectural principles, by Peter
MacPherson, 1856.

1857 **Ginsburg, Christian D.**   The Song of
Songs: Translated from the Original Hebrew, with a
Commentary, Historical and Critical, by Christian D.
Ginsburg.   London: Longman, Brown, Green, Longmans,
and Roberts, 1857.
> Also; The Song of Songs and Coheleth. New York:
> Ktav, 1970.
>> [This is a reprint of the 1857 & 1861 editions.]

1858 **Anonymous**   A metrical translation of the Song of
Solomon, from the original Hebrew, compared with the
ancient versions; to which is added an introduction,
explanatory   of   its   literal   and   spiritual
signification.   London: Rivingtons, 1858.
> [A revised version of "The Song of Solomon, Translated
> into English Verse", published anonymously in 1853.]

1858 **Anonymous**   The Song of Solomon in (various British dialects) from the Authorized English Version. Twenty-six versions by different men.   London: Privately printed for Prince Louis Lucien Bonaparte, 1858-1862.

1858 **Anonymous**   The Book of Canticles, or, Song of Solomon, according to the English version, revised and explained from the original Hebrew. [Frances Rolleston] London: Rivingtons, 1858.
>   Second edition; (Metrical version of the Canticles. To which is added Psalm XLV;) London: 1859.

1858 **Bywater, Abel**   The Song Solomon in the Sheffiel (Yorkshire) dialect; from the authorised English version, by Abel Bywater London: Privately printed for Prince Louis Lucien Bonaparte by George Barclay, 1858.
>   [See Anonymous, Song of Solomon in [various British dialects], 1858.]

1858 **Forster, John George**   The Song of Solomon in the Newcastle dialect; from the authorised English version by J.G. Forster. London: Privately printed for Prince Louis Lucien Bonaparte by George Barclay, [1858].

1858 **Rayson, John**   The Song of Solomon in the Cumberland dialect; from the authorised English version, by John Rayson. London: Privately Printed for Prince Louis Lucien Bonaparte by George Barclay, [1858].

1858 **Richardson, John**   The Song of Solomon in the Westmoreland dialect; from the authorised English version, by the Rev. John Richardson... London: Privately Printed for Prince Louis Lucien Bonaparte by George Barclay, [1858].

1858 **Riddell, Henry Scott**   The Song of Solomon in the Lowland Scotch dialect; from the authorised English version, by Henry S. Riddell. London: Privately Printed for Prince Louis Lucien Bonaparte by George Barclay, 1858.

1858 **Rolleston, Benjamin**   The Book of Canticles; or, Song of Solomon According to the English Version, Revised and Explained from the Original Hebrew, by Benjamin Rolleston. London: Rivingstons, 1858.
>   [Second edition including Psalm XLV was published in 1859.]

1859 **Anonymous**   The Song of Solomon in the living Cornish dialect; from the authorised English

version. London: Privately printed for Prince Louis
Lucien Bonaparte by: George Barclay, 1859.
> [Possibly by Edwin Netherton.]

1859 **Barnes, William**   The Song of Solomon in the Dorset
dialect; from the authorised English version, by
Rev. William Barnes. London: Privately printed for
Prince Louis Lucien Bonaparte by George Barclay,
1859.
> [See Anonymous, Song of solomon in [various British
> dialects], 1858.]

1859 **Dickinson, William**   The Song of Solomon in the
dialect of Central Cumberland; from the authorised
English version, by William Dickenson.   London:
Privately Printed for Prince Louis Lucien Bonaparte
by George Barclay, 1859.
> [See Anonymous, The Song of Solomon in [Various British
> dialects] (Central Cumberland), 1858.]

1859 **Littledale, Henry Anthony**   The Song of Solomon
in the dialect of Craven, in the West Riding of
Yorkshire; from the authorised English version, by
Henry Anthony Littledale. London: Privately printed
for Prince Louis Lucien Bonaparte by: George
Barclay, 1859.
> Revised, 1860.

1859 **Moore, Thomas**   The Song of Solomon in Durham
dialect as spoken at St. John's Chapel, Weardale; by
Thomas Moore. London: Privately printed for Prince
Louis Lucien Bonaparte by: George Barclay, 1859.
> [See Anonymous, The Song of Solomon in [Various British
> dialects] (Durham), 1858.]

1859 **Robson, Joseph Philip**   The Song of Solomon in
the Newcastle dialect; from the authorised English
version, by Joseph P. Robson.   London: Privately
Printed for Prince Louis Lucien Bonaparte by George
Barclay, [1859].

1859 **Staton, James Taylor**   The Song of Solomon in the
Lancashire dialect; as spoken at Bolton; from the
authorised English version, by James Taylor Staton.
London: Privately printed for Prince Louis Lucien
Bonaparte by: George Barclay, 1859.
> Revised, 1860.

> Unauthorized reprint; The Song of Solomon in the
> Lancashire dialect, as spoken at Bolton; from
> the authorised English version; Translated for
> Prince Louis Lucien Bonaparte by James T.
> Staton. Manchester: John Heywood, 1859.

1859 **Weiss, Benjamin**   The Song of Songs Unveiled:
a New Translation and Exposition of the Song of
Solomon by Benjamin Weiss. Edinburgh: William
Oliphant & Co., 1859.

1860 **Anonymous**   The Song of Solomon in the
North Yorkshire dialect; from the authorised English
version, by the author of 'A Glossary of Yorkshire
words and phrases collected in Whitby and the
neighbourhood'.   London: Privately printed for
Prince Louis Lucien Bonaparte by: George Barclay,
1860.

1860 **Anonymous**   The Song of Solomon in the East of
North Riding Yorkshire dialect; from the authorised
English version. [by F.K. Robinson]   London:
Privately printed for Prince Louis Lucien Bonaparte
by: George Barclay, 1860.

1860 **Anonymous**   The Song of Songs in Lowland Scotch;
from the authorised English version.   London:
Privately printed for Prince Louis Lucien Bonaparte
by: Strangeways & Walden, 1860.

1860 **Baird, Henry**   The Song of Solomon in Devonshire
Dialect; from the authorised English version, by
Henry Baird. London: Privately printed for Prince
Louis Lucien Bonaparte by George Barclay, 1860.
     [See Anonymous, Song of Solomon in [various British
     dialects], 1857.]

1860 **Baynes, J. Spencer**   The Song of Solomon
in the Somerset dialect; from the authorised English
version, by J. Spencer Baynes.   London: Privately
printed for Prince Louis Lucien Bonaparte by
Strangeways & Walden, 1860.
     [See Anonymous, Song of solomon in [various British
     dialects], 1857.]

1860 **Gillett, Edward**   The Song of Solomon in the
Norford dialect; from the authorised English verse,
by Rev. Edward Gillett... London: Privately printed
for Prince Louis Lucien Bonaparte: by Strangeways &
Walden, 1860.

1860 **Lower, Mark Anthony**   The Song of Solomon [in]
the dialect of Sussex; from the authorised English
version, by Mark Anthony Lower, M.A., F.S.A. London:
Privately printed for Prince Louis Lucien Bonaparte
by: George Barclay, 1860.

1860 **Monsell, John S.B.**   Songs from the Song of Songs,
and Other Poems, by John S.B. Monsell. Turquay: E.
Cockrem, 1860.

1860 **Phizackerley, James**   The Song of Solomon in the North Lancashire dialect as spoken north of the Wyre; from the authorised English version, by James Phizackerley. London: Privately printed for Prince Louis Lucien Bonaparte by Strangeways & Walden, 1860.

> [See Anonymous, The Song of Solomon in [various British dialects] (North Lancashire), 1858.]

1860 **Pulman, George P.R.**   The Song of Solomon in the East Devonshire dialect; from the authorised English version by, George P.R. Pulman. London: Privately printed for Prince Louis Lucien Bonaparte by Strangeways & Walden, 1860.

> [See Anonymous, The Song of Solomon in [various British dialects] (East Devonshire), 1858.]

1860 **Robson, Joseph Philip**   The Song of Solomon, versified from the English translation of James of England into the dialect of the colliers of Northumberland, but principally those dwelling on the banks of the Tyne, by J.p. Robson. [London: George Barclay] Impensis Ludovici Luciani Bonaparte, 1860.

> Another edition; The Song of Solomon in the Northumberland dialect; from the authorised English version, by J.P. Robson. [London: George Barclay] Impensis Ludovici Luciani Bonaparte, 1860.

1860 **Robson, Joseph Philip**   The Song of Solomon in the Lowland Scotch dialect; from the authorised English version, by Joseph P. Robson. London: Privately Printed for Prince Louis Lucien Bonaparte by George Barclay, 1860.

1860 **Rogers, Charles**   The Song of Solomon in the West Riding Yorkshire dialect; from the authorised English version, by Charles Rogers... London: Privately Printed for Prince Louis Lucien Bonaparte by George Barclay, 1860.

1860 **Stuart, A. Moody**   The Song of Songs. An Exposition of the Song of Solomon...Second Edition, by A. Moody Stuart. London: J. Nisbet & Co., 1860.

> ["This second edition is enlarged by the translation ..." The first edition, dated 1857, was for its text the KJV.]

> Another edition; A Key to the Emblem of Solomon's Song, with a Translation, 1861.

1860 **Wood, R.H.**   The Song of Solomon in Verse. By R.H. Wood. London: Partridge & Co., 1860.

1861 **Anonymous**   The Bride of Christ; or, Explanatory Notes on the Song of Solomon. With introductory preface, by the Author of "Memorials of Hedley Vicars."... [C.M. Marsh; and with the English text, revised.] London: Seeley, Jackson & Halliday, 1861.

1861 **Kite, Edward**   The Song of Solomon in the Wiltshire dialect, as it is spoken in the Northern Division; from the authorised English version, by Edward Kite. London: Privately printed for Prince Louis Lucien Bonaparte by Strangeways & Walden, 1861.

1861 **Withington, Leonard**   Solomon's Song: Translated and Explained in Three Parts. I. The Manuduction. II. The Version. III. The Supplement. By Leonard Withington... Boston: J.E. Tilton & Co., 1861.
     ["...to be literal as possible, but not so literal as not to aim to give the parallel meaning..."]

1862 **Green, George M.**   The Song of Solomon in Saxon-English; from the authorised English version, by George M. Green, (together with the text of the Authorised Version). London: Privately printed for Louis Lucien Bonaparte: by Strangeways & Walden, 1862.

1862 **Henderson, George**   The Song of Solomon in Lowland Scotch; from the authorised English version, by George Henderson. London: Privately printed for Prince Louis Lucien Bonaparte by: Strangeways & Walden, 1862.

1863 **Yates, Edward**   The Song of Solomon, rendered into English verse. By Edward Yates. New York: Calvin Blanchard, 1863.

1864 **Anonymous**   The Song of Songs. An Exposition. [Henry Dunn] London: [Printed for private circulation], 1864.
     [With a translation of the text.]

1864 **Anonymous**   The Song of Songs, translated into English verse. With an introduction from St. Athanasius, notes from Theodoret, and appendix from St. Bernard. London: Rivingtons, 1864.

1864 **Hambleton, Joseph**   The Song of Songs... divided into acts and scenes, with the dialogues apportioned to the different interlocutors, chiefly as directed by... Ernest Renan... Rendered into verse, from the received English translation and other versions. London: Trubner & Co., 1864.

1865 **Houghton, W.**   An Essay on the Canticles, or the
Song of Songs, with a Translation of the Poem, and
Short Explanatory Notes, by W. Houghton.   London:
Trubner & Co., 1865.

1867 **Anonymous**   ...The Song of Songs. A Hebrew pastoral
drama. Not by King Solomon...[In English verse by
H.A. Ouvry]   London: R. Barrett & Sons, 1867.
    Another edition; With notes and illustrations by
Satyam Jayati [i.e. H.A. Ouvry. Together with
the AV, an abridged paraphrase of Jayadeva's
Gitagovinda, and extracts from the Moallacat.
With plates.]   London: Williams & Norgate,
1867.

1867 **Bush, Joseph**   The Canticles or the Song of
Solomon: a metrical paraphrase, with explanatory
notes and practical comments. By Joseph Bush.
London: Hatchard & Co., 1867.

1869 **Rentoul, William Skinner**   A Metrical Version of the
Song of Solomon... (Written for the American edition
of Rev. Moody Stuart's Exposition of that beautiful
inspired Song.) Philadelphia: William S. Rentoul,
1869.
    ["...a literal translation of the Song, so far as
practical..." A. Moody Stuart's Exposition is listed
separately under 1860; not known whether 'the American
edition' was ever published.]

1870 **Green, William Henry**   The Song of Solomon,
Translated from the German, with Additions, by W.
Henry Green.   New York: Charles Scribner's Sons,
1870.
    [See Complete Bibles, 1895 Lange's Commentary.]

    Another edition, 1909.

1870 **Pitman, Isaac**   Rhythmic Version of the Song of
Solomon by Isaac Pitman, 1870.
    [See Wisdom and Poetical Books and Selections, 1870
Francis Barham, The Writings of Solomon.]

1873 **Anonymous**   The Song of Songs, commonly called the
Song of Solomon, or, the Canticle. From the French
of Albert Reville. London: Williams & Norgate, 1873.
    ["In rendering the poem into English, the words of the
ordinary English translation of the Bible have been used
as far as applicable."]

1877 **Anonymous**   Songs of the Semitic in English verse.
By G.E.W. London: Trubner & Co., 1877.
    [The Song of Songs and other selections.]

1878 **Lethbridge, J. Watts**   The Idyls of Solomon:
the Hebrew Marriage Week. Arranged in Dialogue by J.
Watts Lethbridge. London: E.W. Allen, 1878.

1879 **Metcalf, James W.**   The Song of Songs of Solomon.
With Explanations and Reflections Having Reference
to the Interior Life, by Madame Guyon. Translated
from the French by James W. Metcalf. New York: A.W.
Dennett, 1879.

1881 **Clarke, B.S.**   The Song of Songs, arranged
in twelve canticles, and rendered into English blank
verse by B.S. Clarke. With an introduction by H.
Bonar. London: J. Nisbet & Co., 1881.

1881 **Pratt, James**   The Song of Solomon, Rendered
into English Verse ...from the Original Hebrew and
from the Septuagint, by James Pratt.   London:
Griffith & Farran, 1881.

1882 **Blackburn, Walter Garstang**   The Sacred Eclogue,
Being the Poetical Allegorical Descriptions or
Idylls ("Song of Songs") of the Prophet Solomon,
King of Israel; Opening the Spiritual Mystery of
Perfect Nuptial Love. A New Version in English...,
by Walter Garstang Blackburn. CUCL. 1882.

1882 **Briggs, Thomas Pearl**   The Song of Songs. A
Paraphrase, in verse, of Solomon's Song...With an
introduction by Rev. Franklin Johnson. By T.P.
Briggs. Boston: J.H. Earle, 1882.

1882 **Garstang, Walter**   The Sacred Eclogue. Being the
Poetic Allegorical Descriptions, or Idylls, ("Song
of Songs") of the Prophet Solomon, King of Israel;
Opening the Spiritual Mystery of Perfect Nuptial
Love. A New Version, in English, of the Text in the
Biblia Hebraica edit. E. Van der Hooght. Blackburn:
James Douglas, 1882.

1885 **Wrangham, Digby S.**   Lyra Regis. The Book of Psalms,
and other Lyrical poetry of the Old Testament,
rendered literally into English metres...
    [See Old Testament Selections for the complete entry.
    Includes the Song of Solomon.]

1887 **Daland, William C.**   The Song of Songs,
translated from the Hebrew, with occasional notes.
Leonardsville, Ky: Published for the Author, 1887.
    ["While recognizing the dramatic form of the poem, the
    translator has endeavored to preserve as simple a plan
    as possible."]

    Second edition; Alford Center, New York: American
    Sabbath Tract Society, 1888.

["The version has been materially improved, and
many errors which appeared in the former imprint
have been corrected."]

1889 **Strong, James**   Sacred Idyls; a Metrical Version
of Solomon's Song, with Appropriate Explanations, by
James Strong. New York: Hunt & Eaton; Cincinnati:
Cranston & Stowe, 1889.

1890 **Anonymous**   The Book of Job and the Song of Solomon.
Translated into English metre...
[See Wisdom and Poetical books and Selections, 1890
Anonymous, Poetical Parts of the Old Testament.]

1893 **Balfour, Frederic Henry** The Song of Songs, which is
Solomon's. Arranged in Dramatic for Frederic Henry
Balfour. Tokyo: Shueisha Printing Office, 1893.

1893 **Terry, Milton S.**   The Song of Songs; an Inspired
Melodrama Analyzed, Translated, and Explained by
M.S. Terry. Cincinnati: Cranston & Curts; New York:
Hunt & Eaton, 1893.
["The critical reader of our translation will observe at
several places our disregard for the masoretic
pointing."]

1894 **Kelly, William**   The Song of Songs Which
is Solomon's (or Canticles), with Brief Remarks.
London: T. Cheverton, 1894.
[Contains his translation of the text interspersed.
Contained also in The Bible Treasury, 1894.]

1894 **Taylor, J. Hudson**   Union and Communion;
or, Thoughts on the Song of Solomon, By J. Hudson
Taylor. London: Morgan & Scott, 1894.
[With an amended version of the text.]

1895 **Goodwin, T.A.**   Lovers Three Thousand Years Ago as
Indicated by the Song of Solomon by Rev.T.A.Goodwin,
...Chicago: The Open Court Publishing Company, 1895.
["The plan of this book is to eliminate all textual
criticisms and to restore the text to the form which
made the poem a treasure with the ancient Hebrews."]

1895 **Thomson, William M.**   The Song of Songs Translated
from the Hebrew, with a Study of the Plan, the Age,
and the Character of the Poem, by Ernest Renan,
Member of the [French] Academy. Done into English by
William M. Thomson. London: William M.Thomson, 1895.
[Translated from the French work of Renan, 1860.]

1897 **Ellis, John William**   The Song of Songs; Translated
and Arranged, by J.W. Ellis. Columbia, MO.: E.W.
Stephens, Printer, 1897.
["In this translation and metrical arrangement
faithfulness to the original has been the controlling
factor rather than euphony."]

1901 **M'Swiney, James**   Translation of the Psalms and Canticles with Commentary...
[See Wisdom and Poetical books and Selections for the complete entry.]

1901 **Stockard, Sallie Walker**   The Lily of the Valleys, by Sallie Walker Stockard.   n.p.: n.p., 1901.
[Song of Songs.]

1902 **Haupt, Paul**   The Book of Canticles. A new Rhythmical Translation with Restoration of the Hebrew text and explanatory and critical notes by Paul Haupt...   The American Journal of Semitic Languages and Literatures, Vol. XVIII, pp. 193-245; Vol. XIX, pp. 1-32, Jul & Oct, 1902.
Reprinted; Chicago: University of Chicago Press, 1902.

1903 **Bagshawe, Edward Gilpin**   The Psalms and Canticles in English Verse...
[See Bible Selections for the complete entry.]

1904 **Falconer, Hugh**   The Maid of Shulam, by Hugh Falconer.   London: Hodder & Stoughton, 1904.
[Commentary on the Song of Solomon, with an amended version. "The translation aims at fidelity to the meaning and spirit of the original, and, for the sake of lucidity, the various parts of the poem are assigned to different speakers, changes of scene are indicated... a few expressions have been softened..."]

1904 **Pierce, George Winslow**   The Song of Songs, Which is Solomon's Versified by George Winslow Pierce. Norwood, Massachusetts: Plympton Press, 1904.
[402 couplets, one line per page.]

Another edition, 1915.

1905 **Bayne, Fannie Fenton**   The Song of Songs; a translation into English Verse, by Fannie Fenton Bayne.   London: Page & Co., 1905.

1906 **Anonymous**   The Song of Songs which is Solomon's. London: E. Grant Richards, 1906.

1906 **Coutts, Francis**   The Song of Songs. A Lyrical folkplay of the Ancient Hebrews, arranged in Vii scenes...   With illustrations by Henry Ospovat. London & New York: John Lane, 1906.

1908 **Gollancz, Hermann**   The Targum to the "Song of Songs"; the Book of the Apple; the Ten Jewish Martyrs; a Dialogue on Games of Chance (by Leo de Modena), Translated from the Hebrew and Aramaic, by Hermann Gollancz.   London: Luzac & Co., 1908.

1909 **Noyes, G.A.** The Song of Songs Accented in Accordance with the Poetical System, with a Rhythmic Translation by G.A.Noyes. London: Luzac & Co., 1909.
[Hebrew & English.]

1910 **Burne, George H.P.** The Song of Songs; An Attempt to Produce a Rhyming Paraphrase... by George H.P.Burne.
[Typewritten MS. 7 leaves in B.M.]

1910 **King, Mary** The Song of Songs; a Drama of Faithful Love, with Notes and Comments by Mary King. London & Edinburgh: Marshall Brothers, 1910.

1911 **Dearness, William** A Restoration of the Drama of Canticles with copious notes. Also an Essay on the Calf Cult of Northern Israel by William Dearness. Cincinnati: The Ebbert & Richardson Co., 1911.
[Presented in the form of a metrical drama.]

1911 **Smith, Nataniel** The Messages of the Poets: the Books of Job and Canticles and some Minor Poems in the Old Testament...
[See Old Testament Selections for the complete entry.]

1912 **Gordon, Alexander R.** The Poets of the Old Testament...
[See Old Testament Selections for the complete entry. Includes Job, Proverbs, the Thoughts of the Wise, Song of Songs, Vanity, the Songs of Moses and Deborah, and a few Psalms.]

1913 **Cannon, William Walter** The Song of Songs, Edited as a Dramatic Poem, with Introduction, Revised Translation, and Excursuses, by William Walter Cannon. Cambridge: at the University Press, 1913.
["I have added a Revised Translation, taking the AV as the basis... I have availed myself as far as I could, of the fine poetical renderings of the Late Prebendary Kingsbury in the Speaker's Commentary (1871)..."]

1913 **Ray, Charles Walker** The Song of Songs of the King and his Bride; An Interpretation, by Charles Walker Ray. Philadelphia: Published for the Author by American Baptist Publication Society, 1913.
[With a new translation.]

1914 **Jennings, William** The Song of Songs, a New Metrical Translation Arranged as a Drama, with Introduction and Notes by William Jennings. Oxford: Parker & Co., 1914.

1915 **Scott, David Russell** Pessimism and Love in Ecclesiastes and the Song of Songs, with Translations from the Same...
[See Wisdom and Poetical books and Selections for the complete entry.]

1917 **McFadyen, John Edgar**   The Wisdom Books (Job, Proverbs, Ecclesiastes) also Lamentations and the Song of Songs...
>[See Wisdom and Poetical books and Selections, 1916 John Edgar McFadyen, [The Poetical Books of the O.T.].]

1919 **Katz, Gershon**   Shulamit, An Ancient Love-Drama, Known as the Song of Songs. Translated from the Hebrew into English Rhymed Verse, by Gershon Katz. London: Universal Translation and Typewriting Bureau, 1919.

1921 **Jastrow, Morris**   The Song of Songs, Being a Collection of Love Lyrics of Ancient Palestine. A New Translation based on a Revised Text, Together with the Origin, Growth and Interpretation of the Songs, by Morris Jastrow.   Philadelphia & London: J.B. Lippincott Co., 1921.
>["...I follow, with some exceptions, the results reached by...J.W.Rothstein, whose Grundzuege des Hebraischen Rhythmus, represent a most valuable contribution to this very difficult subject."]

>Another edition, 1922.
>>[Three Hundred & Ten Copies of this Book Printed ...by Edwin & Robert Grabhorn...(San Francisco, The Book Club of California).]

1924 **Bushnell, K.C.**   The Supreme Virtue: Loyalty to God's Anointed King. By K.C. Bushnell.   Oakland, Calif.: the Author, 1924.
>[A Historical Exposition of the Song of Solomon, with an emended version.]

1925 **Anonymous**   The Song of Songs, called by many the Canticle of Canticles; Printed and Published at the Golden Cockerel Press at Waltham St. Lawrence in Berkshire in the year MCMXXV. Berkshire: Golden Cockerel Press, 1925.
>["The present rendering of the Song of Songs is not so much a fresh translation as a version of versions of the world."]

1925 **Wright, S. Fowler**   The Song of Songs by S. Fowler Wright. "Poetry", Feb., 1925.
>["...it may seem surprising that I should have attempted a rendering of the Song of Songs in a regular stanzaic form. My aim has been not to offer an alternative translation, but to reconstruct a poem the original of which exists only in disordered and inconsequent fragments; and, in doing this, I have preferred a form of verse that I am least incompetent to handle."]

>First edition; The Song of Songs and Other Poems, 1925.

Second edition; New York: Cosmopolitan Book
Corp., 1929.
[Verso of title page is labeled "First Edition".]

1927 **Bach, Marcus**   Song of Songs (Solomon), by Marcus
Bach. Kansas City, Mo.: n.p., 1927.
["It is the purpose of this new and poetical treatise to
present this exquisite Biblical Love Song in a clear and
inspiring manner."]

1927 **Meek, Theophile James**   The Song of Songs, which
is Solomon's; an American Translation, by Theophile
James Meek. Chicago: University Press, 1927.
[See J.M. Powis Smith and Others, O.T., 1927.]

1928 **Forrest, William Mentzel**   King of Shepherds? The
Song of Solomon newly Rendered and for the First
Time Given as a Complete Drama. Boston: The
Stratford Co., 1928.

1928 **Guerney, B.G.**   Sulamith; a Romance of Antiquity
by Alexander Kuprin, Translated from the Russian by
B.G. Guerney. New York: Privately printed for
subscribers, 1928.
[Incorporates a paraphrase of the Song of Solomon.]

1928 **Margoliuth, David S.**   The Song of Songs, by David S.
Margoliuth. 3 Vols. London: S.P.C.K., 1928.
[Part of a new commentary on the Holy Scriptures by
Charles Gore, etc...From Lilly's 'Canticles', 1948.]

1932 **Patterson, John L.**   The Song of Songs, Arranged
Conjecturally As A Lyrical Drama, Together With An
Interpretative Introduction and Explanatory Notes,
by John L. Patterson. Louisville, Kentucky: Standard
Publishing Co., 1932.
["...little attempt has been made to reconstruct it or
to revise the text..." which borrows various passages
from ERV, ASV, Jewish Publication Society Version.]

1935 **Chamberlain, George Sumner**   The Song of Songs;
A paraphrase explanatory of this mystical book, by
George Sumner Chamberlain. [No place or name] 1935.
[The 'Paraphrase' is mostly devotional Christian
commentary.]

1936 **Oesterley, William Oscar Emil**   The Song of
Songs, the AV, Together with a new Translation, an
introduction and notes, by W.O.E. Oesterley... With
Engravings on Copper by Lettice Sanford. [London:]
Golden Cockerel Press, 1936.
[Based upon an amended text.]

1936 **Richards, James**   De Song of Songs, by Solomon,
put into the Sussex Dialect by Jim Cladpole. [James
Richards] Turnbridge Wells: J. Richards, 1936.

1936 **Smith, Walter Bernard**   A New Church Psalter. Being the Church of England Prayer Book Version of the Canticles and Psalms...
    [See Wisdom and Poetical books and Selections for the complete entry.]

1937 **Ellis, Havelock**   The Song of Songs as a Drama by Ernest Renan, Translated with an Introduction, by Havelock Ellis. Decorated by Bernard Sleigh. Cambridge: City of Birmingham School of Printing; College of Arts and Crafts, 1937.
    [Translation from the French; Introduction dated Sparkes Creek, Scone, N.S.W., Dec., 1878.]

1937 **Golding, Louis** The Song of Songs. Newly Interpreted and Rendered as a Masque. [Completed during April, 1937, at the Corvinus Press. Laus Deo] 1937.
    ["This rendering of the Song of Songs was made in 1928... It will be seen that the strophes in roman letters are the rendering of the text, while those in italics are interposed by the author." A special edition of 178 copies.]

Another edition; London: Rich & Cowan, 1938.

1937 **Ma Than E**   The Song of Songs, put into Basic English, by Ma Than E.   London: K. Paul, Trench, Trubner & Co., 1937.
    [Psyche miniatures. General series, no. 88.]

    [See Complete Bibles, 1949 Basic Bible (Song of Songs).]

1937 **O'Neill, George**   The Psalms and the Canticles of the Divine Office, a new English translation...
    [See Wisdom and Poetical books and Selections for the complete entry.]

1938 **Brooks, J. Barlow**   Solomon's Song of Songs in Lancaster Dialect, by J. Barlow Brooks. Oxford: the Author, [1938? 1939?]

1940 **Woods, T.E.P.**   Shulammith, a Love Story Which is an Interpretation of the "Song of Songs, which is Solomon's" by T.E.P. Woods. Grand Rapids, Michigan: 1940.

1942 **Moorhouse, Harry**   The Crocus of Sharon. A New Metrical Transcript of the Song of Songs, Arranged as a Lyrical Folk-Drama of the Ancient Hebrews in Five Acts, by Harry Moorhouse. Ilfracombe, N. Devon: Arthur H. Stockwell Ltd., 1942.
    [With a critical Exposition.]

1944 **Jackson, J.B.**   Exposition of the Song of Songs, by J.B. Jackson. Sydney: Wholly set up and Printed in Australia by William Homer, 1944.

["...an exact literal translation of the Hebrew text of
the Song of Solomon..."]

1945 **Sola Pool, David de**   The Song of Songs, Which
is Solomon's. Translated from the Hebrew Bible, by
David de Sola Pool. The Menorah Journal, Vol.
XXXIII, No.1, Spring, 1945.
    ["...this English rendering does no violence to the text
    by any of the emendations, omissions, rearrangements or
    reconstructions unnecessarily offered by the 'higher
    critics'... This version reveals the poem as a dramatic
    unity..."]

    Reprinted, 1945.

1946 **Lehrman, S.M.**   Canticles, 1946.
    [See Old Testaments, 1936 Soncino Booksof the Bible.]

1948 **Lilly, Joseph L.**   The Canticle of Canticles, by
William Pouget... and Jean Guitton; Translated [from
the French] by Joseph L. Lilly.   [New York:] The
Declan X. McMullen Co., 1948.
    ["A few translations of the O.T. seem not to coincide
    with the references given, because they were made from
    the Hebrew text."]

1948 **Waterman, Leroy**   The Song of Songs. Translated and
Interpreted as a Dramatic Poem by Leroy Waterman.
Ann Arbor: University of Michigan Press, 1948.

1949 **Richardson, Oliffe**   Two Ancient Love Tales;
the Shulamite and a Brief Tale of the Love of Cupid
and Psyche (Abridged from Apuleius), by Oliffe
Richardson. Fairford, Gos.: Oliffe Richardson, 1949.
    ["The Shulamite' consists of a verse translation of the
    Song of Solomon.]

1951 **Driver, G.R.**   The Ethiopia version of the Song of
Songs, critically edited by Hugh Craswall Gleave.
With English translation and Memoir by G.R. Driver.
London: Taylor's Foreign Press, 1951.
    [Includes the Ethiopia text, English translation and
    apparatus.]

1952 **Wragg, Arthur**   The Song of Songs, with Drawings by
Arthur Wragg.   London & New York: Selwyn & Blount,
1952.
    ["A fragmentary wedding idyll.]

1954 **Gordis, Robert**   The Song of Songs: A Study. Modern
Translation and Commentary. New York: Published for
the Jewish Theological Seminary of America by the
Bloch Publishing Co. "Texts & Studies of the Jewish
Theological Seminary of America, Vol. XX, 1954.
    ["A fresh translation of the Hebrew text with a
    prefatory comment on each song..."]

1957 **DeWitt, S.A.**   The Song of Songs or Shir
A Shirim... A Rhymed and Rhythmed Rendering of the
Prose contained in the KJV of the Old Testament.
New York: Greenburg, 1957.
["Libretto (in search of a Composer)..."]

1958 **Anonymous** ...The Song of Songs Explained by W.Wolf.
[Joseph Leftwich] London: [Printed by L. Honig &
Sons Ltd. for the Author], 1958.
["This volume is made up of translations of my book
'Shit Hashirim, the Song of Songs,' which appeared in
1908 in the German language, and of a collection of my
essays... I am happy that I could entrust the
translation of this book to the expert pen of Mr. Joseph
Leftwich."]

1959 **Schonfield, Hugh J.**   The Song of Songs; Translated
from the Original Hebrew with an Introduction and
Explanations by Hugh J. Schonfield...   New York:
Mentor Books Paperback, 1959.
["I regard it as a wrong approach to the Song that,
because it is included in the Biblical Canon, there must
be a moral in it somewhere to counterbalance the
uninhibited language in which sexual passion is
portrayed... I have...sometimes introduced words to
bring out the sense or complete a line... I have also
occasionally transposed a line or a phrase to preserve
the metre."]

Another edition;   London: Elek   Books   Ltd;
Toronto: The Ryerson Press, 1960

1961 **Barnes, O.L.**   The Song of Songs; a new interlinear
Hebrew-English translation, interlinear grammatical
analysis of every word, accentual dichotomy, revised
Hebrew text, and new critical apparatus and
collation with BH and Snaith, by O.L. Barnes. Also
a Lost Page of Genesis of the Ben Asher Aleppo
Codes.   Newcastle upon Tyne: Progressive Printers
Ltd., 1961.

1962 **Weitzner, Emil**   Humanist Meditations...
[See Old Testament Selections, 1959 for the complete
entry.]

1965 **Donn, Thomas M.**   The Allegory of Divine Love;
Being a Metrical Version of the Song of Songs, With
an Introduction and Notes Vindicating its Original
Allegorical Nature and Purpose, by Thomas M. Donn.
Inverness: printed by Robert Carruthers & Sons
"Courier Office", 1965.

1967 **Seerveld, Calvin G.**   The Greatest Song in critique
of Solomon; freshly and literally translated from
the Hebrew and arranged for oratorid performance.
Palos Heights, Illinois: Trinity College Bookstore;
Toronto: Wedge Press, 1967.

1968 **King, Ronald**   The Song of Songs, with original
screen images designed and printed by Ronald King.
Guildford, Surrey: Circle Press Publications, 1968.
[Limited edition of 150 copies.]

1969 **Mayne, Noel**   Song of Songs, Photographed by Noel
Mayne. London: Skilton, 1969.
[Photography of the nude.]

1970 **Collins, Maureen P.**   Song of Love, Selections
from the Song of Songs, edited by Maureen P.
Collins. With photos by Fortune Monte and Sylvia
Plachy. New York: Association Press, 1970.

1970 **Feldman, Leon A.**   Commentary on the Song
of Songs. Based on MSS and Early Printings with an
Introduction, Notes, Variants, and Comments. By
Abraham ben Isaac ha-Levi TaMaKH.   Van Gorsum
Assem., 1970.
[Studia Semitica Neerlandica, No.9.]

1972 **Suares, Carlo** The Song of Songs; the Canonical Song
of Solomon Deciphered According to the Original Code
of the Qabala... Berkeley & London: Shambalah, 1972.
["Our version of the Song, not as a translation of the
canonical, but as a Midrash, that is, an exposition
based upon its inner cabalistic meaning. Our
commentaries verse by verse, including every time: the
Hebraic text; a phonetic transcription; the text quoted
from the RSV of the Bible; a repetition of the verse
according to the necessity of the verse."]

1973 **Graves, Robert**   The Song of Songs, Text
and Commentary by Robert Graves. Illustrated by Hans
Erni.   New York: Clarkson N. Potter, Inc.;
Distributed by Crown Publishers, Inc.;   London:
Collins, 1973.

1974 **Gordis, Robert** The Song of Songs and Lamentations;
a Study, Modern Translation, and Commentary, by
Robert Gordis. New York: KTAV, 1974.
[A revision, with new material, of the author's The Song
of Songs (1954) and A Commentary on the text of
Lamentations (1958).]

1974 **Valender, James and José L. Morales**   The Song Of
Songs. A mystical exposition by Father Juan Gonzalez
Arintero... Translated by James Valender... and José
L. Morales... Cincinnati, OH: The Dominican Nuns,
Monastery of the Holy Name, 1974.

1975 **Jay, Peter**   The Song of Songs, Translated by Peter
Jay, with an Introduction by David Godstein and
Illustrations by Nikos Stavroulakis. London: Anvil
Press Poetry, 1975.

1976 **Glickman, (S.?) Craig**   A Song for Lovers, Including
a New Paraphrase and a new Translation of the Song
of Solomon, by S., Craig Glickman [Foreword by
Howard G. Henricks].   Downers Grove, Ill.: Inter-
Varsity, 1976.

1977 **Falk, Marcia**   The Song of Songs; Love Poems
from the Bible, Translated from the Original Hebrew,
by Marcia Falk.   New York: Jovanovich, Inc., 1977.
     [Contains Literary comments.]

     Another edition;   Love Lyrics from the Bible;
     Translated and Literary Study of the Song of
     Songs.   Sheffield: The Almond Press, 1982.

1977 **Pope, Marvin H.**   Song of Songs. A New Translation
with Introduction, and Commentary by Marvin H. Pope.
Garden City, New York: Doubleday and Co., Inc.,
1977.
     [See Complete Bibles, 1964 Anchor Bible, Vol. 7c.]

1985 **Fox, Michael V.**   The Song of Songs and the Ancient
Egyptian Love Songs. Michael V. Fox.   The University
of Wisconsin Press, 1985.

Prophets and Selections

???? **Blake, Buchanan** How to Read [the Prophets]; Being the Prophecies arranged Chronologically in their Historical setting. With explanations, maps, and glossary. 5 parts Edinburgh: T. & T. Clark, [189?]-1895.

        189? Part I. The Pre-Exilian Prophets (with Joel). Second edition, 1893.

        1891 [Part II.] How to Read Isaiah; being the Prophecies of Isaiah. [i.e. I. Isaiah]... Second edition, 1892?

        1892 Part III. Jeremiah.

        1894 Part IV. Ezekiel.

        1895 Part V. Isaiah (XL.-LXVI) and the Post-Exilian Prophets.

        [The text contains "...divergences from the Authorized Translation... The aid of the RV, especially its marginal readings, as also the excellent Variorum Bible has been gratefully used..."]

1568 **Cole, Thomas** Ezekiel & Daniel, 1568.
    [See Complete Bibles, 1568 Bishops' Bible.]

1568 **Horne, Robert** Isaiah, Jeremiah, and Lamentations, 1568.
    [See Complete Bibles, 1568 Bishops' Bible.]

1645 **Anonymous** A Bottle of Holy Tears; or, Jeremies Threnes and Lamentations, Metrically and Metaphrastically Laid out in Verse. 1645.

MACK LIBRARY
BOB JONES UNIVERSITY
GREENVILLE, SC

1727 **Lowth, William**   A Commentary upon the Larger
and Lesser Prophets: being a continuation of Bishop
Patrich. By William Lowth...   London: for R.
Knaplock, and Others, 1727.

1836 **Anonymous**   A Literal Translation of the Prophets,
from Isaiah to Malachi. With Notes, Critical,
Philological, and Explanatory. By Lowth, Blayney,
Newcome, Wintle, Horsley. In Five Volumes... A New
Edition.   London: Printed for Thomas Tegg & Son;
Glasgow: R. Griffin & Co.; Dublin: Tegg, Wise & Co.,
1836.
[Prophet selections.]

1866 **Williams, Rowland**   The Hebrew Prophets,
translated afresh from the original, with regard to
the Anglican version, and with illustrations for
English readers by Rowland Williams. 2 Vols. London
& Edinburgh: Williams & Norgate, 1866-1871.
[Part II was edited by Ellen Williams, after Dr.
Williams' death. "It has been thought right to
employ...the ancient versions, particularly the
Septuagint and Vulgate..."]

1866 [Part I] The Prophets of Israel and Judah
under the Assyrian Empire; Joel, Amos,
Obadiah, Hosea, Micah, Isaiah 1-34,
Nahum.

1871 Part II; The Hebrew Prophets During the
Babylonian and Persian Empires; Habakkuk,
Zephaniah, Jeremiah, Lamentations,
Ezekiel 1-4,8, Isaiah LII.13-LIII.12.

1871 **Williams, Ellen**   (Editor)   See Rowland Williams,
The Hebrew Prophets, 1866.

1875 **Smith, John Frederick**   Commentary on the Prophets
of the Old Testament, by the late Dr. Georg Heinrich
August von Ewald... London & Edinburgh: Williams &
Norgate, 1875-1881.
1875 - - Vol. I.   Yoel, 'Amos, Hosea, and
"Zakharya," Ch. ix-xi.

1876 - - Vol. II.   Yesaya, 'Obadaya, and
Mikha.

1878 - - Vol. III. Nahum, Ssephanya, Habaqquq,
"Zakharya," Ch. xii-viv.,
Yeremya.

1880 - - Vol. IV. Hezeqiel, "Yesayah,"

1881 - - Vol. V.   Anonymous pieces. Haggai,
                    Zacharya, Mal'aki, Yona,
                    Barukh, Daniel.

["Dr. Ewald did not shrink from laying a heavy strain on
the language, if he could thereby make it bring out some
peculiarity of the Hebrew... This (English) translation
does the same..." Theological Translation Fund Library.]

1909 **McFadyen, John Edgar**   The Messages of the Prophetic
and Priestly Historians..., 1909.
[See Frank Knight Sanders and Charles Foster Kent, The
Messages of the Bible, Vol. IV, 1900.]

[Prophet selections.]

1909 **Woods, Francis H. and Francis E. Powell**   The Hebrew
Prophets for English Readers in the Language of the
RV of the English Bible, Printed in Their Poetical
Form, with Headings and Grief Annotation Edited by
Francis H. Woods and Francis E. Powell. In Four
Volmes. Oxford: at the Clarendon Press, 1909-1912.
      1909 Vol. 1   Amos, Hosea, Isaiah (1-39) and
                     Micah
      1910 Vol. 2   Zephaniah, Nahum, Habakkuk and
                     Jermiah
      1911 Vol. 3   Obadiah, Ezekiel and Isaiah
                     (XL-LXVI)
      1912 Vol. 4   Haggai, Zechariah, Malachi,
                     Joel, Deutro-Zechariah, Jonah
                     and Daniel

[The Deity is rendered "Jehovah" a few times in the text
and many times in the subtitles.]

1910 **Chamberlin, Georgia Louise**   The Hebrew Prophets
or Patriots and Leaders of Israel: A Text-book for
Students of High School age and above by Georgia
Louise Chamberlin. 3 Vols.   Chicago, Illinois:
University of Chicago Press, 1910-11.
[Text is ASV. "In many cases, however, the translation
has been further revised with a view to making the
selections more clear and comprehensible..."]

Another edition, 1911. (1 Vol.)

1912 **Landman, Isaac**   Stories of the Prophets (Before
the Exile) by Isaac Landman.   Cincinnati, Ohio:
Department of Synagog and School Extension of the
union of American Hebrew Congregations, 1912.
["The author...approaches his subject...from the
dramatic standpoint...he has culled from the lives of
the prophets those striking and intense experiences
which illustrate most powerfully the indomitable spirit

1914 **Buttenweiser, Moses**   The Prophets of Israel From the Eighth to the Fifth Century; Their Faith and their Message by Moses Buttenwieser. New York: The Macmillan Co., 1914.
> ["In translating biblical texts, square brackets are employed in all those cases when there is no exact word-equivalent in the Hebrew original, but where the word is implyed by the syntactical construction." Selections from Jeremiah, Amos, Hosea and Isaiah.]

1916 **Gordon, Alexander R.**   The Prophets of the Old Testament. New York: Hodder & Stoughton, George H. Doran Co., 1916.
> ["...stress is throughout laid upon translations of their most significant utterances, which reproduce as nearly as possible the sense and rhythm of the original..."]

> [Prophet selections.]

1917 **Newman, Louis I. and William Popper**   Studies in Biblical Parallelism. Part I. Parallelism in Amos by Louis I Newman. Part II. Parallelism in Isaiah, Chapters 1-10 by William Popper. Semicentenial Publications of the University of California, 1917.
> [Isaiah, Chapters 1-37 appeared in 1931.]

1929 **Gamoran, Mamie**   The Voice of the Prophets, 1929.
> [See Old Testament Selections, 1924 Anonymous, The Bible Story in Bible Words.]

1932 **Hamond, E.W.**   The Eighth Century Prophets by E.W. Hamond...With a Preface by Dr.Cyril Norwood. London: Student Christian Movement Press, 1932.
> [Selections from Amos, Hosea, Isaiah, and Micah.]

1936 **Hamilton, Edith**   The Prophets of Israel, 1936.

1939 **Leslie, Elmer A.** The Prophets Tell Their Own Story. New York & Nashville: Abingdon-Cokesbury Press, 1939.
> ["...his own translation of the Prophetic Material, using...R. Kittel's Biblia Hebraica.]

> [Prophet selections.]

1939 **Moffatt, James**   The Book of the Prophets, 1939.

1939 **Wordsworth, W.A.**   En Roeh. The Prophecies of Isaiah the Seer, with Habakkuk and Nahum, Introduction, Translation and Notes by W.A. Wordsworth. Edinburgh: T. & T. Clark, 1939.
> [The translation is from the Masoretic and LXX. The Deity is rendered "Yeabe".]

1946 **Faus, W. Arthur**   The Genius of the Prophets. New

[~The Scriptural quotations in the book are based on the familiar KJV for the most part, though many changes have been made for the sake of greater accuracy of meaning and, also, in order that in the poetry the English rhythm will more nearly approximate that of the Hebrew..."]

1948 **Cohen, Abraham** (Editor) The Twelve Prophets. Hebrew Text & English Translation with an Introduction and Commentary by The Rev. Dr. A. Cohen... London: The Soncino Press, 1948.
[See Old Testaments, 1936 The Soncino Books of the Bible.]

1958 **Heaton, E.**   The Old Testament Prophets. Harmondsworth & Baltimore: Penguin Books, 1958.
[Prophet selections.]

1960 **Attwater, Rachel**   The Prophets by Joseph Dheilly...
[See Bible Selections, 1960 Anonymous, The 20th Century Encyclopedia (The Prophets), Vol. 66.]

1961 **Vawter, Bruce**   The Conscience of Israel. Pre-exilic Prophets and Prophecy, by Bruce Vawter. New York: Sheed & Ward, 1961.
[Prophets selections.]

1963 **Phillips, J.B.**   Four Prophets; Amos, Hosea, First Isaiah, Micah. A Modern Translation from the Hebrew, by J.B. Phillips. London: Geoffrey Bles; New York: The Macmillan Co., 1963.
[A translation from the Hebrew into 'the English of today'.]

1964 **Stuhlmueller, Carroll**   The Prophets and the Word of God by Carroll Stehlmueller, C.P. With a Foreward by Bernard Cooke, S.J.   Notre Dame, Indiana: Fides Publishers, Inc., 1964.
["Scriptural quotations, except in those cases where the author has made his own translation, are from the Confraternity of Christian Doctrine translation."]

1966 **Levy, Isaac** The Haptoroth, Translated and Explained by Samson Raphael Hirsch... rendered into English by Isaac Levy. London: Printed by L.Honig & Sons, 1966.

1969 **Bland, Sheldon H.**   Issues of Faith: Understanding the Prophets by Sheldon H. Bland... New York: Union of American Hebrew Congregations, 1969.
["The translations from the Bible are my own".]

1975 **Brandt, Leslie F.**   Prophets Now, by Leslie F. Brandt, with art by Corita Kent.   St. Louis: Concordia Publishing House, 1975.

8
Major Prophets

MAJOR PROPHETS AND SELECTIONS

???? **Hubbard, David A.**   Word Biblical Commentary.
Jeremiah - Lamentations. David A. Hubbard.   Waco,
Tx: Word Books, Publishers, [198?].
> [See Complete Bibles, 1982 Word Biblical Commentary,
> Vol. 23.]

1645 **Anonymous**   A Bottle of Holy Tears; or,
Jeremies Threnes and Lamentations, Metrically and
Metaphrastically Laid out in Verse. 1645.

1784 **Blayney, Benjamin**   Prophecy of Jeremiah and the
Book of Lamentations. A new translation, with notes,
critical, philological, and explanatory. By Benjamin
Blayney.   Oxford: Claredon Press, 1784.
> 2nd edition, 1810.

> [See Prophets and Selections, 1836 Anonymous, A Literal
> translation of the Prophets.]

1850 **Owen, John**   Commentaries on Jeremiah
and Lamentations by John Calvin. Translated from the
original Latin, and collated with the author's
French version.   5 Vols.   Edinburgh: Calvin
Translation Society, 1850-1855.
> [See Bible Selections, 1844 Anonymous, Commentaries on
> the Books of the Bible.]

1909 **Sanders, Frank Knight and Charles Foster Kent**
The Messages of the Earlier Prophets freely rendered
in paraphrase, 1909.
> [See Abridged Bibles, 1900 Frank Knight Sanders and
> Charles Foster Kent, The Messages of the Bible, Vol. I.]

1913 **Price, Ira Maurice**   Jeremiah, Ezekiel and Daniel,
1913.

[See Complete Bibles, 1913 American Baptist Publication
Society, The Holy Bible.]

1940 **Martin, William Wallace** Jeremiah-Ezekiel Prophecies
of Promises to Chosen People; Punishments to Chosen
People; Promises to Other Peoples; Punishments to
Other People. Reconstructed, Retranslated and
Annotated by William Wallace Martin. Nashville: The
Parthenon Press, 1940.

1987 **Harrington, Daniel J. and Anthony J. Saldarini**
Former Prophets, 1987.
[See Old Testaments, 1987 Aramaic Bible, Vol. 10.]

ISAIAH

???? **Childs, Brevard S.** Isaiah and the Assyrian Crisis,
by Brevard S. Childs. Naperville, Illinois: Alec R.
Allenson Inc., [196?].
[Part of 'Studies in Biblical Theology'. Second Series.
3. Includes translations from selected portions of a
reconstructed text.]

???? **Denney, James** A Biblical Commentary on
the Prophecies of Isaiah by Franz Delitzsch, D.D...
Authorised Translation from the Third Edition...In
Two Volumes. London: Hodder & Stoughton, [189?].
[This appears to be a different work than that
translation by Martin, in the O.T. Commentary of 1865-80
(q.v.)]

Another edition; New York: Funk & Wagnalls, n.d.

???? **Ginsberg, H.L.** First Isaiah. Introduction,
Translation, and Notes by H.L. Ginsberg. Garden
City, New York: Doubleday & Co., [19??].
[See Complete Bibles, 1964 Anchor Bible, Vol. 19.]

???? **Jennings, F.C.** Studies in Isaiah. New York:
Loizeaux Brothers Inc., [194?].
[Includes a "free metrical rendering."]

Third printing, 1950.

???? **Judaica Press Publications** The Judaica Books of
the Prophets...Isaiah...
[See Old Testament Selections for the complete entry.]

???? **Strachey, Edward** Hebrew politics in the Times of
Sargon and Sennacherib. By Edward Strachey. [187?].

[Includes a new translation of Isaiah.]

Another edition; Jewish History and politics in the Times of Sargon and Sennacherib: An Inquiry into the historical meaning and purpose of the prophecies of Isaiah... Second Edition, revised with additions. London: W. Ibister & Co., 1874.

1531 **Joye, George**   The Prophete Isaye, translated into englysshe, by George Joye... Printed at Straszburge by Balthassar Beckenth in the year of our Lorde 1531. the x daye of Maye. 1531.
[Actually printed by Martinus de Keyser, Antwerp.]

1609 **Cotton, Clement**   A Commentary upon the Prophecie of Isaiah. London: Felix Kyngston, 1609.

1644 **Boyd, M. Zachary**   The Garden of Zion...
[See Old Testament Selections for the complete entry. Includes Isaiah.]

1653 **Slater, Samuel**   Epithalmium; or, Solomons Song...
[See Old Testament Selections for the complete entry. Includes Isaiah 26.]

1656 **Cowley, Abraham**   Isaiah, chapter 34; in metre. London: H. Mosley, 1656.

1700 **Blackmore, Sir Richard**   A Paraphrase on the Book of Job...
[See Old Testament Selections for the complete entry. Includes some chapters of Isaiah.]

1720 **Fisher, John**   Isaiah, Chapter 34 Paraphrased in Blank Verse. Oxford: 1720.

1726 **Bedingfield, Philip**   A Paraphrase on the Book of Isaiah. Wherein...the whole text and paraphrase, are printed in separate columns, over against each other; and arguments placed before each chapter by Philip Bedingfield. London: Thomas Wotton, 1726.

1736 **Burton, Jo.** Isaiah, Chapter 40, Part of Deuteronomy 28 in verse. Oxford: n.p., 1736.

1753 **Langhorne, William**   Isaiah, some parts of it paraphrased. London: Printed for R. Griffiths, 1753.

1766 **Dodsley, ?** Isaiah, chapters 34 and 35; paraphrased in verse. London: 1766.
[Published in Dodsley's Collection of Poems, Vol. V.]

1776 **Green, William**   Isaiah 52:13 to the end of 53. Cambridge: J. Bentham, 1776.

1776 **Holden, Lawrence**   A Paraphrase on the
Book of Isaiah: with Notes Critical, Historical, and
Practical... In Two Volumes by Lawrence Holden of
Maldon in Essex. Chelmsford: for the Author by S.
Gray, 1776.

1778 **Lowth, Robert**   Isaiah. A New Translation;
with a Preliminary Dissertation and Notes, Critical,
Philosophical and Explanatory. By the late Robert
Lowth... 2 Vols. London: By J. Nichols, for J.
Dodsley & T. Cadell, 1778.
     [Based on the Hebrew of the London Polyglot, and on the
     LXX. "The Arabic Version is sometimes referred to, as
     verifying the reading of the LXX..."]

     [The Deity is rendered "Jehovah" many times.]

     Second edition; 1779.

     First American edition; Boston: Printed and
     Published by Joseph T. Buckingham, 1815.

     One volume edition; London: Printed for W. Baynes
     and Son and H.S. Baynes, Edinburgh, 1825.

     Fourteenth Edition; Carefully Corrected and
     Revised. London: Printed for William Tegg &
     Co., 1848.

     [See Anonymous, A Literal Translation of the Prophets,
     1836.]

1784 **Dodson, Michael**   Isaiah 52:13 to 53:12...
The Unitarian Society for Promoting Knowledge of
Scripture, 1784.

1785 **Butt, George**   Isaiah Versified. London: T. Cadell,
1785.

1785 **Dodson, Michael**   Isaiah 1 to 12. London: J.Johnson,
1790.

1790 **Anonymous**   New Translation of Isaiah; with
notes supplementary to these of Dr. Lowth... and
containing remarks on many perts of his translation
and notes. By a Layman. [Michael Dodson] London: J.
Johnson, Society for Promoting the knowledge of the
Scriptures, 1790.

1793 **Fenton, Elijah**   Isaiah, Part of Chapter
14 Paraphrased in Verse. Miscellaneous Poems and
Translations. Edinburgh: 1793.
     [Reprinted by Anderson British Poets.]

1795 **Anonymous**   A Paraphrase on the Eight Chapters
of the Prophet Isaiah: Wherein it is attempted to
express the Sense of the Prophet, in proper English
Style. Whoso readth, let him understand. Printed at
Worcester, Massachusetts, by Isaiah Thomas, and Sold
at Worcester Bookstore, 1795.
[The chapters paraphrased are 41-48.]

[See Anonymous, A Paraphrase... Isaiah, 1802; 1803;
1803.]

1800 **Fraser, Alexander**   Commentary on Isaiah, Being a
Paraphrase, with Notes, Showing the Literal Meaning
of the Prophecy, 1800.

1802 **Anonymous**   A Paraphrase on Four Chapters of the
Prophet Isaiah: In which it is attempted to express
the Sense of the Prophet, in proper English Style.
By the Author of the Paraphrase on the Eight
Chapters of Isaiah. Northampton: Printed by William
Butler, 1802.
[The chapters paraphrased are 49-52.]

[See Anonymous, A Paraphrase... Isaiah, 1795; 1803;
1803.]

1803 **Anonymous**   A Paraphrase on the Six last Chapters
of the Prophet Isaiah: In which it is attempted to
express the Sense of the Prophet, in proper English
Style. By the Author of the Paraphrase, on the Eight
Chapters of Isaiah, (lately published.)...
Northampton: Printed & Sold by William Butler, 1803.
[See Anonymous, A Paraphrase... Isaiah, 1795; 1802;
1803.]

1803 **Anonymous**   A Paraphrase on Nine Chapters of the
Prophet Isaiah. By the Author of the Paraphrase on
the Eight Chapters of Isaiah. Northampton: Printed
by William Butler, 1803.
[The chapters paraphrased are 52-60.]

[See Anonymous, A Paraphrase... Isaiah, 1795; 1802;
1803.]

1803 **Stock, Joseph**   The Book of the Prophet Isaiah:
in Hebrew and English. The Hebrew text metrically
arranged: the translation altered from that of
Bishop Lowth. With notes, critical and explanatory,
by Joseph Stock. Bath: R. Crutwell, 1803.

1827 **Anonymous**   Isaiah 60, by T.B.M. [Probably Thomas
B. Marsh]. Mormon Elder's Journal, Vol.1, No.2,
Pages 31-32, 1827.

1830 **Jenour, Alfred**   The Book of the Prophet

explanatory notes, and practical remarks; to which
is prefixed a preliminary dissertation on the nature
and use of prophecy by Alfred Jenour. 2 Vols.
London: R.B. Seeley & W. Burnside, 1830.
[He has endeavoured to combine the advantages of a
critical and devotional commentary together with a new
version and a metrical arrangement.]

1830 **Jones, John**   The Book of the Prophet Isaiah.
Translated from the Hebrew text of Van der Hooght.
By the Rev. John Jones. Oxford: W. Baxter for J.
Parker and C.J.C. & F. Rivington, 1830.
Second edition; Oxford: William Graham, 1842.

["The translator has followed the system of the
Masoretic points..."]

1840 **Barnes, Albert**   Notes: explanatory and practical
on the Book of Isaiah; with a new translation... In
three volumes. By Albert Barnes.   Boston: Crocker &
Brewster;   New York: Jonathan Leavitt, 1840.
[Translation is mostly KJV. "In some instance I have
used the words of Lowth or Noyes; and in a single place
I have made use of the translation by Herder, as
rendered by President Marsh. In all cases, however, I
have examined the Hebrew and endeavored to express its
true sense..."]

Second edition; revised, 1845.

Another edition; London: G.Routledge & Co., 1855.

1840 **Henderson, E.**   The Book of the Prophet
Isaiah translated from the original Hebrew; with a
commentary, critical, philological and exegetical.
To which is prefixed, an introductory dissertation
on the life and times of the prophet; the character
of his style; the authenticity and integrity of the
book; and the principles of prophetic interpretation
by E. Henderson... London: Hamilton, Adams, and
Co., 1840.
["I have adopted the more approved method of throwing
the translation into a poetical or rhythmical form...
regulated chiefly by the divisions marked out by the
Hebrew accents..." The full title is taken from the
second edition.]

Second edition, 1857.

1841 **Govett, Robert, Junior**   Isaiah Unfulfilled:
being an Exposition of the Prophet. With a New
Version and Critical Notes. To which are added, two
dissertations: One on the "Sons of God" and "Giants"
of Genesis VI, and the other, a comparative estimate
of the Hebrew and Greek texts. By R. Govett, Jun...
London: James Nisbet & Co., 1841.

1843 **Anonymous**   The Vision of Isaiah concerning
Jreusalem, from chapter xl. to the end; rendered
into verse according to Bishop Lowth's translation.
London: 1843.

1845 **Anonymous**   Isaiah XXXV. The Jewish Chronicle,
Vol. 1, New Series, Page 267, April, 1845.
[Published under the direction of the American Society
of Meliorating the Condition of the Jews.]

Also; The Bible Collector, No. 6, Page 2,
April-June, 1966.

1846 **Alexander, Joseph Addison**   The Earlier (and Later)
Prophecies of Isaiah, by Joseph Addison Alexander.
2 Vols. New York & London: Wiley & Putnam, 1846-
1847.
["A literal translation of the whole text has...been
incorporated..."]

The Prophecies of Isaiah, Earlier and Later...
Reprinted under the editoral superintendence
of John Eadie, LL.D. (Preface dated 1848)
Glasgow: Published by William Collins.

Isaiah illustrated and explained... An
Abridgement of the Author's Critical
Commentary on Isaiah. New York: Charles
Scribner & Co., 1851.

The Prophecies of Isaiah, Translated and
explained. A New and Revised Edition. 2 Vols.
New York: Charles Scribner & Co., 185?

Another edition; 1865.

Commentary on the Prophecies of Isaiah...New
and Revised Edition. Edited by John Eadie. 2
Vols. Edinburgh: Andrew Elliot, James Thin
[T.& T. Clark], 1865.

Another edition; Edinburgh: T.& T. Clark, 1873.

Reprint edition; One Volume. Grand Rapids,
Michigan: Zondervan Publishing House, 1953.

1850 **Pringle, William**   Commentary on the Prophet Isaiah
by John Calvin. Translated from the original Latin,
and collated with the author's French version. 4
Vols. Edinburgh: Calvin Translation Society, 1850-
1853.
[See Bible Selections, 1844 Anonymous, Commentaries on
the books of the Bible.]

1853 **Rae, John**   The Book of the Prophet Isaiah, rendered into English blank verse; with explanatory notes, by John Rae. Sydney: W. & A. Ford, 1853.

1860 **Anonymous**   The Book of the Prophet Isaiah. Dublin: University Press, 1860?

1860 **Sawyer, Leicester Ambrose**   The Holy Bible...
     [See Old Testament Selections for the complete entry. Includes Isaiah.]

1860 **Smithson, J.H.**   A new Translation from the Hebrew, of the Prophet Isaiah: together with an exposition of the spiritual sense of the divine prophecies, from the theological works of Swedenborg by J.H. Smithson.... London: Longman, 1860.

1862 **Whish, J.C.**   A Paraphrase of the Book of the Prophet Isaiah: with notes from various sources by J.C. Whish.   London: Seeley, Jackson & Halliday, 1862.

1865 **Eadie, John** (Editor) See Joseph Addison Alexander, The Earlier ...Prophecies, 1846.

1867 **Martin, James**   The Prophecies of Isaiah, 1867.
     [See Old Testaments, 1865 Biblical Commentary.]

1869 **Glover, O.** The Prophet Isaiah, Chapters I-XXXIII. From the German of H. Ewald. Cambridge: Deighton, Bell & Co., 1869.
     [Translated from "Die Propheten des Alten Bundes."]

1870 **Cheyne, T.K.**   The Book of Isaiah Chronologically Arranged. An Amended Version, with Historical and critical Introductions and explanatory Notes. London: Macmillan & Co., 1870.
     ["The basis of the version is naturally the revised translation of 1611, but no scruple has been felt in introducing alterations, wherever the true sense of the prophesies appeared to require it."]

1871 **Birks, Thomas R.**   Commentary on the Book of Isaiah, Critical, Historical, and Prophetical, including a revised English translation; With introduction and appendices on the nature of scripture prophecy, the life and times of Isaiah, the genuineness of the later prophecies, the structure and history of the whole book, the Assyrian history in Isaiah's days, and various difficult passages. By Rev. T.R. Birks. London, Oxford & Cambridge: Rivingtons, 1871.
     Second edition; revised.   London: Macmillan & Co., 1878.

Another second edition; London: The Church of England Book Society, 1878.

1871 **Pauli, C.W.H.**   The Chaldee Paraphrase on the Prophet Isaiah. Translated by C.W.H. Pauli. London: London Society's House, 1871.
["I have followed the text of the Biblia Magna Hebraica... and the English AV of the Hebrew text, wherever it was possible."]

1873 **Friedlander, Michael**   The Commentary of Ibn Ezra on Isaiah: edited from the MSS. and Translated, with Notes, Introductions, and Indexes.   London: Published for The Society of Hebrew Literature by N. Trubner & Co., 1873-1877.
1873 ...Vol. I   Translation of the Commentary.

1873 ...Vol. II   The Anglican version of the Book of the Prophet Isaiah Amended according to the commentary of Ibn Ezra.

1877 ...Vol. III   ...with notes and glossary.

1877 ...Vol. IV   Essays on the writings of Ibn Ezra.

Reprint of Vol. 1 in English and Hebrew; (Two volumes in one, printed back-to-back) New York: Philipp Feldheim, Inc., 1965?

1874 **American Bible Union**   Isaiah 1-13:22, by Thomas J. Conant. New York: American Bible Union, 1874

1874 **Proby, W.H.B.**   The Ten Canticles of the O.T... Canon...
[See Old Testament Selections for the complete entry. Includes the Song of Isaiah and the Song of Hezekiah.]

1877 **Sharpe, Samuel**   The Book of Isaiah, arranged chronogically in a revised translation... with historical notes, by Samuel Sharpe. London: S.R. Smith.
[Apparently a different work than in his OT.]

1879 **Waddell, P. Hately**   Isaiah frae Hebrew intil Scottis. By P. Hately Waddell. Edinburgh & Glasgow: J. Menzies & Co., 1879.

1880 **Cheyne, T.K.**   The Prophecies of Isaiah. Translated with Critical Notes and Dissertations. 2 Vols. London: Kegan Paul & Co., 1880-1881.
1882 Second Edition.

1884 A New Translation, with Commentary and
     Appendices...Third Edition.   New York:
     Thomas Whittaker.

1886 Fourth Edition. 2 Vols. in one.   London:
     Kegan Paul & Co.

1889 Fifth Edition, Revised. 2 Vols.   London:
     Kegan Paul & Co.

1895 Fifth Edition, Revised. 2 Vols. in one.
     New York: Thomas Whittaker.

1898 Sixth Edition, Revised. 2 Vols.   London:
     Kegan Paul.

1881 **Rodwell, J.M.**   The Prophecies of Isaiah. Translated
     from the Hebrew by J.M. Rodwell. London: F. Norgate,
     1881.
         ["He has...aimed...to be strictly literal and Faithful
         to the Hebrew text...he has retained the parallelisms
         which are a distinct feature of all Hebrew poetry... The
         translation has adhered throughtout to the common
         Masoretic text..."]

         Second edition;   London: Frederic   Norgate;
         Edinburgh: Williams & Norgate, 1886. Reprinted
         from The Journal of Sacred Literature, 5th
         ser., vol. I and II.

         Third edition, 1880.

1883 **Arnold, Matthew**   Isaiah of Jerusalem
     in the Authorized Version with an Introduction,
     Corrections, and Notes by Matthew Arnold. London:
     Macmillan & Co., 1883.

1884 **Sawyer, Leicester Ambrose**   (The Bible) Analyzed...
         [See Bible Selections for the complete entry.]

1889 **Banks, J.S.**   The Prophecies of Isaiah. Exponded by
     Dr. C. Von Orelli... Translated by Rev. J.S.Banks...
     Edinburgh: T.& T. Clark, 1889.
         ["Our only text is the one settled by the Masorete
         editors comparatively late in our era. Wherever,
         therefore, the text is difficult or obscure, we have
         resort, not to different readings, but to the LXX, the
         Targums, and Jerome's version and, finally, to
         conjecture."]

         [The Deity is rendered "Yahweh" many times.]

         Again, 1895.

1889 **Epstein, Eph. M.**   A New Translation of Isaiah 53;
     Together with its Introduction in Isa 52: 13-15.

Gold from Ophir; a new book of Bible readings, original and selected. Kansas City: Gospel Tract Depot, Mitchell & Shiop, p. 70-71, c1889.
[The Deity is rendered "Jehovah"]

1889 **Smith, George Adam**   The Book of Isaiah, 1889.
[See Bible Selections, 1888 Expositor's Bible.]

1890 **Forbes, John**   The Servant of the Lord in Isaiah XL-LXVI. Reclaimed to Isaiah as the author from Argument, Structure, and date. Edinburgh: T. & T. Clark, 1890.

1891 **Blake, Buchanan**   How to Read Isaiah...
[See Prophets and Selections, ???? Buchanan Blake, How to Read...]

1891 **Blake, Buchanan**   How to Read Isaiah (XL-LXVI)...
[See Prophets and Selections, ???? Buchanan Blake, How to Read...]

1895 **Cheyne, T.K.**   Introduction to the Book of Isaiah with an appendix containing the undoubted portions of the two chief prophetic writers in a translation by T.K. Cheyne. London: Adam & Charles Black, 1895.
["...the following translation ...is merely provisional. It is designed to illustrate and exhibit synthetically some of the most important results of the critical discussion in the previous pages..." Note preceding the Appendix.]

1897 **Kelly, William**   An Exposition of the Book of Isaiah. New and Enlarged Edition. By William Kelly. London: T. Weston, 1897.
["As Lectures on Isaiah had long gone out of print, I declined allowing a new edition till I had leisure to prepare a correct version and a somewhat fuller commentary. This is now entitled an Exposition of the Book of Isaiah, being rather a new book than a re-issue." (1897 preface). Apparently the first edition ('Lectures...') did not include a translation, as does 'An Exposition...']

Second Edition; London: F.E. Race, 1913?

Third Edition; London: F.E. Race, 1916.

Fourth Edition; London: C.A. Hammond, 1946.

1897 **Mitchell, Hinckley Gilbert**   Isaiah. A Study of Chapters I-XII. New York & Boston: Thomas Y. Crowell & Co., 1897.
["...a second volume on chapters XIII-XXXIX if I am spared to complete it." Apparently not published.]

1898 **Cheyne, T.K.**   The Book of The prophet Isaiah, a new English Translation Printed in Colors Exhibiting

the Composite Structure of the Book, with
Explanatory Notes and Pictorial Illustrations, by
T.K. Cheyne. New York: Dodd, Mead, and Company,
1898.
[See Old Testament Selections, 1898 Sacred Books of the
Old and New Testament, Part 10. The Polychrome Bible.]

1901 **Flecker, E.**   A New Translation of Isaiah.
With Explanatory Notes, and a History of the Life of
Isaiah. By Rev. E. Flecker ...London: Elliot Stock,
1901.
["...the translation is given in a rhythmical form by
its division into lines, a system which the author found
much help in obtaining the very mind of Isaiah."]

1904 **Ottley, Robert R.**   The Book of Isaiah According to
the Septuagint (Codex Alexandrinus); Translated and
Edited by R.R. Ottley... London: C.J. Clay & Sons;
Cambridge: University Press, 1904-1906.
1904 - - I. Introduction and Translation with
a parallel version from the Hebrew.

1906 - - II. [Greek] Text and Notes.

["...some errors and omissions have been corrected, a
few words altered in the translations, and a few
footnotes added."]

[BMC also lists an edition with two English versions
only, 1907.]

Second edition; 2 Vols., 1909.

1908 **Box, G.H.**   The Book of Isaiah. Translated
from a Text Revised in accordance with the results
of recent criticism; with introductions, critical
notes and explanations, and two maps... Together
with a prefatory note by S.R.Driver... By G.H. Box.
London: Sir I. Pitman and Sons, 1908.
Another edition; New York: The Macmillan Co.,
1909.

Also; London: Sir I. Pitman and Sons, 1916.

1910 **Glazebrook, M.G.**   Studies in the Book of Isaiah.
Oxford: At the Clarendon Press, 1910.
["In the form of the translation I have largely followed
the German of Duhm's great edition, but I owe much also
to Dr. Cheyne's kind permission to borrow phrases from
his admirable version..."]

1912 **Gray, George Buchanan and Arthur S. Peake**
A Critical and Exegetical Commentary on the Book of
Isaiah. I-XXXIX by George Buchanan Gray... XL-LXVI
by Arthur S. Peake... In Two Volumes. Edinburgh: T.
& T. Clark, 1912.

[See Complete Bibles, 1895 International Critical Commentary (Isaiah).]

1912 **Hitchcock, George S.** The First Twelve Chapters of Isaiah. A New Translation and Commentary. By George S. Hitchcock... London: Burns & Oates, 1912.

1913 **Anonymous** The Prophecies and Visions of the Prophet Isaiah. Revised by Snowdrop. London: Lynwood & Co., 1913.

1914 **Buttenweiser, Moses** The Prophets of Israel From the Eighth to the Fifth Century...
[See Prophets and Selections for the complete entry. Includes Isaiah.]

1917 **Newman, Louis I. and William Popper** Studies in Biblical Parallelism...
[See Prophets and Selections for the complete entry.]

1918 **McFadyen, John Edgar** Isaiah in Modern Speech..., by John Edgar McFadyen... London: James Clarke & Co., 1918.
["It will be found, I believe, that so far from obscuring the prophet's thought, the rhythmic form...not infrequently invests it even greater lucidity than sometimes attaches to the familiar prose translations."]

[The Deity is rendered "Jehovah" many times.]

1922 **Sheppard, H.W.** The First Twelve Chapters of Isaiah. A new translation, by H.W. Sheppard. Cambridge: Bowes & Bowes, 1922.

1925 **Levy, Reuben** Deutero-Isaiah; A Commentary; Together with a Preliminary Essay on Deutero-Isaiah's influence on Jewish Thought. Oxford: University Press; London: Humphrey Milford, 1925.
["A new translation of the Hebrew has been attempted and an endeavour has been made in it to indicate by means of accents (') the rhythm of the original."]

1928 **Torrey, Charles Cutler** The Second Isaiah; a new interpretation by Charles Cutler Torrey. New York: Charles Scribner's Sons, 1928.
[Part II is entitled, "Translation with indication of metrical form." Chapters 34-66.]

1930 **Allan, J.B.** The Book of Isaiah. I-XXXIX Vol.1 Translated into Colloquial English by J.B. Allan. London: National Adult Sunday School Union, 1930.
[See Old Testament Selections, 1920 Books of the Old Testament in Colloquial Speech, No. 8.]

1931 **Popper, William** The Prophetic Poetry of Isaiah Chapter 1-37, Translated in Parallelism from a

Revised Hebrew Text, by William Popper. Berkely,
California: University of California Press, 1931.
["Most of the changes introduced into the (Hebrew)
text...have been made in order to restore clarity of
meaning on the basis of regularity of form..." Chapters
1-10 appeared in 1917. See Louis I. Newman and William
Popper.]

1932 **Hamond, E.W.**   The Eighth Century Prophets...
[See Prophets and Selections for the complete entry.
Includes Isaiah.]

1939 **Wordsworth, W.A.**   En. Roeh. The Prophecies of
Isaiah the Seer...
[See Prophets and Selections for the complete entry.]

1940 **Martin, William Wallace**   Isaian Prophecies.
Promises to Chosen People; Punishments to Chosen
People; Promises to Other Peoples; Punishments to
Other People. Reconstructed, Retranslated and
Annotated by William Wallace Martin. Nashville: The
Parthenon Press, 1940.

1940 **Slotki, Israel W.**   Isaiah. Hebrew Text & English
Translation. With an Introduction and Commentary, by
I.W. Slotki. London: The Soncino Press, 1940.
[See Old Testaments, 1936 Soncino Books of the Bible.]

     Also, 1949.

1941 **Kissane, Edward J.**   The Book of Isaiah, Translated
from a critically revised Hebrew text, with
commentary by Edward J. Kissane. 2 Vols. Dublin:
Browne & Nolan, 1941-1943.
          1941 - - Vol. I (I-XXXIX)
          1943 - - Vol. II (XL-LXVI)

          ["In the translation I have aimed at accuracy rather
          than elegance. ...the ruggedness of the original
          sometimes breaks through..."]

1944 **Smith, Sidney**   Isaiah Chapters XL-LV; Literary
Criticism and History... The Schweich Lectures of
the British Academy, 1940. London: Published for the
British Academy by Humphrey Milford, 1944.
["With great regret a paraphrastic translation of the
passages cited has been given..."]

1948 **Coslet, Walter A.**   A Paraphrase of the K.J.V. of
Isaiah 53. By Walter A. Coslet.   The Bible
Versionist, p. 2, July, 1948.
[The Deity is rendered "Jehovah".]

1948 **North, Christopher R.**   The Suffering Servant in
Deutero-Isaiah; An Historical and Critical Study, by

Christopher R. North.   Oxford: University Press;
London: Geoffrey Cumberledge, 1948.
["From the corrected sheets of the first edition",
1950.]

[Part II contains "The [Servant] Songs: Text and
Translation".]

1949 **Stenning, J.F.**   The Targum of Isaiah; Edited with
a Translation by J.F. Stenning...   Oxford: at the
Clarendon Press, 1949.
["The corrected text of Isaiah represented by the
English translation is based on mss to which the editor
had access...(i.e. the Yemen MSS, B.M. or.2211, fols.
156aff, with superlinear punctuation and other Aramaic
documents.)]

Another edition, 1953.

1958 **Bland, Sheldon H.**   Prophetic Faith in Isaiah by
Sheldon H. Bland.   London: Adam and Charles Black,
1958.
["The translations from the Hebrew in this book
(frequently paraphrastic) are my own unless otherwise
designated..."]

1961 **Morgenstern, Julian**   The Message of Deutero-Isaiah
in its Sequential Unfolding, by Julian Morgenstern.
Cincinnati: Hebrew Union College Press, 1961.
["...some textual rearrangement of the address, as it
lies before us in the MT form, is unavoidable..."
English translation of Isaiah 40-48.]

1962 **Anonymous**   Isaiah. Concordant Literal O.T...
[See Old Testament Selections, 1957 Anonymous,
Concordant Literal...]

1963 **Leslie, Elmer A.**   Isaiah; Chronologically arranged,
translated and interpreted. Elmer A. Leslie.   New
York & Nashville: Abingdon Press, 1963.
["I have made my own translation of the entire book of
Isaiah on the basis...which includes the most
significant variant readings of the complete Hebrew MS
of the Book of Isaiah which was discovered in 1947 in a
cave near the NW corner of the Dead Sea."]

1963 **Phillips, J.B.**   Four Prophets; Amos, Hosea, First
Isaiah, Mich...
[See Prophets and Selections for the complete entry.]

1964 **Margoliouth, Rachel**   The Indivisible Isaiah;
evidence for the single authorship of the prophetic
book.   Jerusalem: Sura Institute of Research;   New
York: Yeshiva University, 1964.
["We have used the Bible translation of the Jewish
Publication Society. However...we were obliged, where
necessary to employ our own translation..."]

1964 **North, Christopher R.**   The Second Isaiah; Introduction, Translation, and Commentary to Chapters XL-LV, by Christopher R. North. Oxford: The Clarendon Press, 1964.
> ["The Translation is fairly literal... Occasionally I have paraphrased where...the standard English Version may convey a misleading sense..."]

1965 **Knight, George A.F.**   Deutero-Isaiah; a theological commentary on Isaiah 40-55 by George A.F. Knight. New York & Nashville: Abingdon Press, 1965.
> ["...I have kept as close as possible to the received Hebrew text...I take a conservative view of the MT..."]

1965 **Young, Edward J.**   The Book of Isaiah; The English Text, with Introduction, Exposition and Notes by Edward J. Young. Grand Rapids, Michigan: William B. Eerdmans Publishing House, 1965.
> 1965 - - Vol. I   Chapters 1-18
> - - Vol. II
> - - Vol. III

1966 **Minn, H.R.**   The Servant Songs; Excerpts from Isaiah 42-53; Introduction, Translation and Commentary, by H.R. Minn. Christchurch, Auckland, Dunedin, Invercargill: Presbyterian Bookroom, 1966.
> ["The renderings that follow are reasonably literal. At points a freer translation is given..."]

1968 **Jewish Interpreters**   The Fifty-third Chapter of Isaiah According to the Jewish Interpreters. New York: Ktav, 1968.
> [2 volume work reprint. Vol.2 contains quite a number of translations by Jewish rabbis and commentators.]

1968 **Leupold, Herbert Carl**   Exposition of Isaiah, by H.C. Leupold. 2 Vols. Grand Rapids, Michigan: Baker Book House, 1968-1969.

1968 **McKenzie, John L.**   Second Isaiah. Introduction, Translation, and Notes, by John L. McKenzie. Garden City, New York: Doubleday & Co., 1968.
> [See Complete Bibles, 1964 Anchor Bible, Vol. 20.]

1969 **Stalker, D.M.G.**   Isaiah 40-66, 1969.
> [See Old Testament Selections, 1962 Old Testament Library.]

1971 **Aston, Frederick Alfred**   The Challenge of the Ages; New Light on Isaiah 53. Frederick Alfred Aston. Scarsdale, New York: Research Press, 1971.
> Revised Edition; 1972.

1971 **Buksbazen, Victor**   The Prophet Isaiah: New Translation and Commentary. Victor Buksbazen. Collingswood, NJ: The Spearhead Press, 1971.

1978 **Rosenberg, David**   Light—Works, Interpreted
from the Original Hebrew Book of Isaiah, by David
Rosenberg. New York: Harper & Row, 1978.
    [Selected passages poetically paraphrased]

1979 **Watts, J. Wash**   A Distinctive Translation of Isaiah
with an interpretative outline by J. Wash Watts.
[South Pasadena, Calif.: Jameson Press], 1979.

1982 **Rosenberg, A.J.**   Isaiah, 1982—1983.
    [See Old Testament Selections, ???? Judaica Press
    Publications.]

1985 **Watts, John D.W.**   Word Biblical Commentary. Isaiah
1—33. John D.W. Watts.   Waco, TX: Word Books,
Publisher, 1985.
    [See Complete Bibles, 1982 Word Biblical Commentary,
    Vol. 24.]

1986 **Oswalt, John N.**   The Book of Isaiah: Chapters 1—39,
1986.
    [See Hebrew Scriptures Listing, 1976 New International
    Commentary on the O.T.]

1987 **Chilton, Bruce D.**   Isaiah, 1987.
    [See Old Testaments, 1987 Aramaic Bible, Vol. 11.]

1987 **Hayes, John H. and Stuart A. Irvine**   His Times
& His Preaching. Isaiah, The Eighth—Century Prophet.
John H. Hayes and Stuart A. Irvine.   Nashville:
Abingdon Press, 1987.

1987 **Watts, John D.W.**   Word Biblical Commentary. Isaiah
34—66. John D.W. Watts.   Waco, TX: Word Books,
Publisher, 1987.
    [See Complete Bibles, 1982 Word Biblical Commentary,
    Vol. 25.]

1988 **Giliadi, Avraham**   The Book of Isaiah. A New
Translation with Interpretive Keys from the Book of
Mormon, by Avraham Giliadi. Salt Lake City, UT:
Deseret Books, 1988.

1990 **Ackerman, Susan**   Isaiah 57:3—13. Bible Review,
Vol. VI, No. 1, Feb., 1990, page 40.

JEREMIAH

???? **Ball, C.J.**   Prophecies of Jeremiah, [189?].
    [See Bible Selections, 1888 Expositor's Bible.]

???? **Hubbard, David A.**   Word Biblical Commentary.
Jeremiah - Lamentations...
    [See Major Prophets and Selections for the complete
entry.]

???? **Judaica Press Publications**   The Judaica Books of
the Prophets...
    [See Old Testament Selections for the complete entry.
Includes Jeremiah.]

1534 **Joye, George**   Jeremy the Prophete...
    [See Old Testament Selections for the complete entry.]

1620 **Cotton, Clement**   Lectures upon the First Five
Chapters of the Prophecie of the Prophet Jeremiah...
London: Felix Kyngston, 1620.
    Reprint; London: Edward Brewster, 1658.

1645 **Anonymous**   A Bottle of Holy Tears...
    [See Major Prophets and Selections for the complete
entry.]

1784 **Blayney, Benjamin**   Prophecy of Jeremiah...
    [See Major Prophets and Selections for the complete
entry.]

1850 **Owen, John**   Commentaries on Jeremiah...
    [See Major Prophets and Selections for the complete
entry.]

1851 **Henderson, E.**   The Book of the prophet Jeremiah
and that of the Lamentations, translated from the
original Hebrew, with a Commentary, critical,
philological and exegetical by E. Henderson...
London: Richard Clay, for Hamilton, Adam & Co.,
1851.
    Another edition; Andover: Warren F. Draper;
Boston: W.H. Halliday & Co.; Philadelphia:
Smith, English & Co., 1868.

1860 **Sawyer, Leicester Ambrose**   The Holy Bible...
    [See Old Testament Selections for the complete entry.
Includes Jeremiah.]

1878 **Linton, Henry P.**   The Book of Jeremiah: with
explanatory notes and appendices. London: Philip's
Series of Scripture Manuals, 1878.

1880 **Kennedy, James and David Patrick**   Prophecies of
Jeremiah, 1880.
    [See Old Testaments, 1865 Biblical Commentary.]

1892 **Blake, Buchanan**   How to Read Jeremiah...
    [See Prophets and Selections, ???? Buchanan Blake, How
to Read...]

1906 **Brown, Charles Rufus**   The Book of Jeremiah, 1906.
[See Old Testament Selections, 1906 Anonymous, An American Commentary.]

[The Deity is rendered "Jehovah" many times.]

1906 **Driver, Samuel Rolles**   The Book of the Prophet Jeremiah. A revised translation, with introductions and short explanations. By the Rev. S.R. Driver, D.D... New York: Scribner; London: Hodder & Stoughton, 1906.
["I have given a revised translation of the Book, in the general style of the AV, as clear and exact as English idiom would permit..."]

2nd edition; 1908.

1907 **Gillies, J.R.**   Jeremiah; The Man and His Message by J.R. Gillies. London: Hodder & Stoughton, 1907.

1914 **Buttenweiser, Moses**   The Prophets of Israel...
[See Prophets and Selections for the complete entry. Includes Jeremiah.]

1917 **Morais, Sabato**   Jeremiah, 1917.
[See Old Testaments, 1917 Jewish Publication Society.]

1919 **McFadyen, John Edgar**   Jeremiah in Modern Speech, by John Edgar McFadyen. London: James Clarke & Co., [1919].
[The Deity is rendered "Jehovah" many times.]

1922 **Skinner, John**   Prophecy and Religion; Studies in the Life of Jeremiah. By John Skinner. Cambridge University Press, 1922.
[Lectures in New College, Edinburgh during the Spring of 1920; contains translations of many passages, mostly from the LXX.]

6th reprint, 1951.

1923 **Smith, George Adam**   Jeremiah. Being the Baird Lecture for 1922. By George Adam Smith. New York: George H. Doran Co., 1923.
[Translation and Commentary. "...I have rendered the name of the God of Israel as it is by the Greek and our own Versions - - the Lord..."]

Another edition; London: Hodder & Stoughton Ltd., n.d.

Fourth Edition; Revised and Enlarged. New York & London: Harper & Bros. Publishers, 1929.

1923 **Welch, Adam C.**   The Book of Jeremiah. Translated
into Colloquial English by Adam C. Welch.   London:
National Adult School Union, 1923.
> [See Old Testament Selections, 1920 Books of the Old
> Testament in Colloquial Speech, No. 3.]

> Revised, 1928.

1932 **Gordon, T. Crouther**   The Rebel Prophet: Studies
in the Personality of Jeremiah.   New York & London:
Harper & Bros. Publishers, 1932.
> ["I have laid down the following rules for the
> translation of Jeremiah...1. Poetry must be translated
> as poetry. 2. The stresses of the Hebrew must be
> repeated exactly in the English... 3. The order of the
> words...must be repeated in the English in the same
> order. 4. The sounds of the Hebrew must be translated
> into the same sounds in English as far as possible..."]

1935 **Broadbent, E.H.**   Jeremiah. The Book of the Prophet
with explanatory notes and Paraphrases.   London,
Glasgow & Edinburgh: Pickering & Inglis, 1935.

1939 **Anonymous**   Jeremiah The Prophet by George A.
Birmingham. [J.O.Hannay] London: 1939.
> Another edition; God's Iron, A Life of the
> Prophet Jeremiah by George A. Birmingham.
> (J.O. Hannay M.A., D.Litt.) London: Geoffrey
> Bles, 1956.

> Also; Jeremiah The Prophet. First American
> Edition. New York: Harper & Brothers, 1956.

1940 **Martin, William Wallace**   Jeremiah-Ezekiel
Prophecies...
> [See Major Prophets and Selections for the complete
> entry.]

1949 **Freedman, Harry**   Jeremiah, 1949.
> [See Old Testaments, 1936 Soncino Books of the Bible.]

1952 **Laetsch, Theo.**   Bible Commentary: Jeremiah.   St.
Louis, Mo.: Concordia Publishing House, 1952.

1954 **Leslie, Elmer A.** Jeremiah Chronologically Arranged,
Translated and Interpreted by Elmer A. Leslie.   New
York & Nashville: Abingdon Press, 1954.

1961 **Bland, Sheldon H.**   Jeremiah; Man and Prophet.
Cincinnati: Hebrew Union College Press, 1961.

1965 **Bright, John**   Jeremiah. Introduction, Translation,
and Notes by John Bright.   Garden City, New York:
Doubleday & Co., Inc., 1965.
> [See Complete Bibles, 1964 Anchor Bible, Vol. 21.]

1971 **Corre, A.D.**   The Daughter of my People. Arabic and Hebrew Paraphrases of Jeremiah 8.13-9.23.   Leiden: E.J. Brill, 1971.

1973 **Anonymous**   Hebrew Scriptures Study Sheets. Concordant Version of Jeremiah and Lamentations...
      [See Old Testament Selections, 1957 Anonymous, Concordant Literal...]

1980 **Thompson, J.A.**   The Book of Jeremiah, 1980.
      [See Hebrew Scriptures Listing, 1976 New International Commentary on the O.T.]

1987 **Hayward, Robert**   Jeremiah, 1987.
      [See Old Testaments, 1987 Aramaic Bible, Vol. 12.]

LAMENTATIONS

???? **Hubbard, David A.**   Word Biblical Commentary. Jeremiah - Lamentations...
      [See Major Prophets and Selections for the complete entry.]

1340 **Rolle, Richard**   The Lamentations of Jeremiah. By Richard Rolle. MS c1340.

1534 **Joye, George**   Jeremy the Prophete...
      [See Old Testament Selections for the complete entry.]

1566 **Anonymous**   The Wailyngs of the prophet Hieremiah, done into Englyshe verse. [Thomas Drant]   London: Thomas Marshe, 1566.

1587 **Fetherstone, Christopher**   The Lamentations of Ieremie, in prose and meeter; with apt notes to sing them withall: Togither with Tremelius his annotations, translated out of Latin into English by Christopher Fetherstone, for the profit of all those to whom god hath given an in-sight into spiritual things. Seene and allowed.   London: Printed by Ihon Wolfe, 1587.

1587 **Stocker, T.**   The Lamentations; lamentably paraphrased by Daniel Tousain, and translated... London: For H. Bate, 1587.

1593 **Udall, John**   A Commentarie vpon the Lamentations of Ieremy. Wherein are contained...a literall interpretation of the text out of the Hebrew, with a paraphrasticall exposition of the sense therof... London: Joan Orwin, 1593.

Another edition; London: Peter Short for Thomas
Man, 1595.

Another edition; London: by the assigns of Joane
Man and Benjamin Fisher, 1621.

1600 **Broughton, Hugh**   Books of David...
     [See Old Testament Selections for the complete entry.]

1606 **Broughton, Hugh**   The Lamentations of Jeremy,
     Translated vvith great care of his ebrevv Elegancie,
     and Oratoriovs Speaches: vvherein his six fold
     Alphabet Stirreth all to attention, of God's Ordered
     Providence   in   Kingdomes   confusion.   VVith
     explications from other Scriptures touching his
     story and phrases. [Geneva?], 1608.
     Another edition, 1608.

     [Reprinted with Job, Ecclesiastes & Daniel.] Londson:
     N.Elkins, 1662.

1608 **Anonymous**   The Lamentations of Jeremy: with
     a commentary London: T.C. for Thomas Man, 1608.

1609 **Anonymous**   Meditations upon the Lamentations
     of Jeremy. [Anne Jenkinson] London: W. Hall for R.
     Braddock, 1609.

1621 **Wither, George**   The Hymnes and Songs...
     [See Old Testament Selections for the complete entry.]

1624 **Quarles, Francis**   Sions Elegies. Wept by Ieremie
     the Prophet, And Periphras'd. London: Printed by W.
     Stansby for Thomas Dewe, 1624.

1631 **Donne, John**   The Lamentations of Jeremy; For the
     most part according to Tremelius. London: M.F.,1631.
     [In couplet verse.]

     Another edition; London: by M.F., for John
     Marriott, 1633.

     [Reprinted in "The Complete Poetry and Selected Prose of
     John Donne..." New York: Random House, The Modern
     Library, 1941.]

1636 **Sandys, George**   A Paraphrase... Divine Poems...
     [See Old Testament Selections for the complete entry.]

1644 **Boyd, M. Zachary**   The Garden of Zion...
     [See Old Testament Selections for the complete entry.]

1645 **Anonymous**   A Bottle of Holy Tears...
     [See Major Prophets and Selections for the complete
     entry.]

1647 **Anonymous**   The Lamentations of the Prophet Jeremiah paraphras'd. Suitable to the Exigencies of these times. London: 1647.

1648 **Quarles, John**   Fons Lachrymarum, or a Fountain of Tears; from whence doth flow Englands Complaint, Jeremiah's Lamentations paraphras'd... London: J. Macocke for N. Brooks, 1648.

1650 **Anonymous**   The Psalms, Hymns and Spiritual Songs...
        [See Old Testament Selections for the complete entry. Includes Lamentations]

1652 **Anonymous**   The Lamentations of Jeremiah; in Metre. London: for Stephen Bowtell, 1652.

1661 **Powell, Vavasoure**   ... Or the Bird in the cage, chirping four distinct notes... The Lamentations of Jeremiah in Meeter, in the oridinary measure of singing Psalms. By Vavasoure Powell. London: Printed for L.C., 1661.

1680 **Chamberlaine, James**   Threnodia: or, Lamentations of Jeremiah paraphras'd with a prayer for the Church. London: Printed by R.E. for R.Bentley, 1680.

1683 **Anonymous**   A Paraphrase [in Verse] On the First and Second Chapters of the Lamentations of the Prophet Jermiah. London: printed for Charles Corbett, 1683.

1699 **Chamberlaine, James**   Lamentations of Jeremiah...
        [See Old Testament Selections for the complete entry.]

1708 **Anonymous**   The Lamentations of Jeremiah Paraphras'd. By W.B. [William Brown]   Edinburgh: John Vallange, 1708.

1739 **Anonymous**   David's Lamentations Over Saul and Jonathan; Paraphrased in Verse. <u>Gentleman's Magazine</u>, Vol. IX, page 209, 1739.

1750 **Erskine, Ralph**   A Short Paraphrase upon the Lamentations of Jeremiah. Adapted to the common Tunes. To which is subjoined A twofold Paraphrase of David's Last Words, 2 Sam. xxiii. 3, 4, 5, 6, 7. Viewed 1. As a Direction to Kings; 2. As a Prophecy of Christ. As also a Paraphrase on the First Gospel Promise, Gen. iii. 15. And on the Great Gospel Mystery, 1 Tim.iii.16.   Glasgow: John Newlands, 1750.
        [Reprinted in Erskine's Works, "Scripture Songs. In Two Books." Glasgow: 1766.]

1754 **Erskine, Ralph**   Scripture Songs...

[See Bible Selections for the complete entry. Includes a short paraphrase upon the Lamentations.]

1784 Blayney, Benjamin   Prophecy of Jeremiah and the Book of Lamentations...
[See Major Prophets and Selections for the complete entry.]

1793 Hill, Aaron   Habakkuk 3... David's Lamentation...
[See Bible Selections for the complete entry.]

1820 Perrin, W.   Hebrew Canticles...
[See Old Testament Selections for the complete entry.]

1848 Slight, Henry Spencer   Talmon and Hadassah: a tale of the first Captivity and Destruction of Jerusalem, illustrative of God's judgements on the national sin. Also a metrical version of the Lamentations of Jeremiah. By Henry Spencer Slight. London: n.p., 1848.

1850 Owen, John   Commentaries on Jeremiah and...
[See Major Prophets and Selections for the complete entry.]

1854 Anonymous   The Songs and Small Poems...
[See Old Testament Selections for the complete entry.]

1860 Sawyer, Leicester Ambrose   The Holy Bible...
[See Old Testament Selections for the complete entry.]

1885 Wrangham, Digby S.   Lyra Regis. The Book of...
[See Old Testament Selections for the complete entry.]

1893 Greenup, A.W.   The Targum [of Onkelos] on the Book of Lamentations. Translated by A.W. Greenup. Sheffield: [privately circulated], 1893.

1926 Vivian, Herbert   The Lamentations of a New Jermiah; Translated out of the original tongues: and with the former translations diligently compared and revised. Appointed to be read surreptitiously in churches by Herbert Vivian. London: George Allen & Unwin Ltd., 1926.

1940 Martin, William Wallace   Jeremiah-Ezekiel Prophecies...
[See Major Prophets and Selections for the complete entry.]

1954 Gottwald, Norman K.   Studies in the Book of Lamentations. Chicago: Alec R. Allenson, 1954.
[Starts with "Translation of the Book of Lamentation".]

Also; -- Studies in Biblical Theology [No. 14], 1954. London: S.C.M. Press Ltd.

1972 **Hillers, Delbert R.**   Lamentations. Introduction, Translation, and Notes, by Delbert R. Hillers. Garden City, New York: Doubleday & Co., 1972.
      [See Complete Bibles, 1964 Anchor Bible, Vol. 7A.]

1973 **Anonymous**   Hebrew Scriptures Study Sheets... Concordant Version of Jeremiah and Lamentations...
      [See Old Testament Selections, 1957 Anonymous, Concordant Literal...]

1976 **Levine, E.**   The Aramic Version of Lamentations. New York, 1976.
      [Text and translation.]

1976 **Zlotowitz, Meir**   Lamentations, 1976.
      [See Old Testaments, 1976 ArtScroll Tanach Series.]

EZEKIEL

1788 **Newcome, William**   An Attempt towards an Improved Version, a Metrical Arrangement, and an Explanation of the Prophet Ezekiel. By William Newcome... Dublin: R. Marchbank, for J. Johnson, G.G.J. & J. Robinson, P. Elmsly, 1788.
      [Translation is based on the Hebrew as well as a "...collation of a Coptic version supposed to be of the second century, and...the Pachomian ms of the LXX version, ascribed to the tenth or eleventh century..."]

      [See Anonymous, A Literal Translation of the Prophets, 1836.]

1844 **Anonymous**   Commentaries [on the Books of the Bible]...
      []See Bible Selections for the complete entry. Includes Ezekiel.]

1845 **M'Farlan, James**   A Version of the Prophecies of Ezekiel; retaining, for the most part, in English the same order of expression which occurs in the Hebrew original; by the Rev. James M'Farlan... Edinburgh: Printed for the Author by Oliver & Boyd, 1845.

1845 **McFarlane, James**   Prophecies of Ezekiel, a New Version. Edinburgh: 1845.

1849 **Myers, Thomas**   Commentaries on the Prophet Ezekiel by John Calvin. Translated from the original Latin, and collated with the author's French version. 2

Vols. Edinburgh: Calvin Translation Society, 1849-1850.
[See Anonymous, Commentaries on the Books of the Bible, 1844.]

1851 **Fairbairn, Patrick**   Ezekiel, and the Book of His Prophecy: An Exposition. Edinburgh: T. & T. Clark, 1851.
Second Edition, 1855.
["The exposition has been rendered more uniform by a translation of the whole Book, while in the First Edition this was limited to the more difficult parts..."]

Third Edition, 1862.
[Changes are "...chiefly confined to verbal alterations..."]

Fourth Edition, 1876.

Reprinted; Grand Rapids, Michigan: Zondervan, 1960.

Another reprint; Evansville, Indiana: Sovereign Grace, 1960.

1855 **Henderson, E.**   The Book of the Prophet Ezekiel, translated from the original Hebrew, with a Commentary, critical, philological and exegetical by E. Henderson. London: Richard Clay, for Hamilton, Adam & Co., 1855.
["In presenting the text...to my readers, I have retained the ordinary cast of prose throughout..."]

Another edition; Andover: Warren F. Draper, 1855.

1860 **Sawyer, Leicester Ambrose**   The Holy Bible...
[See Old Testament Selections for the complete entry. Includes Ezekiel.]

1869 **Murphy, A.C. and J.G. Murphy**   The Prophecies of the Prophet Ezekiel Elucidated. By E.W. Hengstenberg... Translated by A.C.Murphy and J.G.Murphy. Edinburgh: Clark's Foreign Theological Library, 1869.

1876 **Martin, James**   The Prophecies of Ezekiel, 1876.
[See Complete Bibles, 1865 Biblical Commentary.]

1894 **Blake, Buchanan**   How to Read Ezekiel...
[See Prophets and Selections, ???? Buchanan Blake, How to Read...]

1899 **Toy, Crawford H.**   The Book of Ezekiel, a new English Translation, with Explanatory Notes..., by C.H. Toy. New York: Dodd, Mead and Co., 1899.
[See Old Testament Selections, 1898 Sacred Books of the Old and New Testaments, Part 12.]

1917 **Schneeberger, H.W.**   Ezekiel, 1917.
[See Old Testaments, 1917 Jewish Publication Society.]

1931 **Levy, Abraham J.**   Rashi's Commentary on Ezekiel
40-48; Edited on the basis of eleven manuscripts...
A thesis submitted in partial fulfillment of the
requirements for the degree of Doctor of Philosophy
in the Dropsie College for Hebrew and Cognate
Learning. By Abraham J. Levy.   Philadelphia: The
Dropsie College for Hebrew and Cognate Learning,
1931.

1936 **Cooke, G.A.**   A Critical and Exegetical Commentary
on The Book of Ezekiel by G.A. Cooke...   Edinburgh:
T. & T. Clark, 1936.
[See Complete Bibles, 1895 International Critical
Commentary.]

1939 **Matthews, I.G.**   The Book of Ezekiel, 1939.
[See Old Testament Selections, 1906 Anonymous, An
American Commentary.]

1940 **Martin, William Wallace**   Jeremiah-Ezekiel
Prophecies...
[See Major Prophets and Selections for the complete
entry.]

1943 **Irwin, William A.**   The Problem of Ezekiel; An
Inductive Study. Chicago, Illinois: The University
of Chicago Press, 1943.
[Includes a reconstructed translation of those portions
of Ezekiel Chapters 1 through 38 which the author
considered genuine.]

1947 **Brownlee, Hugh**   The Book of Ezekiel - The Original
Prophet and the Editors... A Thesis submitted in
partial fulfillment of the requirements for the
degree of Doctor of Philosophy in the graduate
school of Arts and Sciences Duke Univ.   Durham, NC:
Duke University, 1947.
[Part II, "A Tentative Reconstruction of the Book of
Ezekiel in its Original Poetic Forn."]

1950 **Fisch, S.**   Ezekiel, 1950.
[See Old Testaments, 1936 Soncino Books of the Bible.]

1977 **Anonymous**   Concordant Literal O.T...
[See Old Testament Selections, 1957 Anonymous,
Concordant Literal...]

1977 **Eisemann, Moshe and Nosson Scherman**   Ezekiel, 1977.
[See Old Testaments, 1976 ArtScroll Tanach Series.]

1979 **Clements, Ronald E.**   A Commentary on the
Book of the Prophet Ezekiel, Chapters 1-24 by Walter
Zimmerli. Translated by Ronald E. Clements. Edited

by Frank Moore Cross and Klaus Baltzer with the assistance of Leonard Jay Greenspoon. Philadelphia: Fortress Press, 1979.

1983 **Allen, Leslie C.**   Word Biblical Commentary. Ezekiel 20-48. Leslie C. Allen.   Waco, TX: Word Books, Publisher, 1983.
[See Complete Bibles, 1982 Word Biblical Commentary, Vol. 29.]

1987 **Levey, Samson H.**   Ezekiel, 1987.
[See Old Testaments, 1987 Aramaic Bible, Vol. 13.]

DANIEL

???? **Murphy, James G.**   A Critical and Exegetical Commentary on the Book of Daniel. With a New Translation. [186?].
Also; The Book of Daniel; or, the Second Volume of Prophecy. Translated and Expounded, with a preliminary sketch of antecedent prophecy. London: Nisbet & Co., 1884.

Another edition; A Critical and Exegetical Commentary... Andover: Warren F. Draper, 189?

1545 **Joye, George**   The exposition of Daniel the Prophete gathered oute of Philip Melancthon / Johan Ecolampadius / Chonrade Pellicane, and out of Iohan draconite, &c. By George Joye. A Prophecye diligently to be noted of al Emprowrs and Kinges in these laste dayes. Emprinted at Geneue: actually Antwerp?, 1545.
Another edition; Imprinted at London: by Jhon Daie & Wylliam Seres, 1550.

Another; Imprinted at London by Thomas Raynolde, 1550.

1555 **Cotsforde, Thomas**   Daniel, Chapter IX, verse 4-19 in Metre. Geneva: 1555.

1570 **Anonymous** Commentaries of that diuine Ihon Caluine, vpon the Prophet Daniell, translated into Englishe, especially for the vse of the family of the ryght honorable Earl of Huntington, to set forth as in a glasse, how one may profitably read the Scriptures, by consideryng the sence thereof, and by prayer.

[Arthur Golding]   London: Imprinted by Ihon Daye, 1570.
> ["To the reader" signed A.G. "...the one half of the booke of Daniell, coteynyng the first vi chapters ...the which latter part also I do meane (by God's grace) to publish..." Not known whether the remainder was indeed published.]

1596 **Anonymous**   Daniel, His Chaldie Visions and His Ebrevv, both Translated after the Original: and expounded both, by reduction of heathen most famous stories vnto the exact proprietie of his wordes (which is the surest certaintie what he must meane:) and by joyning all the Bible, and learned tongues to the frame of his worke. [by Hugh Broughton]. London: Printed by Richard Field, for William Young, 1596.
> [Text differs from the Genevan, upon which it is based; accompanied by a Commentary.]

> Another edition; Daniel... Imprinted at London by Gabriel Simson, 1597.
>> [Closely resembles the 1596 edition. The only differences being the omission of 'The Faults Escaped' and the addition of a colophon.]

> Also; Daniel with a Brief Explication by Hvgh Brovghton. Printed at Hanaw by Daniel Avbri, 1607.

> In Addition; Daniel reprinted with Job, Ecclesiastes and Lamentations. London: N. Elkins, 1662.

1607 **Broughton, Hugh**   Daniel with a brief Explication by Hvgh Brovghton. Hanaw: Printed by Daniel Avbri, 1607.
> Reprinted with Job, Ecclesiastes, and Lamentations; London: N.Elkins, 1662.

1644 **Brightman, Thomas**   The Revelation with Daniel chapter XI, verses 36-45...
> [See Bible Selections for the complete entry.]

1644 **Huit, Ephraim**   The Whole Prophecie of Daniel explained, by a paraphrase, analysis, and briefe comment... London: Henry Overton, 1644.

1653 **Aspinwall, W.**   Daniel, Chapter VII with a correction of the Translation. London: 1653.

1792 **Wintle, Thomas**   Daniel, an improved version attempted; with a preliminary dissertation and notes, critical, historical and explanatory by Thomas Wintle. Oxford: J. Cooke, 1792.
> Introduction; London: 1807.

[See Anonymous, A Literal Translation of the
Prophets..., 1836.]

1794 **Anonymous**   Remarks on the Book of Daniel...
[See Bible Selections for the complete entry.]

1818 **Bellamy, John**   The Holy Bible...
[See Old Testament Selections for the complete entry.
Includes the Book of Daniel.]

1832 **Thorpe, Benjamin**   Caedmon's Metrical Paraphrase...
[See Old Testament Selections for the complete entry.
Includes Daniel.]

1852 **Myers, Thomas**   Commentaries on the Prophet Daniel
by John Calvin. Translated from the original Latin,
and collated with the author's French version. 2
Vols. Edinburgh: Calvin Translation Society, 1852-
1853.
[See Bible Selections, 1844 Anonymous, Commentaries [on
the Books of the Bible]...]

1864 **Sawyer, Leicester Ambrose**   Daniel, with its
apocryphal additions, translated, arranged, and the
principal   questions   of   its   interpretation
considered, by Leicester Ambrose Sawyer. Boston:
Walker, Wise and Company, <u>American Biblical</u>
<u>Quarterly</u>, January 1, 1864.

1877 **Easton, M.G.**   The Book of Daniel, 1877.
[See Old Testaments, 1865 Biblical Commentary.]

1879 **Seiss, Joseph A.**   Voices from Babylon; or, the
Records of Daniel the Prophet, by Joseph A. Seiss.
Philadelphia: Porter & Coates, 1879.
[Includes "A critically - revised translation of the
Book of Daniel."]

Another edition; New York: Charles C. Cook 1879.

Also; New York: Charles C. Cook, 1915.

1882 **Sawyer, Leicester Ambrose**   (The Bible) Analyzed...
[See Bible Selections for the complete entry. Includes
Daniel.]

1883 **Hunt, Theodore W.**   Caedmon's Exodus and Daniel...
[See Old Testament Selections for the complete entry.]

1895 **Anonymous**   The Book of the Prophet Daniel
Translated... [Ralph Sadler] London: Sheppard and
St. John, 1895.

1899 **Pollard, Josephine**   Ruth, A Bible Heroine; and
Other Stories...
[See Old Testament Selections for the complete entry.
Includes abbreviated stories of Job, Samuel, David &

Saul, Solomon the Wise Man, Elijah, Elisha, Jonah the
Man Who Tries to Hide from God, Daniel.]

1905 **Heller, Nachman**   Daniel and Ezra, the Canonized...
[See Old Testament Selections for the complete entry.]

1906 **Anonymous** Prophetic Suggestions; Being...Revelation
and Daniel...
[See Bible Selections for the complete entry.]

1906 **Wright, Charles Henry Hamilton**   Daniel and His
Prophecies by Charles H.H. Wright. London: Williams
& Norgate, 1906.
[Includes "The Book of Daniel; A New Translation based
on the RV."]

1907 **Blackburn, Francis A.**   Exodus and Daniel, Two Old
English Poems...
[See Old Testament Selections for the complete entry.]

1909 **Porter, Frank Chamberlin**   The Messages of the
Apocalyptical Writers...   [Daniel and Revelations]
[See Abridged Bibles, 1900 Frank Knight Sanders and
Charles F. Kent, The Messages of the Bible, Vol.VIII.]

1909 **Williams, O.T.**   Short Extracts from Old English
Poetry...
[See Old Testament Selections for the complete entry.]

1912 **Rutland, James R.**   Old Testament...schools...
[See Old Testament Selections for the complete entry.
Includes the chief episodes in Genesis, Exodus, Joshua,
Judges, Samuel, Kings, and Daniel.]

1916 **Kennedy, Charles W.** The Caedmon Poems Translated...
[See Old Testament Selections for the complete entry.]

1923 **Craige, W.A.**   Specimens of Anglo-Saxon Poetry...
[See Old Testament Selections for the complete entry.]

1927 **Gordan, Robert K.**   Anglo-Saxon Poetry...
[See Old Testament Selections for the complete entry.]

1927 **Montgomery, James A.**   A Critical and Exegetical
Commentary on The Book of Daniel by James A.
Montgomery... Edinburgh: T. & T. Clark, 1927.
[See Complete Bibles, 1895 International Critical
Commentary.]

Reprinted, 1950.

1929 **Charles. R.H.** A Critical and Exegetical Commentary
on the Book of Daniel. With introduction, indexes,
and a new English translation. Oxford: Clarendon
Press, 1929.

1948 **Lattey, Cuthbert**   Daniel, 1948.

[See Complete Bibles, 1913 Westminster Version.]

1949 **Leupold, Herbert Carl**   Exposition of Daniel, by
H.C. Leupold. Columbus, Ohio: Wartburg Press, 1949.
[With a new translation based on the Masoretic text.]

1949 **Young, Edward J.**   The Prophecy of Daniel;
A Commentary by Edward J.Young. Grand Rapids,
Michigan: William B. Eerdmans Publishing Co., 1949.
["The translation of Daniel herein endeavors to being
out the exact meaning of the Hebrew and Aramaic..."]

1959 **Misrahi, Jean**   A Thirteenth-Century Musical Drama;
The Play of Daniel... Based on the transcription
from British Museum Egerton 2615... Translation from
the Latin Text, by Jean Misrahi. New York: Oxford
University Press, 1959.

1961 **Tubbs, Edward J.** The Book of Daniel, Transliterated
and Translated from the Hebrew and Chaldee Text...
for Diploma Students and Bible-Lovers, by Edward J.
Tubbs. London: Printed for the Author by Norman,
Hopper & Co., Ltd., 1961.

1965 **Porteus, Norman W.**   Daniel, 1965.
[See Old Testament Selections, 1962 O.T. Library.]

1968 **Anonymous**   Concordant Literal O.T...
[See Old Testament Selections, 1957 Anonymous,
Concordant Literal...]

1972 **Nickelsburg, Jr., George W.E.**   Resurrection,
Immortality, and Eternal Life in Intertestamental
Judaism. George W.E. Nickelsburg, Jr. Cambridge:
Harvard University Press; London: Oxford University
Press, 1972.
[Harvard Theological Studies XXVI.]

["Translations of Daniel are my own."]

1978 **Hartman, Louis F. and Alexander A. DiLella**
The Book of Daniel. A New Translation with Notes and
Commentary on Chapters 1-9 by Louis F. Hartman,...
Introduction and Commentary on Chapters 10-12 by
Alexander A. DiLella,...   Garden City, New York:
Doubleday & Co., Inc., 1978.
[See Complete Bibles, 1964 Anchor Bible, Vol. 23.]

1979 **Goldwurm, Hersh**   Daniel, 1979.
[See Old Testaments, 1976 ArtScroll Tanach Series.]

1989 **Goldingay, John E.**   Word Biblical Commentary.
Daniel. John E. Goldingay. Waco, TX: Word Books,
Publisher, 1989.
[See Complete Bibles, 1982 Word Biblical Commentary,
Vol. 30.]

9

Minor Prophets

MINOR PROPHETS AND SELECTIONS

???? **Andersen, Francis I.** Habakkuk, Obadiah, Joel and Jonah. Introduction, Translation, and Notes by Francis I. Anderson. Garden City, New York: Doubleday & Co., Inc., [19??].
[See Complete Bibles, 1964 Anchor Bible, Vol. 25.]

???? **Andersen, Francis I.** Micah, Nahum and Zephaniah. Introduction, Translation, and Notes by Francis I. Anderson. Garden City, New York: Doubleday & Co., Inc., [19??].
[See Complete Bibles, 1964 Anchor Bible, Vol. 24A.]

???? **Andersen, Francis I.** Amos and Hosea. Introduction, Translation and Notes by Francis I. Anderson. Garden City, New York: Doubleday & Co., Inc., [19??].
[See Complete Bibles, 1964 Anchor Bible, Vol. 24.]

???? **Andersen, Francis I.** Haggai, Zechariah and Malachi. Introduction, Translation, and notes by Francis I. Anderson. Garden City, New York: Doubleday & Co., Inc., [19??].
[See Complete Bibles, 1964 Anchor Bible, Vol. 25A.]

???? **Judaica Press Publications** The Judaica Books of the Prophets...
[See Old Testament Selections for the complete entry. Includes the Book of Twelve Prophets.]

1560 **Pilkington, James** Aggeus the prophete declared by a large commentarye. [London: Willyam Seres], 1560.
Another edition; An Exposition vpon Abdias, 1562.

Also; Aggeus and Abdias Prophetes, the one corrected, the other newly added and both at large declared, 1562.

[Reprinted in "The Works of James Pilkington", by the
Parker Society. Cambridge: The University Press, 1842.]

1568 **Grindal, Edmund**   Lesser Prophets, 1568.
[See Complete Bibles, 1568 Bishops' Bible.]

1573 **Norton, Robert**   Certaine Godlie Homilies or Sermons
upon the Prophets Abdias and Ionas: Conteyning a
most fruitefull exposition of the same. Made by the
most excellent lerned man, Rudolph Gualter of
Tigure. And translated into Englishe by Robert
Norton. London: Henrie Bynneman, for Rafe Newberie,
1573.

1594 **Anonymous**   A Frvitfvll Commentarie vpon the
twelue Small Prophets, Briefe, Plaine, and Easie,
Going over the same verse by verse, and shewing
euery where the Method, points of doctrine, and
figures of Retoricke, to the no small profit of all
godly and well disposed Readers, with very necessary
fore-notes for the vnderstanding both of these and
also all the other Prophets. The text of these
Prophets together with that of the quotations
omitted by the Authour, faithfully supplied by the
Translatour, and purged of faults in the Latine
coppie almost innumerable, with a table of all the
chiefe matters herein handled, and marginall notes,
very plentifull and profitable; so that it may in
manner be counted a new Booke in regard to these
additions. Written in Latin by Lambertus Danaeus,
and newly turned into English. [Ihon Stockwood]
Cambridge: Printed by Ihon Legate, 1594.

1659 **Stokes, David**   A Paraphrasticall Explication of
the Twelve Minor Prophets, by David Stokes. London:
for Thomas Davies, 1659.

1785 **Newcome, William**   An Attempt towards an Improved
Version, a Metrical Arrangement, and an Explanation
of the Twelve Minor Prophets. London: Printed for
J. Johnson, G.G.J. & J. Robinson, P. Elmsly, 1785.
Another; Dublin: R. Marchbank, 1785.

Another edition; Now enlarged and improved with
additional Notes, and a comparison of the
chief various renderings of Dr. Horseley, on
Hosea, and Dr. Blayney on Zechariah.
Pontefract: Printed by B. Boothroyd for F.
Burkitt, London, 1809.

Also; London: for Richard Baynes, 1819.

Another edition, 1836.

[See Prophets and Selections, 1836 Anonymous, A Literal Translation of the Prophets.]

1818 **Bellamy, John**   The Holy Bible...
[See Old Testament Selections for the complete entry. Includes the following Minor Prophets; Obadiah, Jonah, Micah, Nahum, Habakkuk, Zephaniah and Haggai.]

1833 **Noyes, George R.**   A New Translation of the Hebrew Prophets, Arranged in Chronological Order. By George R. Noyes. Boston: 1833-1837.
> 1833 - - Volume I. Containing Joel, Amos, Hosea, Isaiah, and Micah. Boston: Charles Bowen.
>
> 1837 - - Volume II. Containing Nahum, Zephaniah, Habakkuk, Obadiah, Jeremiah, Lamentations. Boston: James Munroe & Co.
>
> 1837 - - Volume III. Containing Ezekiel, Daniel, Haggai, Zechariah, Jonah, and Malachi. Boston: James Munroe & Co.

[The Deity is rendered "Jehovah" many times.]

Second edition; with corrections and additions. 3 Vols. Boston: James Munroe & Co., 1843.
> [Vol. I 1843; Vol. II & III 1837.]

Third edition; With New Introduction and Notes. Boston: American Unitarian Association, 1866.

Sixth edition; 2 Vols.   Boston: American Unitarian Association, 1880.

1833 **Pick, Aaron**   A Literal Translation from the Hebrew of the Twelve Minor Prophets; with some notes from Jonathan's Paraphrase in the Chaldee, and critical remarks from R.S. Yarchi, Abenezra, D. Kimchi, and Abarbanel. London: Joseph Shackell, for W. Straker, 1833.
> Second Edition; Carefully Revised and Corrected. London: James Nisbet, 1835.

Another edition; 1838.

1835 **Anonymous**   Songs of the Prophets; with prose remarks and metrical versions. London: Orr & Smith, 1835.

1839 **Barlee, Edward**   An explanatory version of the Minor Prophets, with the text. By the Rev. Edward Barlee. London: R. Clay, for William Pickering, 1839.

1845 **Henderson, E.**   The Book of the Twelve Minor Prophets, translated from the original Hebrew: with a commentary, critical, philological and exegetical by E. Henderson. London: Hamilton, Adam & Co., 1845.
> ["He has constantly had recourse to the collection of various readings made by Kennicott and DeRossi; he has compared renderings of the LXX., the Targums, the Syriac, the Arabic, the Vulgate, and other ancient versions..."]

Another edition, 1858.

1846 **Owen, John**   Commentaries on the Twelve Minor Prophets by John Calvin. Translated from the original Latin, and collated with the author's French version. 5 Vols. Edinburgh: Calvin Translation Society, 1846-1849.
> [See Bible Selections, 1844 Anonymous, Commentaries on the Books of the Bible.]

1853 **Drake, William**   Notes critical and explanatory on the prophecies of Jonah and Hosea, with a summary of the history of Judah and Israel during the period when the prophecies were delivered. Cambridge: Macmillan & Co., 1853.
> [A word-for-word praxis.]

1856 **Moore, Thomas Verner**   The Prophets of the Restoration; or Haggai, Zechariah and Malachi. A new translation, with notes. New York: Robert Carter & Bros., 1856.
> ["I have given first my own translation, which is presented, like that of Newcome, Henderson, Calvin, and others, in metrical form, according to the Parallelism..."]

Reprinted; Commentary on Zechariah. London: The Banner of Truth Trust, 1958.

Also; Commentary on Haggai and Malachi. London: The Banner of Truth Trust, 1960.

1860 **Pusey, Edward Bouverie**   The Minor prophets with a Commentary explanatory and practical and introductions to the several books by E.B. Pusey. Oxford: J.H. & J. Parker; Cambridge: Deighton, Bell; London: Rivingtons, 1860.
> ["In some places...I have put down what I thought an improvement of the English Version..." The facing title page is entitled, 'The Holy Bible with a Commentary...' The preface states, "The New Testament except the Apocalypse, and most of the rest of the Old Testament, have been undertaken by friends, whose names will be published, when the arrangement shall be finally completed..." Apparently this was not done.]

1860 **Sawyer, Leicester Ambrose**   The Holy Bible...
[See Old Testament Selections for the complete entry.
Includes the twelve Minor Prophets.]

1864 **Whish, J.C.**   A Paraphrase of the Books of the
Minor Prophets: with notes from various sources by
J.C. Whish. London: Seeley & Co., 1864.

1867 **Cowles, Henry**   The Minor Prophets; with Notes,
critical, explanatory, and practical. Designed for
both pastors and people. By Henry Cowles. New York:
D. Appleton & Co., 1867.
["The author has aimed to give a translation, more or
less free, or a paraphrase, in all cases where he has
been compelled to differ from the received version..."]

1867 **Stuart, Peter**   (Editor)   See John Bellamy, The Holy
Bible, 1818.

1868 **Martin, James**   The Twelve Minor Prophets, 1868.
[See Old Testaments, 1865 Biblical Commentary.]

1870 **Barham, Francis** A Revised Version of the prophecies
of Hosea and Micah. By Francis Barham.   London:
Fred. Pitman; Bath: I. Pitman, J. davies, 1870.

1873 **Elzas, A.**   The Minor Prophets, translated from the
Hebrew Text with an introduction, and a commentary,
critical, philological and exegetical by A. Elzas.
3 Vols.   London: Trubner & Co., 1873-1874.
1873 ...Vol.1 Hoshea, Joel
1874 ...Vol.2 Amos, Obadiah, Jonah

1882 **Smith, W.R.**   The Prophets of Israel, by W.R. Smith.
London: n.p., 1882.
Second edition; London: Black, 1895.

1893 **Banks, J.S.**   The Twelve Minor Prophets,
Exponded by Dr. C. Von Orelli... Translated [From
the German]. Edinburgh: T.& T. Clark,   1893.
Another edition, 1897.

1896 **Douglass, Benjamin**   A translation of the minor
Prophets. With an occasional brief note introduced.
New York, Chicago, Toronto: Fleming H. Revell Co.,
1896.
["...he has followed the Masoretic punctuation, and the
translation is given as originally written, without any
attempt at revision."]

1896 **Smith, George Adam**   The Book of the Twelve
Prophets..., 1896.
[See Bible Selections, 1888 Expositor's Bible.]

1905 **Harper, William Rainey**   A Critical and Exegetical
Commentary on Amos and Hosea by William Rainey
Harper... Edinburgh: T. & T. Clark, 1905.
[See Complete Bibles, 1895 International Commentary
(Amos and Hosea).]

Reprinted; 1910, 1936.

1908 **Sanders, Frank Knight and Charles Foster Kent**
The Messages of the Later Prophets freely rendered
in paraphrase, 1908.
[See Abridged Bibles, 1900 Frank Knight Sanders and
Charles Foster Kent, The Messages of the Bible, Vol.
II.]

1911 **Smith, John Merlin Powis and Others**   A Critical and
Exegetical Commentary on Micah, Zephaniah, Nahum,
Habakkuk, Obadiah and Joel by John Merlin Powis
Smith... William Hayes Ward... Julius A. Bewer...
Edinburgh: T. & T. Clark, 1911.
[See Complete Bibles, 1895 International Critical
Commentary (Micah, Zephaniah, Nahum, Habakkuk, Obadiah
and Joel).]

[Micah, Zephaniah and Nahum by J.M. Powis Smith;
Habakkuk by William Hayes Ward; Obadiah and Joel by
Julius A. Bewer.]

Reprinted; 1928, 1948.

1912 **Duff, Archibald**   The Twelve Prophets; a Version
in the Various Poetical Measures of the Original
Writings, by Bernhard Duhm, D.D...Authorized
Translation. London: Adam and Charles Black, 1912.

1912 **Mitchell, Hinckley G. and Others**   A Critical and
Exegetical Commentary on Haggai, Zechariah, Malachi
and Jonah by Hinckley G. Mitchell... John Merlin
Powis Smith... Julius A. Bewer... Edinburgh: T. &
T. Clark, 1912.
[See Complete Bibles, 1895 International Critical
Commentary (Haggai, Zechariah, Malachi and Jonah).]

Reprinted, 1937.

1917 **Voorsanger, J.**   Obadia, Jonah, 1917.
[See Old Testaments, 1917 Jewish Publication Society.]

1928 **Smith, George Adam**   The Book of the Twelve Prophets
commonly called the Minor Prophets. In Two Volumes.
By George Adam Smith. With an Introduction and a
Sketch of Prophecy in Early Israel. Revised edition.
New York: Harper & Bros., Publishers, 1928.

1929 **Pilcher, C.V.**   Hosea, Joel, Amos; A devotional
Commentary, by C.V. Pilcher. London: The Religious
Tract Society, 1929.
["Where the RV seemed at all adequate, he has followed
its wording... Where however, the RV seemed
unintelligible or inadequate, the commentator has
followed, generally, the translation of Dr. Ernst
Sellin..."]

1934 **Naish, John and R.B.Y. Scott**   The Books of Micah
and Habakkuk, translated into Colloquial English by
John Naish and R.B.Y. Scott. London: National Adult
School Union, 1934.
[See Old Testament Selections, 1920 Books of the O.T. in
Colloquial Speech, No. 10.]

[Micah by John Naish and Habakkuk by R.B.Y. Scott.]

1937 **Bevenot, Hugh**   Nahum & Habakkuk, 1934.
[See Complete Bibles, 1913 Westminister Version.]

1941 **Martin, William Wallace**   Twelve Minor
Prophets, Complete. The Judean Version, its Author
a Descendent of the Southern Kingdom. Also the
Ephramean Version, its Author a Descendent of the
Northern Kingdom. Reconstructed and Retranslated by
William Wallace Martin. Nashville: The Parthenon
Press, 1941.

1945 **Wolfe, Rolland Emerson**   Meet Amos and Hosea, The
Prophets of Israel by Rolland Emerson Wolfe. New
York & London: Harper & Bros., 1945.
["The translation is fairly literal. At certain places
liberties have been taken, but only in so far as they
are in harmony with the spirit of the Hebrew text."]

1948 **Cashdan, Eli**   Haggai, Zechariah & Malachi, 1948.
[See Old Testaments, 1936 Sonoino Books of the Bible.]

1948 **Goldman, Solomon**   Obadiah, Jonah & Micah, 1948.
[See Old Testaments, 1936 Soncino Books of the Bible.]

1948 **Lehrman, S.M.**   Hosea, Joel, Amos, Nahum, Habakkuk,
and Zephaniah, 1948.
[See Old Testament, 1936 Soncino Books of the Bible.]

1953 **Bullough, Sebastian**   Obadiah, Micah, Zephaniah,
Haggai, Zechariah, 1934.
[See Complete Bibles, 1913 Westminster Version.]

1958 **Deere, Derwood William**   The Twelve
Speak; A Translation of the Books of [the Minor
prophets]...with exegetical and interpretative
footnotes and an introductory section on Prophecy.
By Derwood William Deere... 2 Vols. New York: The
American Press, 1958-1961.

1960 **Morgan, G. Campbell**   The Minor Prophets. The Men
and their Messages, by G. Campbell Morgan. London:
Pickering & Inglis, 1960.

1962 **Heschel, Abraham J.** The Prophets. New York: Jewish
Publication Society of America, 1962.
["The RSV has been used throughout, interspersed
occasionally with my own translation."]

Another edition; New York & Evanston: Harper &
Row.

1974 **Anonymous**   Hosea, Amos, and Micah in Today's
English Version. Justice Now! New York: American
Bible Society, 1974.

1976 **Allen, Leslie C.** The Books of Joel, Obadiah, Jonah,
and Micah, 1976.
[See Hebrew Scriptures Listing, 1976 New International
Commentary on the O.T.]

1977 **Janzer, Waldemar and Others**   A Commentary
on the Prophets Joel and Amos by Hans Walter Wolff.
Translated by Waldemar Janzer, S. Dean McBride, Jr.,
and Charles A. Muenchow. Edited by S. Dean McBride,
Jr. Philadelphia: Fortress Press, 1977.

1984 **Smith, Ralph L.**   Word Biblical Commentary.
Micah–Malachi. Ralph L. Smith. Waco, TX: Word
Books, Publisher, 1984.
[See Complete Bibles, 1982 Word Biblical Commentary,
Vol. 32.]

1987 **Meyers, Carol L. and Eric M. Meyers**   Haggai,
Zechariah 1–8. A New Translation with Introduction
and Commentary. Garden City, New York: Doubleday &
Co., Inc., 1987.
[See Complete Bibles, 1964 Anchor Bible, Vol. 25b.]

1987 **Stuart, Douglas**   Word Biblical Commentary.
Hosea–Jonah. Douglas Stuart. Waco, TX: Word Books,
Publisher, 1987.
[See Complete Bibles, 1982 Word Biblical Commentary,
Vol. 31.]

1987 **Verhoef, Pieter A.** The Books of Haggai and Malachi,
1987.
[See Hebrew Scriptures Listing, 1976 New International
Commentary on the O.T.]

1990 **Robertson, O. Palmer** The Books of Nahum, Habakkuk,
and Zephaniah, 1990.
[See Hebrew Scriptures Listing, 1976 New International
Commentary on the O.T.]

HOSEA

???? **Ainsworth, Henry**   MS form of Hosea...
   [See Bible Selections for the complete entry.]

1771 **Neale, James**   The Prophecies of Hosea, translated,
   with a commentary and notes. London: The Author,
   1771.
      Another edition; Revised and edited with much
      original matter, by W.H. Neale. London: Hope
      & Co., 1850.

1801 **Horsley, Samuel**   Hosea. Translated from the Hebrew;
   with notes, explanatory and critical by Samuel
   Horsley. London: by J. Nichols for James Robson,
   1801.
      Second edition; London: J. Hatchard, 1804.

      [See Prophets and Selections, 1836 Anonymous, A Literal
      Translation of the Prophets.]

1850 **Neale, W.H.**   [See James Neale, Prophecies of Hosea, 1771.]

1853 **Drake, William**   Notes critical and explanatory
   on the prophecies of Jonah and Hosea...
      [See Minor Prophets and Selections for the entire
      entry.]

1869 **Bassett, Francis Tilney**   The Book of the Prophet
   Hosea, literally translated, with introduction and
   notes critical and explanatory. By ...Francis Tilney
   Bassett... London: W. Macintosh; Bath: R.C. Peach,
   1869.

1870 **Barham, Francis**   A Revised Version of the
   prophecies of Hosea and Micah...
      [See Minor Prophets and Selections for the entire
      entry.]

1873 **Anonymous**   Hoshea. The English version revised by
   the Cambridge Hebrew Society. Cambridge: Deighton,
   Bell & Co., 1873.

1873 **Elzas, A.**   The Minor Prophets...
      [See Minor Prophets and Selections for the complete
      entry. Includes Hosea.]

1898 **Anonymous**   Hosea. [Ralph Sadler] London, 1898.

1905 **Harper, William Rainey**   The Structure of the Book
   of Hosea by William Rainey Harper. Biblical World,
   January, 1905.
      ["The translation aims to follow closely the Hebrew
      idiom..."]

Another edition; — —["...issued in a revised form..."]
Chicago: University of Chicago Press, 1905.

1905 **Harper, William Rainey**   A Critical and Exegetical
Commentary on Amos and Hosea...
[See Minor Prophets and Selections for the complete
entry.]

1914 **Buttenweiser, Moses**   The Prophets of Israel From
the Eighth to the Fifth Century...
[See Prophets and Selections for the complete entry.]

1921 **Scott, Melville**   The Message of Hosea, by Melville
Scott. London: S.P.C.K.; New York: Macmillan & Co.,
1921.
["... a new translation of the text as arranged and
emended..."]

1924 **Povah, J.W.**   The Book of Hosea. Translated into
Colloquial English by J.W. Povah. London: National
Adult School Union, 1924.
[See Old Testament Selections, 1920 Books of the Old
Testament in Colloquial Speech, No. 6.]

1929 **Pilcher, C.V.**   Hosea, Joel, Amos...
[See Minor Prophets and Selections for the complete
entry.]

1932 **Hamond, E.W.**   The Eighth Century Prophets...
[See Prophets and Selections for the complete entry.]

1945 **Wolfe, Rolland Emerson**   Meet Amos and Hosea...
[See Minor Prophets and Selections for the complete
entry.]

1963 **Phillips, J.B.**   Four Prophets; Amos, Hosea, First
Isaiah and Micah...
[See Prophets and Selections for the complete entry.]

1966 **Ward, James M.**   Hosea; A Theological Commentary
by James M. Ward. New York: Harper & Row, 1966.
["Where the traditional renderings have been found fully
adequate I have simply followed them..."]

1974 **Anonymous**   Hosea, Amos, and Micah in Today's
English Version...
[See Minor Prophets and Selections for the complete
entry.]

1974 **Stansell, Gary**   A Commentary on the Books of
the Prophet Hosea by Hans Walter Wolff. Translated
by Gary Stansell. Edited by Paul D. Hanson.
Philadelphia: Fortress Press, 1974.

1980 **Andersen, Francis I. and David Noel Freedman**
Hosea. A New Translation with Introduction and Notes
by Francis I. Andersen and David Noel Freedman.
[See Complete Bibles, 1964 Anchor Bible, Vol. 24.]

JOEL

???? **Blake, Buchanan**   The Pre-Exilian Prophets (with
Joel)...
[See Prophets and Selections, ???? Buchanan Blake, How
to Read...]

???? **Garstang, Walter**   Joel, a New English Text; with
notes by Walter Garstang, [188?].

1582 **Ludham, Ihon**   The Homilies or Familiar Sermons of
M. Rodolph Gualther Tigurine vpon the Prophet Ioel.
Translated from the Latine into Englishe.   London:
Thomas Dawson, for William Ponnsonby, 1582.

1735 **Chandler, Samuel**   A Paraphrase and Critical
Commentary on the Prophecy of Joel. London: J. Noon,
1735.

1867 **Rowley, Adam Clarke**   Joel. A translation,
in metrical parallelisms, according to the Hebrew
method of punctuation: with notes and references, by
Adam Clarke Rowley. London: Hamilton, Adams & Co.,
1867.

1869 **Hughes, Joseph**   The Prophecy of Joel: the Hebrew
text, metrically arranged, with a new English
translation and critical notes. 2 Parts London: S.
Bagster & Sons, 1869.

1873 **Elzas, A.**   The Minor Prophets...
[See Minor Prophets and Selections for the complete
entry. Includes Joel.]

1917 **Cohen, Oscar**   Joel, 1917.
[See Old Testaments, 1917 Jewish Publication Society.]

1924 **Duncan, J. Garrow and Others**   The Book of Joel
(J.G. Duncan), Nahum (G. Currie Martin) and Obadiah
(Constance Mary Coltman) Translated into Colloquial
English.   London: National Adult Sunday School
Union, 1924.
[See Old Testament Selections, 1920 Books of the O.T. in
Colloquial Speech, No. 5.]

1929 **Pilcher, C.V.**   Hosea, Joel, Amos...

[See Minor Prophets and Selections for the entire entry.]

1976 **Allen, Leslie C.**   The Books of Joel..., 1976.
[See Minor Prophets and Selections for the entire entry.]

1977 **Janzer, Waldemar and Others**   A Commentary on the Prophets Joel and Amos...
[See Minor Prophets and Selections for the entire entry.]

AMOS

1869 **Drake, William**   Notes on the Prophecies of Amos; with a new translation. By William Drake.   London: Williams & Norgate, 1869.

1874 **Elzas, A.**   The Minor Prophets...Amos, Obadiah...
[See minor Prophets and Selections, 1873 A. Elzas, The Minor Prophets.]

1893 **Mitchell, Hinckley Gilbert Thomas**   Amos: an essay in exegesis. Boston: N.J. Bartlett & Co., 1893.
Revised edition; Boston: & New York: Houghton, Mifflin & Co., 1900.

1904 **Harper, William Rainey**   The Structure of the text of the Book of Amos by William Rainey Harper. Chicago, Illinois: University of Chicago Press, 1904.
["This translation is intended to follow closely the Hebrew idiom, and, inasmuch as it was important to have it correspond line for line, the idiom is sometimes, perhaps, more Hebraic than English."]

1905 **Harper, William Rainey**   A critical and Exegetical Commentary on Amos and Hosea...
[See Minor Prophets and Selections for the complete entry.]

1914 **Buttenweiser, Moses**   The Prophets of Israel...
[See Prophets and Selections for the complete entry.]

1917 **Mendes, Henry Pereira**   Amos, 1917.
[See Old Testaments, 1917 Jewish Publication Society.]

1917 **Newman, Louis I. and William Popper**   Studies in Biblical Parallelism. Part I. Parallelism in Amos...
[See Prophets and Selections for the complete entry.]

1920 **Robinson, Theodore H.**   The Book of Amos. Translated into Colloquial English by Theodore H. Robinson. London: National Adult Sunday School Union, 1920.
[See Books of the Old Testament in Colloquial Speech, No. 1, 1920.]

Revised, 1927.

1929 **Pilcher, C.V.**   Hosea, Joel, Amos...
[See Minor Prophets and Selections for the entire entry.]

1932 **Hamond, E.W.**   The Eighth Century Prophets...
[See Prophets and Selections for the complete entry.]

1936 **Richards, James**   De Sermon of Amos, a cowman and local preacher from Tekoa. Put into the Sussex Dialect by Jim Cladpole. [James Richards] Turnbridge Wells: J. Richards, 1936.

1942 **Reid, Francis W.**   The Book of Amos; Translated from the Hebrew Bible by Francis W. Reid Master of Arts; Labor Warns Luxury, 765 B.C. Berkeley, California: Multigraphed and Bound by Francis W. Reid, Author, 1942.
["Special Edition, One Hundred Copies... Dedicated to the California Christian Endeavor Union."]

1945 **Snaith, Norman H.**   The Book of Amos, by Norman H. Snaith. London: The Epworth Press, Study Notes on Bible Books, 1945-1946.
     1945 - - Part One: Introduction
     1946 - - Part two: Translation and Notes

1945 **Wolfe, Rolland Emerson**   Meet Amos and Hosea...
[See Minor Prophets and Selections for the complete entry.]

1963 **Phillips, J.B.**   Four Prophets...Isaiah, Amos...
[See Prophets and Selections for the complete entry.]

1963 **Weitzner, Emil**   Humanist Meditations...Amos...
[See Old Testament Selections, 1959 for the complete entry.]

1974 **Anonymous**   Hosea, Amos, and Micah...
[See Minor Prophets and Selections for the complete entry.]

1977 **Janzer, Waldemar and Others**   A Commentary on the Prophets Joel and Amos...
[See Minor Prophets and Selections for the complete entry.]

1988 **Hayes, John H.**   His Times & His Preaching.
Amos, The Eighth—Century Prophet. John H. Hayes.
Nashville: Abingdon Press, 1988.

1989 **Richardson, H. Neil**   Amos's Four Visions of
Judgment and Hope. <u>Bible Review Magazine</u>, Vol.V,
No.2, Pages 16—21, April, 1989.

OBADIAH

1560 **Pilkington, James**   Aggeus the prophete...
[See Minor Prophets and Selections for the complete
entry.]

1574 **Anonymous**   Abdias, or Obadiah; interpreted by T.B.
[Thomas Brasbridge]. London: Henry Bynneman, 1574.

1613 **Hinde, William**   The Prophesy of Obadiah, 1613.

1834 **Pick, Aaron**   The Prophecy of Obadiah. London: J.
Wilson, 1834?
[A translation from the Hebrew.]

1874 **Elzas, A.**   The Minor Prophets...Obadiah...
[See Minor Prophets and Selections, 1873 A.Elzas, The
Minor Prophets.]

1924 **Coltman, Constance Mary and Others**   The Books of
Joel...Obadiah...
[See Old Testament Selections, 1920 Books of the O.T. in
Colloquial Speech.]

1970 **Watts, John D.W.**   Obadiah: A Critical Exegetical
Commentary. Grand Rapids, MI: Eerdmans Publishing
Co., 1970.
[Contains a so-called distinctive translation.]

1976 **Allen, Leslie C.**   The Books of Joel, Obadiah...,
1976.
[See Minor Prophets and Selections, 1976 for the entire
entry.]

JONAH

???? **Anonymous**   Jonah; a poetical paraphrase. [Joseph
Mitchell] [172?].
Second Edition; corrected and adorned with
sculptures. To which are also added poetical

paraphrases on several other places of scripture. London: Aaron Ward, 1924.

???? **Davis, Arthur and Herbert Adler**   Service of the Synagogue...
[See Old Testament Selections for the complete entry.]

???? **Mitchell, Joseph**   See Anonymous, Jonah, [172?].

???? **Schliebe, R.H.**   Jonah, n.d.
[Metrical. Unpublished.]

1350 **Anonymous**   Patience: a West Midland poem of the fourteen century. (MS. Cotton Nero A.x)
A metrical version of the Book of Jonah edited with introduction, Bibliography, notes and glossary. By Hartley Bateson. Manchester: Univ. of Manchester Publications, 1912.

Second edition, recast and partly rewritten; Manchester: Univ. of Manchester Publications, 1918.

1531 **Tyndale, William**   The prophete Jonas with an introduccio before teachinge to vnderstode him and the right vse also of all the scripture and why it was written and what is therin to be sought and shewenge wherewith the scripture is locked vpp that he which readeth it can not vnderstode it though he studie therin neuer so moch: and agayne with what keyes it is so opened that the reader can be stopped out with no sotilte of false doctrine of man from the true sense and vnderstondynge therof. Antwerp: M. de Keyser?, 1531.
[The only known copy was discovered in the Library of Ickworth, in 1861, by Lord Arthur Hervey.]

Reproduced in Facsimile. — — To which is added Coverdale's version of Jonah, Introduction by Francis Fry. London: Willis and Sotheran, 1863.

1550 **Hooper, Bishop John**   An oversight and deliberation vpon the holy Prophete Ionas; made, and vterred before the Kynges maiestie, and his moost honorable councell, by Ihon Hoper in lent last past. Comprehended in seue Sermons. Imprinted at London by Ihon Daye, 1550.
Another edition; imprinted at London by Ihon Tisdale, 1551.

1570 **Tymme, Thomas**   Newes from Niniue to Englande, brought by the Prophete Jonas: which newes is plainlye published in the godly and learned

exposition of Maister Iohn Brentius folowing,
translated out of the Latine into Englishe by Thomas
Tymme. London: Henrie Denham, 1570.

1573 **Norton, Robert**   Certaine godlie Homilies... Abdias
     ans Ionas...
          [See Minor Prophets and Selections for the complete
          entry.]

1600 **Abbott, George** [Archbishop of Canterbury]   A Exposition
     upon the Prophet Ionah. Contained in certain sermons
     preached in S. Maries Church in Oxford.   London:
     Richard Field, 1600.

1600 **Abbott, J.**   Jonah, with exposition. London: R.Field,
     1600.

1620 **Quarles, Francis**   A Feast for Wormes. Set forth
     in a poeme of the history of Ionah...   London: Felix
     Kingston, for Richard Moore, 1620.
          [A paraphrase.]

1644 **Boyd, M. Zachary**   The Garden of Zion...
          [See Old Testament Selections for the complete entry.
          Includes Jonah.]

1676 **Anonymous**   The Book of the Song of Solomon (and
     the Book of Jonah)...
          [See Old Testament Selections for the complete entry.]

1700 **Anonymous**   Scriptural Poems. Being several portions
     of Scripture... IV. The Prophecy of Jonah...
          [See Bible Selections for the complete entry.]

1796 **Benjoin, George**   Jonah, a faithful translation
     from the original, with philological and explanatory
     notes; to which is prefixed a preliminary discourse,
     proving the genvineness, the authenticity and the
     integrity of the present text. By George Benjoin.
     Cambridge: J. Burges, Printer to the University,
     1796.
          [A diaglot Hebrew & AV, an original translation, and a
          very literal translation.]

1835 **Sibthorp, R. Waldo**   Pulpit Recollections: being
     notes of lectures on the Book of Jonah... Second
     edition (With a new translation.)   London: R.B.
     Seeley & Burnside, 1835.

1853 **Drake, William**   Notes critical and explanatory on
     the prophecies of Jonah and Hosea...
          [See Minor Prophets and Selections for the complete
          entry.]

1874 **Elzas, A.**   The Minor Prophets...Jonah...

[See Minor Prophets and Selections, 1873 A. Elzas, The Minor Prophets,]

1873 **Mitchell, Alexander**   The Book of Jonah: the text analyzed, translated, and the accents named: being an easy introduction to the Hebrew Language. London: S. Bagster & Sons, 1873.
[Hebrew & English]

1874 **Proby, W.H.B.**   The Ten Canticles of the Old Testament Canon...
[See Old Testament Selections for the complete entry. Includes the Song of Jonah.]

1875 **Mitchell, Stuart**   Jonah, the Self-Willed Prophet. A Practical Exposition of the Book of Jonah. Together with a Translation and Exegetical Notes. Philadelphia: Claxton, Remsen & Haffelfinger, 1875.
["The translation here offered aims not so much at giving a definite interpretation to the text as at putting the reader of English as nearly as possible in the same position as the reader of Hebrew."]

Third edition; Philadelphia: Presbyterian Board of education, n.d.

Reprinted; The Book of Jonah, 1966. La Mirada, California: The Bible Collector, No. 7, July - September 1966.

1878 **Kalisch, Marcus Moritz**   The Book of Jonah, preceded by a treatise on the Hebrew and the stranger. London: Longmans, Green & Co., 1878.

1883 **Redford, R.A.**   Studies in the Book of Jonah; A Defense and an Exposition, by R.A. Redford. London: Hodder & Stoughton, 1883.
[Part II, Chapter I consists of "The Words themselves, Literally Rendered." "...Ewald has rendered the Hebrew very ably in his work on 'The prophets of the Old Testament.' We have kept his translation before us in putting together the following version, without paraphrase or substitution of English for Hebrew idiom."]

1899 **Polland, Josephine**   Ruth, A Bible Heroine; and Other Stories Told in the Language of Childhood...
[See Old Testament Selections for the complete entry.]

1924 **Anonymous**   The Road to Real Success...
[See Bible Selections for the complete entry.]

1924 **Coltman, Constance Mary**   The Book of Ruth and Jonah...
[See Old Testament Selections, 1920 Books of the O.T. in Colloquial Speech.]

1926 **Martin, Arthur Davis**   The Prophet Jonah: The Book and the Sign. London, New York, Toronto: Longmans, Green & Co., 1926.

1938 **Bird, Thomas E.**   Jona, 1934.
[See Complete Bibles, 1913 Westminster Version.]

1951 **Silverman, Morris**   ...High Holiday Prayer Book...
[See Old Testament Selections for the complete entry.]

1961 **Weitzner, Emil**   Humanist Meditations...Jonah...
[See Old Testament Selections, 1959 for the complete entry.]

1970 **Bulla, Clyde Robert**   Jonah and the Great Fish. New York: Thomas Y. Crowell Co., 1970.
[A graceful retelling of the story.]

1975 **Levine, E.**   The Aramic Version of Jonah. Jerusalem, 1975.   [Text and translation.]

1976 **Allen, Leslie C.**   The Books of Joel, Obadiah, Jonah, and Micah, 1976.
[See Minor Prophets and Selections, 1976 for the entire entry.]

1976 **Zlotowitz, Meir**   Jonah, 1976.
[See Old Testaments, 1976 ArtScroll Tanach Series.]

1983 **Vawter, Bruce**   Job and Jonah...
[See Old Testament Selections for the complete entry.]

1987 **Curle, Jock**   The Story of Jonah. Retold by Kurt Baumann. Translated by Jock Curle. Illustrated by Allison Reed. New York, London, Toronoto & Melbourne: North-South Books, 1987.

MICAH

1551 **Gilby, Anthony**   A Commentarye vpon the prophet Mycha. Written by Antony Gilby. Anno Domi. M.D.LI. Imprinted at London: by Jhon Daye, 1551.

1848 **Barham, Francis**   The Bible Revised...
[See Old Testament Selections for the complete entry.]

1870 **Barham, Francis** A Revised Version of the prophecies of Hosea and Micah...
[See Minor Prophets and Selections for the entire entry.]

1876 **Sharpe, John**   Micah, a new translation, with notes for English Readers... and Hebrew students. By John Sharpe. Cambridge: J. Hall & Son, 1876.

1908 **Margolis, Max L.**   The Holy Scriptures, with Commentary; Micah. Philadelphia: Jewish Publication Society, 1908.
    [Intended as the first in a series of O.T. commentaries. This was actually the only one published. Final result was the JPS version of the O.T., 1917.]

1910 **Haupt, Paul**   The Book of Micah, a new metrical translation, with restoration of the Hebrew text and explanatory and critical Notes by Paul Haupt. Chicago: University of Chicago Press, 1910.

1917 **Harris, Maurice H.**   Micah, 1917.
    [See Old Testaments, 1917 Jewish Publication Society.]

1932 **Hamond, E.W.**   The Eighth Century Prophets...
    [See Prophets and Selections for the complete entry.]

1934 **Naish, John and R.B.Y. Scott**   The Books of Micah (John Naish), and Habakkuk...
    [See Minor Prophets and Selections for the complete entry.]

1963 **Phillips, J.B.**   Four Prophets...Micah...
    [See Prophets and Selections for the complete entry.]

1965 **Weitzner, Emil**   Humanist Meditations...Micah...
    [See Old Testament Selections, 1959 for the complete entry.]

1974 **Anonymous**   Hosea, Amos, and Micah...
    [See Minor Prophets and Selections for the complete entry.]

1976 **Allen, Leslie C.**   The Books of Joel, Obadiah, Jonah, and Micah, 1976.
    [See Minor Prophets and Selections, 1976 for the entire entry.]

NAHUM

1879 **Rich, Thomas H.**   A Study of Nahum, by Thomas H. Rich. Boston: D. Lothrop & Co., 1879.
    ["My book is not a new translation, but a metrical paraphrase."]

1907 **Haupt, Paul**   The Book of Nahum; a New Metrical
Translation With an Introduction; Restoration of the
Hebrew Text and Explanatory Notes by Paul Haupt.
Baltimore: The Johns Hopkins Press, 1907.

1911 **Hirshfield, Hartwig**   Jefeth b. Ali's Arabic
Commentary on Nahum, with introduction, abridged
translation and notes. London: Jew's College
Publication, 1911.   [Judeo-Arabic & English]

1917 **Mayer, L.**   Nahum, 1917.
     [See Old Testaments, 1917 Jewish Publication Society.]

1924 **Martin, G. Currie and Others**   The Books of Joel
(J. Garrow Duncan), Nahum (G. Currie Martin), and
Obadiah (Constance Mary Coltman)...
     [See Old Testament Selections, 1920 Books of the O.T. in
     Colloquial Speech.]

1939 **Wordsworth, W.A.**   En Roeh. The Prophecies of
Isaiah the Seer, with Habakkuk and Nahum...
     [See Prophets and Selections for the complete entry.]

1959 **Maier, Walter A.**   The Book of Nahum;
A Commentary by Walter A. Maier.   Saint Louis:
Concordia Publishing House, 1959.

1990 **Robertson, O. Palmer**   The Books of Nahum..., 1990.
     [See Minor Prophets and Selections for the entire
     entry.]

HABAKKUK

1644 **Boyd, M. Zachary**   The Garden of Zion...
     [See Old Testament Selections for the complete entry.]

1646 **Stokes, David**   A Paraphrasticall Explication of the
Prophecie of Habakkuk... Oxford: Leonard Litchfield,
1646.

1650 **Anonymous**   The Psalms, Hymns and Spiritual Songs...
     [See Old Testament Selections for the complete entry.]

1700 **Blackmore, Sir Richard**   A Paraphrase on the Book of
Job; as likewise on...
     [See Old Testament Selections for the complete entry.]

1727 **Broome, Rev.W.**   Habakkuk 3; Part of...
     [See Old Testament Selections for the complete entry.]

1737 **Anonymous**   Habakkuk Chapter 3. <u>Gentleman's</u>
     <u>Magazine</u>, Vol.VII, page 695, 1737.

1747 **Costard, G.**   Habakkuk, Chapter 3, paraphrastically
     translated into verse. Oxford: 1747.

1755 **Green, William**   A New Translation... Habakkuk...
     [See Old Testament Selections for the complete entry.]

1758 **Jones, Lewis**   The Third Chapter of Habakkuk in
     verse. London: Davy, <u>Gentleman's Magazine</u>, August,
     1758.

1762 **Anonymous**   Habakkuk, Chapter 3; (Latter Part)
     in Verse. <u>Gentleman's Magazine</u>, Vol.XXXII, Page 288,
     1762.

1793 **Hill, Aaron**   Habakkuk 3, Part of Psalm 14...
     [See Bible Selections for the complete entry.]

1810 **Clarke, George Somers**   Hebrew Criticism and Poetry
     ...The Patriarchal Blessing of Isaac...Jacob...
     [See Old Testament Selections for the complete entry.]

1874 **Proby, W.H.B.**   The Ten Canticles of the O.T...
     [See Old Testament Selections for the complete entry.]

1881 **Anonymous**   A Revised Version of the Prophecy of
     Habakkuk, by the Hebrew Club in the Divinity School
     of Yale College. New Haven: Tuttle & Co., 1881.

1911 **Stackhouse, George G. V.**   The Book of Habakkuk.
     Introduction, and notes on the Hebrew text, by
     George G.V. Stackhouse. London: Rivingtons, 1911.

1917 **Grossman, R.**   Habbakuk, 1917.
     [See Old Testaments, 1917 Jewish Publication Society.]

1934 **Naish, John and R.B.Y. Scott**   The Books of Micah
     (John Naish), and Habakkuk (R.B.Y. Scott)...
     [See Minor Prophets and Selections for the complete
     entry.]

1939 **Wordsworth, W.A.**   En Roeh. The Prophecies of
     Isaiah the Seer, with Habakkuk and Nahum...
     [See Prophets and Selections for the complete entry.]

1966 **Harris, J.G.**   The Qumran Commentary on Habakkuk.
     London: A.R. Mowbray & Co., Ltd., 1966.
     [Contemporary Studies in Theology, 9. Paraphrase.]

1990 **Robertson, O. Palmer**   The Books of Nahum, Habakkuk,
     and Zephaniah, 1990.
     [See Minor Prophets and Selections for the entire
     entry.]

ZEPHANIAH

1917 **Schlesinger, M.**   Zephaniah, 1917.
[See Old Testaments, 1917 Jewish Publication Society.]

1990 **Robertson, O. Palmer**   The Books of Nahum, Habakkuk,
and Zephaniah, 1990.
[See Minor Prophets and Selections for the entire
entry.]

HAGGAI

1560 **Pilkington, James**   Aggeus the prophete...
[See Minor Prophets and Selections for the entire
entry.]

1586 **Fetherstone, Christopher**   Haggeus, the Prophet.
Where-vnto is added a most plentifull commentary,
gathered out of the publique lectures of...D. Ihon
Iames Gryneus...and now first published. Faithfully
translated out of Latin into English. London: Ihon
Wolfe, for Ihon Harrison the Younger, 1586.

1649 **Rainoldes, T.**   The prophesie of Haggai; interpreted
by T. Rainoldes. London: for William Lee, 1649.

1856 **Moore, Thomas Verner**   The Prophets of the
Restoration; or Haggai, Zechariah and Malachi...
[See Minor Prophets and Selections for the complete
entry.]

1917 **Mendelsohn, S.**   Haggai, 1917.
[See Old Testaments, 1917 Jewish Publication Society.]

1987 **Meyers, Carol L. and Eric M. Meyers**   Haggai,
Zechariah 1-8...
[See Minor Prophets and Selections for the entire
entry.] .

1987 **Verhoef, Pieter A.** The Books of Haggai..., 1987.
[See Minor Prophets and Selections for the entire
entry.]

1988 **Wolff, Hans Walter**   Haggai. Minneapolis: Augsburg
Publishing House, 1988.

ZECHARIAH

1629 **Pemble, W.**   First Nine Chapters of Zechariah, with an exposition.   London: R. Young, 1629.
Again, 1629.

1797 **Blayney, Benjamin**   Zechariah; a new translation; with notes, critical, Philological, and explanatory; and an appendix in reply to Dr. Eveleigh's sermon on Zech. II 8-11. A dissertation on Daniel IX.V.20 to the end. By Benjamin Blayney. Oxford: J.Cooke, 1797.
[See Anonymous, A Literal Translation of the Prophets, 1836.]

1824 **Stonard, John**   A Commentary on the Vision of Zechariah the Prophet; with a corrected translation and critical notes. By John Stonard.   London: C. & J. Rivington, 1824.

1837 **M'Caul, A.**   Rabbi David Kimchi's Commentary upon the Prophecies of Zechariah. Translated from the Hebrew. With Notes, and Observations on the Passages Relating to the Messiah.   London: James Duncan, 1837.

1856 **Moore, Thomas Verner**   The Prophets of the Restoration; or Haggai, Zechariah and Malachi...
[See Minor Prophets and Selections for the complete entry.]

1877 **King, Edward George**   Zechariah. The drama of night visions.   Pt. 1. Vision I. A new translation, with commentary, chiefly from Rabbinical sources. By Edward G. King. Cambridge: Rivingtons, 1877.

1879 **Wright, Charles Henry Hamilton**   Zechariah and his Prophecies, Considered in Relation to Modern Criticism: with a Critical and Grammatical Commentary and New Translation. Eight Lectures delivered before the University of Oxford in the Year 1878, on the Foundation of the Late Rev. John Bampton M.A., Canon of Salisbury. London: Hodder & Stoughton, 1879.
Second edition, 1879.

1956 **Leupold, Herbert Carl**   Exposition of Zechariah, by H.C. Leupold. Columbus, Ohio: Wartburg Press, 1956.
[With a new translation.]

1963 **Unger, Merrill F.**   Unger's Biblical Commentary, Zechariah by Merrill F. Unger. Grand Rapids, Michigan: Zondervan Publishing House, 1963.
[Contains the KJV and Unger's version, with the Deity rendered "Jehovah".]

1987 **Meyers, Carol L. and Eric M. Meyers**   Haggai,
     Zechariah 1-8...
          [See Minor Prophets and Selections for the complete
          entry.]

MALACHI

???? **Gilby, Anthony**   The Prophet Malachi; with
     a commentary, [155?].

1626 **Stock, Richard**   A Learned and Very Usefull
     Commentary upon the whole Prophesie of Malachy....
     By Richard Stock. 1626.
          Another edition; − − and now, according to the
          originall Copy left by him, published for the
          common   good.   Whereunto   is   added,   An
          Exercitation   upon   the   same   Prophesie   of
          Malachy. By Samuel Torshell. London: Printed
          by T.H. and R.H. for Daniel Frere and William
          Wells, 1641.

          Another edition, 1865.

1856 **Moore, Thomas Verner**   The Prophets of the
     Restoration; or Haggai, Zechariah and Malachi...
          [See Minor Prophets and Selections for the entire
          entry.]

1898 **Sadler, Ralph**   Malaki, My Angel. The last book of
     the Hebrew canon. Rendered afresh from the original,
     by Ralph Sadler. London: Sheppard & St. John, 1898.

1917 **Davidson, D.**   Malachi, 1917.
          [See Old Testaments, 1917 Jewish Publication Society.]

1934 **Lattey, Cutbert**   Malachy, 1934.
          [See Complete Bibles, 1913 Westminster Version.]

1987 **Verhoef, Pieter A.**   The Books... and Malachi, 1987.
          [See Minor Prophets and Selections for the entire
          entry.]

10

Apocrypha and Apocryphal Books

1913 **Apocrypha & Pseudepigrapha of the Old Testament**
The Apocrypha and Pseudepigrapha of the Old
Testament in English; with introductions and
critical and explanatory notes to the several books;
edited in conjunction with many Scholars by R.H.
Charles. 2 Vols. Oxford: Clarendon Press, 1913.

Vol. I: [Apocrypha]

I Esdras:	S.A. Cook
I Maccabees:	W.O.E. Oesterley
2 Maccabees:	James Moffatt
3 Maccabees:	Cyril W. Emmet
Tobit:	D.C. Simpson
Judith:	A.E. Cowley
Sirach:	G.H. Box & W.Oesterley
Wisdom of Solomon:	Samuel Holmes
I Baruch:	O.C. Whitehouse
Epistle of Jeremy:	C.J. Ball
Prayer of Manasses:	H.E. Ryle
Prayer of Azariah & Song of the Three Children:	W.H. Bennett
Susanna:	D.M. Kay
Bel and the Dragon:	T.W. Davies
Additions to Esther:	J.A.F. Gregg

Vol. II. [Pseudepigrapha]

The Book of Jubilees:	R.H. Charles (1902)
Letter of Aristeas:	H.T. Andrews
The Books of Adam & Eve:	L.S.A. Wells
The Martyrdom of Isaiah:	R.H. Charles
I Enoch:	R.H. Charles (1893)
The Testament of the XII Patriarchs:	R.H. Charles
The Sibylline Oracles:	H.C.O. Lanchester

The Assumption of Moses: R.H. Charles (1897)
2 Enoch...:   Neville Forbes & R.H.
                             Charles
2 Baruch...:   R.H. Charles (1896)
3 Baruch...:   H. Maldwyn Hughes
4 Ezra: G.H. Box
The Psalms of Solomon: G. Buchanan Gray
4 Maccabees: R.B. Townshend
Pirke Aboth: R. Travers Herford
The Story of Ahikar: J. Rendell Harris, Agnes
                             Smith Lewis & F.C.
                             Conybeare (1898)
The Fragments of a Zadokite Work: R.H. Charles

> [The entire work was reprinted by Clarendon Press in
> 1963; Individual works was reprinted by S.P.C.K.,
> various dates.]

1913 **Ball, Charles James**   Epistle of Jeremy, 1913.
     [See The Apocrypha and Pseudepigrapha, 1913.]

1913 **Bennett, W.H.**   Prince of Azariah & Song of the
     Three Children, 1913.
     [See The Apocrypha & Pseudepigrapha, 1913.]

1913 **Box, G.H.**   4 Ezra, 1913.
     [See The Apocrypha & Pseudepigrapha, 1913.]

1913 **Cook, Stanley Arthur**   1 Esdras, 1913.
     [See The Apocrypha & Pseudepigrapha, 1913.]

1913 **Cowley, Arthur E.**   Judith, 1913.
     [See Apocrypha & Pseudepigrapha, 1913.]

1960 **Anonymous**   The Twentieth Century Encyclopedia of
     Catholicism...
     [See Bible Selections for the complete entry. Includes
     the O.T. Apocrypha.]

1983 **Charlesworth, James Hamilton**   (Editor)
     The Old Testament Pseudepigrapha. Edited by James H.
     Charlesworth.
          Vol. 1 Apocalyptic Literature & Testaments.
          Garden City, N.Y.: Doubleday & Co., Inc.,
          1983.

          Vol. 2 Expansions of the "Old Testament" and
               Legends, Wisdom and Philosophical
          Literature, Prayers, Psalms and Odes,
          Fragments of Lost Judeo — Hellenistics Works.
          Garden City, New York: Doubleday & Co., Inc.,
          1985.

11

Apocrypha

APOCRYPHA AND SELECTIONS

???? **Greenfield, Jonas C.**   Tobit and Judith.
Introduction, Translation, and Notes by Jonas C.
Greenfield. Garden City, New York: Doubleday & Co.,
[197?].
　　　[See Complete Bibles, 1964 Anchor Bible, Vol. 40.]

???? **James, Montague Rhodes**   The Lost Apocrypha
of the Old Testament. London: S.P.C.K., [19??].

1568 **Parkhurst, John**   Apocrypha, 1568.
　　　[See Complete Bibles, 1568 Bishops' Bible.]

1829 **Howard, Luke**   The Apocrypha of the Book of
Daniel; containing the story of Susanna; the prayer
of Azariah, with the Hymn of the Three Children; and
the History of Bel and the Dragon: translated from
the Latin Vulgate; with notes; and a short treatise
on the matter contained in these pieces. London:
The Translator, 1829.

1879 **Anonymous**   The Apocrypha; Greek and English...
London: Samuel Bagster, 1879.
　　　[Bound with Brenton's O.T., 1879. The entire Apocrypha
　　　is KJV except for the Prayer of Manasses, and III & IV
　　　Maccabees. Another edition, Apocrypha only, 1888.
　　　Another edition bound with Brenton's O.T., 1966.]

1880 **Bissell, Edwin Cone**   The Apocrypha of the Old
Testament with Historical introduction, a Revised
Translation, and notes critical and explanatory.
New York: Charles Scribners Sons, 1880.
　　　Another edition; Edinburgh: T.& T. Clark, 1880.

　　　Also; New York: Scribners, 1903.

1884 **Anonymous**   The uncanonical and apocryphal
scriptures, being the additions to the Old Testament
canon which were included in the ancient Greek and
Latin versions, the English text of the AV together
with the additional matter found in the Vulgate and
other ancient versions. London: Whitaker, 1884.

1888 **Wace, Henry**   See Complete Bibles, 1871 Frederick
Charles Cook, The Speaker's Commentary (Apocrypha).

1914 **Clegg, Alfred**   The Bible within the Bible,
including the Apocrypha...
     [See Bible Selections for the complete entry.]

1938 **Goodspeed, Edgar J.**   The Apocrypha. An
American Translation by Edgar J. Goodspeed. Chicago:
University of Chicago Press, 1938.

1939 **Oesterley, William Oscar Emil**   Readings from
the Apocrypha. Selected and Translated, by W.O.E.
Oesterley. London: The Sheldon Press; New York:
The Macmillan Co., 1939.
     ["For the use here made of the RV, thanks are due to the
     delegates of the Clarendon Press..."]

1950 **Anonymous**   Jewish Apocryphal Literature...An
English Translation... New York: By Harper & Bros.
for the Dropsie College for Hebrew and Cognate
Learning, 1950-1958.
     1950 ...The First Book of Maccabees... Sidney
          Tedesche.

     1954 ...The Second Book of Maccabees...Sidney
          Tedesche.

     1953 ...The Third and Fourth Books of
          Maccabees, edited and Translated with
          the Greek text from Alford Rahlf's
          Septuaginta. Moses Hadas.

     1958 ...The Book of Tobit... Frank Zimmerman.

     1957 ...The Book of Wisdom... Joseph Reider.

1957 **Revised Standard Version**   The Apocrypha. Revised
Standard Version...Revised A.D. 1957. Toronto, New
York: and Edinburgh: Thomas Nelson & Sons, 1957.
     [See New Revised Standard Version, 1989.]

     [Two of the translators were Gerald E.Knoff and Paul
     C.Payne.]

1970 **New English Bible**   The New English Bible:
Apocrypha. Library Edition. Oxford and Cambridge:
University Presses, 1970.

1975 **Nevins, Albert J.**   The Deuterocanonical Books. Paraphrased by Albert J. Nevins...   Huntington, Indiana: Our Sunday Visitor, 1975.

1977 **Moore, Carey A.**   Daniel, Esther, Jeremiah: The Additions. A New Translation with Introduction and Commentary by Carey A. Moore.   Garden City, New York: Doubleday & Co., 1977.
[See Complete Bibles, 1964 Anchor Bible, Vol. 44.]

1978 **De Lange, Nicholas** Apocrypha: Jewish Literature of the Hellenistic Age by Nicholas De Lange. New York: Viking Press, 1978.

1987 **Skehan, Patrick W.**   The Wisdom of Ben Sira. A New Translation with Notes by Patrick W. Skehan. Introduction and Commentary by Alexander A. DiLella. Garden City, New York: Doubleday & Co., Inc., 1987.
[See Complete Bibles, 1964 Anchor Bible, Vol. 39.]

1989 **New Revised Standard Version**   The Apocryphal/ Deuterocanonical Books of the Old Testament. New Revised Standard Version. Iowa Falls, Iowa: World Bible Publishers, Inc., 1989.
[See NRSV, 1990.]

[See RSV, 1957.]

BARUCH

1913 **Hughes, H. Maldwyn**   3 Baruch, 1913.
[See Apocrypha and Apocryphal Books, 1913 Apocrypha & Pseudepigrapha.]

1913 **Whitehouse, O.C.**   I Baruch, 1913.
[See Apocrypha and Apocryphal Books, 1913 Apocrypha & Pseudepigrapha.]

1982 **Burke, David G.**   The Poetry of Baruch. A Reconstruction and Analysis of the Original Hebrew Text of Baruch 3:9-5:9 by David G. Burke. Society of Biblical Literature, Septuagint & Cognate Studies, No. 10.   Chico, CA: Scholars Press, 1982.

BEL AND THE DRAGON

1829 **Howard, Luke** The Apocrypha of the Book of Daniel; containing...the History of Bel and the Dragon...

[See Apocrypha and Selections for the complete entry.]

1913 **Davies, T. Whitton**   Bel and the Dragon, 1913.
     [See Apocrypha and Apocryphal Books, 1913 Apocrypha and
     Pseudepigrapha.]

1932 **Anonymous**   The History of the Destruction of
     Bel and the Dragon; cut off from the end of Daniel.
     London: Henderson & Spalding, 1932.

1977 **Moore, Carey A.**   Daniel, Esther...The Additions...
     [See Apocrypha and Selections for the complete entry.]

ECCLESIASTICUS

1550 **Anonymous**   Certayne Chapters of the Prouerbes...
     [See Bible Selections for the complete entry. Includes
     the ix chapter of Ecclesiasticus.]

1550 **Hunnis, William**   Certayne Psalmes chosen out...
     [See Old Testament listing for the complete entry.
     Includes Ecclesiasticus the last]

1639 **Daniel, George**   Ecclesiastics: or the Wisdom of
     Iesus the son of Syrach paraphrased. 1639.

1706 **Anonymous**   Select Moral Books... Ecclesiasticus...
     [See Wisdom and Poetical books and Selections for the
     complete entry.]

1727 **Broome, Rev. W.**   Habakkuk 3...Ecclesiasticus 43...
     [See Old Testament listing for the complete entry.]

1827 **Howard, Luke**   Liber Ecclesiasticus, the Book of
     the Church; or Ecclesiasticus: translated from the
     Latin Vulgate, by Luke Howard...   London: Printed
     for the Translator, by A. and R. Spottiswoode, 1827.

1878 **Anonymous**   The Wisdom of Jesus the Son of Sirach;
     or Ecclesiasticus. By M.W.T. Boston: Roberts Bros.,
     1878.

1897 **Cowley, Arthur E. and A. Neubauer**   Ecclesiasticus
     XXXIX. 15 to XLIX. 11, translated from the original
     Hebrew and arranged in parallel columns with the
     English Revised Version of 1895 by A.E. Cowley and
     A. Neubauer...   Oxford: Clarendon Press, 1897.

1916 **Oesterley, William Oscar Emil**   The Wisdom of Ben-
     Sira (Ecclesiasticus), translation with notes by
     W.O.E. Oesterley. London: S.P.C.K., 1916.
          [See Apocryphal Books, 1916 William Oscar Emil Oesterley
          and G.H. Box, Translations of Early Documents.]

1930 **Marcus, Joseph**   The Newly Discovered Original
     Hebrew of Ben Sira (Eccl. 32:16-34:1). The Fifth
     Manuscript and a Prosodic Version of Ben Sira (Eccl.
     22:22-23:9). Edited from the Hebrew Manuscripts...in
     the Library of the Jewish Theological Seminary in
     America by Joseph Marcus. Philadelphia: The Dropsie
     College for Hebrew and Cognate Learning, 1931.

1932 **Power, Arnold Danvers**   The Wisdom of Jesus, the Son
     of Sirach, commonly called Ecclesiasticus, by Arnold
     D. Power. Chelsea [London]: Ashendene Press, 1932.
          [Based on the AV & RV, "Occasionally a sentence has been
          entirely reconstructed in order more closely to conform
          with what seems most likely to be the original text."]

          Another edition; Ecclesiasticus, or the Wisdom of
          Jesus the Son of Sira, A New Translation...
          London: Hodder & Stoughton, 1939.

1965 **Yadin, Yigael**   The Ben Sira Scroll from Masada;
     with Introduction, Emendations and Commentary by
     Yigael Yadin. Jerusalem: The Israel Exploration
     Society and the Shrine of the Book, 1965.
          [Contains a Hebrew text reconstructed from various
          ancient fragments, and an English translation.]

1974 **Frank, Richard M.**   The Wisdom of Jesus Ben Sirac
     (Sinai ar.155, IXth/Xth cent.) translated by Richard
     M. Frank. Louvain, Belgium: CorpusSCO, 1974.

ESDRAS

1711 **Whiston, William**   Primitive Christianity Reviv'd by
     William Whiston. 5 Vols. London: for the author,
     1711.
          [The Second Book of Esdras.]

1722 **Lee, Francis**   An Epistolary Discourse concerning
     the Books of Ezra, Genuine and Spurious, but more
     Particularly the Second Apocryphal Book under that
     Name...Together with a New Version of the Fifth Book
     of Esdras; translated by Francis Lee. London: G.
     James, 1722.

1820 **Laurence, Richard**   The First Book of Esdras,
     (i.e., the Second Book of Apocryphal Esdras in our
     Bibles); translated from the Ethiopic version by
     Richard Laurence. Oxford: for the author, 1820.

1912 **Box, G.H.**   The Ezra - Apocalypse; Being Chapters
     3-14 of the book commonly known as 4 Ezra or II

MACK LIBRARY
BOB JONES UNIVERSITY
GREENVILLE, SC

Esdras, translated from a critically revised text, with critical introduction, notes and explanations; with a general introduction to the Apocalypse, and an appendix containing the Latin text. London: Sir I. Pitman & Sons, 1912.

1974 **Myers, Jacob M.**   I & II Esdras. Introduction, Translation and Commentary, by Jacob M. Myers. Garden City, New York: Doubleday & Co., 1974.
[See Complete Bibles, 1964 Anchor Bible, Vol. 42.]

1984 **Harper, H.B. George**   H.B. & His/Her Bible Adventures (Human Being)...
[See Bible Selections for the complete entry. Includes I & II Esdras.]

HISTORY OF SUSANNA

1829 **Howard, Luke**   The Apocrypha of the Book of Daniel; containing the Story of Susanna...
[See Apocrypha and Selections for the complete entry.]

1913 **Kay, D.M.**   Susanna, 1913.
[See Apocrypha and Apocryphal Books, 1913 Apocrypha & Pseudepigrapha.]

JUDITH

???? **Greenfield, Jonas C.**   Tobit and Judith...
[See Apocrypha and Selections for the complete entry.]

1698 **Thwaites, Edward**   Heptateuchus, liber Job...
[See Bible Selections for the complete entry.]

1799 **Turner**   History of the Anglo-Saxons. 3 Vols. 1799-1805.
Second edition; n.d.

Third edition, 1820.

[According to Cook's "Judith; an old English Epic Fragment", 1888, Turner's work contains an English translation of Judith.]

1888 **Cook, Albert Stanburrough**   Judith; an Old
     English Epic Fragment; Edited, with introduction,
     translation, complete glossary, and various indexes.
     Boston: D.C. Heath & Co., 1888.
          ["The ms is the well-known Cotton Vitallius A XV of the
          British Museum... The nucleus from which this volume has
          grown is the translation, made by five University
          students of Old English: George D. Boyd, Fanny Cooper,
          Alice K. Grover, Adolph C. Miller, and Catherine E.
          Wilson. This translation I have retouched, and in some
          portions refashioned..."]

          Also; 1903.

          Reprint; Folcroft, PA: Folcroft Library
          Editions, 1974.
               [Reprint of the 1903 edition.]

          Reprint; Norwood, PA: Norwood Editions, 1976.
               [Reprint of the 1898 edition.]

1908 **Pentin, Herbert**   The Apocrypha in the English
     Language. Vol.1. Judith. London: S, Bagster & Sons,
     1908.
          [With an abridged version of the Book of Judith and a
          translation of the Anglo-Saxon Poem "Judith". No more
          published.]

1972 **Enslin, Morton S.**   The Book of Judith. Greek text
     with an English translation, commentary and critical
     notes by Morton S. Enslin. Edited with a general
     introduction and appendices by Solomon Zeitlin.
     Leiden: Brill, 1972.

1985 **Moore, Carey A**.   Judith. A New Translation
     with Introduction and Commentary by Carey A. Moore.
     Garden City, New York: Doubleday & Co., 1985.
          [See Complete Bibles, 1964 Anchor Bible, Vol. 40.]

MACCABEES

???? **Tedesche, Sidney**   The Book of Maccabees. Translated
     by Sidney Tedesche. Illustrated by Jacob Shacham.
     Hartford, Connecticut: Published by Prayer Book
     Press, Inc., n.d.

1550 **Anonymous**   The Thyrde Boke of the Machabees not
     found in the Hebrew Canon, but Translated out of the
     Greke into Latin. London: Gualter Lynne, 1550.

1832 **Cotton, Henry**   The Five Books of Maccabees
in English. With Notes and Illustrations. Edited by
Henry Cotton.   Oxford: University Press, 1832.
["Dr. Cotton has...for the first time, given an English
translation of what are called the fourth and fifth
books..."]

1913 **Emmet, Cyril W.**   The Third Book of Maccabees, 1913.
[See Apocrypha and Apocryphal Books, 1913 Apocrypha and
Pseudepigrapha.]

[Bound with the Fourth Book of Maccabees. See R.B.
Townshend, 1918.]

Another Edition; The Third Book of Maccabees.
London: S.P.C.K., 1918.

1913 **Moffatt, James**   The Second Book of Maccabees, 1913.
[See Apocrypha and Apocryphal Books, 1913 Apocrypha and
Pseudepigrapha.]

1913 **Oesterley, William Oscar Emil**   I Maccabees, 1913.
[See Apocrypha and Apocryphal Books, 1913 Apocrypha and
Pseudepigrapha.]

1918 **Townshend, R.B.**   The Fourth Book of Maccabees...
[See   Apocrypha   and   Apocryphal   Books,   1913
Apocrypha and Pseudepigrapha (Fourth Maccabees).]

[Bound with the Third Book of Maccabees. See Cyril W.
Emmet, 1913.]

[See Apocryphal Books, 1927 Rutherford H. Platt, Jr.,
The Forgotten Books of Eden.]

1926 **Anonymous**   The Fourth Book of Maccabees...
[See Apocryphal Books,   1926 Anonymous, The Lost
Books...]

1950 **Tedesche, Sidney**   First Book of Maccabees, 1950.
[See Apocrypha and Selections, 1950 Anonymous, Jewish
Apocryphal Literature.]

1953 **Hadas, Moses**   III & IV Maccabees, 1953.
[See Apocrypha and Selections, 1950 Anonymous, Jewish
Apocryphal Literature.]

Reprinted;   The   Third   and   Fourth   Books   of
Maccabees edited by Moses Hadas.   New York:
KTAV Publishing House, 1976.

1954 **Tedesche, Sidney**   Second Book of Maccabees, 1954.
[See Apocrypha and Selections, 1950 Anonymous, Jewish
Apocryphal Literature.]

1976 **Goldstein, Jonathan A.**   I Maccabees. A new
translation with introduction, and Commentary by

Jonathan A. Goldstein. Garden City, New York: Doubleday & Co., 1976.
[See Complete Bibles, 1964 Anchor Bible, Vol. 41.]

1983 **Goldstein, Jonathan A.**   II Maccabees. A new translation with introduction, and Commentary by Jonathan A. Goldstein. Garden City, New York: Doubleday & Co., 1983.
[See Complete Bibles, 1964 Anchor Bible, Vol. 41A.]

1983 **Anderson, H.**   3 Maccabees. 1983.
[See Apocrypha and Apocryphal Books, 1983 James H. Charlesworth, The Old Testament Pseudepigrapha.]

1983 **Anderson, H.**   4 Maccabees. 1983.
[See Apocrypha and Apocryphal Books, 1983 James H. Charlesworth, The Old Testament Pseudepigrapha.]

PRAYER OF MANASSES

1537 **Matthew, Thomas**   The Byble...holy Scripture...
[See Complete Bibles for the entire entry. Includes Roger's translation of the Prayer of Manasses.]

1913 **Ryle, H.E.**   Prayer of Manasses, 1913.
[See Apocrypha and Apocryphal Books, 1913 Apocrypha & Pseudepigrapha.]

REST OF ESTHER

1913 **Gregg, J.A.F.**   Addition to Esther, 1913.
[See Apocrypha and Apocryphal Books, 1913 Apocrypha & Pseudepigrapha.]

1977 **Moore, Carey A.**   Daniel, Esther, Jeremiah...
[See Apocrypha and Selections for the complete entry.]

SONG OF THE THREE HOLY CHILDREN

1550 **Hunnis, William**   Certayne Psalmes chosen out...

[See Old Testament listing for the complete entry.
Includes the song of the three children.]

1691 **Walker, T.**   Divine Hymns, or a Paraphrase upon the
Te Deum &c. And the Song of the Three Children or
Canticorum Benedicite omnia opera &c. as they are in
the Book of Common Prayer, by T. Walker. Cambridge:
Printed by J. Hayes for W. Graves, 1691.

1703 **Chudleigh, Mary**   Poems on several occasions;
together with The Song of the Three Children,
paraphrased, by Mary Chudleigh. 2 Pts.   London:
Bernard Linott, 1703.

1724 **Anonymous**   A Paraphrase on the Song of the Three
Children.   In   irregular   stanzas.   [Mark   le   Pla]
London: Edward Lathbury, 1724.

1829 **Howard, Luke**   The Apocrypha of the Book of Daniel;
containing the...the Three Children...
[See Apocrypha and Selections for the complete entry.]

1956 **Anonymous**   The Psalms: A New Translation...
[See Old Testament Selections for the complete entry.
Includes the Song of the three Children.]

TOBIT

???? **Greenfield, Jonas C.**   Tobit and Judith...
[See Apocrypha and Selections for the complete entry.]

???? **Moore, Carey A.**   Tobit. A New Translation with
Introduction and Commentary by Carey A.Moore. Garden
City, New York: Doubleday & Co., Inc., [19??].
[See Complete Bibles, 1964 Anchor Bible, Vol. 40a]

1828 **Howard, Luke**   The Book of Tobias; commonly called
the Book of Tobit: translated from the Latin Vulgate
by Luke Howard. London: The Translator, 1828.

1878 **Neubauer, Adolph**   The Book of Tobit; A Chaldee
text from a unique MS. in the Bodleian Library, with
other Rabbinical texts, English translations and the
Itala.   Oxford: Clarendon Press, 1878.
[Hebrew, Latin, English and Aramaic.]

1913 **Simpson, D.C.**   Tobit, 1913.
[See Apocrypha and Apocryphal Books, 1913 Apocrypha and
Pseudepigrapha.]

1958 **Zimmerman, Frank**   Book of Tobit, 1958.
[See Apocrypha and Selections, 1950 Anonymous, Jewish Apocryphal Literature.]

WISDOM OF SOLOMON

???? **DiLella, Alexander A**.   Wisdom of Ben Sira. A New Translation with Introduction and Commentary by Alexander A. DiLella. Garden City, New York: Doubleday & Co., Inc., [19??].
[See Complete Bibles, 1964 Anchor Bible, Vol. 39.]

???? **Magoon, E.L.**   Proverbs for the People; or, Illustrations of Practical Godliness drawn from the Book of Wisdom. By E.L. Magoon. Boston: [185?].

1400 **Anonymous**   King Solomon's Book of Wisdom. (With Adam Day's "Dreams".)
Reprinted; London: E.E.T.S., 1878.

1550 **Anonymous**   Certayne Chapters of the Prouerbes...
[See Bible Selections for the complete entry. Includes 5th chapter of the Book of Wisdom.]

1597 **Middleton, Thomas F.**   The Wisdom of Solomon Paraphrased by Thomas F. Middleton. London: Valentine Sems, 1597.
[Metrical version.]

1706 **Anonymous**   Select Moral Books of the O.T...
[See Wisdom and Poetical books and Selections for the complete entry.]

1827 **Howard, Luke**   Liber Sapientiae, the Book of Wisdom; commonly called the Wisdom of Solomon: translated from the Latin Vulgate by Luke Howard. London: A. & R. Spottiswoode for the author, 1827.

1906 **Anonymous**   The Wisdom of Solomon...
[See Old Testament Selections for the complete entry.]

1913 **Goodrick, A.T.S.**   The Book of Wisdom with introduction and notes. Edited by the Rev. A.T.S. Goodrick... London: Rivingtons; New York: The Macmillan Company, 1913.
["The text adopted for translation is Swete's, but with occasional corrections from Fritzsche..." "The aim of the Editors is to provide a Series of Commentaries on the Old & New Testament..." This ambitious project, 'The Oxford Church Bible Commentary', apparently interrupted by World War I, includes only Wisdom and Mark. See W.C. Allen, St. Mark, 1915.]

[See Bible Selections, 1913 Oxford Church Bible Commentary.]

1913 **Holmes, Samuel**   Wisdom of Solomon, 1913.
[See Apocrypha and Apocryphal Books, 1913 Apocrypha & Pseudepigrapha.]

1917 **Oesterley, William Oscar Emil**   The Wisdom of Solomon, by W.O.E. Oesterley. London: S.P.C.K.; New York: Macmillan, 1917.
Another edition, 1918.

1957 **Reider, Joseph**   The Book of Wisdom, 1957.
[See Apocrypha and Selections, 1950 Anonymous, Jewish Apocryphal Literature.]

1963 **Geyer, J.**   The Wisdom of Solomon. London: S.C.M. Press, 1963.

1975 **Schoenbechler, Roger**   The Book of Wisdom, an interpretative version in measured rhythm, by Roger Schoenbechler. Minnesota: Liturgical Press, 1975.

1979 **Winston, David**   The Wisdom of Solomon. A New Translation with Introduction and Commentary by David Winston. Garden City, New York: Doubleday & Co., Inc., 1979.
[See Complete Bibles, 1964 Anchor Bible, Vol. 43.]

12

Apocryphal Books

APOCRYPHAL BOOKS AND SELECTIONS

???? **Anonymous**   The Sixth and Seventh Books of Moses; or, Moses' Magical Spirit Art, known as the Wonderful Arts of the old wise Hebrews, taken from the Mosaic Books of the Cabala and the Talmud, for the good of mankind. Translated from the German, word for word, according to old writings. With numerous Engravings. Published for the trade. Printed in United States of America, n.d.

> [For the 8th, 9th, and 10th Books of Moses, see Henri Gamache, 1967.]

???? **Rodkinson, Michael L.**   The Babylonian Talmud; Original Text Edited, Corrected, formulated and Translated into English by Michael L. Rodkinson. n.p.: n.p., [19??].

> First Edition Revised and Corrected. Isaac M. Wise. n.p.: n.p., n.d.
>
> Second Edition; Re-edited, Revised and Enlarged. Boston: The Talmud Society, 1918.

1727 **Whiston, William**   A Collection of the Authentick Records Belonging to the Old and New Testaments. Translated into English... Part I. London: for the author, 1727.

> Some of the contents:
> I.   A Differentiation on the Book of Baruch: to prove that it is a Canonical Book...
> II.   The Epiftle of Baruch to the nine Tribes and a half, with its Poftfcript.
> IV.   The Septuagint Verfion of the Defcription of Ezekiel's Temple...
> V.   A large Differtation on the IVth Book of Efdras, to prove it genuine.
> VI.   A particular Explication of the XI and XII Chapters.
> VII. XVIII Pfalms of Solomon II.

IX.   The IIId Book of Maccabees.
X.   Some Account of the IVth Book, now loft.
XI.   The Epiftle of the Jews of Jerusalem, to
       the Jews in Egypt, 2 Macc.i. and ii.1-18.
XVII. Extracts out of the Book of Enoch.
XIX.   The Teftaments of the XII Patriarchs.
XXI.   Fragments of Apocryphal Books of the Old
       Testament now loft; with notes upon them.

1834 **Anonymous**   Israel's Sojourn in the Land of Egypt.
[Amicus] London: Longmans, Rees & Co., 1834.
[Preface is signed "Amicus".]

1835 **Coit, T.W.**   See Complete Bibles, 1769 Benjamin
Blayney, The Holy Bible.

1835 **Coit, T.W.** (Editor) The Apocryphal Books of the Old
Testament, translated out of thew original tongues,
...compared and revised, by the command of King
James I. Arranged in paragraphs and parallelisms, by
T.W. Coit... Cambridge: Printed and Published by
Manson and Grant..., 1835.

1871 **Baring-Gould, S.**   Legends of the Patriarchs and
Prophets and other Old Testament Characters; from
various sources. 2 Vols. New York: Macmillan & Co.,
1871.
        Another edition; 1 Volume. New York: Hurst & Co.,
        Publishers, n.d.

1889 **Harris, R.**   The Apology of Aristedes by R. Harris.
Philadelphia: Haverford College Studies #6 & 7,
1889.

1891 **Deane, W.J.**   Pseudepigraphica. Edinburgh: 1891.
        [O.T. epigraphica, especially the Sybylline Books.]

1896 **Morfil, W.R.**   The Book of the Secrets of Enoch:
Translated from the Slavonic by W.R. Morfil, and
edited, with Introduction, Notes, and Indices by
R.H. Charles. Oxford: At the Clarendon Press, 1896.
        [See 1927 Rutherford H. Platt, Jr., The Forgotten Books
        of Eden.]

1898 **Conybeare, F.C., J.R. Harris, and Agnes Smith Lewis**
The Story of Ahikar. From the Aramaic, Syriac,
Arabic, Armenian, Ethiopic, Old Turkish, Greek and
Slavonic Versions.   London: 1898.
        [Reprinted in: 'The Apocrypha and Pseudepigrapha...',
        1913; 'The Forgotten Books of Eden...', 1927.]

1901 **Issaverdens, Jacques**   The Uncanonical Writings of
the Old Testament found in the Armenian MSS. of the
Library of St. Lazarus, translated into English by
Jacques Issaverdens. Venice: Monastery of St.
Lazarus, 1901.

[English and Armenian]

1909 **Ginsberg, Louis** Legends of the Jews. Philadelphia: Jewish Publication Society, 1909.
Another edition; 1938.

[See Willis Barnstone, The Other Bible (Haggadah), 1984.]

1909 **Harris, James Rendel** The Odes and Psalms of Solomon; Now first published from the Syrian version by J. Rendel Harris. Cambridge: University Press, 1909.
[Re-edited by Rendel Harris & Alphonso Mingana. Manchester: University Press; London: Longmans, Green & Co.; London: Bernard Quaritch; New York, Bombay, Calcutta & Madras: Longmans, Green.]

1916 - - Vol. I The Text...

1920 - - Vol. II The Translation...

[See Frank Crane, The Lost Books, 1927.]

1913 **Box, G.H. and W. Oesterley** Sirach, 1913.
[See Apocrypha and Apocryphal Books, 1913 Apocrypha & Pseudepigrapha.]

1913 **Charles, R.H.** The Martyrdom of Isaiah, 1913.
[See Apocrypha and Apocryphal Books, 1913 Apocrypha & Pseudepigrapha.]

1913 **Charles, R.H.** The Fragments of a Zadokite, 1913.
[See Apocrypha and Apocryphal Books, 1913 Apocrypha & Pseudepigrapha.]

1913 **Herford, R. Traver** Pirke Aboth, 1913.
[See Apocrypha and Apocryphal Books, 1913 Apocrypha & Pseudepigrapha.]

1913 **Lanchester, H.C.O.** The Sibylline Oracles, 1913.
[See Apocrypha and Apocryphal Books, 1913 Apocrypha & Pseudepigrapha.]

1916 **Oesterley, William Oscar Emil and G.H. Box** Translations of Early Documents; Edited by W.O.E. Oesterley and G.H. Box. 1916-1917.
A series of volumes:
I. The Wisdom of Ben-Sira (Ecclesiasticus), translation with notes by W.O.E. Oesterley. London: S.P.C.K., 1916.

II. The Apocalypse of Baruch, by R.H. Charles, 1917. [See R.H. Charles, 1896.]

III. The Assumption of Moses, by W.J. Ferrar, 1917. [See William John Ferrar, 1917.]

IV. The Apocalypse of Ezra, by G.H. Box, 1917. [See G.H. Box, 1917.]

V. Book of Enoch, by R.H. Charles, 1917. [See R.H. Charles, 1912.]

VI. Book of Jubilees, by R.H. Charles, 1917. [See R.H. Charles, 1902.]

VII. The Testaments of the Twelve Patriarchs, 1917.

1923 **Cowley, Arthur E.**   Aramaic Papyri of the Fifth Century B.C. Edited and translated. Oxford: Clarendon Press, 1923.

1927 **Budge, Ernest A. Wallis**   The Book of the Cave Treasures, a history of the Patriarchs and the Kings, their successors, from the creation to the crucifixion of Christ, translated from the Syrian text of the British Museum MS. Add 25875. By E.A. Wallis Budge. London: Religious Tract Society, 1927. [The Life of Adam and Eve. pp.51 – 74.]

1927 **Crane, Frank**   The Lost Books of the Bible and the Forgotten Books of Eden. Newfoundland: Alpha House, 1927.
[See Willis Barnstone, The Other Bible (The Story of Ahikar), 1984.]

1927 **Platt, Rutherford H., Jr.** (Editor)   The Forgotten Books of Eden, edited by Rutherford H. Platt, Jr. Cleveland, OH: World Publishing Co., 1927.
Another Edition; New York: Bell Publishing Co., 1980.

1945 **Smith, Joseph, Jr.**   The Lost Book of Genesis, translated by Joseph Smith; Edited with an Introduction and Finale, by Linden Dalberg. [Keng, Wash.]: J. Victor, 1945.
["A part of his Bible called 'the Inspired Version.'"]

1951 **Leslau, W.**   Falasha Anthology: Translated from Ethiopic sources, with an Introduction. New Haven: Yale University Press, Yale Judaica Series, Vol. vi, 1951.
["The works included are... The Book of the Angels, The Apocalypse of Baruch, The Apocalypse of Gorgorius, The Testament of Abraham, The Death of Moses..."]

1954 **Rabin, Chaim**   The Zadokite Documents. I. The Admonitions, II. The Laws; Edited with a translation and notes, by Chaim Rabin. Oxford: Clarendon Press, 1954.
Revised, 1958.

1956 **Barrett, Charles K.**   The New Testament Background: Select Documents Edited, with introductions, by C.K. Barrett.   London: S.P.C.K., 1956.
> Reprinted; New York & Evanston: Harper & Row, Publishers, 1961.

1958 **Thomas, D. Winton**   Documents from the Old Testament Times. Translations with introductions and notes by members of the Old Society for Old Testament study and edited by D. Winton Thomas. Edinburgh & London: Thomas Nelson & Sons Ltd., 1958.
> Another Edition;   New York: Harper & Row, Publishers, 1961.

1960 **Doresse, Jean**   The Secret Books of the Egyptian Gnostics. An Introduction to the Gnostic Coptic manuscripts discovered at Chenoboskion. With an English Translation and critical evaluation of the Gospel According to Thomas. [Philip Mairet] London: Hollis & Carter, 1960.
> [Fully revised and augmented by Philip Mairet for the English Edition.]

1961 **Grant, Robert M.**   Gnosticism. New York: Harper & Bros., 1961.
> [See Willis Barnstone, The Other Bible (The Secret Book of John), 1984.]

1961 **Runes, Dagobert D.**   Lost Legends of Israel. By Dagobert Runes. New York: The Wisdom Library, a Branch of the Philosophical Library, 1961.

1965 **Sanders, J.A.**   Discoveries in the Judaean Desert of Jordan   IV   The Psalms Scroll of Qumran Cave 11... by J.A. Sanders. Oxford: at the Clarendon Press, 1965.
> [Translation of Nos. I, II, and III of the Five Syriac Apocryphal Psalms; Sirach 51. Hebrew and English.]

1966 **Fitzmyer, Joseph A.**   The Genesis Apocryphon of Qumran Cave I. Rome: Pontifical Biblical Institute, 1966.
> [Biblica et Orientalia, No.18.]

1967 **Gamache, Henri**   Mystery of the Long Lost 8th, 9th and 10th Books of Moses together with the legend that was of Moses and 44 secret keys to universal power by Henri Gamache. Highland Falls, New York: Sheldon Publications, 1967.

1969 **MacDonald, J.**   The Samaritan Chronicle No.11 (or: Sepher Ha-Yamin) From Joshua to Nebuchadneezar. Berlin: Verlag Alfred Topelmannnnn, 1969.

1974 **Wilson, R. McL.**   Gnosis: A Selection of Gnostic
     Texts. Translated by R. McL. Wilson and Edited by
     Werner Foerster. 2 Vols. Oxford: Oxford University
     Press, 1974.

1975 **Asmussen, Jes P.**   Manichaean Literature.
     Delmar, New York: Scholars' Facsimiles & Reprints,
     1975.
         [See Willis Barnstone, the Other Bible (Manichaean
         Creation Myths), 1984.]

1977 **Bethge, Hans-Gehard and Orval S. Wintermute**   The
     Origins of the World, 1977.
         [See James M. Robinson, The Nag Hammadi, 1977.]

1977 **Bohlig, Alexander and Frederik Wisse**   The Gospel
     of the Egyptians, 1977.
         [See James M. Robinson, The Nag Hammadi, 1977.]

1977 **Bullard, Roger A.**   The Second Treatise of the
     Great Seth, 1977.
         [See James M. Robinson, The Nag Hammadi, 1977.]

1977 **Giversen, Soren and Birger A. Pearson**   Melchizedek,
     1977.
         [See James A. Robinson, The Nag Hammadi, 1977.]

1977 **Layton, Bentley**   The Hypostasis of the Archons
     [Genesis 1-6], 1977.
         [See James M. Robinson, The Nag Hammadi, 1977.]

1977 **Robinson, James M.**   (General Editor)   The Nag Hammadi
     Library in English. Translated by members of the
     Coptic Gnostic Library Project of the Institute for
     Antiquity and Christianity. James M. Robinson,
     Director. San Francisco: Harper & Row..., 1977.
                      Contributors:
         Harold W. Attridge   Hans-Gebhard Bethge
         Alexander Bohlig   James Brashler
         Roger A. Bullard   Soren Giversen
         Charles W. Hedrick   Wesley W. Isenberg
         Thomas O. Lambdin   George W. MacRae
         Dieter Mueller   William R. Murdock
         Douglas M. Parrott   Birger A. Pearson
         Malcolm L. Peel   James M. Robinson
         William R. Schoedel   John D. Turner
         Francis E. Williams   R. McL. Wilson
         Orval S. Wintermute   Frederik Wisse

1984 **Barnstone, Willis** The Other Bible. Edited by Willis
     Barnstone. San Francisco: Harper & Row..., 1984.

1984 **Cook, D.**   Joseph and Aseneth, 1984.
         [See H.F.D. Sparks, The Apocryphal Old Testament, 1985.]

1984 **Hadas, Moses**   The Martyrdom of Eleazar, His Wife,
     and Seven Sons, 1984.

[See Willis Barnstone, The Other Bible, 1984.]

1984 **Kuhn, K.H.**   The Testament of Isaac, 1984.
[See H.F.D. Sparks, The Apocryphal Old Testament, 1985.]

1984 **Kuhn, K.H.**   The Testament of Jacob, 1984.
[See H.F.D. Sparks, The Apocryphal Old Testament, 1985.]

1984 **Pennington, A.**   The Ladder of Jacob, 1984.
[See H.F.D. Sparks, The Apocryphal Old Testament, 1985.]

1984 **Schubert, Kurt**   Manichaean Creation Myths, 1984.
[See Willis Barnstone, The Other Bible, 1984.]

1984 **Shutt, R.J.H.**   Apocalypse of Sedrach, 1984.
[See H.F.D. Sparks, The Apocryphal Old Testament, 1985.]

1984 **Shutt, R.J.H.**   Apocalypse of Esdras, 1984.
[See H.F.D. Sparks, The Apocryphal Old Testament, 1985.]

1984 **Shutt, R.J.H.**   The Vision of Esdras, 1984.
[See H.F.D. Sparks, The Apocryphal Old Testament, 1985.]

1984 **Thornhill, R.**   The Paraleipomena of Jeremiah, 1984.
[See H.F.D. Sparks, The Apocryphal Old Testament, 1985.]

1984 **Vermes, G.**   The Genesis Apocryphon, 1984,
[See Willis Barnstone, The Other Bible, 1984.]

1984 **Whittaker, M.**   The Testament of Solomon, 1984.
[See H.F.D. Sparks, The Apocryphal Old Testament, 1985.]

1984 **Whittaker, M.**   The Life of Adam and Eve, 1984.
[See H.F.D. Sparks, The Apocryphal Old Testament,
1985. The translation of L.S.A. Wells. Revised by M.
Whittaker.]

1985 **Agourides, S.**   Apocalypse of Sedrach. 1985.
[See Apocrypha and Apocryphal Books, 1985 James H.
Charlesworth, O.T. Apocrypha.]

1985 **Attridge, H.**   Philo the Epic Poet. 1985.
[See Apocrypha and Apocryphal Books, 1985 James H.
Charlesworth, O.T. Apocrypha.]

1985 **Attridge, H.** Fragments of Pseudo–Greek Poets. 1985.
[See Apocrypha and Apocryphal Books, 1985 James H.
Charlesworth, O.T. Apocrypha.]

1985 **Sparks, H.F.D.** (Editor)   The Apocryphal Old
Testament. Oxford, U.K.: Clarendon Press, 1985.
["In the 1950's there seemed no serious objection to
this [presenting the material in 'biblical style', i.e.
not in the modern idiom], and all contributors were
instructed accordingly. But as time went on it became
clear that our decision was questionable... The only
alterative was to modernize the others. And I undertook
to do this as part of my overall responsibility... "]

APOCALYPSE OF ABRAHAM

1886 **Gaster, M.**   The Apocalypse of Abraham. From the
     Roumanian Text, Discovered and Translated by Dr. M.
     Gaster. Read 2nd Feb. 1886.

1918 **Box, G.H.**   The Apocalypse of Abraham: Edited, with
     a Translation from the Slavonic Text and Notes, by
     G.H. Box...with the assistance of J.I. Landsman.
     New York: The Macmillan Co., 1918.
     [See Apocryphal Books, 1916 W.O.E. Oesterley & G.H. Box,
     Translations of Early Documents.]

1983 **Rubinkiewicz, R.**   Apocalypse of Abraham. 1983
     [See Apocrypha and Apocryphal Books, 1983 James H.
     Charlesworth, O.T. Pseudepigrapha.]

1984 **Pennington, A.**   The Apocalypse of Abraham, 1984.
     [See Apocryphal Books, 1985 H.F.D. Sparks, The
     Apocryphal Old Testament.]

APOCALYPSE OF BARUCH

1896 **Charles, R.H.**   The Apocalypse of Baruch. Translated
     from the Syriac: Chapters I-LXXXXXVII, from the
     Sixth Cent. MS. In the Ambrosian Library in Milan,
     and Chapters LXXVIII-LXXXVII - The Epistles of
     Baruch - From a New and Critical text based on the
     ten MSS. and published herewith; Edited, with
     Introduction, Notes, and Indices. London: Adam and
     Charles Black, 1896.
     [Bound with the Assumption of Moses.]

     Other editions, 1917,1918,1929.

     [Reprinted in Apocrypha and Pseudepigrapha (q.v.)
     "...improvements and corrections...",1913. Also; See
     Apocrypahal Books, 1916 W.O.E. Oesterley and G.H. Box,
     Translations of Early Documents.]

1984 **Argyle, A.W.**   The Greek Apocalypse of Baruch. 1984.
     (The translation of H.M. Hughes revised by A.W.
     Argyle.)
     [See Apocryphal Books, 1985 H.F.D. Sparks, The Apocrypha
     O.T.]

1984 **Brockington, L.H.**   The Syriac Apocalypse of Baruch.
     1984. (The translation of R.H. Charles revised by
     L.H. Brockington.)
     [See Apocryphal Books, 1985 H.F.D. Sparks, The Apocrypha
     O.T.]

APOCALYPSE OF ELIJAH

1983 **Wintermute, O.S.**   Apocalypse of Elijah. 1983.
[See Apocrypha and Apocryphal Books, 1983 James H. Charlesworth, O.T. Pseudepigrapha.]

1984 **Kuhn, K.H.**   The Apocalypse of Elijah, 1984.
[See Apocryphal Books, 1985 H.F.D. Sparks, The Apocryphal Old Testament.]

APOCALYPSE OF EZRA

1917 **Box, G.H.**   The Apocalypse of Ezra – II Esdras III–XIV. translated from the Syriac text, with brief annotations. London: S.P.C.K., 1917.
[See Apocryphal Books, 1916 W.O.E. Oesterley & G.H. Box, Translations of Early Documents.]

1983 **Stone, M.E.**   Greek Apocalypse of Ezra. 1983.
[See Apocrypha and Apocryphal Books, 1983 James H. Charlesworth, O.T. Pseudepigrapha.]

APOCALYPSE OF MOSES

1895 **Conybeare, F.C.**   On the Apocalypse of Moses. Jewish Quarterly Review, VII, pps. 216–235, 1895.

APOCALYPSE OF ZEPHANIAH

1983 **Wintermute, O.S.**   Apocalypse of Zephaniah...
[See Apocrypha and Apocryphal Books, 1983 J.H. Chralesworth, The O.T. Pseudepigrapha.]

1984 **Kuhn, K.H.**   The Apocalypse of Zephaniah and an Anonymous Apocalypse, 1984.
[See Apocryphal Books, 1985 H.F.D. Sparks, The Apocryphal Old Testament.]

ARISTEAS' EPISTLE

1913 **Andrews, H.T.**   Letter of Aristeas, 1913.
[See Apocrypha and Apocryphal Books, 1913 Apocrypha and
Pseudepigrapha.]

[See Apocryphal Books, 1927 R.H. Platt, Jr., The
Forgotten Books of Eden.]

1926 **Anonymous**   The Letter of Aristeas...
[See Apocryphal Books,   1926 Anonymous, The Lost
Books...]

1951 **Hadas, Moses**   Aristeas to Philocrates (Letter of
Aristeas) Edited and Translated by Moses Hadas. New
York: Harper & Bros. for the Dropsie College for
Hebrew and Cognate Learning, 1951.

1983 **Shutt, R.J.H.**   Letter of Aristeas, 1983.
[See Apocrypha and Apocryphal Books, 1983 James H.
Charlesworth, O.T. Pseudepigrapha.]

ASCENSION OF ISAIAH

1900 **Charles, R.H.**   The Ascension of Isaiah; Translated
from the Ethiopic Version which, together with the
new Greek fragment, the Latin version and the Latin
translation of the Slavonic, is here published in
full. London: Adam and Charles Black, 1900.
Other editions; London: S.P.C.K., 1918, 1919.

[Bound with the Apocalypse of Abraham.]

1984 **Barton, J.M.T.**   The Ascension of Isaiah. The
translation of R.H.Charles revised by J.M.T. Barton.
1984.
[See Apocryphal Books, 1985 H.F.D. Sparks, The Apocrypha
Old Testament.]

ASSUMPTION OF MOSES

1897 **Charles, R.H.**   The Assumption of Moses; Translated
from the Latin Sixth Century MS, the unamended Text
of which is published herewith, together with the
text i its restored and critically emended Form;
Edited, with introductory notes and indices.
London: Adam and Charles Black, 1897.

Other editions, 1917, 1918, 1929.

[Bound with the Apocalypse of Baruch.]

1917 **Ferrar, William John**   The Assumption of
     Moses; Translated. London: S.P.C.K.; New York: The
     Macmillan Co., 1917.
          ["The following translation is made from Clement's Latin
          text published in Lietzmann's Kleine Texte (1904)"]

     Reprinted with a few corrections, 1918.

     Another reprint, 1929.

          [See Apocryphal Books, 1916 William Oscar Emil Oesterley
          & G.H. Box, Translations of Early Documents.]

1984 **Sweet, J.P.M.**   The Assumption of Moses. The
     translation of R.H. Charles revised by J.P.M. Sweet.
     1984.
          [See Apocryphal Books, 1985 H.F.D. Sparks, The
          Apocryphal Old Testament.]

BOOK OF ADAM

1882 **Malan, Solomon Caesar**   The Book of Adam and Eve,
     also called The Conflict of Adam and Eve With Satan,
     A Book of the Early Eastern Church, Translated from
     the Ethiopic, with notes from the Kufale, Talmud,
     Midrashim, and other Eastern Works. By S.C. Malan.
     London & Edinburgh: Williams & Norgate, 1882.
          [Reprinted in the "Forgotten Books Of Eden... Cleveland,
          Ohio & New York City: The World Publishing Co., 1927."]

1913 **Wells, L.S.A.**   The Books of Adam & Eve, 1913.
          [See Apocrypha and Apocryphal Books, 1913 Apocrypha &
          Pseudepigrapha.]

BOOK OF JUBILEES

1885 **Schodde, George H.**   The Book of Jubilees
     Translated from the Ethiopic, by George H. Schodde.
     Bibliotheca Sacra, XLII, Pages 629-645, 1885; XLIII,
     Pages 56-72, 356-371, 455-486, 1886; XLIV, Pages
     426-459, 602-611, 727-745, 1887.
          Reprinted; Oberlin, Ohio: E.J. Goodrich, 1888.

1902 **Charles, R.H.**   The Book of Jubilees, or the Little
Genesis, translated from the Editor's Ethiopic text,
and edited with Introduction, Notes, and Indices.
London: Adam and Charles Black, 1902.
> [Reprinted in the Apocrypha and Pseudepigrapha (q.v.)
> 1913.]
>
> [See Apocryphal Books, 1916 W.O.E. Oesterley and G.H.
> Box, Translations of Early Documents.]
>
> [Apocrypha and Apocryphal Books, 1984 Willis Barnstone,
> The Other Bible.]
>
> Reprint; Jerusalem: Makor, 1972.

1971 **Davenport, Gene L.**   The Eschatology of the Book of
Jubilees. Leiden: Brill, 1971.
> [SPB 20.]

1983 **Wintermute, O.S.**   Jubilees, 1983.
> [See Apocrypha and Apocryphal Books, 1983 James H.
> Charlesworth, O.T. Pseudepigrapha.]

1984 **Rabin, C.**   Jubilees, 1984.
> [See Apocryphal Books, 1984 H.F.D. Sparks, The
> Apocryphal Old Testament.]
>
> [This is the translation of R.H. Charles revised by C.
> Rabin.]

BOOK OF SHEM

1977 **Wisse, Frederik**   The Paraphrase of Shem...
> [See Apocryphal Books, 1977 James M. Robinson, The Nag
> Hammadi Library,]

1983 **Charlesworth, J.H.**   Treatise of Shem...
> [See Apocrypha and Apocryphal Books, 1983 J.W.
> Charlesworth, The O.T. Pseudepigrapha.]

BOOK OF ENOCH

???? **Kenealy, Edward V.H.**   The Book of Enoch, [187?].
> [A speculative entry, based upon the following, from the
> Preface to 'The Testament of Jesus, by Kenealy; Watford,
> 1901' (Preface signed, C.W.H.): "2. Enoch... The prophet
> of Atlantis, now submerged. His priests went as far west
> as the Americas, where the ruins of temples and pyramids

may be seen at this day. His sacred book was republished
by the Twelfth Messenger (i.e., Kenealy). The false copy
was published by Archbishop Laurence." Credence would
hardly be given to such a fanciful statement, except for
the facts: 1) Laurence did publish 'Enoch' in 1821
(subsequent issues in 1833, 1838, 1883) and 2) C.W.H.
also speaks of Adam's "...sacred Apocalypse... The false
copy, called Revelation, is at the end of the Bible. His
sacred book was republished by the Twelfth Messenger."
Kenealy did, in fact publish 'The Book of God: The
Apocalypse...' in 1867. No further confirmation has been
found however.]

1821 **Laurence, Richard**   The Book of Enoch the Prophet:
An Apocryphal production supposed to have been lost
for ages; but discovered at the close of the last
century in Abyssinia, now first translated from the
Ethiopic MS. in the Bodleian Library by Richard
Laurence. Oxford: 1821.

Second edition; J.H. Parker, 1833.

Third edition; Revised and enlarged. John Henry
Parker, 1838.

Another Edition; London: Kegan Paul, Trench &
Co., 1883.

Also; The text now corrected from his latest
notes, with an introduction by the author of
"Evolution   of   Christianity".   Glasgow:
J.Thompson, 1883.

Reprint; Minneapolis: Wizards Bookshelf, 1972,
1973.

Reprint; Thousand Oaks, CA: Artisan Sales, 1980.

1882 **Schodde, George H.**   The Book of Enoch: Translated
from the Ethiopic, with introduction and notes, by
George H. Schodde. Andover: Warren F. Draper, 1882.
Another edition, 1911.

1893 **Charles, R.H.**   I Enoch, 1893.
[See Apocrypha and Apocryphal Books, 1913 The Apocrypha
& Pseudepigrapha.]

1893 **Charles, R.H.**   The Book of Enoch translated
from Professor Dillman's Ethiopic Text emended and
revised   in   accordance   with   [Five]   hitherto
uncollated Ethiopic MSS. and with the Gizeh and
other   Greek   and   Latin   Fragments,   edited   with
Introduction,   Notes,   Appendices,   and   Indices.
Oxford: n.p., 1893.
[Also see 1912.]

1912 **Charles, R.H.**   The Book of Enoch, or 1 Enoch,
     translated from the Editor's Ethiopic Text, and
     edited with the Introduction, Notes, and Indexes of
     the First Edition 1893 wholly recast, enlarged, and
     rewritten. Together with a reprint from the editor's
     text of the Greek fragments. Oxford: The Clarendon
     Press, 1912.
        ["This is not so much a second edition as a new
        book...with a view to this translation, the present
        edition emended Dillman's text in accordance with nine
        hitherto uncollated Ethiopic MSS. in the British Museum,
        and the Greek and Latin fragments which have just come
        to light...published by the University Press in 1906."]

        [Reprinted in the Apocrypha and Pseudepigrapha (q.v.)
        1913. Also; Apocryphal Books, 1917 W.O.E. Oesterley and
        G.H. Box, Translations of Early Documents.]

        Reprint; Jerusalem: Makor, 1973.

        Another edition; London: SPCK, 1974, 1980.

1913 **Forbes, Neville and R.H. Charles**   2 Enoch, 1913.
        [See Apocrypha and Apocryphal Books, 1913 The Apocrypha
        and Pseudepigrapha.]

1928 **Odeberg, Hugo**   3 Enoch; or, the Hebrew Book of
     Enoch. Edited and transated for the first time with
     introduction, commentary and critical notes, by Hugo
     Odeberg.   Cambridge: University Press, 1928.
        Reprint: New York: Ktav Publishing House, 1973.

1978 **Knibb, M.A.**   The Ethiopic Book of Enoch:
     a New Edition in the Light of the Aramaic Dead Sea
     Fragmento by M.A.Knibb; in consultation with Edward
     Ullendorff... II. Introduction, Translation, and
     Commentary.   Oxford: Clarendon Press; New York:
     Oxford University Press, 1978.
        [See Apocryphal Books, 1984 H.F.D.Sparks, The Apocryphal
        O.T.]

1983 **Alexander, P.** 3 (Hebrew Apocalypse of) Enoch. 1983.
        [See Apocrypha and Apocryphal Books, 1983 James H.
        Charlesworth, O.T. Pseudepigrapha.]

1983 **Andersen, Francis I.**   2 (Slavonic Apocalypse of)
     Enoch. 1983.
        [See Apocrypha and Apocryphal Books, 1983 James H.
        Charlesworth, O.T. Pseudepigrapha.]

1983 **Isaac, E.**   (Ethiopic Apocalypse of) Enoch. 1983.
        [See Apocrypha and Apocryphal Books, 1983 James H.
        Charlesworth, O.T. Pseudepigrapha.]

JASHER

???? **Anonymous**   Joseph and Potiphar's Wife (Jasher
44: 1-80) "Showers of Blessing", 681st Issue, Pages
9-12, Sept., 1977.

1751 **Anonymous**   The Book of Jasher. With Testimonies and
Notes explanatory of the Text. To which is prefixed
various Readings. Translated into English from the
Hebrew, by Alcuin, of Britain, who went a Pilgrimage
into the Holy Land. This Book is twice mentioned in
the Holy Scripture. viz. in Josh. x.13., and in 2
Sam. i.18.; in both places it is appealed to as a
Work of Credit and Reputation, and as such was at
that Time had in great Esteem. [Jacob Ilive.
London:] 1751.

> Another edition; The Book of Jasher. With
> Testimonies and Notes, Critical and
> Historical, explanatory of the Text. To which
> is prefixed Various Readings, and a
> Preliminary Dissertation, proving the
> Authenticity of the Work. Translated into
> English from the Hebrew, by Flaccus Albinus
> Alcuinus of Britain, Abbot of Canterbury. Who
> went a Pilgrimage into the Holy Land, and
> Persia, where he discovered this volume, in
> the City of Gazna... [C.R. Bond] Bristol:
> Printed for the Editor, by Philip Rose, 1829.
>> [This edition has a few slight revisions from the
>> 1751 edition.]

[There have been many reprints of the 1829 edition.]

Also; The Book of Jasher: with Testimonies and
Notes, Critical and Historical, Explanatory of
the Text, to which is prefixed, various
readings, and a Preliminary Dissertation,
proving the Authenticity of the Work.
Translated into English from the Hebrew by
Flaccus Albinus, of Britain, Abbot of
Canterbury,... London: Longman, MDCCCXXIX.
[1829]

> Another edition; The Book of Jasher, one of the
> sacred books of the Bible, long lost or
> undiscovered, now offered in photographic
> reproduction of the version by Alcuin. San
> Jose, Calif.: The Rosicrucian Order, AMORC,
> 1934.

[For a complete account of these forgeries, see Thomas
Hartwell Horne's 'Introduction to the Holy Scriptures'

1829 **Bond, C.R.**   See Anonymous, Book of Jasher, 1751.

1840 **Anonymous**   ...The Book of Jasher; referred to in
Joshua and Second Samuel. Faithfully translated from
the Original Hebrew into English. [Mr. Samuel?] New
York: M.M. Noah & A.S. Gould, 1840.
> ["...the Rev. Mr. Horne, in his Introduction to the
> Study of the Scripture, has been at some pains to
> collect a history of the various fabrications of Jasher;
> the most remarkable of which was originally published in
> England, in the year 1750, (or 1751) by a person called
> Ilive, and purported to be a translation from a Hebrew
> work of that name, found in Persia by Alcuin. It was
> republished in Bristol in the year 1829, and a copy is
> now in my possession. It is a miserable fabrication...
> In the same work by Dr. Horne, a slight reference is
> made to the Book of Jasher, written in Rabbinical
> Hebrew, said to have been discovered in Jerusalem at its
> capture under Titus, and printed in Venice in 1613. This
> is the book now translated into English for the first
> time."]

Another Edition; Jasher. The Lost Book of Jasher
10:13 2nd Samuel 1:18. Discovered in Jerusalem
Ruins. Faithfully translated from the Original
Hebrew into English.   Los Angeles, Calif.:
America-Jerusalem Rapid Bible Museum, 1916.
> [Title is taken from the 1926 edition.]

Another Edition; Extracts From the Book of
Jasher, mentioned in Joshua 10:13 and 2 Samuel
1:18.   Los Angeles: L.Danhoff, A.C.Jeffries,
1916.

Another edition; ...Jasher; The Lost Book of
Joshua 10:13; 2nd Samuel 1:18; Discovered in
Jerusalem Ruins; faithfully Translated from
the Original Hebrew into English [Improved
Edition]   Los Angeles, California, U.S.A.:
America-Jerusalem Rapid Bible Mission Unit 1
(Inc.), 1926.
> [The majority of the text is a paraphrase of
> material from Genesis and Exodus, with a little
> from Numbers, Joshua and I Kings.]

1954 **Anonymous** The Book of Jasher; faithfully translated
from the original. Dedicated to the world and all
religions.   Philadelphia: Bible Corp. of America,
1954.

1977 **Anonymous**   Joseph and Potiphar's Wife. Showers of
Blessing", 681st Issue, September, 1977, pages 9-12.
> [See ???? Anonymous for same entry. Shown here for
> convenience in locating the entry. The date of the
> translation is unknown.]

EZEKIEL

1983 **Robertson, R.G.**   Ezekiel the Tragedian, 1983.
[See Apocrypha and Apocryphal Books, 1983 James H.
Charlesworth, O.T. Pseudepigrapha.]

IV EZRA

1892 **Bensly, R.L.**   The Fourth Book of Ezra, with
Introduction by M.R. James. Cambridge: 1892.
[Text and Studies, Vol. III, No. 2, Cambridge.]

1983 **Metzger, Bruse M.**   The Fourth Book of Ezra. 1983.
[See Apocrypha and Apocryphal Books, 1983 James H.
Charlesworth, O.T. Pseudepigrapha.]

ODES OF SOLOMON

???? **Box, G.H.**   The Odes and Psalms of Solomon by
G.H.Box. London: S.P.C.K., [19??].

???? **Harris, Rendel**   An Early Christian Psalter by
Rendel Harris. London: James Nisbet & Co., [190?].
["...these odes, artificially ascribed to Solomon, have
been found in a Syraic M.S..."]

Second impression; 1910.

1909 **Harris, James Rendel**   The Odes... Solomon...
[See Apocryphal Books for the complete entry.]

1912 **Bernard, John Henry** The Odes of Solomon. Cambridge:
n.p., 1912.

1926 **Anonymous**   The Odes of Solomon...
[See Apocryphal Books, 1926 Anonymous, The Lost
Books...]

1973 **Charlesworth, James Hamilton**   The Odes of Solomon,
Edited with Translation and Notes by James H.
Charlesworth. Oxford: at the Clarendon Press, 1973.
Corrected reprint; Missoula, Montana: Scholars
Press, 1977 (1978?)

1983 **Charlesworth, J.H.**   Odes of Solomon, 1983.

[See Apocrypha and Apocryphal Books, 1983 James H. Charlesworth, O.T. Pseudepigrapha. May be same as 1973.]

1984 Emerton, J.A.   The Odes of Solomon, 1984.
[See Apocryphal Books, 1984 H.F.D. Sparks, The Apocryphal Old Testament.]

1985 Pennington, M. Basil and Others   The Odes of Solomon...
[See Early Church Fathers, 1985 M. Basil Pennington and Others, The Living Testament. Also; Apocryphal Books, 1927 Frank Crane, The Lost Books.]

1916 − − Vol. I The Text...

1920 − − Vol. II The Translation...

PSALMS OF SOLOMON

1891 Ryle, Herbert Edward and Montague Rhodes James
Psalms of the Pharisees, commonly called the Psalms of Solomon. The Text Newly Revised from all the MSS. Edited, with introduction, English Translation, Notes, Appendix, and Indices. Cambridge: At the University Press, 1891.

1909 Harris, James Rendel   The Odes... Solomon...
[See Apocryphal Books for the complete entry.]

1913 Gray, George Buchanan   Psalms of Solomon, 1913.
[See Apocrypha and Apocryphal Books, 1913 Apocrypha & Pseudepigrapha.]

1926 Anonymous   The Psalms of Solomon...
[See Apocryphal Books, 1926 Anonymous, The Lost Books...]

1983 Wright, R.B.   Psalms of Solomon, 1983.
[See Apocrypha and Apocryphal Books, 1983 James H. Charlesworth, O.T. Pseudepigrapha.]

1984 Brock, S.P.   The Psalms of Solomon. 1984.
[See Apocryphal Books, 1984 H.F.D. Sparks, The Apocryphal Old Testament.]

TESTAMENT OF ABRAHAM

1892 James, Montague Rhodes   The Testament of Abraham: The Greek text now first edited with an introduction and notes. Cambridge: T & S, 1892.

1892 **Barnes, W.E.**   'Extracts...Testament of Abraham'...
[See M.R. James, The Testament of Abraham, 1892. pp. 135-139.]

1892 **Barnes, W.E.**   'Extracts...Testament of Isaac'...
[See M.R. James, The Testament of Abraham, 1892. pp. 140-151.]

1892 **Barnes, W.E.**   'The Testament of Jacob'...
[See M.R. James, The Testament of Abraham, 1892. pp. 152-154.]

1927 **Box, G.H.** The Testament of Abraham, Translated from the Greek text with introduction and notes...by G.H. Box.   London: S.P.C.K.;   New York: & Toronto: The Macmillan Co., 1927.
[With an appendix containing a translation from the Coptic Version of the Testaments of Isaac and Jacob. S.Gasalee.]

[See W.O.E. Oesterley & G.H. Box, Translations of Early Documents, 1916.]

1983 **Sanders, E.P.**   The Testament of Abraham, 1983.
[See Apocrypha and Apocryphal Books, 1983 James H. Charlesworth, O.T. Pseudepigrapha.]

1984 **Pennington, A.**   The Testament of Abraham, 1984.
[See H.F.D. Sparks, The Apocryphal Old Testament, 1984.]

TESTAMENT OF JOB

1971 **Spittler, Russell Paul**   The Testament of Job: introduction, translation, and notes, by Russell Paul Spittler.   Cambridge, Mass.: n.p., 1971.

1974 **Kraft, Robert A.**   The Testament of Job, according to the SV text/Greek text and English translation edited by Robert A. Kraft... New York: Society of Biblical Literature;   Missula, Mont.: Distributed by Scholars' Press, 1974.

1983 **Spittler, R.P.**   Testament of Job, 1983.
[See Apocrypha and Apocryphal Books, 1983 James H. Charlesworth, O.T. Pseudepigrapha.]

1984 **Thornhill, R.**   The Testament of Job, 1984.
[See Apocryphal Books, 1984 H.F.D. Sparks, The Apocryphal Old Testament.]

TESTAMENTS OF THE THREE PATRIARCHS

1983 **Sanders, E.P. and W.F. Stinespring**   Testaments of
     the Three Patriarchs. 1983.
          [See Apocrypha and Apocryphal Books, 1983 James H.
          Charlesworth, O.T. Pseudepigrapha.]

TESTAMENTS OF THE TWELVE PATRIARCHS

???? **Charles, R.H.**   The Testament of the XII Patriarchs.
     London: A. & C. Black, [190?].
          [Reprinted in Apocrypha and Pseudepigrapha (q.v.) 1913.]

     Another edition; London: S.P.C.K., 191?

     [Also; Published in "The Forgotten Books of Eden...,
     1927.]

1575 **Gilby, Anthony**   Testamentes of the twelue
     Patriarches, the sons of Jacob. Translated out of
     Greek into Latin by Robert Grosthead sometime Bishop
     of Lincoln: And out of his copy, into French and
     Dutch by others, and now Englished. To the credit
     whereof, an ancient Greek copy written in Parchment
     is kept in the Vniversity Library of Cambridge.
     1575.
          Other editions; 1581, 1604, 1706.

     Another edition; London: Printed by E.C. and A.C.
     for the Company of Stationers, 1670.

     [The complete title attributed to 1575, is taken from
     the 1670 copy.]

1975 **Stone, Michael E.**   The Armenian Version of the
     Testament of Joseph: introduction, critical edition,
     and translation by Michael E. Stone.   Missoula,
     Mont.: Published by Scholars Press for the Society
     of Biblical Literature, 1975.

1983 **Kee, H.C.**   The Testaments...Twelve Patriarchs...
          [See Apocrypha and Apocryphal Books, 1983 James H.
          Charlesworth, O.T. Pseudepigrapha.]

1984 **DeJonge, M.**   The Testaments...Twelve Patriarchs...
          [See Apocryphal Books, 1984 H.F.D. Sparks, The
          Apocryphal Old Testament.]

13

New Testament

NEW TESTAMENTS

???? **Anonymous**   Classic Interlinear Translations. The Greek English New Testament being the Original Text, with a Literal Interlinear Translation. Pennsylvania: Handy Book Co., n.d.

???? **Comfort, Philip W. and Robert K. Brown**   The New Greek-English Interlinear New Testament. Wheaton, IL: Tyndale House, [199?].

???? **Cook**   New Testament, Plain Translation by a Student. (Printed in Australia), [????].

???? **Gordon, Robert**   [New Testament] [????].
   [Alexander Geddes, in his <u>Prospectus</u>, refers to a fresh translation of the New Testament by Robert Gordon, the Rector of the Scotch College, Rome, which he had in MS.]

???? **Linn, Samuel P.**   (Editor)   The New Testament of our Lord and Saviour Jesus Christ. Translated out of the Original Greek, together with the Book of Psalms to which is added... The whole edited by Rev. Samuel P. Linn... Philadelphia: John E. Porter & Co., n.d.

???? **Weigle, Luther A.**   (Editor)   The New Testament Octapla; Eight English Version of the New Testament in the Tyndale -King James Tradition. Edited by Luther A. Weigle.   Edinburgh, New York, Toronto: Thomas Nelson & Sons, [19??].
   [Contains: Tyndale (1535 edition), Great Bible (1540 edition), Geneva Bible (1561-1562 edition), Bishops' Bible (1602 edition), Rheims (1582 edition), KJV (1873 edition), ASV (1901) and RSV (1946).]

1380 **Wycliffe, John**   The New Testament. c1380.
   1731 New Testament... Translated out of the Latin Vulgat by John Wiclif..about 1378

To which is Praefixt a History of the several Translations of the H. Bible and N. Testament, &c. into English, both in MS. and Print, and of the most remarkable Editions of them since the Invention of Printing. By John Lewis.... London: John March.

Reprinted; Edited, with preliminary matter, by H.H. Baber. London: Richard Edwards, 1810.

1848 The New Testament in English Newly Translated by John Wycliffe. Circa MCCCLXXX (Now First Printed from a contemporary Manuscript formerly in the Monastery of Sion Middlesex, Late in the Collection of Lea Wilson Esq.) London: for William Pickering; Chiswick: Whittingham.

1879 The New Testament in English, according to the version of John Wycliffe, about A.D. 1380, and revised by John Purvey, about A.D. 1388. Formerly edited by...Josiah Forshall...and...Frederic Madden ... And now reprinted. Oxford: Clarendon Press.

1986 The New Testament in English. Translated by John Wycliffe MCCCLXXXII. Revised by John Purvey MCCCLXXXVIII. Sexcentenary Edition. First Exact Facsimile of the First English Bible with an Introduction by Donald L. Brake. From Rawlinson 259 MSS. in the Bodleian Library Oxford, England. Portland, Oregon: Printed in Great Britain by Kingprint International for International Bible Publications.

[See Romans, 1914 Emma Curtiss Tucker, Wycliffite Epistle to the Romans.]

1525 **Tyndale, William** (The New Testament) [Worms: Peter Schoeffer, 1525.]

[William Tyndale's first edition. Only two of 3,000 copies still exist.]

1836 The New Testament...published in 1526. Being the first Translation from the Greek into English, by that eminent scholar and martyr, William Tyndale. Reprinted verbatim: with a memoir of his life and writings, by George Offor. Together with the proceedings and correspondence of Henry VIII, Sir T. More, and Lord Cromwell. London: Stevens and Pardon, for S. Bagster, 1836.

1837 The New Testament...By William Tyndale ...The Original Edition, 1526, being the First Vernacular Translated from the Greek. With a Memoir of his Life and Writings. To Which are Annexed, the Essential Variations of Coverdale's, Thomas Matthew's, Cranmer's, the Genevan, and the Bishops' Bibles, as Marginal Readings. By J.P. Dabney. Andover [Mass.] and New York: Printed and Published by Gould and Newman, from the London Edition of Bagster, 1837.

1862 The first New Testament printed in the English language (1525 or 1526), translated from the Greek by William Tyndale; reproduced in facsimile with an introduction by Francis Fry, F.S.A. Bristol: Printed for the Editor, 1862.

1871 Another edition; - - photo-lithographed from the unique fragment now in the Grenville Collection, British Museum. Edited by Edward Arber... London: 1871.

1901 The Revelation of St. John the Divine; from the first English translation, MDXXV. Now newly imprinted with Albert Durel's illustrations. Detroit, MI: Cranbrook Press, 1901.

1954 The Newe Testamente: M.D.XXVI W. Tyndale. 4 Vols. Lexington, KY: Anvil Press, 1954-1955.
     [The Four Gospels only. Vols. 1-3 dated 1954; Vol. 4 Dated 1955. 300 copies.]

1976 The New Testament, by William Tyndale, 1526. New York & London: D.Paradine Developments, 1976.
     [A 4-color facsimile reprint. It commemorates the 450th anniversary of the original publication and carries an introduction by F.F. Bruce.]

1989 The Newe Testament by William Tindale. M.D.XXVI. The Quincentenary of Tindale's Birth (1490? to 1990). The first English New Testament published and the first from the original Greek. The text based upon George Offor's reprint, MDCCCXXXVI.

Modern spelling, punctuation and
introduction by John Wesley Sawyer. The
Martyrs Bible series. Volume one.
Milford, OH: John the Baptist Printing
Ministry, 1989.
[Tyndale's first edition. Only two of 3,000
copies still exist.]

1525 **Tyndale, William**   (The New Testament) [Cologne:
Peter Quentell, 1525.]
[Only a fragment, 'The gospell of S. Mathew. The fyrst
Chapter [through] the xxii. Chapter.', still remains in
the Grenville Collection of the British Museum. 3,000
copies of the first ten sheets had been secretly printed
before Tyndale had to flee Cologne to Worms, where he
began his work afresh.]

Complete edition; Worms: Peter Quentell, 1526.

Reprinted; ...New Testament translated by
William Tyndale 1525. Facsimile of unique
fragment of the uncompleted Cologne edition.
Oxford: Clarendon Press, 1926.

1534 **Joye, George**   The new Testament as it was written,
and caused to be written by them which herde yt.
Whom also oure saueoure Christ Iesus commaunded that
they shulde preach it vnto al creatures. The Gospell
of S. Matthew,... Antwerpe: by me Widowe of
Christoffel [van Ruremonde] of Endhoue, 1534.

1534 **Tyndale, William**   The newe Testament dylygently
corrected and compared with the Greke by Willyam
Tindale: and fynes-shed in the yere of oure Lorde
God. A.M.D. & xxxiiij. in the moneth of Nouember.
Antwerp: Marten Emperowr [=De Keyser] 1534.
[This is a carefully revised edition of Tyndale's N.T.,
1525.]

Another edition; London: William Copland, 1549.

Reprinted; The New Testament translated by
William Tyndale. A Reprint of the edition of
1534 with the Translator's Prefaces & Notes
and the variants of the edition of 1525.
Edited by N. Hardy Willis... Cambridge:
University Press, 1938.

Also; Tyndale Commemorative Volume. Reproducing
Substantial Parts of Tyndales Revised New
Testament of 1534 With Some of the Original
Woodcuts. Also an Account of the Author's
Life. Lutterworth Press, 1939.

1535 **Joye, George**   [The New Testament in Tyndale's version, as modified by George Joye.]   Antwerpe: Catharyn Widowe [of Christoffel of Endhoven, 1535.

1535 **Tyndale, William**   The newe Testament yet once agayne corrected by Willyam Tindale: Where vnto is added a Kalendar and a necessarye Table wherin easely and lightelye maye be founde any storye contayned in the foure Euangelistes and in the Acts of the Apostles. Printed in the yere of oure Lorde God. M.D. & xxxv. [Antwerp: Martin de Keyser? for Govaert van der Haghen, 1535.]
[This is also known as the G.H. edition because of the monogram on the second title-page. This revision is considered to be Tyndale's last work.]

["There are three distinct quarto editions of Tyndale's New Testament, all bearing the date 1536, they, agree closely with the G.H. edition, but differ throughout in many small points."]

["There are three, or four, octavo editions of Tyndale's New Testament bearing this date [1536]. While agreeing closely, they differ throughout in many small points. Their text agrees generally with that of the G.H. edition."]

Another edition; The newe Testament in Englyshe and Latyn accordyng to the translacyon of doctour Erasmus of Roterdam. Anno. M.CCCCC. XXXVIII. Ieremie. XXII. Is nat my worde lyke a fyre sayeth the Lorde, and lyke an hammer that breaketh the harde stone? Prynted in Fletestrete by Robert Redman Set for the vnder the Kynges moste gracious lycence. 1538.
[This diaglot contains Tyndale's English N.T. with the Latin of Erasmus. The English agrees generally with the G.H. edition.]

Second edition; London: William Powell, 1548.

Third edition; London: W. Powell, 1549.

Fourth edition, 1550.

Also; ...of the last translacio. By Wylliam Tyndal. [London?: T. Petyt], 1548.
[The text agrees very closely with the G.H. edition.]

Another edition; London: John Day and William Seres, 1548, 1550, 1551?.

Another edition; London: Wyllyam Tylle, 1549.

Another edition; [Antwerp?], 1549.

Also; The newe Testament faythfully translated
by Miles Couerdal. Anno. 1550. Roma . xv . a
Whatsoeuer thinges re wrytten afore tyme, are
wrytten   for   oure   learnynge.   [Zurich: C.
Froschover, 1550.
> [This text agrees closely with the 1536 G.H.
> edition of Tyndale's N.T. and is NOT Coverdale's
> as stated on the title page.]

[See New Testament Octapla, 1962.]

1538 **Coverdale, Myles**   The new Testament of oure
Sauyour Iesu Christ. Faythfully translated & lately
correcte: wyth a true concordaunce in the margent &
many necessary annotations declarynge sondry harde
places coteyned in the text. Eympit in the yeare of
our Lorde. Mdxxxviii Antwerp: Matthew Crom.
> [This work was disowned by Coverdale.]

1538 **Coverdale, Myles**   The New Testament both in Latine
and Englyshe after the vulgare texte: which is red
in the churche. Translated and corrected by Myles
Coverdale: and prynted in Paris, by Franunces
Regnault. M.ccccc.xxxviii in Nouembre. Prynted for
Richard Grafton and Edward Whitchurch cytezens of
London., 1538.
> [Diaglot]

1538 **Hollybushe, Johan**   The newe testament both in
Latine and Englyshe eche correspondente to the other
after the vulgare texte, communely called S.Jeromes.
Faythfullye translated by Johan Hollybushe. Anno.
M.CCCCCXXXVIII. Jeremie. xxii. Is not my worde lyke
a fyre sayeth the Lorde, and lyke an hammer that
breaketh the harde stone.   Prynted in Southwarke by
James Nicolson. Set forth wyth the Kynges moost
gracious lycence.
> [James   Nicolson   published   this   work   after   making
> 'corrections' and substituting the name Hollybushe for
> Coverdale.]

1538 **Matthew, Thomas**   The newe Testament
of oure sauioure Jesu Christ, newly and diligently
translated in to Englysshe by Thomas Mathew with
annotations in ye mergent to helpe the reader to the
vhderstadying of ye Texte. Set forth with the Kynges
moost gratious lycence.   [London: Thomas Gybson],
1538.

1539 **Taverner, Richard**   The Nevv Testament in Englysshe:
after the Greke exemplar: Dilygently translated, and
corrected   by   Rycharde   Tauerner.   M.D.XXXIX.   Cum
Priuilegio ad Imprimendum solum.   London: Thomas
Petyt, for Thomas Berthelet. [1539]
> [There were two editions dated 1539; one in quarto and
> the other in octavo.]

1540 **Grafton, R. and E. Whitchurch**   New Testament
     Translated from the Latin of Erasmus, by R. Grafton
     and E. Whitchurch. London: 1540.

1548 **Tyndale, William**   The newe Testament of oure
     Sauyour Jesu Christ. London: Richard Jugge, 1548.
     [The text is based on the 1534 and the G.H. edition of
     1536, and shows signs of careful editing.]

1549 **Anonymous**   The first tome or volume of the
     Paraphrase of Erasmus vpon the newe testamente. 2
     Vols.   Empriented at London in Fletestrete at the
     signe of the sunne by Edwarde Whitchurche the last
     daie of Januarie. Anno Domini 1548. [=1549]
     ["Among the translators were Nicholas Udall, Thomas Key,
     Miles Coverdale, John Olde, and Leonard Coxe; while
     Princess (afterward Queen) Mary translated the greater
     part of the Paraphrase upon St. John's Gospel. The
     Paraphrase of the Revelation, omitted by Erasmus, was
     the work of Leo Juda, translated by Edmund Alen."]

     Another   Edition;   The   Second   Tome   of   the
     Paraphrase of Erasmus on the New Testament.
     London: Edward Whitchurch, 1549.

1549 **Coverdale, Myles**   [The Newe Testament. Diligently
     Translated by Myles Couerdale and conferred with the
     translacion of William Tyndale, with the necessary
     Concordances truly alleged. An. M.D.XLIX.] London:
     Reynolde Wolfe. (1549)
     [A revised edition of Coverdale's New Testament.]

1552 **Jugge, Richard**   The newe Testament of our Sauiour
     Jesu Christe. Faythfully translated out of the
     Greke. Wyth the Notes and expositions of the darke
     places therein. Mathew. xiij f. Vnio, quem praecepit
     emi servator Iesus, Hic situs est, debet non aliunde
     peti. The pearle, which Christ commaunded to be
     bought Is here to be founde, not elles to be sought.
     London: Rycharde Jugge, 1552?
     [Jugge's revision of Tyndale's version.]

     Other Editions; 1552?, 1553, 1561?, 1566?

1557 **Whittingham, William**   The Nevve Testament of
     ovr Lord Iesus Christ. Conferred diligently with the
     Greke, and best approued translations. Vvith the
     arguments, as wel before the chapters, as for euery
     Boke & Epistle, also diuersities of readings, and
     moste proffitable annotations of all harde places:
     wherunto is added a copious Table.   At Geneva:
     Printed By Conrad Badius. M.D.LVII. (1557)

[Whittingham based this text on Tyndale and compared it to the Great Bible. Even though this work forms the ground work for the Geneva Bible New Testament, it is a distinct work.]

Reprinted; The New Testament... A facsimile reprint of the celebrated Genevan Testament, 1557; with the marginal annotations and references, the initial and other wood cuts, prefaces and index. London: for S. Bagster and Sons, 1842.

1576 **Tomson, Laurence**   The New Testament of Ovr Lord Iesvs Christ translated Out of Greeke By Theod. Beza: Whereunto are adioyned brief Summaries of doctrine vpon the Euangelistes and Acts of the Apostles, together with the methode of the Epistles of the Apostles by the said Theord. Beza: And also short expositions on the phrases and hard places teken out of the large annotations of the foresaid Authour and Ioach. Camerarius, By P Loseler. Villerius. Englished by L. Tomson. Imprinted at London by Christopher Barkar dwelling in Poules Churchyard at the signe of the Tigres head. 1576. Cum priuilegio.
[First edition of Thomson's revision of the Geneva New Testament.]

Another edition; London: Christopher Barkar, 1577.
[This edition agrees closely with the 1576 edition. However, there are slight differences in the text.]

Other Editions; 1578, 1580, 1582, 1583, 1585, 1586, 1587.

[Most editions of the Geneva Bible since 1587 have the Tomson N.T. The New Testament editions are: 1589, 1590, 1592, 1593, 1596, 1597, 1598, 1600, 1601, 1603, 1609, 1611, 1613, 1615, 1616. The Geneva-Tomson Bible editions are: 1587, 1590, 1592, 1594, 1595, 1597, 1598, 1601, 1602, 1606, 1607, 1608, 1610.]

[See Geneva-Tomson-Junius Version, 1599, 1602.]

1589 **Fulke, William**   The Text of the New Testament of Iesvs Christ, translated ovt of the vulgar Latine by the Papists of the traiterous Seminarie at Rhemes. With Arguments of Bookes, Chapters, and Annotations, pretending to discouer the corruptions of diuers translations, and to cleare the controuersies of these dayes. VVhereunto is added the Translation out of the Original Greeke, commonly vsed in the Church of England. With A Confvtation of all svch Agrvments, Glosses, and Annotations, As Conteine

Manifest impietie, of hersie, treason and slander, against the Catholike Church of God, and the true teachers thereof, or the Translations vsed in the Church of England: Both by auctoritie of the holy Scriptures, and by the testimonie of the ancient fathers. By William Fvlke, Doctor in Diuinitie. Imprinted at London by the Deputies of Christopher Barker, Printer to the Qveens most excellent Maiestie. Anno 1589.

> [Rheims and Bishops Versions in parallel columns with very acrimonious notes by W. Fulke.]

2nd edition, 1601.

3rd edition, 1617.

4th edition, 1633.

Another edition; 1843.

1599 **Anonymous**   New Testament. English and 11 other Languages Nuremburg: 1599.

1602 **Geneva-Tomson-Junius New Testament**   The New Testament of ovr Lord Iesvs Christ, Translated out of Greeke by Theod. Beza: With briefe Summaries ... Englished by L. Tomson. Together with the Annotations of Fr. Junius vpon the Reuelation of S. John. Imprinted at London by Robert Barker, Printer to the Queenes most Excellent Maiestie. Anno 1602.

> [Apparently the earliest issued of the Geneva N.T. with Junius' Revelation in place of Tomson's.]

Also, 1610.

1653 **Hammond, Henry**   A Paraphrase, and Annotations Upon all the Books of the New Testament: Briefly explaining all the difficult places thereof. By H. Hammond, D.D.   London: J. Flesher: for Richard Royston, at the Angel in Ivie-lane, 1653.

> Later editions; 1659, 1671, 1675, 1681, 1689, 1702, and 1845.

1685 **Baxter, Richard**   A Paraphrase on the New Testament with Notes Doctrinal and Practical. By plainness and brevity fitted to the use of religious families... and of the younger and poorer sort of scholars and ministers... With an advertisement of difficulties in the Revelations. By Richard Baxter.   London: Printed for B. Simmons and Tho. Simmons, 1685.

> 2nd edition, 1695.

Again, 1810.

[Baxter was imprisoned two years for having the audacity to do this work, and would have remained in prison had not the King remitted his fine.]

1701 **Lloyd, William**   (Bishop of Worcester)   The Holy Bible... Oxford: University-Printers, 1701.
[An improved edition of the KJV.]

1703 **Whitby, Daniel**   Paraphrase and Commentary on the New Testament, 1703.
10th. Edition; 2 Vols. London: Printed by James Mayes, Shoe Lane, for Longman, Hurst, Rees & Orme; Samuel Bagster & Sons; W. Baynes; R. Ogle; Edinburgh: Ogle & Ackman; Glasgow: M. Ogle, 1808.

1719 **Nary, Cornelius**   The New Testament... Newly translated out of the Latin Vulgat; and with the original Greek, and divers translations in vulgar languages diligently compared and revised. Together with Annotations...and Marginal Notes... By C.N., C.F.P.D.   [Dublin?]
[An original version by Cornelius Nary, a Roman Catholic Priest.]

1729 **Anonymous**   The New Testament in Greek and English. Containing the Original Text corrected from the Authority of the most Authentic Manuscripts: and a New Version form'd agreeably to the Illustrations of the most Learned Commentators and Critics: with Notes and Various Readings, and a Copious Alphabetical Index... [Daniel Mace] 2 Vols. London: for J. Roberts, 1729.
[Often wrongly described as William Mace.]

1730 **Anonymous**   Annotations on the New Testament...By R.W. [Robert Witham] D.D...2 Vols. n.p.: n.p., 1730.
["In this original and annotated version, the author professes to explain the literal sense... to show the differences between the Vulgate and the Greek text."]

Reprinted; 2 Vols. 1733. [This is not merely a reissue, but quite a distinct edition.]

1730 **Webster, William**   The New Testament...According to the Ancient Latin Edition. With Critical Remarks... From the French of Father Simon. By William Webster ...London: for John Pemberton and Charles Rivington, 1730.

1731 **Lewis, John** See Anonymous, The New Testament, 1380.

1736 **Lindsay, John**   A critical and practical commentary on the New Testament...compared with the original Greek and the more authentic translations...by John Lindsay. London: R. Penny, 1736.

1738 **Anonymous**   The New Testament... with arguments
of books and chapters; with annotations, and other
helps, for the better understanding the text, and
especially for the discovery of corruptions in
divers late translations, and for clearing up
religious controversies of the present times; to
which are added tables of the Epistles and Gospels,
controversies, and heretical corruptions. The text
is faithfully translated into English, out of the
authentical Latin, diligently conferred with the
Greek, and other editions in divers languages, and
the annotations etc. are affix'd to it by the
English College then resident in Rhemes. The Fifth
edition (the first in filio) adorn'd with cuts...
[Douay?]
> [Cotton suggests this reprint of 1582 was edited by
> Richard Challoner and Francis Blyth.]

1739 **Doddridge, Philip**   The New Testament with
Paraphrase and Notes. 6 Vols.   London: J. Wilson,
1739-1756.

> Another Edition; 6 Vols. London: Printed by
> Assignment from the Author's window..., 1761.

> Also; A new translation of the New Testament...
> extracted from the paraphrase of the late
> Philip Doddridge, D.D., and carefully revised.
> With an introduction and notes [by Samuel
> Palmer].   London: For J. Rivington, W.
> Johnston, R. Baldwin and C. Rivington, 1765.

> Another edition;   The Family Expositor; or a
> Paraphrase and Version of the New Testament;
> With Critical Notes, and a Practical
> Improvement of each Section. In six Volumes...
> by P. Doddridge, D.D. To which is prefixed, A
> Life of the Author, by Andrew Kippis...
> Etheridge's Edition, from the Eighth London
> Edition.   Charlestown, Massachusetts: S.
> Etheridge, Printer; Sold by him at Washington
> Head Bookstore. Sold also by said Etheridge
> and Company, in Boston. 1807.
>> [This harmonized the Gospels. The New Testament
>> paraphrase, separate from the commentary and
>> notes, was published. In 1833, a 1 Vol. Edition of
>> this work, along with a memoir of the Author was
>> Published at Amherst. This was a very popular work
>> and was reprinted many times in various forms.]

> First American Edition; Abridged. 2 Vols. Edited
> by S.Palmer.   Hartford: Printed by Lincoln &
> Gleason, 1807.

> Also; 1 Vol. Edition. New York: Robert Carter &
> Bros., 1857.

1739 **Guyse, John**   The Practical Expositor; Or,
An Exposition of the New Testament, In the Form of
a Paraphrase; with occasional notes In their proper
places for further explications, and serious
Recollections at the close of every chapter... 6
Vols. Edinburgh: Printed by W.Darling..., 1739-1752.
[The Title is taken from the 3th ed., 1775.]

Another edition, 1752.

Third edition; 1775.

Sixth edition; 1818.

1745 **Whiston, William**   Mr. Whiston's Primitive New
Testament. Part I. containing the Four Gospels, with
the Acts of the Apostles. Part II. containing XIV.
Epistles of Paul. Part III. containing VII.
Catholick Epistles. Part IV. containing the
Revelation of John.   Stamford & London: for the
author, 1745.
[This work follows the KJV except where the three Greek
manuscripts (D, D2, and A) dictate a difference in
wording, or addition, or omission.]

1755 **Wesley, John**   Explanatory Notes on the New
Testament by John Wesley... London: William Bowyer,
1755.
[Many modifications of the AV, approximately 12,000
single word changes.]

Reprinted, 1757.

Standard Edition, 1760.

Another edition; 3 Vols.   Bristol: William Pine,
1765.

Fourth edition, 1768.

Abridged edition; City Road, London: Printed and
Sold at the New-Chapel, 1790.

Another edition, 1839.

Also; [Edited by George Croft Cell] London:
Lutterworth Press, 1938.

Anniversary edition, 1953.

Another Edition; London: Epworth Press, 1954,
1976.

First American Edition; Philadelphia: Printed by
J. Crukshank, sold by J. Dickins, 1791.

Other American Editions; New York: Published by
Ezekiel Cooper and John Wilson, 1806; John C.
Totten, Printer. Published by Daniel Hitt and
Thomas Ware, for the Methodist Connection in
the United States, 1812; New York: Published
by J. Soule and T. Mason for the Methodist
Episcopal Church in the United States, 1818;
New York: Published by T. Mason and G. Lane
for the Methodist Episcopal Church..., 1839;
New York: G. Lane and P.P. Sandford, 1844;
Chicago, Philadelphia & Toronto: John C.
Winston Co., 1938; Grand Rapids: Baker Book
House, 1986. Many others.]

1764 **Wynne, Richard**   The New Testament: carefully
collated with the Greek, and corrected; divided and
pointed according to the various subjects treated of
by the inspired writers, with the common division
into chapters and verses in the margin; and
illustrated with notes critical and explanatory. By
Richard Wynne, A.M. 2 Vols. London: Printed for R.
and J. Dodsley in Pall-Mall, 1764.

1765 **Anonymous**   A New Translation of the New Testament
...extracted from the paraphrase of the late Philip
Doddridge... and carefully revised. With an
introduction and notes [by Samuel Palmer]. London:
for J. Rivington, W. Johnston, R. Baldwin and C.
Rivington, 1765.
          [See Philip Doddridge, The N.T..., 1739.]

1765 **Clarke, Samuel and Thomas Pyle**   New Testament.
1765 - 1795.
          Vol. 1 & 2   A Paraphrase on the Four
          Evangelists; wherein, for the clearer
          understanding of the sacred history, The whole
          Text and Paraphrase are printed in separate
          Columns over - against each other. With
          Critical Notes on the more difficult passages.
          Very useful for families. By Samuel Clarke,
          D.D. 2 Vols. London: Printed for G.G. & J.
          Robinson, and Vernor & Hood, London; W.H.
          Lunn, Cambridge; J. Cooke, Oxford; J. Mundell
          & Co., Edinburgh; and the other Proprietors,
          1765.

          Vol. 3 & 4   A Paraphrase on the Acts of the
          apostles, and upon all the Epistles of the New
          Testament. Being A Complete Supplement to Dr.
          Clarke's Paraphrase on the Four Gospels. With
          Notes, and a short Preface to each Epistle;
          showing The Occasion and design of it; with
          the several Arguments set at the Head of each
          Chapter. And a General Index to all the

Principal Matters, Words, and Phrases of the New Testament, excepting the Revelation. For the use of families. In Two Vols. By Thomas Pyle, M.A.... London: Printed for G.G. & J. Robinson, London; W.H. Lunn, Cambridge; J. Cooke, Oxford; J. Mundell & Co., Edinburgh; and the other Proprietors, 1795.

1768 **Harwood, Edward**   A Liberal Translation of the New Testament; being An Attempt to translate the Sacred Writings with the same Freedom, Spirit, and Elegance, With which other English Translations from the Greek Classics have lately been executed...with Select Notes, Critical and Explanatory. By E. Harwood. 2 Vols. London: for T. Becket and Others, 1768.

> [A free translation of the New Testament in the elevated style of English current among many authors of the second half of the eighteenth century. As an example of the 'elegance' of diction may be quoted the opening sentences of the Parable of the Prodigal Son: 'A Gentleman of a splendid family and opulent fortune had two sons. One day the younger approached his father, and begged him in the most importunate and soothing terms to make a partition of his effects betwixt himself and his elder brother — The indulgent father, overcome by his blandishments, immediately divided all his fortunes betwixt them'.]

1770 **Worsley, John**   The New Testament or New Covenant... Translated from the Greek according to the present idiom of the English tongue. With notes and references...By the late Mr. John Worsley...London: Printed by R. Hett, 1770.

> [Published after John Worsley's death and edited by his son, Samuel Worsley, and Matthew Bradshaw,]

1774 **Ashton, James**   The Christian Expositor...The New Testament, 1774.

1783 **Barclay, John**   The Experience and Example of the Lord Jesus Christ...

> [See Bible Selections for the complete entry. Includes the Lord's Prayer.]

1783 **Carpenter**   N.T., 1783.

> [Catholic]

1783 **MacMahon, Rev. Bernard**   The New Testament... with annotations. The Fourth edition of Challoner's revision of the Rheims version newly revised and corrected according to the Clementin edition of the Scriptures. Dublin: D. Graisberry for R. Cross and P. Wogan, 1783.

> [This is the Fourth edition of Challoner's revision of the Rheims version newly revised and corrected. This is MacMahon's first revision of Challoner.]

Another; MacMahon's fourth revision, called "the seventh edition". Dublin: Wogan, 1803.

Also; MacMahon's fifth revision, called "the eighth edition". Dublin: H. Fitzpatrick, Printer and Bookseller to the R.C. College, Maynooth, 1810.

[For the second and third revision of the N.T., see MacMahon's Holy Bible, 1791.]

1790 **Gilpin, William**   An exposition of the New Testament; intended as an introduction to the Study of the Scriptures, by Pointing out the Leading Sense and Connection of the sacred writers. By William Gilpin... London: 1790.
Second Edition; 2 Vols., 1793.

Other editions; 1798, 1811.

1791 **Wakefield, Gilbert**   A Translation of the New Testament: By Gilbert Wakefield...3 Vols.   London: Philanthropic Press, 1791.
[Wakefield used "Jehovah" at Rev. 19:1, 3, 4 & 6.]

Second edition; ...with improvements. 2 Vols. London: Printed by A. Hamilton, for George Kearsley, 1795.

Reprinted; Cambridge, Mass.: Printed at the University Press, by Hillard and Metcalf, 1820.

[In addition the following were translated:]

1781 A new translation of Thessalonians.

1782 A new translation of the Gospel of St. Matthew; with notes... Warrington: W. Eyres.
      Second edition; with improvements. London: George Kearsley, 1795.

      Reprinted; Cambridge: Printed at the University Press, by Hillard and Metcalf, 1820.

1798 A New Translation of Those Parts Only of the New Testament Which are Wrongly Translated in our Common Version.

1820 A Translation of the New Testament...From the Second London Edition.   Cambridge

[Mass.]: Printed at the University Press, by Hillard and Metcalf.

1792 Anonymous   The New Testament of our Lord and Saviour Jesus Christ Translated from the Latin Vulgate. Compared with the Original Greek, with Annotations. Printed in the Year MDCCXCII. [1792]

1795 Haweis, Thomas   A Translation of the New Testament from the original Greek. Humbly attempted with a view to assist the unlearned with clearer and more explicit views of the mind of the Spirit in the Scriptures of Truth. By T. Haweis, LL.B.... London: Printed for T. Chapman, 1795.

1796 Newcome, William   An Attempt toward revising our English translation of the Greek Scriptures, or the New Covenant of Jesus Christ: and toward illustrating the sense by philological and explanatory notes... By William Newcome... 2 Vols. London: for J. Johnson; Dublin: John Exshaw, 1796.
    [This is the first English translation of the Griesbach text. Newcome used the name "Jehovah" a few times in his translation of the New Testament.]

1798 Scarlett, Nathaniel   A Translation of the New Testament from the Original Greek, humbly attempted by Nathaniel Scarlett, assisted by men of piety and literature; with notes.   London: Printed by T. Gillet and Sold by Scarlett; F. & C. Rivington, 1798.
    [There are two 1798 editions; an octavo edition and a pocket edition.]

    [This work is based on a manuscript Translation of the Old Testament by James Creighton, an Anglican Clergyman. Creighton, William Vidler, John Cue and Scarlett met once a week to revise the translation.]

1807 Palmer, S.   See Philip Doddridge, The New Testament, 1739.

1808 Anonymous   The New Testament. An improved version upon the basis of Archbishop Newcome's new translation with a corrected text and notes critical and explanatory.   London: Richard Taylor & Co., 1808.
    [An Anonymous translation edited by Belsham. It is Unitarian.]

    Another edition; London: J. Johnson, Longman & Co., 1808.

    Fifth edition, 1819.

American Edition; The New Testament, in an improved version, upon the basis of Archbishop Newcome's new translation: with a corrected text, and notes critical and explanatory. Published by a Society for Promoting Christian Knowledge and the Practice of Virtue, by the distribution of books... From the London Edition... Boston: Printed by Thomas B. Wait and Co... for W. Wells, 1809.

> [This is the only American edition of Belsham's "Improved Version".]

1810 **Baber, Henry Hervey** New Testament...Edited, with preliminary matter by..., 1810.

> [See John Wycliffe, N.T., 1380.]

1812 **Anonymous** A modern, correct, and close translation of the New Testament; with occasional observations, and arranged in order of time; with a special explanation of the Apocalypse. By the Author of 'The Christian Code' and 'Primitive History'. [W. Williams.] London: 1812.

1812 **Anonymous** The New Testament...translated out of the Latin Vulgat...first published by the English College of Rhemes, Anno 1582. Newly revised... With Annotations... Newcastle upon the Tyne: Preston and Heaton, 1812.

> [Edited by John Worswick, a Roman Catholic priest. "But in reality the text throughout a considerable portion of this book differs entirely from any of the ordinary R.C. editions. In some passages words are added in brackets, e.g. Matt. xvi.7... For some reason these peculiarities occur only in the first part of the New Testament; from Romans iii to the end the book is a mere reprint of Challoner's edition of 1752. But, in the Gospels and Acts Cotton noted no fewer than 395 variations..." Known as the Newcastle N.T.]

1813 **McDonald, Rev. John** The New Testament... Second American from the Cambridge Stereotyped Edition... Revised and Corrected by Rev. J.McDonald... Albany: H.C. Southwick, 1813.

> Another edition, 1816.

1815 **Anonymous** The New Testament of our Lord and Saviour Jesus Christ: translated out of the Latin Vulgate; and diligently compared with the original Greek. Sterotyped from the edition published by authority in 1749. Camden Town: Sterotyped and printed by A. Wilson; London: New Bond Street, and sold by J. Booker, 1815.

> [The text follows Challoner's edition of 1749, but some changes occur in the text of the first three Gospels and at Phil. ii.7. These changes appears to be due to Dr. Thomas Rigby.]

1816 **Thompson, William**   The New Testament, translated from the Greek; and the Four Gospels arranged in Harmony, where the parts of each are introduced according to the natural Order of the Narrative, and the exact Order of Time. With some preliminary Observations, and Notes critical and explanatory. By William Thompson... 3 Vols. Kilmarnock, 1816.
> ["In this version, 'studiously made as literal as possible,' the English idiom is continually sacrificed to the Greek,..."]

1818 **Horrabin, Rev. M.**   The New Testament of Our Lord and Saviour Jesus Christ; Translated out of the Latin Vulgate...edited by M. Sidney and carefully revised by Rev. M. Horrabin. London: P. & F. Hatch, 1818.
> [Roman Catholic. Challoner's revision of 1749 with some modifications influenced by the text of 1750.]

1822 **Alger, Israel**   The New Testament... The Pronouncing Testament...to which is applied, in numerous words, The Orthoepy of the Critical Pronouncing Dictionary; Also, the Classical Pronounciation of the Proper Names as they stand in the Text-Scrupulously Adopted From "A Key to the Classical Pronounciation of Greek, Latin, and Scripture Proper Names. By John Walker, Author of the Critical Pronouncing Dictionary, &c."...To which is prefixed, An Explanatory Key... by Israel Alger, Jun... Printed and Published by Lincoln & Edmands: Boston, 1822.
> Another edition, 1823, 1824, 1825, 1828, 1830, 1836, 1849, 1853.

1823 **Kneeland, Abner**   ...The New Testament, in Greek and English; the Greek According to Griesbach; the English upon the basis of the fourth London edition of the Improved Version, with an attempt to further improvement from the translations of Campbell, Wakefield, Scarlett, Macknight, and Thomson. In Two Volumes. By Abner Kneeland, Minister of the First Independent Church of Christ, called Universalist, in Philadelphia: William Fry, Printer...Published by the editor...and sold by him - Also by Abm. Small..., 1823.
> [Kneeland used the name "Jehovah" a few times in the New Testament.]

> Another edition; The New Testament; Being the English Only of the Greek and English Testament; Translated from the Original Greek According to Griesbach...By Abner Kneeland ... Philadelphia: William Fry, Printer... Published by the editor...and sold by him - Also by Abm. Small..., 1823.

1824 **Anonymous**   The New Testament...Edinburgh: Sir D.
Hunter Blair and J. Bruce, 1824.
[An incorrect edition; e.g. Mark 11:8, 'strayed' for
'strawed'; Luke 6:29, 'forbid' for 'forbid not'; 1 Peter
3:18, 'offered' for 'suffered'.]

1824 **Jones, Elizabeth**   The New Testament; Syriac,
Arabic and English Interlineary, 1824.

1825 **Townsend, George**   The New Testament, arranged in
chronological & historical order, with copious notes
on the principal subjects in theology, the Gospels
on the basis of the Harmonies of Lightfoot,
Doddridge, Pilkington, Newcome, and Michaelis; the
account of the Resurrection, on the authorities of
West, Townson, and Cranfield: the Epistles are
inserted in their places, and divided according to
the Apostles' arguments. By...George Townsend... 2
Vols. London: C. & J. Rivington, 1825.
    1st. American edition;   Boston: Published by
    Perkins and marvin;   Philadelphia: Henry
    Perkins, 1837.
        [Contains the Gospels Harmonized.]

1826 **Campbell, Alexander**   The Sacred Writings of the
Apostles and Evangelists of Jesus Christ, Commonly
Styled the New Testament, Translated from the
Original Greek, by George Campbell, James Macknight,
and Philip Doddridge, Doctors of the Church of
Scotland. With Prefaces to the Historical and
epistolary Books; and an Appendix, Containing
Critical Notes and Various Translations of Difficult
Passages.   Buffaloe, Brooke County, Virginia:
Printed and Published by Alexander Campbell, 1826.
    [The Doctors George Campbell, James Macknight and
    Doddridge will be listed further on in this work and it
    is their translations, having already been combined in
    an English publication, which affected Alexander
    Campbell to provide an improved version of their labors.
    Alexander Campbell came from a Presbyterian background,
    through the Baptists, to formulate the "Disciples of
    Christ', or 'The Church of Christ', or 'Campbellites as
    they are commonly called today. This is considered, by
    many Scholars of eminent refutation, a translation of
    the finest caliber. It is based on Griesbach's text.
    Also known as "Living Oracles".]

    The various important editions are as follows:
        1st. Came from the press April 1826.

        2nd. Carried date 1828 but was not circulated
        until January 1829. Smaller format, smaller type,
        several improvements in wording. The word "into"
        rather than "in" used in Matthew 28:19. Campbell
        was disappointed with the poor binding and
        workmanship.

3rd. Dated 1832 but circulated in 1833. Called 'Family Testament' and was printed with same type as first. Revised & Enlarged. Contained "Preface to third edition" and also "Preface to the Fourth or Stereotyped Edition". This is a more modern version in style and has a greatly increased appendix.

4th. Title indicates it is "Stereotyped from the third edition, revised". However, it is not called the fourth edition. It is a "pocket edition" with less notes and smaller size. It is dated 1833.

5th. Marked Fourth Edition and appeared in 1835. This edition dropped verse numbers for numbering only paragraphs. Was printed by M'Vay and Ewing. There are a few changes in this edition.

6th. This was called Sixth Edition and was published by Forrester and Campbell of Pittsburgh dated 1839 but sold in 1840. This was the last under the supervision of Campbell. This edition represented almost no change. The multitude of later printings were from the plates of this edition, or by a photo process, or reprints of the Pocket edition (4th).
Reprint from 1833 Pocket Edition [by J.A. James].
Another edition; Cincinnati: Printed and Published H.S. Bosworth, 1860.

Reprint of the 1839 edition; Cincinnati: Franklin & Rice, 1870.

Other editions; 1871, 1873, 1874, 1882; Cincinnati & Chicago: Central Book Concern, 1881; St. Louis: Christian Board of Publication, 1914; Nashville: Harbinger Book Club, 1951.

Reprint; Gospel Advocate Co., 1954, 1974.

1827 **Cummings, J.A.**   New Testament of our Lord and Saviour Jesus Christ, with an Introduction giving An Account of Jewish and other Sects; and Notes illustrating obscure Passages, and explaining obsolete Words and Phrases; for the use of Schools, Academies, and private Families. By J.A.Cummings... Second Edition, revised and improved.   Boston: Hillard Gray, Little and Wilkins, 1827.
[No information on the first edition.]

1827 **Nourse, James**   The New Testament...arranged in paragraphs, such as the sense requires... New York: G. & C. Carvill, 1827.
[This is evidently the AV paragraphed. The extent of any revisions or changes of words is questionable.]

1828 **Anonymous**   The New Testament in the Common
Version, conformed to Griesbach's Standard Greek
Text. Boston: Gray & Bowen, 1828.
> [This was edited by John Gorham Palfrey, a Unitarian
> minister and copyrighted by Nathan Hale, and is
> attributed to Hale by some authorities such as Henry
> Cotton.]

> Third Edition, 1830.

1828 **Greaves, Alexander**   Gospel of God's Anointed, the
Glory of Israel, and the Light of Revelation for the
Gentiles: or, the Glad Tidings of the Service,
Sacrifice, and Triumph of our Lord and Saviour Jesus
Christ, the only begotten Son of God; and of the
gracious and mightily operative powers of the Holy
Spirit, which were the first-fruits of that labour
of divine love: being a recent version, in two
parts, of the Christian Greek Scriptures, (commonly
called the New Testament,) in which is plainly set
forth the New Covenant promised by God through Moses
and the Prophets.   London: A. Macintosh, for
Alexander Greaves, 1828.
> [Greaves , a Jewish scholar, first published his work
> anonymously, but in the second edition, later the same
> year, signed the work and dedicated it to his Gentile
> friends.]

1831 **Summer, John Bird**   A Practical Exposition of the
New Testament in the form of lectures. Intended to
assist the practice of domestic instruction and
devotion. By John Bird Summer. London: J. Hatchard
& Son, 1831-1851.
> 1831 - - St. Matthew and St. Mark... (Mark;
> Seventh edition, 1847)

> 1832 - - St. Luke...

> 1835 - - St. John...

> 1838 - - the Acts...

> 1843 - - the Romans and the First Epistle to
> the Corinthians...

> 1845 - - Second Epistle to the Corinthians and
> the Epistles to the Galatians, Ephesians,
> Philippians, and Colossians...

> 1851 - - the Thessalonians, to Timothy, Titus,
> Philemon, and to the Hebrews...

> 1840 - - the General Epistles of James, Peter,
> John and Jude...

- - the Revelation

[The text appears to be KJV; but the accompanying exposition contains many variant readings and paraphrases.]

1833 **Dickinson, Rodolphus**   A New and Corrected Version of the New Testament; or, a minute revision, and professed translation of the original histories, memoirs, letters, prophecies, and other productions of the Evangelists and Apostles: to which are subjoined, a few, generally brief, critical, explanatory and practical notes. By Rodolphus Dickinson. Boston: Lilly, Wait, Colman & Holden, 1833.

[Griesbach text. The translation is quite wordy; there is the appearance of affectation about the choice of words.]

Another edition; The Productions of the Evangelists and Apostles, a faithful and true translation of the Scriptures of the New Testament, with references, subdivisions and an appendix containing notes to the preface and notes on the text. To which is added the Apocrypha. Toronto: William Lyon Machenzie, 1837.

1833 **MacKenzie, William Lyon**   The Productions of the Evangelists and Apostles, 1833.

[A pirated edition of Dickenson's N.T.]

1834 **Anonymous**   The New Testament of our Lord and Saviour Jesus Christ; translated out of the Latin Vulgate, diligently compared with the Original Greek, and first published by the English College of Rheims, Anno 1582. With the Original Preface, Arguments and Tables, Marginal Notes, and Annotations. To which are now added, An Introductory Essay; and a complete Topical and Textual Index. New York: Published by Jonathan Leavitt...; Boston: Crocker and Brewster..., 1834.

[Contains many changes. "We have compared this New York edition... with the first publication of that volume, which was issued at Rheims, in 1582; and, after examination, we do hereby certify, that the reprint is an exact and faithful copy of the original work, without abridgment or addition, except that the Latin of a few phrases which were translated by the annotators, and some unimportant expletive words were undesignedly omitted. The orthography also has been modernized."]

1835 **Caldecott, J.M.**   The Holy Writings of the First Christians, called the New Testament... Chester: J. Parry & Son, 1835.

[The text is 'chiefly taken from the common version but rendered more exactly to the meaning...with notes...' It was printed by J.M. Caldecott, Liverpool, possibly the author.]

1836 **Penn, Granville**   The Book of the New Covenant of our Lord and Saviour Jesus Christ, being a critical revision of the text and translation of the English version of the New Testament, with the aid of most ancient manuscripts unknown to the age in which that version was last put forth by authority.   London: James Moyes, for James Duncan, 1836.
[Penn's name is listed only on the backstrip which reads "Penn's New Testament".]

1837 **Cardwell, Edward**   The New Testament in Greek and English; with a marginal Harmony... Edited by Edward Cardwell. 2 Vols.   Oxford: University Press, 1837.

1837 **Dabney, J.P.**   See William Tyndale, (The New Testament), 1525.

1838 **Cell, George Croft**   See John Wesley, Explanatory Notes on the New Testament, 1755.

1840 **Anonymous**   The New Testament...revised from the authorised version with the aid of other translations and made conformable to the Greek text of J.J. Griesbach by a Layman [Edgar Taylor]. London: C. Whittingham, for William Pickering, 1840.

1840 **Sharpe, Samuel**   The New Testament, translated from the text of J.J. Griesbach. By Samuel Sharpe. London: John Green, 1840.
Second edition, 1844.

Third edition: London: Thomas Hodgson, 1856.

Fourth edition; London: Arthur Hall, Virtue, and Co., 1859.

Seventh edition; London: Williams & Norgate, 1881.

1841 **English Hexapla**   English Hexapla, exhibiting the six important English translations of the New Testament Scriptures:
Wiclif, 1380 [Revised by Purvey, 1394.]
Genevan, 1557 [Whittingham's Testament, 1557.]
Tyndale, 1534
Anglo-Rhemish, 1582 [1st. edition, 1582.]
Cranmer, 1539 [1st. edition of the Great Bible.]
Authorized, 1611...
preceded by an Historical Account of the English Translations.   4   Vols.   London: Wertheimer and Co., for S. Bagster & Sons, 1841.

1842 **Heinfetter, Herman**   The New Testament. 1842-1864.
   1848 A Literal Translation of St. Paul's
        Epistle to the Romans, on definite rules
        of translation. By Herman Heinfetter...
        London: Cradock and Co., 1848.
             [Published in two parts in 1842 and 1848.]

   1849 A Literal Translation of the Gospel
        According to St. John. By Herman
        Heinfetter...

   1849 A literal translation of the Epistles of
        John and Jude... By Herman Heinfetter...

   1850 A Literal Translation of St. Paul's
        Epistles to the Thessalonians, Timothy,
        Titus, and Philemon... Also Galatians,
        Ephesians, Philippians, and Colossians...
        By Herman Heinfetter...

   1851 A literal translation of St. Paul's
        Epistles to the Corinthians. By Herman
        Heinfetter...

   1851 A literal translation of the Epistles of
        Paul the Apostle to the Hebrews, on
        definite rules of translation; and an
        English version of the same: as also of
        the Epistle to the Romans. By Herman
        Heinfetter...   London: Cradock and Co.,
        1851.

   1851 A Literal Translation of the Epistles of
        James and Peter...By Herman Heinfetter...

   1851 A Literal Translation of the Revelation
        ...By Herman Heinfetter...

   1852 A Literal Translation of the Acts... By
        Herman Heinfetter...

   1853 A Literal Translation of the Gospel
        According to Matthew... By Herman
        Heinfetter...

   1853 A Literal Translation of the Gospel
        According to Mark... By Herman
        Heinfetter...

   1854 A Literal Translation of the Gospel
        According to Luke... By Herman
        Heinfetter...

1854 A Literal Translation of the Last Eight
     Books of the New Testament... By Herman
     Heinfetter...

1864 An English Version of the New Testament
     ...from the text of the Vatican
     Manuscript. By Herman Heinfetter ...Sixth
     edition. London: Evan Evans, 1864.
> Another edition; A Literal Translation
> of the New Testament. By Herman
> Heinfetter, 1863.
>
> Another edition; A Collation of an
> English Version of the New
> Testament... from the text of the
> Vatican Manuscript with the
> Authorized English Version. By
> Herman Heinfetter...Sixth edition.
> London: Evan Evans, 1864.

1843 **Clarke, Sir John**   The New Testament, 1843.

1843 **Etheridge, J.W.**   Horae Aramaicae: comprising
concise notices of the Aramean dialects in general
and of the versions of the Holy Scripture extant in
them: with a translation of...Matthew...Hebrews from
the ancient Peschito Syriac, by J.W. Etheridge.
London: Simpkin, Marshall and Co., and John Mason,
1843-1849.
> 1846 A Literal translation of the Four Gospels
>   from the Peschito Syriac...   London:
>   Longman, Green, Brown and Longmans, 1846.
>   [Included in his book, "The Syrian Churches".]
>
> 1849 The Apostolic Acts and Epistles, from the
>   Peschito or Ancient Syriac: to which are
>   added, the remaining Epistles, and the
>   Book of Revelation, after a later Syriac
>   text: translated, with prolegomena and
>   indices, by J.W. Etheridge...   London:
>   Longman, Brown, Green and Longmans, 1849.

1845 **Campbell, George and J. MacKnight**   The New
Testament Translated Out of the Original Greek; The
Four Gospels by G. Campbell, the Epistles by J.
MacKnight, and the Acts and Revelation of the Common
Version... Hartford: J.G. Wells, 1845.

1847 **Anonymous**   The Holy Bible, University
from the Latin Vulgate... with annotations by ...Dr.
Challoner, together with references...   London:
Richardson and Son, 1847?
> [The text is a composite text from the various Challoner
> editions and McMahon's revisions.]

1848 **Komstok, A.**   The New Testament...in Komstok's
purfekt alfabet. Filadelphia: Publict: Bi A.Komstok,
1848.
[Andrew Comstock is A. Komstok.]

1848 **Morgan, Jonathan**   The New Testament...Translated
from the Greek, into Pure English, with Explanatory
Notes, on Certain Passages, Wherein the Author
Differs from Other Translators. By Jonathan Morgan
... Portland: S.H. Colesworthy; Boston: B.B.Mussey;
New York: P. Price;   Philadelphia: J. Gihon;
Cincinnatti [sic]: A.T. Ames; Louisville: Noble and
Dean, 1848.
[Morgan was somewhat freakish from the standpoint of
Phonetic spelling and orthography. It appears that
Morgan was eccentric in his person and that was shown in
his translation as well, which was an alteration of the
AV.]

1849 **Anonymous**   The Good News of Our Lord Jesus, the
Anointed; from the critical Greek text of Tollotson.
Boston: Published by Joshua V. Himes, 1849.
[A revision by Nathan N. Whiting. An 'Immersion'
version. This is said to be the "Millerite N.T."]

1850 **Anonymous**   The New Testament Dictated by the
Spirit. New York: 1850.

1850 **Cone, Spencer H. and William H. Wyckoff** (Editors)
The Commonly Received Version of the New Testament
... With Several Hundred Emendations. Edited by
Spencer H. Cone and Wm. H. Wyckoff... New York:
Published at Private Expense, Sold by Lewis Colsy
New Orleans: Duncan, Hurlbutt & Co., 1850.
[This is an Immerse Version. Mr. Cone, after many years
of service in the American Bible Society and as
President of American and Foreign Bible Society, was
instrumental in founding the American Bible Union. This
work was an attempt to meet the problem raised by the
refusal of the Bible Societies to print "sectarian"
versions. Cone and Wyckoff, Baptists, edited this
"Commonly Received Version of the N.T." with "Immerse"
and several hundred emendations.]

Reprinted; New York: E.H. Tripp, 1851, 1857.

1850 **McMahon, James** The New Testament...Translated from
the Latin Vulgate...Newly Revised and Corrected,
with Annotations, Explanatory of the most Difficult
Passages. Illuminated after Original Drawings. By
W.H.Hewett, Esq... New York: Hewett & Spoones, 1850.
[Rheims Version revised by the Rev. James McMahon. This
is called "The Pictorial Catholic New Testament".]

1851 **Moody, Clement**   The New Testament Expounded
and Illustrated According to the Usual Marginal
References in the Very Words of Holy Scripture,

Together with the Notes and Translations and a Complete Marginal Harmony of the Gospels. London: Longman, Brown, Green, and Longmans, 1851.

1851 **Murdock, James**   The New Testament; or, The Book of the Holy Gospel of Our Lord and Our God, Jesus the Messiah. A Literal Translation from the Syriac Peshito Version. By James Murdock.   New York: Published by Stanford and Swords, 1851.
Reprinted, 1852, 1855.

Also; New York: Robert Carter & Bros., various years from 1858-1879.

Reprinted; Boston: Horace L Hastings, 1892.

Sixth edition, 1893.

Seventh edition; 1896.

In addition; The Syriac New Testament Translated into English from the Peshitta Version. Boston: 1915.

1852 **Taylor, John**   The Emphatic New Testament according to the Authorized Version, compared with the various readings of the Vatican Manuscript...Edited, with an introductory essay on Greek Emphasis, by John Taylor. London: 1852-1854.
1852 - - The Four Gospels. London: Taylor, Walton and Maberly.

1854 - - Acts to Revelation. London: Samuel Bagster & Sons.

1854 - - (one volume) London: Samuel Bagster & Sons.

[The 'various readings' are indicated by footnotes and brackets in the text.]

1855 **Anonymous**   [The New Testament] de Nu Testament ov or Lord and Savyor Jezus Krist. Akordin tw de otorizd verfon. In Fonetik Spelin... Sinsinati: Lonli Bruderz, 1855.

1857 **Bengel, Jotham Albrecht**   English Translation of the New Testament, 1857.

1857 **Giles, J.A.**   [Keys to the Classics] The New Testament, construed from Greek into English literally, and word for word. By The Late Rev. Dr. Giles... London: Cornish & Sons, 1857.

[Number of Volumes is unknown. Vol. II is St. Mark's Gospel.]

1858 **Sawyer, Leicester Ambrose**   The New Testament, Translated from the Original Greek, with Chronological Arrangement of the Sacred Books, and Improved Divisions of Chapters and Verses by Leicester Ambrose Sawyer... [Lithotyped by Cowles and Company, Boston. Press of Allen and Farnham]. Boston: John P. Jewett and Company; Cleveland, Ohio: Henry P.B. Jewett; London: Sampson Low, Son and Company, 1858.
Revised and Improved Edition; Boston: Walker, Wise & Co., 1861.

1861 **Anonymous**   The New Testament of Our Lord Jesus Christ as Revised and Corrected by the Spirits. New York: 1861.

1861 **Kelly, William**   New Testament. 1861-1912.
19?? Lectures on the Gospel of Matthew

19?? Exposition of the Gospel of Mark

19?? An Exposition of the Gospel of Luke

1898 An Exposition of the Gospel of John [with a new translation]. By William Kelly. London: T. Weston.
Revised edition; edited, with additions, by E.E. Whitfield. London: 1908. New edition; London: 1923.

1890 The Acts of the Apostles, with a New Version of a Corrected Text, Expounded. 2 Vols. Exeter: Gospel Depot, [1890].
[The British Museum dates this work as 1895, but our date is taken from the editor's note to the 3rd edition.]

Second edition revised; London: F.E. Race, 1914. Also; London: 1952.

1878 Notes on the first Epistle of Paul the Apostle to the Corinthians, with a New Translation. London: G. Morrish.

1882 Notes on the Second Epistle of Paul the Apostle to the Corinthians, with a New Translation. London: G. Morrish.

1873 Notes on the Epistle of Paul the Apostle to the Romans, with a New Translation. London: G. Morrish.

Reprinted; Sinbury, Penn.: Believer's Bookshelf, 1978.

1865 Lectures on the Epistle of Paul the Apostle to the Galatians, with a New Translation. By William Kelly. London: G. Morrish.
Reprint; Addison, IL: Bible Truth Publishers, 1983.

1901 Lectures on the Epistle of Paul, the Apostle, to the Ephesians, with a new translation. By William Kelly. London: G. Morrish.
Reprint; Addison, IL: Bible Truth Publishers, 1983.

1869 Lectures on the Epistle of Paul to the Philippians, with a New Translation. London: G. Morrish.

1869 Lectures on the Epistle of Paul the Apostle to the Colossians, with a New Translation. By William Kelly. London: G. Morrish.

1893 The Epistles of Paul the Apostle to the Thessalonians. Translated from a correct text, and expounded by William Kelly. London: T. Cheverton.
Second edition; London: F.E. Race, 1912.
Third edition; London: C.A. Hammond, 1953.

1901 An Exposition of the Epistle of Paul the Apostle to Titus and that to Philemon with translation of an amended text. By William Kelly. London: Thomas Weston.

1889 An Exposition of the Two Epistles of Paul the Apostle to Timothy, with a translation of an amended text. Two Parts. London: W. Walters.

1913 An Exposition of the First Epistle to Timothy. With a translation of an amended text. By William Kelly. Second edition, revised. London: F.E. Race.

1913 An Exposition of the Second Epistle to Timothy. With a translation of an amended text. By William Kelly. Second edition, revised. London: F.E. Race.

1905 Exposition of the Epistle to the Hebrews with a new version by William Kelly. London: T. Weston.

1913 Exposition of the Epistle of James, with a translation of an amended text by William Kelly. London: F.E. Race.

1904 The First Epistle of Peter. London: T. Weston.

1906 The Second Epistle of Peter. London: F.E. Race.

1905 An Exposition of the Epistles of John with a new version by William Kelly. London: T. Weston.

1912 Lectures on the Epistle of Jude — translated from a corrected text - by W. Kelly. [With the text.] London: F.E. Race. London: F.E. Race.

1849 The Book of Revelation, Translated from the Greek, with Notes of the Principle Different Readings Adopted in Critical Editions, and Remarks Connected with the Study of the Book. London: J.K. Campbell.

1861 Lectures on the Book of Revelation [with the text]. London, Edinburgh: Williams & Norgate.
    New edition; London: G. Morrish, 1893.

    Also; The Revelation Expounded, with a New Translation. 4th ed. London: F.E. Race, 1901.

    5th ed.; C.A. Hammond, 1921.

1860 Apokalypsis Ioannou. The Revelation of John, edited in Greek, with a new English version, and a statement of the chief authorities and various readings. London: Williams & Norgate.

1893 Lectures on the Book of Revelation. By William Kelly. New Revised edition. London: A.S. Rouse.

1862 **American Bible Union**   The New Testament...
The Common English Version, Corrected by the Final

Committee of the American Bible Union... 2 Vols. New York: American Bible Union, 1862-1863.

The Final Committee consists of:
Dr. Thomas J. Conant   Horatio B. Hackett
E. Rodiger   G.R. Bliss
Dr. A.C. Kendrick

[Part 1 (1862) the Gospels. Part 2 (1863) Acts-2 Corinthians. No separate copy of part 3 (Galatians-Revelation) has been located nor does an examination of THE BIBLE UNION QUARTERLY, for the period, indicate such publication. Another edition; 1863-1864. A one volume edition of the complete N.T. was published in 1864. In 1866, the second revision was published. The 1866 edition had two forms; one using 'Baptize', the other using 'Immerse'. In 1885, the American Baptist Publication Society took over the Text and revised it again; publishing it under the Title: 'The New Testament... American Bible Union Version. Improved Edition.' This also had two forms as that of the 1865 edition. Later this Society published: 'The Holy Bible. An Improved Edition.',in which the N.T. was for the fourth and last time revised.]

Other editions;
        "Pulpit and Family Testament", 1866
        "Merrill Memorial", 1866
        "Willingham Memorial", 1866, 1867
        "Amory Memorial", 1866, 1868, 1870, 1874

1862 **Highton, Rev. H.**   A Revised Translation of the New Testament: with a notice of the principal various readings in the Greek text. By...H. Highton. London: S. Bagster and Sons, 1862.

1863 **Alford, Henry**   The New Testament for English Readers... London: Gilbert & Rivington, 1863.
        Reprinted; Moody Press, Chicago, 1955

1864 **Anderson, Henry Tompkins**   The New Testament. Translated from the Original Greek, by H.T.Anderson. Cincinnati: Published for the Translator, 1864.
        [An 'Immersion' version.]

        Revised; Louisville: John P. Morton & Co., 1866.

        Another edition; Great Bridge, Staffs: C.W. Purser; Birmingham: For David King, 1867.

1864 **Anonymous**   The New Testament... In Fonetic Speling ... Cincinnati: Elias Longley, 1864.

1864 **Wilson, Benjamin**   The Emphatic Diaglott: containing the original Greek text of what is commonly styled the New Testament (According to the Recension of Dr. J.J. Griesbach) with an interlineary word for word

English translation; a new Emphatic Version, based
on the Interlineary Translation, on the renderings
of eminent critics, and on various readings of the
Vatican Manuscript together with illustrative and
explanatory footnotes, and a copious set of
references to the whole of which is added a valuable
alphabetical appendix. By Benjamin Wilson...
Geneva, Illinois: Published by the Author, 1864.
        [According to the Preface (dated Aug 1864) the work was
        issued in parts to subscribers.]

        ["Jehovah" is used eighteen times. Matthew 21:9; 21:42;
        22:37; 22:44; 23:39. Mark 11:9; 12:11; 12:29 (2X); 12:30
        12:36. Luke 10:27; 13:35; 19:38; 20:37; 20:42. John
        12:13 & Acts 2:34.]

Later editions; New York: Fowler and Wells, 1864,
1865, 1866, 1883, 1887, 1890 and 1902.

Another edition; New York: Samuel R. Wells, 1870,
1873.

[In 1902 the text was endorsed by the Watch Tower Bible
and Tract Society and printed by Fowler and Wells.]

Another edition; Brooklyn, New York U.S.A.:
International Bible Students Association,
Watch Tower Bible and Tract Society, 1927.

Another edition; Brooklyn, New York U.S.A.:
International Bible Students Association,
Watch Tower Bible and Tract Society, 1942.
        [Another edition was issued in 1942 in which the
        WB&TS revised the footnote at I John 5:7 but did
        not change the Scripture text.]

1865 **Green, Thomas Sheldon**   The Twofold New Testament:
being a new translation accompanying a newly formed
text. In parallel columns. By...Thomas Sheldon
Green. London: S. Bagster & Sons, 1865.
        [Greek – English diaglot.]

1868 **Rotherham, Joseph Bryant**   The New Testament. 1868-
1872.
        1868 The New Testament of Our Lord and Saviour
             Jesus Christ; a New Translation, in which
             Special Regard has been paid, among other
             Points of Detail, to the Power of the
             Greek Article, to the Forces of the
             Various Tenses, and to the Logical Idiom
             of the Greek Original; with Critical and
             Explanatory Notes (The Text Conformed to
             Ancient Authorities).
                [The Gospel according to Matthew with
                Notes.]

1872 The New Testament: Newly Translated (from the Greek Text of Tregelles) and Critically Emphasised, According to the Logical Idiom of the Original; with an Introduction and Occasional Notes. By Joseph B. Rotherham. London: Samuel Bagster & Sons, 1872.

> Second edition, revised; London: Samuel Bagster & Sons; New York: John Wiley, 1878.

> Revised; New York: J. Wiley & Sons, 1896.

> Third edition, 1897. [Translated from a different Greek text.]

> Another edition; New York: Fleming H. Revell and Co., 1898.

> Also; New York: John Wiley & Sons, 1901.

> [The fourth edition forms part of the Bible, 1902.]

> Fifth edition; London: Sampson Low & Co., 1923.

> [In 1896, Bagster printed an edition with the Watchtower imprint, which was their first venture into Bible publishing and selling. About this time there were also imprints by the American Baptist Publishing Society, Philadelphia and the Standard Publishing Company of Cincinnati.]

1869 **Ainslie, Rev. Robert**   The New Testament: translated from the Greek text of Tischendorf... by Rev. Robert Ainslie...   Brighton: H.& C. Treacher; London: Longmans, Green & Co., 1869.

1869 **Alford, Henry**   The New Testament of Our Lord and Saviour Jesus Christ after the Authorized Version, newly compared with the original Greek, and revised, by Henry Alford. London: R. Clay, Sons, and Taylor, for Strahan & Co. Publishers, 1869.

1869 **Noyes, George R.**   The New Testament: Translated from the Greek Text of Tischendorf, by George R. Noyes, D.D., Hancock Professor of Hebrew and Other Oriental Languages, and Dexter Lecturer on Biblical Literature...   Boston: American Unitarian Association; [Cambridge, Mass.: Printed by John Wilson and Son], 1869.

Reprinted; 1870, 1873, 1878, 1880.

1870 **Anonymous**   A Critical English New Testament: Presenting at one view The Authorised Version and the Results of the Criticism by the Original Text. London: Samuel Bagster & Sons, 1870.

1870 **Bowes, John**   The New Testament Translated from the Purest Greek. By John Bowes. Dundee: Bowes Brothers, 1870.

1871 **Arber, Edward** (Editor)   See William Tyndale, N.T., 1525.

1871 **Darby, John Nelson**   The Gospels, Acts, Epistles, and Book of Revelation: commonly called the New Testament. A new translation from a revised text of the Greek original. Second edition, revised. London: G. Morrish, 1871?
        [The first edition of this N.T. was issued in parts, undated between 1859 and 1867. The third edition appeared in 1884. The fourth edition, 1904.]

        [1865]   The Gospel According to Matthew
        [1865]   The Gospel According to Mark
        [1865]   The Gospel According to Luke
        [1867]   The Gospel According to John

1875 **Davidson, Samuel**   The New Testament. Translated from the Critical Text of Von Tischendorf; with an introduction on the criticism, translation, and interpretation of the book, by Samuel Davidson... London: Henry S. King & Co., 1875.
        Revised edition, 1876.

1877 **Anonymous**   The Englishman's Greek New Testament; giving the Greek text of Stephens 1550, with the various readings of the editions of Elzevir 1624, Griesbach, Lachmann, Tischendorf, Tregelles, Alford, and Wordsworth: together with an interlinear literal translation, and the Authorized Version of 1611. London: S. Bagster and Sons, 1877.

1877 **Blackley, W.L. and James Hawes**   (Editors)   The Critical English Testament, Being an Adaption of Bengel's Gnomon, with Numerous Notes, showing the Precise Results of Modern Criticism and Exegesis. Edited by Rev. W.L.Blackley and Rev. James Hawes. 3 Vols. London: Daldy, Ibister & Co., 1877–1878.
        [Contains a revised translation of Revelation only, no other running translations.]

1877 **Richter, John August**   The New Testament...Revised and corrected from copies of the Sinaitic, Vatican, Alexandrian, and other old copies of the original

Greek... By John August Richter. Invercargill, N.Z.:
Bain & Co., 1877.
> ["Immerse" used for "baptize".]

1881 **American Revised Version**   The New Testament...
revised A.D. 1881. With the readings and renderings
preferred by the American Committee of Revision,
Incorporated into the text, by Roswell D. Hitchcock.
New York: Fords, Howard & Hulbert, 1881.
> Another edition; The New Testament... revised
> A.D. 1881, with the readings and renderings
> preferred by the American Committee of
> Revision incorporated into the text.
> Philadelphia: American Baptist Publication
> Society, 1881.

1881 **Clarke, R.L. and Others** (Editors)   The Variorum
Edition of the New Testament of Our Lord and Saviour
Jesus Christ: translated out of the original Greek;
and with the former translations diligently compared
and revised, by his Majesty's special command. With
Various Renderings and Readings from the best
Authorities, edited by Rev. R.L. Clarke, Alfred
Goodwin and Rev. W. Sanday. London, Edinburgh & New
York: Printed by George Edward Eyre and William
Spottiswoode..., 1881.

1881 **English Revised Version**   The New Testament, 1881.
> [See Complete Bibles, 1881 for the entire entry.]

1881 **Hall, Isaac H.**   The Revised New Testament...
prepared under the direction of the translator.
Philadelphia: Hubbard Bros., 1881?

1881 **Tischendorf, Constantine**   The Sinai and
Comparative New Testament. The Authorized English
Version; with Introduction, and various Readings
from the three most celebrated Manuscripts of the
original Greek Text, by Constantine Tischendorf;
Tauchnitz Edition, Vol. 1000. With the various
readings so inserted in the text, that the whole
Scripture according to either the Sinai, Vatican,
Alexandrian, or the Received Greek, can be read by
itself, while the variations are all compared with
facility. By Edwin Leigh.   New York: Ivision,
Blakeman, Taylor and Co., 1881.
> ["The Gospels" appears on the cover, with a subtitle:
> "Four in One; Sinai, Vatican, Alexandrian: the three
> oldest and best copies. The New Testament as the early
> Christians had it in the Fourth Century...compared with
> the Modern Received Greek of the Sixteenth Century." No
> further record of any additional volumes.]

1881 **Williams, Samuel**   The New Testament...published for Samuel Williams. New York: Fords, Howard & Hulbert, 1881.
> [ERV amended. American Committee's preferences in the text. Immersionist.]

1882 **Curry, Daniel**   The New Testament... containing the old and new versions; the marginal readings of the old version; notes of the new version; notes of the American committee... by Daniel Curry.   New York: 1882.

1883 **Hanson, John Wesley**   The New Covenant: Containing I. An Accurate Translation of the New Testament. II. Harmony of the Four Gospels. III. A Chronological Arrangement of the Text. IV. A Brief and Handy Commentary... By J.W. Hanson... Two Vols. Boston and Chicago: The Universalist Publishing House, 1884–1885.
> [The first American translationfrom Westcott and Hort text. An immersion version.]

Also, 1886.

1883 **Jackson, Cortes**   The New Testament...translated out of the Greek...with apostolic references by Cortes Jackson. Denver, Colorado: Collier and Cleaveland, printers, 1883.
> Again; Cincinnati: Standard Publishing Co., 1889.

1885 **American Baptist Publication Society**
The New Testament ... the Common English version, revised by the American Bible Union. Improved Edition. New York: American Baptist Publication Society, 1885?
> [This N.T. was issued in two forms – one with 'Baptized', the other with 'Immerse'. This work was revised and corrected 1912 by Rev. J.W. Willmarth and published in 1913 as part of the "Holy Bible ...an Improved Edition" Philadelphia: American Baptist Publ. Society.]

> Revision Committee consists of:
> Alvah Hovey (Newton Theological Seminary)
> John A. Broadus (Louisville Theological Seminary)
> Henry G. Weston (Crozer Theological Seminary)

1885 **Dillard, W.D.**   [The New Testament] The Teachings and Acts of Jesus of Nazareth and His Apostles Literally Translated out of the Greek. By W.D. Dillard. Chicago: Privately Printed, 1885.
> ["We propose to render every word in the N.T. Greek into plain vernacular English words... Primarily a re-worded Authorised Version". Dedicated to the "poor, illiterate and unlearned."]

1886 **Pitman, Isaac**   The New Testament...printed
     in an easy reporting style of phonography. By Isaac
     Pitman. London: Frederick Pitman, 1886.

1891 **Sawyer, Leicester Ambrose**   [The New Testament]
     The Bible: Analyzed, Translated and Accompanied with
     Critical Studies, Published in parts of Books,
     Single Books and Collections of Books, by Rev.
     Leicester A. Sawyer... Whitesboro, New York: [T.J.
     Griffiths, Printer, Utica], 1891.
          [This work contains a new translation with improved
          renderings.]

          [See New Testaments, 1858 Leicester Ambrose Sawyer, The
          New Testament.]

1892 **Anonymous**   The New Testament...Revised A.D. 1881...
     Phonetic edition, in reformed spelling. London: L.
     Pitman & Sons, 1892.

1895 **Fenton, Ferrar**   The New Testament...translated from
     the Greek into current English. By Ferrar Fenton.
     London: J.S.Dodington; S.W.Partridge & Co., [1895].
          Revised edition; The New Testament in modern
          English...newly translated direct from the
          accurate Greek text of Drs. Westcott and Hort,
          by Ferrar Fenton...with some critical notes.
          Second edition of the Gospels, and sixth of
          St. Paul's Epistles, translated afresh.
          London and Tombridge: Bradbury, Agnew, and
          Co.; London: for H. Marshall and Son, etc.,
          1900.

          Another edition; Revised, 1905.

          Fourth edition of the Gospels and eighth of
          St. Paul's Epistles translated afresh, 1906.

          Tenth edition; revised, 1930.

          Romans, 1882; Epistles, 1884.

1896 **Stevens, W.**   The New Testament, Authorised Version,
     written in orthic shorthand by W. Stevens,...London:
     C.J. Clay & Sons, 1896.

1896 **Vaughan, H.**   The New Testament of Our Lord
     and Saviour Jesus Christ, according to the Rheims
     Version, revised by Bishop Challoner... London:
     Burns & Oates, 1896.
          [The text is mainly that of Challoner, 1749.]

Another edition; New York, Cincinnati & Chicago: Benziger Bros., Printers to the Holy Apostolic See, 1898.

Revised edition; London: Burns, Oates and Washbourne, 1922?]

1897 **Berry, George Ricker**   The Interlinear Literal Translation of the Greek New Testament with the Authorized Version Conveniently Presented in the Margins for Ready Reference, and with the Various Readings of the Editions of Elzevir 1624, Griesbach, Lachmann, Tischendorf, Tregelles, Alford and Wordsworth. To which has been added A New Greek-English New Testament Lexicon, supplemented by a Chapter elucidating the Synonyms of the New Testament, with a Complete Index to the Synonyms by George Ricker Berry. New York: Hines, Noble & Eldredge, 1897.

> Another edition; Reading, PA: Handy Book Co., n.d.

> Another edition; Chicago: Wilcox & Follett Co., 1946.

> Reprinted; Grand Rapids, Mi: Zondervan Publishing House, 1958, 1960, 1961, 1963, 1965, 1966, 1967, 1968, 1969, 1970, 1971, 1981.

> [Many times reprinted. This is clearly The Englishman's Greek New Testament.]

1897 **Morrow, Horace E.**   The New Testament Emphasized. Based upon a study of the Original Greek Text. By Rev. Horace E. Morrow. Middletown, Connecticut: Charles Reynolds, 1897.

1897 **Weekes, Robert D.**   ...The New Dispensation. The New Testament Translated from the Greek by Robert D. Weekes. New York & London: Funk & Wagnalls Co., 1897.

1898 **Anonymous**   The Twentieth Century New Testament. A Translation into Modern English Made from the Original Greek (Westcott & Hort's Text) By a company of about twenty scholars representing the various sections of the Christian Church. In Three Parts. New York: Fleming H. Revell Company, 1898–1901.

> [This was a 'Tentative Edition' for comment, then a retranslation was done, published simultaneously in New York (Fleming H. Revell Co.) and London (Mowbray House – a one volume revised edition). This work was done by a company of about twenty persons; among whom Mrs. Mary Higgs is named by some to be Chairman.]

The following are some of the translators:
Henry Bazett   T.S.Boulton
W.T.Broad   J.A.B.Clough
W.M.Crook   P.W.Darnford
G.G. Findley   E.D.Gilderstone
J.K.Homer   A.Ingram
Ernest de Merindol Malan

1898 The Five Historical Books

1900 Paul's Letters to the Churches

1901 The   Pastoral,   Personal,   and   General
     Letters; and the Revelation

Again; 1902, 1903, (Revised) 1904.

Boy Scout edition; 1916?

Also; The Gospels and Book of Acts, 1905?

1898 **Horner, G.W.**   The Coptic Version of the New
Testament in the Northern Dialect otherwise called
Memphitic and Bohairic with introduction, critical
apparatus, and literal English translation. 4 Vols.
Oxford: Clarendon Press, 1898-1905.

1901 **American Standard Version**   The New Covenant
commonly called the New Testament of our Lord and
Saviour Jesus Christ translated out of the Greek.
Being the version set forth A.D. 1611 compared with
the most ancient authorities and revised 1881. Newly
edited by the New Testament members of the American
Revision Committee A.D. 1900. Standard edition. New
York: Thomas Nelson and Sons, 1901.
              N.T. Committee consists of:
       E. Abbot (Harvard)   J.K. Burr (Drew)
       T. Chase (Haverford)   J. Hadley (Yale)
       C. Hodge (Princeton)   A.C. Kendrick (Rochester)
       A. Lee (Bishop of Delware)
       M.B. Riddle (Hartford & Western)
       P. Schaff (Union)   C. Short (Columbia)
       J.H. Thayer (Andover, Harvard)
       E.A. Washburn (Calvary Church, New York:)
       T.D. Woolsey (Yale)

1901 **Moffatt, James**   The Historical New Testament.
Being the literature of the New Testament arranged
in the order of its literary growth and according to
the dates of the documents. A New Translation,
edited with prolegomena, historical tables, critical
notes, and an appendix, by James Moffatt...
Edinburgh: T. & T. Clark;   New York: Charles
Scribner's Sons, 1901.
       Second and revised edition; Edinburgh: 1901.

1901 **Nisbet, Murdoch**   The New Testament in Scots; being
Purvey's revision of Wycliffe's version turned into
Scots by Murdoch Nisbet. 3 Vols. Edinburgh & London:
For the Society by William Blackwood, 1901-1905.
[1901, 1903 and 1905.]

1901 **Smith, William Wye**   The New Testament in Braid
Scots, rendered by Rev. William Wye Smith, with a
glossary of Scottish terms.   Paisley: Alexander
Gardner, 1901.
New Edition; revised, 1904.

Third edition, revised, 1924.

1902 **Anonymous**   The 'Revised English' New Testament;
being the authorized version re-revised and
grammatically corrected; with the Words of Jesus in
a distinct type. London: S. Bagster & Sons, 1902.
["An attempt to present the King James' version with
corrections of the grammer and rendering." Prepared by
George Washington Moon. "Preliminary specimen pages of
the Tentative edition shortly to be published by one of
the Life Governors of the British and Foreign Bible
Society, to mark its Centenary in the year 1904." In
1904, a tentative edition was published; See Samuel
Lloyd... and George Washington Moon, 1904.]

1902 **Cooper, James and A.J. MacLean**   The Testament of
our Lord. Translated into English from the Syriac.
With Introduction and Notes by James Cooper... and
A.J. MacLean... Edinburgh: T. & T. Clark, 1902.
[See M.R. James, Apocryphal N.T., 1924; See Burton Scott
Easton, Pastoral Epistles, 1947.]

1902 **Godbey, W.B.**   Translation of the New Testament from
the Original Greek. By Rev. W.B. Godbey. Cincinnati:
M.W. Knapp, Office of God's Revivalist, 1902?
Current Reprint; Schmul Publishing Co., Inc.
P.O.Box 4068, Salem, OH 44460.

1903 **Weymouth, Richard Francis**   The Modern Speech New
Testament. An idiomatic translation into everyday
English from the text of "the Resultant Greek
Testament." By the late Richard Francis Weymouth.
London: J. Clarke & Co., 1903.
Second edition, 1904.

Third edition; Edited and partly revised by
Ernest Hampden-Cook, M.A., 1909.
Reprinted; Grand Rapids: Kregel
Publications, 1978.

Fourth edition; Newly Revised by Several Well-
known New Testament Scholars [S.W. Green,
A.D.J. Farrer and H.T. Andrews], 1924.

Fifth edition; Newly Revised by James Alexander
Robertson, 1929.
> Reprinted; Boston: The Pilgrim Press;
> London: James Clarke & Co., Ltd., 1943;
> New York: Harper & Bros., Publishers,
> 1953?

Sixth Edition; New York: Harper & Bros., 1953.

1904 Lloyd, Samuel and George Washington Moon (Editors)
The Authorized Version of the New Testament in
"Revised English". London: S. Bagster & Sons, 1904.
> Re-issued; The Corrected English New Testament.
> A revision of the "Authorised" Version (By
> Nestle's Resultant Text). Prepared with the
> Assistance of Eminent Scholars and Issued by
> Samuel Lloyd, a Life Governor of the British
> and Foreign Bible Society as His Memorial of
> the Society's Centenary. With Preface by the
> Bishop of Durham... New York: G.P. Putnam's
> Sons, The Knickerbocker Press, 1904.

Also; London: Samuel Bagster & Sons Ltd.,
Printed by Ballantyne, Hanson & Co., 1905.

Another edition; The Workers' Testament Lloyd's
(corrected) New Testament... with Worker's
Notes by William Edgar Geil. London: Samuel
Bagster and Sons, 1906.

1904 Worrell, Adolphus S. The New Testament Revised
and Translated by A.S. Worrell, with Notes and
Instructions designed to aid the earnest Reader in
obtaining a clear Understanding of the Doctrine,
Ordinances, and primitive Assemblies as revealed in
these Scriptures... Louisville: Published by A.S.
Worrell; Philadelphia: The American Baptist
Publication Society, 1904.
> Another edition; The New Testament of our Lord
> and Saviour Jesus Christ a translation by A.S.
> Worrell, M.A. Springfield, Missouri: Gospel
> Publishing House, n.d.

Also; The Worrell New Testament. A.S. Worrell's
Translation with Study Notes. Springfield,
Missouri: Gospel Publishing House, 1980.

1906 Anonymous The New Testament. London: J.M. Dent
& Sons Ltd.; New York: E.P. Dutton & Co. Inc., 1906.
[Everyman's Library edited by Ernest Rhys. Theology &
Philosophy. The New Testament A Chronological
Arrangement by Principal Lindsay. Its not known if this
work is the same as Lindsay's entry.]

1906 **Lindsay, Thomas M.**   The New Testament of Our Lord and Savior Jesus Christ Arranged in the Order in which Its Parts Came to those in the First Century which believed in Our Lord. Edited by Thomas M. Lindsay. London: J.M. Dent & Co.; New York: E.P. Dutton & Co., 1906.
> [It is unknown whether this work is the same as that in the series "Everyman's Library first published in March 1906." This was mainly an AV with minor changes in words, plus italicizing and rearrangement.]

> Other editions; May 1906, March 1907 (revised throughout), October 1911, April 1917, January 1920.

1907 **Young, Robert**   The Book of the New Covenant. Translated according to the Letter and Idiom of the Original Greek. By Robert Young... Edinburgh: George A. Young & Co., Publishers...; New York: Funk & Wagnalls Co., 1907.
> [Revised Edition.]

1909 **Anonymous**   The Bible in Modern English or The Modern English Bible (New Testament). A rendering from the Originals by an American making use of the Best Scholarship and Latest Researches at Home and Abroad. [Frank Schell Ballantine] Perkiomen, Pa.: Perkiomen Press, 1907.
> [3000 copies sold before 10,000 copies were withdrawn due to poor printing.]

> [The name "Jehovah" is used at Acts 2:25, 34.]

1909 **Anonymous**   Evolutionary Edition of the New Testament, translated by an Evolutionist. Part 1. St. Paul: Commonsense Bible Teacher, 1909.
> [Incomplete?]

1909 **Hampdon-Cook, Ernest**   See Richard Francis Weymouth, N.T., 1903.

1909 **Weaver, S. Townsend**   The University New Testament, in modern historical and literary form, for the church, the school, and the home... By S. Townsend Weaver. Philadelphia: University Publishing Co., 1909.

1911 **Horner, G.W.**   The Coptic Version of the New Testament in the Southern Dialect...Sahidic and Thebaic...English translation. 7 Vols.   Oxford: Clarendon Press, 1911-1924.
> 1911 The Coptic Version...The Gospels of S. Matthew and S. Mark.

1911   The Coptic Version...The Gospel of S.
Luke.

1911   The Coptic Version...The Gospel of S.
John.

1922   The Coptic Version...The Acts.

1920   The Coptic Version...The Epistles of S.
Paul.

1924   The Coptic Version....The Revelation.

1913 **Clarke, Sir Edward George**   The New Testament. The
Authorised Version, Corrected. The text prepared by
the Right Hon. Sir Edward Clarke.   London: Smith,
Elder & Co., 1913.
["More current than the AV; more acceptable than the
RV".]

1913 **Courtney, W.L.**   The Literary Man's New
Testament. The books arranged in chronological order
with introductory essays and annotations. By W.L.
Courtney.   London: Chapman and Hall, 1913.
Also, 1915.

1913 **Moffatt, James**   The New Testament; A
new translation in modern speech, by James Moffatt,
based upon the Greek text by von Soden.   London:
Hodder & Stoughton, 1913.

1914 **Cunnington, Edward Ernest**   The New Covenant,
commonly called the New Testament of our Lord and
Saviour Jesus Christ. A revision of the version of
A.D. 1611 by...E.E. Cunnington. London: G. Routledge
& Sons, 1914.
Second Edition; revised: The New Testament
otherwise called: The New Covenant of our Lord
and Saviour, Jesus Christ. A revision of the
version of A.D. 1611.   London: T. Fisher,
Unwin Ltd, 1919.

Other editions; Revised edition. London: 1930;
Revised edition.   Edinburgh: 1930;   Revised
edition.   London: 1935;   Edinburgh: 1935.

In addition; The Adelphi New Testament. Second
Edition: Revised.   London: T. Fisher, Unwin
Ltd., 1919.
[This is a revision of the 1914 edition.]

Further; The Western New Testament.   London:
George Routledge & Sons, 1926.

1914 **Panin, Ivan**   The New Testament from the Greek
     text as established by Bible Numerics. Edited by
     Ivan Panin.   New Haven: Bible Numerics Co., 1914.
          Second Edition; Toronto: Clarke, Irwin & Co.,
          1935.

          Reprinted, Oxford: University Press, 1944, 1945.

          Also; Toronto: Book Society of Canada, 1954,
          1966, 1973, 1979.

1915 **Pullan, Leighton**   (Editor)   See Oxford Church Bible
     Commentary, 1913.

1915 **Weaver, S. Townsend**   The greatest book ever
     written; the New Testament in its inspired literary
     form, authorized version. By S. Townsend Weaver.
     Washington: 1915.

1917 **Lauritzen, Johannes Rudolph**   1517 – October 31,
     1917. In Memoriam (sic) Of Dr. Martin Luther's
     Reformation. The NEW TESTAMENT of our Lord Jesus
     Christ. Translated out of the Original Greek by DR.
     MARTIN LUTHER, 1521 at the Castle 'The Wartburg' and
     Prepared for the English Print; Former Translations
     Diligently   Compared,   Revised   and   Published   by
     JOHANNES RUDOLPH LAURITZEN, Pastor of St. Peter's
     Evangelical Lutheran Church, Knoxville, Tenn., U.S.
     of N.A., 1917.

1917 **Moffatt, James**   The New Testament; A New
     Translation by James Moffatt. New Edition Revised.
     New York: Hodder & Stoughton, George H. Doran
     Company, 1917.
          Another edition; ...Together with the Authorized
          Version. Parallel Edition... London: Hodder &
          Stoughton, 1922 and New York: Harper & Bros.,
          1935.

          Also; The New Testament. A New Translation by
          James Moffatt. New York: Association Press,
          1918.

          Another edition; Together with the AV Parallel
          Edition with Introduction... New York: George
          H. Doran, 1922?

          Again, 1929?

          New Edition; Revised.   London & New York: Harper
          & Bros., 1935.

In addition; The New Testament and the Psalms;... James Moffatt. New York: Harper, 1950?

1918 **Anderson, Henry Tompkins**   The New Testament, Translated from the Sinaitic Manuscript Discovered by Constantine Tischendorf at Mt. Sinai, by H.T. Anderson.   Cincinnati: The Standard Publishing Co., 1918.
   [Different translation from the N.T. dated 1864.]

1921 **Anonymous**   A Plain Translation of the New Testament. By a Student. Melbourne: McCarron, Bird & Co., 1921.

1922 **Ballantine, Frank Schell**   A Plainer Bible for Plain People in Plain America...(New Testament)...from the original   Greek   By   Chaplain   [Frank   Schell] Ballantine...Jersey City: Plainer Bible Press, 1922.
   [Some question as to whether this is a revision of the previous work, or an effort to dispose of the remaining 7,000 vols. of "The Bible in Modern English". In any event, only 50-60 copies of this edition circulated due to water damage of the entire lot in storage at a warehouse. (Simms, Bible in American).]

1923 **Ballantine, William G.** The Riverside New Testament. A Translation from the Original Greek into the English of To-Day. By William G.Ballantine. The Riverside Press...   Boston & New York: Houghton Mifflin Company, 1923.
   [This work was considered "modern yet conservative in literary quality." Ballantine's aim was "to serve as a plate glass window through which the man who does not read Greek will see in English what he would see if he did read Greek."]

   Revised edition, 1934.

1923 **Goodspeed, Edgar J.**   The New Testament. An American Translation by Edgar J. Goodspeed... Chicago: Univ. of Chicago Press, 1923.
   [There have been many editions where the text has not been basically changed. There are a few improvements in the 25th Anniversary Edition of 1948.]

   Other edition, 1926, 1942, 1948.

   Also; The Goodspeed Parallel New Testament. The American   Translation   and   the   King   James Version   in   Parallel   Columns,   with Introductions and explanatory Notes by Edgar J. Goodspeed.   Chicago: University of Chicago Press, 1943.

In addition; The Student's New Testament. The Greek Text and the American Translation. Edgar J. Goodspeed. Chicago: University of Chicago Press, 1954.

1924 **Andrews, H.T.**   See Weymouth, Richard Francis; The N.T. in Modern Speech, 1924 edition, 1903.

1924 **Anonymous**   The New Covenant: a Mutual Arrangement or Testament for a true civilization founded upon brotherly labor, following the Greek title which is usually rendered the New Testament, translated out of the Greek as a Labor Determinative Version, and diligently compared with former with former translations herein revised for the recovery of Biblical labor standards. Jackson, Mich.: Home of the American Labor Determinative Revision Committee, 1924.

1924 **Green, S.W.**   See Richard Francis Weymouth, New Testament (1924 ed.), 1903.

1924 **Montgomery, Helen Barrett**   Centenary Translation of the New Testament Published to Signalize the Completion of the First Hundred Years of the American Baptist Publication Society. Translated by Helen Barrett Montgomery.   Philadelphia: The American Baptist Publication Society, 1924.
[The first woman to produce a modern speech New Testament. The Gospels were published Feb., 1924.]

Other editions; 1928, 1933, 1938, 1940, 1941, 1942.

Another edition; Century Translation, The New Testament in Modern English Translated by Helen Barrett Montgomery.   Philadelphia, Chicago, Kansas City, Los Angeles & Seattle: The Judson Press, 1954.

Another Edition; Nashville: Holman Bible Publishers, 1988.

1924 **Several Well-Known New Testament Scholars**
See Francis Weymouth, New Testament (4th. edition), 1903.

1925 **Overbury, Arthur E.**   The People's New Covenant (New Testament) Scriptural Writings Translated from the Meta-Physical Standpoint by Arthur E.Overbury. Being a Revision Unhampered by So-Called Ecclesiastical Authority. This Version Interprets the New Covenant ...from a Spiritual or Meta-Physical Standpoint, and Recognizes Healing as Well as Teaching as a

Component Part of True Christianity... Monrovia, California: Published and for Sale by Arthur E. Overbury; New York: Didion & Co.; Los Angeles: Hyatt & Lyon, 1925.

[Known as "The Triumphant Christ Version" and is used by the Christian Scientists.]

[This revision is unhampered by the so-called ecclesiastical authority. This version recognizes healing as well as teaching as a component part of true Christianity.]

Another edition; Revised. Los Angeles: Wolfer Printing Co., 1932.

Revised edition, 1943.

1926 **Concordant Version**   Concordant Version, The Sacred Scriptures. Designed to put the English reader in possession of all the vital facts of Divine revelation... [N.T.]
[See New Testament Selections, 1914 Concordant Version of The Sacred Scriptures.]

1927 **Pitman, Isaac**   The New Testament...printed in the advanced stage of Pitman's shorthand. New era edition. London: Sir I. Pitman & Sons, 1927.

1928 **Hamilton, A.**   The Student's Greek Testament, with parallel references and English translation. [Edited by A. Hamilton] London: Hurlbert Publishing Co., [1928]

1929 **LeFevre, George N.**   The Christian's Bible – New Testament. The New Testament of our Lord and Saviour Jesus, the Christ. A Translation from the Greek, chiefly of the Codex Sinaiticus and Codex Vaticanus; These Being the Oldest and Most Complete MSS. of the New Testament. It is not Simply a Translation of Words, but Under the Guidance of the Holy Ghost, His Thoughts, as Recorded in Greek by His Specially Inspired Writers, are Made Known Unto Us. By a Servant of Christ [George N. LeFevre]. Strasburg, Pa.: George N. LeFevre, 1929.

[The Copyright Office dates this 1929. On a sampling of 132 copies, 10% were dated 1928 and the other 90% were dated 1929. Only 500 were printed. (See "The Bible Collector" Journal, No. 35, July–Sept. 1973.)]

[LeFevre used the name "Jehovah" many times in his translation of the New Testament.]

1929 **Martin, William Wallace**   The New Testament critically reconstructed and retranslated, by William Wallace Martin. Nashville, Tennessee: Parthenon Press, 1929–1944.

1929 Epistles (Complete)...separated, arranged
and translated by William Wallace Martin.
2 Vols. Nashville: Press of Marshall and
Bruce Co., [1929].
[Martin divides Romans into two letters,
the author of one was Paul and the other
was Apollos. Hebrews is divided into three
letters, in which the three authors were:
Paul, Apollos, and Barnabas. Martin divides
others into more than one letter as well.]

1937 The New Testament, critically
reconstructed and retranslated. By
William Wallace Martin. Nashville:
Parthenon Press. [1937].

1942 John, The Gospel of the Word. The Gospel
of the Only Beloved Son. Mark, the Gospel
of the word. The Gospel of the Only
Beloved Son. Reconstructed, retranslated,
and annotated by William Wallace Martin.

1942 The Epistles of Paul to the Romans,
Corinthians, Hebrews, and Ephesians; the
Epistles of Apollos to the Romans,
Corinthians, Hebrews, and Ephesians; the
Epistles of Barnabas to the Romans,
Corinthians and Hebrews. Reconstructed,
Retranslated, and Annotated, by William
Wallace Martin.

1942 The Church Organized. [Addresses of Stephen,
Epistles, Revelation, reconstructed, retranslated,
annotated.] By William Wallace Martin.

1944 Gospel of Matthew...

1944 Gospel of...Luke...

1944 Gospels of Matthew and Luke

1929 **Robertson, James Alexander**   See Richard Francis
Weymouth, New Testament (5th. edition), 1903.

1929 **Wolff, George W.**   The New Testament in Blank
Verse. By George W. Wolff.   St. Louis: Becktold
Company, Edition Binders, [1929].

1931 **Lenski, R.C.H.**   A New Commentary on the New
Testament, Interpretation and Translation. R.C.H.
Lenski. 12 Vols. Columbus, Ohio: Lutheran Book
Concern, 1931-1946.
1932 Interpretation of St.Matthew's Gospel.
(1943)

> 1934 The Interpretation of St. Mark's and St. Luke's Gospel. (1946)
>
> 1931 The Interpretation of St. John's Gospel. (1942)
>
> 1934 The Interpretation of the Acts of the Apostle.
>
> 1936 The Interpretation of St. Paul's Epistle to the Romans.
>
> 1935 The Interpretation of St. Paul's First and Second Epistle to the Corinthians.
>
> 1937 The Interpretation of St. Paul's Epistle to the Galatians, to the Ephesians, and to the Philippians.
>
> 1937 The Interpretation of St. Paul's Epistle to the Colossians, to the Thessalonians, to Timothy, to Titus and Philemon.
>
> 1938 The Interpretation of the Epistle to the Hebrews and to the Epistle of James.
>
> 1938 The Interpretation of the Epistles of St. Peter, St. John and St. Jude.
>
> 1935 The Interpretation of St. John's Revelation.
>
> 1935 The Epistle Selections of the Ancient Church. An Exegetical-Homiletical Treatment. A Series of Epistle Texts for the Entire Church Year.
>
> [Matt., Mark and Luke were published by The Wartburg Press, Columbus.]

1932 **Ballantine, Frank Schell**   Our God and Godhealth, our Healer. Godhealth's messengers and Godhealth's message of life and light and love and law, the light of life and the law of love, the wisest wisdom of the wise of all ages: translated from the original Greek, reinterpreted in the thought-forms, language and idioms of America today, and arranged for reading with sustained interest from beginning to end as a modern novel, by Chaplain Ballantine. By Frank Schell Ballantine. Collegeville, Pa.: Craigie Publishing Company, 1932.

1934 **James, Montague Rhodes and Delia Lyttelton**   The Aldine Bible. The New Testament, edited with an

introduction by M.R. James ...assisted by Delia
Lyttelton. Four Vols. New York: E.P. Dutton & Co.,
1934-1936.

> Vol. 1   The Gospels according to St. Matthew
>   and St. Mark, 1934.

> Vol. 2   The Gospel according to St. Luke,
>   and the Acts of the Apostles, 1935.

> Vol. 3   The Pauline and Pastoral Epistles,
>   1936.

> Vol. 4   The Epistle to the Hebrews, The
>   Gospel according to St. John, The
>   Johannian Epistles, Peter, James,
>   Jude, and the Revelation, 1936.

Also; London: J.M. Dent & Sons, 1934.

1934 **Wade, G. Woosung**   The Documents of the New
Testament translated & historically arranged with
critical introductions by G.W.Wade... London: Thomas
Murby & Co., 1934.
> ["G.W. Wade (Editor) attempts to provide an accurate,
> yet not literal, rendering of the Greek text..."]

> [The Gospel according to Matthew was reprinted in 1935;
> the other Gospels were separately reprinted in 1936.]

1935 **Carey, James A**.   New Testament of Our Lord
and Saviour Jesus Christ, Translated from the Latin
Vulgate. Diligently Compared with the Original
Greek... With Annotations and References by Dr.
Challoner, Canon Haydock and Dr. H.J. Ganes, and an
Historical and Chronological Index. With a Preface
of Rev. James A. Carey, M.A... A. Wildermann -
Brepols Publication, Carey's revision of Challoner,
printed in Belgium by Brepols' Catholic Press. New
York: C. Wildermann Co. [n.d.] 1935?
> ["...the corrections made have been introduced only
> where the exiting English seems obviously wrong or
> meaningless."]

Also, 1936, 1937, & 1938.

1937 **Callan, Fr. Charles Jerome** (Editor)
The New Testament ...Translated into English from
the Original Greek by The Very Reverend Francis
Aloysius Spencer, O.P. Edited by Charles J. Callan,
O.P., and John A. McHugh, O.P.... New York: [Printed
by the Statford Press, Inc.] The Macmillan Company,
1937.

1937 **Greber, Johannes**   The New Testament. A
New Translation and Explanation Based on the Oldest

Manuscripts, by Johannes Greber. German text and English translation. New York: John Felsberg, Inc., 1937.

> [The translation from German to English was made by a professional translator and corrected by a committee of American clergymen. Greber was a former Roman Catholic priest who came to believe in a communication with the spirits. Some list Greber N.T. as "Spiritualist New Testament".]

Currently Reprinted; Johanne Greber Memorial Foundation, Teaneck, NJ.

1937 Spencer, Francis Aloysius   The New Testament of Our Lord and Saviour Jesus Christ. Translated into English from the Original Greek by Francis Aloysius Spencer, O.P. Edited by Charles J. Callan, O.P., and John A. McHugh, O.P... [Nilhil Obstat: Arthur J. Scanlan, S.T.D., Censor Librorum. Imprimatur: Patrick Cardinal Hayes, Archbishop of New York. Printed by the Stratford Press, Inc., New York.] New York: The Macmillan Co., 1937.

> Reissued, 1940, 1941, 1943, 1945, 1946, 1948, 1951.

1937 Williams, Charles B.   The New Testament. A Translation in the Language of the People by Charles B. Williams, Professor of Greek in Union University ...Boston: Bruce Humphries, Inc., Publishers, 1937.

> ["The effort has been to translate thoughts and not single words into idiomatic English." Also, his aim was to made the N.T. "readable and understandable by the plain people".]

Another edition; [Slighty revised] Chicago: Moody Press, 1950.

Other editions; Chicago, 1949, 1956; London, 1950, 1952.

1938 Anonymous   The Book of Books. A translation of the New Testament complete and unabridged. [Production supervised by R. Mercer Wilson.] London: R.T.S., The Lutterworth Press, The United Society for Christian Literature, 1938.

1938 Clementson, Edgar Lewis   The New Testament. A Translation. By Rev. Edgar Lewis Clementson. Pittsburgh: The Evangelization Society of the Pittsburgh Bible Institute, 1938.

> [Not published for profit (Financial); Paper bound.]

1938 Willis, N. Hardy (Editor)   See William Tyndale, The newe testament, 1534.

1939 **Copp, Zed Hopeful**   The Book of Life. Home Library. The Interwoven Gospels, The Acts, Revelation, The Epistles, and Gems from Proverbs...
[See Bible Selections for the complete entry.]

1940 **Lamsa, George M.**   The New Testament According to the Eastern Version. Translated from the Original Aramaic Sources by George M. Lamsa... Philadelphia: A.J. Holman Co., 1939.

1941 **Anonymous**   The New Testament in Basic English.
[See Complete Bibles, 1933 Charles K. Ogden, The Bible in Basic English.]

1941 **Anonymous**   The New Testament of Our Lord and Savior Jesus Christ. Translated from the Latin Vulgate. A Revision of the Challoner - Rheims Version. Edited by Catholic Scholars Under the Patronage of the Episcopal Committee of the Confraternity Of Christian Doctrine. Paterson, New Jersey: St. Anthony Guild Press, 1941. [Confraternity Version]
The following are some of the translators:

Edward P.Arbez	Ernest William Barnes
John Barton	Charles Jerome Callan
Edward A.Cerny	J.P.Christopher
John J.Collins	J.S.Considine
Charles J.Costello	Henry Dillon
Edward H.Donze	William A.Dowd
Led. P.Foley	Henry J. Grimmelsman
Charles G. Heupler	Maurice A.Hofer
Mark Kennedy	William H. McClellan
John Ambrose McHugh	Albert Meyer
William Newton	Charles H.Pickar
Thomas Plassmann	

1941 My Daily Reading from the New Testament, Gospels Unified, Epistles Unified...Confraternity of Christian Doctrine...arranged by Rev. Joseph F. Stedman...Confraternity of the Precious Blood...Brooklyn...Montreal: Catholic Society of the Bible. [Selections.]
Another edition, 1942.

Other editions, 1943, 1947.

1950 Special Student Edition; New York: Catholic Book Publishing Co.

Third Edition, 1953.

1956 Official Catholic Edition, Complete and Unabridged appears on the paper cover; Garden City, New York: Doubleday & Co., Inc.

[See Complete Bibles, 1948 Anonymous, Holy Bible...
Confraternity.]

1943 **Stringfellow, Ervin Edward**   The New Testament.
2 Vols. 1943-1945.
       1943 The Gospels, A Translation Harmony and
       Annotations by Ervin Edward Stringfellow,
       A.M... St.Louis: John S. Swift, 1943.
         Second printing, 1948.

       1945 Acts and Epistles, A Translation and
       Annotations by Ervin Edward Stringfellow,
       A.M... Des Moines, Iowa: William C.
       Brown Co., 1945.

1944 **Anonymous**   The Beginnings of the Way. London and
Redhill: United Society for Christian Literature,
Lutterworth Press, 1944.
    ["A new translation has been used for this book. It
    follows almost entirely the recent edition of the New
    Testament entitled The Book of Books..."]

1944 **Anonymous**   The New Testament of our Lord
and Saviour Jesus Christ. Newly Translated from the
Latin Vulgate at the Request of Their Lordships, the
Archbishops and Bishops of England and Wales. [By
R.A. Knox]. Trial edition. London: Burns, Oates and
Washbourne, 1944.
    Two printings issued; New York: Sheed & Ward,
    1944.

    Definitive edition, 1945.

    A Chanticleer Edition, 1946.

    Another edition; New York: Sheed & Ward, 1946.

    An Australian edition; Sydney, Melbourne:
    Pellegrini and Co., 1947.

    Pocket edition, 1954.

    [Numerous printings.]

1945 **Berkeley Version**   Berkeley Version of
the New Testament from the Original Greek with Brief
Footnotes by Gerrit Verkuyl (Editor)... Berkeley,
California: James J. Gillick & Co., 1945.
    [Two of the translators were: Clyde T. Francisco and
    Derwood Wilham Deere.]

    Revised edition; [41 corrections] 1946.
        Another revised edition; [Additional
    corrections] 1947.

Another edition; Corrected notes with original text. Zondervan, 1950 & 1953.

Revised edition; The Modern Language New Testament. The New Berkeley Version. Grand Rapids: Zondervan Publishing House, 1969.

[See Holy Bible. The Berkeley Version in Modern English, 1959.]

1946 Revised Standard Version   (R.S.V., RSV)
The New Covenant commonly called the New Testament of our Lord and Saviour Jesus Christ. Revised Standard Version. Translated from the Greek. Being the Version set forth A.D. 1611. Revised 1881 and 1901, compared with the most ancient authorities and Revised 1946... [Norwood, Mass.: J.S. Cushing Co. – Berwick & Smith Co.]   New York: Thomas Nelson & Sons, 1946.

> The N.T. Committee are as follows:
> Luther A. Weigle (Chairman)
> James Moffatt (Secretary–until 1944.)
> Fleming James (Secretary)
> H.J. Cadbury (Harvard)
> E.J. Goodspeed (U of Chicago)
> W.R. Bowie (Grace Church)
> F.C. Grant (Union)
> M. Burrows (Yale)
> C.T. Craig (Oberlin)
> A.R. Wentz (Lutheran)

["In subsequent editions, none of which are identified as 'revised' or 'second', 'third' etc. editions" there are "minor variations".]

Catholic Edition, 1965.

1947 Arendzen, J.P.   New Testament of our Lord and Savoir Jesus Christ ascending to the Douay version with an introduction and notes by Dr. J.P.Arendzen. London: Sheed & Ward, 1947.

1947 Phillips, J.B. The New Testament in Modern English. 1947–1958.

> 1947 Letters to Young Churches. A Translation of the New Testament Epistles by J.B. Phillips. With an Introduction by C.S. Lewis... London: G.Bles, 1947; New York: Macmillan Company.
> > Another edition; Letters to Young Churches...Epistles, a corrected edition, 1957, 1958, 1968.

> 1952 The Gospels translated into Modern English. By J.B. Phillips.   London:

Geoffrey Bles, 1952; New York: Macmillan Co.

> Another edition; The Gospels, a corrected edition, 1958.

1955 The Young Church in Action. The Acts of the Apostles translated into Modern English by J.B. Phillips. London: Geoffrey Bles; New York: Macmillan & Co.

> Reprinted; Oct. 1955, Dec. 1955, June 1956.

1956 St. Luke's Life of Christ; translated into modern English by J.B. Phillips. London: William Collins Sons & Co.

1957 The Book of Revelation. A new translation of the Apocalypse by J.B. Phillips. London: Geoffrey Bles; New York: The Macmillan Co.

1958 The New Testament in Modern English, translated by J.B. Phillips. New York: Macmillan Co.

> Revised edition; London: Bles, 1960.

Revised Edition; 1972.

Another Edition; The New Testament in Modern English for Schools. Great Britain: Bles; Collins, 1959.

> Reprinted; Oct. 1959, Febr. 1960, May 1960.
> Revised Edition; 1960.
> American Edition; New York: Macmillan Co., 1965.

1947 **Swann, George**   New Testament of our Lord and Saviour Jesus Christ; Translated from the Greek text of Westcott and Hort. By Rev. George Swann... Louisville: [Printed by the Pentecostal Publishing Co.], 1947.

> [Mr. Swann made changes in each edition.]

Second edition, 1949.

Third edition; Louisville, Kentucky: New Testament Publishers, n.d.

1948 **Ford, Thomas Francis and Ralph Ewart Ford**   The New Testament... The Letchworth Version in Modern English. Letchworth, Herts England: Letchworth Printer Ltd., 1948.

> [A modern speech AV of the New Testament.]

NEW TESTAMENT

1949 **Alexander, Albert George**   Interpretation of the Entire New Testament, 1949.

1950 **Anonymous**   The New Testament of our Messiah and Saviour Yahshua. Sacred Name Version. Critically compared with ancient authorities and divers manuscripts. [A.B. Traina] Irving, New Jersey: Scripture Research Association, 1950.
    ["Yahweh" is used many times.]

    Another edition, 1951.

1951 **Anonymous**   The New Testament of our Lord and Saviour Jesus Christ. The Authentic Version. [Claire Pershall] Plattsburgh, Missouri: Brotherhood Authentic Bible Society, [1951].

1951 **Norlie, Olaf Morgan**   The New Testament... in Modern English translated from the original Greek and supplied with an outline, by Olaf Morgan Norlie. [Northfield, Minnesota: Published by the Author], 1951.
    [The N.T. was mimeographed in the unsuccessful hope of finding a publisher.]

    Another Edition; One Way: The Jesus People N.T. A Translation in Modern English. Pasadena, CA: Compass Press, 1961.

1952 **Williams, Charles Kingsley**   The New Testament. A New Translation in Plain English. By Charles Kingsley Williams... London: S.P.C.K. and Longmans, Green and Co., 1952.

1953 **Barclay, William**   The Daily Study Bible. 15 Vols. London. New York: Collins; Edinburgh: Saint Andrew Press; Philadelphia: The Westminster Press, 1953-59.
    1956 Gospel of Matthew. (2 Vols.)
        Revised, (2 Vols.) 1975.
    1954 Gospel of Mark. Revised, 1975.
    1953 Gospel of Luke. Revised, 1975.
    1955 Gospel of John (2 Vols.)
        Revised, 1975.
    1953 Acts of the Apostles. Revised, 1976.
    1955 Letter to the Romans. Revised, 1975.
    1954 Letters to the Corinthians. Revised, 1975.
    1955 Letters to the Galatians and to the Ephesians. Revised, 1976.
    1957 Letters to the Philippians, Colossians, and Thessalonians. Revised, 1975.
    1956 Letters to Timothy, Titus, and Philemon. Revised, 1975.
    1955 Letter to the Hebrews. Revised, 1976.

1954 Letters of James and Peter. Revised, 1976.
1953 The Letters of John and Jude.
     Revised, 1976.
1959 The Revelation of John. (2 Vols.)
     Revised, 1976.

1953 **Moore, George Albert**   The New Testament. A New,
Independent, Individual Translation from the Greek,
by George Albert Moore, Colonel, U.S.A., Rtd.
Issued Serially.   Chevy Chase, MD: The Country
Dollar Press, 1953.
    [Issued serially and accumulatively in only one
    mimeographed edition, "Collector's Edition" of 250
    copies. 1953-1954.]

    [American Bible Society has a separate issue of the
    Gospels, 1953.]

1954 **Bradley, Morton C. Jr.**   The King James Version. The
New Testament in Cadenced form. Designed by Morton
C. Bradley, Jr. Cambridge, Mass.: Bradley Press.
Distributed by Rinehart, New York, 1954.

1954 **Kleist, James A. and Joseph L. Lilly**
The New Testament Rendered from the Original Greek
with Explanatory Notes. Part One: The Four Gospels,
Translated by James A. Kleist, S.J. Part Two: Acts
of the Apostles, Epistles and Apocalypse, Translated
by Joseph L. Lilly.   Milwaukee: Bruce Publishing
Co., 1954.

1955 **Parker, P.G.**   The Clarified New Testament by
Principal P.G. Parker. Lynton, Devon: Published by
The Christian Workers Bible Centre, Printed by
Reliance Printing Works, Halesowen, 1955?

1955 **Schonfield, Hugh J.**   The Authentic New Testament;
edited and translated from the Greek for the general
reader, by Hugh J.Schonfield. Maps and Illustrations
by J.F.Horrabin. London: Dennis Dobson Ltd., Central
Press, 1955.
    [The Limited subscriber's edition (3,500 copies) was
    first published 1955; The general edition was published
    1956.]

    Reprinted; New York: New American Library – A
    Mentor Religious Classic, 1958.

1956 **Wuest, Kenneth S.**   Wuest's Expanded Translation of
the Greek New Testament...Kenneth S. Wuest, Litt.D.,
Teacher of Greek, the Moody Bible Institute. 3
Vols. Grand Rapids, Michigan: William B. Eerdmans
Publishing Co., 1956-1959.
    1956 Vol. I   The Gospels. Also; London:
                  Pickering & Inglis, 1957.

   1958 Vol. II   Acts through Ephesians.   Also;
      London: Pickering & Inglis,
      1958.
   1959 Vol. III Philippians through Revelation.
      Also; London: Pickering &
      Inglis, 1959.

  Another edition; 1 vol. ed. London: 1961.

1957 **Black, Adam & Charles**   Black's N.T. Commentaries.
(General Editor: Henry Chadwick)   London: Adam and
Charles Black, 1957.
   1960 A Commentary on the Gospel According to
    St. Matthew by Floyd V. Filson.
     Reprinted, 1967. Second edition, 1971.

   1960 A Commentary on the Gospel According to
    St. Mark by Sherman E. Johnson.
     Second edition, 1972.

   1958 A Commentary on the Gospel According to
    St. Luke by A.R.C. Leaney.

   1963 A Commentary on the Gospel According to
    St. John by J.N. Sanders.

   1957 A Commentary on the Acts of the Apostles
    by C.S.C. Williams.

   1957 A Commentary on the Epistle to the Romans
    by C.K. Barrett.
     Reprinted, 1967, 1971 & 1973.

   1968 A Commentary on the First Epistle to the
    Corinthians by C.K. Barrett.
     Second edition, 1971. Reprinted, 1973.

   1968 A Commentary on the Second Epistle to the
    Corinthians by C.K. Barrett.

   1957 A Commentary on the Epistle to the
    Colossians by Robert M. Grant.

   1959 A Commentary on the Epistle to the
    Philippians by F.W. Beare.
     Second edition, 1969. Third edition,
    1973.

   1958 A Commentary on the First and Second
    Epistles to the Thessalonians by Ernest
    Best.

   1963 A Commentary on the Pastoral Epistles, I
    & II Timothy, Titus by J.N.D. Kelly.

Reprinted, 1972.

1957 A Commentary on the Epistle to the Hebrews by H.W. Montefiore.

19?? A Commentary on the Epistles Peter and of Jude by J.N.D. Kelly.

19?? A Commentary on the Johannine Epistles by J.L. Houlden.

1957 A Commentary on the Revelation of St. John the Divine by G.B. Caird.

1958 **Amplified New Testament**   Amplified New Testament. [Copyright by the Lockman Foundation.] Grand Rapids: Zondervan Publishing House, 1958.
Another edition; London: Marshall, Morgan & Scott, 1959.

1958 **British and Foreign Bible Society**
A Diaglot New Testament for the use of Translators. [Three volumes completed - Mark 1958, Matthew 1959, John 1960 (corrected, 1961). For private circulation only. Rev. Mr. H.K. Moulton, Deputy Translations Secretary stated that other books of the N.T. will be published regularly in due course. There are four committees engaged on this work, based on different University centers in Great Britain, under the directorship of Professor W. D. McHardy of Oxford; also closely connected with the work: G. D. Kilpatrick, Oxford, Dr. William Barclay and Dr. C. K. Barrett plus other leading British scholars.]
The following were some of the translators:
E.C.Blackman
W.J.Bradnock
J.Hargreaves
George Raymond Beasley-Murray

1958 **Harper's New Testament Commentaries**   Harper's New Testament Commentaries. New York: Harper Bros., 1958-
[Each Commentary contains a clear, new translation of the Greek text into modern English. See Entries for Adam & Charles Black.]

1958 **Johnson, Ashley S.**   The Self-Interpreting New Testament. Compiled and Arranged by Ashley S. Johnson. Grand Rapids: Baker Book House, 1958.
[Reprinted from the original edition printed and issued by the author. (n.d.)]

1958 **Marshall, Alfred** The Interlinear Greek-English New Testament by Alfred Marshall and a Foreword by J.B. Phillips. London: Samuel Bagster and Sons, 1958.
Second edition; London: 1960.

Also; The RSV Interlinear Greek-English New Testament. Nestle's Greek with Alfred Marshall's interlinear. London: Bagster, 1968.

1958 **Tomanek, James L.**   The New Testament of our Lord and Savior Jesus Anointed by James L. Tomanek. Pocatello, Iowa: Printed by Arrowhead Press, 1958.

1958 **Translation for Translators**   The New Testament: A Translation for Translators. London: British and Foreign Bible Society, 1958-196?
[This work, which were 8 1/2 X 14 inches mimeographed sheets, was published "to provide translators with a clear, accurate and straightforward translation of the Greek which could serve as a background for their own work." This work was the forerunner to the Translator's New Testament (1973) and were intended for a limited and temporary use. No longer available.]

1958 Mark (47 pages)
1959 Matthew (74 pages)
1960 John (65 pages)
1961 James - Jude (39 pages)
1962 Luke (81 pages)
1963 1-2 Timothy, Titus, Hebrews (47 pages)
1964 Romans - 2 Corinthians (80 pages)
      Revelation (47 pages)
1963 Acts (83 pages)

1959 **Fraser, John W.**   Calvin's New Testament Commentaries: a New Translation, 1959.

1959 **New International Commentary on the N.T.**   New International Commentary on the N.T. edited by F.F. Bruce.   Grand Rapids: W.B. Eerdmans Publishing Co., 1959-
[16 Vols. known.]

1960 **Roth, Vincent T.**   A Critical Emphatic Paraphrase of the New Testament. By Vincent T. Roth.   Brownsville, Texas: Duplicated by Vincent T. Roth, 1960.
[Roth used the name "Jehovah" many times in his translation of the New Testament.]

Revised, 1963.

[Both the original and the revised edition were privately processed on a spirit process duplicator.]

1961 **Heenan, John J. and Others**   The New Testament. Published in the USA, 1961.   [Roman Catholic]

1961 **New English Bible**   The New English Bible. The New Testament.   Oxford: Oxford University Press, 1961.
[The British and Foreign Bible Society in association with the University Presses, published an edition of St.

John, pp.62; and St. Luke, pp. 64 in 1963.; St. Matthew, pp. 62 and St. Mark, pp. 62 in 1962. B&FBS also issued a Missionary Edition of the N.T. in 1962, not to be sold in the United Kingdom, the United States of America, Canada, Australia, New Zealand and South Africa.]

Second Edition, 1970.

[See Complete Bibles, 1961 New English Bible, for more entry information.]

1961 **Noli, Metropolitan Fan S.**   The New Testament of our Lord and Savior Jesus Christ from the approved Greek text of the Church of Constantinople and the Church of Greece.   Boston: Albanian Orthodox Church in America, 1961.

1961 **Norlie, Olaf Morgan**   Simplified New Testament in Plain English for Today's Reader. Grand Rapids: 1961.   [This may be the same as the 1951 edition.]

Also; The Children's Simplified New Testament in Plain English for Today's Reader. Grand Rapids: 1962.

1962 **Dymond, Dr.**   New Testament. MS. 1962.
[Dr. Dymond used the name "Jehovah" and "YHWH" throughout his translation. Never published.]

1962 **Kraeling, Emil G.**   Clarified New Testament. Vol. 1. The Four Gospels.   New York, Toronto & London: McGraw-Hill Book Co., Inc., 1962.

1962 **Lattimore, Richmond**   The New Testament. 1962-1982.
        1962 The Revelation of John. Translated by Richard Lattimore.   New York: Harcourt, Brace & World.

        1979 The Four Gospels and the Revelation, Newly Translated from the Greek, by Richmond Lattimore. New York: Farrar - Straus - Giroux.

        1982 Acts and Letters of the Apostles. Newly translated from the Greek by Richmond Lattimore.   New York: Dorset Press.

1963 **Beck, William F.**   The New Testament in the Language of Today. By William F. Beck.   St. Louis, Mo: Concordia Publishing House, 1963.
[Uses the most recent manuscripts, especially papyri P66 and P75. It is written in plain, everyday speech for the common reader.]

Slightly Revised, 1964.

Revised again, 1967.

1963 **New American Standard Version**   New Testament, 1963.
     [See Complete Bibles, 1960 for the entire entry.]

1966 **Anonymous**   Today's English Version of the New
     Testament. A Translation made by the American Bible
     Society. New York: The Macmillan Co., 1966.
          [Robert G. Bratcher is the editor. This is a translation
          into "common English", avoiding difficult or technical
          words, regional words or idioms. The line drawings were
          especially prepared by Miss Annie Vallotton. Each
          edition has revisions. Originally published as "Good
          News for Modern Man".]

          Second edition, 1966; Third edition, 1971; Fourth
          edition, 1976.

          Also; "Catholic Edition" and "Dwight D.
          Eisenhower Memorial Edition".

          [Many individual books were published.]

          [See Complete Bibles, 1976 Anonymous, Holy Bible.]

1966 **Anonymous**   The Living Scriptures [by Jay Green]
     A New Translation in the King James Tradition.
     National Foundation for Christian Education, 1966.

1966 **Jerusalem Bible**   The New Testament, 1966.
     [See Complete Bibles for the entire entry.]

1966 **Lovett, C.S.**   The Personal New Testament with
     Lovett's Lights for Laymen. Rephrased by C.S.Lovett.
     [? Vols.] Baldwin Park, CA: Personal Christianity,
     1966-1976.
          1966 Lovett's Lights on I John.

          1967 Lovett's Lights on James.

          1967 Lovett's Lights on Philippians. With
               rephrased text by C.S. Lovett. Personal
               Christianity, No. 5110. (1978 edition)

          1969 Personal Gospel... John. Vol. 3 Chs.
               6:52-9:27. Rephrased by C.S. Lovett.
               Personal Christianity, No. 519.

          1969 Personal Gospel... John. Vol. 4 Chs.
               9:28-13:14. Rephrased by C.S. Lovett.
               Personal Christianity, No. 522.

          1969 Personal Gospel... John. Vol. 5 Chs.
               13:16-17:15. Rephrased by C.S. Lovett.
               Personal Christianity, No. 524.

1970 Vol. Four. John. The Personal New
     Testament with Lovett's Lights for
     Laymen. Rephrased by C.S.Lovett...

1972 Lovett's Lights on Acts.

1975 Lovett's Lights on Romans.

1976 Lovett's Lights on Hebrews.

1967 **Craddock, Edward J.**   The Christ Emphasis New
Testament of our Lord and Saviour. Nashville: 1967.

1967 **Klingensmith, Don J.**   The New Testament
in Everyday English. By Don J. Klingensmith. Fargo,
North Dakota: Kaye's, Inc., 1967–1974
     1967 The New Testament. Volume 1. According to
          Matthew, Mark, Luke–Acts. A Young
          People's Translation. Don J.Klingensmith,
          Chief Editor.
               [The cover reads: The New Testament. Volume
               1... A Great Plains Version by the help of
               Young People in Everyday English.]

          Other editions; 1968, 1969.

     1974 The New Testament in Everyday English, by
          Don J. Klingensmith.
               Another edition, Revised, 1981.

1967 **Taylor, Kenneth** The Living New Testament, 1967.
     [See Complete Bibles for the entire entry.]

1968 **Anonymous**   The New Testament of Our Master
and Saviour Yahvahshua the Messiah (commonly called
Jesus Christ). Restoration of Original Name New
Testament is designed to restore to the scriptures
the Sacred Name of the MOST HIGH and His Son from
the Sacred Original on the Basis of the Rotherham
Version. Revised by Missionary Dispensary Bible
Research. Buena Park, Calif.: Missionary Dispensary
Bible Research, 1968.
     ["Yahweh" is used many times.]

     [See Complete Bibles, 1970 Anonymous, The Restoration of
     Original Sacred Name...]

1968 **Barclay, William**   The New Testament. A New
Translation. 2 Vols. London: Collins, 1968–1969.

1969 **Cressman, Annie** Good News for the World. Bombay:
Soon!, 1969.
     Reprint, 1971.

1969 **Ledyard, Gleason H.**   The New Life New Testament,
     translated by Gleason H. Ledyard.   Canby, Oregon:
     Christian Literature Foundation, 1969.
>   [Ledyard was for many years a missionary to the Eskimos
>   in the Canadian Central Arotic. "The reason for this
>   translation...is to take difficult words that are found
>   in most translations of the Bible and put them into
>   words or phrases that are easy to understand." The
>   vocabulary is limited to 850 words.]

     Also; The Children's New Testament.   Waco &
     London: Word Books, 1969.

     Another Edition; [Slightly revised], 1977.

1969 **Watchtower Bible and Tract Society**
     The Kingdom Interlinear Translation of the Greek
     Scriptures; Presenting   a   literal   word-for-word
     translation into English under the Greek text as set
     out in "The New Testament in the Original Greek –
     The Text Revised by Brooke Foss Westcott D.D. and
     Fenton John Anthony Hort D.D." (1948 Reprint)
     together with the New World Translation of the
     Christian Greek Scriptures, Revised Edition, a
     modern-language translation of the Westcott and Hort
     Greek Text, first published by them in the year 1881
     C.E., with which are included the valuable Foreword
     and the Appendix of the said translation, with
     numerous footnotes and an Explanation of the Symbols
     Used in the Marginal References. Produced by New
     World Bible Translation Committee. –1969 C.E.-
     Brooklyn, New York: Watchtower Bible and Tract
     Society of New York, Inc., International Bible
     Students Association, 1969.
>   Another   edition;   The   Kingdom   Interlinear
>   Translation of the Greek Scriptures.   Three
>   Bible Texts.
> >   [Greek Text Above
> > >   The New Testament in the Original Greek, by
> > >   B.F. Westcott and F.J.A. Hort – 1881
> >   English Text Underneath
> > >   An interlinear word-for-word translation
> > >   into English – 1969
> >   English Text Alongside
> > >   The New World Translation of the Holy
> > >   Scriptures, Matthew through Revelation –
> > >   1984 Revision]
     Rendered from the Original Greek Language by
     the New World Bible Translation Committee. –
     1985 Edition- Brooklyn, New York: Watchtower
     Bible and Tract Society of New York, Inc.,
     International Bible Students Association,
     1985.

1970 **Anonymous**   King James II Version of the New
     Testament. [Jay Green] Byron Center, Mi: Associated
     Publishers and Authors, Inc., 1970.
        [Retains the beauty, majesty and flow of the KJV. It
        removes only the Elizabethan English.]

     2nd Edition; April 1971. (Revised)

     3rd Edition; August 1971. (Revised)

1970 **Anonymous**   New Testament. Judaean and Authorized
     Version. Jerusalem: Judaean Publishing House, 1970.
        [The N.T. without Antisemitism. KJV with modifications.]

1972 **Anonymous**   King James Version New Testament –
     Twentieth Century Edition. [Jay Green]   MacDill
     A.F.B., FL: Tyndale Bible Society, 1972.

1972 **Klingensmith, Don J.** Today's English New Testament.
     By Don J. Klingensmith.   New York, Washington,
     Hollywood: Vantage Press, 1972.

1973 **Estes, Chester**   The Better Version of
     the New Testament, Based on the Greek Text According
     to Eminent Scholars and According to Certain
     Fundamental Principles of Biblical Interpretation,
     by Chester Estes. Muscle Shoals, Alabama: 1973.
        Second edition, 1975.

     Third edition, 1978.

1973 **New International Version** The New Testament, 1973.
        [See Complete Bibles, 1969 for the entire entry.]

1973 **Translator's N.T.**   The Translator's New Testament.
     London: British and Foreign Bible Society, 1973.
        Revised edition: 1979. [See Phil. 2:1]

1975 **Christianity Today**   The Greek – English New
     Testament: King James Version, New International
     Version, Greek   Text,   Literal   Interlinear.
     Washington, D.C.: Christianity Today, 1975.

1976 **Yeager, Randolph O.** The Renaissance New Testament,
     by Randolph O. Yeager. Vol. I. Bowling Green, Ky.:
     Renaissance Press, 1976.

1977 **Adams, Jay E.**   The Christian Counselor's New
     Testament. A New Translation in Everyday English
     with   notations,   Marginal   References,   and
     Supplemental helps by Jay E. Adams. Grand Rapids:
     Baker Book House, 1977.
        Revised, 1980

1978 **Anonymous**   The Simple English Bible - New
Testament. New York, New York: International Bible
Publishing Co., 1978.
Other editions, 1980, 1981.

1978 **Anonymous**   The New Testament: English Version
for the Deaf. Translated from the Greek Text. Grand
Rapids: Baker Book House, 1978.
["The New Testament. A New Easy-to-Read Version, 1978"
published by Baker appears to be the same text.]

[See The Holy Bible: English Version for the Deaf,
1987.]

1978 **Anonymous**   International Children's Version - New
Testament. Fort Worth, Tx.: Sweet Publishing, 1978.
Again; 1981, 1983.

[See Anonymous, Holy Bible. International Children's
Version, 1986.]

1979 **Abbott, John L.**   New Testament: Judgment Hour
Version by John L. Abbott. Queensland, Australia:
Published by the Author, 1979.
Second Edition, 1982.

Third Edition, 1987.

1979 **Adams, Jay E.**   The New Testament in Everyday
English. Jay E. Adams. Grand Rapids: Baker Book
House, 1979.
[Different from "The Christian Counselor's N.T.", 1977.
A few places are Acts 2:37, 43, 44; Acts 4:36...]

1980 **Greenhill, Roy**   The Distilled Bible: New Testament,
by Roy Greenhill. Stone Mountain, Georgia: Paul
Benjamin Publishers, 1980.
[This work is not a paraphrase nor a condensed version
similar to the Reader's Digest.]

1981 **Anonymous**   The Compact Bible - The New Testament...
in Fewer Words. [Edited by Pat Excel] Amboy, Wash.:
Oak Tree Press, 1981.

1981 **Anonymous**   May Your Name be Inscribed in the Book
of Life. Washington, D.C.: The Messianic Vision,
Publisher, 1981.
[A Messianic Jewish Version. Basically the KJV with
names for God and Christ changed.]

1983 **Lorimer, William Laughton**   The New Testament in
Scots. Edinburgh: 1983.

1984 **Anderson, Julian G.**   A New Accurate Translation
of the Greek New Testament into simple Everyday
American English with introduction, maps, pictures,

illustrations, cross-references, and explanatory notes for further study. By Rev. Julian G. Anderson. Naples, Florida: 1984.

1984 **New Century Version**   The Word; New Century Version. N.T. Fort Worth, TX: Sweet Publishing, 1984.

1985 **Schonfield, Hugh J.**   The Original New Testament; Edited and Translated from the Greek by the Jewish Historian of Christian Beginnings, by Hugh J. Schonfield.   San Francisco: Harper & Row, Publishers;   Cambridge, Hagerstown, New York, Philadelphia, London, Mexico City, Sao Paulo, Singapore, Sydney: 1985.

1985 **Witness Lee, John C. Ingalls and Others** The Recovery Version.   Anaheim, CA: Living Stream Ministry, 1985.
     [Others are: Bill Duane, Albert Knock.]

     [See index for all listings of the Recovery Version.]

1986 **Hagan, Lowell and Jack Westerhof**   Theirs is the Kingdom. The New Testament. Lowell Hagan and Jack Westerhof. Illustrations by Paul Stoub.   Grand Rapids, MI: Wm. B. Eerdmans Publishing Co.; Basingstoke, England: Marshall, Morgan & Scott Publications, Ltd., 1986.

1987 **Anonymous**   The New American Bible, Revised New Testament. Nashville: Catholic Bible Press, 1987.

1988 **Giessler, Phillip B**. God's Word to the Nations. The New Testament. Ed. Phillip B. Giessler. Luther Bible Soc. Revision Committee Staff. Cleveland, OH: Biblion Publishers, 1988.

1988 **McCord, Hugo**   New Testament. McCord's New Testament Translation of the Everlasting Gospel. By Hugo McCord. Henderson, TN: Freed-Hardeman College, 1988.

1989 **Cassirer, Heinz W.**   God's New Covenant. A New Testament Translation. Grand Rapids, MI: Wm. B. Eerdmans Publishing Co., 1989.

1989 **Sawyer, John Wesley** (Editor) The Newe Testament..., 1989.
     [See Willim Tyndale, (The New Testament), 1525.]

1989 **Stern, David H.** Jewish New Testament; a translation of the New Testament that expresses its Jewishness by David Stern... Jerusalem, Israel: Jewish New Testament Publications; Clarksville, Maryland: 1989.
     Second Printing; (With Corrections), 1989.

ABRIDGED NEW TESTAMENTS

???? **Cave, William**   [Abridged New Testament]
167? Antiquitates Christianae, or, the Life and Death of the Holy Jesus, [167?].

1676 Antiquitates Apostolicae: or, The History of the Lives, Acts and Martyrdom of the Holy Apostles of our Saviour, And the Two Evangelists, SS. Mark and Luke. To which is added an Introductory Discussion concerning the three great Dispensations of the Church, Patriarchal, Mosaical, and Evangelical. Being a Continuation of Antiquitates Christianae, or, the Life and Death of Holy Jesus. London: Printed by R. Norton, for R. Royston, 1676.

1593 **Coverdale, Myles**   Fruitful Lessons upon the Passion, Burial, Resurrection, Ascension and the Sending of the Holy Ghost Gathered out of the Foure Evangelists. London: Thomas Scarlett, 1539.

1744 **Collet, Samuel**   A Practical Paraphrase on the Epistles of St. Paul to the Romans, and the Galatians, and on The Epistle to the Hebrews. After the manner of the late Reverend Dr. Clark's Paraphrase on the Four Evangelists. London: J. Moon, 1744.

1755 **Anonymous**   The New Testament Adapted to the Capacities of Children. To which is added, an historical account of the Lives, Actions, Travels, Sufferings, and Death of the Apostles and Evangelists. With a Preface setting forth the Nature and Necessity of the Work. Adorned with Cuts; Designed by the celebrated Raphael and engraved by Mr. Walker. [John Newbery] London: for J. Newbery, 1755.

1777 **Chandler, Samuel**   A Paraphrase and Notes on the Epistles of Saint Paul to the Galatians and Ephesians: with Doctrinal and Practical Observations. Together with a Critical and Practical Commentary on the Two Epistles of Saint Paul to the Thessalonians. By the Late Learned Samuel Chandler, D.D. Published from the author's MS. by Nathaniel White.   London: Printed for Edward and Charles Dilly, 1777.

1836 **Craik, Henry**   Improved renderings of those passages of the English version of the New

Testament, which are capable of being more correctly translated. London: Nisbet, 1836.
>Another edition; London: Samuel Bagster & Sons, c1872.

1837 **Anonymous**   A Revision of the common or received English Translation of the Gospel and of the three Epistles of John, the Evangelists and Apostle...being an attempt to render clear and intelligible to the unlearned English reader the more obscure or ambiguous expressions of the Holy Evangelist. London: B. Fellowes, 1837.

1852 **Woodruff, Hezekiah**   An Exposition of the New Testament, or The New Covenant of our Sovereign Saviour. The Anointed. By Hezekiah Woodruff. Auburn [New York]: Henry Oliphant, 1852.
>["It is necessary to a full and complete translation of the original, that it should translate the idiom as well as the words." Omits Mark, Luke and John. The Book of Acts is entitled, "Doings of the Commissioners."]

[The only Gospel included is Matthew.]

1861 **Thorn, Leonard**   The New Testament of our Lord and Saviour Jesus Christ; As Revised and Corrected by the Spirits. Entered...in the year 1861, by Leonard Thorn... New York City: Published by the Proprietors, 1861.
>["...I, Jesus, came in spirit bodily, and revised and corrected the first four books of the new testament, namely, Matthew, Mark, Luke, John and also Revelations..." (Introductory Remarks). "James, Peter, John and Jude all came freely when called, and corrected their writings... Several pages of entirely new matter were by Jesus Christ. This, of course, is intended for spiritualists."]

1865 **Anonymous**   Controversial texts corrected, or, a selections of texts from the New Testament, which... have been made to give countenance to the popular doctrine of the Trinity, the proper Deity of Jesus, and the Atonement... by S.S.   Hull: William Hunt, 1865.

1868 **Anonymous**   The New Testament Narratives, in the words of the Sacred Writers, translated according to the Vulgate. With Notes, maps, etc. London: Burns, Oates & Co., 1868.

1870 **Anonymous**   Greek Testament Studies: or, a Contribution towards a revised translation of the New Testament... by Alquinus. London: B.M. Pickering, 1870.

1888 **Pollard, Josephine**   History of the New
     Testament in Words of One Syllable...with Ninety Six
     Illustrations, by Josephine Pollard. New York: A.L.
     Burt Co., 1888.

1910 **Pryse, James Morgan**   The Restored New
     Testament. 1910-1914.
          1910 The Apocalypse Unsealed: being an
               esoteric interpretation of the Initiation
               of Ionnes... commonly called the
               Revelation of (St.) John, with a new
               translation. By James M. Pryse. Los
               Angeles, California & New York: John M.
               Pryse; London: J.M. Watkins.

          1914 The Restored New Testament. The Hellenic
               fragments, freed from the pseudo-Jewish
               interpolations, harmonized, and done into
               English verse and prose. With
               introductory analyses, and commentaries,
               giving an interpretation according to
               ancient philosophy and Psychology and a
               new literal translation of the Synoptic
               Gospels, [also the Apocalypse] with
               introduction and commentaries. By James
               M. Pryse. London: John M. Watkins; New
               York: John M. Pryse.
                    Second Edition, 1916.

                    Third Edition, 1925.

               ["The prose translation of the Apocalypse is strictly
               literal; that of the composite Gospel formed from the
               Synoptics, although a free rendering, follows the Greek
               text faithfully except in some passages which by their
               pitiable poverty of expression called for expansion, and
               in others which have been so falsified by the
               ecclesiastical forgers that the meaning of the original
               is now but a matter of conjecture." Consists of Part
               First: The Anointing of Iesous (Restored from the
               Synoptic Gospels), The Crowning of Jesus (Metrical
               Version), Selections from the Fourth Gospel, The
               Initiation of Ioannes (Prose Version of the Apocalypse)
               Initiation (Metrical Version of the Apocalypse), Letter
               to the Galatians, Letter to the Korinthians, Letter to
               the Thessalonikans. Part Second: The Synoptic gospels,
               Translated into Modern English, with Comments on the
               Spurious Portions.]

1925 **Loveland, Seymour**   Illustrated Bible Story Book -
     N.T.; Stories retold for little children by Seymour
     Loveland. Chicago & New York: Rand McNally & Co.,
     1925.

1931 **Boggs, Norman Towar**   The Christian Saga, 1931.

1939 **Clarke, W.K. Lowther**   The New Testament
Shortened. London: National Society, 1939.
[AV text abridged with some alterations and change.]

1939 **Schonfield, Hugh J.**   ["...the story of the
beginnings of Christianity..."] London: n.p., 1939
- 1948.
1939 Jesus - a Biography
Reprinted; Banner Books, 1948.

1946 The Jew of Tarsus. An Unorthodox Portrait
of Paul. MacDonald & Co. Ltd.

1948 Saints Against Caesar; the rise and
reactions of the first Christian
community. With the book of Revelation in
a new translation and commentary. London:
MacDonald & Co. Ltd.

["... I have not hesitated to retranslate from the Greek
where an obscurity exists (in the KJV)..."]

1941 **Binsse, Harry Lorin**   The Living Thoughts of St.
Paul. Presented by Jacques Mauritain [Translation
from "La Pensee de Saint Paul"] by Harry Lorin
Binsse. New York & Toronto: Longmans & Co., 1941.
[Extracts from the Epistles and Acts.]

1949 **Arendzen, J.P.**   Paul of Tarsus. Fragments
of an Autobiography ...London: Grail Publications,
1949.
[Extracts from the N.T., partly in paraphrase.]

1951 **Anonymous**   The Way into the Kingdom. London:
Epworth Press, 1951.
[Translation from the N.T., with a commentary.]

1964 **Violi, Unicio J.**   Review Notes and Study Guide
to the New Testament by Unicio J. Violi. New York:
Monarch Press Inc., 1964.
["The quotations are taken from the KJV of the Bible
(1611)... All obsolete and unfamiliar words are
immediately translated in parenthesis. The most complete
commentary to the synoptics is that of Matthew... Since
the other gospels largely repeat details and incidents
in the life of Jesus, the commentary on the Gospels of
Mark and Luke is devoted to the episodes that are not
repeated in all three synoptics." There is also a
commentary on the O.T. in this series, but it contains
no text.]

1967 **Dale, Alan T.**   New World. The Heart of the New
Testament in Plain English.   London: Oxford
University Press, 1967.
Reprinted; 1968, 1969, 1970, 1972.

NEW TESTAMENT SELECTIONS

???? **Hahn, Stanley R.** Soul Winner's New Testament. Using primarily the edition of 1611...together with the translation of Stanley R. Hahn, Th.D., of certain key verses and passages which appear in italics directly beneath the verse and bearing the same number as the verse which contains transliterated words, together with notes. Philadelphia, Pa., U.S.A.: National Bible Press, [195?].

> Revised edition; made especially for the Clift Brannon Evangelic Association. Philadelphia, Pa., U.S.A.: National Bible Press, 1959.
>
> > [Hahn's translation covers those verses including the word "Baptize"; each verse is given in a rather literal translation, with the word "Immerse" instead.]

> Another edition; The Soul Winner's N.T. Translated out of the Original Tongues and with the Former Translations diligently compared - Commonly Known As The Authorized (King James) Version of 1611 AD. Revised. 1972 Tenth Edition made especially for the Clift Brannon Evangelical Association.
>
> > [In this edition the retranslated verses are given in the notes at the foot of each page.]

1066 **Anonymous**   The Four Gospels, the Gospel of Nicodemus, the Embassy of Nathan the Jew to Tiberius, and the Story of Veronica - - all in Anglo-Saxon. Cambridge University Library, Cambridge MS. Ii.2.II, c1066.

1380 **Anonymous**   New Testament ["...nearly half of the N.T., entirely independent of the Wycliffite version." Acts, Epistles (Except Philemon) and Matthew I-VI:13 MS. 1380-1420] 1380-1420.

> 1380 Cambridge, University Library Dd.XII.39 (Midlands Acts)

> 1400 Oxford, Bodleian Library, Douce 250 (Acts, Matthew, Southern Epistles)

> 1400 Cambridge, Selwyn College 108.1.1 (Acts, Matthew, No Midlands Catholic Epistles)

> 1420 Cambridge, Corpus Christi, Parker 434 (Copy of Douce 250)

> 1902 A Fourteenth Century English Biblical version, consisting of a prologue and parts of the New Testament. Edited from the Manuscripts, together with some

introductory chapters on Middle English
Biblical versions (prose translations) By
permission of the Philosophical Faculty
of Upsala... Edited by Anna C. Paues.
Cambridge: University Press, 1902.

1904 A Fourteenth Century English Biblical
Version, from MSS containing a
translation of nearly half of the New
Testament, entirely independent of the
Wycliffite Version. Edited by Anna C.
Paues. Cambridge: University Press, 1904.

[This second edition lacks the
introduction, but contains additional
material in an appendix including a version
of the General Epistles.]

1974 A Fourteenth Century English Biblical
Version. New York: Ams Press, 1974.
[This is a reprint of the 1904 Edition.]

1705 **Stanhope, George**   A paraphrase and comment upon
the Epistles and Gospels appointed to be used in the
Church of England on all Sundays and Holy-Days
throughout the year. By George Stanhope... 4 Vols.
London: S.Keble, R. Sare, 1705-1709.
A new edition, in two volumes. Oxford: University
Press, 1851.

[Many times reprinted.]

1761 **Heylyn, John**   An Interpretation of the
New Testament ...containing Acts of the Apostles and
several Epistles, 1761.

1781 **Wakefield, Gilbert**   A new translation of those
parts only of the New Testament which are wrongly
translated in our Common Version. By Gilbert
Wakefield. 1781.

1789 **Symonds, John**   ...Observations on the expediency
of revising the present English version, by John
Symonds. Cambridge: 1789-1794.
1789 The Gospels... and the Acts of the
Apostles...
1794 The Epistles...

[Contains many corrections of the KJV.]

1807 **Evanson, Edward**   A New Testament; or, the New
Covenant according to Luke, Paul and John. Published
in conformity to the plan of the late Rev. Edward
Evanson. London: Printed by R. Taylor & Co. for
Richard Phillips, and sold by J. Johnson, 1807.

["The translation here given of the authorised
Scriptures is, with some exception, taken from the
venerable Archbishop Newcome's version..." Consists of
the greater part of Luke, Acts, 1 & 2 Corinthians, 1 &
2 Timothy, Titus & Philemon. Edited by Timothy Brown.]

1832 Scholefield, James   Hints for an
Improved Translation of the New Testament by James
Scholefield. n.p.: n.p., 1832.
Re-edited, 1836, 1849.

1836 Anonymous   A Literal Translation of the Apostolic
Epistles and Revelation..., 1836-1839.
1836 The Catholic Epistles and Revelation (A
Literal translation and commentary).
Preface signed W.H. London: C. & W.
Reynell.

1839 A Literal Translation of the Apostolical
Epistles and Revelation, with a
Concurrent Commentary. [William Heberden]
London: Printed for J.G. & F. Rivington,
St. Paul's Churchyard, and Waterloo
Place, Pall Mall, 1839.

1837 Fellowes, B.   A Revision of the Gospel and
Third Epistle of John... London: 1837.

1848 Browne, H.   Homilies on the Gospel According
to St. John, and his First Epistle by S. Augustine,
Bishop of Hippo; Translated, with Notes and Indices.
In Two Volumes. By H. Browne. Oxford: John Henry
Parker; London: F. & J. Rivington, 1848.

1849 Turnbull, Joseph   The Epistles and Revelation.
1849-1858.
1849 The Second Letter of Paul the
Apostle to the Corinthians.
Translated according to the present
English idiom. [Greek and English]
London: The Author.

1851 The Epistle of Paul to the Romans.
An original translation from the
Greek text. London: S. Bagster &
Sons.

1854 The Epistles of Paul the Apostle, an
original translation, with critical
notes and introduction. London: S.
Bagster & Sons.

1858 The Seven Epistles of James, Peter,
John, and Jude, and the Revelation,
translated from the original Greek.

With critical notes, and a dissertation on the authenticity of 1 John v.7,8 respecting the heavenly witnesses. London: S. Bagster & Sons.

1872 The Epistles and Revelation. An Original Translation of the whole of the Epistles and the Book of Revelation, with Critical Notes. London: Samuel Bagster & Sons.

1857 **Green, Thomas Sheldon**   The New Testament translated by Thomas Sheldon Green... London: S. Bagster and Sons, [1857?]
[St. Matthew and Romans, only. No more published in this form; see 1865.]

1861 **American Bible Union**   The Sacred Scriptures.. New York: American Bible Union, 1861.
[All quarto parts issued to date in one "immense" volume.]

1861 **Anonymous**   Facsimiles of Certain Portions of the Gospel of St. Matthew, and the Epistles of Ss. James & Jude, written on papyrus in the first century, and preserved in the Egyptian Museum of Joseph Mayer, Esq. Liverpool. [G.P. Silke] London: Trubner & Co., 1861.
[Greek and English]

1869 **Tischendorf, Constantine**   The New Testament: the authorised English version; with introduction, and various readings from the three most celebrated manuscripts of the original Greek text. By Constantine Tischendorf. Tauchnitz Edition, Volume 1000. Leipzig: Bernhard Tauchnitz; London: Sampson Low, Sons, and Marston, 1869.
["While the text of the English AV is faithfully represented in this edition, such texts as differs from it in the three great authorities (Sinaitic, Alexandrine and Vatican codices) are indicated in the notes."]

1870 **Ellicott, Charles John**   Considerations on the Revision of the English Version of the New Testament.   London: Longmans, Green, Reader, and Dyer, 1870.
[Includes "...some samples of revision, textual and grammatical... The Portions chosen are the Sermon on the Mount, and four of the most difficult chapters of St. Paul's Epistle to the Romans..." St. Matthew Chapters V, VI, & VII; Epistle to the Romans Chapters V, VI, VII, & VIII.]

1877 **Anonymous**   A New Biblia Pauperum.

[Biblia Pauperum means "Bible of the Poor". Only 250 copies were issued.]

Another Edition; A Smaller Biblia Pauperum conteynynge Thyrtie and Eyghte Wodecuttes illvstratynge The Lyfe, Parablis, and Miraclis off Oure Bleffid Lorde and Savioure Jesus Crift,... Iohn Wiclif,...   M.D.CCC.LXXXIV. [1884]

1887 **Tafel, Leonard, Rudolph L. Tafel and L.H. Tafel** Interlinear translation of the New Testament. By Leonard Tafel, Rudolph L. Tafel, and L.H. Tafel. Vol. I. New York: 1887?
[Contains the Gospels, Acts, and the Apocalypse.]

1891 **Stellhorn, F.W.**   A Brief Commentary on the New Testament, by F.W. Stellhorn. Columbus, Ohio: The Lutheran Book Concern, 1891-1899.
    1891 - - Vol. 1. The Four Gospels
    1899 - - Vol. 2. Paul's Epistle to the Romans

[Text is a slightly altered KJV.]

1896 **Anonymous**   The Sermon on the Mount. and other extracts, from the New Testament. A faithful rendering of the original and explanatory notes by Aretas. Reprinted from the _Irish Theosophist_. Toronto: _The Lamp_, 1896.
    Another edition; James M. Pryse. Elliott B. Page & Co., 1899.

    Also; The Sermon on the Mount and Other Extracts from the New Testament; A Verbatim Translation from the Greek, with Notes on the Mystical or Arcane Sense.   New York: Theosophical Society, 1904.

[Includes Matthew IV.23 to VI.27 and other passages from Matthew, Luke, and I Corinthians, also the Epistles of James & Jude. "The (1904) translation has been carefully revised..." A different version from that in Pryse's Restored N.T., 1914.]

1902 **Paues, Anna C.**   See Anonymous, New Testament, 1380.

1902 **Sampson, Gerard**   The Layman's Bible Series... The English text and paraphrases of each verse in parallel columns... 5 Vols. London & Oxford: A.R. Mowbray & Co., 1902-1904.
[John, Romans, Hebrews, and Peter.]

1903 **Forster, Henry Langstaff** [N.T. Selections] 1903-1906.
    1903 The Revelation... Tasmania: H.L. Forster.

1906 St. John's Gospel, Epistles, and Revelation... Adelaide: Hunkin, Ellis and King.

1910 **Wright, Joseph** Grammar of the Gothic Language and the Gospel of Mark. Selections from other Gospels and the Second Epistle to Timothy with Notes and Glossary by Joseph Wright... Oxford: at the Claredon Press, 1910.
[Title taken from the second edition.]

Reprinted; 1917, 1921, 1924, 1937, 1946, 1949.

Second Edition; 1954.
Reprinted; 1958, 1963, 1966, 1968.

1912 **Nutt, David** Epistles and Apocalypse from the Codex Hareianus. London: 1912.

1912 **Strafford, Countess of** Selections of Texts from the Tauchnitz edition of the New Testament. With parallel readings from the Sinaitic, Vatican, and Alexandrian codices. Compiled and arranged by the Countess of Strafford. Revised and enlarged edition. London: Elliot Stock, 1912.

1914 **Concordant Version** Concordant Version of the Sacred Scriptures. Los Angeles: Concordant Publishing Concern, 1914 -1968.
   1914 Paul's Epistle to the Romans with Framework, and Ephesians, Philippians, Colossians, and I and II Thessalonians with Framework.

   1919 The Unveiling of Jesus Christ. (Revelation) Greek with sublinear, version and notes.

   1919 The Unveiling of Jesus Christ. (Revelation) Greek with sublinear and version. Popular Edition. First revision. [No notes. This edition was printed for the International Society of Bible Students now known as the Watchtower, Bible and Tract Society. The Order was canceled before issues were shipped.]

   1919 The Unveiling of Jesus Christ. (Revelation) Version with Notes.

   1922 The Unveiling of Jesus Christ. Third edition.

   1923 Romans - Galatians.

1923 Ephesians – Philemon

1923 Acts – Unveiling (known as vol. 2.)

1924 Hebrews to Jude.

1925 Concordant Version...John's Account.

1926 Matthew, Mark and Luke along with a 4th edition of the Unveiling.

1926 Concordant Version, The Sacred Scriptures. Designed to put the English reader in possession of all the vital facts of Divine revelation without a former knowledge of Greek by means of A Restored Greek Text with Various Readings, conforming, as far as possible, to the inspired autographs; A Consistent Sublinear, based upon a Standard English Version with notes. which are linked together and corrected for the English reader by means of an English Concordance and Lexicon and a complementary list of The Greek Elements.

1927 Pocket Edition [New Testament] Concordant Version. The Sacred Scriptures. An Idiomatic, Consistent English Version, Conforming to the Basic Laws of Language, in that, as far as Possible Each English Expression Constantly Represents its Closest Greek Equivalent, and Each Greek Word is Translated by Exclusive English Rendering...
        [English Text only. 10,000 copies.]

1931 Concordant Version, The Sacred Scriptures. Designed to put the English reader in possession of all the vital facts of Divine revelation without a former knowledge of Greek by means of A Restored Greek Text... A Uniform Sublinear... A Consistent, Emphasized English Version with notes...An English Concordance and Lexicon...Completely Revised, 1930.

1944 Revised International Edition – Concordant Version. The Sacred Scriptures. "New Testament". An Idiomatic, Consistent, Emphasized Version...

1955 Greek Sub - and Superlinear Concordant Version of the Sacred Scriptures, New Testament, A Restored Greek Text with Sublinear.

1966 The Memorial Edition of the Concordant Literal New Testament.

[Also see Old Testament Selections, 1957 Anonymous, Concordant Version.]

1915 **Boddard, Dwight**   The Good News from a Spiritual Realm. Ann Arbor Press, 1915.

1917 **Ballantine, Frank Schell**   Thinking Good is Thanking God. By Frank Schell Ballantine.   Philadelphia: Henry Altemus Company. [1917]

1917 **Ballantine, Frank Schell**   Thinking Right is Living Right. By Frank Schell Ballantine.   Philadelphia: Henry Altemus Company. [1917]

1918 **Buchanan, Edgar Simmons**   (UnJudaized Version) From the Huntington Palimpsest Formerly in the Library of Tarragonagona Cathedral, now in the Collection of the Hispanic Society of America, NY. Deciphered and Translated from the oldest known Latin Text. 3 Vols. London: C.F. Roworth, 1918.
      [Luke, John and Acts.]

1920 **Ballantine, Frank Schell**   Science and Scripture Health; the new medicine (moral and preventive). By Craig MacCameline [Pseud. for Frank Schell Ballantine]. Detroit: The Craigie Publishing Co. [1920]
      [Contains translations of Mark, Philippians, and the first three chapters of the Gospel to John "printed as a modern book for present day American readers."]

      Another edition; Collegeville, Pa.: The Craigie Publishing Co., 1931.

      Also; Some Leaves from my Book, Science and Scripture Health by Frank Schell Ballantine. Collegeville, Pa.: The Craigie Publishing Co., n.d.

1923 **Sommer, D.A.**   Simplified New Testament, authorized version... simplified translations of hundreds of hard passages...Edited by D.A.Sommer. Indianapolis: "Simplified Bible" House, [1923].

1934 **Royds, Thomas Fletcher**   The Epistles and Gospels for the Sundays and chief holy days of the Christian year. A new translation...with some Collects and

Prayers. By Thomas Fletcher Royds. Oxford: Basil Blackwell, 1934.

1936 **Gellibrand, Edward**   Jesus Manifest; by Dmitri Merijkowski... translated [From the Russian]. New York: Charles Scribner's Sons, 1936.
[Contains a translation of miscellaneous N.T. verses.]

1937 **Dana, H. E.**   The Epistles and Apocalypse of John. Kansas City, Kansas: Central Seminary Press, 1937. Again, 1947.

1939 **Grant, Frederick C.**   The Message of Jesus Christ; the tradition of the early Christian communities; restored and translated into German by Martin Dibelius; translated into English by Frederick C. Grant. New York: Charles Scribner's Sons, 1939.

1940 **Boylan, Patrick**   The Sunday Epistles and Gospels with Commentaries and Suggestions for use in Preaching. 2 vols. Dublin: Browne & Nolan Ltd., 1940–1941.

1940 **Wuest, Kenneth S.**   Word Studies...in the Greek New Testament for the English Reader. By Kenneth S. Wuest. Grand Rapids, Michigan: William B. Eerdmans Publishing Co., 1940–1963.

        1940 – – Golden Nuggets...   Third Edition, 1943.
        1950 – – Mark... Also; London: 1956.
        1955 – – Romans... Also; London: 1956.
        1944 – – Galatians...   Other Editions; 1948, 1962.
        1953 – – Ephesians & Colossians...
        1942 – – Philippians...
        1947 – – Hebrews... Also; London: 1956.
        1952 – – Pastorial Epistles...
        1942 – – First Peter... Another Edition, 1963.
        1954 – – In These Last Days. II Peter; I, II, & III John and Jude...   Another Edition, 1963.
        1963 – – Bypaths in the Greek New Testament...
        1942 – – Untranslatable Riches from the Greek New Testament...

[Each volume includes a commentary and a "...fuller New Testament..."]

1945 **Heywood, D. Herbert**   New Era Testament. A Revival of Greek and Coptic Christianity and Platonism. Prepared for World Associations of Churches for Human Welfare and Progress and for the Mental

Scientists Association Church.   Los Angeles:
Metropolitan University Press, 1945.
> [Includes a translation of "The Gospel of Mark...;
> "Sermon on the Mount, from Mathaies Chapter 5, 6 & 7";
> "The Gospel of John, Prologue, Chapters 13, 14 & 15;
> Romans, Twelfth Chapter; and numerous excerpts from...
> The work is based on the assumption that Jesus was a
> member of an Alexandrian medical cult from the Greek
> community of the Decapelis..."]

> Other editions; 1947, 1950, 1949.

> Reprinted; 1950, by D. Herbert Heywood - A
> Revival of Greek and Cepric Christianity...

1946 **Knox, Ronald Arbuthnott**   The Epistles and Gospels
for Sundays and Holydays, translation and commentary
by Ronald A. Knox. New York: Sheed & Ward, 1946.
> [Same as N.T., 1944?]

> Again; 1953.

1953 **Hendriksen, William**   New Testament Commentary...
Grand Rapids, Michigan: Baker Book House, 1953-
> ["A commentary offering the student an introduction, new
> translation, commentary, summary, critical notes, and
> bibliography."]

> 196? - - Matthew
> 1953-4 - - The Gospel of John (two vols.)
> 19?? - - Galatians
> 1966 - - Ephesians
> 1962 - - Philippians
> 1964 - - Colossians & Philemon
> 1955 - - I & II Thessalonians
> 1957 - - Pastoral Epistles (I & II Timothy -
>   Titus)

1956 **Cox, Ronald**   New Testament Narrative based
on the translation ...by Ronald Knox, arranged in a
continuous narrative with explanations by Ronald
Cox... London: Burns & Oates;   New York: Sheed &
Ward, 1956-1958.
> 1958 The Gospel Story...

> 1956 It is Paul Who Writes... The Epistle of
>   St. Paul & of the Acts of the Apostles

> ["Where the Greek is different from the Knox text, I
> have made corrections. The more important of these have
> been made by Mgr. Knox himself..."]

1959 **Bowie, Walter Russell**   The Living Story of the New
Testament. Illustrated by Douglas Rosa. Engelwood
Cliffs, NJ: Prentice-Hall, 1959.

1961 **Badley, J.H.**   A Bible for Modern Readers (and what it means for us). The New Testament selected and rearranged by J.H. Badley... London: James Clarke & Co. Ltd., 1961.

1961 **Harington, Jay**   Paul of Tarsus. Cleveland & New York: Shepherd Books, The World Publishing Co., 1961.
   [A dramatic re-creation of the Acts of the Apostles and the Letters of St. Paul.]

1968 **Siecker, A.**   Challenge; the sayings of Jesus in a modern setting. A. Siecker. New York: Vantage Press, 1968.

1969 **Jordan, Clarence**   The Cotton Patch Version of Luke and Acts. Jesus' Doings and the Happenings. A modern translation with a Southern accent, fervent, earthy, rich in humor. New York: Association Press, 1969.

1971 **Poehlmann, William R. and Robert J. Karris**
A Commentary on the Epistle to the Colossians and to Philemon by Eduard Lohse. Translated by William R. Poehlmann and Robert J. Karris. Edited by Helmut Koester. Philadelphia: Fortress Press, 1971.

1974 **Anonymous**   Walk with Me in Modern English. One chronological story as combined from the Four Gospels and the first chapter of the Book of Acts. Meriden, Conn.: Published by Tampco, 1974.
   [Copyright by The Anointed Music and Publishing Co.]

   Also; An Abridged Version, 1974.

1976 **Bergman, Jerry**   Miscellaneous Verses. MS. Titled: Guilt - A Spiritual or Psychological Problem? by Jerry Bergman,Ph.D., 1976.

1977 **Haugerud, Joann**   The Word for Us; the Gospels of John and Mark, Epistles to the Romans and the Galatians Restated in Inclusive Language, by Joann Haugerud. Seattle: Published by Coalition on Women and Religion, 1977.
   Reprinted, 1981.

1983 **Bauckham, Richard J.**   Word Biblical Commentary. Jude, 2 Peter. Richard J. Bauckham. Waco, TX: Wood Books, Publisher, 1983.
   [See Complete Bibles, 1982 Word Biblical Commentary, Vol. 50.]

14

Gospels

GOSPEL LISTINGS

???? **Gaus, Andy**   The Unvarnished Gospels. Translated by Andy Gaus.
[A contemporary translation of the Greek.]

???? **Anonymous**   Hortus Animae; or, Garden of the Soule: Being a Manual...
[See Bible Selections for the complete entry.]

???? **Funk, Robert**   New Gospel Parallels. 2 Vols. Polebridge Press, [19??].
[The translation is the New Scholars Version.]

???? **Tafel, Leonard, Rudolph L. Tafel and L.H. Tafel** Interlinear Translation of... Gospels...
[See Bible Selections for the complete entry.]

700 **Egbert**   [The Gospels in Anglo-Saxon] c700.

950 **Aldred**   Interlinear Gloss, Lindisfarne Gospels.

1000 **Anonymous**   The Four Gospels. Cotton MS. Otho C.i. Bosworth III, or "Cot", c1000?

1025 **Anonymous**   The Gospels in Anglo-Saxon or Wessex. British Museum, Royal MS: Bibliotheca Regia I.A.xiv, Bosworth V or RL, c1025.

1050 **Anonymous**   The Four Gospels in Saxon. Bodley 441, Bosworth VI, c1050.

1066 **Anonymous**   The Four Gospels,the Gospel of Nicodemus, the Embassy of Nathan the Jew...
[See New Testament Selections for the complete entry.]

1150 **Anonymous**   The Four Gospels in Anglo-Saxon. The Hatton MS. Bodleian, No.38, Bosworth IV or H, c1150.

1300 **Anonymous**   Sunday Verse Gospels.
[Translated from the rhymed French Gospels of Robert Greatham, probably by an Austin canon or parish priest.]

1566 **Beacon, Thomas**   The Gospels for all Sundays. London: Thomas Marshe, 1566.

1569 **Golding, Arthur**   The Gospels for Sunday's and Saints Days. London: Henry Bynneman, 1569.

1571 **Anonymous**   The Gospels of the Fower Euangelistes translated in the olde Saxons tyme out of Latin into the vulgare tounge of the Saxons, newly collected out of the Auncient Monumentes of the sayd Saxons, and now published for testimonie of the same.   At London: Iohn Daye dwelling over Aldersgate. 1571.
["Printed in parallel with the English of the Bishops' Bible of 1568." Preface by John Foxe.]

Another edition; The Gospels of the Fower Evangelistes translated in the olde Saxons tyme out of Latin into the vulgare toung of the Saxons, the Auncient monumentes of the sayd Saxons. London: 1571. [In Saxon and English]

1701 **Clarke, Samuel**   Paraphrase of the Four Evangelists. 2 Vols. London: for the Bookseller, 1701.
[Unknown if same as that dated 1765. See New Testaments, 1765 Samuel Clarke and Thomas Pyle.]

Again; 1795.

1707 **Anonymous**   Moral Reflections upon the [Four Gospels] Translated from the French [of P. Quesnel]. London: 1707-1709.
1707 the Gospel of St. Mark   ["F.T."]

1707 the Gospel of St. Luke
[T. Whittenhall?]

1709 the Gospel of St. Matthew
[T. Whittenhall?]

1709 the Gospel of St. John   [Anon]

1719 **Russel, Richard**   The Four Gospels, with moral reflections, translated from the French of Paschal Quesnel. 4 Vols. 1719-1725.

1749 **Heylyn, John**   Theological Lectures at Westminster Abbey with Interpretation of the Four Gospels, 1749.

1788 **Anonymous**   The Four Gospels, with
a comment, and reflections both spiritual and moral,
by Pasquier Quesnel. Translated from the French.
Revised, corrected, and the Popish errors expunged,
by a Presbyter of the Church of England. [Clement
Crutwell] 2 vols. Bath: S. Hazard, 1788-1790.

1789 **Campbell, George** The Four Gospels, translated from
the Greek, with preliminary dissertations, and notes
critical and explanatory. By George Campbell... 2
Vols. London: For A. Strahan and T. Cadell, 1789.
    1st. American Edition; The Four Gospels,
    translated from the Greek. With Preliminary
    Dissertations, and notes Critical and
    explanatory. By George Campbell...
    Philadelphia: Printed by Thomas Dobson...,
    1796.
        [The Deity is rendered "Jehovah" at Luke 20:43
        footnote.]

    Other editions; Philadelphia: Printed by Thomas
    Dobson, 1796; Philadelphia: Printed by A.
    Bartram, 1799; 4 Vols. Aberdeen: J. Chalmers
    & Co., 1803 -4; 2 Vols. Edinburgh: 1807.

    Revised edition. 3 Vols. London: 1812.

    Other editions; 4 Vols. Boston: Published by W.
    Wells and T.B. Wait, 1811; Aberdeen: D.
    Chalmers & Co., 1814; With Author's Last
    Corrections. Boston: By True and Greene,
    Printers...Published by Timothy Bedington and
    Charles Ewer, 1824; 2 Vols. London: Printed
    for T.Tegg & Son, 1834; 2 Vols. Andover &
    New York: Printed & Published by Gould and
    Newman, 1837.

1801 **Darling, Ralph**   A Poetical Version of the Four
Gospels. Hull: Robert Peck, 1801.
    ["...the writer...has limited himself to the faithful
    expression in verse, of what our learned and pious
    translators of the scriptures have executed in prose."]

1805 **Anonymous** [The Four Gospels]...Translated from the
Original Greek, and illustrated by Extracts from the
Theological Writings of that Eminent servant of the
Lord, the Hon. Emanuel Swedenborg, together with
notes and observations of the translator, annexed to
each chapter. [J. Clowes]
    1805 The Gospel according to Matthew...London:
    I.& E. Hodson.
        Second edition; London: I. & E. Hodson.

    1826 The Gospel according to Mark...
    Manchester: W.& W. Clarke.

Second edition; thoroughly revised, D. Howarth and J.H. Smithson. London: W. White, J.S. Hodson, 1858.

1823 The Gospel according to Luke... Manchester: W.D. Varey.
Second edition; revised. London: Hodson, 1852.

1819 The Gospel according to John... Manchester: J. Gleave
Second edition; Manchester: J. Gleave, 1838.

["...in regard to the translation of the Gospel from the original Greek, the Editor wishes to remark that he has endeavored to make it as literal as possible, consistent with the different idioms of the two languages."]

1807 **Kenrick, Timothy**   An Exposition of the Historical Writings of the New Testament, with reflections subjoined to each section. In Three Vols. Birmingham, England: J. Belcher & Son, 1807.
["The Common translation has been taken as the basis of this exposition, and variations from it are distinguished by the italic characters and inverted commas..."]

Second edition; London: 1824.
["...some verbal alterations and occasional differences of arrangement..."]

Another edition; From the Second London Octavo Edition. Boston: Munroe and Francis, 1828.

1834 **Anonymous**   The Triglott Evangelists, Interlinear: consisting of the Original Greek, from the Text of Griesbach; The Latin taken from Montanus, Beza, and the Vulgate; and the English of the AV, Accommodated to the Greek Idiom: With Grammatical and Historical Notes, Indexes, &c. to which is added, A Grammar containing the Idiomatic Peculiarities of the New Testament. London: Printed for John Taylor by Thomas, 1834.
[Preface is signed "H.H.D."]

1836 **Anonymous**   A new version of the Four Gospels; with notes critical and explanatory, by a catholic. [John Lingard] London: Joseph Booker, 1836.
Another edition; London: C. Dolman, 1851.

1836 **Bradford, Alden**   Evangelical History; or the Books of the New Testament; with a General Introduction, a Preface to Each Book, and Notes, Explanatory and Critical. In Two Volumes. By Alden Bradford   Vol.1

Containing the Four Gospels. Boston: Joseph Dowe, 1836.
> [There is no record of volume two ever being published.]

1841 Anonymous Catena Aurea. Commentary on the Four Gospels, collected out of the works of the Fathers by S.Thomas Aquinus. [Mark Pattison, T.D. Ryder, and J.D. Dulgarius] 4 Vols. Oxford: J.H. Parker, 1841-1845.
> [With the text translated from the Latin. Preface signed J.H.N. (John Henry Newman)]

1842 Thorpe, Benjamin Da Halgan Godspel on Englisc. The Anglo-Saxon Version of the Holy Gospels, edited from the Original MMS, by Benjamin Thorpe. London: J.G.F. & J. Rivington, 1842.
> Another Edition; New York: Wiley & Putnam, 1846.

1846 Greenleaf, Simon An Examination of the Testimony of the Four Evangelists, by the Rules of Evidence administered in Courts of Justice. With an account of the Trial of Jesus. By Simon Greenleaf..., Royall Professor of Law in Harvard University. Boston: Charles C. Little and James Brown, 1846.
> [Contains the Four Gospels as arranged by Archbishop Newcome with the corrections by Dr. Robinson.]

1849 Kenrick, Frances Patrick The Four Gospels, 1849.
> [See Complete Bibles, 1849 for the entire entry.]

1855 Norton, Andrews A Translation of the Gospels. With Notes. By Andrews Norton. 2 Vols. Boston: Little Brown & Co., 1855.
> [Published posthumously by Ezra Abbot and his son, Charles Eliot Norton. The first three chapters of Matthew are omitted.]

> Another edition, 1856.

> Ninth Edition; Cambridge: John Wilson & Son, 1890.

> Sixth edition; John Wilson & Son, 1883.

> [Reprinted several times.]

1858 Cureton, William Remains of a Very Ancient Recension of the Gospels in Syriac, hitherto unknown in Europe, discovered, edited, and translated by William Cureton... 2 Pts. London: John Murray, 1858.
> ["My great object has been to make it as literal as I could...for this purpose, I have retained the order of the Syriac words, so far as it seemed possible to do so without obscurity. It has been my intention also to render always the same Syriac term by the same English word."]

1858 **Knowles, William J.**   Poetical Expression of the
Gospels by William J. Knowles. Boston: Published by
the Author; Henry J. Howland, Printer, 1858.
> ["The Gospels I've presented here, so plain and simple
> too, The little child who reads with care may find the
> sayings true, Should I encouragement receive, the same
> as heretofore, Remaining portions soon will give, which
> I've laid up in store."]

Another edition, 1860.

1860 **Morison, John H.**   Disquisition and Notes on the
Gospels ... Boston: Walker, Wise and Co., 1860-186?
>   1860 - - Matthew (2nd ed., 1861)
>   18?? - - Mark
>   18?? - - Luke
>   18?? - - John

> ["...the text which is here followed in all the
> variations which are of consequence enough to warrant a
> departure from the reading of our Common English
> Version, is Tischendorf's Stereotype Edition of the
> N.T., published in 1850."]

1863 **Brameld, G. William**   The Holy Gospels, translated
from the Original Greek: the spurious passages
explained; the doubtful bracketed; and the whole
revised after the texts of Griesbach, Lachmann,
Tischendorf, Alford, and Tregelles. With notes and
critical appendix. London: Longman, Green, Longman,
Roberts & Green, 1863.

1865 **Bosworth, Joseph** The Gothic and Anglo-Saxon Gospels
in Parallel columns with the versions of Wycliffe
and Tyndale... London: John Russell Smith, 1865.
> Also; London: Gibbrup, 1907.

1869 **Folsom, Nathaniel S.**   The Four Gospels: translated
from the Greek text of Tischendorf, with the various
readings of Griesbach, Lachmann, Tischendorf,
Tregelles, Meyer, Alford, and Others; With Critical
and Expository Notes by Nathaniel S. Folsom.
Boston: A. Williams & Co., 1869.
> ["The translation which I have made is modern in its
> style, with the exception of retaining the personal
> pronouns thou and thee...universally employed in
> prayer..."]

Second edition with an appendix, 1871.
> ["I have made no changes of translation affecting,
> in the slightest degree, any of the passages of
> supposed doctrinal bearing. Here and there a
> stronger word has been put in place of
> another..."]

Third edition; Boston: Cupples,   Upham,   and
Company, 1885.

1871 **Skeat, Walter W.**   The Gospel according to Saint
...in Anglo-Saxon, Northumbrian, and Old Mercian
Versions, synoptically arranged, with collations
exhibiting all the readings of all the MSS; together
with the Early Latin Version as contained in the
Lindesfarne MS., collated with the Latin Version in
the Rushworth MS. Cambridge: University Press, 1871-
1887.
>   1887 - - Matthew (Rev. of Kemble, 1858)
>   1871 - - Mark   Reprinted; Darmstradt:
>   Wissenschaftliche Buchgesellschaft, 1970.
>   1874 - - Luke
>   1878 - - John

1874 **Anonymous**   A True History of Jesus Christ, being
a Detailed Account of the Manner of his Birth, and
of All that he Did and Suffered up to the time of
his Crucifixion. Dictated by Himself. Boston: W.F.
Brown & Co., 1874.

1875 **McClellan, John Brown**   The New Testament of Our
Lord and Saviour Jesus Christ, A new translation, on
the basis of the authorised version, from a
critically revised Greek text, newly arranged in
paragraphs, with analysis, copious references and
illustrations from original authorities, new
chronological and analytical Harmony of the Four
Gospels, notes and dissertations. A contribution to
Christian evidence... In Two Volumes.   London:
Macmillan and Co.; Cambridge: C.J. Clay, 1875.
>   1875 - - Vol.I The Four Gospels. With the
>   chronological and analytical Harmony.

>   - - [Vol. II Never Published]

1876 **Dunwell, F.H.**   The Four Gospels, as interpreted
by the early church: a commentary on the AV...
compared with the Sinaitic, the Vatican, and the
Alexandrine MSS., and also with the Vulgate.
London: W. Clowes and Sons, 1876.

1883 **Tischendorf, Constantine**   The Good News, according
to the original text of the oldest known Greek
manuscript [Codex Sinaiticus] on the basis of the
common English version. By Constantine Tischendorf.
Glasgow: John Thomson, 1883.
[The Gospels in the AV, corrected by C. Tischendorf.]

1885 **Cardale, Edward T.**   The Four Holy Gospels according
to the AV. With variations of Type in the Use of
Capital Letters and with Marginal Notes containing
Selections from Various Readings of the Earlier
English Translators; Also of the AV, and of the

Revisers of 1881, and of Others. By the Rev. Edward T. Cardale... London: Rivingtons, 1885.

1887 **Tafel, Leonard, Rudolph L. Tafel and L.H. Tafel** Interlinear translation of the New Testament...
[See New Testament Selections for the complete entry. Includes the Gospels.]

1888 **Bilton, Ernest**   The Four Gospels translated into Modern English from the Authorised and Revised Versions by Ernest Bilton.   Paisley & London: A. Gardner, 1888.

1891 **Hill, James Hamlyn**   The Gospel of the Lord: an early version which was circulated by Maricon of Sinope as the original gospel; translated by James Hamlyn Hill.   Guernsey: for John Whitehead... by T.M. Richard, [1891?]

1891 **Stellhorn, F.W.**   The Four Gospels...
[See New Testament Selections, 1891 F.W. Stellhorn, A Brief Commentary...]

1894 **Lewis, Agnes Smith**   A Translation of the Four Gospels from the Syriac of the Sinaitic Palimpsest, by Agnes Smith Lewis. London & New York: Macmillan & Co., 1894.
["The text of the Four Gospels discovered by me in the Convent of St. Katherine on Mt. Sinai in 1892, was transcribed...during our second visit to Sinai in 1893. A considerable part however, was still undeciphered when the transcribers were compelled by the pressure of other duties to leave Sinai... I therefore undertook a third journey to the Convent during...1895, in company with my sister, Mrs. James Y. Gibson...who undertook the duty of examining all those parts about which doubts had been expressed... I am therefore in a position to complete the translation which I published last year, through Messrs Macmillan and Co...and to include it in this volume, with a reprint of 98 pages hitherto defective in the Syraic edition published by the Syndics of the Cambridge University Press in 1894."]

Also; Some Pages of the Four Gospels Re-transcribed from the Sinaitic Palimpsest with a Translation of the Whole Text. London: C.J. Clay & Sons, 1896.

New edition; with parts retranslated. Cambridge & Boston: 1896.

1897 **Ballantine, Frank Schell**   Good News. The Four Gospels in a Modern American Dress. By Frank Schell Ballantine.   Scranton: [Press of Tunstall & Wolf.] Good News Publishing Co., 1897.

1898 **Spencer, Francis Aloysius**   The Four Gospels.
A New Translation from the Greek Text Direct, with
Reference to the Vulgate and the Ancient Syriac
Version. By Very Rev. Francis Aloysius Spencer, O.P.
Preface by His Eminence James, Cardinal Gibbons. New
York: William H. Young & Co., 1898.
> ["He has endeavored to represent our Lord and the
> apostles as speaking, not in an antique style, but in
> the language they would speak if they lived among us
> now." In spite of the title, this work appears to be
> based upon the Vulgate than upon the Greek; it is not
> the same work as that which appeared, under the same
> title, in 1901.]
>
> [The Four Gospels, translated from the Latin Vulgate. By
> Francis Aloysius Spencer.' Although all the sources
> consulted say that Father Spencer's translation from the
> Vulgate was published in 1898, no copy of a translation
> based on the Latin text alone has been found. The title
> page for the translation from the Greek was copyrighted
> 1898.]
>
> [Four editions in four years.]

1904 **Buchanan, Edgar Simmons**   The Latin Gospels in the
Second Century. A literal translation into English
of the Latin version current in Proconsular Africa
and Western Europe fifty years after the death of S.
John the Evangelist. Translated from the old Latin
MS.**ff** 2 now in the National Library in Paris. By
E.S. Buchanan. 4 parts.   Sevenoaks: J. Salmon,
[1904-1906]

1904 **Burkitt, Francis Crawford**   Evangelion
da- Mepharreshe: The Curetonian Version of the Four
Gospels, with the readings of the Sinai Palimpsest
and the early Syriac Patristic evidence edited,
collected and arranged by F. Crawford Burkitt. 2
Vols. Cambridge: University Press, 1904.
> [Volume 1 (pp.2-535) contains the text on each left-hand
> page, with the English translation opposite.]

1904 **D'Onstan, Roslyn**   The Patristic Gospels; an
English version of the Holy Gospels as they existed
in the second century... Collated...by Roslyn
D'Onstan. London: Grant Richards, 1904.

1907 **Anonymous**   The Fourfold Portrait of the Heavenly
King as presented in the Gospels; A new translation
of the Gospels side by side with the Authorised and
Revised Versions, quotations from the Old Testament
scriptures, and parallel passages arranged to
facilitate comparison of the gospel narratives; by
Interpreter. [Alford Ernest Bourne] London: Elliot
Stock, 1907.

1909 **Montefiore, Claude Goldsmid**   The Synoptic Gospels;
Edited with an Introduction and Commentary...
Together with a series of additional notes by I.
Abrahams. 3 Vols. London: Macmillan & Co., 1909.
[The notes were not published.]

> Second edition, revised and partly rewritten,
> 1927.
> > ["In the earlier edition, I printed a translation
> > of each gospel as a whole, repeating the
> > translation piecemeal before each section of the
> > commentary. I have omitted the first translation
> > in this (second) edition... The text is usually
> > the text which lies behind the RV."]

1914 **Aurora**   Edgar J. Goodspeed in The Making of
the English New Testament, Chicago, 1925, page 110,
refers to an American version which appeared in
Aurora, Illinois, in 1914. Although a considerable
effort has been made, no further information about
such a version has been obtained.   There was,
however, published in a Aurora [c.1914-1921] The
Unknown God by W. W. Walter, 2 volumes, which
according to the Catalog of the Library of Congress
uses the Authorized Version. Its contents are I.
The teachings of Jesus of Nazareth according to St.
Matthew and St. Mark, and II. The teachings of Jesus
of Nazareth according to St. Luke and St. John.

1914 **Buchanan, Edgar Simmons**   The Four Gospels from the
Latin Text of the Irish Codex Harleianus, Numbered
Harl.1023 in the British Museum Library, in an
English version, with a short introduction, by E.S.
Buchanan. London: Heath, Cranton & Ouseley Ltd.,
1914.
[Text starts with Matt. XXXIII:25.]

1914 **Walter, William W.**   The Unknown God; The
Teachings of Jesus of Nazareth According to... By
W.W. Walter. 2 Vols.   Aurora, Ill: William W.
Walter, 1914-1921.
> 1914 - - St. Matthew and St. Mark; Volume One
> 1921 - - St. Luke and St. John; Volume Two

> ["... the passages from the Bible are taken from the KJV
> and are printed in lightfaced type, followed in each
> instance by the translation in bold type."]

1917 **Buchanan, Edgar Simmons**   The Gospels. Twenty-five
lections from a Spanish Lectionary - palimpsest. An
early Latin manuscript of Tarragona in the
collection of the Hispanic Society of America. With
English translation by E.S. Buchanan. New York &
London: G.P. Putnam's Sons, 1917.

[The title page of the copy in the British Museum has a MS note "Only copy in existence - rest of edition suppressed. E.S.B."]

1918 **Callan, Fr. Charles Jerome**   The Four Gospels. With a Practical Critical Commentary for Priests and Students. New York: Joseph F. Wagner, Inc., 1918.

1920 **Anonymous**   In Memoriam of the Great Translators of the Bible, Dr. Martin Luther and his co-workers 1517-1534. The one-column Edition of the Bible-Workers Four Gospels according to Matthew, Mark, Luke and St. John; Capitalized and Revised. Copyright 1920. Translated out of the Original Greek by Dr. Martin Luther; and prepared for the American Edition by a Large Staff of Lutheran Pastors of the American Lutheran Bible Society. Knoxville, Tenn.: US of NA.
     Another Edition; The Four Gospels...Capitalized and Revised. Translated out of the Original Greek by Martin Luther. Knoxville, Tenn.: American Lutheran Bible Society, 1920.

1920 **Lauritzen, Johannes Rudolph**   The Bible-Workers Four Gospels according to Matthew, Mark, Luke and St. John, Capitalized and Revised, Translated out of the Original Greek by Martin Luther and Prepared for the American Edition by a Large Staff of Lutheran Pastors for the American Lutheran Bible Society, Knoxville, 1920.

1924 **Anonymous**   The Road to Real Success...
     [See Bible Selections for the complete entry. Includes the four Gospels, the Epistles, John 1, and The Book of Jonah.]

1924 **Pitollet, Camille and Pierre Batiffol**   The Oldest Text of the Gospels...By Camille Pitollet and Pierre Batiffol, with an introduction by E.S. Buchanan. New York: n.p., 1924.

1929 **Buchanan, Edgar Simmons**   The Book of the Four Gospels of Our Lord and Saviour Jesus Christ. Translated from a Latin Palimpsest. By E.S. Buchanan. New York: Privately printed, 1929.

1932 **Osborn, Edwin Faxon**   The words and deeds of Jesus, from the records by Matthew, Mark, Luke and John; King James translation adapted to children and arranged for study, without comment, by Edwin Faxon Osborn. Kalamazoo, 1932.

1933 **Lamsa, George M.**   The Four Gospels according to the Eastern Version. Translated from the Aramaic by George M.Lamsa...Philadelphia: A.J.Holman Co., 1933.

Second printing, 1934.

1933 **Torrey, Charles Cutler**   The Four Gospels; A New
Translation. By Charles Cutler Torrey. New York &
London: Harper & Brothers, 1933.
["The Greek text which is here followed is almost always
that of Westcott and Hort... The translation...diverging
from it only where it seems probable, or certain, from
recognition of the underlying Semitic idiom, that the
Greek rendering causes misunderstanding." From the
Preface.]

[There are two editions dated 1933; one edition, at John
1:1 reads,"and the Word was god" (Small g) and the other
edition reads, "and the Word was God" (Large G.]

Another edition; London: Hodder & Stoughton,
1934.

Second edition; New York & London: Harper &
Brothers, 1947.
[John 1:1 reads,"and the Word was god".]

["...continued study of the Greek text and of the
Aramaic underlying it has resulted in a number of
Significant changes in the translation.]

1935 **Anonymous**   The Good News as told by Matthew, Mark,
Luke & John. A Rendering into modern English for the
use of students. Shanghai: Christian Literature
Society, 1935-1940.
1940   St. Matthew...   C. Wilfred Allan

1937   St. Mark...   W.E. Soothill

1940   St. Luke...   E.J. Clark & Doris V.
                            Coombs

1935   St. John...   E.J. Clark & Doris V.
                            Coombs

[This translation is based on the Mandarin Union and
several English translation, and is intended for
English-speaking Chinese. Mark seems to be more lacking
as a translation than the others.]

1938 **Cammack, Melvin Macye**   See John Wycliffe, [Four
Gospels], 1360.
[John Wyclif and the English Bible.]

1938 **Easton, Burton Scott**   What Jesus Taught;
The sayings Translated and Arranged with Expository
Comment.   New York, Cincinnati & Chicago: The
Abingdon Press, 1938.
["In making this translation the researches of
specialists in the Greek text and - especially - of
experts in the Aramaic language have been freely used."]

1940 **Dakes, John A.**   Christ Jesus: the Authentic
     Story of the Founder of Christianity as told by
     Matthew, Mark, Luke and John in the Four Gospels,
     Translated from the Original Greek by John A. Dakes.
     Chicago, Illinois: Avalon Publishing Co., 1940.
          ["In the preparation of this translation, I have
          consulted (fourteen Greek texts, from that of Walton,
          1657 to Westcott & Hort, 1881)..."]

     Another edition, 1954.

1942 **Anonymous**   Gospel of God; The Four Gospels
     in One Gospel of Light; Superet Translation of Jesus
     Christ's Words; Key to the Bible. [Josephine C.
     Trust.   Los Angeles, Calif.: Superet Press], 1942.

1951 **Rieu, E.V.**   The Four Gospels. 1951-1952.
          1951 St. Mark's Gospel; A New Translation from
               the Greek. London: Curwen Press.
                    [The colofon reads: "One thousand two
                    hundred and fifty copies of this edition of
                    St. Mark's Gospel have been printed at The
                    Curwen Press, London, E13, on Arnold and
                    Foster's Grey Mould—made, and bound there
                    for Allen and Richard Lane for Christmas
                    1951..."]

          1952 The Four Gospels. A new translation from
               the Greek by E.V. Rieu.   Harmondsworth,
               Middlesex: Penguin   Books,   Ltd.;
               Baltimore: Penguin Books.
                    ["This is a new translation from the Greek,
                    based... on Codex Sinaiticus. The back of
                    the title page states, "First published
                    1953... Copyright 1953 by Penguin Books
                    Ltd.; Library of Congress Catalog Card
                    Number 53-8747"]

          Other editions, 1953, 1956.

1952 **Phillips, J.B.**   The Gospels translated..., 1952.
          [See New Testament, 1948 for the entire entry.]

1957 **Heenan, John J.** The Word of Salvation; Translation
     and Explanation of I. The Gospel according to Saint
     Matthew by Alfred Durand S.J. and II. The Gospel
     according to Saint Mark by Joseph Huby S.J. III. The
     Gospel according to Saint Luke by Albert Valensin
     S.J. and Joseph Huby S.J. and IV. The Gospel
     according to Saint John by Alfred Durand S.J.
     Translated into English by John J. Heenan. 2 Vols.
     Milwaukee: The Bruce Publishing Co., 1957.
          [Translation of a French text with commentary published
          originally by Beauchesne et ses Fils, Paris. The English
          translation of the text "does not follow strictly any of
          the standard English versions...but stays...close to the
          French translation in order to preserve consistency with
          the commentary..."]

1958 **Meissner, Lawrence**   New Testament Gospels, a Modern
     Translation. By Lawrence Meissner. Portland, Oregon:
     [c.1958]

1961 **Anonymous**   Gud Nius Mak: Raitim [Four Gospels in
     Pidgin English] London, Canberra, Capetown, Toronto,
     Wellington: Published by the British & Foreign Bible
     Society, 1961.
          ["...in Neo Melanesian (Pidgin English) for the
          Territory of New Guinea."]

1962 **Voerman, Arthur H.**   The Story of the Good News; An
     Explanatory Paraphrase of the Four Gospels by Arthur
     H. Voerman.   New York: Exposition Press, 1962.
          ["This is the first volume of a paraphrase of the N.T.
          The rest of the books of the N.T. are in preparation."
          The publisher reports that Mr. Voerman died before any
          more of the work could be published.]

1964 **Anonymous**   Gutnius Bilong Jisas Kraist, Matiu,
     Mak, Luk, John. London, Canberra, Capetown, Toronto,
     Wellington: Published by the British & Foreign Bible
     Society, 1964.

1967 **Williams, Dick and Frank Shaw**   The Gospels in
     Scouse; the Gear story in Liverpoolese, the Language
     of the Beatles, by Dick Williams and Frank Shaw.
     Liverpool, England: Gear Press, 1967.
          [Liverpool Vernacular Gospels.]

1970 **Mercier New Testament**   The Mercier New Testament:
     A Version of the New Testament in Modern English.
     Part I: Matthew, Mark, Luke, and John. Prepared by
     Kevin Condon.   Cork: Mercier Press, 1970.
          [A fresh Catholic translation of the Gospels from the
          Greek in plain, simple modern English. Not Meant to
          compete with the standard English versions, but to lead
          to a greater appreciation and use of them. Illustrated
          by a hundred carefully selected photographs.]

     Second printing; 1971.

     Also; The Alba House New Testament. The
     Accounts of Matthew, Mark, Luke and John.
     Prepared by Kevin Condon. 1970.

1977 **Anonymous**   The Four Gospels; newly translated
     from the Greek. Luton, England: White Cresent Press,
     1977.   [The Marrow Gospels.]

1977 **Marrow, Norman**   The Four Gospels; Newly translated
     from the Greek by Norman Marrow.   Luton, England:
     White Crescent Press Ltd., 1977.

1978 **Brandt, Leslie F.**   Jesus Now, by Leslie F. Brandt, with art by Corita Kent.   St. Louis: Concordia Publishing House, 1978.

1980 **Blackwelder, Boyce W.**   The Four Gospels, an Exegetical Translation, by Boyce W. Blackwelder. Anderson, Ind.: n.p., 1980.

1980 **Tucker, Robert Reed**   The Easy Bible: Matthew, Mark, Luke, John: a literal, fundamental translation translated by Robert Reed Tucker. Canoga Park, CA: R.R.Tucker, 1980.

1983 **Lovasik, Lawrence G.**   The Story of Jesus. By Lawrence G. Lovasik... New York: Catholic Book Publishing Co., 1983.
   [Each story is told in simple and direct words.]

1986 **Stuart, Jamie**   A Scots Gospel, by Jamie Stuart. John Knox Press, 1986.

GOSPELS AND ACTS

???? **Kimber, Benjamin Jones**   The Scriptural Chronological Life of Jesus Christ; As written by Matthew - Mark - Luke - John. Coordinated by Benjamin J. Kimber.   Modesto, CA: Harry's Press, [19??].
   ["Taken from the KJV of the Four Gospels and Acts...Kimber has replaced an occasional word or phrase for clarification..."]

1000 **Aelfric**   West Saxon portions of Gospels-Acts

1568 **Cox, Richard**   Four Gospels and Acts, 1568.
   [See Complete Bibles, 1568 Bishops' Bible.]

1599 **Anonymous**   The Four Gospels and Acts of the Apostles, in English and Eleven Other Languages. Nuremburg: Elias Hutter, 1599.

1761 **Anonymous**   Divers Parts of the Holy Scriptures done into English, chiefly from Dr. J.Mill's Printed Greek copy. With Notes and maps. [Mr. Mortimer] London: Printed for T. Piety, MDCCLXI. [1761]
   [The Four Gospels and Acts. Ascription to "Mr. Mortimer" is by Wilson.]

1789 **Symonds, John**   The Gospels... Acts... Apostles...
   [See New Testament Selections, 1789 John Symonds, ...Observations on the...]

1808 **Anonymous**   The Acts of the Days of the
Son of Man, from the Passion Week to his Ascension.
Philadelphia: Printed by Conrad Zentler..., 1808.
   [This is a harmony, from the Gospels and 1st Chapter of
   Acts, of the last days of the Savior's life.]

1813 **Bradford, Alden**   Evangelical History: or
a Narrative of the Life, Doctrines and Miracles of
Jesus Christ, Our Blessed Lord and Saviour, and of
His Holy Apostles: Containing the Four Gospels and
the Acts: with a General Introduction, and Prefatory
Remarks   to   each   Book   and   Notes, Didactic,
Explanatory and Critical. Designed chiefly for those
who have not leisure to peruse the Larger Works of
Voluminous Commentators. By Alden Bradford. Boston:
Published by Bradford and Read, 1813.
   [Text of John 20:20]

1857 **Cotton, Henry**   The Four Gospels and the Acts of the
Apostles, with short notes for the use of schools
and young persons. By Henry Cotton, D.C.L....Oxford:
John Henry & James Parker, 1857.

1881 **Crickmer, William Burton**   The Greek Testament
Englished, Annotated. By William Burton Crickmer...
London: Elliot Stock, 1881.
   [Contains the Four Gospels and Acts.]

1914 **Clark, Albert**   The Primitive Text of the Gospels
and Acts. Oxford: n.p., 1914.

1915 **Anonymous**   Places of Emphasis in the Gospels and
Acts of the Apostles, according to the Greek, noted
for reading the lesson in Church. T.D.M. [Thomas
Dickin Morris], 1915.

1946 **Black, Matthew**   An Aramaic Approach to the Gospels
and Acts by Matthew Black. With an Appendix on The
Son of Man by Geza Vermes. Oxford: At the Clarendon
Press, 1946.
   Second edition, 1954.

   Third edition, 1967.

   Reprint, 1971.

1947 **Anonymous**   The good news; the story of Christ Jesus
from the Gospel and the Acts in a modern translation
with explanatory notes. [Edited by H.F. Wickings.]
London & Redhill: Lutterworth Press, 1947.

1973 **Christianson, Christopher J.**   The Concise Gospel
and the Acts. A Continuous Narrative Harmonizing the
four Gospels and the Acts. Compiled by Christopher

J. Christianson. Introduction by Larry Christenson. Plainfield, New Jersey: Logos International, 1973.

1974 **Anonymous**   Walk with Me in Modern English. One chronological story as combined from the Four Gospels and the first chapter of the Book of Acts...
[See New Testament Selections for the complete entry.]

GOSPEL SELECTIONS

???? **Anonymous**   The Hellenic New Testament. (Matthew & Mark) n.p., n.d..
["We have tried...to produce a literal and precise translation of the Hellenic (Greek) text."]

1200 **Orm or Ormin**   The Ormulum. Bodleian MS; Junius I, c1200.
- - now first edited from the original manuscript in the Bodleian by Robert Meadows. Oxford: University Press, 1852.

Also; - - with the notes and glossary of Dr. D.M. White. Edited by Rev. Robert Holt. 2 Vols. Oxford: Clarendon Press, 1878.
Reprint; New York: Ams Press, 1974.

[Parts of the Gospels and Acts, paraphrased in poetic Middle English.]

1450 **Anonymous**   The Gospels of SS Matthew...Mark and Luke. Cambridge Univ. MS. Ii.2.12; BM. Egerton 842; Corp. Chr. Parker. MS.32, 1450.

1483 **Anonymous**   The Golden Legende... the legende named in latyn legenda aurea, that is to saye in Englysshe the golden legende...
[See Bible Selections for the complete entry.]

1535 **Gardyner, Bishop Stephen**   [Luke and John]
["I have finished the translation of S. Luke and S. John, wherin I bestowed great labour..." from a letter dated Waltham, June 1, 1535. MS not preserved.]

1539 **Anonymous**   The Manual of prayers / or the prymer in Englyshe & Laten set out at lenght, whose contentes the reader by...
[See Bible Selections for the complete entry.]

1574 **Golding, Arthur**   The Gospels usually read in
the Churches; with an exposition by Nicholas Heming,
translated... London: Henry Bynneman, 1574.

1748 **Trapp, Joseph**   Explanatory notes upon the
Four Gospels, in a new method of the use of all, but
especially the unlearned English reader, in two
parts, to which are prefixed three discoveries by
Joseph Trapp. London: 1748.
          [The design of this work...to correct the AV, and
          explain the diction of the sacred writings, but chiefly
          to reconcile apparently contradictory passages.]

          Another edition; Oxford: 1805.

1817 **Cotter, John Rogerson**   The Gospels of St. Matthew
and St. Mark, paraphrased, 1817-1840.
          1817 The Gospel of Saint Matthew, paraphrased,
               and put into question and answer. Dublin:
               W. Watson.

          1840 The Gospels of St. Matthew and St. Mark,
               paraphrased and put into question and
               answer, on a new plan... Second edition
               revised. London: J.G.F. & J. Rivington.

1834 **Anonymous**   Specimens of a proposed Accurate
Translation of the Four Gospels, from the received
Greek text, on the basis of the AV. [J.G. Tolley]
London: for T. & W. Boone, 1834.

1859 **Shadwell, Lancelot**   The Gospel of Matthew and Mark.
1859-1861.
          1859 The Gospel according to Matthew,
               faithfully rendered into English from a
               revised Greek Text, with notes by
               Lancelot Shadwell. London: Published for
               the Proprietor, by Arthur Hall, Virtue
               and Co.

          1861 The Gospel of Matthew, and of Mark, newly
               rendered into English, with notes on the
               Greek text. London: Walker & Co.

1885 **Anonymous**   The Gospel According to Matthew, Mark
and Luke. Edinburgh & London: Ballantyne, Hanson &
Co., for Kegan Paul, Trench & Co., 1885.

1899 **Grierson, G.A.**   Linguistic Survey of India.
Compiled and edited by G.A.Grierson. Eleven Volumes.
Calcutta: Office of the Superintendent of Government
Printing, India, 1899.
          [This work has variations in different volumes. The
          parable of the Prodigal Son is given in languages and

dialects of India with literal translations into English.]

1905 **Genders, J.W.**   The Holy Bible for Daily Reading. A new arrangement. London: Passmore & Alabaster, 1905.
[Matthew & Mark only]

Another edition; A new revision. 1908.

1910 **Wright, Joseph**   Grammar of the Gothic Language and the Gospel of Mark. Selections from other Gospels...
[See New Testament Selections for the complete entry.]

1913 **Anonymous**   [The Synoptic Gospels] Preliminary Edition. London: W.B. Clive, 1913-1914.
      1913 The Gospel according to S. Mark...
      J.F. Richards.
      1913 The Gospel according to S. Luke...
      T. Walker.
      1914 The Gospel according to S. Matthew...
      T. Walker.

1917 **Buchanan, Edgar Simmons**   The New Bible__Text extracted from the Huntington Palimpsest of Hispanic Society, N.T. Selections from the Gospels.   New York: n.p., 1917.

1919 **Buchanan, Edgar Simmons**   An Unique Gospel Text. (31 selections) from a Latin Palimpsest in the collection of the Hispanic Society of America; Deciphered and Translated...with introductions by B.E. Scriven and J.B. [i.e. Jean Buchanan.] London: Heath Cranton Ltd., [1919].
[So thoroughly larded with the word "spirit" that most passages are unrecognizable.]

1926 **McCormack, R.**   Seven in Scripture. The true text of St. John XVII and other passages from the Gospels restored and established. By R. McCormack.   London & Edinburgh: Marshall Bros., 1926.

1928 **Osborn, Edwin Faxon**   The words and deeds of Jesus from the records by Matthew and John; translated from the Greek into modern English and arranged for study by Edwin Faxon Osborn. Grand Rapids: 1928.

1930 **Montefiore, Claude Goldsmid**   Rabbinical Literature and Gospel. London: Macmillan & Co., 1930.
["A good deal of Rabbinical (and some Gospel) material here translated..."]

1938 **Anonymous**   The Germanisation of the New Testament. By Bishop Ludwig Muller... With a foreword by the

Rev. Dr. H.C. Robbins. London: ["Friends of Europe Publication #64"], 1938.

1940 **Boylan, Patrick**   The Sunday Epistles and Gospels...
[See New Testament Selections for the complete entry.]

1946 **Knox, Ronald Arbuthnott**   The Epistles and Gospels...
[See New Testament Selections for the complete entry.]

1954 **Kyles, Rev. David**   The Parables of Jesus, retold by David Kyles. London: Ward, Lock & Co., 1954.
[Living Story Picture Books Series.]

1956 **Kimber, A.W.**   What Did Jesus Say? London: Blandford, 1956.
["The record, as set out in Chapters 1 to 12, contains nothing more than what Jesus himself said and taught... In some cases...the text has been altered to make the matter clearer...']

1957 **Baskerville, John**   Two New Books for the Bible. Dayton, OH: J.B. Downs, 1957.   [Matthew and Luke.]

1959 **Green, Jay and others**   The Multilinear Translation of the New Testament. Evansville, Indiana: Sovereign Grace Book Club, 1959. [Matthew, Mark and Luke only.]
["This then, is the plan of our present edition:
Line 1.   Robert Stephens Greek Text, 1550
Line 2.   Literal Translation of the Greek Text (The Englishman's Greek N.T., 1877)
Line 3.   A Clarified KJV (Green's own tr.)
Line 4.   The ERV of 1881
Line 5.   The Codex Vaticanus (B) Translated into English (only where it differs.)
There are finally to be four volumes in this work..." Apparently only volume I was issued. Text appears similar to Green's Bible of 1960 & 1962. Jay Green, Elmer Nicholas and Brady Shafer]

1970 **Jordan, Clarence**   The Cotton Patch Version of Matthew and John. A modern translation with a Southern accent. New York: Association Press, 1970.
[Clarence Jordan died suddenly on October 29, 1969. He did not complete the N.T. But he did leave manuscripts of Matthew and the first eight chapters of John.]

1978 **Johnson, Ben Campbell**   Matthew and Mark, a Relational Paraphrase. Ben Campbell Johnson. Waco, Texas: Word, Inc., 1978.

GOSPEL HARMONIES

???? **Anonymous**   Sweet Story of Jesus. New York: Graham & Matlack, n.d.

[Bible Series 047]

???? **Anonymous**   Peep of Day; A Series of Earliest
Religious Instruction, [Mrs. F.L] (Bevan) Mortimer]
New York: H.M. Caldwell Co. Publishers, [188?].
[An abbreviated monotessaron paraphrase for children.]

???? **Bowie, Walter Russsell**   The Story of Jesus
for Young People. Englewood Cliffs, N.J.: Prentice -
Hall, [195?].

???? **Byrne, Laurence E.**   The Life of Christ. Milwaukee:
The Bruce Publishing Co., [195?].

???? **Coles, Abraham**   The Life and Teachings of our Lord
in Verse, [188?].

???? **Gundert, Hermann**   The Life Of Christ in Malayalam,
combined with an English Gospel Harmony, [187?].
[The Vernacular version by Hermann Gundert; the
revisor's preface signed S.G.]

Second edition; Mangalore: Basel Mission Press,
1876.

???? **Ingraham, J.H.**   The Prince of the House of David or
Three Years in the Holy City. Chicago: M.A. Donohue
& Co., [18??].
[The central figure is Jesus the "Son of David", our
most blessed Lord and Saviour. The time of this work
embraces a period of about four years, from the
appearing of John the Baptist to the ascension of our
Lord.]

Reprinted; Geneva, IL: 205 Publications, 19??

Another Edition; New York: A.L. Burt Co.,
Publishers, n.d.

Reprinted; Elgin, IL: David C. Cook Publishing
Co., 1898.

???? **Orchard, John B.**   A Synopsis of the Four Gospels;
Arranged According to the Two-Gospel Hypothesis,
edited and translated by John Orchard. Macon, GA:
Mercer University Press, [19??].

???? **Schmidt, Duane**   The Late J.C., by Duane Schmidt.
Des Moines: Wallace-Homestead Book Co., [????].

???? **Younghusband, Francis**   The Story of Our Lord,
told in Simple Language for Children by Francis
Younghusband. London: Longmans, Green & Co., [189?].

800 **Cynewolf**   Crist [Metrical Gospel Story] c800

1360 **Wycliffe, John**   [Four Gospels] c.1360
     ["It was discovered that Wyclif in his English sermons
     and tracts often had translated large sections of the
     Bible in a consecutive manner. This is particularly true
     of the Gospels, practically the whole of which have been
     pieced together."]

          1869 Select English Works of John Wiclif.
               Edited from the original MSS. Edited by
               Thomas Arnold. Oxford: Clarendon Press.

          1880 The English Works of Wyclif, hitherto
               unprinted, Edited by F.D. Matthew.
               London: E.E.T.S.

          1938 John Wyclif and the English Bible, by
               Melvin Macye Cammack. New York: American
               Tract Society.

1380 **Anonymous**   Harmony of the Gospels. [John Wyclif?]
     BM Reg. 17.c.33; Harl.1862 and 6333; Bodleian 771,
     c1380.

1400 **Anonymous**   Clement Englished. MS XVI.D.2, Library
     of the Dean & Chapter of York, 1400.
          [Dominical Gospel & Paternoster with glosses; described
          in the Bulletin of the John Rylands Library, Vol. 29,
          No. 2, Feb. 1946. The relation between this and other
          translations of Clement's Gospels is not known.]

1400 **Anonymous**   Harmony of the Gospels. Harl. MS 5085
     Holkham Hall 672; Magd.Coll.Pepys 2489; Corp.Chr.286
     ...an English version of Clement of Lanthony's
     Harmony... (Penniman).

     The Pepysian Gospel Harmony, edited by Margrey
     Goates. London: Published for the E.E.T.S. by
     Humphrey Milford, Oxford Univ. Press, Original
     series #157, 1919 & 1922.

     Reprinted; New York: Kraus Report Corp., 1971.

1410 **Love, Nicholas**   Mirrour of the Blessed Lyf of Iesu
     Crist. MS Sherard, Corp. Chr. 142, 1410.
          [...containing paraphrases from the Gospels... Some two
          dozen MSS are extant. (Butterworth).]

     Another edition; Speculum vitae Christi (STC
     3259) Westminster: William Caxton, 1486, 1487.

     Another edition; Wynken de Worde, 1517.

     Reprinted;   edited by L.F. Powell.
     (Bodl.MS.Brasenose E.9) Oxford: 1908.

1553 **Paynell, Thomas**   The Pandectes of the Evangelicall
Lawe, by Thomas Paynell. London: Nicholas Hyll, for
Wm Seres & Abr. Vele, 1553.
      [Four Gospels in narrative.]

1584 **Anonymous**   The Holie History of our Lord
and Savyour Jesus Christe, &c gathered into English
meeter. London: R. Field, 1584.

1584 **Anonymous**   A Harmonie vpon the three Euangelists,
Matthew, Mark and Luke, with the Commentarie of M.
Ihon Caluine: Faithfullie translated out of Latine
into English, by E.P[agit]. Whereunto is also added
a Commentarie vpon the Euangelist S. Ihon, by the
same   authour.   [Translated   by   C.   Fetherstone]
Londini: impensis George Bishop, 1584.
      [Cotton's ascription to 'Ephraem Paget' seems to be in
      error.]

      Another edition; Londini: Impensis Thomas Adams
      [Impreinted at London by Thomas Dawson for
      Thomas Adams], 1610.

1594 **Field, R.**   The Holie History of Our Lord and Savior
Jesus Christ Gathered into English Metre.   London:
1594.

1594 **Holland, Robert**   The holie Historie of our Lord
and Saviour Jesus Christ's natiuitie, life, acts,
miracles,   death,   passion,   resurrection,   and
Ascension by Robert Holland, 1594.

1601 **Anonymous**   The Song of Mary the Mother of Christ,
containing the story of his life and passion, 1601.

1607 **Walsall, Samuel**   The life and death of Jesus Christ
by Samuel Walsall, 1607.

1610 **Paget, Ephrain**   A Harmony of the Evangelists.
London: n.p., 1610.

1634 **Garthwait, Henry**   Montessaron - The Evangel.
Harmonie. Cambridge: T. Buck and R. Daniel, 1634.

1644 **Lightfoot, John**   The Harmony of the Foure
Evangelists: ... The First Part. London: R. Cotes
for Andrew Crooke, 1644.

1649 **Taylor, Jer.**   The Great Exemplar of Sanctity and
Holy Life according to the Christian Institution:
Described in the History of the Life and Death of
the Ever Blessed Jesus Christ the Saviour of the
world. With considerations and Discourses upon the
several parts of the Story; And prayers fitted to

the several Mysteries, by Jer. Taylor.   London:
1649.
> Third edition; In Three Parts.   London: Printed
> by R. Norton for Richard Royston, 1657.

1668 **Cradock, Samuel** The Harmony of the Four Evangelists
...London: Samuel Thompson...and Francis Tyton,
1668.

1671 **Coles, Elisha**   Christologia; or, a Metrical
Paraphrase on the History of our Lord and Saviour
Jesus Christ by Elisha Coles. London: Printed for
Peter Parker, 1671.
> Another edition; The Harmony of the Four
> Evangelists in a Metrical Paraphrase on
> the History of our Lord and Saviour Jesus
> Christ: Dedicated to his Universal Church
> by Elisha Coles. London: 1678.

1680 **Chamberlaine, James** A Sacred Poem wherein the Birth
[Life and Death] of the Holy Jesus are delineated.
Also eighteen of David's Psalms, Paraphras'd.
London: Printed by R.E. for R. Bentley, 1680.

1693 **Wesley, Samuel**   The Life of Oue Blessed Lord and
Saviour Jesus Christ. An heroic poem dedicated to
Her Sacred Majesty... each book illustrated by
necessary notes, explaining all the more difficult
matters in the whole history; also a prefactory
discourse concerning heroic poetry by Samuel Wesley.
London: for Charles Harper, 1693.
> Second Edition; revised by the Author and
> improved with the addition of a large Map of
> the Holy Land; and a Table of Principal
> Matters; with Sixty Copper Plates, by the
> celebrated Hands of W. Faithorn., 1700?
> [From Wesley's 'History of the New Testament',
> 1701.]
>
> Another edition; - - Revised by Thomas Coke,
> 1809.
>
> Also; The Life of Christ. A Poem. Edward T. Roe
> (Editor). Chicago: Union Book Co., 1900.

1701 **Anonymous**   The Harmony of the Four Evangelists:
being the whole text of the four Gospels dispos'd
according to the order of time by John Le Clerc.
With a paraphrase and useful dissertations. London:
Samuel Buckley, 1701.
> [Translated from Le Clerc's 'Harmonia Evangelica'
> published in Amsterdam, 1699.]

1705 **Bonnel, James**   Harmony of the IV Evangelists.
London: James Downing, 1705.
[Originally formed by William Austin, a Roman Catholic,
but reformed and improved.]

1720 **Hailes, Lord Chief Justice**   Harmony of the Four
Evangelists. London: John Coren, 1720.

1733 **Harley, Edward**   The Harmony of the Four Gospels
with a History of the Acts of the Apostles by Edward
Harley. London: J. Downing, 1733.

1750 **Hele, Arthur**   The Four Gospels Harmonized and
Reduced into One... Reading: A. Hele, 1750.

1756 **MacKnight, James**   A Harmony of the Four Gospels,
in which the natural order of each is preserved,
with a paraphrase and notes, by James MacKnight. 2
vols. London: The Author, 1756.
Second edition; corrected and greatly enlarged.
2 Vols. London: William Strahan, 1763.

Third edition; 2 Vols. Edinburgh: By R. Ritchie,
1804.

Fourth edition; London: Longman..., 1809.

Fifth edition; London: Longman..., 1819.

1765 **Greenwood, William**   The Harmony of the Evangelists,
or, the four Gospels connected on the one regular
historical series. London: for John Rivington, 1765.
[In some passages, the author has altered the AV.]

1768 **Smart, Christopher**   The Paraphrase of our Lord and
Saviour Jesus Christ. Done into familiar verse, with
occasional applications, for the use and improvement
of the younger minds. London: for W. Owen, 1768.

1771 **Anonymous**   The Acts of the Days of the Son of
Man; or, the History of our Lord and Saviour Jesus
Christ. Comprehending all that the four Evangelists
have recorded concerning them. London: M. Lewis,
1771.
[Translated from Samuel Lieberkuhn's 'Geschichte unsers
Herrn und Heilandes Jesu Christi.']

1773 **Baker, Rev. Richard**   Harmony of the Four
Evangelists; translated from the original text; with
notes, in four Parts. London & Norwich: n.p., 1773-
1775.
2nd edition, 1783-87.

1780 **Priestley, Joseph**   A Harmony of the Evangelists
in English; with critical dissertations, and an

occasional paraphrase and notes for the use of the unlearned by J. Priestley. London: J. Johnson, 1780.

1782 **Willan, Robert**   The History of the Ministry of Jesus Christ; combined from the narrations of the four Evangelists by Robert Willan. London: by James Phillips, 1782.

1793 **Cranfield, Thomas**   A Harmony of the Gospels... Dublin: 1793.

1795 **Austin, William**   See James Bodnel, Harmony...IV Evangelists, 1705.

1802 **Anonymous**   An English Harmony of the Four Evangelists, generally disposed after the manner of the Greek of William Newcome, Archbishop of Armagh; with a map of Palestine... Explanatory notes and indexes. [Richard Phillips and Thomas Thompson] London: W. Phillips, 1802.
      Another Edition; London:Printed for Samuel Bagster, 1847.

1803 **Rutter, Henry**   Evangelical Harmony; or the History of the life and doctrines of Our Lord Jesus Christ, according to the four Evangelists, by Henry Rutter. 2 Vols. London: Keating, Brown & Keating, 1803.
      ["The text... is that of Bishop Challoner's edition (See Challoner, 1749), though we have frequently had recourse to Dr. Witham's approved version (See Witham, 1730), which occasionally expresses the sense with greater ease and perspicuity."]

      Another edition; The Life, Doctrines & Sufferings of our Blessed Lord & Saviour, Jesus Christ, as recorded by the four evangelists, with moral reflections, critical illustrations, and explanatory notes. The second edition, revised by the author... London: for the Proprietors, 1830.

      Also; − − to which is added the Acts of the Apostles... by Charles Constantine Pise. New York: R. Martin & Co., 1844.
         [Pise's 'Acts of the Apostles' are listed separately, 1844.]

      Another edition; London & New York: Virtue, Emmins & Co., 1845.

      Also; New York: Johnson, Fry & Co., 1845.

1803 **Warner, R.**   The English Diatessaron; or the History of Christ, from the compounded Texts of the Four Evangelists. By R. Warner. Bath: 1803.

Another edition; A Chronological History of our Lord and Saviour Jesus Christ, from the compounded texts of the four holy Evangelists; or, the English Diatessaron. Bath: 1819.

1804 **Boothroyd, Benjamin**   The New Testament, or History of Christ, contained in the four Evangelists, harmonized by the late excellent Philip Doddridge. Improved and explained...by question and answer. Pontefract: The Author, 1804.

1804 **Fellowes, Robert**   The Guide to Immortality; or, Memoirs of the Life and Doctrine of Christ by the four Evangelists; digested into one continued narrative, according to the order of time and place laid down by Archbishop Newcome; in the words of the established version, with improvements, and illustrated with notes. 3 Vols. London: John White, 1804.

1808 **Thompson, Robert** The Gospel History, in a connected series; with notes, by Robert Thompson. London: for T. Hamilton, 1808.
     [A new translation]

1809 **Anonymous**   An English Harmony of the Evangelists, generally disposed after the manner of the Greek of William Newcome...: With a Map of Palestine, divided into Twelve Tribes. Explanatory Notes and Indexes. Philadelphia: Published by Kimber and Conrad..., Brown & Merritt, Printers..., 1809.
     Another edition; An English Harmony of the Evangelists, disposed after the manner of the Greek of William Newcome..., with explanatory notes and indexes, and a new map of Palestine, divided into tetrarchies, and shewing the travels of our Lord Jesus Christ. London: Printed for Samuel Bagster... M.DCCC.XXVII. [1827]

1809 **Coke, Thomas** See Samuel Wesley, The Life..., 1693.

1813 **Chambers, Joseph**   A Harmony of the Four Gospels. Retford: E.G. Woodhead, 1813.

1815 **Fleetwood, John**   The Life of...Jesus Christ. Oxford: Bartlett, 1815.
     Another edition, 1833.

     Also; The Life of our Lord and Saviour Jesus Christ, together with the Lives of his Holy Apostles, Evangelists and other primitive martyrs (rev). New York: Virtue, Emmins & Co., 1877?.

Another edition; The Life of our blessed Lord and saviour Jesus Christ (Rev). Philadelphia: Henry T. Coates & Co., n.d.

1815 **Thomson, Charles**   A Synopsis of the Four Evangelists; or, a regular History of the Conception, Birth, Doctrine, Miracles, Death and Resurrection and Ascension of Jesus Christ in the Words of the Evangelists. By Charles Thomson. Philadelphia: William M'Cullogh, 1815.
["He has employed a literal translation of the very words of the Evangelists without any omission or addition, excepting that he has inserted explanations of peculiar phrases and technical terms between brackets."]

1823 **Wilkins, George**   A Brief, Harmonized, and Paraphrastic Exposition of the Gospel by George Wilkins. Nottingham: G. Stretton, 1823.

1829 **Thompson, John S.**   The Monotessaron; or, the Gospel History, according to the Four Evangelists: Harmonized and Chronologically arranged, in a New Translation from the Greek Text of Griesbach, illustrated by selections from the most eminent commentators, ancient and modern, and by a great variety of original notes and dissertations, exhibiting the latest improvements in Biblical science and criticism, by John S. Thompson. Baltimore: Printed for the Author, 1829.
["...the translation has been made from the best edition of Griesbach, and carefully collated from the ancient Syriac and Latin Vulgate."]

1831 **Anonymous**   A Harmony of the Gospels, on the plan proposed by Lant Carpenter, LL.D. [John G. Palfrey] Boston: Published by Gray & Brown, 1831.

1833 **Ware, Henry**   The Life of the Saviour by Henry Ware, 1833.
Second edition; 1833.
["...several additions and some changes..."]

Eighth edition; Boston: American Unitarian Association, 1892.
[Explanatory paraphrase with most of the speeches redone.]

1838 **Carpenter, Lant**   A Harmony or Synoptical Arrangement of the Gospels, founded upon the most Ancient Opinion respecting the duration of our Saviour's ministry, and exhibiting the succession of events in close Accordance the older of the two Apostolical Evangelists with Dissertations, Notes and tables, 1838.

1841 **Currey, Rev. C.**   The Four Gospels; exhibited as one continued narrative, by an arrangement in parallel columns by C. Currey. London: Rivingtons, 1841.
[New translation?]

1841 **Scott, David Dundas**   The Four Witnesses: being a Harmony of the Gospels on a new Principle. By Dr. Isaac Da Costa of Amsterdam. Translated [from the Dutch] by David Dundas Scott. London: James Nisbet & Co., 1841.
          Another edition; New York: Robert Carter & Bros., 1855.

1845 **Forster, John**   The Gospel Narrative with a Continuous Exposition. London: 1845.
[John Foster?]

1845 **Pringle, William**   Commentary on the Harmony of the Evangelists by John Calvin. Translated from the original Latin, and collated with the author's French version. 3 Vols.   Edinburgh: Calvin Translation Society, 1845.
          [See Bible Selections, 1844 Anonymous, Commentaries on the books of the Bible.]

1848 **M'Clintock, John and Charles E. Blumenthal**
The Life of Jesus Christ in its Historical Connexion and Historical Development. By Augustus Neander Translated from the German edition of 'Das Leben Jesu Christi... by John M'Clintock & Charles E. Blumenthal. Hamburg: Freiderich Perthes, 1845'. New York: Harper & Bros., 1848.
          Another edition, 1864.

1854 **Strong, James**   A New Harmony and Exposition of the Gospels: Consisting of a Parallel and Combined Arrangement On a New Plan, of the Narratives of the Four Evangelists, According to the Authorized Translation; and a Continuous Commentary, with Brief Notes Subjoined. Being the First Period of the Gospel History. With a Supplement, Containing Extended Chronological and Topological Dissertations, and a Complete Analytical Index. By James Strong...   Illustrated with Maps and Engravings. New York: Carleton & Phillips, 1854.
          [The 'Continuous Commentary' is actually an expanded Paraphrase of the narrative.]

          Another Edition; New York: Published by Lane & Scott... Joseph Longking, Printer, 1852.

1862 **Barham, Francis**   Improved Monotessaron: a complete authentic Gospel life of Christ; combining the words of the four Gospels, in a revised version, and an orderly chronological arrangement. London: Rivingtons, 1862.

1867 **Kirk, Edmund**   The Life of Jesus by Edmund Kirk. Boston: Lee & Shepard, 1867.

1869 **Pound, William** The Story of the Gospels in a single narrative, combined from the four Evangelists, showing in a new translation their unity. To which is added a like continuous narrative in the original Greek. 2 Vols. London: Rivingtons, 1869.

1870 **Barham, Francis and I. Pitman**   A Rhymed Harmony of the Gospels... Printed both in the Phonetic and in the customary Spelling, as a Transition Book from Phonetic Reading to the reading of books as now commonly printed. London: Fred. Pitman; Bath: Isaac Pitman, 1870.

1870 **Longfellow, Henry Wadsworth**   Christus: A Mystery, 1870?
          [Contains a fanciful, abbreviated, poetic monotessaron.]

1871 **Beecher, Henry Ward**   The Life of Jesus, The Christ. By Henry Ward Beecher... New York: J.B. Ford and Co., 1871.
          [Also contains "Gospels Consolidated". Preface by F.T.H.]

1871 **Gardiner, Frederic**   A Harmony of the Four Gospels in English, according to the AV, corrected by the best critical editions of the original. Andover: W.F. Draper, 1871.
          ["The text is throughout that of the Authorised or common Version, except where critical labors upon the original text, since that version was made, have established a change in the Greek; and also in a very few instances in which the translation admits of correction by common consent."]

          Another edition; Edinburgh: T. & T. Clark; London: Hamilton, Adams & Co.; Dublin: John Robertson & Co., 1871.

1871 **Gardiner, Frederic**   Diatessaron. The Life of our Lord; in The Words of the Gospels. By Frederic Gardiner... Andover: W.F. Draper, 1871.

1876 **Coleridge, Henry James**   Life of our Life. 2 Vols. London: Burns & Oates, 1876.
          [Incorporating an English translation of the author's harmony of the Gospels.]

1877 **Geikie, Cunningham**   The Life and Words of Christ. New York: American Book Exchange, 1877.

["I have tried to present his acts and words as they would strike those who first saw or heard them, and have added only as much elucidation to the latter as seemed needed. All His Sayings and Discourses are given in full..."]

Another edition, 1879.

1878 **Anonymous**   The Life of Our Lord and Saviour Jesus Christ, arranged in chronological order in the language of the inspired evangelists. With an introduction by the Rev. John Medicraft. London: Elliot Stock..., [1878].
[The Preface is signed "J.M." Still the translator is unknown.]

1879 **Kimball, Elijah H.**   The Four Gospels United into One. Newly Translated from the Original and Rendered into Verse. New York: G.W. Carleton & Co.; London: Trubner & Co., 1879.
["The translation is based on Three Greek MSS., and Robinson's Synopsis... Though generally rhythmical, yet both rhythm and rhyme have been made subordinate to the careful rendering of the original; while the familiar and cherished wording of the present version has been, in the main, preserved."]

1881 **Anonymous**   The Gospels distributed into Meditations for every Day in the Year, and arranged according to the Harmony of the four Evangelists, by L'Abbe Duquesne. Translated from the French and adapted to the use of the English Church. Vol. 1, Oxford: J. Parker & Co.; Vol. 2, London: Rivingtons; Vol. 3, London: Walter Smith, 1881-1884.

1881 **Hare, Robert and Harriet Clark Hare**
Christian Spiritual Bible, containing the Gospel of the Type of the Emanation and God, the only ubiquitous Son; being the Gospel of our Lord in his four Incarnations. Together with the Gospel of our Lady, his altruistic Affinity given through the angel Robert by his intelligences, Robert Hare, M.D., late emeritus professor of Chemistry, etc., and Harriet Clark Hare. Edited by their son and daughter, Philadelphia, A.D. 1881. In Heaven, 1901.
[Contains the Four Gospels and a part of the first chapter of Acts, from the KJV, woven into a consecutive narrative, together with much other matter, both poetry and prose. Intended as a Bible for those who believe in reincarnation.]

1881 **Kirby, W.F.**   The Four Gospels explained by their Writers. With an appendix on the Ten Commandments... edited by J.B. Roustaing. Translated (from the French) by W.F. Kirby. 3 Vols. London: Trubner & Co., 1881.

1884 **Deems, Charles F.**   The Light of the Nations. New York: Gay Brothers & Co., 1884.
> ["I strive to make a harmonious narrative from...the Four Evangelists... There will be found in this book a new translation of the sayings of Jesus... My renderings from the Greek must be judged by scholars..."]

1884 **Foster, Charles**   The Story of the Gospel or Our Saviour's Life on Earth Told in Words Easy to Read and Understand. By Charles Foster... 150 Illustrations.   Philadelphia, PA: Published by Charles Foster Publishing Co., 1881, 1884.

1885 **Hartpence, Wm. R.**   The Unity of the Four Gospels, According the best modern translations from the original Greek, and the most approved chronologies. Cincinnati: Published by the Author, 1885.

1888 **Hemphill, S.** The Diatessaron of Tatian... Now first edited in an English form, with an introduction and appendices. London: Hodder & Stoughton, 1888.

1888 **Hutchings, W.H.**   The Life of Christ, 1888.
> [Translated and edited from St. Bonaventure; from Thornton's booklist.]

1889 **Pittenger, William**   The interwoven Gospels; or, The four histories of Jesus Christ blended into a complete and continuous narrative in the words of the Gospels; according to the revised version of 1881 with the readings and renderings preferred by the American committee of revision incorporated into the text. Compiled by William Pittenger. New York: J.B. Alden, 1889.
> Another edition; The interwoven Gospels and Gospel Harmony... New York: J.B. Alden, 1891.

1890 **Anonymous** The Christ, The Son of God. A Life of Our Lord and Saviour Jesus Christ, by the Abbe Constant Fouard, Translated from the Fifth Edition with the Author's Sanction. [George F.X. Griffith] 1890.
> [Monotessaron with commentary. One volume edition; London, NY, Toronto: Longmans, Green & Co., 1944.]

1891 **Anonymous**   Jesus, the Carpenter of Nazareth by a Layman [Robert Bird] New York: Charles Scribners Sons, 1891.
> ["This life is written in short realistic pictures..." Speeches are often retranslated or paraphrased.]

1894 **Hill, James Hamlyn**   The Earliest Life of Christ, ever compiled from the four Gospels. Being The Diatessaron of Tatian (Circ. A.D. 160) literally translated from the Arabic version and containing the Four Gospels woven into One Story; With an

Introduction and Notes, and Appendix. By J.H. Hill. Edinburgh: T. & T. Clark, 1894.
["A literal translation of the Diatessaron as published by Ciasca...in Rome in 1888."]

Second Edition; Abridged, 1910.

1894 **Kingsley, Florence Morse**   Titus, a comrade of the cross by Florence Morse Kingsley. Chicago: David C. Cook Publishing Co., 1894.
[A fanciful narrative of the life of Christ, with speeches uniquely rendered.]

Another edition; "...thoroughly revised by the author...", 1895.

1895 **Anonymous**   The Four Gospels Harmonized and Translated by Leo Tolstoy; in three parts; Translated from the original manuscripts into English at the request of the author. "The English Editor". Croydon: The Brotherhood Publishing Co.; London: Walter Scott Ltd., 1895-1896.
["A faithful and trustworthy rendering of the Russian original." Printed in Greek and English with a commentary. Of the projected three volumes, only vols 1 & 2 appeared.]

[See Anonymous, The Gospel in Brief, 1896.]

1895 **Pope, Charles H.**   The Gospels Combined; Parallel Passages Blended, and Separate Accounts Connected; Presenting in One Continuous Narrative, The Life Of Jesus Christ as Told by Matthew, Mark, Luke, and John. His Words in Special Type. Compiled by Charles H. Pope. Boston: W.A. Wilde, 1895.
["The language is that of the RV of 1881, with free use of its valuable marginal readings..." The interweaving is so intricate that sentences are often made up from different gospels.]

Third Edition; Boston: Charles H. Pope, 1912.

1896 **Anonymous**   The Gospel in Brief by Leo Tolstoy; Translated from the Russian Original Embodying the Author's Last Alterations and Revisions. "The English Editor".   London: Walter Scott Ltd.; Croydon: The Brotherhood Publishing Co., 1896.
Reprinted in: "The Religious Writings of Leo Tolstoy; Lift up your eyes...". N.Y.: The Julian Press Inc., 1960.

[See Anonymous, The Four Gospels, 1895.]

1896 **Beauclerk, Henry**   Jesus. His life in the very words of the four Gospels. A diatessaron. By Henry Beauclerk. London: Burns & Oates, 1896.

1896 **Blair, J.F.**   The Apostolic Gospel. With a critical reconstruction of the text. (Harmony).   London: Smith, Elder & Co., 1896.

1896 **Hill, James Hamlyn**   The Ephraem Fragments, or the portions of the Diatessaron cited by S. Ephraem the Syrian in the course of a commentary which he wrote upon it. <u>A Dissertation on the Gospel Commentary of S. Ephraem, etc.</u> by James Hamlyn Hill. 1896.

1896 **Hogg, Hope W.**   The Diatessaron of Tatian. New York: The Christian Literature Co., 1896.
    [Contained in "The Ante-Nicene Fathers". Additional Volume [IX]. "Containing the Early Christian Works Discovered since the completion of the Series, and selections from the Commentary of Origen. Allan Menzies, D.D..." Have found no trace of the former part of the series.]

1898 **Fletcher, Anne**   "New Testament Story in Verse". Chicago, Illinois: W.S. Reeve Publishing Co., 1898.
    [Condensed Monotessaron, bound with 'Famous Women of the Bible..." by Henry Davenport Northrop.]

1899 **Breen, A.E.**   A Harmonized Exposition of the Four Gospels. By Rev. A.E. Breen... 4 Vols.   Rochester: The John P. Smith Printing House, 1899-1904.
    Revised; 1908.

1900 **Altemus, Henry**   A Child's Life of Christ in Words of one Syllable. Philadelphia: Henry Altemus Co., 1900.

1900 **Roe, Edward T.**   (Editor)   See Samuel Weslay, The Life ...Jesus Christ, 1693.

1900 **Totten, Charles A.L.**   The Gospel of History: an Interwoven Harmony of Matthew, Mark, Luke and John, by Charles A.L. Totten. <u>Our Race</u>, No. 25-26, 1900.
    Reprinted; Merrimac, Mass.: Destiny Publishers, 1972.

1901 **Anonymous**   The Testament of Jesus. By Kenealy the Twelfth Messenger of God. [Edward V.H. Kenealy] Watford: C.W. Hillyer, 1901.
    [A curious monotessaron, with renderings similar to the ASV, but with many omissions and rearrangements; all miracles are deleted, the story ending with Jesus' burial. The Preface, signed by the posthumous editor, "C.W.H.", excoriates the Christian Church and Jews. He also presents a table of 'Sacred Messengers'.]

1901 **Hall, Thomas Cuming**   The Messages of Jesus According to the Synoptists...
    [See Charles F. Kent and Frank Knight Sanders, The Messages of the Bible, Vol.IX, 1900.]

1902 **Guthrie, William Norman**   The Christ of the Ages in
     words of Holy writ; being the story of Jesus drawn
     from the Old and New Testament, and compiled by Wm.
     Norman Guthrie.   Cincinnati, Ohio: The Western
     Literary Press, [1902.]
          ["Only two or three phrases in it are not actually
          Biblical, and they are from the Book of Enoch... There
          is some measure of rearrangement of words, structural
          inversions, syntactical changes; and these in turn
          needed to be licensed - - wherefore verse seemed
          absolutely necessary... hence the free 'loose' blank
          verse, as used by the later Jacobean dramatists..."]

1903 **Davis, Noah K.**   The Story of the Nazarene
     in annotated paraphrase. By Noah K. Davis. New York:
     Fleming H. Revell Company, 1903.

1903 **Tappan, Eva March**   The Christ Story, by Eva March
     Tappan. Boston & New York: Houghton, Mifflin & Co.,
     1903.
          [Children's monotessaron.]

1903 **Wilkinson, F.H.**   The Gospel of Jesus Christ
     the Son of God in the words of the four Evangelists.
     Arranged,   translated,   and   annotated   by   F.H.
     Wilkinson.   London: Marshall Bros., 1903.

1904 **Koepsel, L.H.**   The Life Supreme. Being the Real and
     True Biography of Jesus Christ. Parsons, Kansas: The
     Foley Railway Printing Co., 1904.
          [Monotessaron based mostly upon the 'Twentieth Century
          Version' of the N.T., 1898 edition.]

1904 **Losch, Henry**   The God-Man, or the Life and Works of
     Jesus, the Christ and Son of God. A Poem in Fifteen
     Parts.   Philadelphia: Ferris & Leach, 1904.
          [Monotessaron]

1904 **Wiener, Leo**   The Four Gospels Harmonized and
     Translated from the Original Russian and edited...
     Leo Wiener. 2 Vols. Boston: Dana Estes & Co., 1904.
          [Greek, KJV, and a free rendering in parallel columns,
          with commentary.]

     Another edition; Volumes I-II combined.   New
     York: Willey Book Co., 1904.

1905 **Smith, David**   The Days of His Flesh, The Earthly
     Life of Our Lord and Saviour Jesus Christ, by David
     Smith. London & New York: Hodder & Stoughton, 1905.
          [Monotessaron; Translation and Commentary.]

     Eighth Edition, Revised, 1910.

1910 **Smith, James**   A Life of Jesus Christ in Modern
     English for the use of schools. Compiled from the

Gospels by Rev. James Smith.   London: Macmillan & Co., 1910.

> 2nd edition, 1920.

1913 **Whipple, Wayne**   The Story-Life of the Son of Man, Nearly a Thousand Stories from Sacred and Secular Sources in a Continuous and Complete Chronicle of the Earth Life of the Saviour by Wayne Whipple. New York, Chicago, Toronto: Fleming H. Revell Company, 1913.

> [An anthology from many sources, with some of Whipple's own translation.]

1915 **Goddard, Dwight**   The Good News of a Spiritual Realm. By Dwight Goddard. Ann Arbor, Michigan: The Ann Arbor Press, 1915.

> ["This book is an interweaving of the Four Gospels into continuous account of the Life and Teachings of Jesus of Nazareth, in which the attempt is made by free translation and paraphrase to bring out clearly the unity and the reasonableness of his system of thought..."]

> Another edition; Paraphrased [& revised] New York, Chicago, Toronto, London, Edinburgh: Fleming H. Revell Co., 1916.

1916 **Bowen, Clayton R.**   The Gospel of Jesus Critically Reconstructed from the earliest sources. Boston: The Beacon Press, 1916.

> ["The English of the translation has been freely adapted from many sources, chiefly, of course from the Standard versions. But, it has been revised and recast throughout..."]

1916 **Damon, Louis A.**   A Story of Jesus the Christ; Chiefly from Bible Texts, Selected from Bible texts by Louis A. Damon. Chicago: Rand McNally & Company, 1916.

> [Monotessaron, based on the KJV with minor changes.]

1916 **Dorn, E.B. Van**   Manifestations in the Life of Christ. Chicago: Mrs. E.B. Van Dorn, 1916.
> [A condensed monotessaron, based on the KJV.]

1916 **Westphal, Alexandre**   Jesus of Nazareth. Harmony of the four Gospels by Alexandre Westphal... This translation is made by a few prisoners, for the use of their companions and others in captivity. Lausanne. An epitome of a two-volume work by Westphal. 1916.

1918 **Anonymous**   By an Unknown Disciple. London: Hodder & Stoughton, 1918.
> [Monotessaron and Narrative; several times reprinted.]

1919 **Goates, Margrey**   The Pepysian Gospel Harmony, 1919.
[See Anonymous, Harmony of the Gospels, 1400.]

1921 **Anonymous**   The Gospel according to Thomas. (A story
of Christ...told for the most part in the...words of
the New Testament.) With an introduction by Will
Hayes. London: C.W.Daniel, 1921.

1921 **Grant, Frederick C.**   The Life and Times of Jesus.
New York & Cincinnati: The Abingdon Press, 1921.
["For the sake of clearness, the Bible text used in this
volume has been paraphrased in modern English. Though
adhering closely to the current versions, the original
has been compared throughout."]

1921 **Higgins, James**   The Story Ever New, Giving the most
interesting events in the life of Jesus Christ as a
text-book in religion for grammar grade children.
New York: The Macmillan Co., 1921.
["The different narratives...are taken from the N.T.
They are expressed in simple yet dignified diction that
can be readily and easily grasped by pupils in the
grammar grades. As a rule, the words of the approved
(Douay?) text have been preserved."]

1922 **Brewster, H.S.**   The Simple Gospel. By H. S.
Brewster. New York: The Macmillan Co., 1922.

1923 **Cook, Neander P.**   The Genuine Words of Jesus,
according to the Older Documents Underlying the New
Testament Gospels. Edited and Newly Translated from
the Greek... including a Sketch of the Life and
Times   of   Jesus.   Based   exclusively   upon   the
Historically Trustworthy Source by Neander P. Cook.
Alhambra & Los Angeles, Calif: The Weimar Press,
1923.
["In translating the original Greek I have followed (so
far as possible) the English versions, but on occasion
have not hesitated to correct or change them... It may
interest the lay reader to know that the bulk of the
gospel of John (certainly its discourses) is held by all
scholars to be unhistorical. Nearly the same is true of
the eschatalogical discourses and material of the other
gospels."]

1923 **Vedder, Henry C.**   The Words of Jesus, Edited
According to Modern Literary Form by Henry C.Vedder.
2 Vols. Girard, Kansas: Haldeman-Julius Company;
Ten Cent Pocket Series No. 112, 1923.

1924 **Cornwell, A.T.**   The Essential Gospel, The
Heart of the Gospel, Thoroughly Translated for Daily
Reading by A.T. Cornwell. Clearwater, Florida:
Published by A.T. Cornwell, 1924.
[A "...simple version of the Gospel only, without
ambiguous words; with every irrelevant circumstance and
comment   which   might   distract   attention,   every

unessential subject of the controversy upon which men
honestly differ, every reference to purely local
conditions – – reverently omitted – – a direct statement
of its essence thoroughly translated into every – day
words and idioms, of the word of truth, transmitted by
God to man through Jesus Christ." Text consists of the
Gospel story paraphrased.]

1924 **Thurber, Robert Bruce**   Bible Stories Series Number
One; The Story of Jesus, by Robert Bruce Thurber.
Nashville, Tennessee, Atlanta, Georgia; Fort Worth,
Texas: Southern Publishing Association, 1924.
[An abridged monotessaron.]

1925 **Moffatt, James**   Everyman's Life of Jesus, A
Narrative in the words of the Four Gospels, by James
Moffatt. New York: George H. Doran Co., 1925
[An interweaving of Moffatt's translation of the four
gospels as they appeared in his N.T. of 1913; the
interweaving creates many new wordings.]

1925 **Smith, David**   Our Lord's Earthly Life, by David
Smith. London: Hodder & Stoughton, 1925.
[Monotessaron narrative with a new, free translation of
speeches; a different work from that in 'The Days of His
Flesh', 1905.]

1926 **Loux, Dubois H.**   A harmony of the Gospels. Jesus'
exaltation of the Fatherhood of God; business new
era version, translated out of the original Greek by
Dubois H. Loux.   Jackson, Michigan: Fellowship of
Declaration, 1926.
[Loux believes that interest-taking is condemned in the
N.T., and so translates it.]

1927 **Gibbons, Helen Davenport**   The Radiant Story of
Jesus by Alphonse Seche; Done into English by Helen
Davenport Gibbons. New York & London: The Century
Company, 1927.
[Monotessaron; mostly KJV with some paraphrase; also
many apocryphal N.T. and some O.T. passages,]

1928 **Gibran, Kahlil**   Jesus the Son of Man. His Words
and his Deeds as Told and Recorded by Those who knew
him. New York: Alfred A. Knopf, 1928.
29th printing; 1973.

1928 **Towne, Edward Owings**   The Philosophy of Jesus...
A narrative of the life and teachings of Jesus of
Nazareth, arranged from the Gospels of Matthew, Mark
and Luke, as newly translated into modern English.
By Edward Owings Towne. New York & London: New Era
Book Corp., 1928.
Another edition, 1929.

1929 **Barnouw, A.J.**   The Liege Diatessaron... Edited
with a textual apparatus by D. Plooij, with the

assistance of C.A. Phillips. English Translation of
the Dutch Text by A.J. Barnouw. Amsterdam: n.p.,
1929.
[A Middle-Dutch version of the Diatessaron of Tatian.]

1930 **Barton, John**   A Catholic Harmony of
the Four Gospels; being an adaption of the Synopsis
Evangelica of Pere M.J.Legrange, with introduction
and notes. London: Burns, Oates & Co., 1930.

1930 **Goodier, Alban**   The Public Life of Our Lord Jesus
Christ; An Interpretation. New York: P.J. Kenedy &
Sons, 1930.
[*"The author...has been content to take the Douay
Version as he finds it, upon it to build his harmony...
he has seldom substituted a translation of his own."*]

1931 **Mathews, Basil**   A Life of Jesus... Thirty-Three
Photographs by the Author. New York & London: Harper
& Brothers, 1931.
[*"...in language real and living for any person who has
ever read or heard anything about (Jesus)..."*]

1932 **Lamsa, George M.**   My Neighbor Jesus in the Light
of His Own Language, People, and Time. By George M.
Lamsa. New York & London: Harper & Brothers, 1932.

1932 **Pierson, Helen W.**   The Life of Jesus, by Helen W.
Pierson. Springfield, Mass.: McLoughlin Bros., Inc.,
1932.
[Children's Montessaron.]

1933 **Reynolds, Andrew J.**   Jesus of Nazareth "The Prince
of Life", by Andrew J. Reynolds. Denver, Colorado:
Fowler-Metzger-Aley Co., 1933.
[Monotessaron; slighty modernized KJV.]

1934 **Dickens, Charles**   The Life of Our Lord. Written for
his children during the years 1846 to 1849...and now
first published. New York: Simon and Schuster, 1934.
[*"It is about sixteen short chapters, chiefly adapted
from St. Luke's Gospel, most beautiful, most touching,
most simple as such a narrative should be."*]

Another edition; Westminster Press, n.d.

Also; New York: Garden City Publishing Co.,
Inc., 1939.

1934 **Durden, C.W.**   The Epic of Jesus. New York, London,
& Edinburgh: Fleming H. Revell Co., 1934.
[Poetical Monotessaron]

1934 **Smith, Louise Pettibone and Ermine Huntress Lantero**
Jesus by Rudolph Bultman. Translated by Louise
Pettibone Smith and Ermine Huntress Lantero. 1934.

[Abbreviated Monotessaron & Commentary, translated from the German.]

Another edition; Jesus and the Word. New York: Charles Scribner's, 1958.

1936 **West China University** Jesus, a Life of Jesus Taken from the Records of Matthew, Mark and Luke...West China University. By Lesslie Earl Willmott, Dryden Linsley Phelps, Lewis Calvin Walmsley, Mary Katherine Willmott, Margaret Hallanbeck Phelps and Constance Kilborn Walmsley. Chengtu, Szechwan, China: The Canadian Mission Press, 1936.
   [A Harmony of the Gospels, a version prepared especially for Chinese students with a study of eight English translations and reference to the Greek text. Partly based on Sherman's "The Records of the Life of Jesus". With the Chinese text.]

1936 **Wheeler, E.** Paraphrased Parables; or, Word-pictures from the New Testament, and a Bible alphabet with chorus comments. By E. Wheeler, etc. London: Missionary Service Bureau, 1936.
   [In verse.]

1937 **Crowley, J.M.** The Gospel Story and Those who wrote it. London: The Faith Press Ltd.; New York & Milwaukee, U.S.A.: Morehouse Publishing Co., 1937.
   ["A Harmony of the Gospels linked together by historical and topographical details, with a preface giving a short historical account of the four Gospels.]

1937 **Daniel, Orville E.** A Combined Harmony of the Gospels by Orville E. Daniel, Ph.D. Cocanada, India: Baptist Book Room, 1937.

1937 **Ebersol, Charles E. and Herman Feldmans** The Four Gospels in one made plain. By Charles E. Ebersol and Herman Feldmans with the counsel of an advisory board of Biblical scholars. Edinburgh: Fleming H. Revell Company, c1937.
   [Passages not made plain by a free translation of the Greek are briefly paraphrased.]

1937 **Waterman, Joseph MacNaughton** Good Tidings according to Matthias by Joseph MacNaughton Waterman. Cincinnati, Ohio: Lambeth Press, 1937.
   ["A delightful and entirely different yet reverent life of Jesus Christ is this narrative supposedly from the facile pen of Matthias, who was chosen by the eleven apostles to take the place of Judas..."]

1938 **Sexton, J.H.** The New Testament: the four Gospels harmonized and woven into one complete story of the doings and teachings of Jesus...Edited by J.H. Sexton. Adelaide: n.p., 1938.

1939 **Anonymous**   The Messages of Jesus by Martin Dibelius
...London: Nicholson & Watson Ltd., 1939.
> [Translation from Dibelius' "Die Botschaft von Jesus
> Christus". Tubinger: Mohr., 1939, by F.C.G. (whose
> initials appear after the Preface).]

1939 **Hunt, Marigold**   A Life of Our Lord. By Marigold.
Drawings by Rus Anderson.   New York: Sheed & Ward,
1939.
> Revised edition; 1959.

1939 **Hurley, Wilfred C.**   Unified Gospel of Jesus,
with Summaries and Notes. The Four Gospels in One
Narrative in Chronological Order...Adapted from Il
Vangelo di Jesu A Gli Atti Degli Apostoli di A.M.
Anzini, 1939.

1939 **Longman, Arnold and Franceys**   The Testament
of Jesus. A Single Narrative of the Great Life.
Arranged and translated from the New Testament
records... with a Foreword by C.H. Dodd. Cambridge:
W. Heffer & Sons Ltd., 1939.

1941 **Troyer, Evelyn**   Listening to the Master, by Evelyn
Troyer ...station N-E-W T-E-S-T-A-M-E-N-T televised.
Los Angeles: n.p., [1941].
> [A paraphrase.]

1942 **Foster, Dorothy Fay** (Editor)   The Life of Christ
Visualized. Artists: Stemler, Lohman, Rolfsen, Fay,
and Frohliger. Editor: Dorothy Fay Foster. 3 Books.
Cincinnati, OH: The Standard Publishing Co., 1942-
1943.

1942 Book One	From Bethlehem's manger to calling of the twelve.
1943 Book Two	The ministry.
1943 Book Three	The triumphal entry to the ascension.

> [Nos. 2051-2053 in the "Bible Visualized" series. "A
> reverent translation of Gospel narrative into continuous
> picture."]

1945 **Thompson, Newton**   The Life of Jesus Christ in
the Land of Israel and among its People by Dr. Franz
Michel Willam, Translated and Adapted into English
from the Fourth Revised and Enlarged German edition
by Newton Thompson. London & St. Louis, MO: B.Herder
Book Co., 1945.

1946 **Eickmann, Walther**   The Evangel; The Good News
of Jesus Christ the Son of God, as told by the Four
Evangelists. The Life of Christ in the Words of the
Bible; translated and arranged. New York: Stratford
House, Inc., 1946.

1946 **Neff, Lawrence W.**   The Three Gospels Printed
Side-by-Side; Compiled by Lawrence W. Neff. Emory
University, Georgia: Banner Press, 1946.
> ["The compilation is essentially a rewrite of the KJV,
> so phrased in current speech as to promote clearness and
> preserve the matchless literary style, with a few
> changes to correct recognized errors of the accepted
> translation." A Harmony of Matthew, Mark and Luke.]

1947 **Anonymous**   The Life of Our Lord Jesus Christ,
Written in Easy English by the Sisters of the Cross.
London: The Sheldon Press, 1947.
> Reprinted; 1957 & 1963.

1948 **Fisher, Fred L.**   A Composite Gospel. Nashville,
Tennessee: Broadman Press, 1948.
> ["The aim was to give a smooth, readable, simple and
> accurate translation which could carry over the meaning
> of the Greek text into English."]

1948 **Langford, Norman F.**   The King nobody wanted. By
Norman F. Lengford. Illustrated by John Lear.
Philadelphia: The Westminster Press, 1948.
> ["Where the actual words of the Bible are used, they are
> from the KJV. But the greater part of the story is told
> in the words of every day."]

1948 **Smith, Elwyn A.**   Men Called Him Master, by Elwyn
A. Smith. Philadelphia: The Westminster Press, 1948.
> ["The Stories...in this book are told in different words
> from those you will find in your Bible, and background
> has been built in from other records of the time..."]

1949 **Crofts, Freeman Wills**   The Four Gospels in One
Story Written as a Modern Biography; With difficult
passages clarified and explanatory notes by Freeman
Wills Crofts. New York, London, Toronto: Longmans,
Green & Co., 1949.
> ["... renders the whole in colloquial English in the
> form of a present-day biography."]

1950 **Greenlees, Duncan**   The Gospel of Jesus...Edited
and newly translated from the four Gospels with
explanatory notes and introduction.   Adyar:
Theosophical Publishing House, World Gospel Series
#4, 1950.

1950 **Heenan, John J.**   Jesus Christ; His Life,
His Teaching and His Work, by Ferdinand Prat S.J.:
Translation from the 16th French edition. 2 Vols.
Milwaukee: The Bruce Publishing Co., 1950.
> [Translation interspersed with extensive commentary.]

1951 **Cary, Edward F.**   The Life of Jesus in the Words of
the Four Gospels. Arranged and translated from the
Greek text of Westcott & Hort by Edward F. Cary.
Poughkeepsie, New York: by Edward F. Cary, 1951.

[Gospel Harmony, resulting from 3 years of work, consultations with N.T. professors and a trip to Palestine.]

1951 **Peterson, Russell A.**   The Synoptic New Testament; a new translation and harmony of the Four Gospels from the original Greek. By Russell A. Peterson. Boston: Meador Printing Co., 1951.

1951 **Roper, Harold**   Jesus in His Own Words, Compiled by Harold Roper. Westminster, Maryland: The Newman Press, 1951.
["...all our Lord's words have been taken from the Westminster Version (1913). Here and there an alternative reading is added in square brackets, and we have replaced the names of English coins...by those in the gospels..."]

1952 **Raemers, William**   Jesus Christ, Saviour of the World, by William Raemers. Glasgow, Scotland: John S. Burns & Son, 1952.
Another edition; St. Paul, Minnesota: Catechetical Guild Educational Society, 1955.

[Abbreviated montessaron, with paraphrase and Catholic commentary.]

1953 **Graves, Robert and Joshua Podro**   The Nazarene Gospel Restored. By Robert Graves and Joshua Podro. London: Cassell & Company Ltd., 1953.
[There is not the slightest evidence that such a document as the 'Nazarene Gospel' ever exited, even orally.]

[Part Three consists of a reconstructed monotessaron, with many startling renderings. Part III (text only) reissued under the title: "The Nazarene Gospel. London: Cassell, 1955.]

Another edition; Garden City, New York: Doubleday & Co., n.d.

1955 **Eleanor, Mother Mary**   Jesus Son of David. By Mother Mary Eleanor. Illustrated by George Pollard. Milwaukee: The Bruce Publishing Co., 1955.
["Most of the words attributed to our Lord in this book were really said by him, except that the thee's have usually been changed to you's. A very few have been invented. The deeds are true, except for the little imagined ones in the hidden life in Egypt and Nazareth."]

1955 **Jackson, H. Parry**   Light of the World; a Harmony of the Gospels in Basic English; edited by H. Parry Jackson. London: Parry Jackson, 1955.

1956 **Anonymous**   The Interlineary Hebrew and English Psalter, in which the construction of every word is indicated, and the root of each distinguished by the use of hollow and other types. London: Samuel Bagster & Sons; New York: Harper & Bros., 1956.

1958 **Cox, Ronald**   The Gospel Story...
[See New Testament Selections, 1956 Ronald Cox, New Testament Narrative...]

1959 **Barrett, Paul**   The Life of Christ by Andres Fernandez.... Translated from the Spanish by Paul Barrett. Westminster, MD: The Newman Press, 1959.

1959 **Beck, William F.**   The Christ of the Gospels; The life and work of Jesus as told by Matthew, Mark, Luke, and John; Presented as one complete story in the language of today by William F. Beck. St. Louis: Concordia Publishing House, 1959.

1960 **Anonymous**   The Twentieth Century Encyclopedia of Catholicism...
[See Bible Selections for the complete entry. Includes Gospel harmonies.]

1961 **Ewing, Upton Clary**   The Essence Christ; A Recovery of the Historical Jesus and the Doctrines of Primitive Christianity. New York: Philosophical Library, 1961.
[Contains Five Books; "Book Two is a Fifth Gospel: a reconstructed version of various N.T. narratives which in effect challenges much of what tradition has unfittingly attributed to Jesus..." Reconstruction based on the Dead Sea Scrolls.]

1962 **Allen, Charles L.**   The Life of Christ (Harmony). Westwood, N.J.: Fleming H. Revell Co., 1962.
["I have left Jesus' words in the language of the KJV...".]

1962 **Shank, Robert**   Jesus - His Story; The four Gospels as one narrative in language for today, by Robert Shank. Springfield, Missouri: Westcott Publishers, 1962.
["...I have sought to be guided by three principles: (1) to be faithful to the meaning of the Greek text; (2) to present a simple and reverent translation; (3) to stay close enough to the KJV to retain a sense of familiarity..."]

1963 **Green, Peter**   The Life of Jesus; Jean Steinmann. Translated from the French by Peter Green. Boston: & London: Little, Brown & Co.; An Atlantic Monthly Press Book, 1963.
[Most of the direct quotes appear to be based on the KJV.]

1964 **Payne, Robert**   The Lord Jesus, by Robert Payne. London, New York, Toronto: Abelard-Schuman, 1964.

[A Novel]

1967 **Stone, Eugene**   Jesus and His Teachings. 1967.
['In clear, simple language for young children.']

1968 **Schraff, Francis and Anne**   Jesus Our Brother - A
Life of Christ for the young, by Francis and Anne
Schraff. Liguori, MO: Liguorian Books Redemptionist
Fathers, 1968.
["...written for the boys and girls of today..."]

1969 **Cheney, Johnston M.**   The Life of Christ in Stereo.
The Four Gospels combined as one. By Johnston M.
Cheney. Edited by Stanley A. Ellison, Th.D...
Foreword by Earl D. Radmacher, MA, Th.D... Portland,
Oregon: Western Baptist Seminary Press, 1969.
["While over twenty translations and versions were
constantly consulted, we have sought to preserve the
beauty of the "King James" version, testing each
rendering by the original"]

Another edition; 1971.

3rd Printing; 1973.

1970 **Miles, Bernard**   God's Brainwave, the story of Jesus
doing the job his old Dad sent him to do, by Bernard
Miles. London: Hodder & Stoughton, 1970.
["I see a real man, the Son of God, born into a working
class home, brave, rebellious, ragged, dirty, often
hungry, footsore and bloodshot-eyed. His twelve mates
are mostly illiterate and as ragged and dirty as he is -
have you seen a fisherman's hands and smelt their
working clothes?" ...retold in the language of the
Chiltern Hills.]

1971 **Emerson, William A.**   The Jesus Story. New York,
Evanston, San Francisco, London: Harper & Row, 1971.

1971 **Moss, Arthur Robinson**   Jesus; a New Translation
of the Four Gospels, Arranged as One. Translated and
Ordered by Arthur Moss. With an Introduction by
Henry de Candole... Derby: Citadel Press; London:
Tom Stacy Ltd., 1971.

1973 **Anonymous**   Jesus. The Four Gospels, Matthew,
Mark, Luke and John, combined in one narrative and
rendered in modern English. [Charles B. Templeton]
New York: Simon & Shuster, 1973.

1974 **Anonymous**   Walk with Me in Modern English...
[See New Testament Selections for the complete entry.]

1974 **Coulter, Frederick R.**   A Harmony of the Gospels
in Modern English. The Life of Jesus Christ by

Frederick R. Coulter. Los Angeles: York Publishing Co., 1974.

1976 **Cox, Ronald**   The Gospel Jesus: The Story in Modern English by Ronald Cox. Nole Plaza, Ind.: Our Sunday Visitor, 1976.

1984 **Cole, Marley** Living Destiny – The Man from Matthew, Mark, Luke, John. Knoxville, TN: Proguides, 1984.

1985 **Millar, John Fitzhugh**   (Editor)   A Complete Life of Christ, edited by John Fitzhugh Millar. Williamsburg, VA: Thirteen Colonies Press, 1985.
    [Translation of the Biblical Material is his own.]

1985 **Pryor, R. Lewis**   One Gospel. Taken literally from the four gospels in the Authorized KJV by the Bible compiled by R. Lewis Pryor.   Jefferson, NC: McFarland, 1985.

MATTHEW

???? **Ainsworth, Henry**   MS form of Hosea, Matthew...
    [See Bible Selections for the complete entry.]

???? **Andrews, Charles Freer**   The Sermon on the Mount. By C.F. Andrews. The Macmillan Company, [196?].
    [Chapter 2 contains a translation of St. Matthew, chapter V, VI & VII, from the Greek.]

    Another edition; The Sermon on the Mount. Foreword by Rabindranath Tagore; Introductory Note by Agatha Harrison. New York: Collier Books, 1962.

???? **Anonymous**   The King and His Kingdom by Matthew. Soul Clinic International, [19??].

???? **Anonymous**   The Gospel of St. Matthew in Greek; with an Interlinal and Analytical Translation on the Hamiltonian System. London: Aylott and Co., [182?].

???? **Anonymous**   The Hellenic New Testament...
    [See Gospel Selections for the complete entry.]

???? **Betts, John Thomas**   Juan de Valdes' Commentary upon St. Matthew's Gospel. By John T. Betts. London: Trubner & Co., [188?].

???? **Hagner, Donald A.**   Word Biblical Commentary.
Matthew. Donald A. Hagner. Waco, Tx: Word Books,
Publishers, [198?].
  [See Complete Bibles, 1982 Word Biblical Commentary,
  Vol. 33.]

???? **Hendriksen, William**   New Testament Commentary...
  [See New Testament Selections, 1953 for entire entry.]

???? **King James I**   His version of 26 Psalms, the Lord's
Prayer and...
  [See Bible Selections for the complete entry.]

1380 **Anonymous** New Testament ["...nearly half of the N.T...]
  [See New Testament Selections for the complete entry.]

1400 **Anonymous**   A Lollard Gloss on S. Matthew. [John
Purvey] MSS: Laud Misc. 235; Trin. Cam. 36 c1400.

1530 **Tyndale, William**   An exposition vppon the v. vi.
vii. chapters of Methew, which thre chapters are the
keye and the dore of the scripture, and the
restoringe agayne of Moses lawe corrupte by the
Scrybes and Pharises, And the exposicion is the
restoringe agayne of Christes lawe corrupte by the
Papistes. Set forth by William Tyndale. 1530.
  Another edition; - - Newly set forth and
  corrected according to his first copye, 1532.

  Reprinted; London: Day, 1573.

  Reprinted; Expositions and Notes on Sundry
  Portions of Holy Scriptures... Edited for the
  Parker Society by the Rev. Henry Walter.
  Cambridge University Press, 1849.

1550 **Cheke, Sir John**   The Gospel of S. Matthew...Ye
gospel bi saint Mark ye first Chapter. MS. CIV;
Corpus Christi, 1550.
  [Unknown whether Gospel of Matthew was ever completed.
  MS of Mark, never published.]

  Another edition; St.Matthew, chapter 1 verses 17
  - 19, chapter 2 verses 16. London: 1705.

  Also; The Gospel according to Saint Matthew and
  part of the first chapter of the Gospel
  according to Saint Mark, translated into
  English from the Greek, with original notes,
  by Sir John Cheke, Knight... Also VII.
  original letters of Sir J. Cheke. Prefixed is
  an introductory account of the nature and
  object of the translation; by James Goodwin...
  London: William Pickering.   Cambridge: C.
  Whittingham, J. and J.J. Deighton, 1843.

MACK LIBRARY
BOB JONES UNIVERSITY
GREENVILLE, SC

1570 **Tymme, Thomas**   A Catholike and Ecclesiasticall exposition of the holy Gospell after S. Mathewe, gathered out of all the singuler and approued Deuines (whiche the Lorde hath geuen to his churche) by Augustine Marlorate, And translated out of Latine into Englishe by Thomas Tymme, Mynister. Sene and allowed according to the order appointed. Imprinted at London by Thomas Marshe, 1570.

1700 **Anonymous**   Scriptural Poems...Christ's Sermon...
[See Bible Selections for the complete entry.]

1709 **Whittenhall, T.**   Gospel of St. Matthew, 1709.
[See Anonymous, Moral Reflections, 1707.]

1722 **Blair, James**   Our Saviour's Divine Sermon on the Mount, contain'd in the Vth, VIth, and VIIth chapters of St. Matthew's Gospel, Explained; And the Practice of it recommended in divers Sermons and Discourses. In five volumes. To which is prefix'd, a Paraphrase of the whole Sermon on the Mount. By James Blair. London: J. Brotherton, 1722-1723.
Second edition; In four volumes.   London: 1740.

1726 **Beausobre & Lenfant**   A New Version of all the Books of the New Testament, with a Literal Commentary on all Difficult Passages. To which are added I. An Introduction to the Reading of the Holy Scriptures intended chiefly for Young Students in Divinity. II. An Abstract or Harmony of the Gospel-History. III. A Critical Preface to each of the Books of the New Testament with a General Preface to all St. Paul's Epistles. Written originally in French by Messieurs De Beausobre and Lenfant, By Order of the King of Prussia. Done into English with Additional Notes. Numb. I (to be continu'd Monthly) contains An Account of the whole Work, with part of the Introduction. London: Printed for J.Batley...and S.Chandler M.DCC.XXVI. (1726.)
[An English translation from the work of two French Protestants. The only portion of the text is 'The Holy Gospel of our Lord Jesus Christ, According to St. Matthew.' Apparently no more was published. "We are not to render word for word, but sense for sense".]

Reprinted, 1727, 1760, 1779, 1819.

Again; A New Version of the Gospel According to St. Matthew. With a Literal Commentary on all the Difficult Passages: to which is prefixed an introduction to the reading of the Holy Scriptures,... Written originally in French, by Messieurs De Beausobre and Lenfant,... London: Printed for G. & W.B. Whittaker, Ave-

Maria Lane; and Deighton & Sons, Cambridge, 1823.

[Reprinted as late as 1837 by Whittaker & Co, London.]

1737 **Anonymous**   A Paraphrase on the 5th, 6th and 7th chapters of Matthew, with proper soliloquies at every period. In a letter from a Father to a Son. [Samuel Collet] London: John Noon, 1737.

1741 **Scott, Daniel**   A new version of St. Matthew's Gospel: with Select Notes, wherein The Version is vindicated, and the Sense and Purity of several Words and Expressions in the Original Greek are settled, and illustrated from Authors of established Credit. To which is added, A Review of Dr. Mill's notes on this Gospel. By Daniel Scott... London: Printed for J. Noon, 1741.
> ["I engage for nothing but Diligence and Impartiality, and have endeavored to keep the Mean between a Version too Paraphrastical, and one too Literal... Whilst we avoid either Extreme, we may safely observe the following rule; That Ambiguities are generally to be retained, and supplemental Words rarely inserted, except when the genius of a Language makes them necessary, or Various Readings render them advisable."]

1766 **Mather, Samuel**   St. Matthew. Chapter VI, 9-13 (An Essay on the Lord's Prayer) Boston: Printed by Kneeland & Adams, for Wharton and Bowes, MDCCLXVI.

1776 **Mather, Samuel**   A New Translation of the Gospel of Matthew by Samuel Mather. Boston: Kneeland & Adams, 1776.

1784 **Anonymous**   The New-England Psalter...
> [See Bible Selections for the complete entry.]

1793 **Hill, Aaron**   Habakkuk 3... Matthew 6...
> [See Bible Selections for the complete entry.]

1799 **Anketell, John**   A Versification of the Book of Job, and Christ's Sermon on the Mount...
> [See Bible Selections for the complete entry.]

1807 **Henshall, Samuel**   The Gothic Gospel of Saint Matthew, from the Codex Argenteus of the fourth century; with the corresponding English, or Saxon, from the Durham Book of the eighth century, in roman characters; a literal English lesson of each; and notes, illustrations, and etymological disquisitions on organic principles. By Samuel Henshall, M.A.... 3 parts London: Printed for the author, and sold by J. White, 1807.
> ["...a very eccentric and discursive publication..."]

1819 **Holden, George**   An attempt towards an
     improved translation of the Proverbs of Solomon,
     from the original Hebrew, with notes, critical and
     explanatory, and a preliminary dissertation, by the
     Rev. George Holden.   Liverpool: Printed for the
     author by W. Robinson and Sons and T. Kaye; London:
     Printed for the author by Longman..., 1819.
          [The translation is the KJV with such alterations only
          as appear to be warranted by a critical interpretation
          of the original Hebrew.]

1830 **Anonymous**   The Received Translation of the Gospel
     of Saint Matthew: with alterations; humbly intended
     as an argument in favor of a revised and corrected
     edition of the AV of the Holy Scriptures...by   ,
     Queen's College Cambridge.   Cambridge: private
     printing, 1830.

1834 **Aislabie, William James**   The Gospel according to
     Matthew, Translated from the Greek by W. J.Aislabie.
     London: J.G. and F. Rivington, 1834.

1836 **Anonymous**   Book of Public Worship, for the use
     of the New Church...
          [See Bible Selections for the complete entry. Includes
          the Sermon on the Mount.]

1839 **Prevest, George** The Homilies of S. John Chrysostom,
     Archbishop of Constantinople, on the Gospel of St.
     Matthew. Translated, with Notes and Indices. By
     George Prevest. Cambridge: Frederick Field, 1839.
          Another edition; Part I. Hom. I-XXV. Oxford: John
          Henry Parker, 1843.

          Also; Part II. Hom. XXVI-LVIII. Oxford: John
          Henry Parker, 1854.

1840 **Cotter, John Rogerson**   The Gospels of St. Matthew
     and St. Mark...
          [See New Testament Selections, 1817 John Rogerson
          Cotter, The Gospels of St. Matthew...]

1842 **Anonymous**   Moral Reflections upon the Gospel of St.
     Matthew, a new edition, revised and corrected from
     the French of Pasquier Quesnel. [Robert Francis
     Wilson] London: James Burne, 1842.
          [Editor's preface signed "R.E.W."; a revision of
          Whittenhall's edition of 1709, based upon Russell's
          translation of the N.T., 1719.]

          Another edition; Devotional Commentary on the
          Gospel of St. Matthew. Translated from the
          French of Uesnel. London: Rivingtons, 1869.

1852 **Pitman, John R.** A Practical Commentary on Our Blessed Lord's Sermon on the Mount; Valedictory Address to His Disciples; and Parables. Together with a Brief Paraphrase and Corrections of the Authorized Version, 1852.

1854 **American Bible Union** Matthew, Chapters 1, 2 (By Orrin B.Judd). New York: American Bible Union, 1854.

1855 **American Bible Union** A Specimen of the Revision of the Gospel of Matthew, Greek Text, common and Revised version, with notes.(Chapters 1-3) [By Orrin B. Judd]. New York: American Bible Union, 1855.
> Another edition; The Gospel According to Matthew; Chapters I., II., III. New York: American Bible Union; Loisville: Bible Revision Association; London: Trubner & Co., 1858.

1855 **Anonymous** Christ's Sermon on the Mount, in verse; with analytical divisions and explanatory notes...by R.A. London: Wertheim & Macintosh, 1855.

1856 **Riddell, Henry Scott** The Gospel of St. Matthew in Lowland Scotch; from the English authorized version, by H.S. Riddell. London: Robson, Levey & Franklyn; Impensis Ludovici Luciani Bonoparte, 1856.

1857 **Green, Thomas Sheldon** The New Testament...
> [See New Testament Selections for the complete entry. Includes Matthew.]

1858 **American Bible Union** The Gospel according to Matthew Chapters I, II, III. Translated from the Greek on the basis of the common English version. With Notes. (By Thomas J.Conant). New York: American Bible Union; Louisville, Ky: Bible Revision Association; London: Trubner & Co., 1858.

1859 **Cookesley, William G.** A Revised Translation of the New Testament... Pt. 1 Containing the Gospel of St. Matthew by W.G. Cookesley. London: Longman & Co., 1859.
> [More published?]

> [This translation is based on the Mandarin Union several English translations, and is intended for English-speaking Chinese. Mark seems to be a less exact translation than the others.]

1859 **Shadwell, Lancelot** The Gospel of Matthew... Mark...
> [See Gospel Selections for the complete entry.]

1861 **Anonymous** Facsimiles of Certain Portions of the Gospel of St. Matthew...
> [See New Testament Selections for the complete entry.]

1862 **Henderson, George**   The Gospel of St. Matthew,
     translated into Lowland Scotch, by George Henderson.
     London: Strangeways & Walden: Impensis Ludovici
     Luciani Bonaparte, 1862.

1863 **Anonymous**   The Gospel according to Saint Matthew.
     A new translation with brief notes, and a harmony of
     the Four Gospels. [John Hensley Godwin] London: S.
     Bagster & Sons, 1863.

1863 **Baird, Henry** The Gospel of St. Matthew, translated
     into Western English as spoken in Devonshire, by
     Henry Baird. London: Impensis Ludovici Luciani
     Bonaparte, printed by Strangeways & Walden, 1863.

1864 **Wemtss, D.**   A Metrical Version of the Sermon on the
     Mount, &c., &c. Melbourne: H.T. Dwight, 1864.

1870 **Anonymous**   The Oldest Gospel. Passages from
     the first Canonical Gospel, supposed to form the
     original Hebrew Gospel written by Matthew the
     Apostle, translated into English; with an
     introduction. London: Williams & Norgate, 1870.

1870 **Ellicott, Charles John**   Considerations on the
     Revision of the English Version...
          [See New Testament Selections for the complete entry.
          Includes the Sermon on the Mount, chapters V, VI, &
          VII.]

1872 **Davies, J.**   St. Matthew's Gospel: the text divided
     into paragraphs, and arranged chronologically...
     London: G. Philip & Son, 1872.

1873 **Dods, Marcus** (Editor) The Works of Aurelius, Bishop
     of Hippo, A New Translation... Edinburgh: T. & T.
     Clark, 1873.
          [Text is KJV with occasional minor deviations.]

          Another edition; The Sermon on the Mount
          Expounded,...William Findlay and The Harmony
          of the Evangelists...S.D.F. Salmon.

1877 **MacNaghten, Steuart**   The Holy Gospel according to
     Matthew. Translated by Steuart MacNaghten. London:
     Harrison & Sons, 1877.

1880 **Nicholson, Edward Byron** A Commentary on the Gospel
     According to Matthew, by Edward Byron Nicholson.
     London: C. Kegan & Co., 1880.
          [This entry is from an advertisement in the back of
          Nicholson's 'The Gospel According to the Hebrews',
          1879.]

1883 **Gardner, Charles**   The Gospel according
     to St. Matthew.   Translated from the Greek text of
     Constantinus De Tischendorff, and other standard
     textual authorities. Chicago: C.H. Jones, 1883.
          ["The old English style has been maintained, so far as
          practicable, and smoothness of diction, while desired
          and sought after, has invariably been sacrificed to
          accuracy of thought..."]

1883 **Guy, Edward Alexander**   The New Covenant. According
     to Matthew, with explanations of the translation,
     and Songs of Deliverance. [By] Edward Alexander Guy.
     Cincinnati: Printed at the Aldine Printing Works,
     [1883.]
          [The New Covenant. Part I. Matthew]

          ["Axioms: 1. Every word ought to be translated. 2. The
          same Greek word ought to be translated uniformly by the
          same English word. 3. The different Greek words ought to
          be translated distinctively by different English words.
          4. The primary meaning of each word ought to be given in
          every possible instance... 5. All supplied words ought
          to be given in italics..." An 'Immersion' version.]

     Another edition; minor revisions, 1888.

1885 **Seymour, C.B.**   The inaugural address of the Kingdom
     of Heaven: being a translation, by C.B. Seymour, of
     the Sermon on the Mount, with a running comment and
     notes.   Louisville: Printed by J.P. Morton and
     Company, 1885.

1888 **Campbell, William**   The Gospel of St. Matthew
     in Formosan (Sinkang Dialect), with corresponding
     versions in Dutch and English. Edited from Gravius'
     edition of 1661.   London: Kegan Paul, Trench,
     Trubner, & Co., 1888

1888 **Davie, George J.**   Commentary on the Holy Gospels.
     Translated and Edited from the original Latin. 2
     Vols. London: John Hodges, 1888.
          [Matthew only.]

1894 **Miles, Eustace H.**   The Teaching of Jesus To-day.
     The Sermon on the Mount rendered from the Greek into
     simpler English, by Eustace H. Miles. London: Grant
     Richards, 1894.

1896 **Anonymous**   The Sermon on the Mount and other
     extracts, from the New Testament...
          [See New Testament Selections for the complete entry.
          Includes Mt IV.23 to VI.27.]

1898 **Harrison, R.L.** The Gospel of Jesus according to St.
     Matthew as interpreted to R.L. Harrison by the light

of the Godly experience of Sri Parananda. London: Kegan Paul, Trench, Trubner & Co., Ltd., 1898.

["...an interpretation...by the light of the spiritual experience of those who are known in India as Jivan-muktas, showing that those Gospels, when rightly understood, are in perfect harmony with the teachings of the Vedanta philosophy of India..." The text is KJV with numerous minor alterations; 'Holy Spirit' for 'Holy Ghost', 'Elijah' for 'Elias', etc.]

Another edition; New York: Theosophical Society, 190?

1898 **Smith, William Wye** ...The Gospel of Matthew in Broad Scotch, rendered by Rev. William Wye Smith. Toronto: Imrie, Graham and Co., 1898.

1900 **Ellis, John S.**   Songs of St. Matthew; A Metrical Paraphrase of His Gospel. By John S. Ellis Illustrated; with pictures of Palestine. [Muncie, Indiana] 1900.

1903 **Anonymous**   The True History and Tragedy of Joshua the Messiah. By Levi Benhalpai. [E.A. Guy] Washington: E.A. Guy, 1903.

[A dramatized version of Matthew's Gospel.]

1905 **Genders, J.W.**   The Holy Bible for Daily Reading...

[See Gospel Selections for the complete entry. Includes Matthew.]

1907 **Allen, Willoughby C.**   A Critical and Exegetical Commentary on the Gospel according to St. Matthew. By Willoughby C. Allen. Edinburgh: T. & T. Clark; N.Y.: Charles Scribner's Sons, 1907.

[See Complete Bibles, 1895 The International Critical Commentary.]

1909 **Waylen, Hector**   Mountain Pathways. A study in the ethics of the Sermon on the Mount. Together with a revised translation and critical notes. By Hector Waylen. With an introduction by F.C. Burkitt. London: Sherratt & Hughes, 1909.

["Mathathiah 4:23 - 7:29"]

Second edition; revised and enlarged.   London: Kegan Paul & Co., 1912.

Third edition, 1922.

1910 **Cunard, F.W.**   The First Judgment... Christians...

[See Bible Selections for the complete entry.]

1913 **Walker, T.**   Matthew, 1913.

[See Anonymous, [The Synoptic Gospels] Preliminary Edition, 1913.]

1914 **Anonymous**   The Gospel according to S. Matthew...
     [See Gospel Selections, 1913 Anonymous, [The Synoptic
     Gospels].]

1918 **Lauritzen, Johannes Rudolph**   The Capitalized and
     Revised American Lutheran New Testament and Psalms.
     The Gospel according to St. Matthew. Based on Dr.
     Martin Luther's Translation from the original Greek,
     carefully compared with former editions, and revised
     by a select committee of Lutheran Divines. Published
     by Johannes Rudolph Lauritzen. Knoxville, 1918.

1920 **Findlay, J. Alexander**   The Sermon on the Mount...
     With a paraphrase. By J. Alexander Findlay. London:
     J.A. Sharp, 1920.

1920 **Hoare, F.R.**   Sayings and Stories. A Translation of
     the Sermon on the Mount and some Parables. By F.R.
     Hoare. London: C.F. Garrood, [1920].

1924 **Loux, Dubois H.**   The New Covenant; A mutual
     arrangement or testament for a true civilization
     founded upon brotherly labor, following the Greek
     title which is usually rendered the New Testament
     translated out of the Greek As a Labor Determinative
     version, and diligently compared with former
     translations herein revised for the recovery of
     Biblical labor standards; I. The Gospel According to
     Matthew. By Dubois H. Loux. Jackson, Michigan: Home
     of the American Labor Determinative Revision
     Committee, 1924.

1927 **Schonfield, Hugh J.**   An Old Hebrew Text of St.
     Matthew's Gospel. Translated, with an introduction,
     notes and appendices by Hugh J. Schonfield.
     Edinburgh: T. & T. Clark, 1927.
          [Translated from "The Gospel of Matthew, until this day
          laid up among the Jews and concealed in their recesses,
          and now at last, from out of their apartments and from
          darkness, brought forth into the light..." which, with
          a Latin translation as published by Martin le Jeune, in
          Paris, 1555. "As far as it was consistent with accurate
          translation, the English of the AV has been
          followed..."]

1927 **Smith, T.D.**   Gospel According to St. Matthew, by
     T.D. Smith. Cambridge: n.p., 1927.

1928 **Dean, Joseph**   St. Matthew, 1928.
     [See Complete Bibles, 1913 Westminster Version.]

1928 **Osborn, Edwin Faxon** The words and deeds of Jesus...
     [See Gospel Selections for the complete entry.]

1928 **Potter, J.W.** The Good Message according to Matthew.
     For the use of Christian Spiritualists. Being an

entirely new and accurate translation. Edited by
J.W. Potter. London: Society of Communion, 1928.

1930 **Bacon, Benjamin Wisner**   Studies in Matthew.
By Benjamin Wisner Bacon. New York: Henry Holt and
Company, 1930.
        Part I.   General Introduction
        Part II.   Special Introduction
        Part III.   Translation   "...from the Critical
                       Greek   Text   with   preceding
                       translations diligently revised and
                       compared...Jehovah is used."
        Part IV.   Themes
        Part V.   Appended notes.

1934 **Williams, Charles Kingsley**   The Teaching of
Our Lord Jesus Christ according to St. Matthew with
several passages from St. Mark and St. Luke. Newly
done into very simple English from the Greek of the
Revised Version. By C. Kingsley Williams. London:
S.P.C.K., 1934.

1939 **Einspruch, Henry**   The Good News According to
Matthew... Translated by Henry Einspruch. Baltimore,
Maryland: The Mediater, 1939.
      ["The present attempt to retranslate the Matthian
      account of the Messiah–Jesus into every–day English was
      undertaken with the sole purpose of restoring the locale
      and atmosphere in which the scenes and actions depicted
      therein took place."]

      [Photographic reproduction, also dated 1939 (printed
      1943?) Brooklyn, NY: American Board of Missions to the
      Jews, Inc.]

      Third Edition; Revised. Baltimore, Maryland: The
Lewis & Harriet Lederer Foundation, 1950.

      Fourth Edition; Revised. Baltimore, Maryland:
The Lewis & Harriet Lederer Foundation, 1964.

1940 **Allan, C. Wilfrid**   St. Matthew, 1935.
      [See Gospels, 1935 Anonymous, The Good News...Modern
      English (Matthew).]

1941 **Graber, J.D.**   The Story of the Gospel of Matthew
(The First of the Books of the New Testament)... The
Story of the Gospel of Matthew in Simple English.
Dhamatari, India: Dhamatari Christian Academy
American Mennonite Missionary, 1941.
      ["...this is not a translation. It is the 'Story of the
      Gospel of Matthew'. The object has ever been to express
      the obvious meaning of the text in the kind of English
      used and understood by the average high school student.
      Literary elegance and euphonious expression have
      purposely been sacrificed for simple clearness."]

1945 **Heywood, D. Herbert**   New Era Testament...
[See New Testament Selections for the complete entry.
Includes Matthew chapter 5, 6 & 7.]

1945 **Herbert, D.**   Sermon on the Mount...
[See New Testament Selections, 1945 D. Herbert Heywood,
New Era Testament.]

1948 **DeWitt, S.A.**   The Sermon on the Mount; Set to rhyme
and rhythm out of the King James Version of the New
Testament ...the Gospel according to Matthew... With
a Foreword by Shaemas O'Sheel. New York: Strathmore
Press, 1948.
[Basis of a "...plan of setting the prose of the Sermon
into rhymed iambics for an oratorio..."]

1952 **Jordan, Clarence** Sermon on the Mount. Philadelphia:
Judson, 1952.
["In this relevant explanation of the Sermon on the
Mount (Matt.5-7) Clarence Jordan seeks to convey the
original ideas of the Greek by using present-day
equivalents of the N.T. words." It is not known whether
this is the same work which appeared in "Practical
Religion..."]

Revised edition, 1970.

1954 **Core, J. Melvin**   Matthew; A common sense
translation. Translated by J.Melvin Core. Mossyrock,
Washington: Hand-typed copy, 1954-1955.

1954 **Scher, Andrew R.**   The Master-speech: the Sermon in
the Mount; a non-sectarian interpretation of Matthew
5-7, with questions and answers for study. By Andrew
R. Scher. New York: The Exposition Press, 1954.

1955 **Cummings, D.**   The Interpretation of the Gospel Law
and Commentary on the Epistle to the Hebrews (both
in extensor) Including Historical and Theological
Knowledge of Great Benefit to the Jews, and a
Supplementary Monograph on Baptism, by Apostolos
Makrakis, Translated out of the original Greek.
Southend-on-Sea, 1955.
Another edition; Chicago, Illinois: The Orthodox
Christian Educational Society, 1955.

[The 'Gospel Law' embraces Matthew V-VII.]

1957 **Baskerville, John**   Two New Books for the Bible...
[See Gospel Selections for the complete entry. Includes
Matthew.]

1957 **Bowman, John Wick and Roland W. Trapp**   The Gospel
from the Mount. A New Translation and Interpretation
of Matthew, ch.5 to ch.7. By John Wick Bowman and

Roland W. Trapp.   Philadelphia: The Westminster Press, 1957.

1958 **Cooper, David L**. Messiah: His Historical Appearance (Matthew). Los Angeles, Calif.: Biblical Research Society, 1958.
["I have endeavored to give a literal translation... At times, it is not wise to follow the original text to slavishly...]

1959 **Connick, C. Milo**   The Beatitudes. Fleming Revell, 1959.
[Published in his 'Build on the Rock'.]

1959 **Tempest, Margaret**   The Lord's Prayer for Children. By Margaret Tempest. London: William Collins Sons & Co., 1959.

1960 **Filson, Floyd V.**   A Commentary on The Gospel According to St. Matthew by Floyd V. Filson. London: Adam and Charles Black, 1960.
[See N.T., 1957 Black's N.T. Commentaries.]

[See N.T., 1958 Harper's N.T. Commentaries.]

Reprinted, 1967.

Second edition, 1971.

1962 **Blessing, Rev. William L.**   Blessing Version...
[See Bible Selections for the complete entry. Includes the first two chapters of Matthew.]

1962 **Noli, Metropolitan Fan S.**   The Poet of Nazareth; A Revised Version of the Gospel of St. Matthew with a Rhythmical Translation of the Sayings and Parables of Our Lord and Savior, Jesus Christ. By Metopolitan Fan S. Noli... Boston, Massachusetts: 1962.
["Now, in order to have a clear idea of Jesus as a poet, his sayings should be translated rhythmically as poetry. That is what I have tried to do in this version, in which about three fourths of St. Matthew's Gospel have been rendered in blank verse, with a few rhymes here and there."]

1963 **Simcox, Carrol E.**   The First Gospel; Its Meaning and Message, by Carrol E. Simcox.   Greenwich, Connecticut: The Seabury Press, 1963.
[The Book of Matthew. "The translation is my own. I have tried to make it good, modern English without the kind of dangerously free paraphrasing which can change the meaning of what was written."]

1966 **Fry, E. McGregor**   A Provisional New Translation of the Lord's Prayer, 1966. <u>The Bible Translator</u>, July, 1967.

1966 **Klingensmith, Don J.**   Today's English New Testament According to Matthew. Don J. Klingensmith, Chief Editor. Mandan, North Dakota: United Printing Inc., [1966].
> Another edition; Fargo, North Dakota: Kaye's, Inc., 1977.
>
> Again, 1979.

1970 **Jordan, Clarence**   The Cotton Patch Version...
> [See Gospel Selections for the complete entry.]

1971 **Albright, William Foxwell and C.S. Mann**
Matthew. Introduction, Translation, and Notes by W. F. Albright and C.S. Mann. Garden City, New York: Doubleday & Co., Inc., 1971.
> [See Complete Bibles, 1964 Anchor Bible (Matthew), Vol. 26.]

1978 **Johnson, Ben Campbell**   Matthew and Mark..
> [See Gospel Selections for the complete entry.]

1981 **Beare, Francis Wright**   The Gospel According to Matthew. Translation, Introduction and Commentary by Francis Wright Beare. San Francisco: Harper & Row, Publishers, 1981.

1987 **Howard, George**   The Gospel of Matthew according to a primitive Hebrew text. Macon, GA: Mercer University Press, 1987.

MARK

???? **Anonymous**   Good News by Mark (in easy English). Chicago: Moody Press, [195?].

???? **Anonymous**   The True Servant- - Mark's Story about Jesus. Toronto: Full Gospel Publishing House, [195? or 196?].

???? **Anonymous**   The Hellenic New Testament...
> [See Gospel Selections for the complete entry.]

???? **Cressman, Annie**   Mark. Toronto: Pentecostal Assemblies of Canada. n.d.

???? **Guelich, Robert A.** Word Biblical Commentary. Mark. Robert A. Guelich. Waco, Tx: Word Books, Publishers, [198?].
> [See Complete Bibles, 1982 Word Biblical Commentary, Vol. 34.]

1707 **F.T.**   Gospel of St. Mark, 1707.
[See Gospels, 1707 Anonymous, Moral Reflections.]

1817 **Cotter, John Rogerson**   The Gospel of Saint Matthew,
paraphrased...
[See New Testament Selections for the complete entry.]

1858 **American Bible Union**   The Gospel according to Mark.
Translated from the Greek on the basis of the common
English version. With Notes. (By N.N. Whiting). New
York: American Bible Union; Louisville, Ky: Bible
Revision Association; London: Trubner & Co., 1858.

1858 **Howarth, D. and J.H. Smithson**   See Gospels,
Anonymous, [The Four Gospels], 1805.

1861 **Shadwell, Lancelot**   The Gospel of Matthew...Mark...
[See Gospel Selections, 1859 Lancelot Shadwell, The
Gospel of...]

1864 **Sawyer, Leicester Ambrose**   First Gospel, being the
Gospel According to Mark: Translated and arranged
with a critical examination of the Book, its life of
Jesus, and his religion, by Leicester Ambrose
Sawyer.   Boston: Boston; Walker, Wise and Company,
1864.
[This translation is revised from that in the N.T. of
1858-61]

1869 **Godwin, John Hensley**   The Gospel according to St.
Mark. A new translation. With critical notes and
doctrinal lessons. London: Hodder & Stoughton, 1869.
[Anonymous?]

1870 **Anonymous**   The Gospel according to St. Mark:
revised from the ancient Greek MSS. unknown to the
translators of the AV; by a member of the University
of Oxford. [Mr. Briscoe?]   London: Spottiswoode &
Co.; Longmans, Green, and Co., 1870.

1881 **Leonard, Henry C.**   A Translation of the Anglo-Saxon
Version of St. Mark's Gospel with Preface and Notes,
by H.C. Leonard. London: J. Clarke & Co., 1881.
Second edition; The Good-News after Marcus'
Telling; A Literal Translation of the Anglo-
Saxon Version of St. Mark's Gospel with
preface and notes...Second Edition.   London:
James Clark, 1894.

1883 **Lindsay, Thomas M.**   The Gospel according to St.
Mark. By Thomas Lindsay. Edinburgh: T. & T. Clark,
1883.

1901 **Menzies, Allan**   The Earliest Gospel. A Historical
Study of the Gospel According to Mark. With a

[Greek] Text and English Version by Allan Menzies...
London: Macmillan & Co., 1901.

1905 **Genders, J.W.**   The Holy Bible for Daily Reading...
[See Gospel Selections for the complete entry. Includes
Matthew.]

1909 **Bacon, Benjamin Wisner**   Beginnings of the
Gospel Story: A Historico- Critical Inquiry into the
Sources and Structure of the Gospel according to
Mark, with expository notes upon the text, for
English readers. By B.W. Bacon.   New Haven,
Connecticut: Yale University Press, 1909.
["The text printed is that of the RV of 1881... Also a
Paraphrase of each section."]

1910 **Wright, Joseph**   Grammar of the Gothic Language...
[See New Testament Selections for the complete entry.]

1911 **Sarasvati, Ramabai**   Mark..., 1911.
[A word-for-word translation; Greek & English]

1913 **Richards, J.F.**   Mark, 1913.
[See Gospel Selections, 1913 Anonymous, [The Synoptic
Gospels].]

1915 **Allen, Willoughby C.**   The Gospel According to St.
Mark with Introduction and Notes by W.C. Allen.
London: Rivingtons; NY: The Macmillan Co., 1915.
["The translation of the text of St. Mark needs much
apology. It is generally bald, and frequently un-English
in idiom. That is intentional. I have tried by a very
literal rendering to suggest the main feature of the
Greek." Part of the Oxford Church Bible Commentary.
Also; see A.T.S. Goodrick, Book of Wisdom, 1913.]

[See Bible Selections, 1913 Oxford Church Bible
Commentary.]

1915 **Milner, G.E.J.**   The Gospel according to St. Mark,
by G.E.J. Milner. London: Oxford University Press,
1915.

1916 **Dean, Joseph**   St. Mark, 1916.
[See Complete Bibles, 1913 Westminster Version.]

1919 **Lauritzen, Johannes Rudolph**   The Capitalized and
Revised American Lutheran New Testament and Psalms.
The Gospel according to St. Mark. Based on Dr.
Martin Luther's Translation from the original Greek,
carefully compared with former editions, and revised
by a select committee of Lutheran Divines. Published
by Johannes Rudolph Lauritzen. Knoxville, 1919.

1920 **Anonymous**   Studies in St. Mark...A new translation
with a questionary. [Various authors] London: J.A.
Sharp; C.H. Kelly, 1920.

[Manuals of Fellowship]

1920 **Ballantine, Frank Schell**   Science and Scripture...
[See New Testament Selections for the complete
entry. Includes Mark.]

1920 **Manuals of Fellowship**   Studies in St. Mark...
A new translation with a questionary. [By Various
authors.] London: J.A. Sharp; C.H. Kelly, 1920.

1921 **Eaton, Robert D.**   Gospel According to St. Mark.
New York: Benziger Bros., 1921.

1921 **Pym, T.W.**   Mark's Account of Jesus. Being a version
of St. Mark's Gospel in 'Common Speech'. Compiled by
T.W. Pym. Cambridge: W. Heffner & Sons, 1921.

1922 **Anonymous**   Jesus of Nazareth. A Biography by John
Mark. London and New York: D. Appleton & Co., 1922.

1924 **Vedder, Henry C.**   The Gospel of Mark, translated
and edited, according to modern literary forms, by
Henry C. Vedder. Girard, Kansas: Haldeman-Julius
Company; Ten Cent Pocket Series No. 625, [1924].
["The aim has been so to transfer Mark's words to
current English, that the reader may get the full force
and significance of the story..."]

1927 **Allen, Rev. Ray**   Mark. By Ray Allen. Zion Herald,
1927?
Second edition; New York: The Foss-Soule Press,
1927

Third edition; That Wonderful Man by John Mark.
"His Name shall be called Wonderful."
Translated by Ray Allen. Being the writing
commonly called the Gospel of Mark. Hornell,
New York: W.H. Greenhow, 1929.

4th. edition; Racine, Wisconsin: Whitman, 1935.

8th. edition; Jesus, That Wonderful Man.
Wisconsin: Racine, 1935.

1929 **Lowrie, Walter**   Jesus according to St. Mark.
An interpretation of St. Mark's Gospel. By Walter
Lowrie. London, New York & Toronto: Longmans, Green
& Co., 1929.

1930 **Anonymous**   The Gospel according to Saint Mark
by the Very Reverend M.J. Lagrange, O.P. Authorized
translation from the French. London: Burns, Oates &
Washburn Ltd., 1930

1930 **Loux, Dubois H.** Mark's Good News; To Every Man
His Work, His Pay, His Rest. Translated by Dubois H.
Loux. Jackson, Michigan: Privately printed, 1930.
[The Book of Mark in Iambic Pentameter.]

1932 **Kleist, James A.** Memoirs of St. Peter or the Gospel
according to St.Mark, translated into English sense-
lines by James A. Kleist. Milwaukee, New York,
Chicago: The Bruce Publishing Co., 1932.

1934 **Richards, James** De Good News according to Mark.
Put into de Sussex dialect by Jim Cladpole. [James
Richards] Turnbridge Wells: J. Richards, 1934.
Second edition, 1934.

1937 **Soothill, W.E.** The Good News. Based upon the story
told by John Mark. Expressed in Every-day language.
By W.E. Soothill. Shanghai: The Christian Literature
Society, 1937.
Third edition, 1939.

[See Gospels, 1935 Anonymous, The Good News as told by
(Mark)...Modern English.]

1938 **Brooks, J. Barlow** Th' Good News accordin' to
Mark. Arrang't an' Thranscrib't... i' th' Lankisher
Dialect by J.B. Brooks. Oxford: The Author, 1938.

1940 **Matheson, Mary L.** St. Mark in Current English,
by Mary L. Matheson. Melbourne, Australia: National
Council of Religious Education, 1940.
[Based on the ERV, compared with the Greek of Prof. John
Gillies of Melbourne University. Aim of the translation
is to tell the "...story so simply that even a child may
follow it," and to "...express the thoughts and emotions
partly obscured by the Elizabethan language..." The
results is a good deal of Paraphrase, sometimes borrowed
from other gospels.]

Another edition, 1942.

1948 **Phair, Francis Noble** The Good News by Mark. The
Gospel of Mark Simplified by Francis Noble Phair.
Chicago: Moody Press, 1948.

1950 **Manson, T.W.** A Primer of Christianity.
Three Volumes in one. London, New York, and Toronto:
Oxford University Press, 1950.
Part I. The Beginning of the Gospel. By T.W.
Manson.
["...a new translation into modern
English of St. Mark (earliest of the
Gospels in date) and extracts from
other books of the N.T., with an
introduction..." Includes John 1:1-
18.]

Part II. The Furtherance of the Gospel. By
R.W. Moore.

Part III. The Truth of the Gospel. By G.B.
Caird.

Reprinted, 1958.

1940 **Wuest, Kenneth S.**   Word Studies...Mark...
[See New Testament Selections, 1940 Kenneth S. Wuest,
Word Studies...]

1945 **Heywood, D. Herbert**   New Era Testament...
[See New Testament Selections for the complete entry.
Includes Mark.]

1951 **Vernon, Edward**   The Gospel of St. Mark. A New
Translation in Simple English from the Nestle Greek
Text. By Edward Vernon. London: Hodder & Stoughton,
[1951].
["The ideal would be a version in which no word would be
employed which could not be readily understood by the
average intelligent child of twelve years and upwards."]

Another edition; New York: Prentice-Hall, Inc.,
[1952].

1953 **Grant, Frederick C.**   The Gospel of Mark.
By Frederick C. Grant. New York: Harper & Brothers,
Annotated Bible Series, 1953.

1953 **Parker, Pierson**   The Gospel before Mark, by Pierson
Parker. Chicago, Illinois: The Chicago University
Press, 1953.
["In the restored K text use is made...of both the
Revised Versions of 1881 and 1901. Departures from these
are sometimes necessary..."]

Second impression, 1955.

1956 **Anonymous**   Saint Mark in Basic English. Cambridge:
University Press, 1955.
[i.e. Feb. 1956.]

1956 **British and Foreign Bible Society**   St. Mark's
Gospel (1:1 - 9:1). Translated into English for the
use of Translators. London: British and foreign
Bible Society, [1956].

1957 **Tatlock, Richard**   A Paraphrase of St. Mark...with
a foreword by the Bishop of Stepney. London: A.R.
Mowbray & Co.; New York: Morehouse-Gorham Co., 1957.
["...a forthright version in contemporary language and
style... Though the version is deliberately more of a
paraphrase than a fresh translation..."]

1959 **Cressman, Annie**   The True Servant: Mark's Story about Jesus. Toronto: Full Gospel Publishing House, 1959.
>[References above are to Good News for the World: the Life and Teaching of Jesus. The New Testament in Worldwide English. Bombay, 1969.]

1960 **Johnson, Sherman Elbridge**   Mark, 1960.
>[See N.T., 1957 Black's N.T. Commentary.]

>[See N.T., 1958 Harper's N.T. Commentaries.]

1962 **Beardslee, John W. Jr.**   Mark: a Translation with Notes by John W. Beardslee, Jr. An occasional Paper published by the Theological Seminary New Brunswick. New Jersey: The Theological Seminary, 1962.
>["In this translation of Mark's Gospel, the blunt vividness of the original stands out... He may take a phrase or a whole sentence to render into English the sense of a single Greek word."]

1963 **Dooley, John L.M.**   The Gospel of Mark in Little Children's Words. Sydney: 1963.

1964 **Anonymous**   The Right Time. Mark's Story about Jesus. New York: American Bible Society, 1964.

1974 **Lane, William L.**   The Gospel according to Mark; the English text with introduction, exposition, and notes by William L. Lane. Grand Rapids: Eerdmans, 1974.

1976 **Price, Reynolds**   The Good News According to Mark. Translated by Reynolds Price. [W.Coast Print Center], 1976.

1977 **Haugerud, Joann**   The Word for Us...the Gospels...

>[See New Testament Selections for the complete entry.]

1978 **Johnson, Ben Campbell**   Matthew and Mark..
>[See Gospel Selections for the complete entry.]

1982 **Rhoads, David and Donald Michie**   Mark as Story. Philadelphia, PA: Fortress Press, 1982.
>Reprint; 1985.

1986 **Mann, C.S.**   Mark. A New Translation with Introduction, and Commentary, by C.S. Mann. Garden City, New York: Doubleday & Co., 1986.
>[See Complete Bibles, 1964 Anchor Bible, Vol. 27.]

1989 **Eyer, Shawn Tiberius**   Mark's Gospel: Insight through metaphor; A New Translation and History of the Gospel According to Mark by S. Tiberius Eyer. n.p.: Privately Printed, 1989.

LUKE

???? **Nolland, John**   Word Biblical Commentary. Luke. John Nolland. Waco, Tx: Word Books, Publishers, [198?].
> [See Complete Bibles, 1982 Word Biblical Commentary, Vol. 35.]

???? **Shalders, E.W. and M.D. Cusin**   A Commentary on the Gospel of St. Luke by F. Godet... Translated from the second French edition, by E.W. Shalders and M.D. Cusin. 2 Vols. Edinburgh: T. & T. Clark, "Clark's Foreign Theological Library", [188?].
> Another edition; - - With preface and notes to the American Edition by John Hall. Second Edition. New York: I.K. Funk & Co., 1881.

> Third Edition, 1890.

> Reprinted; Edinburgh: T. & T. Clark, 1952.

1535 **Gardyner, Bishop Stephen**   [Luke and John]...
> [See Gospel Selections for the complete entry.]

1707 **Whittenhall, T.**   Gospel of St. Luke, 1707.
> [See Gospels, 1707 Anonymous, Moral Reflections.]

1807 **Evanson, Edward**   A New Testament; or, the New Covenant according to Luke, Paul and John...
> [See New Testament Selections for the complete entry.]

1860 **American Bible Union**   The Gospel according to Luke (By N.N.Whiting). New York: American Bible Union, 1860.

1880 **Burgess, George**   The Gospel of St. Luke, with critical notes... Also, Six Charges Delivered to the Clergy of His Diocese. (Now reprinted by particular request.) By George Burgess. New York: Anson D.F. Randolph & Co., 1880.
> [Includes a commentary and a new translation.]

1886 **Lindsay, Thomas M.** The Gospel according to St. Luke. By Thomas M. Lindsay. London: Blackie & Son, 1886.

1893 **Bright, James Wilson**   Euangelium secundum Lucam. The Gospel of Saint Luke in Anglo-Saxon. Edited from the Manuscripts, with an Introduction, Notes, and a Glossary by James W. Bright.... Oxford: At the Clarendon Press, 1893.
> Another Edition; Boston: D.C.Heath, 1906.

Reprinted; Folcroft, PA: Folcroft Library Editions, 1973.

Reprinted; Norwood, PA: Norwood Editions, 1977.

1896 **Anonymous** The Sermon on the Mount... extracts...
[See New Testament Selections for the complete entry. Includes part of Luke.]

1896 **Carter, George** The Gospel according to St. Luke. London: Relfe Bros, 1896.

1896 **Plummer, Alfred** A Critical and Exegetical Commentary on the St. Luke, Together with a New Translation, by A. Plummer. Edinburgh: T.& T. Clark, 1896.
[See Complete Bibles, 1895 International Critical Commentary.]

Reprinted; 1922, 1969.

1897 **Margoliouth, G.** The Palestinian Syriac Version...
[See Bible Selections for the complete entry.]

1899 **Grierson, G.A.** Linguistic Survey of India...
[See Gospel Selections for the complete entry. Includes the Prodigal Son.]

1905 **Anonymous** The Good News to all Nations: a verbal translation and a paraphrase of the Holy Gospel according to Luke. Together with notes of comparison with the records of the other evangelists. [By Thomas Wilkins.] London: Cooper & Budd, 1905.
[One of twelve specimen copies, actually 1906.]

1911 **Castells, F. de P.** The Thoughts of the Master: being the message of the Messiah as handed down by Lucanus and interpreted for the members of his own Bible classes by the Revd. F. de P. Castells. London: Alexander & Shepheard, [1911].
[A paraphrase of Luke.]

1913 **Walker, T.** Luke, 1913.
[See Gospel Selections, 1913 Anonymous, [The Synoptic Gospels] Preliminary Edition.]

1918 **Buchanan, Edgar Simmons** (UnJudaized Version) From the Huntington Palimpsest...
[See New Testament Selections for the complete entry. Includes Luke.]

1919 **Lauritzen, Johannes Rudolph** The Capitalized and Revised American Lutheran New Testament and Psalms. The Gospel according to St. Luke. Based on Dr. Martin Luther's Translation from the original Greek, carefully compared with former editions, and revised

by a select committee of Lutheran Divines. Published
by Johannes Rudolph Lauritzen. Knoxville, 1919.

1923 **Robertson, A.T.**   A Translation of Luke's Gospel.
With Grammatical Notes, by A.T. Robertson. New York:
G.H. Doran Co., 1923.
>   ["The purpose of this translation...is to preserve, as
>   far as practicable, the delicate nuances...of the Greek
>   idiom... The quotations from the Old Testament are given
>   in italics and the book is printed like modern
>   English."]

>   Another edition; Nashville, Tennessee: Sunday
>   School   Board   of   the   Southern   Baptist
>   Convention, 1923.

1924 **Vedder, Henry C.**   The Gospel of Luke, a new
translation, edited, according to modern literary
forms, by Henry C. Vedder. Girard, Kansas: Haldeman
-Julius Company; Ten Cent Pocket Series No. 624,
[1924].
>   ["...it has been found necessary to omit all the purely
>   narrative portion."]

1931 **Stoll, Raymond F.** The Gospel according to St. Luke.
A Study of the Third Gospel with a Translation and
Commentary. By the Rev. Raymond F. Stoll...   New
York & Cincinnati: Frederick Pustet Co. Inc., 1931.

1932 **Packard, E.W.S.**   A Running Commentary on the Gospel
According to St. Luke With Parallel Text, by E.W.S.
Packard. London: Student Christian Movement Press,
1932.

1933 **Williams, Charles Kingsley**   The Life of Our Lord
Jesus Christ, according to St. Luke, together with
some passages from the other Gospels. Newly done
into very simple English from the Greek of the
Revised Version by C. Kingsley Williams... London:
SPCK, 1933.
>   Reprinted, 1936.

1935 **Dean, Joseph**   St. Luke, 1913.
>   [See Complete Bibles, 1913 Westminster Version.]

1937 **Young, P.N.F.**   The Good News of Luke the Physician.
With Commentary by P.N.F. Young. London: Lutterworth
Press, 1937.

1940 **Coombs, Doris V. and E.J. Clark**   The Glad
News as told by Saint Luke's Gospel (using a limited
vocabulary). A Rendering into modern English for the
use of students. Shanghai: Christian Literature
Society, 1940.
>   [See Anonymous, The Good News..., 1935.]

1941 **Klingensmith, Don J.**   The Gospel According to Luke in Everyday English. A translation into the everyday language of Midwestern United States from the Westcott and Hort text of the Greek New Testament. By Don J. Klingensmith... Peoria, Illinois: The Bond Press, 1941.
    Second edition, 1945.

    Another edition; The New Testament According to Luke. A Young People's Translation. Don J. Klingensmith, Chief Editor. Fargo, North Dakota: Kaye's, Inc., 1967, 1968.

    Also; The New Testament According to Luke in Everyday English. Fargo, North Dakota: Kaye's, Inc., 1975.

1948 **Parnwell, E.C.**   The Gospel according to St. Luke. The AV, explained in everyday English, by E.C. Parnwell. London: Oxford University Press, 1948.

1955 **Taylor, G. Aitken**   St. Luke's Life of Jesus, retold in modern language by G. Aitken Taylor. New York: The Macmillan Co., 1955.

1956 **Arndt, William F.**   Bible Commentary – The Gospel according to St. Luke. By William F. Arndt. St. Louis, Missouri: Concordia Publishing House, 1956.

1956 **Phillips, J.B.**   St. Luke's Life of Christ, 1956.
    [See New Testament, 1947 for the entire entry.]

1957 **Baskerville, John**   Two New Books for the Bible...
    [See Gospel Selections for the complete entry.]

1958 **Leaney, A.R.C.**   A Commentary on the Gospel according to St. Luke. By A.R.C.Leaney. London: Adam & Charles Black, 1958.
    [See N.T., 1957 Black's N.T. Commentary; See N.T., 1958 Harper's N.T. Commentaries.]

1966 **Geldenhuys, Johannes Norval**   Commentary on the Gospel of Luke; the English text with introduction, exposition, and notes, 1966.
    [See N.T., 1959 New International Comment. on the N.T.]

1969 **Jordan, Clarence**   The Cotton Patch Version...
    [See New Testament Selections for the complete entry.]

1981 **Fitzmyer, Joseph A.**   The Gospel According to Luke (I-IX). Introduction, Translation and Notes by Joseph A. Fitzmyer. Garden City, New York: Doubleday & Co., Inc., 1981.
    [See Complete Bibles, 1964 Anchor Bible, Vol. 28.]

1985 **Fitzmyer, Joseph A.**   The Gospel According to Luke
(X-XXIV). Introduction, Translation and Notes by
Joseph A. Fitzmyer. Garden City, New York: Doubleday
& Co., Inc., 1985.
[See Complete Bibles, 1964 Anchor Bible, Vol. 28A.]

JOHN

???? **Hamilton, James**   The Gospel of St. John, in Greek:
with an Interlineal and Analytical Translation on
the Principles of the Hamiltonian System.   London:
C.F. Hodgson and Son, and sold by Simpkin, Marshall
& Co.; Adams & Co.; and all booksellers, [182?].
["...with very few exceptions, one word in any language
can be correctly translated by one word only into
another..."]

Fifth edition; carefully revised and much
improved. London: 1847.

Also; The Gospel According to John: in Greek:
to which is appended a Critical Annotation;
also, the authorized English Version of the
Protestant Church, and a comparative view of
the Catholic translation from the Vulgate.
Together with Historic and grammatical Notes
by George William Heilig.   Philadelphia:
Charles De Silver & Sons, 1861. [Another edition,
1887.]

735 **Bede**   John in Anglo-Saxon. c735.
[The existence of this translation is based upon a
letter from Cuthbert to Cuthwine.]

1535 **Gardyner, Bishop Stephen**   [Luke and John]...
[See Gospel Selections for the complete entry.]

1557 **Traheron, Bartholemew**   An Exposition of a parte
of S. Iohannes Gospel made in sondrie readinges in
the English Congregation at Wesel by Bartholemew
Traheron, and now published against the wicked
enterprises of new sterte vp Arians in Englande.
Imprinted Anno 1557.

1574 **Tymme, Thomas**   A Catholike and Ecclesiasticall
exposition of the holy Gospell after S. Iohn.
Gathered out of all the singuler and approued
Deuines (whiche the Lorde hath geuen to his churche)
by Augustine Marlorate, And translated out of Latine
into Englishe by Thomas Tymme, Mynister. Sene and
allowed according to the order appointed. Imprinted

at London by Thomas Marshe, 1574.   [Title is taken from
the 1575 edition.]
    Another edition; London: H. Bynneman, 1575.

1584 **Fetherstone, Christopher**   The Commentaries of Ihon
Caluin vpon the Euangelist S. Ihon...translated out
of Latine. London: Thomas Dawson for George Byshop,
1584.

1630 **Usher, Ambrose**   ["All of the O.T.; and of the
New, the four 1st chapters of St. John's...]
    [See Bible Selections for the complete entry.]

1693 **Clagett, Dr. William**   St. John's Gospel, Chapters
1, 2, 3, 4, 5, 7, 8, with Paraphrase. London: W.
Rogers, 1693.

1693 **Clagett, Dr. William**   The Sixth Chapter of St.
John's Gospel with Notes and Paraphrase.   London:
n.p., 1693.

1800 **Anonymous**   St. John's Gospel; Chapter 1, A New
Translation. Gentleman's Magazine, Page 922, 1800.

1807 **Evanson, Edward**   A New Testament; or, the New
Covenant according to Luke, Paul and John...
    [See New Testament Selections for the complete entry.]

1824 **Hamilton, James**   A Key to the Greek Testament;
Part the First, Comprehending the Text of the Gospel
of St. John, and an Interlineary Translation, with
a Preface Explanatory of the Principles and Practice
of the Hamiltonian System. Executed under the
Immediate Direction of James Hamilton.   London:
Printed by N. Bliss, 1824.

1824 **Hamilton, James**   The Gospel of St. John, in Latin,
adapted to the Hamiltonian System by an Analytical
and Interlineary Translation. Executed under the
immediate direction of James Hamilton. London: The
Author, 1824.
    Also; ...to which is prefixed, a preface
explanatory of that system, and instructions.
Fourth edition. Leeds: F. Hobson, 1828.

1825 **Hamilton, George**   The Gospel of St. John,
in Italian, adapted to the Hamiltonian System by an
Analytical and Interlineary Translation. 2 Parts
London: The Author, 1825.
    Another edition; ...for the use of schools,
private teaching and families. James Hamilton.
London: Souter & Law, 185?.

    Also; a New edition, 1853.

1825 **Hamilton, George**   The Gospel of St. John,
in German, adapted to the Hamiltonian System by an
Analytical and Interlineary Translation. 2 Parts
London: The Author, 1825.
  Second edition, 1828.

1825 **Hamilton, George**   The Gospel of St. John,
in Spanish, adapted to the Hamiltonian System by an
Analytical and Interlineary Translation. 2 Parts
London: The Author, 1825.
  Second edition; James Hamilton. London: William
  Joy, 1830.

1830 **Connellan, Owen**   The Gospel according to St. John,
in Irish, with an interlined English translation;
and a grammatical praxis on the gospel according to
St. Matthew in Irish: accompanied with a short
introduction to Irish pronunciation; and an appendix
consisting of familiar conversations. Dublin: R.M.
Tims, 1830.

1830 **Friederici, E.** The Gospel of St. John, In Greek and
English, interlined, and literally translated: with
a transposition of the words into their due order of
construction; and a dictionary defining and parsing
them. Principally designed for the use of schools.
New York: Published for the author by G.F. Bunce,
1830.

1832 **Fenton, W.**   The Gospel of St. John in French,
with a literal interlineary translation; also a free
translation to all the obscure passages, with notes
on the construction of the language. London: Simpkin
& Marshall, 1832.

1835 **Follen, C.**   Luther's German Version of
the Gospel of St. John, with an interlinear English
translation, for the use of students.   Cambridge,
Mass.: J. Munroe & Co., 1835.

1837 **Aislabie, William James**   The Gospel of John,
Translated from the Original Greek by William James
Aislabie. London: The Author, 1837.

1837 **Fellowes, B.**   A Revision of the Gospel and Third
Epistle of John...
  [See New Testament Selections for the complete entry.]

1847 **Pringle, William**   Commentary on the Gospel
according to John by John Calvin. Translated from
the original Latin, and collated with the author's
French version.   2 Vols.   Edinburgh: Calvin
Translation Society, 1847.

[See Bible Selections, 1844 Anonymous, Commentaries on the books of the Bible.]

1848 **Browne, H.**   Homilies on the Gospel According to...
[See New Testament Selections for the complete entry.]

1857 **Anonymous**   The Gospel according to St. John, after the AV; newly compared with the original Greek and revised, by Five Clergymen. [John Barrow, George Moberly, Henry Alford, W.G. Humphrey, C.J. Ellicott and Edited by Ernest Hawkins] London: J.W. Parker & Son, 1857.
[The Greek is Mill's reprint (1707) of the text of Stephens. KJV and the revision are printed in parallel columns.]

Second edition; London: R. Clay for J. Parker & Son, 1857.

1859 **American Bible Union**   The Gospel of John ... (By J.W. Morton). New York: American Bible Union, 1859.

1861 **Huxtable, M.G.**   Christ, the Light of the World: Biblical studies on...St. John's Gospel. By Rudolph Besser D.D. Translated from the German by M.G. Huxtable. 2 Vols. Edinburgh: T. & T. Clark, 1861-1867.

1862 **Anonymous**   The Gospel according to St. John, containing the French text, with a literal word for word translation... London: James Cornish, 1862.
[Same as that of W. Fenton, 1832?]

1862 **Malan, Solomon Caesar**   The Gospel according to S. John, translated from the eleven oldest versions except the Latin, and compared with the English Bible; with notes on every one of the alterations proposed by the Five Clergymen in their revised version of this Gospel, published in MDCCCLVII. By the Rev. S.C. Malan... London: Joseph Masters, 1862.
[The 'eleven oldest versions' are the Syriac, Ethiopic, Sahidic, Memphitic, Gothic, Armenian, Georgian, Slavonic, Anglo-Saxon, Arabic, and Persian.]

1864 **Anonymous**   The Inspired Writings of Saint John; a new and improved edition of the authorised English translation. London: 1864.

1865 **Anonymous**   Commentary on the Gospel of St. John by E.W. Hengstenberg; Translated from the German. Edinburgh: T. & T. Clark's Foreign Theological Library [Ser 4, Vol 5, 7], 1865.

1871 **Corson, Hiram**   "Anglo-Saxon Version of the Gospel According to St. John." Handbook of Anglo-Saxon and Early English. New York: Holt & Williams, 1871.

1872 **O'Conor, W.A.**   A Commentary on John, with translation. London: 1872.

1873 **Anonymous**   The Universal Syllabic Gospel. The English of the Gospel according to St. John. With English Key... London: W. Hunt & Co., 1873.

1874 **Anonymous**   Commentary on the Gospel according to S. John. By S. Cyril, Archbishop of Alexandria. Oxford: J. Parker & Co.; London: Rivingtons, 1874-1885.
      1874 Vol. 1.   [Philip E. Pusey]

      1885 Vol. 2.   [Thomas Randell]

1874 **Tickle, Gilbert Y.**   The Gospel of John: a metrical rendering by Gilbert Y. Tickle. London: S. Bagster & Sons, 1874.

1876 **Taylor, S., and Others**   Commentary on the Gospel of St. John. With a Critical Introduction. Translated from the Second French Edition of F. Godet... S. Taylor, M.D.Cusin and Frances Crombie. Edinburgh: T. & T. Clark, Clark's Foreign Theological [Library Ser 4, v 51, 53, 56], 1876.
      [Date is that of the Preface.]

      Another Edition; 1881.

1881 **Griffith, Thomas**   The Gospel of the Divine Life. A Study of the Fourth Evangelist by Thomas Griffith. London: Kegan Paul & Co., 1881.
      [Contains also a translation of I John.]

1884 **Sawyer, Leicester Ambrose**   (The Bible) Analyzed, translated...Gospel according to John...
      [See Bible Selections for the complete entry.]

1886 **Anonymous**   St. John's Gospel, in Modern English. 1886?.
      [In the Library of Congress.]

1886 **Dwight, Timothy** (1828-1916)   Commentary on the Gospel of John with an historical and critical introduction by F. Godet... translated from the third French edition, with a preface, introductory suggestions and additional notes. 2 Vols. New York: Funk & Wagnalls, 1886.
      Another edition, 1890.

1887 **Paley, F.A.**   The Gospel of St. John: a verbatim translation from the Vatican MS, With the Notable Variations of the Sinaitic and Beza MS., and Brief Explanatory Comments. By F.A. Paley... London & Aylesbury: Hazell, Watson & Viney; London: for Swann Sonnenschein, Lowrey & Co., 1887.

1888 **Sloan-Duployan**   The Gospel according to S. John. [In shorthand.]   pt.1.   London: Sloan-Duployan Phonography, [1888]

1889 **Alexander, William**   Epistles of St. John, 1889.
            [See Complete Bibles, 1888 Expositor's Bible.]

1895 **MacLean, J.P.**   Introduction to the Study of the Gospel of St. John, together with an interlinear literal translation of the Greek text of Stephens, 1550, with the Authorized version conveniently presented in the margins for ready reference and with the various readings of the editions of Elzevir, 1624, Griesbach, Lachmann, Tischendorf, Tregelles, Alford, and Wordsworth. By J.P. MacLean. Cincinnati: R. Clarke Co., 1895.

1896 **Hitchcock, Roswell Dwight**   The Gospel according to John... Being the version set forth A.D. 1611 ... revised A.D. 1881, with the readings and renderings preferred by the American Committee of Revision incorporated into the text by R.D. Hitchcock. New York: Fords & Co., [1896]

1897 **MacRory, J.**   The Gospel of St. John, with notes critical and explanatory. By J. MacRory.   Dublin: Browne & Nolan, 1897.
            [Latin and English.]

1900 **Gill, William Hugh**   The Incarnate Word; Being the Fourth Gospel Elucidated by Interpolation for Popular use, by William Hugh Gill.   Philadelphia: George W. Jacobs & Co., 1900.

1902 **Harrison, R.L.**   An Eastern Exposition of the Gospel of Jesus according to St. John. Being an interpretation thereof by Sri Rarananda by the light of Jnana Yoga. Edited by R.L. Harrison. London: Wm. Hutchinson & Co., 1902.

Another edition; New York: Theosophical Society.

1902 **Sampson, Gerard**   The Layman's Bible Series...
            [See New Testament Selections for the complete entry. Includes John.]

1904 **Bright, James Wilson**   Euangelium secundum Iohannem.
The Gospel of Saint John in West—Saxon; edited from
the manuscripts, with Introduction and notes by
James Wilson Bright. With a glossary by Lancelot
Minor Harris. Boston: D. C. Heath & Co., 1904.
> Reprinted; Folcroft, PA: Folcroft Library
> Editions, 1973.

> Reprinted; Norwood, PA: Norwood Editions, 1977.

1904 **Wilson, James**   The Gospel of Saint John
in West—Saxon, Edited from the Manuscripts, with
introduction and notes by James Wilson. Boston &
London: D.C. Heath & Co., 1904.

1906 **Forster, Henry Langstaff**   St. John's Gospel,
Epistles, and Revelation...
> [See New Testament Selections, 1903 Henry Langstaff
> Forster, [N.T. Selections]...]

1908 **Riggs, James Stevenson**   The Messages of Jesus
according to the Gospel of John, freely rendered in
paraphrase. By James Stevenson Riggs.   London: In
Bodleian Library, Oxford, 1908.
> [See Abridged Bibles, 1900 Frank Knight Sanders and
> Charles Foster Kent, The Messages of the Bible, Vol. X.]

1908 **Westcott, A.**   The Gospel according to St.
John. The Greek Text (of Westcott and Hort) with an
introduction and notes by the late B.F. Westcott.
[Edited with a translation by A. Westcott]. Two
Vols. London: John Murray, 1908.
> ["I have only altered the text (or marginal text where
> preferred) of the RV in those cases where it seemed that
> its rendering would not have satisfied my Father."]

> Reprinted; Grand Rapids, MI: Baker Book House,
> 1980.

1909 **Pryse, James Morgan**   The Magical Message according
to Ionnes.. a verbatim translation from the Greek
done into modern English with introductory essays
and notes. By James M. Pryse.   New York: The
Theosophical Publishing Company of New York, 1909.
> [This work is mentioned in the Foreword to Pryse's
> 'Sermon on the Mount', 1904.]

1914 **Anonymous**   The Fourth Gospel...and Genesis, a
new translation shewing the...connection that exists
between both books by F.W.H...
> [See Bible Selections, 1913 Anonymous, The Fourth
> Gospel...and Genesis.]

1916 **Walter, William W.** The Sweetest Story Ever Told. By
William W. Walter. Aurora, Ill.: W.W. Walter, 1916.

[The Life of Christ, based mostly upon the Gospel of John.]

1918 **Buchanan, Edgar Simmons**   (UnJudaized Version) From the Huntington Palimpsest...
[See New Testament Selections for the complete entry. Includes John.]

1920 **Ballantine, Frank Schell**   Science and Scripture Health...
[See New Testament Selections for the complete entry. Includes the first three chapters of John.]

1922 **Bell, Ernest A. Dr.**   The Gospel of John, translated and arranged for American Readers. By Ernest A. Bell.   Chicago: Pamphlet [1922.]

1924 **Thompson, Herbert**   ... The Gospel of St. John according to the earliest Coptic manuscript. Edited with a translation by Sir Herbert Thompson.   London: British School of Archeology in Egypt...and Bernard Quaritch, 1924.
[Publications of the Egyptian Research Account and British School of Archaeology in Egypt. No. 36.]

1925 **Concordant Version**   Concordant Version...John's Account...
[See New Testament Selections, 1914 Concordant Version.]

1925 **Robinson, Benjamin W.**   The Gospel of John. A Handbook for Christian Leaders. By Benjamin W. Robinson...   New York: Macmillan Co., 1925.
["In making the translation...I have felt free to adopt any suggestions which came to me from previous translations, the 20th Century N.T., Goodspeed's N.T. and others."]

1926 **McCormack, R.**   Seven in Scripture. The true text of St. John XVII...
[See Gospel Selections for the complete entry.]

1928 **Bernard, John Henry**   A Critical and Exegetical Commentary on the Gospel According to St. John by the Most Rev. and Right Hon. J.H. Bernard... edited by the Rev. A.H. McNeile.. (In two volumes) Edinburgh: T. & T. Clark, 1928.
[See Complete Bibles, 1895 The International Critical Commentary (St. John).]

Reprinted; 1942, 1948.

1928 **Osborn, Edwin Faxon**   The words and deeds of Jesus from the records by Matthew and John...
[See Gospel Selections for the complete entry.]

1929 **Reilly, W.S.**   St. John, 1929.
[See Complete Bibles, 1913 Westminster Version.]

1930 **Blount, Charles F.**   Half-hours with St. John's Gospel...Text, paraphrase & reflections. By Charles F. Blount. Two Parts. London: Burns, Oates & Co., 1930-1931.

1933 **Bacon, Benjamin Wisner**   The Gospel of the Hellenists...edited by Carl H. Kraeling... New York: Henry Holt and Company, 1933.
   [The Gospel of John; "The translation has been made from the critical Geek text with preceding translations 'diligently revised and compared.'"]

1933 **Monges, Maud B.**   The Gospel of St. John by Rudolph Steiner... A cycle of twelve lectures, unrevised by the author, given at Hamburg from 18th to 31st of May, 1908, Translated from the original... by Maud B. Monges. Copyright by Harry Collison, 1933.
   Third edition; New York City: Anthroposophic Press, 1962.

1933 **Selwyn, Edward and E.S. Hoernle**   The Love of Jesus. Being the story of Jesus' trial and death as originally told by the disciple whom Jesus loved. Reconstructed and translated by Edward Selwyn-E.S. Hoernle. London: Hodder & Stoughton, 1933.

1935 **Coombs, Doris V. and E.J. Clark**   The Glad News as told by Saint John's Gospel (using a limited vocabulary). A Rendering into modern English for the use of students.   Shanghai: Christian Literature Society, 1935.
   [See Anonymous, The Good News..., 1935.]

1935 **Counsell, W.H.**   My Notebook on St. John. Cambridge: W. Heffer & Sons, 1935.

1935 **Pass, H. Leonard**   A Study in S. John XII-XVII. By H. Leonard Pass. London & Oxford, 1935.

1936 **Lewis, Richard W. and David L. Cooper**   Simplified Gospel of St. John; the KJV simplified for children, youth and the uneducated... Grand Rapids, Michigan: Eerdman Publishing Co., 1936.
   ["This work is being prepared by the Rev. Richard W. Lewis... It is edited by Dr. David L. Cooper, the founder and president of the Biblical Research Society of Los Angeles, California. The Gospel of John is now in the press of the Eerdman Publishing Company..., to be followed by the N.T., and then the whole Bible." From Simms, 1936. Neither the Biblical Research Society nor Eerdmans knew anything of the work as of 1966.]

1938 **Smith, Edwin J.**   The Basic St. John. By Edwin J. Smith. London: Routledge, 1938.
   [Psyche Miniatures #92.]

1939 **Temple, William**   Readings in St. John's Gospel. By William Temple. Two Vols. London: Macmillan & Co., 1939-1940.
        1939 - - First Series (Chap. I-XII)
        1940 - - Second Series (Chap. XIII-XXI)
        1945 - - (First and Second Series) 1 Vol.

1940 **Bailey, R.F.**   The Gospel of St. John. An Introductory Commentary. By R.F. Bailey. London: Student Christian Movement Press, 1940.

1943 **Norlie, Olaf Morgan**   The Gospel of John translated into modern English. With study outline, paragraphing, capitals for all names of Christ, including pronouns; modern punctuation marks, including quotation marks; and the solemn style, found only in English, eliminated. By Olaf Morgan Norlie. San Antonio, Texas: Life Builders Press, 1943.

1944 **Huizenga, Henry**   The Gospel according to St. John in verse. By Henry Heizenga. Kalamazoo: Religious Publishing House, 1944.

1944 **Matheson, Mary L.**   St. John in Current English, by Mary L. Matheson. Melbourne, Australia: S. John Bacon, 1944.

1945 **Heywood, D. Herbert**   New Era Testament...
    [See New Testament Selections for the complete entry. Includes John chapters 13, 14 & 15.]

1947 **Runyon, Florabelle**   The Light in the Dark from John's Good News. A literal translation of the first part of the Gospel of John (from the Bible). Written so that a ten-year-old child can read it. By Florabelle Runyon. Minneapolis: Osterhus Publishing Co., 1947.

1949 **Hoare, F.R.**   Gospel according to St. John; a translation from the Greek into current English, arranged in its conjectural original order by F.R. Hoare. London: Burns, Oates & Washbourne, 1949.

1951 **Greenlees, Duncan**   The World Gospel Series. 6. The Gospel of the Mystic Christ... Based on a New Translation of St. John's Gospel and several Apocrypha, with Explanatory Notes and Introduction by Duncan Greenlees... Adyar, Madras, India: The Pheosophical Publishing House, 1951.

1953 **Anonymous**   The Amazing Witness. The...American Common Speech Translation of the Gospel of John...

[Ray W. Johnson] Seattle, Washington: The Life
Messengers, 1953.
>Second edition; revised, 1961.

>["Later we hope to be able to offer the entire N.T. in
>this simple and understandable everyday language of the
>American people."]

1953 **Hendriksen, William**   New Testament Commentary...
[See New Testament Selections, 1953 William Hendriksen,
New Testament Commentary...John.]

1954 **Amplified Gospel of John**   Amplified Gospel of
John [Copyright by the Lockman Foundation.], 1954.

>Another edition; The Self-Explaining Gospel (The
>Holy Glad Tidings of John) by Francis E.
>Siewert, 1954.

1955 **Chavasse, Claude**   The Dialogues of Jesus:
An Arrangement of S. John's Gospel made by Claude
Chavasse. London: Faber and Faber, 1955.
>["The English of the RV (or the margin) has been
>followed with (certain few) exceptions..."]

1956 **Phair, Francis Noble**   The Good News by John. The
Gospel of John Simplified by Francis Noble Phair.
Chicago: Moody Press, 1956.
>["It is not a translation but a simplification based on
>the KJV..."]

1957 **Titus, Eric Lane**   The Message of the Fourth Gospel.
By Eric Lane Titus. New York & Nashville: Abingdon
Press, [1957].

1961 **Norlie, Olaf Morgan**   The Gospel of John from
Norlie's Simplified New Testament.   Grand Rapids:
Zondervan Publishing House, 1961.
>[This is a specimen of an intended publication of the
>entire N.T.]

>Also; John. Seattle World's Fair Edition. Grand
>Rapids: 1962.

1961 **Vann, Gerald**   The Eagle's Word; A presentation
of the Gospel according to St. John. With an
Introductory Essay by Gerald Vann.   New York:
Harcourt, Brace & World, Inc., 1961.

1962 **Cressman, Annie**   The Book of John, 1962.

1963 **Sanders, J.N.**   A Commentary on the Gospel According
to St. John, by J.N. Sanders. London: Adam & Charles
Black, 1963.
>[See N.T., 1957 Black's N.T. Commentaries.]

[See N.T., 1958 Harper N.T. Commentaries.]

1964 **Brown, Raymond E.**   The Gospel According to John
     (i – xii) Introduction, Translation, and Notes by
     Raymond E. Brown. Garden City, New York: Doubleday
     & Co., Inc., 1966.
         [See Complete Bibles, 1964 Anchor Bible, Vol. 29.]

1964 **Burne, Patrick**   The Fourth Gospel by Louis Bouyer;
     Translated by Patrick Burne. Westminster, Maryland:
     The Newman Press; Dublin: Hely Thom, Ltd., 1964.
         ["Translation from the French of 'Le Quatrieme
         Evangile', 1955."]

1964 **Raymond, William**   The Good News of Jesus Christ by
     His Follower John. By William Raymond. Mimeographed,
     1964.
         ["In the spring of 1964 Mr. Crawford did the original on
         this translation or paraphrase..."]

         Another edition; The Good News of Jesus Christ by
         His Follower John; Translation by William
         Raymond Crawford; Foreword by Jim Vaus.
         Tarrytown, New York: Tarrytown Publishers,
         1965.

1965 **Mantey, Julius and George Turner**   The Gospel of
     John: An Evangelical Commentary. Grand Rapids,: Wm.
     B. Eerdmans, 1965.

1967 **Haggart, James B.**   The Upward Path...The Gospel of
     John in Modern Language by James B. Haggart. London:
     Covenant Publishing, 1967.
         [The Bible Collector dates it 1968]

1967 **Runes, Dagobert D.**   The Gospel According to Saint
     John; In the words of the King James Version of the
     year 1611. Edited in conformity with the true
     ecumenical spirit of His Holiness, Pope John XXIII
     by Dagobert D. Runes. The message of Jesus is
     offered here without adulteration by hate and
     revulsion against the people of the Savior.   New
     York: Philosophical Library, 1967.
         ["It is my ardent wish to bring out in the near future
         the whole body of the New Testament, cleansed of anti-
         Jewish interpolations..." Many references to Jews either
         have   been   reworded   or   eliminated.   i.e.   John
         7:2,7:11,7:15, 8:31-59 (omitted), 18:35 (omitted).]

1969 **Anonymous**   The Gospel according to John; a
     contemporary translation. New York: New York Bible
     Society, 1969.

1969 **New York Bible Society**   The Gospel According
     to John, a Contemporary Translation. New York: New
     York Bible Society, 1969.

1969 **Wolfram, Walter A. and Ralph W. Fasold**   A Black
     English Translationof John 3:1-21 with Grammatical
     Annotations, <u>The Bible Translator</u>, Vol. 20, No.2,
     Pages 52-3, April, 1969.

1970 **Brown, Raymond E.**   The Gospel According to John
     (xiii-xxi). Introduction, Translation, and Notes by
     Raymond E. Brown. Garden City, New York: Doubleday
     & Co., Inc., 1970.
          [See Complete Bibles, 1964 Anchor Bible , Vol. 29a.]

1970 **Jordan, Clarence**   The Cotton Patch Version of
     Matthew and John...
          [See Gospel Selections for the complete entry.]

1971 **Morris, Leon**   The Gospel according to John; the
     English text with introduction, exposition, and
     notes, 1971.
          [See N.T., 1959 New International Comment. on the N.T.]

1975 **Anonymous**   The Gospel of John. Recovery Version.
     Anaheim, Ca.: Living Stream Ministry, 1975.
          [See N.T., 1985 Witness Lee & Others, N.T.]

1977 **Haugerud, Joann**   The Word for Us; the Gospels of
     John and Mark...
          [See New Testament Selections for the complete entry.]

1983 **Bruce, F.F.**   The Gospel of John, Introduction,
     Exposition and Notes by F.F. Bruce... Grand Rapids,
     Mi: Wm. B. Eerdmans Publishing Co., 1983.

1984 **Matheny, C. Howard**   Good News From God. The Gospel
     of John with Corresponding Scriptures from Matthew
     through Revelation. A Most Accurate Translation from
     the Original Greek into English by C.Howard Matheny.
     Columbia, SC: Published by Author, 1984.

1985 **Levi, Peter**   The Holy Gospel of John. Wilton, CN:
     Morehouse-Barlow, 1985.   [1988?]

1986 **Van Roo, William A.**   Telling about God. Vol. I.
     Promise and Fulfillment. William A. Van Roo, S.J.
     Roma: Editrice Pontificia Universita Gregoriana,
     1986.
          [Analecta Gregoriana. Cura Pontificiae Universitatis
          Gregorianae edita Vol. 242, Series Facultatis
          Theologiae: sectio A, n. 26. Contains his own
          translation of John 1.18.]

1987 **Beasley - Murray, George Raymond**   Word Biblical
     Commentary. John. George R. Beasley-Murray. Waco,
     TX: Word Books, Publisher, 1987.
          [See Complete Bibles, 1982 Word Biblical Commentary,
          Vol. 36.]

15

Acts

ACTS LISTINGS

???? **Bartchy, S. Scott** Word Biblical Commentary. Acts. Waco, Tx: Word Books, Publishers, [198?]. [See Complete Bibles, 1982 Word Biblical Commentary, Vol. 37.]

???? **Callan, Fr. Charles Jerome** The Acts of the Apostles. With a Pastoral Critical Commentary for Priests and Students. New York: Joseph F. Wagner, Inc., [19??].

???? **Owens, Jno. J.** The Acts of the Apostles, by Jno. J. Owens. New York: D. Appleton & Co., [186?].

???? **Tafel, Leonard, Rudolph L. Tafel and L.H. Tafel** Interlinear Translation...Sacred Scriptures... Acts... [See Bible Selections for the complete entry.]

???? **Winter, C.T.** The Child's Acts of the Apostles. A Narrative and Commentary, written in Simple Language, for the Little Ones. By C.T. Winter... London: S.P.C.K.; New York: E. & J.B. Young & Co., [19??].

1380 **Anonymous** New Testament ["...nearly half of the N.T...] [See New Testament Selections for the complete entry. Includes Acts.]

1553 **Tye, Christofer** The Actes of the Apostles, translated into Englyshe Metre, and dedicated to the Kynges moste excellent Maiestye, by Christofer Tye, Doctor in Musyke, and one of the Gentlemen of hys graces moste honourable Chappell, wyth notes to eche Chapter, to synge and also to play vpon the Lute, very necessarye for studentes after theyr studye, to

fyle their wittes, and also for all Christians that
cannot synge, to reade the good and godlye storyes
of the Liues of Christ hys Apostles. Imprinted at
London by Wyllyam Seres, 1553.
[The first fourteen chapters only.]

1572 **Bridges, John**   The Acts of the Apostles; with
homilies by Gualterus Tigurinus, Translated... By J.
Bridges. London: Henry Denham, 1572.

1585 **Fetherstone, Christopher**   The Commentaries of Ihon
Caluin vpon the Acts of the Apostles...translated
out of Latine. London: Thomas Dawson for George
Byshop, 1585.

1761 **Heylyn, John**   An Interpretation of the New
Testament ...containing Acts of the Apostles and
several Epistles...
[See New Testament Selections for the complete entry.]

1789 **Willis, John**   Actions of the Apostles: translated
from the original Greek by John Willis.   London:
Sold by Mess. Robson, Clarke & Faulder, Payne & Son,
White & Son; Cambridge: Mess. Merrills, 1789.
[An attempt to update the KJV.]

1792 **Dalrymple, William**   The Acts of the Apostles made
easy ...by a short paraphrase, notes... Air: J. &
P. Wilson, 1792.

1844 **Beveridge, Henry**   Commentaries on the Acts
of the Apostles by John Calvin. Translated from the
Original Latin, and collated with the author's
French Version.   Edinburgh: Calvin Translation
Society, 1844.
[See Bible Selections, 1844 Anonymous, Commentaries on
the Books of the Bible.]

1844 **Pise, Charles Constantine**   The Acts of the
Apostles, rendered into blank verse, with copious
notes, by Charles Constantine Pise. New York: R.
Martin & Co., 1844.
Another edition; The Acts of the Apostles, in
Four Books, with Copious Notes. London & New
York: Virtue, Emmins & Co., 1845.

Also; New York: Johnson, Fry & Co., 1845.

[All three editions bound with Rutter's "Evangelical
Harmony"; see 1803.]

1844 **Pise, Charles Constantine**   See Gospel Harmonies,
1803 Henry Rutter, Evangelical Harmony.

1851 **Browne, H.**   Homilies of S. John Chrysostom, Archbishop of Constantinople, on the Acts of the Apostles, Translated, with Notes and Indices. By H. Browne. 2 Vols. Oxford: John Henry Parker, 1851-1852

1857 **Alexander, Joseph Addison**   A Commentary on the Acts of the Apostles by J.A. Alexander. 2 Vols. New York, 1857.

1858 **American Bible Union**   The Acts of the Apostles. Translated from the Greek on the basis of the common English version. With Notes. (By Alexander Campbell).   New York: American Bible Union; Louisville, Ky: Bible Revision Association; London: Trubner & Co., 1858.
     Reprinted, Joplin, MD: College Press, n.d. (196?)

1858 **Barker, J.H.**   Apostolic Missions, or the Sacred History amplified and combined with the Apostolic Epistles and contemporary secular history. By J.H. Barker. London: Groombridge & Sons, 1858.
     [A paraphrase of the Acts, supplemented by extracts from the Epistles.]

1861 **Green, Samuel G.**   The Acts of the Apostles: an exposition for English readers, on the basis of Professor Hackett's commentary on the original text... With a new and literal version. 2 Vols. London: J. Heaton & Son, 1861.

1863 **McGarvey, John William**   Commentary on the Acts of the Apostles, with a New Version. By J.W. McGarvey...   Cincinnati: The Standard Publishing Co., 1863.
     [In his 'New Commentary on the Acts of the Apostles', Cincinnati: Standard Publication Foundation, 1892/1961, McGarvey stated,"The RV (1881) has...come to my relief, saving me the necessity of correcting my own revision of the AV which was the basis of my former work."]

     Third edition, 1864.

1870 **Thomas, David**   A Homiletic Commentary on the Acts of the Apostles... including emendative renderings, exegetical remarks by David Thomas.   London: R.D. Dickenson, 1870.

1873 **Ramsden, C.H.**   Apostolic Times and Their Lessons; or, Plain, Practical Readings from the Acts of the Apostles, by C.H.Ramsden. 2 Vols. London: Hatchards, 1873-1874.

1887 **Tafel, Leonard, Rudolph L. Tafel and L.H. Tafel**
Interlinear translation of the New Testament...
[See New Testament Selections for the complete entry.
Includes the Acts.]

1895 **Page, T.E. and A.S. Walpole**   The Acts of the
Apostles. With introduction and notes by T.E. Page
and A.S. Walpole. London: Macmillan and Co., 1895.

1897 **Rendall, Frederic**   The Acts of the Apostles in
Greek and English. By F. Rendall. London: Macmillan
and Co., 1897.
Second edition, 1901.

1900 **Stevens, George Barker**   The Messages of the
Apostles..., 1900.
[See Abridged Bibles, 1900 Frank K. Sanders and Charles
F. Kent, The Messages of the Bible, Vol. XI.]

1912 **Furneaux, William Mordaunt**   The Acts of the
Apostles: a commentary for English readers. Oxford:
Clarendon Press, 1912.
[With a new version of the text.]

1915 **Sitterly, Charles Fremont**   Jerusalem to Rome;
the Acts of the Apostles, a new translation and
commentary with introduction, maps, reconstructions
and illustrations from Christian art. By Charles
Fremont Sitterly. New York & Cincinnati: The
Abingdon Press, 1915.
["...Souter's admirable text (Oxford, 1910) is our
basis..."]

Reprinted, 1922.

1923 **Wilson, J.M.**   The Acts of the Apostles. Translated
from the Codex Bezae, with an Introduction on its
Lucan Origin and importance by Canon J.M. Wilson...
London: S.P.C.K.; Toronto & New York: The Macmillan
Co., 1923.
["The words in thick type are in the Codex Bezae...but
not in our ordinary text."]

1930 **Potter, J.W.**   The Acts of the Holy Apostles.
For the use of Christian Spiritualists. Boston: J.W.
Potter; London: Society of Communion, 1930.

1932 **Anonymous**   After Christ Jesus returned to
Heaven. A shortened edition of the Acts of the Holy
Apostles, in Bible words, as translated from the
original Greek. Sukkar: 1932.
[The Books of Acts.]

1933 **Foakes, F.J. and Kirsopp Lake**   The Beginnings
of Christianity. Part I The Acts of the Apostles,

edited by F.J. Foakes and Kirsopp Lake.   London:
Macmillan & Co. Ltd., 1933.

>   1920 - - Vol.1 Prolegomena I. The Jewish,
>   Gentile Christian Backgrounds
>
>   1922 - - Vol. II Prolegomena II. Criticism
>
>   1926 - - Vol. III The Text of the Acts by
>   James Hardy Ropes...Greek
>
>   1933 - - Vol. IV English Translation and
>   Commentary. Kirsopp Lake & Henry J.
>   Cadbury
>
>   1933 - - Vol. V Additional Notes to the
>   Commentary
>
>   ["The best commentary is a literal translation We have
>   tried to provide this by printing at the top of each
>   page (of vol. IV) a translation which would be as
>   literal as possible while not going beyond the limits
>   permitted by idiomatic English."]
>
>   Another edition, 1965.

1933 **Lattey, Cuthbert**   Acts, 1933.
    [See Complete Bibles, 1913 Westminster Version.]

1935 **Williams, Charles Kingsley**   Stories from the
    Acts of the Apostles. Newly done into very simple
    English from the Greek of the RV. By C. Kingsley
    Williams.   London: S.P.C.K., 1935.

1939 **Black, Matthew**   A Palestinian Syriac Palimpsest
    Leaf of Acts XXI (14-26). By Matthew Black.
    Manchester: The Manchester University Press and the
    Librarian, The John Rylands Library. 1939.
        Reprinted; <u>Bulletin of the John Rylands Library</u>,
    Vol. 23, No. 1, April, 1939.

1946 **Matheson, Mary L.**   Acts in Current English, by Mary
    L. Matheson. Melbourne, Australia: The Book Depot,
    1946.

1953 **Kyles, Rev. David**   Dr. Luke writes again: stories
    from the Acts of the Apostles retold by Rev. David
    Kyles.   Stirling: Drummond Tract Depot, 1953.

1955 **Phillips, J.B.**   The Young Church in Action, 1955.
    [See New Testament, 1947 for the entire entry.]

1955 **Stagg, Frank**   The Book of Acts. The Early Struggle
    for an Unhindered Gospel. By Frank Stagg. Nashville:
    Broadman Press, [1955].

1957 **Byrne, Laurence E.**   Giuseppe Ricciotti; The Acts
of the Apostles; Text and Commentary; Translated by
Laurence E. Byrne... Milwaukee: The Bruce Publishing
Co., 1957.
> ["The Scripture Text used is mainly the Confraternity
> Version with an occasional direct translation of
> Ricciotti's Translation from the Greek."]

Another edition, 1958.

1957 **Rieu, C.H.**   The Acts of the Apostles by Saint Luke,
Translated with an Introduction and Notes, by C.H. Rieu.
Harmondsworth: Penguin Books; [Baltimore, Md:] Penguin Books,
1957.
> Reprinted, 1958.

1957 **Williams, C.S.C.**   Acts, 1957.
> [See N.T., 1957 Black's N.T. Commentary.]

> [See N.T., 1958 Harper's N.T. Commentaries.]

1959 **Phair, Francis Noble**   The Acts of the Apostles.
Easy English Edition by Francis Noble Phair.
Chicago: Moody Press, 1959.

1961 **Harington, Jay**   Paul of Tarsus...
> [See New Testament Selections for the complete entry.]

1967 **Albright, William Foxwell and C.S. Mann**
The Acts of the Apostles. Introduction, Translation,
and Notes by Johannes Munck. Revised by W.F.
Albright and C.S. Mann.   Garden City, New York:
Doubleday & Co., Inc., 1967.
> [See Complete Bibles, 1964 Anchor Bible, Vol. 31.]

1969 **Jordan, Clarence**   The Cotton Patch Version of Luke
and Acts...
> [See New Testament Selections for the complete entry.]

1971 **Anonymous**   The Acts of the Apostles: A Commentary
by Ernest Haenchen. [R.McL. Wilson] Philadelphia:
Westminster Press, 1971.
> [Translation from German into English.]

1974 **Anonymous**   Walk with Me in Modern English.
One chronological story as combined from the Four
Gospels and the first chapter of the Book of Acts...
> [See New Testament Selections for the complete entry.]

1979 **Hazel, John F., Jr.**   Heavy Acts, by Brother
Luke; a Paraphrase of the Acts of the apostles as
Interpreted by John F. Hazel, Jr. Lima, Oh: C.S.S.
Publishing Co., 1979.

1980 **Blaiklock, E.M.**   Acts, the Birth of the Church, A Commentary by E.M. Blaiklock. Old Tappan, N.J.: Fleming H. Revell Co., 1980.

1988 **Bruce, F.F.**   The book of the Acts. Revised Edition. 1988.
> [See N.T., 1959 New International Comment. on the N.T.]

ACTS AND EPISTLES

???? **Morrison, Thomas**   The Acts of the Apostles and the Epistles of Paul arranged in the form of a continuous history. With notes, critical and explanatory, a gazetteer of places, and questions for examination. By Thomas Morrison.   London, Edinburgh & New York: T. Nelson & Sons, 188?
> ["It has been the desire of the author to narrate, in clear and simple language, the progress of the church..."]

1756 **Benson, George**   The History of the First Planting of the Christian Religion: Taken from the Acts of the Apostles, and their Epistles. Together with the Remarkable Facts of the Jewish and Roman History, which affected the Christians, within this Period. In Three Vols. [3 in 1] The Second Edition carefully corrected and with large additions. By George Benson... London: Printed and Sold by J. Waugh and W. Fenner..., 1756.

1890 **Tischendorf, Constantine**   The Apostles: according to the oldest known Greek manuscript, Codex Sinaiticus - original text: or, the Common English version corrected according to the original text of the Sinaitic manuscript: by Constantine Tischendorf. Glasgow: John Thomson, [1890].
> [The Epistles, Acts, and Revelation.]

1956 **Cox, Ronald**   It is Paul... and of the Acts of the Apostles..., 1956.
> [See New Testament Selections, 1956 for the entire entry.]

1959 **Paulinus**   "I Paul"   Middle Green, Langley: St. Paul Publications, [1959].
> [The Acts and Epistles.]

16

Epistles and Selections

???? **Anonymous**   Hortus Animae; or, Garden of the Soule... Containing the Gospels and Epistles...
[See Bible Selections for the complete entry.]

???? **Butler, Barry**   The Letter of Saint Paul to the Galatians and the Letter of James; Written in easy English by Barry Butler. Darwin, N.T. (Australia): Church Missionary Society Chaplain, [19??].
Revised edition; Darwin, N.T. (Australia): Church Missionary Society Chaplain, 1969.

1380 **Anonymous**   New Testament   ["...nearly half of the N.T..."]
[See New Testament Selections for the complete entry. Includes the Epistles except Philemon.]

1539 **Anonymous**   The Manual of prayers / or the prymer in Englyshe & Laten set out at lenght, whose contentes
[See Bible Selections for the complete entry. Includes Epistle selections.]

1570 **Golding, Arthur**   A Postil or Orderly Disposing of Certaine Epistles. Usually read in the Church of God, Upon the Sundayes, Holydayes, throughout the Whole Yeare... Written in Latin by David Chrytraeus and translated into English by Arthur Golding. London: 1570.
Again; 1577.

1580 **Anonymous**   The Commentaries of M. Ihon Caluin vpon the first Epistle of Sainct Ihon, and vpon the Epistle of Iude... Translated into Englishe by W.H. London: Ihon Kyngstone for Ihon Harrison, 1580.

1581 **Newton, Thomas**   The Epistles of St. Peter and St. Jude. London: 1581.

1672 **Cradock, Samuel**   The Apostolic History, 1672.

1705 **Anonymous**   A Paraphrase and Notes on the Epistles... [John Locke, James Peirce, Joseph Hallett, and George Benson] 1705-1752
    A Paraphrase and Notes on the Epistles of St. Paul:

    1705 ...to the Galatians. [John Locke] London: Awnsham & John Churchill.

    1706 ...the First Epistle of St. Paul to the Corinthians. [John Locke]   London: Awnsham & John Churchill.

    1707 ...the Second Epistle of St. Paul to the Corinthians. [John Locke]   London: Awnsham & John Churchill.

    1707 ...to the Romans. [John Locke]   London: Awnsham & John Churchill.

    1707 ...to the Ephesians. [John Locke] London: Awnsham & John Churchill.

    1707 ...Galatians, I & II Corinthians, Romans, Ephesians. To which is Prefix'd an Essay for the Understanding of St. Paul's Epistles, by Consulting St. Paul himself. Second edition, 1709.

            Third edition; London: A. Bettesworth & C. Hitch, 1733.

    1725 ...to the Colossians... (1729, 2nd ed) by James Peirce. London: J.Noon & J. Chandler.

    1725 ...to the Philippians... London: J. Noon & J. Chandler.

    1727 ...the Epistle to the Hebrews. London: J. Noon & J. Chandler.

    1727 ...to the Colossians, Philippians, and Hebrews: after the Manner of Mr. Locke. To which are annexed Several Critical Dissertations... London: J. Noon & J. Chandler.

    1731 ...to Philemon, Ist [&] IId

Thessalonians, Ist [&] IId Timothy, Titus... Attempted in Imitation of Mr. Locke's manner. [George Benson] 6 Parts. London: Richard Ford.

Second edition; A Paraphrase and Notes on Six of the Epistles of St. Paul. viz. I Thessalonians, II Thessalonians, I Timothy, Philemon, Titus, II Timothy. Attempted in Imitation of Mr. Lock's Manner. To which are Annexed, Critical Dissertations on Several Subjects, for the Better Understanding of St. Paul's Epistles. The Second Edition, Carefully Corrected, with Large Additions. By George Benson, D.D. London: Printed for James Waugh..., 1752.

1733 ...The second edition...with a Paraphrase and Notes on the Three last Chapters of Hebrews left unfinished by Mr. Peirce; and an Essay to discover the Author of the Epistle, and the Language in which it was originally written, by Joseph Hallet Jun.

1742 A Paraphrase and Notes on the First Epistle to St. Peter...[George Benson] London: M. Fenner.

174? A Paraphrase and Notes on the Seven, commonly called, Catholic Epistles by James, Peter, Jude and John. Attempted in imitation of Mr. Locke's manner. To which are annexed several critical dissertations.

Second edition; carefully corrected with additions. London: J. Waugh & W. Fenner, 1756.

1787 **MacKnight, James**   A New Literal Translation...of all the Apostolic Epistles, by James MacKnight. 1787-1795.

1787 A New Literal Translation, from the original, of the Apostle Paul's First and Second Epistles to the Thessalonians. With a commentary and notes. By James MacKnight... London: The Author.

1795 A New Literal Translation from the Original Greek, of Apostolical Epistles. With a Commentary, and Notes, Philological, Critical, Explanatory, and

Practical. To which is added, a History
of the life of the Apostle Paul. By James
MacKnight... 4 Vols. Edinburgh: For The
Author.
> [Four columns: 'Old Translation', 'Greek
> Text', 'New Translation', 'Commentary'
> (Paraphrase)]

[Alexander Campbell made a minor revision. See N.T.
listings, 1826 The Sacred Writings...]

Second edition; In Six Volumes. To which is
prefixed, an account of the Life of the
author. London: Longman, Hurst, Rees & Orme;
Edinburgh: William Creech & Ogle and Aikman;
Boston: Published by W. Wells & T.B. Wait &
Co., 1806, 1810, 1816.

Also; 4 Vols., 1816.

Another edition; 6 Vols. London: Printed for
Longman, Hurst, Rees, Orme & Brown..., 1816,
1821.

A New Edition; Philadelphia: Desilver, Thomas &
Co., 1835.

Another edition; Grand Rapids, Michigan: Baker
Book House, 1949.

Reprinted; 6 Vols. in 3. Grand Rapids: Baker
Book House, 1969. [Reprint of the 1821 edition.]

[Many times reprinted.]

1794 **Symonds, John**   The Epistles...
> [See New Testament Selections, 1789 John Symonds,
> ...Observations on the expediency of revising...]

1819 **Anonymous**   The Epistles of St. Paul to the
Colossians, to the Thessalonians, to Timothy, and to
Titus, and the general Epistles of St. James: a new
version from the Greek, and chiefly from the text of
Griesbach, by Philalethes. [John Jones] London:
Richards and Co. for Rowland Hunter, 1819.

1829 **Shuttlesworth, Philip Nicholas**   A Paraphrastic
Translation of the Apostolic Epistles, with notes.
By Philip Nicholas Shuttlesworth. Oxford: W.
Baxter, for J. Parker & C.J. Rivington, 1829.
> Second edition, 183?

Third edition; London: J.G. & F. Rivington, 1834.

Fourth edition, 1840.

1830 **Anonymous**   A Manual. The Apostolic Epistles;
with amendments in conformity to the Dutch version.
[Judge Egbert Benson] New York: Published by the
Translator, 1830.
> [E. Benson was a leader in the American Revolution and
> a representative in the Continental Congress. His object
> in this edition seems to have to give the proper
> translation of the terms for charity and bishop, which
> he renders as love and overseer.]

1837 **Barlee, Edward**   A free and explanatory version
of the Epistles; by the Rev. Edward Barlee. London:
William Pickering, 1837.
> ["He is aware that he has taken great liberties with the
> AV, although not greater than any others have done
> before him; and it was only from the feeling that their
> works were too voluminous for the instruction of the
> poorer classes, that he was induced to offer his to the
> public."]

1838 **Bruce, William**   A Paraphrase and Notes on the
Apostolic Epistles and Apocalypse. By William Bruce.
Liverpool & Dublin: Shaw Bros., 1838.
> [The paraphrase is of the Epistles only.]

1846 **Cox, G.V.**   The Prayer-Book Epistles paraphrased in
verse by G.V. Cox. London: John Olivier, 1846.

1856 **MacEvilly, John**   An Exposition of the Epistles of
St. Paul, and of the Catholic Epistles; consisting
of an introduction to each Epistle, an analysis of
each chapter, a paraphrase of the sacred text
[parallel with the Challoner-Rheims text], and a
commentary... By His Grace the Most Rev. John
MacEvilly... 2 Vols. London: Richardson & Son,
1856.
> Second edition; "...some important verbal
> alterations...", 1860.
>
> Third edition; Enlarged, 3 vols.; Dublin: W.B.
> Kelly, 1875.
>
> Fourth edition; "...considerably enlarged...",
> 1891.
>
> Fifth edition, 189?.
>
> Sixth edition; Enlarged, revised and corrected,
> New York, Cincinnati and Chicago: Benziger
> Brothers; Dublin: M.H. Gill & Son, 1895.
>
> Again; 1898.

1867 **Mombert, J. Isidor**   General Epistles, 1867.
> [See Complete Bibles, 1864 Lange's Commentary.]

1888 **Olden, Thomas**   The Holy Scriptures in Ireland
one thousand years ago: Selections from the Wurzburg
Glosses. Translated by Thomas Olden. Dublin: Hodges,
Figgis & Co., 1888.
[Selections from the Epistles, with the text of the AV.]

1889 **Norton, William**   A Translation, in English Daily
used, of [the Epistles], by William Norton. London:
W.K. Bloom, 1889-1890.
        1889 - - the Peshito-Syriac Text, and of the
              received Greek text of Hebrews, James, 1
              Peter, and 1 John. With an introduction,
              on the Peshito-Syriac text, and on the
              revised Greek text of 1881.

        1890 - - the Seventeen Letters forming part of
              the   Peshito-Syriac   books   of   the   New
              Covenant   writings   which   have   been
              received throughout the East, from the
              Beginning,   as   written   in   Syriac   by
              inspiration of God. A like translation of
              the Inspired Greek text of these letters,
              In a Corresponding Column on each Page.
              Also, An Introduction, giving a history
              of the Peshito-Syriac text, testimonies
              as   to   its   origin   value,   the   readings
              followed in the RV of 1881 which are
              condemned, and those which are sanctioned
              by it, etc.

["Six editions of the Peshito have been compared in
making this translation... I. Walton's Polyglott, 1653-
7; II. Professor Gutbier, Hamburg, 1664... III. Romanist
Maronites, Rome, 1703... IV. Leusden & Schaff, Leyden,
1717...V. Professor Lee (B&FBS) 1816... VI. American
Board of Foreign Missions, New York, 1878..."]

1900 **Hayman, Henry**   The Epistles of the New Testament.
An Attempt to present them in current and popular
idiom by Henry Hayman... London: A. and C. Black,
1900.
["My plan has been to keep with the most careful
fidelity to the thoughts of the Apostles, whilst
claiming a perfectly free hand as regards the language
in which I venture to present them..."]

[Contains the AV on opposite pages.]

Reprint editions; Tulsa, OK: Spirit to Spirit,
1982.
           Vol. 1   Romans & Galatians.
           Vol. 2   I & II Corinthians.
           Vol. 3   Ephesians through Philemon.
           Vol. 4   Hebrews & General Epistles.

1904 **Lenker, John Nicholas**   The Epistles of St.
      Peter and St. Jude; Preached and Explained by Martin
      Luther; Both editions (1523 and 1539) of First Peter
      in one volume, with analysis of each chapter by John
      George Walch. Translated and edited by John Nicholas
      Lenker. Minneapolis, Minnesota: Lutherans in All
      Lands Co., 1904.

1906 **Forster, Henry Langstaff**   St. John's Gospel,
      Epistles, and Revelation...
          [See New Testament Selections, 1903 Henry Langstaff
          Forster, [N.T. Selections]...]

1907 **Mayor, Joseph B.**   The Epistle of St. Jude and
      the Second Epistle of St. Peter. By Joseph B. Mayor.
      London: Macmillan and Co., 1907.

1912 **Nutt, David**   Epistles and Apocalypse...
          [See New Testament Selections for the complete entry.
          Includes the Epistles.]

1918 **Buchanan, Edgar Simmons**   (UnJudaized Version) From
      the Huntington Palimpsest Formerly in the Library of
      Tarragonagona Cathedral, now in the Collection of
      the Hispanic Society of America...
          [See New Testament Selections for the complete entry.
          Includes the Epistles.]

1924 **Gigot, Francis**   1 & 2 Timothy, Titus, 1, 2 & 3
      John, 1924.
          [See Complete Bibles, 1913 Westminster Version.]

1934 **Wand, J.W.C.**   The General Epistles of St. Peter and
      St. Jude. Edited by J.W.C. Wand. London: Methuen &
      Co., Westminster Commentaries, 1934.

1940 **Boylan, Patrick**   The Sunday Epistles and Gospels
      with Commentaries and Suggestions...
          [See New Testament Selections for the complete entry.]

1944 **Wand, J.W.C.**   The New Testament Letters Prefaced
      and Paraphrased by J.W.C. Wand... Melbourne: Oxford
      University Press; London, New York & Toronto:
      Oxford University Press, 1944.
          ["...each letter was translated afresh from the Greek.
          Then it was gone over again, with a view to putting
          it...into less stereotyped phraseology... The result may
          be called either a free translation or a close
          paraphrase."]

          ["Jehovah" is used eight times. Romans 9:29; 11:4;
          12:19; Hebrews 7:21; Jude 5; I Peter 1:2.]

          Another edition; The New Testament Letters,
          prefaced & paraphrased. By J.W.C. Wand.
          Brisbane, Australia, 1943.

Revised and corrected; London, New York, Toronto:
Geoffrey Cumberledge, Oxford University Press,
1946.

Reprinted; 1947, 1950, 1956.

1946 **Knox, Ronald Arbuthnott** The Epistles and Gospels...
[See New Testament Selections for the complete entry.]

1947 **Phillips, J.B.**   Letters to Young Churches, 1947.
[See New Testament, 1947 for the entire entry.]

1955 **Whitehouse, H.E.** 21 Epistles set to Meter, Rime and
Verse... By H.E.Whitehouse. Oakland, Calif.: 1955?
[Mentioned in Whitehouse's Psalms, 1956.]

1956 **Laubach, Frank C.**   The Inspired Letters in Clearest
English. Prepared by Frank C. Laubach. Toronto, New
York, Edinburgh: Thomas Nelson & Sons, 1956.
[The N.T. Epistles, intended for the semi-literate.
Romans–Jude in simple English.]

Sixth printing, 1964.

1962 **Wirt, Sherwood E.**   Open Your Bible to the New
Testament Letters. By Sherwood E. Wirt.   Westwood,
N.J.: Fleming H. Revell Co., 1962.

1963 **Jordan, Clarence**   ...The Koinonia "Cotton Patch"
Version of the Epistles by Clarence Jordan.
Americus, Ga.: Koinonia Publications, 1963-1973.
1963 Letters to Ephesians and Philemon...

     1963 The Letter to the Hebrews or a First-
          Century Manual for Church Renewal...

     1964 Practical Religion or the Sermon on the
          Mount and the Epistle of James...

     1964 Letters to the Georgia Convention
          (Galatians) and to the Alabaster African
          Church   Smithville,   Alabama
          (Philippians)...

     1964 A Letter to the Christians in Atlanta or
          First Corinthians...

     1966 A Second Letter to the Christians in
          Atlanta or Second Corinthians...

     1968 The Letter to God's People in Washington
          or Romans... published, 1967

1967 Letters to God's People in Columbus (Colossians) and Selma (I & II Thessalonians)...

1967 Letters to Young Christians (I & II Timothy and Titus)...

1969 Letters from Partners Rock, Jack and Joe, I and II Peter, I, II and III John and Jude in the Koinonia "Cotton Patch" Version

1968 The Cotton Patch Version of Paul's Epistles (1 Vol.) New York: Association Press

["A colloquial modern translation with a Southern accent, rigorous and fervent for the gospel, inspiring in earthiness, rich in humor." "This translation...is based on the Nestle—Aland Greek text, 23rd edition (1957)." "...a presentation of the N.T. writers' thought as they probably would have expressed it today."]

1973 The Cotton Patch Version of Hebrews and the General Epistles (1 Vol.) New York: Association Press

1964 **Reicke, Bo Ivar**   The Epistles of James, Peter, and Jude. Introduction, Translation, and Notes by Bo Ivar Reicke. Garden City, New York: Doubleday & Co., Inc., 1964.
[See Complete Bibles, 1964 Anchor Bible, Vol. 37.]

1969 **Anonymous**   Letters to Street Christians. [Jack Sparks and Paul Raudenbush] 1969-1971.
1969 The 1st Letter to the Street Christians [Ephesians paraphrased] Berkeley: Christian Information Center.

1969 The 2nd Letter to the Street Christians [I John Paraphrased] Berkeley: Christian Information Center.

1969 The Third Letter to the Street Christians [James Paraphrased] Berkeley: Christian Information Center.

1970 The Letter to Street Christians of Berkeley (I Corinthians).

1971 Letters to the Street Christians by two Brothers from Berkeley. Grand Rapids, Michigan: Zondervan.

[The Epistles paraph ased in the language of the "street
people" of Berkele . E.g/, "Little children, don't let
anything push Go out of his place in your life. Right
on!"]

1974 **Brandt, Leslie F.**   Epistles Now, by Leslie F.
Brandt, with art by Corita Kent. St.Louis: Concordia
Publishing House, 1974.
    Another Edition; 1976.

1986 **Sider, Robert D.**   (Editor)   See John B. Payne and
Others, Collected Works of Erasmus... Paraphrase on
Romans and Galatians, 1984.

Pauline Epistles

PAULINE EPISTLES

???? **Byrne, Laurence E.**   Paul the Apostle. By Laurence E. Byrne. Milwaukee: The Bruce Publishing Co., [195?].
> Another edition; The Letters of St. Paul, 195?.

1350 **Anonymous**   The Pauline Epistles contained in MS. Parker 32, Corpus Christi College, Cambridge; edited by Margaret Joyce Powell.   London: Kegan Paul, Trench, Trubner & Co. for the Early English Text Society, 1916.
> [Extra Series #116. Latin and English.]

1562 **Paynell, Thomas**   The Common Places of St. Paul's Epistles. London: John Tisdale, 1562.

1675 **Anonymous**   A Paraphrase and Annotation upon all Saint Paul's Epistles. [Obadiah Walker, Abraham Woodhead, and Richard Allestry.]   1675-1702.
> 1675 A Paraphrase and Annotations upon the Epistles of St. Paul written to the Romans, Corinthians and Hebrews by Three Oxford Dons. Oxford: at the Theater.
>
> 1684 A Paraphrase and Annotation Upon all the Epistles of St. Paul. At the Theater in Oxford.
>> Another Edition; **Paraphrase and Annotations upon all Saint Paul's Epistles. Done by several Eminent Men at Oxford, Corrected and Improved by the Late right reverend and learned Bishop Fell. The Third Edition, with additions.   London: Printed for R.Smith, 1702.**

Another issue; London, 1703.

1708 The third edition...to which is prefix'd
     some   account of the Author's Lives.
     London: Printed & Sold by C. Smith.

1852 Edited by William Jacobson.   Oxford:
     University Press.

1702 **Fell, Dr. John**   See Anonymous, A Paraphrase &
     Annotations upon St. Paul's Epistles, 1675.

1731 **Benson, George**   Philemon, Thessalonians, Timothy
     & Titus, 1705.
     [See Epistles and Selections, 1705 Anonymous, A
     Paraphrase and Notes on the Epistles.]

1807 **Bevan, Joseph Gurney**   The Life of the Apostle Paul,
     as related in Scriptue, but in which his Epistles
     are inserted in that part of the history to which
     they are supposed...to belong... By Joseph Gurney
     Bevan. London: William Phillips, 1807.

1807 **Evanson, Edward**   A New Testament; or, the New
     Covenant according to Luke, Paul and John...
     [See New Testament Selections for the complete entry.]

1822 **Belsham, Thomas**   The Epistles of the Apostle
     Paul, translated with exposition and notes by Rev.
     Thomas Belsham.. 2 Vols.   London: Printed for the
     author by R. & A. Taylor, 1822.
     Another edition; 4 Vols.   London: R.   Hunter,
     1822.

     Reprinted; Portsmouth: The Unitarian, 1825.

1851 **Conybeare, William John and John Saul Howson**
     The Life and Epistles of St. Paul by the Rev. W.J.
     Conybeare, M.A... and The Very Rev. J.S. Howson...
     2 Vols. London: Longmans, Green and Co., 1851.
     ["...the translation of the Epistles adopted in this
     work is to a certain degree paraphrastic. At the same
     time nothing has been added by way of paraphrase which
     is not virtually expressed in the original Greek." Many
     editions of this work appeared in London, New York:
     Charles Scribner; Hartford: S.S. Scranton Co.]

     Another edition;   1 Vol. Edition.   London:
     Longmans, Green and Co., 1886.

     Also; London & Edinburgh: Marshall, Morgan &
     Scott, Ltd., n.d.   [Translations of the Epistles
     only]

Other editions; one vol. New York: T.Y. Crowell, n.d.. Also; Grand Rapids, Michigan: Wm. B. Eerdmans, 1953.

1852 **Jacobson, William** (Editor) See Anonymous, A Paraphrase and Annotation upon all Saint Paul's..., 1675.

1859 **Scrivener, F.H.** An Exact Translation of the Codex Augiensis; A Graeco-Latin MS. of St.Paul's Epistles, by F.H. Scrivener. 1859.

1866 **Dewes, Alfred** Life and Letters of St. Paul. London: Longmans, Green & Co., 1866-1882.
>1866 A Plea for a New Translation of the Scriptures. With a translation of St. Paul's Epistle to the Romans.

>1882 Life and Letters of St. Paul.

1883 **Fenton, Ferrar** St. Paul's Epistles in Modern English. Translated direct from the original Greek into modern English, with the Apostle's own division of the subject matter restored. By Ferrar Fenton. London: Elliot Stock, 1883.
Other editions, 1884, 1886, 1890, 1900.

>Fourth edition; carefully revised and corrected. London: 1894.

1888 **Pritchard, A.H.** An Exposition of the Epistles of St. Paul by Bernardine A. Piconia Translated and edited from the original Latin by A.H. Pritchard. 3 Vols. London: John Hodges, 1888-189?
>1888 Vol. I. Epistle to the Romans and the First Epistle to the Corinthians
>1890
>189?

1892 **Anonymous** The Gospel of Paul the Apostle. Being an attempt to render into modern English the principal writings of St. Paul and the contemporaneous narrative of his trusty companion Luke the beloved physician. By the author of Vox Clamantis. [Ralph Sadler] London: James Nisbet & Co., 1892.

1898 **Abbott, Lyman** The Life and Letters of Paul the Apostle by Lyman Abbott. Boston & New York: Houghton, Mifflin & Co. The Riverside Press, 1898.
["...in giving extracts from Paul's letters, I have generally followed neither the Old Version nor the New version, but have given a free rendering of my own..."]

MACK LIBRARY
BOB JONES UNIVERSITY
GREENVILLE, SC

1898 **Stevens, George Barker**   The Epistles of Paul
     in Modern English. A paraphrase by George Barker
     Stevens. New York: Charles Scribner's Sons, 1898.
          ["...I have sought to reproduce the thoughts of Paul's
          Epistles, and of the kindred letter to the Hebrews, in
          the language of to-day... with constant reference to the
          original Greek and with the aid of various critical
          helps..."]

          [In the preface to 'The Messages of the Bible' Vol. XI
          (see 1898), Stevens states that text "...is reproduced,
          with some revision, from [the above work.]"]

          Another edition; Wheaton, Illinois: Verploegh
          Editions, 1980.

1901 **Way, Arthur S.**   The Letters of St. Paul to Seven
     Churches and Three Friends. Translated by Arthur S.
     Way... London: Macmillan & Co., 1901.
          ["...not so much a translation in modern English, as one
          in which (1) the meaning of the original shall not be
          obscured by the condensed literality of a word-for-word
          rendering as is adopted in the Authorised Version and
          Revised Version: (2) the connection of thoughts, the
          sequence of subjects, the continuity of the argument,
          shall, by the supply of the necessary links, be made
          clear to the reader..."]

          Another edition; - - with the Letter to the
          Hebrews, 1903.

          Second Edition; with the Letter to the Hebrews,
          Revised, 1904.

          Third Edition, 1911.

          Fourth Edition, Revised, 1919, 1921, 1926.

          Seventh Edition, 1935.

          Eighth Edition;   Edinburgh & London: Morgan &
          Scott, 1950.

          Eighth Edition;   Chicago: Moody Press, 1950,
          1953.

          Reprinted; Letter of Paul, Hebrews and the Book
          of Psalms by Arthur S. Way. Grand Rapids:
          Kregel Publications, 1981.

1904 **Edward, Miss**   The Life and Labours of the Apostle
     Paul, As Narrated by Himself. Arranged... London:
     Hebrew Christian Testimony to Israel, 1904.
          [Selections from the Pauline Epistles, expressed in the
          first person.]

1907 **Chamberlain, J.S. Ffoster**   The Epistles of Paul
the Apostle. By J.S. Ffoster Chamberlain. London:
H.J. Drane, 1907.
Another edition; London: E. Stock, 1907.

1907 **Stevens, George Barker**   The Messages of Paul...,
1900.
[See Abridged Bibles, 1900 Frank K. Sanders and Charles
F. Kent, The Messages of the Bible, Vol. XII.]

1912 **Clarke, Sir Edward George**   The Epistles of St.
Paul. The Authorised Version amended by the adoption
of such of the alterations made in the Revised
Version as are necessary for correcting material
mistranslations, or making clear the meaning of the
inspired writer. The text prepared by the Right Hon.
Sir Edward Clarke.   London: Smith, Elder & Co.,
1912.

1916 **Joyce, Margaret**   The Pauline Epistles Contained
in MS. Parker 32, 1916.

1916 **Powell, Margaret Joyce**   See Anonymous, The Pauline
Epistles, 1350.

1919 **Smith, David**   The Life and Letters of St. Paul,
by the Rev. David Smith... New York: George H.Doran
Co.; London: Hodder & Stoughton, 1919.
[Commentary, accompanied by a translation, which Smith
believed "...should be clothed in modern speech, the
simple homely speech of daily use." Contains Romans,
Galatians, Ephesians, Philippians, Colossians, 1
Thessalonians, 2 Thessalonians, 1 Timothy, 2 Timothy,
Titus, Philemon, and a small portion of Acts.]

Another edition; Letters of St. Paul...new
edition edited by M. Wyatt Rawson. London: C.
Higham & Son, 1942.

1922 **Callan, Fr. Charles Jerome**   The Epistles of St.
Paul. With Introduction and Commentary for Priests
& Students. By Rev. Charles J. Callan, O.P. 2 Vols.
New York: Joseph F. Wagner (Inc.); London: B.
Herder, 1922.
["...whenever our ordinary English version of the
Clementine Vulgate has been found to be out of harmony
with the original Greek text...this has been indicated
and a correct translation given..."]

1925 **Wood, C.T.**   The Life, Letters and Religion of St.
Paul by C.T. Wood.   New York: Scribner's Sons;
Edinburgh: T. & T. Clark, 1925.
[Includes "...a paraphrase of all except a few easy
chapters..."]

1941 **Maritain, Jacques**   The Living Thoughts of St. Paul,
Presented by Jacques Maritain. The Living Thoughts
Library, edited by Alfredo Mendel.   Philadelphia:
David McKay Co., 1941.
> ["For the Epistles as for the Acts, use has been made of
> the Westminster version of the Scriptures..., But
> original translations have been used when occasionally
> it seemed preferable."]

1942 **Deane, Anthony Charles**   St. Paul and His Letters.
London: Hodder & Stoughton Ltd., 1942.
> ["A fairly full paraphrase, written...in the first
> person..." and commentary. "The Epistle to Philemon
> alone, by reason of its brevity, is translated in
> full."]

1942 **Rawson, M. Wyatt** (Editor)   See David Smith, The
Life and Letters of St. Paul, 1919.

1950 **Shepard, J.W.**   The Life and Letters of St. Paul. An
Exegetical Study.   By J.W. Shepard.   Grand Rapids:
William B. Eerdmans Publishing Co., 1950.

1958 **Hudson, James T.**   The Pauline Epistles;
their meaning and message by James T. Hudson...
Introduction, Translation, Marginal Analysis and
Paraphrase. London: James Clarke & Co., Inc., 1958.
> ["...a new translation with the missing steps in Paul's
> thoughts supplied in brackets, and a marginal analysis
> and paraphrase..."]

1965 **Bruce, F.F.**   The Letters of Paul, An Expanded
Paraphrase, Printed in Parallel with the Revised
Version, with Fuller References by Drs. Scrivener,
Moulton & Greenup, by F.F. Bruce. Grand Rapids, Mi:
Wm. B. Eerdmans Publishing Co., 1965.
> Another edition; Exter, Devon, England: The
> Paternoster Press, 1965.

> First American Edition; Palm Springs, CA: Ronald
> N. Haynes Publ. Inc., 1981.

1971 **Blackwelder, Boyce W.**   Letters from Paul, an
Exegetical Translation, by Boyce W. Blackwelder...
Anderson, Ind.: Warner Press, 1971.

1976 **Cross, L.S.** Paul's Letters made easy for devotions.
A Vista-Phrase. The successor to easy versions and
paraphrases. The Concise <u>Picture-Outline</u> Text Helps
You Understand Any Version. By L.S. Cross.
Harrison, Ark.: SonLife Books, 1976.
> Another edition; 1982.

1981 **Bruce, F.F.**   An Expanded Paraphrase of the Epistles
of Paul. [Revised]   Palm Springs, CA: R.N.Haynes

PAULINE EPISTLES SELECTIONS

???? **Barth, Markus**   Colossians and Philemon. Introduction, Translation and Commentary by Markus Barth.   Garden City, New York: Doubleday & Co., Inc., [19??].
[See Complete Bibles, 1964 Anchor Bible, Vol. 34b.]

???? **Beet, Joseph Agar**   A Commentary on St. Paul's Epistles to the Ephesians, Philippians, Colossians and Philemon. London: Hodder & Stoughton, [189?]. 3rd edition; London: 1902.

1581 **Anonymous**   The Epistles to the Galatians and Colossians, with a Commentary by Calvin, Translated by R.V.   London: Tho. Purfoote, 1581.

1733 **Pierce (Peirce), James**   A Paraphrase and Notes on the Epistles of St. Paul to the Colossians, Philippians and Hebrews, With Several critical Dissertations by John Pierce...With a Paraphrase and Notes on the Last Chapter of Hebrews Left Unfinished by Joseph Hallett Junior. London: J. Noon, 1733.
[Several title pages dated 1725-1727.]

1752 **Edwards, Timothy**   A Paraphrase, with Critical Annotations, on the Epistles of St. Paul to the Romans and Galatians. To which is prefixed, an analytical scheme of the whole.   London: S. Birt, for Manister Barnard, 1752.

1819 **Anonymous**   The Epistles of Paul the Apostle; translated from the Greek, and Arranged in the order in which they were probably written; with explanatory notes. Part 1. Edinburgh: for P. Hill, 1819.

1841 **Pringle, William**   Commentaries on the Epistles of Paul to the Galatians and Ephesians... Translated from the original [by John Calvin] Edinburgh: Thomas Clark, <u>Biblical Cabinet</u>, Vol. 30, 1841.
[Not known whether this is the same work as that published by the Calvin Translation Society in 1844.]

1841 **White, John** The Restoration of the Holy Scriptures to their ancient reading, their philosophy and harmony with the state and physical forms of man, in a translation of the Holy Epistle of Paul to the Galatians, and a part of his Epistle to the Romans, with notes critical and explanatory, and a introductory dissertation on the style, intelligence and spirit of the Holy Evangelist John by John

White. London: by J.L. Cox, for Sherwood, Gilbert
& Piper, 1841.

1842 **Johnston, Robert**   Expositions of the Epistles
of Paul to the Philippians and Colossians. By John
Calvin, and D. Gottlob Christian Storr. Translated
from the originals by Robert Johnston. Edinburgh:
Thomas Clark [Biblical Cabinet, Vol. 40], 1842.

1844 **Pringle, William**   Commentary on Galatians
and Ephesians by John Calvin. Translated from the
original Latin, and collated with the author's
French version. Edinburgh: Calvin Translation
Society, 1844.
     [See Bible Selections, 1844 Anonymous, Commentaries on
     the books of the Bible.]

1851 **Lewin, Thomas**   The Life and Epistles of St. Paul,
by Thomas Lewin. 2 Vols. London: Francis & John
Rivington, 1851.
     ["The italics indicate variations from the AV."]

     Second edition; with additions and illustrations,
     1874.

     Third edition; 2 Vols. London: George Bell &
     Sons, 1875.
          ["I have made numerous corrections, and have also
          introduced   much   additional   matter...   The
          Epistles...have been translated as literally as
          possible..."]

     Fourth edition; London: n.d.
          ["The present edition, besides the correction of
          various inaccuracies, has received considerable
          additions..."]

     Fifth edition; London: George Bell & Sons, 1890.

1851 **Pringle, William**   Commentary on Philippians,
Colossians and Thessalonians by John Calvin.
Translated from the original Latin, and collated
with the author's French version. Edinburgh: Calvin
Translation Society, 1851.
     [See Anonymous, Commentaries on the books of the Bible,
     1844.]

1853 **Norton, Andrews**   The Epistles of Paul to
the Romans and the Corinthians, by Andrews Norton.
[MS, Harvard] c1853

1855 **Jowett, Benjamin**   The Epistles of St. Paul to
the Thessalonians, Galatians, Romans. With Critical
Notes and Dissertations by Benjamin Jowett. 2 Vols.
London: John Murray, 1855.

[The Greek text of Lachmann is printed on the left-hand page; "...the authorised English translation... is added on the opposite page with slight corrections; which where they are occasioned by variations of reading, are marked by numbers referring to the authorised text, which is retained beneath."]

Another edition; − − Translation and Commentary... Third Edition, edited and condensed by Lewis Campbell. London: John Murray, 1894.

1857 **Ellicott, Charles John** A Critical and Grammatical Commentary on St.Paul's Epistles to the Philippians, Colossians, and to Philemon, with a revised translation. By C.J. Ellicott... London: John W. Parker & Son, 1857.
["To... the interpretations adopted by the Syriac, Old Latin, and Gothic Versions... I have added reference to the Coptic (Memphitic) and Ethiopic Versions..." Greek & English]

Second edition; Revised and Enlarged. London: Parker, Son & Bourn, 1861.
["...a certain number of alterations have been introduced in the Revised Translation..."]

Third edition; corrected. London: Longman & Co., 1865.

Fourth edition, 1875.

Fifth edition, 1888.

Another edition; Andover [Mass.]: Warren F. Draper; Boston: W.H. Halliday; Philadelphia: Smith, English & Co., 1872.

1857 **Linton, Henry P.** A Paraphrase and notes on the Epistles of St. Paul. London: Wertheim & Macintosh, 1857.

1861 **Anonymous** The Epistles of St. Paul to the Galatians, Ephesians, Philippians, and Colossians, after the AV; newly compared with the original Greek and revised, by Four Clergymen. [Henry Alford, George Moberly, W. Humphrey, C.J. Ellicott] London: Robson, Levey & Franklyn, for Parker, Son & Bourne, 1861.

1866 **Davies, J. Llewelyn** The Epistles of St. Paul to the Ephesians, the Colossians and Philemon: with introductions and notes, and an essay on the traces of foreign elements in the theology of these epistles. London: Macmillan & Co., 1866.

["I am especially indebted to three recent works of the
first importance, - the Greek N.T. of Professors
Westcott & Hort, the RV, and Bishop Lightfoot's
Colossians and Philemon." The Greek in the 2nd ed is
that of Westcott & Hort. Epistle Selections.]

Second edition, 1884.

1882 **Hebert, Charles**   The New Testament Scriptures in
the order in which they were written: a very close
translation from the Greek text of 1611, with brief
explanations. The First Portion: The six primary
Epistles, to Thessalonica, Corinth, Galatia, and
Rome, A.D. 52-58. By the Rev. Charles Hebert...
London: for Henry Frowde, Oxford University Press
Warehouse...Seeley, Jackson and Halliday; Oxford:
E. Pickard Hall, and J.H. Stacy, 1882.
      ["...the use of one English word throughout for every
      Greek word is, as far as possible, maintained..."
      Apparently no more was published.]

1885 **Boise, James Robinson**   Notes on Galatians and
Romans. Chicago: The American Publication Society
of Hebrew, 1885.

1894 **Campbell, Lewis** (Editor)   See Benjamin Jowett, The
Epistles of St. Paul, 1855.

1895 **Abbott, T.K.**   A Critical and Exegetical Commentary
on the Book of Ephesians and Colossians, Together
with a New Translation, by Rev. T.K. Abbott...
Edinburgh: T. & T. Clark, 1895.
      [See Complete Bibles, 1895 International Critical
      Commentary.]

1897 **Vincent, Marvin R.**   A Critical and Exegetical
Commentary on the Epistles of St. Paul to the
Philippians and Philemon by Rev. Marvin R. Vincent
... Edinburgh: T. & T. Clark, 1897.
      [See Complete Bibles, 1895 International Critical
      Commentary.]

Reprinted, 1902.

1898 **Moule, Handley C.G.**   Colossian Studies. Lessons in
Faith and Holiness from St. Paul's Epistles to the
Colossians and Philemon. London: Hodder & Stoughton;
New York: A.C. Armstrong and Son, 1898.
      Another edition; New York: George H. Doran,
      undated.

      Also; Grand Rapids: Zondervan Publishing House,
      n.d.

1898 **Rickaby, Joseph**   Notes on St. Paul: Corinthians,
Galatians and Romans, by Joseph Rickaby.   London:
Burns & Oates Ltd., 1898.
> ["I have printed almost exactly the text of Challoner's
> 1752 edition of the Rheims text... I have often
> endeavored to improve the translation."]

> Revised, 1905.

1900 **Rutherford, William Gunion**   St. Paul's Epistles...
London: Macmillan & Co., 1900-1908.
> 1900 St. Paul's Epistle to the Romans, A new
> translation with a brief analysis by W.G.
> Rutherford.
>> [The name "Jehovah" is used six times at
>> pages 44, 48 & 52.]

>> Reprinted, 1914.

> 1908 St. Paul's Epistles to the Thessalonians
> and to the Corinthians. A new translation
> [from the Greek] By the late   W.G.
> Rutherford... With a prefatory note by
> Spenser Wilkinson.

> Reprinted; Five Pauline Epistles. A new
> translation. William Gunion Rutherford (1853-
> 1907) Malvern, Worcs: Golden Age Limited
> Editions, 1984.

1901 **Harris, John Tindall**   The Writings of the Apostle
by John Tindall Harris. London: Headley Bros., 1901.
> [Thessalonians, Philippians and Hebrews only.]

1908 **Rutherford, John**   St. Paul's Epistles to Colossae
and Laodicea. The Epistle to the Colossians viewed
in relation to the Epistle to the Ephesians. With
introduction and notes, by John Rutherford.
Edinburgh: T. & T. Clark, 1908.
> [Greek and English.]

1909 **McFadyen, John Edgar**   The Epistles to the
Corinthians and Galatians with notes and comments.
By John Edgar McFadyen... New York: A.S. Barnes &
Co., 1909.
> [McFadyen has provided the text in the KJV, and a
> commentary, "...weaving into the course of the
> commentary a translation of my own which stands out
> prominently in black lettering."]

> [The Interpreter's Commentary on the N.T., Vol. VI]

> Another edition; London: Hodder & Stoughton,
> 1911.

1913 **Westcott, Frederick Brooke**   St. Paul and
Justification. Being an exposition of the teaching
in the Epistles to Rome and Galatia. By Frederick
Brooke Westcott. London: Macmillan & Co., 1913.

1914 **Goodier, Alban**   Philippians and Philemon, 1914.
[See Complete Bibles, 1913 Westminster Version.]

1914 **Rickaby, Joseph**   Ephesians and Colossians, 1914.
[See Complete Bibles, 1913 Westminster Version.]

1931 **Radford, Lewis B.**   The Epistle to the Colossians
and the Epistle to Philemon. With introductions and
notes. By Lewis B. Radford. London: Methugn & Co.,
Westminster Commentaries, 1931.

1937 **Bonner, C. Bradlaugh**   The Second Epistle to the
Corinthians, the Epistles to the Galatians, to the
Colossians, to the Ephesians, and the Epistle to
Philemon. New   translation   into   French   with
introduction and notes by Henri Delafosse - Joseph
Turmel. English version by C. Bradlaugh Bonner.
London: Watts & Co., 1937.

1937 **Cornish, Gerald Warre**   St. Paul from the Trenches,
A rendering of the Epistles to the Corinthians and
Ephesians done in France during the Great War. By
Gerald Warre Cornish. With a foreword by John Sidney
Braithwaite.   Boston: Houghton Mifflin Company,
1937.
     Second Edition; Cambridge: 1937.

     Third Edition; Cambridge: 1938 (with captions
     added and With a Foreword by John Sidney
     Braithwaite).

     Also; Cambridge: 1940.

     Fifth Edition;   Tibberton,   Gloucestershire:
     Tantivy Press, 1948.

1948 **Gray, Crete**   The Epistles of St. Paul to the
Colossians and Philemon by Crete Gray. A Lutterworth
Commentary. London & Redhill: Lutterworth Press,
1948.
     [ASV, 1901, with a few changes.]

1952 **Anonymous**   Galatians and the Captivity Epistles,
Philippians, Ephesians, Colossians. [A.M. Cox]
Kingston: the author, 1952.

1954 **Hoerber, Robert G.**   Saint Paul's Shorter Letters
(Galatians, Ephesians, Philippians, Colossians, I &
II Thessalonians, I & II Timothy, Titus, Philemon)

by Robert G. Hoerber. Fulton, MO: Published by the Author, 1954.

1958 **Martin, Hugh**   The Seven Letters. By Hugh Martin. Philadelphia: The Westminster Press, 1958.

1959 **Taylor, Kenneth N.**   Romans for the Children's Hour, with I and II Timothy; A Family Devotions Book ...Illustrated by JoAnne Brubaker. Chicago: Moody Press, [1959].
["Is this an exact translation? No, it is called a paraphrase or adaption"]

Also; Romans for the Family Hour... Chicago: Moody Press.
["...essentially the same book but different editions."]

1961 **Harington, Jay**   Paul of Tarsus...
[See New Testament Selections for the complete entry. Includes the Letters of Paul.]

1964 **Blaiklock, E.M.**   From Prison in Rome; Letters to the Philippians and Philemon. By E.M.Blaiklock. Grand Rapids, Michigan: Zondervan Publishing House; London: Pickering & Inglis, 1964.

1968 **Blaiklock, E.M.**   The Way of Excellence, a New translation and study of 1 Corinthians 13 and Romans 12. E.M. Blaiklock. London: Pickering and Inglis, 1968.
Also: Grand Rapids: Zondervan, 1968.

1976 **Johnson, Ben Campbell**   The Heart of Paul. A Relational Paraphrase of the New Testament. Ben Campbell Johnson. Waco, Texas: Word, Inc., 1976.

1981 **Anonymous**   The Epistles of Paul to Galatians, Ephesians, Philippians, Colossians. Recovery Version. Anaheim, CA: Living Stream Ministry, 1981.
[See N.T., 1985 Witness Lee & Others, N.T.]

1982 **O'Brien, Peter T.**   Word Biblical Commentary. Colossians, Philemon. Peter T. O'Brien. Waco, TX: Word Books, Publisher, 1982.
[See Complete Bibles, 1982 Word Biblical Commentary, Vol. 44.]

1984 **Payne, John B.**   Collected Works of Erasmus. New Testament Scholarship. Paraphrase on Romans and Galatians. Edited by Robert D. Sider. Translated and annotated by John B. Payne, Albert Rabil Jr., and Warren S. Smith Jr. 5 Vols. Toronto, Buffalo & London: University of Toronto Press, 1984.

1987 **Schoder, Raymond V.**   Paul wrote from the Heart. Philippians & Galatians in straight forward English by Raymond V. Schoder... Oak Park, Illinois: Bolchazy - Carducci Publishers, 1987.

ROMANS

???? **Keck, Leander E.**   Romans. A New Translation with Introduction and Commentary by Leander E. Keck. Garden City, New York: Doubleday & Co., Inc., [19??].
> [See Complete Bibles listing, 1964 Anchor Bible, Vol. 33.]

1552 **Hooper, Bishop John**   The Epistle to the Romans. Worchester: John Oswen, 1552.

1568 **Anonymous**   Most Learned and fruitfull Commentaries... of D. Peter Martir Vermilius...vpon the Epistle S. Paul to the Romaness: Wherein are diligently and most profitably entreated all suche matters and chiefe common places of religion touched in the same Epistle. With a table of all the common places, and exposition vpon diuers places of the scriptyres, and an index to finde all the principall matters conteyned in the same. Lately traslated out of the Latine into Englishe by H.B. [H. Billingsley?] London: Iohn Daye, 1568.

1568 **Guest, Edmund**   Romans, 1568.
> [See Complete Bibles, 1568 Bishops' Bible.]

1630 **Usher, Ambrose**   ["All of the O.T.; and of the New, the...]
> [See Bible Selections for the complete entry.]

1666 **Day, William**   A Paraphrase and Commentary upon the Epistle of Saint Paul to the Romans. London: S. Griffin for Joshua Kirton, 1666.
> [With text.]

1705 **Locke, John**   Romans, 1707.
> [See Epistles and Selections, 1705 Anonymous, A Paraphrase and Notes on the Epistles...]

1745 **Taylor, John**   A Paraphrase with Notes on the Epistle to the Romans: To which is prefix'd, a Key to the Apostolic Writings, or an Essay to explain the Gospel Scheme, and the Principal Words and

Phrases the Apostles have used in describing it.
London: Printed and Sold by J. Waugh, 1745.

>Another edition; Dublin: Printed by A. Reilly for
John Smith, 1746.

>Second Edition; London: Printed & Sold by J.
Waugh, 1747.

>Third Edition; London: J. Waugh & W. Fenner,
1754.

>Fourth Edition; London: Rivington, 1769.

1752 **Edwards, Timothy**   A Paraphrase, with Critical
Annotations on the Epistles of St. Paul to the
Romans and Galatians...
>[See Pauline Epistles Selections for the complete
entry.]

1761 **Philips, J.**   St. Paul's First Epistle; in a new
Method, by J. Philips. London: for J. Noon, 1761.

1771 **Adam, Thomas**   A Paraphrase on the Eleven First
Chapters of St. Paul's Epistle to the Romans, 1771.

1811 **Anonymous**   St. Paul's Epistle to the Romans,
Paraphrased. London: for M. Richardson, 1811.

1816 **Fry, John**   Lectures, Explanatory and Practical,
on the Epistle of Saint Paul to the Romans. London:
Ogles, Duncan & Cochran, 1816.

1823 **Anonymous**   Horae Romanae; or, an Attempt
to Elucidate St. Paul's Epistle to the Romans, by an
original translation, explanatory notes and new
divisions. By Clericus. [Robert Cox] London: C.
Baldwyn, 1823.
>A reissue; London: for J.Hatchard, 1824.

1828 **Terrot, C.H.**   The Epistle of Paul the Apostle
to the Romans [in Greek] with an introduction [in
English], paraphrase, and notes, by C.H. Terrot.
London: 1828.

1832 **Stuart, Moses**   Commentary on the Epistle to the
Roman, with a translation and various excursus, by
the Rev. Moses Stuart... Andover: Flagg & Gould,
1832.

>Republished, with prefaces. London: Holdsworth &
Ball, 1833.

>Second Edition; Corrected and enlarged. Andover:
Gould & Newman; New York: H. Griffin, 1835.

Third edition; Corrected and considerably enlarged. London: T. Tegg, 1836.

Fourth edition; London: n.p., n.d.

Fifth edition; London: W. Tagg [sic], 1853.

Third Edition; Edited and revised by R.D.C. Robbins. Andover: Warren F. Draper; Boston: Gould & Lincoln, 1859.

Fourth Edition; New York: Wiley & Halstead; Philadelphia: Smith, English & Co., 1859 and 1862.

Sixth Edition; London: William Tegg, 1857.

1834 **Anonymous**   A Paraphrastic Translation of St.Paul's Epistle to the Romans. By Laicus. London: Simpkin & Marshall, 1834.

1834 **Sibson, Francis**   Commentary on the Epistle to the Romans, by John Calvin; to which is prefixed his Life, by Theodore Beza; translated [from the Latin] by Francis Sibson. London: L.B. Seeley & Sons, 1834.

1840 **Bosanquet, Edwin**   A Verbal Paraphrase of St. Paul's Epistle to the Romans, with brief illustrations from scripture, and the Fathers: being an attempt to convey to the general reader, a corrected view of the Apostle's arguments and expressions. By Edwin Bosanquet. London: James Burns, 1840.

1841 **White, John**   The Restoration... Holy Scriptures... [See Pauline Epistles Selections for the complete entry.]

1844 **Anonymous**   The Epistle of Paul to the Romans; with a preface and brief reflections by Luther. Translated from the German. With a Recommended Notice by the Rev. Thomas Brown. Edinburgh: W.P. Kennedy, 1944.

1844 **Cooper, Basil H.**   An Essay towards a new translation of Epistle of St. Paul to the Romans: on the basis of the AV; with a paraphrase and brief explanatory notes. London: Hamilton Adams & Co., 1844.

1846 **Walford, William**   Curae Romanae. Notes on the Epistle to the Romans, with a revised translation, by William Walford. London: Jackson and Walford, 1846.

1848 **Whitwell, William A.** A Translation of Paul's Epistle to the Romans, with an Introduction and Notes by William A. Whitwell. Boston: William Crosby & Co., H.P. Nichols, 1848.
["The books upon which he has principally depended for assistance are 'Novum Testamentum Graece, by Benjamin Koppe', Loske's Paraphrase, Beausobre and Lenfant's translation of the New Testament..."]

1849 **Owen, John** Commentaries on the Romans by John Calvin. Translated from the original Latin, and collated with the author's French version. Edinburgh: Calvin Translation Society, 1849.
[See Bible Selections, 1844 Anonymous, Commentaries on the Books of the Bible.]

1850 **Ewbank, W.W.** A Commentary on the Epistle of Paul to the Romans; with a new translation and explanatory notes. 2 Vols. London: J.W. Parker, 1850-1851.

1853 **Norton, Andrews** The Epistles of Paul to...
[See Pauline Epistles Selections for the complete entry.]

1854 **Anonymous** An Exposition of St. Paul's Epistle to the Romans. By William Benecke. Translated from the German. London: Longman & Co., 1854.

1854 **Knight, Robert** A Critical Commentary on the Epistle of St. Paul the Apostle to the Romans by Robert Knight. London: Bagster & Sons; Simpkin, Marshall & Co.; Oxford: J.H. Parker; Cambridge: Macmillan & Co.; Atherton: W.C. Holland, 1854.
[Greek & English: "A paraphrase has been added for the purpose of enabling the reader to embrace at a glance the interpretation which is defended in the body of the work."]

1854 **Peile, Thomas W.** A New Translation of the Received Text of the Apostolic Epistles, slighty interpolated, and illustrated by a synoptic and logical paraphrase of the contents of each... Part I. London: Rivingtons, 1854.
[Romans only.]

1855 **Livermore, Abiel Abbot** The Epistle of Paul to the Romans; with a Commentary and revised Translation, and Introductory Essays. By Abiel Abbot Livermore. Boston: 1855.

1855 **Jowett, Benjamin** The Epistles of St. Paul...
[See Pauline Epistles Selections for the complete entry.]

1855 **Purdue, Edward**   A Commentary on the Epistle
to the Romans, with a revised translation, by Edward
Purdue. Dublin: S.B. Oldham, 1855.

1857 **Bromehead, A.C.**   A Popular Paraphrase on St. Paul's
Epistle to the Romans, with notes. By A.C.Bromehead.
London: Bell & Daldy, 1857.

1857 **Green, Thomas Sheldon**   The New Testament...
    [See New Testament Selections for the complete entry.
    Includes Romans.]

1858 **Anonymous**   The Epistle of St. Paul to the Romans,
after the AV; newly compared with the original Greek
and revised, by Five Clergymen. [J. Barrow, G.
Moberly, H. Alford, W.G. Humphrey, C.J. Ellicott]
London: Savill and Edwards, for J.W. Parker & Son,
1858.

1861 **Colenso, John William**   St. Paul's Epistle
to the Romans: newly translated and explained from
a missionary point of view. By the Rev. J.W. Colenso
... Cambridge & London: Macmillan & Co., 1861.
    Second edition; New York: Appleton & Co., 1863.

1870 **Ellicott, Charles John**   Considerations on the
Revision of the English Version...
    [See New Testament Selections for the complete entry.
    Includes Romans V, VI, VII & VIII.]

1871 **Berry, Grove**   A Sequel to "Ritualism", parts I.
and II.: based on "The Epistle to the Romans." (An
attempt at translation of what is known as "The
Epistle to the Romans", preserving the order of the
Greek original, and also aiming at uniformity
therein.) By Grove Berry. London: Longmans & Co.,
1871.

1871 **Challis, James** A Translation of the Epistle of the
Apostle Paul to the Romans, with an introduction and
critical notes by James Challis.   Cambridge:
Deighton, Bell & Co.; London: Bell & Daldy, 1871.

1871 **Latham, John Herbert**   Theories of Philosophy and
Religion compared with the Christian theory as set
forth by St. Paul in his Letter to the Romans, now
newly translated with notes by John Herbert Latham.
London: Longmans & Co., 1871.

1873 **Godwin, John Hensley**   The Epistle of Saint Paul to
Romans. A new translation with notes. London: Hodder
& Stoughton, 1873.
    [Anonymous?]

1877 **Beet, Joseph Agar**   A Commentary on St. Paul's
Epistle to the Romans. By Joseph Agar Beet. London:
Hodder & Stoughton, 1877.

> Second edition; revised.   London: Hodder &
> Stoughton, 1881.

> Another edition; New York: Thomas Whittaker,
> 1881.

> Third edition; with a new appendix.   London:
> Hodder & Stoughton, 1882.

> 9th edition, 1900.

1880 **Cusin, Alexander**   Commentary on St. Paul's Epistle
to the Romans. By F. Godet...Translated from the
French by A.Cusin. Edinburgh: T. & T. Clark, <u>Foreign
Theological Library</u>, New Series Vol. 2, 6, 1880.

> Another edition; ...The Translation Revised and
> edited with an introduction and appendix by
> Talbot W. Chambers. 2 Vols. New York: Funk and
> Wagnalls, 1883.

> ["Prof Godet is careful to give a new (French) version
> of the Greek, corresponding to his view of its precise
> meaning. Sometimes the English Translator (Cusin) has
> observed this... But in general the language of the AV
> has been adopted (in the 1880 edition)... The American
> editor has gone over the pages, and sought to make the
> Apostle's word, as they appear here, an exact
> reproduction of the author's (Godet's) views."]

> Second edition; New York: Funk and Wagnalls,
> 1885.

> Third edition; Edinburgh: T. & T. Clark, 1892.

1882 **Fenton, Ferrar**   St. Paul's Epistles to the Romans.
Translated direct from the original Greek into
modern English, with the Apostle's own division of
the subject matter restored. By Ferrar Fenton.
Batley: A. Wildsmith, 1882.

1882 **Hebert, Charles**   The New Testament Scriptures...
> [See Pauline Epistles Selections for the complete
> entry.]

1883 **Betts, John Thomas**   Juan de Valdes' Commentary
upon St. Paul's Epistle to the Romans now for the
first time translated from the Spanish, having never
before been published in English. By John T. Betts.
London: Trubner & Co., 1883.
> [Text appears to be the KJV, occasionally accommodated
> to the Spanish.]

1885 **Boise, James Robinson**   Notes on Galatians...

[See Pauline Epistles Selections for the complete entry.]

1885 **Gaffney, Charlotte**   Paraphrase of the Eleventh Chapter of the Epistle to the Romans. With some parenthetical Gospel truths. By Charlotte Gaffney. [London: 1885?]

1886 **Chase, D.P.**   The Epistle, of Paul the Apostle, to the Romans. The Authorised Version 1611 arranged in paragraphs, and in dialogues, with notes. By D.P. Chase. London: Rivingtons, 1886.

1886 **Gifford, E.H.**   The Epistle of St. Paul to the Romans, with notes and introduction, 1886.

1893 **Moule, Handley C.G.**   The Epistle of St. Paul to the Romans. By Handley C.G. Moule... New York: A.C. Armstrong & Son; London: Hodder & Stoughton, 1893 [Includes a "running Translation of the Epistle...interwoven with this Exposition."]

[See Bible selections, 1888 The Expositor's Bible.]

Second edition, 1894.

Also; [Undated 20th Century reprint.] London: Pickering & Inglis.

1895 **Sanday, William and Arthur C. Headlam**   A Critical and Exegetical Commentary on the Epistle to the Romans by the Rev. William Sanday... and Arthur C. Headlam... Edinburgh: T. & T. Clark, 1895. [See Complete Bibles, 1895 International Critical Commentary.]

Second Edition, 1896.

Third Edition, 1898.

Fourth Edition, 1900.

Fifth Edition, 1902.

Reprinted; 1905, 1907, 1908, 1911, 1914, 1920, 1925, 1930, 1945, 1949, 1950.

1898 **Rickaby, Joseph**   Notes on St. Paul... [See Pauline Epistles Selections for the complete entry.]

1899 **Stellhorn, F.W.**   Paul's Epistle to the Romans... [See New Testament Selections, 1891 F.W. Stellhorn, A Brief Commentary...]

1900 **Rutherford, William Gunion**   St. Paul's Epistle...
[See Pauline Epistles Selections, 1900 William Gunion
Rutherford, St. Paul's Epistles...]

1902 **Sampson, Gerard**   The Layman's Bible Series...
[See New Testament Selections for the complete entry.
Includes Romans.]

1902 **Williams, William G.**   An Exposition of the Epistle
of Paul to the Romans. By William G. Williams...
Cincinnati: Jennings & Pye;   New York: Eaton &
Mains, 1902.
["...the corrected translation here given makes more
than 1600 additional changes from the (ERV)... I have
attempted in this translation to reproduce for my
readers, literally and exactly, in as good English as
the Greek permits, the Apostle's turn of thought and
turn of expression."]

1904 **Everitt, Herbert**   St. Paul's Journey from Jerusalem
to Rome, being a paraphrase. By Herbert Everitt.
London: S.P.C.K., 1904.

1911 **Grey, H.G.**   St. Paul's Epistle to the Romans. By
H.G. Grey. The Reader's Commentary, 1911.
[Revised Version??]

1913 **Harford, George**   The Gospel According to Saint
Paul Being an Expanded Rendering of the Epistle to
the Romans by George Harford. London, Edinburgh, &
New York: Marshall Brothers, Ltd., 1913.

1913 **Westcott, Frederick Brooke**   St. Paul and
Justification ...the Epistles to Rome and Galatia...
[See Pauline Epistles Selections for the complete
entry.]

1914 **Concordant Version**   Paul's Epistle to...
[See New Testament Selections, 1914 Concordant Version
of the Sacred Scriptures.]

1914 **Lard, Moses E.**   Commentary on Paul's Letter to
Romans: With a Revised Greek Text, Compiled from the
Best Recent Authors, and a New Translation, by Moses
E. Lard.   St. Louis: Christian Board of Publication,
1914.
[Preface dated 1875]

1914 **Tucker, Emma Curtiss**   The Later Version of the
Wycliffite Epistle to the Romans, compared with the
Latin Original: A Study of Wycliffite English.   New
York: Henry Holt & Co., 1914.
[The Text and Notes. Yale Studies in English, Vol. 49.]

1917 **Moffatt, James**   St. Paul to the Romans. Studies
in the Epistle to the Romans. By R.L. Pelly. With a

translation into modern English by Professor James
Moffatt. London: n.p., 1917.

1920 **Lattey, Cuthbert**   Romans, 1920.
[See Complete Bibles, 1913 Westminster Version.]

1920 **Pallis, Alexander**   To the Romans. A Commentary by
Alexander Pallis. Liverpool: Liverpool Booksellers'
Co., 1920.
[With the Greek text and the commentator's English
version.]

1929 **Maltby, W.R.**   The Eighth of Romans. By W.R. Maltby.
London: Epworth Press, 1929.
[Manuals of Fellowship.]

1930 **Isaacs, Wilfred H.**   Translational Studies in the
New Testament... The Epistle of Paul the Apostle to
the Romans. London: 1930?
[A new translation, with notes, extracted from "The
King's Message".]

1933 **Hoskyns, Edwyn Clement**   The Epistle to the Romans
by Karl Barth; Translated from the Sixth German
edition.   London, New York & Toronto: Geoffrey
Cumberledge, Oxford University Press, 1933.
["Taken together the AV, RV, AV mg., RV mg., offer a
wide choice of translations. Where, however, the author
has no support from the English versions, or where he
has paraphrased the Greek, a different fount [sic] has
been used..."]

Another edition, 1968.

1934 **Boylan, Patrick**   St. Paul's Epistle to the Romans.
Translation and Commentary by...Patrick Boylan...
Dublin: M.H. Gill & Son, 1934.
["Exactitude rather than elegance has been aimed at in
the translation (from the Greek)."]

1937 **Williams, Charles B.**   Romans, a Translation in
the Language of the People, by Charles B. Williams.
Chicago: Moody Press, 1937.

1938 **Newell, William R.**   Romans Verse by Verse,
by William R. Newell.   Chicago, Illinois: Grace
Publications, 1938.
["The text used is in general that of the RV... At times
it is necessary to render literally; and, in several
instances to paraphrase..."]

1940 **Nash, C.H.** Christ Interpreted: Paul's letter to the
Romans, the greatest interpretation of Jesus Christ
in all literature; a new translation and commentary
by the Rev.C.H. Nash, foreword by the Right Rev. W.

Wilson Cash. London, Edinburgh: Marshall, Morgan &
Scott, 1940.
> [The title is taken from the 1954 ed.]

> Another edition, 1954.

1943 **Hague, Lois**   Paraphrase of Romans by Lois
Hague. MS located in Biola Library, 1943.

1945 **Heywood, D. Herbert**   New Era Testament...
> [See New Testament Selections for the complete entry.
> Includes Romans 12.]

1948 **Carpenter, S.C.**   A paraphrase of selections from
St. Paul's Epistle to the Romans. By S.C. Carpenter.
London: S.P.C.K. National Society, 1948.

1949 **Griffith, Gwilym O.**   St. Paul's Gospel to the
Romans. Oxford: Basil Blackwell, 1949.
> [Chapter 3 consists of "The Epistle in Paraphrase".]

1950 **Quimby, Chester Warren**   The Great Redemption.
A living commentary on Paul's Epistle to the Romans.
By Chester Warren Quimby. New York: The Macmillan
Co., 1950.

1951 **Pilcher, Charles Venn**   The Epistle of St. Paul to
the Romans; translated in paraphrase together with
an introduction By Charles Venn Pilcher. London:
Lutterworth Press, 1951.

1954 **Mueller, J. Theodore**   Commentary on the Epistle
to the Romans by Martin Luther; A New Abridged
Translation, by J. Theodore Mueller. Grand Rapids,
Michigan: Zondervan Publishing House, 1954.
> ["He depends heavily on Ellwein, and significant
> sections of his translation are not entirely true to the
> original." From Pauck's 'Lectures on the Romans', 1961.]

1955 **Cressman, Annie**   Paul's Letter to the Romans. By
Annie Cressman. Tchien, Liberia: Assemblies of God
Mission, 1955.

1955 **Hunter, Archibald MacBride**   The Epistle to the
Romans; the Law of Love. A.M.Hunter...London: S.C.M.
Press, 1955.
> [Contains his own translation interspersed with the ERV
> & ASV.]

> Reprinted; 1957, 1961, 1968.

1955 **Taylor, Vincent**   The Epistle to the Romans.
By Vincent Taylor. London: The Epworth Press, 1955.
> [Epworth Preacher's Commentaries.]

1955 **Wuest, Kenneth S.**   Word Studies...Romans...
[See New Testament Selections, 1940 Kenneth S. Wuest,
Word Studies...]

1957 **Barrett, Charles K.**   A Commentary on the Epistle to
the Romans. C.K. Barrett. London: Adam and Charles
Black; New York: Harper & Brothers, 1957.
[See N.T., 1957 Black's N.T. Commentaries.]

[See N.T., 1958 Harper Commentaries.]

Reprinted, 1967, 1971 & 1973.

1958 **Anonymous**   The Epistle to the Romans: An Expanded
Translation. [By F.F. Bruce].   The Evangelical
Quarterly, XXX,2 (April-June, 1958), pages 98-103;
XXX, 3 (July- Sept.,1958), pages 161-165; and XXX,
4 (Oct.-Dec., 1958), pages 220-225.
[Covers Romans 1:1-8:39]

1959 **Anonymous**   The Epistle to the Romans: An Expanded
Translation. [By F.F. Bruce]   The Evangelical
Quarterly, XXXI, 1 (Jan.-Mar., 1959), Pages 43-46;
XXXI, 2 (Apr.-June, 1959), pages 99-101.
[Contains Romans 9:1-16:27.]

1959 **Murray, John**   The epistle to the Romans; the
English text with introduction, exposition, and
notes. 2 Vols. 1959-1965.
[See N.T., 1959 New International Comment. on the N.T.]

1959 **Taylor, Kenneth N.**   Romans for the Children's Hour,
with I and II Timothy...
[See Pauline Epistles Selections for the entire entry.]

1961 **Pauck, Wilhelm**   Luther: Lectures on Romans; Newly
Translated and Edited by Wilhelm Pauck.
["...it is necessary in this translation to approximate
as closely as possible the words and the mannerisms of
the Vulgate... I rely therefore, on the Douay and Rheims
edition of the translation..."]

1961 **Rhys, Howard**   The Epistle to the Romans, by Howard
Rhys. New York: The Macmillan Co., 1961.
["The English rendering...that is here offered is
awkward, and on occasion ungrammatical... the aim here
has been accuracy rather than elegance..."]

1962 **Blackwelder, Boyce W.**   Romans, an Exegetical
Translation, by Boyce W.Blackwelder. Anderson, Ind.:
n.p., 1962.

1966 **Ellison, H.L.**   The Mystery of Israel. An Exposition
of Romans 9-11 by H.L. Ellison.   The Paternoster
Press, 1966.

1968 **Blaiklock, E.M.**   The Way of Excellence...
       [See Pauline Epistles Selections for the complete
       entry.]

1974 **Witness Lee, John C. Ingalls and Others** The Epistle
     of Paul to the Romans. Recovery Version. Text and
     references by: Witness Lee, John C. Ingalls, and
     Other Co-workers. Outline and Footnotes by Witness
     Lee. Anaheim, CA: Living Stream Ministry, 1974.
       [Also; see Anonymous, The Gospel of John, 1975;
       Anonymous, Hebrews, 1981; Anonymous, The Epistle of Paul
       to Timothy..., 1981; Anonymous, The Epistle...
       Thessalonians, 1982; Anonymous, The Epistles...
       Galatians..., 1981; Anonymous, The Epistle...
       Corinthians, 1982; The New Testament, 1985.]

1975 **Cranfield, C.E.B.**   A Critical and Exegetical
     Commentary on The Epistle to the Romans by C.E.B.
     Cranfield...In two volumes. Edinburgh: T. & T. Clark
     Ltd., 1975-1979.
            1975 Vol. I Introduction and Commentary on
                 Romans I-VIII.
            1979 Vol. II Commentary on Romans IX-XVI and
                 Essays.

1977 **Haugerud, Joann**   The Word for Us...
       [See New Testament Selections for the entire entry.]

1984 **Payne, John B.**   Collected Works of Erasmus...
       [See Pauline Epistles Selections for the entire entry.]

1988 **Dunn, James D.G.** Word Biblical Commentary. Romans.
     James D.G. Dunn. Waco, TX: Word Books, Publisher,
     1988.
       [See Complete Bibles, 1982 Word Biblical Commentary,
       Vol. 38a (Romans 1-8) and Vol. 38b (Romans 9-16).]

1988 **Morris, Leon**   The Epistle to the Romans. Grand
     Rapids, MI: Eerdmans, 1988.
       [He includes the NIV with some modifications.]

CORINTHIANS

???? **Anonymous**   First Corinthians Thirteen. Burbanks,
     CA: Distributed by Pastor Jerry A. Jones, n.d.
       [Used on the radio program, "Gospelstones", heard on
       KHOF/FM Los Angeles, CA 99.5]

???? **Butler, Barry**   The First Letter of St. Paul to
     the Corinthians; Written in easy English by Barry
     Butler. Darwin, N.T. (Australia): Church Missionary
     Society Chaplain, [19??].

???? **Howe, E. Margaret and John Davis**   Word Biblical
Commentary. I Corinthians. Waco, Tx: Word Books,
Publishers, [198?].
> [See Complete Bibles, 1982 Word Biblical Commentary,
> Vol. 39.]

> [These two are listed on the "New Testament
> Contributors" as translators. However, the spine shown
> in a advertisement picture its states "Richardson"]

???? **Lee, L. Valentine**   The Greatest of These is
Love. The Parson's Page, n.d.
> [No more is known about this work.]

1568 **Goodman, Gabriel**   I Corinthians, 1568.
> [See Complete Bibles, 1568 Bishops' Bible.]

1577 **Tymme, Thomas** A Commentarie vpon S. Paules Epistles
to the Corinthians. Written by M. Iohn Caluin: and
translated out of Latine into Englishe by Thomas
Tymme. London: For Iohn Harrison & George Bishop,
1577.

1706 **Locke, John**   I Corinthians, 1706.
> [See Epistles and Selections, 1705 Anonymous, A
> Paraphrase and Notes on the Epistles...]

1707 **Locke, John**   II Corinthians, 1707.
> [See Epistles and Selections, 1705 Anonymous, A
> Paraphrase and Notes on the Epistles...]

1740 **Anonymous**   1 Corinthians, Chapter 13; Paraphrased
in Verse. Gentleman's Magazine, Vol. X, Page 192,
1740.

1777 **Pearce, Zachary**   A Commentary, with Notes, on
the Four Evangelists and the Acts of the Apostles;
together with a new translation of Saint Paul's
First Epistle to the Corinthians, with a Paraphrase
and Notes. To which are added other Theological
Pieces... To the whole is prefixed some account of
his Lordship's life and character, written by
himself. Published from the original manuscripts, by
John Derby, A.M. In Two Volumes. London: Printed by
E. Cox; for T. Cadell, 1777.
> [Only twelve copies printed.]

1793 **Eusebia**   Poetical Paraphrase of I Corinthians 13.
Gentleman's Magazine, Dec., 1793.

1793 **Pilkington, Matthew**   I Corinthians 13 paraphrased
in verse. In Anderson's Poets. Edinburgh, 1793.

1793 **Prior, Matthew**   I Corinthians 13 paraphrased in
verse, In Anderson's Poets. Edinburgh, 1793.

1825 **Tolley, I.G.**   A Paraphrase of St. Paul's First
Epistle to the Corinthians, with explanatory notes
by I.G. Tolley. London: Hatchard & Son, 1825.

1843 **Cornish, Hubert Kestell**   Homilies of S. John
Chrysostom, 1843.
    [1 Corinthians.]

1848 **Pringle, William**   Commentary on Corinthians by
John Calvin. Translated from the original Latin, and
collated with the author's French version. 2 Vols.
Edinburgh: Calvin Translation Society, 1848.
    [See Bible Selections, 1844 Anonymous, Commentaries on
    the books of the Bible.]

1851 **Thom, J.H.**   St. Paul's Epistles to the Corinthians:
an attempt to convey their spirit and significance,
by J.H. Thom. London: John Chapman, [Catholic
Series], 1851.

1853 **Norton, Andrews**   The Epistles of Paul...
    [See Pauline Epistles Selections for the complete
    entry.]

1855 **Stanley, Arthur Penrhyn**   The Epistles of St.
Paul to the Corinthians. With critical notes and
dissertations. 2 Vols. London: John Murray, 1855.
    [Includes the Greek text, a paraphrase and a new
    translation; also an Appendix, 'The Apocryphal Epistles
    of the Corinthians to St. Paul, and of St. Paul to the
    Corinthians, preserved in the Armenian Church.']

    Second edition, one Vol., 1858.
        ["The changes in this edition are chiefly those of
        compression and correction."]

    Third edition, 1865.

    Fourth edition, 1876.

1858 **Anonymous**   The Epistles of St. Paul to the
Corinthians, after the AV; newly compared with the
original Greek, and revised by Five Clergymen. [J.
Barrow, G. Moberly, Henry Alford, W.G. Humphrey,
C.J. Ellicott] London: Savill and Edwards, for J.W.
Parker & Son, 1858.

1881 **Linton, Henry P.**   The First [& Second] Epistle
to the Corinthians, with explanatory notes and
appendix. London: ["Philip's Series of Scriptural
Manuals"], 1881-1882.

1882 **Beet, Joseph Agar**   A Commentary on St. Paul's
Epistles to the Corinthians. London: Hodder &
Stoughton, 1882.

Another edition; New York: Thomas Whittaker,
1883.

7th edition; London: Hodder & Stoughton, 1902.

1882 **Betts, John Thomas**   Juan de Valdes' Commentary
upon St. Paul's First Epistle to the Church at
Corinth: now for the first time translated from the
Spanish by John T.Betts. 2 Parts London: Trubner &
Co., 1882-1883.

1882 **Hebert, Charles**   The New Testament Scriptures...
[See Pauline Epistles Selections for the entire
entry.]

1886 **Cusin, Alexander**   Commentary on St. Paul's Epistle
to the First Epistle to the Corinthians. By F. Godet
...Translated from the French by A.Cusin. Edinburgh:
T. & T. Clark, Clark's Foreign Theological Library,
New Series Vol. XXVII & XXX, 1886-1887.
Another edition, 1898.

1896 **Anonymous**   The Sermon on the Mount and...I Corinth.
[See New Testament Selections for the entire
entry.]

1898 **Rickaby, Joseph**   Notes on St. Paul: Corinthians...
[See Pauline Epistles Selections for the entire entry.]

1900 **Kennedy, James Houghton**   The Second and Third
Epistles of St. Paul to the Corinthians with some
proofs of their independence and mutual relation, by
James Houghton Kennedy. London: Methuen & Co., 1900.
[Second Corinthians divided in two; Greek and English.]

1908 **Rutherford, William Gunion**   St. Paul's Epistles...
[See Pauline Epistles Selections, 1900 William
Ginion Rutherford, St. Paul's Epistles...]

1909 **McFadyen, John Edgar**   The Epistles to the
Corinthians and Galatians...
[See Pauline Epistles Selections for the entire entry.]

1909 **Rendall, Gerald H.**   The Epistles of St. Paul
to the Corinthians. A study personal and historical
of the date and composition of the Epistles. By
Gerald H. Rendall. London: Macmillan & Co., 1909.

1911 **Robertson, Archibald and Alfred Plummer**   A Critical
and Exegetical Commentary on the First Epistle of
St. Paul to the Corinthians by the Right Rev.
Archibald Robertson... and the Rev. Alfred Plummer
... Edinburgh: T. & T. Clark, 1911.
[See Complete Bibles, 1895 International Critical
Commentary.]

Reprinted; 1914, 1929, 1950.

1912 **Menzies, Allan**   The Second Epistle of the Apostle Paul to the Corinthians. Introduction, text, English translation and notes, by Allan Menzies.   London: Macmillan & Co. Ltd., 1912.

1914 **Lattey, Cuthbert**   I Corinthians, 1914.
[See Complete Bibles, 1913 Westminster Version.]

1915 **Plummer, Alfred**   A Critical and Exegetical Commentary on the Second Epistle St. Paul to the Corinthians by Rev. Alfred Plummer.·.. Edinburgh: T. & T. Clark, 1915.
[See Complete Bibles, 1895 International Critical Commentary.]

1918 **Anonymous**   The Greatest of These; An Indian Paraphrase of I Corinthians 13. <u>The Covenant Weekly</u>, June 24, 1918.

1920 **Anonymous**   Letters from Paulos, a leader in wisdom, to his pupils in Korinthos. Rendered into modern English out of the Symbolism of the ancient Greek by Omikron. London: Kegan Paul, Trench, Trubner & Co. Ltd.; New York: E.P. Dutton & Co., 1920.

1920 **Lattey, Cuthbert and Joseph Keating** II Corinthians, 1920.
[See Complete Bibles, 1913 Westminster Version.]

1921 **Isaacs, Wilfred H.**   The Second Epistle of Paul to the Corinthians. A Study in Translations and an Interpretation by Wilfred H. Isaacs...   London: Oxford University Press, 1921.

1923 **Brown, Ernest Faulkner**   The Indian Church Commentaries —The First Epistle of Paul the Apostle to the Corinthians; 'with introduction and notes by E.F. Brown.   London: S.P.C.K.'   Vepery, Madras: Diocesan Press, 1923.

1930 **Bryant, H.E.**   New Light on an Old Letter; a new version of St. Paul's second letter to the Corinthians with introduction and short notes. By H.E. Bryant. London: Epworth Press, 1930.
Also; London and Cape Coast: The Atlantis Press.

1933 **Bryant, H.E.**   Christianity in Practice, according to St. Paul. Being a paraphrase of the First Epistle to the Corinthians, with notes by H.E.Bryant. London and Cape Coast: The Atlantis Press. [n.d.] [1933?]

1937 **Bonner, C. Bradlaugh**   The Second Epistle to the
Corinthians, the Epistles to the Galatians...
[See Pauline Epistles Selections for the entire entry.]

1937 **Cornish, Gerald Warre**   St. Paul from the Trenches...
[See Pauline Epistles Selections for the entire
entry.]

1941 **Anonymous**   First English Translation of
I Corinthians 13. Consolation, page 19, Dec., 1941.

1958 **Robinson, William Gordon**   The Gospel and the Church
in a Pagan World; a Study in 1 Corinthians. By
William Gordon Robinson. London: Independent Press,
1958.

1959 **Anonymous**   The First Epistle to the Corinthians: An
Expanded Translation. [F.F. Bruce] The Evangelical
Quarterly, XXXI, 3 (July- Sept., 1959), pages 164-
169; XXXI, 4 (Oct.-Dec., 1959), pages 218-224.
[Contains I Corinthians 1:1-8:13.]

1959 **Welch, Mary**   A Physician's Paraphrase of I Cor.
13. Wayside Windows Newsletter, Oct.-Dec., 1959.
Reprinted; Clear Horizons, Summer, 1960.

Reprinted; Bible Collector, Apr.-June, Issue
No.2, 1965.

1960 **Anonymous**   The First Epistle to the Corinthians: An
Expanded Translation. [F.F. Bruce] The Evangelical
Quarterly, XXXII, 1 (Jan.-Mar., 1960), pages 30-33;
XXXII, 2 (Apr.- June, 1960), pages 114-118; XXXII,
3 (July- Sept., 1960), pages 162-169.
[Contains I Corinthians 9:1-16:24.]

1960 **Anonymous**   The Second Epistle to the Corinthians:
An Expanded Translation. [F.F.Bruce] The Evangelical
Quarterly, XXXII, 4 (Oct.-Dec., 1960), pages 227-
231.
[Contains II Corinthians 1:1-3:18.]

1961 **Anonymous**   The Second Epistle to the Corinthians:
An Expanded Translation. [F.F.Bruce] The Evangelical
Quarterly, XXXIII, 1 (Jan.-Mar., 1961), pages 44-48.
[Contains II Corinthians 4:1-7:16.]

1961 **Parks, Emmett F.** Facing Decision with I Corinthians
13. A paraphrase of I Corinthians 13, moulded to
meet a specific need. Philadelphia: American Baptist
Publication Society, Published in Baptist Leader,
March, 1961.

1962 **Heathcote, A.W. and P.J. Allcock**   The First Epistle
of Saint Paul to the Corinthians [by] Jean Hering...

Translated from the Second French Edition.   London: The Epworth Press, 1962.

1962 **Hughes, Philip Edgcumbe**   Paul's second epistle to the Corinthians, 1962.
   [See N.T., 1959 New International Comment. on the N.T.]

1962 **Moule, Handley C.G.**   The Second Epistle to the Corinthians; a Translation, Paraphrase, and Exposition... Edited with Appendices by A. W. Handley Moule.   Grand Rapids, Michigan: Zondervan Publishing House, 1962.

1968 **Barrett, Charles K.**   A Commentary on the First Epistle to the Corinthians, by Charles K. Barrett. London: Adam and Charles Black, 1968.
   [See N.T. 1957 Black's N.T. Commentaries.]

   Second edition, 1971.   Reprinted, 1973.

1968 **Barrett, Charles K.**   A Commentary on the Second Epistle to the Corinthians, by Charles K. Barrett. London: Adam and Charles Black, 1968.
   [See N.T., 1957 Black's N.T. Commentaries.]

1968 **Blaiklock, E.M.**   The Way of Excellence...
   [See Pauline Epistles Selections for the entire entry.]

1976 **Leitch, James W.**   A Commentary on the First Epistle to the Corinthians by Hans Conzelmann. Translated by James W. Leitch. Bibliography and References by James W. Dunkly. Edited by George W. MacRae, S.J. Philadelphia: Fortress Press, 1976.

1976 **Orr, William F. and James Arthur Walther**
   I Corinthians. A New Translation, Introduction with a Study of the Life of Paul, Notes, and Commentary by William F. Orr and James Arthur Walther.   Garden City, New York: Doubleday & Co., Inc., 1976.
   [See Complete Bibles, 1964 Anchor Bible, Vol. 32.]

1982 **Anonymous**   The Epistles of Paul to the Corinthians. Recovery Version.   Anaheim, Ca.: Living Stream Ministry, 1982.
   [See N.T., 1985 Witness Lee & Others, N.T.]

1983 **Caudill, R. Paul**   First Corinthians: a translation with notes by R. Paul Caudill. Nashville: Broadman Press, 1983.

1984 **Furnish, Victor Paul**   II Corinthians. Translated with Introduction, Notes, and Commentary by Victor P. Furnish.   Garden City, New York: Doubleday & Co., 1984.
   [See Complete Bibles, 1964 Anchor Bible, Vol. 32A.]

1986 **Martin, Ralph P.**   Word Biblical Commentary.
     2 Corinthians. Ralph P. Martin.   Waco, TX: Word
     Books, Publisher, 1986.
          [See Complete Bibles, 1982 Word Biblical Commentary,
          Vol. 40.]

1987 **Fee, Gordon D.** The First Epistle to the Corinthians,
     1987.
          [See N.T., 1959 New International Comment. on the N.T.]

GALATIANS

???? **Butler, Barry**   The Letter of Saint Paul...
          [See Epistles and Selections for the complete entry.]

???? **Chadwick, Henry**   The Epistle to the Galatians.   New
     York: Harper Bros., [????].
          [See N.T., 1957 Black's N.T. Commentary, 1957.]

???? **Furnish, Victor Paul**   Galatians. Introduction,
     Translations and Notes. By Victor P.Furnish.   Garden
     City, New York: Doubleday & Co., [19??].
          [See Complete Bibles, 1964 Anchor Bible, Vol. 33A.]

???? **Hendriksen, William**   New Testament Commentary...
          [See New Testament Selections, 1953 for entire entry.]

???? **Martyn, J. Louis**   Galatians; Introduction,
     Translation, and Notes, by J. Louis Martyn.   Garden
     City, New York: Doubleday & Co., [19??].
          [See Complete Bibles, 1964 Anchor Bible, Vol. 33a.]

???? **Zylstra, Henry** The Epistles of Paul to the Churches
     of Galatia. by Herman N. Ridderbos (Translated from
     the Dutch) by Henry Zylstra, [195?].
          Second edition; London: Marshall, Morgan & Scott
          ["New London Commentary on the New Testament"], 1954.

1574 **Anonymous**   Sermons of M. Iohn Caluine vpon the
     Epistle of Saincte Paule to the Galathians. [Arthur
     Golding] Imprinted at London, by Lucas Harison and
     George Bishop, 1574.

1575 **Middleton, Thomas F.**   The Epistle to Galatians with
     Luther's Commentary.   London: Thomas Vantroullier,
     1575.
          Again, 1791.

1581 **Anonymous**   The Epistles to the Galatians...
          [See Pauline Epistles Selections for the complete
          entry.]

1587 **Prime, John**   The Epistle to the Galatians.   Oxford:
Joseph Barnes, 1587.

1705 **Locke, John**   Galatians, 1705.
[See Epistles and Selections, 1705 Anonymous, A
Paraphrase and Notes on the Epistles...]

1752 **Edwards, Timothy**   A Paraphrase, with Critical
Annotations... Romans and Galatians...
[See Pauline Epistles Selections for the complete
entry.]

1805 **Anonymous**   The Epistle to the Galatians; being
a specimen of a new version of the New Testament,
with notes, &c.   London: by T. White, 1805.

1839 **Owen, John**   A Commentary on the Epistle of St.
Paul to the Galatians, faithfully collected from the
lectures of Dr. M. Luther, and again revised...1535.
A new translation, with notes and a sketch of
Luther's Life.   London: Seeley, Burnside & Seeley,
1839.
Another edition, 1845.

1841 **Pringle, William**   Commentaries on the Epistles of
Paul to the Galatians and Ephesians...
[See Pauline Epistles Selections for the complete
entry.]

1841 **White, John**   The Restoration...Holy Scriptures...
[See Pauline Epistles Selections for the complete
entry.]

1848 **Haldane, James Alexander**   An Exposition on the
Epistle to the Galatians, 1848.

1854 **Ellicott, Charles John**   A critical and Grammatical
Commentary on St. Paul's Epistle to the Galatians,
with a revised translation... Greek & English.
London: J.W. Parker & Son, 1854.
Second edition; revised and enlarged, 1859.

Also; With an introductory notice by Calvin E.
Stowe. Andover: Draper, 1860.

Third edition; carefully revised throughout.
London: Longman & Co., 1863.

Fourth edition; Corrected, 1867.

Another American edition; Boston: Draper &
Halliday, 1867.

Fifth edition; revised and enlarged.   London:
Longman & Co., 1889.

1854 **Pringle, William**   Commentary on Galatians
and Ephesians by John Calvin. Translated from the
original Latin, and collated with the author's
French version.   Edinburgh: Calvin Translation
Society, 1854.
> [See Bible Selections, 1844 Anonymous, Commentaries on
> the Books of the Bible.]

1855 **Jowett, Benjamin**   The Epistles of St. Paul...
> [See Pauline Epistles Selections for the complete
> entry.]

1861 **Anonymous**   The Epistles of St. Paul to the
Galatians, Ephesians...
> [See Pauline Epistles Selections for the complete
> entry.]

1862 **Anonymous**   The Epistle of St. Paul to the
Galatians; with Explanatory Notes. By Henry, Bishop
of Grahamstown. Grahamstown: C.T. Campbell & Co.,
1862.

1863 **Gwynne, George John**   A Commentary critical,
exegetical, and doctrinal on St. Paul's Epistles to
the Galatians: with a revised translation. Dublin:
George Herbert, 1863.
> [Greek & English]

1867 **Carey, Stafford**   The Epistle of the Apostle Paul to
the Galatians. With a paraphrase and introduction.
London: William & Norgate, 1867.

1869 **Bayley, E.**   Commentary on Galatians (with
Paraphrase). London: 1869.

1869 **Eadie, John**   A Commentary on the Greek text of the
Epistle of Paul to the Galatians. Edinburgh: T. &
T. Clark; London: Hamilton & Co.; Dublin: John
Robertson, 1869.
> ["The following translation professes only to give a
> tolerably correct version of the epistle..."]

1871 **Godwin, John Hensley**   The Epistle of Saint Paul
to Galatians. A new translation. With critical notes
and doctrinal lessons. London: Hodder & Stoughton,
1871.
> [Anonymous?]

1874 **Edmunds, John**   S.Paul's Epistle to Galatians;
with explanatory notes. Edinburgh: Oliver & Boyd,
1874.

1875 **Anonymous**   A Letter to the Churches of Galatia.
By Paul, first Missionary to them. [J.T. Butlin]
London: Elliot Stock, 1875.

1876 **O'Conor, W.A.**   A Commentary on the Epistle of St. Paul to the Galatians. With a revised text. London: Hatchards, 1876.

1882 **Hebert, Charles**   The New Testament Scriptures...
[See Pauline Epistles Selections for the complete entry.]

1885 **Beet, Joseph Agar**   A Commentary on St. Paul's Epistle to the Galatians. London: Hodder & Stoughton, 1885.
Another edition; New York: Thomas Whittaker, 1885.

5th edition; "With a few corrections and alterations, the work remains as in the former editions.",1897.

6th edition, 1903.

1885 **Boise, James Robinson**   Notes on Galatians...
[See Pauline Epistles Selections for the complete entry.]

1888 **Findlay, C.G.**   The Epistle to the Galatians, 1888.
[See Bible Selections, 1888 Expositor's Bible.]

1904 **Weston, Percy**   Scripture Translation: suggestions and specimens...With revised renderings of Galatians by Percy Weston. London: Bible Training College, 1904.

1909 **McFadyen, John Edgar**   The Epistles to the...
[See Pauline Epistles Selections for the complete entry. Includes Corinthians and Galatians.]

1913 **Westcott, Frederick Brooke**   St. Paul and Justification...the Epistles to Rome and Galatia...
[See Pauline Epistles Selections for the complete entry.]

1920 **Keough, Alexander**   Galatians, 1920.
[See Complete Bibles, 1913 Westminster Version.]

1921 **Burton, Ernest DeWitt**   A Critical and Exegetical Commentary on the Epistle to the Galatians, by Ernest DeWitt Burton. Edinburgh: T. & T.Clark, 1921.
[See Complete Bibles, 1895 International Critical Commentary.]

Reprinted; 1948, 1950.

1924 **Balmer, W.T.**   The Truth of the Gospel. A paraphrase of St.Paul's Letter to the Galatians. By W.T.Balmer. London: Atlantis Press. [1924]

1931 **Machen, J. Gresham**   Notes on Biblical Exposition.
Boston: J. Gresham Machen. Philadelphia, 1931.
[An exposition of Gal. 1:1-3:14 with a translation in
Christianity Today, Vol. 1, No. 9, to Vol. III, No. 10.]

1939 **Waterhouse, J.W.** The Gospel I Preach. Some Comments
on St. Paul's letter to the Galatians with a new
translation and questions for discussion, by J.W.
Waterhouse. London: Epworth Press, ["Manuals of
Fellowship"], 1939.

1942 **Griffith, Gwilym O.**   Racialism and World Faith.
A Study in the Epistle to the Galatians, By G.O.
Griffith. London: Lutterworth Press, 1942.

1944 **Wuest, Kenneth S.**   Word Studies...Galatians...
[See New Testament Selections, 1940 Kenneth S. Wuest,
Word Studies...]

1952 **Anonymous**   Galatians and the Captivity Epistles...
[See Pauline Epistles Selections for the complete
entry.]

1954 **Hoerber, Robert G.**   Saint Paul's Shorter Letters...
[See Pauline Epistles Selections for the complete
entry.]

1957 **Anonymous** The Epistle to the Galatians: An Expanded
Paraphrase. [By F.F. Bruce].   The Evangelical
Quarterly, XXIX, 1 (Jan.- March, 1957), pages 35-44.

1958 **Neill, Stephen**   Paul to the Galatians, by Stephen
Neill. New York: Associated Press; Norwich G.B.:
Page Bros., 1958.
["Quotations, except for a number translated from the
Greek, are from the RSV... In the Paraphrase the attempt
has been made to make every word and phrase in the
Epistle as clear as possible."]

1962 **Graebner, Theodore**   A Commentary on St. Paul's
Epistle to the Galatians by Martin Luther; A New
Abridged Translation. St.Louis, Missouri: Zondervan
Publishing House, 1962.

1969 **Bligh, John**   Householder Commentaries No. 1.
Galatians: a Discussion of St. Paul's Epistle, by
John Bligh. London: St. Paul's Publications, 1969.

1969 **Quesnell, Quentin** The Gospel of Christian Freedom.
New York: Herder & Herder, 1969.
[Paraphrase of St. Paul's Epistle to the Galatians.]

1977 **Haugerud, Joann**   The Word for Us...
[See New Testament Selections for the complete entry.]

1979 **Betz, Hans Dieter**   A Commentary on Paul's Letter
     to the Churches in Galatia by Hans Dieter Betz.
     Fortress Press, 1979.

1981 **Anonymous**   The Epistles of Paul to Galatians...
     [See Pauline Epistles Selections for the complete
     entry.]

1984 **Payne, John B.**   Collected Works of Erasmus...
     [See Pauline Epistles Selections for the complete
     entry.]

1987 **Schoder, Raymond V.**   Paul wrote from the Heart...
     [See Pauline Epistles Selections for the complete
     entry.]

1990 **Longenecker, Richard N.**   Word Biblical Commentary.
     Galatians. Richard N. Longenecker. Waco, Tx: Word
     Books, Publishers, 1990.
     [See Complete Bibles, 1982 Word Biblical Commentary,
     Vol. 41.]

EPHESIANS

???? **Beet, Joseph Agar**   A Commentary on St. Paul's
     Epistles to the Ephesians, Philippians...
     [See Pauline Epistles Selections for the complete
     entry.]

???? **Lincoln, Andrew T.**   Word Biblical Commentary.
     Ephesians. Andrew T. Lincoln. Waco, Tx: Word Books,
     Publishers, [198?].
     [See Complete Bibles, 1982 Word Biblical Commentary,
     Vol. 42.]

1540 **Anonymous**   A Commentary in Englyshe vpon Sayncte
     Paules Epystle to the Ephesyans for the instruccyen
     of them that be vnlerned in tongues, gathered out of
     the holy scriptures and of the olde catholyke
     Doctours of the Churche, and of the beste authors
     that nowe a dayes do wryte. Anno, D. 1540. Per
     Lancelotum Ridleum, Cantabrigensem. [Lancelot
     Ridley] London: Robert Redman, 1540.
     [Text is mostly Coverdale's.]

1577 **Golding, Arthur**   The Epistle to the Ephesians.
     London: L. Harrison & G. Bishop, 1577.

1580 **Fleming, Abraham**   The Epistle of the blessed
     Apostle Saint Paule, which he, in the time of his
     trouble and imprisonment, sent in writing from Rome

to the Ephesians. Faithfvllie Expovnded, Both for the benefite of the learned and vnlearned by Nicholas Hemming, Professor of Diuinitie in the Vniversitie of Coppenhagen in Denmarke. Familiarlie translated out of Latine into English by Abraham Flemming. Heerein are Handled the high mysteries of our salvation, as maie appeare by the Table of common-places necessarilie annexed by the same A.F. Perused and Authorised.   At London: Printed by Thomas East, 1580.
Another edition, 1581

1581 **Anonymous**   An Exposition vpon the Epistle of S.Paule the Apostle to the Ephesians: by S. Ihon Chrysostome, Archbishop of Constantinople. Truely and Faithfully translated out of the Greeke. London: Henry Binneman & Ralph Newberie, 1581.

1705 **Locke, John**   Ephesians, 1707.
[See Epistles and Selections, 1705 Anonymous, A Paraphrase and Notes on the Epistles...]

1776 **Anonymous**   A Liberal and Minute Inspection of the Holy Gospel; Affording An Occasional Paraphrase, with Notes and Emendations, upon the Four Gospels and the Acts... and a Regular Exposition of all the Epistles except the Revelation. London: for the Author, 1776.
[A Specimen comprising only the Epistle to the Ephesians.]

1779 **Callander, John**   An Essay toward a literal English Version of the New Testament, in the Epistle of the Apostle Paul directed to the Ephesians. Glasgow: Andrew Foulis, Printer to the University, 1779.
[Greek and English.]

1841 **Pringle, William**   Commentaries on the Epistles of Paul to the Galatians and Ephesians...
[See Pauline Epistles Selections for the complete entry.]

1854 **Eadie, John**   A Commentary on the Greek text of the Epistle of Paul to the Ephesians. London & Glasgow: R. Griffin & Co., 1854.
Revised edition; revised throughout and enlarged. London: Griffin, Bohn & Co., 1861.

Third edition; edited by Rev. W. Young. Edinburgh: T. & T. Clark, 1883.

Reprinted; Glasgow and Grand Rapids, Mi: Zondervan, 195?.

1854 **Pringle, William**   Commentary on Galatians
and Ephesians by John Calvin. Translated from the
original Latin, and collated with the author's
French version.   Edinburgh: Calvin Translation
Society, 1854.
> [See Bible Selections, 1844 Anonymous, Commentaries on
> the books of the Bible.]

1855 **Ellicott, Charles John**   A Critical and Grammatical
Commentary on St. Paul's Epistle to the Ephesians,
with a revised translation... London: John W. Parker
& Son, 1855.
> Second edition; revised and enlarged, 1859.

> Third edition; corrected. London: Longman & Co.,
> 1864.

> Fourth edition, 1868.

> Fifth edition, 1884.

> Another edition; with the ERV added.   Andover:
> Warren F. Draper, 1897.

1856 **American Bible Union**   The Epistle to the Ephesians
... (By N.N. Whiting).   New York: American Bible
Union, 1856.
> Another edition,   1857

1861 **Anonymous**   The Epistles of St. Paul to the
Galatians, Ephesians, Philippians, and Colossians...
> [See Pauline Epistles Selections for the complete
> entry.]

1866 **Davies, J. Llewelyn**   The Epistles of St. Paul to
the Ephesians...
> [See Pauline Epistles Selections for the complete
> entry.]

1883 **Young, Rev. W.**   See John Eadie, A Commentary...
Ephesians, 1854.

1892 **Findlay, C.G.**   The Epistle to the Ephesians, 1888.
> [See Bible Selections, 1888 Expositor's Bible.]

1895 **Abbott, T.K.**   A Critical and Exegetical Commentary
on the Book of Ephesians and Colossians...
> [See Pauline Epistles Selections for the complete
> entry.]

1900 **Moule, Handley C.G.**   Ephesian Studies; Expository
Readings on the Epistle of Saint Paul to the
Ephesians. London: Hodder & Stoughton; New York:
George H. Doran, 1900.
> ["...pretend only to provide...a careful paraphrase or
> running rendering of the epistle..."]

Also; London: 1902.

1903 **Robinson, J. Armitage**   St. Paul's Epistle to
the Ephesians; A revised text and translation with
exposition and notes, by J. Armitage Robinson.
London: Macmillan & Co., 1903.
Second edition, 1904.

1908 **Rutherford, John**   St. Paul's Epistles to Colossae
and Laodicea...
[See Pauline Epistles Selections for the complete
entry.]

1913 **Hitchcock, George S.**   The Epistle to the Ephesians.
An encyclical of St. Paul. Translated from a revised
Greek text and explained for English readers by
George S. Hitchcock. London: Burns & Oates, 1913.

1914 **Concordant Version**   Paul's Epistle to...
[See New Testament Selections, 1914 Concordant Version
of the Sacred Scriptures.]

1937 **Cornish, Gerald Warre**   St.Paul from the Trenches...
[See Pauline Epistles Selections for the complete
entry.]

1949 **Carver, William Owen**   The Glory of God in the
Christian Calling. A study of the Ephesian Epistle.
By William Owen Carver. Nashville: Broadman Press,
[1949].

1952 **Anonymous**   Galatians and the Captivity Epistles...
[See Pauline Epistles Selections for the complete
entry.]

1953 **Wuest, Kenneth S.**   Word Studies...
[See New Testament Selections, 1940 Kenneth S. Wuest,
Word Studies...]

1956 **Carpenter, S.C.**   A paraphrase of Ephesians. By S.C.
Carpenter. London: A.R. Mowbray & Co.; New York:
Morehouse - Gorham Co., 1956.
["...I have made St. Paul appear to quote modern
writers, e.g., Shakespeare and Matthew Arnold, not to
mention the Book of Common Prayer, if the language
seemed to explain or illustrate his meaning."]

1959 **Barth, Markus**   The Broken Wall, A Study of
the Epistle to the Ephesians. Philadelphia: Judson
Press, 1959.

1966 **Hendriksen, William**   New Testament Commentary...
[See New Testament Selections, 1953 William Hendriksen,
New Testament Commentary...]

1974 **Barth, Markus** Ephesians. Introduction, Translation and Commentary on Chapters 4 - 6 by Markus Barth. Garden City, New York: Doubleday & Co., Inc., 1974.
[See Complete Bibles, 1964 Anchor Bible, Vol.34a.]

1974 **Barth, Markus** Ephesians. Translation and Commentary on Chapters 1 - 3 by Markus Barth. Garden City, New York: Doubleday & Co., Inc., 1974.
[See Complete Bibles, 1964 Anchor Bible, Vol. 34.]

1979 **Caudill, R. Paul** Ephesians: a translation with notes by R. Paul Caudill. Nashville: Broadman Press, 1979.

1981 **Anonymous** The Epistles of Paul to Galatians, Ephesians, Philippians, Colossians...
[See Pauline Epistles Selections for the entire entry.]

1984 **Bruce, F.F.** The epistle to the Ephesians, 1984.
[See Colossians, 1984 for the entire entry.]

PHILIPPIANS

???? **Beet, Joseph Agar** A Commentary on St. Paul's...
[See Pauline Epistles Selections for the entire entry.]

???? **Krall, Kevin** The Epistles of the Christ Spoken Through Paul to the Church at Phillipp. (sic) by Kevin Krall. Tulsa, OK: Spirit to Spirit Publications, n.d.

???? **Reumann, John** Philippians. Introduction, Translation, and Notes by John Reumann. Garden City, New York: Doubleday & Co., [19??].
[See Complete Bibles, 1964 Anchor Bible, Vol. 33b.]

1550 **Rydley, Lancelot** An Exposytion in Englyshe vpon the Epistyll of saynt Paule to Philippias, for the instruction of them that be vnlerned in toges; gathered out of the holy scriptures, and of the olde catholike doctours of the church, & of the best authors that now adayes do write. Canterbury: Ihon Mychell, 1550?

1584 **Anonymous** A Commentarie of M. Ihon Caluine vppon the Epistle to the Philippians... translated out of the Latine by W.B. [William Becket] London: for Nicolas Lyng, 1584.

1725 **Peirce (Pierce), James** Philippians, 1725.
[See Epistles and Selections, 1705 Anonymous, A Paraphrase and Notes on the Epistles...]

1733 **Pierce (Peirce), James**   A Paraphrase and Notes on the Epistles of St.Paul...Colossians, Philippians...
  [See Pauline Epistles Selections for the complete entry.]

1842 **Johnston, Robert**   Expositions of the Epistles...
  [See Pauline Epistles Selections for the complete entry.]

1851 **Pringle, William**   Commentary on Philippians, Colossians and Thessalonians by John Calvin. Translated from the original Latin, and collated with the author's French version. Edinburgh: Calvin Translation Society, 1851.
  [See Bible Selections, 1844 Anonymous, Commentaries on the books of the Bible.]

1857 **Ellicott, Charles John**   A Critical and Grammatical Commentary on St.Paul's Epistles... Philippians...
  [See Pauline Epistles Selections for the complete entry.]

1859 **Eadie, John**   A Commentary on the Greek text of the Epistle of Paul to the Philippians. [Greek & English.] London & Glasgow: R. Griffin & Co., 1859.
  Second edition; edited by Rev. W. Young. Edinburgh: T. & T. Clark, 1884.

1861 **Anonymous**   The Epistles of St. Paul to...
  [See Pauline Epistles Selections for the complete entry.]

1875 **Johnstone, Robert**   Lectures exegetical and practical on the Epistle of Paul to the Philippians with a revised translation of the Epistle and notes on the Greek text by the Rev. Robert Johnstone... Edinburgh: William Oliphant & Co., 1875.
  Reprinted; Grand Rapids, Michigan: Baker Book House, 1955.

1885 **Vaughan, Charles John**   St. Paul's Epistle to the Philippians. With translation, paraphrase, and notes for English readers. By C.J. Vaughan. London: Macmillan & Co., 1885.
  [Greek and English.]

1897 **Moule, Handley C.G.**   Philippian Studies. Lessons in Faith and Love from St. Paul's Epistle to the Philippians. New York: A.C. Armstrong & Son, 1897.
  [Contains a new translation, interwoven with a commentary.]

  Fifth Edition, 1904.

  Another edition; Grand Rapids: Zondervan Publishing House, n.d.

1897 **Vincent, Marvin R.**   A Critical and Exegetical
     Commentary on the Epistles of St. Paul to...
     [See Pauline Epistles Selections for the complete
     entry.]

1901 **Holcomb, James T.**   The Epistle of Paul to the
     Philippians expanded in a paraphrase and explained
     in notes... By James T. Holcomb. New York: American
     Tract Society, 1901?

1914 **Concordant Version**   Paul's Epistle to...
     [See New Testament Selections, 1914 Concordant Version
     of the Sacred Scriptures.]

1918 **Jones, Maurice**   The Epistle to the Philippians.
     By Maurice Jones. London: Methuen & Co., Westminster
     Commentaries, 1918.

1919 **Plummer, Alfred**   A Commentary on St. Paul's
     First Epistle to the Philippians. By Alfred Plummer.
     London: Robert Scott, 1919.

1920 **Ballantine, Frank Schell**   Science and Scripture...
     [See New Testament Selections for the complete
     entry. Includes Philippians.]

1920 **Maltby, W.R.**   St. Paul's Letter to the Philippians.
     A New Translation and a Questionary Edited by W.R.
     Maltby. London: Epworth Press, J.A. Sharp, 1920.
     [Manuals of Fellowship, No. 1.]

1930 **Cockin, F.A.**   What it means to be a Christian.
     A Modern Version of St. Paul's Letter to the
     Philippians. With Six Studies in the Letter by W.S.
     Tindal. London: Student Christian Movement Press,
     1930.

1942 **Wuest, Kenneth S.**   Word Studies...Philippians...
     [See New Testament Selections, 1940 Kenneth S. Wuest,
     Word Studies...]

1946 **Carpenter, S.C.**   A Paraphrase of St. Paul's Epistle
     to the Philippians. By S.C. Carpenter...   London:
     S.P.C.K., 1946.
     ["...the scholar...proceeds to write the Epistle in the
     language of to-day... Lastly, he will take the pains to
     make the thought and argument of St. Paul very clear by
     writing at greater length than the original..."]

     Reprinted; 1947, 1948.

1952 **Anonymous**   Galatians and the Captivity Epistles...
     [See Pauline Epistles Selections for the complete
     entry.]

1954 Hoerber, Robert G.   Saint Paul's Shorter Letters...
[See Pauline Epistles Selections for the complete entry.]

1958 Simcox, Carrol E.   They met at Philippi: A Devotional Commentary on Philippians, by Carrol E. Simcox. New York: Oxford University Press, 1958.
["Dr. Simcox's own translation of each passage is followed by an analysis..."]

1959 Beare, Francis Wright   A Commentary on the Epistle to the Philippians. By Francis Wright Beare. London: Adam & Charles Black; New York: Harper & Brothers, 1959.
[See N.T., 1957 Black's N.T. Commentaries.]

1962 Leitch, James   The Epistle to the Philippians; Karl Barth.   London: SCM Press Ltd.;   Richmond, Virginia: John Knox Press, 1962.

1964 Blaiklock, E.M.   From Prison in Rome; Letters to...
[See Pauline Epistles Selections for the complete entry.]

1980 Anonymous   A Paraphrase of Philippians. Pulpit Helps. September, 1980.

1981 Anonymous   The Epistles of Paul to Galatians...
[See Pauline Epistles Selections for the complete entry.]

1983 Hawthorne, Gerald F.   Word Biblical Commentary. Philippians. Gerald F. Hawthorne.   Waco, TX: Word Books, Publisher, 1983.
[See Complete Bibles, 1982 Word Biblical Commentary, Vol. 43.]

1987 Schoder, Raymond V.   Paul wrote from the Heart...
[See Pauline Epistles Selections for the complete entry.]

COLOSSIANS

???? Barth, Markus   Colossians and Philemon...
[See Pauline Epistles Selections for the complete entry.]

???? Beet, Joseph Agar   A Commentary on St. Paul's Epistles to the Ephesians...
[See Pauline Epistles Selections for the complete entry.]

1548 **Ridley, Lancelot**   An Exposition in Englishe vpon the Epistle of S. Paule, to the Colossians, wherin the letter is purely declared, with many good exhortations... Londini: in aedibus Richardi Graftoni, 1548.
> Another edition, 1549.

1581 **Anonymous**   The Epistles to the Galatians...
> [See Pauline Epistles Selections for the complete entry.]

1581 **Purfoote, Thomas**   The Epistle to the Colossians. London: T. Purfoote, 1581.

1609 **Anonymous**   Ten Sermons tending chiefly to the fitting of men for the worthy receiving of the Lord's Supper... Whereunto is annexed a plaine and learned metaphrase on the Epistle to the Colossians, written by a godly and iudicious preacher. [Ihon Dod - See 1632.]   London: Printed by William Hall for Roger Iackson, 1609.
> Another edition, 1610.
>
> Another edition; - - Newly printed and enlarged. London: T.P. for Roger Jackson, 1620.
>
> Also, 1621.
>
> Another edition, 1634.

1632 **Anonymous**   A plaine and learned Metaphrase on the Epistle to the Colossians, written by a godly and judicious preacher, 1632.
> [Annexed to 1609 Anonymous, Ten Sermons...]

1672 **Anonymous**   XLIX Sermons Upon the Whole Epistle of the Apostle St. Paul to the Colossians. In Three Parts. By that Famous Minister of the Reformed Church in Paris, Mr. John Daille... Translated into English, by F.S.   London: Printed by R.White for Tho. Parkhurst...1672.

1725 **Peirce (Pierce), James**   Colossians, 1725.
> [See Epistles and Selections, 1705 Anonymous, A Paraphrase and Notes on the Epistles...]

1733 **Pierce (Peirce), James**   A Paraphrase and Notes on the Epistles of St. Paul to the Colossians...
> [See Pauline Epistles Selections for the complete entry.]

1819 **Anonymous**   The Epistles of St. Paul to...
> [See Epistles and Selections for the complete entry.]

1831 **Allport, Josiah**   An Exposition of the Epistle
of St. Paul to the Colossians by the Right Rev. John
Davenport... Bishop of Salisbury... originally
delivered, in a series of lectures before the
University [of Cambridge]. Translated from the
Original Latin; with a life of the author and notes
... By Josiah Allport. 2 vols. London: Hamilton,
Adams & Co., 1831.

1831 **Davenant, John**   An Exposition of the Epistle...to
the Colossians, 1831.

1842 **Johnston, Robert**   Expositions of the Epistles of...
          [See Pauline Epistles Selections for the complete
          entry.]

1851 **Pringle, William**   Commentary on Philippians...
          [See Pauline Epistles Selections for the complete
          entry.]

1856 **Eadie, John**   A Commentary on the Greek text of the
Epistle of Paul to the Colossians. [Greek & English]
London & Glasgow: R. Griffin & Co., 1856.
          Another edition; New York: Robert Carter & Bros.,
          1856.

          Second edition; edited by Rev. W. Young.
          Edinburgh: T. & T. Clark, 1884.

          Reprinted; Printed by Klock & Klock in the
          U.S.A., 1980.

1857 **Ellicott, Charles John**   A Critical and Grammatical
Commentary on St. Paul's Epistles to the...
          [See Pauline Epistles Selections for the complete
          entry.]

1859 **Hall, H. Bedford**   The Epistle of Paul the
Apostle to the Colossians. A revised translation by
H. Bedford Hall. London: Bell & Daldy, 1859.

1861 **Anonymous**   The Epistles of St. Paul to...
          [See Pauline Epistles Selections for the complete
          entry.]

1866 **Davies, J. Llewelyn**   The Epistles of St. Paul...
          [See Pauline Epistles Selections for the complete
          entry.]

1894 **Pascoe, J.M.**   ...Paul's letter to the Colossians,
written A.D. 63. Transcribed by J.M.Pascoe. New York
& Cincinnati: n.p., 1894.

1895 **Abbott, T.K.**   A Critical and Exegetical Commentary
on the Book of Ephesians and Colossians...

[See Pauline Epistles Selections for the complete entry.]

1898 Moule, Handley C.G.   Colossian Studies...
[See Pauline Epistles Selections for the complete entry.]

1908 Rutherford, John   St. Paul's Epistles to Colossae...
[See Pauline Epistles Selections for the complete entry.]

1914 Concordant Version   Paul's Epistle to...
[See New Testament Selections, 1914 Concordant Version of the Sacred Scriptures.]

1914 Westcott, Frederick Brooke   A Letter to Asia. Being a paraphrase and brief exposition of the Epistle of Paul to the Believers at Colossae. By Frederick Brooke Westcott. London: Macmillan & Co., 1914.

1931 Radford, Lewis B.   The Epistle to the Colossians...
[See Pauline Epistles Selections for the complete entry.]

1937 Bonner, C. Bradlaugh   The Second Epistle to the Corinthians... Colossians, to the Ephesians...
[See Pauline Epistles Selections for the complete entry.]

1948 Gray, Crete   The Epistles of St. Paul to...
[See Pauline Epistles Selections for the complete entry.]

1952 Anonymous   Galatians and the Captivity Epistles...
[See Pauline Epistles Selections for the complete entry.]

1953 Wuest, Kenneth S.   Word Studies...
[See New Testament Selections, 1940 Kenneth S. Wuest, Word Studies...]

1954 Hoerber, Robert G.   Saint Paul's Shorter Letters...
[See Pauline Epistles Selections for the complete entry.]

1957 Grant, Robert M.   Colossians, 1957.
[See N.T., 1957 Black's N.T. Commentary.]

1958 Anonymous   The Epistle to the Colossians: An Expanded Translation. [By F.F.Bruce] The Evangelical Quarterly, XXX, 1 (Jan.-Mar., 1958), pages 43-48.

1966 Hendriksen, William   New Testament Commentary...
[See New Testament Selections, 1953 William Hendriksen, New Testament Commentary...]

1971 Poehlmann, William R. and Robert J. Karris
A Commentary on the Epistle to the Colossians...

[See New Testament Selections for the entire entry.]

1981 **Anonymous**   The Epistles of Paul to Galatians...
     [See Pauline Epistles Selections for the entire entry.]

1982 **O'Brien, Peter T.**   Word Biblical Commentary.
     Colossians, Philemon...
     [See Pauline Epistles Selections for the entire entry.]

1984 **Bruce, F.F.**   The epistles to the Colossians, to
     Philemon, and to the Ephesians, 1984.
     [See N.T., 1959 New International Comment. on the N.T.]

THESSALONIANS

???? **Bailey, John A.** I & II Thessalonians. Introduction,
     Translation, and Notes by John A. Vailey.   Garden
     City, New York: Doubleday & Co., Inc., [19??].
     [See Complete Bibles, 1964 Anchor Bible, Vol. 32b.]

???? **Malherbe, Abraham J.**   I & II Thessalonians. A New
     Translation with Introduction and Commentary by
     Abraham J. Malherbe. Garden City, New York:
     Doubleday & Co., Inc., [19??].
     [See Complete Bibles, 1964 Anchor Bible, Vol. 32b.]

1550 **Anonymous**   Certayne Chapters of the Prouerbes...
     [See Bible Selections for the complete entry. Includes
     II Thessalonians chapter 3.]

1571 **Iewel, Ihon** An exposition vpon the Two Epistles of
     the Apostle Saint Paul to the Thessalonians, 1571.
     [Text appears to be Genevan with minor changes.]

          Another edition; London: By R. Newberie & H.
          Bynneman, 1583.

          Another edition; London: for Ralfe Neuburie,
          1594.

          Also; London: Ihon Norton, 1611.

          New edition; carefully revised and corrected by
          Peter Hall. London: B. Wertheim, 1841.

          In addition; - - part of the Works of John
          Jewel. Cambridge: University Press for the
          Parker Society, 1847.

1586 **Tymme, Thomas**   The Figure of Antichriste, with
     the tokens of the end of the world... disciphered by

a catholike and diuine exposition of the seconde Epistle of Paul to the Thessalonians by Thomas Tymme. London: For Fraunces Coldocke, 1586.

1594 **Jewell, Bishop John**   An Exposition vpon the Two Epistles of the Apostle Paul to the Thessalonians. London: 1594.

1621 **Jackson, Timothy**   The Second Epistle of St. Paul to the Thessalonians; with an exposition.   London: by E.G., for T. Pavier, 1621.

1819 **Anonymous**   The Epistles of St. Paul to...
     [See Gospel Selections for the complete entry.]

1841 **Hall, Peter**   An exposition... Two Epistles, 1841.
     [See Ihon Iewel, An Exposition...Two Epistles..., 1571.]

1851 **Pringle, William**   Commentary on Philippians...
     [See Pauline Epistles Selections for the entire entry.]

1855 **Jowett, Benjamin**   The Epistles of St. Paul to...
     [See Pauline Epistles Selections for the entire entry.]

1856 **American Bible Union**   The Epistles of Paul to the Thessalonians... by the Translator of II Peter-Revelation (By John Lillie).   New York: American Bible Union, 1856.
     Another edition, 1857.

1858 **Ellicott, Charles John**   A Critical and Grammatical Commentary on St. Paul's Epistles to the Thessalonians, with a revised translation [and Greek text].   London: John W. Parker & Son, 1858.
     Second edition; revised and enlarged. London: Parker, Son & Bourn, 1862.
          ["...traces of regular and deliberate revision on every page..."]

     Third edition; London: Longman & Co., 1866.
          ["A very slight amount of change has been found necessary..."]

     Fourth edition; London: Longman, Roberts & Green, 1880.

     Another edition; Andover: Warren F. Draper, 1893.

1860 **Lillie, John**   Lectures on the Epistle of Paul to the Thessalonians by John Lillie.   New York: R. Carter & Brothers, 1860.

1862 **Thrupp, J.F.**   The Song of Songs, a revised Translation, with introduction and Commentary, by

J.F. Thrupp.   Cambridge & London: Macmillan & Co.,
1862.

1864 **Vaughan, Charles John**   The Epistles of Paul for
English Readers by C.J. Vaughan. Cambridge & London:
Macmillan & Co., 1864.
   [I Thessalonians only.]

1877 **Eadie, John**   A Commentary on the Greek text of the
Epistles of Paul to the Thessalonians... edited by
the Rev. W. Young. With a preface by the Rev.
Professor Cairns.   London: Macmillan & Co., 1877.
   [Contains a phrase-by-phrase translation; Greek &
   English.]

1882 **Hebert, Charles**   The New Testament Scriptures...
   [See Pauline Epistles Selections for the complete
   entry.]

1891 **Anonymous**   A Translation of Two Ancient Epistles
addressed to Certain Inhabitants of Thessalonica in
Macedonia, Circa A.D. 54. London: J. Nisbet & Co.,
1891.

1901 **Harris, John Tindall** The Writings of the Apostle...
   [See Pauline Epistles Selections for the complete entry.
   Includes Thessalonians.]

1908 **Rutherford, William Gunion**   St. Paul's Epistles...
   [See Pauline Epistles Selections, 1900 William Gunion
   Rutherford, St. Paul's Epistles...]

1908 **Milligan, George**   St. Paul's Epistles to the
Thessalonians. By George Milligan. London: Macmillan
and Co., 1908.
   Also; Grand Rapids: Wm. B. Eerdmans Publ. Co.,
   1952.

1912 **Frame, James Everett**   A Critical and Exegetical
Commentary on the Epistles of St. Paul to the
Thessalonians. By James Everett Frame.   New York:
Charles Scribner's Sons, 1912.
   [See Complete Bibles, International Critical
   Commentary.]

   Reprint, 1946.

1913 **Lattey, Cuthbert**   Thessalonians, 1913.
   [See Complete Bibles, 1913 Westminster Version.]

1914 **Concordant Version**   Paul's Epistle to the Romans...
   [See New Testament Selections, 1914 Concordant
   Version of the Sacred Scriptures.]

1918 **Plummer, Alfred**   A Commentary on St. Paul's First
     Epistle to the Thessalonians. By Alfred Plummer.
     London: Robert Scott, 1918.

1932 **Bicknell, E.J.**   The First and Second Epistles to
     the Thessalonians. By E.J. Bicknell. London: Methuen
     & Co., Westminster Commentaries, 1932.

1954 **Hoerber, Robert G.**   Saint Paul's Shorter Letters...
          [See Pauline Epistles Selections for the complete
          entry.]

1955 **Hendriksen, William**   New Testament Commentary...
          [See New Testament Selections, 1953 William Hendriksen,
          New Testament Commentary...]

1958 **Best, Ernest**   A Commentary on the First and
     Second Epistles to the Thessalonians by Ernest Best.
     London: Adam and Charles Black, 1958.
          [See N.T., 1957 Black's N.T. Commentaries.]

1982 **Anonymous**   The Epistles of Paul to the
     Thessalonians. Recovery Version. Anaheim, CA: Living
     Stream Ministry, 1982.
          [See N.T., 1985 Witness Lee & Others, N.T.]

1982 **Bruce, F.F.**   Word Biblical Commentary. 1 & 2
     Thessalonians. F.F. Bruce.   Waco, TX: Word Books,
     Publisher, 1982.
          [See Complete Bibles, 1982 Word Biblical Commentary,
          Vol. 45.]

1991 **Morris, Leon**   The first and second Epistles to the
     Thessalonians. Revised Edition. 1991.
          [See N.T., 1959 New International Comment. on the N.T.]

18

Pastoral Epistles

PASTORAL EPISTLES AND SELECTIONS

???? **Mounce, Robert H.** Word Biblical Commentary. Pastoral Epistles. Robert H. Mounce. Waco, Tx: Word Books, Publishers, [198?].
> [See Complete Bibles, 1982 Word Biblical Commentary, Vol. 46.]

1579 **Tomson, Laurence** Calvins Sermons on the Epistles to Timothie and Titus, 1579.

1828 **Anonymous** The Epistles of St. Paul the Apostle to Timothy and Titus: translated out of the Latin Vulgate... first published by the English College of Rhemes, 1582: newly revised and corrected according to the Clementine edition of the Scriptures with practical and explanatory notes. [W.Curray?] Dublin: W. Curray, Jun. & Co., 1828.

1832 **Eyre, Charles** An Illustration of the Epistles of St. Paul, including an entirely new translation. By Charles Eyre. 2 Vols. London: Sold by Longman, Rees, Orme, Brown and Green; Ipswich: also by J.Raw, 1832.
> ["The work aspires, as a Paraphrase, to have as much fidelity as any translation, and as a translation, to be as beneficially illustrative as any Commentary of Paraphrase extant." Unitarian.]

1856 **Ellicott, Charles John** A Critical and Grammatical Commentary on Pastoral Epistles, with a revised translation. By C.J. Ellicott. London: John W. Parker & Son, 1856.
> Second edition; revised and enlarged. London: Parker, Son & Bourn, 1861.
>
> Third edition; corrected. London: Longman & Co., 1864.

Fifth edition; The Pastoral Epistles of St. Paul:
with a critical and grammatical commentary,
and a revised translation, by C.J. Ellicott...
London: Longmans, Green and co., 1883.

Another edition; Andover [Mass.]: Warren F.
Draper, 1897.

1856 **Pringle, William**   Commentary on Timothy, Titus
and Philemon by John Calvin. Translated from the
original Latin, and collated with the author's
French version.   Edinburgh: Calvin Translation
Society, 1856.
[See Bible Selections, 1844 Anonymous, Commentaries on
the books of the Bible.]

1860 **American Bible Union**   The Epistles of Timothy
and Titus (By N.N.Whiting). New York: American Bible
Union, 1860.

1874 **Fairbairn, Patrick**   The Pastoral Epistles.
The Greek Text and Translation. With Introduction,
Expository Notes, and Dissertations. Edinburgh: T.
& T. Clark, 1874.
["The text of Tischendorf, in his 8th edition, so nearly
coincides with what I take to be the correct one, that
I have adopted it... The AV has never been needlessly
departed from."]

1901 **Lilley, J.P.**   The Pastoral Epistles. A
new translation, with introduction, commentary, and
appendix. By J.P. Lilley. Edinburgh: T. & T. Clarke
[Hardbooks for Bible Classes], 1901.

1916 **Anonymous**   Epistles of Paul the Apostle. 2 Vols.
London: C.F. Clay, Cambridge Univ. Press, 1916.
[Syriac & English; Horae Semiticae No. 11.]

1917 **Brown, Ernest Faulkner**   The Pastoral Epistles. With
introduction and notes by Ernest Faulkner Brown.
London: Methuen & Co., 1917.
[Westminster Commentaries.]

1920 **Parry, R. St. John**   The Pastoral Epistles with
Introduction, Text and Commentary. By R. St.John
Parry. Cambridge: University Press, 1920.

1924 **Lock, Walter**   A Critical and Exegetical Commentary
on The Pastoral Epistles (I & II Timothy and Titus)
by The Rev. Walter Lock... Edinburgh: T. & T.
Clark, 1936.
[See Complete Bibles, 1895 International Critical
Commentary.]

[Contains paraphrases.]

1930 **Isaacs, Wilfred H.**   Translational Studies in the New Testament. The Epistles to Timothy and Titus. Birmingham [England]: Hulbert Publishing Co., 1930?

1932 **Vincent, Boyd**   (pro-The Pastoral Epistles for To-day. A handbook for ably earlier) students and clergymen. By Boyd Vincent. London: Skeffington & Son, n.d. [1932?]

1937 **Falconer, Robert**   The Pastoral Epistles: Introduction, Translation, and Notes, by Sir Robert Falconer. Oxford: Clarendon Press, 1937.

1937 **Scott, E.F.**   The Pastoral Epistles, by E.F. Scott. Edinburgh & New York: n.p., 1937.
   [Mentioned in the bibliography in Easton's Pastoral Epistles, 1947.]

1947 **Easton, Burton Scott**   The Pastoral Epistles. Introduction, translation, commentary and word studies. New York: Charles Scribner's Sons, 1947.
   ["The translation endeavors to turn the original into intelligible modern English, avoiding any attempt at expository paraphrase."]

   Another edition; London: SCM Press, 1948.

1952 **Wuest, Kenneth S.**   Word Studies...
   [See New Testament Selections, 1940 Kenneth S. Wuest, Word Studies...]

1958 **Kent, Homer Austin**   The Pastoral Epistles. Studies in I & II Timothy and Titus. By Homer A. Kent. Chicago: Moody Press, 1958.
   [Includes an "...extremely literal translation of the Epistles..."]

1963 **Kelly, John Norman Davidson**   Pastoral Epistles, 1963.
   [See N.T., 1957 Black's N.T. Commentary.]

   [See N.T., 1958 Harper's N.T. Commentaries.]

1964 **Quinn, Jerome D.**   I & II Timothy and Titus. Introduction, Translation and Notes, by Jerome D. Quinn. Garden City, New York: Doubleday & Co., Inc., 1964.
   [See Complete Bibles, 1964 Anchor Bibles, Vol. 35.]

1972 **Buttolph, Philip and Adela Yarbo**   A Commentary on the Pastoral Epistles by Martin Dibelius and Hans Conzelmann. Translated by Philip Buttolph and Adela Yarbo. Philadelphia: Fortress Press, 1972.

1981 **Anonymous**   The Epistles of Paul to Timothy, Titus,
Philemon. Recovery Version.   Anaheim, CA: Living
Stream Ministry, 1981.
[See N.T., 1985 Witness Lee & Others, N.T.]

TIMOTHY

1579 **Tomson, Laurence** Calvins Sermons on the Epistles...
[See Pastoral Epistles and Selections for the
entire entry.]

1632 **Barlow, John**   An Exposition of the First and
Second Chapters of the Latter Epistle of the Apostle
Paul to Timothie; Wherein the text is logically
resolved; The words also plainly explicated; with an
easie Metaphrase annexed: Thence doctrines arising
are deduced: And by Scripture, Examples, and reason
confirmed...by Iohn Barlow. London: Printed by R.Y.
for Iames Bolen & George Lathum, 1632.

1819 **Anonymous**   The Epistles of St. Paul to the
Colossians, to the Thessalonians...
[See Epistles and Selections for the complete entry.]

1828 **Anonymous**   The Epistles of St. Paul...
[See Pastoral Epistles and Selections for the entire
entry.]

1856 **Ellicott, Charles John**   A Critical and Grammatical
Commentary..., 1856.
[See Pastoral Epistles and Selections, 1856 for the
entire entry.]

1856 **Pringle, William**   Commentary on Timothy, Titus
and Philemon by John Calvin. Translated from the
original Latin, and collated with the author's
French version.   Edinburgh: Calvin Translation
Society, 1856.
[See Bible Selections, 1844 Anonymous, Commentaries on
the Books of the Bible.]

1905 **Moule, Handley C.G.**   The Second Epistle to Timothy.
Short Devotional Studies on the Dying Letter of St.
Paul.   London: The Religious Tract Society;
Philadelphia: The Union Press 1905.
Reprinted; Grand Rapids, Michigan: Baker Book
house, 1952.

1910 **Wright, Joseph**   Grammar of the Gothic Language...
[See New Testament Selections for the entire
entry.]

1930 **Isaacs, Wilfred H.**   Translational Studies in...
　　　[See Pastoral Epistles and Selections for the entire
　　　entry.]

1954 **Hoerber, Robert G.**   Saint Paul's Shorter Letters...
　　　[See Pauline Epistles Selections for the entire
　　　entry.]

1957 **Hendriksen, William**   New Testament Commentary...
　　　[See New Testament Selections, 1953 for the entire
　　　entry. Includes I & II Timothy.]

1959 **Taylor, Kenneth N.**   Romans...the Children's Hour...
　　　[See Pauline Epistles Selections for the entire entry.]

1986 **Kramer, William**   Evolution & Creation; A Catholic
　　　Understanding. Rev. William Kramer...   Huntington,
　　　IN: Our Sunday Visitor Publishing Div., 1986.
　　　[Contains the author's translation of I Tim. 1:7.]

TITUS

1535 **Coxe, Leonard**   The Paraphrase of Erasm Rotherdame
　　　vpon ye Epistle of sait Paule vnto his discyple
　　　Titus. lately translated into Englysshe and fyrste
　　　a goodly prologue. London: Ihon Byddell, 1535.
　　　[Not known whether this translation was revised in the
　　　N.T. of 1548-49]

1579 **Tomson, Laurence**   Calvins Sermons on the Epistles...
　　　[See Pastoral Epistles and Selections for the
　　　complete entry.]

1819 **Anonymous**   The Epistles of St. Paul to the...
　　　[See Epistles and Selections for the complete entry.]

1828 **Anonymous**   The Epistles of St. Paul...
　　　[See Pastoral Epistles and Selections for the complete
　　　entry.]

1856 **Ellicott, Charles John**   A Critical and Grammatical
　　　Commentary..., 1856.
　　　[See Pastoral Epistles and Selections, 1856 for the
　　　entire entry.]

1856 **Pringle, William**   Commentary on Timothy, Titus
　　　and Philemon by John Calvin. Translated from the
　　　original Latin, and collated with the author's
　　　French version.   Edinburgh: Calvin Translation
　　　Society, 1856.
　　　[See Bible Selections, 1844 Anonymous, Commentaries on
　　　the Books of the Bible.]

1930 **Isaacs, Wilfred H.**   Translational Studies...

[See Pastoral Epistles and Selections for the complete entry.]

1954 **Hoerber, Robert G.**   Saint Paul's Shorter Letters (Galatians...Titus...), 1954.
[See Pauline Epistles Selections for the entire entry.]

1957 **Hendriksen, William**   New Testament Commentary...
[See New Testament Selections, 1953 William Hendriksen, New Testament Commentary... Includes Titus.]

PHILEMON

???? **Barth, Markus**   Colossians and Philemon. Introduction, Translation...
[See Pauline Epistles Selections for the complete entry.]

???? **Beet, Joseph Agar**   A Commentary on St. Paul's Epistles to the Ephesians, Philippians, Collossians and Philemon...
[See Pauline Epistles Selections for the complete entry.]

1633 **Attersoll, William**   A Commentarie vpon the Epistle of Saint Pavle to Philemon. Wherein, the Apostle handling a meane and low subject, intreating for a Fraudulent and Fugitive Servant, mounteth aloft to God, and delivereth sundry high Mysteries of true Religion, and practice of Duties. By William Attersoll. London: Printed by Tho. Cotes, and are to be sold by Michael Sparke, 1633.

1856 **Pringle, William**   Commentary on Timothy, Titus and Philemon by John Calvin. Translated from the original Latin, and collated with the author's French version.   Edinburgh: Calvin Translation Society, 1856.
[See Bible Selections, 1844 Anonymous, Commentaries on the books of the Bible.]

1860 **American Bible Union**   Epistle to Philemon ...(By H.B. Hackett). New York: American Bible Union, 1860.

1866 **Davies, J. Llewelyn**   The Epistles of St. Paul to the Ephesians, the Colossians and Philemon...
[See Pauline Epistles Selections for the complete entry.]

1897 **Vincent, Marvin R.**   A Critical and Exegetical Commentary on the Epistles of St. Paul to...
[See Pauline Epistles Selections for the complete entry.]

1898 **Moule, Handley C.G.**   Colossian Studies...
   [See Pauline Epistles Selections for the complete
   entry.]

1931 **Radford, Lewis B.**   The Epistle to the Colossians...
   [See Pauline Epistles Selections for the complete
   entry.]

1937 **Bonner, C. Bradlaugh**   The Second Epistle to the
   Corinthians, the...and the Epistle to Philemon...
   [See Pauline Epistles Selections for the complete
   entry.]

1948 **Gray, Crete**   The Epistles of St. Paul to...
   [See Pauline Epistles Selections for the complete
   entry.]

1954 **Hoerber, Robert G.**   Saint Paul's Shorter Letters...
   [See Pauline Epistles Selections for the complete
   entry.]

1964 **Blaiklock, E.M.**   From Prison in Rome...
   [See Pauline Epistles Selections for the complete
   entry.]

1966 **Hendriksen, William**   New Testament Commentary...
   [See New Testament Selections, 1953 William Hendriksen,
   New Testament Commentary...]

1971 **Poehlmann, William R. and Robert J. Karris**
   A Commentary on the Epistle to the Colossians and...
   [See New Testament Selections for the complete
   entry.]

1982 **O'Brien, Peter T.**   Word Biblical Commentary.
   Colossians, Philemon...
   [See N.T. Selections for the complete entry.]

HEBREWS

???? **Ainsworth, Henry**   MS form of Hosea, Matthew and...
   [See Bible Selections for the complete entry.]

???? **Lane, William L.**   Word Biblical Commentary.
   Hebrews. Waco, Tx: Word Books, Publishers, [198?].
   [See Complete Bibles, 1982 Word Biblical Commentary,
   Vol. 47.]

???? **Robbins, R.D.C.**   See Moses Stuart, St. Paul's
   Epistle...Hebrews, 1828.

1605 **Cotton, Clement**   Hebrewa. London: 1605.

1727 **Peirce (Pierce), James**   Hebrews, 1725.
[See Epistles and Selections, 1705 Anonymous, A
Paraphrase and Notes on the Epistles...]

1733 **Hallett, Joseph**   Hebrews, 1733.
[See Epistles and Selections, 1705 Anonymous, A
Paraphrase and Notes on the Epistles...]

1733 **Pierce (Peirce), James**   A Paraphrase and Notes on
the Epistles of St. Paul to the Colossians...
Hebrews...
[See Pauline Epistles Selections for the complete
entry.]

1755 **Sykes, Arthur Ashley**   A Paraphrase and Notes upon
the Epistle to the Hebrews. To which is prefixed an
enquiry into the author of this Epistle: when it was
wrote: the manner of citing the Old Testament ; and
the method of reasoning in it. With some remarks on
the late Lord Belingbroke's treatment of St. Paul,
by Arthur Ashley Sykes.   London: John and Paul
Knapton, 1755.

1783 **Barclay, John**   The Experience and Example of the
Lord Jesus Christ... Divine Praise...
[See Bible Selections for the complete entry. Includes
Hebrews.]

1783 **Hardy, Samuel**   Necessary for all Christians.
A new translation of St. Paul's Epistle to the
Hebrews, from the Original Greek, with explanatory
notes.   London: Author, 1783.

1783 **Harly, S.**   A New Translation of St.Paul's Epistle to
the Hebrews, with Explanatory Notes. London: 1783.

1819 **McLean, Archibald**   A Paraphrase and Commentary
on the Epistle to the Hebrews, by Archibald McLean.
2 Vols.   London: 1819.
Second Edition; Revised. 2 Vols. London: W.
James, 1820.

1828 **Sampson, George Vaughan**   A Literal Translation of
St. Paul's Epistle to the Hebrews, from the original
Greek, with copious notes. Edited by his son, the
Rev. George Vaughan Sampson.   London: C. & J.
Rivington, 1828.

1828 **Stuart, Moses**   St. Paul's Epistle to the Hebrews.
A New Translation and Commentary. By Moses Stuart.
Andover, Mass.: n.p., 1828.
Another edition; A Commentary on the Epistle to
the Hebrews...Second Edition, Corrected and
Enlarged.   Andover: Flagg, Gould and Newman;
New York: J. Leavitt, 1833.

Second edition; London: H. Fisher, n.d.

Third edition, Corrected and Enlarged; Andover: Warren F. Draper, 1854.

Another edition; Edited and Revised, by R.D.C. Robbins. Andover: Warren F. Draper, 18??

1834 **Anonymous**   The Epistles to the Hebrews. A New translation, in sections with marginal references and notes and an introductory syllabus. [Josiah Conder] London: Holdsworth & Ball, 1834.

1843 **Hinton, John Howard**   The Epistle to the Hebrews: freely rendered, and arranged on the principles of Scripture Parallelism. [London] 1843.

1847 **Craik, Henry**   An Amended Translation of the Epistle to the Hebrews. By Henry Craik. London: Samuel Bagster & Sons, 1847.

1853 **Owen, John**   Commentaries on Hebrews by John Calvin. Translated from the original Latin, and collated with the author's French version. Edinburgh: Calvin Translation Society, 1853.
        [See Bible Selections, 1844 Anonymous, Commentaries on
        the Books of the Bible.]

1857 **American Bible Union**   The Epistle to the Hebrews (By N.N. Whiting). New York: American Bible Union, 1857.

1868 **Kingsbury, Thomas L.**   Commentary on the Epistle to the Hebrews by Franz Delitzsch... translated from the German by Thomas L. Kingsbury. 2 Vols. Edinburgh: T. & T. Clark; London: Hamilton & Co.; Dublin: John Robertson, 1868-1870.

1868 **Ripley, Henry J.**   The Epistle to the Hebrews, with Explanatory Notes: to which are added a condensed view of the Priesthood of Christ, and a translation of the Epistle, prepared for this work, by Henry J. Ripley. Boston: Gould & Lincoln, 1868.

1871 **M'Caul, Joseph B.**   The Epistle to the Hebrews, in a paraphrastical commentary, with illustrations from Philo, the Targums, the Mishna and Gamara, the later Rabbinical writers, and Christian annotators. By Joseph B. M'Caul. London: Longman & Co., 1871.

1872 **Howard, John Eliot**   ...The Epistle to the Hebrews. A revised translation with notes. By John Eliot Howard. London: Yapp & Hawkins, 1872.

1882 **Davidson, Andrew Bruce** The Epistle to the Hebrews. With an introduction and notes. Edinburgh: T. & T. Clark, 1882.

1883 **Rendall, Frederic** The Epistle to the Hebrews in Greek and English. With critical and explanatory notes. London: Macmillan & Co., 1883.
   ["An original and often felicitous translation... " From Goodspeed's 'Epistle to the Hebrews', 1908.]

   Another edition, 1888.

1884 **Lowrie, Samuel T.** An Explanation of the Epistle to the Hebrews. By Samuel T.Lowrie. New York: Robert Carter & Brothers, [1884].

1901 **Harris, John Tindall** The Writings of the Apostle...
   [See Pauline Epistles Selections for the complete entry.]

1902 **Sampson, Gerard** The Layman's Bible Series...
   [See New Testament Selections for the complete entry. Includes Hebrews.]

1904 **Chamberlain, J.S. Ffoster** The Epistle to the Hebrews. Edited by J.S. Ffoster Chamberlain. Cambridge: E. Johnson, 1904.
   [The Editor's version with notes.]

1906 **Rotherham, Joseph Bryant** Studies in the Epistle to the Hebrews. By Joseph Bryant Rotherham. Cincinnati: The Standard Publication Co., 1906.
   ["The whole of the Sacred Text has been given, mainly according to the Author's 'Emphasised' Version (1897), with such occasional modification as seemed (necessary for a) successful exposition."]

1910 **Wickham, E.C.** The Epistle to the Hebrews. With an introduction and notes. By E.C. Wickham. London: Methuen & Co., 1910.
   Second edition, 1922.

   [Westminster Commentaries. Contains a paraphrase.]

1912 **Anonymous** The Epistle to the Hebrews. An experiment in conservative revision. By Two Clerks. [Henry Charles Beeching and Frederick Brooke Westcott] Cambridge: University Press, 1912.

1922 **Boylan, Patrick** The Epistle to the Hebrews. Translation and brief commentary. By Patrick Boylan. Dublin & Vienna: M.H. Gill & Son, 1922.
   [It is not known whether this is the same translation published in the Westminster version of the N.T.]

1924 **Boylan, Patrick** Hebrews, 1924.

[See Complete Bibles, 1913 Westminster Version.]

1924 **Moffatt, James** A Critical and Exegetical Commentary on the Epistle to the Hebrews by James Moffatt... Edinburgh: T. & T. Clark, 1924.
[See Complete Bibles, 1895 International Critical Commentary.]

Reprinted, 1948.

1925 **Wales, Frank H.** The Epistle to the Hebrews. Translation by F.H.Wales...London: Oxford University Press, 1925.

1933 **Isaacs, Wilfred H.** New Testament Epistles in English prose for the general reader. The Epistle to the Hebrews with some interpretative suggestions by Wilfred H. Isaacs. London: Humphrey Milford, O.U.P., 1933.

1933 **Maeder, J.D.** The Epistle of Paul the Apostle to the Hebrews, being a literal translation... By J. D. Maeder. Salisbury, North Carolina: 1933.

1937 **Hudson, James T.** The Epistle to the Hebrews, its meaning and message... Introduction, Translation, Marginal Analysis by James T. Hudson. Edinburgh: T. & T. Clark, 1937.

1939 **Edwin, Herman** The Letter to the Hebrews translated from the Greek text, as edited by Dr.Eberhard Nestle and later completed by Dr.Erwin Nestle. Minneapolis, Minn.: privately multigraphed, 1939.
[Attempted to "...bring out the meaning of the letter, not out of it to produce an acceptable English."]

Another edition; Minneapolis, Minn.: New England Press, 1940.

1940 **Mueller, Herman Edwin** The Letter to the Hebrews. A translation by Herman Edwin Mueller. Directly from the Greek text as originally edited by Dr. Eberhard Nestle and later completed by Dr. Erwin Nestle. Minneapolis: 1940.
Second edition, 1948.

1947 **Newell, William R.** Hebrews Verse by Verse by William R. Newell... Chicago: Moody Press, 1947.
[Commentary and translation. "The text ...is in general the RV... at times it is necessary to render literally and in several instances to paraphrase..."]

Second Edition, 1947.

Third Printing, 1949.

1947 **Wuest, Kenneth S.**   Word Studies...Hebrews...
     [See New Testament Selections, 1940 Kenneth S. Wuest,
     Word Studies...]

1951 **Manson, William**   The Epistles to the Hebrews.
     An historical and theological reconsideration. By
     William Manson. The Baird Lectures, 1949. London:
     Hodder & Stoughton, 1951.
          ["The rendering of the Epistles is from the author's own
          translation..."]

          Another edition; Greenwich, Connecticut: The
          Seabury Press, 1951.

1952 **Wright, Walter C.**   Hebrews. A Guide for Bible
     Students in Busy Days. By Walter C. Wright. Chicago:
     Moody Press, 1952.

1957 **Muller, William A.**   Letter to the Hebrews by
     William A. Muller. Grand Rapids, Michigan: William
     B. Eerdmans, 1957.

1958 **Montefiore, Hugh W.**   Hebrews, 1958.
     [See N.T., 1957 Black's N.T. Commentary.]

     [See N.T., 1958 Harper's N.T. Commentaries.]

1964 **Swetnam, James**   Albert Vanhoye, S.J. A Structured
     Translation   of   the   Epistle   to   the   Hebrews;
     Translated from the Greek and the French by James
     Swetnam. Rome: Pontifical Bible Institute, 1964.

1972 **Buchanan, George Wesley**   To the Hebrews.
     Translation, Comment and Conclusions by George
     Wesley Buchanan.   Garden City, N.Y.: Doubleday &
     Co., 1972.
          [See Complete Bibles, 1964 Anchor Bible, Vol. 36.]

1972 **Kent, Homer Austin**   The Epistle to the Hebrews.
     A Commentary. By Homer A. Kent. Grand Rapids, MI:
     Baker Book House, 1972.
          ["The use of a literal translation at the beginning of
          each discussion is intended as an aid in arriving at the
          author's thought."]

1978 **Wexler, R.**   Hebrews 10:24-25. <u>Women's Household</u>,
     Sept., 1978.

1981 **Anonymous**   Hebrews. Recovery Version. Anaheim,
     Ca.: Living Stream Ministry, 1981.
          [See N.T., 1985 Witness Lee & Others, N.T.]

1990 **Bruce, F.F.**   The epistle to the Hebrews, 1990.
          [See N.T., 1959 New International Comment. on the N.T.]

19

Catholic Epistles

CATHOLIC EPISTLES

1734 **Collet, Samuel** A Practical Paraphrase on the Seven Catholic Epistles, after the manner of Dr. Clark's Paraphrase on the Four Evangelists, 1734.

1749 **Benson, George** ...the seven, commonly called, Seven Catholic Epistles by James, Peter, Jude and John... 174?.
[See Epistles and Selections, 1705 Anonymous, A Paraphrase and Notes on the Epistles.]

1836 **Anonymous** The Catholic Epistles and Revelation. (A Literal translation and commentary)...
[See New Testament Selections, 1836 Anonymous, A Literal Translation...]

1852 **American Bible Union** The Second Epistle of Peter, The Epistles of John and Jude (by John Lillie). New York: American Bible Union, 1852.

1854 **American Bible Union** The Second Epistle of Peter, The Epistles of John and Judas, and the Revelation Translated from the Greek, on the Basis of the Common English Versions, with Notes. [by John Lillie] New York: American Bible Union, 1854.

1855 **Owen, John** Commentaries on The Catholic Epistles by John Calvin. Translated from the original Latin, and collated with the author's French version. Edinburgh: Calvin Translation Society, 1855.
[See Bible Selections, 1844 Anonymous, Commentaries on the Books of the Bible.]

JAMES

???? **Butler, Barry**   The Letter of Saint Paul to...
[See Epistles and Selections for the complete entry.]

???? **Mayor, Joseph B.**   The Epistle of St. James. The
Greek text with introduction, notes, and comments.
By Joseph B. Mayor. London: Macmillan and Co., n.d.
Second edition, revised; 1897.

Third edition, revised; 1910.

Another edition; The Epistle of St. James. The
Greek text with introduction, notes, and
comments, and Further Studies in the Epistle
of St. James. London: Macmillan, 1913.

Reprinted; Grand Rapids, Michigan: Zondervan,
1954.

1577 **Anonymous**   A Learned and fruitfull Commentarie
vpon the Epistle of Iames the Apostle... Written in
Latine by the learned Clerke, Nicholas Hemminge...
and newly translated into English by W.C. [W. Gace]
London: Thomas Woodcocke and Gregorie Seton, 1577.

1591 **Turnbull, Richard**   An Exposition vpon the
Canonicall Epistle of Saint Iames...Divided into 28
lectures or sermons by Richard Turnbull.   London:
Iohn Windet, 1591.
Another edition; — — newly corrected, enlarged,
and amended by the authour. London: Iohn
Windet, 1592.

1630 **Usher, Ambrose**   ["All of the O.T.; and of the
New... Romans, I Corinthians, St. James..."]
[See Bible Selections for the complete entry.]

1700 **Anonymous**   Scriptural Poems. Being several portions
of Scripture...Ruth...VI. The Epistle of James...
[See Bible Selections for the complete entry.]

1819 **Anonymous**   The Epistles of St. Paul to...
[See Epistles and Selections for the complete entry.]

1838 **Anonymous**   Expository lectures on the General
Epistle of James. By the Rev. Bernard Jacobi.
Translated from the German. London: R.T.S., 1838.

1861 **Anonymous**   Facsimiles of Certain Portions of...
[See New Testament Selections for the complete
entry.]

1871 **Johnstone, Robert** Lectures exegetical and practical
     on the Epistle of James with a new translation of
     the Epistle and notes on the Greek text by the Rev.
     Robert Johnstone... Edinburgh: William Oliphant &
     Co., 1871.
          Another edition; New York: Anson D.F. Randolph &
          Co, n.d.

1876 **Bassett, Francis Tilney**   The Catholic Epistles
     of St. James. A revised text. With translation,
     introduction and notes critical and exegetical by
     Francis Tilney Bassett. London: S. Bagster & Sons,
     1876.

1888 **Deems, Charles F.**   The Gospel of Common Sense
     as contained in the Canonical Epistle of James. New
     York: Wilbur B. Ketcham; Edinburgh: James Gemmell,
     1888.
          [Includes a new translation from the Greek.]

1891 **Bazett, Henry** James' Letter. The people's version.
     By Henry Bazett. Bexley Heath: The Author, 1891.

1896 **Anonymous**   The Sermon on the Mount... extracts...
          [See New Testament Selections for the complete entry.
          Includes part of James.]

1904 **Knowling, R.J.**   The Epistle of St. James. With an
     introduction and notes. By R.J. Knowling. London:
     Methuen & Co., 1904.
          Second edition, 1910.

          Third edition, 1922.

          [Westminster Commentaries.]

1916 **Ropes, James Hardy**   A Critical and Exegetical
     Commentary on the Epistle of St.James by James Hardy
     Ropes... Edinburgh: T. & T. Clark, 1916.
          [See International Critical Commentary (James), 1895.]

          Reprinted, 1948.

1924 **Anonymous**   The Road to Real Success...
          [See Bible Selections for the complete entry. Includes
          the Epistles of James.]

1935 **Richards, James**   De Letter of James. Put into de
     Sussex dialect by Jim Cladpole. Turnbridge Wells:
     James Richards, 1935.
          Second edition, 1936.

1936 **Brooks, J. Barlow**   Epistle of James in the
     Lancaster Dialect, by J.B. Brooks. Stalybridge,
     Lancashire: George Whittaker & Sons, [1936? 1937?].

776

1953 **Baird, Thomas Charles**   Now let it work.
The Epistle of St. James: a paraphrase and running
commentary. By Thomas Charles Baird. London:
Manuals of Fellowship, Third Series, edited by
Florence M. Bull and J. Alan Kay No.4, 1953.

1953 **Bird, T.C.**   Now let it work! The Epistle of St.
James. A Paraphrase and running commentary by T.C.
Bird. London: Epworth Press Manuals of Fellowship,
1953.

1964 **Reicke, Bo Ivar**   The Epistles of James, Peter...
[See Epistles and Selections for the complete entry.]

1967 **Estes, George P.**   James, 1967.

1976 **Adamson, James B.**   The Epistle of James, 1976.
[See N.T., 1959 New International Comment. on the N.T.]

1976 **Williams, Michael A.**   James. A Commentary on the
Epistle of James by Martin Dibelius. Revised by
Heinrich Greeven. Translated by Michael A. Williams.
Edited by Helmut Koester. Philadelphia: Fortress
Press, 1976.

1988 **Martin, Ralph P.**   Word Biblical Commentary. James.
Ralph P. Martin. Waco, TX: Word Books... 1988.
[See Complete Bibles, 1982 Word Biblical Commentary,
Vol. 48.]

PETER

???? **Green, Samuel G.**   The Apostle Peter: His Life and
Letters, [187?].
Third Edition; With Maps. London: Sunday School
Union, n.d.

1581 **Newton, Thomas**   The Epistles of St. Peter...
[See Epistles and Selections for the complete entry.]

1650 **Anonymous**   A Paraphrase and Exposition of
the Prophesie of Saint Peter, Concerning the Day of
Christ's Second Coming. The Second Edition corrected
and amended. London: R. Leybourn, for Samuel Man,
1650.

1742 **Benson, George**   1st Peter, 1705.
[See Epistles and Selections, 1705 Anonymous, A
Paraphrase and Notes on the Epistles.]

1851 **Demarest, John T.**   A Translation and Exposition of the First Epistle of the Apostle Peter. New York: John Moffet, 1851.
> ["This differs little from the version in common use", (which is also given).]

1852 **Lillie, John**   II Peter, I, II, & III John, Jude, 1852.
> [See Catholic Epistles, 1852 & 1854 American Bible Union.]

1873 **Lillie, John**   Lectures on the First and Second Epistle of Peter...With an Introduction by Philip Schaff. By John Lillie.   New York: Scribner, Armstrong & Co., 1873.
> ["In the translation...appended to the Lectures, only those variations are taken to the text, on which critical editors, for a century past, may be said to be in agreement."]

1888 **Owen, John W.**   The Letter of the Larger Hope, being a rendering into modern English of the First Epistle of Saint Peter, with illustrations and notes. By John W. Owen. Adelaide: Burden & Bonython, 1888.
> Another Edition; – – With an introduction by the very Reverend G.W. Kitchen.   London: Elliot Stock, 1890.

1894 **Cologan, W.H.**   The Life and writings of St. Peter, With notes. London: Catholic Truth Society, 1894.

1900 **Masterman, J. Howard B.**   The First Epistle of Peter. Greek text. With introduction and notes. By J. Howard B. Masterman. London: Macmillan and Co., 1900.

1902 **Sampson, Gerard**   The Layman's Bible Series...
> [See New Testament Selections for the complete entry.]

1904 **Lenker, John Nicholas**   The Epistles of St. Peter...
> [See Epistles and Selections for the complete entry.]

1907 **Mayor, Joseph B.**   The Epistle of St. Jude...
> [See Epistles and Selections for the complete entry.]

1934 **Wand, J.W.C.**   The General Epistles of St. Peter...
> [See Epistles and Selections for the complete entry.]

1942 **Wuest, Kenneth S.**   Word Studies...First Peter...
> [See New Testament Selections, 1940 Kenneth S. Wuest, Word Studies...]

1943 **Gray, Crete**   Pilgrims in Vanity Fair. A Study of the First Epistle of Peter. With a translation and

questions for group discussion.   London: Epworth
Press, 1943.

1947 **Beare, Francis Wright**   The First Epistle of Peter.
The Greek text with introduction and notes. Edited
and translated By Francis Wright Beare.   Oxford:
Basil Blackwell, 1947.
> 2nd edition; revised. Oxford, 1958.

1954 **Wuest, Kenneth S.**   Word Studies...In Those Last
Days. II Peter, I, II, III John and Jude...
> [See New Testament Selections, 1940 Kenneth S. Wuest,
> Word Studies...]

1964 **Reicke, Bo Ivar**   The Epistles of James, Peter...
> [See Epistles and Selections for the complete entry.]

1965 **Schubert, Dee**   The First Apostolic Letter of Peter
to the Holy Ones Collectively, by Dee Schubert. [La
Mirada,   California: Biola   College   Library,
Typewritten MS], 1965.

1977 **Blaiklock, E.M.**   First Peter; A Translation and
Devotional Commentary. E.M. Blaiklock. Waco, Texas:
Word Books, Publishers, 1977.

1983 **Bauckham, Richard J.**   Word Biblical Commentary.
Jude, 2 Peter...
> [See New Testament Selections for the complete entry.]

1984 **Paul, William E.**   A transphrased paraversion
of I & II Peter. Intended for translator's personal
edification only.   MS. 1984.

1988 **Michaels, J. Ramsey**   Word Biblical Commentary.
I Peter. J. Ramsey Michaels. Waco, TX: Word Books,
Publisher, 1988.
> [See Complete Bibles, 1982 Word Biblical Commentary,
> Vol. 49.]

1990 **Davids, Peter H.**   The First Epistle of Peter.
Eerdmans, 1990.
> [See N.T., 1959 New International Comment. on the N.T.]

EPISTLES OF JOHN

???? **Houlden, J.L.**   Johannine Epistles, [19??].
> [See N.T., 1957 Black's New Testament Commentary.]

1531 **Tyndale, William**   The exposition of the epistles
of St. John. 1531-1538.

1531 The exposition of the fyrste epistle of
     seynt Ihon with a prologge before it.
     Antwerp: Martin Lempereur.

Another edition, 1537.

1538 The exposition of the Epistles of St.
     John.

Another edition; Southwark: James Nicholson,
1539.

Reprinted; Expositions and Notes on Sundry
Portions of Holy Scriptures... Edited for the
Parker Society by the Rev. Henry Walter.
Cambridge University Press, 1849.

1578 **Anonymous**   Marlorat's Catholike exposition vppon
     the two last epistles of John. [A.Golding?] 1578.
     Another edition, 1584.

1580 **Anonymous**   The Commentaries of M. Ihon Caluin...
     [See Epistles and Selections for the complete
     entry.]

1630 **Usher, Ambrose**   ["All of the O.T.; and of the New,
     the four 1st chapters of St. John's Gospel...
     [See Bible Selections for the complete entry.]

1837 **Fellowes, B.**   A Revision of the Gospel and Third
     Epistle of John...
     [See New Testament Selections for the complete entry.]

1848 **Browne, H.**   Homilies on the Gospel According
     to St. John, and his First Epistle...
     [See New Testament Selections for the complete entry.]

1852 **Lillie, John**   II Peter, I, II, & III John, Jude,
     1852.
     [See Catholic Epistles, 1852 & 1854 American Bible
     Union.]

1853 **Mardon, Benjamin**   The Catholic Epistle of John the
     Apostle translated from the Greek text of Lachmann,
     ...with notes critical and explanatory by Benjamin
     Mardon. London: E.T. Whitfield, 1853.

1857 **Graham, W.**   The Spirit of Love; or a Practical and
     Exegetical Commentary on the First Epistle of John.
     London: Benton Seeley, 1857.
     [Greek and English]

1871 **Barham, Francis**   An elucidated translation of St.
     John's Epistles, from the Greek and Syriac, with a

devotional commentary, by Francis Barham. London:
Fred Pitman; Bath: I. Pitman; J. Davies, 1871.

1879 **Pope, W.B.**   The First Epistle of St. John.
A contribution to Biblical Theology. By Erich Haupt.
Translated, with an introduction by W.B. Pope.
Edinburgh: T. & T. Clark, <u>Clark's Foreign
Theological Library</u> (New Series, Vol. 64), 1879.

1884 **Devine, Pius**   Auxilium Praedicatorum; or a Short
Gloss upon the Gospels (Appendix; or a Short Gloss
upon the Epistles of S. John the Evangelist). 3
Vols.   Dublin: M.H. Gill, 1884.
      [Latin & English]

1885 **Westcott, Brooke Foss**   The Epistles of St. John.
The Greek Text with Notes and Essays by Brooke Foss
Westcott. 1885.
      [The Second Edition. "...I have added a continuous
      translation to each section." Apparently the First
      edition had no English text.]

      Third   edition;   ["some   corrections."]   The
      Macmillan Co., 1892.

      Photolithoprinted;   Grand   Rapids;   Michigan:
      William B. Eerdmans Publishing Co., 1952.

1889 **Alexander, William Lindsay**   The Epistles
of St. John. Twenty-one discourses, with Greek Text,
comparative versions, and notes chiefly exegetical.
London: Hodder & Stoughton, 1889.
      [See Bible Selections, 1888 The Expositor's Bible.]

1905 **Walker, Frank J.** The Message of John in colometrical
print, together with a note of ministry. New York:
Johannine Bible Press, 1905.
      [The Epistles of John.]

1906 **Forster, Henry Langstaff**   St. John's Gospel,
Epistles, and Revelation...
      [See New Testament Selections, 1903 Henry Langstaff
      Forster, [N.T. Selections]...]

1909 **Law, Robert**   The Tests of Life; A Study of the
First Epistle of St. John by Robert Law. Edinburgh:
T. & T. Clark, 1909.
      ["The text used is that of Tischendorf's 8th edition;
      but in one passage (5.18) I have preferred the reading
      indicated in our AV and in the Reviser's margin."]

      [This version provides for "...grouping together the
      passages bearing upon a common theme."]

      Second edition, 1909.

["But for a few added notes and a few corrections, chiefly typographical, the second edition is a reprint of the first..."]

1911 **Anonymous**   The "Sine Qua Non" of a Christian. A verbal translation and a paraphrase of the First General Epistle of John the Apostle, with introduction and notes. [Thomas Wilkins] London: Cooper & Budd, 1911.

1917 **Anonymous**   The First Epistle of St. John. Text and notes interwoven. Mainly on the lines of Bishop Westcott. [T.D.Morris], 1917.

1924 **Anonymous**   The Road to Real Success...
[See Bible Selections for the complete entry. Includes I John.]

1933 **Wood, H.G.**   The First Epistle of John by H.G. Wood. With a new translation and questions for discussion. London: Epworth Press, 1933.
[Manuals of Fellowship, Series 2, No. 6]

1936 **Richards, James**   De Love Letters of Old John. Put into de Sussex dialect by Jim Cladpole. [James Richards] Turnbridge Wells: J. Richards, 1936.

1937 **Dana, H. E.**   The Epistles and Apocalypse of John...
[See New Testament Selections for the complete entry.]

1954 **Wuest, Kenneth S.**   Word Studies...In Those Last Days. II Peter, I, II, III John and Jude...
[See New Testament Selections, 1940 Kenneth S. Wuest, Word Studies...]

1973 **Malatesta, Edward**   The Epistle of St. John. Greek text and English translation schematically arranged. Edward Malatesta.   Rome: Pontifical Gregorian University, 1973.

1973 **O'Hara, R. Philip and Others**   A Commentary on the Johannine Epistles by Rudolf Bultmann. Translated by R. Philip O'Hara with Lane C. McGaughy and Robert W. Funk. Edited by Robert W. Funk.   Philadelphia: Fortress Press, 1973.

1978 **Marshall, I. Howard**   The Epistles of John, 1978.
[See N.T., 1959 New International Comment. on the N.T.]

1982 **Brown, Raymond E.**   The Epistles of John. Translated with Introduction, Notes, and Commentary by Raymond E. Brown.   Garden City, New York: Doubleday & Co., Inc., 1982
[See Complete Bibles, 1964 Anchor Bible, Vol. 30.]

1984 **Smalley, Stephen S.**   Word Biblical Commentary.
1, 2, 3 John. Stephen S. Smalley.   Waco, TX: Word
Books, Publisher, 1984.
    [See Complete Bibles, 1982 Word Biblical Commentary,
    Vol. 51.]

JUDE

1538 **Ridley, Lancelot**   An Exposition in the epistell
of Iude the apostel of Christ wherein he setteth
playnly before euery mans eyes false apostels, and
theyr craftes, by ye which they haue longe deceyued
symple christian people. By Lancelot Ridley. London:
Imprinted in the house of Thomas Gybson, 1538.
    Another edition; London: John Gowghe, 1538.

    Also; − − considerably revised.   London:
    Wyllyam Copland for Rychard Kele, 1549.

1580 **Anonymous**   The Commentaries of M. Ihon Caluin...
    [See Epistles and Selections for the entire
    entry.]

1581 **Newton, Thomas**   The Epistles of St. Peter...
    [See Epistles and Selections for the entire entry.]

1591 **Turnbull, Richard**   An Exposition vpon the
Canonicall Epistle of Saint Iude: with the analysis
and resolution, both generall of the whole Epistle,
and particular of euerie Lecture: Diuided into tenne
Sermons or Lectures made and written by Richad [sic]
Turnbull. London: Iohn Windet, 1591.
    Another edition; − − Lately reuised and augmented
    by the author. London: Iohn Windet, 1592.

1825 **Anonymous**   The Catholic Epistle of Jude,
with a paraphrase and notes. [Henry Rutter] London:
Keating & Brown, 1825.

1825 **Rutter, Henry**   See Anonymous, The Catholic Epistle
...Jude, 1825.

1852 **Lillie, John**   II Peter, I, II, & III John, Jude,
1852.
    [See Catholic Epistles, 1852 & 1854 American Bible
    Union.]

1856 **Gardiner, Frederic**   The Last of the Epistles;
a Commentary upon the Epistle of St. Jude, designed
for the General Reader as well as for the Exegetical
Student. Boston: John P. Jewett & Co.; Cleveland,

Ohio: Jewett, Proctor & Worthington;   New York:
Sheldon, Blakeman & Co., 1856.
> [Chapter VII contains "A New Translation of the Epistle.
> The text followed here, as throughout, is that of
> Lachmann."]

1861 **Anonymous**   Facsimiles of Certain Portions of...
> [See New Testament Selections for the complete entry.]

1896 **Anonymous**   The Sermon on the Mount... extracts...
> [See New Testament Selections for the complete entry.
> Includes part of Jude.]

1904 **Lenker, John Nicholas**   The Epistles of St. Peter
and St. Jude...
> [See Epistles and Selections for the complete entry.]

1907 **Mayor, Joseph B.**   The Epistle of St. Jude and...
> [See Epistles and Selections for the complete entry.]

1934 **Wand, J.W.C.**   The General Epistles of St. Peter...
> [See Epistles and Selections for the complete
> entry.]

1950 **Cox, A.M.**   The Epistle of Jude. London: 1950.

1954 **Wuest, Kenneth S.**   Word Studies...In Those Last
Days. II Peter, I, II, III John and Jude...
> [See New Testament Selections, 1940 Kenneth S. Wuest,
> Word Studies...]

1964 **Reicke, Bo Ivar**   The Epistles of James, Peter...
> [See Epistles and Selections for the complete entry.]

1972 **Lawlor, George Lawrence**   The Epistle of Jude, a
Translation and Exposition by G.L. Lawlor. Nutley,
NJ: 1972.
> Another edition; Translation and Exposition of
> the Epistle of Jude by George Lawrence Lawlor.
> Presbyterian and Reformed Publishing Co.,
> 1972.

1983 **Bauckham, Richard J.**   Word Biblical Commentary.
Jude, 2 Peter...
> [See New Testament Selections for the complete entry.]

Revelation

???? **Arnold, Elias**   A commentary upon the Divine Revelation of the Apostle and Evangelist John. By David Pareus... Translated out of the Latine into English by Elias Arnold. Amsterdam: Printed by C.P., [16??].

???? **Aune, David E.**   Word Biblical Commentary. Revelation. Waco, Tx: Word Books, Publishers, [198?].
> [See Complete Bibles, 1982 Word Biblical Commentary, Vol. 52.]

???? **Livermore**   Revelation of John (From the Sinaitic MS), [19??].
> [No more is known.]

???? **Scott, Walter**   Exposition of the Revelation of Jesus Christ, by Walter Scott. 4th Edition. London: Pickering & Inglis, [19??].
> ["We have freely used the labours of many scholarly men in our translation of the text. The New Translation (Morrish, London) [i.e., Darby] has been largely drawn upon."]

> [8th impression of the 4th edition; no date or place.]

???? **Tafel, Leonard, Rudolph L. Tafel and L.H. Tafel** Interlinear Translation of the Sacred Scriptures, with Grammatical and Critical Notes...
> [See Bible Selections for the complete entry. Includes Pentateuch, Gospels, Acts and Revelations.]

1370 **Anonymous**   The Apocalypse.
> [In "A Fourteenth Century English Biblical Version," 1902. Anna C. Paues groups the following mss. into three versions of the work:

a. Harl 874; Magd. Coll. Cambr. 2498; Trin. Coll.
Cambr. 50.
b. St. John's Coll. G.25
c. Reg.17A26; Rylands R.4988; Laud 235;Laud 33]

An English Fourteenth Century Apocalypse
version with a prose commentary. Edited from
Ms. Harley 874 and ten other mss. Elizabeth
Fridner (Editor) Lund, G.W.K. Gleerup (Lund
Studies in English.) 1961.

1545 **Bale, John**   The Image of bothe churches after
the most wonderful and heauenly Reuelation of Sainct
Iohn the Euangelist, contayning a very frutefull
exposicion or paraphrase vpon the same. Wherein it
is conferred with the other scriptures, and most
auctorised historyes. Compyled by John Bale — an
exile also in this life for the faythfull testimonye
of Jesu. Imprinted at London by John Daye & William
Seres, 1545-1550.
[According to Bills, this work is in Latin.]

Edition with the Latin Englished by John Studley.
London: 1574.

Another edition; London: Rychard Jugge, 1548.

Also; 3 Parts. London: John Myer, 1550.

Another edition; [Antwerp?], 1550.

Also; London: Thomas East, 1570.

Again; London: Parker Society, 1849.

1561 **Anonymous**   A hundred Sermons vpon the Apocalips of
Iesu Christe...compiled by...Henry Bullinger. [John
Daus] London: John Day, 1561.
[Cotton lists a 1561 edition, attributing the
translation to "John Davis."]

Another edition; Faythfully corrected and
amended. London: Iohn Daye, 1573.

1561 **Davis, John**   The Revelation. London: John Daye,
1561.

1573 **Bullinger, Henry**   The Revelation Expounded in 100
Sermons. London: John Daye, 1573.

1574 **Anonymous**   A Catholike exposition vpon the
Reuelation of Sainct Iohn. Collected by M.Augustine
Marlorate out of diuers notable writers. [Arthur
Golding] London: H.Binneman for L. Harison and G.
Bishop, 1574.

1574 **Studley, John**   See John Bale, The Image of Both Churches..., 1545.

1592 **Anonymous**   Apocalypsis. A Briefe and learned commentarie vpon the Revelation of Saint Ihon the Apostle and Euangelist, applied vnto the historie of the Catholike and Christian Church. Written in Latine by M. Francis Iunius, Doctor of Divinitie, and professor in the Vniuersitie of Heidelberge. And translated into English for the benefit of those that vnderstand not the Latine. [Thomas Barbar] Imprinted at London by Richard Dexter..., 1592.

> [British Museum Catalogue ascribes to Barbar, based on the initials "T.B.", which appeared in the translator's address in the 1596 edition. In many Genevan Bibles, starting in 1599, this translation of Revelation supplanted that of Thomson. See Complete Bibles, 1599 Geneva-Tomson-Junius Bible.]

> Another edition; The Revelation of Saint Ihon the Apostle and Evangelist, vvith a briefe and learned Commentarie, Written by Franc. Iunius... London: Richard Field, for Robert Dexter, 1594.

> Also; The Apocalyps, or Revelation of S. Ihon The Apostle and Evangelist of our Lord Iesvs Christ. With a briefe and methodicall exposition vpon euery chapter by way of a little treatise, applying the words of S.Ihon to our last times that are full of spirituall and corporall troubles and divisions of Christendome. Lately set forth by Fr. DvIon [i.e., Francis Junius] and newly translated into English for the edification and consolation of the true members of our Lord Iesus Christ in his Catholike Church. [By T.B.] Printed by Ihon Legat, Printer to the Vniverstie of Cambridge, 1596.

> Another edition; The Revelation ...London: R. Field for R. Dexter, 1600.

1593 **Napier, John**   A Plaine Discovery of the Whole Reuelation of Saint John set down in two Treatises: the one searching and proving the interpretation thereof, the other applying the same Paraphrastically and Historicallie to the text. Set foorth by Ihon Napier. L. of Marchistoun younger; whereunto are annexed Certaine Oracles of Sibylla, agreeing with the Reuelation and other places of Scripture. Edinburgh: Robert Walde-Graue, 1593.

> ["The second and principal Treatise, wherein (by former grounds) the whole Apocalyps or Reuelation of S. John, is paraphrastically Expounded, Historically applyed, and

temporally dated with Notes on every difficulty..." With
Genevan text.]

Newlie imprinted and corrected;   [London:] Printed
for Ihon Norton, 1594.

Also; Now reuised, corrected and enlarged by
him. With a resolution of certain doubts...
London: [Andrew Hart] for Ihon Newton, 1611.

The Fifth Edition: corrected and amended.
Edinburgh: Printed for Andro Wilson, 1645.

1596 **Gyffard, George**   Sermons vpon the whole booke of
Revelation. Set forthe... London: Thomas Man & Toby
Cooke, 1596.
    Another edition; London: Richard Fielde, Felix
Kingston, 1599.

1610 **Broughton, Hugh**   A Revelation of the Holy
Apocalypse, by Hvgh Broughton. [Middleburgh?] 1610.
    Another edition, Coloniae.Iu. 1610.

1611 **Brightman, Thomas**   The Revelation. 1611.
    [1615 & 1616. 3rd. edition corrected and amended.
    Leyden: John Classon von Dorpe.]

1616 **James, King, VI of Scotland**   Revelations,
chapter XX, verses 7-10 with an exposition and a
paraphrase on the whole book (from Complete Works)
London: Bill and Barker, 1616.
    [Information is from Cotton.]

    Also; Edinburgh: Henrie Charteris, 1588.

1616 **Stuart, James**   Revelation; Chapter XX. Verses 7, 8,
9 & 10, with an exposition and a paraphrase of the
whole book, by James Stuart. London: Bill & Barker,
1616.
    [From "The Workes of the Most High and Mightie Prince,
    James, &c" According to Richard Montagu, Bishop of
    Winchester, who published the King's collected works,
    the Revelation was written "...before hee was twenty
    yeeres of age."]

1630 **Usher, Ambrose**   ["All of the O.T.; and of the
New... Epistles of St. John, and Revelation...
    [See Bible Selections for the complete entry.]

1639 **Anonymous**   The Book of Revelation paraphrased,
with annotations on every chapter, whereby it is
made plain to the meanest capacity. London: 1639.

1644 **Brightman, Thomas**   The Revelation with Daniel...
    [See Bible Selections for the complete entry.]

1650 **Hall, Joseph**   The Revelation Unrevealed. Oxford:
1650.

1675 **Hayster, Richard**   The Meaning of Revelation, or
a Paraphrase with questions on the Revelation of the
Holy Apostle and Evangelist John the Divine. London:
J.R. [John Redmayne], 1675.
Another edition, 1676.

[Chapters 6-18 only.]

1682 **Woodhead, Abraham**   The Apocalyps (sic)
paraphrased... 2 Parts. n.p.: n.p., 1682.

1689 **Woodhead, Abraham**   Concerning Images and Idolatry
by Abraham Woodhead. Oxford: Printed in the year
1689.
[Includes "The Apocalyps Paraphrased". MS note in the
Bodleian copy: "This Book was never yet published, but
printed by Mr. Obadiah Walker in the stables belonging
to the University College, where the greatest part of
the edition was seized, but Mr. Walker himself gave this
book to Mr. Hudson who gave it here."]

[The British Museum Catalog lists this work as "An
extract out of Bishop Mountague's appeal...concerning
Mohamet. (1682?)"]

1693 **Anonymous**   The Book of Revelation Paraphrased;
with Annotations on each Chapter. Whereby it is made
plain to the meanest Capacity. [Edward Waple]
London: [William Marshall and J. Salusbury], Printed
in the Year, MDCXCIII. [1693]
["...care hath been taken, that no interpretation should
be inserted into the Paraphrase upon the text, which was
not thought to be justly grounded upon the Scriptures
quoted in it."]

Another edition; London: Printed and to be Sold
by Richard Wellington, 1694.

Also; London: James Brown, 1715.

1694 **Cradock, Samuel**   A Brief and Plain Exposition and
Paraphrase of the Whole Book of Revelation,...
London: 1694.
Another Edition; London: T. Parkhurst, 1696.
Also; London: Jonas Brown, 1715.

Also; Glasgow: Robert Chapman and Alexander
Duncan, and Sold by James Young..., 1782.

1706 **Kennett, Basil**   An Essay Towards a Paraphrase
on the Psalms ...a Paraphrase on the Third Chapter
of the Revelations...
[See Bible Selections for the complete entry.]

1719 Daubuz, Charles The Revelation literally translated from the Greek by Charles Daubuz. London: Benjamin Tooke, 1719.
[Text is in Greek and English.]

Another edition; A Perpetual commentary on the Revelation of St. John; With a preliminary discourse, concerning the certainty of the principles upon which the Revelation of St. John is to be understood. London: Benjamin Tooke, 1720.

Also; Newly modell'd, abridg'd, and Render'd plain ... by Peter Lancaster. London: for the author, 1730.

1730 Lancaster, Peter   A Perpetual Commentary on the Revelation of St. John; With a preliminary discourse, concerning the certainty of the principles upon which the Revelation of St. John is to be understood. New modell'd, abridg'd, and render'd plain to the meanest capacity by Peter Lancaster. London: Printed for the Author & Sold by W. Innys, 1730.
[This work, by Charles Daubuz, originally appeared in 1720. According to Cotton, the 1730 edition contains a new translation by Lancaster.]

1735 Pyle, Thomas   The Scripture preservative against Popery, being a paraphrase on Revelation. Which completes the paraphrase of the New Testament in the manner of Dr. Clarke. London: J. Noon, 1735.
Second edition; London: G.G. & J. Robinson, 1795.

1737 Lowman, Moses   A Paraphrase and Notes on the Revelation of St.John. By Moses Lowman. London: John Noon, 1737.
[The text and paraphrase are in parallel columns.]

Another edition; Dublin: Printed by S. Powell for Edward Exshaw..., 1740.

Second edition, 1745.

Third edition, 1773.

Also, 1791, 1807.

[Also many later editions. Also added to Patrick, Lowth, Daniel Whitby's Commentary.]

1754 Erskine, Ralph   Scripture Songs. In Three Parts...
[See Bible Selections for the complete entry. Includes 16 songs from Revelations.]

1757 **Robertson, John**   Bongelius's Introduction to
his Exposition of the Apocalypse; with his preface,
and the greatest part of his conclusion to it; and
also his marginal notes on the text, with a summary
of the whole exposition, Translated from the High
Dutch, by John Robertson. London: n.p., 1757.

1772 **Rowe, Elizabeth**   Miscellaneouc Works...
      [See Bible Selections for the complete entry. Includes
      Revelation 16.]

1789 **Cooke, William**   The Revelation Translated,
and explained throughout, with keys, illustrations,
notes and commentaries; a copious introduction,
argument, and conclusions by William Cooke.
London: G.G.J. & J. Robinson;   Yarmouth: Downs &
March, 1789.
      [Author was a Greek Professor at Cambridge. Severely
      disparaged by Orme]

1790 **Anonymous**   A Paraphrase, Notes, and Observations
upon the Revelation of S. John, the Divine, Apostle
and Evangelist. Part I containing introductions.
London: G.G. & J. Robinson, 1790.
      [The 'Introductions' are extracted from various authors;
      not clear whether the paraphrase is actually included in
      the work, as published.]

1790 **Belcher, W.**   The Galaxy. Consisting of a variety
of sacred and other poetry...
      [See Bible Selections for the complete entry. Includes
      the Revelation.]

1791 **Tucker, Nathaniel**   The Apocalypse Revealed,
wherein are disclosed the arcana there fore-told,
which have hitherto remained concealed, now first
translated from the original Latin of Emanuel
Swedenborg, by Nathaniel Tucker. 2 Vols. Manchester:
C. Wheeler, 1791.
      New Edition; revised & corrected. [John Spurgin
      and Robert Boldock]   London: J.S. Hodson,
      1832.

      New Edition; Revised & corrected by Francis de
      Soyres. London: William Newbery, 1851.

      Another edition; New York: American Swedenborg
      Printing & Publishing Society, 1875.

      Another edition, 1883-1887.

      Another edition; London: Swedenborg Society,
      1940.

1794 **Anonymous**   Remarks on the Book of Daniel, and on the Revelations. Whereby it appears, that Daniel had visions...
[See Bible Selections for the complete entry.]

1794 **Winthrop, James**   An Attempt to Translated the Prophetic Part of the Apocalypse of Saint John into Familiar Language, by divesting it of the Metaphors in which it is involved. By James Winthrop. Printed in Boston: for the Author by Belknap & Hall, MDCCXCIV [1794].
Another edition; A Appendix to the New Testament... Cambridge, Mass.: Hilliard & Metcalf, 1809.

1805 **Woodhouse, John Chappel**   The Apocalypse, or, Revelation of Saint John, Translated; with Notes, Critical and Explanatory. To which is prefixed a Dissertation on the Divine origin of the Book; in answer to the objections of the late Professor J.D. Michaelis. London: Printed for J. Hatchard by J. Brettell, 1805.
[Griesbach's Greek, KJV and new translation in parallel columns.]

[An 1828 edition omits the translation. However, whatever was important in the improved translation is included in the annotations.]

1811 **Anonymous**   The Apocalypse, or Book of Revelation, explained according to the spiritual sense, in which are revealed the arcana which are there predicted, and which have been hitherto deeply concealed. Translated into English from a Latin posthumous work of...Emanuel Swedenborg [by W.H.] and revised by the translator of the Arcana Coelestia [J.C.] (To which is subjoined a summary exposition of the internal sense of the Prophetic Books of the word of the Old Testament, and of the Psalms of David.) [William Hill, translator and John Clowes, revisor] 6 vols. London: J. & E. Hodson, 1811-1815.
Second edition [Revised]; [Francis de Soyres and James Mitchell] London: J.S. Hodson, 1834-1840.

New Edition revised and corrected. de Soyres &c. London: Swedenborg Society, 1854-1871.

Another edition; Revised and retranslated. Isaiah Tansley and James Speirs. London: 1884-1901.

1823 **Brown, J.A.**   The Even-tide, or, Last Triumph of the Blessed and only Postentate, the King of Kings, and Lord of Lords; being a development of the mysteries of Daniel and St. John, and of the Prophecies

respecting the renovated Kingdom of Israel; ...by
J.A. Brown. 2 vols. London: published by J. Offor,
Newgate Street; Longman and Co...., 1823.
[Free paraphrase of the Revelation. pages 363-424.]

1827 **Croly, George**   Apocalypse of St. John or prophecy
on the rise, progress and fall of the church of
Rome; the Inquisition; the revolution in France, the
universal   war,   and   the   final   triumph   of
Christianity. Being a new interpretation. London:
C. & J. Rivington, 1827.
[New York edition same year.]

Other editions; 1828, 1838.

1832 **Boldock, Robert**   See Nathaniel Tucker, The
Apocalypse Revealed ...Swedenborg. (Revised 1832),
1791.

1832 **Pilkington, George** The Revelation of Jesus Christ;
newly translated from the original Greek; with a
plain reading, divesting it of all its metaphors and
notes. By George Pilkington.   Part I.   London:
Effingham Wilson, 1832.
[Chapters I-XI only]

1832 **Spurgin, John**   See Nathaniel Tucker, The
Apocalypse Revealed, 1791.

1834 **Soyres, Francis de and James Mitchell**   See
Anonymous, The Apocalypse (Second Edition Revised),
1811.

1836 **Anonymous**   The Catholic Epistles and Revelation (A
Literal Translation and Commentary)...
[See New Testament Selections, 1836 Anonymous, A Literal
Translation...]

1841 **Fysh, Frederic**   The Revelation of St. John, in
blank verse; with critical and chronological notes.
London: J.W. Parker, 1841.

1843 **Govett, Robert**   The Revelation of St. John literal
and future; being an exposition of that book: to
which are added remarks in refutation of the ideas
that the Pope is the Man of Sin and that popery is
the apostasy predicted by St. Paul. With special
reference to Dr. O'Sullivan on the Apostasy.
London: Hamilton, Adams, 1843.
[Not clear whether this includes a translation; and if
so, whether it is the same as 1861.]

1844 **Tregelles, Samuel Prideaux**   ...The Book
of Revelation in Greek, edited from the ancient
authorities; with a new English version, and various

readings; by Samuel Prideaux Tregelles.   London: S.
Bagster & Sons, 1844.

> Another edition;   The Book of Revelation
> translated from the ancient Greek text.
> London: S. Bagster & Sons, 1849.
>> [English only; translation revised.]

> Also; - - With an historical sketch of the
> printed text of the Greek New Testament... A
> New Edition, with a notice of the Palimpsest
> MS. hitherto unused.   London: S, Bagster &
> Sons, 1859.

> Third Edition, 1881.
>> ["The previous editions of this translation
>> followed the Greek text of the Revelation
>> published by Dr. Tregelles, in 1844. The present
>> edition follows his last edition of the Greek
>> text, published in 1872."]

1847 **Lord, David N.**   An Exposition of the Apocalypse.
New York: Harper & Brothers, 1847.
> [Includes a new translation.]

1848 **Hoare, William Henry**   The Harmony of the
Apocalypse by William Henry Hoare.   London: J.W.
Parker, 1848.
> [A paraphrase.]

1848 **Murray, George Edward**   The Apocalypse in Greek,
arranged in parallelisms; with a literal English
translation, by George Edward Murray.   London: not
published, 1848.
> [A proof copy is in the British Museum. The projected
> edition was never published.]

1849 **Kelly, William**   The Book of Revelation,
translated from the Greek; with notes of the
principal different readings adopted in critical
editions, and remarks connected with the study of
the book by William Kelly.   London: J.K. Campbell,
1849.
> [...The Revelation of John, edited in Greek, with a new
> English Version, and a statement of the chief
> authorities and various readings. London: Williams &
> Norgate, 1861.]

1849 **Wordsworth, Christopher**   The Apocalypse; or,
Book of Revelation; the original Greek text, with
Mss. collation; an English translation and harmony,
with notes; and an appendix to the Hulsean lectures
for 1848 on the Apocalypse by Christopher
Wordsworth.   London: Francis & John Rivington, 1849.
> [The Greek text is twofold: Scholz's and that formed by
> the editor, on the authority of the oldest Mss.]

Another edition; A Harmony of the Apocalypse; or, Book of Revelation; being also a revised English translation of the same, with notes... second edition with additions, 1852.

1851 **Fairbairn, Patrick**   The Revelation of St. John. Expounded for those who search the Scriptures. By E.W. Hengstenberg... Translated from the German. Edinburgh: T. & T. Clark, Clark's Foreign Theological Library. Vol. 22, 26, 1851.
Another edition; New York: Robert Carter, 1852.

1851 **Soyres, Francis de**   See Nathaniel Tucker, The Apocalypse Revealed, (Revised & Corrected), 1791.

1851 **Stuart, Moses**   The Apocalypse by Moses Stuart. 2 Vols. Andover: W.F. Draper, 1851.
Another edition; - - Edited and revised by R.D.C. Robbins, 186?

1852 **Jenour, Alfred**   Rationale Apocalypticum by Alfred Jenour. 2 Vols. London: T. Hatcherd, 1852.
[Revelation translated.]

1852 **Williams, Isaac**   The Apocalypse, with notes and reflections by Isaac Williams. London: F. & J. Rivington, 1852.

1854 **Anonymous**   The Apocalypse or Revelation of Saint John, arranged in Blank verse; with some minor paraphrases chiefly of portions of scripture. Newcastle-upon-Tyne: John Hernman, 1854.

1854 **Lillie, John**   II Peter, I, II, & III John, Jude, and Revelation...
[See Catholic Epistles, 1854 American Bible Union.]

1854 **Soyres, Francis de and James Mitchell**   See Anonymous, The Apocalypse (New Edition Revised and corrected), 1811.

1856 **Anonymous**   The Apocalypse of St. John. A new translation metrically arranged, with Scripture illustrations. [John H. Godwin] London: Jackson & Walford, 1856.

1861 **Matheetees (Robert Govett)**   The Apocalypse Expounded by Scripture (translation interwoven)   4 Vols. London: J. Nisbet & Co., 1861-1865.
[Translation is interwoven with the text.]

Abridged one volume edition; London: C.J. Thynne, 1920.

Another edition; London: C.J. Thynne & Jarvis, 1929.

1861 **Trench, Richard Chenevix** Commentary on the Epistles to the seven churches in Asia, by Richard Chenevix Trench. 1861.   [Revelations 1-3.]

1862 **Anonymous**   Revelations revealed, or the progress of error, and the triumphs of truth (paraphrase). Philadelphia: W.P. Hazard, 1862.

1862 **Pratt, J.H.**   Paraphrase of the Revelation of St. John by J.H. Pratt. London: n.p., 1862.

1863 **Coleman, John B.**   "Revelations" Edinburgh: Nisbet, 1863.

1863 **Vaughan, Charles John** Lectures on the Revelation of John by Charles John Vaughan. 2 Vols. London: 1863.
[First two editions had translations prefixed to the lectures; later editions interwove translations into the body of the lectures.]

Second edition; 1865.

1864 **Clay, Edmund**   An Exposition and Interpretation of the Book of Revelation. Experimental and Practical; According to "The Testimony of Jesus", and the Analogy of Holy Scripture. With a new translation and paraphrase, based on the Critical Commentaries of Dean Alford, Dr. Wordsworth, and Mr. Kelley. London: J. Nisbet & Co., 1864.
[Chapters 1-10; text is KJV with corrections.]

1866 **Blackley, W.L. and James Hawes**   The Critical English Testament Being an Adaption of Bengel's Gnomon, with Numerous Notes, showing the Precise Results of Modern Criticism and Exegesis...
[See New Testaments, 1866 for the entire entry. This contains only a translation of Revelations.]

1867 **Anonymous**   The Book of God: The Apocalypse by ☉ [Edward V. H. Kenealy] 3 Vols. London: 1867-1870.
1867 The Apocalypse of Adam-Oannes by ☉, Greek Text, with a new translation into English. The Seven Thunders, Notes on the Apocalypse, Index. London: Reeves & Turner.

18?? An Introduction to the Apocalypse. London: Trubner & Co.

18?? A Commentary on the Apocalypse [Preface signed ☉] London: Trubner & Co.

1868 **Anonymous**   The Revelation of St. John the Divine, translated from the original Greek... Newly revised by a Catholic Priest. London: G.J. Palmer, 1868.

1869 **Anonymous**   Near, Even at the Doors. Intended to aid the plain man, who may be a prayerful student of the word of God. By a Layman. London: E. Malborough, 1869.   [The Book of Revelation.]

1871 **MacDuff, John R.**   Memories of Patmos; or some of the words and visions of the Apocalypse, by John R. MacDuff. Oxford: 1871.

1872 **Glasgow, James**   The Apocalypse translated and expounded. By James Glasgow... Edinburgh: T. & T. Clark, 1872.

1872 **Seiss, Joseph A.**   The Apocalypse. A Series of Special Lectures on the Revelation of Jesus Christ. With Revised Text. 3 Vols. Philadelphia: Smith, English & Co., 1872.
> [Copyright dated 1865; Preface dated 1869; Many editions in England and the United States.]

> 15th [English] edition;   London & Edinburgh: Marshall, Morgan & Scott, 1937.

> 10th [American] Edition;   Grand Rapids, Michigan: Zondervan Publishing House, 1951.

1874 **Craven, E.R.**   The Revelation of John translated, enlarged and revised by E.R. Craven.   New York: Charles Scribner & Co., 1874.
> [Now in print by Zondervan.]

1875 **Davidson, Samuel**   Dr. Friederich Bleek's Lectures on the Apocalypse. Edited by Lic. Th. Hossbach... translated from the German by Samuel Davidson. London & Edinburgh: Williams & Norgate, 1875.

1877 **Anonymous**   The Apocalypse Revealed; wherein are disclosed The Arcana There Foretold, Which have Hitherto Remained Concealed. From the Latin of Emanuel Swedenborg. The Rotch Edition. Approved by the General Convention. [Translation by T.B.Hayward, and revised by John Worcester]   Philadelphia: J.B. Lippincott & Co., 1877.
> [A new translation with a 'spiritual' commentary.]
> Another edition, 1878.

> Rotch edition, revised. Boston: New Church Union, 1907.

1880 **Hayward, Savill**   A New Translation of the Book of
Revelation. With concise notes. By Savill Hayward...
London: Haughton & Co., 1880.

1880 **Malet, Arthur**   The Book of Revelation...
[See Bible Selections for the complete entry.]

1881 **Browne, H.**   John's Apocalypse, literally translated
and spiritually interpreted. By H.Browne. Consulting
Physician to the Manchester Royal Infirmary.
Manchester: Tubbs, Brook & Chrystal, 1881.
Also; London: Marshall & Co., 1881.

1881 **Huntington, Edward**   The Apocalypse with
a commentary and an introduction on the reality of
prediction, the history of Christendom, the scheme
of interpretation, and the antichrist of St. Paul
and St.John. London: Kegan Paul, Trench & Co., 1881.
["The English text in this volume was made some years
ago from the... Bishop of Lincoln's... critical work on
the Greek text of the Apocalypse published in 1849."]

1882 **Murphy, James G.**   The Book of Revelation; or,
the Last Volume of Prophecy. Translated and Briefly
Expounded. London: J. Nisbet & Co., 1882.

1883 **Sawyer, Leicester Ambrose**   (The Bible) Analyzed...
[See Bible Selections for the complete entry.]

1884 **Tansley, Isaiah and James Speirs**   See Anonymous,
The Apocalypse (Revised and retranslated), 1811.

1885 **Fuller, Samuel**   The Apocalypse of St. John the
Divine, Self-interpreted. A Commentary for English
Readers, with a new translation. By Samuel Fuller.
New York: Thomas Whittaker, Bible House, 1885.

1887 **Tafel, Leonard, Rudolph L. Tafel and L.H. Tafel**
Interlinear translation of the New Testament...
[See New Testament Selections for the complete entry.]

1888 **Gow, William**   The Apocalypse Unveiled, and a Fight
with Death and Slander. By William Gow.   Perth: J.
Young & Sons, 1888.
[Paraphrased.]

1889 **Worcester, Samuel Howard** ...The Apocalypse Explained
...A posthumous work of Emmanuel Swedenborg. 2 Vols.
New York: American Swedenborg Printing & Publishing
Society, 1889.

1890 **Tischendorf, Constantine**   The Apostles: according
to the oldest known Greek manuscript...
[See Acts and Epistles for the complete entry.]

[See Acts and Epistles for the complete entry.]

1891 **Anonymous**   The Apocalypse of St. John;
done into modern English. With Explanatory Notes and
Translations from the Septuagint. By the Author of
Vox Clamantis. [Ralph Sadler] London: [Sheppard &
St. John], Printed for Private Circulation, 1891.
Another edition; London: J. Nisbet, 1891.
[Part 1 of a work entitled, "The Veil Lifted".]

.1891 **Grimes, Edward**   The Apocalypse. A revised version
in English of the Revelation given to the Apostle
John... With notes historical and explanatory. By
Edward Grimes. Newport-on-Usk: [E. Grimes], 1891.

1892 **Briggs, Thomas Pearl**   Revelation a paraphrase and
exposition in verse. Introduction by E. Benjamin
Andrews. By T.P. Briggs. Boston: J.H. Earle, 1892.

1893 **Anonymous**   The Vision of S. John of Patmos, by E.G.
[Edward Greatorex] London: J. Masters & Co., 1893.
[Metrical paraphrase of the book of Revelation.]

1893 **Scott, Thos. Lucas**   The Visions of the Apocalypse
and their Lessons. Being the Donnellan Lectures for
1891-1892, preached before the University of Dublin
... London: Skeffington & Son, 1893.
[Includes a paragraph version of the Revelation of S.
John.]

1896 **Latham, John Herbert**   The Revelation given to
St. John the Divine. An original translation, with
critical and expository comments. By John H. Latham.
London: Elliott Stock, 1896.

1900 **Benson, Edward White**   The Apocalypse. An
introductory Study of the Revelation of St. John the
Divine; being a presentment of the structure of the
book and of the fundamental principles of its
interpretation. By Edward White Benson. [With a
translation of the text. Edited by Margret Benson.]
London: Macmillan and Co., 1900.

1900 **Burlton, Charles H.B.**   A Metrical Version
of the Revelations. By Charles H.B.Burlton. Madras:
Addison & Co., 1900.
Another edition; A Metrical Version of the
Revelation of St. John the Divine. London:
Marshall Bros. 1903.

1902 **Bullinger, E.W.**   The Apocalypse or "The
Day of the Lord". By E.W. Bullinger. London: Eyre
& Spottiswoode, 1902.

1903 **Forster, Henry Langstaff**   The Revelation...
[See New Testament Selections, 1903 for the entire entry.]

1904 **Ager, J.C.**   The Apocalypse Explained according to the Spiritual Sense, in which the Arcana therein predicted but heretofore concealed are revealed; a posthumous work by Emanuel Swedenborg. 2 vols. New York: American Swedenborgian Printing & Publication Society, 1904.

1904 **Ramsay, W.M.**   The Letters to the Seven Churches of Asia, by W.M. Ramsay. New York: n.p., 1904.

1905 **Ottman, Ford C.**   The Unfolding of the Ages in the Revelation of John. By Ford C. Ottman.   New York: The Baker & Taylor Co., 1905.

1906 **Anonymous**   Prophetic Suggestions...
[See Bible Selections for the complete entry.]

1906 **Chamberlain, J.S. Ffoster**   John's Revelation. By J.S. Ffoster Chamberlain.   London: Henry J. Drane, 1906.
[A new version arranged in acts and scenes, with notes.]

1907 **Campbell, J.L.**   The Patmos Letters. London: Morgan & Scott, 1907? 1908?
[Contains his own translation on Rev. chapter 2 & 3.]

1907 **Conybeare, Fred S.**   The Armenian Version of Revelation and Cyril of Alexandria's Scholia on the Incarnation and Epistle on Easter. Edited from the oldest MSS. and Englished by Fred C. Conybeare. London: The Text and Translation Society, 1907.

1908 **Inger, Archie J.**   Revealed translation of John's Revelation, given by the Lord Jesus Christ to Archie J. Inger, and published to the world that all may come into the light of God's truth.   Oakland, California: 1908.
["I, the Lord Jesus Christ, am the writer of this book by revelations, through his [my?] medium, Archie Inger 'Christ', and have interpreted in this last day..."]

Another edition; New York: Fenno, n.d.

Also reprinted; San Francisco: 1956.

1909 **Porter, Frank Chamberlin**   The Messages of the Apocalyptical Writers..., 1909.
[See Abridged Bibles, 1900 Frank Knight Sanders and Charles F. Kent, The Messages of the Bible, Vol. VIII.]

1910 **Gowen, Herbert H.**   An Analytical Transcription of the Revelation of S. John the Divine with Introduction, brief Commentary and a Dictionary of Apocalypse. London: Skeffington & Son, 1910.

1912 **Nutt, David**   Epistles and Apocalypse...
[See New Testament Selections for the complete entry. Includes Revelations.]

1915 **Buchanan, Edgar Simmons**   A New Text of the Apocalypse from Spain. Extracted and translated from the Latin text of the Morgan MS. of the eighth century commentary of the Spanish Presbyter Beatus. By E.S. Buchanan. New York: Paget Literary Agency, 1915.

1915 **Gigot, Francis**   Apocalypse of John, 1915.
[See Complete Bibles, 1913 Westminster Version.]

1915 **Kratzer, G.A.**   Revelations Interpreted by G.A. Kratzer. Chicago: Central Christian Science Institute, 1915.
[Includes the AV and a "Suggested Paraphrase" in parallel columns.]

Second Edition; Revised. (n.d.)

1915 **Whitehead, John**   The Apocalypse Revealed. Wherein are disclosed the Arcana there fore-told, which have hitherto remained concealed. Translated from the Latin of Emanuel Swedenborg... In two volumes... A new translation by John Whitehead.   New York: Swedenborg Foundation, 1915.
Another edition, 1931.

1918 **Anonymous**   The Revelation of Jesus Christ, according to the Sinaitic Text. With Explanatory Notes and Comments. Brooklyn: Watch Tower Bible and Tract Society, 1918.

1918 **Whiting, Charles C.**   The Revelation of John: an interpretation of the book with an introduction and a translation by Charles C. Whiting. Boston: Gorham Press, 1918.
["A translation, as literal as possible, into clear, simple, modern English..."]

1919 **Concordant Version**   The Unveiling of Jesus Christ. (Revelation)...
[See New Testament Selections, 1914 Concordant Version of the Sacred Scriptures.]

["The translation is designedly interpretative and sometimes paraphrastic."]

1920 **Calkins, Raymond**   The Social Message of the Book of Revelation by Raymond Calkins. New York: The Womans Press, 1920.

1920 **Charles, R.H.**   A Critical and Exegetical on The Revelation of St. John with Introduction, Notes, and Indices also The Greek Text and English Translation by R.H. Charles... (In Two Volumes) Edinburgh: T. & T. Clark, 1920.
     [See Complete Bibles, 1895 International Critical Commentary.]

     Reprinted, 1950.

1922 **Charles, R.H.**   The British Academy Lectures on the Apocalypse... The Schweich Lectures 1919. London: Published for the British Academy by Humphrey Milford, 1922.
     [See Complete Bibles, 1895 International Critical Commentary; not known whether this is the same translation.]

1922 **Osborn, Thomas**   The Lion and the Lamb. A drama of the Apocalypse. By Thomas Osborn. New York & Cincinnati: The Abingdon Press, [1922].

1923 **Oman, John**   The Book of Revelation. Theory of the text: Re-arranged text and translation: commentary by John Oman.... Cambridge: at the University Press, 1923.
     Also; The text of Revelation. A revised theology. Greek and English. Cambridge: Cambridge University Press, 1928.
     [(A revision of the 1923 edition.)]

1924 **Farrer, Austin D.J.**   See Weymouth, The N.T. in Modern Speech, 1903.

1924 **Frost, Henry Weston**   Matthew Twenty-Four and the Revelation. An analysis, literal translation and exposition of each. New York, London: Oxford University Press, 1924.

1925 **Bronson, Carl**   The Revealed Testament of John the Disciple. By Carl Bronson. Los Angeles, Calif.: The Wings Publishing Co., 1925.

1926 **Hardie, Alexander**   A Study of the Book of Revelation by Alexander Hardie. Los Angeles: The Times-Mirror Press, 1926.
     ["...almost no changes of the text (from the KJV) have been suggested. The Greek word Zoon has been translated 'beast'; but it properly means 'living being', and it

has been so rendered in this study. However, when
reference is made to the Papacy, another Greek word is
used; namely therion, which means 'wild beast' or
'beast', and it is properly used when speaking of
Romanism."]

1928 **Anonymous**   The Apocalypse Explained...according
to the spiritual sense; in which the Arcana there
predicted but hitherto concealed are revealed. A
Posthumous work of Emanuel Swedenborg. Standard
edition. New York: Swedenborg Foundation, 1928.
[Revelation, chapters I through XiX:10, with extensive
commentary.]

1930 **Bird, Thomas E**.   Apocalypse of St. John... By T.E.
Bird. St. Louis: B. Herder Book Co., 1930.

1932 **Bonner, C. Bradlaugh**   The Book of Revelation. A key
to Christian origins. By Dr. Paul Louis Couchard.
Translated from the French by C. Bradlaugh Bonner.
London: Watts & Co., 1932.
[A translation of Couchard's "L'Apocalypse" with a
translation of the Book of Revelation based upon that by
R.H.Charles.]

1935 **Newell, William R.**   The Book of Revelations, by
William R. Newell. Chicago, Illinois: The Scripture
Press, 1935.
["The Text used is in general that of the RV, which is
more accurate than that of the Old Version. At times it
is necessary to render literally; and in several places
to paraphrase, to make clearer the meaning." Several
times reprinted under the title, "Revelations Verse by
Verse".]

1937 **Dana, H. E.**   The Epistles and Apocalypse of John...
[See New Testament Selections for the complete entry.]

1946 **Giffard, William**   An Anglo-Norman Rhymed
Apocalypse. (13th Century) Oxford: Published for
the Anglo-Norman Text Society by B.Blackwell, 1946.
Reprinted; New York: Johnson Reprint Corp.,
1967.

1947 **Venable, C.L.**   A Reading of Revelation. By C.L.
Venable. Philadelphia: Muhlenberg, [1947].
[A paraphrase.]

1948 **Alexander, Albert George**   Interpretation of
the Revelation of St. John the Divine by Apostolos
Makrakis. Translated from the Original Greek Text by
A.G. Alexander.   Chicago: Hellenic Christian
Educational Society, 1948.
[KJV with some variant readings from the Septuagint.]

MACK LIBRARY
BOB JONES UNIVERSITY
GREENVILLE, SC

1948 **Carpenter, Hilary J.**   The Apocalypse of Saint John.
By R.J. Loenertz, O.P. Authorised Translation by
Hilary J. Carpenter... London: Sheed & Ward, 1948.
["The Douai version...Occasionally ...an alternative
translation has been added in note form giving a
rendering more in conformity...with the critical Greek
text."]

1949 **Farrer, Austin D.J.**   A Rebirth of Images. The
Making of St. John's Apocalypse. By Austin Farrer.
London: Dacre Press, 1949.

1949 **Hoyt, Edyth Armstrong**   Studies in the Apocalypse...
1949.
Other editions, 1950, 1952.

Also; Studies in the Apocalypse of John of
Patmos; A non-interpretative and literary
approach to the last Book of the English
Bible. Based on the Well Known Lecture Series
by Edyth Armstrong Hoyt... Together with a
Free Modern Paraphrase and Glossary Prepared
by a Group of Research Students.   Columbus,
Ohio: Edwards Brothers, Inc., Publishers; Ann
Arbor, 1962.

1950 **Rogers, William Hubert**   The Book of Revelation in
plain language by W.H. Rogers. New York: American
Board of Missions to the Jews; Phoenix, Arizona:
W.H. Rogers, 1950.
["This work is not a translation, transliteration or a
paraphrasing of the Scripture. It is rather metaphorical
truths set forth in the common language of every day
speech." "...the third edition..."]

Another edition; Phoenix, Arizona: for the
Author, 1950.

1951 **Scher, Andrew R.**   The Book of Life opened;
the hidden meaning of the Revelation of St. John the
Devine;   a   non-sectarian   interpretation   with
questions and answers for study. By Andrew R. Scher.
New York: Exposition Press, 1951.   .
[paraphrase]

1955 **Bowman, John Wick**   The Drama of the Book
of Revelation. An Account of the Book... with a New
Translation in the Language of Today by John Wick
Bowman. Philadelphia: The Westminster Press, 1955.
["The translation – better perhaps, the paraphrase – is
my own: in general it follows Nestle's well-known Greek
text..."]

1957 **Caird, G.B.**   A Commentary on the Revelation of St.
John the Divine, by G.B. Caird.   London: Adam &
Charles Black, 1957.

[See Black's N.T. Commentaries, 1957.]

1957 **Phillips, J.B.**   The Book of Revelation, 1957.
[See New Testament, 1947 for the entire entry.]

1958 **Corathiel, Elizabethe**   The Apocalypse of St. John
by Henricus Marin Feret. Translated by Elizabethe
Corathiel. Westminster, Maryland: The Newman Press,
1958.

1958 **Torrey, Charles Cutler**   The Apocalypse of John;
edited and translated by Charles Cutler Torrey. New
Haven, Connecticut: Yale University Press, 1958.

1959 **Bloomfield, A.E.**   All Things New; A Study of
Revelation. By A.E. Bloomfield. Minneapolis, Minn:
Bethany Fellowship, 1959.
["...we have followed basically the A.V."]

1961 **Fridner, Elisabeth** (Editor)   See Anonymous, The
Apocalypse, 1370.

1961 **Niles, D.T.**   As Seeing the Invisible. A Study of
the Book of Revelation, by D.T. Niles. New York:
Harper, 1961.
[With a paraphrase.]

1964 **Farrer, Austin**   The Revelation of St. John the
Divine: Commentary on the English Text. Oxford: At
the Clarendon Press, 1964.
["I have simply made my own revision of the AV, with
much reliance on the RV. My sole object has been to have
an English text which represents the Greek..."]

1966 **Walvoord, John F.**   The Revelation of Jesus Christ;
A Commentary by John F. Walvoord. Chicago: Moody
Press, 1966.
[A Commentary. "...the AV of the Bible has been inserted
before each section...it was considered adequate to
introduce textual changes where these affect the
meaning... The Nestle Greek Text was used with its
critical apparatus..."]

1968 **Minear, Paul S.**   I Saw a New Earth. An Introduction
to the Visions of the Apocalypse. Paul S. Minear...
Washington/ Cleveland: Corpus Books, 1968.

1973 **Durham, Thomas Ernest**   The Book of Revelation;
a private translation from the original Greek into
simple English language, with the meaning of the
symbols given in the chapter headings by Thomas
Ernest Durham. Minneapolis: Denison, 1973.

1974 **Beasley – Murray, George Raymond**   The Book
of Revelation. Greenwood, S.C.: Attic Press, 1974.

1975 **Ford, J. Massyngberde**   Revelation. Introduction, Translation, and Commentary by J. Massyngberde Ford. Garden City, New York: Doubleday & Co., 1975.
[See Complete Bibles, 1964 Anchor Bible, Vol. 38.]

1977 **Mounce, Robert H.**   The Book of Revelation, 1977.
[See New Testaments, 1971 New International Commentary on the N.T.]

21

Apocryphal Books (N.T.)

APOCRYPHAL BOOKS (N.T.)

???? **Anonymous**   The Epistle of Paul the Apostle to the Laodicians. [17??].
>[In his 'Apocryphal N.T.', 1820, Hone states, "The Quakers have printed a translation, and plead for it, as the reader may see, by consulting Poole's Annotations on Col. vi. 16."]

???? **Anonymous**   Pilate's Report to Caesar. Akron, OH: Hamilton Publishing House, n.d.

???? **Aulagnier, Jean**   The Diary of Jesus. Day by Day Account of Jesus Life. Based on Ancient Calendars and on the Writings of Maria Valorta. Kolbe's Publications Inc., 19??.

???? **Bauer, Walter**   The Works and Sufferings of Jesus. [19??].
>[See Wilhelm Schneemelcher, N.T. Apocrypha, pp. 433-443, 1963.]

???? **Dunlop, Margaret**   Apocrypha Sinaitica:...two recensions of the Recognitions of Clement, a Story entitled the Preaching of Peter, and James the son of Alphaeus and Simon the son of Cleophas, with illustrations; in Arabic, transcribed and translated. London: C.J. Clay & Sons; Cambridge University Press, [189?].

???? **Kraft, Robert A.**   The Didache and Barnabas, [196?].
>[See Apostolic Fathers, 196?]

???? **Malan, Solomon Caesar**   Conflicts of the Holy Apostles, [18??].
>[See M.R. James, Apocryphal N.T. , 1924.]

???? **Savoy, Gene**   The Decoded New Testament, the Lost System of Christ is Clarified for the first time in centuries. By Gene Savoy. [197?].

???? **Valtorta, Maria**   The Poem of the Man-God. 5 Vols.   Italy: Oisani, [19??].

???? **Wake, William and Nathaniel Lardner**   The Apocryphal New Testament. Comprising the Gospels and Epistles now extant, that in the first four centuries were more or less accredited to the Apostles and their coadjutors, but were finally excluded from the New Testament canon with... William   Wake... and Nathaniel Lardner... New Edition. London: Simpkin, Marshall, Hamilton, Kent & Co., n.d.

1300 **Anonymous**   The Boy in the Tower. MS. Harley 3954. c1300.
> [Metrical version of an apocryphal story. Reprinted, 1878, in Sammlung Altenglisher Legenden; Reprinted in Apocryphal N.T., 1924 by M.R. James. Oxford: Clarendon Press.]

1400 **Trevisa, John**   The Translacon of Nichodeme out of latyn into englisshe laboured by Mayatre Johan Trevysa, doctour in theologye, at the instaunce of Thomas, some tyme lord of Berkeley. [British Museum MS.16165] c1400
> A black letter edition; London: Julyan Notary, 1507.

> Another edition; Wynken de Worde, 1509.

> Another edition; London: John Skat, 1529.

> [From 'Dialogus inter Militem et Clericum... by John Trevisa' EETS, 1925.]

1650 **Anonymous**   Something concerning Agbarus, Prince of the Edesseans; With his Epistle to Christ; and Christ's Epistle in Answer thereto. Also Paul's Epistle to the Laodiceans, with the manner of his Death, and his Exhortation to his Persecutors. A Catalogue of those scriptures mentioned, but not included in the Bible. London. c1650.
> [Bound with some Quaker tracts; London, 1650.]

1700 **Anonymous**   A Copy of a Letter written by our Lord and Saviour Jesus Christ, and found eighteen miles from Iconium, fifty three years after our blessed Saviour's Crucifixion. Transmitted from the Holy City by a converted Jew. Faithfully translated from the original Hebrew copy now in the possession of the Lady Cuba's family in Mesopotamia... London: Great St. Andrew's St., Seven Dials, c1700.

[A broadside, with many variations.]

1726 **Jones, Jeremiah**   A New and Full Method of settling the Canonical Authority of the New Testament, 1726. Another edition, 1736?

Also; Oxford: Clarendon Press, 1798.

Another edition; 3 Vols. Oxford: Clarendon Press, 1827.

[Contains several apocryphal N.T. books, reprinted by William Hone, 1820.]

1726 **Jones, Jeremiah**   See Anonymous, William Hone, The Apocryphal Books, 1820

1732 **Whiston, William**   The Testimony of Phlegon Vindicated: or, an Account of the Great Darkness and Earthquake at our Saviour's Passion, described by Phlegon. Including all the Testimonies, both Heathen and Christian, in the very Words of the original Authors, during the first Six Centuries of Christianity. With proper Observations on those Testimonies. By William Whiston. London: Sold by Fletcher Gyles...Holborn J. Roberts...Warwick-Lane, 1732.

1820 **Hone, William**   The Apocryphal New Testament, being all the Gospels, Epistles, and other Pieces now extant, attributed in the first four centuries to Jesus Christ, his Apostles, and their companions, and not included in the New Testament by its compilers. Translated from the original tongues, and now first collected into one volume.   London: Printed for William Hone, 1820.
Second edition, 1821.
["To this second edition a small fragment of the Second Epistle of Clement to the Corinthians, accidently omitted, has been added..."]

Third edition, 1821.

Fourth edition, 1821.

Another edition; New York: Dewitt & Davenport, 1849.

From the last London Edition; Boston: Benjamin B. Mussey, n.d.

Another edition; Boston: Published by Bazis & Ellsworth, n.d.

Also; Peter Eckler, n.d.

2nd edition reprint; London: W.Reeves, n.d. (19??)
Another Edition; Cleveland, Ohio; New York
City: The World Publishing Co., 1926.

Eight printing; Cleveland, Ohio; New York City:
The World Publishing Co., 1944.
[Bound with 'The Forgotten Books of Eden...']

Another Edition; The Lost Books of the Bible:
being all the Gospels, Epistles and other
pieces now extant...   New York: Bell
Publishing Co., 1979.
[Reprint of 1926 edition.]

[The first part of the work is plagiarized from Jeremiah
Jones' "New and Full Method..." 1736, and the second
from William Wake's "Apostolic Fathers", 1817.]

[See Apocryphal Books, 1926 Anonymous, The Lost Books of
the Bible.]

1823 **Hone, William**   Ancient Mysteries Described,
Especially the English Miracle Plays, founded on
Apocryphal New Testament Story, Extant among the
Unpublished Manuscripts in the British Museum;
including notices of Ecclesiastical Shows, the
Festivals of Fools and Asses - The British Boy
Bishop - The Decent into Hell - The Lord Mayor's
Show - The Guildhall Giants - Christmas Carols, &c.
With Glossary and Index... With engravings by G.
Cruikshank and others.   London: William Reeves,
1823.

1830 **Smith, Joseph, Jr.**   The Book of Mormon: An Account
Written by the Hand of Mormon upon Plates taken from
the Plates of Nephi... By Joseph Smith, Junior,
Author and Proprietor. Palmyra: Printed by E.B.
Grandin, for the Author, 1830.
[First issued, as divided into chapters and verses with
references, by Orson Pratt, 1879.]

[First issued in double-column pages, with chapter
headings, chronological data, revised foot-note
references, pronouncing vocabulary, and index. Salt Lake
City, Utah, U.S.A.: The Church of Jesus Christ of Latter
Day Saints, 1920.]

[Smith used "Jehovah" for God's name on the last page
only.]

Another edition; paper-back, 1950.

1833 **Cruse, Christian Frederick**   The Ecclesiastical
History of Eusebius Pamphilus... 1833.

Twelfth edition; Philadelphia: J.B. Lippincott & Co., 1865.

1842 **Anonymous**   Pontius Pilate's Account of the Condemnation of Jesus Christ, and his own Mental Sufferings. Extracted from an old Latin manuscript recently found in Vienne. Boston: 1842.
[Reprinted under the title: 'Pilate's Court', 1878; Also reprinted under the title: 'The confessions of Pontius Pilate', 1893.]

1858 **Smith, Gibson**   The Gospel of Jesus: Compiled by his Disciple Matthew; from his own memoranda, and those of Peter, Also the Acts of the Eleven Disciples; the last Epistle of Peter to the Chapelites; the Acts of Paul and the Jewish Sanhedrim; and the contents of the History of Jesus, by Peter. Translated from parchment manuscripts; in Latin, and found in the catacombs under the city of Rome.   South Shaftsbury, Vt.: Published by Gibson Smith, 1858.

1863 **Anonymous**   The Forbidden Books of the Original New Testament. London: E. Hancock, 1863.
[Same as Horne's 'Apocryphal N.T.', 1820?]

1865 **Wright, William**   Contributions to the Apocryphal Literature of the New Testament, collected and edited from the Syriac manuscripts in the British Museum by William Wright. London: 1865.

1867 **Cowper, B. Harris**   The Apocryphal Gospels and other Documents Relating to the History of Christ. Translated from the Originals in Greek, Latin, Syriac,etc. With Notes, Scriptural References and Prolegomena. Second Edition. Edinburgh: Williams and Norgate..., 1867.

1869 **Baring-Gould, S.**   Curious Myths of the Middle Ages. Philadelphia: J.B. Lippincott, 1869.
[Includes some N.T. lore.]

Another edition; London: 1901.

1871 **Sonnini, C.S.**   Never before published; The long lost chapter of the Acts of the Apostles, containing an account of the Apostle Paul's journey into Spain and Britain and other interesting events, translated by C.S. Sonnini From an original Greek manuscript found in the archives at Constantinople; presented to him by the Sultan Abdoul Achmet. London: George J. Stevenson, 1871.
[Goodspeed's 'New Apocrypha' also mentions other editions from London & Toronto: The Covenant Publishing Co.]

Also; "The long Last Chapter of the Acts of the Apostles". Showers of Blessing, 692nd Issue, Pages 16-18, August, 1978.

Another; "Acts of the Apostles". Showers of Blessing, 564th Issue, December, Pages 11-13, 1967.

Also; "The Lost Chapter". Showers of Blessing, 500th Issue, Pages 17-18, Aug., 1962.

Reprinted; Thousand Oaks, CA: Artisan Sales, 1982.

1873 **Walker, Alexander**   The Apocryphal Gospels, Acts and Revelations, Translated by Alexander Walker. Edinburgh: T. & T. Clark, 1873.
[Volume XVI of the 24-volume 'Ante-Nicene Christian Library', edited by Alexander Roberts and James Donaldson, 1867-1872.]

Another edition; Edinburgh: T. & T. Clark; New York: Scribner's Sons, 1890, 1899.

1874 **Anonymous**   Letters to and from Rome in the Years A.D. 61, 62, and 63; Translated by C.V.S.   London: Williams & Norgate, 1874?

1874 **Baring-Gould, S.**   The Lost and Hostile Gospels: An Essay on the Taledoth Jeschu, and the Petrine and Pauline Gospels of the First Three Centuries of which Fragments Remain.   London & Edinburgh: Williams & Norgate, 1874.

1879 **Clough, W.O.**   Gesta Pilati; or the Reports, Letters and Acts of Pontius Pilate, Procurator of Judea, With an Account of his Life and Death: being a translation and compilation of all the writings ascribed to him, as made to Tiberius Caesar, Emperor of Rome, concerning the life of Jesus, his trial and execution.   With   an   introduction   and   notes. Indianapolis: Robert Douglass, 1879.
Second edition, 1880.

["...free from those errors that inevitably creep into all first editions." Translation from "a Coptic-Sahidian papyrus manuscript ...probably dating from the fifth century.]

1879 **Mahan, W.D.**   A Correct Transcript of Pilate's Court. Boonville, MO: 1879.
[32 page pamphlet by Rev. W.D. Mahan.]

[Pontius Pilate's Account of the Condemnation of Jesus Christ, and his own Mental Sufferings. "Extracted from an old Latin MS recently found at Vienne".   Boston:

n.p., 1842. This work appears to be the source for Mahan's 'Pilate's Court'.]

1880 Reprint;   Indianapolis: William   Overton Clough.

1880 The Acta Pilati.   Shelbyville, Indiana: Rev. George Sluter, 1880

[According to Goodspeed, the above work was incorporated into:]

1884 The   Archaeological   and   Historical Writings of the Sanhedrin and Talmuds of the Jews, Translated from the Ancient Parchments and Scrolls at Constantinople and the Vatican at Rome... n.p.: n.p.

1887 The Archko Volume; or, the Archeological Writings of the Sanhedrin and Talmuds of the Jews. (Intra Secus.) These are the Official Documents made in these Courts in the Days of Jesus Christ. Translated by Drs. McIntosh and Twyman, of the Antiquarian Lodge, Genoa, Italy. From Manuscripts in Constantinople and the Records of the Senatorial Docket Taken from the Vatican at Rome, 1887.
> [Title is taken from the Second edition, copyrighted by W.D. Malan, 1887 and 1896. The identity of who the two "Doctors" really are is unclear. Who are McIntosh and Twyman?]

Second   edition;   Philadelphia: Antiquarian Book Co., 1905.

Unabridged Edition; Grand Rapids, Michigan: The Archko Press, 1929.

1892 An Ancient and Interesting Document found in the Vatican at Rome, which purports to be the original report of Pilate, Roman Governor of Judea, to the Emperor Tiberius Caesar: explanatory of the causes which led to the tumult in Jerusalem, in connection with the death of Jesus of Nazareth. Zion's Watch Tower, Vol. XIII, No. 3 & No. 4, Feb., 1892.
> Reprinted; Akron, Ohio: Hamilton Publishing House, n.d.

1895 Caesar's Court... Dalton, Ga.: The A.J. Showalter Co.

1904 The Archko Library, Translated from Ancient Manuscripts at the Vatican of Rome, and the Seraglio Library at Constantinople, by Drs. McIntosh and Twyman. 5 Parts Topeka, Kansas: W.C. Fisk Publisher, 1904.

Volume I.   Melker's Letters to the Sanhedrin.
Volume II.   Gamaliel's Report to the Sanhedrin.
Volume III.   Report of Caiaphas to the Sanhedrin...
Volume IV.   Pilate's Report to Tiberias Caesar.
Volume V.   Herod's Trial Before the Sanhedrin.

Other editions; Philadelphia: 1905, 1913; Grand Rapids, Mich.: The Classic Press, n.d.; Grand Rapids, Mich.: William B. Eerdmans, 1929.

1923 Reprint of 1884 edition; Chicago, Ill., U.S.A.: The de Laurence Company.

1936 Caesar's Court..Cincinnati, Ohio: F.L. Rowe, Publisher.

1879 **Sluter, George**   The Acta Pilati. Important Testimony of Pilate, Recently Discovered, Being his Official Report to the Emperor Tiberius, concerning the Crucifixion of Christ. Shelbyville, Ind.: M.B. Robins, Publisher and Printer, 1879.
["It may perhaps be necessary to guard the reader against supposing this to be the spurious or forged Acta, to which allusion is made by many writers. The best and most complete edition of these is that of Fabricius (Codex Apocryphus, Edition 1703)... They are certainly spurious, and the inventions of a later day... But the Vatican copy, which I here present, is an entirely different paper..."]

1882 **Newbrough, John Ballou**   Oahspe; A Kosmon Bible in the words of Jehovih and his Angel Embassadors. A Sacred History of the Dominions of the Higher and Lower Heavens on the Earth for the Past Twenty-Four Thousand Years...Together with a Synopsis of the Cosmogony of the Universe; The Creation of the Plants... New York: Oahspe Publication Association, 1882.
[Supposedly received while in a trance by Newbrough, who typed the work during many nights. Deals with the history and cosmology of the world; contains sections resembling each of the major world religions. There are 37 sections, or 'books' of which 'God's Book of Eskra'

tells a story of Joshu, strongly reminiscent of the story of Jesus.]

2nd edition; revised. Boston: & London: 1891.

3rd edition; Revised. London: 1912.

Reprinted; London, Sydney & Melbourne: The Kosmon Press, 1926.

Also; Los Angeles & London: The Kosmon Press, 1935.

1884 **Anonymous**   A Collection of Gospels, Epistles, and other Pieces extant from the Early Christian Centuries but not included in the Commonly Received Canon of Scripture;... Translated from the original tongues, and now reprinted. Glasgow: Thomson & Co., 1884.

1884 **Hitchcock, Roswell D. and Francis Brown** ...Teaching of the Twelve Apostles. Recently discovered and published by Philotheos Bryennios, Metropolitan of Nicomedia. Edited with a Translation, Introduction and Notes. New York: Charles Scribner, 1884.

1884 **Romestin, H. De**   The Teaching of the Twelve Apostles. With Introduction, Translation, Notes, and Illustrative Passages. Edited by H. De Romestin... London: Parker & Co., 1884.
     2nd edition, 1885.

1885 **Schaff, Philip**   The Oldest Church Manual called the Teachings of the Twelve Apostles. The Didache and Kindred Documents in the Original with Translations and Discussions of Post-Apostolic Teaching Baptism Worship and Discipline and with Illustrations and facsimiles of the Jerusalem Manuscript, by Philip Schaff. n.p.: n.p., 1885.
     Second Edition, 1886.
        ["...a number of corrections and improvements..."]

     Another edition; The Teachings of the Twelve Apostles, or the Oldest Church Manual...Third Editions. New York: Funk & Wagnalls, 1890.
        ["A few minor corrections have been made in the text."]

1887 **Pick, Bernard**   The Life of Jesus According to Extra-Canonical Sources. By Bernard Pick. New York: John B. Alden, Pub., 1887.
        ["We have prepared the present volume...making the English translation of Cowper and Walker our basis."]

[Canonical narratives, arranged in continuity from the birth of Jesus to the ascension.]

Another edition; The Extra-Canonical Life of Christ. New York & London: Funk & Wagnalls, 1903.

1889 **Budge, Ernest A. Wallis**   The Book of the Bee, by Bishop Shelomon of Khilat, Armenia; edited and translated from the Syriac Text ...Volume I, Part II of the Semetic Series of Anecdota Axoniensia. By Ernest A.Wallis Budge. Oxford: The Clarendon Press, 1889.

1889 **King, C.W.**   The Gnostics and their Remains. By C.W. King. London: 1889.

1893 **Shehadi, B.**   The Confession of Pontius Pilate... alleged to have been first written in Latin, by Fabricius Albinus...and translated into Arabic by Jerasimus Jared, late Bishop of Zahleh, in Lebanon. By B. Shehadi. New South Wales, Australia: n.p., 1893.
        [The source for this work was 'Pontius Pilate's Account of the Condemnation of Jesus Christ, and his own Mental Sufferings', Boston: 1840. See Anonymous, A Correct Transcript..., 1879.]

Reprinted; E. Orange, NJ: n.p., 1917.

1894 **Connelly, J.H. and L. Landsberg**   Life of Saint Issa, Best of the Sons of men... New York: G.W. Dillingham, 1894.
        Another edition; New York: R.F. Fenno, 1926.

[Translation from the French by Nicholas Notovich.]

1894 **Crawford, F. Marion**   Life of Saint Issa, Best of the Sons of Men. New York: Macmillan, 1894.
        [Translation from the French by Nicholas Notovich]

1894 **Ghandi, Virchand R.**   The Unknown Life of Jesus Christ. From an Ancient Manuscript, Recently Discovered in a Buddhist Monastery in Thibet by Nicholas Notovich, Translated from the French and Edited with an Introduction and illustrations by Virchand R. Ghandi, B.A., Bombay, India. Revised by Prof. G.L. Christie, B.A. of the University of Paris. Chicago: Virchand R. Ghandi, 1894.
        Another edition; London: 1895.

1894 **Loranger, Alexina**   The Unknown Life of Jesus Christ by the discoverer of the manuscript, Nicholas Notovich. Translated from the French by Alexina

Loranger. New York & Chicago: Rand McNally & Co.,
1894.

1895 **Crispe, Violet**   Life of Saint Issa, Best of the
Sons of Men. London: Hutshinson, 1895.
[Translation from the French by Nicholas Notovich]

1895 **Mamreov, Peter F., Anna F. Mamreov and B.A.F.
Mamreov**   Iesat Nassar; the Story of the Life
of Jesus the Nazarene. New York: Sunrise Publishing
Co.; London: Gay & Bird, 1895.
["While founded on strictly Christian and Jewish secular
and ecclesiastical histories, as also on traditions and
legends of oriental and occidental nations, the
personages who figure in the tale are presented as
everyday mortals..."]

Another edition; Boston: Meader Publishing Co.,
1957.

1896 **James, Montague Rhodes**   Apocrypha Anecdota...
Cambridge Texts and Studies. Cambridge: 1896-1897.
1896 - - First Series
1897 - - Second series

1896 **Keane, A.H.**   The Antichrist Legend, from the
German of W. Bousset, with Prologue by A.H. Keane.
London: 1896.

1896 **Robinson, Forbes**   Coptic Apocryphal Gospels.
Translations Together with the texts of some of them
by Forbes Robinson. Cambridge: University Press,
1896.
[One volume of: Texts and Studies: Contributions to
Biblical and Patristic Literature, J.A. Robinson,
editor; 1891-1952.]

1897 **Grenfell, B.P. and Arthur S. Hunt**   Sayings of Our
Lord from an early Greek Papyrus discovered and
edited with a translation and commentary. New York:
H. Frowde, 1897.
["...printed with some alterations...from the
forthcoming publication of the two texts in the
Oxyrhynchus Papyri, Part IV, Nos. 654 and
655...reprinted from the revised text and translation
given in the Oxyrhynchus Papyri, Part I,, no. 1."]

Also; Egypt Expiration Fund, Graeco-Roman
Branch; New Sayings of Jesus and Fragment of a
lost Gospel from Oxyrhynchus; Edited, with a
translation and commentary, by Berard P.
Grenfell... and Arthur S. Hunt... With one
plate and the text of the 'Logia' discovered
in 1897. New York, London, Toronto, Melbourne
& Bombay: Oxford University Press; Published
for the Egypt Exploration Fund, 1908.

Another edition; Oxford: 1908.

1899 **Budge, Ernest A. Wallis**   The History of the
Blessed Virgin Mary and The History of the Likeness
of Christ which the Jews of Tiberias made to mock
at: the Syriac texts edited with English
translations by E.A.Wallis Budge. 2 Vols. London:
Luzac, 1899.
Reprinted; New York: AMS Press, 1976.

1899 **Gaster, M.**   The Chronology of Jerameel; or,
the Hebrew Bible Historiale. Being a collection of
Apocryphal and Pseudo-epigraphical books dealing
with the history of the world from the creation to
the death of Judas Machabeus. Translated for the
First Time from an unique Manuscript in the Bodelian
Library. London: Printed and Published under the
Patronage of the Royal Asiatic Society, 1899.

1900 **Brodrick, M.**   The Life and Confession of Asenath
the Daughter of Pentephres of Heliopolis, narrating
how the all - beautiful Joseph took her to wife.
London: n.p., 1900.
[Prepared by, from Notes supplied by the late Sir Peter
Le Page Renouf.]

1901 **Budge, Ernest A. Wallis**   Contendings of the
Apostles. [Ethiopic text and translation) 2 Vols.
1901.
[See M.R. James' Apocryphal N.T., 1924.]

1902 **Lewis, Agnes Smith**   Studia Sinaitica No. XI
- Apocrypha Syriaca. The Protovengalium Jacobi and
Transitae Mariae... London: C.J. Clay & Sons;
Cambridge University Press, 1902.
[Protovengalion of James and the Assumption of Mary,
with a translation.]

1903 **Donehoo, James DeQuincy**   The Apocryphal and
Legendary Life of Christ; Being the Whole Body of
the Apocryphal Gospels and Other Extra Canonical
Literature with Pretends to tell of the Life and
Words of Jesus Christ, Including Much Matter Which
has not Before Appeared in English. In Continuous
Narrative Form, with Notes, Scriptural References,
Prolegomena, and Indices. New York: The Macmillan
Company; London: Macmillan & Co., 1903.

1904 **Archko Volume**   See Anonymous, A Correct Transcript,
1879.

1904 **Greene, Henry Copley**   The Childhood of Christ -
translated from the Latin... with original text of
the manuscript at the Monastery of St. Wolfgang.

New York: Scott-Thaw Co.; London: Burns & Oates, 1904.

> [Taken from 'L'Evangile de la Jeunesse de Notre-Seigneur Jesus-Christ d'apres S. Pierre.' by Catulle Mendes: Paris, Armand Colin, 1894. In his 'Apocryphal New Testament, 1924, M.R. James describes this as "...a sentimentalized compilation from Provangelium, Pseudo-Matthew, the Latin Thomas, and the Arabic Gospel..." describing it further as a 'modern forgery'.]

1904 **Guthrie, Kenneth Sylvan**   The Long-Lost Second Book of Acts, Setting forth the Blessed Mary's Teachings about Reincarnation, Discovered and translated by Kenneth Sylvan Guthrie.   Medford, Massachussets: Prophet Publishing House, 1904.

1904 **Lewis, Agnes Smith**   The Arabic Version of the Acta Apocrypha Apostolorum. Edited and translated... With Fifth century Fragments of the Acta Thomae in Syriac.   London: C.F. Clay & Sons;   Cambridge University Press, 1904.

1904 **McIntosh and Twyman**   See Anonymous, A Correct Transcript (The Archko Volume), 1879.

1907 **Anonymous**   The Crucifixion and Resurrection of Jesus, by an Eye-Witness. A Discovered MSS. of the old Alexandrian Library giving, almost complete, a remarkable and lengthy letter, full, graphic, and apparently truthful account by an Eye-Witness and friend of Jesus, an elder of the Essene Order, to which Jesus belonged, showing Jesus did not die on the cross, but six months later. With much additional and explanatory matter concerning the Essenes and the Crucifixion Story.   Chicago: Indo-American Book Co., 1907.

> [Vol. II of the "Supplemental Harmonic Series".]

Another edition; Los Angeles, Calif.: Holmes Book Co., [1919].

> [A note, at the beginning of the 1919 edition, was written by Dr. Elsie Louise Morris of Los Angeles.]

1908 **Anonymous**   The Aquarian Gospel of Jesus the Christ. The Philosophic and Practical Basis of the Religion of the Aquarian Age of the World and of the Church Universal. Transcribed from the Book of God's Remembrances, Known as the Akashic Records, by Levi... [Levi H. Dowling] London: L.N. Fowler & Co.; Los Angels: E.S. Dowling, 1908.

> [Frequently reprinted.]

1908 **Chandler, Walter M.**   The trial of Jesus from a Lawyer's Stand point by Walter M. Chandler... 2 Vols. New York: The Empire Publishing Co., 1905.

[Contains an unidentified "Acts of Pilate".]

1908 **Howard, Velma Swanston**   Christ-Legends, by
Selma Lagerof, translated from the Swedish by Velma
Swanston Howard. New York: Henry Holt, 1908.
[Gathered from diverse Oriental sources and retold for
young Swedish readers.]

1908 **Radford, L.B.**   The Epistle to Diognetus, by L.B.
Radford. London: S.P.C.K.; New York: E.S. Gorham,
1908.
["Early Church Classics".]

1909 **Pick, Bernhard** The Apocryphal Acts of Paul, Peter,
John, Andrew and Thomas by Bernhard Pick. Chicago:
The Open Court Publishing Co.; London: Kegan Paul,
Trench, Trubner & Co., 1909.

1910 **Crum, W.E.**   Rustafjaell's Light of Egypt. 1910.
[Contains translation of Coptic apocryphal N.T. books;
from M.R. James' 'Apocryphal N.T.', 1924.]

1913 **Budge, Ernest A. Wallis**   Coptic Apocrypha in the
Dialect of Upper Egypt. By E.A.Wallis Budge.
[From M.R. James' 'Apocrypha N.T.', 1924.]

1913 **Smith, David**   Unwritten Sayings of our Lord.
By the Rev. David Smith...   London, New York: &
Toronto: Hodder & Stoughton, [1913].
[Contains "A Fragment of a Lost Gospel".]

Second Edition, n.d.

1914 **Schmoger, C.E.**   The Lowly Life and Bitter
Passion of Our Lord Jesus Christ and His Blessed
Mother Together with the Mysteries of the Old
Testament from the Visions of Venerable Anne
Catherine Emmerich, As Recorded in the Journal of
Clement Brentano, and edited by Very Rev. C.E.
Schmoger, C.SS.R. - With Permission of the Superiors
of His Order and the Approbation of the Right Rev.
Bishop of Ratisbon - From the Fourth German Edition
by the Translator of the Life of Anne Catherine
Emmerich... Volume I through IV.   Lille-Paris-
Bruges; Desclee, deBrouwer & Co.; New York: The
Sentinal Press, 1914.

1915 **Anonymous**   A Book of the Childhood of Christ
Depicted by the Old Masters. New York: Frederick A.
Stokes Co., Publishers. 1st. Edition, September,
1915.
Reprinted; October, 1915.

1916 **Ferrier, J. Todd**   The Logia or Sayings of the
Master as spoken by him; recovered in these days, as

was foretold by him. London: The Order of the Cross, 1916.

[A Spiritualist paraphrase; Deity is addressed as 'Father-Mother'.]

Second edition, 1926.

Third edition, 1946.

1917 **Hanish, Otoman Zar-Aduslo**   Yehoshua Nazir; Jesus the Nazarite; Life of Christ by Otoman Zar-Aduslo Hanish. Los Angeles: Mazdaznan Press, 1917.

1918 **Brooks, E.W.**   Joseph and Aseneth: The Confession and Prayer of Aseneth, Daughter of Pentephres the Priest. By E.W. Brooks. New York: The Macmillan Co., 1918.

[See Translations of Early Documents. London: S.P.C.K., 1918.]

1920 **Barton, William E.**   Four Hitherto Unpublished Gospels... John the Baptist, Andrew the Brother of Simon Peter, Judas Iscariot, James the Brother of Jesus by William E. Barton... New York: George H. Doran Co., 1920.

1920 **Robinson, J. Armitage**   Barnabas, Hermas and the Didache, by J. Armitage Robinson. London: S.P.C.K.; New York: Macmillan, 1920.

1920 **Seaborne, Frederick**   The Lost New Testament Book Restored Through Spirit Agency Professedly a Continuation of the Acts of the Apostles Down to the Death of St. Peter and St. Paul, by Luke, and Given to the World by Spirit Theophilus, Through the Hand of the Psychic, 1920.

[A modern Apocrypha.]

Reprint; Mokelumne Hill, Ca.: Health Research, 1971.

1920 **White, Hugh G. Evelyn**   The Sayings of Jesus from Oxyrhynchus by Hugh G.Evelyn White. Cambridge: 1920.

1921 **Martin, James**   The Empty Tomb; the disappearance of Jesus as related in the letters of Caiaphas, the High Priest. New York: Harper & Bros., Publishers, 1921.

[Published in Great Britain under the title, 'Letters of Caiaphas to Annas'.]

Another edition, 1960.

1922 **Maclean, A.J.**   An English Translation of the
     Teachings of the Twelve Apostles, by A.J. Maclean.
     London: S.P.C.K., Texts for Students, No. 13a, 1922.
        ["The   translation   is   Dr.   Bigg's   (very   slightly
        revised)...brought up to date by Dr. A.J. Maclean..."]

        Reprinted, 1936, 1948.

1924 **James, Montague Rhodes**   The Apocryphal
     New Testament, being the Apocryphal Gospels, Acts,
     Epistles, and Apocalypses with other narratives and
     fragments newly translated by Montague Rhodes James
     ... Oxford: Clarendon Press, 1924.
        Corrected, 1953, 1963, 1972.

        [Reprinted many times.]

1926 **Anonymous**   The Lost Books of the Bible being
     all the Gospels, Epistles, and other pieces now
     extant attributed in the first four centuries To
     Jesus Christ, His Apostles and their Companions. Not
     included, by its compilers, in the Authorized New
     Testament; and, the recently discovered Syriac MSS.
     of Pilate's Letters to Tiberius, etc. Translated
     from   the   original   tongues...   New   York: Alpha
     Publishing Co., 1926.
        [See William Hone, Apocryphal N.T., 1820.]

        Another edition; New York: Lewis Copeland Co.,
        1930.

        [Also; copyrighted by Gebbie & Co., 1890 & David McKay,
        1901.]

1929 **Schonfield, Hugh J.**   The Lost "Book of the
     Nativity of John" A Study in Messianic Folklore and
     Christian Origins With a New Solution of the Virgin
     Birth Problem. By Hugh J. Schonfield. Edinburgh: T.
     & T. Clark, 1929.
        ["Part II is simply a tentative reconstruction of the
        lost book..."]

1931 **Anonymous**   "The Letter from Heaven". Strange New
     Gospels by Edgar J. Goodspeed. Chicago: University
     of Chicago Press, 1931.
        Reprinted; Anglican Theological Review, Vol. 15,
        1933.

        Reprinted; The Letters from Heaven. Famous
        Biblical Hoaxes or, Modern Apocrypha by Edgar
        J. Goodspeed. Grand Rapids, Mi.: Baker Book
        House, 1956.

        [The reconstructed text, for the 1931 edition, came from
        old cherished broadsides. Rev. Desmond Morse-Boycott's

(in London) was dated soon after 1700 and printed in London.]

1931 **Goodspeed, Edgar J.**   Strange New Gospels. Chicago: University of Chicago Press, 1931.

1933 **Owen, Edward Charles**   Some Authentic Acts of the Early Martyrs. London: SPCK, 1933.
[See Willis Barnstone, The Other Bible (The Passion of Perpetua & Felicity), 1984.]

1935 **Anonymous**   The New Gospel Fragments; With One Plate. Oxford: University Press for the Trustees of the British Museum, 1935.
[Reprinted 1951 and 1955 Lithographically. Includes "...the Greek text as revised since the appearance of the Editio princeps (of the Fragments of an unknown Gospel; i.e., Egerton Papyrus 2.)"]

1935 **Bell, Idris and T.C. Skeat**   Fragments of an Unknown Gospel; text also in The New Gospel Fragment. London: British Museum, 1935.

1937 **Schonfield, Hugh J.**   According to the Hebrews; A New Translation of the Jewish Life of Jesus (the Toldoth Jeshu), with an inquiry into the nature of its sources and special relationship to the lost Gospel according to the Hebrews, by Hugh J. Schonfield. London: Duckworth, 1937.
[Translation of the History of Jesus the Nazarene according to the Hebrew Codex Strasburg.]

1937 **Szekely, Edmond and Purcell Weaver**   The Gospel of Peace of Jesus Christ, by the Disciple John. Aramaic and ancient Slav texts compared and edited by Edmond Szekely. London: C.W. Daniel Co.; Surrey: Lawrence Weaver, 1937.
["The content of this book is only a fragment – about an eighth – of the complete mss which exist in Aramaic in the Library of the Vatican and in the ancient Slav in the Royal Library of the Habsburgs (now the property of the Austrian Government)."]

Another edition; The Essene Gospel of John... (reprint).   [Tecata, California:] Essene School of Life, 1942.

1940 **Boldt, Herman J.**   The Crucifixion and Resurrection of Jesus, by an eye-witness... Retranslated from the German. A Letter of a Contemporary of Jesus. By Herman J.Boldt. 1940.
[Taken from K.H.Venturini's Natural History of the Great Prophet of Nazareth (1800–02) "a romantic reconstruction."]

1941 **Rimmer, Harry**   Crying Stones. By Harry Rimmer... Grand Rapids, MI: Wm.B.Eerdman Publishing Co., 1941.

[Contains a translation of the Didache.]

4th edition, 1946.

1945 **Heard, Gerald**   The Gospel According to Gamaliel
by Gerald Heard. New York & London: Harper & Bros.,
1945.

1945 **Metzger, Bruce Maning**   St. Paul and the Baptized
Lion. <u>Princeton Seminary Bulletin</u>, Nov., 1945.
   [See An Introduction to the Apocrypha. Bruce M.
   Metzger... New York: Oxford University Press, 1957.
   Contains "St. Paul..."]

1949 **O'Shea, Denis**   Mary and Joseph. Their Lives and
Times. Milwaukee: The Brace Publishing Co., 1949.

1953 **Barns, J.W.B.**   St. Paul and the Baptized Lion.
Oxford: 1953.

1956 **Goodspeed, Edgar J.**   Famous "Biblical" Hoaxes.
Originally entitled, Modern Apocrypha. By Edgar J.
Goodspeed.   Grand Rapids, MI: Baker Book House,
1956.
   [Contains some excepts from some of the Apocryphal Books
   he covers in this work.]

1957 **Fuller, Reginal H.**   Unknown Sayings of Jesus
by Joachim Jeremias... Translated from the German.
1957.
   Second edition; London: S.P.C.K., 1964.

   ["The second edition is translated from the third
   edition of Unbekannte Jesusworte, published in
   1963...and revised from the second German edition by
   Professor Jeremias..."]

1958 **Lloyd, Roger**   The Private Letters of Luke. Great
Neck, New York: Channel Press, 1958.

1959 **Blinzler, Josef**   The Trial of Jesus. The Jewish
and Roman proceedings against Jesus Christ described
and assessed from the oldest accounts by Josef
Blinzler translated from the second revised and
enlarged edition by Isabel and Florence McHugh.
Westminster, Maryland: The Newman Press, 1959.

1960 **Hibberd, Wulston** The New Testament Apocrypha, 1960.
   [See Bible Selections, 1960 Anonymous, Twentieth Century
   Encyclopedia of Catholicism, Vol. 72.]

1963 **Higgins, A.J.B.**   New Testament, edited by
Wilhelm Schniemelcher. English Translation by A.J.B.
Higgins. Edited by R. McL. Wilson.   Philadelphia:
Westminster, 1963.

1963 **Schneemelcher, Wilhelm and R. McL. Wilson**
New Testament Apocrypha. Edited by Wilhelm
Schneemelcher. English translated by R. McL. Wilson.
2 Vols. Philadelphia: The Westminster Press, 1963.
Reprinted, 1966.

1966 **Luk, A.D.K.**   Life and Teaching of Jesus and
Mary. Oklahoma City: A.D.K. Luk Publications, 1966.

1974 **Gurney, A.R., Junior**   The Gospel According to Job.
A novel by A.R. Gurney, Jr. New York, Evanston, San
Francisco, London: Harper & Row, Publishers, 1974.
[This work "blends the past with the present, Bible
times with the American scene, the Holy Family with
every family."]

1976 **Bruns, J. Edgar**   The Forbidden Gospel. J. Edgar
Bruns. San Francisco: Harper & Row Publishers, 1976.
["A 'Fifth Gospel' reconstructed from authentic ancient
sources that gives an unorthodox picture of Jesus and
his teachings."]

1976 **Charlesworth, James Hamilton**   The Pseudepigraphy
and Modern Research. Missoula, Montana: Scholars
Press, 1976.

1977 **Attridge, Harold W.**   The Dialogue of the Savior),
1977.
[See Apocryphal Books, 1977 James M. Robinson, The Nag
Hammadi.]

1977 **Hedrick, Charles W.**   The Second Apocalypse of James,
1977.
[See Apocryphal Books, 1977 James M. Robinson, The Nag
Hammadi.]

1977 **MacRae, George W.**   The Apocalypse of Adam, 1977.
[See Apocryphal Books, 1977 James M. Robinson, The Nag
Hammadi.]

1977 **MacRae, George W. and R. McL. Wilson**   The Gospel of
Mary, 1977.
[See Apocryphal Books, 1977 James M. Robinson, The Nag
Hammadi.]

1977 **MacRae, George W. and William R. Murdock**
The Apocalypse of Paul, 1977.
[See Apocryphal Books, 1977 James M. Robinson, The Nag
Hammadi.]

1977 **Mueller, Dieter**   The Prayer of the Apostle Paul,
1977.
[See Apocryphal Books, 1977 James M. Robinson, The Nag
Hammadi.]

1977 **Parrott, Douglas M. and R. McL. Wilson**   The Acts of
Peter and the Twelve Apostles, 1977.

[See Apocryphal Books, 1977 James M. Robinson, The Nag Hammadi.]

1977 **Parrott, Douglas M.**   Eugnostos the Blessed and The Sophia of Jesus Christ, 1977.
[See Apocryphal Books, 1977 James M. Robinson, The Nag Hammadi.]

1977 **Peel, Malcolm L.** The Treatise on Resurrection, 1977.
[See Apocryphal Books, 1977 James M. Robinson, The Nag Hammadi.]

1977 **Schoedel, William R.** The First Apocalypse of James, 1977.
[See Apocryphal Books, 1977 James M. Robinson, The Nag Hammadi.]

1977 **Turner, John D.**   The Book of Thomas the Contender, 1977.
[See Apocryphal Books, 1977 James M. Robinson, The Nag Hammadi.]

1977 **Williams, Francis E.** The Apocryphon of James, 1977.
[See Apocryphal Books, 1977 James M. Robinson, The Nag Hammadi.]

1977 **Wilson, R. McL.**   The Gospel of Mary, 1977.
[See George W MacRae and R. McL. Wilson, Apocryphal Books, 1977 James M. Robinson, The Nag Hammadi.]

1977 **Wilson, R. McL.**   The Acts of Peter and the Twelve Apostles, 1977.
[See Douglas M. Parrott and R. McL. Wilson, Apocryphal Books, 1977 James M. Robinson, The Nag Hammadi.]

1977 **Wisse, Frederik**   Letter of Peter to Philip, 1977.
[See Apocryphal Books, 1977 James M. Robinson, The Nag Hammadi.]

1977 **Wisse, Frederik**   The Apocryphon of John, 1977.
[See Apocryphal Books, 1977 James M. Robinson, The Nag Hammadi.]

1978 **Savoy, Gene**   The Lost Gospel of Jesus: The Hidden Teachings of Christ. Authorized Millennium Edition by the Most Rev. Gene Savoy... Reno, Nevada: The International Community of Christ, Church of the Second Advent, 1978.
Again; 1979.

1982 **Cameron, Ron**   The Other Gospels. Non-Canonical Gospel Texts. Edited by Ron Cameron. Philadelphia: Westminster Press, 1982.

1982 **Miller, Calvin**   The Philippian Fragment. Downers Grove, Illinois: Inter-Varsity Press, 1982.

1984 **Meyers, Marvin W.**   The Secret Teachings of Jesus. Four Gnostic Gospels translated, with an introduction and notes, by Marvin W. Meyers. New York: Vantage Books, 1984.

1985 **Baarda, T.**   The Sentences of the Syriac Menander. 1985.
     [See Apocrypha and Apocryphal Books, 1985 James H. Charlesworth, O.T. Pseudepigrapha.]

1985 **Burchard, C.**   Joseph and Aseneth. 1985.
     [See Apocrypha and Apocryphal Books, 1985 James H. Charlesworth, O.T. Pseudepigrapha.]

ACTS OF ANDREW

1924 **James, Montague Rhodes**   The Acts of Andrew, 1924.
     [See Apocryphal Books (N.T.), 1924 Montague Rhodes James, The Apocryphal N.T.]

1924 **James, Montague Rhodes**   The Acts of Andrew and Matthias (Matthew), 1924.
     [See Apocryphal Books (N.T.), 1924 Montague Rhodes James, The Apocryphal N.T.]

ACTS OF PAUL

1924 **James, Montague Rhodes**   The Acts of Paul, 1924.
     [See Apocryphal Books (N.T.), 1924 Montague Rhodes James, The Apocryphal N.T.]

ACTS OF PETER

1924 **James, Montague Rhodes**   The Acts of Peter, 1924.
     [See Apocryphal Books (N.T.), 1924 Montague Rhodes James, The Apocryphal N.T.]

ACTS OF JAMES

1974 **Anonymous**   A Nativity from the Apocryphal Book
     of James: Translated for Christmas 1974. [Reynolds
     Price] [n.p.: Rooster Press, 1974.]

ACTS OF THE APOSTLES

1871 **Wright, W.**   Apocryphal Acts of the Apostles;
     Edited from Syriac manuscripts in the British Museum
     and Other Libraries [sic] with English Translation
     and Notes by W. Wright. 2 Vols. 1871.
          [Syriac text and translation, vol. 2 of M.R. James'
          Apocryphal New Testament, 1924.]

     Reprinted; Amsterdam: Philo Press, 1968.

ACTS OF THOMAS

1924 **James, Montague Rhodes**   The Acts of Thomas, 1924.
          [See Apocryphal Books (N.T.), 1924 Montague Rhodes
          James, The Apocryphal N.T.]

1962 **Klijn, A.F.J.**   The Acts of Thomas; Introduction-
     Text-Commentary by A.F.J. Klijn. Leiden: E.J. Brill,
     1962.
          ["Supplements to Novum Testamentum", Vol. V.]

APOCALYPSE OF PAUL

1924 **James, Montague Rhodes**   The Apocalypse of Paul,
     1924.
          [See Apocryphal Books (N.T.), 1924 Montague Rhodes
          James, The Apocryphal N.T.]

APOCALYPSE OF PETER

1924 **James, Montague Rhodes**   The Apocalypse of Peter, 1924.
> [See Apocryphal Books (N.T.), 1924 Montague Rhodes James, The Apocryphal N.T.]

1975 **Brown, S. Kent and C. Wilfred Griggs** The Apocalypse of Peter: Introduction and Translation. <u>BYU Studies</u>, V. 15, No. 2, Pages 131-145, Winter, 1975.

1977 **Bullard, Roger A.**   Apocalypse of Peter, 1977.
> [See Apocrypha and Apocryphal Books, 1977 James M. Robinson, The Nag Hammadi.]

ARABIC GOSPEL OF INFANCY

1924 **James, Montague Rhodes**   The ...Gospel of Infancy, 1924.
> [See Apocryphal Books (N.T.), 1924 Montague Rhodes James, The Apocryphal N.T.]

EPISTLE OF BARNABAS

1817 **Wake, William**   The Catholic Epistle of Barnabas, 1817.
> [See Early Church Fathers, 1817 William Wake, The Genuine Epistles...]

1926 **Anonymous**   The General Epistle of Barnabas, 1926.
> [See Apocryphal Books, 1926 Anonymous, The Lost Books...]

EPISTLE OF JESUS CHRIST

1867 **Cowper, B. Harris**   The Letter of Jesus to Abgar, 1867.

[See Apocryphal Books (N.T.), 1867 B. Harris Cowper, The
Apocryphal Gospels.]

1924 **James, Montague Rhodes**   The Epistle of Jesus
Christ, 1924.
[See Apocryphal Books (N.T.), 1924 Montague Rhodes
James, The Apocryphal N.T.]

GOSPEL ACCORDING TO THE HEBREWS

1879 **Nicholson, Edward Byron**   The Gospel According to
the Hebrews. Its Fragments Translated and Annotated
with a Critical Analysis of the External and
Internal Evidence Relating to it, by Edward Byron
Nicholson. London: C. Kegan & Co., 1879.
[Includes 33 fragments from ancient Greek and Latin
sources, mostly related to the book of Matthew; contains
'Corrections and Supplementary Notes', dated 1881.]

1963 **Vielhauer, Philipp and George Ogg**   The Gospel of
the Hebrews, 1963.
[See Apocryphal Books (N.T.), 1963 Wilhelm Schneemelcher
and R. McL. Wilson, N.T. Apocrypha.]

[See Apocryphal Books (N.T.), 1982 Ron Cameron, The
Other Gospels.]

GOSPEL OF NICODEMUS

1066 **Anonymous**   The Four Gospels, the Gospel...
[See New Testament Selections for the complete entry.]

1400 **Anonymous**   The Middle-English Harrowing of Hell
and Gospel of Nicodemas. MS., c1400.
...Now first edited from all the known
manuscripts, with introduction and glossary.
By William Henry Hulme. London: EETS, by K.
Paul, Trench, Trubner & Co. Ltd., 1907.

1507 **Anonymous**   Here Begynneth the Treatys of Nycodemus
Gospell. London: n.p., 1507.
Again; 1509, 1512, 1529, 1532, 1537.

1698 **Thwaites, Edward**   Heptateuchus, liber Job...
[See Bible Selections for the complete entry.]

1867 **Cowper, B. Harris**   The Gospel of Nicodemus, or
     Acts of Pilate, 1867.
          [See Apocryphal Books (N.T.), 1867 B. Harris Cowper, The
          Apocryphal Gospels...]

1867 **Cowper, B. Harris**   The Latin Gospel of Nicodemus,
     Part I., or, Acts of Pilate, 1867.
          [See Apocryphal Books (N.T.), 1867 B. Harris Cowper, The
          Apocryphal Gospels...]

1907 **Hulme, William Henry**   See Anonymous, The Middle-
     English Harrowing..., 1400.

1924 **James, Montague Rhodes**   The Gospel of Nicodemus...
          [See Apocryphal Books (N.T.), 1924 Montague Rhodes
          James, The Apocryphal N.T.]

1926 **Anonymous**   The Gospel of Nicodemus...
          [See Apocryphal Books, 1926 Anonymous, The Lost Books of
          the Bible...for the complete entry.]

1963 **Scheidweiler, Felix and A.J.B. Higgins**   The Gospel
     of Nicodemus, 1963.
          [See Apocryphal Books (N.T.), 1963 Wilhelm Schneemelcher
          and R. McL. Wilson, N.T. Apocrypha.]

1974 **Lindstrom, Bengt**   A late Middle English version
     of the Gospel of Nicodemus edited from British
     Museum Ms. Harley 149 by Bengt Lindstrom. Uppsala
     & Stockholm: Distributed by Almquist & Wiksell,
     1974.

GOSPEL OF PETER

1893 **Harris, James Rendel**   A Popular Account of the
     Newly-Recovered Gospel of Peter by J. Rendel Harris.
     London: Hodder & Stoughton, 1893.
          [An apocryphal Passion-story, translated.]

1894 **Anonymous**   The Gospel According to Peter. A Study
     by the author of 'Supernatural Religion' [Cassels]
     London and New York: Longmans, Green & Co., 1894.
          [With the Greek text and a translation.]

1897 **Robertson, J.A.**   The Gospel of Peter, by J.A.
     Robertson. Edinburgh: T. & T. Clark, 1897.
          [An additional volume of the 'Ante-Nicene Library',
          1867-1872.]

1924 **James, Montague Rhodes**   The Gospel of Peter, 1924.

[See Apocryphal Books (N.T.), 1924 Montague Rhodes James, The Apocryphal N.T.]

1963 **Maurer, Christian and George Ogg**   The Gospel of Peter, 1963.
[See Apocryphal Books (N.T.), 1963 Wilhelm Schneemelcher and R. McL. Wilson, N.T. Apocrypha. Also; Apocryphal Books (N.T.), 1982 Ron Cameron, The Other Gospels.]

GOSPEL OF PHILIP

1932 **Dowden, Hester**   The Gospel of Philip the Deacon - Claiming to be a reconstruction of the original document burned in Athens about the time of Philip's mission (say A.D. 36-40), through the recall of the spiritual Memories of the Past which ever persist, and are available to mental sympathy. Received by Frederick Bligh Bond through the hand of Hester Dowden --- First Complete Edition, Embodying the narrative of the Holy Nativity, and the Messianic Constellation, the Passion, and the Resurrection of Christ, the Pentecostal gifts and the story of Sangreal, the Sole personal Relic of the Master remaining on Earth. With Nine Appendices. New York: Macoy Publishing Co., 1932.

1962 **Wilson, R. McL.**   The Gospel of Philip. Translated from the coptic text, with an Introduction and Commentary by R. McL. Wilson. New York & Evanston: Harper & Row, Publishers, 1962.
[From a second century Gnostic work found in the Nag Hammadi tomb.]

[Also, see Apocryphal Books (N.T.), 1963 Wilhelm Schneemelcher and R. McL. Wilson, N.T. Apocrypha.]

1977 **Isenberg, Wesley W.**   The Gospel of Philip, 1977.
[See Apocryphal Books, 1977 James M. Robinson, The Nag Hammadi.]

GOSPEL OF THE TWELVE APOSTLES

1901 **Ouseley, Gideon Jasper Richard**   The Gospel of the Holy Twelve; known also as the Gospel of the Perfect Life. Edited by a Disciple of the Master, from

Eastern and Western sources. Paris: The Order of
Atone-ment, and United Templars Society, 1901.

> ["...Gospel of the holy Twelve was communicated to
> (Ouseley) in numerous fragments at different times, by
> Emmanuel Swedenborg, Anna Kingsford, Edward Maitland,
> and a priest of a former century (i.e., Placidus, a
> Carmelite, c1326.) By them it was translated from the
> original (which was 'preserved in one of the
> Monasteries...in Thibet') and given to (Ouseley) to be
> supplemented...where indicated, from the Four Gospels
> (A.V.) revised where necessary by the same..."]

Another edition; The Gospel of the Holy Twelve;
An original and complete Gospel written down
and published by the late Rev. G.J. Ouseley;
New Edition, with Introduction and Notes by E.
Francis Udny. London: Edson (printers) Ltd.,
1923.

> [Considerably revised.]

Also; The Gospel of the Holy Twelve; Known also
as the Gospel of the Perfect Life. Translated
from the original Aramaic and edited by the
Rev. Gideon Jasper Richard Ouseley (Samuel
Hopgood Hart, editor). Santa Ana, Costa Rica:
Teofilo de la Torre, 1954.

Another edition; - - edited by a Disciple of the
Master, with former editions compared and
revised (Ronald Hentland, editor). London:
John M. Watkins, 1956.

1963 Wilson, R. McL.   The Gospel of the Twelve, 1963.
> [See Apocryphal Books (N.T.), 1963 Wilhelm Schneemelcher
> and R. McL. Wilson, N.T. Apocrypha.]

GOSPEL OF THOMAS

1867 Cowper, B. Harris   The Gospel of Thomas, 1867.
> [See Apocryphal Books (N.T.), 1867 B. Harris Cowper, The
> Apocryphal Gospels...(contains three different
> translations.)]

1924 James, Montague Rhodes   The Oxyrhynchus Sayings of
Jesus, 1924.
> [See Apocryphal Books (N.T.), 1924 Montague Rhodes
> James, The Apocryphal N.T.]

1924 James, Montague Rhodes   The Gospel of Thomas, 1924.
> [See Apocryphal Books (N.T.), 1924 Montague Rhodes
> James, The Apocryphal N.T.]

1930 **Robinson, Benjamin Willard**   The Sayings of Jesus.
     Their background and interpretation by Benjamin
     Willard Robinson...   New York & London: Harper &
     Bros. Publishers, MCMXXX [1930].

1959 **Guillaumont, A. and others**   The Gospel According to
     Thomas Coptic Text Established and Translated by A.
     Guillaumont, H. CH. Puech, G. Quispel, W. Till and
     Yassah Abd Al Masih. Leiden: E.J. Brill; New York:
     Harper & Bros., 1959.

1960 **Anonymous**   The secret books of the Egyptian
     Gnostics; An introduction to the Gnostic Coptic
     Manuscripts discovered at Chenoboskion. With an
     English translation and critical evaluation of the
     Gospel according to St. Thomas. [Philip Mairet] New
     York: Viking Press, 1960.

1960 **Schoedel, William R.**   The Secret Sayings of Jesus
     by Robert M. Grant in collaboration with David Noel
     Freedman; With an English Translation of the Gospel
     of Thomas by William R. Schoedel. Garden City, New
     York: Doubleday & Co., Inc., 1960.

1963 **Wilson, R. McL.**   The Gospel of Thomas, 1963.
     [See Apocryphal Books (N.T.), 1963 Wilhelm Schneemelcher
     and R. McL. Wilson, N.T. Apocrypha, pages 278-313.
     Another translation by Wilson can be found on pages 511-
     522.]

1977 **Lambdin, Thomas O.**   Gospel of Thomas, 1977.
     [See Apocryphal Books, 1977 James M. Robinson, The Nag
     Hammadi.]

     [See Apocryphal Books (N.T.), 1982 Ron Cameron, The
     Other Gospels.]

1990 **Eyer, Shawn Tiberius**   The Gospel According to
     Thomas; Translated from the Ancient Coptic by Shawn
     Eyer. Ms. 1990.

GOSPEL OF TRUTH

1960 **Grobel, Kendrick**   The Gospel of Truth.
     A Valentinian Meditation on the Gospel. Translation
     from the Coptic and Commentary. London: 1960.

1961 **Isenberg, W.W.**   The Gospel of Truth, 1961.
     [See Apocryphal Books, 1961 Robert M. Grant,
     Gnosticism.]

1963 **Wilson, R. Mcl.**   The Gospel of Truth, 1963.
[See Apocryphal Books (N.T.), 1963 Wilhelm Schneemelcher
and R. McL. Wilson, N.T. Apocrypha, pages 233-241.
Another translationby Wilson can be found on pages 523-
531.]

1977 **MacRae, George W.**   The Gospel of Truth, 1977.
[See Apocryphal Books, 1977 James M. Robinson, The Nag
Hammadi.]

GOSPELS OF INFANCY

1697 **Sike, Henry**   The First Gospel of the Infancy of
Jesus Christ. 1697.
[See Apocryphal Books (N.T.), 1820 William Hone, The
Apocryphal N.T.; Also, 1924 Montague Rhodes James, The
Apocryphal N.T.]

1924 **James, Montague Rhodes**   The ...Gospel of Infancy,
1924.
[See Apocryphal Books (N.T.), 1924 Montague Rhodes
James, The Apocryphal N.T.]

1926 **Anonymous**   The Gospels of Infancy...
[See Apocryphal Books, 1926 Anonymous, The Lost
Books...]

1963 **Higgins, A.J.B.**   Infancy Gospels, 1963.
[See Apocryphal Books (N.T.), 1963 Wilhelm Schneemelcher
and R. McL. Wilson, N.T. Apocrypha.]

MACK LIBRARY
BOB JONES UNIVERSITY
GREENVILLE, SC

22

Dead Sea Scrolls

1951 **Brownlee, W.H.**   The Dead Sea Manual of Discipline. Translation and Notes. By W.H. Brownlee. New Haven, CT: Bulletin of the American Schools of Oriental Research, 1951.

1951 **Burrows, Millar** The Dead Sea Scrolls. By M.Burrows. New York: The Viking Press; London: Secker & Warburg, 1951.
> [See Apocryphal Books, 1984 Willis Barnstone, The Other Bible (The Manual of Discipline).]
>
> [See Apocryphal Books, 1984 Willis Barnstone, The Other Bible (The Damascus Document).]
>
> [See Apocryphal Books, 1984 Willis Barnstone, The Other Bible (The War of the sons of Light with the sons of Darkness).]

Other editions; 1955, 1956, 1957.

1956 **Allegro, John M.**   The Dead Sea Scrolls by John M. Allegro. Baltimore, Maryland: Penguin Books, 1956.
> [With revisions, 1958.]

1956 **Gaster, Theodore H.**   The Dead Sea Scriptures, in English Translation with Introduction and Notes by Theodore H. Gaster. Garden City, New York: Anchors Books; Doubleday & Co., Inc., 1956.
> Revised and enlarged edition; 1964.

1962 **Vermes, G.**   The Essene Writings from Qumran by G. Vermes. Cleveland & New York: Meridian Books; The World Publishing Co., 1962.
> ["...rendering into English a French text (by A. Dupont-Sommer) which is itself a translation from Hebrew or Aramaic..."]

1962 **Vermes, G.**   The Dead Sea Scrolls in English by G. Vermes. Baltimore, Maryland: Penguin Books, 1962.
Another edition; New York: Penguin Books, 1975.

Another edition; Sheffield, England: Sheffield Academic Press, 1987.

1965 **Anonymous**   Scrolls from the Wilderness of the Dead Sea. A catalog of the exhibition, The Dead Sea Scrolls of Jordan, Arranged by the Smithsonian Institution in cooperation with the Hashemite Kingdom of Jordan and the Palestine Archeological Museum. Published for the American Schools of Research by the University of California, 1965.
[Contains translations of a number of fragments.]

1967 **Sanders, J.A.**   The Dead Sea Psalms, 1967.
[See Hebrew Scripture Selections, 1967 for the entire entry.]

23

Josephus

1602 **Lodge, Thomas**   The Works of Josephus, 1602.

1700 **L'Estrange, Roger**   The Works of Josephus. Oxford: 1700.

1737 **Whiston, William**   The Works of Flavius Josephus the learned and authentic Jewish historian and celebrated warrior, to which are added seven dissertations concerning Jesus Christ, John the Baptist, James the Just, God's command to Abraham, etc.. translated by William Whiston. 1737.
[Many times reprinted.]

1862 **Traill, Dr. R.** Jewish War (Josephus). London: 1862.

1889 **Shileto, A.R.**   The Works of Flavius Josephus: Whiston's translation revised by A.R. Shileto. 5 Vols.   London: G. Bell, 1889-1890.
[This work is a part of Bohn's Standard Library.]

1919 **Thackeray, H. St. J.**   Selections from Josephus Translated by H. St. J. Thackeray. London: Society for Promoting Christian Knowledge;   New York: The Macmillan Co., 1919.

1926 **Thackeray, H. St. J. and Others**   Josephus with an English Translation by H. St. J. Thackeray, M.A... In Nine Volumes.   London: William Heinemann Ltd.; Cambridge, Mass.: Harvard University Press, 1926-1965.
[Loeb Classical Library]

   1926 Vol. 1   The Life Against Apion. By H. St. J. Thackeray. Reprinted; 1956, 1961, 1966.

1927 Vol. II   The Jewish War, Books I-III by
H. St. J. Thackeray. Reprinted; 1956, 1961,
1967.

1928 Vol. III   The Jewish War, Books IV-VII by
H. St. J. Thackeray. Reprinted; 1957, 1961,
1968.

1930 Vol. IV   Jewish Antiquities, Books I-IV
by H. St. J. Thackeray. Reprinted; 1957,
1961, 1967.

1934 Vol. V   Jewish Antiquities, Books V-
VIII by H. St. J. Thackeray and Ralph
Marcus.... Reprinted; 1935, 1950, 1958,
1966.

1937 Vol. VI   Jewish Antiquities, Books IX-XI
by Ralph Marcus. Reprinted; 1951, 1958,
1966.

1943 Vol. VII   Jewish Antiquities, Books XII-
XIV by Ralph Marcus. Reprinted; 1957, 1961,
1966.

1963 Vol. VIII Jewish Antiquities, Books XV-
XVII by Ralph Marcus. Completed & edited
by Allen Wikgren. Reprinted; 1969.

1965 Vol. IX   Jewish Antiquities, Books
XVIII-XX by Louis H. Feldman...

1931 **Eislen, Robert**   The Messiah Jesus and John
the Baptist According to Flavius Josephus; Recently
Rediscovered 'Capture of Jerusalem'.   New York:
Lincoln MacVeagh, 1931.
    [English Edition by Alexander Haggerty Krappe]

1934 **Thackeray, H. St. J. and Ralph Marcus**   Josephus.
Jewish Antiquities. Books V-VIII, 1934.
    [H. St. J.Thackeray and Others, Josephus, 1926.]

1937 **Marcus, Ralph**   Jewish Antiquities, Books IX-XI,
1937.
    [See H. St. J. Thackeray, Josephus, 1926.]

1942 **Szekely, Edmond Bordeaux**   The Essenes, by Josephus
and his contemporaries, by Edmond Bordeaux Szekely.
Tecate, Calif., U.S.A.: Essene School of Life, 1942.
    ["This booklet contains the complete, authentic
    reconstruction by Josephus Flavius... of the original
    purity, simplicity and harmony of the free, creative
    life of the famous "Essene Republics..."]

1943 **Marcus, Ralph**   Jewish Antiquities, Books XII–XIV, 1943.
[See H. St. J. Thackeray, Josephus, 1926.]

1959 **Williamson, G.A.**   Josephus; The Jewish War, translated with an introduction by G.A. Williamson. 1959.
Reprinted; Baltimore, Maryland: Penguin Books, 1960.

1963 **Marcus, Ralph**   Jewish Antiquities, Books XV–XVII. Completed & edited by Allen Wikgren, 1963.
[See H. St. J. Thackeray, Josephus, 1926.]

1965 **Feldman, Louis H.**   Josephus. Jewish Antiquities. Books XVIII–XX. 1965.
[See H.St.J.Thackeray, Josephus, 1926.]

1966 **Thackeray, H. St. J.and Ralph Marcus**
Josephus. The Jewish War and Other Selections from Flavius Jospehus translated by H. St J. Thackeray and R. Marcus. London: The New English Library Ltd., 1966.
[The Great Histories edited by M.I. Finley.]

1982 **Cornfeld, Gaalya** (General Editor)   Josephus; The Jewish War. Newly translated with extensive commentary and archaeological background illustrations. Gaalya Cornfeld, General editor; Benjamin Mazar, Paul L. Maier, consulting editors. Grand Rapids, MI: Zondervan Publishing House, 1982.

1988 **Maier, Paul L.**   Josephus; The Essential Writings. A Condensation of 'Jewish Antiquities' and 'The Jewish War'. Translated and Edited by Paul L. Maier. Illustrated. Grand Rapids, MI: Kregel Publications, 1988.

24

Early Church Fathers

???? **Apostolic Fathers**   The Apostolic Fathers,
A New Translation and Commentary, 6 Vols., [196?].
          Vol. 1   Introduction   Robert M. Grant.

          Vol. 2   I & II Clement   R.M. Grant &
                                            Holt H. Graham.

          Vol. 3   The Didache & Barnabas
                                        Robert A. Kraft.

          Vol. 4   Ignatius of Antioch R.M. Grant.

          Vol. 5   Polycarp, Martyrdom of Polycarp,
                      Fragment of Papias
                              William R. Schroedel.

          Vol. 6   Hermas   Graydon F. Snyder.

???? **Grant, Robert M.**   Ignatius of Antioch, [196?].
          [See Apocryphal Books (N.T.), 196? The Apostolic
          Fathers.]

???? **Grant, Robert M. and Holt H. Graham**   First and
      Second Clement, [196?].
          [See Apocryphal Books (N.T.), 196? The Apostolic
          Fathers.]

???? **Schroedel, William R.**   Polycarp, Martyrdom of
      Polycarp, Fragment of Papias, [196?]
          [See Apocryphal Books (N.T.), 196? The Apostolic
          Fathers.]

???? **Snyder, Graydon F.**   Hermas, [196?].
          [See Apocryphal Books (N.T.), 196? The Apostolic
          Fathers.]

1668 **Elborowe, Thomas**   The famous epistles of Saint
Polycarp and Saint Ignatius, with the Epistle of
Saint Barnabus, 1668.

1670 **Cave, Dr.**   The Epistle of Polycarp to the
Philippians.
        [In his 'Apocryphal N.T.', 1820, Hone states,"There is
        also a translation by Dr. Cave attached to his life of
        Polycarp."]

1817 **William, Late Lord Archbishop of Canterbury**
The Genuine Epistles of the Apostolical Fathers,
            St. Barnabas,   St. Polycarp,
            St. Ignatius,   St. Clement,
            The Shepherd of Hermas;
...for about a Hundred and Fifty Years after Christ.
Translated and Published, with a Preliminary
Discourse, by the Most Reverend Fathers in God,
William, Late Lord Archbishop of Canterbury.
[William Wake] Fifth Edition. London: Printed for
Samuel Bagster..., MDCCCXVII. [1817]

1849 **Cureton, William**   Corpus Ignatianum: a complete
collection of the Ignatian Epistles. 1858.

1867 **Ante-Nicene Christian Library**   Ante-Nicene
Christian Library. Edited by Alexander Roberts and
James Donaldson. 24 Vols. Edinburgh: 1867-1872.
        Another Edition; The Ante-Nicene Fathers.
        Translations of the Writings of the Fathers
        down to A.D. 325. Buffalo, NY: 10 Vols. The
        Christian Literature Publishing Co., 1885.

1869 **Lightfoot, Joseph Barber**   The Apostolic Fathers.
1869-1890.
        1869 S. Clement of Rome. The two epistles to
        the Corinthians. A revised text with
        introduction and notes. London.

        1890 Part I. S. Clement of Rome. 2 Vols.
        London: Macmillan & Co.

        1885 Part II. S. Ignatius, S. Polycarp. 3
        Vols. London: Macmillan & Co.
                Second edition; 3 Vols.   London:
                Macmillan & Co., 1889.

        Another edition; The Apostolic Fathers by J.B.
        Lightfoot. Edited and completed by J.R. Hamer.
        Grand Rapids, MI: Baker Book House, 1956.
                [Many reprints.]

1889 **Anonymous**   The Apostolic Fathers... [W. Burton]
London: Griffith Farran Okeden & Welsh, William

Heineman, Ltd., Harvard University Press, The Macmillan Co., 1889.

> Part I. The Epistles of SS. Clement of Rome and Barnabas, and the Shepherd of Hermas with an introduction...

> Part II. The Epistles of St. Ignatius and St. Polycarp, The...Martyrdom of St. Polycarp, The teaching of the twelve apostles, The Epistle to Diognetus, An essay on the right use of the fathers.

> ["The translation... is that of Archbishop Wake, with the exceptions of some portions of the epistles of Clement, translated by the present editor (W.Burton)..."]

1890 **Schaff, Philip and Henry Wace**   The Nicene & Post-Nicene Fathers, 1890-1892.

> 1892 - - First Series, 14 Vol. By Philip Schaff. New York.

> 1890 - - Second Series, 14 Vol. By Philip Schaff and Henry Wace. New York.

1898 **Bigg, Charles**   Early Church Classics. The Doctrine of the Twelve Apostles. Translated into English with Introduction and Notes by Charles Bigg... London: Society for Promoting Christian Knowledge, 1898.

1900 **Srawley, J.H.**   An English Translation of the Epistles of St. Ignatius with full introduction and notes, by J.H. Srawley. London: S.P.C.K., 1900.
Reprinted with notes; 1919, 1935.

Reprinted without notes, 1934, 1954.

1912 **Lake, Kirsopp**   The Apostolic Fathers with an English Translation.   London: Loeb Classical Library, 1912-1913.

> 1912 - - Vol. 1
> 1913 - - Vol. 2
>> Another edition; Vol. 2. London: William Heinemann; NY: G.P. Putnam's Sons, 1917.

Another edition; London: William Heinemann, 1930.

Also; 2 Vols. Cambridge, Mass.: Harvard University Press, 1950-1952.

1937 **Clarke, W.K. Lowther**   The First Epistle of Clement to the Corinthians. Translations of Early Documents. 1937.

846 EARLY CHURCH FATHERS

1946 **Ancient Christian Writers** Ancient Christian Writers. The Works of the Fathers in Translation edited by Johannes Quasten... and Joseph C. Plumpe ... The Catholic University of America, Washington, D.C. 17 Vols. Westminster, Maryland: The Newman Bookshop, 1946-1953.

1946 **Grant, Robert** Second Century Christianity. A Collection of Fragments, 1946.

1946 **Kleist, James A.** The Epistles of St. Clement of Rome and St. Ignatius of Antioch, newly translated and annotated by James A. Kleist... Westminster, Maryland: The Newman Bookshop, 1946.
[See Ancient Christian Writers, 1946.]

1947 **Glimm, Francis X.** The Fathers of the Church; New Translation. New York: Christian Heritage Inc., 1947.

1948 **Kleist, James A.** The Didache, The Epistle of Barnabas, the Epistles and the Martyrdom of St. Polycarp, the Fragments of Papias, the Epistle to Diognetus; Newly Translated and Annotated by James A. Kleist. London: Longmans, Green & Co., Ancient Christian Writers, Vol. six, 1948.
["First published in the library edition 1948... pocket edition first published 1957. The Library edition is published in U.S.A. and Canada by the Newman Press, Westminster, MD, U.S.A."]

1950 **Goodspeed, Edgar J.** The Apostolic Fathers; An American Translation. London: Independent Press, 1950.
[A modern translation of the letters of Clement, the Shepherd of Hermas, the Martyrdom of Polycarp, and eight other writings of the early fathers.]

1953 **Richardson, Cyril C. and Others** The Library of Christian Classics. Early Church fathers Newly translated and edited by Cyril C. Richardson... In collaboration with Eugene R. Fairweather..., Edward Rochie Hardy..., Massey Hamilton Shepherd, Jr... Philadelphia: The Westminster Press, 1953.
Another Edition; Early Christian Fathers. Newly translated and edited by Cyril C. Richardson. In collaboration with Eugene R. Fairweather, Edward Rochie Hardy, Massey Hamilton Shepherd. New York: Collier Books, Macmillan Publishing Co., 1970.

1956 **Hamer, J.R.** See Joseph Barber Lightfoot, The Apostolic Fathers, 1869.

1962 **Carol, Sister Ann**   The Pageant of Literature. Early Christian Writers. Sister Ann Carol, O.P... New York: The Macmillan Co., 1962.
> ["The selections in this book...all very in style, mood, and subject matter, but the authors of these sections are unanimous in their love of God".]

1968 **Staniforth, Maxwell**   Early Christian Writings. The Apostolic Fathers. Translated by Maxwell Staniforth. Baltimore, Maryland: Penguin Books, 1968.
> Another edition; Early Christian Writings. The Apostolic Fathers. Translated by Maxwell Staniforth. With introduction and new editorial material by Andrew Louth. Baltimore, Maryland: Penguin Books, 1987.

1972 **Anonymous**   The Fathers of the Church; A New Translation. 122 Vols. Washington, D.C.: The Catholic University of America Press, 1972-1989.

1985 **Pennington, M. Basil and Others**   The Living Testament. The Essential Writings of Christianity since the Bible. M. Basil Pennington, Alan Jones, Mark Booth.   San Francisco: Harper & Row, Publishers, 1985.

25

Koran

???? **Bell, Richard**　　　　The Qur'an. Translation, with a Critical Rearrangement of the Surahs by Richard Bell. 2 Vols., [19??].

???? **Ross, Alexander**　　　　The Koran. By Alexander Ross. [16??].
> [In the introduction 'To The Reader' preceding his own translation of the Koran, George Sale mentions an earlier English version which "...is no other than a translation of (a 17th century French version by Andrew du Ryer), and that a very bad one: for Alexander Ross, who did it, being utterly unacquainted with the Arabic, and no great master of the French, has added a number of fresh mistakes of his own to those of Du Ryer; not to mention the meanness of his language, which would make a better book ridiculous."]

1734 **Sale, George**　The Koran: Commonly called the Alcoran of Mohammed. Translated in English immediately from the Original Arabic, with explanatory notes taken from the most approved Commentators. To which is prefixed a Preliminary Discourse, by George Sale. London: C. Ackers, 1734.
> [Many times reprinted.]

1846 **Anonymous**　　The Biblical Legends of the Musselmans, from the German by G. Weil. New York: Harper, 1846.

1861 **Rodwell, J.M.**　　　　The Koran, Translated from the Arabic... with notes and index (the Suras arranged in chronological order.) n.p.: n.p., 1861.
> Second edition; by E.H. Palmer (Sacred Books of the East, Vol.vi., ix.) 1876.

> Reprint; Everyman's Library edited by Ernest Rhys. Philosophy & Theology. The Koran with introduction by Rev. G. Margoliouth, M.A.

London: Published by J.M. Dent & Sons Ltd.,
1909.
> Reprinted, 1911, 1913.

[Many times reprinted.]

[The above information is taken from G. Margoliouth's
Introduction to Rodwell's Koran in the edition by J.M.
Dent & Sons, 1909.]

1882 **Lane-Poole, S.**   The Speeches and Table-Talk of the
Prophet Mohammed, etc., chosen and translated, with
introduction and notes. By S. Lane-Poole. 1882.
[From G. Margoliouth's introduction to Rodwell's Koran,
1904; consists of selections from the Koran.]

1900 **Palmer, E.H.**   The Koran (Qur'an) Translated by E.H.
Palmer.   Oxford   University   Press   [The   World
Classics], 1900.
Another edition, 1928.

1905 **Khan, Mohammed Abdul Hakim**   The Holy Quran,
translated... with short notes. By Mohammed Abdul
Hakim Khan., 1905.
[From G. Margoliouth's introduction to Rodwell's Koran,
1904.]

1928 **Ali, Muhammad**   Translation of the Holy
Quran (without Arabic text) With Short Notes and
Introduction by Muhammad Ali, M.A., LL.B.   Lahore,
India: Ahmadiyya Anjuman-I-Ishaat-I-Islam, 1928.

1930 **Pickthall, Marmaduke**   The Meaning of the Glorious
Koran; An Explanatory Translation, by Marmaduke
Pickthall. New York: Alfred A. Knopf, 1930.

1934 **Abdullah Yusuf Ali**   The meaning of the Glorious
Quran. Text, Translation and Commentary By Abdullah
Yusuf Ali. 2 Vols. Cairo, Egypt: Dar Al-Kitab Al-
Masri, 1934.
> Another Edition;   The   Holy   Qur'an;   Text,
> Translation and Commentary by Abdullah Yusuf
> Ali. Printed in the United States of America
> By the American International Printing Co.,
> Washington, D.C., 1946.
> [Copyright 1946 by Khalil Al-Rawaf]

1949 **Lamsa, George M.**   The Short Koran Designed for
Easy Reading. Edited... George M. Lamsa. Chicago &
New York: Ziff-Davis Publishing Co., 1949.

1955 **Arberry, Arthur J.**   The Koran Interpreted by Arthur
J. Arberry... Combined in One Volume... New York:
The Macmillan Co., 1955.

1956 **Dawood, N.J.** The Koran. Translated with notes by N.J. Dawood. Penguin Books, 1956.

    1st. revision; 1959.

    2nd. revision; 1966.

    3rd. revision; 1968.

    4th. revision; 1974.

    [Reprinted many times.]

1958 **Jeffery, Arthur** The Koran: Selected Suras. Translated from the Arabic by Arthur Jeffery and decorated by Valenti Angelo. New York: The Heritage Press, 1958.

1966 **Leaney, A.R.C.** The Rule of Qumran and Its Meaning: Introduction, translation and commentary. Boston: A.R.C. Leaney, 1966.

1986 **Shakir, M.H.** Holy Qur'an. Translated by M.H.Shakir. Elmhurst, New York: Tahrike Tarsile Qur'an Inc., 1986.

Bibliography

1776 **Anonymous**   A List of Various Editions of the Bible, and Parts thereof, in English; From the Year 1526 to 1776; From a Manuscipt (No. 1140) in the Archiepiscopal Library at Lambeth, much enlarged and improved. [Mark Cephas Tutet. London: Bowyer], 1776.

1822 **Anonymous**   Catalogue of editions of the Holy Scripture and other Biblical works in the Library of the British and Foreign Bible Society. London: British and Foreign Bible Society, 1822. [17 pages]
   Another edition, 86 pages, 1832.
   Another edition, 5000 titles, 1857.
   Another edition, 1903.

1965 **Anonymous**   General Catalog of Printed Books: Photolithographic edition to 1955. London: Published by the Trustees of the British Museum, 1965.
   Vol. 17; Bible; Complete Bible - OT
   Vol. 18; Bible; --NT
   Vol. 19; Bible; --Appendix

1844 **Barnes, Albert**   Notes critical, illustrative, and practical on the Book of Job... new translation. By Albert Barnes. London: Wiley & Putnam, 1844.
   [Includes an exhaustive bibliography of versions of Job.]

   Another edition; carefully revised by John Cumming. London: George Routledge, 1847.

   Another edition; New Improved edition by Albert Barnes. New York: Leavitt & Allen, 1854.

Another edition; carefully revised by John Cumming. London: George Routledge, 1847.

Another edition; New Improved edition by Albert Barnes. New York: Leavitt & Allen, 1854.

1903 **Darlow, T.H. and H.F. Moule**   Historical Catalogue of the Printed Editions of the Holy Scriptures in the Library of the British and Foreign Bible Society by T.H. Darlow and H.F. Moule. 4 Vols. London: British and Foreign Bible Society, 1903-1911.
Reprinted; Kraus Reprint Corporation, 1963.

1876 **Dore, John Read** Old Bibles or an account of various Versions of the English Bible by J.R. Dore. London: Basil M. Pickering, 1876.
Another edition; Old Bibles: An Account of the Early Versions of the English Bible... Second Edition, with the preface to the version of 1611 added at the request of the late Right Rev. Christopher Wordsworth... Printed and Published by Eyre and Spottiswoode, 1888.

1886 **Dore, John Read**   Early Versions of the Old and New Testaments examined by the York College... selected from the Library of J[ohn] R[ead] Dore. Huddersfield: Society rosicr. in Anglia, 1886.

1965 **Ehlert, Arnold D.** (Editor)   The Bible Collector: Issued Quarterly by the International Society of Bible Collectors. La Mirada, California: 1965-1984.

1961 **Harris, Frank L**. English Translations of the Bible. A Preliminary Short-Title List. 1961.
[51 Sheets; Approx. 350 items.]

1968 **Herbert, A.S.**   Historical Catalogue of printed Editions of the English Bible, 1525-1961; Revised and Explained from the Edition of T.H. Darlow and H.F. Moule, 1903. By A.S. Herbert. London: The British and Foreign Bible Society; New York: The American Bible Society, 1968.

1961 **Hills, Margaret T.**   The English Bible in America; A Bibliography of Editions of the Bible and New Testaments Published in America 1777-1957. By Margaret T. Hills. New York: American Bible Society and The New York Public Library, 1961.
Second Edition; Revised, 1962.

1985 **Johnson, Carl** (Editor)   Bible Collectors' World: Issued quarterly. 1985-

Bibliographical Notes by Edmund Bailey O'Callaghan. Albany, New York: Munsell & Rowland, 1861.
> Reprinted; Detroit, MI: Gale Research Co., 1966.

1913 **Pick, Bernard** Translations of the Bible; A Chronology of the Versions of the Holy Scriptures Since the Invention of Printing – Written for the American Bible Society by Bernard Pick. New York: American Bible Society, 1913.

1926 **Pollard, A.W. and G.R. Redgrave** A Short-Title Catalogue of Books Printed in England, Scotland, and Ireland and of English Books printed abroad, 1475–1640. By A.W. Pollard and G.R. Redgrave. London: The Bibliographical Society, 1926.

1952 **Pope, Hugh and Sebastian Bullough** English Versions of the Bible by Very Rev. Hugh Pope, O.P.; Revised and Amplified by Rev. Sebastian Bullough, O.P. t. London:ouis, MO. & London: B. Herder Book Co., 1952.

1859 **Shea, John Dawson Gilmary** A Bibliography Account of the Catholic Bibles, Testaments and other portions of Scripture, translated from the Latin Vulgate and printed in the United States by John Dawson Gilmary Shea. New York: Cramoisy Press, 1859.
> Also; Ann Arbor, MI: University Microfilms, 1974.

1936 **Simms, P. Marion** The Bible in America; Versions that have played their part in the making of the republic by P.Marion Simms. New York: Wilson–Erikson Inc., 1936.

1945 **Wing, Donald** Short Title Catalogue of Books Printed in England, Scotland, Ireland, Wales, and British America and of English Books Printed in Other Countries 1641–1700; Compiled by Donald Wing of yale University Library; In Three Volumes. New York: Printed for the Index Society by Columbia University Press, 1945 thru 1951.

1892 **Wright, John** Early Bibles in America by John Wright. New York: Thomas Whitaker, 1892.
> Third Edition; Revised and Enlarged. New York: Thomas Whitaker, 1894.

Index of Translators, Editors, and Translations

MACK LIBRARY
BOB JONES UNIVERSITY
GREENVILLE, SC

About the Author

WILLIAM J. CHAMBERLIN is Director of The Bible Museum and Biblical Research Foundation. He has published widely on rare translations of the Bible and is editor of *The Bible Researcher.*